The Blackwell Encyclopedia
of the
Russian Revolution

Edited by
Harold Shukman

Copyright © Basil Blackwell Ltd 1988, 1994
Editorial organization © Harold Shukman 1988, 1994

First published 1988
This paperback edition, revised and updated 1994

Blackwell Publishers
108 Cowley Road
Oxford, OX4 1JF, UK

238 Main Street
Cambridge
Massachusetts 02142, USA

British Library Cataloguing in Publication Data

A CIP catalogue record for this book is available from the British Library.

Library of Congress Cataloging in Publication Data

The Blackwell encyclopedia of the Russian revolution / edited by
    Harold Shukman.
        450 p.
        Includes bibliographical references and index.
        ISBN 0–631–19525–4 (pbk).
        1. Soviet Union—History—Revolution, 1917–1921—Encyclopedias.
    I. Shukman, Harold.
    DK265.B54   1995
    947.084′1′03—dc20   94–11241
                                                                             CIP

Typeset in 9 on 11 pt Plantin Light
by Columns of Reading
Printed and Bound in Great Britain by
Hartnolls Limited, Bodmin, Cornwall.

Contents

Contents

Preface

Before addressing the historical background of this paperback edition of the Encyclopedia, we wish to note with deep regret the deaths of two of our authors. On 2 June, 1988, only a few weeks before the publication of the Encyclopedia, Robert McNeal was killed in an automobile accident in Massachusetts. On 1 August, 1990, Michael Glenny died suddenly in Moscow.

Since the publication of this book in the summer of 1988, the perception of the events to which it was devoted has undergone a significant change. If in 1988 the Russian Revolution could still be viewed as having launched the process that resulted in the creation of the world's second super-power, by 1994 that creation is no more. In the years between 1988 and now, the Soviet state engendered by the Revolution entered a period of terminal decline, diseased by corruption, a flawed ideology, an irrational economic policy and unsustainable strategic goals. In the years immediately following this book's publication, moreover, the forces that had led to the virtual dismemberment of the territory of the former Russian Empire during the Civil War of 1918–21, and that had remained latent throughout the seventy years of Communist rule, erupted with such energy by the end of the 1980s that they succeeded in completely undoing the work of Soviet reunification. The Soviet Union has disintegrated and the Communist Party of the Soviet Union has evaporated, which means in effect that, for all those interested in studying the Russian Revolution, from which both drew their legitimacy, to engage now in its description and analysis is no longer to question the origins of an existing political entity. The Russian Revolution has at last passed into history.

Russian historians were relatively slow to respond to the liberal policies that were a dominant feature of the last years of the Soviet regime, the Gorbachev era, the period of *glasnost* – openness – perhaps best paraphrased as the time for telling the truth. So much Soviet writing about the Revolution had been saturated by the ideological demands of the Stalin period, and because of the purges of the 1930s by the 'depopulation' of modern Russian history, that the process of reassessment was bound to take some time. Indeed, in 1988, liberally-minded historians were complaining to each other that the job of recovering the Soviet past was being done by playwrights and novelists. What they had in mind were the (unstaged) plays of Mikhail Shatrov about the February Revolution and the peace negotiations at Brest-Litovsk, which were imagined dramatized debates between the chief *dramatis personae*, and Anatoly Rybakov's *Children of the Arbat*, a fictionalized account of the background to the purges of the 1930s.

The 'repopulation' of the field, however, was addressed relatively soon. Beginning with Bukharin in January 1988, by the middle of that year all of the purged Bolsheviks had been posthumously rehabilitated: since Trotsky, the chief (though absent) defendant at the purge trials, had technically not been purged and processed by Stalin's 'judicial' machinery, he could not be judicially rehabilitated; he has, however, been the subject of at least two studies published in Russia, a two-volume biography by Dmitri Volkogonov and a short but pointed sketch by Vitaly Startsev. In addition, in 1989 a two-volume collection appeared, entitled

Rediscovered Names (*Vozvrashchennye imena*), which included articles on such figures as Bukharin, Kamenev, Zinoviev, Rykov and Rakovsky, based chiefly on memoirs and reminiscences, but also with some original archival material. In 1993 the Great Russian Encyclopedia publishing house – formerly Soviet Encyclopedia – published *Russian Political Activists of 1917* (*Politicheskie deyateli Rossii 1917*), a biographical dictionary covering personalities from a wide range of parties and groups, and also handling such touchy subjects as Lenin and Trotsky with laudably balanced judgment. The root-and-branch reassessment of Lenin, however, has had to wait for another two-volume work by Volkogonov, based on the Lenin archives, due out in Russia in the summer and in the West in the autumn of 1994.

The opening up of the modern history archives in Russia has been something of an intermittent process. The archives of the Communist Party in various locations and various parts have been renamed: the Central Party Archives are now called the Russian Centre for the Preservation and Study of Contemporary Historical Documentation, or RTsKhIDNI, in its Russian acronym; while the former Central Committee archives are now known as the Russian Centre for the Preservation of Contemporary Documentation, or RTsKhSD. One of the richest and most varied repositories, the former Central Archives of the October Revolution (TsGAOR) has been merged with the Central State Archives of the Russian Federation and is called by the latter name (TsGARF). The former Special Archive, consisting of the national archive collections of the countries of Western Europe occupied by the Germans in the Second World War, and including, for instance, French security reports on the activities of Russian revolutionaries in Paris before and during the First World War, is now called the Centre for the Preservation of Historical Documentary Collections. Finally, one of the treasure-houses of Party history, the archives of the Moscow Party Organization, which contains, *inter alia*, the personal dossiers of the largest and most active membership group in the former Soviet Union, is now known as the Scientific and Informational Centre for the Political History of the City of Moscow.

In August 1991, virtually in its first act after the failed coup against its authority, the Russian government brought all these repositories under the single authority of the State Archive Service, or Russian Archive Commission (Rosarkhiv). In view of the inevitable disruption caused by such vigorous reorganization and changes of personnel, it is still too early to expect an abundant or systematic archival publication programme. Nevertheless, much valuable material is now appearing in various new journals devoted to the publication of extracts from the archives, most notably *Istoricheskii arkhiv* and *Istochnik*, and a new series of miscellanies called 'Unknown Russia' (*Neizvestnaya Rossiya*). It is the aim of all of these publications to spread their range of interest as wide as possible, with the result that they are bringing to light documents relating to the entire span of Russian history, from the medieval period to the end of the Soviet era. Well-established history journals which have survived from the previous regime reflect a similar trend. 'Questions of the history of the CPSU' (*Voprosy istorii KPSS*), which used to be published under the auspices of the Party Central Committee, in October 1991 was obscurely renamed 'The Centaur' (*Kentavr*) – perhaps to reflect the blatantly obvious fact that the Party was no longer a single, unambiguous species – and is now physically a very much reduced version of its predecessor. It can, however, be relied on to publish new material on the history of the Party of interest to scholars.

In the West, where Russian scholarship has been devoted to the analysis and interpretation of original sources, rather than the reproduction of the raw material, there have been numerous valuable additions to the library of the Russian Revolution. While it is not feasible here to produce an exhaustive inventory, nor practical to add to the Further Reading lists within the body of the Encyclopedia, the following works represent a core of up-to-date research to which any reader wishing to deepen his or her knowledge of the subject is recommended to turn:

Acton, E.: *Rethinking the Russian Revolution*. London: Edward Arnold, 1990; Connaughton, R.:

The Republic of the Ushakovka: Admiral Kolchak and the Allied Intervention in Siberia, 1918–1920. London: Routledge, 1990; Dabom, J.: *Russia: Revolution and Counter-revolution, 1917–1924.* Cambridge: Cambridge University Press, 1991; Elwood, R.C.: *Inessa Armand: Revolutionary and Feminist.* Cambridge: Cambridge University Press, 1992; Freeze, G.L.: *From Supplication to Revolution: A Documentary History of Imperial Russia.* Oxford: Oxford University Press, 1988; Galili y Garcia, Z.: *The Menshevik Leaders in the Russian Revolution: Social Realities and Political Strategies.* Princeton: Princeton University Press, 1989; Kemp-Welch, A., ed.: *The Ideas of Nikolai Bukharin.* Oxford: Oxford University Press, 1992; Koenker, D. and Rosenberg, W.: *Strikes and Revolution in Russia, 1917.* Princeton: Princeton University Press, 1989; Lincoln, W. Bruce: *Red Victory: A History of the Russian Civil War.* London: Sphere Books, 1990; McAuley, M.: *Bread and Justice: State and Society in Petrograd, 1917–1922.* Oxford: Oxford University Press, 1991; Melancon, M.: *The Socialist Revolutionaries and the Anti-war Movement, 1914–1917.* Columbus: Ohio State University Press, 1990; O'Connor, T.E.: *The Engineer of Revolution: L.B. Krasin and the Bolsheviks.* Oxford: Westview, 1992; Pipes, R.E.: *The Russian Revolution, 1899–1919.* London: Harvill Press, 1990, and its sequel, *Russia Under the New Régime*, published in 1994; Service, R.: *Lenin: A Political Life.* vol. 2, London: Macmillan, 1991; Stites, R.: *Revolutionary Dreams: Utopian Visions and the Experimental Life in the Russian Revolution.* New York: Oxford University Press, 1989; Volkogonov, D.A.: *Stalin: Triumph and Tragedy.* Transl. and ed. Shukman, H. London: Weidenfeld and Nicolson, 1991; Volkogonov, D.A.: *Lenin: His Life and Legacy.* Transl. and ed. Shukman, H. London: HarperCollins, 1994.

The purpose of this Encyclopedia is to describe and analyse the events of 1917 in Russia, as well as their background and origin, and to show how they affected the political, economic, social and ethnic structures of the old empire and gave rise to the new order. The Encyclopedia does not attempt to cover Russian society in its totality; it includes studies of revolutionary organizations, but not those of parties and bodies whose programmes and tactics were based on negotiation, reconciliation and evolution, rather than revolution. The period of reform beginning in the 1860s is taken as a starting point, and the coverage terminates roughly with the end of the Civil War in 1921, by which time the Bolsheviks had eliminated any serious threat from their internal political enemies. The multi-national character of the Russian Empire and the Soviet Union emerged with unprecedented (and unsurpassed) force during the events of 1917–21, and this is acknowledged in the wide-ranging treatment of revolution in the borderlands.

Depth can be added to the evolution of ideas and institutions, as well as the playing out of events, by the study of the lives of individual figures. A series of biographies has been included in the Encyclopedia, covering characters from all parties, as well as a number of leading figures of the old regime and the non-revolutionary parties (such as Nicholas II, Gapon, Guchkov, Lvov, Rasputin, Stolypin, Witte) whose activities compel their inclusion in a work devoted to the Revolution.

The Encyclopedia is designed as a source of reference for students and teachers of modern Russian history and politics and for the general reader wishing to extend and deepen an interest in this central event of twentieth-century history. Because an alphabetical arrangement of entries would lead to unnecessary duplication of material and possible confusion, the Encyclopedia has been arranged in an approximate chronological sequence, and the scheme of entries is clearly set out in the more than usually detailed contents list.

Each entry is intended to be complete in itself, but where it might be helpful to consult other entries, cross-references are printed in small capitals in the text. There is a general index at the end of the volume through which the reader can trace all references to a specific individual or topic. Most entries are followed by suggestions for further reading. Changes in this edition include the correction of typographical errors and the addition of a number of entries in the Biographical Section.

I owe thanks to the past and present staff of Basil Blackwell who have been involved in the conception, formation and production of this book: Janet Godden, Jo Hadley, Elizabeth Lake, Ann McCall, René Olivieri, Alyn Shipton and, above all, Carol Le Duc, whose alertness and commitment eliminated many of the flaws a less diligent editor might have let slip through. To Mary Hunt I am grateful for keying all the material in the hardback edition, and to Halina Boniszewska I am indebted for her help and the care with which this paperback edition has been prepared. My greatest debt of gratitude is to my contributors. Some responded to my invitation by recruiting additional authors, some made valuable suggestions for the content of the book, some contributed illustrations and, most important, all of them simplified my work by their professional approach, none more so than Felix Patrikeeff, who spotted gaps and expertly filled them with enviable despatch. The value of this book rests on the intrinsic quality of my contributors' expertise, which I have done my best to enhance.

Harold Shukman
March 1994

Acknowledgements

The illustrations in this book are reproduced by courtesy of the following: Richard Abraham, London, figures 2, 7, 14, 15 and 50; BBC Hulton Picture Library, London, figure 53; Bibliothèque Nationale, Paris, figure 55; Bodleian Library, Oxford, figure 44; Bulgarian National Library, Sofia, figure 74; Madame Colette Chambelland, Paris, figures 34, 35, 49, 56 and 58; Francis Conte, Paris, figure 68; from *Crapouillet* (1937), figure 3; Culver Pictures, figure 11; Dennis Dobson, London, figure 39; Michael Futrell, British Columbia, figure 71; Peter Gatrell, Manchester, figures 12 and 13; Sidney Harcave, New York, figures 10, 64, 73 and 79; Hoover Institution Archives, Stanford, figures 4 and 26; Houghton Library, Harvard, figures 24 and 69; Richard G. Hovannisian, UCLA, figures 54, and 75 (photographs, Bodleian Library); Imperial War Museum, London, figure 18; International Institute of Social History, Amsterdam, figures 45, 47, 48, 60, 61, 65, 77 and 80; David King, London, figures 5, 16, 17, 21, 22, 46 and 66; Boris Koreneff, Polytechnik, Australia, figure 38; George Leggett, London, figures 52, 63 and 76; from *Ace of Spies* (1967) by Robin Bruce Lockhart, figure 70; Robert McNeal, Massachusetts, figure 28; John Milner, Newcastle, figure 42; John Murray, London, figures 1 and 36; Museum of Modern Art, New York, figure 43; Barbara Norton, Pennsylvania, figure 57; Oxford University Press, figure 37; Oriental Research Partners, Cambridge, Massachusetts, figure 62; Pasternak Trust, Oxford, figure 27; Central Archive, Central Committee, Polish United Workers' Party, Warsaw, figures 8 and 9 (photographs, Richard Abraham); Harold Shukman, Oxford, figure 6; Sotamuseo, Helsinki, figures 32 and 33; Süddeutscher Verlag, Munich, figure 25; Richard Taylor, Swansea, figures 19, 20, 40, 41 and 59; Ukrainian Congress Committee of America, New York, figures 31 and 72; Ukrainian Free Academy of Sciences, New York, figures 29, 30, 51 and 78; Roger Viollet, Paris, figure 67; Wide World, London, figure 23.

Part 1 illustration: Street demonstration in Petrograd, 23 February 1917.
Part 2 illustration: Contemporary photomontage of the Bolshevik leaders of the Revolution (among whom Joseph Stalin does not appear).
Both by courtesy of David King, London.

The editor and publisher would also like to thank Martin Gilbert, London, for producing the map which appears as endpapers at the back of the book.

Contributors

Richard Abraham **RA**
London

Edward Acton **EDJLDA**
University of Liverpool

John Biggart **JB**
University of East Anglia

Edward Braun **EB**
University of Bristol

William E. Butler **WEB**
University College London

Francis Conte **FC**
Sorbonne, Paris

Nadia Diuk **ND**
Washington DC

Linda Edmondson **LE**
University of Birmingham

R. Carter Elwood **RCE**
Carleton University, Ottawa

John Erickson **JE**
University of Edinburgh

Michael Futrell **MHF**
University of British Columbia

Peter Gatrell **PWG**
University of Manchester

Israel Getzler **IG**
Hebrew University of Jerusalem

Graeme Gill **GJG**
University of Sydney

Michael Glenny **MVG**
Colchester

Sidney Harcave **SH**
State University of New York at Binghamton

Stephen F. Jones **SFJ**
*School of Slavonic and East European Studies,
University of London*

John Keep **JLHK**
University of Toronto

Peter Kenez **PK**
University of California, Santa Cruz

David Kirby **DGK**
*School of Slavonic and East European Studies,
University of London*

Baruch Knei-Paz **BK**
Hebrew University of Jerusalem

Lionel Kochan **LK**
Universty of Warwick

George Leggett **GHL**
London

David Longley **DAL**
University of Aberdeen

Evan Mawdsley **EM**
University of Glasgow

Martin McCauley **MMcC**
*School of Slavonic and East European Studies,
University of London*

Robert McNeal **RHMcN**
University of Massachusetts

John Milner **JM**
University of Newcastle-upon-Tyne

Barbara T. Norton **BTN**
Widener University, Pennsylvania

Alec Nove **AN**
University of Glasgow

Madhavan K. Palat **MKP**
Jawaharlal Nehru University, India

Felix Patrikeeff **FP**
Oxford

Contributors

Michael Perrins **MP**
University of Lancaster

D. Pospielovsky **DP**
University of Western Ontario

Azade-Ayse Rorlich **A-AR**
University of Southern California

Nurit Schleifman **NS**
Tel Aviv University

Gerald Seaman **GS**
University of Auckland

Robert Service **RS**
School of Slavonic and East European Studies, University of London

Harold Shukman **HS**
University of Oxford

Lewis Siegelbaum **LS**
Michigan State University

S. A. Smith **SAS**
University of Essex

Richard Taylor **RT**
University College of Swansea

Henry J. Tobias **HJT**
University of Oklahoma

Nicolas Walter **NW**
London

Howard White **HJW**
London School of Economics and Political Science

Alan Wood **AW**
University of Lancaster

Editorial Notes

Topography

The map bound as end-papers to this volume shows the entire area of the Russian Empire and Soviet Republic as it was between the 1860s and about 1921 – the period embraced by the Encyclopedia. Main cities and towns mentioned in the text are shown, as are the Trans-Siberian Railway and its branches, the main rivers and ethnic and borderland territories.

Marxism/Social Democracy

The terms Marxist and Social Democrat appear to some extent interchangeably in the text. The tsarist regime banned political organizations but not political philosophies. Thus, Marxists and those inclined towards Marxism were found among various groups. However, Social Democrats were the *organized* Marxists who composed the Russian Social Democratic Labour Party. Its Russian initials, RSDRP, are used throughout the Encyclopedia.

St Petersburg, Petrograd, Leningrad

The capital of the Russian Empire bore the name Sankt Peterburg, in its German form, until the outbreak of the First World War in August 1914, when it was Russified to become Petrograd, which it remained until Lenin's death in 1924. It then became and remained Leningrad until April 1993, when it reverted to its original name of St Petersburg.

Transliteration

It is impossible to transliterate Russian accurately, except by means of diacritical marks which require their own glossary. As long as there is no difficulty in recognizing Trotsky or Alexander, there seems little merit in insisting on Trotskii, Trotskiy or Trockij, and Aleksandr. Similarly, Peter has been used rather than Pyotr, Fedor rather than Fyodor. Such symbols as ' for the soft-sign have been dropped – we have become accustomed to seeing *glasnost* without it. However, in Further Reading and any bibliographical references, whole endings and soft-signs appear, as do any other apparatuses necessary to ensure the proper identification of a work.

In the presentation of Ukrainian names, their accepted appearance in Western usage has been adopted.

Dates

At the end of the sixteenth century most of Europe adopted the Gregorian or New Style Calendar, while the Russians retained the Julian or Old Style Calendar. By the nineteenth century Old Style dates lagged twelve days behind New Style; by the twentieth century the difference was thirteen days. For some time around the turn of the century, it became the custom (in Russian newspapers and private correspondence, for instance) to use both styles. Finally, on 14 February 1918, the Soviet government decreed that 1 February 1918, Old Style, was to become 14 February 1918,

New Style, and henceforth all dates were in conformity with the Gregorian calendar. The revolution itself, however, continued to be celebrated as the 'October Revolution'. In ambiguous cases, we have shown whether a date is Old Style, (OS), or New Style (NS).

Pseudonyms

Persecution by the tsarist police made pseudonyms commonplace among professional revolutionaries. As writers and underground organizers, both leading and minor activists changed their identities frequently, until their reputation in the movement (usually through journalistic activity) necessitated their establishing a single fixed label. (Curiously, with rare exceptions, women revolutionaries seem to have retained their real names throughout.) Following the Revolution, members of the Soviet government continued to use their old underground names: thus its head was Lenin, who added his pseudonym when signing decrees – V. I. Ulyanov (Lenin); the first president of the Comintern was Zinoviev, not Radomyslsky; the Red Army was organized by Trotsky, not Bronstein; and the eventual successor to Lenin was Stalin, not Dzhugashvili.

Since Jews (more than other minorities) were numerous in the Russian revolutionary movement, a pseudonym offered the added advantage of ethnic anonymity, and Jews therefore probably represent a disproportionate number among those with aliases.

Throughout the Encyclopedia, personalities are referred to by their most commonly-known names. Their other names, whether real or 'adopted, are given in the biographical entries and included in the Index as cross-references.

Historical facts about Russia's revolutionary past have been greatly enriched in the last two years or so by a flood of new and occasionally sensational writing, more in the Soviet popular, rather than academic, press. The Encyclopedia has attempted to reflect this; some previously obscure dates of death and (posthumous) rehabilitation are now known, such as those of Bukharin revealed in February 1988. However, where dates remain unknown, this is clearly stated, and where they are dubious, the given dates are accompanied by a question mark.

PART I

Introduction

The Russian Revolution of 1917, an event of incomparable importance no less in world history than in Russian history, was itself both an effect and a cause. It was the effect of a relatively short phase of government-inspired reforms; a relatively long tradition of political revolutionary organization; and the collapse of an exhausted administrative system under the impact of the FIRST WORLD WAR. It was the cause of failed imitations in Central Europe in the aftermath of 1918, of a re-play after the Second World War which has produced the present-day map, and of social, political and economic experiment in many countries of the Third World, and it resulted in the creation of an original system of administration whose chief features – centralized government and a command economy – remain in place today.

The government of Alexander II, emerging from Russia's defeat in the Crimean War, embarked in the 1860s and 1870s on a policy of reform designed to modernize the economy, to generate a large class of educated administrators and professionals, to introduce a degree of local autonomy into the provincial and municipal administration, to update the creaking legal system, and to 'de-feudalize' the army by making military service compulsory for all classes of the population. However, all these aims, worthy in themselves, were undertaken to bolster the strength of the state, not that of society. From the middle of the nineteenth century a pattern of reform and reaction, modernization and backwardness, is discernible in Russian social and political history; by the end of the century, in every section of society the stresses of change are unmistakable. The 1905 REVOLUTION graphically brought these tensions out onto the streets, but the state was strong enough to withstand the trauma. It was a trauma, however, that was far less in magnitude than the one inflicted by the First World War, a test of strength that of all the empires only the British survived intact, the Russian, the German, the Austro-Hungarian and the Ottoman all collapsing to create the new map of Europe and the Middle East.

Empires and regimes do not fall from economic or military stress alone: the internal ferment of ideology, the idea of reform and drastic change must also be present if the debilitated system is to be replaced by something more viable or vigorous. Across a broad front of educated opinion, ideas of change gathered force and the polarization of Russian society widened.

Emancipation of the serfs inspired ideas of universal civil rights, for there was no franchise in Russia, no free press, free speech or assembly, no representation. The autocracy of the tsar ruled through a centralized bureaucracy, backed up by a powerful police force. As the empire grew in size, marching eastwards from its European provinces to the Pacific, this administration plainly thinned out, but it redoubled its efforts in European Russia (and even abroad) to keep in check the growing number of forces ranged against it.

The local government institutions introduced under Alexander II embodied a degree of elective local representation in the zemtsvo, and planted the seed of universal representative government in the minds of the educated young people who worked in them and who were committed to their progressive role. It was at this level that WOMEN first found a practical social role in Russia, mainly as doctors and teachers in the villages, though they quickly widened their horizons to embrace revolutionary and political organization. Reformed law courts and the legal profession engendered ideas of law being made by elected representatives of the people, that is, of an elected legislature.

Alexander II also greatly increased the number of high schools and universities and institutions of higher learning, since a reformed and modernizing Russia would need large numbers of educated people to expand industry and commerce and staff the growing needs of the administration. While these expectations were largely met and graduates went on to become managers and entrepreneurs, doctors, lawyers and civil servants, the universities were also hothouses of seditious ideas and organization, even during the heyday of the reforms. Attempts made by student revolutionaries on the tsar's life, beginning in 1866 and succeeding in 1881, made a reactionary response almost inevitable, and politically the period from 1881 up to 1905 is one of almost unrelieved gloom against a background of unprecedented industrial growth and economic success. The ideology of monarchism narrowed and became more an ideology of defence which was uncreative and undynamic. Reform-minded bureaucrats, far-sighted enough to warn of approaching calamities, were overwhelmed by defensive conservatives who feared that further change would only bring further demand for change and end in disaster.

The events of 1905, taking place during a war against Japan that had gone disastrously for Russia, forced the tsar to concede a measure of representation, a pseudo-parliament, the State Duma. Like his grandfather's reforms, however, this half-hearted reform became a stick for his own back, for reports of debates in the chamber which voiced fierce criticism of the government and its failures, and even of scandals at court, now began to appear in the relatively free press. Publicity was something new for the Russian autocracy, and even the divinely-appointed tsar could not remain sacrosanct in the face of publicity showing him to be all too human. The scandalous presence of the lecherous charlatan, RASPUTIN, at the court of Nicholas II, well before the outbreak of the war, only accelerated the erosion of the tsar's image.

According to Marx the socialist revolution occurs at the peak of industrial development, when the ruling class owns a monopoly of capital and the enormously increased working class has reached the end of its tether. Russia in the early years of this century, however, was a country where eighty-six per cent of the population lived not in industrial towns but in the countryside. The great majority of these were PEASANTS who had been struggling since 1861 to make a success of agriculture, with varying results. At the time of emancipation and chiefly in the old gentry-estate regions, peasants had been provided with too little land at too high a price and under the restraint of collective ownership in communes; the burden of debt grew and the standard of living fell. In the newer grain-producing areas peasant plots were larger, private ownership had been encouraged, and the methods were more modern and efficient; the peasants' standard of living was higher and the complaint of land hunger less strident. Russia's vast peasant population, in other words, was not an undifferentiated mass: yet, illiterate and poor, emancipated but not liberated, the eternal supplier of conscripts for Russia's vast army, it was permeated by a sense of grievance.

To an overwhelming extent it was from this vast, backward peasantry that Russia's industrial workforce was recruited. The government of Alexander II and still more so that of his son, Alexander III, was determined to bring Russia into the nineteenth century, to strengthen her economy for the competition with the British, French and German empires that loomed ahead. Lacking native capital, the government borrowed heavily from abroad, offering high returns, government guarantees, high import tariffs to protect foreign investment. Massive grain exports and high domestic taxes helped to finance this arrangement and by 1897 the balance of trade was such that the ruble could be put on the gold standard.

Part of this rapid process was the sudden increase in the number of industrial WORKERS of all kinds, men uprooted from overcrowded, impoverished villages and thrust into gaunt workers' barracks in large cities and towns, taught the rudiments of machine work and factory labour under the crudest conditions. Although no new social or legal category of 'worker' was created to include them in the social hierarchy – nobility, clergy, lower middle class and peasantry – Russia's factory force quickly learned the practices of factory workers elsewhere, including that of self-help, organization, trade unions, strike funds, political consciousness.

'Consciousness', or ideology, was a dominant feature of modern Russian history. From the 1860s, POPULISTS, and after the turn of the century their successors, the SOCIALIST REVOLUTIONARIES, attempted to render the peasants aware that their position would only improve if they organized themselves collectively to take their fate into their own hands. These efforts largely failed. The peasants found politics, especially socialist politics, irrelevant. The peasants' goals were individual in character: the break-up of the agricultural commune and the attainment of more land for the family's holdings. MARXISM's appeal to the workers – 'You have nothing but your chains to lose' – fell on more fertile ground, for Russian workers as yet had no stake in the economy they were building under appalling conditions of work, in terms of hours, pay and amenities.

The successful application of such ideas was first carried out in the Russian Empire not by Russian Marxists, but by POLISH MARXISTS and Jewish Marxists organized later as the JEWISH BUND. These groups felt doubly disadvantaged, as exploited labour and oppressed nationalities, for the tsarist regime was nationalistic, anti-Semitic and hostile to all but the most backward of its minority peoples. Thus, by the turn of the century, the working class of much of the empire had learnt the ways of illegal trade unions and much of those of underground political organization.

Revolutionaries and labour organizers were not alone in bringing enlightenment to the workers: part of the credit belongs, if inadvertently, to the regime itself, notably to its police force, both uniformed and secret (the OKHRANA). The regime had been aware from the outset that workers, crowded together in manifestly poor conditions, could quickly become a source of unrest and civil disturbance. The Paris Commune of 1871 was a recent memory for the police authorities as much as it was for the Socialist International. The surveillance that existed chiefly to monitor and frustrate the activities of the organized revolutionaries also therefore became a feature of workers' lives, and strikes often became demonstrations as the heavy hand of the state helped to defend the bosses' interests.

1905 is commonly called the dress rehearsal for 1917 and the parallel is apt in many ways. There was the almost total confrontation of society with the regime, the most widespread and open call for political change ever seen in Russia, the unprecedented crowds that would become a feature of the capitals in 1917. The Russo-Japanese War, like the First World War, meant that many more men than usual were uniformed and armed, and while this would be a key feature of 1917, in 1905 it was partly the state's inability to recall large forces from the Far East to restore order, that forced Nicholas II to make concessions. Though the regime recovered from the events of 1905, its mood was one of defensiveness thereafter: how many such onslaughts could it withstand and survive?

For labour politics, 1905 was also a turning point. The Petrograd Council of Workers' Deputies, or the SOVIET, came into being as a general strike committee, an extension of past economic experience with a political dimension. Was it the embryo of workers' government? Putting the question implied the answer. To the SOCIAL DEMOCRATS, that is the young Marxists who had tried to organize them in the 1890s, the workers owed at least their awareness that only by combining their efforts could they achieve an improvement in their lot. But the workers had responded badly to the split in the ranks of the Social Democrats into BOLSHEVIKS and MENSHEVIKS in 1903, for it implied a demand to divide their own fragile efforts along these new sectarian lines. In 1905 the workers felt they could focus their efforts without proclaiming allegiance to a party: the Soviet carried no partisan labels, though many Social Democrats and Socialist Revolutionaries were involved in its actions and statements.

The strain of modern war for which Russia was not prepared, the heightened pressure of politicians of the opposition parties in the Duma which focused increasingly on the personal behaviour of the royal family and exploited their fatal friendship with Rasputin, the politicians' denunciations of the government's inefficiency, and indeed the inefficiency itself, all proved too great a weight for the absolutist structure. In February 1917 demonstrations against food and fuel shortages in the capital got out of hand; mutinous troops joined the demonstrators, the government lost its head, and a PROVISIONAL GOVERNMENT, consisting mainly of liberal Duma politicians, took over. Isolated from all his supporters the tsar abdicated, his successor declined the crown and the Romanov dynasty came to a close.

The new government, liberal and democrat in spirit, immediately enacted civil and political equality, freedom of speech and the press, an unusual step in the middle of a major war and one that as much as anything led to the Provisional Government's downfall eight months later.

The workers' and revolutionaries' experience of 1905 was revived during the FEBRUARY REVOLUTION, the Petrograd Soviet coming into being at virtually the same moment as the Provisional Government. Claiming to represent the Petrograd workers' and soldiers' committees which mushroomed in the rear and at the front, the Soviet exercised a power that became the hallmark of 1917 in Russia: the power of popular democracy standing in judgement over the liberal government's actions.

The government that had come into being in order to improve on the tsar's war effort and to bring Russia victory, was on a collision course with popular opinion almost from the start. While Russians wished for victory, the abdication of the tsar had been popularly perceived as the beginning of the end of the war, since the tsar, as supreme commander, had been so clearly identified with its continuation. Therefore, as long as the Provisional Government prosecuted an active war effort, it was a target for anti-war agitation.

The thought that the war might end without giving birth to the socialist revolution had obsessed LENIN. Never had the international working class been so armed, never had the war aims of the imperialists been so plain to see. The IDEA OF WORLD REVOLUTION, sparked in one country and igniting elsewhere, seemed realistic when Europe was entering its third year of war and manpower and economic resources were being consumed at a horrific rate. But in Russia, as in all the other belligerent countries, Lenin's defeatist propaganda made no headway before February 1917: however unpopular the war might be, defeatism was not an attractive alternative, and in any case, the Russian secret police did not slumber during the war. Returning to Petrograd in April 1917 with the help of the German government, Lenin at once put his ideas into practice, and by the summer desertion and fraternization were a feature of frontline life for the Russian soldier. The great army of peasants-in-uniform, while impervious to socialist propaganda, readily understood the call to stop fighting and to return to their villages to claim their share of the land from the now powerless landlords. In this way the still small force of Russia's working class, whom the Bolsheviks claimed to lead as the vanguard of the socialist revolution, had the tacit support of the unwitting majority. Much of the energy and militancy of the soviets in 1917 derived from this alliance.

As the Russian army disintegrated, the Provisional Government lost its grip on the military leadership. Fearing a right-wing *putsch*, its leader, KERENSKY, turned to the soviets, arming them against an attack. No attack came but the Bolsheviks, who were growing in number in the soviets, were now armed. The government had thus virtually destroyed its own military support, and power, as TROTSKY put it, was lying in the streets waiting to be picked up. On October 25 (OS) and in the name of the soviets, not of any party, the Bolsheviks carried out the OCTOBER REVOLUTION.

The ideas of civil liberty, which had aroused educated Russian opinion and mobilized workers, had found an echo among most of the Russian Empire's national minorities where it re-emerged as national liberation. Among the minorities in the European provinces (Poles, JEWS), the UKRAINE, the BALTIC (Latvians, Estonians, Finns), TRANSCAUCASIA (Armenians and Georgians), and among the widespread Muslim population of the Volga and Central Asia, (Tatars, Uzbeks, Kazakhs, Turkmens and Tadzhiks), the idea of national progress was involved with changing to varying degrees the relationship of the group with the Russian state. The February Revolution, and even more so the Bolshevik takeover, appeared to have provided the opportunity for such change to occur, and it was therefore inevitable that much of the fighting during the CIVIL WAR would take place on territory claimed by one or another of these minorities.

The Bolsheviks had not seized power solely in order to take Russia out of the war, though that had been and would remain their immediate priority. They had seized power in order to transform backward Russia into the first communist society in history and one, moreover, whose survival could well depend on similar revolutions taking place elsewhere. Various stages would have to be gone through before that condition was reached, of course. First, in an overwhelmingly peasant country the Bolsheviks were aware that their only natural allies were the workers. Therefore the workers' state, the dictatorship of the proletariat, would start the process. Political and armed opposition would be eliminated through the combined effects of the Civil War and the political police (VECHEKA); social enemies, the middle classes who had not emigrated by 1921, would be reduced by economic discrimination as the working class was favoured and advanced; the Russian ORTHODOX CHURCH, along with other alternative spiritual resorts, would be severely repressed; the peasants would at first be coerced through the policy of WAR COMMUNISM, and then, under the New Economic Policy of March 1921, seduced into feeding the state. The institutions created by the Bolshevik government to effect these policies, and indeed the administrative *style* of those institutions guided by the new government, the Council of People's Commissars, would retain both the structure and atmosphere of the state that remained long after Lenin had departed the scene in 1924.

Our approach has been to describe the condition and development of each topic before 1917, and to examine its fate during and in the aftermath of the October Revolution: 1917 is our rough benchmark. The chief focus of this *Encyclopedia*, therefore, rests on the period beginning with the emergence of the revolutionary movement and ending with the defeat of the Bolsheviks' political enemies in 1921. It would have been possible, for example, to begin with the Decembrist Uprising of 1825 as the first effort in Russia to overthrow the sovereign and introduce the ideas of the French Revolution, and to end at the collectivization of agriculture in 1930 as the demise of the peasant problem launched essentially in the 1860s. But the Decembrists did not create the revolutionary movement and so their Uprising does not really represent a 'beginning', and collectivization – brutal and thorough though it was – was almost at once diluted by the restoration of the private plot in order yet again to recruit peasant aid, and so does not really represent an 'ending'. Furthermore, to have gone further back and further forward would have meant producing an encyclopedia of Russian and Soviet history, and this was not our intention. Readers will nevertheless find that in many entries, both articles and biographies, the cut-off is not sharp, and that the momentum of events or of a life is often allowed its natural span.

The idea of 'revolution' had also gone beyond the sphere of national liberation, economic management and political reorganization into the realm of the arts. While many Russian writers, of whom the most significant was Dostoevsky, had dreaded the advance of the socialist idea and what they saw as its dehumanizing, anonymous energy, others espoused its humanitarian concern for the underdog and its egalitarian assault on privilege and bourgeois hypocrisy. Of the writers of the nineteenth and twentieth centuries who were on the side of the revolution, GORKY, BLOK and MAYAKOVSKY have been chosen here to represent those most involved in the practices of the revolutionary movement and the 1917 revolution itself.

The attitudes of painters, sculptors, theatre directors and composers were similarly aroused by hopes of social and spiritual renewal through the violent breakdown of the old order. Modern artists – Russian modernists were among the avant-garde of European art even before 1914 – identified their own iconoclasm, their own obsession with the fundamentals of art, with the social iconoclasm of the revolution. The symbols of the revolution during the phase we deal with here are indeed those of the modernist movement, whether in the design of the Hammer and Sickle or of Lenin's Mausoleum. It turned out that the artists had misread the cultural intentions of the new regime: a regime whose organizing principle was that of centralization and command found conservative artists more to their taste, both aesthetically and politically, and the modernists were quickly submerged either in industrial design and photography, or emigration. Their contribution nevertheless left an indelible mark of excitement and experimentation during the first phase and Soviet art never again showed comparable signs of life (see CULTURAL REVOLUTION; ART; THEATRE; CINEMA; MUSIC; BALLET).

An aspect of the revolution itself was the wave of EMIGRATION it triggered, varied as much in the social background of the refugees, or émigrés as they were to become known, as in the directions they took, and here the story is allowed to run its natural course even though it carries us beyond the main period dealt with.

The second part of the book contains a selection of biographies arranged alphabetically, partly to include some of the best known and most important figures in each of the topics dealt with in a main article, partly to present a cross-section of personalities whose names may be virtually unknown, but whose lives convey something of the way people either came to be revolutionaries or were involved in the revolution, and to reveal the range of intellectual and other influences that came to bear on their lives. This selection owes as much to the preferences of individual contributors as it does to the Editor's initiative.   HS

Historical Interpretations of the Revolution

The OCTOBER REVOLUTION occupies the strategic centre of contemporary history. Its repercussions and the issues it raised were of momentous importance, for East and West, for the developed and undeveloped world alike. As a result, different interpretations of the events of 1917 have served to mould, reinforce and entrench sharply conflicting views of the modern era as a whole, and few fields of history have remained more heavily politicized. The main line of historiographical development may be traced by examining three broad schools of thought – Soviet, liberal and 'libertarian'. Yet since the 1960s a number of scholars working in the West have begun to break the mould and have developed a fourth school, the revisionist. They have carried out a wealth of painstaking research while consciously seeking to resist the presuppositions of the established camps.

The Soviet view

For Soviet historians, the Great October Socialist Revolution is the greatest event in history. It dealt a stunning blow to the system of exploitation of one man by another on which the established order had rested; it opened the way for the construction of socialism in an area covering one sixth of the globe; and it created a powerful base of support for progressive movements across the world.

The revolution, in the Soviet view, provides irrefutable proof of the laws of history discovered by Marx and 'creatively developed' by LENIN. It presents the prototype of the transformation for which all capitalist societies are destined (see THE IDEA OF WORLD REVOLUTION). Capitalism in the advanced countries had, by the end of the nineteenth century, reached its highest and last stage – imperialism. The contradictions between bourgeois society based on private ownership and the market economy on the one hand, and the enormous productive power of large-scale factory industry on the other, had reached the point of explosion. The class struggle between bourgeoisie and proletariat became ever more intense: mounting economic crises followed in rapid succession and spilled over into the catastrophe of the FIRST WORLD WAR. The necessary economic and social conditions had been created for the overthrow of capitalism and the construction of socialism.

Just as Lenin had foreseen, revolution broke out initially not where imperialism was most strongly developed but 'at the weakest link in the imperialist chain': Russia. Here, imperialism had developed alongside a semi-feudal agrarian structure and the bourgeoisie had proven too feeble to overthrow the absolute monarchy. The first revolution on the Russian agenda, therefore, was the bourgeois-democratic overthrow of tsarism and abolition of feudal remnants. But by taking the lead in the bourgeois-democratic revolution of February, the proletariat, in alliance with the poor peasantry, was able to push straight forward towards the socialist revolution.

Moreover, as Lenin had insisted, the success of the revolution depended on the presence not only of the appropriate 'objective' social and economic conditions, but also of the necessary 'subjective' conditions. Here the critical role belonged to the BOLSHEVIK PARTY. This

Marxist party 'of a new type' united the most advanced sections of the working class in a democratic but centralized and disciplined body, free from the bourgeois reformism which sapped western workers' movements. It was the party which raised the 'spontaneous' protest of the proletariat into a fully class-conscious and organized socialist revolutionary movement. And it was precisely because Lenin's party was informed by Marx's scientific understanding of the historical process and the objective interests of the proletariat that it was able to provide unerring strategic and tactical guidance. Under the party's leadership, according to this view, the proletariat established hegemony over the mass movement which brought the tsarist regime to its knees in 1905 and overthrew it in February 1917. This foredoomed the attempts of the PROVISIONAL GOVERNMENT to consolidate the rule of the bourgeoisie. During 1917 the vanguard party opened the eyes of the more backward sections of the proletariat and the working masses to the reactionary nature of the petit-bourgeois and liberal parties, drew the poor peasants into alliance with them, and carried through the epoch-making OCTOBER REVOLUTION. With Soviet democracy established, the party led the people to triumph over the forces of counter-revolution and foreign imperialism and proceeded to the construction of socialism.

To outsiders, the Soviet view is rendered implausible by the fact that it is upheld by the overt exercise of political control. As early as 1920 a special commission on the history of the party and the October Revolution was set up and empowered to gather all relevant documentary material – from the archives of the party to those of the OKHRANA. Access to the archives was jealously guarded, and censorship of 'counter-revolutionary distortions' was instituted. During the 1920s, the memoirs and documentary editions published reflected a relatively wide range of Marxist approaches (see SKVORTSOV; CULTURAL IMPACT OF THE REVOLUTION). But at the end of the twenties dissentient voices, castigated by STALIN as 'hopeless bureaucrats' and 'archive rats', were silenced. By 1938 the *Short History of the Communist Party* (known as *Short Course*) had enshrined the most simplistic and rigid line of interpretation: Stalin's own role was inflated out of all proportion, the treachery of his various defeated rivals was traced to their earliest participation in the party, and the MENSHEVIKS and SOCIALIST REVOLUTIONARIES were dismissed as malicious saboteurs. It was unthinkable to cast doubt on the authorized version: major facets of the revolution became too dangerous for scholars to touch and the flow of documentary publications all but dried up.

The Stalinist phase did virtually irreparable damage to the reputation of Soviet historiography. A body of 'scholars' who tolerated such flagrant abuse of documentary evidence forfeited all credibility. Following Stalin's death in 1953, however, historiography shared in the general thaw in cultural life. The *Short Course* was withdrawn and Stalin

cut down to size. Access to archives was eased, and a flood of new and less tendentiously edited documentary collections began to appear. Memoirs from the twenties, for long consigned to oblivion, began to be used again; the number, professional competence and self-confidence of historians in higher education rose rapidly, and knowledge of the work of western scholars increased significantly. On secondary issues, the party line has gradually become less monolithic and clear-cut. New evidence introduced to bolster the orthodox view in one field frequently carries unforeseen implications for orthodoxy in another and impels more nuanced interpretation. The account given has to carry conviction with a better-educated, more discriminating public, and to provide a solid base for the growing number of review articles and monographs devoted to exposure of 'bourgeois falsifications' emanating from the West.

As a result, since 1956 new studies have been undertaken on every aspect of the revolution. There has been much more sophisticated treatment of the pre-revolutionary economy and the case for including Russia among the countries which had entered the imperialist phase of capitalism. Quantitative methods have been applied to social developments not only at the centre but also among the national minorities. There has been more careful analysis of the relative weight of 'spontaneous' and 'conscious', party-organized protest, of the change of political consciousness among workers in different cities and individual factories, among soldiers in different sections of the front and rear, among peasants in different regions of the country. Treatment of the SRs, the Mensheviks, and even the Kadets and the Right has been less polemical and based more closely on archival material. The Bolshevik Party has remained hallowed ground, but immense energy has been devoted to substantiating the claims made on its behalf, to tracing its growing influence across the country, and there has even been somewhat more critical discussion of divisions within it. Successive new syntheses on the history of the revolution have appeared, and with each edition they have tended to become more detailed, subtle and refined.

The basic propositions of the Marxist-Leninist interpretation remain firmly in place. Lenin's works continue to be regarded as the fundamental source for the study not merely of his own activity, but of any and every aspect of the revolution. Soviet historians continue to work under the supervision of a complex web of party bodies ultimately responsible to the Central Committee. Access to the more sensitive archives is still narrowly restricted, and blatant distortions, such as the underrating of the role of TROTSKY, remain. Monographs treating potentially contentious areas tend to be published in very restricted editions, and individual historians who advance unwelcome ideas run the risk of public reprimand and expulsion from the profession. Yet, while Soviet historiography has not ceased to celebrate the Revolution as the supreme vindication of

Marxism-Leninism and the source of legitimacy of the Central Committee today, its standards of scholarship have earned for it a new respect.

The liberal view

In the West, the historiography of the revolution has long been dominated by liberal scholars. The liberal tradition is rooted in an approach to history fundamentally at odds with that of Marxism-Leninism. The historical process is regarded as altogether too rich and complex to be reduced to the laws of historical materialism and the dictates of class struggle. 'Classes' are in reality neither homogeneous nor tidily defined and their 'objective interests' are far from self-evident. The significance of class struggle is often outweighed by that of countervailing divisions – cultural, religious, national. The century since Marx's death has belied his expectation that advanced industrial society would witness ever sharper polarization between bourgeoisie and proletariat, and falsified the Soviet claim that October blazed the trail for which all humanity is destined.

Nowhere does the liberal approach more directly contradict that of Marxism-Leninism than in its treatment of the political process. Political struggle is seen as a more or less autonomous factor in the historical process. The leading actors in the historical drama are credited with an independence and causative role of their own. It is those at the summit who make the decisive moves in history, who provide the key to any historical situation. They are to be understood as human beings, and not as representatives of this or that class interest. It was the actions, the policies, the judgement, motives, principles and ambitions, the skill and lack of it of NICHOLAS II and MILYUKOV, KERENSKY and Lenin which were decisive.

The corollary of this emphasis on the crucial importance and autonomy of the political leadership is the liberal treatment of the role of the masses as essentially subordinate. In a backward, largely illiterate society such as late Imperial Russia, the intervention of the masses tended to be anarchic and destructive. They oscillated between passivity and elemental violence, inspired by blind resentment and irrational hope. Ignorant, politically immature, with no grasp of the real issues at stake, they were guided by the vagaries of rumour or the propaganda and rabble-rousing of rival political activists. In the liberal view, although harsh material conditions may have predisposed the Russian masses to revolt, the occasion and the outcome of their intervention depended upon the interplay between the leading figures on the political stage.

The revolution, therefore, far from conforming to universally valid laws of history, was the product of an historical conjuncture fortuitous in itself and unique to Russia. It is to be explained in large measure in terms of the impact of total war upon a country at the most delicate stage of modernization. The militancy of the working class reflected the early stage of industrialization, the speed with which peasants were being drawn into ill-prepared cities, the primitive rebelliousness of undisciplined youth and disoriented peasant-workers. The restiveness of the peasantry arose from the country's agricultural backwardness at a time of population explosion. The dramatic collapse of the tsarist regime owed much to the fatal blend of intransigence and incompetence of Nicholas II. The failure of the liberals and moderate socialists resulted from the inept if well-meaning policies of their leaders, the continuing strain of the war, and the lack of political experience and sophistication of the masses. October was the product of unscrupulous manipulation by a conspiratorial revolutionary elite led by a man consumed with the lust for power. The claim that the Bolshevik triumph was an expression of the will of the Russian masses is as ill-founded as the belief that it was the ineluctable outcome of intensifying class struggle.

Just as Soviet historians see in post-revolutionary developments confirmation of their interpretation, so for liberal historians the Soviet record bears out the undemocratic nature of the Bolshevik victory. From the barbarous excesses of the CIVIL WAR and suppression of all rival parties, through Stalin's collectivization, forced industrialization, and Great Terror, to the dictatorial means used to install Communist regimes in Eastern Europe after 1945, the regime has epitomized all that is authoritarian. Even when Stalin's successors edged towards détente, ran down the labour camps, and showed a new concern to reduce overt coercion, the party dictatorship born in October continued to rely on methods of social control which denied the most basic civil liberties.

Liberal historiography has focused upon the political and ideological antecedents of the revolution, the ideas and activities of the government and the liberal, moderate socialist and Bolshevik parties, rather than on social and economic developments. In the early decades, much use was made of the memoirs which began to pour forth in the 1920s, from figures at court and in the army, from foreign diplomats and correspondents, and from political leaders across the political spectrum. And it was those of liberal and moderate socialist leaders, men like Milyukov and Kerensky, which exerted greatest influence. In part, of course, this simply reflected the fact that Soviet archives were closed to western scholars, while during the Stalin era the documents and memoirs published in the Soviet Union were sparse and manifestly tendentious. But even the much richer Soviet collections issued in the twenties were given relatively little attention. A number of documentary collections, some of them drawing on Soviet publications, were compiled by western scholars, but they tended to bear the strong imprint of liberal editorship and to concentrate on political rather than socio-economic material. When access to primary sources began to improve from the late 1950s and 1960s, the range of liberal studies broadened, significant new ground being broken in the treatment of events outside Petrograd and among the national minorities. But the major contours of the liberal approach remained unchanged. Although by the mid 1980s the western consensus based on the traditional liberal interpretation had broken down, many of the most eminent scholars in the field remained firmly committed to it and it continued to inform conventional wisdom among non-specialists.

The libertarian view

A third view of the revolution has been developed by writers on the far left of the political spectrum. Historians belonging to this 'libertarian' current are inspired by a vision of human potential for social harmony and individual fulfilment of which history has witnessed no more than the faintest inkling. Here the centre-stage of the revolution is occupied by the masses, ordinary men and women, anonymous workers, peasants and soldiers. Their rejection of the authority of tsar, bourgeoisie and moderate socialists alike, and their sustained assault upon the State and private property, is celebrated as one of the greatest expressions of man's striving after true liberty. Protest which Soviet historians dismiss as 'spontaneous' and unreflecting, and which liberal historians see as mindless and destructive, libertarians regard as the central drama of the revolution. But the mass movement which had swept away tsarism and the Provisional Government was mastered, curbed and ultimately crushed by Lenin and his party. The Bolshevik triumph marked not the fulfilment but the failure of the revolutionary promise of 1917.

This point of view was articulated in the immediate aftermath of the revolution by anarchist writers (see ANARCHISM) who championed the resistance to Bolshevik rule which culminated in the KRONSTADT REVOLT of 1921. But criticism of October from the Left was at first muted by the Soviet image as the centre of the world revolutionary movement. After 1945, however, that image rapidly became tarnished. The xenophobia and repression associated with Stalin's last years belied the Soviet Union's internationalist pretensions and the successive rebellions against Soviet-backed regimes – in East Germany in 1953, in Poland and Hungary in 1956, in Czechoslovakia in 1968 and in Poland in the early 1980s – progressively undermined the allegiance of foreign radicals to the USSR. This bristling empire built on the bones of peasants and political prisoners and denying the most fundamental rights to the workers themselves seemed more and more a mere mirror image of the capitalist system. Critiques of the bureaucratic and oppressive nature of Soviet-style 'socialism' from within Eastern Europe began to coalesce with the variety of western radical currents dubbed the 'New Left'.

Two themes stand out in libertarian treatment of the revolution. The first concerns the issue of self-management by workers and peasants. It is the distribution of power at the point of production that is regarded as the critical question, the acid test of socialism. Wherever those who produce are subordinated to those who manage production, society will be marked by division, the masses oppressed, and human potential stunted. Attention has focused in particular upon the FACTORY COMMITTEES, the grass-roots organizations which began to be formed immediately after February, and which represent, in the libertarian view, the aspiration of the Russian proletariat to take control of their own lives. After October there was a fierce but unequal struggle between the workers' movement for self-management and the Bolsheviks' determination to absorb the Factory Committees into the trade unions, establish rigid party control over the trade unions, and concentrate managerial power in the hands of the centralized State. And once the State had established the right to appoint management from above, the division between officials and workers at the bench rapidly widened. The crucial power was torn from the hands of the proletariat and the Bolsheviks were free to extend hierarchical control over the peasantry, the army, the press and political life.

The second major concern of libertarian writers is to trace the roots of what they regard as the elitist, coercive nature of the regime established by the Bolsheviks. Far from representing the vanguard of the proletariat, as it claimed, the party represented an entirely different class – that of 'intellectuals'. This new class embraced on the one hand the 'marginal intelligentsia' of Imperial society, and on the other the middle-ranking officers and bureaucrats of the old regime. In their different ways both sought forceful economic modernization of backward Russia, and both aspired to monopolize power over the distribution of wealth in the new society. Sincere though the ideals of Lenin and his allies may have been, Marxism served as a mystifying ideology and masked even from its strongest supporters the real ambitions of its intelligentsia. And after the revolution the two strata merged to form a ruling class which repressed and exploited workers and peasants as brutally as did the capitalists of the West.

The libertarian view is still barely acknowledged by Soviet historians, and is treated by most western historians as academically not wholly respectable. For its adherents, however, this unholy alliance is evidence of the common interest of the Soviet and the western establishments in suppressing a revolutionary vision which threatens both.

The revisionist view

So sharply have the battle-lines been drawn between the Soviet, liberal and libertarian schools of thought that fruitful debate between them has been all but impossible. Adherents of each have tended to discount the work of the others as the product of brainwashing, special-pleading or wishful-thinking.

The emergence of a 'revisionist' school among western historians was made possible by the easing of tension between East and West from the mid 1950s. To question the liberal account was no longer tantamount to endorsing Communist rule. Disenchantment with the liberal establishment characteristic of the 1960s began to find expression in the work of a new generation of scholars at major universities and research institutes. They began to apply to the revolution the techniques and approaches, the concern with social history and with quantitative methods, already being widely applied in less politically sensitive fields. Moreover, following the Second World War, there was a great expansion of Russian studies in the West – in the USA, Britain, France, West Germany and, rather later, in Israel and Japan. The number of Russian and Soviet specialists increased dramatically. In no country was a concerted research plan adopted, but the resources became available for more detailed social, economic and institutional study of the revolution. Scholars began to make full use of the primary material published in the Soviet Union in the 1920s; the cultural thaw within the Soviet Union increased western readiness to take seriously new research by Soviet scholars; from the late 1950s a series of cultural exchange agreements between the USSR and the major western democracies facilitated scholars' access to Soviet libraries and, to a much more limited extent, to archives.

As yet, the 'revisionists' have set about dismantling separate aspects of the traditional liberal view rather than replacing it with any comprehensive new synthesis. They have called into question the likelihood of stable capitalist and western-style democratic development in Russia even without the advent of the First World War. They have devoted much closer attention to the aspirations and dynamics of mass discontent. They have treated with new respect Bolshevik claims to popular support. Soviet historians, while regarding some aspects of this new work as evidence of progress in western historiography, have continued to reject the bulk of it as a new species of 'bourgeois falsification'. Adherents of the traditional liberal view have questioned the reliability of the sources on which this work is based and criticized it for re-establishing 'old pro-Bolshevik legends' about the period. Yet many 'revisionist' arguments have begun to gain a wide measure of acceptance amongst western specialists.

The major thrust of this recent research has been in two directions. First, it has begun to examine the revolution 'from below', to penetrate beneath the world of high politics to developments in the factory, in the village, in the armed forces. Detailed monographs, based on the contemporary press, on memoirs, on resolutions passed in villages, at factory gates and in soldiers' committees, have dealt with the way in which the revolution was viewed by workers, peasants, soldiers and sailors. This approach has challenged

the assumption that the revolution can be understood primarily by examining the major actors on the political scene. It takes seriously the aspirations of the masses themselves; it credits them with an independence, sense of direction and rationality of their own; it suggests that the masses acted upon the political leaders as much as being acted upon by them. One implication is that the root cause both of the fall of tsarism and the failure of the liberals and moderate socialists lies much deeper than in the traditional liberal interpretation. Another is that the view of October as the product of a truly mass revolutionary movement is not so wide of the mark. Equally, however, revisionist work refutes many aspects of the Soviet portrayal of the Bolshevik Party – the depth of its influence before February, its organizational coherence during 1917, and its popularity after October. Indeed a major concern of the revisionists has been to explain how the seemingly irresistible popular and egalitarian movement of 1917 gave rise so rapidly to a monolithic Bolshevik dictatorship for which they hold no brief at all.

This is the problem addressed by the second major thrust of revisionist research: detailed analysis of the mass organizations – soviets, soldiers' committees, factory committees, peasant committees, trade unions, Red Guards, and the Bolshevik Party itself – which burgeoned during the revolution. It explores the roles played by these organizations. It traces the relationships between them. It examines the way in which their democratic processes worked, and the differences in power and outlook between their executive committees and their rank-and-file membership. Much of this work has yet to be drawn together into a coherent synthesis. But it points towards an understanding of the revolution which, while lending support to specific features of each of the three traditional schools of thought, supersedes them all.   EDJLDA

Further Reading

Baron, S.H. and Heer, N.W. eds.: *Windows on the Russian Past: Essays on Soviet Historiography since Stalin.* Columbus, Ohio: 1977.

Heer, N.W.: *Politics and History in the Soviet Union.* Cambridge, Mass.: 1971.

Menasche, L.: Demystifying the Russian Revolution. *Radical History Review* 18 (1978) 142–54.

Mints, I.I. et al: *Kritika osnovnykh kontseptsii sovremennoi burzhuaznoi istoriografii trekh rossiiskikh revolyutsii.* Moscow: 1983.

Naumov, V.P. ed.: *Sovetskaya istoriografiya fevral'skoi burzhuazno-demokraticheskoi revolyutsii. Leninskaya kontseptsiya istorii Fevralya i kritika ee fal'sifikatorov.* Moscow: 1979.

Suny, R.G.: Towards a Social History of the October Revolution. *American Historical Review* 88 (1983) 31–52.

Russian Society and Institutions before and after 1917

The first section of the Encyclopedia surveys the principal institutions and strata of society which played a part in the events leading up to the revolution of 1917 and in the revolution itself. Obviously, Russian society comprehended more groups than those surveyed in this section, but the peasantry, the workers, the army, the women's movement, the Church and the secret police played sufficiently important parts in the chain of revolutionary events to merit separate discussion.

Seeking to stabilize the autocracy, Alexander II launched reforms which only encouraged a desire for more radical change, including representation, democracy and the abolition of the autocracy itself. To turn back the tide, Alexander III, after his father's assassination, imposed a harsh regime of repression which drew on traditional Russian values of conservatism, Christian piety and nationalism. In response, Russian society became increasingly polarized as a revolutionary movement arose, based on the internationalist platform of Marxism, which found its natural allies among the nascent national liberation movements of the anti-Russian ethnic minorities of the Empire.

Russia's vast peasant population, eighty per cent of the total, was becoming restive. While some had gained from the emancipation of 1861, the majority had too little land and too much debt. The 1905 REVOLUTION was even more violent in the countryside than in the towns. The FIRST WORLD WAR increased the pressure on the peasant economy by mobilizing their manpower, but it also armed a vast number of men who by 1917 were ripe for agitation which called on them to lay down their arms and return to their villages to claim the land that the Bolsheviks were promising. Peasant-Bolshevik comradeship, however, was shortlived. By its policy of WAR COMMUNISM, the Soviet government imposed draconian demands for food and soon the peasant economy almost ceased to exist. In 1921 Lenin recognized the need to make concessions to the peasants and his New Economic Policy temporarily reintroduced a market economy for small producers.

One of the goals of the emancipation had been to recruit labour into new industries. By the end of the nineteenth century the number of workers in all branches of the urban and industrial economy had duly grown rapidly and in terms of coal output, iron, steel, oil and wheat production, Russia had become a factor on the world markets, but at great social cost to the workers. Bereft of family and village life, Russia's new working class of ex-peasants, illiterate, unskilled and ignorant, were poorly paid and housed, harshly treated and felt themselves uprooted. They were moreover regarded by the police as a potential source of unrest. Workers' organizations were to the fore in the 'dress rehearsal' of 1905, and the OCTOBER REVOLUTION created the first 'Workers' State'. It was not long before discord arose between the workers' organizations and the BOLSHEVIKS over what this term was to mean in practice.

Women also had their grievances. Illiteracy, economic exploitation and inferior status made fertile soil for protest. Prompted by the reforms of Alexander II, the early stirring of a women's movement soon diversified into a wide range of activities, including women's education, philanthropy and in due course political organization. In many respects, 1917 yielded the results women wished for.

A tool of the State since the early eighteenth century, the Russian Orthodox Church lacked the intellectual independence and vigour to counter the spread of new ideas, and it became increasingly identified with a backward-looking, defensive regime. Attempting to remain politically neutral in the CIVIL WAR, the Church inevitably became a focus of comfort and spiritual reassurance in the hard times of 1917 to 1921. Its position, however, was ultimately made untenable by a combination of Bolshevik militant atheism and the activities of its émigré elements.

A modernized, industrialized Russia that would hold its own with the other great powers also needed a modern army to march in step with society. Alexander II's reforms abolished the recruitment of peasants for twenty-five years, and instituted universal conscription for far shorter periods. By greatly increasing the re-cycling of citizens and soldiers, the government hoped to keep the army in step with social change, to create a 'nation-in-arms'. While in peacetime the army remained predominantly peasant, the Russo-Japanese War and more dramatically the First World War drew all levels of society into the ranks. While regular officers lamented and were demoralized by the tsar's abdication in March 1917, many young conscripted officers were elated. As for the ordinary ranks, the sudden collapse of authority prepared them for Lenin's agitation, and on the issue of war and peace (in Lenin's immortal phrase) they voted with their feet.   HS

The Peasants and Revolution: 1900–1921

On the eve of the fall of the tsar, some eighty-six per cent of the population of the Russian empire lived in the rural areas. The vast majority of these people were peasants, engaged in small-scale agriculture and living in innumerable small villages scattered throughout the country. If for no reason other than the physical size of this group, the actions and attitudes of the peasants were bound to have a major impact on the course of Russian development during the first two decades of this century.

Background

The position of the peasantry at the turn of the century was a direct reflection of the terms of the Emancipation Act of 1861. This legislation had been designed to liberate the peasants from serfdom, in the process passing much of the land into their hands. But the terms of the emancipation were profoundly disappointing to many peasants. Much of the best quality land remained in the hands of non-peasant landowners, while the land which the peasants did gain had to be purchased through a process of annual redemption payments. In the traditional grain-producing areas, in the central agricultural and in the middle Volga regions, the area of land the average peasant household held after emancipation was less than it had cultivated prior to 1861. Furthermore their holdings were often unbalanced, with too little meadow and pasture compared with arable land. The combined effects of growing indebtedness as the peasants fell behind in their redemption payments, the low levels of agricultural technology and the disruptive effects of the traditional inheritance and tenure arrangements mediated through the repartitional PEASANT COMMUNE, led to significant deterioration of peasant living standards throughout much of these traditional growing areas. In these regions where peasant agriculture remained technically backward and controlled by the repartitional peasant commune, peasant agriculture stagnated in the half century following emancipation.

This fate did not befall all peasant agriculture. In the newer grain-producing regions of the UKRAINE, north Caucasus, SIBERIA and Kazakhstan, the standard and output of peasant agriculture improved. Here peasant plots were larger, the repartitional commune was much weaker than in the traditional areas, and the pressures of land hunger were less intense. The predominance of private over communal tenure facilitated technological innovation, which was a major spur for the development and growth of peasant agriculture here.

Despite the improvements in the newer grain-producing regions, the period following emancipation saw many of the peasants bitter and disappointed. Land hunger remained unassuaged and may even have been heightened in the traditional producing areas. Standards of living were continually under pressure, as was the maintenance of a traditional life-style. Particularly important in this regard was the decline of peasant handicraft in the face of competition from the rise of industry in the towns which made the peasants even more reliant on a market economy and on income gained through sale of their produce in that market. Many peasant households were also reliant on capital remitted by members of the household who worked on either a seasonal or permanent basis in the expanding factory network in the towns. This human link reinforced the economic link by which the market was to pull the futures of the towns and the countryside closer together.

1905

The accumulated frustrations and tensions thus generated erupted in THE 1905 REVOLUTION. The peasants believed that the solution to their difficulties lay in seizing that land which lay outside their control. This was a misperception because the problems of peasant agriculture stemmed from the structure of that agriculture (see PEASANT COMMUNE). Nevertheless in 1905–7, peasants across Russia seized land which they believed to be theirs by right. Acting on the principle that land should belong to those who worked it, the peasants dispossessed private landowners of their land, livestock and implements, often destroying their houses and killing those landowners in the process. The authorities lost control in the countryside, with the organs of local government unable to exercise authority in the villages. The government had to restore order in the rural areas by force: many peasants were killed, and by 1907 the unrest had subsided.

Attempted reform

In an attempt to avoid future rural unrest, the government undertook major reforms, including the encouragement of large-scale peasant migration to the newer areas of Siberian settlement and, more important, the restructuring of

Figure 1   Peasant women at work.

agriculture by destroying the peasant commune. The commune was seen, in the light of 1905, as a major force for peasant revolution which needed to be undermined if stability was to be brought to the rural areas. Under the guidance of P. A. STOLYPIN, the government embarked on the so-called 'wager on the sturdy and the strong'. This was a series of measures designed to facilitate the separation of individual peasants from the commune, by enabling an individual householder to consolidate his diverse strips into a single holding and obtain hereditary tenure over his farm. Peasants could thus escape the stultifying control of the commune and set up their own, independent farm. This seemed, in principle, to be a major blow at the power and position of the repartitional commune and a move in the direction of greater innovation in Russian agriculture.

But the success of the Stolypin reforms was limited. More than eighty per cent of peasants remained within the traditional institution, and even the 'separators' who did consolidate and separate their arable land from the commune, often retained their dwelling in the village and kept usage rights in the undivided land, pastures, meadows and forests. Their separation from the commune was by no means complete. Moreover their act of separation was met with significant resentment by many who remained within the commune, for the consequent disruption could lead to a decline in the quality of the land held by those remaining. Furthermore the separators' stronger economic position often enabled them to acquire extra land through rental and purchase more easily than those remaining in the commune. Paradoxically, the Stolypin reforms and the separation may have strengthened the commune: those still within its confines saw reinforcement and reimposition of the communal principle as the only means of defending their economic interests against the attack posed by separation.

In the years following 1905, the peasants sought to expand their control over the land which they did not possess through widespread rental and purchase. By 1914 the peasants owned and rented some ninety per cent of the exploitable land in European Russia. But this did not satisfy their land hunger; primitive farming methods and continuing debt ensured that many peasants remained unable to meet their commitments as well as produce the desired surplus on a consistent basis.

The First World War

Initially, the war had a positive effect on the peasant economy. But the basis of such prosperity was weak. The longer the war dragged on, the more difficult became the plight of peasant agriculture. Tools and implements were wearing out and could not be replaced because of the demands of the war effort. The front continued to drain manpower and animals from the farm, leading to labour shortages. The loss of animals also created shortages of natural fertilizer which, in the absence of imported mineral fertilizer, was necessary for continuing high yields. Inflation ate into the peasants' savings while the introduction of a government grain monopoly with fixed prices in late 1916 severely restricted the incomes of grain producers without at the same time imposing similar restraints on their main items of expenditure; while their cost of living rose, peasant producers found their main source of income pegged. As February 1917 approached, the economic basis of peasant agriculture was steadily eroding.

1917

The fall of the tsar stimulated peasant expectations across the country. Like all social groups, they interpreted the tsar's fall as signalling an end to the old injustices and the beginning of a period in which they would realize their long-held aspirations. Initial peasant demands focused principally on three areas: land, food supply and local administration. Peasant meetings across the country adopted resolutions and decisions calling for the passing of land into the hands of those who worked it. This constituted a direct attack on non-peasant land-ownership in principle. On food supply, both peasant producers and consumers demanded a more effective form of regulation of the domestic grain market. The effect of the government's grain monopoly had been to dry up supply as producers refused to market their grain because it yielded no profit. They preferred to hold their grain back and drive up prices; this resulted in significant grain shortages in consuming areas. The new government was expected to remedy this situation. The third area of concern was local administration, and here the peasants demanded that control over the countryside be taken out of the hands of the established urban-based authorities and passed over to the peasants themselves. Existing local authorities were seen as alien to the peasant way of life and to peasant interests, more representative of the private landowners and towns than the multitude of villages scattered throughout the Russian countryside. However the reaction of the new PROVISIONAL GOVERNMENT in Petrograd to these demands produced only frustration and resentment.

On the land question, the government's approach was two-pronged. It endeavoured to increase productivity by expanding human labour power and access to agricultural equipment. It encouraged the use of refugees, prisoners-of-war, military reservists, youth and unemployed factory workers, although in practice this had little impact in the villages. Factories were also encouraged to increase the production of agricultural machinery, but again to little effect.

The second prong of the government's land policy related to land-ownership and disposition. Here the main emphasis was on the need to avoid hasty and ill-considered change in the structure of land relations. Instead of taking the land into their own hands, the peasants were called on to leave tenure arrangements unchanged pending a detailed survey which would provide the basis for a final resolution of this queston by the CONSTITUENT ASSEMBLY. In order to carry out this policy, the Provisional Government established land committees, whose essential brief was to collect data and, as far as possible, maintain existing land relations. Although the government's attempts to freeze land relations permitted some modifications, most particularly the nationalization of imperial lands and a decision of 12 July making legal provision for private landowners to dispose of their land, the major focus of policy was to retain the status quo. But this policy was unacceptable to the peasants; not only were they being denied both legal and actual control over the land they regarded as theirs, but private landowners were being given a way of disposing of their land which, the peasants feared, could place it beyond the scope of any future reform.

The government's position on the regulation of food supply was equally unacceptable to the peasants. On 25 March the government introduced a grain monopoly whereby all grain, except what the producer needed for his own use, was to be surrendered to the state at a fixed price set sixty per cent above that prevailing at the time. Grain not surrendered was subject to requisition. The government also publicly recognized the need to establish fixed prices on those articles of prime necessity which the peasants needed, but no meaningful steps were taken in this regard. Food committees were established to implement this policy, although the responsibilities of these bodies were soon expanded to include the protection of crops against damage resulting from peasant unrest. Despite doubling the fixed price at the end of August, the government was unable to encourage producers to market their grain in the desired quantities; with grain prices fixed and no restriction on the prices of other goods, grain producers had no incentive to surrender their grain. Even the operation of food rationing could not long delay the inevitable food crisis.

On the question of local administration, the government's response was also unsatisfactory. Little effort was made to expedite the introduction of new organs of local administration. Once again, the government's intention was to conduct a holding operation until 'local organizations on correct democratic bases' could be formed, but this involved making substantial use of the existing mechanism and personnel. Such an arrangement, with its links with the past and staffed by people like zemstvo (local government) board chairmen, landowners and prominent citizens from the towns, could not gain the confidence of the peasantry. The local organs appeared to them as alien, urban outposts in the countryside.

The peasant response to the dashing of their hopes and expectations was violent and effective. The initial trust in and support for the Provisional Government rapidly eroded as its procrastination became evident. Increasingly, peasants turned towards open seizure of land, accompanied as the year wore on by higher levels of personal violence and the destruction of crops, implements and houses; if early in the year peasant control over land was established peacefully by refusal to pay rent on land they were already using, within two months of the fall of the tsar this had become insignificant compared with the open seizure of property. Levels of the seizure of timber and the placing of embargoes on people felling trees remained high throughout most of the year, while the seizure of crops was particularly prevalent from July onward. Grain producers refused to market their grain, preferring to destroy it or distil it into alcohol than surrender it to the authorities. The authority of the towns was rejected as the peasants turned inward, looking for guidance to their own village-based institution, the commune and the PEASANT ASSEMBLY. Bodies established by urban politicians, such as soviets, land committees and food committees, were ignored as the peasants looked to their own institutions for guidance.

The timetable of peasant unrest in the main followed the cycle of peasant life. Thus the lighter demands of fieldwork during the times of peak unrest compared with the lower levels of unrest during the busy times of late May and early June when many peasants were occupied in hay-making and the gathering-in of fodder, and late July and August when they were harvesting crops, preparing the soil and planting for next season.

The effect of peasant unrest was important for the course of the revolution. The process of land seizure completely destroyed non-peasant land-ownership in the countryside. Non-peasant landowners, along with those who had separated from the repartitional commune under the Stolypin reforms, were expropriated: the control of traditional peasant organs was restored throughout much of the rural areas. This was accompanied by a general equalization of land-holdings so that the processes of levelling and restoration of communal norms negated the effect of the changes fostered by Stolypin. The refusal by peasant producers to market their grain led to major food shortages in the rural consuming areas and in the cities. The resultant uncertainty and hunger were major factors in the radicalization of the popular mood in the capital which was so important for Bolshevik success (see BOLSHEVIK PARTY). A further factor was the mounting unemployment resulting from factory closures, a development to which the peasants contributed through their seizure of timber and

consequent choking off of the fuel supply to the factories. The rural areas had thrown off control by the cities. Peasant communities became a law unto themselves, looking inward to their own institutions and turning their backs on the authority based in the towns. The interrelationship between town and country had broken down.

The Bolsheviks and the rural-urban gulf

Upon coming to power, the Bolsheviks sought to heal the rift with the countryside by placing an official seal on the peasant seizure of land. One of their first measures was the Decree on Land formally abolishing private ownership of land and passing control over it to the citizens through the district land committees and peasants' soviets pending the Constituent Assembly. Although not vesting legal title to the land in the peasants, the decree seemed to give them what they long demanded: control over all of the land. This may have won the Bolsheviks some support in the villages, although the elections to the Constituent Assembly showed how small that support was: the majority of the peasants voted for the SOCIALIST REVOLUTIONARIES, with the Bolsheviks getting little support from the rural areas. But the new government's position on the land question may have been instrumental in the outcome of the CIVIL WAR: the bulk of peasant support seems to have gone to the Bolsheviks because to the peasants the Whites seemed to promise restoration of the old order in the countryside.

But support for the Bolsheviks was clearly qualified by the peasants' reaction to some of their policies. The most important of these was WAR COMMUNISM introduced in mid 1918. Characterized most graphically for the peasants by the armed requisitioning of produce, the elimination of the market and private trade and the attempt to foster class warfare in the villages, War Communism was bound to evoke peasant opposition. Committees of the Poor were established in June 1918 in an attempt to divide the villages between rich and poor, to build up party support among the latter, to establish party control in the villages and to assist in the collection of surplus produce. However the effectiveness of these bodies was seriously compromised by the propensity of many in the villages to unite against what was seen as the common foe from outside. The Committees of the Poor could not displace the authority of the existing village-based institutions, and were incorporated into the local soviets in November 1918. Peasant reaction to the economic policies of War Communism was predictable: they sought to sell their produce on the black market, to withhold supplies from state procurement agencies, and to reject the authority of the urban-based government. By 1920 this opposition had grown into open unrest and guerrilla warfare, with major outbreaks in the Ukraine and Tambov province.

The New Economic Policy (NEP)

The continuing rural rejection of urban authority and the

economic and social chaos to which this contributed forced the Bolsheviks to retreat from the policies of War Communism. In March 1921, NEP was introduced. Through the introduction of a stable tax in kind (later changed to a financial tax) and the restoration of market forces as the chief dynamic of the economy, the peasants were given a greater degree of certainty in their economic life and some control over their economic future. They now settled down to work within a system which gave them much of what they had demanded in 1917. As in the revolutionary year, the peasants had demonstrated to the government that its authority was more formal than actual in the countryside. An urban-based and urban-oriented party could not establish effective authority without the wholesale restructuring of rural affairs. This was not done until the end of the 1920s.   GJG

The All-Russian Soviet of Peasants' Deputies

This was to be the peak organization of the peasants' soviets which emerged throughout the country during 1917. Preparations for an all-Russian Congress were begun soon after the fall of the tsar, with the Peasants' Union and the SOCIALIST REVOLUTIONARIES playing a prominent part.

The Congress was convened in Petrograd on 4 May 1917 (OS). It consisted of 1,115 delegates elected by the lower level soviets. There were 537 SRs, 136 non-party, 329 of unknown affiliation, 103 SDs, six Trudoviks and four Popular Socialists. The SRs' strong position, buttressed by the support of many of the formally uncommitted, enabled them to exercise a significant influence on the proceedings and to gain a commanding position on the executive committee elected at the congress. Most of the delegates were not peasants from the fields, but non-peasant intellectuals who evinced an interest in rural matters.

Despite the non-peasant nature of the delegates, the congress decisions appear broadly to have reflected the state of opinion of the villages at the time. The congress resolutions also had a distinct SR flavour, and most of them were in tune with PROVISIONAL GOVERNMENT policy. They gave basic support to a continuation of the war pending a just peace without annexations, and to the grain monopoly with fixed prices, rationing and the improved supply of consumer goods. On the land question, the congress was closer to the position of Agriculture Minister, V. M. CHERNOV, than it was to government policy. It favoured the abolition of private ownership in land and its distribution on an equal basis to all who worked it, with

Figure 2   1st Congress of Peasant Soviets, 4 May 1917.

control over all aspects of the land being vested in the land committees pending final resolution of this question by the CONSTITUENT ASSEMBLY. However while these resolutions may have reflected the peasant mood in May, in the absence of another congress prior to the Bolshevik seizure of power, this organ was out of step with radicalized peasant opinion by October.

The congress elected an executive committee to conduct its business between congresses and to represent the peasants' soviets in the capital. It consisted of thirty members, of whom twenty-five were SRs, who were mainly on the right wing of the party and therefore unsympathetic to Chernov's radical proposals. Many also had close links with the Provisional Government. The conservative disposition of this body ensured that, as the peasants became more militant, the executive committee became increasingly irrelevant to events in the countryside.

A further congress was convened after the Bolsheviks had seized power and, once the Bolsheviks had achieved dominance in it, it decided to merge with the All-Russian Soviet of Workers' and Soldiers' Deputies.   GJG

The Peasant Assembly

The peasant assembly (skhod) was the commune or village organ of self-government. It was a non-elected body consisting of the heads of the constituent households, which resolved most issues through a process of wide-ranging debate, sometimes followed by a vote. It was the chief decision-making organ of the peasant community, and its writ encompassed all aspects of peasant life. It exercised certain judicial functions, controlled the use of communal land (including determining the timetable for fieldwork), organized certain public services and amenities (including education and welfare for the aged, orphaned and handicapped), collected and used funds for common purposes, apportioned land and taxation obligations and punished arrears. The assembly normally elected an elder (starosta) and a variety of other officials for a three-year period to carry out its executive functions. A similar body was formed at the parish (volost) level to deal with inter-communal matters.

The assembly was seen by many observers as an example of primitive democracy at work. However it rarely matched such expectations in practice. In most instances it was dominated by a few of the more active, wealthy or powerful peasants who used it to consolidate their own positions. However during 1917 it became a major forum of peasant discussion and decision making. As the peasant mood was radicalized, conservative leaders in the assembly were

replaced by more extreme elements, often recently returned from the front. As a result the assembly remained in the forefront of village affairs; even after the OCTOBER REVOLUTION it was usually the real decision-making body in the villages, if under the guise of the soviet.   GJG

The Peasant Commune

The origins of the peasant commune (mir or obshchina) are obscure. The nineteenth-century Slavophiles argued that its origins lay in the traditions of the Russian peasants and that it was the form through which they sought to organize village life. Others have suggested that it was a more recent development, dating only from the eighteenth century when the monarchy introduced it principally as a means of gathering taxes. What is certain is that the commune was strengthened at the time of the emancipation of the serfs in 1861. Following emancipation, it was the major administrative body in the rural areas, being made collectively responsible for the financial obligations of its members, both in terms of the redemption dues and the state taxes. To enforce this responsibility, the commune was given sweeping powers over the mobility of its members; personal departure from the repartitional commune required the approval of both the communal PEASANT ASSEMBLY and the head of the household, while total withdrawal from the commune also required the surrender of the land and the settling of outstanding financial obligations. In the hereditary commune, withdrawal required simply the settling of financial obligations, but given the over-valuation of the land at the time of emancipation, this was rarely easy. Separation from the commune was in practice, therefore, very difficult.

There were two types of commune, the repartitional and hereditary. In the former, arable land was owned by the community and redistributed periodically by the commune as the size of the constituent households changed. In the latter land was allocated permanently to households at the time of emancipation. In both types of commune households usually also owned a kitchen garden while meadowland, pastures and forests remained in common usage. The different types of tenure made little practical difference to the physical disposition of land-holdings; even in the hereditary commune, an individual household's land was usually not consolidated. Arable land was held in strips, scattered around the village to ensure that each household got access to land of varying quality. Such an arrangement, allied to the continuing three-field system and the absence of collective cultivation (each household worked alone on its own fields) was very wasteful, while the redistribution of plots severely reduced the incentive to innovate in the repartitional commune. The repartitional commune was the dominant form throughout most of Russia, although the hereditary commune was strongest in the newer grain-producing areas of the south-west and parts of the south-east of European Russia. It was also strong in the north-west. Commune and village did not always coincide, but most communes corresponded to villages or small peasant settlements. Early this century the typical commune had about 100 households and 2000 acres of land.

The STOLYPIN reforms constituted a major attack upon the commune but had little effect. When peasant unrest unrolled in 1917, it was fiercest in those areas dominated by the repartitional commune. This was the main vehicle of peasant action and the chief forum for general discussion and debate in the countryside. Organizations that were independent of the commune tended to wield little influence in the rural areas. One of the main results of 1917 was the reimposition of communal norms, reflected most graphically in the re-absorption of the separators into the commune. By 1920 only some four per cent of peasant households in thirty-nine provinces of European Russia were outside the communal structure.   GJG

Further Reading

Atkinson, Dorothy: *The End of the Russian land Commune, 1905–1930.* Stanford: Stanford University Press, 1983.

Gill, Graeme J.: *Peasants and Government in the Russian Revolution.* London: 1979.

Keep, J.L.H.: *The Russian Revolution. A Study in Mass Mobilization.* London: 1976.

Maynard, John: *The Russian Peasant and other Studies.* London: 1943.

Milyutin, V.P. ed.: *Agrarnaya revolyutsiya,* 4 vols. Moscow: 1928.

Pershin, P.A.: *Agrarnaya revolyutsiya v Rossii.* Moscow: 1966.

Robinson, G.T.: *Rural Russia Under the Old Regime.* New York: 1932; repr. 1962.

Shanin, Teodor: *The Roots of Otherness: Russia's Turn of Century.* London: 1985.

The Workers: February–October 1917

By 1917 there were around 3.5 million workers in the factories and mines of Russia, 1.26 million workers and employees in transport, and 1.25 million workers in construction. The number of wage workers of all types totalled about 18.5 million, or 10 per cent of the population. In Petrograd and its suburbs there were 417,000 industrial workers, of whom 65 per cent were metal workers, 11 per cent textile workers and 10 per cent chemical workers. In Moscow there were about 420,000 workers, of whom one third were textile workers and one quarter metal workers. In the Central Industrial Region as a whole there were over one million workers, of whom 61 per cent were textile workers. In the Urals 83 per cent of

the 350,000 industrial workers were employed in mining and metallurgy. The UKRAINE had a workforce of around one million, of whom the main contingents were miners in the Donbass (280,000) and metallurgical workers in the southern industrial region. Other regions with sizeable concentrations of workers included the BALTIC, the Volga, TRANSCAUCASIA and SIBERIA (Omsk, KRASNOYARSK, Chita). The regional concentration of the working class in Russia was complemented by its concentrations in large units of production. In Petrograd over 70 per cent of workers were in enterprises of more than 1,000 workers; in the Ukraine two thirds of the workforce were in enterprises of more than 500 workers, and the situation was similar in the Urals. This concentration of the industrial labour force was critical in facilitating its mobilization in 1917, and gave the working class a political weight out of proportion to its rather small numbers.

The expansion of industry during the FIRST WORLD WAR and the conscription of between one fifth and one quarter of the workforce created many openings for newcomers to industry. Peasants were drawn by the prospect of lucrative work in industry (in 1917 31 per cent of workers owned land), and women came into the factories as husbands and brothers were called up (in 1917 the proportion of women workers was 40 per cent). Perhaps as many as two thirds of the workforce, therefore, were newcomers often with only limited experience of urban life and strong ties to the countryside. They were a different breed from the skilled men who had worked in industry for many years, who earned reasonably good wages, who were fairly well-educated and politically aware, and who were to be found particularly in the metal industry in Petrograd. Long experience of industrial militancy had imbued them with a strong sense of class unity and a deep antagonism to the tsarist state and the propertied classes.

Despite a rising level of strikes and revolutionary activity during the war, no one predicted the outbreak of revolution in February 1917. The revolutionary events began in the capital on 23 February (8 March NS) when thousands of women workers and housewives, angry at the bread shortage, took to the streets to celebrate International Women's Day, ignoring pleas from labour leaders to stay calm. The next day 200,000 workers came out on strike. By 25 February huge armies of demonstrators were clashing with troops, and the revolution had commenced. On 27 February the climax came when whole regiments of the Petrograd garrison mutinied. On the same day certain labour leaders, mainly MENSHEVIKS, announced the formation of a provisional executive committee of the Petrograd Soviet, and Duma leaders set up a Provisional Committee to maintain public order. On 28 February the Executive Committee of the Petrograd Soviet of Workers' and Soldiers' Deputies was formally instituted, and a soviet was also inaugurated in Moscow. The next day, after talks with the Soviet, the PROVISIONAL GOVERNMENT was established in which the Soviet Executive Committee decided not to participate. On 2 March NICHOLAS II abdicated, and six days later he was arrested. Thus was autocracy swept away and 'dual power' created.

In Petrograd a majority of workers, trusting in the Soviet as their representative and unwilling to risk dissension in the revolutionary ranks, backed the policy of the Menshevik and SOCIALIST REVOLUTIONARY leaders of the Executive Committee of giving conditional support to the government 'in so far' as its policies corresponded to the interests of the revolution. They did not disguise their lurking distrust of the Duma politicians now in power. On the burning question of the war, workers also backed the policy of the Executive Committee. In the resolutions which were passed by general meetings of workers in all the major factories, the government was urged to work assiduously for a democratic peace, based on a renunciation of indemnities and territorial annexations. LENIN characterized the mood of workers at this stage as one of 'revolutionary defencism', i.e. they were prepared to continue fighting to defend revolutionary Russia from Austro-German militarism.

On returning to work after 6 March, workers in Petrograd proceeded to dismantle the autocratic structure of management in the factories. Hated foremen and administrators fled or were expelled. Factory rule books, with their punitive fines and humiliating searches, were torn up. Factory committees were created to represent workers' interests to management. The Petrograd Society of Factory and Works Owners, in conciliatory mood, formally agreed with the Soviet Executive Committee on 10 March to recognize the committees and to implement the eight-hour working day. Workers also succeeded, through localized action, in achieving increases in their monthly earnings of between 30 per cent and 50 per cent, to compensate for the wartime rise in the cost of living. Outside the capital, the employers were less prepared to make concessions, particularly in respect of the eight-hour day.

The first sign of a rift between workers and the Provisional Government came in April when MILYUKOV's note to the Allies was made public. Workers and soldiers surged on to the streets on 20–21 April and there were clashes with middle-class counter-demonstrators. Workers' resolutions demanded the immediate formulation of peace terms and the renunciation of secret treaties. When six socialists from the Executive Committee entered the government in early May, most workers welcomed this as a move which would allow greater soviet control over the 'capitalist ministers'. In Petrograd, however, a minority, mainly skilled metal workers from the Vyborg district, condemned the coalition as a 'ministry of compromise with the bourgeoisie'. From this time, too, certain metal works in Moscow, mainly in the Zamoskvorechye district, began to pass resolutions calling for the transfer of power to the soviets. Petrograd, however, remained in the van of political developments.

As the summer progressed, wider layers of Petrograd workers, including the unskilled and women workers, became more radical, partly in response to political events, but chiefly because of the deepening economic crisis which increasingly threatened workers' livelihoods. This rising tide of militancy came to a head on 3–4 July when soldiers and workers demonstrated to force the 'ten capitalist ministers' to resign and compel the Central Executive Committee (so named since the First All-Russian Congress of Soviets) to form a government. As many as 400 were killed or wounded and leading Bolsheviks were arrested. The 'July Days' thus resulted not in a soviet government, but in KERENSKY's government taking a sharp turn to the right. While dramatizing the hostility felt by workers and soldiers towards the government, the 'July Days' also highlighted their ambivalence towards the moderate socialists who led the Soviet. The Central Executive Committee had declined to take power, as the demonstrators insisted, since it believed in the necessity of cooperating with the propertied classes, and this left workers uncertain as to the way forward. They felt isolated, and baulked at the prospect of a division in the ranks of 'revolutionary democracy'.

The economic crisis engendered a mood of militancy also outside Petrograd, at first apparent among skilled workers but soon arising among other groups. In Moscow an analysis of workers' resolutions reveals that from May onwards, the economy supplanted the war as the issue which most exercised workers. Economically-based militancy was quickly politicized, however, for workers blamed the crisis in industry and the threat to jobs on capitalist 'sabotage', and condemned the Kerensky government for failing to tackle the problems of most concern to them: the collapse of the economy, the war, food supply and the land question. This militancy expressed itself in the movement for WORKERS' CONTROL and in the burgeoning strike movement.

During the late summer and autumn, strikes increased dramatically and spread outwards from Petrograd and the Central Industrial Region to all corners of the former Empire. In July the number of strikes rose to half a million and thereafter grew consistently to reach 1.2 million by October. These strikes, originally economic, acquired an increasingly political character, with the posting of armed guards on factory gates to prevent removal of goods and equipment and the occupation of factories. Surprisingly, the autumn saw a decline in the number of strikes in Petrograd and Moscow, but this was due to a recognition that they could serve as an excuse for employers to shut down unprofitable enterprises. As strikes multiplied and as workers' control of production intensified, employers everywhere began to take a tough line towards the labour movement, by locking out recalcitrant workers, by laying off employees, cutting back on orders and investment and by clamouring for the Menshevik minister of labour, M. I. Skobelev, to quash the pretensions of organized labour.

It was above all the KORNILOV rebellion that allowed the Bolsheviks to capitalize on the growing polarization between the upper and lower classes. The spectre of a military dictatorship seemed to highlight the bankruptcy of the policy of conciliation with the propertied classes which had been pursued so earnestly by the Mensheviks and Right SRs. In the wake of the Kornilov rebellion, whose defeat in part was due to the effective mobilization of railway and telegraph workers, the BOLSHEVIK demand for power to be transferred to the 'representatives of the proletariat and peasantry' was endorsed for the first time by the Petrograd and Moscow Soviets (31 August and 5 September respectively), and by eighty other soviets during the first half of September. An examination of worker resolutions from the main industrial centres reveals enthusiastic support for Bolshevik attacks on the bourgeois-landlord government, the capitalist system and the imperialist war, and ubiquitous calls for the transfer of power to the soviets, workers' control of production and the arming of the Red Guards (see WORKERS' MILITIAS AND RED GUARDS. In Moscow, where social polarization was not as acute as in Petrograd, over 50,000 workers passed resolutions in support of soviet power, including many textile workers in the month of October. Even in Petrograd, however, it seems that only a minority of resolute, or possibly foolhardy, workers looked to the violent overthrow of the coalition government as the means to establish soviet power. Memories of the July Days had still not faded and most workers feared the prospect of political isolation and civil war.

The announcement on the morning of 25 October that the Provisional Government had been overthrown was undoubtedly welcomed by a majority of workers. It is true that some opposed what they saw to be an illegal seizure of power which threatened to engulf Russia in civil war, but such sentiments were confined mainly to printers, railway workers, postal and telegraph employees, white-collar workers and professionals. Yet though they welcomed a soviet government, most workers had no clear idea about its precise political form and functions. Some called for a 'homogeneous revolutionary democratic government', which would be based on a broader range of democratic organizations than the soviets alone, but which would rule out any attempt to cooperate with the propertied classes. More popular were calls for a 'homogeneous socialist government', which looked to the parties within the Central Executive Committee of the Soviets to form a government based on the soviets. It quickly became apparent that there was no basis for any political agreement between the socialist parties within the soviet, and the foundations of a one-party state were set in place.

It is often argued that workers played an essentially destructive and anarchistic role in the Russian Revolution, and that the Bolsheviks won their following by manipulating the base instincts of the masses. Bolshevik agitation undoubtedly played a crucial role in radicalizing the masses, but the Bolsheviks did not create popular discontent. This arose out of the workers' own experience of economic and social upheavals and political events. In the spring of 1917 most workers hoped that the Provisional Government would defend the interests of the common people, achieve a speedy peace settlement and give land to the peasants. Instead the Provisional Government appeared to uphold the interests of the propertied classes, by seeming to prolong the war, postpone a settlement of the land question and, above all, connive in the 'sabotage' of industry that was being perpetrated by the capitalist class. The contribution of the Bolsheviks was to provide an explanation of worker grievances in terms of class analysis and to relate the urgent problems of daily life to a wider social and political order. The Bolsheviks won support because their analysis and proposed solutions seemed to make sense, whereas those offered by the moderate socialists, which had commanded general assent in the early months, came to seem increasingly false. A worker from the Orudiinyi (gun) plant, Petrograd, where formerly Bolsheviks were not even allowed to speak at factory meetings, said in September: 'the Bolsheviks have always said: "It is not we who will persuade you, but life itself." And now the Bolsheviks have triumphed because life has proved their tactics right.'   SAS

Further Reading

Hasegawa, T.: *The February Revolution: Petrograd 1917*. Seattle: University of Washington Press, 1981.

Keep, J.L.H.: *The Russian Revolution: A Study in Mass Mobilisation*. London: Weidenfeld & Nicolson, 1976.

Koenker, D.: *Moscow Workers and the 1917 Revolution*. Princeton: Princeton University Press, 1981.

Mandel, D.: *Petrograd Workers and the Fall of the Old Regime*. London: Macmillan, 1983.

Rabinowitch, A.: *The Bolsheviks Come to Power*. New York: Norton, 1976.

Factory Committees: February–October 1917

In the wake of the FEBRUARY REVOLUTION workers throughout Russia formed factory and works committees, railway line committees and mine committees to represent their interests to management. Initially, these committees were strongest in the state-owned defence plants of Petrograd, where the flight of the former military administrators during the revolution forced the committees to take charge of the plants on a temporary basis. This also happened in a number of former state enterprises in the Urals and in the Pipe Works in Samara. In the private sector the committees at first functioned like trade unions, fighting to win the eight-hour day, to increase wages, to reform the internal regime of the workshops and to oversee hiring and firing of workers. Outside of Petrograd the factory owners were less than happy at the appearance of these committees, but the legalization of the committees by the PROVISIONAL GOVERNMENT on 23 April 1917 gave them little choice but to try to work with these new organizations.

The committees quickly developed an enormous volume of business, much of it handled by specialized sub-committees. They dealt with matters as diverse as the security of the factory, food supply, 'culture and enlightenment', health and safety, the improvement of working conditions, labour discipline, checking that workers had officially been excused conscription, campaigning against drunkenness, liaison with the local soviet or garrison. Much of their business was of a fairly trivial kind: for example, on 28 July at the Baltic works in Petrograd the committee discussed what to do with a consignment of rotting fish. Yet precisely because of the concern with everyday life, workers regarded the committees as 'their' institutions, closer to them than the trade unions or soviets. As the economic crisis began to bite, and particularly once trade unions were operating effectively, the committees turned away from matters to do with the defence of workers' wages and conditions and began to devote themselves to establishing WORKERS' CONTROL of production. The Soviet historian, Z. V. Stepanov, has counted 4,266 acts by 124 factory committees in Petrograd between 1 March and 25 October and calculates that 1,141 acts related to workers' control of production and distribution; 882 concerned organizational questions; 347 concerned political questions; 299 concerned wages; 241 concerned hiring and firing and the monitoring of conscription, etc.

Factory committee members were initially elected on a non-political basis, but as politics hardened along party lines, members began to be elected on party slates. In the early months, the moderate socialists dominated the committees as they did all labour organizations. Being the institutions closest to the mass of workers, however, the committees were the first to register the radicalization that was occurring in popular attitudes. Already at the First Conference of Petrograd Factory Committees in early June the BOLSHEVIKS were in the ascendant, winning 290 votes for their resolution on control of the economy, as against 72 votes for the MENSHEVIK resolution and 45 votes for the ANARCHIST resolution. The clear-cut support of the Bolsheviks for workers' control of production led to the moderate socialists being recalled from the committees and Bolsheviks being elected in their stead. Even before the KORNILOV rebellion the committees had become the Bolsheviks' firmest base of support within the labour movement.

It is reckoned that 2,151 factory committees were in existence by October, of which 687 were in enterprises of more than 200 workers. To coordinate their activities in the sphere of workers' control these committees had developed higher level organizations, of which there were 95 by October. Of these 75 brought together committees on a city or regional basis, and 20 on an industrial basis. By far the most important was the Petrograd Central Council of Factory and Works Committees (CCFC), set up at the First Conference in June, which was transformed into the supreme national body after the All-Russian Conference of Factory Committees (17–22 October). The CCFC employed some 80 people by October in its various commissions, departments and sections, all vainly trying to restore order to the economy and thus preserve jobs. It was under firm Bolshevik control and played a major economic role in the first months of Bolshevik power (see DEMISE OF WORKERS' CONTROL IN INDUSTRY).   SAS

Further Reading

Smith, S.A. ed. and annot.: *Oktyabr'skaya Revolyutsiya i Fabzavkomy*. New York: Kraus International, Millwood, 1983.

———— : *Red Petrograd: Revolution in the Factories, 1917–18*. Cambridge: Cambridge University Press, 1983.

Stepanov, Z.V.: *Fabzavkomy Petrograda v 1917 godu*. Leningrad: 1985.

Workers' Control: February–October 1917

Workers' control of production and distribution was principally an attempt by the FACTORY COMMITTEES to dam the rising tide of economic disorder which became apparent in the summer of 1917. Although sometimes seen as an anarcho-syndicalist bid to oust the capitalists from their factories, it was in fact motivated less by ideology than by a practical concern to stave off factory closures and save jobs. Faced by shortages of fuel, raw materials and spare parts, spiralling costs, declining productivity and a heightened tempo of labour militancy, industrialists began to scale down their operations and to lay off workers. It is reckoned that 568 enterprises shut down between March and July, and a further 251 in August and September. By that month, 200 mines had been closed in the Donbass. In response to such 'sabotage', the factory committees tried to preserve jobs by imposing a measure of 'control' – in the sense of inspection or supervision – over the employers.

At first workers' control was restricted mainly to overseeing the activities of management and was defensive in character. It has been calculated that up to July workers' control was practised in 378 enterprises, with a total workforce of 832,000, mainly in the metal industries but also in textiles and mining. Two thirds of the acts of workers' control involved such things as the factory committees restructuring the internal regime of the enterprise, supervising the hiring and firing of workers, participating in the deployment and protection of labour or organizing food supply. Already, however, committees were also seeking to procure scarce supplies and to monitor their use by management. As the economic crisis deepened, workers' control became more offensive and cut more into the rights of managers to manage. During the late summer and autumn the committees began to intervene in the technical side of production and to demand access to order-books and financial accounts. It is reckoned that by October workers' control was in force in 573 factories and mines with a combined workforce of 1.4 million (41 per cent of the industrial proletariat). It was most widespread in Petrograd, where it operated in 96 enterprises (with a workforce of 289,000), and Moscow, where it operated in 114 enterprises (with a workforce of 194,000).

In a minority of cases, workers' control developed in an extreme direction, with workers arresting or expelling managers or seeking to run enterprises by themselves. This was particularly so in the UKRAINE and the Urals, where capitalist opposition to the demands of labour was very tenacious. In the Ukraine, for example, attempts to shut down production led factory committees to take over plants such as the Gelferich-Sade, the Steam-Engine and the General Electric companies in Kharkov. And in the Donbass miners arrested managers and occupied the mines until late September when troops put an end to these activities with considerable bloodshed. Nevertheless one should not exaggerate the extent of such extreme forms of workers' control. It is reckoned that only 4.3 per cent of 2,094 acts of workers' control in the months of July to October involved factory committees actually running enterprises.

The movement for workers' control of production essentially arose independently of any political party. The MENSHEVIKS and SRs disapproved of it as a strategy for dealing with disruption in industry, since they believed that spontaneous initiatives by workers in individual enterprises could only exacerbate economic disorder. Instead they argued for 'state control', i.e. planned, centralized all-embracing control of the economy by the government, the seeds of which had already been sown during the war. The Bolsheviks, too, believed that only action by the state could restore order to the economy, but they refused any support for the initiatives of the PROVISIONAL GOVERNMENT, since they believed that, as a government of capitalists and landlords, it would seek to restore order at the expense of the working class. The BOLSHEVIKS thus supported workers' control of production, but some in the party remained sceptical regarding its effectiveness. LENIN construed workers' control in the narrow sense of 'account-ing and inspection' and sought after October to integrate it into a centralized system under government control.   SAS

Further Reading

Itkin, M.L.: *Rabochii kontrol' nakanune Oktyabrya*. Moscow: 1984.
Selitskii, V.I.: *Massy v bor'be za rabochii kontrol'*. Moscow: 1971.

Smith, S.A.: *Red Petrograd: Revolution in the Factories, 1917–18*. Cambridge: Cambridge University Press, 1983.

Trade Unions: February–October 1917

The 1905 REVOLUTION led to a relaxation in the laws prohibiting trade unions, and during 1906–7 they grew rapidly. They barely survived police repression during the subsequent period of reaction, and their revival in 1912–14 was curtailed again with the outbreak of war. Former activists hastened to re-establish them after the FEBRUARY REVOLUTION, founding 91 unions in March and April, and by May another 30 had affiliated to the Petrograd Central Bureau of Trade Unions, and 38 to its Moscow counter-part. In far-away Irkutsk some 8,000 workers had enrolled in 20 unions by summer, and in Baku 27 unions were operating, including a seamen's union of 4,800 and an oil workers' union of 3,000. By the time of the Third All-Russian Trade Union Conference, 21–8 June, there were 976 unions in existence with a total membership of 1.4 million. The largest of these was the metal workers' union with 400,000 members, followed by the textile workers with 178,500. Trade union growth continued through the summer and autumn, so that by October 2,000 unions were said to be active with a membership of over two million.

In the early weeks of the revolution it was artisans who took the lead in creating trade unions. In manufacturing industry, particularly in metal-working, unions were rather slow to get off the ground, partly because factory committees successfully took up the defence of workers' interests. Indeed in regions such as the Donbass and the Urals unions never achieved influence comparable with that of the factory and mine committees. Many of the first unions were local in character, or else confined to a particular craft. In Petrograd, for example, foundry workers, machinists and electricians had separate organiz-ations before combining with the metal workers' union. The policy of union leaders, however, regardless of party affiliation, was to establish a few large unions embracing all the workers in a particular branch of industry, irrespective of their trade. Despite craft resistance in some quarters (for example from wood-turners), this policy enjoyed consider-able success even before the BOLSHEVIKS came to power.

The coexistence of unions and factory committees led to clashes regarding their respective spheres of competence. At the First Conference of Petrograd Factory Committees (30 May–5 June), to the chagrin of committee activists, trade union spokesmen argued that there was not room for two organizations, and that the committees should become the primary cells of the unions. At the Second Conference (7–12 August) the Bolshevik trade-union leader, A. L. Lozovsky, was more conciliatory. His resolution, passed by conference, proposed that trade unions defend the wages and working conditions of their members, whilst the committees regulate production. After the OCTOBER REVOLUTION, however, this division of labour once again became an issue of contention, when trade unions claimed the right to regulate production.

By the summer the factory committees had largely withdrawn from wage bargaining, and it was left to the unions to try to repair the depredations of price inflation, by negotiating collective wage contracts, or 'tariffs', with the employers' organizations. Twenty-five contracts were signed in Petrograd up to October, the most significant being that between the metal workers' union and the metalworking section of the Society of Factory and Works Owners, which was signed only after two months of protracted and bitter negotiation. These tariffs were, however, a depressing failure, for no sooner had they been signed than inflation rendered the wage increases nugatory. Nevertheless in these contracts the unions sought to strengthen the position of the low-paid and to overcome sectionalism, and this helped to increase the prestige of the unions in the eyes of their members.

Nationally, the MENSHEVIKS were the most influential party within the trade union movement, but the Bolsheviks built up their influence at the expense of the moderate socialists in the course of 1917, as they did in other mass organizations. At the Third All-Russian Trade-Union Conference in June, among the delegates were 73 Bolsheviks, 36 Mensheviks, 31 non-aligned Social Democrats, 35 SRs etc. Conference elected a Temporary All-Russian Central Council of Trade Unions, consisting of 13 Bolsheviks, 13 Mensheviks and three SRs. In some unions Bolshevik fortunes rose from the late summer, as the politics of conciliationism became more discredited. Of the delegates to the first national conference of textile workers in late September, 48 were Bolsheviks, 10 Mensheviks, four SRs and two belonged to no party. At the first national congress of metal-workers in January 1918 75 delegates were Bolsheviks, 51 were non-party, 20 were Mensheviks, seven were Left SRs, six Right SRs etc.

'Bolshevization' was, however, by no means universal within the trade unions. The printers' union remained a redoubt of Menshevism, and unions such as those of chemical workers and glass workers remained under moderate control. The All-Russian Executive Committee of Railway Workers, representing a federation of largely autonomous line committees and unions based at the principal intersections, was dominated by white-collar employees of right-wing socialist views. In spite of being politically less reliable than the factory committees from the Bolshevik point of view, it was nevertheless the unions rather than factory committees which the Bolsheviks sought to utilize after October.   SAS

Further Reading

Gaponenko, L.S.: *Rabochii klass Rossii v 1917 g.* Moscow: 1970.
Smith, S.A.: *Red Petrograd: Revolution in the Factories, 1917–18.*
Cambridge: Cambridge University Press, 1983.
Stepanov, Z.V.: *Rabochie Petrograda v period podgotovki i provedeniya oktyabr'skogo vooruzhennogo vosstaniya.* Moscow: 1963.

Workers' Militias and Red Guards in 1917

Workers' militias were established on a local basis during the February Revolution to protect factory property and to uphold law and order in the working-class districts. They arose spontaneously, without the intervention of political parties, though inspired in part by the socialist ideal of a citizenry-in-arms. They clashed with the new all-class, non-partisan militias which were set up by local authorities under the auspices of the PROVISIONAL GOVERNMENT. In the next months, the authorities, with the backing of the moderate socialists on the Soviet Executive Committee, sought to disband the workers' militias, but in Petrograd, at least, the latter continued to compete with the new civil militia, in a microcosm of 'dual power'.

As the unpopularity of the government grew, more politicized formations – the Red Guards – were created, committed to struggling against counter-revolution and to defending the gains made by workers since March. These Red Guards were backed by the factory committees and more militant city-district soviets and had the support of the BOLSHEVIKS. In the teeth of fierce opposition from the Soviet leadership, the development of the Red Guards was slow, and the failure of the July Days set them back considerably. Their rapid growth came with the KORNILOV rebellion which spurred workers to obtain and learn to use weapons. By October there may have been as many as 200,000 Red Guards throughout Russia.

During the OCTOBER REVOLUTION, in contrast to February, masses of workers did not come out on to the streets to clash with armed soldiers and police. The armed forces of the Provisional Government in Petrograd had already been won over to the SOVIETS, so the task of the insurgents was merely to occupy key centres and disarm the last supporters of the old regime. The Bolsheviks actually discouraged mass participation in the insurrection, but they did rely on the powerful network of Red Guards. These consisted mainly of young men who, though by no means solidly Bolshevik, were determined to establish soviet power. Nevertheless, within a few months, the new government concluded that the Red Guards were unsuitable as the core of a regular army. Their spontaneous and local character and their paucity of numbers seemed incompatible with the apparent need for a centralized, disciplined and efficient army. By the spring of 1918 the Red Guards had either dwindled away or been absorbed into TROTSKY's new RED ARMY.   SAS

Further Reading

Startsev, V.M.: *Ocherki po istorii Petrogradskoi Krasnoi gvardii i rabochei militsii.* Moscow: 1965.

Wade, R.A.: *Red Guards and Workers' Militias in the Russian Revolution*. Stanford: Stanford University Press, 1984.

Workers and the Bolshevik State: October 1917–March 1921

Contrary to their expectations before coming to power, the BOLSHEVIKS discovered that, far from being able to utilize the power of the state in order to bring some order into the economy, the galloping economic disorder threatened to destroy their tenuous hold on state power. The crisis in the economy, already severe before October, grew steadily worse. The collapse of fuel and raw materials supplies, the exhaustion of plant and plummeting labour productivity, the disruption of the transport system, the loss of territory and the decline in grain marketings not only added hugely to the problems of the Bolshevik government in defending itself against external aggression, but engendered a level of peasant and worker disaffection which threatened the security of the regime from within.

From the moment the Bolsheviks seized power their slender social base of support began to disintegrate. On suing for peace, they began to demobilize the war industries and this, together with the more general decline of manufacturing and extractive industries, led to a rapid increase in the number of workers laid off and a sharp fall in the number in employment. By the autumn of 1918 there were fewer than 2.5 million industrial workers in Russia, and only 1.2 million by the middle of 1920. The dissolution of the proletariat went further, however, in precisely those centres where the working class had played a key political role in 1917. In Petrograd the industrial workforce shrank in size from 384,600 in 1917 to 101,840 in mid 1920. In Moscow it shrank from 205,900 to 89,000 in the same period. In the Urals the workforce fell from 339,600 in January 1918 to 154,714 in January 1921. Moreover the cutbacks were unevenly distributed by branch of industry. The metalworking industries, where labour militancy had been most pronounced during 1917, suffered a huge haemorrhage of workers in the first months of 1918, but thereafter this slowed considerably. In contrast, the number of textile workers held up for most of 1918, but by mid 1920 had fallen to 27 per cent of its 1913 level. In other industries, such as tailoring, leather or food, numbers remained stable or even increased.

In the winter of 1917–18 the speedy demobilization of the war industries and the acute food shortages caused tens of thousands of workers to leave the towns and return to the countryside in search of land and food. To some extent, the working class which was left behind was less proletarian ('*déclassé*', in Soviet jargon) than in 1917, since the number of urbanized, skilled and literate workers, i.e. the more class-conscious elements, had fallen considerably. Nevertheless a core of such workers remained in all industrial centres (to a greater extent in Moscow than in Petrograd),

and this was particularly so in regions such as the Central Industrial Region or the Urals, where the traditional ties of industrial workers to the land, paradoxically, helped to preserve the working class. As we shall see, however, workers failed to maintain that unity as a social group and power as a political force which they had achieved in 1917.

The CIVIL WAR brought worsening working conditions and plummeting real wages. The Bolsheviks sought to introduce rationality into wage policy, but the catastrophic fall in the value of the ruble rendered their efforts futile. The Second All-Russian Congress of Trade Unions (January 1919) opted for a national tariff for all categories of labour, dividing all employees into three categories, each subdivided into twelve grades. The maximum for a technical specialist was fixed at 3000 rubles; the wage of the highest-paid skilled worker was fixed at 1150 rubles, and that of the lowest grade of unskilled labourer at 600 rubles. This five-to-one ratio was actually an attempt to uphold wage differentials, which had been much eroded by this stage, but the decreasing importance of money wages reinforced trends towards wage equalization. By the end of 1920 the real value of the money wage was only 2.3 per cent of its 1913 level, but if one includes food rations, work-clothes and free communal services, then the real value of the 'wage' was about one third its prewar value. The economist, S. G. Strumilin, reckoned that the money element accounted for 52.6 per cent of the average 'wage' in 1918; 20.7 per cent in 1919; 7.4 per cent in 1920.

During the Civil War workers came to rely on the authorities for the fulfilment of their most basic needs. The government, however, was unable to meet these at anything like an adequate level, particularly in the sphere of food supply. In the autumn of 1920 a factory worker received on average per month between roughly five and seven pounds of bread, instead of the norm of 27. And the attempt by the government to give preferential rations to strategically important sectors created further problems, by encouraging all workers to press for the better rations. In late 1918 one-quarter million workers in 250 defence plants, were put on a military ration; in the next year this was extended to many non-defence plants. By the end of 1920 some 2.7 million workers qualified for special rations. Yet on average only one fifth or one quarter of this special ration could be met. Workers had no choice but to engage in illicit trade or barter household possessions for food.

The constant search for food, the necessity of doing side-line work to supplement family income and the higher rates of illness as a consequence of a deteriorating diet, resulted in staggering levels of absenteeism in industry and exacerbated the already acute problem of low productivity. It was reckoned that one third of all working days in 1920 were lost through absenteeism. The government introduced a panoply of tough measures to combat absenteeism and low productivity, though their effectiveness seems to have been limited. By 1920 piece rates, which Lenin had

25

been urging since the spring of 1918, were once again ubiquitous.

The steady deterioration in the workers' economic position created severe political problems for the Bolshevik government, as many of the same economic discontents that had helped propel them into power were by the spring of 1918 strengthening opposition. In Petrograd it was the Treaty of Brest-Litovsk which proved to be the turning-point. The MENSHEVIKS gained a new lease of life by giving political shape to labour disaffection regarding job losses and food supply. Arguing that the SOVIETS no longer represented worker interests, since they were subject to manipulation by the ruling party, the Mensheviks set up conferences of worker deputies which, in addition to lambasting the economic policies of the government, criticized its growing habit of suppressing those not compliant with its wishes. Similar conferences were created in Moscow, Nizhni Novgorod, Kineshma, Tula and elsewhere. In Petrograd the active core of opposition to the government came from metal workers hardest hit by unemployment, especially those in the state defence plants, from printers and from the Nevsky district of the city, long a bastion of the SRs. The shooting of workers, in nearby Kolpino, who demonstrated against the shortages of food and jobs, unleashed a wave of protest not only in Petrograd but in numerous provincial towns. This particularly dramatic example of official brutality and the expulsion of Mensheviks and SRs from the Central Executive Committee of the Soviets in mid-June strengthened the anti-Bolshevik mood in sections of the Petrograd working class. The Mensheviks sought to capitalize on this by planning a general strike for 2 July, but a combination of repression by the authorities and indifference in the working class ensured that it did not actually take place.

Outside the former capital, the spring and early summer of 1918 also witnessed a revival of the moderate socialists. In new elections to 19 provincial city soviets in the Central Industrial Region (Kaluga, Kostroma, Ryazan, Tver, Tula and Yaroslavl), in the southern black-earth provinces (Orel, Kursk, Tambov), in the Volga basin (Nizhni Novgorod, Kazan, Saratov) and in Penza, Vologda and Archangel, Bolsheviks lost control to the moderates. Aware of the precariousness of their power and fearing, with some justification, that victories for the moderate socialists would open the gates to White counter-revolution, the Bolsheviks proceeded to root out opposition with ruthless despatch. Their determination was strengthened by the assassinations of the popular agitator, V. Volodarsky, in Petrograd on 20 June, and of the German ambassador, Count von Mirbach by the Left SRs on 6 July. Recalcitrant soviets were disbanded, and authority vested in executive committees, the VECHEKA or special emissaries.

In the course of 1918 political opponents within the trade unions were also gradually brought into line. The printers' union continued as a stronghold of Menshevism well into 1920 in Moscow and Samara. In the glass workers' union and chemical workers' union the Bolsheviks gradually wrested control from the Mensheviks in the course of 1918, although the Moscow branch of the chemical workers' union was dominated by non-party elements and Mensheviks until 1921. In the communication workers' union, Left SR and Menshevik influence was undermined with difficulty, particularly among post and telegraph workers and in Moscow. The declining fortunes of the opposition parties within the trade-union movement can be seen in their falling representation at national trade-union congresses. Between the First Congress in January 1918 and the Third in April 1920 the proportion of Menshevik delegates fell from 16 per cent to 3 per cent and the proportion of delegates from other socialist parties from 10 per cent to 4 per cent. The proportion of non-party members, however, rose from 8 per cent to 18 per cent.

It is difficult to assess the extent to which the decline of the socialist opposition to the Bolsheviks was due to government repression or to their inability to consolidate working-class support once full-scale civil war had flared up in June. It is beyond dispute that the Bolsheviks made it difficult for the opposition parties to operate in the soviets and trade unions, even though they were not illegal. On the other hand, it is apparent that, even before the onset of major civil war, opposition to the Bolsheviks was largely economic in its roots and, in Petrograd at least, there seems to have been little enthusiasm for the overthrow of the soviet system and the re-convening of a CONSTITUENT ASSEMBLY, as advocated by the SRs, or the more nebulous political objectives of the Mensheviks. Once civil war was in full spate, although the majority of the Mensheviks and Left SRs opted for the Reds as the lesser evil, it was not easy for them in practice to dissociate themselves from the Right SRs and the minority of Mensheviks who were pledged to bring down the Bolshevik regime by force, nor to refute Bolshevik allegations that their encouragement of labour protest gave comfort to the Whites. The outbreak of civil war may well have served not to foster working-class disaffection for the Bolsheviks but, initially at least, to rally already discontented workers to the regime, in its life-and-death struggle against the Whites.

While many thousands of workers continued enthusiastically to support the Soviet regime during the Civil War in spite of all hardships, it is difficult to gauge the extent and meaning of such support. It is nevertheless manifest in several forms. Tens of thousands of workers volunteered to enlist in the RED ARMY, to join food detachments or to take up responsible positions within the government or party apparatus. In August 1920 a census of the five million-strong Red Army and RED NAVY showed that workers comprised 15 per cent of army units and 29 per cent of naval units, and metal workers comprised by far the largest element among them. There are no global data on the numbers who took part in seizing grain, as this was very much a seasonal operation, but in the second half of 1918 and first quarter of 1919 at least 20,000 workers took part in the food detachments. Finally, although the proportion of workers within the Communist Party fell between 1918 and 1921 from 57 per cent to 41 per cent, the absolute numbers rose from 65,400 to 240,000 (these were, of course, workers by origin, and not necessarily by current occupation). In Petrograd 12,697 workers, or 11 per cent of the industrial labour force, were party members at the end of 1920. In Moscow and Perm the corresponding figures were 8.8 per cent and 8.7 per cent; party saturation was lowest on the railways and in areas of light and small industry, such as Vladimir and Tula.

Given the disastrous industrial conditions under WAR COMMUNISM, it is hardly surprising that there were periodic outbursts of worker unrest; yet little is known about them. The spring of 1919 saw a bout of short strikes in Moscow (centred on the Bogatyr chemical works), Ivanovo-Voznesensk and Tula, where strikes at the state armaments plant halted production for five days, and where the authorities distributed grain, arrested leaders and launched a party recruitment drive. At the Putilov works in Petrograd striking workers demanded free trade in grain, and the authorities intervened to dismantle the shop committees which were said to be led by SRs. An investigating commission reproached management for its 'inability to approach the worker as a teacher to a pupil and, where necessary, as an administrator to a subordinate'. The most serious strike of this period, however, occurred at Astrakhan in March, in the wake of a rebellion by the local garrison. As many as 2,000 people may have been killed by troops sent to quell the uprising. After the spring of 1919 there were sporadic strikes such as those that broke out in the workshops of the Moscow-Kursk railway in December 1919 and January 1920, in which Left SRs were implicated. Most industrial disputes in 1919–20, however, did not issue in stoppages; they no longer concerned wages in the main, but complaints of inadequate food rations or demands for release from work in order to search for food.

Not until the severe winter of 1920–21 did the bottled-up tensions of three years of civil war finally explode in a wave of labour unrest, peasant rebellion and acrimonious in-fighting within the Communist Party (see BOLSHEVIK OPPOSITIONS). On 22 January 1921 the government announced yet another cut in the bread ration after food trains were held up in Siberia and the Northern Caucasus. Three weeks later strikes and demonstrations broke out in Moscow, the key demands of which were for higher rations, 'free trade' and the abolition of grain requisitioning. Some calls were raised for civil and political freedoms. No sooner had the unrest in the capital subsided than it spread to Petrograd. On 23 February workers at the Pipe Works demanded an increase in rations and an immediate distribution of shoes and winter clothing. Their demands

were taken up in other enterprises. As the local party leader, ZINOVIEV declared martial law and strikers at the Pipe Works and the Laferme tobacco factory were locked out. The Mensheviks put out leaflets which called for freely elected soviets and independent trade unions, the restoration of civil liberties, and an end to terror and the release of political prisoners; SRs called for a Constituent Assembly. Regular troops and officer cadets broke up demonstrations and made widespread arrests, but the authorities also distributed extra rations and allowed workers to leave the city to search for food. By early March nearly all the strikes had been suppressed, but a greater threat loomed in the shape of the uprising at KRONSTADT.

Labour protest during the Civil War failed to dent government policies, reflecting weakness of a working class both diminished in numbers and lacking the social cohesion and organizational strength characteristic of 1917. Labour organizations had been instrumental in bringing the Bolsheviks to power but had quickly been incorporated into the new regime. They could thus no longer serve as a fulcrum for a protest movement directed against that regime. The factory committees had been absorbed into the trade unions, the unions were threatened with 'statization' and the power of the soviets had been supplanted by party and military formations. Labour unrest certainly embarrassed a government that claimed to represent proletarian interests but it did not seriously impede the policies of that government. In fact, the passive (and sometimes active) resistance of the peasants was probably a much greater constraint on government action than worker opposition, for the war could not be won without food.

The weakness of labour protest was due partly to small numbers, partly to lack of organization and the fact that the collapse of industry had sapped the economic strength of the working class, but chiefly due to its very nature: the collapse of the economy, by pitting one group of workers against another in the competition for jobs and food, encouraged particularism and localism in worker resistance and discouraged the kind of class-wide activities which had been so much a feature of 1917. Finally, the political context fostered a kind of 'economism'. In 1917 it had been possible to blame the economic ills of the working class on the capitalists or the PROVISIONAL GOVERNMENT. Now there was no longer a clear target for labour protests nor a clear political solution to the economic ills of labour. Certainly, workers saw their woes springing from the policies of War Communism and demanded their abandonment, but they baulked at the prospect of a head-on clash with the architects of those policies. The Mensheviks and SRs, within the limited arena permitted them, urged just such a confrontation, but workers remained sceptical that the political panaceas offered by the moderates could deliver food and jobs. In the last analysis, they felt that Bolsheviks alone provided a bulwark against the restoration of the capitalist order, and this belief deflected any attempt

27

to develop a new political solution to labour's economic ills.

Meanwhile, faced with the dissolution of that class which had brought it to power, the Bolshevik party consoled itself with the thought that the proletarian revolution could be saved only if the party exercised a dictatorship on behalf of the idealized proletariat, and over the actual one. In 1921, however, most Bolsheviks still perceived the threat to the revolution as external; few could see the danger of a corrosion of the revolution from within, via the atrophy of independent labour and popular organizations and the bureaucratization of state and party.   SAS

Further Reading

Baevsky, D.A.: *Rabochii klass v pervye gody sovetskoi vlasti, 1917–21 gg.* Moscow: 1974.

Brovkin, V.: The Mensheviks' political comeback: the elections to the provincial city soviets in spring 1918. *Russian Review* 42 (1983) 1–50.

Gimpelson, E.G.: *Sovetskii rabochii klass, 1918–20 gg.* Moscow: 1974.

Rosenberg, W.: Russian labour and Bolshevik power after October: social dimensions of protest in Petrograd, November 1917–June 1918'. *Slavic Review* 44 (1985).

Schapiro, L.: *The Origin of the Communist Autocracy.* New York: Praeger, 1965 (orig. 1955).

The Demise of Workers' Control in Industry

One of the first measures enacted by the Bolshevik government was the Decree on Workers' Control published on 14 November 1917. This recognized the right of workers in all enterprises to control all aspects of production, to have access to all spheres of administration, and the right of the lower organs of workers' control to make their decisions binding on the employers. The Decree did not spell out in precise detail the scope of workers' control, and this quickly proved to be a bone of contention between the Central Council of Factory Committees and the short-lived All-Russian Council of Workers' Control, set up by the Decree, in which the trade unions had the loudest voice. The CCFC urged that workers' control no longer be seen as mere 'inspection and accounting', but as active intervention in production, as a measure leading to eventual workers' self-management within a system of state-owned industry. For their part, the trade unions advocated a much narrower interpretation of workers' control and urged that enterprise control commissions be strictly subordinate to the control-distribution commissions of the relevant trade unions and to central direction generally.

At the grass roots, FACTORY COMMITTEES and their control organs quickly discovered that escalating economic problems forced them to adopt ever more radical forms of workers' control. Many factory owners began to run down their operations, to refuse new orders and sell off stock. Such acts of 'sabotage' caused the control organs to

intervene decisively in all aspects of administration and production, and desperately to seek out scarce supplies of fuel, raw materials and spare parts, new orders and funds to pay wages, in a vain effort to stave off closures. Where owners did abandon or seek to close down their enterprises, the control organs attempted to take over the running of them. Such takeovers were, in general, motivated more by a practical concern to save jobs than by anarcho-syndicalist ideology. In Petrograd province between November and March 1918, only 27 factories were taken over, and in nearly all cases, this was seen as a temporary measure until the enterprises were taken into state ownership. Factory seizures were more common where workers took over small light-industrial enterprises, especially food-processing plants, for example in the Middle and Lower Volga, Vyatka, the Western provinces and the central black-earth region.

Many leading BOLSHEVIKS, particularly in the trade unions, looked askance at the 'syndicalist' excesses of the factory committees, pointing out that, in the competition for scarce resources, factory committees ended up defending the interests of their particular enterprise against those of others. By the end of 1917 the party leadership was generally agreed that the trade unions alone, as organizations embracing whole branches of industry, could tackle the mammoth problems of regulating the economy. It was thus agreed at the First All-Russian Trade Union Congress in January 1918 that the factory committees should cease to exist separately from the trade unions, and that the committees should become the basic cells of the unions within each workplace. Although the CCFC was hardly enamoured of this shot-gun marriage, the factory committees consented to be absorbed into the unions, since they recognized that there was no room for two organizations vying to restore order to the economy. Nevertheless throughout the CIVIL WAR, trade-union leaders continued to complain periodically about the aspirations of some factory committees to independence of the unions.

If the factory committees lost out to the unions in less than six months of Bolshevik power, they could yet be satisfied that one of their major objectives was realized far sooner than they dared hope in October. For the CCFC, from the first, had urged the government to move rapidly towards a planned socialist economy, by undertaking sweeping nationalization of industry and full state regulation of the economy. Most of the Bolshevik leaders, however, favoured a system of 'state capitalism', i.e. state control of strategic sectors with extensive private ownership of industry under government supervision and workers' control. This proved unviable, for a tide of 'nationalizations from below' welled up in response to deepening turmoil in industry. Factory committees, local soviets and local national economic councils (*sovnarkhozy*), having taken control of enterprises threatened with closure, tried to force the authorities to take them into state ownership. Between

November and March 1918, 863 warrants were issued to dispossess owners of industrial enterprises, many of which were in the Urals, and of these, 775 were issued by local bodies (mainly soviets). In the face of such pressure from below, the resistance of the Supreme Council of National Economy (VSNKh) to nationalization began to weaken, and on 23 June, sweeping nationalization of industry was announced.

At the Sixth (and final) Conference of Petrograd Factory Committees on 25 January 1918 a resolution calling for the immediate nationalization of industry argued for workers' management of enterprises under state ownership. At the First Congress of Sovnarkhozy (25 May–4 June 1918), however, a resolution to ensure that two thirds of the members of the management boards of nationalized enterprises were elected by the workforce was defeated, in favour of one allowing only one third of the members to be directly elected, and emphasizing strict subordination of management boards to the central organs of VSNKh. Even this limited form of workers' collegiate management was unacceptable to LENIN who, in the interests of raising labour productivity, was now preaching the virtues of dictatorial management by one person. Up until the end of 1919, however, he met with stiff resistance from trade unions and factory committees. In 1919 only 10.8 per cent of Russian enterprises, for which there is information, were run by individual managers; by the autumn of 1920 this had risen dramatically to 82 per cent.

By the end of the Civil War not much was left of that vigorous movement for workers' control which had been spearheaded by the factory committees in 1917. Talk of workers' control was not entirely absent, but it was now deemed to be institutionalized in the form of workers' inspectorates (trade-union bodies responsible for monitoring affairs in critical sectors such as rail transport and food supply) and state control organs, charged with auditing the affairs of government departments. Within the workplace an authoritarian structure of management had been restored – though not without considerable resistance – in which professional managers and technical specialists held the upper hand over labour organizations. It is tempting to see this as a consequence of the Bolsheviks' deep-rooted preference for centralization and technical expertise, and to see in their support for workers' control in 1917 little more than political opportunism; but although ideological predispositions undoubtedly played a part in bringing workers' control to an end, the principal causes of this outcome must be located in the terrifying difficulties wrought by economic collapse and civil war.   SAS

Further Reading

Drobizhev, V.Z.: *Glavnyi shtab sotsialisticheskoi promyshlennosti.* Moscow: 1966.

Sirianni, C.: *Workers' Control and Socialist Democracy: The Soviet Experience.* London: Verso, 1982.

The Militarization of Labour and the Role of Trade Unions

With the outbreak of full-scale civil war industry was converted into a supply organization for the RED ARMY, and industrial policy became a component of military strategy. Centralized direction and planning of industry, which was the hallmark of WAR COMMUNISM, had significant consequences for labour, in particular, because increasing efforts were made to place workers under military discipline. It was the policy of labour 'militarization' which served as the catalyst for a fierce debate within the Bolshevik party from 1920–21, which came into focus on the question of the role of the trade unions in a workers' state.

The Code of Laws on Labour promulgated in December 1918 imposed the 'duty to work' on all the able-bodied between the ages of 16 and 50 (see SOVIET LEGAL SYSTEM). In the course of 1919 the acute shortage of labour, especially of skilled labour, in such critical sectors as transport, fuel production and defence production, led to growing numbers of workers being put on a military footing: in April 1919, for example, coal miners were prohibited from leaving their jobs. On 29 January 1920 SOVNARKOM proclaimed the introduction of general labour conscription: all were now liable to be called up for stints of work in food and fuel procurement, road construction, cartage etc. It was also decreed that military and naval units could be mobilized for civilian reconstruction, and 'labour armies' were formed. It is estimated that in the first half of 1920 nearly six million people were drafted to work in the timber industry. The militarization of labour was a response to problems of labour supply, labour turnover and labour indiscipline. It may not in fact have been as widely practised as the plethora of decrees would suggest, but even when it was successfully implemented it may not have solved the acute problems of the regime in ensuring an adequate supply of efficient labour. Labour turnover, for example, continued to run at a high level: data on 35 defence plants show that between September 1919 and August 1920 whilst 38,500 workers were taken on (mainly conscripts), 35,000 left their jobs.

The Chief Committee for General Labour Conscription of the Council of Defence, together with its local organs, was principally responsible for labour mobilization, but labour unions were also encouraged to play an active part. Although some rank-and-file trade unionists may have welcomed militarization as a solution to their intractable local difficulties, union leaders generally regarded it with suspicion. For they were neither convinced that militarization was effective, nor that it was for them as trade unions to implement it. It was the attempt to execute far-reaching militarization of labour on the railways that brought trade-union opposition to a head.

By the winter of 1919–20 the situation on the railways

was chaotic, with individual lines competing for scarce supplies of fuel and food, local bodies ignoring central directives, and absenteeism running at 20 per cent to 40 per cent between January and March 1920. In March 1920 TROTSKY took over the commissariat of transport with a view to centralizing control of the transport system and intensifying labour discipline. As the railway workers were already under military discipline, his first act was to reorganize the party's activities on military lines, by creating the Chief Political Administration for Lines of Communication (Glavpolitput), an organization of the 'political department' type. Trotsky got the wheels turning, but only at a cost of enormous friction with the leaders of the railroad union. In August, with the backing of the party leaders, Trotsky ousted the heads of the union, and established the Provisional Central Committee for Transport (Tsektran), a combination of commissariat, labour union and political organ, responsible for the entire rail and water transport system. This body not only short-circuited the leadership of the railroad union, it undercut the authority of the All-Russian Central Council of Trade Unions and thus brought the trade unions as whole into confrontation with the party leadership.

Opposition to government policies had been growing within the trade unions for a considerable time, initially over the question of one-man management, and then over the issue of militarization of labour. At the root of this opposition was a sense that party leaders were riding roughshod over the rights of the unions. At the Ninth Party Congress in March 1920 SHLYAPNIKOV's call for a 'separation of powers' between party, soviets and trade unions was rejected and, subsequently, BUKHARIN and RADEK were installed in the All-Russian Council of Trade Unions to represent the party leadership. Increasingly the conflict came to centre on the role of the trade unions within a workers' state. (See BOLSHEVIK OPPOSITIONS.)

This issue had arisen as early as the First All-Russian Trade Union Congress in January 1918 when the Mensheviks had vigorously defended the independence of the trade unions from the state. It resurfaced at the Second Congress in January 1919, which endorsed the notion of a gradual 'statization' of the trade unions, as their functions broadened and merged with those of the state industrial administration. In the meantime, however, the trade unions' functions and powers remained unclear. If the state, as the principal employer, also represented the interests of labour, did the unions have any functions left? If so, did these functions include defending the material interests of their members, or were they confined to implementing government industrial policy? And what degree of independence from the state should the unions enjoy? Trotsky gave forthright answers to these questions: the task of the unions was to raise labour productivity and they should abandon any pretensions to autonomy. This provoked the wrath of trade-union leaders, for example

M. P. Tomsky, and at the conference of trade unions in November 1920 an acrimonious debate broke out, which increasingly became public.

In the three months preceding the Tenth Party Congress in March 1921, a number of 'platforms' were circulated concerning the role of the trade unions. Trotsky, Bukharin and six other members of the Central Committee accused the railroad union of acting like a capitalist trade union and called for the 'planned transformation of the unions into apparatuses of the workers' state'. The defenders of the trade unions accused their opponents of wanting to emasculate them altogether, whilst on the far left, a group emerged under the name of the 'Workers' Opposition', which linked the issue of trade-union autonomy to a far-reaching critique of bureaucratization within the state and party. Its leaders were Shlyapnikov and KOLLONTAI and they went so far as to advocate that the administration of the economy be carried out through the trade unions. The Lenin-Zinoviev 'platform of ten' was essentially a compromise, though there is some evidence that Lenin was basically in favour of the Trotsky-Bukharin proposals. This platform rejected the rapid statization of the trade unions, arguing that they should serve as a link between the party and immature masses and as 'schools of communism'. It was this platform which was adopted by 336 votes, against the 50 cast for Trotsky's platform and the 18 cast for the Workers' Opposition, at the Tenth Party Congress.   SAS

Further Reading

Carr, E.H.: *The Bolshevik Revolution 1917–23*, vol. 2. London: Pelican, 1966 (orig. 1952).

Daniels, R.V.: *The Conscience of the Revolution: Communist Opposition in Soviet Russia*. New York: Clarion Books, 1969.

The Women's Movement before 1917

First developed during the early reforming years of Alexander II's reign, the women's movement had two sources of inspiration: feminist ideas which had slowly been taking hold in western Europe and North America in the previous two decades and the wave of enthusiasm for social change which arose among educated Russians after Tsar Nicholas I's death in 1855.

The ideas behind the women's movement in Russia, as elsewhere, derived from the rationalism of the Enlightenment and the egalitarian and libertarian ideology of the French Revolution, though it took half a century for the implications for women to become apparent. The radical proposals of the utopian socialists in France caused a flutter in the 1830s and 1840s, and George Sand's novels, with their sexually emancipated heroines, were widely read and emulated; but outside small socialist communities the concept of female equality was generally lampooned as outlandish and contrary to nature until the middle of the nineteenth century.

Precisely why attitudes began to change is still not entirely clear. In western Europe and North America, the rapid growth of an urban middle class, the formation of a female proletariat, the expansion of education, increasing mass participation in politics, the development of liberal and socialist ideologies, and possibly demographic factors, all contributed to disturb prevailing conventions.

In Russia, the catalyst was the abrupt political change after Nicholas I's death and the reforms which ensued. The government's declared intention of freeing the serfs unwittingly encouraged dreams of other forms of emancipation: of children from parents, women from fathers and husbands, and ultimately, of society from the patriarchal state. The government further stimulated women's aspirations in 1858 by extending the gymnasium system of secondary education to girls (with some restrictions), thus unintentionally establishing the grounds for women's higher education.

The issue of sexual equality became an integral part of the current political debate: the 'woman question' was treated at length by male radical publicists (Chernyshevsky, Mikhailov, Pisarev, Dobrolyubov, Lavrov) and by some liberals (notably N. I. Pirogov in his 'Questions of Life'). Few women in the 1850s and 1860s gave public utterance to their discontents and aspirations though by this time they had taken the first steps to organize. Their absence from the journals is not easily explained. Financial resources were a significant factor: one woman who did find her way into print, Mariya Vernadskaya, co-edited a journal with her husband. In true laissez-faire spirit, she told women to stop being dependent, stand on their own two feet and go out and earn a living.

The women's movement in Russia had much in common with women's movements in the West. All made a critical break with past assumptions by asserting the equality of the sexes in intellect, moral worth and social value. In practical terms, they helped to create new opportunities for women outside the home, promoting higher education, professional training and access to paid occupations. But correspondingly, they contributed to new concepts of child-development, emphasizing the importance of schooling and the mother's role, thus initiating a potential conflict between the urge towards female autonomy and the consciousness of a need for self-sacrifice in the interests of the next generation. The radical solution to this conflict was to make society collectively responsible for child-rearing. It is noteworthy that in the entire course of the women's movement, in Russia as elsewhere, the potential role of fathers in child-care was hardly explored.

As in the West, those involved in the movement were mainly educated women from the privileged classes – in Russia, more often from the gentry than from the less-significant merchant class, but also including women from clerical families, and a few of peasant origin. As in the West, they shared the intelligentsia's 'repentant' response

to society's ills in the wish to serve society, expressed in outlets ranging from philanthropy to radical politics.

The distinguishing feature of the Russian movement was the sharp division between radicals and reformers. The reformers used restraint and compromise. Working within the law they raised petitions, lobbied ministers and exploited personal connections to reach influential figures. Concentrating on philanthropy and higher education they may have achieved more than with a more comprehensive programme, given tsarist conservatism. Philanthropy was already an acceptable form of public activity for women, while in higher education they could count on support from individual professors and even from university administration (in 1863 all but Moscow and Dorpat faovured women's admission). From the end of the 1860s, feminist lobbying resulted in public lectures, preparatory courses and finally university-level courses for women (1872 in Moscow), all existing on public goodwill, organization and funding. Women were admitted to courses for 'learned midwives' at the Medical Surgical Academy in St Petersburg (1872), extended to full-length medical courses in 1876. In 1878 the first formally constituted higher courses for women opened in St Petersburg followed by Moscow, Kiev and Kazan. Though outside the university system and not giving rights to state service and rank which men enjoyed, these courses were in practice women's universities.

The feminists' philanthropic enterprises were intended both to help the beneficiaries become self-sufficient and to give their organizers practical experience of administration and public life. They were run, as far as was then possible, on democratic lines and minimum regulations. The most successful venture was a Society to Provide Cheap Lodgings (founded in 1861) which in twenty years became a major charity in St Petersburg. Other charities included a society to raise funds for women attending the higher courses (1878) and refuges to save poor women from prostitution.

While for many the 'woman question' could be resolved by the attainment by peaceful means of the right to study, work and live independently, for others the issue of emancipation had an entirely subversive significance. Both for radicals and for their extreme conservative opponents, the 'woman question' was associated with the destruction of the existing social order. Arch-conservatives predicted the collapse of the family and social disorder if women were admitted to university; radicals, too, saw the liberation of women as only the beginning of a transformation of society. Up to the mid 1860s, the revolt of radical women was primarily a personal one: rejection of parental authority and social convention. Numerous young women arranged 'fictitious marriages' with men sympathetic to the cause, in order to leave home; they cut their hair short, wore simple, unadorned clothing, smoked in public, went out unchaperoned, and experimented with communal living arrangements and collective workshops (arteli), as much for practical as for ideological reasons. Such communes and workshops became a veritable fad after Chernyshevsky popularized and idealized them in his didactic novel, *What is to be done?* (1863).

Within a few years, this personal, 'nihilist' rejection of cultural norms became more overtly political. As the fragile tolerance of unorthodoxy, which marked the early years of Alexander II's reign, gave way to increasing hostility and extremism on both sides, nihilist women (if they did not retreat from public activity altogether) tended either to gravitate towards more moderate feminism or, more commonly, to move into active revolutionary circles. The point of departure in many cases was the desire to train for a profession which could be of use to 'the people'. The most popular choices were teaching and medicine. Some attended the courses which started during the seventies in Russia; others went abroad, particularly to Zurich (104 by 1873, one third of the Russian colony) where many became involved in radical and revolutionary émigré politics. Although at first they tended to cluster in women's discussion circles, where they could study political texts and learn to 'think rationally', most then joined mixed groups and left the 'woman question' behind. Radical men (and increasingly women) in the seventies felt either that it was irrelevant to the revolutionary struggle or that it would be resolved after the revolution, with other social questions. In their own circles, sexual equality was taken for granted.

Several hundred women became involved in POPULISM, forming a sizeable minority of all activists (15 per cent of all those arrested). But though some began their revolutionary work among female factory workers, none addressed the specific needs or grievances of women and explained this failing in terms of these women's backwardness. From the early 1870s to the late 1890s, revolutionary thinkers and propagandists (Populist and later Marxist) paid minimal attention either to the 'woman question' or to female workers and peasants, and even after 1900 their response was marked by ambivalence.

Like all reform movements in Russia, feminism occupied an uneasy position between two warring extremes, and was given short shrift by both. In the increasingly restrictive environment of Alexander II's reign, every manifestation of independent initiative came under suspicion: not only the Populists' 'going to the people', but entirely non-political enterprises like a publishing cooperative initiated by three pillars of the feminist establishment in the mid-sixties, fund-raising activities, proposals to form women's groups, and so forth.

The highly publicized involvement of women in revolutionary politics reinforced existing prejudices against feminism. While this might have unintentionally beneficial effects – notably the government's decision to expand women's higher education in Russia to stem the flow of radical women to Switzerland, and its subsequent decision to establish the higher courses on a formal basis under the Ministry of Education – its negative effects were insidious. Both the government's restrictiveness and the revolutionaries' loss of interest meant that the issue of women's equality was reduced, in essence, to the expansion of secondary and higher education, the entry of women into the medical and teaching professions, some limited rights to state service, and carefully supervised philanthropy.

The split between feminists and radical women became complete. After 1878, radicals were totally committed to the terrorism of People's Will. Women occupied a unique position in the movement, prominent not only in numbers (one third of the organization's executive) but also in the reverence with which they were held. Though much of the women's work in the terrorist campaign was routine, if still dangerous, a few women were involved in planning and carrying out the final attempt which killed the tsar on 1 March 1881.

The susceptibility of the women's movement to fluctuations in the political climate was graphically illustrated after the assassination. The expansion of higher education for women was halted: medical courses were suspended for over a decade, and only the St Petersburg higher courses remained open. For most of the 1880s, the movement lay dormant; after the death of Alexander III (1894) and the revival of public initiative, feminists began tentatively to organize again, though even their modest proposals collided with bureaucratic obstruction. However, government support for women's education permitted the higher courses to re-open, followed in 1897 by a newly established Women's Medical Institute.

Even by 1900, however, the women's movement still signified little more than education and philanthropy. Its appeal was limited to educated women of moderate views, who were hampered either by personal aptitude or official restriction in grappling with the social and economic changes that had brought thousands of women into the proliferating factories, and exacerbated the already acute problems of low pay (between half and two thirds the men's rates), dangerous working conditions, appalling housing and poor diet, ill-health, high infant mortality, abandoned children, alcoholism, prostitution, etc. And given the suppression of all open political life, Russian feminists had not yet embraced political and civil rights in their programmes.

Women in revolutionary organizations were hardly better equipped to make a popular appeal to women. Though committed to sexual equality and considering themselves equals of their male comrades, they had inherited the Populists' disdain for 'narrow' separatism and piecemeal reform, and found confirmation in Marx's hostility to class-divisive strategies. Seeing women workers effectively disabled by their lowly status in the hierarchy of skill and pay, their poor literacy rates, their dual burden of work and family, and their psychological and physical subordination to men, few revolutionaries could detect any revolutionary potential there, and women's apparent lack of responsiveness to propaganda only confirmed this view.

However, a small number of working-class women had broken through these prejudices, and through the hostility of their own men, to participate in workers' circles in various industrial centres early in the 1890s. Although the Marxist agitational circles which succeeded them in the mid-nineties were far less welcoming, these women's experience, combined with female participation in industrial strikes (some initiated by women) provided evidence that the female proletariat was not the uniformly inert mass their male counterparts often insisted. Even so, Russian SOCIAL DEMOCRATS made little effort to win over women. A pamphlet by KRUPSKAYA, 'The Woman Worker' (1901) inspired by Bebel and by Clara Zetkin's work in Germany, was the sole contribution on women to the social-democratic literature until 1905, and only then did the party's tactics in relation to women's organizations become a live issue. However, both Social Democrats and SOCIAL-IST REVOLUTIONARIES included equal political and civil rights of men and women in their programmes (1903 and 1904 respectively) without apparent discord, unlike some socialist parties abroad, and unlike the constitutionalist groups of the liberation movement in Russia.

The 1905 REVOLUTION brought about a transformation in the women's movement. For the first time, political rights were put on the agenda and political organization was employed to win them. The cause of this abrupt change was the political crisis precipitated by the Russo-Japanese war and the eruption of demands for a constitution by the liberation movement, of which feminists counted themselves a part. Sharing its goals, they assumed that its demand for a CONSTITUENT ASSEMBLY extended to both sexes. Their discovery that this assumption was false and that proposals for women's suffrage met resistance and ridicule (as well as strong support), led a group of liberationists to found a Union of Equal Rights for Women, which became one of the founder members of the Union of Unions in spring 1905. Their goals were diverse: to unite women of all classes, nationalities and religions in defence of their rights; to press the liberal and socialist opposition into a commitment to female equality; and to force the government to grant political and civil rights, to increase protective legislation for women at work, give peasant women equal rights in land distribution, introduce coeducation in schools and universities, and give women access to state and public employment.

The union made a striking impact during 1905. Its membership, 6,000–8,000 by the autumn, included liberals and moderate socialists, as well as some SDs and SRs. It had sections in St Petersburg, Moscow and 17 provincial branches, reaching peasant and working-class women, and attempting to organize domestic servants. Its principal achievement was to force liberals to make a commitment to women's suffrage which survived the defeat of the 1905

Revolution. However, the union's propaganda elicited no response from the government, which consistently refused to consider the issue right up to 1917.

The 1905 Revolution had a galvanizing effect on other women's groups, and simultaneously revealed the schismatic tendencies inherent in the women's movement. At the end of 1904 a new journal, *Zhenskii vestnik* (Women's Messenger, 1904-1917), appeared, edited by M. I. POKROVSKAYA, a feminist highly critical of the liberation movement, who espoused separatist tactics. A year later she founded the Women's Progressive Party which was weakened at its inception by the breakaway of a still more separatist group.

Feminist activity among working-class women in the major industrial centres provoked Social Democratic women to think more seriously about the separate organization of women. A few, notably KOLLONTAI, were alarmed by the interest which female factory workers were displaying towards such organizations. Particularly significant was the women's section set up in Father Gapon's Assembly of Russian Factory Workers at the end of 1904, and four working women's clubs which attracted large attendances in St Petersburg during 1906, before being closed down by the police. In addition, women had called for separate female representation on the Shidlovsky Commission early in 1905, and took an active part in the strike movement during the year.

While a perceptive observer would have recognized that even the Union of Equal Rights, the first feminist organization to make a direct appeal to working women, had only tenuous links with the factories, the absence of any social-democratic organization for women raised the serious possibility that feminists might fill the vacuum and entice women workers into activity hostile to the male-dominated labour movement. Since social-democratic influence even among male workers in 1905 was unstable, Kollontai and her colleagues argued that it was doubly important to give women a reason to identify with party work. The argument attracted little support from either MENSHEVIK or BOLSHEVIK organizations. Kollontai's group was accused of promoting feminism, an accusation particularly galling to Kollontai herself, one of the most virulent critics of feminism from 1905 to 1917. In 1907, without official party approval, her group set up a legal Mutual Aid Society for Working Women in St Petersburg, which thrived for several months before falling victim to quarrels between its intelligentsia and its working-class members. She was also largely responsible for assembling a working women's delegation to the first Russian women's congress in 1908, a major event sponsored by feminist organizations, which attracted much publicity and debate. Kollontai was forced to go abroad immediately afterwards and did not return until 1917.

The party organizations continued to ignore working women until the revival of the labour movement, following the Lena massacre in 1912, prompted a new interest. Why this change occurred has still to be agreed: perhaps a delayed response to the sharp increase of women in the labour force from 1905; the rise in the number of strikes initiated by women, beginning in 1910; the intervention of LENIN, prompted by Krupskaya and Inessa ARMAND, who sensed both the potential support which women might offer the revolution, and their capacity to hinder it if their interests were threatened or their needs unmet. The influence of SD and SR women, both on factory women and on their respective parties, is also a matter of disagreement: some historians have argued a decreased female influence in revolutionary parties, especially as the RSDRP became more 'proletarianized'; this must be balanced against the new awareness among many SD and SR women of female factory workers' special interests, and these revolutionaries' subsequent initiatives to organize working-class women.

In 1913, International Women's Day (inaugurated in Germany in 1910) was celebrated for the first time in Russia, and again in 1914. That year saw the publication of a Bolshevik and Menshevik journal specifically aimed at women, neither of which survived more than a few issues. In addition, both factions' newspapers began to give more space to women's issues and to letters from women.

Meanwhile, the threat of a feminist takeover of factory or peasant women had disappeared, when the liberation movement disintegrated in 1906–7. The Union of Equal Rights survived until 1908, succeeded by a more narrowly feminist League of Equal Rights which remained the main women's organization until the OCTOBER REVOLUTION. The achievements of the women's movement after 1905 were to keep women's issues before the public and to sponsor legislation in the Duma. Using the greater scope for public assembly between 1906 and 1914, women's organizations staged three major congresses: the 1908 congress, one in 1910 on prostitution, and the last in 1912 on women's education. They also used their well-wishers in the Duma (Kadets, Trudoviks, and a few Octobrists) to get legislation passed on inheritance, legal separation of spouses and a married woman's right to her own internal passport. All attempts to introduce legislation on women's suffrage failed.

On the outbreak of the FIRST WORLD WAR most feminists became patriots, like the liberal intelligentsia generally; any pacifist sentiments remained strictly private. As in the West, middle-class women volunteered for war work in military hospitals and at the front; feminist organizations contributed by setting up their own hospitals. There was some substitution of men by women in white-collar jobs and the professions, but less than feminists expected and much less than occurred in manual occupations. In Petrograd, the proportion of women in industry rose from 25.3 per cent in 1913 to 33.3 per cent in 1917; in Moscow, from 39.4 per cent in 1914 to 48.7 per cent in

1917. A comparable or greater increase took place in the agricultural labour force.

The war saw little intensification of the revolutionary parties' interest in working women, despite their increased significance in the WAR ECONOMY. But in the final crisis of tsarism, goaded by severe food shortages and rocketing prices, they proved to be a spontaneous revolutionary force, independent of feminists or Social Democrats. On International Women's Day, 23 February 1917, women workers came out on strike and, joining crowds of women impatiently queueing for bread, set off the chain of events which led to the tsar's abdication. Thus working women, the 'inert mass', the 'backward stratum' of the proletariat, inadvertently led workers and soldiers into the February Revolution.   LE

Women in 1917 and After

The immediate goals of the feminists were first attained in 1917: equal political rights; belated recognition by the Bolsheviks that working women were actively involved in political protests and strikes; the unofficial establishment of women's sections in the Bolshevik organization; and, after the Bolshevik coup, the appropriation of the symbols of women's liberation by the Soviet regime and the disintegration of the 'bourgeois' women's movement.

The February Revolution did not in itself guarantee women's political rights: both PROVISIONAL GOVERNMENT and SOVIET were willing to temporize on the issue until the war ended. Feminists gave them no chance to do so. They launched a barrage of propaganda which culminated on 19 March (NS) in a procession to the Tauride Palace of 40,000 women, who refused to disband until women were promised the vote. Resistance crumbled and the marchers went home satisfied. Four months later, the electoral law for the Constituent Assembly was ratified, giving equal voting rights to all men and women over twenty (excepting convicts, deserters, the insane and the imperial family). Women were also given full voting rights in local elections.

Legislation was passed equalizing women's rights in the civil service, the legal profession, schools and higher education. Welfare legislation was hardly begun, but night work for women and children was restricted. Changes in the laws on marriage and the family were indefinitely postponed.

Feminists, untouched by Leninist defeatism, now channelled their energies into the war effort. They proposed labour conscription of women and applauded WOMEN SOLDIERS; leading feminists played host to Mrs Pankhurst, sent to Russia by Lloyd George to promote the Allies' cause. Existing feminist societies re-grouped into the Republican Union of Democratic Women's Organizations, a coalition of liberals and non-socialist radicals, which also drew in Mensheviks and SRs.

The extent of non-Bolshevik influence on working-class

women during 1917 is impossible to gauge. Given the subsequent eclipse of the women's movement and the disappearance of feminist records, it is hard to shift the later Soviet interpretation which portrays an unbridgeable gap between the bourgeois, pro-war feminists and the angry, unsatisfied mass of women workers. In any event, the feminist campaign for the vote in March coincided with meetings and demonstrations of working women also calling for rights. Kollontai saw this as evidence that the feminists had 'captured the minds of working women', and immediately renewed her pressure on the Petrograd party to pay attention to women's issues.

Others, Bolshevik and Menshevik, had already arrived at the same conclusion. On 13 March, Vera Slutskaya, an erstwhile opponent of separate sections, proposed and won the creation of a Bureau of Women Workers in the Bolshevik organization, and the revival of *Rabotnitsa* (The Woman Worker), founded in 1914. For the rest of the year, Bolsheviks competed with Mensheviks, SRs and 'bourgeois' feminists for the allegiance of working-class women (factory workers, servants, laundresses, soldiers' wives), most successfully in Petrograd, less so in Moscow. Mensheviks and SRs benefited from the sharp reaction against the Bolsheviks after the July Days; otherwise, the surviving evidence points to an increasing influence of a better-organized Bolshevik party apparatus for urban working-class women. None of the organizations, feminist or revolutionary, paid much attention to peasant women.

Bolshevik activity among women in Petrograd reached a peak in October, in preparation for a conference of working women, scheduled for 27 October (OS) but held early in November. In the meantime, Bolshevik medical students had been training factory women for medical brigades, which on the night of the armed uprising were despatched around the city. A number of women had also joined the Red Guards and took part in the storming of the Winter Palace, during which a few were killed.

Women and Bolshevik rule

The central issue preoccupying those involved in the Bolshevik organization of women during 1917 was how to use them in the revolutionary struggle. This was complicated by a disagreement among activists as to the purpose of agitation among women. Was it to raise the consciousness of a backward element in order to neutralize its hostility and give it a reason to identify with the Bolsheviks, or was it to bring under party control an already active proletarian women's movement? The official party line emphasized women's backwardness; female activists stressed their revolutionary potential. In reality, an effective Bolshevik strategy had to take account of both. But even if this were successful, the result would always be an instrumental approach to the 'woman question': to use the particular needs and particular oppression of women for the sake of the revolution. The more idealistic aspect of

women's liberation (epitomized in Social Democracy by Kollontai and Armand) was subordinated to the struggle for power.

An additional problem was the very existence of women's sections. Separate agitation among women had been reluctantly agreed by the party in the spring of 1917, but it was repeatedly stressed that such work should under no circumstances lead to autonomous sections. Slutskaya's proposal for a bureau was not fully realized; instead, *Rabotnitsa* became the focus of Bolshevik work with women. Thus from the very beginning of Bolshevik rule there existed a noticeable ambivalence towards the 'woman question': a theoretical commitment to women's liberation via socialist revolution, but a distaste for separate organization and an unwillingness to accept that women's interests were not always identical with, or protected by, men's interests. There was also the inherited and often unconscious assumption that issues relating to women were always of secondary importance. These factors combined with the insecurity of Bolshevik power, of foreign intervention and the CIVIL WAR, desperate shortages and economic collapse, to push the dream of women's liberation into the remote future. In the circumstances it was remarkable that the new regime honoured its commitment to women, to the extent of issuing decrees which, on paper at least, affected the everyday lives of millions of women.

Political and civil rights: Already guaranteed by the Provisional Government, these were confirmed with some modification by the Soviet government: women of the former privileged classes were actually deprived of citizenship, and the concept of citizenship itself was widened to include economic and social rights and responsibilities. Women as well as men thus became liable for labour conscription, though in practice it was not imposed equally on both sexes. Correspondingly, the right to work was enshrined by law; in reality, women's unemployment rose disproportionately in the twenties, after the introduction of NEP. Women were guaranteed equal pay for equal work, but violations of the principle were widespread. Similarly, women were to enjoy (with men) an eight-hour day, and were additionally banned from night work, overtime and underground labour. In practice, these restrictions were frequently ignored.

Family and marriage legislation: Here the impact was greater. The remaining disabilities which restricted women's freedom within marriage were swept away, women were given equal rights to hold land, to enjoy full membership of the rural commune, and to act as head of the household. Civil registration of marriage, replacing ecclesiastical marriages, gave equal authority to husband and wife and removed discrimination against illegitimate children. Restrictions on divorce were lifted. Abortion was legalized in 1920 to reduce mortality from illegal abortions, rather than from a belief in a woman's freedom of choice.

Indeed, the assumptions made by revolutionary policy-makers, even those like Kollontai who considered themselves sexually emancipated, were remarkably conservative. While they made heroic efforts to protect the health of mothers and children in a period of social upheaval and scarcity, they hardly questioned the assumption that all women should have children and that these children should be cared for by women. Exceptions to this rule might be made for individual heroines too engrossed in the fight for the revolution's survival to think of personal relationships, but the mass of women were expected to fulfil their social duty and reproduce. Bolsheviks talked grandiloquently about the emancipation of women from household drudgery and childcare, but their solution was to place these functions in the hands of a female collective – nurseries, kitchens, refectories, laundries, etc., all run by women. The socially more radical possibility that men might take on traditionally female roles at home (as women were expected to take on men's at work) was never explored.

To a considerable extent this social conservatism reflected the outlook of the 'masses' whom the revolution was intended to serve, but this cannot be the sole explanation, in view of the Bolsheviks' determination to mould a new Soviet citizen and their lack of squeamishness about trampling on old prejudices and customs.

Women's party organization: The long-running battle within the party over the existence of separate women's sections was resolved in 1919 by the formation of the Women's Section of the Central Committee Secretariat, otherwise known as Zhenotdel (or, derisively, Tsentrobaba). Local sections were established throughout the country, with the task of breaking down women's hostility to the new regime's measures, and organizing them under the wing of the party. Zhenotdel performed many functions during its early years, combining propaganda and political recruitment, with social services. Its staff set up communal dining rooms, crèches and kindergartens, cared for thousands of orphans and abandoned children, promoted women's literacy, and carried the sexual and social revolution into the Muslim communities of CENTRAL ASIA. During the twenties its importance dwindled, especially after the death of Armand and Kollontai's removal from the political scene. In 1930 it was suddenly closed down.

The liberation of women was proving far more complex than any pre-war Bolshevik had ever envisaged. The introduction of NEP resulted in sharply increased female unemployment and further cuts in the welfare provisions which had already been trimmed by the Civil War. Paradoxically, it was only with STALIN's forced industrialization that women were fully mobilized into the workforce, a double paradox, since this period also saw the reversal of the emancipatory precepts of the Bolsheviks. Stalinist policies resulted in full female participation in the economy and simultaneously the resurrection of traditional, 'bourgeois' concepts of home, family, good wives and self-sacrificing mothers.

LE

Further Reading

Atkinson, Dorothy, Dallin, Alexander and Lapidus, Gail Warshofsky eds.: *Women in Russia*. Stanford: Stanford University Press, 1977.

Donald, Moira: Bolshevik Activity amongst the Working Women of Petrograd in 1917. *International Review of Social History* 27 (1982) 129–60.

Edmondson, Linda Harriet: *Feminism in Russia, 1900–1917*. London: Heinemann Educational Books; Stanford: Stanford University Press, 1984.

Engel, Barbara Alpern: *Mothers and Daughters. Women of the Intelligentsia in Nineteenth Century Russia*. Cambridge: Cambridge University Press, 1983.

Glickman, Rose L.: *Russian Factory Women. Workplace and Society, 1880–1914*. Berkeley: University of California Press, 1984.

Lapidus, Gail Warshofsky: *Women in Soviet Society; Equality, Development and Social Change*. Berkeley: University of California Press, 1978.

Stites, Richard: *The Women's Liberation Movement in Russia. Feminism, Nihilism and Bolshevism, 1860–1930*. Princeton: Princeton University Press, 1978.

Women Soldiers: 1917–1921

Russia has a tradition of women soldiers, such as Nadezhda Durova, who served as a Cossack during the Napoleonic Wars. In 1917, the idea of volunteer women's battalions came from Sergeant Maria BOCHKAREVA. Her own 300-strong Women's Battalion of Death was designed to shame the men into continuing the war. It attracted the support of M. V. Rodzyanko, General L. G. KORNILOV and Mrs Emmeline Pankhurst. It saw action on the South-West Front, capturing 2,000 prisoners, but was disbanded in the face of BOLSHEVIK hostility. Other women's battalions formed by the PROVISIONAL GOVERNMENT carried out guard duties in Moscow and Petrograd. The 1st Petrograd Women's Battalion remained with the Provisional Government in the Winter Palace until its capture by Bolshevik forces on 25/26 October 1917. Allegations that the Bolsheviks then raped them were probably unfounded.

Women served on both sides during the CIVIL WAR. The Soviet government conscripted women doctors and recruited Communist women volunteers for guard duties in the rear. By 1920 there were 66,000 women in the RED ARMY; the combatant minority serving alongside men. In 1919 Nina Rostovtseva was awarded the Order of the Banner of Labour for saving her comrades from capture by White forces.

RA

Further Reading

Botchkareva, M.L.: *Yaska: My Life as Peasant, Officer and Exile.* New York: Stokes, 1919.

Bochkarnikova, Maria: Boi v Zimnem Dvortse. *Novyi Zhurnal* 68 (1968).

Bryant, Louise: *Six Red Months in Russia.* New York: Doran, 1918.

Chirkov, P.M.: *Reshenie zhenskogo voprosa v SSSR (1917–1937 gg).* Moscow: 1978.

Heldt, Barbara: Nadezhda Durova: Russia's cavalry maid. *History Today* 33 (1983).

Pankhurst, Emmeline: In *Britannia*, 13 July, 16 November 1917.

Solonevich, Boris: *Zhenshchina s Vintovkoi.* Buenos Aires: 1955.

The Russian Orthodox Church

Historically and canonically the Orthodox Church is made up of autonomous dioceses, a group of which usually forms a national or local church with a senior archbishop at the top who often bears the title of Patriarch. The Patriarch administers the local church with a council of bishops and periodic local councils, and in a close 'symphonic' cooperation with the king or emperor of the given state.

Peter the Great overturned this by forbidding the election of a new patriarch after the death of Patriarch Adrian in 1700, and abolishing the institutions of local councils and bishops' councils, replacing all this in 1721 by a synod, technically under the emperor himself. But the virtual head of the Synod from then until 1917 became the Over-Procurator, a lay bureaucrat – in fact a military officer for most of the first 120 years of the system – responsible only to the tsar, not to the church. The Synod members were not elected but appointed by the tsar and the Over-Procurator, and had no power prerogatives whatsoever in this strange new department of the state where on each level of administration the real power was in the hands of lay bureaucrats responsible to the Over-Procurator, not to the diocesan bishop or the 'supreme' Synod of Bishops. As a state department the church also lost the traditional prerogatives to disapprove of certain government actions or policies and to plead with the tsar on behalf of the oppressed.

Thus in the eyes of the nation, and particularly of the growing radical intelligentsia – atheistic as a matter of course and therefore disinterested in investigating the real situation – the church was seen as a reactionary institution condoning serfdom. Consequently, with the growth of the influence of the radical intelligentsia on Russian society at large in the last four decades of the nineteenth century, the moral prestige of the church declined.

In this growing radical secularism the church's struggle for the restoration of autonomy and conciliarism found very little response or sympathy in the lay liberal elements and, in contrast to society, the church failed to gain much from the reformist era of the 1860s.

It would be wrong to see the whole synodal period as total stagnation. The church achieved considerable gains in its missionary endeavours among the natives of Siberia and Alaska, as well as in Japan, China and Korea. The nineteenth century revival of the monastic elderhood had not only a great moral impact on the population and especially on leading figures of Russian culture (for example Dostoevsky, Gogol, Leontiev), but also, in cooperation with the early Slavophils, it brought about a revival of the original Orthodox theology of the Church Fathers, all but buried by the Roman and Protestant theological onslaughts of the previous two centuries. On the eve of the 1917 revolution the church ran some 37,000 primary schools, 58 seminaries, thousands of orphanages, old age homes, hospitals and other charitable and educational institutions.

1905

The turn of the twentieth century witnessed the return to the church of some leading members of Russian radical (mostly ex-Marxist) intelligentsia, bringing the church somewhat out of its isolation. The liberal Metropolitan ANTONI (Vadkovsky) of St Petersburg supported a moderate workers' movement including the one led by Father George Gapon which was to end so tragically in 'Bloody Sunday' 1905. Supported by S. Yu. WITTE and the liberal neophyte intelligentsia, Metropolitan Antoni appealed to NICHOLAS II to restore the patriarchal-conciliar system and a self-governing church infrastructure. Nicholas reacted only by permitting a pre-conciliar commission whose sessions of 1906–7 gave full support from the envisaged reform. But the tsar refused to grant permission for a constituent local council. Having the example of the hostile Duma, particularly the first two assemblies in which a considerable number of the elected deputies from the ranks of the parish clergy (in contrast to the bishops) joined or supported the radical parties, Nicholas may have feared that a more democratic church, less dependent on the state, would to some extent dissociate itself from the monarchy. Instead, his edicts of toleration (30 April 1905 and 30 October 1906), granting the non-Orthodox religions in the Empire freedom of activities, conversions, and the status of legal person, further disadvantaged the Orthodox Church. It alone now was prevented from running its own affairs having no legal person status and thus remaining under the complete control of the tsarist government. Yet in the eyes of the masses the Orthodox Church appeared as a mighty institution basking in the sun of the Empire. This was the image cultivated by the propaganda of the radicals to undermine the prestige of the church.

Their devotion to RASPUTIN showed that the last royal couple was attracted to pseudo-mystical charlatans rather than to the traditional Orthodox sainthood personified in the *startsy* (holy men). Every clergyman, every bishop who dared to criticize Rasputin was penalized, mostly by removal from his see and banishment to a distant monastery. Eventually the Synod was filled with either Rasputin's protégés or bishops who kept silent out of cowardice. Thus with the growing radical anti-Rasputin propaganda the prestige of the church was also suffering.

The other aspect that lowered the moral authority of the church on the eve of the 1917 revolutions was its support for the Russian and Serbian cause in the FIRST WORLD WAR. As the war grew ever more unpopular among the common masses, so did the church and its clergy.

Having been precluded by Nicholas II from organizing itself as an autonomous self-governing body on all levels of its internal life – from the parish to the central administration – being held together administratively only by the state, and formally headed by the emperor, the church was decapitated and internally disorganized, once the tsar had abdicated and the old state collapsed. The church faced the revolution in a most disadvantaged situation created by the stubbornness and petrification of the old regime and its crowned head.

1917–1922

The tsar's blockage of church reform attempts alienated even his hand-picked Synod, so that on the eve of his abdication it rejected the Over-Procurator's request to appeal to the nation to support the monarchy. Moreover, on 16 March it advised the Grand Duke Michael to refuse the crown unless elected by a CONSTITUENT ASSEMBLY. On 4 August the Synod acclaimed the democratic revolution as 'the hour of the general freedom of Russia . . .'

As early as March 1917 local spontaneous diocesan assemblies of clergy and laity adopted resolutions supporting the PROVISIONAL GOVERNMENT and requesting that the Synod permit the election of bishop-candidates by such assemblies.

The Synod and, after 28 August 1917, the All-Russian Local Council (Sobor) consistently supported the Provisional Government. It appealed to the armed forces to ignore the BOLSHEVIKS' anti-war propaganda, and to the nation to avert the threatening CIVIL WAR by keeping civic peace and order. The only major dispute between the church and the Provisional Government was over the nationalization of parochial schools (Law of 3 July 1917).

The Synod, on 12 April 1917, restored the right of diocesan assemblies to elect diocesan bishops. Such assemblies confirmed popular bishops but removed the most reactionary, Rasputin-connected ones, replacing them with particularly popular arch-pastors, notably in Moscow and Petrograd.

The FEBRUARY REVOLUTION at last allowed the church to convoke the cherished Sobor, which opened in Moscow on 28 August with 588 delegates representing all ranks of clergy and the laity. Reflecting the prevailing anti-monarchist mood, the Council wavered between a reformed synodal system (but independent of the state) and a

patriarchal-conciliar one. As the Bolshevik threat became real, the pro-patriarchal support began to grow, culminating in the election on 13 November of the Moscow Metropolitan TIKHON as Russia's first patriarch since 1700. The pro-patriarchal party argued that the church should have a personified leader to face the new militantly atheistic dictatorship. Once it had become clear that the pro-patriarchists were winning, the opposition walked out and would eventually evolve into a pro-Marxist schism under the name of Renovationists or the 'Living Church'.

Continuing its sessions, the Sobor reformed the church into a hierarchical federation of self-governing dioceses, based on a network of self-governing parishes and a graduated electoral system. It passed by-laws on the regularity and prerogatives of diocesan, metropolitan and local councils; stressed the importance of the sermon, introducing the institution of lay ministry to assist the clergy, particularly with preaching and teaching. The Sobor restored autonomy and internal democracy of the monasteries. The seminaries that would be created in place of the ones being closed by the Bolsheviks were to be established in monasteries, which would have become catalysts of a Christian identity of the nation in the theomachistic state (along the lines of Poland after the Second World War), had it not been for a near-total destruction of monasteries by the Bolsheviks in the first decade of their rule.

Other acts of the Sobor broadened the role of women on parish and diocesan level. Deliberation was begun on reintroducing a female diaconate, when the Sobor had to disperse in September 1918. The Bolshevik state had confiscated all assets of the Church and the very building in which the sessions had been taking place.

Had the church been allowed to convoke the Sobor at least ten years earlier, it would have had the time to brace the church for the trials to come. At this late hour the chaos of the Civil War and the mounting anti-church terror precluded the implementation of most of the Sobor's acts. Yet, the new responsibility granted to the parish councils saved the church from disintegration upon the almost total collapse of the central Church administration caused by periodic arrests of bishops and the state-supported subversive schisms.

The Sobor and the Patriarch took no sides in the encroaching Civil War, appealing only for an end to the bloodshed. Tikhon categorically refused to give even a secret blessing to the White Armies: the church could not support fratricide, especially since its members fought on both sides. Upon the Bolshevik victory in the first stage of the Civil War the Sobor appealed to the victors for clemency and forgiveness (24 November 1917 NS). On 1 February 1918 the Patriarch anathematized the Bolsheviks for the Red Terror, instructing the parish clergy and laity to defend their parishes by peaceful resistance and mass public prayers. On 21 July 1919, at the height of the White victories, the Patriarch appealed to the Orthodox flock to be merciful and forgiving to 'the persecutors of the church'.

On 8 October, when the Whites were only about 200 miles from Moscow, Tikhon called on the clergy not to take sides, to keep aloof from politics and political parties. The Church, he stressed, was not placing its hopes in any foreign intervention or any military force. None of them could save Russia until the nation repented and turned to God. The encyclical freed the clergy from any political obligations as the Soviet 1918 CONSTITUTION had separated the Church and the State; but as citizens, all Christians owed civic duty and loyalty to the powers that be.

LENIN's Government, however, chose an open offensive against the Church, beginning with the 5 February 1918 (NS) Decree on the Separation of Church from the State and School from the Church which totally disenfranchised the Church, depriving it of legal person status, of all real estate (including the temples for worship), of the right to own any property or hold bank accounts. It forbade the teaching of religion in any general schools, even in private ones, whether to children or adults. Adults could learn theology only in seminaries training potential clergy.

In this first stage of his struggle against religion, Lenin acted in the full Marxist faith that religion, as part of the superstructure, would die away once deprived of its material base.

The result was the very reverse of Lenin's expectations. Churches that had stood almost empty only a year before, began to be filled to bursting in 1918–19. Mass public church processions attracted hundreds of thousands of worshippers, up to 30 per cent of the population of Petrograd, for instance. In response to the Government's campaign to nationalize church property, which began with the creation of a special Liquidation Department of the Commissariat of Justice on 19 April 1918, parishioners reacted by forming church defence groups and intensifying public processional worship.

The regime, which had already fired on many a church procession killing hundreds of people, now responded with organized arrests and executions of clergy, monastics and leading lay church activists. According to incomplete data released by the Church, in the course of 1918–20 no less than 28 bishops, several thousand parish priests and monastics and over 12,000 lay men and women were murdered. As the Civil War front fluctuated, clergy and lay believers were shot for blessing the Whites or offering prayers for their victory. Such acts did not meet the Patriarch's approval as clearly spelled out in the above-cited encyclical of 8 October 1919.

Meanwhile in the territories occupied by the White Armies, autonomous Higher Church Administrations were formed by means of local Church Councils. The most important was the Provisional Higher Church Administration of South Russia. Tikhon recognized that body's appointments and ordinations, but not its politics. Realizing the impossibility of maintaining regular contacts with the periphery in the growing chaos and terror, the Patriarch in his encyclical of 20 November 1920 permitted peripheral groups of bishops to form temporary autocephalies, should contact with Moscow be lost or become impossible. The encyclical could relate only to the canonical territory of the Moscow Patriarchate, not to the territories of the Patriarchs of Constantinople or of Serbia, where most of the White émigrés would find asylum by 1921 and where, falsely claiming legitimacy on the grounds of the above encyclical, a group of émigré bishops organized in 1921 a Higher Russian Church Administration Abroad, renamed the Bishops' Synod of the Russian Orthodox Church Abroad in 1922. This body claimed to be a free representative of the captive Patriarch, and thus proclaimed, implicitly in his name, purely political aims of an anti-Bolshevik crusade (appealing to the western allies to undertake one), restoration of the Romanovs, among other things. This greatly aggravated the fate of the Church in Russia.

All the Patriarch's attempts to dissociate himself and the Russian Church from the acts of the 'Karlovcians' (so called after the town of Karlovci in Serbia where the émigré 'Synod' installed itself) by calling on them to dissolve themselves (encyclicals of 5 May 1922 and 1 July 1923, and his posthumously published Testament of 7 April 1925) failed to impress the Lenin Government. Having failed to destroy the Church by depriving it of its material base, the Soviets were now using the tactic of 'divide and rule' by singling out the Orthodox Church for attack, claiming that it was being persecuted not as a religious faith but as a counter-revolutionary institution of the tsarist past bent on restoring the monarchy. A link with the monarchist 'Karlovcians', however flimsily construed, could not have provided a better pretext for the persecutions.

In line with this argument the regime stimulated a split in the Church. In 1921–22 the most convenient pretext was the great famine when, according to an internal secret memo by Lenin, an opportunity availed itself to place the Church in such a situation as to make it possible to present it to the nation as a heartless, greedy institution. Indeed, first the government cut short and banned all Tikhon's initiatives to organize aid to the famine-stricken. Instead, the government ordered all Church valuables to be forcibly confiscated. The Church agreed to give up all remaining valuables voluntarily, except the vessels used in the Eucharist. It proposed instead to collect from the parishioners their worth in voluntary donations. But the government wanted a confrontation, as outlined in Lenin's memo, which ordered forced confiscations of the Eucharistic vessels as well, causing 1,414 armed clashes and the murder or subsequent executions of at least 8,100 clergy and monastics of all ranks and several times as many members of the laity.

The alleged refusal of the Church to aid the famine-stricken was the excuse for the leftist clergy to create the

'Living Church' (Renovationist) schism after the convenient imprisonment of the Patriarch by the GPU (see VECHEKA) on 6 May 1922.

While refusing the Patriarchal Church any form of regular existence (for example the right to publish, to have seminaries), the government granted these rights to the schismatics, as well as the Protestants and Muslims, though not to the Jews (see JEWISH RELIGION). The Soviet law issued in 1922 permitted the internal exile of unwanted persons for up to three years without trial, arrest of almost all bishops loyal to the Patriarch, and most prominent parish priests; and the handing over to the Renovationists of over two thirds of the churches. But the laity remained mostly loyal to the Patriarch. The Renovationists became an administration with clergy and temples but without flock. The Patriarchals were a Church of the people and packed churches, but without an administration.

Under direct international pressure, the government was forced to release the Patriarch from prison in June 1923, whereupon most of the clergy returned to him. Seeing the Renovationists' failure to attract the masses, the government eventually lost interest in them. When the holocaust of collectivization and terror of 1928–39 (with some breathing spells in between) began, the regime ceased to differentiate between religions and their loyalties. The Renovationists eventually fell victim to the terror as much as the Patriarchals and members of all other religions. Renovationists would not reappear among the Churches revived in the Second World War, but this is beyond the scope of this essay. DP

The 'Living Church' or Renovationist Schism

The immediate predecessor of the Renovationist Schism was the St Petersburg Union for Church Renovation whose founders, thirty-two married priests, presented a memorandum to Metropolitan Antoni (Vadkovsky) of St Petersburg, requesting wide-ranging reforms within the Church, including abolition of the monastic monopoly of episcopal consecrations. They argued that the function of monasticism was contemplation, not administration, and that bishops should be chosen primarily from among regular, although well educated, married clergy. They opposed the institution of a Patriarch, preferring conciliar mixed bodies of bishops, lower clergy and laity. The programme also included the usage of the spoken Russian instead of Church Slavonic, liturgical reforms, broader participation of the Church in social activism and various collectivist-socialist concepts.

Although the liberal Metropolitan accepted their memorandum as one of the working programmes for the future Sobor agenda, the authors' open sympathy for the 1905 REVOLUTION, explicit anti-monarchism and support for the leftist parties in the first two Dumas, forced the Synod to ban the group once the revolution was suppressed.

After the OCTOBER REVOLUTION the vast majority of believers, common masses as well as the intelligentsia, turned away from any prospect of cooperating with or approving of the Bolsheviks as irreconcilable militant atheists and Church persecutors. In contrast, the revived Renovationists proclaimed Lenin a great liberator of humanity from exploitation and social injustice, and argued that Marx's atheism was merely a reaction to the bourgeois adulteration of religion in the nineteenth century. Once the Church has purged itself of its internal and psychological ties with the past, they argued, the Bolsheviks would cease persecution, finding in the renovated Church an ally and co-worker in building socialism.

The movement found very little response in the nation, because one of the chief motives for the post-revolutionary religious revival was disappointment with and reaction to Bolshevism. A Church praising the Bolsheviks was unacceptable to most believers, especially those returning to the Church after 1917. Finding no support in the nation, the Renovationists were forced to rely on Bolshevik (in the final analysis VECHEKA) support for their existence. Once this was provided it would be the less principled, security-seeking elements who joined it, often those priests who had participated in the extreme right and anti-Semitic organizations under the tsar, and whom now the Cheka could easily blackmail. The other founding elements of the movement were power-ambitious married priests, because the schism opened to them the road to episcopal consecrations and leadership. Since the Renovationists allowed divorce and remarriage of the clergy, they attracted also compromised clergy. All these factors further lowered their prestige and forced them into ever greater cooperation with and dependence on the Cheka. This in turn led to a near-complete isolation of the movement from the mass of believers, sealing their fate but compromising also the healthy part of their original reform programme. The consequence of the Schism is an extremely conservative Church of today's Soviet Union, in place of the reform-oriented dynamic Church conceived by the 1917–18 Sobor. DP

Further Reading

Cunningham, James: A Vanquished Hope. The Movement for Church Renewal in Russia, 1905–1906. Crestwood, NY: St Vladimir's Seminary Press, 1981.

Levitin, Anatoli and Shavrov, Vadim: Ocherki po istorii russkoi tserkovnoi smuty, 3 vols. in 1. Glaube in der 2 Welt. Kuesnacht: 1978.

Manuil (Lemeshevsky), Metropolitan: Russkie pravoslavnye ierarkhi s 1893 po 1965 gody. Samizdat, Kuibyshev: 1966. First 3 volumes reprinted as Die russische orthodoxen Bischoefe von 1893 bis 1965, trans. and ed. by Prof. Dr Fairy von Lilienfeld. Erlangen: 1979–84.

Pospielovsky, Dimitry: The Russian Church under the Soviet

Regime, 1917–1982, 2 vols. Crestwood, NY: St Vladimir's Seminary Press, 1984.

Regelson, Lev: *Tragediya russkoi tserkvi, 1917–45*. Paris: YMCA Press, 1977.

Stepanov, Vladimir (Deacon Vladimir Rusak): *Svidetel'stvo obvineniia: Tserkov' i gosudarstvo v Sovetskom Soyuze*, 3 vols. Moscow: Samizdat, 1980.

Struve, Nikita: *Christians in Contemporary Russia*. London: Harvill Press, 1967.

———— ed.: *Russkie pravoslavnye ierarkhi: Ispovedniki i mucheniki*. Fotoal'bom, Paris: YMCA Press, 1986.

Zybkovets, V.K.: *Natsionalizatsiya monastyrskikh imushchestv v Sovetskoi Rossii (1917–1921)*. Moscow: 1975.

The Imperial Army in War and Revolution

Between 1914 and the beginning of 1918 Russia mobilized over fifteen and a half million men, a number far in excess of the operational army's capacity to deploy or properly to arm and supply. Total losses are estimated at over seven million, including over one million dead, four million wounded and almost two and half million taken prisoner.

As in 1905, apart from the fear of being despatched to the fronts, the miserable conditions of army life, exacerbated by war, and concern for the well-being of their families and farms, were the major causes of discontent among the troops. Even in January and February 1917 political protest in the army had not reached the proportions of that of the civilian population. In Petrograd during the last days of February soldiers comprised a minority of demonstrators and their sympathies were expressed in their widespread refusal to fire upon the crowds. As late as October over six million men were serving in the trenches and the incidence of desertions, mutinies and demonstrations against further offensives which had begun to occur at the end of 1916 accelerated only in July, August and September 1917 and was most marked after the OCTOBER REVOLUTION.

The army changed radically in the course of the war. Professional officers continued to occupy the more senior positions but the carnage of 1915 resulted in platoon and company commands passing increasingly to reserve officers or ensigns hastily trained in special six-months courses. Though for the most part patriotic and proud of their new status, few, like their men, had any respect for the old regime.

The ranks also underwent a profound transformation. The regiments and garrisons of the rear, where the soldiers' revolution first took root, were swamped by an influx of raw conscripts as basic training was progressively reduced to a mere six weeks by 1917. The sixteen reserve Guards infantry battalions stationed within the city of Petrograd, for example, contained almost 100,000 men. Three quarters of these conscripts were peasants, eighty per cent were at best semi-literate, a fact to which the revolutionary parties attributed the low political awareness of the common soldier.

Veterans and evacuees, who naturally resisted attempts to return them to the fronts, constituted a particularly disruptive element in the garrisons and played a key role in spreading opposition to the war among their colleagues and in the countryside. The Petrograd and Moscow military districts alone contained at least 133,000 evacuees and in some units for which data are available like the volatile 62nd, 183rd and 185th reserve infantry regiments of the Nizhni Novgorod garrison they comprised between one quarter and one third of the total complement.

Moreover, in 1915 the war ministry had begun to call up many older men who had received deferments or exemptions before 1914 and in 1917 after the summer offensive forty-year-old troops were no longer released in significant numbers to work on their farms. These measures caused much resentment and contributed to the increasing rate of desertions.

Estimates of the number of reservists ordered to the fronts between March and October 1917 vary from 1,500,000 to over three million. Some units refused to move until forced to do so and many individuals deserted in transit. Of the 12,000 men of the 57th and 204th reserve infantry transferred in June 1917 from the Moscow district, for example, front line staffs were reportedly able to account for the arrival of only half. Such exaggerated desertion rates were, however, the exception rather than the rule. In spite of widespread war-weariness the numbers of inexperienced and reluctant conscripts sent to the fronts massively increased between June and September and fatally weakened such resilience as the active army still possessed.

Democratization and collapse: The course of the Russian army's disintegration passed through a number of distinct stages. On 1 March the executive committee of the newly constituted Petrograd soviet issued its first order to the garrison in response to soldiers' demands that their relations with their officers should be formalized on a democratic basis. The news of the emperor's abdication broke the following day. These events destroyed at one stroke the basis of officer authority. Henceforth, officers had to appeal to patriotic sentiment or to the dubious legitimacy of the Provisional Government to secure the obedience of their men.

Order No. 1 instructed all units of the garrison to elect soldiers' committees and delegates to the soviet on the basis of one per company or cavalry squadron. Officers were to treat their subordinates with respect as befitted citizens. Later in the year the exact definition of which matters were to be resolved by the committees and which by officers became the subject of a succession of codicils issued by the Provisional Government and the Stavka (High Command), none of which had much practical effect.

The order was meant to apply solely to the Petrograd garrison but its provisions were rapidly copied in other garrisons and at the fronts. The Provisional Government and the Stavka unsuccessfully resisted the committees' demands that officers should be elected, but realized that the spread of committees throughout the army could not itself be prevented. On 30 March the commander in chief, M. V. ALEXEEV, sanctioned the election of committees in companies, regiments and armies on the basis of a draft prepared by General A. A. POLIVANOV in consultation with the Petrograd soviet three weeks earlier. The higher committees were to be elected in a ratio of one officer to two soldiers, a move evidently designed to re-establish officer control. As a result officers actually came to preside over a large proportion of the soldiers' committees.

Alexeev's instructions were, with minor amendments, confirmed by war ministry order no. 213 of 16 April, which attempted to limit the role of company committees to determining the economic welfare of the unit. On the other hand officers lost many of their disciplinary powers to company and regimental courts.

Such stability as Alexeev's scheme had brought to the army was shattered in May and June by a combination of political crisis in the Provisional Government following P. N. MILYUKOV's note on Russia's war aims and the mass re-inforcement of the fronts for the impending summer offensive. The influx of reservists brought in its wake the wholesale re-election and radicalization of the committees. In addition, in order to boost his own popularity among the troops, the new war minister, A. F. KERENSKY, had extended Polivanov's earlier definition of soldiers' rights. These now included the freedom of political discussion and persuasion and the right to join political organizations. Kerensky thus removed any legal foundation upon which commanders might have stemmed the flood of BOLSHEVIK and ANARCHIST propaganda sweeping the army. In April alone the Bolsheviks printed 150,000 copies of *Soldatskaya Pravda* (Soldiers' Truth), half of which found their way to the fronts.

Although the offensive failed and defeatism and fraternization became more widespread, the slogan of 'revolutionary defencism', to which Kerensky, the liberals and moderate socialists as well as the right adhered, was still sufficiently persuasive to enable the government to suppress the Bolshevik-inspired armed demonstrations in Petrograd and elsewhere on 16 and 17 July (NS). The garrison was undecided and in spite of pervasive grass-roots Bolshevik agitation a mass of individual soldiers rather than entire units came out on to the streets of the capital.

The prospect of a military dictatorship, the extension of the death penalty to the rear and the curtailment of soldiers' liberties implicit in General KORNILOV's abortive expedition against Petrograd strengthened support for the Bolsheviks during September but to an extent which was uneven and difficult to determine with any exactitude. In June the

Bolshevik leadership had reported the existence of forty-three garrison organizations of the party with a further ten in which Bolsheviks and MENSHEVIKS were co-operating. The number of party members among the troops was estimated at 26,000. By October there were at least ninety-five organizations in the rear and over four hundred were claimed to exist at the fronts giving a membership of 50,000 with perhaps 40,000 sympathizers.

Estimates such as these should be treated with caution. Some Bolshevik military organizations in the rear, like that of Mozhaisk near Moscow, contained almost as many workers as soldiers. The distribution of seats on garrison soviet executive committees is also an uncertain guide: while in August and September Bolsheviks, left SRs and Menshevik Internationalists became dominant, the desire to give all revolutionary parties minimum representation regardless of the size of their following, was still evident. Bolshevik support in the active army was unevenly spread. Party influence was strongest on the northern and western fronts, particularly in units like the XII army with its two brigades of LATVIAN RIFLEMEN, within which the Bolsheviks established a so-called 'left bloc' in co-operation with Latvian social democrats. On the south-western front the Bolsheviks were much less popular and they commanded minimal support on the Rumanian front as the election returns for the CONSTITUENT ASSEMBLY of January 1918 demonstrate.

The overwhelming majority of troops expressed no party allegiance or at least until the autumn of 1917 accepted the leadership of the SOCIALIST REVOLUTIONARIES. Officers similarly tended to support the defencist right wing of the SR party and among senior officers sympathy for the Kadet party was fairly common, demonstrating that the majority had readily assimilated the idea of a national democratic army. All attempts by officer organizations to unite with their worker and soldier counterparts were, however, rebuffed. The left, while accepting the right of individual officers to stand for election, did not hesitate to portray officer soviets such as those in Petrograd, Moscow, Kazan and Novgorod and patriotic officer unions as potential centres of counter-revolution.

In the case of soldiers' organizations the opposite was often true. In major industrial towns the trend throughout 1917 was for soldiers' soviets to become 'sections' of their worker counterparts and thus to concede civilian control over the affairs of the garrison. A similar pattern emerged on the northern and western fronts. In April the first congress of the western front resolved that it should become part of 'the all-Russian organization of soviets' together with the Minsk city soviet. In the same month a similar meeting of the Pskov city soviet organizations presented an immense advantage to parties like the Bolsheviks. Whichever party succeeded in dominating the key industrial soviets commanded an influence over the army out of all proportion to its actual following. In

Figure 3   The end of the war: 'The soldiers vote with their feet.' (Lenin)

contrast among the hundreds of small rural garrisons and
on the south-western, Romanian and Caucasian fronts far
removed from Russia's industrial centre, the Socialist
Revolutionaries and to some extent the Mensheviks held
sway until the final collapse of the army in the first months
of 1918.

Kerensky's attempted suspension of order no. 213 after
the summer offensive, his connivance in restoring discipline by punitive measures and subsequent *volte-face*
during the Kornilov affair and his formation of a supreme
'directory' in September, destroyed his credibility, already
at a low ebb, among the troops. This did not mean,
however, unqualified support for the new Soviet regime, in
spite of the obvious attractiveness of slogans for bread,
peace and land. LENIN's coup in Petrograd and similar
action in other centres under the direction of soviet
military-revolutionary committees were carried out by a
well-organized but mixed bag of Red Guards, armed
workers and small pro-Bolshevik army and naval units. At
the fronts, despite some token resistance to the enemy, may-
hem and desertions rendered very many units incapable

of either opposing or effectively supporting the soviet
Bolshevik-Left SR coalition. In the rear, any garrison units
(much depleted after the mass re-inforcement of the fronts)
which opposed or were ambivalent towards the new regime
were disarmed or disbanded. After the dispersal of the
Constituent Assembly in January 1918 armed opposition to
Lenin's government was frequently tolerated by the local
troops until it was ruthlessly suppressed by pro-Bolshevik
detachments drafted in from other areas.

The soldiers' revolution of 1917 was largely anonymous,
anti-belligerent and libertarian to the point of licence. The
key to Bolshevik success lay not so much in winning the
army's active support for the party's supremacy but in
exploiting its latent political neutrality.

Politicization of the General Staff: 1904–1914

The experience of 1904 and 1905 gave renewed impetus to
the reform movement within the Russian officer corps,
exemplified in a flood in 1906 of official and unofficial
pamphlets, articles and books critical of past military
deficiencies. The focus of the movement naturally became

the State Duma, reluctantly conceded by NICHOLAS II in 1905 in order to pacify liberal opinion and empowered to fund government programmes including almost all areas of military expenditure.

The first and second Dumas were quickly dissolved for their obstruction of government policy but the third, elected in November 1907 on an illegally altered franchise, was dominated by an unstable patriotic centre-right coalition sympathetic to the army's requirements. From its inception the most prominent of the members of this coalition, A. I. Guchkov, leader of the Octobrist party and chairman of the Duma defence commission, set out to cultivate political friendship among reformist officers serving in the ministry and General Staff. Among Guchkov's confidants were the war minister, A. F. Rediger, Generals Polivanov, A. S. Lukomsky, assistant war minister 1915–1916, V. I. Gurko, later commander of the western front, and G. N. Danilov, from 1910 to 1914 quarter-master general and a close colleague of General Alexeev, chief of staff from 1915 and commander-in-chief from February to May 1917.

Throughout 1908 and 1909 Guchkov openly attacked the bureaucratism and departmental intrigue which characterized much of Russia's military administration. Not least, he condemned the unwarranted interference of members of the imperial household in the army's professional business and used the Duma's control over credits to bolster the influence of his military friends, collectively known as the 'Young Turks', in the policy deliberations of the ministry.

Guchkov's ulterior motives were probably to secure the military's practical accountability in the Duma, leaving the emperor as little more than a figurehead, but he was careful not to impugn Nicholas personally and never publicly questioned the principle of monarchy. Nevertheless, his criticisms infuriated Nicholas. In 1909 Rediger was replaced by cavalry General V. A. Sukhomlinov, a firm supporter of the prerogatives of the emperor and of the undivided authority of his ministers.

Disgraced in 1915 and subsequently tried for his allegedly criminal negligence, Sukhomlinov worked for the progressive removal or transfer of officers whom he suspected of 'Young Turk' sympathies from the ministry, general staff and its academy, culminating in Polivanov's dismissal in 1912.

The FIRST WORLD WAR, however, enhanced the fortunes of the 'Young Turks'. The huge losses and the shortages of rifles and artillery which the Russian army experienced early in 1915 served to discredit their opponents and to open the way to positions in the high command for the erstwhile reformers. In spite of the fact that Guchkov's power base in the Duma had disintegrated in 1910 through defections and later in the loss of seats, the associations which he had formed in the army were to endure and, against the background of a rising chorus of liberal demands for a GOVERNMENT OF PUBLIC CONFI-DENCE which bound the Duma leadership and the high command together in persuading Nicholas to abdicate in 1917.

The generals and the abdication of Nicholas II

The strikes and demonstrations which took place in Petrograd between 23 and 26 February 1917 were joined on 27 February by troops of the garrison. None of the civic and military authorities was prepared and there were few if any reliable units to resist the movement. Most officers were unwilling to risk disciplinary action and the military district command was isolated and demoralized.

On the same night the council of ministers convened for the last time and issued an appeal to the emperor at general headquarters in Mogilev to prorogue the Duma and despatch troops from the fronts to suppress the disturbances. The president of the Duma, the Octobrist M. V. Rodzyanko, simultaneously sent a proposal that the emperor's brother, Grand Duke Michael, should be appointed plenipotentiary in the city with a view to forming a cabinet responsible to the Duma. Nicholas refused to grant that authority and having announced his intention to return to Petrograd to take charge of affairs himself, prorogued the Duma and instructed General N. I. Ivanov to proceed with a punitive force to the capital.

Both Ivanov and the chief of staff, General Alexeev, were uneasy about the prospect of armed repression and although Alexeev continued to draw loyal troops from the fronts to reinforce Ivanov's expedition, he was persuaded that political concessions offered the best chance of pacifying the discontent.

Nicholas departed for Tsarskoe Selo by a circuitous route on 28 February (OS). In Pskov on 1 March he was met by General N. V. RUZSKY, who, faithfully reflecting the views of Alexeev, attempted to convince Nicholas that he should appoint a liberal Duma ministry. By midnight Ruzsky was under the impression that he had succeeded, Rodzyanko was briefed and Ivanov's troops were halted at Tsarskoe Selo.

Rodzyanko, however, now somewhat disingenuously claimed that matters had got out of hand. He told Ruzsky that he had ordered the arrest of the majority of the council of ministers and that only the emperor's abdication in favour of a regency under the Grand Duke Michael would save the dynasty and ensure the smooth transfer of power to a new administration.

On the morning of 2 March Alexeev transmitted to the commanders of the fronts and the Baltic and Black Sea fleets a summary of Ruzsky's consultations with Rodzyanko, citing his own fears for the cohesion of the army, were Nicholas not to abdicate. The construction of Alexeev's message left little possibility that the response would be negative. Confronted with what amounted to a breach of their personal oath of allegiance on the part of his most senior generals, Nicholas resignedly agreed and

Rodzyanko and Alexeev were informed, though not without an attempt by members of the emperor's immediate suite to persuade Nicholas to reconsider and to delay the telegrams.

In the evening Nicholas received two prominent Duma representatives, A. I. Guchkov and V. V. Shulgin, who similarly urged him to abdicate. However, having been given no assurance that he might remain with his son, Nicholas suddenly stated his intention of abdicating both for himself and his heir and produced a signed antedated decree to that effect. In spite of the dubious legality of this act, any prospect of a regency or the monarchy's survival in Russia collapsed at a stroke. The implications for the legitimacy of all government authority, including the military high command, were profound and unforeseen.

Unlike the socialists of the Soviet and the radical elements of the Duma, Rodzyanko, Alexeev, Ruzsky and their military colleagues had not initially sought the emperor's abdication. Fearful of precipitating unnecessary bloodshed and isolated from Petrograd, they accepted too readily Rodzyanko's interpretation of events and they were, moreover, largely ignorant of the rivalries and divisions within the Duma leadership, which coloured his statements. Nicholas and his entourage were genuinely unpopular, in many quarters hated, but much of this was the result of the court scandals of 1916 which had been exploited in a persistent campaign of denigration by Duma liberals and to which the generals had turned a blind eye or, in individual cases, tacitly supported.

They and the majority of the Duma leadership underestimated the degree to which Nicholas despised the elective institution which he had been forced against his instincts to concede in 1905, nor had they bargained for the sense of personal duty, however incompetently executed, and devotion to family which informed his actions. As a result, with the Duma prorogued never again to re-assemble, the generals had perforce little to fall back upon but to recognize a Provisional Government which enjoyed neither popular trust not accountability to an elected body.

That Alexeev and his fellow commanders had consciously chosen to put considerations of patriotism and the preservation of the army above those of personal loyalty is beyond dispute, but in many respects they had both deceived themselves and had been deceived by others. Their adventure into the world of dynastic and party politics, for which their experience had hardly prepared them, served only to precipitate the destruction of that national unity of effort which they had hoped to bring about.

The Petrograd garrison and the Bolsheviks

At the beginning of 1917 the provisional committee of the Duma estimated that the Petrograd garrison contained 171,000 officers and men with a further 152,000 stationed in outlying towns which could be considered part of the Petrograd conurbation, such as Tsarskoe Selo, Pavlovsk, Gatchina and Oranienbaum. To these should be added perhaps 100,000 wounded and evacuees.

The core of the garrison comprised the 200,000 men of the Guards and army reserve infantry, 20,000 artillerymen and a cavalry force numbering 8,400, most of them COSSACKS. Although proportionately fewer workers were drafted into the army from Petrograd than from other industrial centres, they accounted for a significant destabilizing element, especially in technical and specialist units. In addition, 11,000 skilled worker-soldiers were employed in the artillery and munitions factories of the city.

Given the symbolic importance of the capital for the rest of the country, the attitudes of the garrison were vital to the extent to which governments, tsarist, Provisional, or Soviet, were able to cope with the revolutionary train of events. The 1st machine-gun regiment, the greater part of which Kerensky had ordered to the front, initiated the disaffection among the troops on 2 and 3 July. In the mass demonstration of the following day they were joined by sections of the Finland, Moscow, Grenadier and 180th army reserve infantry regiments in which the Bolsheviks were most strongly represented, the 6th sappers battalion and one or two artillery training companies.

However, the demonstrators did not succeed in attracting the Guards infantry battalions nor anything more than a minority of army reservists. Only some 1,300 turned out, for example, of the 10,000 strong 180th. The demonstration involved over 50,000 servicemen but a significant proportion of these were sailors.

Despite the allure of Bolshevik slogans, party membership among the troops was relatively weak. By the end of July the party's military organization in Petrograd numbered some 1,800 and there were another 4,000 followers organized in the so-called 'Pravda club'. In October there were perhaps some 6,000 members and the party had managed to establish nuclei in thirteen of the sixteen Guards battalions which had hitherto been largely impervious to its influence.

At the meeting of the Petrograd Bolshevik committee on 15 October one of the party's military organization, V. I. Nevsky, claimed the garrison would come out 'squarely for the Soviet' against Kerensky though he doubted the support of other troops in the environs of the city. However, N. V. KRYLENKO, member of the Bolshevik military bureau and subsequently commander-in-chief, reported to a meeting of the central committee immediately after that there was a sharp division of opinion among the party's military representatives concerning the soldiers' readiness to take up arms against the Provisional Government. In spite of this, Lenin insisted that active preparations for an armed uprising should be undertaken by a special party 'centre'.

On 16 October, at TROTSKY's suggestion, the Soviet set

up a military-revolutionary committee ostensibly to organize the defence of the city. Four days later the committee's first plenary session, of which the Bolshevik 'centre' was part, resolved to create a network of commissars throughout the garrison. Most of these proved to be Bolsheviks and on 23 October they were endowed with full power in the name of the Soviet. The committee thus usurped the authority of the Petrograd military district commander, Colonel G. P. Polkovnikov, and by-passed the SR and Menshevik dominated military section of the Soviet central executive committee.

The existence of commissars in fifty-one units was reported on 24 October. In reality, commissars had taken over in about a third of the 380 military units, institutions, parks and arsenals identified in Petrograd by the Duma committee in March and by the beginning of November over three hundred had been appointed.

For several weeks after the demise of Kerensky's government THE MILITARY-REVOLUTIONARY COMMITTEE became the effective government of the capital but Bolshevik control over the garrison remained precarious. The Semenovsky Guards and 2nd machine-gun regiments, for example, sent resolutions to the committee, proposing a government composed of all revolutionary parties. Others refused to obey N. I. Podvoisky's order to move out against General P. N. Krasnov's punitive expedition or to undertake active duty until the immediate convocation of a CONSTITUENT ASSEMBLY, a demand which also found a ready response among troops at the front.

On the other hand, any specifically anti-Bolshevik sentiment within the garrison was neutralized by the party's public commitment to peace and demobilization and, subsequently, by the short-lived coalition with the left SRs which held out for the troops the prospect of a more broadly based democratic socialist order. The garrison's neutrality gave Lenin the initial breathing space he required.   MP

Further Reading

Denikin, A.I.: *The Career of a Tsarist Officer: Memoirs 1872–1916.* Minneapolis: 1975.

Frenkin, M.: *Russkaya armiya i revolyutsiya, 1917–18.* Munich: 1978.

Fuller, W.C. Jnr.: *Civil Military Conflict in Imperial Russia, 1881–1914.* Princeton, NJ: 1978.

Golub, P.A.: *The Bolsheviks and the Armed Forces in Three Revolutions: Problems and Experience of Military Work.* Moscow: 1979.

Katkov, G.: *Russia 1917: The February Revolution.* London: 1967.

Korablev, Yu.I.: *Voennye organizatsii partii bolshevikov v 1917 godu.* Moscow: 1986.

Schapiro, L.: *1917. The Russian Revolutions and the Origins of Present-day Communism.* Harmondsworth: 1984.

Sobolev, G.L.: *Petrogradskii garnizon v bor'be za pobedu oktyabrya.* Leningrad: 1985.

Wildman, Allen K.: *The End of the Russian Imperial Army: The Old Army and the Soldiers' Revolt, March–April 1917.* Princeton, NJ: 1980.

The Milyutin Reforms

Russia's misfortunes in the Crimean war demonstrated that her army was seriously deficient in leadership, administrative competence and up to date weaponry. The tenacity and courage of many of its officers and men were unable to compensate for antiquated methods of conscription and training, which had never managed to yield sufficient numbers of experienced reservists, and for a supply system which inadequately fed, clothed and armed its men.

Taking advantage of the new Emperor Alexander II's reformist mood, the newly-appointed war minister, Dmitry Alexeevich MILYUTIN embarked upon a seventeen-year programme of military reforms in the teeth of a persistent traditionalist opposition. In 1862 Milyutin introduced the first of a system of military districts, each of which possessed its own semi-independent commander, staff, military council and specialist departments (engineers, artillery, medical, etc.). The military districts were of two types: districts having a common border with another power (Warsaw and the Caucasus, for example) contained in peacetime the bulk of active units, and their commanders, designated governors-general or viceroys (*namestniki*), were also often the head of the local civilian administration. The primary function of the internal districts was to maintain and train reserved units for the reinforcement of border districts and their commanders fulfilled a largely supervisory and administrative coordinating role.

The advantage Milyutin perceived in his system of districts was a reduction in the costly over-centralization of military administration combined with great flexibility in mobilization and deployment. Although the system collapsed in 1917, the efficacy of Milyutin's ideas was demonstrated by the fact that the BOLSHEVIKS resurrected it in 1918 and it remains the basis of Soviet internal military organization to this day.

Two further reforms were, however, of potentially revolutionary significance, although the implications were not widely realized at their inception. The poor quality of many Russian officers Milyutin attributed to their low level of both general and technical education, and to the fact that traditionally they had been inducted from a restricted social base. Consequently, he introduced a system of military schools designed to furnish the army with a cohort of professional officers of mixed social origins. In May 1863 the specialist senior classes of all but four of the elite cadet corps were reorganized into separate military schools, while the lower classes became general high schools (*gimnazii*), the intention being to transfer them to the civilian sector, although this never in fact took place.

Of greater significance was Milyutin's expansion of the network of officer (Junker) schools based in the military districts. These offered a specialist two-year military course to candidates who possessed general secondary educational qualifications and provided the bulk of regular officers for regiments of the line. Their expansion, together with a policy of promoting more non-commissioned officers, meant that by the end of the century officer service had become an essentially 'middle-class' occupation. Although poor conditions of service continued to discourage the most gifted or idealistic young Russians from pursuing a military career, the reform contributed to an improvement in both the numbers and professionalism of Russian officers. In 1874 the army had 29,000 officers, by 1894 almost 37,000 and by 1904 over 41,000.

Small groups of students who were familiar with the texts of revolutionary writers had existed in the cadet corps in the early 1860s but their influence was negligible. Strict discipline prevailed in both the military and Junker schools and the discussion of political issues was forbidden. Even during the upheaval of 1905 there is little evidence of revolutionary activity among the officer corps despite their widespread demoralization. If, however, the professionalism of the Russian officer engendered political inertia, it lay at the root of a long-term fundamental shift in the relationship between the autocracy and its military servants. The principle of personal service to the emperor, accompanied by a patriarchal and religious ideology, which had for centuries sustained the omnipotence of the ruler, began to be eroded in favour of a primary allegiance to the nation state. The political developments which followed the 1905 revolution accelerated the process. When in 1917 the autocracy collapsed with the abdication of NICHOLAS II, few officers greeted its demise with the same concern and regret as they were later to witness the disintegration of their regiments and what they considered the humiliation of their country.

Milyutin's crowning achievement was the introduction in 1874 of universal male military service. Hitherto the ranks had been filled through annual levies upon the lowest orders of society and the system was as inefficient as it was inhuman, for it did not provide any significant reserves. From 1874 all twenty-year-old men became liable for six years active service in the armed forces and nine years in a civilian reserve (the period of active service was later reduced to three years) with more generous arrangements for volunteers and those with secondary or higher education. Exemptions and deferments could be granted on the basis of family impoverishment, physical disability or occupation.

Universal military service met with stubborn resistance from the landed gentry and the traditionalist military establishment. That the new system of conscription persisted is testimony to the persuasiveness of Milyutin's argument that it was essential to Russia's survival as a power. In 1874 the army contained 742,000 troops of whom some 186,000 were local militia or auxiliaries. During the 1880s the figure varied between 820,000 and 850,000 and had reached just over one million by 1898. This increase was accompanied by the creation of a viable reserve of second-line units in the military districts and an ever-expanding reservoir of trained civilians upon which to draw.

Albeit a convinced monarchist, Milyutin had little sympathy for unmerited privilege. His vision of a new bond between autocrat and a more equal nation, which the 1874 reform exemplified, could not, however, be translated into reality as long as Alexander II and his successors sought to preserve the old social hierarchy and to bolster the pre-eminence of the gentry. The reform implied that soldiers had citizens' rights commensurate with their duties, rights which the autocracy was reluctant to concede.

Under Alexander III and Nicholas II the war ministry ceased to be the engine of social change that it had been in the 1860s and 1870s. Preferment continued in the army to fall to those of gentry origin, the ordinary population never came to regard military service as a necessary duty and harsh discipline, petty restrictions and vestiges of the old patronizing attitudes of the military establishment towards the common soldier served as a constant source of aggravation.

The army in 1905: A wave of major demonstrations and illegal meetings swept through the garrisons and mainly second-line units in the last months of 1905 and continued on a lesser scale into the spring of 1906. No part of the empire was unaffected. Incidents of mass insubordination occurred among troops stationed as far apart as Brest-Litovsk, Grodno, Ekaterinoslav, Chita, Krasnoyarsk, Irkutsk, Tiflis, Batumi, Sukhumi, Kars and Kerch. Specialized units like sapper, artillery, telegraph and railway detachments were particularly vulnerable to the influence of political propaganda since they were usually located in the vicinity of fortresses or urban settlements. Mutinies in Tashkent and Baranovichi and the mass political demonstration of the 3rd brigade of sappers in Kiev in November 1905 probably owed their origins to civilian revolutionary agitation, but overall specifically political revolutionary activity among the troops was remarkably limited and the army did not collapse into anarchy. The Guards, cavalry, Cossacks and front-line regiments continued on the whole to obey orders and most incidents of disaffection in the army were quelled without bloodshed.

There are several explanations why political protest was less prevalent in the army than among sections of the civilian population. Conscripts as a rule were posted to areas far removed from their home towns or villages in order to minimize the risk that they might develop a community of interest with the local population. The majority of ordinary soldiers were of peasant origin, many barely literate, and without ready access to the liberal or oppositionist press, probably had little understanding of political developments. Although the 1905 October manifesto and the prospect of elections to a State Duma evoked in some units considerable interest, rarely did a political programme emerge from their meetings. The troops had little love for the autocracy and the government but they as yet could conceive of no alternative order.

Conditions of service and the unsavoury duties they were called upon to perform figured prominently in the petitions and slogans thrown up in the course of the unrest. The Russo-Japanese war had literally impoverished the army and it is therefore not surprising that demands for the better provision of tea, sugar, food and linen were commonplace. Other causes of complaint were the brutality of individual officers, inadequate leave and restricted recreational facilities (public theatres, for example, were out of bounds for privates but not for officers) and the tedium and harshness of barrack life.

Two issues in particular posed an immediate threat to the cohesion of the army as the last remaining bulwark of the regime. Indiscriminate over-conscription to raise the Manchurian armies had resulted in large numbers of reservists stranded in the Far East and Siberia or swelling the volatile garrisons of European Russia. With the end of hostilities their natural desire was to be returned to civilian life, but logistical difficulties and the tendency of the civilian authorities to call out troops at the least sign of popular unrest meant that their return was frequently seriously delayed. This, together with the widespread use of field courts-martial, proved a major cause of resentment and the idea began to take root that these duties were neither honourable nor strictly legal. During 1905 almost 125,000 men were called out to combat strikes or agrarian disorders and at least 18,000 were posted to guard public buildings and institutions. 1906 witnessed only a minor improvement. The war ministry under A. F. Rediger recognized the danger of using troops as a substitute for an inadequate police but was overruled in the council of ministers until the revolutionary wave had subsided.

The shock of defeat at the hands of the Japanese, whom most officers had regarded with condescension at the beginning of the war, had led to many hundreds of resignations. Normal peacetime deployment of the troops continued for three years to be disrupted by the internal security requirements of the regime and for two years proper field exercises and manoeuvres were severely restricted.

According to most contemporary military observers, Russia was incapable of waging war until 1909, by which time the deleterious effects of the Russo-Japanese conflict and the revolution were being overcome.　　　MP

Further Reading

Beskrovnyi, L.G.: *Russkaya armiya i flot v XIX veke.* Moscow: 1973.

Fuller, William C. Jr.: *Civil-military Conflict in Imperial Russia, 1881–1914.* Princeton, NJ: Princeton University Press, 1985.

Mehlinger, H.D. and Thompson, J.J.: *Count Witte and the Tsarist Government in the 1905 Revolution.* Bloomington and London: Indiana University Press, 1972.

Miller, Forrest A.: *Dmitrii Miliutin and the Reform Era in Russia.* Charlotte, NC: Vamderbilt University Press, 1968.

Zayonchkovskii, P.A.: *Voennye reformy 1860–1870 gadov v Rossii.* Moscow: 1952.

The Russian Navy

Russia's position as the world's third largest naval power was lost in the Russo-Japanese War of 1904–5. At Tsushima and Port Arthur the Russian navy lost eleven battleships and fifty-eight smaller ships. Naval reconstruction received a high priority and contributed to the industrial boom of the late Imperial era (and to the weakness of the Russian Army). But the other powers were building ships even more rapidly, and when war broke out again in 1914 Russia was still far behind her rivals.

One factor leading to revolutionary conditions in the fleet was increased mechanization. This made the fleet a conscript force with a significant (if not predominant) factory-worker component and an unusually large number of literate men. There was inevitable tension between this rank and file and the aristocratic officer corps; the shortage of career non-commissioned officers was a related problem. Harsh discipline was used to keep control, but if this failed the results could be disastrous. A second factor was the concentration of sailors in ships and naval bases; this made explosions, when they came, very violent. Two new elements in 1905 were the general growth of the revolutionary movement and the naval disorganization which followed the Pacific defeats.

The most spectacular event was the mutiny of the battleship *Knyaz Potemkin Tavricheskii* in June 1905, but there were also riots and rebellions at Kronstadt (October) and Sevastopol (November). In July 1906 the socialists were able to set off uprisings at Sveaborg (near Helsinki) and aboard the cruiser *Pamyat Azova*. The authorities had to resort to extreme measures to regain control. These, and the revolutionary experience of 1905–6, contributed to the future volatility of the lower deck.

Imperial Russia entered the war much inferior to the German Navy in the Baltic. The cruisers and destroyers achieved success in a mining campaign against the German coast, but the Baltic battleships, including four new dreadnoughts, were tied up in harbour, where their morale deteriorated. The situation was better in the Black Sea, despite the arrival of the German battle-cruiser *Goeben*.

Two dreadnoughts commissioned in 1915 gave the Russians superiority and kept the Black Sea Fleet active.

1917

With 1917 it quickly became clear that the Baltic Fleet was one of the most revolutionary forces in Russia. One hundred officers and men were killed in the February Revolution. There was a massacre of officers at Helsinki, the base of six of the fleet's seven battleships. Things were even worse at the Kronstadt training base, near Petrograd, where the authorities lost all control.

The mutinies had many of the same causes as in 1905, but there was also the wartime extension of service, the Baltic-German origins of many officers, and the demoralizing inactivity; the least active ships and bases were more rebellious than those that had been directly involved in the fighting. The small SR and Marxist underground had been rounded up in 1915–16 by the tsarist police, so the mutinies were a spontaneous response to the February Revolution rather than an organized revolt; the best evidence of this is the weakness of the revolutionary parties, especially the BOLSHEVIKS, in the months after February.

One strand of events in 1917 was the demand for more democratic control of service life. The PROVISIONAL GOVERNMENT and even some of the more realistic officers tried to compromise by making concessions, but more and more power was claimed 'from below' by the naval committees, first at ship level and then on a wider basis. Some Bolshevik leaders saw democratization primarily as a means of weakening the Provisional Government; most of the sailors, however, believed that the fleet could be run on ultra-democratic lines. Throughout, the Baltic Fleet was the most affected. Radicals like P. Ye. Dybenko dominated Tsentrobalt, the Central Committee of the Baltic Fleet, from an early stage. Democratization weakened the fleet's combat readiness, and when the Germans attacked the islands in the Gulf of Riga they met little effective resistance.

The other (related) development was the spread of political parties and the sailors' participation in the base soviets. The Bolsheviks were weak at first; the SRs were the strongest faction in the battle fleet at Helsinki, and even at Kronstadt there was a large 'non-partisan' element. Nevertheless the Bolsheviks, thanks to active party workers like F. F. RASKOLNIKOV, made headway, especially in Kronstadt, and even the sailors who belonged to other parties were on the extreme left.

In June there was a crisis about whether or not Kronstadt would obey the orders of the Petrograd government. In the July Days, the demonstrations following the June offensive and the ministerial crisis, the Kronstadters played a conspicuous part; government counter-measures did not resolve the problem and led to greater alienation. Then the KORNILOV affair destroyed what little authority remained to the officers.

By October the Bolsheviks were able to manipulate much of the Baltic Fleet. They would win 58 per cent of the fleet vote in the November CONSTITUENT ASSEMBLY elections (compared with 39 per cent for the SRs), and they controlled the key democratic naval institutions. The Kronstadt sailors helped capture the Winter Palace, the cruiser *Avrora* fired a blank shell, and men and ships that arrived from Helsinki helped fend off KERENSKY's weak attempts to counter-attack. The sailors were probably not decisive in the armed uprising of the OCTOBER REVOLUTION, but they were highly visible and gave important moral support.

The other fleets were less radical than the Baltic Fleet, given different conditions and their distance from civilian revolutionary centres. In the Black Sea Fleet, much the largest force after the Baltic Fleet, the Bolsheviks would in November take only 21 per cent of the vote, compared with 42 per cent for the SRs and 25 per cent for Ukrainian nationalists. Democratization made much less progress in the early months, but the energetic KOLCHAK was eventually forced to resign command in the Black Sea. Similar developments took place in the small Northern Flotilla (in Murmansk and Archangel) and the Siberian Flotilla (in Vladivostok).   EM

Further Reading

Bushnell, J.: *Mutiny amid Repression: Russian Soldiers in the Revolution of 1905–1906*. Bloomington: Indiana University Press, 1965.

Mawdsley, E.: *The Russian Revolution and the Baltic Fleet*. London: Macmillan, 1978.

Mitchell, D.W.: *A History of Russian and Soviet Sea Power*. London: Andre Deutsch, 1974.

The Okhrana

The term is popularly applied to the tsarist political police in its entirety, although institutionally it constituted but one factor of several in charge of internal security under the directorship of the Police Department. Established in stages since 1880, the Sections for Safeguarding Public Security and Order came to be known simply as Okhrana or Okhranka.

The other main investigative body under the Police Department was the Separate Corps of Gendarmes which was established in 1826 following the Decembrist uprising, when an urgent need for a permanent police force seemed to emerge. The Third Section, founded by Nicholas I as part of His Majesty's Private Chancery, was invested with broad but vague powers, charged with supervising all areas of life, not only the arrest and interrogation of criminals who engaged in anti-state activity, but also to take preventive measures. For this purpose its operational arm consisted of the Separate Corps of Gendarmes and a network of a relatively small number of spies. The Corps of Gendarmes was a prestigious, autonomous elite unit, imbued with a strong sense of *esprit de corps* and answerable to its chief only. Its officers were recruited from among the best Guards cadets and offered a rapid advancement course. The Corps continued to maintain its autonomy even after 1880 when, for reasons of efficiency, it was resolved to unify the political with the general police apparatus under the Ministry of the Interior, while a newly created Police Department was to direct the amalgamated bodies. The Third Section was abolished, its tasks were transferred to the Special Section which was to handle all undercover activity throughout the Empire.

The Corps of Gendarmes, however, remained the operational arm of the police. In the course of its existence it had acquired its own institutional interests. As civilians the Minister of the Interior and the Director of the Police Department encountered difficulties in exercising their authority over the Corps of Gendarmes, whose officers adhered proudly to military tradition. The extensive autonomy granted to the Corps of Gendarmes by law restricted the authority of the Director of the Police Department to interfere in its affairs, especially as the Corps of Gendarmes came under the budgetary aegis of the Ministry of War. The problem of hierarchical discipline was further aggravated by the remoteness from St Petersburg of the Corps' area of activity.

A centralized anti-revolutionary struggle led by the Police Department was becoming essential with the growth of the revolutionary movement; the mere administrative abolition of the Third Section while preserving the autonomy of the Corps could not suffice. Additional investigative bodies were required, whose subordination to the Police Department could be ensured. At this point the Okhrana sections were set up. Their activity was also co-ordinated by the Special Section.

The Okhrana sections were first established in the industrial centres of St Petersburg, Moscow and Warsaw, thus reflecting the growing concern of the authorities at the fast developing movement of the urban workers, who were increasingly becoming a target for revolutionary propaganda. New Okhrana sections were opened parallel to the spreading of the revolutionary activity, until 1907 locally and later also at district level, for closer supervision and co-ordination of the investigative operations. They consisted mostly of organizing an elaborate network of undercover agents in all social sectors.

Since both the Corps of Gendarmes and the Okhrana sections were now fulfilling the functions of a political police force, the duplication necessitated a formal division of their tasks. Thus the Okhrana was to expose political crimes before they were committed, while the Corps was to investigate the crimes after their perpetration.

The formal definition notwithstanding, the division of authority remained to a large extent theoretical. Competition and friction which had previously characterized relations between the Third Section and the Ministry of the Interior, now dominated the relations between the Okhrana sections and the Gendarmerie, deteriorating rapidly to the level of fierce rivalry and sometimes reaching the point of outright enmity. Nor could the division of responsibility prevent a considerable overlap between the spheres of activity and the two bodies. Gendarmes were engaged in the Internal Agency (as undercover activity was officially known) almost to the same extent as the Okhrana. Their agents were active at times in the same organizations and used by their respective employers to scuttle each other's achievements. Nevertheless the Okhrana sections and their undercover agents had become the main arm of the Police Department in its attempts to penetrate the revolutionary movement.

Since underground conditions forced most party centres to function outside Russia, the Okhrana section that was established in the Russian embassy in Paris in 1885 acquired the utmost importance. It was in charge of all surveillance of revolutionary activity in Europe, as well as in North America; including party conferences, which for the most part were held abroad, banned literature and most importantly, weapons smuggled from Western Europe into Russia (see THE SCANDINAVIAN CONNECTION). Many émigré colonies existed in West European cities, since a good many revolutionaries fled from Russia to avoid arrest.

At the head of each Okhrana section stood a chief who had several case officers under him, each in charge of directing a number of undercover agents. The case officer was their contact man, he received their information and dealt with them personally. A few very important undercover agents were allowed to operate under the personal directive of the chief and in direct contact with him only. In the large Okhrana sections the agents were grouped according to their organizations and handled by a special officer for each party.

Apart from undercover agents who constituted the Internal Agency, an Okhrana section normally also had an External Agency, i.e. detectives whose surveillance of the revolutionaries was not carried out from within their organizations, but rather from outside by tailing the suspects. The External Agency included several kinds of detective. Most of them tailed revolutionaries on the basis of daily directives. Others were 'supervisors' – top detectives who usually supervised events in a specific region. They examined passports of suspects and assigned surveillance units as required. They kept an eye on people who frequently entertained strangers and they watched students' and workers' apartments.

Particular tasks were assigned to the St Petersburg Okhrana which necessitated special groups of detectives not to be found elsewhere. The security of the Imperial family, ministers and other high-ranking figures was entrusted to the 'Protection Unit'. The Special Detachment specialized in identification by sight of important revolutionaries. Detectives of this detachment were sent abroad in groups from time to time to spot revolutionaries under the guidance of the Foreign Agency. The St Petersburg Okhrana also employed detectives whose task was to locate strangers who were staying in hotels or in furnished rooms in the capital, without having registered with the police, as required by law.

A bureau and archives were also the main components of each Okhrana section. In St Petersburg there were two of each: a general bureau and archives which dealt with all attendant aspects of the Police Department's activity and a secret bureau and archives which covered all clandestine matters pertaining to revolutionaries and undercover agents. The archives assembled physical data on revolutionaries, while the library amassed illegal revolutionary literature.

While the working conditions of the Okhrana Foreign Agency differed from those inside Russia, its basic organization and working arrangement were similar to those in other sections. The Foreign Agency also had permanent representations in key centres like London or Berlin. The latter was considered especially important, since it served as a transit route for revolutionaries travelling to and from Russia.

The External Agency was the most vulnerable point in the operations of the Okhrana Agency abroad. By its very nature more overt and more easily exposed, time and again it served the French socialist opposition as an instrument with which to attack the government for allowing and co-operating in the infringement of French sovereignty by a foreign power. To conceal and camouflage this activity, and so as not to conflict formally with the law, it was reorganized in 1913 as a private detective agency. Two French nationals ran it as partners, their chief client being the Foreign Agency in Paris. Finances originated entirely in the Police Department in St Petersburg. Beside surveillance, the detectives were often given the task of tailing revolutionaries on their way to Russia, and identifying them to the Russian police at the moment of crossing the border.

From 1906 to 1907 the detectives of the External Agency abroad were engaged in observing and monitoring arms smuggling from Europe to Russia. Special detectives, stationed in European ports in England, France, Belgium, Holland and particularly Copenhagen, reported by telegraph directly to the Police Department in St Petersburg on the departure of any ship carrying arms.

Each Okhrana section in Russia had several secret retreats where case officers could meet their agents. Employees of the sections rented the flats and were responsible for their maintenance. They had to be particularly reliable, since they met the agents and knew some of them personally. The meetings themselves took place in the guest room. The tenant was to receive both the undercover agent and his officer and leave when they began to talk. Though similarly organized the sections varied greatly in their importance and size, those in the capitals naturally playing the leading role. However, their relative weight depended significantly on their chiefs and on the use to which they chose to put the information and power that they had amassed.

NS

Further Reading

Agafonov, V.K.: *Zagranichnaya okhranka: sostavleno po sekretnym dokumentam zagranichnoy agentury i departamenta politsii.* Petrograd: 1918.

Johnson, R.J.: Zagranichnaya agentura: the tsarist political police in Europe. *The Journal of Contemporary History* January/April (1972).

Martynov, A.P.: *Moya sluzhba v otdel'nom korpuse zhandarmov: vospominaniya.* Stanford: 1972.

Monas, S.: *The Third Section: Police and Society in Russia under Nicholas I.* Cambridge, Mass.: 1961.

Vassilyev, A.T.: *The Ochrana: The Russian Secret Police.* London: 1918.

Agents Provocateurs

This was a general term applied by the revolutionaries to people who furnished the authorities with information on subversive actions while they themselves took part in it; a formal distinction between members and non-members of revolutionary parties in the service of the police. By contrast, in police usage an agent provocateur was only a person in their service whose loyalty was not exclusively to them i.e. a person suspected of serving in the OKHRANA for revolutionary purposes. Thus neither of these meanings necessarily implies the dictionary definition of 'tempting to overt action'.

The formal emphasis notwithstanding, the term refers to a wide police penetration of the revolutionary movement as well as other public sectors from top to bottom. There were, however, significant differences in types of police agents: party members who maintained permanent and regular contact with the police were officially termed 'undercover agents'. They usually received a steady monthly salary, supplemented at times by special bonuses for information of particular value. They took part in the entire range of the revolutionary activity sometimes reaching positions of leadership in their organizations. Most prominent among them were E. A. AZEF, head of the SR Combat Organization and R. V. MALINOVSKY, a confidant of LENIN, member of the Bolshevik Central Committee and head of their faction in the fourth Duma.

On the other hand, informers who for the most part were not members of any party or organization, did not pass on information regularly and systematically. They reported on matters which had come to their knowledge indirectly and were known in the police as 'auxiliary agents'. They were poorly and irregularly paid, usually in a piecemeal fashion and according to the value of each single report. They might have overheard at work the time and place of a workers' meeting, or they might be on the fringe of a revolutionary circle and were occasionally or partially informed about revolutionary activity.

Cases are known, however, of undercover agents who, while not affiliated to any specific party, had access to abundant valuable information which enabled them to report on several organizations at one and the same time. They were labelled by V. Agafonov as encyclopedists. B. Batushansky was one such. As a dentist especially popular among revolutionaries, his clinic became a kind of political centre, making it possible for him to report about the local intelligentsia, the Social Democrats and the Socialist Revolutionaries.

Instances of revolutionaries who, as part of an anti-police method of struggle, penetrated its ranks with the consent and knowledge of their organization, are extremely rare. In fact the only known example is that of N. Kletochnikov. He became a clerk in the St Petersburg police, and for two years supplied his party with names of undercover agents operating within its organizations. Contacts with the police on one's own initiative were strictly forbidden though several people did claim to have done so. D. BOGROV, the anarchist who murdered P. A. STOLYPIN at the theatre in Kiev in 1911, is a case in point. The true nature and circumstances of his action are controversial to this day. In 1910 A. Petrov, a Socialist Revolutionary, assassinated A. Karpov, the St Petersburg Okhrana chief, causing an uproar in the party over the role played by the Central Committee in this affair.

No exact data exist on the overall numbers of the Internal Agency, as the agents were collectively known to the police. It is thought that their number ran into the thousands reaching a peak in 1912 with 26,000 informers. It is clear, however, that most of them were not members of any party or organization, but adventurers of various sorts who offered to sell or barter to the police information that they had come by. An analysis of partial data suggests that the group of salaried agents active in the revolutionary movement constituted about one third of the overall number and did not exceed a few thousand. The deep impact that they had left on all parts of the revolutionary movement, however, which all the available documentation attests, is therefore due not so much to their numbers as to their moral, social and political effect.

Between 1905 and 1912 the agents' value for the police was measured in terms of their connection with terrorist activity in general and with central terrorism in particular, and in terms of how close an agent was to the centre of organizational revolutionary activity. For this reason the police directed most of their material and human resources toward penetrating the ranks of the SRs and ANARCHISTS.

It was only prior to 1904 and again towards 1912, when the SR and anarchist threat was much in decline, and subsequently when virtually no targets remained for infiltration by the Internal Agency, that the police were able to give deeper thought to revolutionary activity in industry. In 1906, a year of peak revolutionary activity, the highest concentration of undercover agents was among the anarchists, where the number was three times that of the SR agents and more than six times the number among SDs. However, undercover agents in the SR party earned three times the amount earned by their SD counterparts, while the latters' salary was less than half that of the anarchist agents. The data testify to the fact that centralized terror was the main target for police activity and finances, although peripheral terror of the anarchist sort acquired wider penetration. This also accounts for the great number of anarchist agents and their relatively low pay.

Most of the undercover agents in the revolutionary parties were coerced into cooperation with the police in the course of their imprisonment. The police sought to turn to their own advantage the fear felt by the prisoner under interrogation, and they therefore found it more productive not to concentrate on experienced veterans who fell into their hands, but rather on those who had not yet been hardened by daring revolutionary acts. Members of socially or economically weak groups seem to have felt more insecure and therefore more vulnerable to police intimidation. Thus although the general social profile of the undercover agents is similar to that of their respective parties, there seems to be an over-representation of Jews and workers among them.

Fear and shock cannot of course serve as an exclusive explanation, additional conditions were required to tip the scale, 'the characteristic permitting the deal' in the words of one police chief. Those who were seduced into becoming informers were described by Agafonov as being of weak character and insufficiently resolute faith, individuals who felt that they had been wronged and persons who sought an easy life. Pay was manifestly of major significance. The wages of workers in St Petersburg in 1913 ranged from 20 to 100 rubles a month. The police paid their undercover agents on a much wider scale, starting at about 40 rubles, averaging around 100 rubles, but going as high as 150 and 500 (see ZHUCHENKO), and rocketing to 2000 in the case of Azef. Notably the most valuable undercover agents were not those who were coerced into treason but those who volunteered to serve on their own accord, agents like Azef, Ya. Zhitomirsky, B. Dolin or Z. Zhuchenko, all of them considered among the finest of the Okhrana agents who remained in service for many years. S. Beletsky, a former Director of the Police Department (December 1912–January 1914), maintained that most of the prisoners whose previous revolutionary activity had been marked by a deep commitment rarely provided information of any value, because their new role as undercover agent weighed heavily upon them.

When a prisoner expressed his readiness to become a paid collaborator he was handed over to the Okhrana personnel, who took down his confession and his statement of repentance. The prisoner was then pardoned and released, the confession serving as a guarantee that he would not change his mind. To dispel suspicion of party comrades or of other prisoners, an escape was often staged. In one case an escape was so convincing that a policeman and a warder were tried in its wake and sentenced to hard labour!

Some police chiefs tried to affect the promotion of their agents in their parties to gain them access to important sources of information. Various ways were chosen to raise an agent's prestige in the eyes of his comrades, most commonly by providing him with funds to further certain party goals. M. Gurevich initiated and published the first legal Marxist organ *Nachalo* (The Beginning) with police money. In the case of Malinovsky, police falsified documents in order to provide him with the clean past he needed in order to stand for election to the Duma on behalf of the Bolsheviks, and they arrested anyone who stood in his way.

It had been assumed that the police made use of their undercover agents to influence intra-party developments. A few attempts were indeed made, notably by Beletsky who, on his own admission acting on the principle of divide and rule, employed Malinovsky to widen the split between the Bolsheviks and the Mensheviks to avoid any prospects of reunification (see MALINOVSKY). The same approach typified the Police Department in 1905 *vis à vis* the SRs and the MAXIMALISTS. It seems, however, that these are isolated instances. Apart from the fact that, due to its structure, the Police Department was ill-suited for such widely concerted manipulations, its overriding interest was to gain information that would lead to immediate liquidation, very often at the expense of long-range benefits. The capture of a battle squad, the seizure of an explosives laboratory, or the discovery of a printing-press were regarded as especially noteworthy achievements, attracting most efforts of police chiefs who would often share the prize with the agent who made their success possible.

Making arrests based on an agent's information, or providing him with funds for particular purposes, had to be done very cautiously, as these served as the most common triggers of suspicion. Failure to explain financial resources could constitute proof of a member's contact with the police. In case of such rumours or suspicions a commission of inquiry would be set up. Sometimes the inquiry was based almost exclusively on the testimony of the suspect himself. Sometimes evidence was obtained from comrades who had known him for long periods in the revolutionary movement. Inquiries usually focused on financial questions, escapes from prison, knowledge of secret details which became known to the police, or a person's survival from his group's downfall. No aspect of a suspect's life

remained unexposed. Standing for party investigation was a severe personal ordeal, for it required the suspect to reveal and explain every detail of his private life without contradicting either his own previous statements or evidence given by other persons whose testimony remained secret. He was not permitted to evade any question. Normally he was suspended from all party activity for the duration of the inquiry. It was extremely difficult for anyone to clear his name. Once accused, even when not found guilty, rumours and suspicions continued to circulate. Furthermore, new evidence, unavailable earlier because of the nature of underground activity, was always expected to emerge. If, on the other hand, guilt was proved, it was made public throughout the revolutionary press. In many cases suspects escaped before they were tried, some committed suicide to avoid being exposed. Bela Lapina took her own life because she was unable to prove her innocence. Deliberate false accusations were not uncommon, the inquiries dragging on for years and reopening every time new evidence came up. The anarchist Nikolai Rogdaev fell victim to such slander for more than ten years. The anarchists and the Polish Socialist Party usually executed their traitors. The SRs did so in Russia but not abroad, and many of their agents, Azef included, were allowed to escape.   NS

Further Reading

Bobrovskaya, T.: *Provocateurs I have Known.* London: 1931.

Elwood, R.C: *Roman Malinovsky: A Life without a Cause.* Newtonville, Mass.: 1977.

Nicolaevsky, B.: *Azeff the Spy: Russian Terrorist and Police Stool.* New York: 1934.

Schleifman, N.: *Undercover Agents in the Russian Revolutionary Movement.* London: 1988.

The Zubatov Movement

Also known in its time as 'Police Socialism', Zubatovshchina denotes an experimental effort by the tsarist autocracy to mobilize a labour movement that was to be non- or anti-socialist and possibly even counter-revolutionary. The word is derived from the name of Sergei Vasilyevich ZUBATOV, the principal and most successful advocate of the theory and practice of this idea during his tenure as head of the security police (OKHRANA) of the Moscow region at the turn of the century.

The experiment consisted of a three-fold mobilization of workers: in Moscow on the basis of industrial dispute, in the Jewish Pale (chiefly Minsk and Odessa) as a political party to compete with the BUND, and in St Petersburg on the basis of leisure-time activity. It was throughout envisaged as a competition with the dangerously successful social democratic mobilization of workers; it was therefore premised on working-class activism, organization, and leadership, all engendered by the workers themselves, and manipulated rather than imposed by the State. It thus amounted to sponsoring a labour movement, but one with a non-socialist ideology and leadership: as such it was almost revolutionary in the context of tsarist practice. The experiment began in 1900 and petered out in the revolution of 1905-7.

The factory dispute: The reform was launched in Moscow under Zubatov's immediate control, with the support of his immediate superior D. F. TREPOV, the police chief of Moscow city, and under the patronage of the Grand Duke Sergei Alexandrovich, the governor-general of Moscow and the tsar's uncle. The police would first encourage workers to submit complaints of violations of the law and of the contract without extending to demands for changes in either. Trepov would then contact the factory manager or the inspector on the telephone or through a worker emissary to negotiate and have the grievance redressed at once if possible. Workers responded enthusiastically, and this phase lasted until May 1902 when Yuli Guzhon of the Guzhon and Mussi plant of the Association of Silk Mills, challenged Trepov, complained to S. Yu. WITTE, the finance minister, and had Trepov restrained in St Petersburg. A group of workers, leaders in their own constituency, were selected to handle the complaints, ensure their legality, and negotiate with managers and factory inspectors. They were Fedor Slepov, Mikhail Afanasyev, and Nikifor Krasivsky, all non-socialists but respected nonetheless. They were each paid a monthly maintenance by the police in sums ranging from 20 to 100 rubles (i.e. about the range of a worker's monthly wage). They were not police spies, however (see AGENTS PROVOCATEURS). They did not supply intelligence leading to arrests, indeed they refused to do so when later asked, and their subsidies were publicly acknowledged. This group then formed the core of the Society for Mutual Help for Workers in Mechanical Production, set up in May 1901 with Trepov's approval. Between 1902 and 1904 a series of similar bodies were set up in other trades such as textiles, tobacco, engraving, confectionery etc. But the core group remained the same, and constituted another body informally and later formally called the *Sovet* (Council) of Workers of the City of Moscow. This body, led by Slepov and Afanasyev, in effect came to represent the Moscow workers under Zubatov's influence. It was extensive enough for him to use 50,000 workers to demonstrate on 19 February 1902, the anniversary of the peasants' emancipation, and to lay a wreath at the foot of Alexander II's statue in the Kremlin; for the rest they disputed with and challenged socialist agitators among workers. Such was mobilization on the basis of industrial dispute, through which a major all-city organization of workers in Moscow was created and acted as a rival to any socialist group.

The Jewish experience: In the Jewish Pale of Settlement workers were ideologically mobilized against the Bund, which was then most active in the area, and organized into a rival political party. This time the leaders were found by Zubatov's personal evangelism among arrested Bundists, the most significant converts being Alexander CHEMERISKY, Manya VILBUSHEVICH, and Yosif Goldberg in Minsk, and Meer Kogan and Khunia (Genrikh Isaevich) SHAEVICH in Odessa. Their conversion was genuine, not venal as much subsequent and post-revolutionary testimony has asserted. They mobilized workers against the Bund, concentrating on the single 'Economist' charge (see ECONOMISM) that the Bund had sacrificed the material interests of the workers to its own political ambitions. They were then encouraged to demand proper enforcement of the law, to hold mass meetings and conduct strikes for the purpose, by the chief of the gendarmes in Minsk, Colonel Nikita Vasilyev, and by the local administration in Odessa, all on instructions from the Department of Police in St Petersburg. Finally they were brought together in the Independent Jewish Labour Party (IJLP) in Minsk in July 1901, and in its Odessa branch, the Independent Labour Group, with a manifesto and political programme that was clearly 'economist'. These bodies conducted strikes in both cities until the summer of 1903 when the experiment was called off, in Minsk because it was getting dangerously close to Zionism, and in Odessa because it was unable to neutralize the general strike of 17 July of that year. It differed from Moscow by being a political party (the first official one in Russia, and long before the revolution of 1905), rather than an organization to handle industrial disputes.

Leisure activities: The third facet of the reform was the mobilization of workers' leisure time. Begun in 1901, it became the residue in Moscow from the Guzhon crisis of 1902 to the revolution of 1905, but it was the substance in St Petersburg, from autumn 1903 under the stewardship of Father Grigory Gapon until the radical mobilization of December 1904. Since both industrial dispute and party politics were fraught with serious consequences, this was found to be the safest area of workers' activism. It consisted of popular enlightenment (not training) and rational recreation. Enlightenment, chiefly in Moscow, consisted of public lectures on bread-and-butter issues such as working hours, labour law, insurances, and so forth by the academic intelligentsia, most notably Professor I. Kh. Ozerov of Moscow University. From the Guzhon crisis of 1902 even this was deemed too radical, and the topics were strictly limited to history, literature, science, and religion, by conservative scholars and churchmen. In St Petersburg, Gapon provided the same, both before and after the registration of his Assembly of Russian Factory Workers of the City of St Petersburg in February 1904, but in an altogether unsystematic and dilettantish manner. Rational recreation, the other aspect of the mobilization of leisure, consisted largely of weekly social events, for example family dance parties, musical soirées, an occasional excursion etc., in both Moscow and St Petersburg. In Moscow it was very closely supervised by both Zubatov and Trepov, with written applications and permission being required for each event; in St Petersburg Gapon was not so supervised by either Major-General Fullon, the governor of the city, or by Prince P. D. Svyatopolk-Mirsky, the Minister for Internal Affairs. Recreation in Moscow therefore remained innocuous, even in 1905; in St Petersburg on the other hand it became the means to the radical mobilization from the autumn of 1904.

Results: The whole experiment is customarily described as a failure, but it could as well be seen as an uncertain beginning. In Moscow it was withdrawn, or rather modified, after Guzhon protested; only leisure management remained, if in a conservative vein. Unlike in St Petersburg, these unions and gatherings did not become the basis of a radical mobilization even in 1905, and these Zubatovite unions continued their meetings into at least April of that year before fading out. The IJLP in Minsk was abruptly terminated, not for anything that it had done, but because the new Minister for Internal Affairs, V. K. PLEHVE, was apprehensive of the Zionist, and therefore separatist implications of an explicitly Jewish workers' body. In Odessa, the Independents were dissolved in July 1903 for their failure to avert the general strike of that month and not for any sin of commission. Only in St Petersburg did the experiment turn about face with Gapon switching sides and mobilizing the workers to the point of a confrontation with the Autocracy, even if behind icons and royal portraits, in the petition and the march to the Winter Palace on 9 January 1905 (see 1905 REVOLUTION).

Ideas: The general system of ideas which informed these experiments may be examined through the book lists supplied to workers, through Zubatov's statements and through the theoretical exercises of his publicist collaborator, L. A. TIKHOMIROV. The books were the standard reading of the radical intelligentsia, with a markedly left-liberal to reformist-socialist orientation. The authors were Sydney and Beatrice Webb, Werner Sombart, S. N. Prokopovich, and Eduard Bernstein, all socialists of the Fabian, 'Katheder', legal-marxist, and evolutionary strains. The other authors were the contemporary industrial relations experts of Europe, Wilhelm Kulemann from Germany, and Paul de Rousiers and Louis Vigouroux of France. Their theories were derived from the experience of developed, not developing capitalism, of political democracy, powerful labour movements, and unified working classes in each of the advanced capitalist countries of USA, England, France, and Germany. They saw these features as the sole protection from the menace of social democracy, which was Zubatov's reason for choosing their works. The ideology thus presented in these readings was not in the least conservative, nationalist, theological, xenophobic, or proto-fascist; it was instead highly radical in tsarist conditions with implied extensive liberal reforms and stopping short only of revolution itself. Zubatov's own ideas reflected the same, but less explicitly so. He spoke throughout as a loyal servant of Autocracy and extolled the virtues of monarchy; but for the rest he spoke of the equilibrium of classes in conflict, of the competitive struggle for power, of social forces rather than conspiracies, and finally even of his desire for an evolutionary and progressive capitalism, with the Autocracy merely mediating conflict. Only his idiom tended to conservative apologia for Autocracy, but his message was modern and reformist. As for his publicist collaborator, L. A. Tikhomirov, the renegade member of People's Will and later editor of the conservative *Moskovskiya Vedomosti* (Moscow Gazette), his principal theoretical concern was to see the working class as another *soslovie* (social estate), and pillar of Autocracy in the manner of the gentry and peasantry, and to integrate them fully through corporate status, for example in unions, co-operatives etc., all amounting to a distinct and recognizable variety of European conservatism. The thrust of this reform therefore was radical, rational, secular, and limitedly pluralist, but not revolutionary, and equally not nationalist, chauvinist, religious, or corporativist, save in the lecture programme in Moscow after 1902. Only Father Gapon seemed to make concessions to Christian and national feeling, but even so more to provide for himself as a priest in the movement and to satisfy the police; yet eventually the most radical events occurred under his leadership.

Conclusions: The general significance of these events may be examined with regard to the labour movement, and to the state. In the history of the labour movement it signified the tentative acceptance of the fact by the Autocracy, and of its necessity and inevitability; it marked the shift from the repression of the movement itself to that of the social democratic leadership of the movement, which was characteristic of the years 1907–14. Further, it witnessed the birth of the soviet form of labour organization, a uniquely Russian contribution to labour history. The soviets, as they emerged in the revolution of 1905–7, were essentially non-party, non-doctrinal, general representative bodies of the working class of a city. As such, the Council or soviet of the Workers of the City of Moscow and Gapon's Assembly of Russian Factory Workers of St Petersburg were just such city-wide soviets, undifferentiated representations of the working class of the city rather than of just an industry or a craft as unions necessarily are. These were non-revolutionary or counter-revolutionary soviets; and the Gaponite body became something very like a revolutionary soviet also in its final days as it championed the Putilov strike, conducted the general mobilization of the workers of the city, and took them on the march to the Winter Palace. In the history of the tsarist state, Zubatovshchina signified the first full-scale attempt by the Autocracy to mobilize a class in modern fashion, to the extent of resorting to party politics, as in Minsk and Odessa, and as in the electoral and party politics of the Duma years, 1906–17. It marked the shift from the traditional reliance on the historic institutions of the Autocracy to seeking mass legitimacy, but as yet only in the particulars of unionism and not in the universals of an electoral system. This kind of an Absolutism seeking a democratic legitimacy is called Bonapartism, especially in Soviet historiography; the Zubatovite reform thus adumbrated the inauguration of the Bonapartist state of the inter-revolutionary years, 1906–17. The importance of this reform lay in this dual aspect, in its fashioning a new and unique form of labour organization, the soviet, and in its launching the Bonapartist State. MKP

Further Reading

Palat, Madhavan K.: Police socialism in Tsarist Russia, 1900–1905. *Studies in History* 2.1 (1986 New Delhi) 71–136.

Pospielovsky, Dmitry: *Russian Police Trade Unionism: Experiment or Provocation?*. London: 1971.

Schneiderman, Jeremaiah: *Sergei Zubatov and Revolutionary Marxism*. Ithaca and London: 1976.

Tidmarsh, Kiril: The Zubatov idea. *American Slavic and European Review* 19 (1960) 335–46.

Tobias, Henry J.: *The Jewish Bund in Russia; From its Origins to 1905*. Stanford: 1972.

The Revolutionary Movement

It was not until after the middle of the nineteenth century and the reforms of Alexander II that a revolutionary movement began to emerge. Common to its different trends was the belief that society and the political system must be re-ordered on a democratic, or popular, basis.

While the revolutionaries of the 1870s, first as POPULISTS and later as SOCIALIST REVOLUTIONARIES (PSRs), concentrated their efforts on the peasants, their successors, the MARXISTS, organized themselves as the RUSSIAN SOCIAL DEMOCRATIC LABOUR PARTY (Russian initials RSDRP) and focused their attention on the new factory proletariat. The emergence of LENIN brought to the surface differences of political philosophy and party organization which caused the RSDRP to split into BOLSHEVIK and MENSHEVIK wings. A significant movement among the JEWS paralleled these developments and led to the formation of the BUND, while POLISH MARXISTS became similarly organized. At the same time, the ANARCHISTS, representing a long Russian tradition, became more active, both on the level of humanistic propaganda and, more commonly and spectacularly, bomb-throwing.

The era of the political party, albeit of the Russian type, had arrived and with it a tendency to factional splits, particularly rife among émigrés, who were mostly intellectuals. Inside Russia activists who were more concerned with protecting their meagre resources and limited scope for action were impatient of party squabbles. As Russia entered the twentieth century her political temperature was rising and now was not the time for ideological hair-splitting. Soon events would render party divisions almost meaningless, as workers took to the streets and peasants plundered and set fire to landlord property.   HS

Populism

The term *narodnichestvo*, from *narod*, the people, is properly applied only to certain revolutionary activists from the intelligentsia who, in 1875–8, sought to help peasants to express their own aspirations for social change instead of trying to instil socialist ideas 'from above' by propaganda and personal example. However, the term is commonly applied to the entire agrarian socialist movement in Russia, from its origins in the ideas of A. I. HERZEN (1812–70) and other Romantic thinkers of the 1840s to the extinction of the SOCIALIST REVOLUTIONARIES, in 1917 Russia's largest political party, at the hands of the BOLSHEVIKS during the CIVIL WAR.

The radical intelligentsia was rooted in the psychological alienation experienced by sensitive and cultured *dvoryane* (privileged state servitors, 'gentry') whose western-style education familiarized them with progressive ideals but who were then confronted in daily life with the multiple injustices of absolutism and serfdom. The reforms initiated by Alexander II, after Russia's defeat in the Crimean War, aroused great public enthusiasm, which gave way to

dissatisfaction once their necessarily limited scope became evident. Students at several universities formed discussion circles, and in autumn 1861 staged protest demonstrations in St Petersburg to which the authorities reacted with exaggerated nervousness. The illegal distribution of inflammatory fly-sheets led to the arrest (July 1862) on trumped-up charges of N. G. CHERNYSHEVSKY (1828–89), chief editor of *Sovremennik* (The Contemporary). While in prison awaiting trial he wrote a novel, *What's to be Done?*, which provided disaffected young Russians with an attractive model of an alternative life-style. Emancipated from family ties and the constraints of conventional morality, the 'new people' (women as well as men (see WOMEN'S MOVEMENT BEFORE 1917)) should harden themselves psychologically and physically for a revolutionary struggle against all traditional authorities. Atheism, utilitarianism, and 'a fanatical, ascetic belief in science' (Billington, p. 393) were the key concepts. The character of Bazarov in I. S. Turgenev's novel *Fathers and Sons* sympathetically caricatured the radical student sub-culture, but earned the writer angry criticism. Many regarded Chernyshevsky, exiled to Siberia, as a martyr to the people's cause. Others took their lead from the eccentric rebel and apostle of anarchism, M. A. BAKUNIN (1814–76), or else followed the individualistic 'rational egoism' of D. I. Pisarev (1840–68).

Efforts to set up a nation-wide clandestine organization, Land and Liberty (Zemlya i Volya), in 1862–3, and to help the Polish insurgents, were unsuccessful. As the public mood swung to the right, the radicals lost ground. This trend accelerated when in 1866 a student, D. V. Karakozov, attempted to assassinate the tsar. Left-wing intellectuals were widely (if misleadingly) written off as 'nihilists'. F. M. Dostoevsky, in *The Possessed* (1872), would draw attention to the spiritual perils inherent in revolutionary fanaticism, basing his indictment on the criminal traits exhibited by S. G. NECHAYEV (1847–82) and his followers.

The movement's reputation was salvaged by P. L. LAVROV (1823–1900), whose *Historical Letters* (1868–9) stressed the moral debt which 'critically thinking individuals' owed to the common people whose sacrifices made their education and privileges possible. From 1869 onwards activists in St Petersburg, Moscow, Kiev, Vilna and other centres set up clandestine societies for self-education, based on the circulation of prohibited literature. A notable part was played by emancipated Jewish youths who were both attracted and repelled by their hostile Russian environment. M. A. NATANSON (1850–1919), a medical student from Vilna province, was the driving spirit behind a circle formed in St Petersburg in 1869, which two years later merged with another to form one named after N. V. Chaykovsky (1850–1926); at its peak it had some fifty members. The circle of A. V. Dolgushin, which moved to Moscow in 1873, was closer ideologically to Bakunin (and Nechayev) than to Lavrov; its members advocated fomenting insurrections among the peasants, whom they saw as instinctive rebels. The more reflective 'Lavrists' thought such revolts required prior preparation by propaganda, but were attracted to these ideas.

The search for a 'correct' tactical line, and other quasi-philosophical issues, aroused passionate debate, but in the summer of 1874 adherents of both tendencies came together in a striking 'movement to the people'. Several hundred (perhaps as many as 2,500) idealistic young men and women forsook the comforts of civilization to live among the common people, ostensibly as teachers, medical auxiliaries or artisans, but actually as propagandists for social change. Part pilgrimage, part amateur development project, the campaign failed in the short term. Some 700 participants were arrested, some of them handed over to the authorities by the very people they wanted to serve.

Nevertheless the experience heightened the radicals' sense of solidarity and led them to rethink their tactics. First, greater attention had to be given to urban workers and artisans, who had often shown themselves more receptive to the radical message than peasants. In Odessa

E. O. Zaslavsky set up a short-lived South Russian Workers' Union (1874–5), which intervened in industrial disputes. Second, the surviving activists realized that their movement needed a tighter organizational structure.

Land and Liberty: In 1876 a Northern Revolutionary-Populist Group took shape in the capital, which later took the better known name of Land and Liberty (there was no continuity with the earlier eponymous body). Its chief initiators were Natanson and A. D. Mikhailov (1853–1929). On 6 December 1876 its leaders staged the first public demonstration in Russian history. They also devised a programme that de-emphasized ultimate objectives in favour of 'those popular claims and demands that exist at the moment' (Venturi, p. 573). The empire was to be dissolved; two thirds of the land was to be transferred to the peasants, organized in self-governing communes; minimal powers were to be reserved to the future central government. But this happy state was to be established by revolutionaries whose organization, although not devoid of democratic features, had a markedly centralist character. Rank-and-file activists, known as *derevenshchiki* (villagers, as they were now often settled more permanently in the countryside), were under the direction of a nucleus of militant leaders, many of them ex-political prisoners, skilled in the arts of survival 'underground'.

Such arrangements had long been advocated by P. N. TKACHEV (1844–86), a former associate of Nechayev (and of Polish insurrectionists); but his daring notion that a conspiratorial elite of professional revolutionaries should actually seize state power did not commend itself to his Populist comrades, who stood for action by the people, not just on its behalf. Nevertheless the idea of political action gained ground, even though it contradicted their scornful attitude towards politics as a trivial pursuit of conventionally-minded individuals, abhorrent to true social revolutionaries.

Terrorism: Such anarchistic reasoning had lost its appeal for radicals now increasingly embroiled in a violent struggle with the authorities. Beginning in southern Russia, this soon spread to other centres. In part it was a response to repressive measures. Activists helped political prisoners (notably Prince P. A. KROPOTKIN) to escape from jail. The first instance of armed resistance to arrest (curiously, by another prince!) occurred in August 1875. The following year some 'southerners' tried to kill a workman turned police informer. Land and Liberty had a 'Disorganizing Section' which included an explosives expert and a spy in the political police (Third Department; see OKHRANA). Revolutionaries in Kiev employed deceptive techniques (a bogus Imperial charter) in a plot to provoke a peasant insurrection nearby. Mass trials of arrested radicals fuelled a desire for revenge. In January 1878, the day after sentences were announced in the great 'trial of the 193',

Vera I. ZASULICH (1849–1919) shot and wounded the governor of St Petersburg, General F. F. TREPOV, to avenge a prisoner whom he had ordered to be flogged. Although clearly guilty, a jury acquitted her and comrades frustrated her re-arrest. The effect was sensational: liberal public opinion turned strongly against the government; the terrorists gained confidence and perpetrated further coups: the assassination of the Kiev police chief (May), the Third Department head (August), and the governor-general of Kharkov (February 1879). The next target, predictably, was the tsar himself (April 1879). The shot missed and his assailant, A. K. Solovyov, was hanged – as were several other activists.

On the technical plane the revolver gave way to the bomb. Politically, Land and Liberty yielded to the People's Will (Narodnaya Volya) group, for that summer the organization split. A minority, led by G. V. PLEKHANOV (1857–1918), clung to the old propagandist tactics (see BLACK REPARTITION). The majority succumbed to the lure of terrorism. The new body was semi-fictitious, for real power lay with its Executive Committee whose members were pledged to sacrifice their lives for one another, if need be, and could not quit 'until its ends have been achieved, i.e. the existing government has been destroyed' (Venturi, pp. 651–2). It had an inner core of eight members. Its conspiratorial activities were of course enshrouded in secrecy but its aim, tsaricide, was publicly revealed. For most leaders this became an end in itself but some, including A. I. ZHELYABOV (1850–81), entertained residual hopes that the assassination would spark a popular upheaval or that the new ruler might make constitutional concessions – although according to Populist theory such an eventuality could have benefited only 'bourgeois' liberals, not the masses. The rank-and-file members (several hundred) of the People's Will – it took the title 'party' in 1880 – played a mainly passive role, but it also had many more unaffiliated sympathizers who promoted its goals indirectly. It ran a clandestine printing-press and, from autumn 1880, established a 'military organization' with contacts in the armed forces.

On 5 February 1880 a workman, S. N. Khalturin (1856–82), who in 1878–9 had helped to found a Northern Society of Russian Workers, but later was converted to terrorism and secured employment in the Winter Palace, set off a powerful dynamite charge under a hall where Alexander II was expected to be present. Eleven people were killed and fifty-six injured, but the tsar was not hurt. Several subsequent attempts likewise failed. On 27 February 1881 Zhelyabov was arrested. But security precautions were amateur. Before police could uncover the conspirators, among them three women, they acted. On 1 March Alexander II, who had just authorized measures that heralded a liberalization of the government structure, was driving to his palace when a bomb was thrown at his sleigh. He stopped to talk to the injured, whereupon he was fatally injured by another bomb; the man who threw it, I. Hryniewiecki, died too.

Zhelyabov and four comrades were hanged; another died in prison. The remaining activists were soon rounded up, although proclamations were issued in the Executive Committee's name later in the year. The organization was infiltrated by police spies and forfeited its positive public image. The assassination had proved wholly self-destructive. It set back political progress for a generation. Nevertheless the appeal of terrorism lived on, resurfacing in both main revolutionary parties in the early twentieth century.

Cultural populism: Populism was also a sociological, economic, philosophical, historiographical and literary phenomenon. Lavrov and N. K. MIKHAILOVSKY (1842–1904) developed a theory of 'sociological subjectivism' which offered a justification for action by intellectuals on the lower classes' behalf. The harmful division of labour, attributed to 'capitalism', would be overcome as mankind progressed to a higher stage of social development marked by co-operation instead of competition. The belief that Russia could attain socialism by following a 'special path', avoiding the evils of modern industrialism, rested largely on untested assumptions about the collectivistic potential of the peasant commune (*obshchina*), with its practice of periodic land redistribution among individual householders. As experience showed Russian peasants to be no less self-interested than other mortals if given the opportunity, this belief waned; in the 1880s the 'Legal Populists' (S. N. Yuzhakov et al.) pressed rather for state intervention to protect small-scale 'popular' enterprises from factory competition. Although the movement had obvious pseudo-religious features, its adepts preached a materialistic and atheistic world-view that owed much to contemporary scientific advances and sociological theorizing in the West. In an age of grand universalist schemes it was tempting to apply biological findings to human society without exercising sufficient scholarly caution. As enthusiastic 'westernizers', the Populists generally underestimated the weight of inertia and tradition in Russian political culture and social life, and so were led to idealize the common people and the liberating possibilities of Revolution. In this they followed their Romantic predecessors, for all their overt commitment to a scientific approach. Populist literature, however, is less 'romantic' than 'realist': its most obvious trait is a truthful, if emotionally laden, depiction of popular suffering – for a deep moral concern for 'social justice' was the wellspring of narodnik thought. Populism's significance today lies in its having grappled with issues that, other things being equal, confront many nationalist movements or regimes in developing countries – not least the place of revolutionary violence in efforts to further the cause for human betterment.   JLHK

Further Reading

Billington, J.H.: *Fire in the Minds of Men: Origins of the Revolutionary Faith*. New York: 1980.

Naimark, N.M.: *Terrorists and Social Democrats: The Russian Revolutionary Movement under Alexander III*. Cambridge: 1983.

Pipes, Richard: Narodnichestvo: a semantic inquiry. *Slavic Review* 23 (1964) 441-58.

Venturi, F.: *Roots of Revolution: A History of the Populist and Socialist Movements in Nineteenth-Century Russia*. London: 1960; New York: 1961, repr. 1966.

Walicki, A.: *A History of Russian Thought from the Enlightenment to Marxism*, trans. H. Andrews-Rusiecka. Oxford: Oxford University Press, 1980.

Wortman, Richard: *The Crisis of Russian Populism*. Cambridge: 1967.

Black Repartition

This term denotes the general expropriation of landed property owned by 'non-toilers' and its redistribution among peasant small-holders in egalitarian fashion. The goal of some communally-minded peasants, aggrieved at the limited scope of the 1861 emancipation, it was taken up by the POPULISTS and later by the SOCIALIST REVOLUTION-ARIES, and was largely achieved by the agrarian revolution of 1917–18. The term was adopted in 1879 as the name of the minority faction in the expiring Land and Liberty organization who disapproved of terrorism and adhered to the old tactical line of first building up a mass base by propaganda and agitation. The group had little influence and in 1880 the leaders, notably G. V. PLEKHANOV, emigrated. An economic determinist, Plekhanov became convinced that the village commune was breaking down as capitalism penetrated the countryside, and that the urban working class was replacing the peasantry as the most potent force for social revolution, as in the West. This eased the group's acceptance of Marxism, formalized by the appearance of the LIBERATION OF LABOUR group in 1883.   JLHK

Marxism in Russia

The 'scientific socialism' elaborated in Western Europe by Karl Marx and Friedrich Engels was imported into Russia as a ready-made system of thought (ideology) that was attractive to certain radical intellectuals disenchanted with POPULISM, the native brand of socialism. It did not arise organically among industrial workers as a conscious expression of their perceived 'class interests' in the struggle against capital, as Marxist theory presupposed. This was because Russia's socio-economic and political development lagged behind that of the West, especially in three respects. First, the relatively few industrial workers ('proletarians') were, at least until the 1890s, essentially peasants in origin and outlook. Secondly, the survival of the egalitarian land-redistributive commune (*obshchina*) convinced many pro-

gressive-minded intellectuals that Russia had to follow a 'special path' to socialism; the Populists respected Marx but considered that his teachings required major modification before they could be applied to Russia. Thirdly, the empire lacked a strong, politically active middle class ('bour-geoisie') with an interest in securing civil liberties and constitutional rights; despite the 'great reforms' of the 1860s the government was still based on absolutist principles and political discourse stifled.

Marx saw tsarism as the bulwark of reaction throughout Europe and yearned for its overthrow. He strongly supported the People's Will terrorists in 1879–81 and was even willing to concede that, should their campaign of political assassinations trigger a proletarian revolution in Europe, the land commune might indeed, as Populists held, serve as the basis for social regeneration in Russia. His pragmatic stance embarrassed G. V. PLEKHANOV and his émigré comrades in the BLACK REPARTITION group, who had renounced terrorism and were becoming converted to a more doctrinaire interpretation of Marxism.

In September 1883 they broke off negotiations for a co-operative journalistic enterprise with some Populist fel-low-émigrés and reconstituted themselves as the LIBERA-TION OF LABOUR group. They made it their task to formulate the theoretical precepts that should guide a Marxist social-democratic labour party when one could be formed, and to this end launched a polemical offensive against their Populist rivals. They dismissed them as 'utopians' and reactionaries who objectively stood for the propertied elements in the peasantry, for as they saw it the penetration of capitalism into the Russian countryside was inexorably polarizing the communally-minded rural dwellers into richer and poorer elements. Only the uprooted industrial workers, 'with nothing to lose but their chains', could spearhead a popular revolution. Although numerically small, the Russian proletariat was rapidly acquiring a consciousness of its class interests and potential strength. Socialists should patiently build up their mass support, not waste their energies in terrorist coups, which could not accelerate the pace of historical development anyway, since as Marx had taught this was governed by impersonal laws. Russia first had to pass through a stage of bourgeois rule, on western lines, which would substitute constitutional democracy for absolutism and promote capitalist progress. But the organized proletariat could limit the duration of this phase and ensure that the 'bourgeois-democratic revolution' took a very radical form. Much depended on the international context: if proletarian revolution came about in the West, developments in Russia would be greatly speeded up. But a fully socialist society, governed by a 'proletarian dictatorship', could be established only by the combined efforts of workers in all countries. Russia's early Marxist theorists underestimated the force of nationalism: Plekhanov was a convinced 'westernizer' who envisaged that socialism would overcome Russia's legacy of backwardness and integrate her into the

Figure 4   Poster celebrating 1 May.

mainstream of European civilization.

At the founding congress of the Second (Socialist) International (1889–1914), where Plekhanov represented Russia, he proclaimed this faith in a Russian workers' revolution. He earned the respect of foreign comrades, although some thought him over-optimistic. It was harder for the Russian Marxist leaders to establish firmly their influence at home, for they were all but isolated from the few surviving clandestine radical discussion circles, and to many activists their teaching seemed too abstract or partisan. In practice the first Social Democrats in Russia often co-operated closely with the Populists, ideological reservations notwithstanding. By the early 1890s, however, circles with a distinctly Marxist orientation had come into existence in several cities, especially in the south (Odessa, Kharkov, Kiev) as well as on the middle Volga (Kazan, Nizhni Novgorod). In general, though, the Great Russian heartland of the empire and the russified regions of the Ukraine lagged behind the national-minority regions of the west, where Poles, Jews, and later Latvians all demonstrated greater militancy and organizing ability. This was partly the consequence of the discrimination to which they were subjected.

In St Petersburg the first Marxist 'propagandists' (leaders of circles) were D. N. Blagoev, a Bulgarian, and P. V. Toczyski, a Pole; other activists included M. I. Brusnev, L. B. KRASIN and V. A. Shelgunov. Only the latter was of proletarian background and here, as elsewhere, relations between intellectuals and workers within the clandestine circles were sometimes strained. The intellectuals sought to prepare 'Russian Bebels' – (August Bebel was a founder of the German S.D. party) – by giving their charges a smattering of education with a radical political emphasis; the workers sometimes proved keener to advance their careers than to become soldiers of the revolution. Police surveillance and harassment prevented the small underground groups from maintaining more than episodic connections with one another.

The transition 'from propaganda to agitation', i.e. to greater activism and to involvement in labour disputes, began in the west. At Vilna (now Vilnius) in 1894 Yu. O. MARTOV and A. KREMER produced a tract, *Ob agitatsii* (On Agitation), in which they argued that through industrial action workers would learn to appreciate the necessity to engage in political struggle, since the authorities generally backed the employers in upholding 'order' in the factories (see BUND). In St Petersburg S. I. RADCHENKO's circle (to which V. I. LENIN belonged) was at first cool towards the new tactics, fearing exposure, but many of the younger workers favoured them. In 1895 Martov arrived bearing a mimeograph and soon convinced Lenin and other comrades to help guide an incipient strike movement among the capital's textile workers. Before much could be accomplished the leaders were arrested, but their organization survived for some time under the clumsy title UNION OF STRUGGLE FOR THE EMANCIPATION OF THE WORKING CLASS. It could claim some credit indirectly for the concessions which the strikers eventually won (1897), although their leaders came mainly from the ranks, and, in the following years, the Social Democrats in the capital (and in Moscow) had to lie rather low or emigrate. K. M. Takhtarev took a quasi-syndicalist stand in his paper *Rabochaya mysl* (Workers' Thought) and this aroused misgivings among the orthodox theorists. They took no part in the preparations for the founding congress of the Russian Social-Democratic Labour Party (RSDRP) at Minsk in March 1898, which were conducted mainly by B. L. Eidelman of Kiev with the assistance of the relatively powerful Jewish Bund. This attempt at unification proved premature, since all members of the party's newly elected Central Committee but one were promptly arrested.

Meanwhile, helped by a modest relaxation of the censorship, Marxism had been making headway among the radical intelligentsia. To many it seemed to offer a more 'scientific' alternative to Populism in solving the 'accursed questions' of Russia's historical destiny, in so far as the masses' plight, highlighted by a catastrophic famine in 1891–2, could plausibly be attributed to the growing pains inescapable from early capitalism. The two economists

P. B. STRUVE and M. I. Tugan-Baranovsky discerned positive features in Russia's current rapid industrial expansion and her growing role in world markets. They were criticized by the Populist thinker N. K. MIKHAILOVSKY for an apparently amoral readiness to swim with the tide of events and 'to drown the muzhik in the factory boiler'; no cause, however progressive, was worth sacrifice of the interests of real individuals. Plekhanov entered the lists, under a pseudonym, with an exposition of Marxist dialectical and historical materialism, in which he argued that acceptance of objective historical regularities actually left individuals ample freedom to help shape the course of events. The Marxists were not united in this debate: both Plekhanov and Lenin thought that Struve erred in playing down the ultimately revolutionary connotations of capitalist progress. But these differences remained concealed from eager young radicals who were impressed by the Marxists' more self-confident approach and by the growing power of organized labour, as demonstrated in Russia and the West. By 1896–7 periodicals with a Marxist orientation were appearing in St Petersburg and Samara.

But Struve found Marxist philosophy sadly wanting and, turning to Kant to supplement it, ended by negating it. His growing concern for the autonomy of the individual, free to choose between good and evil (seen as objective ethical categories), shocked the orthodox as 'metaphysics' and clearly could not be reconciled with historical materialism. The so-called 'Legal Marxists' (a misnomer!) also questioned classical Marxist sociological and economic doctrines, rejecting revolution in favour of evolution and casting doubt on the labour theory of value and the impoverishment of the proletariat. In this way they anticipated the better-known German 'revisionists', notably Eduard Bernstein. They went on to become liberals and, eventually, conservative nationalists and believers in Orthodox Christianity.

Plekhanov stood by the old certainties, at least in public. At a congress of the International (1900) he took a more radical stand even than Karl Kautsky, acknowledged leader of the left-wing German Social Democrats. He was also alarmed at 'revisionist' tendencies introduced among the Russian Marxist émigrés by S. N. PROKOPOVICH and his wife E. D. KUSKOVA. After gentler methods had failed, he resolved on a schism within their organization, now called the League of Russian Social Democrats Abroad (not to be confused with the Union etc.).

The new deviation was christened ECONOMISM. It embraced at least three discrete tendencies, but these refinements were lost from view in the heat of the polemic. The orthodox leaders gained heart from the verbal support they received from Lenin and a group of comrades exiled to Siberia. When he and MARTOV were released in 1900 they emigrated and set up a new periodical together with Plekhanov and his associates. Its title, *Iskra* (The Spark), reflected their conviction that they could, through propa-

ganda from abroad, create a united Social Democratic party pledged to militant orthodox Marxism which could ignite the flames of social revolution in Russia. The first step, they believed, was to purge the clandestine circles (now known as committees) of the so-called 'Economist' heresy. This was not too difficult since it was in any case largely a figment of their imagination; moreover, heterodox tendencies among Russian Marxists at home and abroad were weakened by the knowledge that a broadly-based opposition movement was emerging in Russian society, directed against the autocracy: this was the long-heralded 'bourgeois-democratic revolution'. *Iskra*'s drive for control of the new party, which it in effect established at the Second Congress of the RSDRP (1903), became part of a much more grandiose strategy of mobilizing all discontented elements under the revolutionary Marxist banner, overcoming all the 'reactionary' forces in Russian public life, and winning state power – essentially the strategy which Lenin's BOLSHEVIKS would apply in 1917, for which the 1905 REVOLUTION served, in Lenin's words, as a 'dress rehearsal' (See SOCIAL DEMOCRACY and LENIN).   JLHK

Further Reading

Baron, S.H.: *Plekhanov: The Father of Russian Marxism*. Stanford and London: 1963.

Keep, J.L.H.: *The Rise of Social Democracy in Russia*. Oxford: 1963.

Kindersley, R.: *The First Russian Revisionists: A Study of Legal Marxism in Russia*. Oxford: 1962.

Naimark, N.M.: *Terrorists and Social Democrats: The Russian Revolutionary Movement under Alexander III*. Cambridge, Mass: 1983.

Pipes, R.E.: *Social Democracy and the St Petersburg Labor Movement, 1885–1897*. Cambridge, Mass.: 1963.

——— : *Struve: Liberal on the Left, 1870–1905*. Cambridge, Mass: 1970.

Wildman, A.K.: *The Making of a Workers' Revolution: Russian Social Democracy, 1891–1903*. Chicago and London: 1967.

The Liberation of Labour Group

The first organization of Russian Marxists was founded by G. V. PLEKHANOV, the leading spirit in the BLACK REPARTITION group, and four associates (P. B. AXELROD, V. I. ZASULICH, L. G. DEICH, and a man named Ivanov who soon died) in Geneva in September 1883. Its basic theoretical precepts (see MARXISM IN RUSSIA) were the work of Plekhanov; Axelrod's contribution lay primarily in his efforts (1898) to formulate more precisely the correct tactical relationship between Social Democrats and 'bourgeois' liberals. The arrest in Germany (1884) and subsequent extradition to Russia of Deich, the only practical conspirator among them, isolated the émigrés from potential followers in Russia; another reason was the abstract, didactic and polemical tone favoured in their writings.

Apart from his major tracts (*Socialism and Political Struggle*, 1883; *Our Differences*, 1884) and much topical political journalism, Plekhanov devised two programmatic documents which anticipated that formally adopted in 1903 by the RSDRP (Russian Social-Democratic Labour Party), whose leaders saw it as the lineal descendant of the Liberation of Labour group. There was indeed continuity, both intellectually and organizationally, for the party adopted the same intransigent ideological approach to politics.

Already in the 1880s the group's exclusiveness aroused criticism among more recent, and generally younger, radical émigrés, who felt that their practical experience as propagandists should earn them a share in policy-making. In 1888 Plekhanov agreed to the establishment of a League of Russian Social Democrats Abroad, mostly consisting of students, which his group joined as a corporate body with the right to edit (and thus control) its publications. In 1894 the group, which was short of funds, formally merged with the League on the understanding that its literary output should become more 'agitational' and popular in character. Its failure to act on this principle fuelled opposition, which soon took an ideological form. In 1898, at the League's first congress, Plekhanov and Axelrod renounced their editorial role in the hope of overawing the dissenters; but they managed very well without them, and put out the journal *Rabochee Delo* (Worker's Cause). In 1900, at the League's second congress, Plekhanov provoked a schism and in effect revived the Liberation of Labour group under a new title, 'Revolutionary Organization "Social Democrat"'. This existed only on paper and in October 1901 was absorbed into the Foreign League of Revolutionary Social Democracy, a body controlled by the hard-line editors of *Iskra*, led by V. I. LENIN, which played a major part in ensuring that the re-established RSDRP adopted Leninist organizational precepts.

JLHK

Further Reading

Baron, S.H.: *Plekhanov: The Father of Russian Marxism*. Stanford and London: 1963.

Frankel, J.: Volontarisme, maximalisme: le Groupe Osvobozhdenie truda, 1883–92. *Cahiers du monde russe et soviétique* 9 (1968) 294–323.

Keep, J.L.H.: *The Rise of Social Democracy in Russia*. Oxford: 1963.

Tyutyukin, S.V.: Gruppa "Osvobozhdenie truda" i sovremennaya burzhuaznaya istoriografiya. *Voprosy istorii* 12 (1983) 19–33.

Ziemke, T.: *Marxismus und Narodnichestvo: Entstehung und Wirkung der Gruppe 'Befreiung der Arbeit'*. Frankfurt: 1980.

Union of Struggle for the Emancipation of the Working Class

This body, which existed in St Petersburg from 1895 to 1897, is of significance as the first organization which gave Russian Social Democrats a footing in the country's labour movement (excluding national-minority regions). Yu. O. MARTOV chose the name in December 1895 for a clandestine body comprising several circles of radical intellectuals (notably those of S. I. RADCHENKO and Martov himself) and a Central Workers' Group. The latter had been established in the summer of 1895 by working-class activists in the metallurgical industry. The League was directed by a five-man 'inter-regional bureau' and three subordinate regional (i.e. city-ward) bureaux, with partly interlocking membership; all its seventeen members were intellectuals. It attempted to focus workers' grievances by writing and distributing agitational leaflets and to co-ordinate industrial action by men in different factories or industrial branches. Such action was undertaken most dramatically by textile-workers, of whom 30,000 came out on strike in May 1896. Contemporaries were startled by this evidence of Russian labour's growing militancy. The strikers did not attain their objectives owing to opposition by employers backed by the finance ministry of S. Yu. WITTE, but a law of 2 June 1897 did limit the length of the working day (to eleven and a half hours) and made overtime working conditional on voluntary agreement. The League was closely watched by the police, who in December 1895 and January 1896 (before the great strike!) arrested some fifty leading activists, including Martov and V. I. LENIN. In the spring of 1896 the main leader was the future Menshevik F. I. DAN but it was by then less effective; and in August 1896 the main role passed to K. M. Takhtarev, who decided to emigrate in 1898. He had always wanted the League to be a genuine workers' organization, but his anti-intellectual, syndicalist line scandalized the more orthodox Social-Democratic leaders.

JLHK

Further Reading

Pipes, R.E.: *Social Democracy and the St Petersburg Labor Movement, 1885–1897*. Cambridge, Mass.: Harvard University Press, 1963.

Economism

Pejorative name given by revolutionary Russian Social-Democratic leaders ('the orthodox'), notably G. V. PLEKHANOV and V. I. LENIN, to dissenting tendencies within the nascent RSDRP (Russian Social-Democratic Labour Party) between 1898 and 1903. The term originated in the notion, advanced by none other than Yu. O. MARTOV, the future MENSHEVIK leader, in 1893 that 'economic' (i.e. industrial) action would soon convince workers, once they encountered resistance to their demands from the state authorities as well as from employers, to take up political struggle to better their lot and to accept the party's precepts. The tactic was employed with some success by Social-Democratic activists (including Lenin) in agitation in St Petersburg during the textile-workers' strikes of 1895–7, and elsewhere; but subsequently it became almost an article of faith among certain younger leaders (for example B. N. Krichevsky).

Three distinct currents of opinion were subsumed under the label 'Economism'. First, K. M. Takhtarev, in the newspaper *Rabochaya Mysl* (Workers' Thought), 1897–1901, took a somewhat syndicalist (trade-unionist) line. He expressed scepticism about radical intellectuals' claims to direct the labour and socialist movement in Russia and concentrated on practical steps to improve workers' living conditions. Second, B. N. Krichevsky and other editors (P. F. Teplov, A. S. Martynov) of *Rabochee Delo* (Workers' Cause), 1899–1902, were 'middle-of-the-roaders'. Their journal was the organ of the League of Russian Social-Democrats Abroad, a body mainly comprising émigré students. It conducted propaganda activity in Russia on a fairly extensive scale for the time, and more effectively than the self-styled 'orthodox', who were jealous of its success and in 1902 crushed it. Its 'line' was identical to that subsequently adopted by the MENSHEVIKS: for instance, it backed the revolutionary interpretation of Marxism against Bernstein's 'revisionist' criticism, but thought his views should be aired. Third, a few intellectuals, notably S. N. PROKOPOVICH and his wife E. D. KUSKOVA, argued that, since it was easier to secure economic gains than political reforms in absolutist Russia, Marxists should continue to provide leadership in industrial disputes but soft-pedal socialist propaganda in the workplace, instead co-operating with other opponents of autocracy, such as liberals, to win a constitution. Not until workers had learned to appreciate political freedom should they be approached with revolutionary slogans. The 'orthodox' misinterpreted this suggestion, which was repudiated by adherents of the other two tendencies as betrayal of proletarian class interests. They made much of an address given by Kuskova in St Petersburg, of which they obtained an unofficial, distorted transcript, and labelled it 'Credo'. The document served to dramatize the perils of non-conformity. The anti-Economist campaign had all the elements of a witch-hunt and helped Lenin to impose his own ideas on the RSDRP during the *Iskra* period.

JLHK

Further Reading

Brennan, J.F.: The origins of economism in St Petersburg. *Canadian Slavic Studies* 4 (1970) 162-82.

Frankel, J.: Economism: a heresy exploited. *Slavic Review* 22 (1963) 263-84.

———— : trans. and ed.: *Vladimir Akimov on the Dilemmas of Russian Marxism, 1895–1903*. Cambridge: Cambridge University Press, 1969.

Keep, J.L.H.: *The Rise of Social Democracy in Russia*. Oxford: Oxford University Press, 1963.

The Russian Social Democratic Labour Party (RSDRP)

Many Russian revolutionaries in the 1880s, inspired by the 'father of Russian Marxism', G. V. PLEKHANOV, abandoned their POPULIST ideas for MARXISM, called themselves Social Democrats and set up small groups, or propaganda circles in various Russian towns. With the aim of forming a Russian social democratic party in due course, their immediate purpose was to transform the outlook of the Russian workers, educating them as a class-conscious, politically mature elite whose role would be to carry the message of socialist revolution into the factories. Successful to some extent, this practice also had the effect, however, of arousing in many of the 'half-intellectual' workers so trained a desire to escape from the factory drudgery and either become revolutionaries themselves or further their self-improvement elsewhere. Moreover, factory workers were hardly more willing than the peasants of the 1870s to absorb socialist ideas taught in the abstract. They were ready to take direct action for their immediate needs and were organizing strikes with some success on their own initiative. In the face of these trends, the Marxists adopted a new approach, which was summarized in a pamphlet called 'On Agitation' (1893–4) originally written in Yiddish but soon made available in Russian. Large, open-air assemblies were held, it was hoped out of police view, where workers were 'agitated' to coordinate their demands for specific, small economic gains. In time, the argument ran, as the workers acquired greater awareness of their economic interest, and of the natural alliance between the factory-owners and the state, they would become politically aware.

The idea of mass agitation, which had succeeded in the early 1890s among workers in the Pale of Jewish Settlement (see THE BUND), was conveyed by Yu. O. MARTOV from his exile in Vilna to the Social Democrats of St Petersburg when he returned there in 1895. In the capital, with LENIN and others, Martov took part in establishing the UNION OF STRUGGLE FOR THE EMANCIPATION OF LABOUR and several successful strikes were organized before both he and Lenin were arrested and exiled to Siberia.

By the mid 1890s a network of contacts and a flow of information and mutual assistance, albeit intermittent and interrupted by the OKHRANA, had been established, and with émigré help the drive to form a Social Democratic party in Russia had taken root in many of the main cities and industrial centres. In 1897 the social democratic organizations of the Pale of Jewish Settlement amalgamated to become the General Jewish Workers' Union, or Bund, and this encouraged a number of Russian committees to convene the First Congress of the Russian Social Democratic Labour Party in March 1898 in Minsk. Ironically the sole intellectual contribution to this exercise, the party Manifesto, was written by P. B. STRUVE, until recently a

'Legal Marxist' but shortly to emerge as leader of the liberal constitutionalist movement. Of the nine delegates, all but one (a Bundist) were arrested within two weeks and the process of building the party inside Russia was temporarily halted. Further attempts were made and failed, either through police interference or conflict within the movement, and the next party congress to be convened inside Russia was the Sixth, in mid 1917.

With many of the intellectuals and practical organizers either abroad or in Siberian exile, social democratic organizations in Russia declined and the focus of interest moved to Western Europe and the ideological plane. Political circumstances in Germany, such as the repeal of anti-socialist laws, had opened up wider opportunities for the working class to participate in the political process, in socialist parliamentary activity and the legal struggle to improve the labour laws. Eduard Bernstein, a leading German socialist thinker, was re-examining Marxist theory, in particular the notion of class war which was now seen as a barrier to collaboration between workers and middle class liberals in their common aim of achieving a democratic republic. In Russia, where no parliament existed and the organization of the workers was besieged by police persecution, Bernstein's ideas both paralleled and provoked several new trends.

One idea, exemplified by Ekaterina KUSKOVA and her husband S. N. PROKOPOVICH, and which became known as the ECONOMISM, argued that Marxist theory itself demanded the constant revision of social analysis; that working class organization – such as that exemplified in the ideas of the pamphlet 'On Agitation' – had opened up a path of gradual progress which premature political organiz-ation by the Marxists threatened to close; that social democrats should continue their assistance to the workers in economic agitation only and, rather than waste human resources trying to form a revolutionary party, they should throw in their political lot with the liberals in the struggle for a constitution, a path which both advocates of this line themselves were soon to adopt. Their departure from social democracy was made easier by the hostility their ideas had aroused in Plekhanov's Group.

Kuskova outlined her ideas for discussion by the UNION OF RUSSIAN SOCIAL DEMOCRATS ABROAD in a document published without her knowledge in Rabochee Delo (Workers' Cause), and a copy of it was sent to Lenin in Siberia by his sister, Anna, who gave it the title 'Credo'. Rabochee Delo did not depart from the 'orthodox' line which called for the political organization of the working class, but personal and organizational rivalry with Plekhanov inevitably drew the charge of 'revisionism'.

The idea that Marxist revolutionaries should either devote themselves to helping the workers organize trade unions or fall in line behind the political leadership of liberals was anathema to those calling themselves orthodox. Plekhanov attacked the new ideas and reiterated the fundamental principle that the workers would only be able to guarantee their democratic freedoms if they took the leading role in struggling for them. Meanwhile, in his Siberian exile, Lenin vehemently joined the battle. In his eyes support for the liberals amounted to disarmament of the revolution. As for the workers, he asserted that they were incapable of seeing beyond the horizon of trade unionism, that only intellectuals, armed with Marxism, could inject them with political revolutionary aims. To restore the movement to its revolutionary path, all socialist elements must unite and stay clear of alliances with the liberals; all heretical, that is critical, points of view were to be excluded from the social democratic press, and the workers were to be given the message that the overthrow of tsarism took precedence over demands for the eight-hour day and similar matters.

Iskra

The chief weapon in this battle was a newspaper which served not merely as a collective propagandist and collective agitator, but also as a collective organizer. Iskra (The Spark) formulated the party programme in an orthodox vein and served as the focus and organizational centre for calling the Second Party Congress. While Martov remained in Russia to recruit supporters and set up local facilities, Lenin went to Geneva to plan strategy with Plekhanov. Their meetings went badly. Like other social democrats abroad before him, Lenin found Plekhanov remote from the Russian scene, arrogant and impossible to deal with, and he therefore set up his part of the operations in Munich and conducted the editorial business by correspondence.

Local response to the first issue of the newspaper, in December 1900, was enthusiastic, but two obstacles stood in the path of Iskra's organizational ambition. The first was the natural reluctance of local underground organizers to allow outside interference in their activities. Many Russian social democrats still recognized the moral authority of the Union of Social Democrats Abroad and its organ Rabochee Delo. On the other hand, the Union's organization was unable to sustain regular contact with the localities, nor even to maintain the regular issue of its newspaper. Iskra's success in both respects was a crucial factor in the struggle for allegiance.

The second obstacle was the Bund whose committees were proliferating throughout the Pale beyond the Polish and Lithuanian provinces and into present-day Ukraine. The conflict arose because the Bund claimed sole represen-tation of the Jewish workers in the party and the restructuring of the party on federal principles, while Iskra recognized no boundaries between different sections of the working class of the Empire and was adamant that all parts of the party should come under the immediate control of the central committee, a principle directly at odds with the idea of federation on territorial, ethnic or any other grounds. Apart from the larger issue of national minorities and their political organization, this clash brought to the surface the fact that Jews were disproportionately numerous and prominent among both intellectuals and organizers in the 'Russian' party, and therefore the demand that a separate organization be recognized for the Jewish workers in the party threatened the party's universal appeal. In overcoming these obstacles, Lenin developed the ideas that became the organizing principles first of *Iskra*, then of the Bolsheviks and later the Communist Party. In *What is to be done?* (1902), he advocated a centralized organization, run by a small, disciplined group of highly professional revolutionaries.

Between 1901 and 1903, thanks to its regular appearance and reliable delivery to the localities, by its readability and forceful message, and the technical assistance its agents furnished to local groups in the form of passports and literature, *Iskra*, both the newspaper and the organization, forged an increasing following inside Russia. But no committee could continue to enjoy these services until it had publicly and in the pages of *Iskra* renounced *Rabochee Delo* as the official organ of the party, recognized *Iskra* in its stead, and accepted *Iskra's* (i.e. Lenin's) plan for a new, centralized party structure. The purpose of the Second Congress was to put the finishing touches to this process and to formalize the position of *Iskra* as ideological and organizational centre of the party.

Second Congress, 1903: By the summer of 1903, Lenin's agents had most of the arrangements in their hands and *Iskra* had sufficient support to convene the Second Party Congress. Of the fifty-seven delegates who met, first in Brussels and then, after a week of police harassment, in London, *Rabochee Delo* had been granted three votes and the Bund five. Lenin felt assured of at least 80 per cent support. As a precaution against 'accidents', some of the few real worker delegates from Russia were first mustered in Switzerland, where the issues were clarified for them and the importance of discipline drilled into them by Lenin, TROTSKY and other ideological stalwarts.

For the first two weeks of the Congress (which ran for four), Lenin had things almost all his way. His draft of the party programme was passed with little dissension; the Bund had been isolated and its ideas on national organizations and party structure roundly rejected; *Rabochee Delo* had been discarded in favour of *Iskra* as the central organ of the party. Rifts had, however, appeared: the 'compact majority' had been divided in half over nationality issues that had barely been touched on before but, more important for party unity, the sixteen delegates who formed the inner circle of *Iskra* itself were divided, Martov and Lenin were in open conflict, each proposing a different definition of party membership. Lenin, with great consistency, was for a small party of professional revolutionaries with a large fringe of non-party sympathizers and

supporters. Martov was for making members of all who recognized the party programme and were willing to obey central leadership, though he too, as a convinced Iskraist, advocated the need for a protected and conspiratorial inner nucleus. The rift had been progressive since over the previous two years Martov had viewed with growing distaste Lenin's duplicitous methods. The split merely exposed the incompatibility of their style and political temperament.

Martov's position on membership was upheld by 28:23 votes, thanks to the Bund and *Rabochee Delo* who saw in it a watering-down of *Iskra's* practices that had led to their present isolation. However, these two groups departed when some two weeks into the month-long Congress the rest of the delegates threw out their claims to represent respectively the Jewish workers and the party abroad. Lenin hence emerged with a majority. Thereafter he adopted the term 'majorityites' for his following, and dubbed his opponents the 'minorityites', or BOLSHEVIKS and MENSHEVIKS in Russian. He then set about re-staffing the party's central institutions to reflect the new line-up of forces: amid emotional clamour he proposed the exclusion from the *Iskra* editorial board of the revered P. B. Axelrod, V. I. Zasulich and A. N. Potresov, 'its least productive members'. Martov saw this as a device to remove opposition to Lenin and refused to serve without them, leaving only Plekhanov and Lenin; the Russian central committee was composed entirely of Bolsheviks, and a council to settle disputes was formed of two Iskraists, two central committee members, and one member elected by Congress. Shortly after the Congress, however, Plekhanov insisted that the original board of six be restored, whereupon in November 1903 Lenin resigned in a unique act of self-denial and thus surrendered *Iskra* into the hands of the Mensheviks.

From Lenin's point of view the Congress that was to have crowned his efforts and ratified his ideas was a disaster and he gave full vent to his disappointment in a post-congress analysis entitled 'One step forward, two steps backward'. Henceforth, the Bolsheviks were defined as 'hard', dedicated to ideological orthodoxy and organizational homogeneity, while the Mensheviks were vilified as 'soft', vacillating, liable to let sentiment and personal feelings cloud their judgement.

Despite its lack of achievement, the Congress was a turning-point in the history of Russian social democracy. It had exposed a difference over the sort of party the delegates wanted, and hence over their attitude in a revolutionary situation to alliance with other groups, such as the liberals or the SOCIALIST REVOLUTIONARIES. It had also revealed differences in the place within the party programme which the social democrats wished to give to issues of nationality. And it threatened to divide Russian social democracy into two hostile groups just when the government was about to become embroiled in a costly and unpopular war with

Japan, and when social tension in Russia was mounting towards the momentous events of 1905.

Inside Russia, however, party workers were less willing to endanger their limited success by dividing their resources for what, to them, seemed obscure reasons. As a result of this scepticism, between late 1903 and the eve of the FIRST WORLD WAR, but particularly during the events of 1905, many social democrat organizers and rank and file maintained their identities as joint or united committees. Paradoxically, it was a kind of natural 'Leninism', an overriding imperative to secure the integrity of their underground organization, that motivated this resistance to the sectarian division Lenin wanted. Equally, however, their 'Menshevik' reluctance to accept total control from the centre undermined the Mensheviks as a coherent wing of the party. In *Iskra* the official line, propounded by Martov and F. I. DAN, jostled with Plekhanov's views to the right and Trotsky's to the left, and Menshevism continued to evolve more as a broad tendency than as a political party.

Meanwhile, Lenin set about establishing the Bolsheviks, not as a faction but as the party itself. The first step was to start a newspaper. With the literary support of the Marxist philosopher A. A. BOGDANOV, the journalist and future Commissar of Education A. V. LUNACHARSKY, the future diplomat V. V. Vorovsky, and the practical help of L. B. KAMENEV, L. B. KRASIN, G. M. Krzhizhanovsky and G. E. ZINOVIEV, in December 1904 Lenin published the first issue of *Vpered* (Forward). Using his Bureau of Committees of the Party Majority as a substitute Central Committee, (from which he was expelled for this action), Lenin concentrated all his efforts and in April–May 1905 succeeded in convening a congress of Bolsheviks which he called the Third Party Congress. Many of the delegates were uneasy, having expected that a reunion with the Mensheviks was to take place, and Lenin was forced to pass a resolution calling for such a move to be initiated.

The Mensheviks, meanwhile, held their own meeting in Geneva, which they called a conference in recognition of the fact that it was not representative; they formed their own central committee which they called an Organizing Committee, and used the meeting virtually to relinquish their party authority in the belief that Lenin was working for unity. Plekhanov resigned from *Iskra* in protest against such appeasement. The Bolsheviks, however, had no such intentions. If forced by the party mood of the moment to seek unification, Lenin and his close associates intended to revert to Iskraist methods: either a Menshevik committee would submit to the new party authority, i.e. the Bolshevik Central Committee, or a Bolshevik body would be set up in rivalry, the existing committee would be declared defunct and the Bolshevik committee proclaimed legitimate. Events in Russia and the powerful current of solidarity among social democrats rendered most of these calculations obsolete.   HS

Further Reading

Deutscher, Isaac: *The Prophet Armed: Trotsky, 1979–1921*. London: Oxford University Press, 1954.

Haimson, Leopold H.: *The Russian Marxists and the Origins of Bolshevism*. Cambridge: Harvard University Press, 1955.

Keep, J.L.H: *The Rise of Social Democracy in Russia*. Oxford: Oxford University Press, 1960.

Kolakowski, L.: *Main Currents of Marxism*; vol. I, *The Golden Age*. Trans. from Polish by P.S. Falla. Oxford: Oxford University Press, 1978.

Pipes, Richard E.: *Social Democracy and the St Petersburg Labor Movement, 1885–1897*. Cambridge: Harvard University Press, 1963.

Schapiro, Leonard: *The Communist Party of the Soviet Union*. London: Methuen, 1970.

Shukman, Harold: *Lenin and the Russian Revolution*. London: Batsford, 1967; repr. Longman, 1977.

Wolfe, Bertram D.: *Three Who Made a Revolution*. New York: Dial Press, 1948.

The Union of Russian Social Democrats Abroad

The Union of Russian Social Democrats Abroad (Soyuz russkikh sotsial-demokratov zagranitsei) was founded in Geneva, Switzerland during the winter of 1894–95. It was established by G. V. PLEKHANOV, P. B. AXELROD, V. I. ZASULICH, and L. G DEICH in response to demands from recent Russian Social Democrat émigrés for a share in the LIBERATION OF LABOUR GROUP's publication work. The purpose of the new organization was to produce popular and semi-popular literature for dissemination to workers inside Russia (see MARXISM IN RUSSIA).

The Union Abroad functioned initially as an adjunct of the Liberation of Labour Group, which controlled entry into the new organization and supervised all its operations. Among those recent Social Democratic émigrés (referred to as 'youngsters') who played a prominent role in the Union's activities during its early years were V. A. Buchholtz, T. M. Grishin (Kopelzon), V. P. Ivanshin, B. N. Krichevsky, E. D. KUSKOVA, A. S. Martynov (Piker), S. N. PROKOPOVICH, P. F. Sibiryak (Teplov) and I. N. Somov. (V. P. Akimov (Makhnovets) would be a key figure in the organization after 1900.)

The Union Abroad was soon publishing a variety of propaganda leaflets and brochures; by early 1896, it had begun to print the semi-popular miscellany, *Rabotnik* (The Worker), along with a supplement, *Listok 'Rabotnika'* (The Worker's Flysheet), chronicling the development of the Russian labour movement and providing news of the country's industrial unrest. Editorial control of the Union's publications rested with Axelrod and Zasulich; the 'youngsters' were responsible for supplying articles and funds, and also for overseeing the distribution of the printed material through Warsaw, Vilna and Minsk.

Despite some disagreements over administrative policies – particularly editorial policy – the Union Abroad functioned relatively smoothly for several years. Eventually, however, demands by the 'youngsters' for greater independence from the Liberation of Labour Group created tensions within the organization and led to a confrontation with the Group in the winter of 1897–98. Tensions were heightened further the following spring when two of the most vocal 'youngsters', Kuskova and Prokopovich, challenged not only the Group's administrative policies but also their authority as the leaders of Russian Social Democracy, thereby transforming what had been a purely organizational dispute into a major political conflict.

The final months of 1898 witnessed an intensification of the conflict within the Union Abroad as the Liberation of Labour Group launched a polemical attack against the 'youngsters', charging them with the heresy of 'ECONOMISM'. When the First Congress of the Union Abroad convened in November, the battle lines were clearly drawn. Confronted with significant opposition to their policies, the Liberation of Labour Group relinquished their editorial and administrative control of the organization. Shortly thereafter, the 'youngster's replaced *Rabotnik* and its supplement with *Rabochee Delo* (Workers' Cause) and a supplement, *Listok Rabochego Dela*, which were under their own editorial control.

Throughout the year 1899, an increasingly bitter political-ideological battle consumed much of the time and energy of the Union's membership. The conflict between the Liberation of Labour Group and the 'youngsters' reached its climax at the Second Congress of the Union Abroad in April when the Group and their supporters withdrew from the organization. Although the Union continued to function for several more years, its members remained largely diverted from their original purpose by the continuing conflict, which by this time had spread to Russia as well. In July 1903, the Union Abroad was dealt a final blow by the decision of the RUSSIAN SOCIAL DEMOCRATIC LABOUR PARTY, at its Second Congress, to designate *Iskra* (The Spark) and its organization as the only legitimate voice of Russian Social Democracy.   BTN

Further Reading

Ascher. A.: *Pavel Axelrod and the Development of Menshevism.* Cambridge, Mass: Harvard University Press, 1972.

Baron, S.H.: *Plekhanov, The Father of Russian Marxism.* Stanford: Stanford University Press, 1963.

Frankel, J. ed. and trans.: *Vladimir Akimov on the Dilemmas of Russian Marxism, 1895–1903.* Cambridge: Cambridge University Press, 1969.

Norton, B.T.: Eshche raz ekonomizm: E.D. Kuskova, S.N. Prokopovich and the challenge to Russian Social Democracy. *The Russian Review* 45.2 (1986) 184–207.

Wildman, A.K.: *The Making of a Workers' Revolution: Russian Social Democracy, 1891–1903.* Chicago: Chicago University Press, 1967.

The Bolshevik Party: 1905–April 1917

The Russian Social Democratic Labour Party (RSDRP) and particularly its Bolshevik faction were unprepared for revolution when widespread unrest turned into open revolt in many parts of Imperial Russia during 1905. The great hopes which the *Iskra* editors had once entertained for a unified party, a centralized organization and a common programme of action had been shattered by the Menshevik-Bolshevik split at the Second Party Congress in 1903. V. I. LENIN, despite his apparent victory, was the real loser. Shortly after the congress, he quarrelled with G. V. PLEKHANOV, lost control of *Iskra* as well as the other central bodies of the party, and was left isolated abroad. His solution was to seek new adherents among the confused members of the Social Democratic underground and new allies in the émigré community. He found the latter in men like A. A. BOGDANOV and A. V. LUNACHARSKY with whose help he set up a factional newspaper, *Vpered* (Forward), and took steps to call another congress that would create an all-Bolshevik rather than a united Social Democratic Party. So obsessed was he with the calling of his Third Congress, which duly met in London during April 1905, that he failed to take adequate notice of the revolutionary events in Russia. Indeed, he and many other émigré leaders did not return to Russia until November of that year.

1905

The absence of central and unified direction hindered Bolshevik efforts during 1905. Leadership often passed into the hands of students or ANARCHIST elements. New alliances – frequently with nationalist or peasant groups not to mention with the MENSHEVIKS – were formed on the spot without reference to party leaders abroad. New tactics, such as exploiting non-party trade unions and Soviets of Workers Deputies which had sprung up during the course of 1905 or condoning the 'expropriation', i.e. robbery, of tsarist banks, were adapted to fit local conditions. Unrest tended to be spontaneous and local rather than coordinated and national. It was precisely this lack of coordination by a revolutionary party either in time or in place that eventually allowed the tsarist authorities to crush the revolution piecemeal. Symptomatic of these problems was the Moscow Insurrection in December 1905. Initiated by the Bolshevik-dominated Moscow Committee without adequate consultation with the party leadership, the insurrection failed to attract sufficient worker support or sympathy from the Moscow garrison and lacked the necessary arms and detailed planning to stand any chance of success. By the time it was crushed on 17 December by troops sent in from St Petersburg, over 1,000 people had perished.

The common revolutionary cause during 1905, however, served to unify Mensheviks and Bolsheviks in the underground and they in turn brought pressure on the party hierarchy to do likewise. It was this pressure, plus the need to devise new policies to accommodate the revolutionary gains and tsarist concessions in Russia, that resulted in the calling of the Fourth or Unification Congress in Stockholm in April 1906. Of the 112 voting delegates who attended the congress, only forty-six were 'former Bolsheviks'. This advantage allowed the 'former Mensheviks' to take over the new Central Organ, *Sotsial-demokrat*, and the Central Committee as well as having most of the tactical and programmatic decisions go in their favour. Lenin's response was to use his new Bolshevik 'Centre' (which was established contrary to the unitary spirit of Stockholm) and his new factional newspaper *Proletarii* to solicit delegates and exert pressure for the convocation of a Fifth Congress. When it met a year later in London, he did indeed have a slight plurality but it was only with the support of the Polish and Latvian delegates that he was able to reverse some of the decisions taken in Stockholm.

The London Congress marked the high-water mark of pre-war Russian Social Democracy. The 342 delegates at the congress claimed to represent 150,000 party members belonging to 145 local organizations. The SOCIAL DEMO-CRATIC DUMA FRACTION in the Second Duma, which was meeting concurrently with the congress, numbered 65 deputies (eighteen of them Bolsheviks) and was a major irritant to the tsarist government. Many of the 652 trade unions, which had grown up spontaneously during 1905 and now were functioning legally for the first time, had Social Democratic leadership. United and illegal party committees existed in most of the major Russian cities and often were successful in publishing underground news-papers as well as putting out periodic leaflets and conducting propaganda circles for workers. Abroad, the split which had incapacitated Social Democracy after 1903 was seemingly healed and the party once again had a common Central Committee and a Central Organ to provide unified guidance.

Post-1905

In reality this numerical strength and factional cooperation was chimerical and short-lived. One month after the London Congress, Prime Minister P. A. STOLYPIN dis-solved the Second Duma, arrested most of the Social Democratic deputies and changed the election law to cut party representation by more than two thirds. During 1908 and 1909 trade union membership declined drastically as a result of bureaucratic obstructionism and police interven-tion. The police also infiltrated local party committees, closed underground newspapers, and arrested party opera-tives. The number of strikers, which had stood at almost three million in 1905, declined to 46,600 in 1910. By the end of that year, not a single underground newspaper was being published in tsarist Russia. L. D. TROTSKY esti-mated that party membership had dropped to 10,000 of whom only about a tenth probably considered themselves

Bolsheviks. Among those who left revolutionary activity in large numbers were the intelligentsia who had provided so much of the guidance and expertise for Social Democracy since its inception. This exodus had the advantage, however, of causing the RSDRP gradually to become a workers' party in fact as well as in name. The central party institutions also suffered during the 'period of Stolypinist reaction'. London was the last party congress to be held for more than a decade. The Central Committee which it had elected, and whose members were supposed to operate inside tsarist Russia, was so decimated by arrests and 'retirements' that it met only twice in the two and a half years following the Fifth Congress. Factional disagreements between the Menshevik and Bolshevik editors of the Central Organ were of such an intensity that only one issue of *Sotsial-demokrat* appeared in 1907 and 1908.

In reaction to these reverses and contrary to the spirit of the Unification Congress, the émigré leaders of Russian Social Democracy reverted to their own factional interests and to re-thinking their operational strategies in light of their experience in 1905 and the new opportunities which it created. Yu. O. MARTOV and F. I. DAN gave expression to Menshevik views through their *Golos Sotsial-demokrata* (Social Democrat Voice) published in Geneva and Paris. Trotsky and Plekhanov, while continuing to pay lip-service to party unity, each had his own following and his own factional journal, the Viennese *Pravda* and *Dnevnik Sotsial-demokrata* (Social Democrat Diary). Lenin concentrated his efforts on the Bolshevik 'Centre', which served as a factional Central Committee, and on his émigré newspaper *Proletarii*.

Internal Bolshevik dissension Inside Bolshevik ranks there was far less unanimity and blind acceptance of Lenin's leadership between 1907 and 1910 than Soviet historians would have us believe. All Bolsheviks were agreed on the primacy of the underground organization and on the need to continue the pre-1905 practice of using illegal news-papers and propaganda circles to increase the workers' revolutionary consciousness. Lenin argued, however, that it was also necessary to take advantage of the concessions granted by the government to reach a broader section of non-party workers. The election campaigns to the State Duma, for instance, as well as the Duma forum itself, should be exploited as a legal means for carrying out revolutionary agitation. Trade unions should be used as 'front organizations' through which workers could be organized and indoctrinated by party members who had penetrated these bodies. Other Bolsheviks, however, led by Lenin's former lieutenant A. A. Bogdanov, argued that these were 'constitutional illusions' that would lead workers to believe that they could achieve revolutionary change by legal means. Contrary to official party policy, they urged workers to 'boycott' the elections to the First and Third Dumas, they agitated for the 'recall' of Social

Figure 5 Lenin (left) playing chess, Capri 1908, with Bogdanov (right); Gorky looking on (hand on chin).

Democratic deputies or at least the delivering of an 'ultimatum' insisting that the fraction subordinate itself to the moribund Central Committee. Social Democrats working in trade unions or seeking to organize worker delegations to legal congresses frequently found their efforts undermined by left-wing Bolsheviks controlling local party committees and opposed to these legal ventures.

There also were disagreements over the continued use by the left Bolsheviks of paramilitary tactics developed during 1905 and of 'expropriations' of tsarist banks and post offices. While these might have been justified during a period of revolutionary upheaval, the party officially condemned them as 'anarchistic methods of struggle' at the Stockholm and London Congresses. Lenin was in an ambiguous position: while he gave lip-service to the party's decrees, he appreciated the money which these robberies

put into the Bolshevik coffers. When these expropriations were subsequently used in part for help to finance a separate left-Bolshevik school for underground workers at Capri and a separate factional newspaper called *Vpered*, Lenin joined the chorus in denouncing them. The fact that he disagreed with Bogdanov on philosophical matters and with other left Bolsheviks such as Lunacharsky on appeals involving religion only exacerbated differences over tactics and organization.

The situation came to a head at an expanded meeting of *Proletarii*'s editorial board in June 1909. Lenin got his colleagues to condemn left Bolshevism (or Vperedism as it came to be known) and to expel Bogdanov from the faction. While the Vperedists remained active in western Europe for another three years and organized a second factional school at Bologna in 1910, their uncompromising theories were increasingly irrelevant in Russia itself where tsarist authorities had all but destroyed the underground organization.

The same *Proletarii* meeting that expelled Bogdanov revealed another fissure in the Bolshevik ranks. Some of the newer members of the Bolshevik 'Centre', particularly those with close ties to party operations in Russia, reflected local opinion that renewed émigré factionalism was harmful to the party and contrary to local practice. They insisted that the Bolsheviks seek closer ties with Trotsky's *Pravda* and that efforts be made to 'conciliate' differences with the Mensheviks. The sentiments of these 'conciliator' Bolsheviks found much support at a plenum of the Central Committee held in Paris during January 1910. Lenin was attacked for the continued expropriations carried out by some of his former associates; for his unethical acquisition of $140,000 from the estate of N. A. Shmidt; and for the Tiflis banknote scandal and other financial machinations. He was forced by the plenum to turn over his factional treasury to three impartial German Social Democratic 'trustees'. In the name of party unity, he agreed to close down both the Bolshevik 'Centre' and *Proletarii* as well as accepting Menshevik-Bolshevik parity in the Central Organ and in the Foreign Bureau and the Russian Board of the Central Committee. In each instance, the deciding votes rested with representatives of the various 'national' groups – the BUND, the Latvian and the Polish Social Democrats – whose support Lenin increasingly had reason to doubt.

His response to defeat at the 1910 Plenum was similar to his reaction to isolation after the Second Congress in 1903: he decided once again to build an all-Bolshevik party, a 'party of the new type' that would be composed solely of 'like-minded individuals' and would pay no further heed to 'idiotic conciliationism'. He was aided in these endeavours by the withdrawal of Martov and Dan from the new editorial board of *Sotsial-demokrat* thus leaving the Central Organ in his and G. E. ZINOVIEV's hands. He side-stepped the Foreign Bureau and Russian Board of the Central Committee by creating a bogus Committee of Foreign Organizations and a Russian Organizing Commission. And he trained a new generation of underground workers at his own factional school in Longjumeau, outside Paris, to staff these bodies and to provide delegates for an all-important 'Sixth' Party Conference to be convened in Prague during January 1912.

Only eighteen delegates showed up in Prague but sixteen of these were 'like-minded' Bolsheviks. Despite their questionable mandates and the absence of all the non-Bolshevik leaders of Russian Social Democracy, this small gathering declared itself to be 'an all-party conference of the RSDRP – the highest organ of the party'. As such, the delegates took it upon themselves to change the party rules and to elect new Bolshevik-dominated central bodies. They also declared that the so-called 'Liquidator' wing of the Menshevik faction had 'once and for all placed itself outside the party' and threatened that all other groups not operating through the Bolshevik Central Committee would be unable to 'use the name of the Russian Social Democratic Labour Party'. In this way Lenin equated Bolshevism with Russian Social Democracy and took control of what purported to be the central organs of the party without overtly alienating local party members who still had great faith in the supposed benefits of party unity.

Lenin's pragmatism: Lenin, better than his rivals, was aware of the upswing in labour unrest which began in Russia after 1911. In June 1912, shortly after the massive strikes in protest against the shooting of the Lena gold miners, the Bolshevik leader turned his back on émigré factionalism and moved his headquarters to Austrian Galicia. There, close to the Russian frontier, his Central Committee met at least twelve times during the next two years. Much of its attention was focused on the elections to the Fourth Duma and on the operations of *Pravda*, the Bolsheviks' new legal daily newspaper in St Petersburg. Lenin recognized that these legal organizations as well as the revived trade unions and the new worker insurance councils offered a better way of agitating and guiding the urban masses than did the underground party structure which had been very slow to revive from the repression of the Stolypin era. He also used these years in Galicia to rethink and to make more attractive Bolshevik policies concerning the national minorities and the Russian peasantry and to sanction the publication of *Rabotnitsa* (Woman Worker), a legal newspaper aimed at proletarian women. While these new policies may have been short on content and sincerity, they nevertheless reflected Lenin's opportunism and flexibility, especially in comparison to Menshevik repetition of old and out-worn doctrines. The fact that he was more attuned to the mood of the Russian masses after 1912 was evident in the gains the Bolsheviks made in the Duma, in elections to trade union directorates and insurance councils, and in the greater popularity of their legal newspapers.

To consolidate these gains and to complete the schismatic work of the Third Congress and Prague Conference, Lenin made plans for the convocation of a Sixth Party Congress to be held in August 1914. In May of that year, however, R. V. MALINOVSKY, a member of the Bolshevik Central Committee and the leader of the Bolshevik Duma fraction, suddenly resigned from the Russian parliament amid rumours that he was an agent of the tsarist secret police. Shortly thereafter, the International Socialist Bureau called a meeting of ten Russian factions to discuss yet again the possibility of Social Democratic unity. Lenin, who was sure to be censored for having engineered the split of the party's Duma fraction in late 1913 and on the defensive because of the Malinovsky affair and his fractious efforts to retrieve Bolshevik money from the German 'trustees', refused to attend this meeting in Brussels. His uncompromising statement, read in his absence by Inessa ARMAND, so incensed the other delegates that it forged a much stronger anti-Bolshevik coalition and very possibly might have led to his expulsion from the Socialist International. In the face of these unexpected developments, Lenin had to postpone his planned congress and he lost sight once again of revolutionary events in St Petersburg where, on the eve of the First World War, discontented workers threw up barricades in the streets and challenged the authorities.

The war

While the war spared Lenin further ignominy before the International, it initially had a deleterious effect on his party. Almost all legal and illegal organizations in Russia were closed down and their leaders arrested; police suppression and popular patriotism brought the strike movement and worker unrest to a temporary halt; and all contact was lost with the party hierarchy abroad. Lenin, from his new base of operations in Switzerland, denounced the war and those leaders of the RSDRP and the Socialist International who supported it. He felt that the defeat of Russia was the 'lesser evil' and that the imperialist war should be transformed into a civil war. The Bolsheviks promoted conferences of socialist youth and socialist women in Bern and of anti-war socialists in general at Zimmerwald and Kienthal. In each instance, Lenin's defeatist views were in a decided minority but he succeeded in making them better known and the longer the war lasted the more attractive they became to a wide variety of socialists throughout Europe.

The February Revolution

The Bolsheviks and certainly Lenin had little to do with either the abdication of NICHOLAS II or the establishment of a bourgeois PROVISIONAL GOVERNMENT in February 1917. In these new conditions and cut off from the party leadership in Switzerland, a reconstituted Russian Bureau of the Central Committee, headed by A. G. SHLYAPNIKOV, attempted to provide a modicum of coordination and guidance for Bolshevik forces in Petrograd. Its early calls for the overthrow of the Provisional Government and for an end to the war were supported neither by the party's Petersburg Committee nor by L. B. KAMENEV and I. V. STALIN who took over local leadership when they returned from Siberian exile in mid-March. Bolshevik policy now became one of qualified support for the Provisional Government and for the continuation of a defensive war as well as exploring possible means of unity with the Mensheviks.

Lenin, isolated from events in Petrograd, had to sit in Switzerland for almost a month until the Germans finally agreed to put a 'sealed' railway car at his disposal and to haul thirty-two Russians, including nineteen Bolsheviks, across Germany so that they could take a boat to Sweden and then a train back to Petrograd. When Lenin stepped

off at the Finland Station on 3 April and the next day in his famous 'April Theses', he denounced the policies of the local Bolsheviks. He attacked any form of defensive war, any type of support for the Provisional Government, and any notion of unity with the Mensheviks. He called instead for 'all power to the Soviets'. It took his colleagues three weeks to see the error of their ways. At the Seventh or April Conference, Lenin's precepts were overwhelmingly endorsed and a new Central Committee was elected with him at its helm. Lenin, who had created the Bolshevik Party at the Third Congress in 1905 and had reconstituted it at the Prague Conference in 1912, recaptured control of his party at the April Conference in 1917. Six months later, this party seized control of Petrograd and ultimately of Russia itself.   RCE

Further Reading

Elwood, R.C.: *Russian Social Democracy in the Underground: A Study of the RSDRP in the Ukraine, 1907–1914*. Assen: 1974.

Geyer, Dietrich: *Kautskys Russiches Dossier: Deutsche Sozialdemokraten als Treuhänder des russichen Parteivermögens 1910–1915*. Frankfurt: 1981.

Istoriya kommunisticheskoi partii Sovetskogo Soyuza, tom II: 1903–1917. Moscow: 1966.

Resolutions and Decisions of the Communist Party of the Soviet Union. Vol. I: *The Russian Social Democratic Labour Party, 1898–October 1917*. Toronto: 1974.

Schapiro, Leonard: *The Communist Party of the Soviet Union*. New York: 1959.

Swain, Geoffrey: *Russian Social Democracy and the Legal Labour Movement, 1906–14*. London: 1983.

The Social Democratic Duma Fraction

The group of Social Democratic deputies elected to the first four State Dumas (1906–17) who used the Russian parliamentary body primarily as a forum for revolutionary agitation.

When NICHOLAS II announced his intention in October 1905 to convene a legislative assembly elected on the basis of a broad franchise, most Social Democratic leaders advocated a boycott of the proposed Duma. They argued that it would pervert the revolutionary consciousness of the Russian workers by creating 'constitutional illusions' about the possibility of achieving lasting change through parliamentary means. The Bolsheviks in particular felt that the proper course was to intensify revolutionary pressure for the overthrow of the tsar and the convocation of a truly constituent assembly.

Many rank-and-file party members, however, took part in the early elections to the First Duma in the spring of 1906 and helped to return the most radical candidates available. Belatedly recognizing their misreading of the situation, the Mensheviks decided to participate in the remaining elections in the Caucasus and succeeded in electing five of their followers as deputies. These joined thirteen non-party deputies with Social Democratic sympathies to form the first Social Democratic Duma Fraction. Several weeks later the Duma was dissolved. Both wings of Social Democracy accepted the fact that the Second Duma would indeed offer a legitimate forum for revolutionary agitation and thus participated actively in the election of sixty-five deputies – thirty-six Menshevik, eighteen Bolshevik and eleven unaffiliated Social Democrats – during January 1907. On the pretext that this new and enlarged fraction was fomenting unrest in the Russian army, Prime Minister P. A. STOLYPIN dissolved the Second Duma in June, arrested many of the Social Democratic deputies, and radically altered the election law to the disadvantage of the party's constituents. This, plus worker apathy and a resurgence of boycottist sentiment in Bolshevik ranks, resulted in a Social Democratic Fraction of only nineteen deputies in the Third Duma. Of these, four consistently voted the Bolshevik position, four occasionally did so, while the other eleven usually affiliated with the Mensheviks. Despite a revival of interest in the Duma by the party leadership and a growth of worker unrest throughout Russia, the elections to the Fourth Duma in October 1912 returned only seven Menshevik and six Bolshevik deputies.

Because the Bolsheviks in particular tended to elect young, relatively uneducated and inexperienced worker-deputies, leadership of the united fraction in all four Dumas passed, by default as well as by majority, to the few Menshevik *intelligenty* elected each session: Noah ZHORDANIA in the First Duma, I. G. TSERETELI in the Second, E. P. Gegechkori and N. S. Ckheidze in the Third, and Chkheidze (the only Social Democrat to be elected twice) in the Fourth. To compensate for the intellectual deficiencies of his deputies, LENIN often wrote speeches for them to deliver or summoned them abroad to receive first-hand instructions. Both factions utilized the services of sympathetic lawyers and professionals in St Petersburg who could provide the technical advice and political acumen which the deputies frequently lacked.

The Social Democrats viewed the four Dumas as opportunities for revolutionary agitation rather than as means for constructive labour legislation. The election campaigns themselves offered a chance to promote the party's programme and to organize the Russian workers. Inside the Duma, the fraction concentrated on attacking government bills, promoting amendments that had no chance of adoption, participating in long procedural wrangles, embarrassing the government through votes of no confidence and interpellations of ministers, calling attention to worker complaints, and generally disrupting orderly legislative activity.

Increasingly, the party also took advantage of the legal guarantees extended to the Duma and its members to promote Social Democratic goals outside the Duma. Duma speeches, for example, could be reprinted verbatim in the legal press. This led to close ties being established between the fraction and such papers as *Zvezda* (Star), *Pravda* and *Luch* (Ray). Deputies would raise money for party papers, serve as editors and publishers, and through their speeches in the house provide agitational material which might otherwise be banned by the censor. The parliamentary immunity given to the Social Democratic deputies also allowed them to make contact with worker groups outside the Duma without fear of arrest, to visit legal congresses and worker enlightenment societies, to intercede in strikes, and to serve as messengers throughout Russia for the illegal party.

Lenin especially came to recognize the enhanced potential of the fraction as an agitational and organizational force outside the Duma. In order to free himself from the constraints imposed by the Menshevik majority and in conformity with the final split in the party abroad, he ordered his deputies in the Fourth Duma to form a separate Russian Social Democratic Workers Fraction. This group, which was established in November 1913 and was headed by deputy R. V. MALINOVSKY, for a brief period became the coordinating body for all legal and illegal Bolshevik activity in Russia. Its extra-parliamentary functions were curtailed, however, in May 1914 when rumours spread that Malinovsky was a police agent and he was forced to resign from the Duma to the great embarrassment of his colleagues. Later that year the remaining Bolshevik deputies were arrested for their opposition to Russia's involvement in the war. The Mensheviks' Social Democratic Fraction continued to function until the February Revolution offered them a chance to sit on the dais of the Petrograd Soviet rather than on the backbenches of the moribund Duma.   RCE

Further Reading

Badayev, A.: *The Bolsheviks in the Tsarist Duma.* London: 1932.

Levin, Alfred: *The Second Duma: A Study of the Social-Democratic Party and the Russian Constitutional Experiment.* New Haven, Conn.: 1940.

Arrest and Trial of Bolshevik Duma Deputies

Although the Bolshevik deputies had supported the statement against the war, read to the 'historic' session of the Duma of 26 July 1914 (OS) by the MENSHEVIK deputy V. I. Khaustov, and had left the chamber with the Menshevik and Trudovik deputies so as to avoid voting for war credits, they were in reality as confused in their attitude to the war as was every other socialist party. Whereas A. E. Badaev, deputy for Petrograd, wanted to mobilize the Petrograd workers in a strike against the war, G. I. Petrovsky, deputy for Ekaterinoslav, was inclined to heed Vandervelde's appeal for support for the Allied war effort (see VANDERVELDE TELEGRAM). At the end of September, F. N. Samoilov, deputy for Ivanovo-

Voznesensk who had been in Switzerland for health reasons when the war broke out, returned to Russia with LENIN's 'Theses on the War'. These proved so controversial that a first meeting to discuss them had to be abandoned so that the deputies could tour the country to sound out rank and file party opinion. On their return from these tours, the deputies met L. B. KAMENEV, the editor of *Pravda*, and a number of leading Petrograd Bolsheviks to try to reach agreement on Lenin's 'Theses'. During this meeting, on 4 November, they were arrested.

Petrograd was under military jurisdiction and initially the government wanted to have them tried by a military court and face the death penalty for treason, but in the end the more moderate alternative of a civil trial was adopted. This took place in February 1915, and the deputies were defended by an impressive team of lawyers, including A. F. KERENSKY, and N. D. Sokolov. The deputies' behaviour at the trial gave rise to much criticism and contributed to the demoralization of the Bolshevik party at the time, as most of them tried to dissociate themselves from the party. Only M. K. Muranov, deputy for Kharkov, won praise from Lenin for his conduct in court. The deputies and Kamenev were found guilty and condemned to exile in Siberia in perpetuity. Neither the arrests, nor the trial and sentences evoked any significant unrest in the working class or support from the Duma.

DAL

Further Reading

Lenin, V.I.: What had been revealed by the Trial of the RSDRP Labour Group. In *Collected Works*, vol. 21. London: 1964.

Samoilov, F.N.: *Protsess bol'shevistskoi fraktsii chetvertoi Gosudarstvennoi dumy.* Moscow/Leningrad: 1927.

The Scandinavian Connection

That the Scandinavian countries - thanks to their geographical proximity to Russia, a traditional mistrust of the tsarist regime, and developing constitutional and democratic systems – represented potential routes for clandestine communications and transport between Russian radicals and revolutionaries living in Western and Central Europe and their fellows in Russia was perceived already by HERZEN, Ogarev and BAKUNIN in London during the Polish uprising in 1863, when Ogarev prepared a comprehensive though premature plan and Bakunin spent several months in Stockholm. During the following decades the growth of socialist movements and trade unions in Scandinavia, and at the turn of the century the upsurge of Finnish nationalism in response to attempted russification (see the BALTIC), increased the number of those sympathetic, and sometimes helpful, to opponents of tsarism; one such was the outstanding Swedish socialist leader, Hjalmar Branting (1860–1925), who was an early helper

and who later was often willing to use his influence in support and protection.

Between 1898 and 1905 this collaboration of Russian revolutionaries, Finnish nationalists and socialists, and Scandinavian (particularly though not only Swedish) socialists, developed on a large scale, from the occasional forwarding of letters and parcels to the bulk import into Russia of revolutionary literature and attempts to ship cargoes of weapons; several Russian and other parties and factions participated, though more than scanty information is available only about the shares of BOLSHEVIKS and Finnish nationalists, as only they subsequently compiled detailed (though selective) accounts. The principal figures in this period were the Bolshevik V. M. Smirnov (1876–1952), a Russian-language teacher at the University of Helsinki (after 1917 for many years Soviet consul-general in Sweden), and the Finnish patriot Konni Zilliacus (1855–1924, father of the British politician of the same name).

There seem to have been enough helpers on both sides of the Baltic – socialist workers, intellectuals, booksellers – to facilitate this flow of revolutionary literature printed in Western and Central Europe (such as, from the end of 1900, LENIN's organ *Iskra*) to its principal destination St Petersburg; with the strong anti-tsarist mood prevalent in Finland, Finnish officials such as customs men, and railway employees, might help or at least ignore; the powers of the Russian police and other authorities in Finland were limited, in accordance with Finnish, not Russian, law; and Smirnov was an enterprising and efficient manager.

The main problem was shipping the goods across the Baltic; smuggling by steamship passengers and crew members was possible in limited quantities, but risky. Greater regularity was attained in 1902, when Smirnov made an agreement for transport with the experienced journalist and adventurer Zilliacus, who since 1900 had been publishing in Stockholm a weekly dedicated to sustaining Finnish resistance to russification, and was willing to assist any group working against the tsarist regime. Zilliacus had a yacht specially built for the job, and according to his own account during many voyages carried altogether sixteen tons of literature (his own and others') to Finland (some then forwarded to Russia). This was no small quantity; underground newspapers were usually printed on extremely thin lightweight paper, a copy of Zilliacus's own paper weighing less than three grams.

Among other routes at this time perhaps the most remarkable lay far in the Arctic, directly between Vardö in the extreme north of Norway and Archangel (by-passing Finland), thanks to long-established relations between Norwegian and Russian fishermen and the presence as postmaster in Vardö of a well-known Norwegian socialist.

After the outbreak of the Russo-Japanese War early in 1904, unrest in Russia and increasing revolutionary activity (culminating in the initially successful but soon crushed revolution during the later months of 1905) led Bolshevik,

Finnish nationalist and a variety of other organizations to switch their main efforts from the transport of literature to the acquisition and transport of arms. Two leading Bolsheviks deeply involved in this were L. B. KRASIN and M. M. LITVINOV, both subsequently prominent Soviet diplomats.

The most famous gun-running voyage was that of the *John Grafton* through the Baltic during the summer of 1905, a daring but ill-prepared enterprise that also marked the climax of the Japanese wartime policy of encouraging revolution in Russia; after the misgivings of high Japanese authorities had been overcome, at the end of April 1905 one million yen were made available for this purpose – a striking anticipation of the similar German policy a decade later. The key figures were again Zilliacus, who later described the affair in his memoirs (in Swedish and Finnish), and (in the background) Colonel Motojiro Akashi (1864–1919), former military attaché in St Petersburg, whose report compiled soon afterwards became known in Japan and about whom there is a considerable Japanese literature.

The Japanese contacts during 1904–5 included not only Russians (both Bolsheviks and SOCIALIST REVOLUTION-ARIES), Finns and Swedes, but also Poles and Georgians, and British and other West European and American sympathizers and intermediaries (including the elder George Kennan, and that perhaps most globally roving of all Russian revolutionaries Dr Nicholas Russel, already and subsequently active in many parts of East Asia and the Pacific). The cargo collected in London by the summer of 1905 (principally 15,500 rifles, two and a half million cartridges, and three tons of explosives) did after many anxieties and mishaps reach the northern coast of Finland in the *John Grafton*, but after two small consignments had been landed most was lost when the ship ran on to a reef and had to be blown up.

During the long decline of revolutionary activities after the collapse of the 1905 REVOLUTION, surviving Russian activists in their Western and Central European refuges were still concerned to maintain confidential links with Russia – none more than Lenin, always devoted to information, instruction and organization, which at day-to-day level were taken care of by his wife KRUPSKAYA. Her published correspondence shows for example that during the lean years 1908–9 she spent much time establishing a route for correspondence to and from, and the transmission of literature to, Russia, organized in Copenhagen by the Bolshevik Mikhail Kobetsky (1881–1937, subsequently for many years Soviet representative in Denmark), who recruited Danish socialist helpers in the same way as Swedes had long been used.

From 1912 to 1914 Lenin lived in Austrian Poland, close to the Russian frontier, and underground communications with Russia were concentrated there. After the outbreak of war he moved to Switzerland and, with Poland and its

direct routes a theatre of military operations, set about reactivating the potential of the Scandinavian countries (neutral in the war, like Switzerland), choosing as his principal agent the resourceful Bolshevik worker Alexander SHLYAPNIKOV (1885–19–?), who began the job in Stockholm in October 1914. Branting, now an influential political figure, provided invaluable support and protection; but much help came particularly from younger Swedish socialists such as Fredrik Ström (1880–1948, secretary of the Swedish socialist party 1911–1916), Zeth Höglund (1884–1956), and Karl Kilbom (1885–1961), who were increasingly critical of Branting's cautious leadership and sympathetic towards Bolshevism (all three subsequently took part in the foundation of the Swedish Communist Party, which they all sooner or later left; their voluminous memoirs written long afterwards must be used with caution).

Shlyapnikov's closest comrade in Scandinavia however was the much better-known Russian socialist (at this time approaching Bolshevism) and pioneer feminist Alexandra KOLLONTAI (1872–1952); soon expelled from Sweden for fiery anti-militaristic articles and speeches, she settled in Norway. Unlike the intelligent but self-taught proletarian Shlyapnikov she was cosmopolitanly cultivated and an eloquent polemical publicist. The pair collaborated in the principal tasks of organizing underground communications and indoctrinating the Scandinavian extreme left, and during their Scandinavian years enjoyed (so far as distance and frontiers permitted – she was barred from Sweden, but he could go in and out of Norway) an intimate relationship.

The vital Finnish link in the wartime chain from Lenin in Switzerland through Scandinavia to Petrograd (as St Petersburg was now called) was capably handled by the Finnish socialist Karl Wiik (1883–1946), who had met Lenin several years before. Specializing in international contacts, knowing everybody, meticulously reliable, Wiik was an ideal collaborator, and his unpublished memoir written soon afterwards constitutes a prime source, substantially confirming the frank and detailed account published by Shlyapnikov a few years later.

Despite much complaining in the many published letters of Lenin and Krupskaya to Shlyapnikov, it is clear that he succeeded in maintaining some connection between Lenin and such Bolshevik groups as existed inside Russia, and during some periods managed to forward substantial quantities of Bolshevik publications. Owing to wartime hazards, normal maritime routes between Sweden and Finland were disrupted, and the principal link for all purposes between Russia and the West was by rail, with the small northern Swedish town Haparanda on the Finnish frontier mushrooming into a notorious way-station of international intrigue. Shlyapnikov was constantly on the move throughout Scandinavia (in the Arctic he reconnoitred as far as Vardö, finding evidence of the activity there a decade before), made trips to both Britain and the

USA in search of funds (which he hoped to raise among Jewish circles in exchange for material on the harsh treatment being meted out to the Jews in Russia), and accomplished two long clandestine expeditions into Russia.

Beneath the level represented by the efforts of Shlyapnikov, Kollontai, Wiik and their helpers were, however, underground layers much more obscure, complex, controversial and politically dangerous. During the war years, the neutral capitals Stockholm and Copenhagen became centres not only for diplomacy and espionage but also for attempted infiltration and financing of revolutionary organizations by agents, intermediaries or allies of the German authorities who since the first winter of the war had been interested in the possibility of crippling Russia by promoting revolution there. The situation was complicated by Stockholm and (particularly) Copenhagen having become also hothouses of every kind of financial and commercial enterprise, from mere profiteering through black marketeering to downright smuggling, by merchants of many nationalities, trading in all directions where profit lay (into and out of both Russia and Germany, as well as the neutral countries), and in all kinds of goods (from essential raw materials such as coal and rubber to clinical thermometers and contraceptives; drugs and medical supplies were particularly favoured as they combined high value with small bulk).

(For treatment of German policy, see REVOLUTIONIERUNGSPOLITIK, and of its most spectacular advocate and exponent Alexander HELPHAND (PARVUS).) There follows here an account first of a Scandinavian episode in which the central figure was the Estonian nationalist and former Bolshevik Alexander Kesküla (1882–1963), and then of the wartime doings in Scandinavia of the Polish Bolshevik Jacob Fürstenberg (as he spelt his name in Scandinavia) (1879–1937).

After participation in (and organization of) revolutionary activities in Estonia during 1905–7 as a Bolshevik, Kesküla emigrated in 1908 and spent several years at German and Swiss universities. A man of intellect and culture, and no longer a Bolshevik, from his first visit to the German minister in Bern in September 1914 he endeavoured to impress on German authorities his conviction of Lenin's pre-eminence as a revolutionary leader, and was successful enough to receive from them between then and October 1916 sums he subsequently reckoned as having totalled some quarter of a million marks. Much of this was used for his Estonian concerns, but some he infiltrated into Lenin's organization in Switzerland through his collaborator, also Estonian, Arthur Siefeldt, still a Bolshevik and close to Lenin's circle, who at the same time provided Kesküla with inside Bolshevik information which Kesküla then processed for the Germans. Camouflaged financial assistance to the Bolsheviks was just one preliminary step towards the realization of Kesküla's grandiose vision: a revolution in Russia would make possible an independent Estonia, and perhaps a Swedish-Finnish-Estonian federation as one of several bulwarks to keep Russia out of Europe (see also RAKOVSKY).

In 1915 Kesküla settled in Stockholm, soon becoming a sinisterly mysterious and elusive figure to the resident Bolsheviks and their Scandinavian sympathizers; he scorned the flamboyant panache of Helphand (Parvus), but his cool elegance and indirectly manipulative style seemed more threatening. Shlyapnikov had now been joined in Stockholm by other Russians, notably the Bolshevik intellectuals BUKHARIN and Pyatakov.

In the winter of 1915–16 among the Russians and the local extreme left in Stockholm Kesküla's infiltration (he was able to have Bolshevik literature printed for them) led to a labyrinthine imbroglio which – partly because subsequently famous Swedish politicians and the subsequently even more famous Bukharin were deeply and ambiguously involved – long remained in the obscurity, if not total oblivion, seemingly desired by most. Futrell's initial elucidation has been developed by the exhaustive archival research of Björkegren (see Further Reading).

In March 1916 the Swedish conservative government was alarmed by rumours of Russian revolutionaries' involvement in an outspokenly anti-militaristic congress organized by the Swedish left socialists; three of the latter were imprisoned, and several Russians, including Bukharin and Pyatakov, were expelled and retreated to Norway. Suspecting that provocation and betrayal had been engineered by Kesküla, the Russians sought the Estonian's instruments. Two were found: an obscure Bolshevik Jacob Bogrovsky, secretary of the group that included Shlyapnikov, Bukharin and Pyatakov, had accepted money from Kesküla; he was expelled from the party. The other was a Danish left-socialist journalist living in Stockholm, close to most of the Russians and Swedes concerned, and an acquaintance of Kesküla; on behalf of all of them and on his own journalistic business he had made two journeys to Russia, using contacts provided and gathering information. In August 1916 in Copenhagen he was interrogated by a group of Russians (including Bukharin) and Swedes; despite his vigorous defence, suspicions of him were regarded as so strong that he was in effect permanently barred from more than auxiliary participation in the socialist movement to which he was devoted.

This Dane was Alfred Kruse (1888–1958), who spent the remaining four decades of his life vainly seeking rehabilitation from high socialist authorities both Scandinavian and Soviet. Sincere but imprudent and perhaps naive, he was made a scapegoat to cover both Kesküla's hoodwinking of the Stockholm Bolsheviks and (as recently shown by Björkegren) errors and leaks by both Russians and Swedes. This sad story provides a remarkable study of political victimization, and an instructive insight into Bolshevik psychology.

As for Kesküla, later in 1916 his relations with the

Germans ceased; he continued to work for his quixotic Baltic vision, but without the results he desired, and retired to private life.

Much information from unpublished Scandinavian sources has also long afterwards emerged concerning Jacob Fürstenberg (also known in Polish as Hanecki, in Russian as Ganetsky). Of prosperous Warsaw bourgeois origin, from 1902 he was a full-time revolutionary. Though it was sometimes convenient to stress his membership of the Polish social democratic party, he was an experienced and reliable Bolshevik, a veteran of the underground, highly valued by Lenin, who (as Lenin himself wrote in 1921 in a letter of recommendation for Fürstenberg) 'observed him closely in the years 1912–14, when we lived in Cracow together'. Then, from early 1915 until immediately after the February Revolution of 1917 (when Fürstenberg was in Stockholm and Lenin urgently contacted him), he disappeared from the published correspondence of Lenin and Krupskaya, and from published Bolshevik records. Light has been thrown on this missing period of his life through an unfortunate accident (or, depending on viewpoint, the commendable zeal of Danish officials, who unexpectedly opened some packing-cases).

In January 1917 Fürstenberg was arrested in Copenhagen, accused of exporting medical goods without the necessary licences, and subjected to gruelling examination by Judge Viggo Thorup, the respected and feared chief of a special commission engaged in combating the international commercial jungle of Copenhagen, where since the summer of 1915 Fürstenberg had been head of a thriving export-import firm dealing with Germany and Russia.

Commercial papers from his office were seized, and they, together with the protocol of Thorup's examination, document the maze of wheeling and dealing which for over a year Fürstenberg had profitably navigated. So intricate was the maze, and so skilful a prevaricator was this Bolshevik businessman, that in the end his offer to make a modest payment (the value of certain smuggled goods) and leave Denmark, not to return without permission, was accepted by the commission. So he moved to Stockholm, where lived his close collaborator throughout his commercial career (his collaborator's name, like other names in these Copenhagen documents, on the instructions of Danish legal authorities may not be published; it is not a name occurring in this article), and became once more (if, indeed, he had ever ceased being) Lenin's man of confidence, organizing Lenin's communications with Shlyapnikov (now in Petrograd) and the Scandinavian side of Lenin's return to Russia through Germany.

The commercial papers show that though Fürstenberg probably was not (in British or American currencies) a millionaire, he had certainly done very well with thermometers and contraceptives; by Bolshevik standards he must have been extremely wealthy.

Fürstenberg succeeded in keeping one explosive name – Helphand (Parvus) – out of his examination; but the obvious assumption is confirmed by a document surviving in Berlin – the agreement by which the initial capital of Fürstenberg's company was provided half by Helphand and half by another notorious political and financial operator working with and for the Germans, Georg Sklarz.

After the crisis caused by the Russian PROVISIONAL GOVERNMENT's allegations in the summer of 1917, Lenin vehemently defended Fürstenberg within the Bolshevik central committee, declaring that Fürstenberg 'earned his bread as an *employee* (Lenin's emphasis) in a trading firm of which Parvus was a shareholder. He told me so. This is not refuted.'

Whatever Lenin said or wrote, how much he really knew about Fürstenberg's business may never be known; likewise how much he really cared about whatever he did know (bearing in mind earlier replenishments of Bolshevik coffers by robbing banks). Some leading Bolsheviks evidently had doubts about Fürstenberg; Shlyapnikov clearly loathed him. However, the Bolshevik described in Danish commercial reference books of 1915–16 (presumably not available to the central committee in Petrograd in 1917) as chairman of the board of directors of Handels- og Eksportkompagniet A/S must have rejoiced in Lenin's staunch support. Subsequently, he had a fairly distinguished career in Soviet finance, commerce and diplomacy, ending in the late 1930s; like so many old Bolsheviks, he was a victim of Stalin's terror. His last post seems to have been the directorship of the Museum of the Revolution – a responsibility the ambiguous appropriateness of which he perhaps savoured.

After the OCTOBER REVOLUTION, experience and contacts gained through the pre-revolutionary Scandinavian connection contributed to the two-way clandestine communications (out of as well as into Soviet Russia) of the Comintern networks, parts of which utilized Scandinavia.   MHF

Further Reading

Björkegren, Hans: *Ryska Posten*. Bonniers, Stockholm: 1985 (in Swedish).

Futrell, Michael: *Northern Underground*. Faber, London: 1963.

——— : Colonel Akashi and Japanese contacts with Russian revolutionaries in 1904–5. In *St. Antony's Papers*, vol.20. *Far Eastern Affairs* 4. Oxford: Oxford University Press, 1967.

Nish, Ian: Japanese Intelligence and the approach of the Russo-Japanese War. In *The Missing Dimension*, ed. Christopher Andrew and David Dilks. London: Macmillan, 1984.

Revolutionierungspolitik and Alexander Helphand (Parvus)

Already in November 1914 it was clear to Germany's leaders that their hopes of rapid victory had not been realized, and they began to consider possibilities for resolving their problem of waging war simultaneously on the Eastern and Western fronts through removing one of their opponents by political means. As probes both in East and West towards a separate peace brought little satisfaction, attention was paid to the less conventional idea of crippling the Russian Empire through support of revolutionary groups both socialist and nationalist. After the OCTOBER REVOLUTION of 1917 LENIN's government did indeed take Russia out of the war (though from the German point of view this was too late to be decisive). To what extent (if at all) the German policy of internally weakening Russia during 1915–17 (*Revolutionierungspolitik*) was significantly effective, and particularly to what extent (if at all) it materially contributed to Bolshevik activities in Russia during the months between the February and October Revolutions of 1917, have remained vexedly controversial ever since – even after the opening (after the Second World War) of surviving German archives, where the policy and some of its implementation are evident, but identifiable results of much consequence mostly not.

From early in the war German officials in neutral countries were visited and at times almost besieged by anti-tsarist revolutionaries, prophets, preachers and adventurers of numerous nationalities, seeking German aid for their schemes; one grandiose though ineffective outgrowth has been reconstructed by Zetterberg (1978). As regards fostering specifically Russian revolutionary activity, two collaborators with the Germans offered real knowledge and some expertise as well as imagination. One, the Estonian Alexander Keskula, seemed to most an elusive phantom but did aid the Bolsheviks at least a little during 1915 and early 1916. The other was very different: the flamboyant Alexander Helphand (1867–1924), a Russian Jew. Growing up in cosmopolitan Odessa and studying politics and economics at the University of Basle, he became a Marxist and during the 1890s was a prolific and pugnacious socialist journalist in Germany (adopting in 1894 the pen-name Parvus). His attacks on Bernstein's revisionism were admired by leading Russian Marxists such as PLEKHANOV, Lenin and MARTOV. In 1900 he and Lenin met in Munich and for a time collaborated in Lenin's organ *Iskra*, but Helphand soon shared the MENSHEVIKS' distaste for Lenin's relentless struggle for power in the party.

Early in 1904 the Russo-Japanese War began. Helphand saw (more clearly than other Marxists at the time) that the disruptions of war could open the way to revolution in Russia and then in other countries. At this time he met TROTSKY, and a brief but intense intellectual friendship developed, in which Trotsky was particularly influenced by Helphand's conception of the mass strike as the starting-point for revolution (see PERMANENT REVOLUTION).

In October 1905 Helphand went to Russia and joined Trotsky in the leadership of the St Petersburg Soviet, which for a few intoxicating weeks seemed to be taking over power – but their concentration on fanning class struggle alienated the bourgeoisie, soldiers mostly obeyed orders, and the government was able to liquidate the Soviet. Arrested in April 1906, Helphand soon escaped from Siberia and resumed his career as a Marxist writer in Germany, never returning to Russia. However, Helphand's reputation was permanently tarnished by allegations (furiously voiced by Maxim GORKY) of his embezzlement of funds from a socialist publishing house. This confusion was never fully elucidated, but in 1910 Helphand moved to Vienna, and then to Constantinople where he became a specialist on Balkan affairs and a very rich man through business of which the exact nature remains unclear. It was in south-eastern Europe that he learned the intricacies and glimpsed the potential of blending and manipulating politics, commerce and finance.

So it was no shabby journalist but a figure of wealth and influence who in January 1915 told the German ambassador in Constantinople that 'the interests of the German government are identical with those of the Russian revolutionaries'. A few weeks later Helphand unfolded to high officials of the Foreign Ministry in Berlin a comprehensive plan for subversion of the Russian Empire by aiding anti-tsarist movements, both socialist and nationalist, with special emphasis on preparing a mass strike of industrial and railway workers, and on the organizational potential of the Russian Social Democrats who must however be unified, with Lenin's Bolsheviks playing a key role. At the end of March, Helphand received one million marks from the German Foreign Ministry. Even larger sums were soon assigned, as the German foreign minister noted, for 'revolutionary propaganda in Russia'.

In May 1915 Helphand arrived in Switzerland, now displaying an opulent panache (matching his bloatedly corpulent figure), rare if not unique in left-wing annals, reportedly astounding and infuriating impoverished socialists with his zestful enjoyment of expensive cigars, champagne breakfasts and colourful female company. He met Lenin; and was rebuffed. This was a serious reverse; he would have to develop his own machinery for Russian operations. So for the next two years he made Copenhagen (then the liveliest centre of international intrigue of all kinds) his main base.

There, he impressed the German minister Brockdorff-Rantzau; master-minded international commercial deals; set up a so-called Institute for the Study of the Social Consequences of the War, staffed largely by Russians; floated his own German socialist newspaper (*Die Glocke*); and together with a notorious German agent Georg Sklarz financed an import-export firm (trading between Germany and Russia via Scandinavia) which prospered splendidly until in January 1917 its managing director was arrested for contravening Danish regulations and expelled from Denmark. This commercial enterprise may have provided cover for political operations in Russia. Its managing director was the Polish Bolshevik Jacob Fürstenberg, previously and subsequently one of Lenin's most trusted henchmen. Just what was the understanding – if there was one – between Lenin and Fürstenberg during this lucrative episode remains unknown.

Likewise unknown remains who (if anyone) was doing what (if anything) on Helphand's behalf in the political sphere in Russia. Certainly he promised revolutionary events in Russia in January 1916, and in late December 1915 received from the Germans one million rubles 'for the support of the revolutionary movement in Russia'; large strikes did indeed occur in Russia in January and February, but they petered out. Helphand was already rich, there was little reason for him to be a trickster, but from the lush emporium of Copenhagen he had evidently miscalculated the actuality of wartime Russian factories; his credibility with the Germans was severely damaged, and for a year support of Russian revolutionaries had low priority with German authorities.

The February Revolution of 1917 brought drastic changes. At the beginning of April the German Foreign Ministry assigned five million marks for political purposes in Russia. After intricate negotiations, in which Helphand had some part, Lenin was transported (in the famous 'sealed' train) from Switzerland through Germany and Sweden to Russia. During the following months, under Lenin's leadership, the Bolsheviks in Russia directed an immense propaganda at Russian workers and soldiers. Whence came the money to pay for this flood of print is unclear.

In the middle of July, the Russian PROVISIONAL GOVERNMENT published material allegedly showing that Lenin and his comrades were German agents, and Lenin went into hiding to escape arrest. This material consisted principally of apparently commercial telegrams concerning commodities and payments, exchanged between Fürstenberg in Stockholm and associates in Petrograd; according to the Provisional Government they were camouflage for financing the Bolsheviks. This is indeed possible, but it is also possible that these commercial messages were simply such, for it is now known that Fürstenberg recently had been (in Copenhagen) and probably still was (in Stockholm) a big businessman, his withdrawal from Denmark merely a temporary setback.

The Bolshevik triumph in the October Revolution transformed the situation (and undercut Helphand, who until the final German defeat continued attempting to influence German-Russian affairs and then lived mostly in Germany until his death). However, the curiosity of Fürstenberg's Bolshevik comrades was not easily overridden by Lenin. The published minutes of the Bolshevik central committee for the period August 1917 to February 1918 show that Fürstenberg's 'controversial affairs' (as the editor described them) were discussed at eight meetings, though the content of these discussions was omitted.

In the spring and summer of 1917, Lenin in Russia depended for confidential contact with the outside world on his representation in Stockholm, consisting of Fürstenberg and two other Polish Bolsheviks, K. B. RADEK and V. V. Vorovsky. Two socialists in Stockholm at the same time were the German Gustav Mayer and the Swiss Carl Moor.

In his memoirs (*Erinnerungen*, 1949 published in Zurich and Vienna) Mayer told something of how a high official of the German Treasury entrusted him with a task of extreme importance and absolute secrecy, which proved to be acting in Stockholm as a cut-out or post-box for another German official specializing in delicate Russian affairs, at the same time as Mayer was in close touch with Fürstenberg and Radek. Mayer himself, and German documents, indicate that Moor was deeply involved in similar tasks.

Subsequently, in September and December 1917, two documents signed by the German State Secretary Kühlmann refer to 'continual support' of the Bolsheviks and 'a steady flow of funds' to them from German sources 'through various channels and under different labels'.

For many years this whole question was seen, misleadingly, in narrowly and conventionally political terms. Such figures as Mayer and Moor may indeed have functioned as financial intermediaries. However, the recent partial uncovering of some areas in the lusty sprawling demi-monde of wartime international trade cultivated by the socialist Helphand and the Bolshevik Fürstenberg compels the realization that funds (of whatever origin) could have been camouflaged in countless ways; that Fürstenberg, given capital by Helphand and Sklarz, then became rich probably largely by his own efforts; and that, as Helphand and Fürstenberg understood – as, surely, professional revolutionaries in general do understand – revolutionary politics, and *Revolutionierungspolitik*, are often generated in secrecy and pursued with concealment and deception and may leave authentic trace only when something goes wrong. Afterwards, the victors tailor their history to suit their public image.

In the many-layered and multi-faceted world of this article, the historian's aim of discovering 'what actually happened' is probably an unrealizable ideal; relevant German documents are sometimes annotated 'the matter was settled by word of mouth', and Bolsheviks would sometimes have even weightier reasons for eschewing written record. It must be accepted that in these matters 'what actually happened' can almost certainly never be fully known, and may well never be known sufficiently for even approximately satisfactory elucidation.

See also THE SCANDINAVIAN CONNECTION.   MHF

Further Reading

Fischer, Fritz: *Germany's Aims in the First World War*. London and New York: Chatto & Windus, 1967.

Futrell, Michael: *Northern Underground*. London: Faber, 1963.

Haas, Leonhard: *Carl Vital Moor*. Benzinger: Zürich & Köln, 1970.

Katkov, George: *Russia 1917: The February Revolution*. London: Longman, 1967.

————: German political intervention in Russia during World War I. In *Revolutionary Russia*, ed. Richard Pipes. Cambridge, Mass.: Harvard University Press, 1968.

Zeman, Z.A.B. ed.: *Germany and the Revolution in Russia 1915–1918*. London: Oxford University Press: 1958.

Zeman, Z.A.B. and Scharlau, W.B.: *The Merchant of Revolution*. Oxford: Oxford University Press, 1965.

Zetterberg, Seppo: *Die Liga der Fremdvölker Russlands 1916–1918*. Helsinki: The Finnish Historical Society, 1978.

The Mensheviks

It was the 'organizational question' and LENIN's ruthless bid for personal domination of the party that, at the Second Congress of the Russian Social Democratic Party (RSDRP) in 1903, brought about the break between Yuli MARTOV and Lenin, and the split between Martov's supporters, henceforth called Mensheviks ('Minoritarians'), and Lenin's, the BOLSHEVIKS ('Majoritarians'). Against Lenin's concept of an elitist, highly centralized party of professional revolutionaries, the Mensheviks posed their dream of a broadly-based, social democratic workers' party as large and inclusive as tsarist conditions of illegality would permit.

Yet it was the two groups' radically different revolutionary strategies and attitudes to power, elaborated during the experience of the 1905 REVOLUTION, that turned the Menshevik-Bolshevik feud into an irreconcilable and permanent split. As against Lenin's 'revolutionary-democratic dictatorship of the proletariat and the peasantry' and TROTSKY's strategy of PERMANENT REVOLUTION – both predicated on a socialist assumption of power – the Mensheviks staunchly upheld PLEKHANOV's doctrine of 'bourgeois revolution' and its operational complement – socialist abstention from power.

Expecting the 'political domination' of the bourgeoisie to follow the fall of tsarism, the Mensheviks assigned to social democrats and the proletariat the role of 'extreme revolutionary opposition' which, entrenched in such 'organs of revolutionary self-government' as workers' councils (SOVIETS), trade unions, cooperatives, town dumas and village councils, would harass and pressure the bourgeois government into pursuing 'democratic' policies. The bourgeoisie in power would thus be pushed into realizing the 'minimum programme' of Russian social democracy until political liberty and capitalist development had prepared backward Russia for proletarian revolution and the achievement of the 'maximum programme' – socialism.

The Mensheviks' fear of a premature accession to power was grounded in the Marxist notion that a certain level of social-economic development and political liberty were the necessary objective conditions for a socialist revolution, and that only bourgeois-capitalist society could provide them. That fear was reinforced by a narrow-Marxist class theory of the state from which they drew the lesson that 'the capture of the state machine by our party is thinkable only by mandate of the working class', and only for the realization of socialism. Since petty-bourgeois, peasant Russia lacked the will for such a mandate, the party had no right to seize power and use it 'to neutralize the resistance of the petty-bourgeoisie to the socialist aspirations of the proletariat' (A. Martynov).

In this spirit the Mensheviks played a leading role in most of the soviets of the larger towns during the latter part of the 1905 REVOLUTION, and notably in the St Petersburg soviet, in all attempts at setting up trade unions, non-affiliated workers' organizations and in P. B. AXELROD's campaign for a Workers' Congress.

Menshevik tactics: 1906–1914

The Mensheviks proved better equipped than their Bolshevik and SR rivals to take advantage of the new opportunities for open, legal activity in trade unions, cooperatives, workers' educational, insurance and medical associations, the committee of the SD fraction of the Duma, and a now legalized but harassed socialist press. Their successful tactics led to a Menshevik majority at the Fourth (Unification) Congress of the RSDRP in 1906 and the Central Committee it elected. Thus, Menshevik resolutions urging a positive attitude to Duma elections and an agrarian programme of municipalization were adopted. Formulated by P. P. Maslov, the Menshevik agrarian programme, taking account of regional differences and determined not to strengthen the centralized Russian state, envisaged the handing over of confiscated state and private lands (excluding peasant lands) to democratically elected organs of local government for leasing to peasants on an individual basis, excepting large modernized estates which would be managed on a collective basis.

The Mensheviks' tactics of shifting party work largely into the legal arena made good sense both during the difficult years of the STOLYPIN regime and during the three years of heightened labour conflicts which preceded the FIRST WORLD WAR. Still, apart from the short interval between the 1906 Fourth Congress and the 1907 Fifth Congress, the Mensheviks never succeeded in capturing the party institutions. Hankering after party unity with the Bolsheviks, the Menshevik leaders abroad, Martov, F. I. DAN and A. S. Martynov, let slip the one chance they had at the 1910 party plenum in Paris to bring the Bolsheviks (discredited by the 'expropriation' scandals and divided among themselves) to heel or drive them out of the party. But with the Paris plenum placated by their promise to obey party resolutions and rules the Bolsheviks, in January 1912 in Prague, declared themselves the Party, elected an all-Leninist Central Committee and split the SD fraction in

Figure 6   Axelrod, Martov and Martynov in Switzerland(?) 1915.

the Duma. The Mensheviks could only convene a conference of non-Bolshevik SD organizations, including the Jewish BUND, Trotsky's *Pravda* group, the Latvian SDs, and the secessionist wing of the Polish Socialist Party (PPS Lewica) to elect an Organizational Committee (election of a Central Committee would have acknowledged the Bolshevik secession) and appeal to the Bureau of the Socialist International to discipline the Bolsheviks and impose party unity on them.

While dissident factions were generally tolerated in the Menshevik camp and some sort of collective leadership was practised, giving the Mensheviks a more intellectual and democratic complexion but a more amorphous organization, the basic division during the period 1906 to 1914 was between a right wing, situated mainly in Russia, of *praktiki* (practical workers) led by P. A. Garvi, K. M. Ermolaev and I. A. Isuv – allied with a group of intellectuals around the *Nasha Zarya* (Our Dawn) journal (edited by A. N. Potresov, V. O. Levitsky (Martov's brother) and N. Cherevanin (F. Lipkin) in St Petersburg) – and a left wing of Menshevik leaders and activists abroad, led by Martov, Dan, and Martynov, who edited the *Golos Sotsial-demokrata*

(Social Democrat Voice), first in Geneva and then in Paris.

The right wing, denounced by the Bolsheviks as 'Liquidators' of the party, wrote off the underground party committees as outdated, 'spy-ridden nests of provocation' and the Bolsheviks as demoralized and out-of-limits. But the left wing, to ensure the social-democratic character and objectives of legal party activity, wanted it to be linked to an underground skeleton of 'Initiative Groups' (led by S. O. Ezhov – another of Martov's brothers – Yu. Larin and Eva Broido), and strove for unity with the Bolsheviks, thus antagonizing the *praktiki*. On the periphery of the Menshevik camp were Plekhanov's so-called 'Party Mensheviks' who joined the Bolsheviks in denouncing the *praktiki* as 'Liquidators', and Trotsky's *Pravda* Group, who tried to mediate and sought party unity.

Although the First World War produced new divisions and alignments and put Plekhanov's small *Edinstvo* (Unity) group of patriotic 'defensists' outside the Menshevik camp, the basic division between left and right was now in terms of internationalism and defensism. On the left were the émigré Menshevik-Internationalists, (Martov, Axelrod, Martynov), who played a significant role in the Zimmerwald movement. They were supported in Russia by the so-called 'Siberian Zimmerwaldists', (I. G. TSERETELI, Dan, V. Voitinsky), the various Initiative Groups and the Menshevik fraction in the Duma, (led by N. S. Chkheidze). On the right was Potresov and Levitsky's *Nasha Zarya* group of 'self-defensists' who were allied with the Labour Group of the WAR INDUSTRIES COMMITTEE, led by the Mensheviks K. A. Gvozdev and B. O. Bogdanov.

February–October 1917

Having survived the war entrenched in such legal organizations as the Labour Group, cooperatives, and the Duma fraction, the Mensheviks had a head start when the FEBRUARY REVOLUTION came, and as early as 27 February (OS) they had initiated the foundation of the Petrograd Soviet. In tandem with their SR allies, the Mensheviks founded and controlled the large majority of Russia's soviets until September. While Chkheidze was chairman of the Petrograd Soviet (until he was ousted by Trotsky in September), immediately Tsereteli arrived in Petrograd on 19 March it was he who became the *de facto* leader of the Menshevik–SR bloc which dominated the Soviets. Their leadership was confirmed at the delegates' conference of 138 soviets in March and reconfirmed at the First Congress of Soviets in June and in the composition of the Central Executive Committee (TsIK) which it elected. Tsereteli, M. I. Skobelev, Dan and Voitinsky, the Bundist M. I. LIBER and the SRs A. R. GOTS, N. D. AVKSENTIEV, and V. M. CHERNOV, together shaped the grand policy of the Menshevik–SR bloc on the central questions of peace and power.

Tsereteli's peace policy of 'revolutionary defensism' meant that democratic Russia must continue waging a 'defensive' war (without territorial claims) until the combined pressure of the Russian government and European socialist opinion (to be mobilized at a conference of socialist parties in Stockholm) induced the Allies to declare their readiness to negotiate a 'democratic' peace, 'without victors and vanquished'. If initially, during the 'dual power' which ended in the April crisis, the Mensheviks' policy on power meant the soviets' conditional-critical support of the Provisional Government from without, it was Tsereteli who brought the Menshevik-SR bloc to join the reconstituted Provisional Government on 6 May, in order to endow it with that 'plenitude of power' which only the powerful soviets could give. Tsereteli's and the Mensheviks' policy of socialist collaboration with 'all the vital forces of the country', notably the bourgeois liberal Constitutional Democratic party (Kadets), which led to the formation of three consecutive coalition governments (on 6 May, 24 July, 25 September), was dictated by practical considerations: the need for a broad national government to cope with the war, the economic crisis and threatening anarchy. It had little to do with the Menshevik addiction to the doctrine of bourgeois revolution which prescribed a militantly oppositional role, as a small faction of Menshevik-Internationalists, led by Martov, N. N. SUKHANOV, Martynov and (the Bundist) R. A. ABRAMOVICH, constantly reiterated, and it ruled out coalition as 'Millerandism'. Martov's call on 3 July to end coalition with the bourgeoisie and form a broadly socialist government was never heeded, for Martov and his Menshevik-Internationalists never succeeded in wresting party control from Tsereteli and his 'revolutionary defensists': at the Menshevik (Unification) Congress late in August, Martov still failed to gain the support of more than one third of the delegates.

The Mensheviks' pursuit of class collaboration, when hardly any of their demands were realized, suggests a singular misreading of the rapidly changing socio-political situation which, from June onwards, was marked by sharpening class-conflict and political polarization. Thus, the radicalization and increasing bolshevization of the workers and soldiers organized in the soviets was clearly visible in the 'July Days', the sharp right turn and anti-sovietism of the liberal bourgeoisie, notably the Kadets, was fully evident at the Moscow State Conference in mid-August, even before it erupted in the KORNILOV mutiny at the month's end. In that situation, coalitionism was a sure prescription for losing that near-hegemony in the soviets which the Mensheviks, thanks to their impressive performance during the early, formative months of the revolution, had acquired. True, seeing their influence in the soviets slipping, the Mensheviks in August and September tried to shift their power-base into the democratized town dumas. But these bodies never seriously rivalled the soviets which, after the defeat of Kornilov, were on the upsurge, had become bolshevized and, in many towns, were turning into local organs of power. The October elections to the Second Congress of Soviets, in which the Mensheviks were reduced to a small minority, completed the sad story of Menshevik failure even before the Bolshevik seizure of power sealed it.

After the October Revolution and in exile

It was a defeated Menshevik party which came back to Martov on the morrow of the October revolution and, at its Extraordinary Congress in November adopted his policies and accepted his leadership. A month earlier Martov's and Abramovich's desperate bid to prevent the Bolsheviks 'going it alone' and establishing a minority dictatorship had led them to negotiate, unsuccessfully, the creation of a broad socialist government 'from the Popular Socialists to the Bolsheviks'. The sole 'ultimative' demand which they set, and which the Bolsheviks promptly rejected, was 'the cessation of political terror'. The same policy of mediation continued after the dissolution of the CONSTITUENT ASSEMBLY and during the 'democratic' phase of the CIVIL WAR (until October 1918) when, as a neutral 'third force', they tried to halt civil war between SRs and Bolsheviks.

Attempted Menshevik mediation reached its climax in the 1919–1920 period of the Civil War, when the Mensheviks loyally supported the Soviet regime as 'the defender of the revolution' against White counter-revolution and foreign intervention, but 'implacably' denounced Bolshevik despotism in a vain attempt to bring about its democratization. The story came to a tragic end in 1921 when the Mensheviks were finally driven into exile or underground.

While a small Menshevik underground survived in Russia until the early 1930s, the large majority of exiled Menshevik leaders and activists settled in Berlin and, after the Nazis' rise to power in 1933, in Paris, and, in 1940, New York.

Led by Martov and Abramovich, and, after Martov's death in 1923, by Dan and Abramovich – who continued Martov's political line of shunning both the Bolshevik regime and counter-revolution – they built their émigré party organization and were active on the left wing of European social democracy in 'fraternal solidarity' with the German Independents (USPD) and the Austro-Marxists. While at first the Mensheviks were a constituent party of the short-lived Vienna Union of Socialist Parties (the so-called Two-and-a-Half International), after its demise in 1923, they played a significant role in the Second International, out of proportion to their weakness as a defeated SD party-in-exile.

Their lasting achievement was the fortnightly *Sotsialisticheskii vestnik* (Socialist Messenger), founded by Martov at the end of 1920 and since October 1922 the Central Organ of the RSDRP, published at first in Berlin (February 1921–March 1933), then in Paris (May 1933–June 1940) and finally in New York (November 1940–December 1963) where its last number cited its closure as due to 'the inexorable laws of biology' that had robbed it of its last editor and contributors.

This small band of intelligent and knowledgeable former revolutionaries, now condemned to live on the sidelines, formed a unique brains trust of political analysts (Dan, Abramovich, David Dallin, Garvi), economists (Dallin, A. Yugov, Olga Domanevskaya), experts on Soviet trade unions, cooperatives, youth movements, Jewish affairs and literature (Solomon Schwarz, A. Kefali, Grigorii Aronson, Boris Sapir, Vera Alexandrova) and historians (Dan, Boris Nicolaevsky). Distancing themselves equally from the frantic anti-communism of much of the Russian emigration and the naive and permissive pro-Sovietism of large sections of the European left, the Mensheviks in exile created in *Sotsialisticheskii vestnik* a unique, analytical-critical running commentary on the Soviet Union and archive on the Russian revolutionary movement.   IG

Further Reading

Ascher, A.: ed.: *The Mensheviks in the Russian Revolution*. New York: 1976.

Bourguina, Anna: *Sotsial-demokraticheskaya menshevistskaya litera-ture. Bibliograficheskii ukazatel*. Stanford: Hoover Institution, 1968.

Getzler, I.: *Martov: A Political Biography of a Russian Social Democrat*. Cambridge: Cambridge University Press, 1967.

Haimson, L.H.: ed.: *The Mensheviks: From the Revolution of 1917 to the Second World War*. Chicago and London: 1974.

Martow, J.: *Geschichte der russischen Sozialdemokratie. Mit einem Nachtrag von Th. Dan – Die Sozialdemokratie Russlands nach dem Jahr 1908*. Berlin: 1926.

The Mezhrayonka

The formation of the Mezhrayonka, (Russian abbreviation of the Interdistrict Committee of the RSDRP), in Petrograd in November 1913, represented a grass roots effort to find common ground between rival party factions following the failure of the Central Committee Plenum of January 1910 to reconcile BOLSHEVIK and MENSHEVIK groupings, the Leninists' attempt to present their Prague Conference of January 1912 as being a constitutional 'Sixth' Conference of the RSDRP, and the failure of the 'August Bloc' in Vienna in 1912 to find an alternative basis for unity.

As the basis for a merger with the Mensheviks' Initiative Group and the Bolsheviks' Petersburg Committee, the Mezhrayonka, led by K. K. Yurenev, proposed the resolutions of the RSDRP Congresses of 1906 and 1907 and the All-Russian Paris Conference of 1908, later adding the resolutions of the Plenum of January 1910. Their activities encountered hostility from both sides, but by the eve of the FIRST WORLD WAR the Mezhrayonka, though organizationally weak, had recruited about 1,000 members in St Petersburg of whom about 60 per cent were former Bolsheviks and the remainder Mensheviks.

Mobilization and police repression incapacitated the Mezhrayonka between 1914 and 1916, but by the time they resumed their activities in the spring of that year 'Internationalism' provided a basis for an informal working alliance with the Petersburg Committee, the Initiative Group (Petrograd's Defencist Mensheviks had rallied around the Workers' Group of the Central WAR INDUSTRIES COMMITTEE) and the SR MAXIMALISTS. As yet, however, the radical socialists did not command mass support among workers and soldiers and in the elections to the Petrograd Soviet on 28 February 1917 they obtained only 10 per cent of approximately 600 seats.

In February, at a time when the Bolsheviks were internally divided on the question, Yurenev took the lead in the Executive Committee of the Petrograd Soviet, together with the SR, P. A. Alexandrovich, in proposing the transformation of the Soviet into a Provisional Revolutionary Government. The advocacy of this policy by LENIN in April 1917 brought closer a realignment on the left and, following an All-City Conference of the Mezhrayonka from 7–11 May, an Organization Bureau was formed of three Bolsheviks and two members of the Mezhrayonka, which convened a joint Congress of the RSDRP 'Internationalists' from 26 July to 3 August 1917. This Congress assumed the title 'Sixth Congress of the RSDRP'.

In combining with the Leninists the Mezhrayonka brought into the new party not only their Petrograd organization but a cohort of distinguished émigré internationalists. Following an abortive attempt at cooperation with PLEKHANOV's *Edinstvo* (Unity) group in the summer of 1914, the Mezhrayonka had established contact in early 1915 with the *Nashe Slovo* (Our Word) group in Paris, who also conceived of themselves as a 'third force'. V. A. ANTONOV-OVSEENKO, S. A. Lozovsky, D. Z. MANUILSKY and TROTSKY had written articles for the Mezhrayonka journal *Novaya Zemlya* (New Land) (publication was prevented by the police) and until the February revolution liaison between the two groups had been maintained by M. S. URITSKY who had remained in Stockholm.

For members of the *Nashe Slovo* and *Vpered* groups and for unattached internationalists returning to Russia the Mezhrayonka provided an alternative rallying point to Lenin's Bolshevik fraction. On his arrival in Petrograd in May Trotsky was met by a delegation which included Uritsky and L. M. Karakhan of the Mezhrayonka. LUNACHARSKY, MANUILSKY, LEBEDEV-POLYANSKY, IOFFE, Chudnovsky, Uritsky and Volodarsky were among those who joined. Between June and September 1917 the editorial board of the Mezhrayonka journal *Vpered* (Forward) was staffed by these recruits from abroad.

The decision of the closing session of the July Congress to assume the title 'Sixth Congress of the RSDRP' reflected Lenin's policy since 1912 of appropriating the RSDRP insignia and of reconstructing the party on the left. Yurenev, reluctant to offend the Menshevik Internationalists whose affiliation he sought even at this late stage, had proposed the title of 'Petersburg Congress of the RSDRP'. Soviet usage, which adds 'Bolsheviks' in parenthesis to the letters RSDRP, implicitly acknowledges that this congress marked a further break with the Mensheviks, but creates the impression of a rallying by the Mezhrayonka to the platform of the Leninists, whereas the new 'Bolshevik Party' was from its inception a coalition.

Former members of the Mezhrayonka played a prominent part in the OCTOBER REVOLUTION and in the later development of the Soviet regime. While the cohesion of the group after July should not be exaggerated, its importance as a source of Bolshevism to be distinguished from that of Lenin may be seen in the preference of Trotsky and Volodarsky for a 'Soviet' as opposed to a 'Party' revolution; in the preparedness of Lunacharsky in the Vikzhel negotiations to envisage a government without Lenin; in the opposition of Uritsky and Ioffe to the Brest Peace; in the PROLETKULT activities of Lebedev-Polyansky; and in the left orientation of many of its former members in the early years of the Soviet regime.   JB

Further Reading

Hasegawa, T.: *The February Revolution: Petrograd 1917.* Seattle and London: University of Washington Press, 1981.

The Socialist Revolutionaries: 1902–1922

The Party of Socialist Revolutionaries (PSR or SRs) was the most widely supported of the Russian POPULIST organizations in the two decades preceding the overthrow of tsarism and the consolidation of BOLSHEVIK rule in Russia. In 1917, the PSR became the most popular political party in Russia; several of its leaders occupied ministries in the PROVISIONAL GOVERNMENT, and it secured the largest block of seats in the CONSTITUENT ASSEMBLY. The failure of the PSR to secure an immediate peace and radical land reform led to a schism in the party and the defeat of both its wings at the hands of the Bolsheviks.

The emergence of the PSR

The assassination of Tsar Alexander II in March 1881 was followed by the eradication of both main Populist organizations (Narodnaya Volya and Zemlya i Volya). This was all the more successful as Populist morale was seriously weakened by the absence of the mass uprising they had hoped would follow the tsar's assassination. The surviving Populist leaders were exiled, either to the West (where G. V. PLEKHANOV's group moved away from Populism to establish itself as the guardian of Russian MARXIST orthodoxy), or to SIBERIA. In Russia itself, an emasculated Populism survived as a purely literary current, under the leadership of N. K. MIKHAILOVSKY (1842–1904), widely known as a 'subjectivist' sociologist because of his objections to Marxist determinism. Mikhailovsky founded the prestigious journal *Russkoe Bogatstvo* (Russian Wealth), recruiting a panel of gifted collaborators (A. V. Peshekhonov, V. A. Myakotin etc.), whose empirical studies of rural conditions and suggestions for practical improvements in Russian peasant farming provided much of the raw material for future SR theory and agrarian policy.

By the mid 1890s, several socialist revolutionary circles had emerged in Russia, partly in consequence of the Populist-Marxist debates of those years and fostered by veteran Populists (E. E. BRESHKO-BRESHKOVSKAYA, M. A. NATANSON etc.), who returned to Russia following the expiry of their terms of exile. In the late 1890s they began to coalesce into regional groupings. In 1896 a Northern Union of Socialist Revolutionaries was established by A. A. Argunov. In the following year it transferred the focus of its activities from Saratov to Moscow, where, with the assistance of the *Russkoe Bogatstvo* group, it published the first number of the SR *Revolyutsionnaya Rossiya* (Revolutionary Russia). In 1897 the first conference of South Russian SRs took place in Voronezh. Despite repeated arrests, it gradually consolidated its organization. The third major regional grouping was the Minsk-based Workers Party for the Political Liberation of Russia (led by Breshkovskaya and G. A. GERSHUNI), which was particularly successful in recruiting the Jewish workers of Western Russia (see BUND). Competition between exile groups in London, Paris and Switzerland was partly overcome when members of all factions met in Paris in 1900 at the funeral of P. L. LAVROV. The resulting Agrarian Socialist League set out to provide Russian workers and peasants with political literature and to familiarize Russian socialists with the debates of the Second Socialist International. It became the ideal platform on which V. M. CHERNOV, who arrived in the West in 1899, could synthesize an agreed programme for the whole Socialist Revolutionary movement. Chernov and M. R. GOTS (in Western Europe), and Gershuni and Breshkovskaya in Russia, finally prevailed on nearly all the socialist revolutionaries to fuse into one Party of Socialist Revolutionaries in the Winter of 1901–02. *Revolyutsionnaya Rossiya*, now edited by Chernov and Gotz in Switzerland, became the central organ of the PSR, while the Paris-based *Vestnik Russkoi Revolyutsii* (Messenger of the Russian Revolution), edited by N. S. Rusanov and I. A. Rubanovich, became the PSR theoretical journal.

Political terror

A belief in the necessity of terrorism as the principal method of struggle was a legacy inherited by the PSR from Narodnaya Volya. The previous generation of Russian Populists had argued that in an autocratic state, in which authority was personal and in which all but the tsar were denied political rights, the struggle against injustice and oppression must take the form of a personal duel between the Autocrat (and his immediate representatives), and enlightened members of the intelligentsia acting as surrogates for the will of the people. Under the PSR, this rationalist justification for terrorism was reinforced by a pseudo-religious apotheosis of the terrorist as a saviour who gave up both life and soul for the good of the People. The PSR also hoped that terror would deter the government from repression, disorganize the state apparatus and force the masses to think about politics. Terror would thus complement agitation and propaganda among the masses. Despite some opposition within the PSR, Gershuni was permitted to create a virtually autonomous Combat Group (*Boevaya Organizatsiya*).

Class analysis and the PSR programme

Chernov re-cast traditional Populist ideology in the light of Marxist class analysis, allowing it to be embraced by the European socialist tradition and securing the admission of the PSR to the Socialist International in 1904. Where earlier Populists had argued a straightforward opposition between the Autocrat and an undifferentiated 'People', Chernov accepted the existence of social class interests, but argued that all the 'labouring people' shared an identical class interest, not by virtue of the orthodox Marxist criterion (relationship to the means of production), but by the fact that their income derived from their own labour (relations of distribution). Chernov did not contest the avant-garde role of the urban working class in revolutionary struggles, but insisted that a democratic revolution must involve the PEASANTS (the vast majority of the Russian people), whilst both required enlightenment from the intelligentsia (altruistically self-selected, according to all Populists, from all social classes). An eclectic reading of the letters of Marx and Engels, buttressed by the work of western Revisionists on agriculture, employed to deny Marxist, especially LENIN's, claims that the Russian peasantry was being split into a bourgeois upper-crust, petty-bourgeois small proprietors and proletarian landless farm workers. Where traditional Populists had hoped that the Russian revolution would lead directly to a specifically Russian socialism based on the *obshchina* (see PEASANT COMMUNE), Chernov now accepted that it would inaugurate a transitional phase (though not just a bourgeois democratic republic as most Marxists still supposed), in which socialism would emerge in the agrarian sector by means of the 'socialization of the land', which would set strict limits to the possible expansion of industrial capitalism. This concept, or rather slogan, was effective in securing the PSR peasant support, but neither Chernov nor any other PSR theoretician was able to specify how in practice the party would steer between the dangers of nationalisation (which would strengthen the state) and agrarian revolution (which might destroy it).

The PSR copied the fraternal European parties in defining Maximum and Minimum demands. (The Minimum Programme would take immediate effect after the Revolution; the Maximum at some uncertain future date.) The Minimum Programme incorporated the democratic reforms demanded by all socialist parties and by all the Russian opposition. They also spelt out SR demands for the industrial workers. These amounted to the introduction of progressive taxation, protective measures (for example, the eight-hour day and minimum wages), trade union rights, municipal works and the socialization of enterprises on condition this did not strengthen the state bureaucracy. Both Social Democratic critics, and 'Maximalists' within the PSR noted that while the party offered the peasants effective control over one of the means of production (land), it merely offered to protect the industrial workers against excessive exploitation. The Programme confirmed the identity of the PSR as a party of intellectuals in search of a peasant following.

First steps of the PSR

Between 1902 and 1905, the PSR succeeded in gaining the support of a large proportion of the Russian opposition by its success in assassinating a series of highly unpopular officials. It was less successful in consolidating its organization inside Russia and in galvanizing mass support for revolutionary uprisings.

The first victim of SR terrorism was N. P. Bogolepov, Minister of Education, who was assassinated in 1901 by P. V. Karpovich for ordering the conscription into the army of student demonstrators. In the following year S. V. Balmashev assassinated the Minister of the Interior D. S. Sipyagin. Then, in July 1904, at the height of the Russo-Japanese War, Sazonov scored the greatest success of the PSR Combat Group with the assassination of V. K. von PLEHVE, the minister of the interior and the most influential of Nicholas II's ministers.

Despite incessant police harassment and constant arrests (see OKHRANA), the PSR was able to build up a network of 40 local committees served by 10 underground presses by 1904. Attempts to create a Central Committee inside Russia were frustrated by the secret police; relations between members of this shadowy 'Central Committee' and the more stable Foreign Committee Abroad were tense. PSR propaganda succeeded in reaching university students, some of the rural intelligentsia and some sections of the working class (railwaymen etc.). A potential for rural radicalism was demonstrated by peasant uprisings in Poltava and Kharkov Provinces in 1902, but only in some districts of Saratov Province could PSR agitators address the peasants directly.

SRs in the 1905 Revolution

The assassination of reactionary minister of the interior Plehve by the SR terrorist Sazonov in 1904, and of Grand Duke Sergei Alexandrovich, Governor-General of Moscow by I. P. Kalyaev in February 1905, brought the Party immense prestige. It was to the PSR that Father Gapon turned after the 'Bloody Sunday' massacre of peaceful petitioners on 9 January 1905. In June the PSR led a rising in Odessa in support of the mutinous battleship *Potemkin*. The PSR-led Railway and Post and Telegraph Unions played a crucial role in the October 1905 general strike which forced the tsar to grant civic freedoms. N. D. AVKSENTIEV became one of the leaders of the Petersburg Soviet and the PSR fought side by side with the RSDRP in the December Uprising in Moscow. Though the First Party Congress in Imatra, Finland, in January 1906 resolved to boycott the Duma elections, the peasantry took part with enthusiasm, electing 104 radical 'Trudovik' (Labour) deputies. When the First Duma was dissolved in July 1906, the PSR tried unsuccessfully to coordinate risings in the Baltic Fleet (see I. I. BUNAKOV-FONDAMINSKY), and, via the PSR-controlled All-Russian Peasant Union, among the peasantry. In the Second Duma elections in February 1907 the PSR gained 34 seats, while the sympathetic Trudoviks maintained their previous strength. Surprisingly, the PSR was strongly supported in the largest St Petersburg factories and in the Baku oil industry. For a party with a

negligible organized presence inside Russia before 1905, these were substantial achievements.

The PSR's hopes for a unified Russian socialist party were vigorously rebuffed by the RSDRP, which used its head start among the proletariat to establish its hegemony over nearly all the trade unions. The more modest project of a unified Populist party also failed. The traditional literary collaboration of the PSR with the editors of *Russkoe Bogatstvo* (Russian Wealth) (A. V. Peshekhonov, V. A. Myakotin, N. F. ANNENSKY) reached its apogee in the weeks following the October Manifesto in 1905, but foundered on the insistence of the littérateurs on purely legal methods of struggle at the Imatra Congress. Peshekhonov and his colleagues went on to found a separate Popular-Socialist Party, which was influential in the cooperative movement but had little mass support. The PSR Central Committee's insistence on the central direction of 'terror' and on labelling localized 'economic terror' as 'pogrom-like' led to the emergence of an 'agrarian terror' faction, led by M. I. Sokolov and subsequently known as 'MAXIMALISTS'. Their anti-intellectualism found virulent expression in the writings of E. Yu. Lozinsky and in the powerful Moscow organization which bitterly resented the tutelage of the PSR oligarchs in exile. By early 1906, a quasi-anarchist party of SOCIALIST REVOLUTIONARIES-MAXIMALISTS had seceded from the PSR, determined to pursue both political and social revolution by terrorist means.

Reaction and demoralization: 1907–1914

The predominance of high-principled intellectuals, whose formative experience antedated the era of mass politics (more marked in the PSR than in the other opposition parties), proved a serious handicap to the party after 1906. The PSR CC took pride in the fact that the 1905 Revolution had demonstrated the necessity of simultaneous worker and peasant risings, but failed to see that a new era of imperfectly democratic, but genuinely pluralist politics demanded new tactics. They persisted in relying on centralized terror and armed uprisings to bring about democracy and social revolution; they regarded the new opportunities for legal parliamentary and trade union work with (respectively) contempt and condescension. They persisted in demanding the socialization of all land and its communal exploitation, though political and market forces were rapidly destroying the cohesion of peasant communes (see PEASANTS). Support for armed uprisings in the countryside and armed forces was squandered in senseless isolated actions in 1907. Thereafter, the PSR's peasant sympathizers relapsed into enforced passivity, and the Social Democrats used bread and butter issues to consolidate their hold over the proletariat. Of the generation of radical students mobilized by the Revolution, only V. I. and B. N. Lebedev and A. F. KERENSKY achieved leading rank within the PSR by 1917, two of them as ministers

Figure 7   A. V. Peshekhonov (right) and N. D. Avksentiev.

with minimal encouragement from the PSR Central Committee.

The party's commitment to 'terror' effectively debarred the PSR from legal politics after 1907, but when the Maximalists failed to assassinate P. A. STOLYPIN in August 1906, while injuring his children, 'terror' began to rationalize repression rather than weaken government resolve. By 1908, it was obvious that a police agent was active within the PSR central Fighting Organization. When the CC refused to take effective action, Valerian and Iulya Agafonov organized a dissident group of PSR exiles in Paris. The exposure of Evno AZEF, head of the Fighting Organization, as the spy, and the iconoclastic novels of his deputy, B. V. SAVINKOV, that followed, finally discredited 'terror'. In 1911, Avksentiev led the Pochin (Initiative) group's campaign for the PSR's full participation in the Duma and trade unions. The CC rebuffed them and it was purely as an individual, and under the Trudovik label, that Kerensky entered the Fourth Duma in 1912. By imitating BOLSHEVIK tactics, Kerensky was able to re-invigorate SR work in the trade unions, himself becoming chairman of the Shopworkers' congress in 1913. Party leader Chernov did nothing to counter the erosion of party discipline.

Patriots, Centrists and Internationalists: 1914–1917

With the outbreak of war, the homesick and francophile SR leaders in Paris (Avksentiev, Bunakov-Fondaminsky, Savinkov) and in Siberian exile (Breshkovskaya, A. R. GOTS) adopted an unconditionally patriotic position in their journal *Prizyv* (The Call). Chernov and Natanson moved to Berne, Switzerland, to maintain a 'Centrist' position at the international socialist conferences at Zimmerwald (1915) and Kienthal (1916). Inside Russia, the PSR was decapitated by arrests, but in the summer of 1915, Kerensky and V. M. ZENZINOV made an ambitious attempt to re-unite all the Populists under one umbrella and to trigger a working class revolution around such 'bourgeois' institutions as the Union of Zemstvos and Towns and the Duma. When this movement failed, Kerensky and Zenzinov retreated to more patriotic positions and resumed contact with the Paris PSR. The leadership of the working class PSR fell into the hands of P. A. Alexandrovich, whose internationalist views were rapidly leading him to Lenin's conclusion that the world war should be converted into an international class war.

The PSR in government

The February Revolution established the preconditions for the PSR to participate in government and for the creation of a unified Populist party. In practice, the Popular–Socialists, after merging with the Trudoviks, maintained a distinct existence, while a new left-wing 'heresy', even more disruptive than the Maximalists, emerged within the PSR. As the Russian state grew weaker, parallel Ukrainian and Muslim SR leaderships emerged, demanding radical policies on the form of the future Russian state and on moves for peace. These centrifugal developments mirrored the disappointing performance of the PSR as ministers and as Soviet leaders.

The PSR ran the Ministry of Justice (A. F. Kerensky) from March to April; Agriculture (V. M. Chernov, deputy minister N. I. Rakitnikov; S. L. Maslov), and War and Marine (Kerensky, deputy ministers V. I. Lebedev and Savinkov) from May to October; Interior (Avksentiev) in July and August. As compared with the Kadet and MENSHEVIK ministers, they were conspicuously lacking in solidarity. Kerensky's attempt to establish mild penalties for desertion from the front led to his scandalous non-election to the PSR CC in June, while Savinkov's ultra-patriotic and dubious dealings with General KORNILOV led to his expulsion from the PSR in September. Chernov's tenure of the crucial Ministry of Agriculture was marked by equivocation, administrative incompetence and feuding with Peshekhonov's Ministry of Food Supply. From September 1917, ex-minister Chernov led a bitter campaign against his former colleagues within the PROVISIONAL

GOVERNMENT from the columns of the PSR central organ *Delo Naroda* (The People's Cause).

Between June and October 1917, the PSR was the largest faction in the All-Russian Central Executive Committee of Workers' and Soldiers' Soviets and virtually monopolized the equivalent committee of Peasants' Soviets. By entering a Coalition with the Mensheviks and Kadets in May 1917, the PSR abdicated its political direction into the hands of an inner group or 'Star Chamber' of Mensheviks and PSR in the Petrograd Soviet and a secret 'inner cabinet' in the Provisional Government, comprising the Menshevik Leader, I. G. Tsereteli, and three members of the POLITICAL FREEMASONRY, Kerensky, the left-wing Kadet, N. V. Nekrasov, and the industrialist M. I. Tereshchenko. These groups determined that there would be a further military offensive, backed up by an international socialist conference in Stockholm and an Inter-Allied Conference to agree democratic war aims. They also agreed to postpone all radical social reform, including land reform, until after the election of a democratic CONSTITUENT ASSEMBLY, which (they hoped) would only convene after an Allied victory. These policies were vigorously promoted by a patriotic SR faction led by 'grandmother' Breshkovskaya and A. A. Argunov, editor of *Volya Naroda* (People's Will) (supported by Allied subsidies). Their failure, and Kerensky's alleged complicity in the 'Kornilov Affair' in August, massively enhanced the popularity of a left-wing SR faction, aligning itself with the Bolsheviks and led by 'grandfather' Natanson, ex-terrorist Maria Spiridonova, and Boris Kamkov.

Civil war and emigration

The armed resistance to the Bolshevik coup in Petrograd and Moscow was led and coordinated by right-wing PSR, through the All-Russian Executive Committee of Peasant Soviets (Avksentiev etc.) and the Committees of Public Safety in Petrograd and Moscow (V. V. Rudnev). They successfully forced the party centre (Chernov etc.) to expel the left-PSR in November 1917. With their departure, the right-PSR were masters of the party machine but their own unpopularity with the masses obliged them to use Chernov as a figurehead at the sole meeting of the Constituent Assembly on 5 January 1918 (OS). The dissolution of the Assembly by the Bolshevik–Left SR Soviet government averted an uncomfortable demonstration of the fact that while the PSR, with 380 seats, had a majority in the Assembly, it could not command a majority for its policies on the war and the future constitution of the Russian state. The PSR used the dissolution of the Constituent Assembly and the Treaty of Brest-Litovsk as justifications for demanding Allied military intervention against the Bolsheviks in the summer of 1918. The North Russian and Samara-Ufa governments of that summer and autumn were essentially PSR governments. The Samara government was headed by five SR members of the Constituent Assembly

(M. I. Brushvit, P. D. Klimushkin, I. P. Nesterov, B. K. Fortunatov, V. K. Volsky), hence its title KOMUCH (an acronym in Russian of Committee of the Constituent Assembly). Following a conference at Ufa, a Directory was established under Avksentiev. A warning by the CC of the PSR of dangers from the Right gave Admiral KOLCHAK a pretext for his coup d'état in November 1918. Despite this setback the SRs continued their anti-Bolshevik activities from abroad, and were especially active in supporting the KRONSTADT RISING. In 1922, the leading SRs in Russia (A. R. Gots etc.) appeared in the first great 'show trial', accused of causing millions of deaths during the Civil War. International socialist pressure averted the death penalty, though most of the SRs in Russia perished during Stalin's purges. In exile, Chernov's 'centre' feuded with Kerensky and the right-wing SRs, each blaming the other for the debâcle. Chernov's own claims to represent the PSR abroad were eventually exposed as fraudulent. The last major gathering of right and centre PSR in the emigration occurred at the funeral of 'Babushka' Breshkovskaya in Prague in 1934.

The Left–SR tragedy

There were few direct links between the 'Maximalists' of 1906 (who resumed a vestigial existence in 1917–18) and the Left SRs. The basis for the future Left SR Party lay in the collaboration between SR internationalists (Natanson, Alexandrovich) and Bolsheviks during the War. During 1917 the left-wing SRs made no attempt to create a separate party though, like the right-wing SRs, they coordinated factional activities around the journals *Novy Put* (New Path) and *Znamya Truda* (Labour Banner).

In September 1917, the left-wing PSR captured the Petrograd Committee of the PSR and expected soon to control the whole party. These hopes were dashed when, following the walkout from the Second Congress of Soviets by the PSR and Mensheviks, the CC of the PSR expelled from the party the 179 left-wing SRs who remained. The new All-Russian Central Executive Committee of Soviets contained 62 Bolsheviks, 29 left SRs, 1 SR Maximalist and 9 others. On 10 November 1917, an Extraordinary Congress of Peasant Soviets met in Petrograd. Its left SR majority voted to support the Bolshevik government and to create a joint All-Russian Central Executive Committee of Soviets. Shortly thereafter, Natanson presided over the inaugural congress of the Party of Left Socialist-Revolutionaries (Internationalists), at which Spiridonova gave the keynote speech. On 24 November, 7 LSRs joined the government (A. L. Kalegaev, V. A. Karelin, P. P. Proshyan, I. Z. Steinberg, V. E. Trutovsky, etc.). At the 2nd Congress of Peasant Soviets two days later, Spiridonova narrowly defeated Chernov to chair the congress. The PSR then abandoned the Congress to create their own parallel body.

Of the 420 SR deputies to the Constituent Assembly,

some 40 were LSRs who supported the Bolsheviks by walking out when the Assembly refused to endorse the programme of the Bolshevik–LSR government. Alexandrovich then joined the VECHEKA on the LSR's behalf. On 13 January 1918, the LSRs secured the final amalgamation of the 3rd Congress of Peasant Soviets with the 3rd Congress of Worker and Soldier Soviets. The LSRs had helped the Bolsheviks to overcome all democratic obstacles to a monopoly of power.

Spiridonova was initially inclined to support the Brest-Litovsk Treaty as the lesser evil, but the LSRs, alarmed also by growing Bolshevik hostility to the middle peasants, decided to oppose it and in March 1918, they withdrew from the government. On 6 July, during the 5th Congress of Soviets, the LSRs Blyumkin and Andreyev assassinated Count Mirbach, the German Ambassador, while the LSR leaders mounted a half-hearted coup against the Bolsheviks. The LSR members of the Cheka were shot and the party leaders rounded up. Natanson made his peace with the Soviet government but, after many years of exile, Spiridonova was shot in 1941.　　　　　RA

Further Reading

Gusev, K.V.: *Partiya eserov: ot melkoburzhuaznogo revolyutsionarizma k kontr-revolyutsii. Istoricheskii ocherk.* Moscow: Mysl', 1975.

Hildermeier, Manfred: *Die Sozialrevoluzionäre Partei Russlands: Agrarsozialismus und Modernisierung im Zarenreich (1900–1914).* Cologne/Vienna: Böhlau Verlag, 1978.

Janssen, Marc: *Een Showproces onder Lenin: Het vorspeel van de Grote Terreur.* Haarlem: The Hague, 1980.

Perrie, Maureen P.: The Agrarian Policy of the Socialist-Revolutionary Party. From its Origins through the Revolution of 1905–07. Cambridge: Cambridge University Press, 1976.

Radkey, Oliver H.: *The Agrarian Foes of Bolshevism. Promise and Default of the Russian Socialist Revolutionaries, February to October 1917.* New York: Columbia University Press, 1958.

————— : *The Sickle under the Hammer. The Russian Socialist Revolutionaries in the Early Months of Soviet Rule.* New York: Columbia University Press, 1963.

The Maximalists

Beginning in 1904 as an extremist faction within the Party of SOCIALIST REVOLUTIONARIES (PSR), and formulating the essentials of a 'communalist' programme in their *Volnyi diskussionnyi listok* (Free Discussion Supplement) of May 1905 and in *Kommuna* in December 1905, the SR Maximalists broke from the mother party after its first congress (January 1906), soon constituting themselves as the Union of SR Maximalists.

Denounced by the SRs and excluded for having adopted 'anti-parliamentarism as a dogma', the Maximalists were also so opposed to political parties that they called themselves the Union of SR Maximalists, and so anti-bourgeois and anti-capitalist that they rejected every revolutionary strategy which included a 'bourgeois revolution' and capitalist development as a 'natural road to socialism'. Taking for their slogan 'Straight at the Target', they aimed at an urban and agrarian social revolution to establish a Republic of Toilers, their half-way house (analogous to the Marxist 'dictatorship of the proletariat') to fully-fledged socialism.

The Republic of Toilers would socialize all urban and agrarian property and transform it into producers' units, with a system of producers' representation in which workers and employees in workshops, factories and plants would elect their base committees and deputies to the local Soviet of Workers' Deputies, while peasants in the villages would send their deputies to the Peasants Associations. Local soviets would elect deputies to regional soviets, with the federal structure crowned by a Central Soviet serving both as parliament and government of the republic. Direct elections and continuous accountability of deputies, including the instant right of recall, were to ensure the deputy's close and responsive link with his electors.

Rejecting political parties as organizing people not as producers but on the basis of shared opinions, and terming trade unions as no more than 'organs of economic struggle' under capitalism, the SR Maximalists, under the impact of the 1905 REVOLUTION and its soviets, developed a theory and system of soviet democracy pure and simple.

As radical voluntarists and great believers in direct action, the SR Maximalists tried, even after the defeat of the 1905 Revolution, to hasten the advent of the social revolution by 'energetic terrorist acts and partisan warfare' in towns and villages which they hoped would initiate a 'general armed uprising'. But this proved their undoing, as their terrorist exploits (including a most daring and lucrative bank robbery early in 1906, and an unsuccessful and ugly attempt on the life of STOLYPIN in August 1906) and many other 'expropriations' which bordered on outright banditry, led to their demoralization. The majority of their leaders and activists were captured and executed and in 1908 the Union collapsed.

The Russian revolution of 1917 saw a revival of SR Maximalism, when it appeared in Petrograd and Shlisselburg in March and in KRONSTADT in May. By August, Kronstadt's SR Maximalists, led by Grigori Rivkin, Arseni Zverin and Anatoli Lamanov, formed one of the largest factions in the Soviet, equal to the Bolsheviks. The Union's second conference, held on the eve of the OCTOBER REVOLUTION, brought together some 16 town organizations with an active membership of 3,000. Preaching the gospel of soviet democracy and of instant land seizure, the SR Maximalists were closely allied with the BOLSHEVIKS against the SR-Menshevik bloc and for All Power to Soviets, and, as members of the Red Guards and of MILITARY-REVOLUTIONARY COMMITTEES, enlisted in the October seizure of power. But they did not take kindly to the Bolshevik post-October terror, and protested against the arrests of Kadet leaders and the closure of bourgeois newspapers.

Preaching 'revolutionary war', the Maximalists denounced the Brest-Litovsk peace as 'shameful capitulation'. But, more than anything else, they attacked the Bolsheviks' 'urban war on the village' – their term for the Bolsheviks' food requisitioning policies (see WAR COMMUNISM) – and by July 1918 had moved so close to the Left SRs as to think seriously of merger, even though they would not support the Left SR uprising.

What finally turned the majority of SR Maximalists, led by Grigori Nestroev, Rivkin and Zverin, against the Bolsheviks was the overt bolshevization and emasculation of the soviets in the wake of the purge of the VTsIK of 14 June 1918 and the centralization of the Soviet regime laid down in the Constitution of July 1918.

A July 1918 issue of *Maksimalist* carried a denunciation of the 'Commissarocracy' and of the 'most cruel despotism' of the 'party dictatorship'. From July 1919, the paper carried on its masthead the slogan 'All Power to Soviets and not to Parties', linking it with an incessant call for 'freely elected Soviets'. In December 1919, the entire Council of the Union and many Maximalist leaders (including Rivkin and Zverin) were arrested by the VECHEKA on trumped up charges. A pro-Communist minority, led by N.V. Arkhangelsky, A.I. Berdnikov and F.Yu. Svetlov, had already seceded in May 1919, calling itself the Union of Maximalists and publishing *Golos Maksimalista* (Maximalist Voice). Finally, in April 1920, that minority joined the Communist Party.

Whatever the reason (they do seem to have toned down their critique of the regime), the SR Maximalists were re-legalized early in 1921 and allowed to publish *Maksimalist* until late in the year. The journal still proclaimed 'All Power to Soviets and not to Parties' from its masthead, still clamoured for free elections to the soviets, but now also denounced the NEP as the 'road to compromise' with capitalism. Having been in a 'bloc of left revolutionary populism' with the Left SRs since 1920, they merged with them in September 1922, and, by the mid 1920s seem to have disappeared from the Soviet scene, although *Znamya Borby* (Banner of the Struggle), the joint publication of the 'United Party of Left SRs and Union of SR Maximalists', edited by Nestroev and Aron Steinberg, was published in Berlin until the end of the 1920s.   IG

Further Reading

Getzler, I.: All power to Soviets: maximalist ideology and Kronstadt practice. In *Community as a Social Ideal*, pp. 82–98, ed. E. Kamenka. London: 1982.

Hildemeier, M.: *Die Sozialrevolutionäre Partei Russlands*. Cologne and Vienna: 1978.

Nestroev, G.: *Iz dnevnika maksimalista*. Paris: 1910.

Non-Party Democratic Coalitions

For many of Russia's revolutionary intelligentsia, ideology was secondary to their general commitment to political liberation and democratization. This enabled them to join forces with like-minded individuals of diverse ideological orientations in non-party coalitions to promote political freedom and democratic reform. The coalitions they created generally consisted of liberals as well as radicals united in a small, tightly knit organization surrounded by a broad, amorphous group of allies and sympathizers. The activities of these organizations had a profound effect on the course of Russia's revolutionary development.

The Conspirators

The organization known as the Conspirators (Zagovorshchiki) had its origins in a radical student circle established in Kazan in 1883–84 by two medical students, M. D. Fokin, a former member of the People's Will, and D. D. Bekaryukov, who had ties to BLACK REPARTITION. By 1885, the Kazan organization had become the centre of a broad network of more than twenty circles of 'self-education' stretching as far as Kiev, Kharkov, Riga, and St Petersburg.

Although Fokin and Bekaryukov shared a POPULIST orientation, their democratic sympathies and appreciation of Russia's political situation prevented them from adopting any clearly defined ideological position. They were convinced, moreover, that efforts to foment revolution were both premature and dangerous. Consequently, the organization they founded sought simply to prepare the ground for the future political upheaval. The Conspirators' programme thus called for democratic reform in government, improved labour laws for factory workers and more land for the peasants.

During the first decade of its existence, approximately seventy-five or eighty individuals of varying ideological inclinations took part in this revolutionary organization. Relatively little is known, however, about the Conspirators' highly secret activities. Rejecting the then popular tactics of terrorism, they seem to have occupied themselves exclusively with spreading propaganda and with training revolutionary leaders through their network of 'self-education' circles.

The Conspirators protected themselves from police detection by elaborate rules of organization and operation. Only young radical intelligentsia were allowed into the central group, whose composition remained secret. All who belonged to the organization were bound to a strict code of political and social behaviour. And members were also expected to devote themselves selflessly to the revolutionary cause and to undertake 'systematic, long-term conspiratorial work' wherever they might go.

According to the testimony of several participants, the Conspirators formally disbanded by agreement of the membership in 1893. It is possible, however, that this dissolution was bogus, staged for the benefit of the OKHRANA. For there is some evidence to suggest that the organization in fact simply moved its centre to Moscow and continued to function for another decade, using various public organizations and learned and professional societies as 'fronts' until disbanding in 1903.

The People's Right Party

The People's Right Party (Partiya 'Narodnogo prava') was not a party in the usual sense. Founded in Saratov in 1893, at a time when political parties were still illegal in Russia, it consisted of former Populists as well as a few liberals, all of whom viewed their organization as a non-sectarian nucleus around which the country's entire oppositional movement might unite.

The initiative for the creation of the People's Right Party came from former Populist M. A. NATANSON who sought to provide an alternative to the Populist revolutionary programme and to the discredited terrorist tactics of the People's Will. The Manifesto of the People's Right Party, composed with the assistance of the well-known Populist writer N. K. MIKHAILOVSKY and adopted unanimously at the constituent congress, expressed vague socialist aspirations to guarantee the material needs of the people. So, too, did A. I. BOGDANOVICH's more systematic programme statement, 'The Urgent Question', written the following spring and approved by the Party's Council. Yet, for the People's Rightists the *sine qua non* of socialism was the 'people's right' of constitutional government and civil and political liberties, as well as the right of self-determination for the empire's minority nationalities. Insistence on political change as the first priority of oppositional work distinguished the People's Right Party from earlier revolutionary organizations, and they challenged not only the injustices of autocracy but the very right of autocracy to exist.

Throughout late 1893 and early 1894, the People's Rightists devoted most of their energy to creating allies among other revolutionary contingents in Russia, and even established links with the Russian Free Press Fund in London. Assistance from the Polish Socialist Party (see POLISH MARXISM) and the St Petersburg Group of Narodnaya Volya enabled them to set up a printing press in Smolensk and make preparations for another in St Petersburg where Mikhailovsky was to edit a new oppositional journal.

Eschewing the tactics of terrorism, the People's Right Party sought to use public opinion as its main weapon against the regime. The principal tactic for this novel strategy was the publication of propaganda aimed at arousing and uniting all segments of the opposition. The Party's journal, to be patterned after HERZEN's *Kolokol* (Bell), was intended to provide uncensored political news and commentary to help mobilize public opinion. Although

its first issue was prepared for press, the journal did not see the light of day.

The Party's rejection of conspiratorial methods as inimical to their campaign to influence public opinion made it relatively easy for the OKHRANA to uncover their activities. On 21 April 1894, the police moved simultaneously in St Petersburg, Moscow, Orel, Smolensk, Kharkov, Nizhni Novgorod, and elsewhere to close down the Party's press and arrest fifty-five people, including Natanson and most of the other leaders. Although some People's Rightists who eluded police soon resumed publication of oppositional literature under the Party's imprimatur, the arrests of April 1894 in fact marked the end of the People's Right Party. Of its 112 known members a number, including O. V. Aptekman, V. M. CHERNOV, V. P. Ivanshin, Natanson, and P. F. Nikolaev, were to become prominent figures in the socialist parties that emerged at the end of the decade. Others, such as N. F. ANNENSKY, V. Ya. BOGUCHARSKY, V. V. Khizhnyakov, V. G. KOROLENKO, P. N. MILYUKOV, and A. V. Peshekhonov, would provide inspiration and leadership for subsequent non-party democratic coalitions.

The Union of Liberation

The Union of Liberation (Soyuz osvobozhdeniya), organized at the beginning of the twentieth century, continued the tradition of an illegal network of oppositional elements committed to non-violent struggle against autocracy. Even more broadly based than the People's Right Party, the Union of Liberation was composed of Populists and MARXISTS as well as non-sectarian radicals and liberals.

The Union had its origins in the coalescence of zemstvo-constitutionalists on the one hand, and various elements of the radical intelligentsia on the other, as both groups sought more effective means of conducting their struggle for Russia's liberation. This coalescence, inspired in large part by the example of the People's Right Party, was marked by the appearance in June 1902 of the illegal journal *Osvobozhdenie* (Liberation). Edited by former Marxist P. B. STRUVE, it was printed in Stuttgart and smuggled into Russia in an effort to awaken and mobilize public opinion against the government. The journal's moderate-constitutionalist programme, formulated by Struve and former People's Rightist Milyukov, encouraged the creation throughout the country of circles of 'Friends of Liberation'. These circles in turn were transformed into the Union of Liberation following a decision by a number of leading 'Friends' at a clandestine meeting near Schaffhausen in Switzerland in July 1903.

The Union of Liberation was formally established at a constituent congress in St Petersburg on 3–4 January 1904. Elected to its first Council were the liberals P. D. Dolgorunkov, N. N. Kovalevsky, N. N. Lvov, I. I. Petrunkevich, and D. I. Shakhovskoy; and the radicals Annensky, Boucharsky, S. N. Bulgakov,

A. V. Peshekhonov, and S. N. PROKOPOVICH, three of whom were former members of the People's Right Party.

The goal of the Union of Liberation, according to the programme adopted at the constituent congress, was the abolition of autocracy and the establishment of a democratically-elected representative government to ensure full political and civil rights to all citizens. Political change, therefore, was the Union's first priority, although it was expected that social and economic reforms would follow. A subsequent programme statement, adopted at the Union's Third Congress on 25–28 March 1905 (the Second Congress took place on 20–22 October 1904), indicated that these reforms were to include agrarian reform, labour legislation, autonomy for Russia's national minorities and judicial and educational reform.

Recognizing 'no enemies on the left', the Union of Liberation pursued contacts with all oppositional elements. But like the People's Rightists and the Conspirators, the Liberationists rejected terror in their battle against the regime. In an attempt to exert influence and recruit sympathizers to their cause, they penetrated various learned and professional societies and public organizations, including the Imperial Free Economic Society, the Mining Institute, the zemstvos and the consumer cooperatives. Through these 'front' organizations, the Union of Liberation was able to direct much of the political discontent that surfaced among the educated elements of Russian society during the course of the Russo-Japanese War.

In November 1904, the Union of Liberation launched a banquet campaign to promote the adoption of constitutionalist and democratic resolutions by various groups and organizations across the country. St Petersburg Liberationists also took advantage of recently relaxed censorship restrictions to establish the newspaper *Nasha zhizn* (Our Life) which, under the editorial supervision of E. D. KUSKOVA, V. V. Vodovozov and others, assumed a major role in popularizing the Union's political message. An effort was made, in addition, to draw the masses, particularly the working class, into action under the Union's auspices.

The Union of Liberation intensified its activities after Bloody Sunday (see 1905 REVOLUTION). In the spring of 1905, it initiated the formation of all-Russian political-professional unions and was instrumental in uniting them shortly thereafter into the Union of Unions. Through the latter the Liberationists orchestrated much of the civil disobedience and many of the demonstrations that culminated in the general political strike of October 1905.

With the issuing of the October Manifesto of 1905 the Union of Liberation disbanded. The majority of its more than 1600 members joined the Constitutional Democratic Party, the groundwork for which had been laid at the Fourth Congress of the Union of Liberation on 23–25 August, to continue the struggle for change legally and openly. Many Liberationists would also play a leading role in another non-party democratic coalition and repeat their efforts to democratize Russia during the revolutionary circumstances of 1917.

Political Freemasonry

The political Freemasonic organization, which was apparently known after 1910 as the Grand Orient of the Peoples of Russia (Velikii vostok narodov Rossii), was a highly conspiratorial coalition of Populists, Marxists, non-sectarian radicals and liberals that closely resembled the Conspirators as well as the Union of Liberation.

Russian political Freemasonry emerged sometime during the first decade of the twentieth century – perhaps as early as 1901–2 – with some connection to French Freemasonry. By 1910, however, the Russian political Masonic organization had severed all foreign ties and established itself as an irregular type of Masonry. A purely political organization, it abandoned all Freemasonic mystical doctrine as well as most ritual, admitted women to its ranks and maintained only that inner discipline necessary to ensure the highest degree of personal and political integrity among its members, all of whom were sworn to absolute secrecy about the organization and its activities.

By 1914, if not earlier, a vast network of Masonic lodges had been created, extending from St Petersburg and Moscow to such provincial capitals as Kiev, Samara, Saratov, Tiflis, and Kutais. These lodges were independent of one another. Their activities were only loosely guided by a general programme, formulated in the organization's secret Supreme Council and presented by its Secretary General at annual national conventions.

Political Freemasonry recruited only public figures who were known for their influence and authority in various circles of progressive society. The 300–350 individuals reported to have participated in the organization included many of the country's most prominent political figures. Among the important party people were A. I. Guchkov of the Octobrist party; A. I. Konovalov, Count A. A. Orlov-Davydov and Savva Morozov of the Progressive Party; the Constitutional Democrats (Kadets) N. V. Nekrasov, Prince V. A. Obolensky and M. I. Tereshchenko; the Popular Socialist A.A. Demyanov; the Trudoviks L. M. Bramson and P. N. Pereverzev; the SOCIALIST REVOLUTIONARIES A. F. KERENSKY and B. V. SAVINKOV; the MENSHEVIKS N. S. Chkheidze and M. I. Skobelev; and the BOLSHEVIKS S. P. Sereda and I. I. SKVORTSOV-STEPANOV. Well-known non-party participants in the organization included liberals V. I. Bauman and S. A. Kotlyarevsky and radicals M. A. Aldanov, Bogucharsky, KUSKOVA and Prokopovich.

Dedicated to the peaceful achievement of political democracy, broad social reform and autonomy for national minorities, the political Freemasonic organization worked energetically to draw Russia's large apolitical majority into the oppositional movement. Like the People's Rightists and the Liberationists, the Masons sought to mobilize public opinion against a repressive regime. To this end, they infiltrated such government institutions as the zemstvos, the city dumas (including the State Duma) and the military, using these, along with various learned and professional societies and other organizations created specifically for the purpose, as 'fronts' for their activities.

From its inception, the political Masonic organization sought to establish itself as the coordinating centre for the entire oppositional movement. This effort intensified early in 1914 when Moscow Masons established the so-called Information Committee to provide closer contacts between liberal and socialist parties. In September of the same year, employing tactics reminiscent of the Union of Liberation in 1905, the political Masonic organization also initiated a campaign to organize the intelligentsia into non-party unions.

Following the outbreak of the FIRST WORLD WAR, political Freemasonry modified its programme to emphasize cooperation with the regime in order to ensure Russia's military victory. By early 1915, however, the Masons were increasingly alarmed about the government's apparent inability to prosecute the war successfully. Efforts to organize the intelligentsia unions were renewed, as were attempts to create a broad united front of all oppositional parties. It is likely that political Masonry had a hand in the formation of the Progressive Bloc (1915) and in the oppositional campaign which the Bloc conducted along with the Voluntary Organizations during 1915–16. In the spring of 1916, the political Masonic organization began to urge the establishment of a responsible ministry and to draw up lists of candidates for a new cabinet. While some Masons – notably Guchkov, Nekrasov, Tereshchenko, and Konovalov – went so far as to plot the abduction and overthrow of the emperor, political Masonry as a whole remained aloof from such schemes.

Fearing the consequences of a popular uprising in wartime, the political Masonic organization sought throughout 1916 and early 1917 to steer the country's mounting unrest toward a peaceful and orderly resolution. Precisely what part political Freemasonry played in the FEBRUARY REVOLUTION is still unclear. There is evidence to suggest, however, that it had a crucial role in all negotiations about the organization of authority following the abdication of NICHOLAS II. Certainly Masonry exerted a major influence on the selection of the PROVISIONAL GOVERNMENT and on the formulation of its programme. At least six of the twelve men originally chosen for ministerial posts in the new government were political Masons, and there was a significant contingent of them in each of that government's subsequent cabinets.

The fate of political Freemasonry, like its origins, remains obscure. The coalition began to disintegrate with the onset of revolution in February 1917, due to political and social differences among its members. Part of the organization apparently continued to function, however, and took an active part in Russian politics until 1918, if not longer.   BTN

Further Reading

Galai, S.: *The Liberation Movement in Russia, 1900–1905*. Cambridge: Cambridge University Press, 1973.

Naimark, N.: *Terrorists and Social Democrats: The Russian Revolutionary Movement under Alexander III*. Cambridge, Mass. and London: Harvard University Press, 1983.

Norton, B.T.: Russian Political Masonry and the February Revolution of 1917. *International Review of Social History* 28.2 (1983) 240–58.

Anarchism

The combination of the theory of society without the state, and community without government with the practice of direct action and mutual aid, developed as a coherent ideology – or rather, an overlapping set of related ideologies – in Western Europe and North America during the late nineteenth century; but it existed as a revolutionary tendency at other times and in other places. In Russia anarchist tendencies may be traced in the earliest manifestations of opposition to the tsarist regime, and there was a distinct anarchist movement among exiles in Western Europe from the 1860s and within the Empire from the 1900s, which played a small but significant part in the revolutions of 1905 and 1917 and in the CIVIL WAR of 1918–21, but which was forcibly suppressed by the Bolshevik regime in the early 1920s.

Background

Several long and strong libertarian traditions already existed in Russian political thought and action: the persuasive theory (held both by Slavophiles and by Westerners) that the tsarist state was an alien growth, a Scandinavian or Greek or Tatar or German transplant on Slav soil; the ever-present memory of the popular risings of the past, especially those of Razin in the 1670s and Pugachov in the 1770s; the persistent practice of free collective organization in such popular institutions as the PEASANT COMMUNE or the workers' cooperative workshop (*artel*); the equally persistent practice of free collective organization in the non-conformist religious sects.

The growing revolutionary movement in Russia was therefore particularly receptive to anarchism when it emerged as a separate strand in the European socialist movement during the 1860s; and this favourable stance was reinforced because the best-known anarchist in Western Europe at that time was Mikhail BAKUNIN, a veteran of Russian POPULISM as well as of European socialism and Slav nationalism. Russian Populism already contained strong libertarian tendencies derived from such foreign writers as Fourier and Proudhon and such exile leaders as HERZEN and Bakunin himself. (The brief career of

NECHAYEV in 1869–72 contributed little to this tendency – since his particular stance was Jacobin rather than anarchist – except for the involvement of Bakunin and the Herzen circle.) As a result of all these factors, there was a growing shift towards anarchism in the Russian revolutionary movement during the 1860s and 1870s, both among activists in Russia and among exiles in the West.

In Russia the individuals and organizations involved included Orlov, who led an early apostolate to the peasants from Kazan in 1863; KROPOTKIN and some of his colleagues in the Chaikovski Circle in 1872–74; several members of the Union of South Russian Workers in Odessa and of the Workers' Group in St Petersburg in 1873–75; many of the Ukrainian Buntars during the mid 1870s; several members of the All-Russian Social-Revolutionary Organization in Moscow in 1875, and several of the leading defendants in the Trial of 50 in 1877 and in the Trial of 193 in 1877–8; several members of the South Russian Workers' Union in Kiev in 1879 and 1880–81 and of the Northern Union of Russian Workers in St Petersburg in 1876–80 (the leaders included AXELROD and PLEKHANOV, who began as Bakuninists and later became Marxists); several members of Zemlya i Volya (Land and Liberty) in 1876–79 and more especially of its non-terrorist fraction BLACK REPARTITION in 1879–81. Indeed, anarchism was one of the ends which were universally accepted by Populists at that time.

In the West the main focus for Russian anarchism was the Bakunin circle in Switzerland (which also became the main source of the international anarchist movement). There were several Russian-language periodicals and other publications from the late 1860s and a few Russian organizations from the early 1870s: Zhukovsky's *Narodnoye Delo* (The People's Cause) (1868), Ralli's *Rabotnik* (The Worker) (1875–6), and *Obshchina* (The Commune) (1878), Bakunin's Russian Fraternity in Zürich (1872) and Ralli's Revolutionary Commune of Russian Anarchists in Geneva (1873). One of Bakunin's most important works, *Gosudarstvennost i anarkhiya* (Statehood and Anarchy, 1873) was written for Russian consumption, but after his death in 1876 and the increasing suppression of the Populist movement in Russia during the late 1870s, most of the exiles in the West turned their attention to the international anarchist movement, the best-known of them being Kropotkin, who succeeded Bakunin as the most influential anarchist propagandist.

The low-point of Russian anarchism, as of Russian Populism and socialism in general, came during the repression following the assassination of Alexander II in 1881. When anarchism began to revive a decade later, however, it fell behind the rival currents of the SOCIALIST REVOLUTIONARIES (SR) and SOCIAL DEMOCRATS (SD), and it never again exercised a comparable influence in the revolutionary movement.

One new element was the appearance from the late 1880s of a distinct Tolstoyan movement based on the Christian anarchist pacifist ideology recently developed by the best-known writer in the country. Although Tolstoy himself repudiated the title of anarchism, several of the individuals and communities using his name were in effect part of the anarchist movement during the next thirty years.

During the 1890s there were some attempts in the West to revive anarchist propaganda by word. Atabekyan, a follower of Kropotkin in Switzerland who produced both Armenian and Russian publications, started an Anarchist Library in Geneva in 1892; and a similar effort was made a few years later by the Geneva Group of Anarchists. The work was put on a firmer basis in 1902, following the publication in London of a Russian edition of Kropotkin's main political book, *The Conquest of Bread* (1892), with the resonant title *Khleb i Volya* (Bread and Liberty). In 1903 this title was adopted by another follower of Kropotkin in Geneva, Gogeliya (Orgeyani), who formed a group and started a periodical with the same name.

At the same time the first specifically anarchist groups began to appear inside Russia; the earliest known organization was the Borba (Struggle) group formed by Jewish seceders from the Marxist BUND in Belostok in 1903. Throughout the following decade there was a growing dialectical relationship between the exile groups producing literature in the West and sending it into Russia, and the native groups distributing the literature and sending back material. Some Yiddish as well as Russian publications were produced, especially by the thriving Jewish anarchist movements in Britain and the United States. The publications thus circulated were dominated by the writings of Kropotkin and Bakunin, but there were several other Russian authors and also translations of the leading French and Italian anarchists.

1905

The new anarchist movement had little to do with the beginning of the 1905 REVOLUTION, but it was radically stimulated by it; and it could even be said that this was objectively an anarchist episode: the military mutinies, peasant risings and workers' strikes (culminating in a general strike), leading to the establishment of soldiers' and workers' councils (SOVIETS) and of peasant communes and the initiation of industrial and agrarian expropriation, all closely following anarchist propaganda over several decades. At any rate, from 1905 there was a full-scale anarchist movement in Russia.

Anarchist groups were formed in most large towns in the western provinces and in the two capitals, mostly by dissidents from the SRs and SDs. Most such groups described themselves as anarchist communist, but there was a deep division between the moderate Kropotkinian members of Bread and Liberty in Moscow and Kiev on one side and the extreme organizations such as the Jewish Chernoe Znamya (Black Banner) of the Pale of Settlement and the Russian Beznachalie (Rulelessness) of St

Petersburg. The former concentrated on propaganda by word and only occasionally resorted to propaganda by deed, whereas the latter favoured expropriations and assassinations ending in 'motiveless' terrorism. In the larger towns there were also several individualists, including some of the ablest writers among the anarchists. And in industrial areas there soon developed anarcho-syndicalist organizations following the French model, accepting the basic principles of anarchist communism but concentrating on trade-union activity and strongly condemning terrorism. Apart from the separate strand of Tolstoyanism, another specifically Russian type of libertarianism was the anti-intellectual ideology of J. W. MACHAJSKI (Volsky), whose book *Umstvennyi Rabochii* (The Intellectual Worker), published in part in 1898 and in full in 1904–5, argued that a socialist revolution would lead not to a classless society but to a new ruling class of intellectuals, and whose followers formed a group called Rabochii Zagovor (The Workers' Conspiracy) which attracted dissident anarchists and socialists from 1905 onwards.

From 1906 the anarchists were persecuted along with all other revolutionaries, and their movement was driven underground or abroad. An Anarchist Red Cross was formed by western exiles in 1907 to help prisoners and refugees, and five exiles attended the International Anarchist Congress in Amsterdam the same year. the Russian movement was slowly rebuilt from 1911, with strong support in Western Europe and the United States including several organizations and periodicals. Most of the new organizations were anarchist communist and followed Kropotkinian lines, but this pattern was broken in 1914 when he became the best-known anarchist who supported the Allies in the FIRST WORLD WAR; few of his colleagues in the West supported him, but many of his followers in Russia did so, and this split the movement at a critical moment, most of the opponents of the war shifting to anarcho-syndicalist organizations.

1917

The revived anarchist movement had as little to do with the beginning of the revolutionary upheaval of 1917 as other revolutionary tendencies, but anarchists did take part in the propaganda and demonstrations which led to the February Revolution, and the following year marked the high-point of the movement. Anarchists were active in many soviets and unions, and anarcho-syndicalists in many FACTORY COMMITTEES, especially in the heavy industry of Petrograd, among the bakers, printers, railmen and leatherworkers of Moscow, the Donets miners, and the cementworkers and dockers of the Black Sea ports. The anarchist communist daily *Burevestnik* (Stormy Petrel) reached a circulation of 25,000 in Petrograd, and the anarcho-syndicalist weekly *Golos Truda* (The Voice of Labour) had a comparable circulation first from Petrograd and then from Moscow. Anarchist Federations were established in

Petrograd and Moscow, and national conferences were held from July 1917 onwards. The total number of activists has been estimated at about 10,000 throughout the country in 1917–18, but there was of course no permanent organizational framework, and it is impossible to guess how many people either thought of themselves as anarchists of one kind or another or else proceeded along anarchist lines.

Post-October

The anarchists were strongly opposed to the PROVISIONAL GOVERNMENT, and many worked together with the BOLSHEVIK fraction of the SD Party and the Left SRs to destroy it. Anarchists were involved in the June demonstrations and the July Days in Petrograd, and then in the resistance to KORNILOV in August 1917. When Kropotkin returned in June he was almost isolated from the movement by his support of the KERENSKY regime and the continuing war effort. Anarchists supported the OCTOBER REVOLUTION, so far as it involved the elimination of bourgeois democracy, but they opposed the new Soviet government and called instead for a 'Third Revolution' to establish a genuine social revolution following the two political revolutions. They opposed the negotiations with Germany and Austro-Hungary and the Brest-Litovsk Treaty, and called instead for partisan warfare and the extension of revolution beyond national frontiers.

Nevertheless, many anarchists did continue to support the Bolsheviks, either from necessity or from genuine conviction, especially during the Civil War. These 'Soviet Anarchists' or 'Anarcho-Bolsheviks' preferred to work with rather than against the only apparently revolutionary force in the country which seemed likely to succeed, and such early 'fellow-travellers' included several of the leading figures among the moderate anarchist communists and anarcho-syndicalists. The more consistent anarchists welcomed the official policies of ending the war and distributing land and industry to the peasants and workers, but opposed the increasingly restrictive methods of the new regime. As early as March 1918 they were denouncing the 'statization' of the economy and the new class of the 'commissarocracy', and in reply the Bolshevik government launched physical attacks on anarchist centres from April 1918. By August 1918 the anarchists were describing the economy alternately as 'state capitalism' and 'state communism', and from that time their conferences were suppressed and their publications closed.

During 1918 many anarchists fled south to UKRAINE, where the Nabat (Alarm) Confederation of Anarchist Organizations from 1917 tried to develop a 'united' anarchism bringing together anarchist communists, anarcho-syndicalists, individualists and other varieties into a single movement to avoid both sectarianism and collaborationism. An Anarchist Black Cross was formed to help prisoners and refugees. Close links were established with sympathetic partisans in the area, especially the Revolutionary Insurgent Army of Ukraine which was led by the anarchist MAKHNO. But gradually the Bolsheviks gained control of the whole country, and all anarchist organizations and activities were suppressed. In February 1921 the funeral of Kropotkin in Moscow was the occasion for the last open anarchist demonstration. In March 1921 the suppression of the KRONSTADT rising was the occasion for the suppression of all left-wing dissent. In August 1921 Makhno was forced to leave Russia. By the beginning of 1922 the anarchist movement was effectively destroyed.

Anarchists were among the first left-wing victims of the Bolshevik dictatorship. Many were killed, and many suffered in the prisons and the new concentration camps (see VECHEKA). Most of the leaders eventually escaped from Russia, and continued the movement in exile, especially in Germany and France and later in the United States and Mexico. Russian exiles were involved in the formation of the anarcho-syndicalist International Working Men's Association in Berlin at the end of 1922. ARSHINOV, a leading anarchist communist who had been closely associated with Makhno, proposed an 'Organizational Platform' which would re-form the movement as a political party in 1926, but he gained little support. The surviving anarchists inside Russia were nearly all destroyed in the Purges of the 1930s, while those in exile gradually died, though they kept a periodical going in the United States until after the Second World War, and a few are still alive.   NW

Further Reading

Arshinov, Peter: *History of the Makhnovist Movement*, trans. Lorraine and Fredy Perlman. Detroit: Black & Red; Chicago: Solidarity, 1974.

Avrich, Paul, ed.: *The Anarchists in the Russian Revolution*. London: Thames & Hudson, 1973.

———— : *The Russian Anarchists*. Princeton, NJ: Princeton University Press, 1967.

Malet, Michael: *Nestor Makhno in the Russian Civil War*. London: Macmillan, 1982.

Venturi, Franco: *Roots of Revolution*, trans. Francis Haskell. London: Weidenfeld & Nicolson; New York: Knopf, 1960.

Voline: *The Unknown Revolution*, trans. Holley Cantine and Fredy Perlman. Detroit: Black & Red; Chicago: Solidarity, 1974.

The Bund

The Yiddish term for union, also referred to as the Jewish Bund, formally adopted the name General Jewish Workers Bund in Russia and Poland at its founding congress in October 1897. At its Fourth Congress in 1901 the title was augmented and rearranged to read General Jewish Workers Bund in Lithuania, Poland and Russia.

The Bundists defined themselves as an organization of and for the Jewish working masses, and indeed its rank and file membership was the artisanry and factory workers among the Jews. The leadership, however, originated in the more or less russified Jewish intelligentsia who grew up after the educational reforms of the 1860s (see JEWS). Many of them reached the age of social awareness in the years of reaction after 1881. Attracted by Russian culture and yet thwarted by the state's discriminatory behaviour against the Jews, many turned to radical ideologies prevailing among the Russian intelligentsia.

In the later 1880s and early 1890s they were attracted to MARXISM. Living in the midst of heavy concentrations of Jewish workers and artisans in towns such as Minsk and Vilna in the Pale of Settlement, their attention was drawn to the condition of these labouring masses, who became the focal point of their thought and action. They discovered incipient forms of workers' organizations already in operation among these artisans and felt compelled to rethink their methods.

By 1893, they had formulated the tactics of mass agitation, i.e. using everyday economic grievances to foster organization and produce class consciousness. Guided by A. I. KREMER, Yu. O. MARTOV, the future MENSHEVIK leader, and others, they circulated the manuscript 'On Agitation', which dealt with these tactics locally, but attracted attention as well in St Petersburg. It was published as a pamphlet three years later (see RUSSIAN SOCIAL DEMOCRATIC LABOUR PARTY).

Their continuing work among the Jewish workers finally led Kremer and his co-workers into the problems of dealing with Jewish workers concretely. They had to take account of the fact that to reach them in large numbers, they could not employ the Russian language but would have to use Yiddish, the spoken idiom of the Russian Jews. Moreover, they had to take account of the prevailing conditions under which Jewish workers worked for Jewish employers and lived under the restrictions dictated by the state. By 1895 the notion of a separate Jewish working class organization was formulated. It was Martov who publicly laid out this notion in a speech later published under the title 'The turning-point in the Jewish workers movement'.

The formation of the Bund took place amid a flurry of organizational efforts among Social Democratic groups between 1895 and 1897. Seeking to establish their own identity, while becoming part of the general workers movement, delegates from Minsk, Vilna, Warsaw, Belostok, and Vitebsk met in Vilna from October 7–9, 1897 (NS). Well acquainted personally, they did not regard what they were doing as a bold departure. The organization they were creating would not do more than ease practical tasks, such as publishing illegal papers and gaining greater security, representing the Jewish workers' interests before broader non-Jewish groups, and acting as a presence on behalf of equal rights for Jews.

The advanced state of their organization, compared with Russian Social Democratic groups, enabled the Bund to play a leading part organizing a broader Social Democratic movement. In March 1898, the founding congress of the

Russian Social Democratic Workers (or Labour) Party (RSDRP) took place in Minsk, a Bund stronghold. Three of the nine delegates at the congress were from the Bund, which joined the new Party as an autonomous part with the assumed right to deal with problems related specifically to Jewish workers, a definition that incurred no criticism at the time and attracted little attention.

The First Congress of the RSDRP proved to be ill-starred, a series of arrests following the departure of the assembled delegates. As a result, the Bund remained fairly well isolated as an organization in the following years. Between 1897 and 1901 it continued to grow, spreading into new towns, adding membership, sympathizers, and creating a press which gave it a considerable opportunity to spread its message among its natural constituency. *Di Arbeiter Shtime* (The Workers Voice), became its central organ and *Der Yiddisher Arbeiter* (The Jewish Worker) its organ published abroad. In addition, a number of local papers appeared during these years.

The visibility of the Bund brought it into contact with other organizations. The relationship of the Russian-Jewish intelligentsia with the Polish socialists had been troubled even before the formal creation of the Bund. The Bundists' preference for Russian culture and the strong plank of the Polish Socialist Party (PPS) for a Polish republic placed the two movements on a course of troubled relations as the identity of the Bund became clearer (see POLISH MARXISM). The Zionist Congress at Basel in 1897 and the appearance of Theodore Herzl's *Judenstaat* a year before, induced the Bundists to consider the question of Jewish identity in stronger terms than hitherto. How much this was attributable to the Bund's experience with the Poles, how much to the rise of ZIONISM, and how much to the influence of the environment in which the Bundists themselves worked is difficult to measure. The debates of the Austrian Social Democrats in 1899 also focused on ethnic identity and nationality and how socialists in multinational states should respond.

The national question

By the Bund's Fourth Congress in 1901, the national question had become a major issue, and going beyond the long standing claim to equal rights for Jews, the Fourth Congress considered a plank for equal national rights: recognition of the Jews not merely as citizens but as Jewish citizens. It also called for the organization of Russia in the future into a federation of nationalities with autonomy for each.

Concern with national identity led to a reexamination of the Bund's relations with the moribund RSDRP, and the conclusion that the All-Russian party become a federation of equal national parts. The effect of these discussions was to delineate the Bund more clearly as a party of Jewish workers and to provide a framework (however sketchy) for its continued work among the Jewish workers, not merely as workers, but also as Jews.

The ethnic doctrine which evolved became known as 'national cultural autonomy'. It espoused the right of national groups to exist if they so chose and to have equality in practising and developing their cultural life. They should have the right to their own educational institutions, courts, and cultural expression. Moreover, given the absence of specific territorial boundaries for the Jews, as well as the difficulty of drawing distinct boundaries for many ethnic groups in western Russia, these rules were to exist without territorial boundaries. A general legal framework, however, was to be the guide for the entire society.

Relations with the RSDRP

The Bund's ideas on the national question and party reorganization brought it into sharp conflict with elements of the Russian Social Democratic movement which were in the process of rebuilding the RSDRP from about 1901 with their most visible feature the newspaper *Iskra*. Intent on having a unified centre without reference to nationality, the Russians brought the matter to a head at the Second Congress of the RSDRP in 1903.

Under the leadership of LENIN at the Second Congress, the rebuilt Party prevented the Bund from asserting any of its major demands either in terms of federation or as sole representative of the Jewish workers. Feeling themselves reduced to the position of a mere technical committee and, from that perspective, on the verge of virtual destruction, the Bundists split with the Party in an emotional moment which took on traumatic dimensions for them. For all practical purposes the differences which had emerged during the years 1901–1903 became the basis of a virtually permanent split between the Russian Social Democrats and the Bund, even as the Russians themselves split into BOLSHEVIKS and MENSHEVIKS at the same Congress.

Despite the difficulties of their position within the Social Democratic camp in Russia, the Bundists lost little in their efforts to develop as a movement among the Jewish workers. In the years between 1901 and 1905 they estimated their membership had reached 30,000 with an untold number of sympathizers. It published newspapers in Yiddish, Russian, and Polish. After 1903 it even began to attract imitators among children who formed their own unofficial organizations. After the Kishinev pogrom of 1903, self-defence groups grew up, dedicated to resisting the pogrom-makers and to protect peaceful demonstrations.

The Bund also became international in its scope to some extent. The emigration of scores of thousands of Jews, many of them either members or sympathizers, gave the Bund a constituency in the United States and England and a source of funds, channelled through its Foreign Committee, formed in London in 1898, which also served as a publication point for its journals. During these years the

Foreign Committee also became a repository of Bundist and other publications which became the foundation for the Bund Archives, transferred from Western Europe at the beginning of the Second World War to New York, where it still exists.

1905

The Bund reached its peak during the 1905 REVOLUTION from which, like many revolutionary organizations, it expected enormous results. Convinced that a democratic order could arise, it called for a constituent assembly and strove to maximize the workers' demands. Like the rest of the Social Democrats, the Bund boycotted election to the First Duma. Expecting the revolutionary wave to grow even after the defeat of the Moscow uprising in December 1905, the Bund published a daily newspaper, consecutively entitled *Der Veker* (The Alarm), *Di Folkstsaitung* (The People's Paper), and *Di Hofnung* (Hope) between December 1905 and November 1907, calling for further revolutionary effort.

After the dissolution of the First Duma, the Bund rescinded its policy of boycott and entered the election campaign for the Second Duma. During 1906 the Bundists, in the interests of a united Social Democratic front, rejoined the RSDRP at its Fourth Congress. The reunification, however, was never strong and many of the differences which had plagued Bolshevik, Menshevik and Bundist since 1903 continued to exist.

The Bundists, like the entire socialist left, suffered a decline after the dissolution of the Second Duma and the adoption of a new electoral law in June 1907 which favoured the conservative parties. The Bund witnessed a considerable shrinkage of its membership through emigration or reduced commitment. The end of the revolution also saw its press activities cut back, its ability to organize or participate in union activities diminished, and its material means severely reduced. Beset by problems even in its legal activities, the Bund sought to foster cultural work in Yiddish among the workers on the ground that national cultural autonomy would be the goal of the Jewish masses of Russia. Publication of journals continued, more sporadically than before 1905. Political and economic work, however, suffered most through the years 1907–1914.

The FIRST WORLD WAR disrupted the frontier areas of western Russia where the Bund was centred, and as a result, the areas where it had its greatest strength suffered materially. The Bund did what it could to relieve these conditions, but its splintered condition and the scale of need meant little could be achieved. The Bund's attitude toward the war was expressed at the Zimmerwald Conference in 1915, where it adopted the majority platform, calling for peace without annexations and indemnities, and the doctrine that the demands of the proletariat, as an international class, superseded the national demands of the war based on patriotism.

1917

The collapse of tsarism was a moment of exaltation for the Bundists, even under the trying conditions of the war. In Petrograd in April 1917, the Tenth Bund Conference resolved not to participate in the PROVISIONAL GOVERNMENT but to aid it insofar as it fulfilled the gains of the revolution, i.e. the Bund conformed to the general line of the SOVIET. Not for the first time, the Bund called for a special commission of the RSDRP and the national socialist parties to hammer out a national programme.

During the period February to October 1917, the Bund was aligned with the Mensheviks and SRs in the Soviet – its spokesman was Mark LIBER – and, like them, opposed the Bolshevik seizure of power which they viewed as a tragedy for the revolution. The Eighth Congress of the Bund, meeting in December 1917, concluded that in a Russia economically unprepared for social revolution, the programme of the Bolsheviks would end in failure. They held to the position that the limits of the revolution lay in radical democratization which would provide the conditions for socialism in the future. For the present, they called for an end to the war, the turning over of land to the peasants, and a solution of Russia's nationality problems.

Under the Soviets

The CIVIL WAR also created deep rifts within the parties of the left, and the Bund did not escape damage in this respect. By its Eleventh Conference in March 1919 strong differences and splits had entered the ranks, signalling the end of their vaunted unity. The Bund had shifted its position from full democratization to support for a dictatorship of the Soviets, although they still opposed the notion of a Bolshevik dictatorship by that minority. Jewish workers were told, however, to join the Soviet army to fight the reactionary forces. In the UKRAINE, a Communist Bund (Kombund), formed under the guidance of M. Rafes, unsurprisingly backed the Soviet regime rather than the anti-Semitic PETLIURA government.

By the autumn of 1919 the issue had moved to a point where Central Committee discussions centred on leaving the RSDRP and entering the Comintern. The Twelfth Conference in April 1920 took a position that the Bund had to drop its opposition to the Soviet regime, while still maintaining its organization and its obligations to the Jewish workers. A minority, led by R. A. ABRAMOVICH, which favoured the traditional Social Democratic position, charged the majority with rejecting the Bund and Bundism. From that point on one may speak of a real split in the Bund. The majority left the RSDRP and sought to join the Communist Party as autonomous organizations of the Jewish proletariat.

The uprooting of the Jewish population which resulted from the war in the western provinces altered the traditional bases of Bundist strength. A large area of the old Pale of Settlement was under German occupation and areas previously forbidden to Jews had acquired considerable Jewish populations as a result of mass evacuations. While many of the old leaders remained at the top, many of the local organizations were new and represented a new membership lacking past loyalties and traditions. In these circumstances the Bund's central institutions were weakened and its regional configurations in Poland, Belorussia, and the Ukraine, as well as Russia proper, acquired greater significance.

Poland represented a special problem for the Bundists from early on in the war. As a zone of military operations the Bundists there were cut off from other parts of the Empire and had to rely on their own resources. Despite problems with the occupying Germans, the degree of freedom for organizational work permitted the population led to the growth of trade unions and a considerable effort at cultural work.

The separation of the war zone from the empire became permanent with the armistice in November 1918. The creation of an independent Poland of necessity broke the unity of form which had characterized the Bund since its inception. The new Polish Bund, although its roots and directions were grounded in the heritage of the old Bund, became an independent entity, which made its own way in the political and economic world of inter-war Poland.

HJT

Further Reading

Frankel, Jonathan: *Prophecy and Politics: Socialism, Nationalism and Russian Jews, 1862–1917*. Cambridge: 1981.

Gitelman, Zvi Y.: *Jewish Nationality and Soviet Politics: The Jewish Sections of the CPSU, 1917–1930*. Princeton, NJ: 1972.

Johnpoll, Bernard K.: *The Politics of Futility: The General Jewish Workers of the Bund of Poland, 1917–1943*. Cornell: 1967.

Mendelsohn, Ezra: *Class Struggle in the Pale: The Formative Years of the Jewish Workers' Movement in Tsarist Russia*. Cambridge: 1970.

Tobias, Henry J.: *The Jewish Bund in Russia: From Its Origins to 1905*. Stanford: 1972.

Polish Marxism: 1880–1919

The Russian revolutionary movement was influenced by the development of Marxism in Poland in a number of ways. Poland was a conduit for the interchange of Marxist theory and revolutionary practice between Russia and Europe; Polish Marxist organizations were allied with Russian revolutionary organizations in the struggle with the common enemy, Russian Autocracy; Polish Marxists made a significant contribution to the debate about the aims of the Russian Revolution, and the organizational forms and tactics required to achieve them; many individual Polish Marxists played significant roles in the Russian revolutionary movement and in the construction of the Soviet State after 1917.

As a result of the three partitions of Poland (1772, 1793, 1795) and the 1815 Congress of Vienna, Poland was divided between Prussia, Austria and Russia. The majority of the ethnically Polish lands and the whole of the ancient Grand Duchy of Lithuania became part of the Russian Empire, though the Polish lands were given autonomy as the 'Kingdom of Poland'. The Polish *szlachta* (gentry) refused to abandon its dream of independence and rebelled in 1830 and 1863. The result of the first revolt was the abolition of autonomy; the result of the second, the liberation of the serfs on terms favourable to the peasantry and ruinous to the gentry, and a programme of enforced Russification that mirrored the Germanization in the Prussian partition. Only the Poles of Austrian-ruled Galicia could still develop their culture in relative freedom. In Russian Poland, an expanding bourgeoisie adopted a form of Positivism that allowed them to enjoy the profits derived from the opening up of central Russian and Asiatic markets to Polish industry without qualms. The substantial Jewish population (over a third of the Warsaw proletariat in 1896) was divided over Polish independence, especially as Poles as well as Russians participated in the 1881 anti-Semitic pogroms triggered by the Russian authorities in revenge for the assassination of Alexander II.

Nationalism or Socialism: Limanowski and Waryński

Marx and Engels had always appreciated the role played by Polish nationalists in weakening Russian Autocracy while Nicholas I was the 'gendarme of Europe'. When in 1880, Polish socialists in exile met in Geneva to mark the 50th Anniversary of the 1830 Rising, they sent a message concluding 'Long Live Poland!' The most Marxist of the Polish participants, Ludwik Waryński (1856–89) scandalized the gathering by denouncing Polish patriotism. 'We are compatriots', he told them, 'members of one great nationality more unhappy than Poland – the nation of the proletarians.' The nationally-minded socialists, led by Bolesław Limanowski (1835–1935) formed the Lud Polski group, while in September 1882, Waryński founded the International Social-Revolutionary Party 'Proletariat'; though 'Marxism' did not yet exist as a complete doctrine, this was arguably, the first Marxist party in Russia. The internationalism of 'Proletariat' soon found expression in a formal alliance with People's Will. Waryński's arrest in 1883 marked the beginning of the end for 'Proletariat'.

The PPS and SDKP: A decade later, Polish socialists reconsidered the organization of a socialist party under changed circumstances. The chances of revolution in Russia now seemed remote, while tension between Russia and the Teutonic Empires made the idea of Polish independence less utopian. The theoreticians of the Polish Socialist Party (Polska Partia Socjalistyczna: PPS), proclaimed in Paris in 1892, Stanisław Mendelson (1857–1913), his wife Maria Jankowska (1850–1909) etc., were

Figure 8 Leon Jogiches

close friends of Engels. Apart from its demand for Polish independence, the PPS Programme was comparable to that of the model German Social-Democratic Party (SPD), and the PPS was immediately welcomed into the Socialist International. In 1893 Mendelson travelled to Poland to make contact with the underground network established in Wilno by Józef PIŁSUDSKI (1867–1935).

Leo JOGICHES (1867–1919), Rosa LUXEMBURG (1870–1919), Julian Marchlewski (1866–1925) and Adolf Warszawski (Warski) (1868–1937) might have joined the PPS as an internationalist faction, but for the vindictiveness with which Mendelson pursued their mentor Marcin Kasprzak (1860–1905), a veteran of 'Proletariat', with accusations of treason. At the 1893 Zurich Congress of the Socialist International, Mendelson's Galician comrade Ignacy Daszyński (1866–1936) extended similar insinuations to Luxemburg herself. Jogiches and Luxemburg therefore founded the rival Social-Democracy of the Kingdom of Poland (SDKP). The title indicated their determination not to clash with All-Russian parties by recruiting in Lithuania,

Belorussia and UKRAINE. Luxemburg argued that the demand for Polish independence was no longer a Marxist demand, but, most Polish exiles rallied to the PPS. Proletarian support at home was more evenly divided, but after a wave of arrests in 1894–95, the Warsaw SDKP Committee disbanded calling on its supporters to join the PPS.

Within the PPS, the influence of Piłsudski and Witold Jodko-Narkiewicz (1864–1924), for whom Marxist ideas were only of interest in so far as they rationalized the national struggle, grew, though the PPS still found room for such serious Marxists as K. Kelles-Krauz (1872–1905). In 1900 S. Trusiewicz (Zalewski) (1870–1918) and F. Dzierżyński DZERZHINSKY (1877–1926) refounded the SDKP as the SDKP i Litwy (SDKPiL, i.e. of Poland and Lithuania), arguing to begin with for Lithuanian and Polish autonomy within a Russian confederation. Within the SDKPiL divisions on the national question were sharpened when in 1903 it was invited to attend the 'Second Congress', in effect the founding congress of the Russian Social Democratic Labour Party (RSDRP). Luxemburg and Jogiches were determined not to join a party pledged to 'the self-determination of peoples', but many comrades, led by Cezaryna Wojnarowsky (1861–1911), another veteran of 'Proletariat', felt that to refuse to join the All-Russian Party was to betray the very internationalism the SDKPiL claimed to stand for. In 'Organizational Questions of Russian Social Democracy' (1903), Luxemburg defended her position by accusing LENIN of Jacobin elitism.

The 1905 Revolution: schism in the PPS

The 1905 REVOLUTION broke out in response to a war between Russia and a foreign power (Japan), as the PPS had hoped, but it was the proletariat who bore the brunt of a struggle conducted along class lines, as the SDKPiL had foretold. Piłsudski's attempts to provoke a guerrilla war with Japanese aid had only limited success in 1904, but over the following two years, Polish workers took an active part in the struggles against the Russian Autocracy and its Polish bourgeois allies. They responded to 'Bloody Sunday' in St Petersburg with a general strike in Warsaw and Lodz. In April, the Puławy garrison mutinied with Polish encouragement. On 1 May a general political strike took place. It was followed by an uprising in Lodz on 21 June in which Polish, Jewish and German workers belonging to the PPS, SDKPiL and BUND fought side by side compelling their leaders to cooperate. The Poles took part in the October–November general strikes that forced NICHOLAS II to grant civic freedoms, and mounted a strike in sympathy with the December rising in Moscow. Poland tied up some 250,000 Russian soldiers, many of whom mutinied as a result of Polish incitement in the autumn of 1905.

The emergence of mass working-class politics had an

Figure 9   Cezaryna Wojnarowska.

immediate effect on the PPS. Its left-wing 'youth', Marian Bielecki (1879–1912), Marianna Koszutska (Kostrzewa) (1876–1939), and Maksymilian Horwitz (Walecki) (1877–1938), who favoured class politics and a federal solution to Russo-Polish relations, gained a majority in the PPS. When in 1906. Piłsudski's PPS Military Organization refused to accept the directives of the PPS Central Workers' Committee, the party split into a Marxist PPS-Left (PPS-Lewica) and a socialist-nationalist PPS-Revolutionary Fraction (PPS-Frakcja Rewolucyjna), which relied on terror and planned a guerrilla war against Russia.

Marxist theory in Poland

Polish thinkers played an important part in the reception and adaptation of Marxist ideas. Ludwik Krzywicki (1859–1941), a member of 'Proletariat', subsequently became an academic social anthropologist. His eclectic applications of Marxist method to sociology did much to familiarize Polish society with major tenets of Marxism. Stanisław Brzozowski (1878–1911), a novelist and literary critic, was one of the first to assert that there was a disjunction in Marxism between the 'voluntarism' of the young Marx and the 'determinism' of Engels. Kazimierz Kelles-Krauz, the major theoretician of the PPS left-wing, sought to reconcile Marxism with neo-Kantian philosophy. His defence of

'historical materialism' was modified by his 'law of Revolutionary Retrospection' according to which revolutionary movements always look to the past for alternative social norms. Rosa Luxemburg's multifarious activities included a significant contribution to Marxist economics. In *The Accumulation of Capital* (1903), she argued that capitalist expansion depended on the existence of pre-capitalist markets and that capitalism was bound to collapse when they eventually disappeared. An aberrant anarchist version of Marxism was created by Jan Wacław MACHAJSKI (V. Volsky) (1867–1926), whose *Intellectual Worker* (1905) argued that socialism would be the dictatorship of the intelligentsia, exploiting the proletariat by virtue of its monopoly of 'intellectual capital'. In 1905, his Anarchist-Communist 'International' Group attracted considerable short-lived working-class support.

Polish revolutionary Marxists also contributed to the All-Russian debate about the nature of the Russian Revolution. Until 1906, Rosa Luxemburg denied the peasantry any role in the revolution, insisting on the then Marxist orthodoxy that the proletariat was the sole revolutionary class, fated by Russian backwardness to complete the democratic revolution on its own. Unlike the MENSHEVIKS, she believed that the proletariat might have to take power, but she felt that it would not hold on to it unless there was a simultaneous proletarian revolution in western Europe. She was implacably opposed to using the centrifugal force of nationalism to undermine tsarism and saw no place for feminist demands outside the Marxist programme for the liberation of the proletariat. Luxemburg's close friend, Alexander HELPHAND (Parvus) (1867–19), later a notorious collaborator with the German Foreign Ministry, worked with TROTSKY in the Petersburg Soviet during the 1905 Revolution and co-authored his famous theory of PERMANENT REVOLUTION.

SDKPiL schism: the feud with Lenin

One result of the 1905 Revolution was that the Russian and Polish parties became much clearer about their affinities. Though Piłsudski had conducted 'expropriations' like the BOLSHEVIK underground during the revolution, the PPS-Revolutionary Fraction gravitated to the SOCIALIST REVOLUTIONARIES thereafter. The PPS-Left worked with the Mensheviks and the BUND, while the SDKPiL moved closer to the Bolsheviks. After 1906, the working class supporters of the PPS were increasingly alienated by Piłsudski's indifference to their struggles and between 1907 and 1909, Franciszek Wieczorek and others, tired of the tutelage of intellectuals, created their own Polish Socialist Workers Party (RPPS) until it was broken up by arrests. In 1911, the veteran PPS leader, Feliks Perl (1871–1927), led a PPS-Opposition (PPS-Opozycja) faction in protest at Piłsudski's progressive abandonment of socialism.

In 1907, Jogiches and Rosa Luxemburg attended the Fourth Congress of the RSDRP in London. As a result of the short-lived unification of Bolsheviks, Mensheviks and Poles, Jogiches acquired an arbitrating role in the Russian party. When in 1911, Lenin finally broke with the Mensheviks, Jogiches found his power removed. A bitter feud broke out between the Berlin Chief Administration of the SDKPiL and the Bolsheviks. Rosa Luxemburg was able to use her Western European contacts to such effect that by 1914, Lenin was threatened with expulsion from the Socialist International unless he rejoined the Mensheviks in a united RSDRP. Lenin retaliated by fostering opposition inside Poland to Jogiches' authoritarian leadership of the SDKPiL. This opposition also derived from disagreements with the Jogiches-Luxemburg line on trade unions, the peasant question and relations with the PPS-Left. In 1911, this led to a formal split between a minority of those loyal to the Berlin leadership and a majority of 'splitters' in the Warsaw Committee. Karl RADEK (Sobelson) (1885–1939), Jakub Hanecki (Furstenberg) (1879–1937), Jozef Unszlicht (UNSHLIKHT) (1879–1937) became 'splitters'. Dzierżyński sympathized with them but remained loyal to Jogiches and Luxemburg.

The war

The Russian defeats of 1914–15 detached Poland from Russia, while the German High Command proscribed political activity in occupied Poland. As a result, the Polish proletariat, which had played a key role in 1905–6, played only a peripheral role in the 1917 Russian revolution. In Berlin, the SDKPiL leaders (Jogiches, Luxemburg, Marchlewski) joined Karl Liebknecht to create the 'Spartacist League'. This was a small group of internationalists who acted as a ginger group within the Independent Social-Democratic Party (USPD), which split from the SPD in 1917. During the war, Lenin continued to consolidate his relations both with the 'splitters' and with Horwitz (Walecki) of the PPS-Left, whom he met at the international socialist conferences at Zimmerwald and Kienthal in Switzerland.

The foundation of the KPD and KPRP

Many of the 'splitters' took a leading part in the Bolshevik Revolution and assumed major responsibilities in the new Soviet state. Thus, Radek became head of the Communist International, Hanecki head of the State Bank, etc. Dzierżyński became head of the new regime's political police, the VECHEKA. Rosa Luxemburg, in 'protective custody' in Germany, responded enthusiastically to the first news of both Russian revolutions, but in the summer of 1918 she wrote a scathing indictment of Lenin's policies in *The Russian Revolution*. On her release in November 1918, she and Liebknecht were visited by Radek with Lenin's instructions to secede from the USPD and to form a new Communist Party of Germany (KDP). The infant party was immediately crippled by the suppression of the ill-prepared 'Spartacist Rising' in January 1919 and the subsequent

murder of Luxemburg, Liebknecht and Jogiches. Meanwhile, in December 1918, Warszawski (Warski) had opened the First Congress of the Communist Workers' Party of Poland (KPRP) in Warsaw. Horwitz and Maria Koszutska were two of the former PPS-Left members of the new Central Committee, which had an equal number of former SDKPiL members. The legacy of the SDKPiL was evident in the new party's refusal to seek peasant allies and its refusal to accept Polish independence.

Internationalism in retreat: 1918–1921

With the collapse of the Central Powers in November 1918, an independent Polish state became an immediate possibility. A feverish struggle for power broke out. On 2 November, Daszyński established a PPSD (Galician socialist) government in Cracow and then in Lublin. On 5 November, the SDKPiL and PPS-Left began to organize soviets of workers' deputies (RDR). Piłsudski had cut his ties with the PPS, but his military exploits and subsequent imprisonment by the Germans had made him a national hero. When he returned from Magdeburg on 10 November, he was invested as Provisional Head of State in Warsaw. Daszyński made way for a provisional cabinet headed by Piłsudski's nominee, the right-wing PPS leader Jędrzej Moraczewski (1870–1944). The Moraczewski cabinet promised a series of social reforms (the eight-hour day, equal rights for all including women etc.) and prepared for a democratic Constituent Assembly (Sejm). In January 1919, Piłsudski sacked Moraczewski to appease the Polish Right and the Allies before the Versailles peace conference. The elections took place on 26 January, despite attempted coups by the Communists and the Right. The KPRP boycotted the elections, while the PPS and PPSD polled less than 20 per cent of the vote, gaining only 35 of the 432 seats in the Sejm. At the April 1919 Unification Congress in Cracow, the old PPS united with the PPSD and the socialists of the former Prussian partition. The new PPS committed itself to parliamentary democracy and gradual social reform. Its new Central Workers' Committee (CKR) included Perl, Norbert Barlicki (1880–1940) and Mieczysław Niedzałkowski (1893–1940) (old PPS), Daszyński (PPSD) and Józef Biniszkiewicz (1875–1940) (PPS of Prussia).

After breaking ranks with the Communists over a general strike in March, the PPS leadership resolved to withdraw from the all-party soviets and to create their own parallel system which would seek to represent the workers without challenging the powers of the Sejm. A group of radicals led by Tadeusz Żarski (1896–1934) refused to accept this decision. They were eventually expelled from the PPS and founded their own PPS-Opposition Party (PPS-Opozycja). They demanded an independent Polish Soviet Republic and they sought affiliation to the Comintern, but when the RED ARMY arrived at the gates of Warsaw in August 1920, they dropped their demand for Polish independence and joined the KPRP. With the turning of the military tide, Piłsudski was able to secure the incorporation of substantial areas of Lithuania, Belorussia and the Ukraine in independent Poland; a situation accepted by the Soviet government in the 1921 Treaty of Riga. Independent and at peace, Poland provided barren terrain for Polish Marxism. The semi-legal KPP (as it became) still sought the hugely unpopular goal of (re-)incorporation in the USSR, while the PPS stood by parliamentary democracy, though half the population found even Piłsudski too radical. A tragic epilogue to the quarrelsome history of Polish Marxism occurred in 1938 when STALIN suppressed the KPP, sending a large proportion of its leaders to die in prisons and camps.   RA

Further Reading

Daniszewski, Tadeusz, Tych, Feliks et al.: *Historia Polskiego Ruchu Robotniczego 1864–1964*. Warsaw: 1967.

Dziewanowski, M.K.: The Polish revolutionary movement and Russia, 1904-1907. *Harvard Slavic Studies* 4 (1957).

Kolakowski, Leszek: *Main Currents of Marxism: The Golden Age*, vol. 2. Oxford and New York: Oxford University Press, 1978.

Nettl, J.P.: *Rosa Luxemburg*, 2 vols. London: Oxford University Press, 1966.

Polski Słownik Biograficzny, Kraków-Wrocław etc: Polska Akademia Nauk (in progress), 1935– .

Strobel, G.W.: *Die Partei Rosa Luxemburgs, Lenin und die SPD*. Wiesbaden: Steiner, 1974.

Tomicki, Jan: *Polska Partia Socjalistyczna, 1892–1948*. Warsaw: 1983.

The Road to Revolution

Two major events in the twentieth century provided both the context and the impulse for the revolutions of 1917 – the 1905 Revolution and the First World War.

Economic expansion and territorial ambition in NORTHERN CHINA drew Russia into war with Japan in 1904 at a time when the unsolved domestic problems of the nineteenth century had reached their peak. All levels and sections of the population were clamouring for the tsar's positive response to their demands. Democratic freedoms were demanded by organized liberals and given physical force by a wave of strikes, culminating in the general strike of October. The formation of a workers' soviet, or council, in St Petersburg to cooordinate the workers' action, later gave rise to the designation of 1905 as the 'dress rehearsal' for 1917.

Stunned by the broad front of criticism and attack, NICHOLAS II was forced to concede a form of popular assembly, the Duma. Right-wing opinion was outraged: the Russian tsar had been made to bow to the western-inspired, false god of democracy. Blaming the Jews for this fall from grace, BLACK HUNDREDS (hooligan gangs with official support at the highest levels) unleashed violent riots (pogroms) against Jewish communities as part of an effort to rally the 'true' Russian people to their fatherland's cause. The police and the army meanwhile crushed the revolution.

The deepening split in Russian society was reflected in the new assembly, the State Duma. Russia entered the First World War with a wide gulf of mutual suspicion between the state and the elected representatives of the people. The conduct of the war quickly became the arena of conflict between these two camps, as the tsar attempted to limit the opposition's involvement in the war effort and the opposition became increasingly strident in its attacks on the government's fatal incompetence. Scandal at Court, political confrontation and economic crisis converged in the winter of 1916–1917 and set the stage for the first revolution of 1917.   HS

The 1905 Revolution

The Revolution of 1905 was the first mass rising against the regime in the history of Russia. It was the product of the collision between an emperor, NICHOLAS II, who was determined to preserve the abolutist regime to which he had acceded in 1894 – one that relied primarily on the RUSSIAN ORTHODOX CHURCH, the landed nobility, and the peasantry for strength and employed police power to stifle dissent – and those calling for change, under the influence of social, economic, and psychological forces resulting from westernization and industrialization.

Chief among those challenging the status quo was the intelligentsia, a stratum increasingly alienated from the regime, a stratum that set the agenda for much of 'society', as the educated class chose to call itself. Within 'society' liberal ideas were gaining acceptance, at first among a segment of the landed nobility and by the late nineties among the burgeoning ranks of doctors, lawyers, teachers, and other professionals, who tended to be more assertive and radical than the liberal nobles.

Even more radical was the bulk of university students who for nearly a decade were to be the standard-bearers of dissent and the reservoir from which most of the revolutionary leadership was drawn. Also contributing to the impetus for change were the millions of non-Russians among whom the drive for national rights was becoming more intense as the century drew to a close. Labour, which was to be the driving force in 1905, had not yet joined the ranks of political dissenters, but it was speaking up on economic issues by engaging in strikes in defiance of the law. Even among the peasantry, which both friend and foe of the regime considered to be unshakeably monarchist, there were signs of restiveness, particularly among those being pushed off the land.

The government added to its own difficulties by unwise steps taken during this period. Among these were a reckless policy in the Far East that would drive Japan to war, a disastrous scheme known as the Zubatovshchina (see ZUBATOV MOVEMENT) to insulate labour from radical influences, attempts at Russifying Armenians (see TRANS-CAUCASIA) and Finns (see BALTIC) that turned friends into enemies, and the tightening of the screws on Jewish subjects (see JEWS).

By the early 1900s opposition was on the increase: labour strikes, student strikes, a virtual state of anarchy in Finland, the proliferation of liberal and socialist organizations among Russians, Poles, Jews, Finns, Letts, Armenians, and Georgians, also a growing resort to terror by some revolutionaries. The government replied with sterner police measures and these were often answered by assassination of those who carried out such measures.

After D. S. Sipyagin, minister of the interior, was killed by a revolutionary in 1902, the emperor replaced him with V. K. PLEHVE, a man noted for his firmness. Firm though he was, he tried at the beginning of his tenure to win the cooperation of moderate opponents. After failing, he increasingly resorted to repressive measures to stop what he recognized as a revolutionary tide. Because he personified the police state, was identified with the attempt to Russify Finland and blamed for the shocking anti-Jewish pogrom in Kishinev in 1903, he quickly became the most hated official in Russia – no mean feat.

Plehve was not daunted by hostility, but his efforts to cope with unrest were unavailing. His brief tenure was marked by the most serious strikes yet seen in the country, peasant attacks on landlord property in the Ukraine, student unrest, and assassinations. A sign of the times was the formation of the UNION OF LIBERATION, which sought to form a common front of opposition groups.

Matters grew worse with the outbreak of war in January 1904. It was a conflict for which Russia was ill-prepared. Nonetheless, the emperor was convinced that the Japanese would be taught a lesson in short order. Instead the war turned out to be long and disastrous for Russia both at home and abroad. True, there was a modest show of patriotic support and certainly most Russians wanted their country to win, but what enthusiasm there was at first soon gave way to indifference or outrage at the ineptitude of the army and navy, and on the left there was a strong conviction that the worse the war went for the regime the better it was for its cause.

Under such circumstances the assassination of Plehve in July 1904 turned out to be a critical point for the regime. The emperor's instinct was to replace the fallen minister with someone cut from the same pattern, but at court and among higher officials there was strong pressure to find a successor who would be able to conciliate 'society', one who would rely on conciliation rather than on coercion. Such a man, it was argued, was Prince P. D. Svyatopolk-Mirsky, whom the emperor was induced to appoint.

What followed was the first phase of the revolution,

known as 'the political spring', a thaw in the government's policies that was to lead to more open expression of dissent and to rising expectations among the opposition. The prince erroneously assumed that if he could satisfy moderate liberals, i.e. those seeking to cooperate with the government, all would be well. The result was the decree of 12 December 1904, which, among other things, promised adherence to the rule of law, relaxation of press controls, greater religious freedom, but nothing whatsoever of what the most moderate liberals considered a *sine qua non*, namely some form of representative government. Even if the decree had satisfied them it is doubtful that the course of revolution would have been stopped. In any case the decree was received with contempt by virtually all of the opposition, this at a time when illegal activity was on the rise. 'The political spring' was over. Svyatopolk-Mirsky asked to be relieved of his post, a wish that was soon granted.

Within a few weeks the government did a major service for the cause of revolution by providing it with 'a bloody shirt' to wave. At the beginning of 1905 the Assembly of St Petersburg Factory Workers, an organization spawned by the Zubatovshchina, took the bit in its teeth by organizing a strike at the Putilov plant that soon spread throughout the shops and factories of the city. Father Gapon, the leader of the group, betrayed the government's trust in him by leading the strike and seeking to use the occasion to win basic economic and political reforms. He and his aides, some of them close to the revolutionaries, prepared a petition for reform which he, leading a procession of strikers and their families, was to present to the emperor at the Winter Palace on 9 January (OS), a Sunday.

A firm ruler would have received the petitioners, torn up the petition, scolded Father Gapon, and told the procession to disperse. But Nicholas II was not made of such stuff. He chose not to receive the petitioners and approved the plan submitted by his ministers to deploy troops and police to intercept them before they could reach the palace and order them to disperse. Thus, on 9 January the unarmed strikers and their families were intercepted and ordered to disperse. When they ignored the order and tried to push on they were forced to flee by cavalry and mounted police and by infantry using live ammunition, leaving perhaps 800 dead and many more wounded. That day became known as 'Bloody Sunday'. Had the government deliberately set out to dishearten its friends, to convince waverers that it was beyond redemption, and provide ammunition to its enemies, it could not have devised a more effective line of conduct than the one it followed on 9 January 1905, which opened the next phase of the revolution: the government in retreat, the opposition marshalling its forces to overthrow 'autocracy'.

The immediate response to what was widely condemned as a calculated massacre of innocents by the 'butcher' Nicholas II was an outburst of industrial strikes such as the

country had never seen before, the closing down of higher schools by student strikes, expressions of outrage from all sides, a show of solidarity among those of differing views and social position in expressing the belief that the regime was intolerable. Although the government did not crumble in the face of such attack, it was unnerved.

The widespread conviction that one could no longer live with the regime was no passing flash of anger. Labour was now ready to strike for political as well as economic reasons, ready to do battle with the police, while high-school and university students – the academic year in effect over – were using their leisure to work with liberal and socialist organizations. As for the revolutionary leaders, they interpreted what had begun after 9 January as the long hoped-for 'bourgeois-democratic' revolution that should result in a democratic republic governed by the 'bourgeoisie', operating under the close scrutiny of the proletariat. (LENIN took a slightly different view.) In practical terms this meant that most socialists cooperated with the liberals. On the basis of rather skimpy evidence, it should also be noted that the revolutionaries welcomed the peasantry as an ally.

The reaction to 'Bloody Sunday' compelled the emperor to make further concessions which, he hoped, would satisfy the 'well-intentioned' among the opposition. On 18 February he announced his agreement to the creation of an elected State Duma that could offer advice on proposed legislation, but no more than advice. On the same day he issued a decree granting the right of petition. Meanwhile, the work was proceeding on implementing the decree of 12 December 1904 and transforming the council of ministers, a body that had rarely met and then under the chairmanship of the emperor, into something like a cabinet. In the government's eyes a great deal was being conceded. In the eyes of almost all of the opposition the concessions were negligible.

As for Nicholas II, he believed that he had done enough and could now get on with giving his attention to the war, which he was resolved to fight 'to the last kopek and the last soldier'. Then came the news that the Baltic Fleet, which had been sent half-way round the world to the Far East, had been destroyed at Tsushima by the enemy on May 14. By ths time the Japanese were ready to negotiate. Nicholas II was not, until his military advisers informed him that while victory on land was still possible, if Russia lost another major battle there could be adverse consequences at home, a likelihood that was underscored by bitter strikes that broke out after news of Tsushima reached Russia. Most reluctantly Nicholas II agreed to negotiations and, with possibly greater reluctance, appointed S. Yu. WITTE as his chief plenipotentiary.

Figure 10 St Petersburg street scene in 1905, typical of those in many Russian cities, where workers, students and citizens of all kinds joined in demonstrative anti-government protest.

On the home front the struggle continued. In May the Union of Liberation, acting in concert with some socialists, formed the Union of Unions under the leadership of P. N. MILYUKOV. This was a federation of recently formed associations of lawyers, engineers, school teachers, professors, doctors, pharmacists, veterinarians, journalists, agronomists, railwaymen, peasants, feminists, and Jewish activists seeking equal rights, all linked together in the struggle to force the government to call a constituent assembly that would give Russia a democratic constitution. In a sense the organization sought to become 'the general staff' of the opposition. This was not to be, but it did provide some focus for those arrayed against the government.

During the late spring and summer the struggle grew sharper, especially in areas with large non-Russian populations. In Odessa, for instance, street fighting reached such a point that the authorities declared martial law on June 15, the very day on which the battleship *Potemkin*, under the control of its mutinous crew, arrived in port. Although the mutineers failed in their efforts to win over the other ships of the Black Sea Fleet and to fuse their struggle with that of the revolutionary forces in the city, both the mutiny and the bloody strife in the streets of Odessa were signs of things to come.

During this period the bitter struggle between the opposition and the government see-sawed, the one determined to force capitulation, the other confused, sometimes loosening its grip, but never losing it. By late summer, however, the government felt that it was gaining the upper hand, bringing in reliable troops to regain control of the streets, meanwhile expecting that the implementation of its promised reforms would divide the opposition and that ending the war would strengthen its hand at home. The opposition, on the other hand, although still firm of will, had no reasonable hopes of imminent victory. Lenin called for armed revolt and, in fact, revolutionaries were arming themselves (see THE SCANDINAVIAN CONNECTION), but neither he nor any other revolutionary leader had the following with which to mount a 'final' offensive against tsarism. Help for the opposition came, when it did, like manna from heaven, in the form of an unplanned general strike that enveloped the country in October.

Plainly a storm was in the making on the eve of October: labour was still militant, unappeased by what it had achieved and by what had been promised; in many provinces peasants were ready to fight, not for the overthrow of autocracy but for more land; demoralization was spreading in the armed forces; and a good part of the middle class was still firm in its hatred of the regime.

The general strike

It was in this setting that the general strike broke out. It began with a printers' strike in Moscow on 19 September, to be followed by an upsurge of strikes in that city and St

Petersburg. The tempo picked up dramatically in the first days of October when railway workers in Moscow, the hub of the country's railway network, stopped work. Within days railway workers all over the country joined them. In city after city, as railwaymen left their trains they inspired strikes: first, workers went out on strike, then teachers, pharmacists, journalists, actors, shop assistants, even schoolchildren, all it seemed, except the bureaucracy, the police and the troops, joined the strike, demanding the end of autocracy. Urban life was so paralysed that even the railway line to Peterhof, where the emperor was in residence, no longer operated, a government ship the only means by which officials could reach him from the capital unless they chose to walk or ride. In St Petersburg, Moscow, and several other cities strikers, under the leadership of socialists and with the blessings of the Union of Unions, formed SOVIETS which in the beginning were no more than strike committees, but which took on limited governmental authority, for example by decreeing the eight-hour day, labour's major demand.

What was the government to do? At this juncture Nicholas II turned to Witte, who had succeeded brilliantly at Portsmouth, USA, in getting better terms of peace than expected and who was considered by many in the government and even at court as the only one who could help the regime get itself out of the morass. He told the sovereign that he could either yield to historical inevitability and give the people civil and political rights, including the right to be partners in the making of laws, or give unlimited authority to a general to crush the strike. As would be expected, Nicholas's preference was for the latter but he agreed to the former when his close advisers informed him that the use of force could lead to civil war, with no assurance of victory. So on 17 October Nicholas II issued a manifesto granting personal inviolability, freedom of conscience, speech, assembly, and association to his subjects and promising that in future laws would be enacted with the concurrence of a popularly elected State Duma. The next day he appointed Witte to be chairman of the Council of Ministers (in effect prime minister), with authority to carry out the provisions of the manifesto. Russia was now a constitutional monarchy in all but name.

Witte was confident that the manifesto would satisfy enough of the 'reasonable' elements in 'society' to permit civic peace to be restored. The manifesto was widely and enthusiastically greeted as marking the beginning of a new era, one of freedom and democracy. And, despite the urging of the revolutionaries to continue the strike, most

Figure 11   Nicholas II opening the Duma and State Council in 1906.

strikers resumed work so that within days life returned to near-normalcy. Clearly, the manifesto led to the end of the general strike, though not to the end of the civil strife.

The revolutionaries as well as the militant wing of the liberals led by Milyukov were determined to continue the struggle for a constituent assembly. Labour, although not at the beck and call of the revolutionaries, was still in a rebellious mood. The peasantry was now making itself heard for the first time: in central Russia, in the Baltic provinces, in the Caucasus peasants looted and burned landlord property and fought back against local authorities trying to protect the landlords. In the army discipline was breaking down, particularly among the troops returning from the front, with mutinies, the formation of soldiers' soviets, fraternization with strikers. The navy for the first time experienced a mutiny led by an officer, Lieutenant P. P. Schmidt. With some justice Soviet historians call the period that followed 17 October 'the high tide' of the revolution, but the sense of solidarity that had bound all of the opposition together before 17 October was gone and the revolutionaries were unable to combine the still active rebellious and revolutionary forces.

Now advantage was slowly accruing to the government. Most of the erstwhile liberal landed nobility was shifting to the right and joining other nobles in supporting the government. Much of the middle class was now more concerned with the restoration of law and order than exacting further concessions from the government. And the BLACK HUNDREDS were trying to rally support for the government, claiming to be the voice of the 'true' Russia.

Very slowly the government under Witte began to gain the upper hand. In November and December it dispatched punitive expeditions to deal with peasant unrest, also to open traffic on the Trans-Siberian Railway and restore discipline among the troops marooned along that line on their way home from Manchuria. The revolutionaries, with some support from the militant liberals, fought back, most dramatically by calling a new general strike in November. But this one was unsuccessful, ending with the arrests of the leaders (among them L. D. TROTSKY) of the St Petersburg Soviet, which had tried to direct the revolutionary movement. In reaction to the arrest, a new call for a general strike was issued in December. In Moscow, one of the few cities where the call was heeded, the strike turned into an armed uprising that was suppressed by the Semenovsky Guards with heavy artillery and exceptional brutality. True, there were still to be clashes between strikers and police, peasant riots, and assassinations galore for the next eighteen months, but the last hope of the revolution was gone with the end of the Moscow uprising. Some years later Empress Alexandra put it in her way that although everyone had thought Witte to be very clever, it was the COSSACKS who, in the end, 'once more had to save the state'.

For the revolutionaries, 1905 was an unfinished 'bour-geois-democratic' revolution from which there were many lessons to be learned and later applied. In 1920 Lenin was to write: 'Without the "dress rehearsal" of 1905, the victory of the OCTOBER REVOLUTION would not have been possible'.   SH

Further Reading

Bushnell, John: *Mutiny and Repression: Russian Soldiers in the Revolution of 1905–1906*. Bloomington, Indiana: Indiana University Press, 1985.

Cunningham, James W.: *A Vanquished Hope. The Movement for Church Renewal, 1905–1906*. Crestwood, NY: St. Vladimir's Seminary Press, 1981.

Engelstein, Laura: *Moscow 1905*. Stanford: 1982.

Harcave, Sidney.: *First Blood: The Russian Revolution of 1905*. New York: Macmillan, 1964.

Pervaya russkaya revolyutsiya 1905–1907 gg.: problemy i sovremennost. Leningrad: Izdatel'stvo Leningradskogo Universiteta, 1976.

Schwarz, Solomon M.: *The Russian Revolution of 1905: The Workers' Movement and the Formation of Bolshevism and Menshevism*. Chicago: University of Chicago Press, 1967.

Trotsky, Leon: *1905*. New York: Vintage Books, 1971.

Black Hundreds

'Black Hundreds' is a generic and pejorative term applied to such ultra-rightist organizations as the Russian Assembly, the Union of Russian Men, the Russian Monarchist Union, the Union of the Russian People, the Union of the Archangel Michael, and the Society for the Active Struggle against Revolution and Anarchy. Except for the first of these, which was established in 1900, the others appeared in 1905 or shortly thereafter in response to the revolution. All bitterly attacked the liberal and socialist movements and everyone connected with them. Although they differed among themselves in social composition and tactics they shared the belief that the opposition movement was the work of elements alien to the 'true' Russia by birth or disposition, notably the 'zhidy', i.e. 'Yids' (their epithet of choice for JEWS), the Poles, and members of the intelligentsia. Also, they shared the view that what the country needed was to return to the Russia of yore, when that land, so they argued, had been well governed in accordance with the principles of autocracy, orthodoxy, and nationality: orthodoxy meaning the RUSSIAN ORTHODOX CHURCH and nationality meaning the ethnic Russians. It followed that they condemned the October Manifesto, which they regarded as the work of a tool of the 'zhidy', Sergei WITTE.

The Black Hundreds had the blessing and occasionally the financial assistance of a government desperate for assurance that the 'true' Russian people was on its side and for whatever help such organizations could give in fighting the revolutionaries. Despite some claims of membership in the millions, the evidence points to a narrow base of support for the Black Hundreds that came, when it did, from the landed nobility, the imperial court, the officer corps, the police, the Russian Orthodox Church, the lower middle classes and, oddly enough, from some Baltic Germans. In all fairness it should be noted that many of the government were appalled by the Black Hundreds, that the church was divided in its attitudes toward these organizations, and that many who accepted the ideology of the Black Hundreds rejected the use of violence.

The largest and most notorious of the Black Hundreds organizations was the Union of the Russian People, organized shortly after 17 October 1905, by A. I. Dubrovin, a St Petersburg physician, with the goal of forming a mass organization. A man somewhat given to fantasies, Dr Dubrovin and his associates published newspapers, pamphlets, and leaflets that were nearly always inflammatory and usually irresponsible. They organized demonstrations in support of the government and established 'fighting bands', many of their members recruited from the underworld, that mounted or incited physical attacks on Jews and, occasionally, on students, and also tried to disrupt the work of leftist groups. The URP is thought to have been responsible for two attempts on the life of Witte and the assassination of two Jewish liberal deputies to the first Duma, Yollos and Herzenstein.

Much of Dr Dubrovin's influence derived from the goodwill shown him by the emperor, to whom he was introduced by the Grand Duke Nikolai Nikolaevich. Moreover, the URP profited from the cooperation of several major municipal and provincial officials as well as from secret subsidies provided by the Ministry of Interior. Nonetheless, the fortunes of the URP began to decline in 1907 as a result of Dr Dubrovin's extreme behaviour which, among other things, led one of his associates, V. M. Purishkevich, to form a rival organization, the Union of Archangel Michael, which thereafter received the Ministry of Interior's subsidies.

The Black Hundreds remained in existence till the end of the tsarist regime. As for Dr Dubrovin, he was put to death by the Bolsheviks in 1918.   SH

The Religious-Philosophical Movement

This movement was the inspiration of three influential figures in Russian cultural life during the revolutionary period. Zinaida Gippius (1869–1945) was a poetess and religious philosopher of remarkable talent. She created space for personal and spiritual values in poetry and literary criticism, which had got into a utilitarian, materialist rut in the later nineteenth century. Her husband, Dmitri Merezhkovsky (1865–1941) was an equally portentous, though less talented historical novelist and critic, who familiarized the Russian intelligentsia with the Italian Renaissance. Their intimate friend and fellow-resident, Dmitri Filosofov (1872–1940), was formerly the friend and fellow-journalist of Sergei (Dyagilev) Diaghileff on the staff

of *Mir Iskusstva* (The World of Art). Together the three 'Merezhkovskys' constituted a 'mystical union', achieving great influence over the Russian intelligentsia.

'The Merezhkovskys' hoped for a religious revolution, even perhaps a 'Third Revelation', which would transform the negative attitude of the intelligentsia towards religious values. In 1902 they secured the reluctant assent of K. P. Pobedonostsev, Procurator of the Holy Synod, for a series of Religious-Philosophical Assemblies, which met in St Petersburg in 1902–03, bringing together progressive clergy and leading members of the intelligentsia. 'The Merezhkovskys' published the proceedings in their journal *Nash Put* (Our Way). In 1903, the assemblies were abruptly stopped.

The support of the Orthodox hierarchy for anti-Semitic pogroms in 1905 precluded further collaboration with the intelligentsia. After 1906, a Religious-Philosophical Society continued to debate the role of religion in society under the leadership of Nikolai Berdyaev (1874–1948), though 'the Merezhkovskys' continued to play an intermittent part. Following the 1905 REVOLUTION, 'the Merezhkovskys' became notorious as patrons of a group of younger 'decadent' writers, though they achieved some influence over the SOCIALIST REVOLUTIONARIES by befriending B. V. SAVINKOV, I. I. BUNAKOV-FONDAMINSKY and A. F. KERENSKY. In 1917, 'the Merezhkovskys' were strong supporters of General L. G. KORNILOV. They continued their interest in religious-philosophical ideas in emigration and died in France.   RA

Further Reading

Karlinsky, S. ed.: *A Difficult Soul: Zinaida Gippius*, intro. V. Zlobin. Berkeley: University of California Press, 1980.

Lowrie, D.A.: *Rebellious Prophet: A Life of Nicolai Berdyaev*. New York: 1960.

Pachmuss, Temira ed.: *Intellect and Ideas in Action: Selected Correspondence of Zinaida Hippius*. Munich: Wilhelm Fink, 1972.

Schiebert, P.: Die Petersburger religiös-philosophischen Zusammenkünfte von 1902 und 1903. *Jahrbücher für Geschichte Osteuropas*, Neue Folge, Bd. 12, 1964.

The First World War and the Revolution

The First World War began for Russia with a fine show of patriotism. Strikes virtually ceased and workers who a week before had been fighting with the police in the streets of St Petersburg, took part in patriotic demonstrations and fell to their knees to sing the national anthem when the tsar appeared on a balcony of the Winter Palace. NICHOLAS II appealed for an end to internal controversy and for Russia to stand united against the enemy. An 'historic' meeting of the State Duma, convened a week later, gave the government an overwhelming vote of confidence, the only note of discord coming from the small group of twenty-two socialist deputies (ten Trudoviks, seven MENSHEVIKS and five BOLSHEVIKS), who made statements hostile to the government and walked out of the chamber to avoid taking part in the vote.

Yet the show of unity and patriotism covered deep mutual suspicion. Although the tsar saw Austria's actions in the Balkans as a threat to Russia's status as a great power and although, once war was declared, there is no evidence that he looked for some kind of compromise with Germany, the Duma liberals appeared to consider genuine patriotism to be their preserve and suspected him of being pro-German. These suspicions were based on the known views of many of his advisers (for example the Durnovo Memorandum of February 1914, translated in Dmytryshyn), on the perception of the aggressive Far Eastern policy as a substitute for a pan-slavist policy in Europe, and on the way the tsar had tried to avert war with Germany until the last moment. Nicholas may have been sincere in his appeal for national unity but the Duma liberals believed, with more justification in this case, that his ministers were not. Since the assassination of P. A. STOLYPIN in 1911, the tsar had become increasingly intolerant of what he regarded as the Duma's interference in his affairs and had appointed to the council of ministers a number of men like I. L. Goremykin, N. A. Maklakov and I. G. Shcheglovitov who were known for their hostility to the Duma. In the first year of the war these men sought to use the idea of national unity behind the tsar as a means to reduce the Duma's role and, if possible, to abolish it altogether. However, it would be wrong to see the council of ministers as entirely opposed to reform or to the Duma, for it also contained ministers like A. V. Krivoshein who sought to use the war crisis to persuade the tsar to continue Stolypin's work of creating a more democratic Russia.

On the other hand, although the Duma opposition was probably genuinely patriotic and genuinely saw Russia as the protector of orthodoxy and slavdom, the tsar had reason to believe that their anxiety to help owed something to the intention to turn any government failure to their advantage, and it is still not clear how disinterested their motives were. Political calculation did play a part in their display of national unity insofar as they feared that open opposition in wartime might sting the tsar into allowing the anti-Duma group in the cabinet to have its way, whereas a wartime political truce might help Krivoshein to gain the upper hand. Furthermore, the Duma parties were in disarray, and hoped that an end to party strife would given them time to heal their own inner rifts.

It is difficult to gauge the patriotism of the urban working class in the early months of the war. However the absence of strikes or of any significant anti-war demonstrations, and the lack of conviction carried by the attempts of Soviet historians to demonstrate working class opposition to the war, suggest that it was patriotic, or at least not hostile to the war. The peasantry was reserved in its attitude. Although there are more recorded incidents of peasant than of working class opposition to conscription, these were fewer than in previous wars (and the relative calmness is often ascribed to the tsar's decision to ban the sale of vodka). However, there are also fewer recorded incidents of any positive peasant support for the war than there are of working class support and, although the peasant soldiers did their duty and died at the front, many witnesses sum up peasant indifference in the words 'We are from Kaluga, and the Germans will not get that far'.

The socialists' refusal to support the war in the Duma made them appear firmly opposed to the general patriotism. In reality they were confused and demoralized. The demonstrations of urban patriotism, the hostility with which the workers met their anti-war propaganda, the news that the German Socialists had voted in the Reichstag to support the war against 'barbaric Russia', and that prominent Russian émigrés like G. V. PLEKHANOV and International leaders like E. Vandervelde (see VANDER-VELDE TELEGRAM) supported the Allied war effort, destroyed the hope of Russian socialists of all tendencies that the war would be prevented by an international strike. A furious debate began during which three attitudes emerged. The first proposed to cease active opposition to the government during the war, arguing that this would deprive the government of any excuse to attack the labour movement, which would thus remain intact until after the war, when the regime would be seriously weakened. The second position was that, whereas a victory for France and Britain over Germany would be a victory for democracy over reaction, a Russian victory over Germany would be a victory for reaction. Thus socialists should hope for victory for the western Allies, but not for Russia. The third demanded absolute opposition to the war effort of all belligerent nations, and the conversion of the international war into a civil war. The first was the position ultimately adopted by A. F. KERENSKY, the second was put forward by the prominent Menshevik A. N. Potresov, the third was LENIN's view and had few supporters inside Russia initially, but gained in popularity after the summer of 1915.

However, in most cases, factional affiliation was no guide to the position of any individual socialist, and members of all factions could be found among the supporters of each position. These differences meant that the Russian socialists were incapable of formulating any distinctive policy, and further contributed to the temporary fall in working class militancy. The walkout of the 'historic' Duma session was the last gesture of any significance they were to make for some time. A little more than two months later, L. B. KAMENEV, the editor of *Pravda*, and the five Bolshevik deputies were arrested (see ARREST OF BOLSHEVIK DUMA DEPUTIES). As the Bolshevik Duma group was far from united it can hardly have been seen as a serious threat to the war effort, and this may have been an attempt by the minister of the interior, N. A. Maklakov, to provoke an incident that could lead to the dissolution of the Duma, or at least be a warning to the other parties to toe the line. It met with no response inside or outside the Duma, and seemed further proof that all organized opposition had collapsed. With the exception of those socialists who later took part in the workers' groups of the WAR INDUSTRIES COMMITTEES, the socialists remained ineffectual until the FEBRUARY REVOLUTION.

The early campaigns: Russia's initial showing in the war was mixed. The major defeats at Tannenberg/Soldau and the Masurian lakes had been accepted because they had been seen as the price honourably paid for an ill-prepared but necessary offensive to stop the Germans from taking Paris, and because they had been counter-balanced by successes on the Austrian front, in particular the capture of Galich and Przemysl. However, by the end of 1914, the Russian army was short of munitions, and a German counter-offensive forced the Russians to abandon not just newly conquered Galicia but, by the summer of 1915, the whole of Poland. Riga seemed about to fall, Petrograd and even Moscow threatened. The Russian army retreated in an orderly way, but the retreat seemed endless and defeat inevitable. Rumours swept the army and the country in general. The emperor, the empress, leading members of the court and of the government, the minister of war, certain military leaders, any one with a German name, and many who came into none of these categories, were suspected of pro-German sympathies and even of treason. There were ugly incidents like the anti-German pogrom in Moscow in May 1915. In fact, although Russian military planners, like those of every belligerent country, had made a serious error of judgement in assuming that the war would be a short one, there is no evidence of any pro-German sympathies of treason. V. A. Sukhomlinov, the war minister, simply had not planned for so great a need for ammunition, and the shortage of shells for the artillery proved to be particularly serious. He was dismissed in June 1915, but more drastic action seemed necessary if Russia was not to be destroyed.

From union sacrée *to confrontationist politics:* At first, the Duma opposition did not appear to wish to take advantage of the political opportunities offered by the government's difficulties, but seemed genuinely prepared to cooperate. Thus, despite the already apparent shell shortage in the winter of 1914, the Duma leaders accepted a session of a mere three days in January 1915, to vote for the credits to re-equip the army. Throughout the spring, however, they increasingly came under pressure from their own rank and file to oppose the government more strenuously. Radical leadership of the Duma passed temporarily from the Kadets to the Progressists, a party composed mainly of representatives of the industrialists, who began to press for a 'real' Duma session and a 'government responsible to the Duma'. At a conference in June, by substituting the vaguer formula

of a 'GOVERNMENT OF PUBLIC CONFIDENCE', P. N. MILYUKOV barely managed to avert Kadet support for this slogan, which could have led to a show-down with the tsar. By the late summer of 1915, the policy of cooperation with the government appeared to be bearing fruit. The tsar had called for a session of the Duma 'in order to listen to the voice of the Russian people', and this opened on 19 July (OS), the first anniversary of the beginning of the war. Five Special Councils, which included Duma members as well as government officials, had been set up to deal with urgent defence matters and, with the exception of the prime minister I. L. Goremykin, the reactionary members of the government had all been replaced by people more acceptable to the Duma. It was thus a very reluctant Milyukov who was pushed by his party towards confrontationist politics.

The non-Duma liberals: The problem was that the Duma was not the only liberal power base. When war broke out, the tsar granted leave and considerable funds for the reconstitution of the All-Russian Union of Towns and the All-Russian Union of Zemstvos (the Zemgor), which had played such a big part at the time of the Russo-Japanese War. These were again given an important role in organizing ancillary support for the armed forces, in particular Red Cross services and supply. Although the Ministry of the Interior was to make repeated efforts to reduce the influence of the Zemgor, their conspicuous contribution to the war effort made them difficult to attack and their leaders, Prince G. E. Lvov of the Zemstvos and M. V. Chelnokov of the Union of Towns, came to wield considerable political influence. These two organizations were soon joined by a third when a network of War Industries Committees was set up in May 1915 to mobilize Russian industry for the war effort. These organizations were more outspoken and more radical in their opposition to the government than was the Duma. During 1915, as the front moved nearer Petrograd, the three non-parliamentary organizations became the focus of opposition and, more boldly than the Duma, aimed to substitute themselves for their government counterparts.

The Progressive Bloc: It was largely to counterbalance this that all parties from the Left Kadets to the Progressive Nationalists, with the support of the Trudoviks and Mensheviks formed the Progressive Bloc inside the Duma. In August the Bloc presented its programme to the tsar, and felt assured that it would be accepted as it was supported by a majority in the council of ministers. Instead, in September 1915, on the advice of Goremykin, alone, the tsar reversed his policies of the past few months, prorogued the Duma and dismissed the pro-Duma members of the government. He also snubbed the Zemgor by refusing to meet their representatives. Both forms of opposition appeared to have come to nothing.

Nicholas II takes command: The tsar's change of attitude towards the liberal opposition was most probably the result of his decision in August 1915 to assume personal command of the armed forces. In the exalted mood that accompanied this decision, he probably saw the formation of the Progressive Bloc as proof that the Duma politicians were more interested in taking power from the throne than in winning the war. In this he was probably mistaken, and by rejecting the Progressive Bloc he strengthened the non-Duma opposition, ironically, as his political doubts about them were possibly more justified. Helpful to the war effort though the Zemgor appeared, there were many who argued that their job could be done just as efficiently by government bodies. Also the fact that the children of the privileged sought services in the Zemgor as a way of escaping service in the army, the so-called 'Zemstvo hussars', had become a scandal. Even the motives of the industrialists in forming the War Industries Committees could be seen as owing as much to the desire of Russian industry to profit more from the war as to a desire to work for the country.

The attitude of the High Command: The tsar's decision to assume command of the army was opposed by his cabinet, and met with mixed feelings in the army itself. Even before the war, the relationship of the army high command to the throne had become ambiguous (See IMPERIAL ARMY IN WAR AND REVOLUTION). Defeat by the Japanese in 1905 had been ascribed to incompetent Russian command and the high morale and motivation of the Japanese troops. An influential section of the Russian officer corps saw the role played by the personal involvement and patronage of members of the Romanov family as the greatest obstacle to the professionalizing of the Russian command, and similarly saw the democratizing of the country, particularly through the Duma, as the best way of providing the ranks with the personal patriotism they believed essential to a modern army. Thus, although Grand Duke Nikolai Nikolaevich had been personally popular, his patronage of senior officers thought to be incompetent was not. On the other hand, although Nicholas' assumption of command was in itself a continuation of the kind of amateurish interference the modern professional officers resented, his appointment of General M. V. ALEXEEV as chief of staff (i.e. effectively commander of the army), was welcomed. Alexeev was held in high esteem as a very competent general, and indeed one of the ironies of the last and much criticized eighteen months of Nicholas II's reign is that the Russian army did rally, the retreat was halted, the shell shortage was overcome, the army went back onto the offensive in 1916, and, on the eve of the revolution, was better equipped than it had been at any time in the war. Perhaps the single most telling pointer to what had been achieved is the fact that the Russian army suffered over half its total casualties during the first year of the war, i.e. in the period before the tsar and Alexeev took over.

The last eighteen months: Liberal historians have generally seen the tsar's decision to assume command of the army as the turning point for the regime, in that it left the government of the country in the hands of the empress Alexandra Fedorovna, RASPUTIN and sinister 'dark forces'. As the soldiers died pointlessly at the front, corrupt minister 'leapfrogged' corrupt minister in a struggle for power: the ultimate proof that the government was incapable of winning the war and worthy only of the accusations made by V. A. Maklakov that the tsar was a 'mad chauffeur', or by Milyukov that the ministers were either guilty of treason or of folly, and that this degeneration led to the regime's collapse in February 1917. Monarchist historians, on the other hand, have managed to show that Rasputin's influence on the government was negligible, that there is no evidence for the existence of any 'dark forces' or treachery, and have explained the same events in terms of a liberal plot. Thwarted of their hopes for political power by the successes of 1916 which proved that the autocracy could run the war efficiently, the liberals turned to rumour and slander that so undermined the government, that when it was challenged in February 1917, none was prepared to stand for it. Neither of these approaches is satisfactory.

The collapse of 1917 was paradoxically the consequence of the success of the regime in meeting the military challenge, at the expense of civilian Russia: a traditionally Russian situation. The success in feeding the army meant that food supplies to the towns broke down as the transport system, and especially the railways collapsed under the strain, despite the existence of food supplied in the countryside. The enormous expansion of industry to meet the requirements of the army, drew large numbers of peasants into the cities, especially Petrograd, at a time when the transport system was unable to bring food in from the countryside, and this together with the influx of refugees from Western Russia caused conditions to worsen considerably. All these things combined to raise prices three times from 1914 to 1916, while wages only doubled. At the front, the high mortality among officers had led to a lowering of the quality at junior level. The troops were becoming weary of a war which seemed to lead nowhere, but appeared endless. Their morale was further sapped by news of hardship at home, so that rumours of betrayal ('the Russian army is led by Germans who lead Russian soldiers to their death so that Germany can win the war more easily', and 'the gentry officers are deliberately leading the peasant soldiers to their death so that they can get their land back') were readily believed. At a time when the war was bringing so much suffering to so many, the profits that industrial success was bringing to industry seemed particularly offensive, and rumours of corruption, some of them true, were widespread. Yet, despite the undoubted sufferings, the underground socialist parties were able to win only negligible support. The regime fell, in the end, as the result of food shortages in the capital, combined with the refusal of the soldiery to turn their rifles on those with whose sufferings they fully sympathized, and the hopes of the High Command that a democratic Russia would be more likely to win the war.   DAL

Further Reading

Dmytryshyn, B. ed.: *Imperial Russia: a Source Book 1700–1917*. Hinsdale: 1974.

Katkov, G.: *Russia 1917: the February Revolution*. London: 1967.

Kitanina, T.M.: *Voina, Khleb, Revolyutsiya*. Leningrad: 1985.

Oldenburg, S.S.: *Last Tsar*, vol. 4. *The World War, 1914–1918*. Gulf Breeze: 1978.

Pearson, R.: *The Russian Moderates and the Crisis of Tsarism, 1914–1917*. London: 1977.

Stone, N.: *The Eastern Front 1914–1917*. London: 1975.

Wildman, A.K.: *The End of the Russian Imperial Army*. Princeton, NJ: 1980.

Government of Public Confidence

This political demand became the watchword of the Progressive Bloc in the two years before the revolution of February 1917. It was a watered-down version of the traditional liberal demand for a ministry responsible to the Duma, first formulated at the Kadet Party congress in October 1905. The Kadets pursued this throughout the existence of the First State Duma, and indeed, at one stage, were actively negotiating with the tsar's representatives for the formation of a Kadet ministry. After the dissolution of the First Duma, however, although the demand remained official party policy, the Kadets were no longer quite so assiduous in pressing for a ministry responsible to the Duma, as they had lost their parliamentary majority and would no longer be part of it.

In April 1915, the issue arose again when the Duma's medical committee demanded the recall of the Duma, and the establishment of a 'politically responsible ministry'. This call was taken up by the Progressist Party who looked as though they would wrest the leadership of the Duma opposition from the Kadets, as the demand met with considerable response. P. N. MILYUKOV, whose leadership was associated with a conciliationist policy towards the present government, came under attack at a Kadet conference in June, but was nonetheless able to gain acceptance for a new, vaguer demand for a 'Government of Public Confidence' on the grounds that, although in effect this would mean a ministry more responsible to the Duma, the formula would be more attractive to the man in the street. In fact, the new formula gave Milyukov more room to manoeuvre *vis-à-via* the existing cabinet, who could envisage a 'Government of Public Confidence' appointed by the tsar. In August, the Progressive Bloc was formed by the majority of the Duma parties, with the support of the more liberal members of the government, with the aim of eventually forming a ministry from its members, and Milyukov's formula 'Government of Public Confidence' was adopted as its main demand. Although the Progressive Bloc was thwarted in its ambitions by the tsar's dissolution of the Duma and sacking of the liberal ministers, a 'Government of Public Confidence' continued to be the main demand of the liberal opposition until the February revolution.   DAL

Further Reading

Hosking, Geoffrey.: *The Russian Constitutional Experiment*. Cambridge: 1973.

Pearson, Raymond.: *The Russian Moderates and the Crisis of Tsarism 1914–1917*. London: 1977.

Startsev, V.I.: *Russkaya burzhuaziya i samoderzhavie v 1905–1917 gg*. Leningrad: 1977.

The Vandervelde Telegram

On 11 August (29 July OS) 1914, Emile Vandervelde, the chairman of the International Socialist Bureau, recently appointed minister of state by the King of the Belgians, sent a telegram to the Russian Social Democratic Duma deputies urging them to support the war effort. He had been asked to do this because his name was well-known to Russian socialists of all tendencies, as he had played an active part in the attempts made by the Second International to reconcile the different Russian socialist factions, and had visited Russia in June 1914. Vandervelde's telegram became widely known throughout Russia, as it was published in the press and typewritten copies were circulated in the factories, but it did not have the desired effect, serving only to divide the Russian labour movement further and add to its demoralization.

Meetings held by all socialist groups to discuss the telegram throughout August and September failed to reach agreement, as Vandervelde had supporters and opponents in all groups. (His BOLSHEVIK supporters included the deputy G. I. Petrovsky and A. G. SHLYAPNIKOV.) At the end of September LENIN's 'Theses on the War' were brought into Russia, considerably strengthening the position of the anti-war section of the Bolshevik Party. Yet even then it proved impossible to reach agreement.

Only in three groups was any kind of agreement ultimately reached, none of which supported Vandervelde. After the September meeting the Bolsheviks drew up a new draft, and local party organizations were consulted. On 1 November they held another meeting, in theory to approve a reply stating that the struggle against the government must go on. All those participating in the meeting were arrested. However, a few days previously Shlyapnikov had taken the draft to Sweden to send to Lenin who published it in *Sotsial demokrat* although he did not completely approve of it. *Nasha Zarya* (Our Dawn), a MENSHEVIK group, stated that it was impossible for Russian socialists to support the government in the way western socialists did, but that they would undertake not to oppose the war effort. The Menshevik Duma deputies declined to send any reply at all.   DAL

Further Reading

Tyutyukin, S.V.: *Voina, mir, revolyutsiya.* Moscow: 1972.

Vandervelde, E.: *Souvenirs d'un militant socialiste.* Paris: n.d.

The War Industries Committees

Created at the ninth congress of the Association of Industry and Trade in May 1915, the War Industries Committees were the last of the major 'public' organizations to emerge during the FIRST WORLD WAR, the Union of Towns and Zemstvo Union having been formed shortly after the outbreak of hostilities. The immediate inspiration for the committees' formation was the shortage of munitions experienced by the Russian Army. This shortage, which had existed since the beginning of the war, took on crisis dimensions in the spring and summer of 1915 when the Russian army was forced to retreat from Austrian Galicia and Russian Poland. Raising serious doubts about the tsarist authorities' ability to administer the war economy and sustain the war effort, the crisis was at once political and economic, and in so far as it pointed to the need to mobilize the industrial working class for production, it had obvious social implications as well (see ECONOMY AND THE WAR).

Initially, the Central War Industries Committee, located in Petrograd, was controlled by the Association of Industry and Trade and its relations with government and military officials reflected the cautious 'business-like' approach of the Association's executive. Three delegates from the central committee (N. S. Avdakov, Kh. Maidel, and V. V. Zhukovsky) all long-standing and active members of the Association, were co-opted by the Special Council for the Supply of Munitions under the war minister, and several million rubles worth of orders were assigned for distribution by the committee to armaments factories. But at the first congress of the new organization in July 1915, its leaders and their policies were rejected by the majority of the 231 delegates representing 85 district and local war-industries committees. In the forefront of this successful challenge to the Association's domination were Moscow-based textile manufacturers who had already consolidated their position in the Moscow district committee. Many of them, including the chairman of the Moscow committee, P. P. Ryabushinsky, had been active in the Progressist Party and before the war had advocated a 'forward' foreign policy for a Russia which they were determined to make 'Great'. Their privileged place within the new organization was ensured by the election of two prominent Muscovites, A. I. Guchkov and A. I. Konovalov, as chairman and vice-chairman of the central committee.

By February 1916 when the committees held their second congress, they numbered 226, divided into 34 district and 192 local committees. With the exception of the Moscow committee which could contract directly with the central military departments, orders were obtained by the central committee and distributed to district committees and thence to individual private enterprises, those run by the committees themselves, or to their local branches for further distribution. Most of the district and some of the local committees contained sections reflecting the predominant economic activities of the areas in which they operated. Hence, the Urals district committee in Ekaterinburg supported sections devoted to mining, cottage industry, fuel, raw materials, food supply, and the labour question. The Moscow committee by contrast consisted of twenty-one sections, the most active of which were involved with textiles, shell production, and the evacuation and resettlement of factories and equipment located in areas near the front. Presiding over more than 50 local committees throughout the central industrial region and publishing a monthly journal filled with technical information and reports from all parts of the empire, the Moscow committee under Ryabushinsky rivalled the central committee as the authentic voice of the entire organization.

A survey, conducted in late 1915 and covering slightly less than half of the committees, revealed that 31.4 per cent of members (1,378) were representatives of commercial-industrial organizations, 17.1 per cent (751) consisted of zemstvo and city officials, and 16.2 per cent (711) represented scientific and technical organizations. The coalescence of these groups around the issue of mobilizing the productive forces of the country for the war effort was significant. Prior to the war, they had been either dependent on or subordinated to, respectively, foreign and state capital, the central state bureaucracy, and foreign technical and managerial personnel. But the war caused a sharp reduction in foreign capital investment in industry while at the same time requiring massive industrial redeployment and technological innovation. It also brought on the political crisis of mid 1915 because of state officials' unwillingness or inability to accommodate themselves to the new situation.

The emergence of the War Industries Committees, therefore, may be seen as the response by Russia's nascent national bourgeoisie not only to a crisis but to the opportunities which that crisis offered. Provincial producers were attracted to the committees by the possibility of receiving war orders and priority in obtaining raw materials, machinery and technical assistance necessary for their fulfilment. Scientific, technical and professional personnel, drawn from the universities and polytechnics, various branches of the Imperial Technical Society and industry itself, viewed the committees as offering scope for research and development appropriate to war in the industrial age. Indeed, much of the work done during the war in such relatively new fields as pharmaceuticals, telecommunications, and aeronautical instruments was to be the product of this institutional link between science and industry. Finally, the more politically oriented leaders of the organization sought to ally it with other public organizations, the Progressive Bloc in the Duma, and representatives of the industrial working class. Their aim was to reconstitute the political structure which they deemed essential for victory in the war, the maintenance of domestic peace, and economic prosperity after the war.

But the forces amassed by the War Industries Committees were insufficient to overcome those arrayed against them. The attempt to assume control of the military procurement system and to determine credit, labour, raw materials and fuel requirements accordingly, antagonized not only the large Petrograd firms with long established bureaucratic connections, but the military bureaucracy itself. The campaign for a 'GOVERNMENT OF PUBLIC CONFIDENCE' in which the committees' leaders figured predominantly both as advocates and ministerial candidates foundered when the Duma was prorogued and the Progressive Bloc split over the issue of whether to engage in extra-parliamentary protest. It also ironically contributed to the economic marginalization of the committees, as the government responded by stripping them of many privileges and powers they had initially enjoyed. Hence, the various regulatory bureaux and commissions founded by the committees were one by one absorbed or superseded by state institutions in which the committees' representatives constituted small minorities.

The result was that by February 1917 the central and Moscow committees had placed orders worth slightly less than 500 million rubles, or only seven per cent of the value of all orders distributed by the military departments. For certain articles capable of being assembled by small and medium-sized enterprises such as grenades, mortar and high explosive shells, the committees' share was considerably higher. But difficulties in supplying skilled workers and the means of production meant that many orders were eventually cancelled, went unfulfilled, or were only partially fulfilled.

In many ways the most interesting and revealing failure of the committees was their attempt to exercise hegemony over the working class through their sponsorship of Workers' Groups. Although 58 such groups had been elected by factory workers as of February 1917, relations between them and the committees were, as a rule, stormy. Moreover, the proposed reforms which they jointly sponsored, such as the establishment of conciliation boards and factory elders, and the legalization of trade unions, alienated large sections of the business community, exposed the committees and the MENSHEVIK-dominated groups to police harassment, and highlighted the BOLSHEVIKS as the only party unequivocally opposed to class collaboration and 'defensism'.

Finding itself increasingly isolated from its social base, the central workers' group under K. A. Gvozdev abandoned its opposition to mass action in late 1916 and drew up plans for a march to the Duma to coincide with its reopening. Simultaneously, Guchkov began sounding out various liberal activists and military officers about the possibility of a palace coup. Both these actions were effectively nipped in the bud, the former by the arrest of the Central Workers' Group on January 26/27, 1917, and the latter by the February Revolution. Yet, both the Workers' Groups and the War Industries Committees managed to contribute to the constellation of forces that emerged after the overthrow of the monarchy. The factory cells created by the workers' group continued to agitate in the factories after the police dispersed the march to the Duma on February 14. These cells are generally credited with being among the first to call for the election of SOVIETS. Gvozdev and two other members of the central workers' group were released from prison during the February days and subsequently took an active part in the Central Executive Committee of the Petrograd Soviet. Guchkov, after having obtained the tsar's signature on the abdication decree, took up his position as war minister, becoming one of four members of the War Industries Committees to assume ministerial portfolios in the PROVISIONAL GOVERNMENT.

The committees themselves urged unconditional support of the Provisional Government and its prosecution of the war to a victorious conclusion. They thereby antagonized the Workers' Groups which, in any case, had been made redundant by the formation of soviets, factory committees and trade unions. As the revolutionary disintegration of industry proceeded in 1917, those industrialists who had earlier placed their hopes in the committees turned to the more militant employers' unions to defend their interests. At the same time, there was a shift in the committees' orientation away from mobilizing industry for war production towards questions relating to demobilization and the post-war economy. By October, the dominant force within the organization was the 'third element', especially scientific and technical personnel. Having opposed the Bolshevik seizure of power in Petrograd, the committees were placed under the control of the Supreme Council of the National Economy in January 1918 and renamed National Industries Committees. In this way, many technical experts made the transition to working as 'specialists' in the Soviet state.

The War Industries Committees can be interpreted as the organizational expression of a class fraction – Russian industrialists – that proved incapable of imposing its vision of a Great Russia onto the rest of society and translating its contribution to the war effort into effective state power. To the extent that the organization and its activities were perceived by tsarist officials as a challenge to the latter's authority, effective administration of the war economy remained elusive. To the extent that the space it provided for working class representation was contingent on support for the war effort, such cooperation remained limited, strained, and ultimately unacceptable to many workers. The contribution that the War Industries Committees made to the Revolution and its outcome was thus the result of these ironies.   LS

Further Reading

Haumann, Heiko: *Kapitalismus im zaristischen Staat 1906–1917*. Konigstein: 1980.

Izvestiya Moskovskogo voenno-promyshlennogo komieteta. Issues 1–51 (1915–18).

Korbut, M.K. ed.: Gvozdevshchina v dokumentakh. *Izvestiya obshchestva arkheologii, istorii, i etnografii pri Kazanskom gosudarstvennom universitete* 34 (1929) 221–70.

Menitsky, I.A. ed.: K istorii Gvozdevshchiny. *Krasnyi Arkhiv* 67 (1934) 31–92.

Sidorov, A.L.: *Ekonomicheskoe polozhenie Rossii v gody pervoi mirovoi voiny*. Moscow: 1973.

Siegelbaum, Lewis: The Workers' Groups of the War Industries Committees: who used whom: *Russian Review* 34.2 (1980) 150–80.

—— : *The Politics of Industrial Mobilization in Russia, 1914–17*. London and New York: Macmillan/St Antony's College Oxford, 1983.

Trudy Vtorogo s'ezda predstavitelei voenno-promyshlennykh komitetov, 26–29 fevralya 1916 gg. Petrograd: 1916.

Zagorsky, S.: *State Control of Industry in Russia during the War*. New Haven: Yale University Press, 1928.

The Economy and the War

On the eve of the World War, the Russian economy had completed more than five years of uninterrupted growth. Total production of goods and services grew by 30 per cent between 1908 and 1913, and by 17 per cent per capita. Large-scale industrial production grew faster still, the result of sustained consumer demand and, especially, of expenditures on rearmament. The output of rye, wheat and other cereals also grew in excess of the growth rate for the economy as a whole. The cultivation of relatively recently settled land (north Caucasus, western Siberia) gave good yields. However, other sectors of the economy showed fewer signs of dynamism. For example, the numbers of livestock failed to keep pace with the growth of the population. In the traditional food-producing regions (notably the central black-earth region), peasants converted meadow land to arable in order to feed the extra mouths, and so less land was available there to graze cattle.

Other aspects of pre-war economic development would give rise to acute difficulty in wartime. The growth of industrial production disguised the fact that some branches crucial to modern war economies (such as basic chemicals and machine tools) were still in their infancy. Russia relied heavily on imports of these items. The major centre of engineering, St Petersburg, also depended heavily upon imported coal, which would have to be transported from the UKRAINE in the event of interruption to foreign supplies. There were also elements of weakness in agriculture. In the central industrial region and the northwest, agricultural producers had begun to diversify into technical crops (such as flax) and potatoes. While this was a positive development in one respect, it also entailed the regular delivery of grain from the central black-earth region. So long as this supply could be guaranteed, the balance of agricultural production was fairly stable. But a major shock, such as famine or war, could easily upset this balance.

From the military point of view, the outlook for tsarist Russia in July 1914 appeared to be favourable. True, the major rearmament programme was not due to be completed before 1917, and the supply of heavier calibres of artillery left a lot to be desired. But the Russian Army entered the war with supplies of rifles, light artillery and ammunition that corresponded to expert military assessments of the likely scale and duration of a European war. In any case, Russia had what contemporaries believed to be two crucial advantages over her potential enemies, namely a seemingly inexhaustible reserve of manpower and a secure supply of foodstuffs, which could not be compromised by any blockade by land or sea.

'Shell shortage' and its implications

As in other belligerent countries, the first signs of trouble with the Russian war effort emerged in the form of a shell shortage. 'The expenditure of shell has reached unheard-of proportions', wrote the Commander-in-Chief, Grand Duke Nikolai, in September 1914. The military leadership demanded immediate supplies of shell from the Main Artillery Administration (GAU), the agency responsible for procurements, with the result that stocks ran dangerously low by the end of the year. As the panic spread, the specialist arms factories, many of which were state-owned, faced charges of incompetence or corruption. Private entrepreneurs were accused of holding out for higher prices. In truth, the industrialist became the scapegoat for the military's failure to predict the likely volume of munitions consumption. In the same way, the shortage of rifles was attributed to industrial greed or administrative error, rather than to lack of military foresight.

Against this background, politicians such as A. I. Guchkov and M. V. Rodzyanko lost no time in criticizing the GAU and the Minister of War, to whom the Artillery Administration was responsible. By the beginning of 1915, those industrialists who stood outside the normal small circle of arms contractors launched a savage indictment of the War Ministry for its failure to broaden the base of military production: 'We need all factories and workshops to become one gigantic factory, working only for the Army', wrote the Moscow industrialist and banker P. P. Ryabushinsky in 1915. In May, at the Ninth Annual

Figure 12 'Buy 5½% War Loan – An abundance of shell is an investment in victory.'

Congress of the Confederation of Russian Trade and Industry, delegates agreed to establish a Central War Industry Committee. The purpose of this committee would be to act as a clearing-house for orders to enterprises producing munitions and other military goods, and to control the allocation of inputs of raw material to such firms. In short, these industrialists aimed to devise an alternative, unofficial system of procurement that would succeed where the government had failed.

The crisis in shell supply thus had immense political as well as economic repercussions. The War Ministry reacted to political pressure by conceding the need for a Special Council for Artillery Supply (May 1915), on which the Duma and private industry were to have seats. Faced with continuing complaints that this body was too limited in scope, the government then established a SPECIAL COUNCIL FOR STATE DEFENCE (in August 1915), which had overall responsibility for military production. Three other coun-

cils, for transport, fuel and food supply, also began work in August. In these circumstances, the economic and administrative role of the new WAR INDUSTRIES COMMITTEES became of limited significance. Yet, in order to deflect such criticisms as had already been levelled at the GAU and the War Ministry (and thus, by extension, at the tsarist government as a whole) the bureaucracy had to demonstrate its ability to solve the problem of military production and supply.

The war economy in full swing: 1915–1916

The newly-formed Special Council continued to assign orders to the state sector, but on a greatly enhanced basis. For instance, the Sestroretsk Gun Works, which had no outstanding orders on its books in the autumn of 1914, suddenly received instructions to produce at least 15,000 rifles each month, considerably in excess of its pre-war capacity. In the private sector, the major engineering giants such as Putilov and the Kolomna Company grasped new and lucrative orders for shell, diverting their workforce from existing non-military commitments. But since military consumption remained intense, and since foreign deliveries were unlikely to arrive in the short term, many more industrial enterprises were enlisted in munitions production. The most notable bureaucratic effort in this respect was undoubtedly the VANKOV ORGANIZATION.

By 1916 the production of munitions had been put on a satisfactory footing. To some extent, the vast increase in output was accomplished by the construction of new factories and by improvements in productivity. But most of the additional military output entailed the redirection of available resources from civilian to military production. To put it crudely, more guns meant less butter.

The tsarist government showed no real awareness of the needs of the civilian economy. To the extent that it intervened in industry, the government confined itself to laying claims to the resources that were required directly for the war effort. For example, the Metals Committee, formed in December 1915, was charged with the supervision of metal supplies to factories working for national defence and (in September 1916) with fixing prices for such metal. But this regulation did not apply to those producers who did not work for the military, such as the factories and artisans who manufactured consumer goods and agricultural implements. Only in 1917 did the new PROVISIONAL GOVERNMENT recognise that civilian consumers should not be ignored, but by then the economic crisis had become too deeply entrenched.

Overall, the output of large-scale industry reached a peak during 1916. According to one estimate, industrial production in that year was 22 per cent higher (in 1913 prices) than in the last full year of peace. But this increase concealed profound shifts in the composition of output. Whereas in 1913 nearly 70 per cent of all industrial production was consumed by households, by 1916 that proportion had fallen to 58 per cent. Military requirements in 1916 absorbed 25 per cent of industrial production, compared with five per cent in 1913. In some branches, notably engineering, the increase in the proportion of military production was much higher. In this sector, military production increased at the expense of the output of investment goods, such as locomotives and, especially, agricultural equipment. By 1917 there were acute shortages of both products, as well as shortages of basic household goods.

The labour market in wartime: The number of workers in large-scale industry increased by more than 10 per cent between 1913 and 1916. Many workers were, of course, conscripted into the army, but the number was more than offset by the employment of people who were unemployed in 1914. Workers who had lost their jobs during the temporary slump at the outbreak of war formed one such category. In addition, industry made use of other unemployed labour, notably women and juveniles. In 1913, women accounted for less than a third of the industrial labour force; by 1916 the proportion had risen to two fifths. Finally, refugees and prisoners-of-war were put to work, the latter in the most arduous occupations, such as mining and construction. Prisoners also worked as agricultural labourers.

Conscription affected industry adversely, because it deprived factories of scarce skilled labour. Some steps were taken early in 1915 to return skilled men to defence work, although with great reluctance on the part of army leaders. In May, the Special Council for Artillery Supply introduced exemption certificates, which allowed munitions factories to retain skilled labour. But the system was open to abuse: FACTORY COMMITTEES claimed after the February Revolution that there were many fraudulent certificates issued to white-collar workers and even to 'café proprietors'.

The tsarist government maintained no overall supervision of the labour market beyond these measures. Nor did the government have any policy on wages. Money wages in defence-related industry broadly kept pace with inflation until 1917, whereas wages in industries such as foodstuffs, woodworking and printing lagged behind price rises. The results of an industrial census in 1918 indicated that the real wages of munitions workers rose by 23 per cent between 1913 and 1916, but that wages in non-defence industry declined by 16 per cent. However, no workers escaped the consequences of price inflation in 1917. Real wages even for the most favoured groups were at least 25 per cent below their 1913 level.

The transport problem: Transport difficulties during the war reflected in part a decade of under-investment after 1900, especially in railway rolling-stock. After 1914, the burden on the existing lines became intolerable: coal now

had to be shipped from the Donbass to the north west; the evacuation from Poland in 1915 created havoc in the western region; and, to cap it all, the military authorities habitually held on to freight wagons, which should more properly have been returned to the rear. Although additional track was built, the construction of locomotives and rolling-stock could not keep pace with the volume of traffic. Existing stock deteriorated rapidly under the strain. The shortage of metal hampered attempts to repair freight wagons and between the middle of 1916 and the middle of 1917 the number requiring repair doubled. Finally, the government failed to ensure that the railways were supplied with adequate fuel. In these circumstances, the railways were simply not equipped to deal with the additional tasks that the war heaped upon them.

Fiscal and monetary policy: The tsarist government had great difficulties in financing its war effort. Energetic measures were taken to engage the financial assistance of foreign powers, but internal sources covered at least four fifths of total wartime expenditures. The government relied only to a small extent on new sources of taxation, which in any case failed to offset the loss to the Treasury caused by the decision to scrap the state vodka monopoly for the duration of the war.

In practice, the government resorted to the issue of additional paper currency and to domestic borrowing. The pre-war link between currency issue and gold reserves was quickly abandoned. Notes in circulation increased from 1,500 million rubles in July 1914 to 9,100 million in January 1917. The emission of paper currency continued at a still faster rate under the Provisional Government, and the total notes in circulation stood at 17,000 million rubles on the eve of the OCTOBER REVOLUTION. At the same time, the government placed short-term debt with the State Bank and with the major commercial banks in Petrograd. The Russian public did not show great enthusiasm for wartime issues of government stock. The much vaunted 'Liberty Loan' of the Provisional Government proved no more popular with investors than did tsarist bonds.

The government created additional purchasing power in wartime, in order to obtain the resources required for the war effort. But the government failed to reabsorb this purchasing power, either by means of taxation or by loans. The result was an inflationary spiral and lack of confidence in the currency, with was to have grave repercussions for internal trade.

Food production and food supplies: The problem of food supply proved much more intractable than that of munitions production. In principle, the supply of food should not have posed such tremendous difficulties. So far as one can tell from the imperfect statistics, the agricultural sector did not contract until 1916 and even then, on paper, there was sufficient grain in the country at large to feed

(a)

Figure 13 (a) '5½% War Loan –
The aim of the loan is
to hasten victory over
the enemy.'
(b) '5½% War Loan –
Active participation in
the war loan is every-
one's patriotic duty.
All for victory.'
(c) '5½% War Loan – If
you have any near
ones in the ranks, help
them by buying the
bonds.'

(b)

(c)

Russian civilians and soldiers alike. But reality was much more complex.

The grain harvest in European Russia in 1914 corresponded closely to the average in the pre-war years (1909–1913). The harvest in 1915 exceeded pre-war production by around ten per cent. However, in 1916 estimated production of grain was ten per cent lower than the pre-war average. Trends in other branches of agriculture are even more difficult to unravel. It seems likely that the production of technical crops (flax, cotton, sugar) declined, but that the number of livestock did not decline, or at least declined by much less than has previously been thought.

Large-scale farmers experienced particular difficulty in wartime, because their hired labour force was depleted by conscription. Landowners were unable to substitute capital equipment for labour, because agricultural equipment was itself in short supply. But it is also clear that peasants reduced their sowings for the 1916 harvest and that this behaviour played the crucial part in the contraction of grain production in 1916 and 1917.

During 1914 and 1915, the tsarist government intervened in the grain market, by fixing the price of grain required for the army and requisitioning stocks in the event of the owners' refusal to sell. There was at this stage plenty of grain available for government procurements, not least because exports had abruptly ceased. Indeed, substantial surpluses of grain accumulated in the villages, which peasants were unable to unload. Consequently, during the first two years of the war, peasant farmers ate more bread, fed grain to their livestock and distilled grain illicitly.

This higher level of peasant household consumption continued into 1916. But in that year peasants cut back on the sown area and the harvest contracted. For the first time, serious shortages of food began to build up in the towns and at the front. In principle, the decline in output was more than offset by the cessation of exports (15 per cent of the grain harvest had been exported before the war). But peasants now refused to part with their stocks of grain at the prices being offered. In 1916 the government continued to stipulate that grain be procured for the army at fixed prices. The peasants calculated, quite rationally, that the incentives to market grain were distinctly unfavourable. There were few manufactured goods to purchase in exchange for their grain, and such goods were in any case not available at fixed prices. The alternative possibility, that peasants acquire paper rubles and retain them until goods were available to buy, made no sense to them at a time of rapid currency depreciation (see PEASANTS).

Government food supply policy was confused and uncoordinated, at least until the middle of 1916. Local officials could in theory regulate food prices, but in practice the market was unregulated. After November 1915, the Special Council for Food Supply had the power to set maximum prices for foodstuffs, and it exercised this power extensively, so far as government procurements were concerned. Financial penalties were to be imposed for refusing to sell at a fixed price. In the face of serious shortages in 1916, the tsarist government embarked upon a more extensive control of the grain trade. In January 1916, officials finally acknowledged that the state had a duty to procure grain for the ordinary consumer, as well as for the army. In June, the government set up a Central Flour Bureau, with the aim of fixing the price of flour and likewise the price of grain delivered to the flour mills. By the autumn, fixed prices applied to all major foodstuffs, including meat, sugar and flour, whether bought by the state or by the household consumer.

Towards the end of 1916, the new chairman of the Special Council for Food Supply, A. A. Rittikh, introduced a grain levy. The purpose of this was to establish the precise quantity of grain required by the state and thence to assign delivery quotas to each province. The scheme foundered upon a mixture of local provincial opposition and evasion by food producers. The new Provisional Government quickly established a complete grain monopoly (25 March 1917), thereby appropriating all grain that was not required for the producers' own consumption, and for seed and fodder. Local food supply committees had the responsibility for monitoring procurements. The government raised the purchase price in March, and doubled the price in August, when it became evident that food was still being withheld. Local officials were now empowered to use force if necessary, an ominous anticipation of the system of *prodrazverstka* (requisitioning detachments) under WAR COMMUNISM.

The crisis in 1916–1917: The government procured 3.8 million tons of grain in 1914–15 and 5.6 million tons in 1915–16. In 1916–17 the Special Council for Food Supply proposed to treble the quantity of state procurements, but the government probably managed to obtain only eight million tons, or around 15 per cent of the total harvest. Although this was three times the level of state procurements in 1914–1915, it was woefully insufficient in 1916–1917, given the requirements of the army and the urban population, now unable to obtain grain in the normal manner.

Confronted by appalling shortages in 1916, the government gradually approved the introduction of rationing. There was, however, no universal system of rationing under the tsarist regime. Local municipal authorities, (in some cases the police), issued ration cards for selected commodities as and when they thought fit. Eventually, in April 1917, the Provisional Government introduced a comprehensive rationing scheme, administered by the local food supply committees.

The food crisis manifested itself in long queues at the shops and in exorbitant prices on the open or black market. No urban centre escaped the problem of food shortage in 1916 and 1917. In Petrograd, during January 1917, the daily number of wagon loads of grain fluctuated between one and twenty, whereas the officially stipulated minimum had been put at thirty. It was against this background that the February Revolution took place. The urban population struggled throughout 1917 to obtain the basic necessities of life, and the soldier could never be sure of the quality and quantity of his daily ration.

Conclusion

The tsarist government, confronted by the political and economic challenge of a shell shortage in 1914–15, staked everything on a resolution of that problem. To the extent that munitions production mushroomed during 1915 and 1916, the tsarist government 'succeeded'. But the cost of such a limited outlook and policy must be judged catastrophic. Investment in basic sectors of the economy, such as transport, housing and agriculture, was virtually at a standstill. The production of consumer goods declined. Against this background, peasant food producers retreated into subsistence. The tsarist regime had overcome one crisis, only to be plunged into the yet more intractable crisis of food supply in 1916–17. This was the bitter legacy of the tsarist government to its short-lived successor.   PWG

The Special Council for State Defence

The supreme body for the direction of the war effort in the rear during the FIRST WORLD WAR, the Council was set up by imperial decree on 17 August 1915, along with three other councils for fuel supply, transport and food supply. Each council had the relevant government minister as its chairman (respectively, the minister of war, industry, transport and agriculture). The Special Council for State Defence had the right to accept or reject the recommendations of the other councils. It included representatives from the Duma and the State Council, as well as from the new 'voluntary organizations' (see WAR INDUSTRIES COMMITTEES.) However, the Council did not have to answer to the Duma. The chairman had the right to take the final decisions on matters of policy, even if they conflicted with the views of the council as a whole.

The Special Council disbursed orders for military items and advanced cash to enterprises in receipt of such orders. It had the power to determine contract prices and to fix the prices of raw materials. The council could requisition materials and sequestrate an entire enterprise (as it did the Putilov Company). It could inspect the books of enterprises that held government contracts. Finally, the council ordered goods from abroad, by allocating foreign currency to special purchasing committees in London and New York.

By the end of 1916, the Special Council supervised nearly five thousand separate industrial enterprises, which together accounted for two million workers. The War Minister delegated his authority to twelve regional commissioners. They, like the council itself, remained in existence until 1918, when the entire apparatus of regulation was absorbed into the Supreme Council for the National Economy (Vesenkha).   PWG

The Vankov Organization: 1915–1918

General S. N. Vankov (1858–1937) was head of the Bryansk Arsenal in 1914. At the beginning of 1915 he proposed to make use of a new technique for the manufacture of high-explosive shell, for which the army had an insatiable appetite. Enlisting the support of the Artillery Administration and the technical assistance of a team of French specialists, Vankov assigned orders for the different components of shell to a wide range of subcontractors, most of whom had no previous experience of munitions work. Shell casings were produced by steel works in south Russia; high-technology items, such as fuses, were either produced by the Optical Company of Petrograd or imported from France. The maverick entrepreneur N. A. Vtorov filled the shell with explosives at his new factory in Moscow.

The Vankov organization produced around one half of all high-explosive shell in Russia. It also made the major contribution to the production of barbed wire. It was a self-contained organization, whose achievements were made possible by concentrating upon a single, standardized item, capable of mass manufacture. Vankov thought of himself as the director of a 'giant industrial enterprise', free from the supervision of officialdom and from the control of bankers. He had virtually complete autonomy in matters of specification, material supplies and pricing. Vankov believed that bureaucracy and private enterprise alike could learn from his experience: the former, because he had shown the need to eliminate 'red tape', the latter, because he demonstrated industry's capacity to improve its productivity.

The organization was eventually dissolved in 1918. Vtorov committed suicide after the October Revolution, but Vankov subsequently worked for Vesenkha, the Supreme Council for the National Economy, as an expert in metallurgy.   PWG

Further Reading

Antsiferov, A.N.: *Russian Agriculture during the War*. New Haven, Conn.: Yale University Press, 1930.

Davies R.W. ed.: *From Tsarism to the New Economic Policy*. London: Macmillan, 1988.

Haumann, H.: *Kapitalismus im zaristischen Staat, 1906–1917*. Königstein: Hain, 1980.

Siegelbaum, L.H.: *The Politics of Industrial Mobilization in Russia, 1914–1917: A Study of the War-Industries Committees*. London: Macmillan/St Antony's College Oxford, 1983.

Struve P.B. et al.: *Food Supply in Russia during the World War*. New Haven, Conn.: Yale University Press, 1930.

Zagorsky, S.O.: *State Control of Industry in Russia during the War*. New Haven, Conn.: Yale University Press, 1928.

1917 and After: Political Developments

Concerted political opposition, food riots and the mutiny of garrison troops in the capital in February 1917, combined with the reluctant defection of his army commanders, forced NICHOLAS II to abdicate and the Romanov dynasty came to a close. It was replaced by a liberal PROVISIONAL GOVERNMENT which undertook to prosecute the war to victory for Russia and to prepare democratic elections to a CONSTITUENT ASSEMBLY which would decide the form of the future state.

Simultaneously, a SOVIET of workers' and soldiers' deputies came into being which undertook to monitor the actions of the new government and to see that they did not harm the interests of the working class. This supervisory role was extended into the ranks of the army with disastrous consquences for normal discipline.

Against this background, LENIN, returning from Swiss exile in April 1917, raised the banner of socialist revolution. The soviets were enjoined to take power in the name of the workers; the soldiers were agitated to make their own peace with the Germans by coming out of the trenches and fraternizing across the barbed wire; the peasants were encouraged not to wait for the Constituent Assembly to satisfy their land hunger, but to take what they regarded as their birthright by force. The Provisional Government proved unable to maintain itself in power, facing as it did mounting economic chaos and political challenge, and in October it lost power to the Bolsheviks.

Quickly moving to take Russia out of the war by a separate peace with Germany, the Bolshevik government soon found itself confronted by a series of new military enemies. These were drawn from elements of the post-Imperial army that had fought under the Provisional Government and they represented a wide spectrum of political aims, ranging from those of the FEBRUARY REVOLUTION to restoration of the monarchy. Also ranged against the Reds, as the Bolsheviks soon came to be known, were ethnic groupings in the borderlands who seized the opportunity of a confused Russian state to win a new status for their own national minority. The Russian CIVIL WAR was the violent manifestation of anti-Russian feeling that had long been suppressed by the old regime. This section also summarizes the nature and effects of the economic policy of 'WAR COMMUNISM', which the new regime pursued to feed and clothe its RED ARMY.

Having crushed their military enemies, the Bolsheviks then discovered that within their own ranks were leading members whose socialist conscience was troubled by the party's policies, whether in relation to the inner democracy of the party itself, or the international proletariat, or the Russian working class. This opposition was violently expressed in the revolt at KRONSTADT in March 1921, a watershed in Soviet history. This section also examines the nature of Soviet PROPAGANDA, as one of the regime's means of winning friends; and concludes with the EMIGRATION, which was the most graphic demonstration of the regime's failure in that area.

HS

The February Revolution

The abdication of Tsar NICHOLAS II, leading to the end of the Romanov dynasty, and the formation of the PROVISIONAL GOVERNMENT and SOVIET of workers' and soldiers' deputies, constituted the February Revolution of 1917.

The strains exerted on the tsarist administration with increasing force, as the war progressed, came from various directions. Economically, Russia was unfit to bear the weight of modern war and supplies of food, fuel and transport reached a crisis in the winter of 1916–17, with galloping inflation and widespread discontent the inevitable results. In military terms, the army's physical condition in terms of material looked promising at the end of 1916, but the consumption of manpower, the steady rise in the age of new conscripts, and (of crucial importance) the presence of disgruntled veterans and impressionable recruits in vast numbers in the capital Petrograd, placed a question mark over the army's future. In political terms, the war had created an even wider gulf between the tsar and Russia's elected politicians. The tsar had taken charge of the army in September 1915, leaving the government under the erratic care of his wife, the Empress Alexandra. The empress's German origin and the charlatan Rasputin's presence at court created wild rumours of 'treason in high places', weakening the monarchy's image to such an extent that right-wing monarchists were driven to murdering Rasputin in December 1916.

Denunciations of the government's inefficiency grew strident, and when in late February food riots coalesced with troop mutinies to produce a crisis, the government lost control of the situation. A provisional government was formed by mainly liberal politicians. Simultaneously, the Petrograd Soviet, a central council of workers' and soldiers' committees, was formed to monitor the new government in the political and other interests of the working class.

Meanwhile at Pskov, where the tsar's train, en route to the capital, had been halted by striking railway workers, General ALEXEEV urged him to abdicate in favour of his son. At the same time, Guchkov and Shulgin, emissaries sent by the Provisional Government with the same aim, arrived at Pskov. Nicholas meanwhile had decided that he would hand over to his brother, Grand Duke Michael, rather than his haemophiliac son, Alexei, and Shulgin and Guchkov concurred.

On their return to the capital, however, the two monarchist emissaries were confronted by a highly charged mood of republicanism, most vocally expressed by Alexander KERENSKY, the only non-liberal member of the new government and a SOCIALIST REVOLUTIONARY whose membership of the new government, moreover, had been enthusiastically endorsed by the Soviet. Kerensky now warned Grand Duke Michael that his safety could not be guaranteed, given the mood of the masses. Michael therefore declined the crown and the dynasty came to a close.

State power had ceased to exist. The liberal-democratic caretaker government, while it was prepared to introduce democratic legislation, was also committed to carrying on the war to an Allied victory. The Soviet represented those who felt the war had ended with the fall of the tsar. This major difference created an arena of conflict that, more than any other, would provide the opportunity for LENIN's seizure of power.

Chronology of the 'February Days'

The days in late February and early March 1917 (OS) in which the autocratic government of the tsars was overthrown.

Wednesday, 22 February: Strike and lock-out at the giant Putilov factory in south-west Petrograd.

Thursday, 23 February: (International Women's Day) Women workers led demonstrations into the centre of Petrograd protesting at bread shortages.

Friday, 24 February: Demonstrations gathered momentum. Troops attempted to disperse crowds without bloodshed.

Saturday, 25 February: Crowds became bolder. Nicholas II ordered immediate suppression of disorder.

Sunday, 26 February: In afternoon and evening fighting along Nevsky Prospect and in Znamensky Square. First rumours of mutinies. Tsar ordered prorogation of State Duma.

Monday, 27 February: Mutiny of a training battalion of Volynsky Guards, who then marched to other barracks for support. By evening, 70,000 soldiers had mutinied. Duma submitted to prorogation but private meeting of fraction leaders created a 'Provisional Committee of the Duma for the restoration of order, and so forth . . . Mutinous soldiers then arrived at the Tauride Palace demanding that the Duma condone their mutiny. That evening, moderate socialists convened a Provisional Executive Committee of the Petrograd Soviet of Workers' Deputies also in the Tauride Palace.

Tuesday, 28 February: Surrender of Tsarist forces in Petrograd. Election of workers' deputies began throughout the city.

Wednesday, 1 March: Duma Committee decided to form a Provisional Government. Alarmed at refusal of officers to support revolution, Soldier Section of Petrograd Soviet issued 'Order No. 1' undermining traditional military discipline (see Figure 14 opposite). (See also IMPERIAL ARMY.)

Thursday, 2 March: Formation of Provisional Government with the agreement of the Petrograd Soviet. On the advice of the Army High Command, Nicholas II abdicated in favour of his brother.

Friday, 3 March: Abdication of Grand Duke Michael. End of the Romanov Dynasty.   RA

Provisional Government

The name adopted by the Russian central government between the abdication of Nicholas II, the last Tsar, and his brother Grand Duke Michael on 2 and 3 March 1917, and the Bolshevik seizure of power in Petrograd on 25 October (NS 7 November), 1917.

The nature of the Provisional Government

The institutional continuity of the Provisional Government was personified by A. F. KERENSKY and M. I. Tereshchenko, who served in it from March to October, but it was in reality a series of governments of differing political complexions. The liberal Kadets and the MENSHEVIKS (who accepted the current Marxist orthodoxy

Figure 14   The authors of Order No. 1.

suggesting that Russia was unripe for socialism), both agreed that the government following the overthrow of 'Tsarism' must be a 'bourgeois' government. The Kadet leader, P. N. MILYUKOV, was also strongly in favour of a constitutional monarchy, but his hopes were dashed when Grand Duke Michael heeded the advice of Kerensky and other members of the Provisional Committee of the Duma, and declined the crown. The form of the future Russian State was left to the decision of a democratically elected CONSTITUENT ASSEMBLY. Negotiations then took place between Milyukov, on behalf of the Duma Committee, and N. N. SUKHANOV and others, representing the provisional Executive Committee of the Petrograd Soviet of Workers' Deputies. They agreed on the creation of a 'bourgeois' Provisional Government. Several of the prospective ministers were acutely aware that the mutinous soldiers and workers of the capital might not accept their authority so they insisted that two socialists be invited to join them. Mindful of the scandal caused by the socialist Alexandre Millerand who had joined a French 'bourgeois' government in 1899, and the subsequent resolution of the Socialist International, the Menshevik N. S. Chkheidze, declined.

However Kerensky, an SR who had led the Trudoviks (Labour Group) in the Fourth Duma, accepted the post of Minister of Justice. Milyukov assumed that he, as leader of the largest 'bourgeois' party, would dominate the government, as its nominal head was Prince G. E. Lvov, the figurehead of the Union of Zemstvos and Towns, but an administrator rather than a politician. The government included four Kadets and only one socialist, while several other members had previously belonged to the conservative Octobrist Party. These calculations ignored the influence exercised by Kerensky, both as a representative of the Petrograd Soviet, and as a leading member of the Russian POLITICAL FREEMASONRY, which included his fellow-ministers, Nekrasov, Tereshchenko and Konovalov.

The First Provisional Government: 3 March–5 May 1917
The First Provisional Government (Table 1) was acclaimed with such euphoria that its members assumed that its good faith would be accepted indefinitely. In theory its mandate derived from the support of the revolutionary people, which would expire with the convocation of a Constituent Assembly elected on the basis of a democratic electoral law

Table 1 The First Provisional Government

Minister (Party)	Ministry
Prince G. E. Lvov (Independent)	Prime Minister
A. F. Kerensky (Trudovik/SR)	Justice
P. N. Milyukov (Kadet)	Foreign Affairs
A. I. Guchkov (Octobrist)	War and Marine
A. I. Konovalov (Progressist)	Trade and Industry
M. I. Tereshchenko (Independent)	Finance
N. V. Nekrasov (Kadet)	Transport
V. N. Lvov (Octobrist/Centre)	Procurator of the Holy Synod
A. A. Manuilov (Kadet)	Education
A. I. Shingarev (Kadet)	Agriculture
I. V. Godnev (Octobrist)	State Comptroller
V. D. Nabokov (Kadet)	Secretary to the Cabinet

incorporating universal and equal franchise, direct representation and secret ballot. The government pledged itself to ensure its speediest possible convocation. In practice all the members of the First Provisional Government assumed that the elections would be postponed until the war had been won, both on practical grounds and because they hoped that the tide of radicalism would recede. In fact, the mandate of the first Provisional Government was effectively removed within two months by a public dispute over war aims between its members. As the socialist exiles and political prisoners returned to Petrograd, they goaded Kerensky into a violent debate with Milyukov. Milyukov whipped the government into supporting his policy of fighting for the destruction of the Central Powers and a punitive peace. The publication of the so-called 'Milyukov note' of 18 April 1917, implying Russia's continuing commitment to the destruction of Austria-Hungary and punitive reparations against Germany, triggered public demonstrations in the capital remembered as the 'April Days'. On 20 April the Kexholm Guards demonstrated against Milyukov before the Mariinsky Palace. No sooner had they been dispersed by the moderate socialist leaders of the Soviet than a Kadet counter-demonstration appeared. BOLSHEVIK-led Red Guards and military units then staged a mass mutiny.

Order was slowly restored, but General L. G. KORNILOV, Commander-in-Chief in Petrograd, was denied permission to use force and he sought an immediate return to the front. The 'April Days' were followed by the 'April Crisis' around the composition of the Provisional Government. An informal agreement to topple Milyukov was reached between the Menshevik and SR leaders of the Soviet, the Allied Embassies and the Masonic members of the government. Milyukov's position was rendered untenable by the resignation of Guchkov. Negotiations between the Duma Committee and the Kadet Party on the one side, and the Executive Committee of the Petrograd Soviet on

the other, resulted in the proclamation on 5 May 1917 of the 'First Coalition'. The new government was to be subject to the joint tutelage of the Kadet Central Committee and the Petrograd Soviet. Shortly afterwards, a secret 'inner cabinet' comprising the Freemasons, Kerensky, Tereshchenko and Nekrasov, together with the Menshevik leader, I. G. TSERETELI, was established to co-ordinate strategy on war and peace.

The First Coalition: 5 May–2 July 1917

The success of the First Coalition Government (Table 2) was dependent on the success of the offensive (The Kerensky Offensive), launched on the South West Front in Galicia on 18 June. When the offensive failed to gather momentum the government began to fall apart. On 2 July 1917 the Kadet ministers resigned in protest at the inner cabinet's concession of autonomy to the UKRAINE. This was followed by the so-called 'July Days' (3–5 July 1917), when Bolshevik and anarchist soldiers, sailors and civilians attempted to seize power in Petrograd. This attempt was

Table 2 The First Coalition Government

Minister (Party)	Ministry
Prince G. E. Lvov (Independent)	Prime Minister
A. F. Kerensky (SR)	War and Marine
M. I. Tereshchenko (Independent)	Foreign Affairs
N. V. Nekrasov (Kadet)	Transport
I. G. Tsereteli (Menshevik)	Posts and Telegraphs
V. N. Chernov (SR)	Agriculture
P. N. Pereverzev (Trudovik)	Justice
V. N. Lvov (Centre)	Holy Synod
A. A. Manuilov (Kadet)	Education
A. I. Konovalov (Progressist)	Trade and Industry
A. I. Shingarev (Kadet)	Finance
M. I. Skobelev (Menshevik)	Labour
A. V. Peshekhonov (Popular Socialist)	Food
Prince D. I. Shakhovskoy (Kadet)	Welfare
A. V. Godnev (Centre)	State Comptroller
A. Ya. Galpern (Menshevik)	Secretary to the Cabinet

unsuccessful, partly because Minister of Justice Pereverzev leaked documents gathered by the intelligence services purporting to show that Lenin was a German agent (see REVOLUTIONIERUNGSPOLITIK). Pereverzev's unsocialist behaviour scandalized the All-Russian Central Executive Committee of Soviets and the government was forced to sack him. The government was simultaneously abandoned by its Prime Minister, Prince Lvov who felt he lacked the toughness required in dealing with disorder, and by Tsereteli who preferred to combat Bolshevism in the Soviets. On 7 July Kerensky became Prime Minister of a socialist 'rump' government, which staggered on until 21 July. During this period, Nekrasov resigned from the

Kadet Party and tried to create a Radical Democratic Party to compete with the Kadets for bourgeois support. Kerensky's supporters in the SR Party, especially the veteran Katerina BRESHKOVSKAYA, tried to stem the rising tide of pacifism and agrarian radicalism among the SRs by creating a cohesive faction around the newspaper, *Volya Naroda* (The Will of the People). Kerensky's efforts to solve the 'July Crisis' in the government were thwarted by ultimata delivered by the Kadet Party, the new all-Russian Central Executive Committee of Soviets and the SRs. The crisis was compounded by the demands made by General Kornilov on his promotion to the Supreme Command on 18 July. On 21 July Kerensky resigned and took several days leave. In his absence a conference of bourgeois and Soviet leaders was held in the Malachite Hall of the Winter Palace. It resulted in a Second Coalition whose members were henceforth accountable only to the cabinet. The new government hoped to rally public support at a State Conference due to assemble in Moscow in August.

The Second Coalition: 25 July–27 August 1917

The positive achievements of the Second Coalition (Table 3) were overshadowed by the semi-public feuding between the Prime Minister and the Supreme Commander, known to history as the 'Kornilov Affair'. Kornilov's demands for a free hand from government interference, for the restoration of the death penalty in the army, for the militarization of factories and railroads and for the creation of a dictatorial government, were at first kept to a small circle but rumours of tension persisted. The Moscow State Conference (12–15 August 1917) brought together bourgeois and socialist forces but failed to bridge the gap. It was further exacerbated by military reverses including the fall of Riga (21 August). Kerensky himself terminated the Second Coalition on 27 August 1917 by demanding the resignation of all the ministers so that he could dismiss Kornilov, whom he now accused of mutiny. Kerensky was now legally dictator. To assist him he co-opted a 'Directory' of two ministers and the two service chiefs to reimpose discipline on the armed forces and to face down the Soviets whose authority had increased tremendously as a result of the role they had played in rallying working class resistance to Kornilov.

The Directory: 1–27 September 1917

Infuriated by the evidence that Kornilov had tried to restore traditional modes of authority, the mass of the soldiery and workers in Petrograd re-affirmed their support for the soviets. They also demanded radical social reforms, new peace initiatives and the rehabilitation of the Bolsheviks implicated in the 'July Days'. In addition, the Menshevik and SR leaders of the VTsIK were determined to make the Provisional Government submit to some kind of public accountability, forcing Kerensky to shelve a proposed Third Coalition between modern socialists and

Table 3 The Second Coalition Government

Minister (Party)	Ministry
A. F. Kerensky (SR)	Prime Minister
	War and Marine
N. V. Nekrasov (Radical Democrat)	Deputy Prime Minister
	Finance
N. D. Avksentiev (SR)	Interior
M. I. Tereshchenko (Independent)	Foreign Affairs
V. M. Chernov (SR)	Agriculture
A. M. Nikitin (Menshevik)	Posts and Telegraphs
A. V. Kartashev (Independent, pro-Kadet)	Religion
P. P. Yurenev (Kadet)	Transport
F. F. Kokoshkin (Kadet)	State Comptroller
A. V. Peshekhonov (Trudnovik-Popular Socialist)	Food
S. F. Oldenburg (Kadet)	Education
A. S. Zarudny (Trudovik-Popular Socialist)	Justice
I. N. Efremov (Radical Democrat)	Welfare
M. I. Skobelev (Menshevik)	Labour
S. N. Prokopovich (Menshevik)	Trade and Industry
B. N. Savinkov (SR)	Deputy Minister of War
V. I. Lebedev (SR)	Deputy Minister of Marine

bourgeois independents, and operate with a Directory (Table 4) pending the outcome of a Democratic Conerence of democratic, socialist and working class organizations which met on 14–20 September. It collapsed in farce when it failed to decide on whether or not to permit socialists to join Kadets in a new coalition. Kerensky was now free to announce a list of his own choice. A notable omission was Nekrasov, blamed by the Kadets for Kerensky's breach with Kornilov. He retired from the government to become Governor-General of Finland, leaving Konovalov as Deputy Prime Minister.

Table 4 The Directory

Minister	Office
A. F. Kerensky	Prime Minister
	Supreme Commander-in-Chief
M. I. Tereschenko	Minister of Foreign Affairs
A. M. Nikitin	Minister of Posts and Telegraphs
General A. I. Verkhovsky	Minister of War
Rear-Admiral D. N. Verderevsky	Minister of Marine

The Third Coalition: 27 September–25 October 1917

The Third Coalition (Table 5) led a beleaguered existence as Lenin prepared to overthrow it at the Second All-Russian Congress of Soviets scheduled for 20 October. Leaks from the Shablovsky Commission appointed by

Table 5 The Third Coalition Government

Minister (Party)	Office
A. F. Kerensky	Prime Minister
	Supreme Commander-in-Chief
A. I. Konovalov (Kadet)	Deputy Prime Minister
	Trade and Industry
M. V. Bernatsky (Kadet)	Finance
M. I. Tereschenko (Independent)	Foreign Affairs
General A. I. Verkhovsky	War
Admiral N. D. Verderevsky	Marine
S. N. Tretyakov (Kadet)	Chairman of the Economic Council
S. L. Maslov (SR)	Agriculture
A. M. Nikitin (Menshevik)	Posts and Telegraphs
K. A. Gvozdev (Menshevik)	Labour
P. N. Malyantovich (Trudovik)	Justice
A. V. Liverovsky (Trudovik)	Transport
A. V. Kartashev (Independent)	Religion
S. S. Salazkin (Kadet)	Education
N. N. Kishkin (Kadet)	Welfare
S. N. Prokopovich (Menshevik)	Food
S. A. Smirnov (Kadet)	State Comptroller

Kerensky to investigate the 'Kornilov Affair' suggested that Kerensky himself was deeply implicated in a plot to suppress the soviets and discredited the government across the political spectrum. The Germans took the islands at the mouth of the Gulf of Riga, advancing to within 200 miles of the capital. Several national minorities openly planned to secede. Industry was beginning to collapse. A virtual peasant war broke out on the land threatening further reductions in food supplies for the urban population. The government looked in vain for support to the Provisional Council of the Russian Republic (or 'Pre-Parliament'), which opened on 7 October. Once more the Kadets debated the issues inconclusively with the moderate socialist representatives of local government, trade unions, cooperatives and soviets. Unable to break new ground in either foreign or domestic policy without forfeiting what remained of its support, the Provisional Government clung to power in the hope of surviving until the convocation of the Constituent Assembly. This was rendered less likely by its own earlier action in postponing the elections from 17 September to 12 November. Forewarned of Bolshevik plans for a coup by ZINOVIEV and KAMENEV, the government assumed that the Bolsheviks could easily be cowed as they had been in July. With the Bolshevik capture of the ministers in the Winter Palace on 25/26 October 1917, the Provisional Government was effectively at an end. Kerensky's attempts to rally troops from the Northern Front ended in ignominious failure. A committee of assistant ministers of the Provisional Government continued to command the allegiance of the Petrograd civil servants for some days. Efforts to form an alternative provisional government at Army GHQ at Mogilev were abortive, while the anti-Bolshevik risings in Moscow and Petrograd on 28–29 October 1917, ignored the fallen Provisional Government.

Achievements and failures of the Provisional Government

Several leading members of the Provisional Government, and many of its socialist supporters, had endorsed the aims of the international socialist conference in Zimmerwald, Switzerland (1915) with its famous formula demanding an immediate peace 'without annexations or contributions' (reparations). This led many western leaders to suspect the Provisional Government of plotting a separate peace with the Central Powers. In fact the government never wavered in its commitment to the 1914 Treaty of Paris which forbade the conclusion of a separate peace by any of the Allies. The reasons for this fidelity were numerous. The ministers hoped that the struggle with the external enemy would reduce internal social tensions. They feared that a separate peace would provoke a civil war with all its catastrophic social and economic consequences. They identified socialist internationalism with Leninist radicalism, which was repugnant to the Kadets because of their class interests, and to Kadets and moderate socialists alike because of their commitment to the installation of Western European political culture in Russia. The war and blockade had wrought havoc on the Russian economy and the ministers regarded western finance as vital during the war and the period of post-war reconstruction. Some ministers had a strong sense of identification with the constitutional regimes in Britain, France and the USA and believed that victory in the common struggle would entrench a similar form of government in Russia. There was overwhelming evidence that Germany intended to impose a Carthaginian peace on Russia. There was also the danger that if Russia sued for a separate peace, the Allies would outbid her by suggesting to the Germans that they make small concessions in the West (for example Alsace-Lorraine) for large ones in the East (for example the Ukraine).

In the First Provisional Government Milyukov accepted the 'secret treaties' between the Allies, providing, among other things, for the partition of Turkey, the independence of Bohemia, the Italian annexation of Dalmatia and punitive reparations against Germany. He made no secret of his desire for Russian annexation of the Straits at the mouth of the Black Sea (Dardanelles and Bosporus). Kerensky insisted that Russia renounce all annexations and press the Allies into agreeing to offer the Central Powers peace on 'Zimmerwaldist' terms. With the creation of the First Coalition in May, this appeared to be the policy of the whole government. It was to be achieved first by a

Figure 15   Kerensky reviewing the Petrograd garrison, 6 May, 1917. Kornilov second from right.

successful offensive against the Germans which would raise Russia's stock all round, inclining the Central Powers towards more reasonable terms; secondly by the review of Allied War aims at a conference summoned for the purpose at Russian insistence; and thirdly by pressure put on all the belligerents by their own socialist parties which would coordinate their policies at an international socialist conference in Stockholm. After the failure of the offensive, foreign minister Tereshchenko did his best to block all peace moves, to postpone the Allied Conference and to sabotage the Stockholm Conference. Neither conference met until after the fall of the Provisional Government. These manoeuvres became public knowledge in the late summer and Milyukov attacked his successor (in the Pre-Parliament) for pursuing his policies by covert means, a charge Tereshchenko found hard to deny. In October Kerensky sent a desperate secret appeal to Lloyd George to offer a general peace on terms the Germans were bound to reject, so as to encourage the Russian soldiers to remain in the trenches during the winter. This secret diplomacy was wrecked by the unexpected intervention of General Verkhovsky, whose demand for an immediate general peace

(20 October) caused a scandal and led to his own suspension as Minister of War.

The armed forces: By the spring of 1917 the Russian Army and Navy numbered some 10,000,000 men. They were engaged in fighting the Central Powers from Latvia in the north to Romania in the south, in the Caucasus, and also by sea in the Baltic and Black Seas. From 1915–17, Nicholas II was Supreme Commander-in-Chief, though he accepted the operational advice of his Chief-of-Staff, General M. V. Alexeev. After the tsar's abdication, his uncle Grand Duke Nikolai Nikolaevich briefly assumed the Supreme Command until republican sentiment forced his replacement by General Alexeev. Alexeev's resistance to new army regulations ('the means by which the army I command will be destroyed') and his pessimism about Russia's ability to conduct offensive operations resulted in his replacement in May by General A. A. Brusilov. At the same time there was a purge of monarchist officers. Many career officers resented these changes as an affront to the honour of their caste. Their fear of humiliation at the hands of their men made most officers sympathetic to the

129

demands of General Kornilov after his promotion to the Supreme Command in July.

The Russian Army in 1917 was a microcosm of the male half of the socially and ethnically diverse Russian Empire. With the collapse of traditional military discipline the fate of Russia lay in the hands of the 'peasants in grey greatcoats' as the rank-and-file soldiers were known. The Provisional Government was particularly intimidated by the proximity of the Baltic Fleet, the Northern Front (especially the LATVIAN RIFLEMEN) and the Petrograd garrison, all strongly influenced by Bolshevism. The more moderate, and more remote, South West Front and Black Sea Fleet were unable to offer an effective counterweight.

On 1 March 1917, while the outcome of the FEBRUARY REVOLUTION was still in doubt, the Soldier Section of the Petrograd Soviet promulgated its famous 'Order No. 1', broadcast to the army at the front, and providing for the election of committees in all army units, egalitarian forms of address and full civil rights for soldiers off duty. War Minister Guchkov appointed a commission under General A. A. Polivanov to overcome the resulting confusion. Its draft regulations incorporated many provisions of 'Order No. 1' and despite the objections of the Supreme Command, were eventually promulgated as 'The Declaration of the Rights of the Soldier' on 11 May 1917 over the signature of Kerensky, the new War minister. Following the German counter-offensive at Tarnopol on 6 July the government, under heavy pressure from General Kornilov, gradually withdrew rights conceded in the Declaration. The reaction to General Kornilov's mutiny swept away these restrictions and by October 1917 large sections of the armed forces were demanding the right to elect their own commanders.

As early as April 1917 Guchkov had favoured the recruitment of volunteer units of Czechs, Poles and other national minorities. At first Kerensky opposed the splitting of the army on national lines, though he himself sanctioned the formation of exclusively volunteer battalions. After the failure of the offensive, the recruitment of volunteer battalions was accelerated. After Kerensky's assumption of the Supreme Command in September his successor as minister of war, General Verkhovsky, planned a radical reduction in the size of the conscript army and prepared to change the crews of the Bolshevized Baltic Fleet when the sea froze. A secret plan for anti-Bolshevik 'Revolutionary Guards' under General P. N. WRANGEL came too late to save the government. Its last *de facto* Supreme Commander, General N. N. Dukhonin, was beaten to death by Bolshevik soldiers on 20 November 1917 when he refused to agree to a unilateral cease-fire.

Internal affairs: Prior to the February Revolution, tsars had granted very limited political rights to their subjects which discriminated according to caste, wealth, ethnicity, religion and gender. The programme of the First Provisional Government committed it to the democratization of all aspects of political and social life. By the law of 20 March all adult citizens became equal; after intensive lobbying by liberal feminists (see WOMEN: 1917 AND AFTER), the government agreed that this implied equal rights for women also. Electoral lists were drawn up and in August the first democratic elections were held for city dumas and rural zemstvos. Meanwhile 'revolutionary' commissars were sent to supervise the work of career civil servants in the provinces. The pinnacle of the democratic edifice was to be the All-Russian Constituent Assembly. In practice the government was driven to infringe the omnicompetence of the Constituent Assembly, most notably by proclaiming Russia a Republic after the 'Kornilov Affair'.

The Provisional Government hoped to replace the repressive and authoritarian police and penal systems of tsarist Russia with systems that were participatory, liberal and accountable. The former police forces were replaced by militia units under local control; in radical working class districts they quickly became known as 'Red Guards'. Jury trial was restored for all criminal offences and some reactionary judges purged. The 'Governing Senate' remained Russia's supreme court but it was rejuvenated with liberal jurists such as L. I. Petrazhitsky and O. O. Gruzenberg.

As a revolutionary regime, the Provisional Government lost no time in issuing an amnesty for all political offenders (except those convicted of treason in wartime), and in ordering the speedy return of the Siberian exiles. In March the death penalty was abolished. This measure was dictated by the continuing prestige of Tolstoyan ideas among the intelligentsia, by the unanimous vote of the First State Duma in 1906, and by the desire of the ministers to avert a descent into vengeful barbarism. Little thought was given to its implications for discipline at the front. A commission was set up under N. K. Muraviev to investigate the crimes of the fallen regime.

From the First Coalition onwards the Provisional Governments included a minister of welfare, charged with pioneering a rudimentary system of social welfare. In July the RUSSIAN ORTHODOX CHURCH was disestablished and – for the first time since 1721 – permitted to elect its own Patriarch. Relations between the State and the Orthodox Church and the other religious cults were now entrusted to a Ministry of Religious Affairs. The Provisional Government also began the transformation of the educational system along liberal and egalitarian lines.

Agriculture and food supply: The agrarian disturbances of 1905–6 had left little doubt that the peasantry would seize state and gentry land the moment central authority was weakened. The Provisional Government had to face additional problems caused by the war. The armed forces had mobilized millions of young men and draught animals, while young women and older men had gone into war production in industry. There was a fundamental shift in the relative strengths of consumers (many of them armed) and producers. At first the producers, both gentry and peasant, responded patriotically enough to the challenge and by 1916 record grain yields were returned. The tsarist government's levy system took a proportion of the surplus at near market prices leaving the producers free to make additional profits on the remainder. However, as the war went on, the producers found it increasingly difficult to buy goods with paper money. The blockade by the Central Powers and the conversion of Russian industry to war production meant that there was a shortage of goods and a corresponding reduction in the incentive to produce the surpluses with which to purchase them. During 1917 these shortages were exacerbated by breakdowns in the overburdened railway system.

The February Revolution was triggered by rioting against bread shortages by the working class women of Petrograd and the Provisional Government was acutely vulnerable to consumer pressure. On 25 March a state monopoly over grain surpluses replaced the levy, and at prices rapidly overtaken by inflation. When it became clear that the result would be a serious reduction in grain deliveries, the government at first insisted that there would be no price increase (4 August), and then doubled the grain price (27 August). The food shortages of the winter of 1917–18 were caused as much by the defects of the transport system, yet the Provisional Government was blamed both for food shortages and for its infrequent and mostly abortive attempts to sequestrate grain by force.

Economic mismanagement was compounded by administrative chaos and political in-fighting between legalistic and radical populists in the Provisional Government. (The legalists were also those most interested in food production while the radicals wanted early moves towards the expropriation of gentry land.) The seeds of intragovernmental tension were sown by A. I. Shingarev, the Kadet minister of agriculture in the First Provisional Government, who created parallel hierarchies of partly-elected land committees and supply committees. In the Coalition, supply came under the jurisdiction of a new Ministry of Food Supply headed by the agricultural economist and Popular-Socialist A. V. Peshekhonov, while Agriculture was entrusted to the radical SR, V. M. CHERNOV who was supported from outside the government by the Peasant Soviets. The re-election of the zemstvos on democratic lines came too late to help Peshekhonov.

On 16 and 27 March, the Provisional Government nationalized lands belonging to the imperial family, but would not countenance further expropriations. However, on 12 July it prohibited land sales to prevent landlords evading future land reform. Four days later Chernov used administrative powers to authorize local land committees to intervene in land use; shortly afterwards the government was obliged to narrow the criteria for such intervention. By

September the government was sending troops to disperse peasant expropriators.

Labour and industry: The Provisional Government faced equivalent dilemmas in the industrial sphere. Its initial sympathy for the industrial working class disappeared as inflationary wage settlements and the erosion of labour discipline sapped war production. On 15 March it conceded the eight-hour day in munitions plants and it was, at first, sympathetic to demands for a minimum wage. By late April it was seeking to limit the powers of FACTORY COMMITTEES, and on 22 August it re-affirmed the right of management to shed labour and deduct pay for meetings in work time. In the autumn Kerensky demonstratively co-opted the head of the Moscow Stock Exchange to run economic policy, while the Menshevik minister Nikitin contemptuously rejected the plea for a national holiday on May Day as a sectional demand.

Nationalities: The Provisional Government's abolition of ethnic discrimination brought it widespread popularity, especially among geographically dispersed minorities such as the JEWS and Tatars (see CRIMEA AND VOLGA TATARS). The geographically compact border nationalities were more interested in autonomy, and it was not long before some of their leaders raised the demand for secession from the Russian State. In theory the nationalities question was to be left to the decision of the Constituent Assembly. However, the Poles had been encouraged to expect better treatment; to encourage Polish resistance to the occupying Central Powers, the Provisional Government promised them qualified independence on 16 March. The Finns denied the competence of the Russian Constituent Assembly on the grounds that their own democratically-elected assembly had inherited the powers of the fallen Emperor-Grand Duke, while there were no plans for their participation in the Russian Constituent Assembly.

In the First Provisional Government, Milyukov (who hoped for the annexation of Constantinople) co-existed with Kerensky (who publicly offered the Estonians their independence). A consensus emerged in response to events. The 'July Crisis' was precipitated by concessions made by the 'inner cabinet' to the Ukrainian Central Rada (see UKRAINE: REVOLUTION AND CIVIL WAR) and exacerbated by a unilateral attempt by the Social-Democratic majority of the Finnish assembly to re-define Russo-Finnish relations. The Provisional Government dissolved the Finnish assembly and clipped the powers of the Rada, insisting, for example, that four of its seven members be non-Ukrainians. On the eve of the October Revolution Tereshchenko publicly denounced the idea of independence for the BALTIC countries on the arguably 'imperialist' grounds that this would return 'Russia' to the unsatisfactory status she had endured prior to Peter the Great.

RA

131

Further Reading

Broder, R.P. and Kerensky, A.F. ed.: *The Russian Provisional Government of 1917: Documents*, 3 vols. Stanford, Ca.: Stanford University Press, 1961.

Ferro, Marc: *The Russian Revolution of February 1917*. London: Routledge & Kegan Paul, 1972.

——— : *October 1917. A Social History of the Russian Revolution*. London: Routledge & Kegan Paul, 1980.

Keep, J.L.H.: *The Russian Revolution. A Study in Mass Mobilization*. London: Weidenfeld, 1976.

Mints, Izaak I.: *Istoriya Velikogo Oktyabrya*, 3 vols. 2nd edn. Moscow: Nauka, 1977–79.

Radkey, Oliver H.: *The Agrarian Foes of Bolshevism: Promise and Default of the Russian Socialist Revolutionaries February to October, 1917*. New York: Columbia University Press, 1958.

Rosenberg, William G.: *Liberals in the Russian Revolution: The Constitutional Democratic Party, 1917–1921*. Princeton, NJ: Princeton University Press, 1974.

Sidorov, A.L. et al. eds.: *Velikaya Oktyabrskaya Sotsialisticheskaya Revolyutsiya: Dokumenty i materialy*, 14 vols. Moscow: Institut Istorii AN SSSR, 1957–63.

Local Power in 1917

The FEBRUARY REVOLUTION spread rapidly across Russia as a series of local seizures of power. On 28 February commissars of the Provisional Committee of the State Duma in Petrograd had assumed control of the telegraph network: a message was flashed to all railway stations announcing the formation of a new government by the State Duma, followed by a flood of news-agency and private telegrams detailing events in the capital. News spread swiftly, despite some efforts to suppress it, and within a matter of days tsarist civil authorities were overthrown throughout the Empire.

In the towns power was assumed by a network of locally-organized committees, most commonly styling themselves 'Committees of Public Organizations' or 'Committees of Public Safety'. Often elected local-government bodies took the lead in their creation, defying the governors and police and endorsing the actions of the Duma, This was most common in the larger towns where the municipal duma would contain a bloc of 'progressive' anti-tsarist councillors. Elsewhere local liberal or socialist groups would take the initiative. At the same time socialist groups and factory workers began to organize SOVIETS. Either at the order of the local committee or soviet, or on their own initiative, supporters of the revolution began to arrest tsarist officials, to occupy government buildings, and to disarm policemen at their posts. In many towns this had a genuinely popular character, as students and workers were joined by professional people, traders and even businessmen. Many policemen and senior officials fled or went into hiding, while junior officials hastened to pledge loyalty to the revolution. The police force and the gendarme corps

effectively ceased to exist: their personnel were rounded up and sent off to fight at the front. Out of all the governors in the Empire, only one governor-general and one city commandant remained temporarily in office.

As most towns in the Empire had some sort of garrison, the attitude of the Army was crucial to the success of the revolution. In some places the soldiers mutinied and broke out of their barracks. In others the officers were able to prevent this by declaring for the revolution, and the whole garrison would parade through the town in celebration. In either case, the soldiers were quick to set up their own garrison committees or soviets: the unquestioned authority of officers vanished with the old order.

In the smallest towns and in the countryside, the news took slightly longer to spread and the revolution sometimes needed prompting by emissaries from larger centres. Even so, the old tsarist authorities did not long survive. In the countryside the PEASANTS began to drive out the police and repudiate the authority of the land captains, changing unpopular peasant elders and establishing their own elected committees at village and sub-district level.

This great upheaval was relatively bloodless, and was marked by an atmosphere of general excitement and optimism. However, by destroying traditional bases of authority and the existing apparatus of coercion, it inaugurated a prolonged struggle to build and hold local power.

The Committees of Public Organizations

The Committees of Public Organizations which assumed power in towns all over the Empire generally began as very small, informal groups of important local figures. They almost always included representatives of the municipal duma and local heroes of 'society' (such as veterans of the First and Second Dumas, or army officers shunted into the reserve under suspicion of liberalism). They invariably grew rapidly to include representatives of local unions and societies, the district zemstvo, local garrison, workers. The committees of district and provincial capitals began to assume jurisdiction over their whole district or province, at first in a somewhat declaratory fashion, but later by inclusion of delegates from lesser towns and the peasantry.

The committees, with few exceptions, may be thought of as representing a social and political coalition in marked contrast to the 'dual power' of Petrograd. The 'enfranchized strata' of tsarist society may have created them, but their expansion afforded a plurality of seats to the 'democratic elements' (meaning principally workers', soldiers' and peasants' organizations and the socialist parties). The local sovereignty of the committees was recognized by both sides, each sending representatives to participate in executive and directive organs. This local unity ultimately proved fragile, but the rate of its decay should not be exaggerated.

In the first days of the revolution, the committees took

control of the urgent questions of food supply and preservation of order, and imposed their supervision over other aspects of civil administration. The Moscow Committee of Public Organizations, one of the largest, within a week had appointed 27 commissars, 14 commissions and 3 councils, taken over the city commandant's administration, and was monitoring the public services provided by the municipal duma. One of the greatest problems was policing: during the upheaval volunteer 'militias' of students, workers and tradesmen had kept a sort of order, but it was more difficult to establish a more permanent force. Local committees tried to establish a 'militia' on a regular basis, but were desperately short of money and recruits. The committees also made it their business to 'democratize' government and public agencies in their area by assigning to them representatives of the 'democratic elements'. The existing municipal duma and zemstvo were obvious targets, having been elected on very limited franchises. None of these agencies was able to resist committee control. Ironically, the first serious challenge to the committees' power came from above – from the PROVISIONAL GOVERNMENT.

Policy of the Provisional Government

The Provisional Government, despite its official optimism adopted a somewhat cautious policy towards the local committees. Operating with very little knowledge of what was happening outside the capital, the government's first concern was to create for itself reliable local agents to replace the tsarist governors. Its second concern was to stave off anarchy by replacing 'revolutionary' organs with a new 'legal' institutional structure. In this the predominantly Kadet government displayed a certain ideological adherence to the unitary and relatively centralized state. Its attitude was also coloured by its experience of 'dual power' in Petrograd and by a growing desire to pre-empt a socialist-dominated CONSTITUENT ASSEMBLY, by presenting it with a ready-made framework of laws and institutions.

The government caused an outcry amongst the local committees by appointing the zemstvo chairmen as its local 'commissars': the committees insisted on appointing the proposed provincial, district and town commissars themselves. The government compounded the problem by insisting on the right of its commissars to direct and supervise the work of the committees. It also created 'inspectors of militia' to ensure central control over the building of a professional policing agency. It strove to limit the practice of 'democratization' of local institutions, was dilatory about arranging finance for the committees while denying their right to levy local taxes, and placed many other curbs on their powers.

In practice many of these issues were settled amicably, and the government succeeded in creating a more regular hierarchy of province, district and town committees and

commissars. However, its attitude weakened the committees just as they were beginning to face major social problems. The government was determined to replace the committees as swiftly as possible by a new 'legal' system of local government, based upon the zemstvo and municipal duma elected on a fully-democratic basis. A Conference on the Reform of Local Government was set up at the Ministry of Internal Affairs, and a stream of legislation began to emerge in April. The principle of elected local government agencies was extended to all parts of the Empire. Municipal duma elections were held between May and August. Elections to a new sub-district level zemstvo commenced in late August and were only partially completed by December; the new zemstvo at district or province level met (if at all) between November and January. Once the new organs were elected, the committees were supposed to disband, but this did not always occur.

The government further complicated the picture by creating a plethora of 'special agents' for procurement and other aspects of economic administration, and by establishing hierarchies of food supply committees and land committees. The result was the co-existence for most of 1917 of a variety of 'recognized' agencies and a host of 'private' ones, such as soviets.

Fragmentation of local power

The fragile coalition represented by the local committees began to decay in the face of mounting social and political tension. This was not a uniform process throughout the Empire (see SPREAD OF BOLSHEVISM TO THE INTERIOR) but a pattern can none the less be observed.

National political developments were important: the April Crisis raised the war issue throughout the country, the July Days the prospect of anarchy, and the KORNILOV Affair the prospect of counter-revolution. Local newspapers were sufficiently organized to cover national events in some detail, if only in the form of telegraph reports. Local activists took their cues from developments in Petrograd, the same pattern was expected to reproduce itself locally. The rapid growth of political parties and other mass organizations helped the sharing-out of the experience and ideas of the centre, as did the human tide of travelling delegates and agitators and deserters sweeping across the country.

Local social and political conflict also tended to follow a common pattern. Wherever there was an army garrison, for example, the same issues surfaced, rooted in the common experience of conscript soldiers. The first civil disturbances in the towns after the February Revolution almost always involved garrison troops – running riot, seeking out deserters or draft-dodgers, arresting officers or officials. They were concerned for allowances payable to soldiers' wives, and for the release of men for agricultural labour. Gradually their disturbances took on a more anti-war character: troops refused to leave the towns (where they normally spent the winter) to go for spring training, they refused to depart for the front in the normal rotation of units, they rebelled against the restoration of the death penalty and the use of shock battalions, they were incensed by the Kornilov Affair. Similar processes of radicalization can be discerned amongst WORKERS in the face of economic collapse. Both workers and soldiers came to reject the authority of any but their own organizations: soviets, FACTORY COMMITTEES, garrison committees. The peasantry began to reject all outside authority, retreating into village self-government and causing immense economic disruption. The growth of separatism amongst members of national minorities was marked, leading to demands for separate national military units and to the creation of their own local organizations. (See section titled SPREADING THE REVOLUTION.)

By July there were clear signs of disintegration, but the situation was stabilized by the success of the SOCIALIST REVOLUTIONARIES and MENSHEVIKS in gaining control of most of the local institutions of power. They controlled most of the local committees, provided a good proportion of the government commissars, dominated most local soviets and garrison committees, and were very successful in the municipal duma elections. The July Days in Petrograd found little response in the provinces, as a result. However, the events of July and August proved disastrous. The Provisional Government floundered as opinion amongst the upper strata of society began to move to the right. Failure to achieve progress on peace, prevent economic collapse, or pursue social reform, was compounded by increasing resort to repression. As the government rapidly lost support, the authority of its local agents crumbled. Finally, the Kornilov Affair destroyed the credibility of any coalition in the eyes of the 'democratic elements', as was made clear at the Democratic Conference in September.

The immediate response to the Kornilov Affair in the 'democratic' camp was the creation of variously-titled 'Committees to Save the Revolution', in defiance of Provisional Government orders. These bodies had a grim significance in the almost universal exclusion of Kadets from membership. They declared themselves to be the supreme local authority, conducted arrests and searches, dismissed Kadet government commissars. Many refused to disband after the emergency was over, some later becoming MILITARY-REVOLUTIONARY COMMITTEES during the BOLSHEVIK takeover.

After the Kornilov Affair, there was a further fragmentation of power as the SR and Menshevik grip on the organizations of the 'democratic elements' was challenged from below. Government authority was repudiated outright in particular localities. Such 'republics' had occurred earlier in the year (most notably in KRONSTADT, Nizhni Novgorod and Tsaritsyn in the spring and summer), but now became widespread. Agrarian violence escalated. The

Provisional Government began to assign significant numbers of troops to its commissars for the restoration of order, although there is little evidence that they proved reliable. The extent of anarchy should not be exaggerated: most towns maintained relative order, even in October, but the 'official' organs of power had little real authority. During the OCTOBER REVOLUTION municipal duma leaders (socialist and liberal) set up new Committees to Save the Revolution to oppose the Bolsheviks, and it took several months for soviet power to become widely established. The Bolsheviks at first pursued an ambivalent policy towards elected local government organs, but in January 1918 the People's Commissariat for Internal Affairs directed that they be liquidated in favour of local soviets.   HJW

Further Reading

Andreev, A.M.: *Mestnye Sovety i organy burzhuaznoi vlasti (1917 gg)*. Moscow: 1983.

Raleigh, Donald J.: *Revolution on the Volga: 1917 in Saratov*. Ithaca, NY: 1986.

Rosenberg, William G.: *Liberals in the Russian Revolution: The Constitutional Democratic Party, 1917–1921*. Princeton, NJ: 1974.

Startsev, V.I.: *Vnutrennyaya politika Vremennogo pravitel'stva (pervogo sostava)*. Leningrad: 1980.

The Soviets

Attempts to connect the Russian soviets with earlier forms of lower class radical democracy – such as the medieval communes, Cromwell's soldier councils of 1647, the sansculottes sections of the revolutionary commune of Paris of 1792–4 and the Paris Commune of 1871 – have been useful only in so far as they have opened up a historical perspective and framework for a comparative study of radical democracy and its institutions.

But Russian soviets, as distinct from trade unions and socialist parties, were *sui generis*, and can be traced no further back than the 1905 REVOLUTION. Chiefly it was from the October General Strike to the December uprising in Moscow that workers in some 45–50 towns all over Russia elected deputies to local city-wide strike committees. These became the representative organs of the entire working class in a given locality, and were commonly known as Soviets (Councils) of Workers Deputies. The only soviets with some Russia-wide significance and authority were in St Petersburg and, to a lesser extent, in Moscow.

1905

Distinctive of the 1905 soviets was their introduction of *de facto* representation of the working class; their emergence from direct elections in factory assemblies (in St Petersburg 500 workers elected one deputy, in Moscow – 400, in Odessa – 100, in Kostroma – 50); their subordination to the assemblies which retained the right of accountability, including instant recall over their deputies; and their widely acknowledged status and authority as 'workers' parliaments' and, occasionally, even as 'our own workers' government'.

While the 1905 soviets were a much admired exercise in workers' self-government and participatory democracy in a country lacking parliamentary institutions, they were equally impressive as combat organizations fighting for workers' economic and political interests more effectively than the fledgeling trade unions and the relatively small, divisive socialist parties. Such success, however, led to an over-estimation of the soviets' national role and strength and to an under-estimation of the stamina and repressive powers of the tsarist regime.

Thus, what began modestly as an 'organization of the local proletariat for the successful struggle for the betterment of its economic and legal position' (Statute of the soviet of Kostroma), climaxed in St Petersburg and a number of provincial soviets at the end of October in an unrealistic attempt to enforce an eight-hour working day. That in turn led to the isolation of the soviets from the rest of oppositional society and to the ignominious defeat of the November strike.

In parallel, the soviets' successful enforcement of the freedom of the press, assembly and association, and their armed prevention of pogroms in St Petersburg (October), Baku (November) and Odessa (December), led not merely to their assumption of some governmental functions in St Petersburg, Samara, Taganrog and Rostov, but to outright seizures of power in Novorossiisk, Chita, Baku and KRASNOYARSK. The bloody repression of the December uprisings in Moscow and Rostov sealed the fate of the soviets.

The professed political aim of all soviets was not, however, 'soviet power', but the convocation of a CONSTITUENT ASSEMBLY and the establishment of a democratic republic. Nor did any of the socialist parties, who were represented on the soviets, ever demand soviet power. The soviets, however, did have some influence on the revolutionary strategy of the MENSHEVIK and BOLSHEVIK wings of Russian social democracy and a lasting impact on that of the SR MAXIMALISTS.

The Mensheviks viewed the soviets as part of their dual-power strategy in Russia's bourgeois revolution. This assigned to soviets, municipalities, trade unions and workers' congresses the role of local organs of revolution. After the overthrow of tsarism, these institutions were to form a militant opposition to the expected liberal bourgeois government. Still with a bourgeois revolution in mind and a commitment to a parliamentary republic, the minimalist Mensheviks did not see in the soviets possible forms of workers' government and participatory democracy.

As for the Bolsheviks, before 1917 neither LENIN nor TROTSKY is on record as having developed a theory of soviets as an alternative to a constituent assembly. Trotsky

seems to have come closest to a concept of soviet democracy as workers' self-government à la Paris Commune. He extolled the soviets as 'the embryo of revolutionary power', but the function he assigned to them was limited to 'laying the foundation of a new order until the convening of a constituent assembly'. He did not specify what, if any, functions they might have afterwards.

Lenin, the party-minded centralist and suspicious of workers' spontaneity, was wary of soviets as organs of workers' self-government, but valued them as 'indispensable organs of insurrection' and 'rudiments of revolutionary power'. But he expected that victorious uprising would inevitably create other (unspecified) organs.

The Socialist Revolutionaries were a minority in most soviets, but fiercely resisted Bolshevik attempts to impose their own agenda. In their call for the creation of 'soviets of workers, peasants and soldiers', which would include all 'toiling people', they anticipated the soviets of 1917.

It was the SR Maximalists alone who in 1905 developed a fully fledged ideology of soviet power and democracy. Rejecting parliamentarism, political parties and even trade unions, they championed a 'communalist' or soviet 'Republic of Toilers', giving grounds for their claim of 1917 to have been the originators of 'All Power to Soviets'.

1917

Founded largely by members of the socialist intelligentsia, commonly Mensheviks and independent socialists, the soviets of 1917 came into being after February.

The Petrograd Soviet of Workers' and Soldiers' Deputies became the pioneer and leading authority of the soviet movement when it was convened on 27 February by a Provisional Executive Committee consisting of intellectuals, party workers and Duma deputies, mostly Mensheviks. Earlier that day, the Committee had invited workers in plants and factories and soldiers of the mutinous garrison to elect and send delegates to the first session of the soviet in the Tauride Palace.

The newly elected Executive Committee reported the foundation of the Petrograd soviet, consisting of 'the elected representatives of plants and factories, of revolutionary military units, as well as of democratic and socialist parties and groups', thus setting the pattern for the creation of soviets all over Russia. By May there were already 400 soviets in all the larger towns, in August 600, and on the eve of the OCTOBER REVOLUTION 900.

Paralleled later by a congress of peasant soviets, the Petrograd soviet's authority was reinforced and legitimized by a conference of more than 150 soviets, convened in Petrograd at the end of March, and by the First Congress of Soviets, which convened in June when its 1,090 delegates represented more than 400 soviets and some twenty million workers and soldiers.

The distinguishing features of the 1917 soviets were the prominence of the soldier element, the leading role of the socialist intelligentsia, and the implantation of a political party system which climaxed in the contest between a Menshevik-SR bloc and the Bolsheviks for the control of the soviets, ending in Bolshevik victory.

The mode of representation adopted from the beginning favoured the soldiers: allowing every battalion (250 men) one deputy, as against one deputy for every 1,000 workers in Petrograd (500 in Moscow and between 300–400 in most other soviets); it rewarded the garrisons for the crucial role they had played in the revolution, while the garrisons in turn provided the soviets with military backing.

The leading role played by socialist intellectuals and parties in the foundation of soviets, and in their executives and commissions, resulted in their ultimate domination of the soviets. While this weakened the participatory democracy and self-government of the rank and file of workers and soldiers, nevertheless by recognizing rival socialist parties and accepting the formation of rival political caucuses in the soviet plenum, it also created the mechanics of democratic procedures and control in the election of deputies and office-holders. The resultant political pluralism prevented the manipulation of soviets by any one single political party or group.

While the soviets, in the absence of a national parliament and the delayed appearance of democratized municipal dumas, constituted quasi-parliaments of the 'revolutionary democracy' and a battleground for the political contest between the Menshevik-SR bloc and the irreconcilable Bolshevik opposition, they did not perceive themselves as an alternative to the Constituent Assembly. Indeed all soviets were staunchly committed to the Constituent Assembly and its 'speediest convocation' and, until well after the October Revolution, that included Bolshevik-dominated soviets such as Krasnoyarsk and Eniseisk or the radical soviet of Kronstadt.

The early political history of the soviets is largely the success story of the Menshevik-SR bloc. It reached its apogee in the Congress of Peasant Soviets late in May when 537 SR delegates confronted 14 Bolsheviks, and at the First Congress of Soviets in June where 285 SR delegates and 248 Menshevik delegates faced a Bolshevik opposition of 105 delegates. This dominant position was, however, frittered away, largely as a result of the Menshevik-SR coalition policies which alienated many of their supporters in the soviets so that, by September 1917, the Bolsheviks gained majorities in many of the urban soviets, including those of Petrograd and Moscow.

The Second Congress of Soviets convened on 26 October marked the beginning of a process by which the soviets were turned into agents of the central government of Peoples' Commissars. By means fair, foul and terrorist, Bolshevik majorities were secured and on 14 June 1918 Menshevik and SR deputies were expelled, followed on 9 July by the Left SRs. This process culminated in the Soviet CONSTITUTION OF THE RSFSR of July 1918, which defined the soviets as 'the local organs of the state', whose primary task was 'the implementation of all the decrees of the relevant higher organs of the state', and in the resolution of the 8th Party Congress of March 1919 which urged 'the complete dominance (of the Communist Party) in the state organizations of today – the soviets'. IG

Further Reading

Andreev, A.N.: *The Soviets of Workers and Soldiers Deputies on the Eve of the October Revolution, March–October 1917.* Moscow: 1967.

Anweiler, Oskar: *The Soviets: The Russian Workers, Peasants and Soldiers Councils, 1905–1921.* New York: 1974.

Ferro, Marc: *Des Soviets au Communisme Bureaucratique.* Paris: 1980.

Getzler, Israel: 'The Bolshevik Onslaught on the Non-Party "Political Profile" of the Petersburg Soviet of Workers" Deputies October–November 1905'. *Revolutionary Russia*, vol. 5, December 1992. Frank Cass: 1992.

Keep, John L.H.: *The Russian Revolution: A Study In Mass Mobilization.* New York: 1976.

The October Revolution

The PROVISIONAL GOVERNMENT was overthrown in Petrograd on 25 October 1917 (OS). A blank shot fired from the cruiser *Avrora*, anchored in the river opposite the Winter Palace, gave the signal for Bolshevik Red Guards, led by V. A. ANTONOV-OVSEENKO, to seize the government's last, symbolic stronghold of power. The meagre forces at KERENSKY's disposal, consisting only of a handful of cadets and WOMEN SOLDIERS, put up brave but hopeless resistance and during the night of October 25/26 the Palace fell almost without bloodshed. Coordination of the action had been entrusted to the Petrograd Soviet's MILITARY-REVOLUTIONARY COMMITTEE; and its success allowed the announcement to be made to the Second All-Russian Congress of Soviets that power in the country had been transferred to the soviets. The Congress of Soviets took swift measures to establish a new administration which was to be called the Council of People's Commissars (Sovnarkom). The position of premier, or 'chairman', was given to Vladimir Ilyich Lenin (see LENIN'S GOVERNMENT 1917–1923).

Since April 1917 the BOLSHEVIK party's policy had been to crush the Provisional Government; the main uncertainty among Bolsheviks had arisen over timing. On 10 October, their Central Committee met to consider the matter. Lenin, returning incognito from his hiding place in Finland, urged immediate insurrection, but even many left-wing Bolsheviks were unsure of their support among Petrograd workers. Nor did the BOLSHEVIKS yet hold all the urban SOVIETS outside Petrograd and Moscow; and their influence in both the Russian countryside and non-Russian areas remained small.

The right wing in the Bolshevik Central Committee argued that the party would find itself politically vulnerable as soon as it grabbed power. Both ZINOVIEV and KAMENEV

Figures 16 and 17   Winter Palace after seizure.

felt that Lenin vastly exaggerated the likelihood of sympathetic revolutions quickly breaking out elsewhere in Europe: a Bolshevik-led socialist regime in Petrograd, in their view, would quickly collapse. Many liberal, conservative and reactionary circles in Russia at the time held the same view. Lenin was criticized, too, on the grounds that an instant seizure of power would be seen as an attempt to set up the dictatorship of a single party. TROTSKY, who had joined the Bolsheviks in midsummer 1917, took this last objection to heart and proposed that the moves against the Provisional Government should be timed to coincide with the Second All-Russian Congress of Soviets later in the month. Like Lenin, Trotsky maintained that the elections in the urban soviets were running in favour of the Bolsheviks. A vote was taken. Lenin carried the day by ten votes to two.

The Central Committee decision was not sufficient to guarantee the acquiescence of broader sections of the party. A second meeting was therefore called for 16 October to which party representatives from the Petrograd city committee and other regional bodies were invited. Again the vote went in Lenin's favour, this time by nineteen to two (with four abstentions).

The reasoning behind Lenin's policy deserves attention. He and his supporters assumed that they were living in the age of European socialist revolution. The breaking of any link in the chain of worldwide capitalism should therefore be every socialist's aim; for it would enable the other links the more easily to be sundered. Furthermore, there could be no 'democratic peace' in Europe unless it was preceded by continental socialist revolution. Left to themselves, the capitalists of whichever of the two warring coalitions won the Great War would impose a treaty that would conflict with the interests of several of Europe's peoples. The Europe-wide installation of socialist regimes, by contrast, would facilitate the social and economic reconstruction of the continent in political harmony. Russia would be a major beneficiary. Indeed Lenin argued that utter material ruin awaited the old Romanov empire if the Provisional Government stayed in power. Only a socialist administration and socialist policies could stave off the economic collapse. A mixture of reforms from above (including the nationalization of large-scale industry and finance as well as the expropriation of the landed gentry in favour of the peasants) and popular initiative from below (including WORKERS' CONTROL in the factories and peasant land seizures) needed to be undertaken. Lenin also maintained that forces on the Russian political far right would gain the upper hand if no preventive action were undertaken.

Thus considerations of revolutionary duty were entwined with those of pragmatism. There was a feeling, too, that problems existed only to be solved, and that those difficulties which seemed enormous would prove amenable to treatment once the energies of the revolutionary 'masses' were applied to them.

The revival in the Bolshevik party's fortunes had been dramatic. Since early July 1917 Lenin, its major leader, had been hunted by the police and had taken refuge in Finland. Other central leaders like Kamenev and Trotsky had been arrested. Yet the party had never been completely suppressed. In truth, Karensky had not seriously sought to achieve this end. Outside Petrograd the effect of the July Days had not been unduly bothersome; Bolshevik party committees had continued to participate openly in public life. The Central Committee, moreover, did not cease its operations, and the central party press resumed activity. The temporary loss of Lenin and a few others did the party no lasting harm. The Bolsheviks had a large supply of talented organizers at the local as well as the central level. What difficulties they had in midsummer, furthermore, were dispelled in the aftermath of the KORNILOV mutiny. New Bolshevik party members were being registered in their thousands in September and early October. The Bolsheviks could justifiably claim to constitute the only substantial political alternative to the status quo.

Meanwhile even sections of the Kadet party regarded Kerensky as doomed and looked to sterner and more right-wing policies to save Russia. His government had become dangerously isolated from its middle-class supporters. His administrative hold on the provinces was weakening fast. Several towns, like Tsaritsyn and KRONSTADT, were practically socialist mini-states. Bolsheviks were steadily piling up victories in the re-elections of urban soviets in northern, central and south-eastern Russia.

The planning of the uprising was mainly in Trotsky's hands. Operating through the Petrograd Soviet's Military-Revolutionary Committee, he was able to demonstrate that the preparations were not an exclusively Bolshevik affair, for Left Socialist Revolutionaries also belonged to the Committee. Last-minute endeavours were made by the Provisional Government to thwart the insurrection. Bolshevik newspaper offices were raided. But Kerensky lacked a strong local contingent of troops. These Trotsky had in abundance. Moreover the armed forces at the frontline were averse to being drawn into civil political conflicts. Foreign support, too, was unavailable to Kerensky. The Bolsheviks were later to express their relief that the exigencies of the fighting on the Western front made it impossible for the British and French governments effectively to intervene on Kerensky's side. Trotsky certainly handled the situation with skill, but the odds against the Military-Revolutionary Committee's success on 25 October were not long.

Greater difficulties began as soon as the Provisional Government had fallen. The announcement of the presentation of power to the Second Congress of Soviets appalled the MENSHEVIKS and SOCIALIST REVOLUTIONARIES (SRs) attending the Congress; they had backed the Provisional Government in the previous months and most of them repudiated Bolshevik assertions that a purely socialist administration could solve the country's problems. A minority within these two anti-Bolshevik parties favoured the formation of such an administration. The left-wing Menshevik MARTOV had come round to such a viewpoint, and his associates in the Menshevik party were gaining ground. The left wing of the SRs, despairing of pulling its party along with it, formed a separate Party of Left SRs in September. But only the Bolshevik delegates to the Congress of Soviets were entirely happy with the seizure of power. The Mensheviks and SRs strode out of the hall in protest, leaving the Left SRs who declined the invitation to join the new government. Consequently Sovnarkom was initially composed solely of Bolsheviks. Lenin was annoyed that he could not persuade the Left SRs to join; but it entirely accorded with his wishes that the Mensheviks and SRs had walked out. On no account did he want them in his government.

Lenin and Trotsky put this case forcefully at Bolshevik Central Committee meetings in November 1917, but they failed to convince several other members of the Bolshevik Central Committee and Sovnarkom. The composition of the revolutionary government became a sticking point. The Bolshevik Central Committee sessions of 10 and 16 October had sanctioned measures for a seizure of power but had omitted to specify the desirable make-up of the new administration. The debate now came to the fore. Lenin found several leading members of his party ranged against him on the grounds that, if there was to be a soviet government, then other socialist parties including the Mensheviks and the SRs ought to be included in it. In their view, a 'homogeneous socialist government' was required. This was also a widespread opinion among factory workers and other lower social strata which had voted for the Bolsheviks in the soviets before October. The exact proportion of the pro-Bolshevik voters who held this view is unknown; but it must have been substantial. The Mensheviks and SRs made use of their chances. The Railwaymen's Union was led by Mensheviks, and its central executive body reacted to the Bolshevik seizure of power by threatening to hold a rail strike until a 'homogeneous socialist government' was formed. Faced by the intransigence of Lenin and Trotsky, moreover, several leading Bolshevik advocates of political compromise with other socialists resigned collectively from their People's Commissariats. They comprised not only such notable right-wingers as V.P. Milyutin and V.P. Nogin but also A. G. SHLYAPNIKOV.

Lenin kept his head. Decrees on peace and on the land were issued within 24 hours of the seizure of power. Messages were dispatched to Bolsheviks in the country to establish their own soviet power; and, although Sovnarkom rushed troops to key areas such as Moscow, Lenin emphasized that local soviets should if at all possible undertake the transfer of power mainly with their own local resources.

Much effort was put into spreading the message of the Second Congress of Soviets. Bolshevik newspapers increased their print-runs. Agitators were sent into the smaller townships and the countryside where the Bolshevik programme was little known. Poster ART appeared in profusion. The images of the Bolshevik party leaders became more familiar to the public. As the network of Russian urban soviets declared allegiance to Sovnarkom, the campaign of PROPAGANDA increased. TRADE UNIONS and FACTORY COMMITTEES enhanced it. Bolsheviks in Petrograd and in the provinces faced their problems confidently. Peasants were seizing land; workers were taking over their factories (see PEASANTS; WORKERS). The early strikes by civil servants in the old ministries collapsed. A truce was arranged on the Eastern front, and fraternization ensued between Russian and German troops. A European socialist revolution was thought imminent. Not all Russian troops remained on active service; but their desertion from the army was no great concern to the government at this juncture, since it was hoped that they would carry a pro-Bolshevik message back to their native villages. The triumph of Sovnarkom over the counter-revolution seemed complete. Kerensky assembled forces under General Krasnov to mount an offensive but they were defeated by soldiers and Red Guards loyal to the soviet authorities.

Lenin held firm. He was encouraged by the apparent vindication of his revolutionary optimism as much popular support for Sovnarkom remained and as 'soviet power' spread to other regions of the country (see SPREAD OF BOLSHEVISM). In any case, the Menshevik and SR leaderships categorically refused to join a government which included Lenin and Trotsky. The railway strike collapsed. Kadet newspapers were banned by the Bolsheviks, and the Mensheviks and SRs were harassed. Meanwhile the Left SRs had second thoughts about a coalition with the Bolsheviks and entered negotiations with them in November; and gradually, in the winter of 1917–1918, there occurred a return of those Bolsheviks who had walked out of the Bolshevik Central Committee and the Sovnarkom.

These few weeks in Russian history after 25 October 1917 were momentous: no previous national government had ever been constituted by socialists alone. Even the regime's bitterest opponents acknowledged that an event of epochal significance had taken place. There were disagreements among Bolsheviks as to how fast socialism itself could be introduced. Lenin argued that the country's economic condition ruled out the possibility of an instant socialist reformation, and that elements of capitalism needed time to mature in Russia; he declared that, in comparison with Germany, Russia was still 'backward'. Others such as BUKHARIN maintained that a comprehensive socialist programme of reconstruction should be immediately imposed. But all of them at least agreed that a start should be made. On the other hand, there were many socialists, not only in Russia, who contended that what had happened had little to do with socialism. They denied that a popular uprising had occurred in October; describing it instead as a coup d'état by a single fanatical party. The violence attending the birth of the first socialist state quickly became massive. The Bolsheviks talked openly about the need for a 'dictatorship of the proletariat' supported by the peasantry; and the repressive measures against other sections of the population were drastic (see VECHEKA).

Not even the adversaries of the Bolsheviks in the October Revolution had anticipated how great the country's travail would soon become. Food supplies fell precipitely, and peasants would not release grain in return for a quickly depreciating currency. Raw materials to the factories contracted. Enterprises closed in ever larger numbers. Transport was disrupted. The national economy was isolated from world trade; financial support from abroad vanished. Capital flowed out of the country. The German and Austro-Hungarian governments maintained their military menace to the young Soviet republic and in March 1918 were to compel the signature of the treaty of Brest-Litovsk. Political support at home did not come up to the Bolshevik party's expectations. Less than a quarter of the electorate voted for the Bolsheviks in the CONSTITUENT ASSEMBLY elections.

The picture was not entirely sombre. The Bolsheviks also could point a brighter aspect in their situation. They were not without their positive achievements. Mass political participation was encouraged by them. Workers were promoted into positions of public responsibility; and the peasants, at least for a while, were allowed to organize themselves as they wished. A zeal for the construction of a better world than that of capitalism was fostered. Yet a CIVIL WAR was on the horizon. Perhaps Russia after the fall of the Romanovs would have plunged into a bloodbath in any event; but the Bolsheviks by their acts of intolerance had made it even likelier.   RS

Further Reading

Abramovich, R.: *The Soviet Revolution, 1917–1939.* New York: 1962.

Ferro, M.: *October 1917.* London: 1980.

Getzler, I.: *Martov: A Political Biography of a Russian Social Democrat.* London: 1967.

Keep, J.H.L.: *The Debate on Soviet Power. Minutes of the All-Russian Central Executive Committee of Soviets, October 1917–January 1918.* Oxford: 1979.

———— : *The Russian Revolution: A Study in Mass Mobilisation.* London: 1976.

Mandel, D.: *The Petrograd Workers and the Soviet Seizure of Power.* London: 1984.

Rabinowitch, A.: *The Bolsheviks Come To Power.* New York: 1976.

Service, R.: *The Bolshevik Party in Revolution: A Study in Organisational Change.* London: 1979.

Sukhanov, N.: *The Russian Revolution*, ed. J. Carmichael. Oxford: 1955.

Trotsky, L.: *History of the Russian Revolution.* London: 1967.

The Constituent Assembly

The idea of a 'Constituent Assembly' for Russia was derived from the French revolutionary assemblies of 1789–91 and 1848. Yet for all their interest in the French Revolutions, the Russian intelligentsia expressed little interest in a Constituent Assembly until the formation of People's Will Narodnaya Volya in 1879. People's Will popularized the idea by demanding that Alexander II hand over power to an 'All-People's Constituent Assembly' as a precondition for a ceasefire in their campaign of terror. Thenceforth, the demand formed part of the programme of all Russian POPULIST organizations. Bourgeois-liberal groups, such as the Union of Liberation and the Kadet (Constitutional-Democratic) party were more circumspect, agreeing with the principle, but accepting that constitutional government might be reached in stages in agreement with the monarchy. G. V. PLEKHANOV developed Marxist reservations about a Constituent Assembly at the 1903 London Congress of the RSDRP, insisting that *'salus revolutionis suprema lex ... if the elections seemed to us unsuccessful, we should try to dissolve it (the Assembly) not after two years, but if possible, after two weeks.'*

On 9 January 1905, huge processions of workers led by Father Gapon converged on the Winter Palace in St Petersburg. They bore a petition demanding 'the election of a constituent assembly on the basis of universal, secret, and equal suffrage'. The massacre of the petitioners apotheosized their demands which were immediately adopted by all the revolutionary opposition, though the Kadets and Marxists still maintained their reservations. These reservations were sharpened over the winter of 1905–06, when the Marxists glimpsed a 'superior' form of democracy in the SOVIETS, while many Kadets were prepared to give the First State Duma a chance to succeed. The crushing of the revolution and Prime Minister STOLYPIN's anti-democratic coup (3 June 1907) dashed all these hopes. Still, the idea of a Constituent Assembly was deep-rooted and during the First World War, A. F. KERENSKY and V. M. ZENZINOV tried to create a spontaneous 'Constituent Assembly' at meetings of bourgeois and working class organizations.

With the collapse of the Imperial regime in February 1917, all Russian parties proclaimed their support for a Constituent Assembly, in whose favour Grand Duke Michael had abdicated and to whose speedy convocation the PROVISIONAL GOVERNMENT was committed. Yet the assembly did not meet for a further ten months. The reasons for this fatal delay were first, the government's preoccupation with the war and internal political crises; second, the prior need to prepare new electoral lists and reorganize local government on a democratic basis; and third, the predominance of Kadet lawyers fearful of the radical results of a precipitate election in the preparatory Juridical Commission. The government's postponement of the election from 17 September to 12 November brought it considerable odium, BOLSHEVIK agitators insisting that only a Soviet government could guarantee the convocation of the Constituent Assembly.

The elections: Russia's only multi-party election took place in November 1917 in a country girding its loins for civil war and lacking an acknowledged central government. The full results were never established yet nearly 41.6 million votes were counted (see Table 6).

Table 6 Estimated results of Constituent Assembly election, November 1917

Party	Votes cast (millions)	Seats won
PSR	15.8*	299
Ukrainian SRs etc.	4.9	81
Other national minority SRs	c. 1.0	19
Mensheviks	1.36	18
Popular-Socialists etc.	0.5	4
Ukrainian SDs		2
Kadets and Right	3.2	17
Other national parties	c. 2.5	56
Left SRs	*	39
Bolsheviks	9.84	168
Totals	41.68	703

*The PSR lists were prepared before the party schism so the PSR and LSR votes are indistinguishable.

The results were a bitter disappointment to those Bolsheviks who had looked to the Constituent Assembly to legitimize their coup, but Lenin had no doubt about the superiority of Soviet democracy and prepared to meet the Constituent Assembly head on. On 26 November the opposition was reduced by the arrest of several Kadet deputies while a quorum of 400 was established ensuring that the assembly would not meet until Bolshevik power was consolidated.

The tragic session: On 5 January 1918 (OS), the Constituent Assembly gathered in the Tauride Palace, Petrograd. Welcoming demonstrators were shot down by Bolshevik Red Guards in scenes reminding Maxim GORKY of 'Bloody Sunday' 1905. (SR plans for a larger armed demonstration had been shelved following an abortive attempt to assassinate LENIN on 1 January.) Drunken sailors under

the anarchist-communist A. G. Zhelezhyakov filled the galleries. Over SR protests, the Assembly was opened by Ya. M. SVERDLOV, the Bolshevik head of state, who invited the deputies to support the measures taken by the Soviet government: the expropriation of the landlords and bourgeoisie; the introduction of a universal labour obligation; the formation of the RED ARMY; the ceasefire and peace negotiations with the Central Powers; the denunciation of foreign debt; the recognition of Finnish and Armenian independence etc. In the election of President, the Soviet government candidate, Maria A. SPIRIDONOVA, leader of the Left SRs, received 151 votes as against 244 for V. M. CHERNOV, leader of the PSR. Chernov proposed the continuation, with only slight modification, of the policies of the moderate left under the fallen Provisional Government, adding that each act of the Constituent Assembly should be confirmed by referendum. The MENSHEVIK Leader, I. G. TSERETELI followed with a penetrating analysis of the pitfalls awaiting the Bolsheviks. When the Assembly refused to rubber-stamp the programme of the Soviet government, the Bolsheviks and Left SRs denounced it and walked out. The majority then passed a law socializing the land, a declaration to the Allies urging their agreement to a democratic general peace while the ceasefire continued, and a resolution proclaiming Russia a democratic, federal republic. Zhelezhyakov dispersed the deputies in the early hours of 6 January. The Assembly was dissolved by decree of the Bolshevik-Left SR Soviets on the same day on the grounds that it could 'only play the role of justifying the struggle of the bourgeois counter-revolution for the overthrow of Soviet power'. That night two leading Kadet deputies were beaten to death by Bolshevik sailors.

Postscript: After the revolt of the Czechoslovak Legion in Siberia, an anti-Bolshevik SR Provisional Government was set up in Samara on 6 June 1918, entitled the COMMITTEE OF MEMBERS OF THE CONSTITUENT ASSEMBLY (KOMUCH). Early in 1921 an Assembly of Members of the Constituent Assembly gathered in Paris. Both organizations attempted to legitimize the 'democratic counter-revolution' against Bolshevism.   RA

Further Reading

Malchevskii, I.S, ed: *Vserossiiskoe Uchreditel'noe Sobranie.* Moscow and Leningrad: Gosizdat, 1930.

Radkey, Oliver H.: *The Election to the Russian Constituent Assembly of 1917.* Cambridge, Mass.: Harvard University Press, 1950.

Vishniak, M.V.: *Vserossiiskoe Uchreditel'noe Sobranie.* Paris: Sovremennye Zapiski, 1932.

The Civil War: 1917–1921

November 1918 divided the Civil War into two halves. First the Central Powers' defeat transformed the strategic situation, and then the right-wing coup of Admiral KOLCHAK changed the political complexion of the counter-revolution. Centre-left civilian forces took the leading role in 1918: the former MENSHEVIK, I. I. Maisky, described this as the era of 'Democratic Counter-Revolution'. In 1919 and 1920 the Communists' main enemies were of a different kind, the conservative and nationalist officers of the 'White' movement.

The 'Democratic Counter-Revolution': October 1917–November 1918

Phase 1 October 1917–May 1918: 'The Triumphal March of Soviet Power': The first year can be sub-divided by the May 1918 Czechoslovak uprising. Some historians do not treat the October–May period as civil war at all, but contemporaries used the term; indeed LENIN maintained (for a short time) that it had been won by March 1918. Certainly there was considerable fighting. During the phase up to May, pro-Communist forces benefited from the popularity of the new Soviet government and its promises, but they also used armed force to consolidate their hold on urban central Russia and spread Soviet power to the periphery. Lenin called this the 'Triumphal March of Soviet Power', and it did result in nominal control over most of the former Empire. (Another apt term was the 'Railway War'; the campaign was fought by small detachments along the railway lines.)

The main campaigns were against the COSSACK regions and the UKRAINE, where Soviet power had been rejected on political or ethnic grounds. In the east the Orenburg Cossacks under Ataman (Chieftain) A. I. Dutov were quickly crushed by detachments from the Urals and central Russia. In the south the Red forces of V. A. ANTONOV-OVSEENKO were victorious in a wide-ranging winter campaign against the Don Cossacks of Ataman A. M. Kaledin and the Ukrainian Directory. The early Civil War culminated in the assertion of Soviet control over the Don and the bloody capture of Kiev. By late February 1918 anti-Communist forces held no major centres. Even Finland was dominated by a Red Finn government (see BALTIC); TRANSCAUCASIA was the one region still distinct from Soviet Russia.

The brief renewal of war with the Central Powers in February 1918 and the signing of the peace of Brest-Litovsk ended the 'Triumphal March'. The advance of German, Austrian, and Turkish forces broke the Communist hold on most of the periphery. Between February and mid-summer 1918 they entered Estonia, Latvia, Belorussia, the Ukraine, Finland, and the Transcaucasus; this was the most important foreign intervention in the Civil War. Berlin preferred a (weak) Soviet government to any alternative and did not threaten central Russia; nevertheless, the Central Powers led indirectly to new fighting.

Phase 2 May 1918: the Czechoslovak uprising: The starting point for the second phase was an uprising by the Czechoslovak Corps. This corps, 40,000 men recruited by the tsarist government mainly from Austro-Hungarian POWs, was trying to make its way from Russia to the Western Front after the Brest peace. In May 1918 it suddenly rose in revolt. The Czechoslovaks achieved extraordinary success; within three or four months the Soviets had lost the vast territory east of the Volga. The rising was due not to an Allied conspiracy but to the Czechoslovaks' friction with local Soviets; it succeeded, above all, because the Communist grip on the periphery and even on the industrial Urals had, for all the success of the 'Triumphal March', been very weak.

The Volga campaign: The first real front was formed on the Volga. The main anti-Communist forces were the western elements of the Czechoslovak Corps, although Komuch (see COMMITTEE OF MEMBERS OF THE CONSTITUENT ASSEMBLY), the SR government at Samara, did create a 'People's Army'. The total forces were only a few thousand, but they quickly took the Urals and advanced up and down the Volga from Samara. The most striking successes were at Simbirsk and Kazan where, in July–August 1918, the newly-formed Eastern Army Group (Front) of the RED ARMY crumbled (partly thanks to the mutiny of its Left SR commander, Colonel M. A. Muraviev). TROTSKY was sent to rally the Volga forces, and a critical decision was made to transfer troops from the western 'Screens' (facing the Germans) to the Volga. Throughout the campaign the Reds had more troops than their enemies, but army and party reinforcements and improving organization were needed to give them effective supremacy. Spearheaded by the pro-Soviet LATVIAN RIFLEMEN and commanded by the Latvian Colonel I. I. Vatsetis, the Eastern Army Group retook Kazan and Simbirsk in September 1918. In October Samara was recaptured, and by November the Reds were approaching the Urals passes.

Neither Komuch nor its successor, the PROVISIONAL ALL-RUSSIAN GOVERNMENT, had been able to assemble effective forces or win the active political support of the local population; in the end the right seized power and installed Kolchak.

Allied intervention: The Allied role in 1918 is often exaggerated, but it too came indirectly from Brest-Litovsk and the Czechoslovak uprising. The Austro-German-Turkish advance encouraged Allied counter-movement. Small Allied detachments were landed at Murmansk, Vladivostok, Archangel, and Baku, and an uprising by B. V. SAVINKOV in Yaroslavl had Allied encouragement. But Allied intervention in 1918 had three salient features: it was motivated more by the War than anti-Bolshevism, it was small in scale (except for the Japanese presence on the Pacific coast), and it was remote from important Soviet centres.

Don and Kuban: Although this was not clear in mid 1918, the south-east was potentially more important than the Volga front. Unlike Komuch the south-eastern counter-revolution survived to become the most dangerous anti-Communist region. After the Austro-German sweep through the Ukraine the Don Cossacks, now under Ataman P. N. Krasnov, cleared their region and advanced beyond its borders, most notably towards Tsaritsyn (later Stalingrad, now Volgograd). The battles for Tsaritsyn are famous, but the survival of the 'Red Verdun' was due less to the efforts of STALIN, who was the man on the spot, than to Red numerical superiority. Further south the VOLUNTEER ARMY of General DENIKIN was still only a small force but it took control of the Kuban region.

Allied intervention played no part in the south-east in 1918, but the Germans did screen the Don perimeter and give the Cossacks arms. The key factor in the south-eastern Vendée, however, was the Cossack tradition; this provided a large number of trained, well-disciplined, and highly mobile soldiers.

Conclusion: The Cossacks and the Volunteers were at this time a regional threat, remote from the Soviet heartland. The Volga front seemed much more of a direct challenge to Moscow. If the Communists were forced to make changes in their government and their economic policies in 1918, this came about not because of an attack by counter-revolutionary 'Whites' (which only happened in 1919) or large Allied detachments (which never happened), but because of a campaign fought by small numbers of Czechoslovaks acting in the name of moderate socialists.

The 1918 counter-revolution was not successful. The 'Democratic Counter-Revolution' lacked the organizational skill, population resources and military talent needed to wage an effective campaign. The Communist government, even at its most embattled, held a vast territory of a million square miles, with 60 million people and most of the surviving resources of the old army. By the end of 1918 the Red Army had about 500,000 soldiers, and was already bigger than any of the armies it would face in the following year.

Whites versus Reds: November 1918–1922

The second half of the Civil War also falls into two phases. From November 1918 to April 1920, the anti-Communist armies, now fully 'White' in character, were at their most successful; in this phase they also suffered decisive defeats. After April 1920 they held out for half a year in the Crimea and Transbaikal but no longer threatened Soviet power; by the end of 1922 the last White footholds in the Far East had fallen.

Phase 3 November 1918–April 1920: the West and the South-West Fronts: The Central Powers' defeat in November 1918 was followed by a Soviet offensive. This offensive was intended partly to retake regions occupied by the Germans and Austrians, and partly to give military support to Central European revolutions. The Red Army drive into the BALTIC Provinces, Belorussia, and the Ukraine was ultimately unsuccessful. Most of the Red Army was committed to other fronts, and the Soviets often had to rely on locally-raised partisans; their most spectacular crisis came from Ataman N. A. Grigoriev's mutiny in the Ukraine. A vast territory had to be occupied. The national minorities on the periphery were sometimes able to raise effective forces on their own. Outside forces played a role too; French intervention at Odessa (December 1918–April 1919) was unsuccessful, but in the Baltic and Belorussia small Allied, German, Scandinavian, and Polish forces were effective.

The Eastern Front: The first true 'White' offensive came in March 1919, in the east. The Red Army had destroyed the forces of Komuch and rolled the survivors back towards the Urals; Admiral Kolchak took power in November 1918, but the eastern anti-Bolsheviks seemed a spent force. Moscow concentrated its troops against the Don Cossacks, and was surprised when Kolchak attacked. His western Army quickly took back much of what had been lost in the previous autumn, and threatened the vital Volga crossings.

White forces were inadequate. New White divisions forming deep in Siberia were still not ready. The Reds were able to hold the eastern side of the Volga and then counter-attack. The Whites were forced in May to pull rapidly back, and the Reds regained the initiative and pursued a constant offensive to the east. (This was only after the cautious desire of Glavkom (acronym for Main Commander-in-Chief of the Red Army) Vatsetis to stop before the Urals had been over-ruled and the Eastern Army Group commander, S. S. Kamenev, given his head.) Kolchak's armies attempted to regain the initiative at Chelyabinsk on the far side of the Urals, but were outfought. By August the Whites had been pushed onto the Siberian steppe; with the loss of the Urals they ceased to threaten the Soviet heartland and lost their only industrial base. In September–October the Whites counter-attacked but failed to trap the Red forces; the Reds in turn took the initiative in October, bypassed what was left of the Kolchak's field armies, and dashed forward to take Omsk (14 November 1919).

Kolchak had done little to win over support in 'his' zone. In any event, his core Siberian region had a population of only eight million, compared to over sixty million in the Soviet zone. Kolchak also had far fewer Cossacks and experienced officers than did the southern Whites. He assembled an army of about 100,000 combat troops in the early part of 1919, but by the early summer the Red Eastern Army Group had been built up to a 2:1 or 3:1 superiority in manpower.

North Russia: The White situation in Murmansk and

Figure 18   North Russian Expeditionary Force, Murmansk: White Finnish Deserters and British escort.

Archangel was like that in SIBERIA: a large backward area and a small population. Unlike Siberia the front in the north was static, partly due to the climate, the impassable terrain, the vast distances, and the small forces on either side. The unusual factor was the dominant Allied role, but the largest British offensive (in the late summer of 1919) was only at regimental strength, and was nominally intended to cover withdrawal. The British left in the autumn; in March 1920 small Red forces moved up the railways and finished off the remaining Whites.

The Baltic: Finland and the new Baltic states observed a policy of neutrality or limited hostility to Soviet Russia in 1919. The small White Russian NORTH-WESTERN ARMY under General N. N. YUDENICH threatened Petrograd, but it was defeated and interned in Estonia in November 1919.

South Russia: The campaign in south Russia was, in military terms, the most significant of the whole Civil War. In the winter of 1918–19 the Red high command (correctly) put its main effort into capturing the Cossack regions in the south-east (rather than in the advance to the west). Although the Red Army's winter offensive succeeded in

taking much of the Don Cossack Region and weakening the Don Army, it did not complete this task and potential was left for a counter-attack. Meanwhile the Volunteer Army under Denikin finished off the Soviet governments in the north Caucasus, destroying the much larger 'Caspian-Caucasus Army Group' (this was perhaps the most decisive Red defeat).

The Whites and Cossacks, on their own, cleared a large base in the Don-Kuban-north Caucasus area; the decisive factor was not the support of Allied or even quasi-Allied troops (like the Czechoslovak Legion) but rather the Cossack tradition and the military talents of the Volunteer Army. In January 1919 the Don Cossacks were forced to accept fusion into the ARMED FORCES OF SOUTH RUSSIA (AFSR), under Denikin; this confirmed the hegemony on the conservative Great Russian officer corps in south Russia, just as Kolchak's coup had done in Siberia.

The bad state of the Don Cossack army forced the Volunteers to fight in the Donbas industrial area. Under General V. Z. Mai-Maevsky, they repelled several Red offensives by numerically superior armies. In May 1919 the southern Whites were able to take the offensive, bursting out of the Don-Donbas region in all directions. By the end of June the Volunteer Army had captured the major city of the eastern Ukraine, Kharkov, and a bridgehead over the Dnepr at Ekaterinoslav; the Don Army had recaptured most of the Don Cossack Region; and the Caucasus Army had finally taken Tsaritsyn.

Various factors explained these remarkable White successes. The Reds on the southern front were fighting a long way from their central Russian heartland, and when the AFSR offensive began they were overextended and based in the unstable Ukraine and the northern Don Region. Ruthless Red policies of 'de-cossackization' had alienated the Cossack population (see COSSACKS). British tanks were an important moral factor at Kharkov and Tsaritsyn (although only a small amount of Allied aid had reached operational units by this time). Most important was the disorganization of the larger Soviet forces. The breakout was achieved by 45–50,000 AFSR combat troops against about 80,000 Reds. The Reds might have overcome their qualitative weaknesses by sending more troops to the south, but they were faced by Kolchak's spring offensive. The June–July 1919 crisis resulted in a major shake-up in the Soviet high command, including a reduction of the role of Trotsky and the dismissal of I. I. Vatsetis; S. S. Kamenev became the new Red Army Glavkom.

The Whites had to pause in July 1919 after their long advance. General Baron P. N. WRANGEL argued later that Denikin should have shifted forces from the eastern end of his front to the centre and attacked immediately, but this would have been physically difficult and the Reds were already counter-attacking. The Red drive provoked the greatest strategic controversy of the Civil War. Vatsetis had preferred the safe course – emphasizing the centre of the Red southern front and covering Moscow; any counter-offensive would push the Whites south-east, back towards the Don. Kamenev, the new Glavkom, wanted instead to attack towards the Don Cossack centres from the eastern end of the front. This plan had a number of advantages: first, it would cut off White forces in the Ukraine; secondly, prevent any link with Kolchak; and thirdly, allow the quick redeployment of troops from the Eastern Army Group. Kamenev got his way. His counter-offensive began in August, but made relatively little progress: troops had to be diverted to counter a White cavalry raid under General K. K. Mamontov, and the path of the advance was stubbornly defended by the Cossacks.

A diversionary Red offensive in the centre of the front also failed in August 1919. The AFSR grasped the initiative for the first time since June and with this posed the greatest military threat to Soviet power. The Volunteer Army took first Kursk and then Orel, and advanced with little opposition towards the Tula arsenal and Moscow itself. The flanking armies were also making progress, on the left into the north-west Ukraine, and on the right into the provinces north of the Don Cossack Region. Meanwhile in western Siberia Kolchak had been able to stabilize his front, and in

the Baltic Yudenich suddenly moved towards Petrograd. The critical moment came at the end of October and the beginning of November 1919.

In the end Denikin's army was halted and pushed back by Colonel A. I. Egorov's Southern Army Group. Kamenev's strategy had been replaced by a simple defence of the front's centre. The cavalry corps of S. M. Budenny, which emerged in a gap between Volunteer Army and Don Army, played an important if unplanned role, but the most important factor in the turn-around was the weakness of the Whites.

Denikin fought from a weak political and military position. His regime failed to win over the population or to create an effective administration; the lack of time and the already-anarchic state of south Russia are also elements that should not be forgotten. At the height of his success Denikin controlled over forty million people, but over half of these were only briefly under his control; his core region, the north Caucasus and the Don, had a population of less than ten million, a sixth of the core Soviet zone. His AFSR front-line strength of 100,000 in October 1919 faced about 150,000 Reds, and the enemy had large manpower reserves.

The Whites retreated in November–December 1919 back into the Don Region. A new factor was the confident Red use of cavalry, now massed in Budenny's Cavalry Army. Denikin was able to make a brief stand behind the Don River in January 1920, but the Reds, latterly under M. N. TUKHACHEVSKY, were able to turn their flank in a winter campaign and drive on through the Kuban to the coast. Part of the AFSR escaped by sea from Novorossiisk to the Crimea, but the main Cossack base area had been lost.

The Allies: The role of the Allies in 1919 might have been greater, given the opening of the Baltic and Black Seas. Direct Allied military involvement, however, was even less than in 1918. There were Allied garrisons in non-Soviet regions like the Pacific coast and the Transcaucasus, but only on the remote Archangel-Murmansk front did Allied troops engage the Red Army; Kolchak, Denikin, and Yudenich fought without any Allied ground troops (although a few aircraft and tank crew were involved). The Allies did play an important role as arms suppliers, and British arms alone exceeded Soviet production. On the other hand the Whites made their first major advances in the Volga-Urals region and in the north Caucasus before Allied equipment became available on a large scale.

1919 Conclusion: The Reds won the critical campaign partly because of their enormous numerical advantage; this came from keeping control of the same heartland they had held in 1918. Their improving state structure enabled them to ensure internal control. By the end of 1919 their potential numerical superiority had been transformed into a Red Army of three million men, nominally twenty times larger than Denikin's AFSR. Throughout most of 1919 the Whites were at least 400 miles from Moscow, and even Denikin's October offensive never ·got closer than 250 miles. The Whites were unable to coordinate their operations, owing to geography and the pressures on each front. In military terms the Whites under Kolchak, Denikin, and Yudenich were better organized than the 'Democratic Counter-revolution' had been; in political terms, however, they had even less chance of winning over the population. The White leaders thought of a popular 'upsurge' in their favour, but did nothing to bring it about. The Soviet side also faced internal disorder, but in general the Reds' social policies, including a new emphasis on the 'middle peasant', gave them popular support. And in the polarized Red-White struggle of 1919, the Reds gained much support from the centre.

Phase 4 April 1920–1922: The Crimea: After the Novorossiisk débâcle Wrangel replaced Denikin. His forces survived in the Crimea because the Reds desired to achieve a settlement with the Allies, underestimated White potential, and were preoccupied by the war with Poland. Wrangel broke out of the Crimea in June but early in November 1920 was forced to carry out a large and final White evacuation. There were now no organized anti-Communist forces in European Russia.

Siberia: The armies of Kolchak disintegrated as they pulled back to Lake Baikal; the Supreme Ruler himself was executed. Few White troops crossed Lake Baikal. In the summer of 1920 the Reds' small Siberian forces were held up by the Transbaikal Cossacks under Ataman Semenov, but in the autumn the Whites withdrew to the Pacific coast where they survived for two years under Japanese protection. When the Japanese pulled out at the end of 1922 the Whites too were forced into exile (see REVOLUTION IN SIBERIA).

Conclusion

The three-year Civil War was largely an internal event, a by-product of the Bolshevik Revolution. The cost was great: about 800,000 military deaths from combat and disease. This was half Russian military deaths in the World War, but the total population loss over the Civil War era – from fighting, internal repression and, most important, disease caused by post-revolutionary conditions – was perhaps 7–10 million people; economic damage was also very great. The effect on Soviet political psychology is even harder to calculate, but it was certainly high.   EM

Further Reading

Chamberlin, W.H.: *The Russian Revolution.* New York: Macmillan, 1935.

Kenez, P.: *Civil War in South Russia.* Berkeley: University of California Press, 1971; 1977.

Khromov, S.S. et al. eds.: *Grazhdanskaya voina i voennaya interventsiya v SSSR: Entsiklopediya.* Moscow: Sovetskaya Entsiklopediya, 1983.

Lehovich, D.V.: *White against Red: The Life of General Anton Denikin.* New York: Norton, 1974.

Mawdsley, E.: *The Russian Civil War.* Winchester, Mass.: Allen & Unwin, 1987.

Armed Forces of South Russia (AFSR)

The AFSR was the largest White force, a coalition of the southern White armies. Most important were the Volunteer Army and the Don Army; in the autumn of 1918 these fought separate campaigns, but in January 1919 the Volunteers' General DENIKIN became Main Commander-in-Chief of the AFSR. By the summer of 1919 the AFSR front comprised the Kiev District (General A. M. Dragomirov), the Volunteer Army (General V. Z. Mai-Maevsky), the Don Army (General V. I. Sidorin), and the Caucasus Army (General P. N. WRANGEL). Total front-line strength was about 100,000. The AFSR received large Allied (mostly British) supplies in the latter part of 1919 but its strategy was not well coordinated. The AFSR advanced rapidly on Moscow in the autumn of 1919, then fell apart in the rapid retreat to the Don-Kuban region in the winter. With the evacuation to the Crimea and the resignation of Denikin the AFSR ceased to exist.   EM

Committee of Members of the Constituent Assembly (Komuch)

This was an SR-dominated government which existed in the Volga town of Samara in the summer and autumn of 1918; Komuch was the most important anti-Bolshevik organization in 1918, and the high point of centre-left opposition to the Soviet regime.

Komuch was formed on 8 June 1918 as a result of the capture of Samara by Czechoslovak soldiers. From the beginning the dominant role was played by the SOCIALIST REVOLUTIONARIES, and it was natural that they should stress the CONSTITUENT ASSEMBLY where they had had a majority. Komuch was unable to get effective political support in the Volga provinces, given the apathy of the peasants and the hostility of the right and the left. Nevertheless armed forces acting under Komuch's nominal command, the Czechoslovak Legion and the 'People's Army' of Colonel V. O. Kappel, were able to achieve striking victories against demoralized Soviet forces, culminating in the capture of Kazan in August 1918.

Military and political weakness led to retreat in the face of Red Army counter-attacks; Samara fell in October, although by this time Komuch had largely surrendered its powers to the PROVISIONAL ALL-RUSSIAN GOVERNMENT. A number of former Komuch leaders, most notably V. K. Volsky and the Menshevik I. I. Maisky, went over to the Soviet side after the coup of Admiral Kolchak.   EM

The North-Western Army

The smallest of the active White armies originated in the Northern Army, created under German protection at Pskov (south-west of Petrograd) in October 1918; after the German defeat this force withdrew into Estonia. In May 1919, commanded by General A.P. Rodzyanko and now called the Northern Corps (although only of brigade strength), it crossed into Petrograd Province to secure a non-Estonian base. A second offensive began in September 1919, as DENIKIN moved toward Moscow from the south. The North-Western Army (as it became known in July) was now under YUDENICH, and it reached Petrograd's suburbs in late October. It had been impossible, however, to raise more than 14,400 men; the Allies, suspicious of the German-created force, provided little equipment. Given the local Soviet strength (73,000 men) the North-Western Army's advance was remarkable, but in November 1919 it was disarmed and interned in Estonia.   EM

The Provisional All-Russian Government

Based in the Urals-western Siberia area, this was the only attempt to create a civilian anti-Bolshevik government on a national scale; it only lasted for eight weeks, from 23 September to 18 November 1918.

The PA-RG was formed as a result of the Ufa State Conference (8–23 September 1918); the two main bodies involved, the SR Komuch (see COMMITTEE OF MEMBERS OF THE CONSTITUENT ASSEMBLY) and the more conservative Provisional Siberian Government compromised over various issues, including the form of the future government and the role of the Constituent Assembly. The compromise executive, the five-man Directory, was in practice made up of N. D. Avksentiev, V. M. Zenzinov (SRs), V. A. Vinogradov (Kadet), P. V. Vologodsky (Siberian Regionalist), and General V. G. Boldyrev. The PA-RG finally moved to Omsk in Siberia which, combined with the military defeat of Komuch, strengthened the conservatives; the PA-RG Council of Ministers was dominated by veterans of the Provisional Siberian Government. The PA-RG was unable to create a real base, and neither the right nor the left was happy with the compromise; the arrival of V. M. CHERNOV pushed the SRs to the left and angered the right. The PA-RG was overthrown by a military coup on 18 November, and the War Minister, KOLCHAK, was installed as leader, although claiming the national authority of the PA-RG. (See REVOLUTION IN SIBERIA.)   EM

The Volunteer Army

The most effective single force on the White side, the Volunteer Army was originally set up by ALEXEEV in the Don Cossack Region at the end of 1917. After the successful Soviet Don campaign the Volunteers, under the operational command of KORNILOV, moved south to find a new base. The First Kuban Campaign (also called the 'Ice March') failed; Kornilov was killed and replaced by DENIKIN. After regrouping in the newly anti-Bolshevik Don, the Volunteers won a Second Kuban Campaign; during the winter of 1918–19 the Volunteers cleared the whole north Caucasus.

With their pro-Allied orientation the Volunteers were able to assert their control over the Cossacks, although the Volunteer Army became only a component of the ARMED FORCES OF SOUTH RUSSIA. Denikin now led the AFSR, and V. Z. Mai-Maevsky replaced him as head of the Volunteer Army. The Volunteers were the spearhead in the AFSR offensives in 1919, taking first Kharkov and then Kursk and Orel. Although militarily effective on the attack, the army was undisciplined, took part in looting, and fell rapidly back after the November battles. Mai was dismissed; the army was reduced to a corps, and then disbanded. WRANGEL did not revive the name in 1920, because he felt it had been discredited.   EM

The Jäger Movement

The outbreak of war in 1914 revived the Finnish activist movement, which now pinned its hopes on German support for Finnish independence. In the autumn of 1914, a small group of activists in Stockholm and Berlin established contact with the German High Command. Agreement was reached early in 1915 on basic military training for two hundred Finnish volunteers; this was soon revised to two thousand men, enrolled in the 27th Jäger Battalion of the Royal Prussian army. Although the Russian authorities succeeded in breaking up the underground network through Finland in 1916, over fifteen hundred men managed to make their way to Germany for military training. The Jägers were subjected to Prussian military law and discipline, and were deployed on the Riga front, where they saw action in the winter of 1916–17. Pressure by Finnish activists finally persuaded the Germans to remove the battalion from the line, to be held in reserve for use in Finland.

Plans for the return of the Jägers to train Finnish units were broached by the Finns in the autumn of 1917, but the prospects of a separate peace with Russia persuaded the German High Command to proceed cautiously. The main body of the Jägers did not return to Finland until February 1918, when the battalion was finally disbanded.

Relations between the Prussian-trained Jägers and the older generation of ex-Imperial Russian army officers around General Mannerheim were poor from the outset, though the Jägers provided much-needed expertise in the creation of a fighting force. The conflict between the two generations of officers continued after the civil war, with the Jägers gaining the ascendancy by the mid 1920s.

DGK

The Latvian Riflemen

The advance of the German army into the Baltic provinces in 1915 persuaded the Russian authorities to accede to pressure from Latvian Duma deputies and civil organizations and to authorize the creation of two Latvian Rifle Battalions. By 1917 these had grown in strength to one reserve and eight regular regiments. The Riflemen fought several battles on the Riga front in the winter of 1916–17, suffering heavy casualties.

In the spring of 1917 the Soviet of Latvian Riflemen's Deputies shifted from a broadly defencist position to outright opposition to the PROVISIONAL GOVERNMENT. The Second Congress in May elected a new executive committee on which Bolsheviks were in a dominant position. However, the resolution of 17 May, calling for the transformation of the war into a class war, provoked protests from the troops, and was modified by the Third Congress.

After the fall of Riga to the Germans in August 1917, the Riflemen fell back into unoccupied Latvian territory and played an important part in taking control of the XII Army, thereby neutralizing the possibility of an attack on the Bolshevik regime in Petrograd. At the end of November, a special unit of selected Latvian troops was sent to Petrograd to carry out guard and police duties at the Smolny Institute. Latvian troops played a significant role in the early days of the OCTOBER REVOLUTION in Petrograd, though their involvement in the dissolution of the Constituent Assembly has perhaps been exaggerated. Latvian Riflemen were also thrown into battle on the civil war front, though from March 1918 regiments were demobilized and reformed as voluntary units of the new Red Army. In April 1918 a Latvian Riflemen's Soviet Division was established, commanded by General Jukums Vacietis (Vatsetis).   DGK

War Communism

This term is used to describe and define the period roughly from mid 1918 until March 1921, when the Soviet government, under LENIN's leadership, adopted a policy of requisitioning farm produce (so-called *prodrazverstka*), sought to ban all private trade, nationalized almost all industrial establishments, tried to achieve central control over production and allocation of goods, partially replacing money (which was rapidly depreciating) by accounting in kind. The words 'sought' and 'tried' in the above sentence are essential, because real life at no time conformed fully to the government's intentions. Thus L. N. Kritsman, in his pamphlet on 'The Heroic period of the Russian revolution', described the economic system then prevailing as 'the most complete form of proletarian natural-anarchistic economy', and also claimed that in world history there was never a time when so large a proportion of the people had engaged

in trade (though it was illegal). Controls were confused and contradictory, reliable and efficient controllers highly scarce, the official distribution network frequently broke down, various official bodies duplicated each other. Local soviets and party officials often acted independently, disregarding Moscow's instructions. Lenin many times deplored the tendency to issue orders that were in fact not carried out.

It is none the less possible to speak of a system which may be labelled 'war communism'. It profoundly influenced, and was influenced by, the CIVIL WAR. It formed the behaviour patterns of thousands of Bolshevik officials, as they struggled to create some sort of order out of chaos, and found ruthless methods to be the only way. Life became cheap. To shoot someone was to 'waste' him (*v raskhod*). The VECHEKA, forerunner of the KGB, was the effective sword of the revolution. For a few months the Bolsheviks shared power with the Left Socialist-Revolutionaries, but the latter walked out, and even (ineffectually) rebelled in July 1918. The MENSHEVIKS survived, despite some arbitrary arrests and harassment, until 1921, but to all intents and purposes the one-party state was established by mid 1918.

Was all this the consequence of the ideas and policies with which the Bolsheviks had come to power in the OCTOBER REVOLUTION? This conclusion could be challenged by reference to the policies propounded prior to that date. Thus, for example, before October there was nothing to suggest that the Bolsheviks believed in a one-party state, and indeed several Bolsheviks (such as Rykov, Nogin) actually resigned in protest when Lenin announced that they would try to rule without the participation of other socialist parties. The Bolsheviks (along with other left-wing groups) had been on record as opposing the death penalty. As for economic policy and doctrine, this had been a mixture of demagogic slogans and short-term expedients. Marxist doctrine on economics of socialism had been little developed, in Russia or elsewhere, beyond vague and utopian notions on an undefined sort of socialist planning for the good of society. In his most utopian work, *State and Revolution*, Lenin wrote:

> We, the workers, shall organize industrial production on the basis of what capitalism has already created . . . We shall reduce the role of state officials to that of simply carrying out instructions as responsible, revocable, modestly paid 'foremen and accountants', of course with the help of technicians of all sorts . . . The function of control and accountancy, becoming more and more simple, will be performed by each (citizen) in turn, will become a habit and finally die out as a *special* function of a special section of the population . . . To organize the *whole* economy on the lines of the postal service, so that foremen, technicians and accountants, as well as *all* officials,

shall receive salaries no higher than workers' wages, all under the leadership of the armed proletariat, that is our immediate task.

Again, in his 'Can the Bolsheviks retain state power?' written on the eve of the revolution, we have such statements as: '. . . Capitalism has so simplified the work of accounting and control, has reduced it to a comparatively simple process of bookkeeping, which any literate person can do.' But in the same work he wrote that 'the important thing will not be even the confiscation of the capitalists' property, but . . . workers' control', plus 'a fair tax'. Indeed Lenin had also written: 'Everyone agrees that the immediate introduction of socialism in Russia is impossible', and also that 'there was not and could not be a definite plan for the organization of economic life'.

After war communism had been abandoned, A. A. BOGDANOV said 'they had tried to act cautiously, but military-revolutionary necessity . . . compelled them, life compelled them, to act as they did'.

It could thus be argued that Lenin and his comrades had no blueprint corresponding to the war communism model, that they were driven into it by circumstances. This view can be sustained only if the 'circumstances' can be made to include the consequences of the Bolsheviks' own attitudes and policies. Thus, for example, while their original programme, in its vagueness, might appear to be compatible with a mixed economy, with nationalization confined to 'banks and syndicates', the Bolsheviks' own slogans ensured that the remaining capitalists, private managers, traders, were placed in an impossible position. 'Workers' control' was an ambiguous term which could mean merely the power to inspect the accounts, but in practice there were many instances of crude seizure of factories, and many employers were driven out or just fled. Indeed there were decrees trying to stop unauthorized nationalization 'from below'.

In the case of the peasants the situation was more complicated. It must be recalled that the exigencies of war had driven the tsarist government in 1916 to introduce a state monopoly of grain purchases, and in fact peasant unwillingness to sell at the officially-fixed prices contributed to the food shortages which touched off the riots that brought down tsarism. The PROVISIONAL GOVERNMENT also tried, ineffectually, to secure enough produce to feed the towns (see PEASANTS AND REVOLUTION). Bolshevik ideology did not prescribe confiscating or requisitioning: it prescribed some sort of 'product exchange'. But the collapse of the economy meant that there was little to offer. There were strong pressures to keep prices of food from rising and, as in other warring countries, free-market sales came to be seen as black-market 'speculation' even by many non-Bolsheviks. Lenin at first believed that he could count on support from the poor peasants in fomenting 'class war in the villages', and that this would help in

obtaining food. But peasant solidarity was too strong, and the *kombedy* (committees of poor peasants) were soon abandoned.

It might seem inappropriate to blame the Bolsheviks for the Civil War, since after all it was launched by their enemies. Yet it was a Bolshevik slogan to 'turn imperialist war into civil war'. They adopted, quite deliberately, policies which rendered civil war inevitable.

Even before it began, under the Treaty of Brest-Litovsk the Soviets were forced to abandon large territories of the former Empire, including the Ukraine. The armies of DENIKIN, KOLCHAK, Yudenich, the Czech Legion, plus foreign interventionists, occupied large areas, and destroyed railway lines and bridges when they retreated. Supplies of fuel, materials, food, were highly irregular and precarious. To save Bolshevik rule it was plainly necessary to mobilize and to centralize, to impose on a country already exhausted after nearly four years of war the priority of supplies to the RED ARMY. So there were strong, urgent, purely practical reasons for extending central control over production and allocation, and for the extension of requisitioning. Similarly, the Cheka's activities and powers, and the increasing use of the death penalty, seemed to be justified by the emergency situation, given the precariousness of the Bolsheviks' hold on power.

It may therefore be seen that war communism had two interrelated and mutually reinforcing causes: a set of ideological presuppositions (anti-employer, anti-trader, belief in planning, a negative view of the market) and war emergency. Furthermore, the war emergency gave additional impetus to, and appeared to justify, the more extreme manifestations of the ideology. For example, hyper-inflation occurred in many countries under anti-marxist regimes, as for instance in Germany and Hungary, but in Soviet Russia Bolshevik zealots, such as Preo-brazhensky and Larin, saw in the rapid devaluation of money a stage in the progress towards communism, when money would disappear. There were anti-black-market measures in other countries in wartime, but no-one else tried to outlaw all trade. The party's 1919 programme, drafted under Lenin's guidance, included such words as: 'undeviatingly replace trade by planned distribution', and 'the most radical measures preparing the abolition of money', so that zealotry affected the bulk of the party. The Hungarian historian, L. Szamuely, argues with reason that 'the state deliberately aimed at eliminating every element of market relations from economic activity'. As already mentioned, the state monopoly of grain purchases was inherited from pre-revolutionary wartime legislation, and Lenin favoured some ill-defined form of barter, with the state paying the peasants in industrial goods. It was civil war and ruin which turned 'product exchange' into requisitioning. Similarly, while Bolshevik theory did incline its believers towards labour conscription under the slogan 'who does not work shall not eat', material incentives were lacking under conditions of hunger and economic disruption. Together with the fact of breakdown and emergency, this led to theories about 'militarization of labour', propagated in 1920 by both TROTSKY and BUKHARIN, but which both tried quickly to forget once 'war communism' had been abandoned. It is also appropriate to add that the ideologically-inspired excesses committed by the Bolsheviks at this period contributed significantly to economic disruption and chaos, which seemed to justify these very methods.

Lenin himself several times stated that mistakes had been made, Bukharin spoke of 'illusions', excesses were admitted, with the ready excuse that this 'was forced on us by extreme want, ruin and war'.

By 1920 most workers received their meagre rations free of charge, paid no rent, travelled free on the overcrowded tramcars. State enterprises were subject to detailed orders from above about what to produce and to whom to deliver, and no money passed. Side by side with this the state continued to print enormous quantities of rapidly depreciating rubles (to avoid the monetary designation they came to be known as *sovznaki* (soviet tokens)), which helped to fuel a flourishing illegal market which was known as Sukharevka, after the name of a Moscow square in which sales were made. There was a big expansion of barter deals – especially of clothing, furniture, samovars, anything – against food brought in illegally from the countryside. The peasants resisted requisitioning, hid their produce from the squads sent to seize it, but in the last resort many were prepared to support or tolerate the Bolsheviks for fear of the victory of the Whites who would (they feared) bring back the landlords. Lenin was wise enough to leave land redistribution in peasant hands. Even though he would have preferred to set up state or collective farms, he knew that this was quite impracticable in the circumstances. This contrasted with policies pursued by more dogmatic communists during the revolution in (for instance) the BALTIC states and in Hungary, when they failed to support peasant demands for land and suffered the consequences.

By May 1920 only one White army, that of WRANGEL in the Crimea, remained in the field. In that month the Poles chose to attack. After successfully counter-attacking, the Red Army was itself defeated in front of Warsaw. When that war ended and Wrangel was driven out of the Crimea (September 1920) the 'war' justification of war communism was ended too. The people were hungry, cold, exhausted. Most urban residents had fled to the countryside. Disease was rampant. Most industries had stopped for lack of materials, fuel, labour. The peasants were unwilling to produce for the requisition squads, and now that the Whites no longer threatened, rebellions broke out. The shock of the sailors' KRONSTADT REVOLT, which took place during the Tenth Party Congress (in March 1921), was the last nail in the coffin of war communism. Yet Lenin and the bulk of his comrades had intended to continue with the methods of war communism during this period of reconstruction. In October 1920 he was telling the Soviet authorities in the UKRAINE to confiscate money and implements from so-called *kulaks* (richer peasants) and to collect all grain surpluses over and above basic needs. Even as late as December 1920 Lenin was still advocating the continuation of requisitioning, and his government set up so-called 'sowing committees' intending to compel the peasant households to sow and to harvest. But by March 1921 he had seen the necessity of relaxing pressure, substituting a tax in kind for requisitioning, and allowing peasants to keep or freely to sell the remainder. Thus was born the New Economic Policy (NEP). He had a hard time persuading the party to accept this. Perhaps but for the shock of the Kronstadt rebellion, he might not have succeeded.

So what was war communism? Lenin himself was ambivalent. On the one hand it had been all-out assault, like the first attack of the Japanese on the fortress of Port Arthur; that attack too had failed but it was a necessary learning process, so that success would come when the attack would be resumed. NEP was then to be seen as a necessary but painful temporary retreat (*reculer pour mieux sauter*). But Lenin also and repeatedly spoke of NEP as the right road, one which would have been followed in 1918 but for the exigencies of war. It would be followed 'seriously and for a long time'.

So the two interpretations of war communism are not only of interest to historians today. They played an important role in explaining what followed. Those among the Bolsheviks who believed (or, like Bukharin, came eventually to believe) that war communism had been an error, that NEP was after all the right road, would try to follow Lenin's injunction to cling to NEP 'seriously and for a long time'. Those for whom war communism was a glorious period, an all-out offensive against the class enemy, who saw NEP as a forced and hateful retreat, would try to resume the offensive and smash the market-based compromise on which NEP rested. By 1929, this second group, under STALIN, was in the ascendant, with consequences that are well known. AN

Further Reading

Dobb, M.: *Russian economic development since 1917*. London: 1951.

Gimpelson, E.: *Voennyi kommunizm*. Moscow: 1977.

Malle, Silvana.: *The Economic Organization of War Communism*. Cambridge: 1985.

Nove, A.: *An Economic History of the USSR*. London: Pelican, 1972.

Szamuely, L.: *First Models of Socialist Economic Systems*. Budapest: 1974.

Bolshevik Oppositions

The Bolshevik government was confronted by a series of internal party revolts of varying force virtually as soon as it had seized power. Both the intellectual ideologists and the hardened underground practical revolutionaries who now found themselves at the centre of power, voiced their disquiet at LENIN's pragmatism and at the growing evidence of bureaucratic abuses associated with the political monopoly wielded by the Communist Party, and also formed themselves into opposition platforms from which they sought to change policy.

Left Communists

An opposition faction within the Bolshevik party which came to prominence in 1918 through its advocacy of extreme left-wing positions on issues ranging from revolutionary war to economic and social policy. Its activities were largely confined to the year 1918 but it constituted at the time the most impressive group of oppositionists to the party leadership. At the head of the Left Communists stood N. I. BUKHARIN and among its other leaders were K. B. RADEK, E. A. Preobrazhensky, V. M. Smirnov, A. M. KOLLONTAI, and N. Osinsky (V. V. Obolensky). Some of these and others became later associated with other opposition groups in the party.

In general terms the Left Communists may be described as 'ideological fundamentalists' who subscribed to a radical interpretation of Communist doctrine and of the manner in which it should be pursued and implemented by the new Soviet government. Their first major clash with Lenin occurred over the issue of the peace negotiations at Brest-Litovsk. They opposed withdrawal from the War and advocated instead its continuation as a revolutionary confrontation whose aim would be to encourage and foment revolution in Germany and elsewhere. This, of course, was anathema to Lenin who sought a peace agreement at almost any price. When Lenin received in March 1918 a large majority supporting his position, the Left Communists abstained from voting. They had been dealt a powerful blow indicating already the limited extent of their standing in the party. They subsequently abandoned their advocacy of revolutionary war but continued to subscribe to their radical social views. In four issues of the journal *Kommunist* which appeared in Moscow between April and June 1918, they criticized Lenin and the party for succumbing to the temptations of careful pragmatic and unadventurous policies, urging instead the direct pursuit of socialist measures. Amongst the latter were large-scale nationalization, the extension of democracy within party and state, workers' control of the economy, and the rejection of any compromises or understandings with Russian or foreign capitalist interests. Their views on such matters as cultural policy, the family and education were also radical. However pristine ideologically, the weakness of the Left Communists' programme was that most of it was unrealistic and, if implemented in the conditions then prevailing in Soviet Russia, would lead to even greater chaos. Not only the ultra-realist Lenin realized this; most of the party was in no mood for ideological adventures. In any case, the Left Communists were themselves soon drawn into the exigencies of the situation. Thus, Bukharin and others took an active part in the suppression of a rebellion in July 1918 by the Left SOCIALIST REVOLUTIONARIES and later supported the terror campaign against opposition to the Bolsheviks. By the autumn of 1918, faced by the growing reality of a hostile party, Bukharin, Radek and others openly admitted their errors, thus effectively bringing their faction to an end. However, the end of the Left Communist members themselves was to come later: in December 1927, at the Fifteenth Congress, they were expelled from the party, together with other former or persisting oppositionists, and in the 1930s most of them disappeared in the purges.

Democratic Centralists

An opposition group which arose in the Bolshevik party in 1920 with a view to restoring party democracy. Although their position overlapped with that of the WORKERS' OPPOSITION which had come into being at the same time, the Democratic Centralists were less concerned with the interests of workers than with the rights of party members to voice their opinions and enjoy such organizational provisions as would make these opinions influential in central party institutions. The group was made up mainly of intellectuals and among its spokesmen were N. Osinsky (V. V. Obolensky), T. B. Sapronov and V. N. Maximovsky. The Democratic Centralists, as their name would indicate, did not reject the principle of centralism which had governed party organization; nor were they amenable to the extension of democratic principles to political life in general. They did pay some lip-service to trade unionism, to workers' participation in economic management, and to the dangers inherent in the bureaucratization of economic life. But the thrust of their opposition to the Bolshevik leadership lay in the emphasis they placed on preserving democratic procedures within the party itself. They deplored, for example, the creation of 'political departments' which would replace local party committees and thus stifle both initiative and opinion from below. Sapronov eloquently warned Lenin that such tendencies would ultimately result in the destruction of the party Central Committee itself and in the appointment of a 'single commander' over the whole of the Soviet state. Not surprisingly, the Democratic Centralists were enthusiastic supporters of the SOVIETS and proposed various reforms which would restore their effectiveness as democratic institutions. But for the most part their programme was too vague to be translated into realistic measures and too much at odds with the trends in the party to have any impact. They were denounced by Lenin in 1921 and, in 1927, at the Fifteenth Party Congress, the Democratic Centralists were among the multitude of opposition groups which were expelled from the party. Their leaders perished in the purges of the 1930s.

Workers' Opposition

A group formed in 1920 within the Bolshevik party and led by trade unionists who espoused extreme left-wing views on matters of party organization, economic administration and social policy. Amongst its leaders were A. G. SHLYAPNIKOV, A. M. Kollontai (who published its programme at home and abroad as *The Workers' Opposition*), S. Medvedev and Yu. Kh. Lutovinov. The name Workers' Opposition was coined not by the group itself but by Lenin in the course of his attacks upon it. The group never established an organization outside the party but it had wide support among trade unions throughout the country and particularly among the metalworkers. Its programme, if such it was, contained what Lenin and others branded as utopian and idealistic elements. Its members deplored the spread of bureaucratization in party and state in general and the tendencies, then coming into being, of placing the management of economic concerns in the hands of specialists. They advocated decentralization, party democracy, and workers' self-control of management and economic production. They were considered, not incorrectly, as 'anarcho-syndicalists' by the Bolshevik leadership. They never constituted a real threat to Lenin but their appeal to the 'proletarian' conscience of the party, their common ground with other opposition groups and their readiness to mobilize support from Communist organizations abroad proved an embarrassment to the party. They were censured at the Tenth Party Congress in March 1921 which among other things banned party factions, but in 1922 they published a 'Declaration', addressed to a Comintern conference, in which they decried the harassment to which their members were being subjected and the refusal of the Bolshevik party to countenance any of their plans and efforts on behalf of workers' democracy. The reaction in the party was immediate: they were condemned as a threat to party unity, declared an illegal faction, and threatened with expulsion. Thereafter the activities of the Workers' Opposition declined, although it was not until 1926 that the last of their leaders capitulated in full, admitting their 'errors' and renouncing every attempt not to abide by party decisions. Most of the leaders of the Workers' Opposition – a notable exception was Kollontai – disappeared in the Stalinist purges of the 1930s.   BK

Further Reading

Daniels, R.V.: *The Conscience of the Revolution: Communist Opposition in Soviet Russia*. Cambridge, Mass.: 1960.

Kollontai, A.M.: *The Workers' Opposition*. Chicago: 1921.

Schapiro, Leonard: *The Origin of the Communist Autocracy*. Cambridge, Mass.: 1955.

Propaganda

It is conceded by friend and foe alike that at the time of the Revolution and Civil War the Bolsheviks were immensely better than their opponents in getting their message across, winning converts, and mobilizing people. It is also evident that this unquestioned superiority was one of the major causes of ultimate Bolshevik victory. But exactly how the Bolsheviks were better able to bring their ideas to the Russian people and what were the sources of Bolshevik strength in this area of politics are less clear.

Bolshevik attitude to mass persuasion

The simplest explanation of Bolshevik superiority in propaganda is that the revolutionaries saw the significance of the matter most clearly and therefore made the most concerted and sustained efforts. In this respect the contrast between them and their main enemies, the White leaders, was extraordinary. The White leaders were all military men who had acquired a narrow understanding of politics as something subversive and to be avoided by proper soldiers. The generals were accustomed to a way of life in which superiors commanded and inferiors obeyed. Although they believed in the justice of their cause just as firmly as the revolutionaries believed in theirs, their political and social views were unarticulated.

By contrast, the Bolsheviks were revolutionaries. In their underground work their chief task was to acquire followers, to persuade others of the correctness of their views. Their Marxism dictated that there was a universally valid interpretation of history. Those possessed of the priceless weapon of theory could predict and therefore influence events. Under these circumstances, the teaching of Marxism, i.e. propaganda, was not only not reprehensible, but on the contrary a necessary and noble task.

The Bolshevik Party was largely LENIN's creation and his ideas greatly influenced Soviet attitudes to propaganda. First of all, unlike Marx and the Western European socialists, Lenin was sceptical of the workers' ability to understand their true self-interest. In other words, the Bolsheviks were condescending towards the Russian people, including the workers, and condescension is a valuable asset in a successful propagandist. Secondly, in his writings Lenin always stressed the importance of organization. In 'Where to begin?' (1901), he argued that organization and propaganda were two sides of the same coin: a well-organized network would facilitate the work of propaganda and the very process of carrying out agitation would help the task of organization. This Leninist insight was to prove invaluable. Thirdly, Lenin believed that one should not fight ideas with ideas, for the bourgeoisie, with is greater resources, could buy newspapers and journalists and was bound to win. The implication of his position, as it was first fully developed in 'What is to be done?' (1902) was that in order to to neutralize the advantages enjoyed by the enemy, the socialists were entitled to use any methods. The admissibility of censorship was already inherent in Lenin's writings fifteen years before the Revolution.

Propaganda Methods

During the era of the PROVISIONAL GOVERNMENT the propaganda methods used by the Leninists were fundamentally similar to those of the other revolutionaries. All attempted to bring their message to the people by publishing newspapers and sending agitators to factories and regiments. Many Bolsheviks expressed themselves simply and forcefully but of course so did many SOCIALIST REVOLUTIONARIES and MENSHEVIKS.

The Leninists were greatly out-gunned by their enemies. The pro-government parties were much better financed, had a much larger newspaper network at their disposal that the Bolsheviks had. Nor did the government recoil from mild repression. For example, the circulation of Bolshevik newspapers in the Army was severely restricted, and the main newspaper, *Pravda*, was periodically closed down.

The history of Bolshevik propaganda, properly speaking, begins with the OCTOBER REVOLUTION, which gave the Bolsheviks the power of the state to further their propaganda effort. The situation was novel: no previous government had ever attempted such ambitious goals in transforming not only society, but humanity itself. The distinguishing characteristics of Soviet propaganda emerged and may be summarized as follows. First, the Soviet regime was not merely willing but able to suppress conflicting interpretations of political events. It did so much more consistently and to a greater extent than its opponents. Shortly after coming to power the Bolsheviks eliminated the free press. Secondly, the government developed its policies with their propaganda implications very much in mind. It combined the establishment of local government institutions with carrying out agitation. The party was remarkably resourceful in finding new ways to reach the people, such as sending out agitation automobiles, trains and ships. Thirdly, the regime took advantage of its organizational supremacy to suppress

Figure 19 The first agit-lorry cinema in Petrograd, c. 1920.

autonomous organizations and to create institutions through which it was able to penetrate segments of the population which might otherwise have remained unreachable. Fourthly, the Leninists attempted to use for political purposes works of art, such as film and literature. At this time, however, the party did not extend its monopoly over cultural life, which remained free and heterogeneous. (See entries in THE CULTURAL IMPACT OF THE REVOLUTION.)

The Press

The Soviet press came into being in an historically unprecedented situation: it was created and protected by a one-party revolutionary state. This fact essentially determined its character. Once relieved of the pressure of competition, the Bolshevik press developed characteristics that were unique at the time. The decisive development was the almost immediate suppression of the free, i.e. non-party, press.

Neither Lenin nor anyone else had ever envisaged the actual circumstances in which the Bolshevik revolution would be victorious. Since the Bolsheviks had assumed that their victory would come only when the overwhelming majority of the people supported their cause, they had not foreseen the need for censorship. On the other hand, the Bolsheviks were not liberals and they had little faith in formal freedoms. In particular, they had considered talk about the freedom of the press as bourgeois hypocrisy; Lenin repeatedly pointed out that in bourgeois society the writer depended on those who financed him.

Lenin fully approved the short-lived attempt of the Petrograd Soviet to close down the reactionary monarchist press in March 1917. When the Soviet reversed itself a few days later, Lenin had only contempt for it. In the period of the Provisional Government Lenin inconsistently advocated both the closing down of some of the major papers of the bourgeois parties and the confiscation of all paper supply and redistribution among political parties according to their strength in major cities.

After the Bolsheviks struck in October 1917, their MILITARY-REVOLUTIONARY COMMITTEE immediately forbade the publication of 'counter-revolutionary', i.e. anti-Bolshevik papers. This ban, however, was meant to be only temporary. A few days later the Bolshevik-dominated Executive Committee of the Soviet (Ispolkom) discussed the question whether the ban should be indefinitely extended. The passionate debate which took place on 17 November (NS) touched on the nature of the revolutionary order. Lenin and his followers argued that the press was a weapon, no different from bombs, and therefore the task of the revolutionaries was to deprive their enemies of this potential strength. Lenin, in particular, was convinced that any show of liberalism would be fatal to the survival of the revolution. His opponents, who included not only Left Socialist Revolutionaries but also some prominent

Bolsheviks, argued that the revolution was fought for supreme moral values, and that repression would dishonour the movement. They expressed confidence that their worker followers would understand the issues once these were fairly presented to them. In this crucial debate Lenin won.

Victory did not, however, mean the immediate establishment of Bolshevik monopoly. First of all, though Lenin was determined not to allow the presentation of hostile views, he did not yet appreciate that such a step would ultimately lead to allowing one and only one interpretation of any single political event. In November 1917 not even Lenin desired as total a suppression of non-Bolshevik voices as he soon achieved. Secondly, it would have been politically unwise, even if desired, to move against all enemies at once. It was better first to call only for the suppression of the non-socialist papers. Finally, and most important, the Bolsheviks did not have the strength to carry out systematic repression.

The first eight to nine months of Bolshevik rule was a twilight period of the free press. The new authorities harassed their opponents' press ever more mercilessly: they deprived them of the right to carry advertisements; they set up revolutionary tribunals to deal with papers that dared to print hostile articles; and, most important, the Red Guard confiscated invaluable paper supply and printing-presses. The new Bolshevik network of newspapers was thus based on property confiscated from the opposition.

In the first months repression was haphazard. Some newspapers got away with printing truly inflammatory articles on the one hand, while others were closed down for small and formal violations on the other. The situation differed from city to city. In Moscow, for example, until the government's transfer there in March 1918, considerable liberalism was shown by the local authorities. Often newspapers which were closed down could re-open after a perfunctory change of title. The situation changed in the middle of 1918. An abortive Left Socialist Revolutionary rising in July, attempts on the lives of Bolshevik leaders including Lenin, and the spread of the Civil War persuaded the Bolsheviks to take ever more repressive measures. In the middle of 1918 all non-Bolshevik newspapers disappeared from territories controlled by the Bolsheviks.

What kind of press did the Bolsheviks create in a political environment in which their monopoly over interpretation of facts was assured? There was general agreement among contemporaries that the press functioned poorly. The revolutionaries faced difficult problems: there was a paper famine. In 1920, for example, the country produced only 6.7 per cent of the paper produced in 1913. The foreign-made printing-presses broke down and could not be repaired. At the height of the Civil War the size and circulation of major papers depended on how much paper was available on a particular day. Some newspapers did not accept private subscriptions, but attempted instead to service institutions in the hope of a wider readership. Shortage of paper and difficulty in distributing at a time of civil strife meant that on occasion even district capitals received the central newspapers only three or four times a month.

But even aside from the technical difficulties, the Bolshevik papers were hardly impressive instruments of propaganda. Although most revolutionary leaders were experienced journalists, now they bore responsibilities that seemed more important to them. Lenin had to exhort his followers to write for the popular press. At a time of shortage of journalists and paper, the Soviet regime did not utilize its scarce resources well. It bowed to pressure from local organizations and allowed a proliferation of news-papers. The local papers that appeared regularly were incompetently written and edited. The technical quality of all newspapers was low: the print was often illegible and most newspapers could not reproduce photographs.

During the Civil War the Bolsheviks often discussed among themselves what kind of press the revolutionary regime needed. In an important article, Lenin argued that there was no need for long discussions of events of domestic and foreign policy, and instead primary attention should be paid to concrete questions of economic reconstruction. Indeed, as Lenin implied, nobody remained to polemicize with! The major issues of political life were no longer open to debate and thereby the public sphere was drastically narrowed.

Reaching the peasants

Given the extent of economic and political disintegration and the low level of development of the communication system, the Bolsheviks and their opponents alike faced serious difficulties in bringing their message to the Russian people. The Bolsheviks, however, showed impressive ingenuity.

The new regime determined that the Bolshevik point of view would be heard in the villages. The party organized a network of agitators whose job was to explain its policies to the peasants in the most favourable light. The agitators were either Communist workers or, more frequently, demobilized soldiers who had been won over in the course of 1917 and who were now returning to their native villages. The agitators' most important task was to acquaint the peasantry with the Land law, passed immediately after the take-over, that allowed the peasants to seize landlord-land and cultivate it as their private property. In drawing up this decree, Lenin was conscious of its propaganda implications, and he regarded it as the most important instrument in gaining the goodwill of the peasantry.

The Soviet regime was able to mobilize approximately 50,000 agitators during the first year of its existence, almost all of them from the lower classes. The were poorly trained, they had only a vague understanding of Marxist ideology and even of Bolshevik strategy, but their background gave them a particular advantage in reaching their fellow villagers.

In early 1918 Ya. Burov published a pamphlet for agitators which provides a good source for understanding Bolshevik thinking about propaganda at the time. Burov, as an old Bolshevik, drew no line between organization and propaganda. He advised the soldiers that on their arrival in the village they should reconnoitre, find out who the influential people were, what the peasants were thinking and how well they understood the government's policies. After this preparatory work the agitator was to gain the confidence of the three or four most influential people in the village and call a village assembly, where, with the aid of his local helpers, he should try to ensure the passing of pro-Bolshevik resolutions, remaining in the background as much as possible himself. Once the local soviets were safely in pro-Bolshevik hands, the agitator was to carry out the same task at the district level. Burov also gave practical advice to the agitators such as where to get help, and how to respond to ticklish questions such as the reasons for the dispersal of the CONSTITUENT ASSEMBLY.

The Bolsheviks constantly experimented with novel methods of bringing their message to the people. Many of these methods did not amount to much, but in combination they must have made a difference. One such method of little practical value was contained in a decree passed by the Soviet government in December 1918, according to which literate peasants were obliged to read the regulations of the government and other selected material to the illiterates. The local soviets were ordered to send periodic reports on the progress of the work. In remote villages, however, where the need for spreading information about govern-ment policies was most felt, Communist strength was so limited that the party could not enforce its will. In contemporary literature there is hardly any reference to such readings and one must conclude that they took place only rarely.

Since the government's apparatus in the villages was abysmally weak, and the new authorities were not in a position to remedy the situation quickly, a particularly imaginative method of agitation was to send agents by ship and train into the countryside, combining governmental and propaganda work in the process. In addition to many agitators, the trains and ships carried representatives from various commissariats, from the party Central Committee and Komsomol, the youth organization. The trains were equipped with small libraries and printing-presses for producing newspapers and pamphlets. While representa-tives from commissariats established contact with the local agencies in order to supervise their work and provide help, agitators gave lectures to the peasants and engaged individuals in conversation. To attract as large an audience as possible, the trains and ships carried projectors and showed films to eager spectators. Since the great majority of peasants had never encountered this modern miracle, the

Figure 20 Interior of agit-train coach, South-Western Front, 1920.

drawing power of the films was great. Agitators used motor-cycles to reach villages that were not on the railway or a major river. If contemporary reports are accurate, 2–3 million people attended meetings organized in this way, and 2 million attended film shows.

The Bolsheviks also established *agitpunkty* (agitational points) at railway stations. At the time of the Civil War passengers often had to wait days for their train. The agitation points, which had propaganda libraries, lecture halls, film projectors, took advantage of these 'captive audiences'.

Mass organizations

A Bolshevik innovation in the art of mass persuasion was the creation of mass organizations, whose task was to act as connecting links between the policy makers and the population at large. In a sense, the party itself was such a

mass organization since one of its main tasks was to indoctrinate. The trade unions, after the Bolsheviks captured them, also undertook to educate the workers in the spirit of Communism. (See WORKERS AND THE BOLSHEVIK STATE.)

Two major organisations that had no other function but agitation were Komsomol, the youth organization and Zhenotdel, which was to mobilize women (see WOMEN: 1917 AND AFTER). During the Civil War these organizations were still in an embryonic form and acquired mass membership only in the peaceful years of the 1920s. Nevertheless, by popularizing policies developed elsewhere, the two organizations contributed to the Bolshevik victory. They enabled the regime to tailor its propaganda for special audiences and thereby extended the party's reach.

These bodies served another purpose, less evident but no

less important: they provided a sphere of activity for thousands of enthusiasts. The Reds were much more successful than their enemies in mobilizing new talent, people who in the past had been left out of the political life of the country.

The Civil War was a period of self-definition for the mass organizations. On the one hand their success depended on their ability to understand and articulate the mentality and particular concerns of their constituency. Without a degree of autonomy their legitimacy was in doubt. On the other hand the party leadership was concerned that these organizations might become advocates for their constituents. The leaders refused to concede that on selected issues the interests of the young and of women might diverge from the public good, as determined by the party. The Communist regime would tolerate no independent intermediaries between itself and the individual citizen.

Propaganda and culture

The Leninists regarded the backwardness of the Russian people as the major obstacle to building socialism. A manifestation of this backwardness was illiteracy, and to overcome this, in spite of difficult times, the government organized an impressive campaign which served both as a spur to further achievement and as an indoctrination tool. The party sponsored the publication of literacy textbooks that reduced Communist doctrine to the simplest level. As the workers and peasants learned to read and write, they memorized sentences such as 'The defence of the Revolutionn is the duty of the working classes', or 'We are building a new world without tyrants and slaves'. Textbooks bore headings such as: 'What should the poor do in the village?, 'The Tsar, the priest and the kulak', and so forth. In the unsettled circumstances it is doubtful that the campaign was as successful among the workers and peasants as it was among the soldiers of the Red Army.

The Bolsheviks were unequivocally in favour of culture, as long as 'culture' meant only the spread of literacy. Their relationship with the producers of high culture, however, was ambivalent (see CULTURAL REVOLUTION). On the one hand they respected 'culture' and 'art' and had no doubt of the significance of ideas. The realised that they needed the services of intellectuals for the creation of a socialist society, and in the short run they wanted the help of artists in spreading the Communist message. On the other hand the Leninists had a distaste for values which they associated with the intelligentsia, such as moral scruples, interminable disputes and avoidance of action. While the regime gave generous support to some intellectuals, it did not create an environment in which freedom of thought could long flourish.

Some branches of art were easier to exploit than others. Singing revolutionary songs at meetings and parades was a necessary part of such events. The Bolsheviks understood mass psychology. In an interesting speech at a Komsomol congress, BUKHARIN pointed out that the average person, when marching in parades and taking part in singing revolutionary songs, felt part of a large and powerful whole. He therefore recommended singing and parades as agitational tools.

The poster is the quintessential form of propaganda; it is the ultimate in reduction. Its production was relatively cheap, and at a time of great paper shortage, thousands could be reached at small cost. It is generally agreed that the Bolshevik graphic artists were better and more imaginative than their counter-revolutionary counterparts. Even after the passage of seven decades, some of the Soviet posters are still striking (see ART).

The Bolsheviks well appreciated the propaganda potential of film, especially in a country where illiteracy was still about 60 per cent. Furthermore, film had a modern aura and was therefore particularly appealing. The government invested scarce resources in making newsreels with blatant propaganda texts. Young Soviet film-makers also developed a new genre, *agitka*. These were very short, didactic films, often animated posters (see CINEMA).

The government made extraordinary efforts to revive the publishing industry. It bought paper and machinery abroad, and on occasion even contracted foreign firms to print Russian books abroad. The state printed large editions of agitational pamphlets and the Marxist classics. However, it also allowed the publication of non-political literature and even of books that had a veiled anti-Marxist content. During the infancy of the Soviet state, extensive censorship coexisted with a broad heterogeneity in the world of literature and scholarship.   PK

Further Reading

Kenez, Peter: *The Birth of the Propaganda State: Soviet Methods of Mass Mobilization, 1917–1929*. New York: Cambridge University Press, 1985.

Pethybridge, Roger: *The Spread of the Russian Revolution: Essays on 1917*. New York: St Martin's Press, 1972.

———— : *The Social Prelude to Stalinism*. New York: St Martin's Press, 1974.

Tumarkin, Nina: *Lenin Lives! The Lenin Cult in Soviet Russia*. Cambridge, Mass.: Harvard University Press, 1983.

The Kronstadt Revolt: 1921

Situated on Kotlin Island in the Gulf of Finland some 20 miles from St Petersburg, Kronstadt was founded by Peter the Great at the beginning of the eighteenth century to protect his new capital and 'window to the west' from the sea. By the beginning of the twentieth century Kronstadt had grown into a major fortress and naval base, the chief training and repair centre of the Baltic fleet, and a considerable mercantile port for timber exports and coal imports. Its civilian population exceeded 60,000, of whom 50,000 were registered inhabitants and another 10,000 to

15,000 unregistered, while its garrison numbered 20,000 soldiers and sailors. By February 1917 the garrison consisted of 20,000 soldiers and another 12,000 sailors, of whom more than 7,000 were in training units.

While the bomb which killed Alexander II in 1881 was prepared by a Kronstadt naval officer and member of Peoples' Will, Nicholas Sukhanov, it was only from 1902 that revolutionary cells are known to have existed in the torpedo and gunnery training detachments.

1905 and after

Long pent-up anger at appalling conditions erupted in late October 1905, after 50 soldiers were arrested for demanding implementation of their rights in the wake of the tsar's manifesto. Their mutiny degenerated into a rampage of arson, pillage and drunkenness that was only put down two days later by troops from St Petersburg. Despite tsarist leniency, on 2 November the St Petersburg Soviet proclaimed a general strike and Kronstadt's reputation as the hearth of revolution had been made.

The insurrection of 19 July 1906 was planned by the SR-dominated United Committee of the Kronstadt Military-Revolutionary Organization with the BOLSHEVIKS, led by D. Z. MANUILSKY, as junior partners. It was to have coincided with revolts in the three other Baltic fleet bases (Sveaborg, Reval and Libau), but was poorly prepared and armed, and was put down within a few hours by local troops: nearly 1,500 were imprisoned, 180 sent to hard labour, and 36, mostly sailors, executed.

The already harsh Kronstadt regime was tightened further, reaching its apogee under Vice-Admiral Robert Viren, who was supported by the chief of the gendarmerie and almost the entire officers' corps, notably the naval officers. Viren's system was successful in silencing organized revolutionary activity among Kronstadt's workers and in tracking down revolutionary cells in naval and army units. It proved powerless, however, as Viren realised in September 1916, in preventing the disaffection of the entire garrison, and he therefore pleaded for the dismantling of most of the garrison.

1917

The FEBRUARY REVOLUTION began in Kronstadt with a bloody squaring of accounts during the night of 1 March with Viren, some 50 of the most hated commanders and officers and another 30 gendarmes, policemen and police spies, shot by firing squads, and some 350 others including senior officials, incarcerated in Kronstadt's notorious dungeons.

Within 10 days the sailors, soldiers, workers, clerks and teachers elected their own Soviet of 280 deputies who in turn elected an Executive Committee of 35 members. All officers were elected by their units, senior officers and the control commissions which flanked them were elected by the Soviet plenum, and every base committee was elected by the work-place or unit assembly.

In Kronstadt there was no 'dual power'. Soviet power rested on a broad political base of left-wing Soviet factions ranging from the MENSHEVIKS (increasingly Internationalists and led by P. Malyshev a cadet instructor, P. Ediet a petty-officer, and V. A. Valk a sawmill foreman), the SRs (increasingly Left SRs led by the sailors A. Brushvit and B. Donskoi, and the *intelligent* G. Smolyansky), a large radical Non-Party group (by August proclaimed Union of SR MAXIMALISTS and led by the student and Soviet chairman Anatoli Lamanov and the sailor and poet A. Nemm) to the Bolsheviks (led by F. F. RASKOLNIKOV, S. G. Roshal, A. M. Lyubovich and, replacing Raskolnikov after the July Days, I. Flerovsky and Lyudmilla Stal; apart from the signalman Lyubovich, the Bolshevik leaders were all professional revolutionaries and imports). From August, there was also a small, vociferous ANARCHIST faction split into Anarcho-Syndicalists led by Efim Yarchuk, and Anarcho-Communists led by I. S. Bleikhman. Though at the outset the SRs formed the largest faction, by May they had been outnumbered by the Bolsheviks and, by August, by the SR Maximalists now led by G. Rivkin, A. Zverin and Lamanov, with neither of these two factions having an absolute majority. While the SR Maximalist ideology of pure sovietism may have appealed more to Kronstadters, they increasingly accepted Bolshevik political leadership for its superior organization and determination, and Kronstadters of all factions, including Menshevik-Internationalists, followed the Bolsheviks into the OCTOBER REVOLUTION and distinguished themselves in the seizure of power and, subsequently, as crack Red troops in the CIVIL WAR. However, a Bolshevik majority was achieved only as late as June/July 1918. after the Mensheviks and Left SRs had been expelled from the Soviet by decree from outside.

The revolt

Utterly disillusioned by the Bolshevik 'commissarocracy', the Kronstadt garrison rose in March 1921, but now with the SR Maximalist slogan 'All power to Soviets and not to parties!'

While their discontent was fuelled by the economic crisis of WAR COMMUNISM, the large-scale strikes and arrests of Petrograd workers in February 1921, the malaise and dissensions in the Communist Party, and the privileges and high living of its functionaries and commissars, it was the paralysis of the local Communist Party apparatus that enabled Kronstadt's disaffected sailors, many of them Communist Party members, to organize and assemble on 27 and 28 February 1921 on board the battleship *Petropavlovsk*. On 1 March a mass meeting on Anchor Square endorsed a 15-point resolution, drafted and moved by S. Petrichenko, senior naval clerk, and the sailor P. Perepelkin, both from the *Petropavlovsk*, the only dissenters being visiting government functionaries.

Figure 21   Members of the Kronstadt uprising.

Appealing to the left-wing audience of Russia, including disillusioned Communists, the *Petropavlovsk* resolution, together with a more explicit sequel, the 'Appeal of the Revolutionary Committee to the Railwaymen' of 5 March, amounted to nothing less than a demand for the peaceful dismantling of the Communist police state, the abolition of War Communism, and the internal reform of the Soviet system. The key political demand was for immediate new elections to the Soviets by secret ballot based on 'equal franchise' (that is without the current discrimination in favour of workers as against peasants by one to five) in which all left socialist parties and Anarchists would be legalized and compete freely and equally. Communist political departments and special military units, Chekas (see VECHEKA) and 'all privileges of Communists' were to be abolished. All socialist political prisoners were to be equalized rationing; workers' wages were to be paid 'in gold and not in paper trash'.

The economic demands called for the 'disenserfment' of workers and peasants; the right to move from one job to another, and the disbandment of TROTSKY's notorious 'labour armies'; peasants must be free to use the land as they wished, and craftsmen so to practise their crafts, in neither case using hired labour; free consumer cooperatives, not the state, should manage food supplies and equalized rationing; workers wages were to be paid 'in gold and not in paper trash'.

All attempts at negotiations with the Communist authorities met with a tight blockade of the island and with the adamant demands of Trotsky (People's Commissar for War and Navy) and ZINOVIEV (the Petrograd party boss) for unconditional surrender, otherwise 'you will be shot like partridges'.

Therefore, a Conference of Delegates (one third of whom were Communists) elected by naval crews, army units, workshops and Soviet institutions convened on 2 and 4 March and elected a Provisional Revolutionary Committee of 15 which, chaired by Petrichenko and consisting of six

civilians and nine sailors, began to implement the *Petropavlovsk* programme. Aided by the resignation of 784 party members, the formation of a collaborationist, provisional bureau of the RKP and the imprisonment of over 200 Communist diehards, including the chairman of the regional party committee, it made a clean sweep of Communist Party domination. Earlier, some 200 party members, including 20 Chekists, had escaped over the ice to the Krasnaya Gorka fort.

When RED ARMY units failed to subdue Kronstadt, thousands of Communist Party members, including nearly 300 Tenth Party Congress delegates, carried with them, or drove at gun point, some 45–50,000 troops under generals M. N. TUKHACHEVSKY, S. S. Kamenev and V. K. Putna, and on 17 and 18 March made the final and successful assault.

The brutal suppression of Kronstadt, and the establishment there of a tough Communist regime under a military commandant, former Kronstadt sailor P. E. Dybenko, and a revolutionary troika – L. Bregman, P. Vasiliev, and A. I. Gribov – was followed by a vicious campaign of slander and delegitimation.

Early attempts to connect Kronstadt's Revolutionary Committee and/or its chief military officer Major General A. Kozlovsky with White Guardist counter-revolution failed dismally. The specious labelling of the Kronstadt sailors of March 1921 as 'accidental elements' or recently recruited 'Ukrainian peasant lads', purveyed by Trotsky and K. B. RADEK, however, has held sway in Soviet historiography and bedevilled western scholarship.

Personnel lists of the two major battleships which spearheaded the uprising, and of other materials recently studied, however, show that the large majority of the Kronstadt sailors of March 1921 were both veterans of the 1917 revolution and ethnically Great Russians, that the majority of the Revolutionary Committee had been active in 1917, as had all three editors of the *Izvestiya* published by the Revolutionary Committee, including Anatoli Lamanov, who wrote its SR Maximalist ideological articles and was subsequently executed as the ideologist of the uprising.

For the student of history Kronstadt during its golden age (March 1917 to June 1918) stands out as a fully-fledged soviet democracy; the student of Communism, however, will identify in the March 1921 uprising the first major example of left-wing protest from below against Communist domination.   IG

Further Reading

Avrich, Paul: *Kronstadt 1921.* Princeton, NJ: Princeton University Press, 1970.

Getzler, Israel: *Kronstadt 1917–1921.* Cambridge: Cambridge University Press. 1983.

Mawdsley, Evan: *The Russian Revolution and the Baltic Fleet.* London: 1978.

Figure 22   The Red Army attacking Kronstadt, March 1921.

Saul, Norman E.: *Sailors in Revolt*. Kansas: 1978.

Semanov, S.N.: *Likvidatsiya antisovetskogo Kronshtadtskogo Myatezha 1921 goda*. Moscow: 1973.

Sivkov, P.Z.: *Kronshtadt*. Leningrad: 1972.

The Emigration

The Bolshevik seizure of power was the start of the most violent and radical upheaval in Russian history, leading to a series of 'waves' of politically-inspired emigration, the latest of which has not yet (1987) wholly subsided.

It is customary to identify three such waves. The 'First Wave' was the exodus of those who, broadly speaking, had constituted the 'Establishment' of the former regime, and who could not or would not accept the social and political consequences of the OCTOBER REVOLUTION and the defeat of the various 'White' armies in the CIVIL WAR. This outflow began sporadically in 1918, increasing in volume until it was stopped in 1926 by the Soviet government's almost total ban on further emigration. Socially, the 'First Wave' was largely drawn from the property-owning, official and professional classes, many fleeing for their lives, either from the formal threat of reprisals as 'counter-revolutionaries' (see VECHEKA) or from arbitrary terrorism by individuals or mobs venting their age-old resentment on the former bosses, priests, landowners, judges, officers, policemen or civil servants. Apart from these 'ex-officio' enemies, as it were, there were at least as many who emigrated for reasons of principle or because they felt there was no place for them in the new, crude-seeming and apparently unstable Bolshevik Russia: politicians from moderate socialists to monarchists; academics and schoolteachers; doctors, lawyers and engineers; musicians, artists and ballet dancers; journalists and writers (although some, such as Maxim GORKY, Alexei Tolstoy and Ilya Ehrenburg returned and successfully pursued their literary careers in the USSR). Nor were all the 'First Wave' émigrés from privileged, educated or prosperous backgrounds: in the 'White' armies of General DENIKIN, Baron WRANGEL and Admiral KOLCHAK, for example, the rank and file included some tens of thousands who were by origin peasants, craftsmen, COSSACK farmers. After a few years in emigration, many of these returned to Russia, while others eventually settled in Europe, the Americas, the Far East and Australia, usually as farm labourers, industrial workers or small traders.

There are no reliable, global statistics indicating either the total numbers or a breakdown of the social and ethnic origins of 'First Wave' émigrés from Russia. The League of Nations Office of Refugees did make an attempt to compile such figures, but these were so incomplete as to be of little value, being based on the often haphazard records of the host-countries who sheltered the émigrés. Many of these were either newly-created independent states (for example Yugoslavia, Poland, Latvia, Lithuania, Estonia, Finland, Czechoslovakia) or underdeveloped, poorly-administered lands such as China and Iran, none of which were equipped with adequate means to monitor a large influx of refugees who very often entered the initial host-country by clandestine routes. A frequent pattern of emigration was for refugees to flee first of all to a neighbouring country and then sometimes months, sometimes years later, to re-emigrate to more hospitable places and better economic prospects.

A majority of those Russian refugees who emigrated via SIBERIA to the Far East, for instance, went initially to Manchuria, thanks to the fact that the Russian-owned CHINESE EASTERN RAILWAY ran across Manchuria on an extra-territorial strip which included the city that housed the railway's workshops and administrative centre, HARBIN, which by 1920 had been a Russian city for over twenty years. From there, after a stay sometimes lasting ten years, Russian émigrés dispersed into China; the luckier ones then found ways of moving onward, usually via Hong Kong or Shanghai, to the USA or Australia and New Zealand.

Emigration from European Russia took place by various means, the route often depending on the military situation in the Civil War, on whether certain exit points from Russia were in 'Red' or 'White' hands, or on political factors, i.e. the attitudes of the frontier states, some of whom (Poland; Romania) tended to be anti-Russian in sentiment and therefore unwelcoming to Russian émigrés of any political colour, while others (Finland; Estonia; Latvia; Georgia under the MENSHEVIKS and UKRAINE until their reincorporation into Soviet Russia in 1921 and 1922) were more liberal towards the entry or passage of refugees. In Southern Russia the port of Odessa saw a steady flow of emigration until the city finally fell into 'Red' hands, while the only truly mass emigration, numbering over a quarter of a million, took place in November 1920 from the

Crimea, when Wrangel's 'White' army was finally driven into the sea after a rearguard action that held off the RED ARMY long enough to permit the seaborne departure of both Wrangel's troops (145,000) and large numbers of civilians (120,000). This epic of evacuation was made possible by the presence of an Anglo-French naval squadron as well as substantial remnants of the RUSSIAN NAVY, together with numerous commandeered and chartered merchant vessels. This huge, motley flotilla then steamed to Istanbul (then under Allied occupation), where the bulk of the Russian refugees, military and civilian, were first quarantined and then disembarked. An exception to this arrangement was the most illustrious of the émigrés, the Dowager Empress Maria Fedorovna (the former Princess Dagmar of Denmark), who was the aunt of King George V of Great Britain. She was taken in the British flagship to Malta, whence she travelled to Denmark, there to end her days in the place of her birth.

Less well-connected refugees, however, had a harder time. The 'Wrangel' (ex-Black Sea) fleet was offered refuge by France in the Tunisian port of Bizerta until a solution to its proper ownership could be found. Apart from skeleton crews of seamen, it carried large numbers of civilians and the cadets from the 'White' Russian naval academy at Sebastopol. All were disembarked, and on land the officers, the former academy instructors and their wives set up a school, in spartan conditions, at which the cadets were given an adequate education, until France accepted all those who wished to emigrate further. The older warships were sold for scrap, while the more modern ones were eventually acquired by the Soviet government and recommissioned in the Red Fleet.

The biggest problem raised by the evacuation, however, was Wrangel's army. Believing that with Allied support he could return to Russia and overthrow the Soviet regime, Wrangel was determined to keep his force intact. Obliged to feed, accommodate and control this large body of somewhat demoralized troops, the Allied occupation authorities in Turkey found it in their interest, too, to keep these men under their officers in disciplined units. Some were put under canvas on the Gallipoli peninsula, others into camps on the Aegean island of Lemnos. A number of them accepted Soviet offers of an amnesty and returned to Russia, though a majority chose to remain in emigration. Meanwhile Wrangel and his emissaries obtained agreements from the Bulgarian, Yugoslav and French governments which allowed entire battalions, companies and such like, to emigrate to those countries as civilians while retaining their cohesion as units. The administrative convenience of this method suited the host-countries, who were suffering from severe manpower shortages caused by wartime casualties and from other economic effects of the war or of the post-war redrawing of frontiers.

The Russian civilian émigrés who thronged Istanbul, mostly destitute, existing on the meagre handouts of Allied relief agencies, gradually moved on to other countries willing to receive them. Foremost among these was Yugoslavia, where thanks to the strongly pro-Russian sentiments of King Alexander I (a pre-1914 graduate of Russia's elite military school, the Cadet Corps) they were welcomed, especially those with qualifications suitable to provide much-needed expertise in the new state's deficient professional cadres, in industry, on the railways, in medicine, as lawyers and in commerce. Wrangel himself moved to Yugoslavia, where he formed the Russian All-Services Union (ROVS), ostensibly an ex-servicemen's association but in reality a shadow command-network of the 'White' forces, through which contact was maintained with all former officers and (if possible) with their 'units'. The Soviet authorities took ROVS very seriously; sustained and largely successful efforts were made to penetrate it with Soviet agents. After Wrangel's death in 1928 his two successors at the head of ROVS, Generals Miller and Kutepov, were both abducted from Paris and were never seen again.

Germany's invasion of the Soviet Union in June 1941 caused a conflict of loyalty in all Russian émigrés: many gave their moral and material support to the USSR out of Russian patriotism (including Denikin), while the diehard anti-Bolshevik element hoped to return to a non-Soviet Russia in the wake of a German victory. With this aim, two principal groups of the former 'White' Russian forces remaining in Yugoslavia threw in their lot with the Germans. These were émigré Cossack units led by General Krasnov, and a division-sized formation of other 'White' veterans under General Skorodumov, known as the Russian Corps, and consisting of lightly-armed infantry units which the Germans used chiefly to guard their bases and lines of communication, though in the fluid conditions of guerrilla warfare these duties often brought the Russian Corps into direct action against Tito's communist partisans.

Czechoslovakia, like Yugoslavia a Slav country newly created under the Versailles settlement, was another which opened its gates to Russian émigrés, a policy strongly advocated by the republic's Russophile but anti-Bolshevik first president, Thomas Masaryk, with the aim, as in Yugoslavia, of superseding the many Germans who had held responsible positions under Austria-Hungary and of replacing them with 'brother Slavs'. Ample employment was available to qualified émigrés; the Czech state enabled the refugees to maintain several high schools with a Russian curriculum (with Czech or Slovak as obligatory second languages). Russian professors gave courses at the Charles University in Prague, where a Russian Faculty of Law was instituted, allowing those who only spoke Russian to gain degrees. An entire section of the university library was devoted to Russian books, documents and manuscripts, which became the largest and most valuable collection of such material outside the USSR, until on Stalin's orders it was removed in its entirety in 1945 and transported to Moscow. The Russian émigré community suffered considerably under German occupation, many being deported to forced labour in Germany; a similar fate awaited the remainder when, in 1945, most of them were rounded up by Soviet 'repatriation commissions' and sent to Siberian labour camps.

For the large number of Russians who emigrated via the formerly Russian territories of Poland, the Baltic States and Finland, their immediate destination was Germany, where a liberal immigration policy gave unrestricted entry and where, at first, inflation made living cheap for those with even modest funds in stable currencies, gold, jewellery and other realizable assets. Until 1924, when the German mark was stabilized and inflation halted, 'Russian Berlin' was the political, intellectual and artistic 'capital' of the Russian emigration, with a lively cultural life, an extensive Russian-language press and numerous publishing-houses (including one owned by Maxim Gorky), which not only printed the first works of such émigré writers as Vladimir Nabokov but also published books under contract for Soviet publishing organizations, at a time when the paper-making and printing industries in Soviet Russia were in dire straits. Berlin also witnessed the foundation of Smena Vekh (Change of Landmarks), the first movement among émigré Russian intellectuals to advocate reconciliation with the Soviet regime and return to Russia; two distinguished writers who put this idea into practice were Alexei Tolstoy and Andrei Bely. Political life in 'Russian Berlin' was extremely active, chiefly consisting of fierce if sterile arguments on dead issues between the rumps of pre-1918 Russian political parties, who ranged from Mensheviks to monarchists. That such passions still ran high was shown in 1922 when a Russian monarchist ex-officer shot at MILYUKOV, leader of the centrist Kadet Party in exile, and killed instead V. V. Nabokov, his party colleague and father of the writer. It was in Berlin, too, that British right-wing interests paid a group of Russian monarchist émigrés to forge the notorious 'ZINOVIEV letter', hinting at Comintern penetration of British institutions, a plot that helped to bring down the first Labour government.

After 1924, when the cost of living rose sharply for refugees in Germany, re-emigration from Berlin began, accelerated after 1932 by Hitler's rise to power. Most Russians moved westward, joining the large community in France, while others went further, some to French and Belgian colonies in Africa, others to the USA and Latin America. Throughout the 1920s, France's traditionally liberal attitude to immigration combined with several factors – the need to replace manpower lost in the war; a series of right-wing governments hostile to the Soviet Union; long-standing cultural links between France and Russia; a relatively low cost of living – to provide easy entry for Russian refugees, until by the late 1930s the Russian colony in France was one of the largest and most socially diverse to be found in any host-country. It included distinguished figures in the arts and letters, such as Ivan Bunin, the first Russian to win the Nobel Prize for literature (1933); the bass Fedor Chaliapin; Sergei Diaghilev who, though he and his Ballets Russes had left Russia before the revolution, chose not to return home; and Marina Tsvetaeva, considered by many the greatest Russian poet of this century.

Although with a few exceptions the Russians who came to France as émigrés did not prosper economically and were never truly integrated into French society, their children took good advantage of the French educational system and made successful careers. In France, as in other countries, the émigrés' main focus of group cohesion and mutual aid was the RUSSIAN ORTHODOX CHURCH, despite the division between those who accepted the Patriarch of Moscow's authority and the 'autocephalous' who acknowledged only the Patriarch of Constantinople. The most divisive factor, however, experienced perhaps more keenly by Russian émigrés in France than elsewhere, was the German attack on the Soviet Union. Some, notably former 'White' officers, volunteered for service in the German army on the Eastern Front. A greater number, however, felt a sense of gratitude and loyalty to France, identified themselves with the Allied cause and became active in the French Resistance, many perishing and not a few showing outstanding bravery. The wave of Russian patriotic feeling, engendered by the Soviet contribution to the Allied victory in 1945 and much fostered by Soviet diplomats in France and by the Communist Party, persuaded many émigrés to return to the Soviet Union, taking their French-born children with them.

Of the larger European countries, Britain was perhaps the most lukewarm towards receiving Russian émigrés, although those with influential connections, adequate funds or firm employment prospects, women married to British subjects or those backed by a financial guarantor were allowed right of entry or transit. Numerically small, the Russian émigré colony was assimilated with considerable ease into British society.

Contrary to the general impression that the USA positively encouraged immigration, the American quota for Russian immigrants in the first decade after 1918 was small, and entry was also linked to the 'sponsor' system. Hence, the USA tended to be a country of 'secondary emigration', especially in the 1930s, when the Depression and rising political tensions in Europe, together with a liberalization of American immigration laws under Roosevelt's administration, induced many Russian émigrés to cross the Atlantic. Once admitted, their biggest problems were then economic, and former aristocrats and generals found themselves working as manual labourers in order to survive. Those with technical training, artistic talents or academic qualifications were generally able to find work; many proved to be notable scholars and teachers in American universities. When the USSR was drawn into the Second World War, the Russian émigré colony in America responded by contributing generously to funds for both civil and military aid to the Soviet Union.

Of all the achievements of the 'First Wave' of Russian emigration, ultimately its greatest contribution to the rest of the world has been greatly to increase the spread – by scholarship, composition, painting, authorship and performance – of an awareness and appreciation of Russian music, literature and art. For the one link between the Russian émigrés and their fellow-Russians in the homeland that remains unbreakable by political or ideological schism is their deep, unalterable love for their native language and culture. MVG

Post-October Institutions

Totally without experience in the practice of government, the BOLSHEVIKS set out to establish their administration according to the only organizing principle they recognized, namely that of centralism. LENIN's well defined, and in October 1917 well tested, ideas on party structure were applied to government. Since power had been seized in the name of the SOVIETS, it was the soviets which became the new organs of administration, although, as in October 1917, power was in the hands of the Bolshevik Party, (renamed the Russian Communist Party (Bolsheviks) in 1919).

From the outset, the new regime took steps to protect itself from its political enemies by state bureaucratic means reminiscent of those characteristic of the tsarist system. In its rapid growth, far greater scale and violence, however, the Soviet state quickly overtook its predecessor.

Predictably, as an internationalist revolutionary workers' state, the Soviet regime agitated in favour of world revolution. At the same time, it tried to establish itself as a legitimate state among the world powers, and mechanisms and policies were created to help the government walk this tight-rope.

Faced almost at once with the CIVIL WAR, the new regime established and equipped the Red Army and Red Navy in perhaps the most successsful effort of organization it undertook.

Similarly, although the dictatorship of the proletariat was meant to supplant and replace the need for law, as it was understood and expressed in bourgeois society, the new regime, led by the former lawyer Lenin, immediately codified its first acts in the form of new laws and a new legal system was quickly established. The promulgation of a new Constitution as early as 1918 also suggests that on the morrow of the revolution, the style of the new regime was made plain: this was not going to be a free-wheeling regime of improvisors, but a systematic arrangement of institutions for the government of the new state and society in accordance with principles defined and promulgated from a single central authority.

HS

Lenin's Government: 1917–1922 (Sovnarkom)

When the Second All-Russian Congress of Soviets of Workers', Soldiers' and Peasants' Deputies convened in Petrograd late on 25 October (7 November 1917 NS), the PROVISIONAL GOVERNMENT *de jure* still held power. Early the following morning, Lenin informed the Congress that the Provisional Government was under arrest. Thereupon a proclamation of Soviet power was passed. The Congress took 'power into its hands . . .' All power had passed 'to the soviets of workers', peasants' and soldiers' deputies' whose duty it was to 'establish genuine revolutionary order'. Reconvening in the evening of 26 October the Congress passed a motion, proposed by its chairman, L. B. KAMENEV, establishing a Soviet government, the Council of People's Commissars (Sovnarkom). It consisted of fifteen members with V. I. LENIN as its chairman. A. I. Rykov was responsible for internal affairs; V. P. Milyutin for agriculture; A. G. SHLYAPNIKOV for labour; V. P. Nogin

for trade and industry; A. V. LUNACHARSKY for education; I. I. SKVORTSOV-STEPANOV for finance; L. D. TROTSKY for foreign affairs; A. I. Lomov for justice; A. I. Teodorovich for food supplies; N. P. Avilov for posts and telegraphs and I. V. STALIN for nationalities. A Committee for Military and Naval Affairs was collectively to be the responsibility of V. A. ANTONOV-OVSEENKO, N. V. KRYLENKO and P. E. Dybenko but were joined one day later by N. I. Podvoisky. Separate commissariats for the army and navy were established in November 1917. Keenly aware of parallels with the French Revolution, the Bolsheviks may have been concerned to eliminate the possibility of Bonapartism and appointed four men to run the armed forces.

In order to underline the new order members of the government were referred to as commissars and not as ministers. However the division of responsibility was remarkably similar to the ministerial structure of the old

Imperial regime. Besides being temporary until the convocation of the CONSTITUENT ASSEMBLY, Sovnarkom revealed traces of a different mode of rule. Running particular branches of state affairs was to be 'entrusted to commissions' whose membership was to ensure that the Congress programme was carried out in close 'unity with the mass organizations of working men and women, soldiers, sailors, peasants and office workers'. Government power was 'vested in a collegium of chairmen of these commissions, i.e. Sovnarkom'. Hence government was to consist of a web of commissions, linked through their members to the new revolutionary organizations. Each commissar was to be chairman of his respective commission but in reality this collective system of decision-making never established itself due to the chaotic nature of the times. The reason for retaining the old ministerial division of responsibility may have been the pressing need to take over the old ministries and gain some experience of administration before attempting anything more radical. Moreover, Lenin and the Bolsheviks regarded the possession of power as more important than the structure of government.

The term Sovnarkom caught the public imagination and local soviets began establishing their own Sovnarkoms and were often very reluctant to merge with the national government. Moscow, for instance, was still clinging on to its own Sovnarkom when the government moved into the Kremlin in March 1918.

During the first few months of Soviet power it was not Sovnarkom but the MILITARY-REVOLUTIONARY COMMITTEE which ensured the survival of the new order. This led A. A. IOFFE to refer to the MRC, rather than Sovnarkom, as the 'first proletarian government'. Often MRC commissars were sent to ministries to combat opposition and to recruit new officials. In theory this should have been the responsibility of the corresponding commissariats of Sovnarkom. This state of affairs ended on 18 December 1917 (NS) when the MRC was dissolved and its functions distributed among various bodies.

Opinion in the Bolshevik Party was divided on the nature of the first Soviet government. Some, like Lenin, believed that it should be Bolshevik-dominated so as to ensure effective government. Others thought that a broadly based coalition socialist government was desirable. In order to placate this tendency Lenin would have liked to include a few Left SRs in the first Sovnarkom, but negotiations broke down over their demand for a coalition socialist government. Such was the pressure for a coalition government that Lenin was obliged to reopen negotiations but soon secured a majority in the Party Central Committee (CC) to break them off. This led to the resignation of three commissars: Rykov, Nogin and Milyutin. Since two other commissars, Skvortsov-Stepanov and Lomov, had failed to take up their appointments – they were in Moscow – replacements had to be found for five of the original fifteen

members within a week of Sovnarkom's inception. Elections to the Constituent Assembly revealed a clear majority for the Right SRs, under CHERNOV, and this caused Lenin to change course. Since the Left SRs had in the meantime dropped their demand for a grand socialist coalition, the way was clear for a Bolshevik-Left SR coalition government – the only coalition government the Soviet Union has ever known. On 30 November 1917 (NS), the Left SRs were offered Agriculture and on 23 December six more Left SRs joined Sovnarkom: I. Z. Steinberg (Justice); V. E. Trutovsky (Local Government – a new commissariat); P. P. Proshyan (Posts and Telegraphs); V. A. Karelin (State Properties – also new); and V. A. Algasov and V. M. Mikhailov (commissars without portfolio but voting members of the commission of the Commissariat of Internal Affairs).

The first coalition government was de jure still temporary, but when the Constituent Assembly was dispersed on 19 January 1918 (NS) the word provisional was dropped. The Third All-Russian Congress of Soviets, convening shortly afterwards, appropriated the Constituent Assembly's writ and set in motion the drafting of a constitution.

Not unexpectedly there were many conflicts within Sovnarkom over the exact jurisdiction of the various commissariats among Bolsheviks and between Bolsheviks and Left SRs. The Left SR Commissar for Justice attempted on many occasions, always unsuccessfully, to bring the activities of the VECHEKA and the investigative commissions of the Revolutionary Tribunal under the control of the commissariat. The Bolshevik commissar of internal affairs clashed with the Left SR commissar of local government on the structure and control of local government bodies. However the greatest conflict arose over whether peace should be signed with Imperial Germany. The Bolsheviks were split three ways. Lenin regarded peace as imperative irrespective of the cost, which he saw as temporary since the coming socialist revolution in Germany would sweep the Kaiser's government away. BUKHARIN and the Left Communists favoured a revolutionary war and others such as Trotsky sat on the fence and argued that the German army was incapable of advancing very far. Why not just wait for revolution in Germany? The Left SRs all came down on the side of revolutionary war. After acrimonious debate Lenin's proposal to accept the stiff German terms was finally accepted by the CC on 23 February 1918. Thereupon the Bolsheviks Alexandra KOLLONTAI (Welfare); Dybenko (Naval Affairs); N. Osinsky (Chairman of VSNKh) and V. M. Smirnov (Trade and Industry) withdrew from the government and were joined by Trotsky, commissar for foreign affairs, but he was quickly found another post. When the Treaty of Brest-Litovsk was ratified by the Fourth All-Russian Congress of Soviets in March 1918 all the Left SR representatives in the government promptly departed. They were replaced by

Bolsheviks and thus the pattern of one party government was reaffirmed and has remained ever since. The influence of the Left SRs on government was limited and they left no lasting imprint. The exposed position of Petrograd led to a decision to move the party, soviet and government organs to the relative safety of Moscow. On 10 March 1918 Sovnarkom left the 'new' Russian capital Petrograd, for the 'old' Russian capital, Moscow, and on arrival set up office in the Kremlin.

Sovnarkom was only one of the centres of the new revolutionary power. The Bolshevik Party's CC, the Central Executive Committee of the Soviets and the Military-Revolutionary Committee were the most important of the others. All these bodies were to be found in one building, the Smolny Institute, and this resulted, initially, in leading actors identifying with the revolutionary regime rather than with a particular institution. Since the leading members of Sovnarkom were also leading figures in the other key bodies there was much overlapping of functions. Also the various commissars remained in Smolny in the immediate aftermath of the revolution and did not begin to move out into their commissariats until December 1917. This permitted many informal meetings when a problem had to be solved.

Sovnarkom convened almost daily until the end of December and thereafter less frequently. Such a workload was impossibly heavy for the leading lights with their multifarious functions and it became accepted practice for deputies to attend in their place.

Lenin proved to be an effective if somewhat severe chairman. Punctilious in detail, he demanded that agenda items be notified to the secretary beforehand in writing. In January 1918, exasperated by late comers, he instituted a system of fines, five rubles for being half an hour late, ten rubles for being an hour late, unless advance notice had been given in writing.

The growing burden of work soon led to Sovnarkom divesting itself of minor matters, beginning with finance, to a Little Sovnarkom. In February 1918 this body was renamed the Commission of the Sovnarkom and it became more significant as time passed. If a matter could not be resolved in the minor body it was to be placed on the agenda of the Full Sovnarkom.

By the time the capital had been moved to Moscow, Sovnarkom had established itself as the principal decision-making body in the Soviet state. The Party CC had more power and authority but, as yet, no executive to implement its preferences and the CEC, to which Sovnarkom was nominally subordinate, never developed an effective executive apparatus.

Sovnarkom under Lenin falls naturally into three periods. First was the Petrograd period; second the Civil War period beginning in the summer of 1918 and ending in early 1921 and third the early NEP period.

The move to Moscow brought into being a predomi-

nantly new apparatus. By late 1918 only three members, Lenin, Stalin and Lunacharsky, were still in office, while Trotsky and Rykov headed different commissariats. Hence five sixths of the commissars in Moscow were new to their jobs. The nationalization of industry in June 1918 led to the need to coordinate economic activity from the centre, the rapid expansion of the Cheka and RED ARMY and those organs concerned with requisitioning food resulted in the recruitment of a large central government apparatus. Civilian and military specialists were particularly in demand. As a rule the more senior the official the more likely he was to have worked in an administrative capacity before the revolution. The number of Bolshevik Party members in senior positions was about 10 per cent in August 1918 but in the Cheka, for example, it was 52 per cent of all officials at that time. In the most sensitive commissariats, Foreign Affairs and Nationalities, 49 per cent and 39 per cent respectively of senior officials were Bolsheviks. At the other end of the scale was Finance which had less than 2 per cent. The balance changed little during the civil war and the civil service continued to be guided, in the main, by administrators from a previous era. They in turn passed on their bureaucratic skills and work habits to a new generation of communist officials.

Whereas Sovnarkom had been convening almost daily after its inception, it was meeting weekly by 1921. This was due largely to a devolution of decision-making to the Little Sovnarkom and the Council of Labour and Defence (STO). Trotsky was a notorious non-attender of meetings and as a general rule the more important the commissar in the state the less likely he was to turn up at meetings in person, sending his deputy instead.

The first head of Sovnarkom's Chancellery was V. D. BONCH-BRUEVICH, who enjoyed a special relationship with Lenin, having worked with him in Switzerland. Possessing great administrative ability he gathered around him a staff which not only serviced Sovnarkom but also initially Little Sovnarkom and STO. The Chancellery's activities included preparing the agenda for meetings and checking the implementation of decisions. All material for consideration by the government had to pass through the Chancellery and it was to see that items were correctly formulated and the necessary consultations between bodies carried out beforehand. It exerted considerable influence over the order of business and was also to convene special commissions to look into specific matters. Nikolai Gorbunov took over from Bonch-Bruevich in October 1920.

Lenin proved himself a first class leader, administrator and chief executive of Sovnarkom. Between October 1917 and the end of 1921 he concentrated his main efforts on government business and clearly found it very fulfilling. In order to spend so much time on state affairs he deliberately neglected party work. In 1921 60 per cent of his extant letters, memoranda and telegrams were addressed to government agencies or officials and only 14 per cent to

Figure 23   Stalin, Rykov, Kamenev and Zinoviev, 1920s.

central party agencies or officials. As chairman Lenin deployed his skills of being able to assess the situation expertly, deciding what tactics had to be adopted to achieve the intended goals, building the minimal coalition to achieve the maximal effect and always favouring a majority vote over continuing the debate in search of a consensus. However the workload began to take its toll. In July 1921 he was obliged to apply for a month's leave but could not stay away from state affairs.

No effort was made during his lifetime to replace him as chairman of Sovnarkom and when USSR Sovnarkom was set up in July 1923 he was elected its chairman. Measures to lighten his workload had been taken, such as strengthening the powers of Little Sovnarkom in 1921 when it was decreed that all business should first go through it except for foreign policy and defence issues. However absence of the *vozhd* (leader) was bound to lead to demarcation disputes between the Full Sovnarkom, Little Sovnarkom and STO. When Lenin withdrew for a time in 1921, Rykov was appointed vice-chairman but he, in turn, fell ill in late 1921 and was away three months during which time A. D. Tsyurupa replaced him. Since the latter was not a leading Bolshevik, and Lenin and Rykov were incapacitated, the Full Sovnarkom suffered and gradually it became an organ which allowed key decisions to be taken in the Politburo and then acted on them. One reason for this was that as long as Lenin was there he was the link between Sovnarkom and the Politburo. Rykov was not a member of the Politburo when he took the chair and Tsyurupa did not have the standing or self-confidence to play the role. L. B. Kamenev, party leader in Moscow, unofficially took over the task but he did not hold a government portfolio. Not surprisingly he had little success. After the Eleventh Party Congress in 1922 Lenin tried to restore the authority and importance of Sovnarkom but failed. It was the party machine which was growing inexorably in influence at the

expense of the government. Hence Lenin devoted himself, unstintingly, to an institution, which eventually failed to perform the functions that he had envisaged for it. The first Bolshevik leader proved incapable of halting the decline of the government's authority. Hence it can be argued that Lenin failed as chairman of Sovnarkom.

MMcC

Further Reading

Bonch-Bruevich, V.D.: *Vospominaniya o Lenine*, 2nd edn. Moscow: 1969.

Carr, E.H.: *The Bolshevik Revolution 1917–1923*, 3 vols. London: Macmillan, 1966.

Chamberlin, W.H.: *The Russian Revolution 1917–1921*, 2 vols. London: Macmillan, 1935.

Lewin, M.: *Lenin's Last Struggle*. London: Pluto, 1969.

Rigby, T.H.; *Lenin's Government: Sovnarkom 1917–1922*. Cambridge: Cambridge University Press, 1979.

Schapiro, L.B.: *The Communist Party of the Soviet Union*. London: Methuen, 1960.

Committee Memberships of the RSDRP(b)

The RSDRP(b) was always an hierarchical party. The struggle for leadership was reflected in the listing of full and candidate members of the Central Committee (CC). The CC was the key body at the Sixth (1917) and Seventh (1918) Congresses. Hence the listing of membership was in hierarchical order. The Secretariat followed this practice. However at the Eighth Congress (1919) another procedure was adopted. The Politburo (the inner cabinet) became the key party body. Its full and candidate members were given in hierarchical order as were those of the Auditing Commission and the Orgburo, the other new bodies. However the full members of the CC were listed alphabetically (according to the Russian alphabet) but the candidate members were listed hierarchically.

At the Ninth Congress (1920) the Politburo, Orgburo, Secretariat and the Central Control Commission were listed in hierarchical order but whereas candidate members of the CC were listed in hierarchical order, full members of the CC are mixed alphabetically and hierarchically.

At the Tenth Congress (1921) the Politburo and Secretariat are given hierarchically but the Orgburo is in alphabetical order. Full members of the CC are mixed but candidate members are given hierarchically.

At the Eleventh Congress (1922) the Politburo, Secretariat and candidate members of the Orgburo are in hierarchical order but full and candidate members of the CC are mixed. The Central Control Commission and full members of the Orgburo are in alphabetical order.

How does one account for this extraordinary situation? The establishment of the Politburo, Orgburo and Auditing Commission in 1919 which, together with the Secretariat, formed the inner core of the leadership, weakened the CC.

Full members were listed alphabetically but candidate members were in hierarchical order. One explanation for this would be that in a party riven with factionalism, no agreement on the hierarchy of CC members could be reached. This would also appear to be the reason why at the Tenth Congress Orgburo members are listed hierarchically whereas full members are mixed alphabetically and hierarchically. The Eleventh Congress presents a similar varied picture.

However, the inner core of the leadership is throughout listed hierarchically (with the exception of full Orgburo members at the Tenth and Eleventh Congresses) and the listing is the one preferred by Lenin. When he fell ill a struggle ensued to decide who took precedence.

Committee memberships listed below are those provided in the stenographic account of each Congress. Alphabetical ordering is indicated by ★, hierarchical by ★★. All dates are New Style.

Sixth Congress: 26 July–3 August 1917

Central Committee (voting members)★★ Lenin, V. I.; Kamenev, L. B.; Nogin, V. P.; Stalin, I. V.; Rykov, A. I.; Sergeev (Artem), F. A.; Milyutin, V. P.; Krestinsky, N. N.; Berzin, Ya. A.; Muranov, M. K.; Zinoviev, G. E.; Trotsky, L. D.; Kollontai, A. M.; Sverdlov, I. M.; Bukharin, N. I.; Uritsky, M. S.; Bubnov, A. S.; Smilga, I. T.; Dzerzhinsky, F. E.; Sokolnikov, G. Ya.; Shaumyan, S. G.
Candidate Members (non-voting)★★ Dzhaparidze, P. A.; Kiselev, A. S.; Preobrazhensky, E. A.; Stasova, E. D.; Ioffe, A. A.; Lomov, G. I.; Skrypnik, N. A.; Yakovleva, V. N.

For political leadership of Party activities the CC meeting on 5 November 1917 established a seven man Politburo. (However there is no evidence that it ever functioned as such.)★★ Lenin, V. I.; Zinoviev, G. E.; Kamenev, L. B.; Trotsky, L. D.; Stalin, I. V.; Sokolnikov, G. Ya.; Bubnov, A. S.

Secretariat★★ Sverdlov, Ya. M. (executive secretary); Stasova, E. D. (secretary).

Seventh Congress: 6–8 March 1918

Central Committee (voting members)★★ Lenin, V. I.; Sverdlov, Ya. M.; Bukharin, N. I.; Stalin, I. V.; Smilga, I. T.; Lashevich, M. M.; Dzerzhinsky, F. E.; Trotsky, L. D.; Zinoviev, G. E.; Sokolnikov, G. Ya.; Krestinsky, N. N.; Stasova, E. D.; Shmidt, V. V.; Vladimirsky, M. F.; Sergeev (Artem), F. A.
Candidate Members (non-voting)★★ Ioffe, A. A.; Stuchka, P. I.; Berzin (Vinter), Ya. A.; Lomov-Oppokov, G. I.; Kiselev, A. S.; Petrovsky, G. I.; Uritsky, M. S.; Shlyapnikov, A. G.

Secretariat★★ Sverdlov, I. M. (executive secretary); Stasova, E. D. (secretary).

Eighth Congress: 18–23 March 1919

Central Committee (voting members)★ Beloborodov, A. G.; Bukharin, N. I.; Dzerzhinsky, F. E.; Evdokimov, G. E.; Zinoviev, G. E.; Kalinin, M. I.; Kamenev, L. B.; Krestinsky, N. N.; Lenin, V. I.; Muranov, K. M.; Radek, K. B.; Rakovsky, Kh. G.; Serebryakov, L. P.; Smilga, I. T.; Stalin, I. V.; Stasova, E. D.; Stuchka, P. I.; Tomsky, M. P.; Trotsky, L. D.
Candidate Members (non-voting)★★ Sergeev (Artem), F. A.; Vladimirsky, M. F.; Mitskyavichus-Kapsukas, V. S.; Shmidt, V. V.; Bubnov, A. S.; Danishevsky, K. Kh.; Smirnov, I. N.; Yaroslavsky, E. M.

Auditing Commission★★ Kursky, D. I.; Lunacharsky, A. V.; Tsivtsivadze, I. V.

Politburo (voting members)★★ Lenin, V. I.; Trotsky, L. D.; Stalin, I. V.; Kamenev, L. B.; Krestinsky, N. N.
Candidate Members (non-voting)★★ Kalinin, M. I.; Zinoviev, G. E.; Bukharin, N. I.

Orgburo★★ Stalin, I. V.; Stasova, E. D.; Serebryakov, L. P.; Krestinsky, N. N.; Beloborodov, A. G.; Muranov, M. K.; Kamenev, L. B.; Dzerzhinsky, F. E.; Rakovsky, Kh. G.; Trotsky, L. D.; Kalinin, M. I.

Secretariat★★ Krestinsky, N. N.; Stasova, E. D.

Ninth Congress: 29 March–5 April 1920

Central Committee (voting members)★★ and ★ Andreev, A. A.; Bukharin, N. I.; Sergeev (Artem), F. A.; Zinoviev, G. E.; Kalinin, M. I.; Rakovsky, Kh. G.; Dzerzhinsky, F. E.; Rudzutak, Ya. E.; Rykov, A. I.; Kamenev, L. B.; Krestinsky, N. N.; Lenin, V. I.; Preobrazhensky, E. A.; Radek, K. B.; Serebryakov, L. P.; Smirnov, I. N.; Stalin, I. V.; Tomsky, M. P.; Trotsky, L. D.; Evodimov, G. E.
Candidate Members (non-voting)★★ Petrovsky, G. I.; Yaroslavsky, E. M.; Muranov, M. M.; Milyutin, V. P.; Stuchka, P. I.; Nogin, V. P.; Gusev, S. I.; Pyatnitsky, I. A.; Beloborodov, I. A.; Zalutsky, P. A.; Molotov, V. M.; Smilga, I. T.

Central Control Commission★★ Dzerzhinsky, F. E.; Muranov, M. K.; Preobrazhensky, E. A. and representatives of the Moscow, Petrograd, Ivanovo-Voznesensk and Nizhni Novgorod Party organizations.

Politburo★★ Lenin, V. I.; Trotsky, L. D.; Serebryakov, L. P.; Preobrazhensky, E. A.; Stalin, I. V.; Kamenev, L. B.; Bukharin, N. I.

Orgburo★★ Stalin, I. V.; Rykov, A. I.; Serebryakov, L. P.; Krestinsky, N. N.; Preobrazhensky, E. A.

Secretariat★★ Preobrazhensky, E. A.; Serebryakov, L. P.; Krestinsky, N. N.

Tenth Congress: 8–16 March 1921

Central Committee (voting members)★★ and ★ Sergeev (Artem), F. A.; Bukharin, N. I.; Voroshilov, K. E.; Dzerzhinsky, F. E.; Zinoviev, G. E.; Kalinin, M. I.; Kamenev, L. B.; Komarov, N. P.; Molotov, V. M.; Ordzhonikidze, G. K.; Petrovsky, G. I.; Radek, K. B.; Rakovsky, Kh. G.; Rudzutak, Ya. E.; Rykov, A. I.; Stalin, I. V.; Kutuzov, I. I.; Lenin, V. I.; Mikhailov, V. M.; Frunze, M. V.; Shlyapnikov, A. G.; Tomsky, M. P.; Trotsky, L. D.; Tuntul, I. Ya.; Yaroslavsky, E. M.
Candidate Members (non-voting)★★ Chubar, V. Ya.; Kirov, S. M.; Shmidt, V. V.; Zelensky, I. A.; Uglanov, N. A.; Pyatakov, G. L.; Safarov, G. V.; Zalutsky, P. A.; Milyutin, V. P.; Kuibyshev, V. V.; Gusev, S. I.; Osinsky, N.; Smirnov, I. N.; Kiselev, A. S.; Sulimov, D. E.

Politburo (voting members)★★ Lenin, V. I.; Trotsky, L. D.; Zinoviev, G. E.; Stalin, I. V.; Kamenev, L. B.
Candidate Members (non-voting)★ Molotov, V. M.; Kalinin, M. I.; Bukharin, N. I.

Secretariat★★ Molotov, V. M. (executive secretary); Yaroslavsky, E. M. (secretary); Mikhailov, V. M. (secretary).

Orgburo (voting members)★ Komarov, V. P.; Mikhailov, V. M.; Molotov, V. M.; Rykov, A. I.; Stalin, I. V.; Tomsky, L. D.; Yaroslavsky, E. M.
Candidate Members (non-voting)★ Dzerzhinsky, F. E.; Kalinin, M. I.; Rudzutak, Ya. E.

Eleventh Congress: 17 March–2 April 1922

Central Committee (voting members) ★Andreev, A. A.; Bukharin, N. I.; Voroshilov, K. E.; Dzerzhinsky, F. E.; Zelensky, I. A.; Zinoviev, G. E.; Kalinin, M. I.; Kamenev, L. B.; Korotkov, I. I.; Kuibyshev, V. V.; Lenin, V. I.; Molotov, V. M.; Radek, K. B.; Rakovsky, Kh. G.; Rudzutak, Ya. E.; Rykov, A. I.; Sapronov, T. V.; Smirnov, I. N.; Sokolnikov, G. Ya.; Stalin, I. V.; Tomsky, L. D.; Trotsky, L. D.; ★★Frunze, M. V.;

Chubar, V. Ya.; Ordzhonikidze, G. K.; Petrovsky, G. I.; Yaroslavsky, E. M.
Candidate Members (non-voting★ Bubnov, A. S.; Gusev, S. I.; Kirov, S. M.; Komarov, N. P.; Kiselev, A. S.; Mikoyan, A. I.; Rakhimbaev, A. R.; Payatakov, G. L.; Safarov, G. I.; ★★ Lebed, D. Z.; Lepse, I. I.; Lobov, S. S.; Manuilsky, D. Z.; Badaev, A. E.; Mikhailov, V. M.; Smilga, I. T.; Sulimov, D. G.; Shmidt, V. V.

Central Control Commission (voting members)★ Varentsova, O. A.; Korostelev, A. A.; Solts, A. A.; Chentsov, I. D.; Shkiryatov, M. F.
Candidate Members (non-voting)★ Muranov, M. K.; Samoilov, F. N.

Politburo (voting members)★★ Lenin, V. I.; Kamenev, L. B.; Trotsky, L. D.; Stalin, I. V.; Zinoviev, G. E.; Rykov, A. I.; Tomsky, M. M.
Candidate Members (non-voting)★★ Bukharin, N. I.; Molotov, V. M.; Kalinin, M. I.

Secretariat★★ Stalin, I. V. (secretary general); Kuibyshev, V. V. (secretary); Molotov, V. M. (secretary).

Orgburo (voting members)★ Andreev, A. A.; Dzerzhinsky, F. E.; Kuibyshev, V. V.; Molotov, V. M.; Rykov, A. I.; Stalin, I. V.; Tomsky, M. P.
Orgburo Candidates (non-voting)★★ Kalinin, M. I.; Rudzutak, Ya. E.; Zelensky, I. A.   MMcC

Commissars and Commissariats of Sovnarkom under Lenin

Sovnarkom was formed on 8 November 1917 and was composed only of Bolsheviks. Many Bolsheviks and other socialists would have preferred a coalition socialist government. Some Bolshevik commissars did not take up their posts and others soon resigned. The first and only coalition government in the history of the Soviet Union (Bolsheviks and Left Social Revolutionaries) took office on 25 December 1917 but the signing of the Brest-Litovsk Treaty led to the Left SRs leaving the government on 16 March 1918. Some commissariats, such as transport, had many heads due to the contentious nature of the problems involved. The more important the commissariat, the more likely a leading Boshevik was to head it. Full composition is given in Table 7 on p. 170; all dates are given New Style.   MMcC

Defence Council

Established 13 December 1917 (NS) with full powers to mobilize the human and material resources of the country in the interests of defence, the decisions of the Defence Council, (full name Council of Workers' and Peasants'

Table 7 Commissars and Commissariats of Sovnarkom under Lenin

Office	Name	Date		
Chairman	Lenin, V. I.	8 Nov. 1917	to	7 July 1923
(Chairman: USSR Sovnarkom		7 July 1923		21 Jan. 1924)
Deputy Chairman of Sovnarkom and/or	Rykov, A. I.	26 May 1921		21 Jan. 1924
STO	Tsyurupa A. D.	Dec. 1921		21 Jan. 1924
	Kamenev, L. B.	Sept. 1922		21 Jan. 1924
PC for Foreign Affairs	Trotsky, L. D.	8 Nov. 1917		18 Feb. 1918
	Chicherin, G. V.	30 May	}	
	de facto	18 Feb.		21 Jan. 1924
PC for Internal Affairs	Rykov, A. I.	8 Nov. 1917		17 Nov. 1917
	Petrovsky, G. I.	30 Nov. 1917		30 Mar. 1919
	Dzerzhinsky, F. E.	30 Mar. 1919		1922
PC for Local Government	Trutovsky, V. E.	25 Dec. 1917		16 Mar. 1918
PC for Nationalities	Stalin, I. V.	8 Nov. 1917		7 July 1923
PC for Justice	Lomov, G. I.	8 Nov. 1917	never acted	
	Steinberg, I. Z.	25 Dec. 1917	to	16 Mar. 1918
	Stuchka, P. I.	20 Mar. 1918		4 Sept. 1918
	Kursky, D. I.	4 Sept. 1918		1928
PC for State Control	Essen, E. E.	3 Dec. 1917		9 May 1918
	Lander, K. I.	9 May 1918		9 Apr. 1919
	Stalin, I. V.	9 Apr. 1919		7 Feb. 1920
PC for Rabkrin	Stalin, I. V.	7 Feb. 1920		27 Dec. 1922
	Tsyurupa, A. D.	27 Dec. 1922		
PC for Finance	Skvortsov-Stepanov, I. I.	8 Nov. 1917	never acted	
	Menzhinsky, N. R.	2 Feb. 1918 }		
	de facto	12 Nov. 1917 }	to	Mar. 1918
	Gukovsky, I. E.	21 Mar. 1918		16 Aug. 1918
	Krestinsky, N. N.	16 Aug. 1918		{ Dec. 1922
	de facto		until	{ Oct. 1921
	Sokolnikov, G. Ya.	Dec. 1922 }	to	21 Jan. 1924
	de facto	Jan. 1922 }		
PC for Labour	Shlyapnikov, A. G.	8 Nov. 1977		Oct. 1918
	Shmidt, N. N.	Oct. 1918		21 Jan. 1924
PC for Welfare	Kollontai, A. M.	12 Nov. 1917		23 Feb. 1918
PC for Social Security	Vinokurov, A. N.	20 Mar. 1918		8 Dec. 1919
(merged with Commissariat for Labour				
8 Dec. 1919–21 Apr. 1920)	Vinokurov, A. N.	21 Apr. 1920		1923
PC for Education	Lunarcharsky, A. V.	8 Nov. 1917		30 Dec. 1922
PC for Health	Semashko, N. A.	11 July 1918		30 Dec. 1922

Table 7 *continued*

Office	Name	Date'	
PC for Posts and Telegraphs	Avilov, N. P.	8 Nov. 1917	4 Jan. 1918
	Proshyan, P. P.	4 Jan. 1918	16 Mar. 1918
	Podbelsky, V. N.	11 Apr. 1918	25 Feb. 1920
	Lyubovich, A. M.	Mar. 1920	28 May 1921
	Dovgalevsky, V. S.	28 May 1921	30 Dec. 1922
PC for Properties of the Republic	Karelin, V. A.	25 Dec. 1917	16 Mar. 1918
PC for Agriculture	Milyutin, V. P.	8 Nov. 1917	17 Nov. 1917
	Kolegaev, A. L.	8 Dec. 1917	16 Mar. 1918
	Sereda, S. P.	28 Mar. 1918	2 Mar. 1921
	Yakovenko, V. G.	9 Jan. 1922	30 Dec. 1922
PC for Food Supplies	Teodorovich, I. A.	8 Nov. 1917	31 Dec. 1917
	Shlikhter, A. G.	31 Dec. 1917 ⎫	
	de facto	2 Dec. 1917 ⎭	25 Feb. 1918
	Tsyurupa, A. G.	25 Feb. 1918	11 Dec. 1921
	Bryukhanov, N. P.	11 Dec. 1921	21 Jan. 1924
PC for Transport	Elizarov, M. T.	21 Dec. 1917	20 Jan. 1918
	Rogov, A. G.	24 Feb. 1918	9 May. 1918
	Kobozev, P. A.	9 May 1918	25 July 1918
	Nevsky, V. I.	25 July 1918	17 Mar. 1919
	Krasin, L. B.	17 Mar. 1919	23 Mar. 1920
	Trotsky, L. D.	23 Mar. 1920	Dec. 1920
	Emshanov, A. I.	Dec. 1920	14 Apr. 1921
	Dzerzhinsky, F. E.	14 Apr. 1921	21 Jan. 1924
PC for Trade and Industry	Nogin, V. P.	8 Nov. 1917	17 Nov. 1917
	Smirnov, V. M.	7 Feb. 1918	16 Feb. 1918
	Krasin, L. B.	13 Nov. 1918	11 June 1920
PC for Foreign Trade	Krasin, L. B.	11 June 1920	21 Jan. 1924
Chairman of VSNKh	Osinsky, N.	25 Dec. 1917	28 Mar. 1918
	Rykov, A. I.	28 Mar. 1918	28 May 1921
	Bogdanov, P. A.	28 May 1921	1923
		1923	21 Jan. 1924
Committee on Military and Naval Affairs	Antonov-Ovseenko, V. A. ⎫		
	Krylenko, N. V. ⎬	8 Nov. 1917	Nov. 1917
	Dybenko, P. E. ⎭		
	Podvoisky, N. I.	9 Nov. 1917	Nov. 1917
PC for Army	Podvoisky, N. I.	Nov. 1917	28 Mar. 1918
PC for Navy	Dybenko, P. E.	Nov. 1917	28 Mar. 1918
War Commissar (Military Commissar for Army and Naval Affairs)	Trotsky, L. D. (also Chairman, Military Revolutionary Council of the Republic)	28 Mar. 1918	21 Jan. 1924

Defence), were to be implemented unconditionally by all agencies and institutions, central and local, and all citizens. All workers in transport, food supplies and war industries were placed under strict military discipline and the unification of administration in this area was to be the primary concern of the Defence Council. Hence in the realm of the war economy it had a status and authority equal to that of SOVNARKOM. Its members reflected its significance: V. I. LENIN, chairman; I. V. STALIN, acting as the representative of the CEC; L. D. TROTSKY, chairman of the Revolutionary Military Council; V. I. Nevsky, commissar for railways; N. P. Bryukhanov, commissar for food supplies and L. B. KRASIN, chairman of the Extraordinary Supplies Commission. The creation of the Defence Council had little immediate effect on the chaotic state of the military economy and this led in July 1919 to the appointment of A. I. Rykov, chairman of VSNKh, as Extraordinary Plenipotentiary of the Defence Council for the Provisioning of the RED ARMY and NAVY (Chusosnabarm), with subordinate agencies on each front. In August, Chusosnabarm – acronyms of this length and complexity were a feature of the period and even became the butt of many jokes – established a War Industries Council to centralize war industry production. Chusosnabarm was very effective in increasing the flow of war material to the front. The Defence Council's writ covered a wide range of activities. In 1919, 40 per cent of its published decrees touched directly on military affairs; 13 per cent on fuel supplies; 10 per cent on transport; 8 per cent on industry and the remaining 29 per cent embraced such disparate matters as the post office, agriculture and finance. The Defence Council organized for victory and Mikhail FRUNZE, in 1924, maintained that without it the Reds would scarcely have won the Civil War.

In early 1920 with the CIVIL WAR almost over, the Bolsheviks turned their attention to the shattered economy and on 15 January the Defence Council transformed one of the armies in the Urals into a Labour Army and gave it essentially agricultural tasks. Those with special skills, if they could be spared, were transferred to local industrial plants. A Revolutionary Council of the Labour Army was set up to run affairs and disputes could be referred to the Defence Council. There were many acrimonious conflicts caused in no small degree by Trotsky's commitment to labour armies. Another army was established in the Ukraine and smaller ones appeared elsewhere.

When the decree on universal labour service was published in January 1920 the task of administrating it fell to the Defence Council and this led to a change in name. At the Ninth Party Congress, in March 1920, Lenin stated that it was henceforth to be called the Labour and Defence Council (STO).

The virtual elimination of the market economy under WAR COMMUNISM led to economic and administrative confusion as no mechanism to coordinate and guide economic activity existed. VSNKh was quite incapable of playing such a role, but the Defence Council succeeded in marshalling those sectors germane to its interests. This however left non-priority sectors dissatisfied. The Ninth Party Congress called for a comprehensive national economic plan to be drawn up, but the Congress could not agree which organization should coordinate the plan and ensure its fulfilment. STO was a strong candidate. In November 1920 Trotsky advocated that STO be transformed predominantly into a Council of Labour and this happened a month later. STO was to draw up the economic plan for the RSFSR and present it for approval to the CEC, lead the work of the national economic commission according to the plan and supervise its implemenation.

Hence it was to become the main agency for the reconstruction of the economy, but it was also to retain its defence responsibilities. Was it to develop into an economic cabinet equal or superior to Sovnarkom, or a commission with wide-ranging powers but subordinate to Sovnarkom? Lenin favoured the latter solution and this was adopted. STO had under its control a host of regional and local bodies. When Gosplan (see STATE GENERAL PLANNING COMMISSION) was set up in February 1921 it was attached to STO which was to nominate its members.

At the end of the Civil War, STO was poised to become the General Staff of a planned economy, but the arrival of the New Economic Policy (NEP), which again permitted the market economy to function, inevitably reduced its functions. It almost entirely dropped its concern with military matters in 1921 and 1922 and concentrated on labour, industrial and transport problems. Sovnarkom dominated decision-making on economic matters, but it was STO which was primarily responsible for executing those decisions.

When the Defence Council was transformed into STO, membership rose from six to nine and Lenin, Stalin and Trotsky, as before, dominated. In September 1921 the People's Commissariats for Finance and Foreign Trade were added to its brief.

MMcC

State General Planning Commission (Gosplan)

Established 22 February 1921 to map out priorities for the economic development of the country, it was also Gosplan's responsibility to reconcile and coordinate the plans of the various state agencies: e.g. the State Commission for the Electrification of Russia (Goelro). An annual national economic plan was to be elaborated and the ways and means of realizing the plan elucidated. Gosplan was attached to STO which was also to nominate its members. The first chairman of Gosplan was G. M. Krzhizhanovsky. The retreat from WAR COMMUNISM to NEP reduced the role of Gosplan and it was only after 1928 that it became really significant.

MMcC

Military Revolutionary Committee (MRC)

An *ad hoc* committee set up by the Petrograd Soviet of Workers' and Soldiers' Deputies on 12 October 1917 (OS) to monitor and if necessary to countermand any move by the Provisional Government to transfer the more revolutionary troop units from the capital. Its formation was proposed to the Petrograd Soviet by the 18-year-old Left SR P. E. Lazimir who had acted on a Bolshevik suggestion, since the latter did not wish to be seen to be proposing an organization with military aspirations. Lazimir became its first chairman. It consisted of leading members of the Petrograd Soviet and representatives of soldiers' and sailors' organizations, factory committees, trade unions and the military organizations of the revolutionary parties. Its membership was fluid but always under the control of the Bolsheviks, headed by L. D. TROTSKY, as chairman of the Petrograd Soviet. On 16 October (OS) five Bolshevik CC members (Bubnov, DZERZHINSKY, STALIN, SVERDLOV and URITSKY) were instructed to join the MRC. Its recruits were called commissars and their task was to ensure that troops would act on MRC orders. On 24 and 25 October (OS) key bodies were occupied by those loyal to the MRC – military and naval units and detachments of Red Guards – all coordinated from the Smolny Institute, i.e. the same building which housed the Bolshevik Party CC. Trotsky, as chairman of the Petrograd Soviet, was able to sign orders for weapons and have them delivered to the Red Guards.

After taking power, the Bolsheviks depended on the MRC to protect and extend their influence. Some haphazard military opposition, including at attempt by KERENSKY, aided by General Krasnov and his COSSACKS to retake the capital, was summarily dealt with. The MRC began to take on civil administrative tasks and by 28 October (OS) 185 commissars had been placed in charge of various civil bodies. An immediate task was to increase the flow of food supplies to Petrograd, made worse by the strike of railwaymen. Brutal methods were employed to gain control of the available food supplies in the capital and squads were dispatched to the surrounding countryside to requisition more. The first Sovnarkom decree, on the press, was enforced by the MRC which closed down several newspapers critical of the seizure of power, made their facilities available to the Bolsheviks and ensured that the scarce supplies of paper went to the appropriate institutions. MRC activities covered an extraordinarily wide range from ensuring border security, to granting exit visas and residence permits and the allocation of housing.

Formally attached to the CEC, the MRC functioned more like a surrogate government during the first few weeks of the revolution. Its membership was always in flux and at one time counted 82 members, dominated by Bolsheviks and Left SRs, but also including a few ANARCHISTS. The MRC was dissolved on 18 December 1917 (NS) and its functions distributed among the various commissariats.   MMcC

Commissariat of Worker-Peasant Inspection (Rabkrin)

Established on 7 February 1920 as the successor to the People's Commissariat of State Control which had functioned since 3 December 1917 (NS), Rabkrin's first head was I. V. STALIN who had also been the last commissar of state control. Its main function was to check the activities and the effectiveness of the work of all state bodies on behalf of SOVNARKOM. This was an almost impossible task as each commissariat and agency jealously guarded its rights and privileges. TROTSKY jibed that everyone knew that Rabkrin was full of officials who had made a mess of a 'real' job. On 27 December 1922 Stalin was replaced by A. D. Tsyurupa. LENIN was greatly exercised by the failure of Rabkrin to discipline officials and he was planning to reorganize and strengthen Rabkrin at the XII Party Congress in March 1923, but ill health prevented him from doing so.   MMcC

Supreme Council of the National Economy (VSNKh)

Established on 14 December 1917 (NS) and attached to Sovnarkom, the task of VSNKh (also sometimes Vesenkha) was to organize the national economy and state finances, to prepare general norms and plans for the regulation of the economic life of the country, and coordinate and unify the activities of the local and central regulating organs (committees on fuel, metals, transport, food supply committees and others) that were attached to the People's Commissariats, the All-Russian Soviet of Workers' Control, the factory committees and the trade unions. It had authority to confiscate, requisition, sequester and amalgamate various branches of industry, commerce and other enterprises in the field of production, distribution and state finance. Its membership consisted of representatives of the All-Russian Soviet of Workers' Control, People's Commissariats and experts who however had no vote. As of June 1918 it became in effect the commissariat of nationalized industry. There were local National Economy Councils (SNKhs) to run industry. During the CIVIL WAR the main function of VSNKh was to provide the RED ARMY with war material and clothing and under NEP factories producing similar products were grouped together in trusts, but still managed by VSNKh. Headed by N. Osinsky (V. V. Obolensky) December 1917–March 1918; A. I. Rykov March 1918–May 1921; P. A. Bogdanov May 1921–1923.   MMcC

Party-State Institutions

'The key question in any revolution is the question of power in the state', wrote LENIN in 1917. Hence after the seizure of power Bolshevik party members concentrated their efforts and energies on work in state institutions.

Lenin and the leading members of the Central Committee (CC) ran SOVNARKOM. Lenin, STALIN and TROTSKY dominated the DEFENCE COUNCIL. Bolshevik party organizations expanded rapidly and Communists were expected to play a leading role in soviets, trade unions and factory committees.

The party did not possess a nation-wide organization, coordinated from the centre. The Secretariat, headed by Ya. M. SVERDLOV, was small, understaffed (most were women), overworked and quite incapable initially of imposing the centre's view of affairs. One reason for this was that the CC itself was invariably split on major issues. Immediately after the OCTOBER REVOLUTION the issue of whether the Bolsheviks alone should form the government or whether a grand socialist coalition should come into being led to the resignation of three members, L. B. KAMENEV, V. P. Nogin and G. E. ZINOVIEV. A much more serious rift was caused by the desire of Lenin to seek a peace treaty with Imperial Germany. The CC was split three ways with the Left Communists, headed by N. I. BUKHARIN, arguing strongly in favour of revolutionary war. Trotsky favoured sitting on the fence, 'neither war nor peace', and waiting for revolution in Germany. Dissent at the top was mirrored lower down. The signing of the peace treaty at Brest-Litovsk in March 1918 led many party bureaux to dissociate themselves from the leadership in Moscow. The Moscow regional bureau, for example, advocated that all true Bolsheviks should sever their links with the CC. Ukrainian Bolshevik officials resolved that party committees should remain independent of the CC in Moscow because the centre had conceded German autonomy over the UKRAINE. Eventually Moscow weathered the storm despite many party committees favouring revolutionary war. The stark fact was that very few soldiers were willing to fight. The confrontation over the peace issue damaged the organizational cohesiveness of the party as committees opposed to Brest-Litovsk despatched their representatives to argue their case elsewhere. The centre, in turn, sent its emissaries to repair the damage and to win over the waverers. The situation was made more difficult by Bukharin, A. S. Kiselev and G. I. Lomov declaring that they would have nothing to do with a CC which had concluded such a dishonourable peace. It was some time before they could be brought back into the fold.

The organizational identity of the party was in danger of being obliterated during the first year of Bolshevik rule. Lenin, the *vozhd* (leader), preferred to concentrate his efforts on state administration and gradually devoted less and less time to party business. All the leading Bolsheviks, except Bukharin and Elena STASOVA, who devoted their energies to CC work, had responsible state functions. It was very difficult to convene a plenary session of the CC and much informal backstage discussion went on. Party committees at the provincial, regional and town level began to enjoy their power and resisted attempts by the centre to regulate their activities. It was common for soviet, trade union and factory committees to pass resolutions contrary to central party policy. On the other hand many local party committees requested the centre to provide them with instructors and guidance as to how they were to carry out their duties. The trend towards centralization had set in before the onset of the CIVIL WAR and even Left Communists, such as Bukharin, accepted this draft.

The Civil War transformed the party's attitude to military affairs. Whereas before the Revolution it had ridiculed the martial arts and the subordination of soldiers to their officers, it now began doing away with the custom of soldiers electing their own officers. Discipline was praised once again. Trotsky had his way and recruited high ranking ex-tsarist officers for the infant RED ARMY. The Bolsheviks went a step further and abolished elective party bodies in the armed forces.

Prior to the onset of the Civil War there were few party cells in the countryside but the need to recruit men to the colours led to rural committees springing up everywhere and by the summer of 1919 almost every rural district had a party body. The desperate military solution led to a change of heart among Bolsheviks about subordination and every committee accepted that an agency at each level should coordinate activities. The newly found authority of especially the provincial committees was such that in some cases subordinate bodies declined to act until instructions from the centre were received. The exigencies of the moment demanded rapid decision-making and this curtailed public debate.

In order to increase Bolshevik support in non-Russian areas it became the practice to set up local communist parties. Turkestan was first followed by the Ukraine, Lithuania, Latvia and Belorussia. Since the All-Russian Communist party had no intention of becoming a federal party these new bodies merely became regional appendages. They were created to allay suspicion that the Bolsheviks were Great Russian chauvinists in a new garb. The Red Army needed every recruit and contribution it could muster. It was quickly accepted that the new parties should be organized hierarchically.

The new found authority of the higher party organs was not accompanied by an expansion of the central apparatus. When the Secretariat moved to Moscow in March 1918 Stasova stayed behind in Petrograd. Sverdlov had his wife Klavdiya appointed his deputy and her task was to cope with routine party business and only to refer contentious issues which involved matters of principle to her husband. During 1918 there was never more than a dozen full time assistants to cope with the expanding workload despite Klavdiya's efforts to subdivide the activities into sections and recruit more staff. Sverdlov implemented his decisions through the apparatus of the All-Russian Central Executive Committee and the CC's resolutions were handed to Sovnarkom to execute.

Centralization was given considerable impetus in 1918 when the CC simply dissolved the Moscow regional committee and the Northern regional committee. The Urals regional committee was also abolished and replaced by a Siberian bureau which was to run party work in Siberia and the Urals (see REVOLUTION IN SIBERIA), its membership was to be appointed by Moscow. The Turkestan CC was made subordinate to a Turk Commission appointed by Moscow (see REVOLUTION IN CENTRAL ASIA). The Ukrainian CC was obliged to elect to its committee two members proposed by the centre. The pretext was Moscow's unhappiness with the Ukrainian party's attempt at insurrection against the Germans in the summer.

No provincial committee was dissolved or had to accept Moscow nominees. However, the centre decided, often arbitrarily, how many activists would be transferred to work in the Red Army. Provincial as well as regional and town committees accepted that the trend towards centralization was both sensible and ineluctable, partly due to the lack of resources at the local level. Food was a constant problem and if a committee could not procure enough it turned to the centre hoping it would be allocated some. Committees also needed information, instruction and help of all kinds and their very weakness and insecurity led them to cast their eyes on Moscow. Also if the party was going to develop a clear organizational identity of its own it needed a hierarchical system.

A determined advocate of greater direction from the centre was L. M. Kaganovich who proposed that since the CC was so overburdened, two committees should be established to act in its stead between meetings. One should be responsible for political and the other for organizational affairs. The Secretariat would also have to be expanded and to build up a file on local party committees, their personnel and activities. This is almost exactly what the central leadership did decide to do in January 1919 when the Political Bureau (Politburo) and Organizational Bureau (Orgburo) were established. However the small number of top Bolshevik personnel meant that everyone would still have to perform a variety of functions. It was a vain hope to expect those elected to the Politburo and Orgburo to concentrate their energies exclusively on party affairs.

Proposals for stronger party guidance from the centre came from two sources: those like Kaganovich who wanted vigorous centralization of decision-making and the transformation of local committees into transmission-belts of the central will, and others who favoured both greater centralization and more democracy from below. The latter group, based in Moscow and known as the Democratic Centralists (DCs), wanted a considerable increase in the number of directives from the centre and detailed files on all local party personnel (see BOLSHEVIK OPPOSITIONS). At least five CC members should devote all their energies to central party work. The Secretariat was to expand its activity and arbitrate in local disputes, if necessary imposing its own solution. A party inspectorate should be created and given the task of travelling the country checking on local committees.

The death of Sverdlov shortly before the Eighth Party Congress in March 1919 was a terrible blow. Lenin called him irreplaceable; at least two men would be needed to take over his functions. His organizational duties fell to Zinoviev. The DCs correctly foresaw that the Politburo would gradually usurp much of the power of the CC, but how was this to be avoided? Their only proposal was to increase the size of the Politburo and the CC. The DCs favoured local autonomy in the election of committees and in order to make the central leadership accountable to local aspirations, periodic conferences would be necessary. Desirable as these proposals were, the likelihood of their being accepted during a desperate Civil War was remote. The centre would brook no opposition and declared that party bodies which challenged its decisions were helping to undermine the war effort.

Party membership fluctuated wildly in 1918 and 1919, partly due to the desire of the party to rid itself of 'opportunistic' elements. In April 1919 a full-scale purge was set in motion and the Secretariat estimated that membership had fallen to about 150,000 in August 1919. Doubtless many had deserted the ranks fearing a White victory in the Civil War and others perished at the front. With the Civil War almost won the party launched a campaign in September 1919 to recruit good proletarians and peasants and by March 1920 the Secretariat was stating that membership had risen to 600,000. Given the small pool of workers from which to recruit new members, it was inevitable that the majority of new entrants would be of peasant and even bourgeois origin. Women especially were targeted for recruitment (see WOMEN: 1917 AND AFTER). The low educational standards of almost all new members and their lack of contact with Marxism combined to make the membership more docile than ever. The desire to be instructed was very great and favoured 'one-man management' of party committees. This trend was accelerated by the military example especially as Sovnarkom and the Defence Council sent their representatives into the countryside to speed up conscription and the flow of food to the cities and the armed forces. The VECHEKA was not known for taking local sensibilities into account. The agents of the centres, in order to fulfil their tasks, chose their own local auxiliaries and rode roughshod over local committees, if they stood in their way.

At the Eighth Party Congress five full and three candidate members were elected to the Politburo and five to the Orgburo, but the exigencies of the times ensured that plenary sessions, to be held fortnightly, became fewer and fewer. Less than half the CC members carried out their functions exclusively in the capital. The inevitable result was that the CC began to lose its dominant position and to cede authority to its own creatures. It was the Politburo,

Figure 24   1 May 1919, Red Square. Lenin, centre, with Dzerzhinsky standing behind, and Krupskaya third to left (half-face).

concerned with the commanding heights of domestic and foreign policy, and acting in the name of the CC between plenums, which quickly established its authority. The Orgburo was not so effective and in December 1919 its membership was reshuffled with Stalin losing his position. There was no precise dividing line between Politburo and Orgburo functions, but the Politburo took it upon itself to intervene in Orgburo affairs at will and this was reinforced by a CC decision to permit the Politburo to veto Orgburo decrees and resolutions if necessary.

The Secretariat, under Stasova and her deputy Klavdiya Sverdlova, increased its activities and counted some two hundred staff. Five departments were set up, but this did not transform it into an effective arm of the CC. A major problem was that its duties often coincided with those of the Politburo and Orgburo and on such occasions the Secretariat remained the junior partner. After all, no party heavyweight worked in the Secretariat.

The activities of the centre during 1919 gradually eroded the autonomy of the local committees. As Moscow appointed its own people to party and other positions throughout the country (normally merely informing the local committees of its decision and not bothering to consult them), the skeleton of what became known as the nomenklatura system took shape. Sometimes posting communists away from the capital had the added advantage that it was a useful way of getting rid of a troublesome comrade. Gradually Moscow became bolder and disbanded local committees which would not heed its writ. This reached right up to the republican level. The Ukrainian CC, elected in March 1920, was quickly dissolved since it was deemed to be dominated by oppositionists.

By the time the Ninth Party Congress convened in April 1920 the Civil War had almost been won and the pent-up resentment of the local committees at the treatment they were receiving from the centre could surface. The DCs vociferously argued their case but were stronger on what they objected to than proffering solutions. A particular target was the Orgburo. Nevertheless they were out of tune with the times. The mass of Bolshevik officials gained from one-man management of committees and the strict hierarchical control of subordinate bodies. The DCs lost and none of their members was elected to the new CC. Cognizance was taken, however, of the heavy-handed bureaucratic style of control from the centre and Stasova was sacrificed. She was also not elected to the CC. Well known for her advocacy of increasing centralization, she was not diplomatic enough to defuse the situation. N. N.

Krestinsky, E. A. Preobrazhensky and L. P. Serebryakov were put in charge of the Orgburo and Secretariat to forge a middle course between abrasive centralization and local autonomy.

Such pious hopes were not fulfilled. Although the Secretariat's staff rose to about 600 in late 1920, it failed to calm rank and file resentment of central policy. Krestinsky and Serebryakov were often ill, thus Preobrazhensky was hopelessly overburdened. A department of agitation and propaganda was set up to explain central party policy to the rank and file, but was never effective, since Preobrazhensky did not appear to be very enthusiastic. Political departments were set up by Trotsky and his associates as trouble shooters in the economic field. These agencies rode roughshod over the local party committees and usurped their functions. In the Donbass, for example, the political department supervised the resurrection of the coal industry and dominated economic activity. Trotsky was keen on transforming Red Army units into labour armies and favoured the militarization of labour in key economic sectors. The need to mobilize resources for the war against Poland in 1920 only widened the gulf between the top and the bottom of the party.

A party conference in September 1920 saw the DCs and the Workers Opposition (WO) vent their spleen on what they regarded as the increasing authoritarianism emanating from the centre (see BOLSHEVIK OPPOSITIONS). Zinoviev denied that there was a problem and spoke of the need for iron discipline. The centre was aided by the animosity which existed between the DCs and the WO. The WO accused the DCs of behaving just like other party officials in their own areas. It was especially opposed to the system of material benefits which officials received, making them less responsive to the needs of the average party member. The WO wanted workers to have a greater say in local economic and social decision-making. The centre took this to mean that soviets and trade unions should usurp some of the party's power. Predictably the WO lost and Zinoviev's views prevailed. However, compromise was in the air and a Central Control Commission was established to monitor bureaucratic behaviour. Dropping the centre's nominee on local party committees was to cease. Such moves, however, were only tactical, the strategic goal of strict accountability to the centre had not been lost sight of. Soon a CC decree was published making the chairman responsible for the activities of his committee. His title was changed to that of secretary. At least on paper there now existed the makings of a professional party apparatus, beholden to the centre. The interests of the apparatus and the rank and file members were clearly far apart and growing even wider.

The row between the DCs, the WO and the centrists raged on and rent the party apart. The Tenth Party Congress, convened in March 1921, was soon confronted with the KRONSTADT REVOLT. This was a profound shock to the party as the naval base's sailors had been considered among the 'reddest of the red'. Lenin excoriated the WO and declared its programme a 'deviation' from party policy. The resolution 'On Party Unity', passed by the Congress, outlawed factionalism and threatened those, including members of the CC, who continued to oppose central policy with expulsion from the party. The resolution 'On the Anarcho-Syndicalist Deviation' rendered the WO's activities illegal. A purge was launched to rid the party of those who were critical of the central leadership and those of low moral stature. By the end of 1921 about a quarter of the membership had been expelled. By 1923 about two thirds of party members occupied administrative posts and only one in seven was a manual worker. Bureaucrats now ruled the party.

At the Tenth Congress Krestinsky lost his full Politburo seat to Zinoviev who, in turn, was succeeded as a candidate member by V. M. MOLOTOV. Molotov also became head of the Secretariat. Krestinsky, Preobrazhensky and Serebryakov were removed from the Orgburo and replaced by Lenin supporters. V. M. Mikhailov and E. M. Yaroslavsky joined the Secretariat, both being critics of Trotsky's economic ideas.

Lenin's concentration on Sovnarkom and his illnesses from late 1921 onwards meant that there was no one with sufficient authority and skill to coordinate the activities of the central party apparatus. Stalin stepped into the breach in 1922, aided by Molotov's lack of success as head of the Secretariat. Stalin was instrumental in expanding the function of the Orgburo and it began to play a more and more active role in the appointment of local officials. Stalin was made Secretary General of the CC at the Eleventh Party Congress in April 1922 and as such took over the Orgburo and the Secretariat. The expansion of his power and influence was favoured by Lenin's ill health. Gradually the Politburo concentrated on weighty matters of the moment and, for example, relinquished the task of appointing local party officials up to the provincial level to the Secretariat. The gulf between the Politburo and the CC widened and the latter gradually lost its significance. Feuding between the Orgburo and the Secretariat rapidly declined as Stalin was a member of both. Stalin, the arch centralizer, was able to deploy his administrative and political skills to put flesh on the bones of the system which had emerged under Lenin.

When Lenin died in 1924 the dominance of the party apparatus was unquestioned. However such a state of affairs had not been envisaged in October 1917 and had Lenin lived he would have redressed some of the balance by strengthening the government vis-à-vis the Politburo. In October 1917 the soviets were poised to provide the backbone of the administration and party members were directed to work in them. However it was Sovnarkom which developed the infrastructure to implement its own decrees. Had it not been for the Civil War it is possible that the party apparatus would not have grown and acquired its own identity. The exigencies of the Civil War and the need for war material, food and conscripts willy-nilly imposed the wishes of the centre and it transpired that the best vehicles to enforce these predilections were party organs. The low level of legitimacy of the party was also a major factor. The fear of a weak party devouring itself in internecine strife favoured authoritarianism at central and local level and the trend towards one person being responsible for a local committee grew inevitably out of this. Whereas the Bolsheviks waxed eloquent about the creative potential of the proletariat and middle and poor peasantry immediately after October, by 1920 the party bureaucratic elite had shed all faith in them. They persistently referred to the ignorant masses, devoid of class consciousness. Lenin, in October 1921, went so far as to state that the Russian industrial working class had become déclassé and had ceased to exist as a proletariat. Under such circumstances the party, in order to survive, had to impose consciousness from without.

Democratic centralism had given way to bureaucratic centralism by 1921, but it was Stalin who when he took over as Secretary General accelerated the process. The administrative structure of the party inevitably became the norm for all state bodies. There too bureaucratic centralism became the goal.　　　　　　　　　　　　　　　MMcC

Further Reading

Carr, E.H.: *The Bolshevik Revolution 1917–1923*, 3 vols. London: Macmillan, 1966.

Fotieva, L.A.: *V.I. Lenin – rukovoditel' i tovarishch*, 2nd edn. Moscow: 1973.

Keep, J.L.H.: *The Russian Revolution: A Study in Mass Mobilization*. London: Weidenfeld & Nicolson, 1976.

Nove, A.: *An Economic History of the USSR*. London: Penguin, 1960.

Service, R.: *The Bolshevik Party in Revolution 1917–1923*. London: Macmillan, 1979.

Foreign Policy and Diplomacy: 1917–1924

A commission for foreign affairs was created as part of the Council of People's Commissars by a decree of the Second All-Russian Congress of Soviets of Workers' and Soldiers' Deputies (7–9 November 1917 NS). A few days later, after discussion between LENIN and TROTSKY, this Commission was renamed People's Commissariat for Foreign Affairs (acronym: Narkomindel). Despite its new title the government considered that it would only be a sort of diplomatic chancery attached to the Central Committee. With the mood ushered in by the New Economic Policy (1921) it was recognized that traditional diplomacy had its virtues and the Foreign Commissariat acquired a new significance. It was transformed into a centralized apparatus of Soviet Foreign Policy after November 1923 by the new CONSTITUTION which created the USSR and suppressed the Foreign Commissariats existing officially in the other Soviet republics (more particularly so in the UKRAINE under Ch. G. RAKOVSKY).

After the Bolshevik seizure of power, Trotsky was appointed Commissar for Foreign Affairs and kept this function until March 1918. I. A. Zalkind, one of Trotsky's assistants, who was deputed to put things in order in the former ministry, extracted the keys of the archives and safes containing the ciphers and secret documents. A proclamation was then issued saying that if the employees of the ministry did not come to work on the morning of November 13, they would be discharged without pension. The diplomats immediately decided to join the strike organized by government employees against Soviet power to show openly their distrust of the new regime.

As in the foreign services of European countries, the Russian Ministry of Foreign Affairs had long been a fief of the aristocracy: out of 550 career diplomats, 32 were princes and 39 were barons. Whether appointed under NICHOLAS II or the PROVISIONAL GOVERNMENT, they could hardly approve of Bolshevik plans for Russia; nor would they accept a foreign policy which aimed at a separate peace with Germany and a break with the Allies. Thus even if the Bolsheviks had wished to maintain some diplomats to keep things going, it was practically impossible to do so: only a dozen of them remained together with the courtiers and servants. Neither was the new power capable of bringing Russian diplomatic missions under its control. The situation abroad was indeed paradoxical and many representatives of the Provisional Government were able to keep their credentials for a number of years; B. A. Bakhmetyev was ambassador to the USA until 1922; the ambassador to Yugoslavia remained until 1940. V. A. Maklakov organized a 'Council of Ambassadors' in Paris which was composed of Russian representatives abroad.

To counteract these activities, it was agreed to try and appoint as official representatives of the Soviet power Bolsheviks or fellow travellers who happened to be in various countries: V. V. Vorovsky in Sweden, L. K. Martens in the United States, P. Simonov in Australia. G. V. CHICHERIN was appointed to the Court of St James while he was still imprisoned in Brixton Gaol for his activities against the war. Foreigners were also recruited: the Scottish syndicalist John Maclean became consul in Glasgow, and John REED was supposed to have the same function in the USA.

At first it was clear that Trotsky's idea was to eradicate the 'bourgeois' diplomacy inherited from the previous regime. He only thought of his role at the head of the new Commissariat in terms of world revolution, and declared on taking office: 'I will issue a few revolutionary proclamations to the peoples of the world and then shut up shop'. The first 'diplomatic act' of the new government was to publish a hundred secret files selected by the sailor N. Markin for translation into Russian. Nine volumes of documents were

Figure 25   Soviet delegation arriving at Brest-Litovsk, early 1918; Ioffe (centre, facing front), Kamener and Karakhan (to right, talking).

published at the turn of 1918 purportedly to unveil the 'filthy machinations of imperialist diplomacy' which were said to have caused the war.

The paradox of the first socialist state – apparently confined to isolation by its radical aims, but convinced that its fight could only be victorious – struck many Bolshevik leaders. For them, isolation was the 'professional risk' of a revolutionary state; yet they were convinced that this isolation could not last because it was 'chemically' impossible for the two blocs – capitalist and socialist – to remain side by side without interaction. On the other hand the first socialist state must survive until the international revolution, 'until the moment when the united international proletariat rises and fights against united international capital' (Rakovsky, 1918). On the other hand the internal dynamics of the Soviet state was to kindle the energies of the world proletariat (see IDEA OF WORLD REVOLUTION).

From the start the domestic determinants were thus an essential drive for Soviet international behaviour. Lenin drew far reaching conclusions from this situation, predicting the inevitability of 'terrible clashes' between the two

systems, while STALIN emphasized the 'world significance of the October revolution'. He certainly was one of the first Bolsheviks to realize that its impact had created a 'new revolutionary front' running 'from the proletariat of the West through the Russian revolution to the oppressed peoples of the East' (November 1918).

In such conditions diplomacy could only be conceived as a means of 'active wait and see'. During the peace negotiations with Imperial Germany at Brest-Litovsk (December 1917–March 1918), some Soviet leaders admitted without flinching: 'It should not be forgotten that we find ourselves in a period of discussions, and that precisely at this moment bluff and deceit constitute one of the tools of diplomacy'. Whatever the discussions with Foreign powers, Lenin himself gave only 'fragmentary remarks' to the new diplomats, 'reckoning that these treaty talks were temporary, immaterial, necessary . . . only to prolong the breathing space'.

Yet Lenin's concern for the safety of the state led him to put the Central Committee in direct charge of the negotiations with Germany. This enabled him to oppose both Trotsky's 'active internationalism' at Brest-Litovsk and the inconsistencies of the first Soviet diplomats.

As soon as Chicherin was freed from his British gaol (January 3, 1918), he returned to Russia to become Trotsky's Deputy Commissar a few days later. He was put in charge of creating a new diplomatic service. Indeed, besides the workers and sailors who had been recruited by Zalkind for their recent actions in the take-over but who had no idea of what a diplomatic note was, it became vital to select a number of professional revolutionaries who had lived abroad. They came from among the Marxist intelligentsia who had studied law or medicine in France, Switzerland or Germany; they often spoke several languages apart from Russian and had a decent knowledge of foreign countries. They were particularly aware of the political situation of those countries in which they had lived long enough to take part in their socialist movements. Yet this was not enough to make a diplomat, and for the first few years Lenin took care to choose personally the staff he needed for negotiations and representation abroad. On the whole he had no great confidence in them, he thought they were too 'talkative' and told them: 'A diplomat must be capable of keeping silent or of talking without revealing anything'.

On the eve of the Genoa conference in 1922 he admitted: 'We have taken very great pains in the Central Committee to appoint a delegation of our best diplomats (we now have a fair number of Soviet diplomats, which was not the case in the early period of the Soviet Republic)'. He would remember the case of Karl RADEK who was a specialist in voluntary *faux-pas* in the interviews he gave to foreign journalists, boasting for example that the Soviet Embassy in Berlin in 1918 was the 'staff headquarters for the German revolution'.

Along with Chicherin and M. M. Litvinov, the first leading Soviet diplomats were A. A. IOFFE, L. M. KARAKHAN and L. B. KRASIN. These few names typify the ethnic, social and political variety of Narkomindel members during the 1920s. Less than half were Great Russians; three quarters came from the middle class, a whole group from the nobility and a few from the highest aristocracy (such as the Chicherin himself who was *vieux-jeu* in many ways). Most of them had opposed Lenin systematically before October 1917: the great majority had been close to the MENSHEVIKS, others to the SOCIALIST REVOLUTIONARIES or even to the Kadets. The only woman was Alexandra KOLLONTAI, who in 1923 became the world's first woman ambassador. Among early Soviet diplomats one could find foreign social-democrats such as the Pole Julian Marchlewski or the Rumanian Christian Rakovsky. Both felt they were true internationalists, and Rakovsky was obviously proud to be a 'citizen of the world', echoing Anacharsis Cloots during the French revolution.

During the Civil War and Allied intervention Soviet Russia was almost totally isolated. (The only state which did not sever diplomatic relations with Soviet Russia was Afghanistan.) At that time, diplomacy was of little use and often quite irrelevant: the Collegium of the Narkomindel only met three days a week, and the Foreign Commissar wrote proclamations which could have been authored by ZINOVIEV, the head of Comintern. Thus in 1919, during the revolutionary movements in Bavaria, Chicherin declared: 'We may rest assured that the day is not far off when revolutionary Socialist allies will join forces with us and will give support to the Bavarian Republic against any attack . . . In absolute unity we carry on our revolutionary struggle for the well-being of all the workers and exploited peoples.'

In such circumstances, every favourable contact with foreigners was important: this explains the role which such early fellow-travellers as the American John Reed or the Frenchman Jacques Sadoul played for the young Soviet state.

After 1921, when political and commercial relations were being rapidly reestablished with western Europe, the Foreign Commissariat became a major institution. It soon endeavoured to acquire credibility by insisting on a strict separation between diplomatic, military and Comintern activities. Its apparatus in Moscow already numbered 1300 persons whereas it had had little more than 100 at the end of 1917. If the Soviet state had only eight permanent legations abroad in 1921, it already had 17 by the following year.

On November 12, 1923, the Central Executive Committee of the USSR approved a new charter for the Commissariat of Foreign Affairs. Article III indicated that the Commissariat was composed of six basic entities working under a People's Commissar. Two major departments, East and West, divided the world into two major zones with several subdivisions. Administrative services and a Secretariat were assisted by financial and juridical sections. A Press department was in charge of publishing a journal called *Mezhdunarodnaya zhizn* (International Life), collections of documents and reports. It also played the role of censor for foreign correspondents in Russia. The Collegium was a most important organ as it had to prepare collectively the proposals to be made to the Central Committee and then to the Politburo.

Until 1922, Lenin was the real head of Soviet Foreign policy. He carefully prepared the Genoa conference which marked the entry of Soviet Russia into international life, and issued a number of recommendations which looked very much like strict orders to the delegation of Soviet diplomats.

The Rapallo Treaty which was signed at that time between Germany and Soviet Russia was essential to help the two 'pariahs' of Europe to get closer; in Lenin's eyes it also had the distinct advantage of driving a wedge between capitalist countries, and of procuring financial and technical aid for Russia. Members of the Soviet delegation such as

Chicherin, Krasin and Rakovsky were instrumental in bringing the rapprochement to fruition, but when they proposed giving more political or economic concessions than had been decided in Moscow, Lenin immediately threatened to recall them to Moscow.

After March 1923 and the third stroke which paralysed Lenin, Trotsky became the main leader of Soviet foreign policy for the next two years. As if having learned the lessons of Brest-Litovsk, Trotsky later showed the greatest care for the security of the Soviet state. This was clear during the Soviet-Polish war in 1920, the Georgian affair in 1921, and when France occupied the Ruhr in January 1923. In May of the same year, he advocated a compromise with Lord Curzon, when the British Foreign Secretary sent an ultimatum to the Soviet authorities. He also agreed to Chicherin's proposals for separating diplomatic and Comintern activities.

This Soviet moderation was soon to be rewarded by the diplomatic recognition of the USSR by Italy, England and France (1924). Besides the political advantage, these *de jure* relations gave Russia the possibility of establishing commercial links with industrialized countries which could provide credits and technical help. The wish to diversify relations and not to rely exclusively on Germany, was evident, though it provoked some tension within Narkomindel. Whereas Litvinov adopted a balanced position in relations with European powers, Chicherin would mainly favour the German alliance. This was for him the best counterweight to France on the continent, even if the arch enemy of Russia, in Europe as well as Asia, remained the British Empire.

By that time the struggle for power within the Politburo was influencing the recruiting of Soviet diplomats. In the decisive years 1923–7, Stalin's ascent to power was partly due to his ability to put his followers in crucial positions within the Soviet apparatus, while he knew how to evict leading opponents. Rakovsky was sent to England and France as Soviet representative; Antonov-Ovseenko was appointed ambassador to Czechoslavakia and Latvia; L. B. KAMENEV was sent to Rome in the crucial year 1927.

Once Soviet leaders were made diplomats and had to leave the centres of decision-making, their room for manoeuvre was severely limited. They felt they were exiled, considered themselves victims of administrative repression but could not imagine what was in store for them during Stalin's rule. Almost two thirds of the Soviet ambassadors and leading members of the Narkomindel, followers and opponents alike, were to be purged in the late 1930s to make room for a Stalinist generation which remained in power until recent years.   FC

Further Reading

Bakhov, A.S.: *Na zare sovetskoi diplomatii.* Moscow: 1966.

Conte. F.: *Un révolutionnaire-diplomate: Christian Rakovski (L'Union soviétique et l'Europe 1922–1941).* Paris: La Haye, 1978.

Debo, R.K.: *Revolution and Survival: The Foreign Policy of Soviet Russia (1917–1918).* Toronto: Toronto University Press, 1979.

Gorokhov, I., Zamyatin, L. and Zemskov, I.: *G.V. Chicherin: diplomat leninskoi shkoly.* Moscow: 1966.

Haupt, G. and Marie, J-J.: *Les bolchéviks par eux mêmes* (Encyclopédie 'Granat'). Paris: Maspéro, 1969.

Uldricks, T.J.: *Diplomacy and Ideology: The Origins of Soviet Foreign Relations, 1917–1930.* London: Sage Publications, 1979.

Zalkind, I.A.: NKID v semnadtsatom godu. *Mezhdunarodnaya zhizn* 10 (1927) 12–20.

———— : Iz pervykh mesyatsev NKID. *Mezhdunarodnaya zhizn* 15 (1927) 55–61.

The Vecheka

The All-Russian Extraordinary Commission for Combating Counter-Revolution and Sabotage, colloquially called the Vecheka or Cheka after the initials of its shortened Russian title, was established by a Council of People's Commissars (Sovnarkom) resolution on 7(20) December 1917, six weeks after the Bolshevik Party's October coup d'état. Its tsarist political police predecessor, the OKHRANA, had been dissolved, and the regular police decentralized, following the February Revolution. Between 25 October and early December, the Military Revolutionary Committee (initially under the Petrograd Soviet, but from 29 October attached to the All-Russian Central Executive Committee of the Congress of Soviets – VTsIK) had exercised responsibility for revolutionary order, with Felix DZERZHINSKY, forty-year-old veteran Polish revolutionary and member of the Bolshevik Party's Central Committee, prominent in organizing security measures. Appointed chairman of the Vecheka, Dzerzhinsky provided the concept, and shaped the apparatus, of the new agency.

LENIN's pre-October purpose had been to replace those habitual props of government – the standing army, the regular police, and the bureaucracy – by a visionary universal part-time people's militia composed of workers and peasants; if, during his first year in power, he not only restored all three institutions on a professional basis, but also presided over the vigorous growth of the political police, this ideological retreat was dictated by necessity. To achieve his aim of imposing single-party rule under the slogan 'Dictatorship of the Proletariat' in the face of opposition from the bourgeoisie, the military caste, most of the intelligentsia, many trade unions, the huge peasantry, the socialist parties, and even part of the presently disillusioned proletariat (all this against the background of raging Civil War, foreign intervention, chaos and famine, and without benefit of world revolution), Lenin had no option but to rely on professionalism, centralization and discipline in army, bureaucracy and regular police. He also found it increasingly necessary to rely on a political police, which alone could subdue internal resistance and implement the mass terror required for the survival and consolidation of the Soviet regime. *Pravda* of 22 November

1917 carried Lenin's declaration: 'The state is an instrument for coercion . . . we desire to transform the state into an institution for enforcing the will of the people. We want to organize violence in the name of the interests of the workers.' A sentiment echoed by Dzerzhinsky, in *Svoboda Rossii* (Russia's Freedom) of 9 June 1918:

> We stand for organized terror – this should be frankly stated – terror being absolutely indispensable in current revolutionary conditions . . . We terrorize the enemies of the Soviet government in order to stifle crime at its inception. Terror serves as a ready deterrent.

Improvised by Lenin for the suppression of an escalating public service strike, and originally envisaged as a temporary, primarily investigative agency, attached to the Sovnarkom – cabinet of the Soviet government – the Vecheka swiftly acquired the sanctions of arrest and imprisonment; in late February 1918, on the strength of Lenin's proclamation of a state of emergency entitled 'The Socialist Fatherland is in Danger', it appropriated the right to sentence and execute by way of summary justice. The first, not undeserving, victim of Vecheka execution was 'Prince Eboli', a Petrograd robber and blackmailer masquerading as a Chekist, shot on 24 February. Throughout its existence the Vecheka lacked judicial status and powers, all its actions bearing an administrative character; it functioned as an 'extraordinary' agency, outside the constitutional fabric of government. The Vecheka's sphere of interest, originally embracing counter-revolution, sabotage, press, the liberal Kadet Party and the Right Socialist Revolutionaries (Right SRs), quickly broadened to include economic malpractice, misuse of authority and banditry.

In mid March 1918 the Vecheka moved with the government from Petrograd to Moscow, establishing its Lubyanka headquarters near the Kremlin. During 1918 it developed a country-wide network of territorial Chekas at provincial and district level. The first national conference of Chekas met in June; subsequently a Corps of Vecheka Troops was constituted (with a battalion posted to each Provincial Cheka), Frontier Chekas and Railway (later Transport) Chekas emerged, and at the turn of 1918/1919 the Vecheka assumed responsibility for security in the RED ARMY through a system of Special Departments attached to higher army formations. By 1 January 1919 the Vecheka's strength probably stood at around 37,000 men.

The Vecheka and the Left Socialist Revolutionaries

From mid December 1917 the Bolsheviks governed in coalition with the Left Socialist Revolutionaries (LSRs), whose representatives entered the Vecheka on 8 January 1918, occupying key positions in its directing Collegium; they unaccountably remained in the Vecheka after their party's withdrawal from coalition government in mid March. The LSR insurrection in Moscow on 6 July was launched by the LSR-dominated Vecheka Combat Detachment; both Dzerzhinsky and Vecheka headquarters were captured by the rebels. However, on 7 July the revolt was quelled, and the Vecheka began to execute political adversaries (hitherto it had only executed criminals) starting with Dzerzhinsky's LSR deputy, Alexandrovich, and other LSR Chekists. Meanwhile the death penalty under the law, abolished after the February Revolution, was restored on 16 June 1918; it was applied by Revolutionary Tribunals – never by the Chekas which solely exercised summary justice.

The Vecheka and the Red Terror

While Lenin had consistently opposed, as being counter-productive, individual acts of terrorism, he favoured coordinated terror tactics in support of insurrection (as in the 1905 REVOLUTION), and advocated the use of mass terror for the consolidation of a revolutionary regime, on the analogy of the French Revolution. Some spontaneous violence had accompanied the outbreak of the February and October Revolutions. In late November 1917 Lenin had declared the liberal Kadet Party to be 'enemies of the people', and in December he encouraged the masses to take the law into their own hands. For Lenin Soviet law was a convenience, only to be used by the Dictatorship of the Proletariat when this suited its interests. Lenin's formulation on this point was explicit: 'The scientific concept of dictatorship means nothing else but this: power without limit, resting directly upon force, restrained by no laws, absolutely unrestricted by rules.' Deliberate large-scale Bolshevik terror, hitherto restrained by the LSRs, was first employed in summer 1918, in the suppression of peasant risings provoked by the oppressive grain requisitioning campaign (see WAR COMMUNISM), and in the mass execution of captured rebels after Boris SAVINKOV's abortive Yaroslavl insurrection in July. On the night of 16/17 July, the deposed Tsar NICHOLAS II and his family were executed without trial by a Cheka squad in Ekaterinburg, on orders from Lenin.

Mass terror erupted immediately after the assassination of the Petrograd Cheka chief, Moisei URITSKY, and the coincidental wounding of Lenin, on 30 August 1918. The Sovnarkom 'Decree on the Red Terror', enacted on 5 September, authorized the Vecheka to isolate class enemies in concentration camps, and to shoot 'all persons involved in White Guard organizations, plots and insurrections', precipitating a torrent of executions. Lenin's doctrine of class war, in which the victory of the proletariat justified any means for its attainment, was taken by Chekists to extreme conclusions; Dzerzhinsky's lieutenant, Martyn LATSIS, urged that prisoners of the Chekas should be judged not by their actions but according to their social origins: 'We are not waging war against individual persons. We are exterminating the bourgeoisie as a class' (in *Krasnyi* (Red) *Terror*, Kazan, 1 November 1918.) The Vecheka executed hostages in large numbers in order to paralyse the will of hostile sections of the population. Concentration camps, standing under exclusive Vecheka control, were introduced in mid 1918 for the isolation of class enemies, but came to include refractory workers, criminals, and 'politicals' drawn from opposition socialist parties. The separate system of forced labour camps was instituted by a decree published on 15 April 1919; such camps were organized by Provincial Chekas, and were then administered by the People's Commissariat for Internal Affairs (NKVD). Primarily intended to hold workers who infringed labour regulations, by 1920 the eighty-four forced labour camps in the RSFSR contained 25,226 detainees of various categories, besides 24,000 Civil War prisoners. But such statistics are meaningless, since in the early 1920s both types of camp were cleared from time to time by mass extermination of inmates.

Cheka clients were also held for long periods in prisons, in execrable conditions, exposed to brutal interrogation, torture, and the ever-present fear of execution. The local Cheka Collegium would meet in secret session and pronounce verdicts on completed investigation cases by a simple majority vote, in the absence of the accused; execution followed very many of these summary 'trials'. Mass executions in prisons were triggered off by the approach of White Armies, or by the imminence of an amnesty. After the evacuation of Wrangel's defeated army in late 1920, his suspected supporters in the Crimea, many of them selected simply on the basis of their occupation or social origin, were massacred by the Chekas on a scale amounting to genocide. Many atrocities were also perpetrated by the Whites in the Civil War, but these were not directed at hostages or at entire categories and classes.

Criticism of the Chekas

The application of terror in late 1918 and early 1919 involved the Vecheka in conflict on four fronts: first, with the NKVD to whose executive departments of Provincial and District Soviets local Chekas were formally attached while taking their orders from the central Vecheka, such dual subordination engendering severe friction; second, the People's Commissariat for Justice (NKIu) which resented the competing system of punitive Chekas operating, without judicial procedures, parallel to the NKIu's Revolutionary Tribunals; third, elements within the Communist Party critical of the cruelty and arbitrariness of Cheka activity and of the presence of criminals in the Chekas' ranks; fourth, government departments, many of whose key bourgeois 'specialist' personnel were detained by Chekas as suspects or hostages. On all four counts the Chekas were publicly attacked, being depicted as a 'state within the state', apparently not accountable to any external authority; founded by an unpublished Sovnarkom resolution, the Vecheka functioned without systematic supervision, and unregulated by laws. The Party now moved to bring it under control: a statute, enacted on 28 October 1918, attempted to define the Vecheka's purposes and powers, but left its relationship with the Soviets and Revolutionary Tribunals unresolved. On 20 January 1919 the District Chekas were dissolved by decree, but were presently replaced by political bureaux of District Militias (regular police) fulfilling Cheka orders. Moreover, in mid March 1919, Dzerzhinsky was appointed People's Commissar for Internal Affairs, whilst remaining Vecheka chairman, thereby contriving to coordinate NKVD and Vecheka activity and to safeguard Chekist interests. In mid February, the Vecheka's right to pass sentence was transferred to the Revolutionary Tribunals, but the Chekas were still entitled to sentence and execute in territory under martial law, and to confine people in concentration camps.

Party control over the Vecheka

Meanwhile the Party's Central Committee came to the Vecheka's defence, declaring in *Izvestiya* on 8 February 1919 that 'the Chekas were founded, exist and work solely as the direct organs of the Party, under its direction and supervision'. Upon the creation of the Politburo in March 1919, a Politburo member (initially BUKHARIN, later STALIN) was deputed to sit on the Vecheka Collegium, with right of veto. Formally, Lenin was the Vecheka's master, in his dual capacity as Party leader and Sovnarkom chairman; he kept a close grip on Vecheka affairs, visiting its Lubyanka headquarters, and defending the service in public. Only Dzerzhinsky and SVERDLOV, chairman of VTsIK, were privileged to have instant access to Lenin. Dzerzhinsky, who represented the political police in the Party's Central Committee until his death in July 1926, took pains to identify the Vecheka with the Party, claiming in February 1920 that it was the institution with the highest proportion of Communists – nearly fifty per cent – in its ranks, and that it served as 'the best, the sharpest, and the most effective weapon of the workers' dictatorship' (see Belov, 1958).

After his additional appointment in April 1921 as People's Commissar for Transport, Dzerzhinsky had to delegate to his Vecheka deputy, I. S. UNSHLIKHT, a Polish Communist like himself. Very many non-Russian Communists, especially Latvians, Jews and Poles, served in the Vecheka at various levels, including such prominent Chekists as PETERS and Latsis (Latvians), MENZHINSKY and Redens (Poles), Uritsky and Yagoda (Jews).

Organizational development

During the Civil War and beyond, the versatile Vecheka adapted its structure to operational requirements. Provincial Chekas maintained security supervision over the local population, recruiting a multitude of informers, investigating subversive stirrings, and suppressing risings. Cheka Special Departments, attached to the Red Army, operated in military front zones, eliminating local threats and seeing to security within the Soviet armed forces, whose parallel system of political commissars watched over the loyalty of ex-tsarist officers serving as 'military specialists'. The central Special Department and its subordinate units helped to uncover important military and political conspiracies such as the National Centre in 1919, the Tactical Centre in 1920, and the Petrograd Combat Organization in 1921. Transport Chekas cooperated with Railway Security Troops and Railway and River Militias in guarding vital railway and waterway networks against sabotage. The Frontier Troops, nearly 100,000 strong, stood under Vecheka control during November 1920–October 1921; in September 1922 they were reconstituted as a Separate Frontier Corps under GPU direction.

The Corps of Vecheka Troops was absorbed in May 1919 by the newly created Internal Security Troops (VOKhR) which on 1 September 1920 became the Internal Service Troops (VNUS), both these bodies being formally subordinated to the NKVD, whilst standing operationally under Vecheka command. Upon disbandment of VNUS, in January 1921, Vecheka Troops emerged as a purely Cheka organ. These various security forces were prominent in combating 'political banditry', i.e. the large-scale peasant and nationalist insurrections endemic in the countryside, such as the Tambov Revolt (1920–21), MAKHNO's anarchist guerrilla activity in the Ukraine (1919–21), and widespread resistance by the COSSACKS of the Don, and by the Basmachi in Central Asia, these being some of the more important manifestations of hostility to the Communist regime. In 1920 Dzerzhinsky, as Commander of the Rear of the South-West Front in the Ukraine, made massive use of VOKhR troops to secure the internal front in the Soviet-Polish War.

The Vecheka's Foreign Department, established in December 1920, was charged with gathering intelligence abroad. During the NEP period, the Counter-Espionage Department watched foreign embassies and trade missions, and penetrated émigré organizations in the west; long-term classic deception operations culminated in the capture, on Soviet soil, of Savinkov in 1924, and of the British Intelligence agent, Sidney REILLY, in 1925.

The Vecheka's function of economic security, originally concerned with the extirpation of black market activity, bribery and corruption, expanded with the advent of NEP; its Economic Administration, formed in January 1921, guarded against sabotage of the economy, but also aspired to oversee the fulfilment of economic targets. The Vecheka's Secret (previously Secret-Operational) Department concentrated on suppression of political dissent, infiltrating, arresting and systematically destroying the opposition socialist parties – the MENSHEVIKS, Right and Left SRs, also the ANARCHISTS and BUNDISTS, harassing the dwindling independent trade unions and the Orthodox Church, persecuting the liberal intelligentsia, and muzzling the non-Party press. Writing in late 1920,

Latsis (1921) put the Vecheka's aim as being the total supervision of Soviet society: 'The work of the Vecheka must extend over all those spheres of Soviet life where counter-revolution has taken root. And that means that there is no sphere of life exempt from Vecheka coverage.' The Vecheka proved itself to be such a well-disciplined, efficient and versatile machine, that it became an indispensable, all-purpose tool of Party and government, operating in such extraneous fields as: labour conscription; countering of epidemics; fuel procurement; dealing with army desertion; crime; control of firearms; famine relief; and even succouring the shelterless *besprizornye* – children orphaned by Civil War and famine, whose marauding gangs posed a menace to public order. The Vecheka's reputation for ruthlessness stood it in good stead in its varied dealings with individuals and institutions.

Formally, the Vecheka's writ ran solely in the Russian Republic, but in practice its authority extended over the Chekas of the nominally independent republics of the Ukraine, Belorussia, and Transcaucasia, such Chekas being modelled on and directed by the Vecheka. In late 1920, Vecheka manpower totalled around 100,000, and by mid 1921, when it included nearly 140,000 Vecheka Troops and almost 100,000 Frontier Troops, it probably amounted to some 260,000 personnel. Upon the pacification of some of the most troublesome areas of insurrection, a rapid reduction ensued: by December 1921 the Vecheka's strength had dropped to 143,000, and by May 1922 its successor, the GPU of the RSFSR, stood at 105,000 men. The Civil War had been won in late 1920, but many problems remained, among them economic exhaustion, industrial discontent, and widespread peasant rebellion. The KRONSTADT REVOLT signalled the bankruptcy of War Communism. At the Tenth Party Congress, in March 1921, Lenin introduced NEP, yielding economic concessions, but tightening political and security controls. The Vecheka was still sorely needed; however, for the normalization of political and trade relations with capitalist countries, Lenin's new emphasis on 'revolutionary legality', in place of the arbitrary operation of 'revolutionary conscience' and 'revolutionary expediency', required the disappearance or disguise of the Vecheka, with its fearsome reputation and identification with terror.

The Vecheka succeeded by GPU

A decree of 6 February 1922 replaced the Vecheka by the State Political Administration (GPU), which was integrated in the NKVD of the RSFSR as part of the regular machinery of state. Dzerzhinsky continued to direct the NKVD; in effect, the Vecheka organization, although reduced in size, remained in being under another name. The GPU did not inherit (though it swiftly acquired) the Vecheka's extra-judicial powers of meting out summary justice and of confinement in concentration camps. Significantly, in mid May 1922, Lenin wrote to his Commissar of Justice, Kursky; 'The law should not abolish terror; to promise that would be self-delusion or deception; it should be substantiated and legalized in principle, clearly, without evasion or embellishment.'

The subordination of the political police to the NKVD was short-lived; article 61 of the USSR CONSTITUTION, adopted on 6 July 1923, elevated the GPU, now renamed OGPU (Unified GPU), to the equivalent status of a unified People's Commissariat, independent of the NKVD, attached direct to the Sovnarkom of the USSR, and functioning in constituent republics (exceptionally, in Transcaucasia, the Cheka retained its title until 1926, when it became the Transcaucasian GPU). The political police had become a permanent and prominent feature of the Soviet state.

The Vecheka compared with Okhrana

The Vecheka continued a long tsarist political police tradition, but differed both quantitatively and qualitatively from its immediate predecessor, the Okhrana; the latter, relying on the Special Corps of Gendarmes, 15,000 strong, was dwarfed by the vast Vecheka apparatus. Over the last fifty years of tsarist rule, some 14,000 executions had occurred, the great majority in retaliation for the several thousand political assassinations following the 1905 Revolution; however the Okhrana, standing under the Police Department of the Ministry of the Interior, possessed few extra-judicial powers, and was not authorized to execute. By contrast, the Chekas of the various Soviet republics were directly responsible for perhaps 140,000 executions, and maybe another 140,000 deaths in the suppression of insurrections, these being very tentative estimates, in the nature of educated guesses. Both security organizations achieved considerable success: the Okhrana in penetrating and neutralizing the revolutionary parties, which had no hand in the spontaneous revolution of February 1917; the Vecheka in its vital contribution to the survival of the beleaguered Soviet regime. The Vecheka adopted many of the operational methods favoured by the Okhrana, such as the use of AGENTS PROVOCATEURS.

Most of Dzerzhinsky's senior Chekists, some no longer serving in the security apparatus, perished in Stalin's purges. Nearly all have been rehabilitated, and an intensive cult of Lenin's political police has been practised since the late 1950s, helping to obliterate the terror-tainted reputation of the secret police under Yagoda, Ezhov and Beria, and to legitimize the KGB (whose personnel proudly call themselves Chekisty) by tracing its descent from the idealized Cheka created by Lenin. And indeed many of the organizational features of today's KGB can be traced back to the Vecheka, the prototype of a new breed of twentieth-century security organs, serving authoritarian or totalitarian regimes.   GHL

Further Reading

Belov, G.A. et al. eds.: *Iz istorii Vserossiiskoi Chrezvychainoi komissii 1917-1921 gg.* Moscow: Sbornik dokumentov, 1958.

Gerson, Lennard D.: *The Secret Police in Lenin's Russia.* Philadelphia: 1976.

Latsis, M. Ya.: *Chrezvychainye komissii po borbe s kontrrevolyutsiei.* Moscow: 1921.

Leggett, George: *The Cheka: Lenin's Political Police.* Oxford: 1981.

Sofinov, P.G.: *Ocherki istorii Vserossiiskoi Chrezvychainoi komissii (1917–1922 gg).* Moscow: 1960.

Wolin, Simon and Slusser, Robert M. eds.: *The Soviet Secret Police.* New York and London: 1957.

The Red Army

On the morrow of the OCTOBER REVOLUTION the new regime found itself virtually naked to its enemies. Hitherto it had been a prime objective of the BOLSHEVIKS to neutralize, if not actually to cripple an army, the elephantine IMPERIAL RUSSIAN ARMY which might well have trampled them underfoot. It was to this end that the Military Organization (acronym: Voenka) of the Bolshevik Central Committee in Petrograd bent its energies, only to find after November that the interests of sheer survival demanded the opposite, building rather than undermining an army, one not only capable of fighting but effective enough to defeat 'armed counter-revolution', the enemies of the Soviet regime. It was a task for which, as LENIN readily admitted, neither ideological nor political preparation of any kind had been made.

The 'military' Bolsheviks who made up the Military-Naval Committee empowered by the Second Congress of Soviets – Dybenko, Krylenko and Antonov-Ovseenko – were agitators rather than experts, intent on taking over the military administration and speeding the 'democratization' of the old army which still loomed large on the scene. Bolshevik forces were at best a motley aspect, consisting of the Red Guard, variously estimated at anything from 50,000 to 200,000 men, but poorly armed, indifferently trained and ill-disciplined, together with the Bolshevik sailor squads, the dour LATVIAN RIFLEMEN, ex-prisoners of war clustering into their own 'International Legion' and sundry local militia units.

The new government, pursuing its peace formula, succeeded in arranging a truce on the Eastern Front, thus gaining a little time but by no means disposing of the danger. 'Democratization' and desertion steadily sapped the Imperial army, with the front facing the Central Powers thinning drastically. Slowly but surely the need to organize 'the Soviet defence effort' – talk of an 'army' had an ugly reactionary ring to it, the notion of a standing army being as ideologically odious as it was politically unacceptable – brought Lenin to instruct N. I. Podvoisky to call a 'special defence conference' to discuss 'mechanisms' for a proposed Soviet military force. The time for decisions was at hand.

The commitment to 'democratization' of the old army (election of officers and the wholesale transfer of power to the Soldiers' Committees) was giving way to talk of actual demobilization: internally counter-revolution was organizing and arming, externally the armistice on the Eastern Front was patently fragile. With L. D. TROTSKY dispatched to Brest-Litovsk to win more time by spinning out the negotiations with the Central Powers, the 'military' Bolsheviks and select senior Imperial Army officers (already pinpointed early in December by Lenin as 'military specialists', to supply military expertise for a revolutionary army) pondered, propounded and propagandized.

With preparations afoot in mid December 1917 for the All-Army Demobilization Conference, already three proposals were being examined: the General Staff plan to cut the Imperial army to its pre-war level and to use it as the basis for a 'mixed military system'; the Petrograd Red Guard General Staff plan to organize a force of two corps; and M. S. KEDROV's design for a 'Socialist Guard' raised exclusively among the workers, excluding the peasantry. Krylenko, the first Bolshevik Commander-in-Chief, also set about forming a 'People's Guard', consisting of one corps recruited from 'tested revolutionaries', every man a volunteer. Meanwhile the Demobilization Conference voted (by 153 votes) for the creation of a 'Socialist Army', with the Petrograd Soviet also supporting the idea of a 'Socialist army' organized on the principle of elective command, mutual comradely respect and discipline – fine phrases but on the day of that declaration, January 4, 1918, reality intruded brutally with the news that the Rumanian front was falling apart, desertion was clogging the railways and the front needed men. Lenin discussed the matter most urgently with Podvoisky, Dybenko, N. M. Potapov and K. A. Mekhonoshin, proposing an emergency mobilization of the Red Guard in Petrograd and Moscow and plans to raise ten corps (300,000 men) in the coming week.

Front commands, with commissars and soldiers' committees taking the lead, also set about setting up their own 'revolutionary armies', a kaleidoscope of units as variegated as their designations: the Revolutionary Red Army, the National Socialist Guard, the Red People's Guard, the Internationalist-Socialist Army, the National-Revolutionary Guard. But the consciousness of the need for a 'new' army, based on the voluntary system and 'mutual comradely respect' ran deep, breaking decisively with the 'old system'. From the welter of names and the profusion of units the Third Congress of Soviets on January 25–26, 1918 approved the plan for a 'new' army and a draft decree on 'The Worker-Peasant Red Army' (RKKA), an army of the dictatorship of the proletariat, composed of workers and toiling peasants. The draft decree now awaited the surgery of Lenin's pen, which made its particular excisions, eliminating the stipulation about voluntary enlistment and obliterating his earlier preferences for a militia system,

based on 'economic reasoning'. Now survival came first, displacing utopianism. On January 28, 1918 the decree was duly published and the Red Army finally came into existence, at least on paper.

Armies, however, feed on men not phrases and effective fighting forces need above all trained manpower, of which perhaps only some 50,000 were presently available to the Bolsheviks. The sailor squads might be ruthless but scarcely counted as an army, the Latvian riflemen were dispersed in the UKRAINE and on the Eastern Front, the Red Guards mustered 30,000 men but only a third could be considered effective. Volunteers to the fledgeling Red Army failed to materialize: men were galloping home. Organizing by 'detachments' brought chaos to the command system. The newly created 'All-Russian Collegiate for the Organization and Administration of the Worker-Peasant Red Army', run by Krylenko, Mekhonoshin, Podvoisky, V. A. Trifonov and K. K. Yurenev, plus commissars and former officials of the old War Ministry, failed to scoop up men but the fronts emptied and volunteers merely trickled in.

The resumption of the German advance on February 18, 1918 provided a terrifying jolt, bringing the 'military question' into desperate relief and imperilling Petrograd itself. The Petrograd Soviet hurriedly raised the Committee for the Revolutionary Defence of Petrograd and hunted about for reinforcements: the 'military' aspect of the defence was assigned to the Extraordinary Petrograd Military District Staff, converted early in March into the Supreme (or Higher) Military Soviet (VVS) manned by voenspets – the euphemism of 'military specialists' for ex-Imperial officers in Bolshevik service – and as such the first true Soviet command group. On March 3, 1918 the Soviet delegation signed the rapacious Treaty of Brest-Litovsk: Lenin weathered the storm of outrage and disaffection, rejecting the idea of a 'national war' against the Germans which would only mean arming the regime's internal enemies, while Trotsky now moved in as People's Commissar for Military Affairs (War Commissar), displacing Krylenko and ushering in ruthlessly realistic policies to build an effective Soviet fighting force.

Volunteers did not materialize, elective command brought chaos, units and organizations poached and pilfered men. The idea of a 'militia army' died hard and even in March 1918 there were violent protests (as there were to be again in March 1919) about the use of the voenspets. But Lenin aimed for a million-man army and Trotsky set about reaching this target, drawing in more ex-officers, centralizing command and creating a proper military administrative machine. Meanwhile the VVS planned in formal military terms, setting up 'screens' on the western and northern frontiers run by a Military Soviet manned by an ex-Imperial officer flanked by two commissars. This proved to be a workable model, widely adopted elsewhere.

Recruitment at the end of March 1918 had brought in 153,678 men. Arrogant and uninhibited, Trotsky set about changing the entire military scene. In April 1918 universal military training for the 'toiling masses' was enacted to train reserves: the military build-up was put under the control of the All-Russian Supreme Staff, the VVS split into administrations for operations and organization, the apparatus of political control, introduced 'military commissars' (as opposed to 'military-political commissars') responsible for 'revolutionary discipline' and the supervision of the *voenspets*, run now through the All-Russian Bureau of Military Commissars. This administrative rationalization was the first step towards the great centralization of September 1918 but in the early summer of 1918 the Soviet republic had yet to survive great and growing crises. The volunteer system had flopped: the *voenspets* of the VVS were pressing for systematic mobilization: Party stalwarts were calling increasingly for a 'powerful, well equipped, manoeuvrable regular army'. With the revolt in May 1918 of the Czechoslovak Legion in the east, flimsy Soviet armies flung aside in the Ukraine, German troops moving on to the Don and White troops under Krasnov and DENIKIN concentrating, the Soviet republic had to fight or go under: on 29 May 1918 compulsory military service was introduced for the working class.

In Moscow the first mobilization was an undoubted success: in the east, where men were desperately needed, it was a fiasco. At the end of June 1918 M. N. TUKHACHEVSKY took command of the 1st Revolutionary Army (1st Red Army) at Inza. On its own initiative the 1st Red Army early in July 1918 carried out its local mobilization of ex-Imperial officers, a move followed on July 29 with Trotsky's controversial Order No 228 introducing general mobilization of ex-officers, accompanied by a special mobilization of worker ex-NCOs: ultimately 48,409 ex-officers and 214,000 ex-NCOs were drafted into the Red Army, augmented by doctors, vets and administrative personnel, all rendering indispensable service. In that summer systematic mobilization produced 540,123 men and 17,800 NCOs for the Red Army over a three-month period. All the ingredients of an effective military system – manpower, administration, command, training and supply – were gradually making their appearance.

With his newly formed Red divisions fused from 'detachments', Tukhachevsky brought the Red Army its first victories on the Eastern Front. Military orthodoxy marched on apace; centralization was coming to dominate. On September 4 1918, at Trotsky's behest, the Republic Revolutionary Military Council (RVSR) took over the central direction of the Red Army and its attendant affairs, with Trotsky at its head and I. I. Vatsetis, ex-Imperial colonel, the Soviet Commander-in-Chief. A multi-million man Red Army was now in the making, only to encounter the furiously impassioned protests of the 'Military Opposition' at the Eighth Party Congress in March 1919, incensed

at the hijacking of 'their' army: Lenin himself supported the use of *voenspets* and the creation of a regular army, Trotsky survived but his armour was dented in an encounter which was only a prelude to subsequent debates and divisions on the future of the Soviet military system.

On 1 October 1920, with the Soviet-Polish war ending in serious Soviet reverses, the mobilized strength of the Red Army was 5,498,000 men, with 2,587,000 in reserve armies, 391,000 in Labour Armies, all amounting to 800,000 effectives (400,000–500,000 riflemen). The military anatomy of the Soviet Republic had changed dramatically in the course of the civil war: 20 Fronts (and 'sectors') had been set up, involving 16 field armies (38 in all, counting redesignations and the short-lived 'armies' which flitted over the scene), 26 national and local armies (such as the Estonian and Turkestan armies), two cavalry armies (1st and 2nd), nine cavalry divisions, 64 independent cavalry brigades, 83 rifle divisions (including redesignations and divisions raised afresh), eight corps and seven Labour Armies. In addition to the Far East, the National-Revolutionary Army (NRA) of the Far Eastern Republic (DVR) fought from 1920 to 1922 on three Fronts – the Amur, East Baikal and the Eastern. Operating under Soviet command were also two fleets (Baltic and Black Sea) plus 33 flotillas on inland waterways.

Having survived its baptism of fire and for all the tumult and the shouting over its structure, composition, military command and political control, the Red Army had incontestably come to stay.   JE

Further Reading

Britov, V.V.: *Rozhdenie Krasnoi Armii*. Moscow: 1961.

Direktivy komandovaniya frontov Krasnoi Armii (1917–1922), vols 1–4. Moscow: Voenizdat, 1971–1978.

Erickson, J.: The origins of the Red Army. In *Revolutionary Russia*, ed. R. E. Pipes. Cambridge, Mass.: Harvard University Press, 1968.

Fedotoff-White, D.: *The Growth of the Red Army*. Princeton, NJ: Princeton University Press, 1944.

Grazhdanskaya voina: Materialy po istorii Krasnoi Armii. Moscow: 1923.

Klyatskin, S.M.: *Na zashchite oktyabrya. Organizatsiya regulyarnoi armii i militsionnoe stroitel'stvo v Sovetskoi respublike, 1917–1920*. Moscow: 1965.

The Red Navy

In January 1918 the 'Workers' and Peasants' Red Fleet' (RKKF) was officially created, but in fact the six months after the OCTOBER Revolution saw the shattering of most of the old navy. This came in part from revolution, extreme democratization, and the dispersal of officers and sailors.

The sailors were not really a controllable force even for the BOLSHEVIKS, and the Soviet authorities had to fight to keep a measure of control. The old Navy Ministry was dissolved but no effective instrument put in its place. In the Baltic Tsentrobalt came under the influence of non-Bolshevik forces, most notably the ANARCHISTS, and in any event this democratic forum was unable to solve the great problems of the time. In the end appointed commissars replaced the elected committees, but not before much turmoil – notably the mutiny in the Baltic 'Destroyer Division' (May 1918) and the execution of the Baltic commander, Captain A. M. Shchastny.

The general course of the early Civil War was also disastrous for the Red Navy. The Central Powers and the Allies, when they began operations on Russian territory, naturally affected the coastal periphery first. The Northern and Siberian Flotillas fell under Anglo-French and Japanese control by mid 1918. The Black Sea Fleet was in the path of the Austro-German advance into the Ukraine in 1918; when the Germans reached the main naval base of Sevastopol in June a few major ships were taken east to Novorossisk and scuttled by Soviet crews. Many others, in deteriorating condition, remained in German hands; when the Allies reached the Black Sea after November 1918 they scuttled or took over the most effective vessels.

Only the Baltic Fleet survived in Soviet hands, and that was largely thanks to the remarkable 'Ice Crossing' in early 1918, when the forward-based units were evacuated through the frozen Gulf of Finland from Reval and Helsinki to Kronstadt and Petrograd. Even the Baltic Fleet, however, suffered from poor maintenance, and a lack of skilled crews and fuel. The loss of the artillery-mine position in the western Gulf of Finland exposed Kronstadt and Petrograd to attack.

The Civil War

The sailors played a prominent part in the Civil War from the very beginning, first in the battles in Petrograd and in Moscow, and then helping to spread the revolution to other parts of Russia. Both the Baltic and Black Sea Fleets provided large numbers of infantry and armoured train detachments for the desperate battles of 1918. The sailors were a vital factor not as a water-borne force, but as a group of men with a strong corporate sense and revolutionary esprit de corps.

With the stabilization of Soviet rule towards the end of 1918 and the formation of more regular forces, the fleet's role changed. Professional commanders of the Red Navy were appointed, Captain V. M. Altfater (1918–19), Captain E. A. Berens (1919–20), and Admiral A. V. Nemitts (1920–21). Ad hoc naval detachments became less important, except for the 1919 battles around Petrograd. The specifically naval role of the sailors was stressed, although more in river flotillas than sea-going ships. The first major force appeared on the Volga in the autumn of 1918 and improvised flotillas of smaller warships and converted river boats had a significant auxiliary role in the Civil War battles. Most important were the Northern Dvina flotilla, the detachments on Lake Ladoga, the Volga and Kama flotillas, and the Caspian flotilla. The only blue-water force was the Active Detachment (DOT) of the Baltic Fleet, but it was very much reduced by the lack of fuel and the dispersal of men, ships, and equipment to the inland flotillas. A numerically weaker British flotilla was able to blockade the Baltic Fleet in 1918–20. A raid on Tallin (Estonia) in December 1918 cost the Reds two big destroyers, and the cruiser Oleg and a number of destroyers and auxiliaries were lost to mines and British torpedo boats (several of which raided Kronstadt).

The Whites never developed significant naval forces. The remains of the Black Sea fleet was used for coastal bombardment but it was not efficient; with the evacuation of the Crimea by WRANGEL in late 1920 the surviving ships were interned in Tunisia. The Reds' main opponents were small British flotillas on the Northern Dvina, Lake Onega, and the Caspian.

The navy's difficulties, the general economic crisis, and a traditional naval dissatisfaction with authority led in 1921 to the Kronstadt Revolt and the deactivation of the last Red Fleet. In general, little of value survived the crisis of the Revolution and the Civil War. Many ships had been lost in the fighting or scuttled; others had been simply left to rot or disarmed to provide artillery for the army and the flotillas. Three battleships, five cruisers, and a few destroyers and submarines were the only inheritance of the Soviet regime from its tsarist predecessor, and even these ships would not be ready for some years after the Civil War. The crews of the old navy had been dispersed, but they had in the meantime made a major contribution to the victory and consolidation of Soviet power.   EM

Further Reading

See under RUSSIAN NAVY.

The Soviet Legal System

The OCTOBER REVOLUTION transpired without a carefully preconceived theory of law or legislation. Marx and Engels had been preoccupied in their writings primarily with the State and law of their own day. A transition period was foreseen during which the pre-existing capitalist order would be transformed into a communist society, but neither its duration nor possible substages of development were postulated. Politically, Marx said, the transition period would be the 'revolutionary dictatorship of the proletariat'. In his *State and Revolution* Lenin developed the notion, acknowledging that a proletarian State would be essential to complete the revolutionary process of crushing the bourgeoisie but also anticipating that the process of the dying out or withering away of State and law would commence at once. Much of Soviet legal theory has since been engaged with these contradictory processes and the relative weight to be accorded to each. Crucial to subsequent theoretical dialogue have been the perceptions of what actually transpired during 1917–20 and why, with respect to legal developments.

Widely overlooked is the fact that within hours after historical decrees were enacted by the new Soviet Government on peace, on land reform, and the like, Decree No. 7 on the procedure for the adoption and publication of laws was approved: orderly administration of the proletarian State could not proceed in the absence of a scheme for confirming the official nature of and disseminating the legislative directives of the new regime. Normative acts were described as 'proletarian commands' to be obeyed because they expressed the will of the new ruling class. A highly centralized form of government within a federated structure began to emerge. Initial expectations that an untrained, often illiterate, proletariat and peasantry could simply assume the responsibility for administering a State system proved to be illusory.

Extra-legal events were paramount among the concerns of the new leadership. A debilitating but necessary peace, costly in losses of population, territory, and resources, was negotiated with Germany. The Allies retaliated by threatening intervention along Soviet Russia's vulnerable Arctic, Pacific, and Crimean coasts. CIVIL WAR was being waged against sundry opposition and nationalist forces within the former Russian Empire. Industrial collapse and famine afflicted large expanses of the country. On the other hand, law and the legal system became the principal vehicles for articulating and transmitting revolutionary social policies, both those intended to 'dismantle' the *ancien régime* and those intended to build a new society.

The dismantling and restructuring processes simultaneously at work in 1917–20 have been variously interpreted against the background of the New Economic Policy (1921–8) and post-NEP policies. Some have viewed the legal history of 1917–20 as an era primarily dedicated to dismantling the old Imperial order and experimenting *ad hoc* with the minimum legal measures required for transition. In this view NEP constituted a regrettable but essential tactical reversal of the dismantling of State and law, a partial restoration of capitalist elements whose fate was otherwise sealed by initial proletarian legislation. Others have regarded the NEP as a logical continuation and development of the revolutionary measures of 1917–20. The NEP codifications, according to this interpretation, were a consolidation and systematization of revolutionary achievements and by no means a retreat or compromise; the NEP was held to be a necessary next step in the class struggle to achieve socialism.

Concepts of law and legal institutions

The proposition that a proletarian State could dispense with law and a legal system completely and immediately, if it enjoyed any real support, was promptly debunked. A. V. LUNACHARSKY, hardly an admirer of lawyers and legal education, eloquently defended in *Pravda* (1 December 1917) the establishment of a new system of Soviet courts. The courts would, he believed, assist in the formulation of a proletarian legal consciousness, in the creation of its own ideal of court and legal code, in the promulgation of laws 'incomparably higher than the decayed, ossified law of the old system'. By legal consciousness Lunacharsky meant the 'presentiment of new legal forms and relationships' which correspond to the new economic conditions created by the Revolution. The creation of a new civil and criminal law, a new State structure, new agencies of power, including judicial organs, he argued, would strengthen the Revolution and give shape to the new revolutionary consciousness.

As People's Commissar for Enlightenment, Lunacharsky had a major role in the closure of university law faculties in 1918 and the formation of law departments within the faculties of social sciences. Such academic or theoretical legal commentary as emerged in 1917–20 appeared in a journal (thirteen issues, 1918–21) issued by the People's Commissariat of Justice, *Proletarskaya revolyutsiya i pravo* (Proletarian Revolution and Law). In the very first issue A. G. Goikhbarg, a distinguished civil lawyer, pursued the theme. Granting that law would ultimately disappear, he said, does it mean that immediately after the outbreak of proletarian revolution the creation of new socialist relationships can be left to the natural course of events, that an unregulated transition from the 'anarchistic arbitrariness' of bourgeois individualism to the harmonious freedom of socialism would occur? A negative response he held to be self-evident. In the transition period some branches of law would flourish and others would fade into extinction.

Writing in the same issue M. Kozlovsky, a criminal law specialist, saw no need to develop general preventive measures against crime. In the short-term criminal repression would be a measure of self-defence, of terror and isolation, against encroachments, whereas in the long term life itself would lead to communism under which crime will have been eradicated because the objective economic inequalities underlying criminality will have disappeared. A detailed legal code to be used in the struggle against crime, said Kozlovsky, would be tantamount to devising an ingenious utopian system. He preferred to give the revolutionary masses an opportunity to demonstrate their own law creativity.

Expressing a view of law he was soon to modify, P. I. STUCHKA wrote in 1919 on behalf of the 'law-creating role' of the proletarian revolution as well as its destructive work. The socialist upheaval is not 'simply a leap into the unknown', but a transition period requiring a special transitional law, partly because a social system cannot be transformed overnight and partly because the old system remains in existence as a past tradition in the minds of the people. Responding to the accusation that two years after the October Revolution there still was no written proletarian law in the sense that the *Code Civil* had followed the French Revolution, Stuchka declared that such a written proletarian code would never exist in the Soviet Union. Proletarian law was a transitional law.

Dismantling of pre-revolutionary law

On 25 October 1917 the new Soviet government succeeded to a multiplicity of legal orders operating simultaneously within the former Russian Empire. Imperial legislation coexisted with local or regional legislation, canon law, customary law of great varieties, and even tribal law. In the early months after the revolution the leadership found it necessary to proceed with caution between two groups of Marxists: those of a more conservative orientation who favoured a gradual dismantling of the old system, and those of an anarchistic orientation who opposed almost every proposal for the preservation or introduction of legal institutions. Accordingly, Decree No. 1 on the Courts (November 1917) authorized people's courts to refer in judgments to old laws unless they had been repealed by the revolution or were contrary to a revolutionary legal consciousness. In the original draft Decree, prepared by Stuchka, the repeal of all the laws of the overthrown governments was contemplated; at LENIN's behest the provision was attenuated. That same Decree abolished the pre-revolutionary Procuracy and courts and dissolved the Russian Bar. The Notariat survived until March 1918; in November of the same year the Soviet courts were expressly forbidden to make any reference to pre-revolutionary legislation (until November 1918 the 1864 Russian Imperial Code of Civil Procedure could be applied unless contrary to Soviet decrees). A host of individual decrees gave effect to other facets of the dismantling process: land, industry, transport, banks, communications, housing, and other instruments and means of production were confiscated or nationalized. The law faculties were formally abolished in 1918 and their functions assumed by secondary-level faculties of social sciences.

Genesis of proletarian law

Measured by modern Soviet standards of systematization and codification, the period 1917–20 represented a torrent of individual decrees episodic in nature, inconsistent, even incapable of realization. There were literally many thousands annually issued by the central authorities, multiplied several-fold if other Soviet republics and local soviets were taken into account. The form of the statute book was indebted to prerevolutionary patterns. However, the intended legal force of these proletarian commands was left in no doubt: in November 1918 the Seventh All-Russian Congress of Soviets adopted a Decree 'On the Precise Observance of Laws' requiring official and citizen alike to have full regard to the new legal order.

Both the suspicion of or antipathy toward codification in any event and the turbulence of the times militated against comprehensive legislation, reinforced by the expectation that the transition period would be a brief one, and hence modern Soviet characterizations of the early decrees as fragmentary and rudimentary are not inappropriate. Often they seemed to outline a programme of action incapable of immediate full implementation, and in many cases (for example land reform) their implementation depended more upon the autonomous 'revolutionary creative efforts' of local soviets and commissions than the letter of the law.

There were nevertheless several legislative acts of the period that contained fundamental changes of policy and even in a couple of instances bore the designation 'code'. Legislation on the courts was fundamental not merely in that it abolished the old system but also in shaping the new order. Decree No. 1 on the Courts (24 November 1917) gave to every Soviet citizen the right to appear as defence counsel, created people's courts based on the principle of electivity of the judge and lay assessors and on the principle of collegiality, wherein each case is heard by a judge and two lay assessors. Prosecution likewise was left to the aggrieved citizen. Some of these provisions were modified by Decree No. 2 on the Courts (15 February 1918), particularly the introduction of colleges of individuals attached to local soviets for the purpose of acting as prosecution or defence counsel for a fee (later reorganized several times by 1920). The simple hierarchy of courts laid down in 1917 needed to be augmented by intermediate superior instances, the powers of cassational instances enlarged, and the functions of people's assessors elaborated.

Marriage and family was an area which the new regime was irrevocably committed to secularize, but it was not easy to ignore the legal consequences of pre-revolutionary legislation. Two decrees of 18–19 December 1917 established that the Russian Republic recognized only a civil marriage, entrusted the keeping of vital statistics to State agencies, and made equivalent the legal rights of children born within or without wedlock. Divorce was placed within the competence of local courts and marriage registry sections. On 16 September 1918 the decrees were superseded by a lengthy Code of Laws on Acts of Civil Status, Marriage, Family, and Guardianship comprising 246 articles and some appendices. Here there was no lack of detail, although the legislation was silent on the legal status of *de facto* marriages. Nor was there any attempt to call into question the validity of marriages concluded prior to 20 December 1917 if such marriages met the requirements of the laws of the Russian Empire.

Land legislation is a good example of a substantial Basic Law (27 January 1918) implementing a fragmentary programmatic Decree (26 October 1917) augmented by a series of subsequent legislative acts modifying or elaborating the Basic Law, most notably the Law 'On Socialist Land Tenure and On Transition Measures to Socialist Land Cultivation' (14 February 1919). The Basic Law contained 53 articles; its formulation regarding 'socialization', however, fell technically short of nationalization. Although 'any ownership in land, minerals, waters, forests, and living forces of nature' was abolished forever, title to land was not specifically vested in the State. The Basic Law was quite specific about the principle of equal distribution and who enjoyed the right of land use. The law of 14 February 1919 was even lengthened (138 articles) but still fell short of asserting State ownership to land. Priority was given in this enactment to collective forms of working the land, with detailed regulations for the administration of State farms.

In the realm of foreign trade, on 22 April 1918 the RSFSR resolved to 'nationalize' foreign trade, although there was no confiscation of property involved, and conduct foreign trade on the basis of the State monopoly. Here the decree was brief, even cryptic, and took some considerable time to implement. It nevertheless remains in force down to the present day, one of the few from the period to have so endured.

A constitution in modern States is commonly the first order of business after a social revolution. There is nothing to suggest, however, that the Bolshevik leadership considered a constitution to be essential or even desirable in the early days after October 1917, nor that it harboured any sympathy for the view that a constitution should restrain the State. The heritage of an absolutist autocracy and the Basic Law of 1906 contributed mightily to an irresistible pressure across the entire political spectrum in Russia that a constitution must be drafted. On 28 January 1918 the Third All-Russian Congress of Soviets instructed the Central Executive Committee to propose the draft principles for a constitution. After some delays these eventually were produced and on 10 July 1918 the Constitution of the RSFSR was adopted.

Labour conditions and social insurance were dealt with piecemeal in early Soviet legislation. An eight-hour workday was introduced and later an annual two-week holiday, pensions were increased, unemployment, disability and sickness insurance introduced, and labour inspectorates reorganized. On or about 9 December 1918 (the archives provide no precise date) the RSFSR Code of Laws on Labour was adopted. The Code superseded all antecedent legislation and extended to persons who worked for remuneration and to enterprises in both the socialized and private sectors. Under the Code every individual between the ages of 16 to 50, unless permanently disabled, had a 'labour duty', that is, a duty to work. Persons within this age group (excluding the ill and pregnant women within eight weeks before and after birth) but not engaged in socially useful labour could be compulsorily recruited for employment by local soviets. The Code allowed individuals to work in their particular speciality at the established rates; equal pay for equal work was proclaimed. Transfer, dismissal, work hours, labour productivity, and labour safety also were regulated in the Code. To a significant extent, however, the Code was devised to support a policy of labour enlistment rather than of voluntary relationships.

Criminal offences were established individually by a number of early decrees, commencing with the Decree on Land. Jurisdiction over criminal legislation was vested by the 1918 RSFSR Constitution in the All-Russian Congress of Soviets and the All-Russian Central Executive Committee, but no provision was made for the adoption of a criminal code. In fact, the rudimentary step toward a criminal code emanated from the People's Commissariat of Justice which on 12 December 1919 approved a set of Leading Principles of Criminal Legislation of the RSFSR. These dealt cursorily in 27 articles with the concept of crime and punishment, attempt, preparation, types of punishment, and related matters. Soviet legal science widely regards the Leading Principles as having formulated the first definition of crime under Soviet law, requiring that an act be evaluated both formally (was it contrary to law?) and materially (was it dangerous to society?).

Soviet legislation of this period governing the confinement of prisoners was strongly affected by doctrines of class warfare (see VECHEKA). The emphasis was upon isolating elements hostile to the regime, not rehabilitation or re-education, and it required some years before a policy of correctional reform through labour came to predominate. The provisional Instruction of 23 July 1918 issued by the People's Commissar of Justice 'On Deprivation of Freedom as a Means of Punishment and the Procedure for Serving Such' outlined in 31 short articles the basis for assigning prisoners to various types of institutions, the kinds of work they were to perform, the rules for internal order, disciplinary sanctions, and the structure of the Chief Administration for Places of Confinement. Individuals sentenced by the Cheka often were sent to forced-labour camps under decrees of 15 April and 17 May 1919. On 15 November 1920 a substantial (232 articles) Statute on General Places of Confinement was approved, but it dealt with only those places of confinement within the jurisdiction of the People's Commissariat of Justice.

By 1919–20 the Civil War reached its critical stage and the central authorities were at pains to centralize their authority *vis-à-vis* local provinces. This trend was reflected in the legal system by measures introduced in January 1919 to bring local commissariats of justice under the closer supervision of the RSFSR people's commissariat. Each provincial unit was to be headed by a chief who was appointed by the central authorities, and the latter would also carry the local units on the central budget. Complete central subordination was avoided by forming a 'college' within each local unit containing representatives from the provincial soviet. In the interests of uniformity in the application of law, the People's Commissariat of Justice intensified the issuance of directive circulars and instructions and demanded the regular filing of reports by inferior agencies.

As the period comes to a close, dissatisfaction with the pre-existing scheme is expressed in the RSFSR Decree on the People's Court of 21 October 1920. The Decree separated the functions of prosecution, defence, and civil representation, placing the prosecution responsibility in a new department to be organized by the provincial department of justice. The scheme of defence counsel was reorganized yet again under the Decree, and local soviet authority over the structure of the judiciary on its territory was reduced.

The flexibility and scope for local initiative so cultivated by the early approach to law were, by the end of 1920, in rapid decline as the pressures for uniformity, due process, and centralization intensified.

Continuity and change

In retrospect there were opportunities during this period for Soviet law to have developed radically different forms of law in addition to altering the substance, forms that might have been regarded as hastening the transition to a society where law was unnecessary. A combination of revolutionary legal consciousness and court-made law would have been one possibility, and indeed in individual cases undoubtedly occurred. But local court-made law was not generalized as a source of law; rather it was viewed as an exceptional measure when written legislation was unavailable or non-existent. And notwithstanding the rich Russian heritage of peasant customary law, court-made law would not have commended itself perhaps in a milieu where central authority and direction were crucial for the deployment of national resources. Lenin and his colleagues, moreover, had been nurtured in a legal tradition closer to the continental European model than to the Anglo-American, although the latter was widely admired in Russia and emulated in selected aspects. Their instinct and experience was to adapt old forms to new circumstances and stress the substance of the change. (See 'Lenin as a lawyer', under LENIN.)

The Revolution of October 1917 proved to be a Russian Revolution which broke in formal terms with the pre-existing legal order. But law is not merely the statute book at any moment of time; it is an accumulation of historical experience, values, terminology, attitudes shaped in the course of human affairs over many centuries – elements which no functioning society can simply 'abrogate' by legislative fiat irrespective of how drastic a revolution it may undergo.   WEB

Further Reading

Berman, H.J.: *Justice in the USSR*, rev. edn. Cambridge: Harvard University Press, 1963.

Butler, W.E.: *Soviet Law*. London: Butterworths, 1983.

Gsovski, V.: *Soviet Civil Law*. Ann Arbor: University of Michigan Press, 1948.

Hazard, J.N.: *Settling Disputes in Soviet Society*. New York: Columbia University Press, 1960.

Huskey, E.: *Russian Lawyers and the Soviet State*. Princeton, NJ: Princeton University Press, 1986.

Kucherov, S.: *The Organs of Soviet Administration of Justice*. Leiden: Brill, 1970.

Makepeace, R.: *Marxist Ideology and Soviet Criminal Law*. London; Croom Helm, 1980.

Constitution of the RSFSR: 1918

On 28 January 1918 the Third All-Russian Congress of Soviets instructed the Central Executive Committee (TsIK) to submit a draft basic principles for a constitution of the Russian Federated Republic (RSFSR) to the next session of the Congress. Nothing in the writings of Marx, Engels, or LENIN suggested that a constitution for a revolutionary government was necessary or desirable. But in the Russian context, where for more than a century the Russian intelligentsia had dreamed of a liberal constitution and the Decembrists, among others, prepared drafts and the 1905 REVOLUTION had led to the Basic Law of 1906, the pressures were irresistible. Not until April 1918, however, did the TsIK form a constitutional commission composed of fifteen members under the chairmanship of Ya. M. SVERDLOV. STALIN and BUKHARIN likewise were members and the commission included two left communists and three representatives of the MAXIMALISTS and the Left SOCIALIST REVOLUTIONARIES.

Although the commission was instructed to submit a draft constitution to the Fifth Congress of Soviets in July, work proceeded slowly. When the Central Committee of the Party discussed the matter on 26 June, it was evident the draft would not be ready. After discussion, Sverdlov persuaded his comrades to allow those portions of the draft most polished to go forward, and on 3 July the draft was referred to a Party subcommittee chaired by Lenin which made some final emendations. Placed before the Fifth Congress of Soviets a week later, the Constitution received unanimous approval virtually without discussion. Final editing of the text was left to the TsIK – a usual practice – and the Constitution became law on 19 July 1918.

Among the Bolshevik leadership various rationales were offered for the Constitution. Since the CONSTITUENT ASSEMBLY had been dispersed by force in January 1918 and had been expected one day to adopt a constitution, the Fifth Congress of Soviets in a sense had completed that mandate. Sverdlov, however, had stressed the role of a constitution in post-revolutionary construction during which the competence and function of State organs required definition and elaboration. In so far as the Constitution recorded the achievements and aspirations of the Revolution, it was viewed as a means of propagandizing the Revolution at home and abroad.

The international appeal of the Constitution was accentuated by the decision to incorporate as Part I the text of the

Declaration on the Rights of Toiling and Exploited People originally adopted in January 1918 by the Third All-Russian Congress of Soviets (Articles 1–8, RSFSR Constitution). Couched as 'General Provisions' were the articles laying down the purpose of the Constitution and the class character of the basic rights and duties of citizens. Here the exuberance, the thrust, and the cutting edge of the Revolution are most in evidence. The Constitution is designated as a transitional document to establish a dictatorship of the urban and rural proletariat and the poor peasantry for the purpose of 'crushing completely' the bourgeoisie, eliminating the exploitation of man by man, and creating socialism. All power was vested in the entire working population of the country united in the city and rural Soviets. The nationality principle was acknowledged as a basis for creating a federated Russian Republic. The principle of parliamentary supremacy was endorsed (Article 12) by placing supreme power in the All-Russian Congress of Soviets and, in the interval between congresses, in the TsIK.

Articles 13–23 of the RSFSR Constitution concerned individual rights and duties: separation of Church from State (see RUSSIAN OORTHODOX CHURCH) and school from church, speech and press, assembly association, and education. Foreigners resident in the RSFSR were given all political rights so long as they were members of the working class or peasantry who did not employ hired labour. They also could obtain Russian citizenship and seek political or religious asylum. Duties were several, above all the duty to work and to defend the fatherland. Equality or rights of all citizens irrespective of race or nationality was guaranteed, but the conditional nature of all rights was accentuated in Article 23: the RSFSR may deprive individuals and groups of those rights used to the prejudice of the socialist revolution.

The balance of the Constitution (Parts III–IV) was concerned with State structure and symbolism. Part III outlined the structure of Soviet power, both central and local. Population ratios for the election of deputies were fixed, the frequency of sessions of the All-Russian Congress of Soviets was established at twice-yearly (later changed to one annually); the TsIK was consolidated as the highest legislative, executive, and supervisory agency of the RSFSR, directing in a general way the activities of the Government and all inferior soviets. The TsIK was to unify and coordinate all legislative and administrative work and supervise the implementation of the Constitution, and other legislation. The latter function included examining and approving draft decrees submitted by the Government as well as originating its own decrees. Moreover, the TsIK formed the Sovnarkom (Council of People's Commissars), which was charged with the general direction of all affairs of the RSFSR (see LENIN'S GOVERNMENT).

Members of the Council of People's Commissars headed the individual people's commissariats, of which originally there were seventeen.

The competence of the All-Russian Congress of Soviets and TsIK was enumerated in seventeen subpoints to Article 49, but these were not deemed to be clauses of limitation, merely exemplary. Article 50 further conferred competence on 'any other matter which they deem within their jurisdiction'.

Analogous provisions of electoral representation were laid down for regional, provincial, district, and rural district agencies. Their functions were to implement all instructions of the respective superior agencies of Soviet power, adopt all measures for the cultural and economic development of their territories, resolve all purely local matters, and coordinate the activities of all soviets of their territory. Each soviet enjoyed a right to supervise the respective inferior soviet.

The franchise was restricted. Article 65 enumerated seven categories of persons denied the right to vote or to hold elective office. These included persons hiring labour for profit, individuals living on non-labour income, private traders and commercial middlemen, monks and clergymen of all religious denominations, employees and agents of the Imperial police or secret service or members of the former ruling dynasty in Russia, convicted criminals, and the usual restrictions on the mentally ill.

Budgetary policy under the Constitution was said to have the fundamental aim of expropriating the bourgeoisie and promoting the general equality of citizens in the production and distribution of wealth. A general State budget combining State revenues and expenditures was created and the central government determined which revenues would accrue to the general budget and which to the local. Soviets were empowered to levy taxes and duties exclusively for local requirements. Local soviets were to submit semi-annual and annual estimates of revenues and expenditures and rely upon central appropriations to meet general State needs. If funds were inadequate, local soviets were to apply to the respective people's commissariat for a supplemental credit.

Part VI made provision for the Arms and the Flag of the RSFSR.

For all the haste in drafting and the conceded lacunae in many provisions, the RSFSR Constitution of 1918 laid down an approach to State structure and to the equation of individual and collective rights that has served as the point of departure for all subsequent socialist constitutions in the Soviet Union and abroad. All succeeding USSR constitutions (1924, 1936, 1977) are treated in Soviet legal doctrine as lineal descendants, and the influence of the RSFSR model upon the constitutions of Mongolia, the Chinese Soviet Republic (1931–34), Eastern Europe, the Chinese People's Republic, other socialist legal systems, and some third-world countries is widely acknowledged.   WEB

Further Reading

Unger, A.L.: *Constitutional Development in the USSR*. London: Methuen, 1981.

Spreading the Revolution

The Marxist idea of socialist revolution was that wherever it first occurred it would be followed by similar developments elsewhere. Both by the anticipated process of cause and effect, and emulation, neighbouring capitalist regimes would succumb to the forces of stress. In 1917, after nearly three years of exhausting war for imperialist gain, this was not an unrealistic blueprint. The war had strained the belligerent powers to breaking point. In February 1917 the Russian empire gave way and within a year or two central and eastern Europe were similarly convulsed, though with different results.

In Russia it quickly became evident that the national minorities of the empire understood the idea of socialist revolution differently from those in power in the capital. While the new regimes, successively the PROVISIONAL GOVERNMENT and the BOLSHEVIKS, were trying to establish their authority over the territory of the defunct Russian empire, the national liberation movements among the minorities began to assert their own particular interests. Nationalism, which Marxists deplored because it divided and imposed backward notions on the international working class, now emerged as a competing force. Around the entire border of the old empire, among the Finns and other Baltic peoples, among the Jews who mostly inhabited the north-western and western provinces, along the former Polish lands of the western frontier and south and east into the territory inhabited by Ukrainians and Cossacks, on into Georgian and Armenian Transcaucasia, Muslim Central Asia and the Volga region, and across the vast expanse of Siberia, along the Trans-Siberian Railway to the Russian Pacific Far East in Northern China, the former Russian political and economic interest was challenged by those awakened by the Revolution. The Revolution now had either to concede that national liberation to the point of independence was a legitimate aim which would lead to the break-up and drastic reduction of Russian territory, or find some satisfactory explanation for continued political and economic control from Moscow.

This section examines the idea of World Revolution, the spread of the revolution first into the interior of Russia itself, the development of the borderlands and the growth of national and ethnic self-awareness before 1917, the effects of 1917 on these elements and their relationship with the new Soviet state up to the end of the CIVIL WAR.

HS

The Idea of World Revolution

As with much of Marxian social thought, the notion of world revolution is bound by the compelling logic of universalism. Marx's search for the universal has its roots in the Baconian and Cartesian proposition that it is possible to know nature and use this knowledge to master and change it. This he extended to history and the development of society; eventually resulting in Marx and Engels final law of motion of history and succession of societies. The concept of general laws of development, as Marx himself observed, is not always readily acceptable, but in it he found the support of Hegel's view of history moving towards a final aim and the presence of this universal principle in the unconscious of the actors involved in the process. For Marx and Engels, the final stage – and goal –

of development was that of Communism. The transition to that final state was through a process of evolution (the passage from one mode of production to another) and revolution (the inevitability of socialist revolution). In this sense, the world revolution is the final universal liberation of mankind; the advent of socialism on a world scale.

The difficulty for Marx's heirs was how to relate this theoretical scheme to the specific conditions of a single country and, more troublesome still, how this final transition was to occur when mankind was characterized by a high degree of uneven economic and social development both nationally and internationally. Marx overcame the problem of uneven development by using a simple, perhaps simplistic, formula: Europe's capitalist development, together with the expansion of European capitalism throughout the world, was in the process of creating a single world economic system; an idea he put forward in the *Communist Manifesto*:

> National differences and conflicts between peoples are already tending to disappear with the development of the bourgeoisie, freedom of trade, world markets, uniformity of industrial production and corresponding standards of living. Proletarian rule will cause them to disappear even more. United action . . . is one of the first conditions for the liberation of the proletariat.

However, he also suggested that convulsions in the non-European part of this system could react on Europe and even provoke revolutions there. To facilitate a smooth exchange of ideas and a sense of fraternity, Marx added that '. . . Communists everywhere will work towards the linking up of the democratic parties of all countries and their understanding of one another.'

Despite the superficially clear goals and prescriptions, Marx's legacy was not an easy one to unravel. His work on Asia and the colonial sphere showed a patchiness uncharacteristic of his otherwise exhaustive style of analysis. His views on the peasantry were dismissive of that class's revolutionary potential. Above all, Marx eventually entertained the likelihood of exceptions to (or 'short cuts' in – Russia being the notable example) an otherwise rigid law of development.

Lenin on world revolution

Writing in the period of High Capitalism, LENIN attempted to give substance to Marx's broad outline of the world economy and its path to socialism. In *Imperialism: the Highest Stage of Capitalism* (1916), he sharpened the political dimension of the Marxian division between Europe and the non-European world by highlighting the increasing scramble by the producing nations for a shrinking field of markets. His conclusion that this period of imperialism was the highest stage of capitalism placed revolution ahead of the natural economic process by suggesting that the capitalist stage in world history was rapidly drawing to a close and the era of revolution approaching. Lenin's analysis of imperialism, however, also had the effect of vilifying capitalism. This idea was not altogether in line with Marxian thinking. Capitalism was the supplier of culture in the broadest sense of the word – including the assimilation of modern production processes – and the material abundance necessary for the emergence of socialism. In this light, imperialism becomes the vehicle for the early transmission of capitalism to economically more primitive states, thereby speeding up the evolution of a truly homogeneous world economy.

Zimmerwald: Lenin's rethinking of capitalism's place in the Marxist world-view was accompanied by the radicalization of his views on the role of socialist parties and the International in the historical process. Fraternal association of democratic parties was not sufficient: the imperialist World War had to be turned into a war against the bourgeoisie. As the Second International had collapsed at the outbreak of the war, Lenin took the opportunity of calling for a new International: one that might adopt his ideas on the coming revolutionary struggle in the final phase of capitalism. His first attempt to sway the international socialists (through Bolshevik representatives at their Congress) failed, as did subsequent attempts at the International Women's Conference (presided over by Clara Zetkin in Berne, March 1915) and the International Socialist Youth Congress (chaired by Willi Münzenberg, April 1915). Finally, Lenin took his views in person to the Zimmerwald Conference (near Berne, September 1915). Although the well-known leaders of the Second International were absent and the groups present (particularly the German, Polish and Russian socialists) were unfavourably disposed to that International, Lenin did not secure a majority. He did, however, gain the support of a large minority (the Internationalisten der Tat or 'Zimmerwald Left-Wing' which included TROTSKY, ZINOVIEV and RADEK) for the idea of a new International and an airing for his thoughts on the war. Lenin persisted: at the Kienthal Conference in April 1916 he again failed to secure the necessary majority, but support for his position had begun to snowball. The Gruppe Internationale (predecessor of the German Spartakus League) sided with him in one of the votes; Paul Frölich gave him the left-wing Bremer Linke group's unreserved backing, as did the conference's chairman, Münzenberg. In Germany itself, Rosa LUXEMBURG had already taken up Lenin's proposals and led the Gruppe Internationale in accepting that a new workers' international had to be formed to organize unified action of the proletariat of all countries.

1917 and after: All this acted as a considerable fillip to Lenin's own efforts at home. On his return to Russia in April 1917 he stated in his April Theses that '. . . (the Bolsheviks) must not *wait* but must immediately found a Third International.' This was to be done, moreover, '. . . in a bold, honest, proletarian, Liebknecht way . . .' By appending the name of Liebknecht, Lenin imparted both a note of pedigree (Wilhelm Liebknecht had been a member of the 1st International) and a ready reference to the new-found support of the German left (Karl Liebknecht was a devoted internationalist and a member of the Spartakus League). The Bolsheviks had become part of the advance guard of international socialism. The Bolshevik seizure of power in October 1917 further shifted the initiative in Lenin's favour. The fact that socialist revolution in Russia was erected on the weakest of foundations simply meant that the need for a new International was all the more urgent and logical (especially so after the proposed 3rd

Zimmerwald Conference, scheduled to meet at Stockholm the month before – a meeting that might have allowed the more moderate socialists to regroup – had been aborted by the Allied governments): the opportunity presented by the Russian upheaval had to be seized and the initial breach in the wall of capitalism held open. The Bolshevik Party was now at once the vanguard and the weakest link of the international socialist transformation. (Trotsky, in January 1918, spoke proudly of how the Revolution had already lasted five days longer than the Paris Commune.)

The Bolsheviks' belief in world revolution was underpinned by an act of faith born of the need to extend the Russian revolution. At its core was the certainty – as with Marx – that the next, and vital, stage of the revolution was to be in the developed countries of Europe. Nor did this attitude alter drastically with the demoralizing collapse of the Spartakist uprising in Berlin in January 1919, or after the failure of communist attempts at power in Hungary, Bavaria and Vienna in the same year. In its practical form, however, world revolution represented a rallying cry which helped to disguise compromises made by a government determined to hold on to power at any cost: policies of realism were, in effect, papered over by the rhetoric of utopianism. Such compromises were not without their critics within party ranks. When the harsh treaty terms of Brest-Litovsk were accepted in return for a cessation of hostilities, N. I. BUKHARIN warned of the possible dangers to Soviet Russia's role as a revolutionary force on an international scale. He saw the only correct course as being a revolutionary war against German imperialism and cautioned that '. . . opportunists do not take account of the most important fact that the organization of a struggle grows in the very process of struggle . . . .' The RED ARMY that Bukharin regarded as the spearhead of this offensive (or 'export' of revolution) became, under Trotsky's tutelage, and in his own words '. . . The bulwark . . . against all attacks from within and without (and) . . . is inseparable from the Soviet state'. (Manifesto of the Communist International, 1 March 1919. In Trotsky, 1973.)

Trotsky on world revolution

This revolved around his own theory of PERMANENT REVOLUTION and the Leninist ideas on the role, and primacy, of the party, which Trotsky absorbed in 1917. Despite his imaginative application of Marxian principles to the issue of revolution and backwardness (which can be regarded as having provided the theoretical framework, and justification, for a Bolshevik revolution in Russia), Trotsky sacrificed the further elaboration of this theory for the more catholic approach of consolidating the revolution while looking to the advanced European states for the final salvation of the Socialist Revolution. When, prompted by the stark failure of the string of uprisings in 1919, Trotsky adjusted his views on world revolution, it was on the basis

of a simple reversal of his previous position: rather than the advanced nations being the sentinel of revolution, it was the least developed that would take the lead. Moreover, he became increasingly convinced that Lenin's approach to party organization and discipline was a necessary corollary to the successful spread of revolution. (Trotsky was sure that the German party's failure was due to its mass-based character having compromised its revolutionary qualities.)

Comintern

It was because of the Leninist perception of the party's character that Rosa Luxemburg, while encouraging the formation of a new International, had been loath to allow the Bolshevik Party to lead the new organization or allow the German party to submit to Bolshevik policy. Her misgivings were to have broader implications: most liberation movements in less developed countries were nationalist and mass-based in character, relying greatly on the peasantry and indigenous bourgeoisie. When the new international – or the Comintern – was formed in March 1919, Bolshevik ideas on party-building and the revolutionary process predominated. It was soon clear that this was at the expense of the colonial revolution. An early sign of this came at the Congress of the Peoples of the East (Baku, September 1920). There was an air of expectancy at the congress: the Bolsheviks' slogans and early official pronouncements on self-determination had promised a great deal to the 'enslaved masses' of the East. A major factor in the Bolshevik success in the periphery of the Russian empire – notably with the Muslims of CENTRAL ASIA – had, after all, been these outpourings and the PROVISIONAL GOVERNMENT's inability to satisfy the aspirations of the minorities. However, despite Zinoviev's call – as president of the Congress – for a holy war against imperialism, the senior Bolsheviks were able to offer few realistic solutions to the problems facing communist representatives of their own

Figure 26   Italian delegation in Petrograd. The woman is Angelica Balanoff, with Zinoviev (left) and Bombacci (right).

Figure 27 1st Congress of the Communist International (Comintern), Moscow, March 1919.
Left to Right: ?, Rakovsky, Lenin, Lunacharsky, ?, Trotsky and, far right, Zinoviev. Painting by Leonid Pasternak.

national minorities, let alone those of colonial states still under the imperialist yoke. Rather than providing a genuine basis for the minorities and colonies to pursue national and social liberation, the Congress reinforced the general sentiment expressed at the Comintern's Second Congress (July/August 1920): liberation movements remained a supportive element to world revolution and possessed no revolutionary possibility in their own right (despite the European revolution being at an impasse).

At the Third Congress (June/July 1921), Trotsky acknowledged that world revolution was several years away, rather than a few months as he had thought in 1919. The session concluded that the European bourgeoisie was stronger and the European proletariat more susceptible to the influence of the powerful Social Democratic labour organizations than had been thought. Nevertheless, the principal factor in the world revolution remained the proletariat of the advanced capitalist states, although attention to the location of the next upturn in revolutionary fortunes shifted to the rivalries of America and Britain, or America and Japan, and the likelihood of a new world war resulting from them. The next two congresses (November/December 1922 and June/July 1924) revised little of the substance of the 1921 congress. Finally, the Fifth Plenum

of the Comintern Executive (March 1925) confirmed that 'the period of revolutionary upsurge had ended'.

Two years later Bukharin, reporting on the Comintern to the Fifteenth Congress of the CPSU (December 1927), bemoaned the weakness in the theory of revolution shown by communist parties and the lack of intellectuals in their leading circles. This, he concluded, was a major shortcoming of the Comintern. In fact, there was strength in these areas, but it was based on principles unacceptable to Bolshevist interpretation. The views of revolutionists such as the Indo-Chinese Ho Chi Minh were of great potential value to colonial revolution, but were given scant attention by the congresses. Only the Indian communist M. N. Roy was able to present a serious challenge to the Eurocentric policies of the Comintern. The reason for Roy's prominence, however, was not so much his intellectual calibre as his skill at using language and concepts familiar to the Bolsheviks. Even then, he made little headway in altering the Comintern's charted course. Moreover, the Bolshevik outlook itself became increasingly ambiguous, not only to the members of the Comintern but to the Bolsheviks themselves. Lenin, writing his final article in February 1923, expressed pessimism about the Russian and world revolutions. The only hope, he concluded, was in the struggle of the oppressed peoples of Asia, the exploitation of contradictions between imperialists and the rapid industrialization of Russia. The subsequent debate over the correct course drew into its sphere the member parties of the Comintern. The sudden shifts and turns in the debate were difficult enough to fathom in Moscow itself; most foreign communist parties had little choice but to observe the struggle as outsiders and choose a 'correct' line. The result was divisiveness, confusion and, in the case of the Chinese Communist Party, disaster (in the process of defeating the Trotskyist position, STALIN had pressed for the merger of the Chinese Communist Party with the right-wing Kuomintang in the creation of an early 'united front'. After leader Chiang Kai-shek had purged the CCP in Guangzhou (Canton), in March 1926 and massacred its members in Shanghai a year later, Stalin attempted to rectify the situation by encouraging a communist rising in Guangzhou in December 1927, resulting in the almost total destruction of the Chinese party.)

Stalin on world revolution

The rise of Stalin brought with it a final decline of the Comintern from conference hall to lecture theatre. His approach to the question of world revolution, while introducing his own peculiar style of *Realpolitik*, transformed the Bolsheviks' earlier makeshift solutions to theoretical difficulties into Stalinist 'iron laws of history'. At its heart was the need to preserve and further the gains of the Russian revolution. His introduction of the law of uneven capitalist development – which concluded that a successful revolution could lead to the building of socialism in a single country by exacerbating the contradictions existing between unequally developed capitalist states – removed the need to look to world revolution for the transition to socialism. The world revolution could instead be built brick by brick under the leadership of the dictatorship of the proletariat. Less than a year after the Sixth Congress of the Comintern (in July 1928), the construction of socialism began in earnest. The next, and final, congress was convened seven years later (although the Comintern was dissolved only in May 1943), after the CPSU had declared the 'victory of socialism' in the Soviet Union. In the interim, Stalin's references to the Communist International had almost completely ceased, while the main report (delivered by G. M. Dimitrov) to the Seventh Congress made no mention of world revolution. Marxist theory of world revolution had run its course.   FP

Further Reading

Carrère d'Encausse, H. and Schram, S.R.: *Marxism and Asia*. London: Allen Lane, 1969.

Claudin, Fernando: *The Communist Movement: From Comintern to Cominform*. London: Penguin, 1975.

Daniels, Robert V.: *A Documentary History of Communism*, vol. 2. Hanover: University Press of New England, 1984.

Knei-Paz, Baruch: *The Social and Political Thought of Leon Trotsky*. London: Oxford University Press, 1979.

Marek, Franz: *Philosophy of World Revolution*. London: Lawrence & Wishart, 1969.

Trotsky, L.: *The First Five Years of the Communist International*, vol. 1, pp. 43–54. London: New Park Publications, 1973.

Permanent Revolution

The term 'permanent revolution' is commonly associated with Leon TROTSKY – and rightly so for it was he who turned it into a major theoretical framework for the analysis of 'socialist' revolutions in backward societies such as Russia and China. But it was not Trotsky who first coined the term, even in relation to his own 'theory of the permanent revolution', nor was he the first to raise such general notions as came to be associated with it. The idea of a continuous revolution, transforming the lives of men and eventually culminating in a socialist society, originated in French socialist circles in the first half of the nineteenth century; the idea may be discerned in the revolutionary views of Blanqui, and the words 'la révolution en permanence' even appear in a work by Proudhon (*Idées révolutionnaires*, Paris, 1849, p. 255). But such French notions were more an expression of a radical ethos than a coherent theoretical viewpoint, a vague if passionate declaration of rebellion without any concrete analysis of its socio-political exigencies.

More to the point is the use of the term by Karl Marx. It occurs for the first time in his writings in an article of 1843 ('On the Jewish Question') and again in the book, *The Holy Family*, co-authored with Engels. In both cases its significance is largely figurative, in the manner of the French socialists. In 1850, however, it takes on a more specific meaning: first in the context of the events in Germany where Marx speaks of making 'the revolution permanent', of the German workers adopting the 'battle cry' of 'the revolution in permanence' (see the *Address of the Central Committee to the Communist League*); and second in the context of the events in France, where the revolutionary socialism of the French workers is identified as a 'declaration of the permanence of the revolution' (*The Class Struggles in France, 1848–1850*). In the latter case, Marx's intention appears to have been to characterize the French situation as ripe or propitious for a socialist seizure of power, uninterrupted by any further intermediate 'bourgeois-democratic' stage since the socio-economic, as well as the political, conditions in France had already transcended that stage. This was a radical view but it was not out of keeping with Marx's general chronology of revolution, given his assumptions about France's development.

The application of the notion of permanent revolution to Germany is more interesting for in numerous writings of 1850 and before Marx readily admitted that Germany was politically and economically backward (compared with

England and France) for its bourgeoisie had as yet failed to win a dominating position in society. There was at the very least, therefore, a hint here that Marx envisaged the possibility of a combining of revolutionary stages, a speeding up certainly of the transition from relative backwardness to radical socialism. Two years earlier, in the *Communist Manifesto*, he had also argued that because of the 'much more developed proletariat' in Germany, the bourgeois revolution there 'will be but the prelude to an immediately-following proletarian revolution'. In the event, of course, nothing of the kind transpired in Germany and the idea of a permanent revolution does not recur in Marx's writings thereafter. It may, however, be read into some of his speculations, towards the end of his life, about the prospects of revolution in Russia where he raises, not without some hedging and reservations, the possibility that if a radical revolution were to occur in Russia and if it were to act as a 'signal' for a general European conflagration, then Russia might be able to avoid or by-pass a bourgeois stage.

In retrospect, one could easily draw a link between Marx and Trotsky in view of the rudiments at least of a notion of permanent revolution which the former had laid down. But there is no evidence that Trotsky was in this respect influenced by Marx. The inspiration, in fact, for what came to be known as the 'theory of the permanent revolution' came from a different source, from one Alexander HELPHAND who in a series of articles in *Iskra* during 1904, under the pseudonym Parvus, had argued that Russia was the 'weakest link' in the 'capitalist chain' and thus, paradoxically, could bring the whole of the capitalist world down with it. Even more paradoxically, Parvus believed that the peculiar, uneven socio-political conditions prevailing in Russia made her all the more ripe for a radical transformation. Trotsky had first met Parvus in the spring of 1904 and they spent some days together in January 1905 discussing the unfolding events of that year. By now Trotsky was convinced, as he would later testify in his autobiography and elsewhere, that Parvus's instincts had been right and that the latter had recognized the beginnings of a major twentieth century phenomenon, one which Trotsky would thereafter identify as 'the revolution of backwardness'.

In effect, it is this concept of a revolution of backwardness that was at the source of the theory of permanent revolution, though the latter term is not one which Trotsky originally used. When he first formulated the theory, in 1905–1906, he spoke of an 'uninterrupted revolution' and according to Trotsky himself it was the MENSHEVIK A. S. Martynov who had first, apparently in 1908, applied the term 'permanent' in describing Trotsky's views. Be that as it may, the terminology is of little significance since thereafter Trotsky would adopt this seemingly notorious coinage wholeheartedly.

The notoriety is somewhat misplaced, however, for Trotsky's notion of permanence had nothing to do with the spectre of what some have interpreted as an unabated appetite for eternal rebellion. The theory of the permanent revolution was rather a sociological analysis of the peculiarities of Russian history which, particularly in the nineteenth century, had evolved in accordance with what Trotsky called the 'law of uneven and combined development': uneven, because economic and social change was intensive but narrow, disrupting yet circumscribed; combined, because the consequent contradictions and anomalies necessitated policies which drew together the backward and the modern and pulled in a direction and with a force that made governmental half-measures ineffective. Thus partial industrialization had created a significant working class, large urban centres, a revolutionary intelligentsia and radical political demands and activities, even while leaving virtually untouched the predominantly agrarian and primitive character of Russian society. Since such changes as took place were largely at the initiative and under the tutelage of the state, the bourgeoisie remained small and powerless and liberalism merely an idea having no social roots. But such contradictions were the very source of instability, for the two worlds that had come into being could not co-exist indefinitely, particularly in an era of revolutionary thought and agitation within the European arena, an arena in which Russia had pretensions to be a contestant. Given the shift of power from the countryside to the cities, the radicalization of the workers, the necessities of war and further industrial development, the growth of new political movements and organizations – given all this, the only resolution, Trotsky believed, was not a bourgeois revolution but a 'permanent', i.e., uninterrupted, revolution combining bourgeois-democratic goals with the more advanced proletarian-socialist aspirations. Russian backwardness was therefore inescapably creating a peculiarly twentieth-century pattern of revolution whereby a leap into the modern world would emerge as a concrete historical necessity.

This was the kernel of the theory. But it needs to be added that Trotsky had few illusions about the difficulties involved. He freely admitted that the Russian peasantry would stop short of following the workers to the end of their radical path and he thus stipulated the simultaneous need for revolutionary workers' governments in the West which would support the new proletarian regime in Russia and so neutralize the power of the peasantry. The permanent revolution would thus become dependent on world revolution. And eventually, in 1917, he also admitted that only an organization such as the Bolshevik party could provide the leadership and the link between the historical possibilities and the political reality of the combined revolution.

What finally transpired in 1917 appeared to Trotsky to be a vindication of his theory. But the course of his own personal tribulations thereafter may be seen as a reflection of the limitations of the theory itself. Whatever the perspicacity of his sociological analysis of backwardness, clearly the actual course of events was also determined by the political instrument by means of which the OCTOBER REVOLUTION of 1917 was carried out (not surprisingly Lenin in April of that year for the first time gave his blessing, albeit modestly, to the idea of an uninterrupted revolution). It would thus prove impossible henceforth to sever the link between backwardness and Bolshevism. And since the world revolution did not materialize, the doctrine of 'socialism in one country' triumphed instead. As Trotsky was to learn bitterly in exile, it would thus prove impossible henceforth to sever the link between the Russian Revolution and Stalinism. Nevertheless, from a larger historical perspective, it would be unjust not to observe that the 'permanent revolution', if that is what 1917 and the events thereafter were, did bring forth a new form of collectivist society, not one dreamt of by either Marx or Trotsky, but such as can only be described as unprecedented, if no longer unique. BK

Further Reading

Knei-Paz, Baruch: *The Social and Political Thought of Leon Trotsky.* Oxford: Oxford University Press, 1978.

Marx, Karl: *Address of the Central Committee to the Communist League* and *The Class Struggles in France, 1848–1850.* In Marx-Engels: *Selected Works*, vol. 1. Moscow: 1955.

Trotsky, Leon: *The History of the Russian Revolution*, ch. 1. London: 1965.

——— : *The Permanent Revolution* and *Results and Prospects.* London: 1962.

Vestuti, Guido: *La Rivoluzione permanente: uno studio sullapolitica di Trotsky.* Milan: 1960.

The Spread of Bolshevism to the Interior: 1917–1918

The OCTOBER REVOLUTION made the Bolsheviks masters of Petrograd and its environs within a few days and at surprisingly little cost to human life. But the former Russian empire embraced vast territories of varying ethnic and socio-economic make-up; some provinces close to the front line were under military administration; everywhere the governmental authorities were in disarray. The extension of Bolshevik dictatorship to these different areas during the winter of 1917–18 was much more than a smooth, uniform process – 'the triumphant advance of Soviet power', as it is labelled in Soviet historiography. In each town or region events took a variegated course, shaped by a host of local factors, and any generalizations are risky. Yet it may be said that violence was usually latent rather than actual, that psychological, not physical, pressures were crucial in effecting the transfer of power, and that conciliatory tendencies were marked. The old political institutions offered some resistance to their replacement by

new ones under Bolshevik control, which were themselves diverse: party cadres, soviet executives, factory committees, armed Red Guards (militiamen), radicalized military units, etc. The institutional changes were accompanied by new policies designed to destroy the social basis of potential opponents (see VECHEKA) and to mobilize the masses in support of the RED ARMY in the incipient CIVIL WAR.

The railways

A key role in developments was played by the railways. The national railway union executive (acronym: Vikzhel) tried to arbitrate between the moderate socialists (MENSHEVIKS, Right and Centre SOCIALIST REVOLUTIONARIES) and the 'maximalists' (BOLSHEVIKS and Left Socialist Revolutionaries). Convinced that only a 'homogeneous' socialist coalition government (i.e. one excluding 'bourgeois' representatives) could avert a civil war, Vikzhel called a general strike (28 October OS). The threat brought about negotiations, which broke down after a few days but did lead indirectly to a broadening of the dictatorship on 15 November by the admission of some Left SR leaders to the Council of People's Commissars (Sovnarkom: see LENIN'S GOVERNMENT). Radicalized elements from the Petrograd and Moscow rail networks, encouraged by an egalitarian pay scale, dominated an extraordinary congress of the union (19 December OS), but overplayed their hand, suffered an adverse vote (4 January) over the dissolution of the CONSTITUENT ASSEMBLY, and responded by dissolving Vikzhel. A new executive (Vikzhedor, different acronym, same meaning) loyal to the Bolsheviks soon took its place, but it enjoyed little influence and syndicalist or 'localist' tendencies proliferated among Russia's railwaymen throughout the civil war years; where chaotic conditions hindered troop movements, the Red Army authorities imposed their own priorities, often at bayonet-point. (Some railwaymen helped to man the central agencies.)

The army

Military considerations were uppermost all along Russia's western border and (with different results!) in COSSACK territories. Anti-war sentiment, powerfully reinforced by the new government's 'peace decree', was a dynamic force that undermined both the army's regular formal structure and that of the commissars and soldiers' committees that had been appointed or sanctioned by the PROVISIONAL GOVERNMENT. The process went furthest in the north (and in the Baltic Fleet). On the Northern Front (I, V, XII Armies) only a slender majority of committees at corps level or below still took a 'revolutionary defensist' line, and the senior commanders wanted above all to prevent their forces from falling apart; they certainly had little love for A. F. KERENSKY. At an extraordinary congress at Venden (15 November) of XII Army troops, two-thirds backed the maximalists. On the Western Front (II, III, X Armies) the Bolshevik soldier A. F. Myasnikov virtually seized control of Minsk on 25 October, on hearing of the Bolsheviks' success in Petrograd. His men made sure that no 'counter-revolutionary' forces could leave for the interior, but that an armoured train with Red reinforcements duly arrived. Within weeks Myasnikov found himself front commander. At GHQ (Mogilev) the new Commander-in-chief, Lieutenant-General N. N. Dukhonin, played for time, refusing to start armistice talks as the Bolsheviks demanded. He got little support from the All-Army Committee, which on 7 November came out for a coalition government under the left-centre politician V. M. CHERNOV, now discredited; and power passed to the local soviet even before Ensign N. V. KRYLENKO arrived to depose him (whereupon he, Dukhonin, was lynched) and to take his place.

On the South-Western Front (XI, VII, Special Armies) bolshevization was inhibited by the presence of Ukrainian troops undergoing regroupment on national lines, and in late December pro-Rada soldiers arrested many Bolshevik activists (see UKRAINE). National feeling was even more of a factor on the most southerly Romanian front (VIII, IX, IV, VI Armies). Russian troops had to fight their way back from the Bukovina, and in Bessarabia they encountered stiff opposition from Romanian as well as Ukrainian troops; a confused armed struggle broke out which culminated in Romanian occupation of that territory.

In most rear areas soldiers were more easily won over to Bolshevism, for the young reservists were keen to avoid the horrors of the front. Already on 24 October, men of the 35,000-strong garrison at Kazan took over the town in protest at military discipline and helped to establish a short-lived 'Kazan Republic' whose shaky authority rested upon military support.

Relatively few soldiers, however, involved themselves in such revolutionary acts. The normal response to chaos and the breakdown of supplies was to desert – at first individually and then by whole units. Tens of thousands made their way home, by the infrequent and overcrowded trains, by cart or even on foot. The peasants among them wanted their share of the land being redistributed in the great Agrarian Revolution. Deserters often adopted maximalist affiliations to try to legitimize their defection and other illegal acts (for example stealing food in order to survive). They powerfully reinforced the civilian 'commissars' – cadres of urban workers and others – who were helping to establish the new order in the provinces.

Regional variations

In considering the (non-militarized) interior, we may distinguish between several regional categories. (For the borderlands, see UKRAINE; BALTIC; COSSACKS; CENTRAL ASIA; SIBERIA; TRANSCAUCASIA.)

Central industrial region: The 'battle for Moscow' (26 October–2 November OS) was bloodier than that for Petrograd and cost about 1,000 lives. This was because the local Bolshevik leaders (V. P. Nogin; N. I. BUKHARIN led a left-wing faction) were, in Leninist terminology, 'conciliators' and did not set up a MILITARY-REVOLUTIONARY COMMITTEE (MRC) to seize power until 25 October. Hostilities were interrupted by several peace-making efforts. Opposition to the takeover came from the municipal Duma and the military authorities. Only after the struggle was over did the Bolsheviks merge the hitherto separate soviets of workers' and soldiers' deputies; a local Soviet government emerged under the history professor M. N. Pokrovsky. Initially there was greater toleration of dissenting views in Moscow than in Petrograd, but in December encroaching censorship and the imposition of martial law prompted a thirteen-day strike of printers and journalists. Once Moscow became the seat of LENIN's government in March 1918 the screw was tightened further.

Workers from the surrounding areas had helped the Bolsheviks to win control of the new capital. The labour force here was socially homogeneous and traditionally militant. At Ivanovo-Voznesensk, a major textile centre, Bolsheviks won 64 per cent of the vote in the Constituent Assembly elections and were in control by August. The transition was generally smooth, although at Yaroslavl soldiers staged a drunken riot (pogrom).

Urals industrial region: Here too the Bolsheviks had established their primacy during the summer and could take over most major centres swiftly (the exceptions include Perm and Zlatoust, which held out for two and four months respectively). There was more violence than in the centre, reflecting the region's cultural backwardness and the antagonism between Russian industrial workers, Cossacks (under Ataman A. I. Dutov) and native Bashkirs. Workers' armed militias overshadowed the local soviets.

Large commercial centres: The less industrialized urban centres of the Volga valley (and Siberia) had a more diversified labour force and a substantial middle class; on both sides local autonomist and 'conciliatory' tendencies were strong. Brief armed confrontations of an almost symbolic character gave way to an uneasy stalemate until external pressures tilted the balance in favour of the Bolsheviks.

Smaller district centres: Here social tensions were least acute, political conflict subdued, and revolutionary change delayed until induced by agitators from outside. Among the maximalists peasant-oriented Left SRs were often stronger than Bolsheviks, and only once these two parties split (March 1918) did 'proletarian dictatorship' become a reality.

The countryside: Bolshevik presence was minimal in the villages unless they lay close to towns or railway lines. The agrarian revolution was mainly the work of communal (*obshchina*) authorities and owed little to revolutionary cadres. The new power structure gained hold only during the civil war, with the arrival of cadres to carry out food requisitioning (see WAR COMMUNISM), stimulate 'class struggle' among the peasants, and conscript them into the Red Army.

Institutions: The Imperial local government bodies (municipal Dumas, zemstva) swiftly lost effectiveness during 1917; the police and courts scarcely functioned. District zemstva were introduced in some places but wielded little authority. Municipal Dumas were re-elected on a broader franchise, with many voters indifferent to their policies; their executives were usually coalitions of the centre and moderate left, and some cities even came under maximalist governments. The plethora of semi-official bodies (for example land and food supply committees) with vaguely defined powers made for further confusion (see LOCAL POWER).

After October three major developments took place. First, soviet plenums were convoked rarely, so that the locus of power increasingly inclined towards cadre elements and against delegates (or voters); often a triumvirate did duty for a whole soviet. Second, mergers were effected between workers' soviets and those of soldiers (and sometimes also of peasants), in such a way as to ensure extremist predominance. Third, local soviets were brought under tighter control by regional soviets and also by central government organizations. Refractory bodies would be dissolved on the grounds that they had become unrepresentative or disloyal, elections falsified, and opposition spokesmen intimidated or expelled (see LENIN'S GOVERNMENT).

If necessary the maximalists could muster lower-echelon organizations, such as FACTORY COMMITTEES, to 'swamp' electoral gatherings or assemblies and so ensure that their decisions were 'correct'. These bodies often had armed militia units at their disposal and comprised fanatics with libertarian or syndicalist tendencies; but their national organization, set up only days before the Bolshevik coup, was soon absorbed into the machinery for controlling the economy, headed by the SUPREME COUNCIL OF THE NATIONAL ECONOMY (VSNKh). Likewise the trade unions, some of which had Menshevik sympathies, were neutralized by reorganization into industrial branches and co-opted into the economic bureaucracy. The new state order creaked badly and its multiple organs often got in each other's way, but during the civil war the urgent need for military efficiency led to a certain administrative streamlining.

Conclusions

In 1917–18 the Bolsheviks ruled by a mixture of coercion and persuasion. They quickly set up a security apparatus (VECHEKA), whose tentacles stretched into the provinces,

and they instituted a system of drumhead revolutionary tribunals; they also established a much more thorough censorship of the media than that of the tsars, closing down allegedly 'bourgeois' or moderate socialist newspapers, and simultaneously expanded the Bolshevik party's own apparatus for PROPAGANDA and agitation. Progressive measures were adopted (for example in the social welfare field) that could not be implemented but served to illustrate socialism's potentialities. More prosaically, allocation of scarce resources (for example food, housing) to actual or likely supporters was a means of winning their loyalty at a time when money was becoming worthless and normal trade channels drying up.

These social advantages offset the negative effects on production – and thus on popular morale – of such measures as the nationalization of banks and industrial enterprises, which brought much dislocation. Increased economic hardship did not automatically lead to a loss of revolutionary zeal. Many hitherto deprived workers and peasants took comfort in the elimination or harassment of their old enemies in the possessing classes, and threw in their lot with the victors, to the extent of joining the party (or its affiliated bodies) or enrolling in the Red Army. The vast majority of the population, however, preoccupied with sheer survival, stood aside from the struggle for as long as they could and kept their political options open. JLHK

Further Reading

Brovkin, V.: The Mensheviks' political comeback: the elections to the provincial city soviets in spring 1918. *Russian Review* 42 (1983) 1–50.

———: The Mensheviks under attack: the transformation of soviet politics, June–September 1918. *Jahrbücher für Geschichte Osteuropas* 32 (1984).

Frenkin, M.S.: *Russkaya armiya i revolyutsiya, 1917–1918.* Munich: 1978.

Keep, J.L.H.: *The Russian Revolution: A Study in Mass Mobilization.* London and New York: 1976.

Radkey, O.H.: *The Election to the Russian Constituent Assembly of 1917.* Cambridge, Mass.: 1950.

Scheibert, P.: *Lenin an der Macht: das russische Volk in der Revolution, 1918–1922.* Weinheim: 1984.

The Cossacks

In the fifteenth century runaway serfs and other wanderers began to form communities on the sparsely populated steppe south of the Muscovite and Polish states and north of the land controlled by the Ottoman Empire. By the sixteenth century two main groupings had taken shape, one on the River Dniepr, the other on the Don. Proud that they were subject to no monarch, these communities governed themselves by an assembly, called the *rada* on the Dniepr and *krug* on the Don, which elected a leader called the *hetman* or *ataman* (see ATAMANS). Engaged in brigandage, service as mercenary fighters, hunting and fishing, the Cossacks could not retain their independence as the Polish and, especially, the Russian states extended their control southward over the steppe. Between approximately the mid-seventeenth and mid-nineteenth centuries the Cossacks were subordinated to the Russian state, but this regime retained the Cossacks as a legal social estate because they could provide inexpensive troops and could hold down newly-won border areas. In the reign of Alexander II a new system of administration was established over the Cossacks, which in its main lines lasted until the Revolution.

Male Cossacks were subject to four years active military service and eight years in a kind of ready reserve that engaged in annual training. The majority of these troops served in the cavalry and were responsible for providing their own horses, as well as uniforms and cold weapons. The Cossack communities were obliged to pay for firearms and the administrative overhead of the entire system. These substantial expenses supposedly were compensated by the untaxed use of land allocated by the state to the Cossack communities and certain other economic privileges, but by the early twentieth century the costs of this military service were seriously outstripping the revenues of both individual Cossack households and the Cossack communities. The burden of maintaining reserve Cossack formations on active duty for counter-revolutionary actions during the 1905 REVOLUTION, combined with the realization by the regime that the Cossacks were a vital internal security force, led to some attempts to deal with the deteriorating economic situation in 1906–1914. But these were insufficient to placate strong Cossack feeling that their military service to the regime was inadequately requited. The majority of Duma deputies elected by Cossacks were liberals, and there was a considerable revival of the myth of the free, democratic Cossack tradition, undercutting the image of the Cossack as arch-loyal servitor of the monarchy. This did not impair the willingness of the Cossacks to fight Russia's foreign enemies in the FIRST WORLD WAR. By 1917 well over 300,000 Cossacks had been mobilized, and casualties were high among them, a major strain on a total population that was somewhat over 4 million in 1914.

Cossacks were by that time organized into eleven communities, each of which constituted a *voisko*. In previous centuries there had been many other Cossack communities, but in the course of time the state had closed down some, amalgamated others and created some new ones. By the twentieth century the eleven *voiskos* were scattered from the river Don in European Russia to the river Ussuri in Manchuria, occupying large tracts of land that the state had allocated for them. This did not, however, mean that only Cossacks were allowed to live in Cossack territory. Especially in the *voiskos* of European Russia the non-Cossack population, largely peasant, and also worker in some cities or mining areas, outnumbered the Cossacks. In the largest *voisko*, for example, the Don, in 1910 there

were about 1.4 million members of the Cossack estate and almost 1.8 million non-Cossacks. In the next largest *voisko*, the Kuban, the non-Cossacks also outnumbered the 1.2 million Cossacks by about the same proportion. In the adjacent Terek *voisko*, however, about 80 per cent of the population was non-Cossack. In none of the other *voiskos* did the non-Cossacks constitute as much as half of the total population. Relations between Cossack and non-Cossack were hostile.

The Astrakhan *voisko* consisted of small enclaves of land scattered along the Volga from its delta to the area of Saratov, numbering under 40,000 Cossacks by 1914. The Ural *voisko* had a considerable tract of land on the river of the same name and a tradition of obstreperous behaviour, which was related to the adherence of a large majority of these Cossacks to the Old Believers' heresy. The Ural Cossacks abutted the Orenburg *voisko* which lay along the upper reaches of the river Ural, touching the Siberian *voisko*, which consisted of a thin cordon around the northern periphery of much of Russian Central Asia. The small Semirechye *voisko*, which was barely larger than the Astrakhan, consisted of small enclaves near the Chinese frontier in Central Asia. Proceeding east there was then a gap in the line of Cossack lands, although there were a few Cossacks of Enisei and Irkutsk Provinces, who were recognized as *voiskos* only in 1917. The Russian border with China was held by the three most easterly *voiskos* starting around Lake Baikal, the Zabaikal *voisko*, the Amur and the Ussuri.

As an administrative unit the *voisko* was subordinated to non-Cossack officers and civil servants of the war ministry, and its own chief executive was in each case a non-Cossack officer. Only ceremonial vestiges of the traditional Cossack assembly remained, although the regime did permit the establishment of elected bodies to deal only with the land shortage, following the 1905 revolution. This rankled, at least in the *voiskos* that had some direct historic links with the earlier epoch of the autonomous and internally democratic community. The most important of these were the two largest *voiskos*, the Don and Kuban, each of which remembered links with the era of independence. In the case of the Kuban this was largely through the presence of people of Ukrainian descent, who still spoke that language. They were descended from Zaporozhian Cossacks of the Ukraine, whom Catherine the Great had transferred to the Kuban.

1917

Harbouring their numerous grievances toward the monarchy, the Cossacks welcomed the FEBRUARY REVOLUTION. Some units took part in the attempted suppression of crowds at the opening of the disorders, but they were unenthusiastic. Although Cossacks were not among the mutinous regiments, both in Petrograd and their own regions they quickly took advantage of the opportunity provided by the end of the monarchy to assert their interests as a separate estate. With the permission of the PROVISIONAL GOVERNMENT, the Cossacks of the Petrograd garrison, the core of which consisted of three Don regiments, convened an 'All-Cossack Congress'. This body opened in the capital on 23 March (OS), consisting of representatives from all the *voiskos*. It elected as its chairman a colonel of the Orenburg Cossacks, M. P. Dutov, and took a generally patriotic, liberal stance, supportive of the Provisional Government. It was, however, far from wishing to eliminate the Cossacks as an estate, as part of the democratic revolution, and it established a 'Union of Cossack Voiskos' to defend their special interests. This goal was reinforced by a second such Congress, which met on 1–13 June, including over 600 delegates and again electing Dutov as chairman. In the wake of this Congress the Cossack Union began to publish a newspaper, *Volnoe Kazachestvo* (The Free Cossacks), which attempted to maintain liaison with all the *voiskos*.

Similar manifestations of Cossack self-interest appeared in the several *voiskos*. As usual, the Don, the largest and senior community, led the way. On 7 March the ataman of the Don who had been appointed by the tsar was ousted and replaced by an acting ataman, a Don Cossack Colonel Voloshinov. A 'Union of the Don Cossack Voisko' appeared and helped to convene a convention of delegates on 16 April, which called for the revival of the traditional assembly, the *krug*, along with an elected ataman. The *krug*, consisting of about 500 delegates from within the Don and 200 from mobilized units, opened in the Don capital of Novocherkassk on 26 May. It elected a distinguished Don Cossack general, A. K. Kaledin, as ataman and established both a 'Great Krug' as the main legislature of the Don Cossacks and a 'Small Krug' that would act in the intervals between the sessions of the larger body. Many Cossacks wanted to exclude members of other estates from the new political institutions, and almost all Cossacks were determined to retain the land granted their estate by the tsars. Kaledin supported the principle of granting non-Cossacks equal political rights in the Don, but was unable to persuade all of his compatriots that this was the right policy.

A similar pattern prevailed in most of the other *voiskos*: the atamans whom the tsar had appointed were replaced with elected ones, an assembly was elected, and there was conflict with non-Cossack residents. In the Kuban the *rada* (Ukrainian for council, or soviet, it was a name that evoked the Ukrainian roots of many of the Kuban Cossacks) at first included the non-Cossacks, but in July these were excluded because of their demands for the elimination of various Cossack privileges. There was inconclusive talk of some form of amalgamation of the liberated Cossack *voiskos*. Kaledin met with his counterparts from the Kuban and Terek Cossacks, and there was talk about electing him 'campaign ataman', the archaic title of the field commander of the Don troops, of all mobilized Cossacks.

The appearance of strong Cossack particularism in 1917 had mixed implications for the Provisional Government. On one hand, the sense of martial tradition among the Cossack troops, their relative willingness to obey their officers, was a great asset at a time when the discipline of so much of the armed forces was in decline. Moreover, the new Cossack ideology of liberation in the main recognized the legitimacy of the Provisional Government. This was forcibly demonstrated in the July uprising, when Cossack units in Petrograd played an important role in supporting the Provisional Government and suppressing rebellious soldiers and sailors. The Cossacks suffered some casualties in this encounter, and KERENSKY recognized their importance to his security by attending the elaborate funeral services for the fallen Cossacks (see Figure 28, opposite). On the other hand, the independence of the Cossack *voiskos* was a particularly dangerous example of the general decline of the authority of the central government in the outlying regions. A striking example of this problem emerged in connection with the KORNILOV affair. General Kaledin had given an arch-conservative speech at the State Conference, so he was suspected by Kerensky of complicity in Kornilov's attempted coup. But the Don *voisko* refused to surrender him to Petrograd, maintaining that its ataman could be tried only by the krug, as had been the custom in olden times.

Furthermore, the renewal of Cossack independence was compatible with a degree of radicalization, especially among troops on active duty. While not prone to mutiny and desertion, these soldiers, like others, elected committees and engaged in meetings on various levels. They, too, were exposed to BOLSHEVIK anti-war propaganda, and there were even some radical activists among the Cossacks. Some of these established a 'Central Soviet of Cossacks', the organ of which was called *Golos Rabochego Kazaka* (The Voice of the Working Cossack). It attempted to compete with the 'Union of the Cossack Voiskos' for the loyalty of the estate. Although it failed to win over the majority of the Cossacks, the troops at the front generally opposed the war. When delegates from among these men returned to their *voisko* lands to participate in assemblies there, their relatively radical stance at once distinguished them from the older Cossacks, mainly senior officers, who were the leaders. The radical inclination of many rank-and-file Cossacks was manifest during the Kornilov affair, when they showed as much receptivity to anti-Kornilov propaganda as other troops. In a number of Cossack regiments that were supposed to participate in the move on Petrograd the men placed their officers under arrest. In the *voisko* lands, however, the officers who had established themselves as the new local authorities were able to retain their authority. By the late summer and fall there was even a shift toward the right among the Cossack populace in the *voiskos*, owing to their growing apprehension that the Revolution threatened their historic privileges.

Figure 28   Cossack funeral.

Had the I, IV, and XIV Don regiments, garrisoned in Petrograd, wished to defend the Provisional Government, they would have been an appreciable force in the small-scale military operations that in fact determined possession of the city. But they took a neutral attitude to Kerensky's appeal for action, for the most part remaining in their barracks near the St. Alexander Nevsky Monastery, at the opposite end of the Nevsky Propect from the Winter Palace. Other Cossack troops did, however, make the last serious military effort on behalf of the Provisional Government. After Kerensky had departed Petrograd on 25 October he ordered the Cossack General P. N. Krasnov to lead the III Cavalry Corps against the Bolsheviks in the capital. This officer was able to collect only the IX and X Don regiments and a few squadrons of Siberian Cossacks, with which he took Tsarskoe Selo, a little over ten miles south of Petrograd, disarming various pro-Soviet troops on the way. Krasnov ordered this small force to attack Petrograd on October 30, hoping that the Cossack units in the city, and perhaps other troops, would fight along with them. They had only advanced about four miles when they met a much larger force of Red Guards, soldiers and sailors. In the ensuing skirmish the Cossacks lost three killed and 28 wounded, the pro-Soviet forces several

hundred, but Krasnov realized that he lacked the means of carrying out his plan and withdrew.

The revolutionary State and the Cossacks

The Bolsheviks were not fundamentally well-disposed to the Cossacks. Their reputation of serving the tsars, their support for the Provisional Government and the very notion of a separate, privileged estate all militated against Bolshevik sympathy toward the continuation of a Cossack identity. But the Bolsheviks needed troops, especially cavalry and at least did not want the Cossacks to side with the Whites in the Civil War. Lenin spoke of a parallel between the Vendée as a base of counter-revolution during the French Revolution and the Cossack lands of the South in Russia. The Soviet government therefore was willing to make some temporary concessions to Cossack particularism.

As for the Cossacks themselves, they were seriously divided. Most officers and also wealthy or tradition-minded Cossacks were consistently anti-Bolshevik, but not necessarily compatible with the White leaders. Some ordinary Cossacks, especially those who were not well off or who had become strongly opposed to the First World War, were amenable to Bolshevik propaganda. In most Cossack

205

voiskos there were attempts, following the OCTOBER REVOLUTION, to establish separate Cossack administrations, and in the Don and Kuban these became more or less independent states (see Don and Kuban regions below). While these enjoyed considerable support from the Cossack populace, they uniformly had antagonistic relations with the non-Cossacks.

From its inception the Soviet regime attempted to woo Cossack sensibility. The Supreme Central Executive Committee of Soviets on 4 November (OS) 1917 established a Cossack Committee (in September 1918 renamed Section), which attempted to supervise the establishment of Cossack soviets, stressing that they did not plan de-cossackization, i.e. the ending of separate Cossack identity, and that 'working Cossacks' should form their own Soviets. This principle was embodied in a decree of 31 May 1918, which also allowed Cossacks to retain their existing land allotments, even though these were usually larger than peasant farms. In May–June 1918 the Soviet regime began to attempt to form separate Red Cossack military units. This policy succeeded only to a limited extent. The RED ARMY showed scant respect for the Cossacks in areas that they occupied, often requisitioning food without distinguishing 'kulak' from 'working' Cossack, and non-Cossacks were enabled to settle old scores. In almost every Cossack area there was an anti-Bolshevik reaction following the initial establishment of Soviet power. On the other hand, the Bolsheviks were able to capitalize on the friction between Cossacks and Whites, and in many areas were able to win some Cossacks to their underground organizations. In the summer of 1919, when the Soviet state faced a serious threat from the South, it reiterated its claim that it did not aim at ending a separate status for the Cossacks. But once the Red Army had won back this region, the Soviet state no longer needed to make such concessions. In February–March 1920 Lenin and Kalinin addressed a 'First All-Russian Congress of Working Cossacks', stressing not their separate status but the need to restore the economy. A decree of 25 March 1920 then abolished the separate Cossack Soviets that had been announced in 1918 and established the usual institutions of the RSFSR on former Cossack territory.

Don region

As a result of the disintegration of central authority, the region of the Don attained something resembling independent statehood for about two years following the October revolution. The basis for this development was the presence of the Don Cossack population, over 1.5 million people in 1917. The idea of free Cossacks had revived in the early twentieth century and in 1917 had become manifest in the revival of the elected krug, or assembly, along with an elected ataman, General Kaledin. But this had neither asserted nor aimed at sovereign statehood before the October Revolution. That event, however, changed

Kaledin's outlook. He announced his non-recognition of the Soviet government and invited its opponents to come to the Don to organize resistance. This implied that his long-term intention was to support the restoration of some sort of Russian state, not to seek complete independence for the Don Cossacks. But in the short term there was no such state for him to recognize, and so on 7 November (OS) 1917 Kaledin proclaimed the independence of the Don and called for a meeting of the krug to shape a new government.

This body supported Kaledin and his policies, including the establishment of a cabinet that was 50 per cent non-Cossack and the planned convocation of a constituent assembly for the Don state. Headed by Kornilov, the small VOLUNTEER ARMY of anti-Bolshevik officers had taken refuge in the Don and helped Kaledin seize Rostov on 15 December 1917, ousting Soviet authorities there. But from this point the new-fledged Don state declined. On 10 January 1918 more radical Cossacks, headed by F. G. Podtelkov, a Left SOCIALIST REVOLUTIONARY, proclaimed the Kaledin government deposed in favour of a Military Revolutionary Committee. Faced with this rival force, the approach of Red Army forces and the unwillingness of most Don Cossack units to fight for his government, Kaledin committed suicide on 12 February. His state survived him briefly, for a 'little krug' met in Novocherkassk on 17 February and elected A. M. Nazarov ataman. But Red Army units and the Don Military Revolutionary Committee took over the region and executed Nazarov on 3 March.

The Red Army cooperated, somewhat uneasily, with the Military Revolutionary Committee in establishing an independent 'Don Soviet Republic', which was proclaimed on 23 March 1918 following the convocation of 'congresses of Soviets' in the several districts of the Don region. This regime proved even less durable than its predecessor, however, for the harsh rule of the Communist forces soon turned most Cossacks against the Don Soviet Republic. Anti-Communist military units appeared in the countryside, and on 21 April a 'Provisional Don Government' emerged. It was able to capture Novocherkassk and there convene on 11 May a 'krug for the salvation of the Don', which was exclusively Cossack. It elected as ataman General Krasnov, acceding to his demand for dictatorial powers until the next krug should meet. Krasnov, who had been a loyal officer of the Russian Empire and not particularly an advocate of Cossack interest in his previous career, now became an ambitious Cossack nationalist. He called the new state 'The All-Great Don Voisko' and claimed for it greatly expanded boundaries. He established cooperative relations with the Germans, who had appeared to the west of the Don as a result of the Treaty of Brest-Litovsk, received weapons from them and even addressed grandiloquent letters to the Kaiser. The Don Soviet Republic was dispersed, Podtelkov was executed on 19

May, and by August most of the Don region was cleared of Red forces.

Krasnov's attachment to the Germans turned out to be a serious liability. The Volunteer Army was staunchly anti-German, and it emerged from a terrible ordeal in the winter of 1918 in the Kuban as a greatly strengthened force. Its new leader, General A. I. DENIKIN, wanted Cossack support, but found Krasnov a highly uncongenial ally. With the defeat of the Germans in November 1918 and the beginnings of Allied aid to the Whites, Krasnov's position weakened. Faced by a majority of opponents in the krug that convened on 14 February 1919, Krasnov resigned as ataman. His elected successor was the Don Cossack General A. P. Bogaevsky, whose policy was one of cooperation with Denikin. Despite various tensions between Cossack particularism and the Russian nationalism of the Whites, the Don Cossacks provided a considerable part of Denikin's army in its major campaigns of 1919. But the collapse of his front in November spelled the end of the independent Don. When the Red Army completed its conquest of the Don region in January 1920, the Don government retreated to the Kuban and participated in a Supreme Krug in Ekaterinodar, which included delegates from the Terek and Kuban Cossacks. This was the last significant effort to assert the idea of the Don as a state independent of Russia.

Kuban region

During the turmoil following the October Revolution the Kuban region established a semblance of independent statehood, which lasted until 1920. This was based on the Cossack population, which was divided in to two groups, the larger known as the 'Black Sea Cossacks', the designation given them in the time of Catherine the Great, who transplanted these Ukrainian-speaking people to the Kuban. The others were known as 'Line Cossacks', the name derived from their service on the frontier of the Caucasus mountains in earlier times.

In the period of the Revolution the former were more independent-minded, aiming at an eventual federal reconstitution of Russia, the latter more inclined to accept the goal of a 'united Russia', espoused by the Volunteer Army.

A 'Temporary Voisko Government', headed by Ataman A. P. Filomonov, a Line Cossack, appeared after the October Revolution. This included an elected 'Legislative Rada', in which various factions contended. In January 1918 the more radical young Cossacks who had returned from the war obliged Filomonov to include some non-Cossacks in his cabinet. This, however, was insufficient to appease the non-Cossack population of the region, which was less prosperous than the Cossacks and generally supported a 'Kuban Soviet Republic' that appeared in April as a rival to the Cossack state.

In the spring of 1918 Red Army units operating in the area north of the Caucasus forced the Cossack government to retreat to the Don region, where they reached an agreement with the White Russian Volunteer Army. The Whites grudgingly accepted the Cossack state, which agreed to support the military operations of the Volunteer Army. Their combined forces prevailed in the Kuban in the summer of 1918, taking the main city, Ekaterinodar, on 16 August and ending the 'Kuban Soviet Republic'. But conflict between the two main Cossack factions troubled the Kuban state. The continued commitment of the 'Black Sea Cossacks' to the idea of federation, which they attempted to promote at the Paris peace conference, led Denikin to support a military coup in November 1919. Ataman Filomonov resigned and was replaced by N. M. Uspensky, a supporter of the Volunteer Army.

In December 1919 the Kuban government joined with representatives of the Terek and Don voiskos in forming a 'Supreme Krug', which aimed at the establishment of a 'South-Russian Union'. But the advance of the Red Army, which occupied the Kuban in the spring of 1920, ended any possibility of independent Cossack statehood.

RHMcN

Further Reading

Yermolin, A.P.: *Revolyutsiya i kazachestvo*. Moscow: Nauka, 1982.

Kenez, Peter: *Civil War in South Russia, 1918*. Berkeley: University of California Press, 1971.

— : *Civil War in South Russia, 1919–1920*. Berkeley: University of California Press, 1977.

Longworth, P.: *The Cossacks. Five Centuries of Turbulent Life on the Russian Steppe*. New York: Holt, Rinehart & Winston, 1969.

McNeal, R.H.: *Tsar and Cossack, 1855–1914*. London: Macmillan, 1987.

Tschebotarioff, G. P.: *Russia, My Native Land*. New York: McGraw-Hill, 1964.

The Jews in the Revolution: 1907–1921

Russian Jewry with virtual unanimity, gave an enthusiastic welcome to the FEBRUARY REVOLUTION. It could not be otherwise, for the institutionalized anti-semitic policy of the tsarist regime had in no way abated in the years preceding its outbreak. Although the pogroms that marked the years 1903–1906 were not repeated, all the policies that limited Jewish residential, property and occupational rights continued in force. Moreover, the action of the authorities in 1913 in staging a show trial of Mendel Beilis in Kiev on a charge of ritual murder emphasized the undiminished influence of anti-Jewish forces in ruling circles. Beilis was eventually acquitted but the prolonged proceedings brought further obloquy on the government from liberal circles both inside and outside Russia. Those limited political rights possessed by the Duma, reluctantly conceded in response to the abortive 1905 REVOLUTION, offered scant help to Russian Jewry. The Duma, especially after 1907, was not much more than an impotent vehicle for the ventilation of protest and grievances. The Jewish condition was marked by abject poverty, especially in the Pale of Settlement, where petty trade and artisanry were on the brink of collapse. This situation was exacerbated by the high rate of population growth. Russian Jewry increased six-fold over the course of the nineteenth century: from one to six million approximately. To some extent emigration served as a means of alleviating the pressure of surplus population and between 1898 and 1914 about one and a quarter million Jews did leave Russia (mainly for the United States). But this process, despite its magnitude in relative terms, could not seriously affect the dimensions of the absolute problem. The growing impoverishment and destitution of the mass of Russian Jewry was accompanied by the emergence of a Jewish middle-class, especially after the liberal reforms of the 1860s and incipient Russian industrialization. This new class was composed of large-scale merchants, industrialists, private bankers and professional men. They lived mainly in St Petersburg and Moscow, outside the Pale of Settlement or in such major cities as Kiev and Odessa. Although most Jews remained politically unattached, class-differentiation, combined with deep division in political, cultural and religious outlook, brought with it a growing loss of confidence by the mass of Russian Jewry in their traditional leaders, moneyed or religious.

Political organization

The formation of the Marxist BUND in 1897 was one symptom of this, likewise the growing Zionist movement which formed an important component of world ZIONISM from its inception, also in 1897. At the first all-Russian Zionist conference in Minsk (1902), 500 delegates represented some 75,000 subscribers to party funds. By this time there were already in existence a religious Zionist party, the Mizrachi (1901) and a socialist Zionist party, the Poalei Tsion (1900). The latter had a Palestine orientation which, especially after 1906, it conceived in terms of the class-struggle on classical Marxist lines, as formulated by Ber Borochov (1881–1917). The latter's theories, an attempt to combine Zionism with the ideology of the class-struggle, had an influence in both camps. Borochov foresaw no long-term future for the Jewish masses in Eastern Europe. But emigration to America or elsewhere was also no solution, for the Jewish newcomers would inevitably be reduced to the same kind of marginal economic existence that they already led in Europe. Palestine, on the other hand, would inevitably and spontaneously attract the Jewish bourgeoisie which would develop the country's productive resources. These in their turn would foster a genuine Jewish proletariat equipped to wage the class struggle.

Socialist, but non-Marxist, were the Tseire Tsion (1903) which formed the mainstay of the Halutz (pioneer) movement in Russia. The quasi-revolutionary years 1904–7

contributed greatly to the political awareness of Russian Jewry and resulted in a notable change of direction by the mainstream Zionist movement: at the all-Russian Helsinki conference (1906) it revised its earlier stand against general political action in Russia and, under the slogan 'Gegen-wartsarbeit' (work in the Diaspora), developed a synthesis of work in and for Palestine combined with the defence of Jewish civil and national rights in Russia. These included the democratization of the empire, autonomy for national minorities, the convocation of an all-Russian Jewish national assembly and the acknowledgement of Yiddish and Hebrew as Jewish national languages.

The decade 1907–1917 also generated a number of middle-class, territorialist and Zionist parties. These included the People's Party organized by the historian Simon Dubnow; the Jewish Democratic Party founded by Leon Bramson, which was close to the Russian Trudoviki; the People's Group and the League for the Attainment of Equal Rights (M.M. Vinaver and M. Slyozberg, close to the Kadets). Zionist and Socialist parties included the Zionist-Socialist Workers Labour Party (SS) which rejected the Palestine solution as unrealistic and sought Jewish re-settlement through migration to some other specific territory in which to build a Jewish socialist order and in this way solve the Jewish problem; and the Jewish socialist Labour (Workers') Party (SERP) which rejected both the territorialist and Palestine solutions in favour of an extra-territorial national autonomy in Russia subject to an elected national assembly (or Seim) with jurisdiction in cultural, political and economic matters. These two latter groupings merged into the United Socialist Party (the Fareinigte) in the spring of 1917). Their joint membership at that time was estimated at 13,000. Another variety of socialist-Zionist ideology was offered by Aaron David Gordon whose 'religion of labour', under the influence of Tolstoy and Russian POPULIST ideology, replaced the class-struggle by a co-operative ethos and mutual love. Not until 1912 did a specifically anti-Zionist grouping among traditionalist Orthodox Jewry come into existence. This was the Agudat Israel, founded at Kattowitz (a German initiative under the inspiration of Jacob Rosenheim of Frankfurt) and attended by a large delegation of Russian rabbis and laymen.

The First World War

Despite unremitting discrimination, Russian Jewry by and large rallied to the flag in 1914. *Novy Voskhod* (New Dawn) declared that Russian Jewry was 'inseparably allied with our mother country where we have been living for centuries and from which there is no power that can separate us, neither persecution nor oppression'. In the Duma, the Jewish deputy N. M. Friedman gave voice to the 'enthusi-asm' with which the Jews were marching to the battlefield, 'shoulder to shoulder with all the peoples of Russia; there are no forces that can tear the Jews away from their fatherland to which they are bound by bonds centuries old'. By 1917 it is estimated that between 600,000 and 800,000 Jews were serving in the Russian army.

The motive was not simply patriotism but also the hope that Jewish service and devotion would encourage some alleviation of tsarist policy. This hope was to be disappointed. Indeed, it is true to say that Russian Jewry was regarded by the military authorities as a disloyal and unreliable element. Thus, to the inevitable hardships and shortages of wartime were added accusations of espionage, smuggling, treason. It was symptomatic of the atmosphere created that in July 1915 all periodicals published in Hebrew and Yiddish were suppressed on the grounds that they created unnecessary difficulties for the censorship. But the suffering produced by the policy of expelling Jews *en masse* from the war zones was pre-eminent. This was first applied in 1914–15 in Galicia, following the Russian early successes there, and then extended to the north-western fronts: in April 1915, 40,000 Jews were deported from Riga and the province of Courland and in May 120,000 from the city and province of Kovno. Following on the retreat of the Russian armies from Poland and consequent further Jewish expulsions it is estimated that the total number of Jewish refugees reached about half a million. The military authorities justified their actions by claiming the Jews were giving help to the German enemy. But the civilian authorities were forced to reckon with the additional burden imposed thereby on the already strained resources of the interior. In 1915 Jewish notables intervened with the ministry of the interior, and at the council of ministers in July and August 1915 several ministers challenged the accusations of treachery made against the Jews and expressed fears for the stability of the home front on being overwhelmed by a mass of destitute and embittered Jews. 'Pogroms, starvation and epidemics must be expected,' declared Prince Shcherbatov, minister of the interior. 'All this makes it necessary for us to permit the entry of forcibly evacuated Jews to areas beyond the Pale of Settlement, at least on a temporary basis.' A few days later the minister informed the governors of all the Russian provinces that 'in view of the extraordinary wartime situation and until the general review of the laws governing the Jews I am . . . granting permission to Jews to reside in all urban communities, with the exception of the capitals and areas under the jurisdiction of the Ministry of the Imperial Court and the war ministry'. Thus were abrogated for the duration of the war the provisional regulations confining Jewish residence to the Pale of Settlement, an enduring feature of Russo-Jewish life since the end of the eighteenth century.

At the same time, the council of ministers relaxed entry restrictions to educational institutions for injured or sick Jewish soldiers and their children and to the legal profession. The exigencies of war also brought certain Jewish industrialists in 1915 closer to the government through their participation in the WAR INDUSTRIES COMMITTEES. Gregory Weinstein of Odessa even became a member of the State Council – to the great disgust of the Empress who found it 'revolting'. But all these enforced symptoms of change did virtually nothing to alleviate the plight of those Jews forcibly evacuated and dispossessed. Equally ineffective was 'An Appeal for the Jews' published in 1915 by a large group of leading Russian intellectuals, scholars and publicists in which they pleaded that equal rights be extended to the Jews.

Jewish self-help: The resources of Russian Jewry's Central Committee for the Relief of Jewish Sufferers – EKOPO – were strained to the uttermost. In 1916 it was supporting over one quarter of a million Jews. The kindred body ORT (Society of Artisan and Agricultural Labour among the Russian Jews) sponsored technical and vocational schools, workshops (employing 15,000) and a network of some seventy employment agencies. OZE, a health and welfare body, worked through a network of hospitals, clinics and dispensaries.

1917

Not until the February revolution broke out did Russian Jewry enjoy any serious improvement in its status. By this time its composition had radically changed. About 40 per cent were living in areas occupied by the Germans, cut off moreover from major cultural centres such as Warsaw and Vilna. There remained in Russia about 3,440,000 Jews distributed as follows (in round figures): Ukraine, 2,104,800; Belorussia, 690,000; European Russia, 532,000; Asiatic Russia, 155,000.

This much depleted Jewish population displayed astonishing vigour and activity in the period between the two revolutions both in the general and the specifically Jewish field. This was of course the fruit of the political freedom introduced by the liberals and democrats who took power in the name of the PROVISIONAL GOVERNMENT. All sections of organized Jewish opinion greeted with acclaim the fall of tsarist autocracy. In a declaration the Jewish deputies in the Duma spoke warmly of the new opportunities created for the solution of the grave problems confronting Russian Jewry. The Zionists referred to the 1906 Helsinki programme (see above) which could now be implemented in 'the conditions of freedom of a new Russia'. The Bund proclaimed that 'together with all the rest of the population the Jewish working class has entered a period of new life. The force of the revolution, the force of the all-Russian proletariat has brought freedom also to the Jewish people'.

The Provisional Government did not disappoint these hopes and one of its first actions was to issue a decree abolishing all the disabilities from which the Jews suffered. Some Jewish middle-class elements in the capitals amongst whom M. M. Vinaver of the Kadet party was prominent, argued that the decree should take the form of a general abolition of all modes of religious, national and other discrimination and not mention Jews in particular. This was basically the formula adopted when, on April 2 (NS) 1917, the Provisional Government decreed that 'all the limitations on the rights of Russian citizens imposed by hitherto existing laws on the basis of religion, creed or nationality are hereby revoked'. This was three days before the Passover festival – so great was the enthusiasm generated that in certain families, not necessarily assimilated, the decree was read as a complement to the Haggadah.

This was the prelude to widespread and open participation by Jews in general Russian political life, in continuation of a pre-revolutionary trend. Not only did this apply in the case of the Bolshevik leadership (though much less in the case of the Bolshevik rank and file) but also that of the Kadets, where Vinaver was appointed a senator and a member of the commission to draft the law on elections to the CONSTITUTUENT ASSEMBLY. Other prominent Jewish Kadets were Slyozberg, Gruzenberg and Hessen, and Bramson was active in the Trudoviki. In the Right SOCIALIST REVOLUTIONARIES Osip Minor, elected mayor of Moscow, was prominent; also Abram GOTS, deputy-chairman of the all-Russian Soviet of Workers and Peasants; and Mark Vishnyak, secretary of the Constituent Assembly when it met at the beginning of 1918. To the Left SR leadership belonged Mark NATANSON and I. W. Steinberg, commissar for justice in the first Soviet Government. The MENSHEVIK leadership included Yu. O. MARTOV, A. S. Martynov, F. I. DAN and P. B. AXELROD. Jewish members of the Provisional Government with the rank of Deputy-Minister included S. V. Lurie (Kadet) and S. M. Schwarz and A. M. Ginsburg-Naumov (Mensheviks). All the Jewish parties of the left had representatives in the Petrograd Soviet.

Towards the end of the year it was clear, at least in those parts of Russia not occupied by the Germans, that among the Jewish parties, the Zionists were predominant. In the elections to the Constituent Assembly in November 1917, for example, 498,198 votes went for the Jewish parties. The Zionist and religious parties secured 417,215 of these, to which must be added the 20,583 cast for Poale-Tsion. The Bundists and other non-Zionist and socialist parties won only 31,123 and 29,322 votes respectively. But, of course, these figures do not take account of the indeterminate number of those Jews voting for non-Jewish parties.

In the field of Jewish politics proper, journalists, writers and politicians took full advantage of the opportunities created by the new post-February freedom. All could emerge from the underground and in some cases return from abroad. An upsurge of publicistic activity in Yiddish, Hebrew and Russian marked the new era – so did the formation of several small religious parties – 'Tradition and Freedom' in Moscow; 'Eternity of Israel' in Petrograd; 'Unity of Israel' in Kiev and elsewhere. The founding

convention of the first demanded national autonomy, a guarantee of Saturday as the rest-day and governmental financial aid for the Jewish communities (*Kehillot*). Other religious political groupings (e.g. Shomrai Yisroel – Guardians of Israel) meeting in common in July 1917 pressed such political demands as the eight-hour day, the right to strike, freedom of conscience, land distribution on the SR model and the encouragement of religious education. Conferences of Jewish teachers, cooperatives, friends of Hebrew – these were but a few of the examples of the use to which freedom was put.

But by the same token, this situation also allowed the full dimension of the differences inside Russian Jewry to come to the fore. A minor but telling example: early in March 1917 when a Council of United Jewish Organizations in Kiev was founded, the socialists ostentatiously quit the first session. They explained that neither in its composition nor its political stance could the Council claim to represent the Jewish masses. However, there was in all Jewish circles from the earliest days of the revolution sympathy for the convocation of an all-Russian Jewish congress which could represent the collective Jewish community to the authorities and elaborate a mode of national autonomy. An appeal was issued as follows: 'Citizens, Jews! The Jewish people in Russia now faces an event which has no parallel in Jewish history for two thousand years. Not only has the Jew as an individual, as a citizen, acquired equality of rights – which has also happened in other countries – but the Jewish nation looks forward to the possibility of securing national rights. Never and nowhere have the Jews lived through such a serious, responsible moment as the present – responsible to the present and the future generations'.

But divided views marked the protracted discussions concerning the aims and precise agenda of the proposed congress. The Zionists championed the view that the congress must debate Palestine and the Jewish claim thereto. Other parties insisted that the position of the Jews elsewhere (e.g. Poland, Rumania) also be debated, but this was contested by the Bundists who sought to limit the agenda to issues directly affecting the Jews of Russia. A preliminary conference to decide the matter was held in July. It was formed of four representatives locally elected from each of the thirteen cities with no fewer than 50,000 Jews; representatives of the local political parties and their headquarters and the three Jewish deputies from the former Duma. This conference decided that its agenda would include the formulation of a scheme of Jewish self-rule in Russia; definition and guarantee of the Jewish national minority; determining the principle of transitional communal organization for Russian Jewry; consideration of the Jewish situation in Poland, Palestine, Galicia, Romania, etc. Elections were held in the autumn of 1917 and demonstrate, though the Congress never in fact met, the state of Jewish political opinion. Thus from 193 communities of nine provinces in the Ukraine, the Zionist parties won 36 per cent of the delegates; the Bundists 14.4 per cent; the Akhdus (United-religious) 10 per cent; United Jewish Socialist Workers' Party (the Fareinigte) 8.2 per cent; the Poale Tsion Party 6.3 per cent, and the Folkspartei 3 per cent. A similar panorama of opinion was revealed at the elections to the all-Russian Congress of Russian communities which met in Moscow in June 1918 and represented thirty-nine Jewish communities. The 'community centre' created by the Congress comprised 16 Zionists; 6 Bundists; 5 Agudat Israel; 4 non-party; 3 United Socialists; 3 Poale Tsion; 2 Volkspartei and 1 member of the People's group. This organization, explained the Zionist, L. Levite, was intended to develop into a community centre that would constitute the first step towards the creation of a system of Jewish national autonomy in Russia. Recalling the failure to convoke the all-Russian Congress and the unlikelihood of any imminent convocation, Levite hoped that the present congress would be regarded as the only practicable form of Jewish unity in present circumstances. But of course these circumstances now included the Bolshevik regime which did not permit of any form of central Jewish organization or autonomy.

LK

Zionism

Before the FEBRUARY REVOLUTION, Zionism had operated under severe legal handicaps and its expansion thereby hampered. The removal of these was the prelude to a position of dominance. Following a series of local assemblies, an all-Russian Zionist conference met at Petrograd at the end of May, 1917. Present were 552 delegates representing 140,000 subscribers (as compared with 26,000 in 1913) in 700 communities. Henceforth Zionist parties dominated the elections to the all-Russian Jewish Congress and the Jewish community conference in 1918. A Zionist-sponsored educational society 'Culture' (Tarbut) was active supporting some 250 Hebrew-language schools throughout the country. By September, 1917, thirty-nine Zionist periodicals were appearing in Yiddish, ten in Hebrew and three in Russian. In Moscow, a Hebrew daily, *Ha'Am* (The People), was published. Preliminary steps towards the establishment of a Hebrew theatre (Ha'Bima) were also taken. In the Russian armed forces the first moves were taken towards the formation of a General Federation of Jewish Soldiers in Russia under the leadership of Josef Trumpeldor. This would *inter alia* afford defence against pogroms. Trumpeldor, after the Bolshevik coup, devoted himself to the Halutz movement the aim of which was to train young Jews for agricultural settlement in Palestine. He was elected chairman at the organization's first conference in 1919 where he demanded military training for the Halutz members. The issue of the Balfour Declaration in November, 1917, which was extensively publicized in Russia by the British government, naturally

gave great impetus to Zionist activity. It was welcomed with enthusiasm and demonstrations, and meetings in Jewish centres such as Moscow, Kiev and Odessa were organized in honour of the Declaration. In the spring of 1918 a 'Palestine Week' was successfully conducted in hundreds of Jewish communities. It was still possible for emigration bureaux to operate and those established in Petrograd, Minsk and in the Ukraine (centred in Odessa) functioned freely. When the Soviet regime came into existence it faced a widespread Zionist movement with strong grass-roots support and an estimated membership of 300,000 drawn from some 1,200 local groups. Nevertheless at a Zionist conference held in Moscow in May, 1918, attended by sixty delegates, it was thought wise to disregard the internal Russian aspects of the Helsinki programme and to adopt a resolution calling for strict neutrality in Russian internal politics – this, in order to disarm any suspicions held *vis-à-vis* Zionism by the new Bolshevik rulers. The conference also acclaimed the Balfour Declaration as the first step towards the international recognition of Jewry's claim to Palestine.

Bolsheviks and Jews

BOLSHEVIK policy in regard to the Jews emerged as an amalgam of Marxist internationalism and the struggle against the BUND. An early symptom of the clash came in 1903 when LENIN rejected the Bund's claim to the exclusive right to the representation of the Jewish proletariat. He dismissed the idea of a Jewish 'nationality' as:

. . . definitely reactionary not only when expounded by its consistent advocates (the Zionists), but likewise on the lips of those who try to combine it with the ideas of the Social Democracy (the Bundists). This idea of a Jewish nationality runs counter to the interests of the Jewish proletariat, for it fosters among them, directly or indirectly, a spirit hostile to assimilation, the spirit of the 'ghetto'.

In 1913 STALIN took up the same theme in his essay 'Marxism and the National Question', written at Lenin's behest. Stalin argued that all that remained of the Jewish nation was:

. . . their religion, their common origin and certain relics of national character . . . But how can it be seriously maintained that petrified religious rites and fading psychological relics affect the 'fate' of these Jews more powerfully than the living social, economic and cultural environment that surrounds them? And it is only on this assumption that it is generally possible to speak of the Jews as a single nation.

Therefore the attempt of the Bund to preserve a species of Jewish individuality was not only retrogressive in attempting to reverse a process of inevitable assimilation. It also created a barrier to the unity of the proletariat as a class.

On the other hand, the Declaration of the Rights of Nationalities, issued in November, 1917, a few days after the Bolshevik coup, promised free development to all national minorities and ethnic groups within Russia and the removal of all national privileges and restrictions.

This could not, however, overcome the gap between the Bolsheviks and the Jewish parties. Not only did those Jewish parties who were aligned in one way or another with the Mensheviks, SRs or Kadets denounce the Bolshevik coup, but this rejection extended also to the Bund. The latter's central leadershp unanimously condemned the coup as the minority action of a few adventurers backed up by small contingents of soldiers and armed workers. It was a blow to freedom and to the status of the CONSTITUENT ASSEMBLY election, which were scheduled to take place in a mere three weeks. The Bund called for a new socialist coalition which would summon the Constituent Assembly, pass the land to the land committees and initiate peace negotiations.

However, even before the new Bolshevik regime was consolidated in power, it became clear that at least a fresh framework had been created within which the fate of Russian Jewry would be decided. This was formed of the Jewish Commissariat (Evkom) and the Jewish sections of the Communist party (Evsektsiyas) formed in January, 1918 as sub-divisions of the People's Commissariat for National Affairs. Semyon Dimanshtein, a pre-revolutionary Bolshevik with considerable experience of Jewish life in Russia, headed Evkom. His task, in general terms, was to bring about the reconstruction of Jewish life on a socialist basis, to convert the Jewish masses to Bolshevism, to give a socialist direction to Jewish schools and to fight anti-Semitism, pogroms, and such like. But sheer physical welfare and relief work also had to take high priority. Existing organizations such as EKOPO, ORT and OZE were grouped into an allegedly non-political body, Idgezkom (Jewish United Committee), which not only carried on with the work of its constituent bodies but also distributed food and clothing parcels and medicines from the United States (especially the Jewish Distribution Committee) and facilitated emigration. This was on a selective basis and was permitted in the main to those Jews with close relatives abroad. The political activity of Evkom and the Evsektsiyas brought them into conflict not only with the various Jewish socialist parties but also with the organised forces of religion and Zionism.

The struggle against Zionism: By the end of 1918 little had been achieved and Isaak Naidich, a leading Zionist and vice-chairman of the Moscow Jewish Council declared that the Evkom 'which at first proclaimed the combating of Zionism . . . as one of its chief tasks has up to now accomplished nothing of consequence'. The fact is that for most of 1918 Evkom lacked the resources and personnel

required to make much impact on the fractured and fragmented Russo-Jewish population. But in August, 1918 Dimanshtein sought to achieve better coordination with the Evsektsiyas, to raise the morale in his organization and to acquaint the leadership with local activities. Despite some opposition in the Bolshevik Central Committee, Dimanstein secured permission to organize a conference of the Jewish Commissariat and section that met in Moscow in October, 1918. It consisted of 31 Bolsheviks, representing provincial commissariats, and 33 non-Bolsheviks most of whom were teachers in Yiddish schools. The latter threw the conference into confusion by demanding that educational supervision be transferred from the jurisdiction of Evkom to that of the Jewish Kehillas. They demanded that speeches be made in Yiddish rather than Russian and protested at the decision to limit their voting rights to educational matters. There were also complaints at the 'nationalistic' proposal that Jewish communists should promote Jewish agricultural settlement. Eventually Dimanstein explained that the Jewish sections had a double task: to agitate among the Jewish workers and to 'carry out the dictatorship of the proletariat in the Jewish street'. A resolution was passed declaring that:

> . . . all institutions hitherto operating in the Jewish quarter, like the 'communities' and the rest, no longer have any place in our life . . . All such institutions and establishments are harmful to the essential interests of the broad Jewish masses whom they lull by saccharine songs of alleged Jewish democratism. The Jewish worker relies upon the victory of the proletariat during the OCTOBER REVOLUTION. He takes power into his own hands and declares the dictatorship of the proletariat within Jewish society.

This was the prelude to a more or less sustained campaign against Zionism, denounced by Evsektsiya as 'counter-revolutionary'. Thus early in February–March, 1919 it was reported that Zionist offices were being occupied and Zionist periodicals banned. This was in the main the result of local initiative by Evsektsiya members and local Jewish communists rather than government instructions, and reflected the fact that the former, drawn largely from the Bund, were now in a position to settle old political scores with their ideological opponents. They also had to demonstrate to the Bolsheviks that they had forsworn all vestiges of Jewish nationalism. The central government on the one hand had in 1919 to concentrate its efforts on the struggle against counter-revolution and foreign intervention, leaving it little time to deal with the internecine Jewish struggle. On the other hand, it was in May, 1919 that the Yiddish newspaper, *Petrograder Togblatt* (Petrograd Daily), official organ of the Zionist Central Committee, was suspended.

In June, 1919 the second conference of Evkom and

Evsektsiya groups in Moscow demanded the disbandment of 'the counter-revolutionary . . . clerical and nationalistic Zionist organization [which was] an instrument in the hands of Entente imperialism in its war against the proletarian revolution'. The conference also resolved to close all Hebrew schools, in particular those of the Tarbut (Culture) alignment which were Zionist-orientated. It was explained by the Jewish communists that the struggle against Hebrew was not against a language as such but against the ideology of Zionism, that of the class enemy, the bourgeoisie.

In response to Evkom policy, in July the Central Committee of the Zionist organization turned to the All-Russian Central Executive Committee (VTsIK) requesting authorisation as a legal movement. It argued that Zionist activities were solely aimed at transforming Jewish petty traders into farmers and artisans of Palestine, and avoided any reference to Zionist ideology. The Presidium of the VTsIK responded affirmatively, arguing that no decree of the VTsIK or of the Council of People's Commissars had declared the Zionist party to be counter-revolutionary and that the cultural and educational activities of the Zionist organization did not conflict with the decision of the Communist party. Thus the Presidium instructed all Soviet organizations not to hinder the Zionists in their activities.

But this was a provisional release that only held good so long as no other Soviet organization denounced Zionism as a counter-revolutionary organization. Thus the repression of the movement proceeded by fits and starts, with intervals of relaxation. In July the Ukrainian Commissariat for Internal Affairs, located at Kiev, by agreement with the Evsektsiyas and Komfarband, (a union of groups replacing the short-lived Jewish Communist Party), closed 'all bourgeois-Zionist and Jewish clerical, political, economic, educational and cultural societies and organizations'. Their funds were seized and the officials required to halt all activities, hand over their records and undertake not to continue their activities under another name. In September 1919, Zionist offices were closed in Leningrad and Moscow, officials arrested and various Zionist periodicals suppressed. This latter measure remained in force but the others were rescinded within two months. The same sort of alternating policy characterized the circumstances surrounding the all-Russian Zionist Convention of April, 1920 in Moscow. It was permitted at first to function normally, the provincial delegates travelling to the capital with officially authorized documents. But after two days a unit of the VECHEKA, led by a young Jewish woman, arrested about three-quarters of the 109 delegates. They were charged, not with belonging to an illegal movement but with holding an unauthorized conference and maintaining contacts with counter-revolutionary forces in Russia and abroad, for example Admiral KOLCHAK and American Zionists. Again, after a short period of imprisonment most of the arrested Zionists were released, as a result of

interventions by two members of the American Joint Distribution Committee, in Moscow at the time. The Zionist Central Committee now decided to go underground and during the 1920s a 'Central Bureau' sought to coordinate the activities of local Zionist groups.

However, Evsektsiya pressure on the Soviet government was unremitting and at its third conference in 1920 it proclaimed that there was 'no longer any ground for a cautious attack on Zionism. It is necessary to put an end to the vacillation of the official attitude towards the general Zionist party and to all its cultural and economic organizations. It is essential that a total liquidation be carried out.'

This declaration also did not bring consistency into the government's Zionist policy. But it did become a guide-line for Evsektsiya's continual harassment of Zionists during the later 1920s. The Evsektsiya's struggle against Zionism was part and parcel of its role in the language war – Hebrew vs. Yiddish. The latter correspondingly triumphed, though Ha'Bima, the Hebrew theatre founded in Moscow in 1917, continued to function. Hebrew writers, on the other hand, came under persistent harassment at the hands of Evsektsiya which even frustrated efforts by Maxim GORKY to secure their right to emigrate. Eventually, F. E. DZERZHINSKY, head of the Vecheka, intervened on the writers' behalf and in June 1921 a distinguished group of Hebrew writers and intellectuals left Russia. They included the poets Bialik and Tchernichovski and the historian B. Z. Dinaburg (Dinur).   LK

Jewish Religion After the Revolution

From the first, Judaism was under attack from the Soviet regime following the decree of January 1918 which separated Church from State and school from Church. Its most damaging provision, so far as concerned Jewish religious practice, was the prohibition of religious education. However, the Soviet Government's first act that directly affected Jewish religion was the abolition of the *kehilah*, as the embodiment of organized Jewish communal life. This was resolved at the first conference of Evkom and Evsektsiya in 1918 and formally promulgated the following year by the Nationalities Commissar, Stalin. The consequent fragmentation of religious Jewry was to some extent alleviated because they were the main recipient of American relief or the main vehicle for the distribution of aid from the 'Joint'. The Soviet government itself showed initially a certain hesitation about attacking Judaism, for this smacked too closely of the practices of tsarism. Moreover, it did not wish to antagonize the Jews unduly. Memories of the Beilis trial were also still vivid. In any case, religious sentiment was still strong – even in the editorial offices of *Emes* (Yiddish for Truth, i.e. *Pravda*), a central press organ of the Evsektsiya, the printers refused to work on the High Holy Days 1921. When the attack

213

came it was wielded mainly by Jewish communists and it encountered the strongest resistance. A notable example was the closure of one of the synagogues in Vitebsk in 1921 when physical force had to be used against the assembled worshippers. The Lubavitcher Rebbe, Rabbi Joseph Isaac Schneersohn, though unremittingly harassed by the Evsektsiya, organized an underground network of cheders and yeshivas, together with teachers and cantors, which survived his own departure from the Soviet Union in 1928.

Evsektsiya fought by means of propaganda, undisguised force and simulated acquiescence in the demands of the Jewish masses. It utilized all forms of mass persuasion, at places of work and communal centres, meetings, lectures, anti-religious demonstrations, articles, public debates. Show trials, occasionally compared to medieval disputations, were a notable and widely publicized feature of the campaign. One famous 'trial' of the Jewish religion was conducted in Kiev at New Year 1921. After its unmasking as a bourgeois creation, aiming to maintain the masses in a state of ignorance and servility, it was duly sentenced to death. The trial was held, appropriately enough, in the same auditorium as the Beilis trial. Other trials, for example in Vitebsk in 1921, were held of the *cheder* (primary Hebrew-religious school), *yeshiva* (seminary) in Rostov in 1921, ritual slaughter and circumcision. At the same time Jewish religious officials such as rabbis, ritual slaughterers, circumcisers and cantors were subjected to particular discrimination i.e. they were stripped of civil rights, and limited in their access to food rations, jobs, public housing and in educational opportunities for their children. In 1921 the western provinces – Gomel, Minsk and Vitebsk – were the main theatre of the anti-Jewish demonstrations. They later spread to the Ukraine.

Evkom and Evsektsiya had no success in giving positive content to their anti-religious campaign. But the emphasis on Yiddish was an important contribution to the efflorescence of Soviet Yiddish literature in the 1920s. It was the language of instruction in schools and at the Jewish academic institutes in Kiev, Minsk, Moscow and Odessa research was conducted in Yiddish language, folklore and literature. Theatrical troupes developed a wide Yiddish repertory (see MOSCOW STATE JEWISH THEATRE) and a range of Yiddish periodicals appeared in the main Jewish centres. But here too Evsektsiya clashed with those writers who sought for a degree of literary autonomy (while accepting the revolution), for example the Shtrom group in Moscow, composed of David Hofshtein, Dobrushin, Kushnirov and others.   LK

The Jews in the Ukraine

In this region the Jewish population of approximately one and a half million were exposed to the full force of competing ideologies and rival nationalisms. The Ukrainian national movement which before the war had been suppressed by the tsarist government, from 1917 to 1920 underwent a resurgence as nationalist leaders of all political leanings sought to bring about some form of self-rule, coupled with a social revolution by the Ukrainian peasantry against a ruling class dominated by foreigners, that is by Russians, Poles and Jews. These groups were primarily represented in the urban centres and in the industrialist, bureaucracy and land-owning circles (see UKRAINE). The FEBRUARY REVOLUTION gave tremendous impetus to the movement for Ukrainian independence, a movement viewed with some concern by Ukrainian Jewry which saw itself as having more in common with the remainder of Russian Jewry than with the largely Ukrainian peasantry. However, in July 1917, the Ukrainian Central Council (the Rada), in which the Jewish socialist parties were represented, operating under the PROVISIONAL GOVERNMENT with its (mixed) commitment to national autonomy, appointed three vice-secretaries in charge of Russian, Jewish and Polish affairs and granted the Jews broad national, political and cultural autonomy. In November, 1917 when the Third Universal proclaimed the Ukrainian People's Republic, the Jewish representatives voted in favour but with some hesitation, fearing that this would weaken revolutionary unity. Meanwhile, in January, 1918, the Rada issued a decree, the first article of which guaranteed to:

> . . . each of the nations living within the boundaries of the Ukrainian People's Republic . . . the right to national personal autonomy, that is to independent organization of its national life through the organs of a national association, the authority of which extends over all its members within the confines of the Ukrainian People's Republic. None of the nations can ever be deprived, or be restricted in the exercise, of this right.

The vice-secretariats were simultaneously raised to the status of ministries. But a few days later, when the Fourth Universal proclaimed complete Ukrainian independence from Russia, the BUND and the MENSHEVIKS voted against. The Poale Tsion, Fareinigte and the right wing Jewish parties abstained. Although Arnold Margolin, a notable lawyer from Kiev and for a time Ukrainian deputy minister for foreign affairs, could justifiably declare that the Ukrainian Republic had bestowed more rights on the Jews than any other European country, the majority of Ukrainian Jewry remained uncommitted to the cause of Ukrainian independence. It was feared that the latter might be taken over by anti-Semitic elements, a fear grounded in the history of Ukrainian Jewry since the seventeenth century. The anti-Jewish attacks led by Khmielnitsky in 1648–49 were followed by those of the Haidamaks in the eighteenth century and by the pogroms of the 1880s and 1900s. The Bund was in an especially difficult and delicate position in so far as it claimed national minority rights and cultural autonomy for the Jews, while denying these rights to other nationalities.

These fears proved justified beyond even the blackest anticipations, for in 1918–19 the Jews of the Ukraine were massacred on a scale that recalls later German policy. In 1917 the danger was already apparent and in December the Central Rada was urged by Moishe Zilberfarb, the vice-secretary for Jewish affairs, to take action against pogroms. Bundist representatives in the Rada itself tried to persuade their colleagues to adopt resolutions condemning pogroms. The Rada, however, feared to distance itself from its local organs and to flout the anti-Jewish views of its mass supporters. In fact, even in the central Rada itself there were signs of anti-Semitism – for example, when it was suggested in January, 1918 that those war-refugees who had settled in Kiev in the period of mass wartime expulsions be removed from the city. Most such refugees were in fact Jewish.

By way of counter-measures some efforts were made by Jewish soldiers to organize a form of self-defence against pogroms. This initiative met with opposition from the Jewish socialists and the Folkspartei who feared it might only encourage anti-Semitism. Zionist and religious leaders welcomed the proposal. PETLIURA, the Ukrainian national-ist leader was in agreement. Where such Jewish defence units were in fact founded – most notably the well-armed units 400–600 strong in Odessa – they took a major part in averting pogroms.

Elsewhere events moved rapidly against the Jews, during all the turbulent changes of regime. During the spring of 1918 under the German occupation and the rule of their protégé Hetman SKOROPADSKY, there was an intensifica-tion of anti-Semitism. The new regime revoked the decree of January 1918 and tried to restore the anti-Jewish disabilities of tsarist days. This had some effect in arousing pro-Bolshevik views among the Jews. When German troops withdrew and the Skoropadsky regime fell, power in the Ukraine passed to the Directory in Kiev headed by Petliura and to the Bolsheviks in Kiev. In these complex circum-stances of national conflict, civil war and counter-revolu-tion, the Jews fell victim to the anti-Semitism of the past, inflamed by the conflicts of the present and the efforts of the clergy to regain power by exploiting anti-Semitism as a political weapon. The armies of Petliura perpetrated the worst massacres; the White armies of DENIKIN and WRANGEL were hardly less guilty. In 1918 alone the Ukraine was the scene of at least thirty major anti-Jewish outbreaks. In 1919 and until 1921 the massacres continued, reaching a total of about two thousand. It is calculated that during the period 1917-21 some 30,000 Jews were killed and a further 120,000 died from injuries or illnesses directly attributable to the pogroms. This was about 10 per cent of Ukrainian Jewry. About half a million Jews were rendered homeless and destitute through the destruction of homes and property. The longer term consequences were shown in the thousands of homeless Jewish children wandering the streets, cities and villages of the Ukraine in the early 1920s and in the absolute and relative decline of the Jewish population.

This catastrophe must necessarily have political con-sequences. Troops of the RED ARMY were certainly not guiltless in respect of pogroms. There were major out-breaks at Glukhov and Novgorod-Seversk in 1918 with little counter-reaction by the Bolshevik authorities. In 1920 Red Cavalry units (many of whom had earlier served with Denikin's forces) carried out a number of pogroms e.g. at Kremenchug and Lyubar. But certain repressive measures were taken by the Bolshevik command (disarming the guilty regiment, dismissal of others) and, in general, Red Army units displayed a far higher degree of self-control than the White military and political authorities. This inevitably inclined the Jewish population to sympathize with Bolshevism and, justifiably, to regard the Red Army as their saviour from the attacks of Petliura, Denikin and Wrangel. In fact special recruitment agencies were estab-lished to channel Jewish volunteers into Red Army cadres. This provoked a certain amount of debate on the desirability or otherwise of separate Jewish Red Army units. There was apparently some conditional sympathy for the idea from TROTSKY and the Politburo but it was not proceeded with on any noticeable scale. The opposition of the Yevsektsiya may have contributed to this.   LK

The Jews in Independent Lithuania

Pre-war Lithuanian Jewry, following the revolutions of 1917 and the end of the FIRST WORLD WAR, was divided among the new independent states of Lithuania, Belorussia and Poland. The Jews of independent Lithuania (according to the census of 1923) numbered 153,743, equal to 7.5 per cent of the total population. They were primarily an urban element (about 16 per cent lived in the capital Kovno) engaged in the export-import trade, retail trade and crafts, with a small professional component. Politically, their position was characterized by an interesting but short-lived experiment in autonomy. The Tariba (Lithuanian National Council), established under German auspices in the autumn of 1918, included a ministry for Jewish affairs headed at first by Dr Vygodsky, chairman of the Vilno Jewish community and then by Dr Soloveitchik of Kovno, a prominent Zionist. There were also two other Jewish ministers in the Tariba. Together they enumerated their political aims: first, full political and economic equality including recognition of Yiddish as the Jewish language; secondly, proportional representation of Jews in the legislative, executive and judiciary; thirdly, autonomy in respect of culture and social security, to be operated through the local Jewish communities (kehilot) and the Jewish National Council.

This programme was accepted by the new Lithuanian

government which guaranteed Jews 'the right of national cultural autonomy'. By the autumn of 1917 nearly 80 communities had been organized and democratically elected and in January 1920 they held their first conference attended by 139 delegates. The latter in turn elected the Jewish National Council of 34 members. Its attention was largely turned to the needs of war refugees returning from Russia and with repairing the ravages of war. The National Council received financial aid from the 'Joint' and other Jewish organizations. It was also active in the struggle against anti-Semitism, and the defence of Jewish cooperatives and agricultural enterprise.

In March 1920 the *kehilas* received legal recognition as public, statutory bodies, enjoying the right to impose taxation on their members as a means to fulfilling a very wide range of communal-national responsibilities – religious, educational, cultural and philanthropic. They registered births, deaths, marriages and divorces. Every Lithuanian citizen, certified as a Jew, was *eo ipso* a *kehila* member. Elections were conducted on the basis of proportional representation and equal suffrage. The second Congress of Kehilas met in Kovno in February, 1922, with 130 delegates from which a Jewish national Council was elected. It was composed of 16 Agudah members; 11 Zionist-Socialist; 7 General Zionists; 4 Religious Zionists; 2 Folkspartei. The Left Poale Tsion and the communists refused to participate in the National Council. A particular concern was the school curriculum and parental rights in determining the religious and political content of education. The system of Jewish autonomy aroused enthusiasm in Lithuania and abroad – especially when the Government committed itself to the acceptance on entering the League of Nations in May 1922. But the new Lithuanian constitution, whilst recognizing the national rights of minorities, removed the draft clauses providing for ministries for the national minorities and for the latter's rights to use their national language in public affairs. Max Soloveitchik, the Minister for Jewish National Affairs, resigned and left the country at the end of 1922. It was clear that the heyday of Jewish national autonomy in Lithuania was over.   LK

Further Reading

Baron, S.W.: *The Russian Jew under Tsars and Soviets*. New York and London: 1976.

Dinur, B.Z.: *Biymai Milkhama uMahpekha*. (Hebrew: In days of war and revolution). Jerusalem: 1960.

Frumkin, J. et al. eds.: *Russian Jewry, 1917–67*. New York and London: 1969.

Gitelman, Z.Y.: *Jewish Nationality and Soviet Politics*. Princeton, NJ: 1972.

Greenbaum, A.A.: Soviet Jewry during the Lenin-Stalin period. *Soviet Studies* 16.4, 16.5 (1965).

Kochan, L. ed.: *The Jews in Soviet Russia since 1917*. Oxford: Oxford University Press, 1973.

The Ukraine before 1917

In 1897, there were 22 million Ukrainians, or 17.9 per cent of the total population of the Russian Empire, concentrated in nine provinces: Volynia, Podolia, Kiev, Chernigov, Poltava, Kharkov, Ekaterinoslav, Kherson and Tavrida.

Most of the European Ukrainians had come under tsarist rule by the end of the eighteenth century and by the second half of the nineteenth century they were well subsumed into the provincial administrative system of the Russian Empire, apart from some three million under Austrian Imperial rule.

The Ukrainians in Russia maintained a distinct cultural identity even though the last traces of a separate political structure had disappeared with the abolition of the Hetman state in the 1780s. The term 'Ukraina', which had been used variously to denote the COSSACK lands and territories of the Ukrainians, gradually fell out of use. The official designation 'Malorossiya' (Little Russia) replaced it and continued in popular usage to denote the cultural separateness of the people after it was superseded by names of provinces. The term 'Ukraina' began a slow revival towards the end of the nineteenth century as national consciousness grew and was incorporated into the term Ukrainophile which referred to people active in Ukrainian concerns.

The most striking characteristic of the Ukrainian population was its predominantly rural constituency. The 1897 census showed an urban population of 3 million in the Ukrainian provinces. Ukrainians constituted only 30.3 per cent of this total while Russians made up 34 per cent and JEWS 27 per cent. Moreover, the Ukrainian share of the urban population had been declining steadily: in Kiev, for example, Ukrainians declined from 59.8 per cent to 22.2 per cent by 1897, while Russians increased from 15.1 per cent to 54.2 per cent over the same period.

De-urbanization was the result of restrictions by Polish then Russian rulers on previously free Ukrainian burghers and craftsmen. While Ukrainians migrated to become farmers and later serfs, Russians were drawn to the larger towns as the imperial administration grew, and it was mainly Russian workers from the agriculturally unprofitable north who entered the newly expanding industry of the Donbas. Such gentry as there had been either merged into the Russian Table of Ranks to maintain its titled privileges or had become impoverished and thus indistinguishable from the surrounding Ukrainian peasantry. The Entrepreneurs were foreign and lacked links to the society. By the late nineteenth century the Ukraine was a colonial dependency, econonomically, as the provider of raw materials, and in its social structure.

The lack of a significant urban Ukrainian population had a profound effect on the development of the national movement. Constraints on education in the native Ukrainian idiom further hampered social and economic development. By the early 1900s the standard of education was considered to be among the lowest in Europe, and the cultural and educational environment, for example publishing, was hardly developed, with the result that Ukrainian intellectual life evolved fitfully. The leadership of a progressive national movement fell by default exclusively to the small groups of Ukrainian intelligentsia.

The pre-revolutionaries: origins and development of the Ukrainian national movement

The first pre-revolutionary group to put forward a Ukrainian political programme was the secret society, the Brotherhood of Saints Cyril and Methodius (1846). Its members and sympathizers resided mostly in St Petersburg and included the historian, Mykola Kostomarov; the writer, Panteleimon Kulish; the editor, Vasyl Bilozersky; and the poet, Taras SHEVCHENKO. They all, variously, supported the broad aim of an autonomous Ukraine within a democratic Slavic federation. The society was uncovered and its members arrested by the tsarist authorities in 1847. Although the Brotherhood accomplished little in concrete terms, its ideals and the few documents it produced are commonly acknowledged to mark the beginning of the modern Ukrainian national movement.

The focus now moved to ethnographical and historical studies of the Ukrainian population, encouraged, unwittingly to some extent, by the government in its attempts to strengthen the sense of Rus or 'Russian' heritage on the Right Bank against Polish influence. Songs and peasant traditions in ethnographical studies inspired the next generation of activists towards POPULIST concerns.

Throughout the 1860s the active members of the Ukrainian intelligentsia maintained a network of loosely structured secret groups, the Hromada (Society) organizations which, though mainly cultural in their outlook and never large in membership, formed the seedbed of political ideas. In 1873 some Kiev members, eager to legalize their activities and supported by the governor-general, helped to establish the South-Western Section of the Imperial Russian Geographical Society. All but two of the founder members were also members of the clandestine Ukrainian Hromada. The Section collected ethnographic and statistical materials from the surrounding territories, conducted a successful census in Kiev in 1874 and accomplished an ambitious publications programme during its short existence.

The activity of some members of the South-Western Section, notably the socialists Mykhailo DRAHOMANOV, Serhii Podolinsky and Nikolai Ziber, alerted the authorities to a potential source of sedition. An investigation commission resulted in the Ems Ukase which imposed a wide-ranging ban on the Ukrainian language: publishing and the performance of plays in the language was prohibited, the South-Western Section was closed down together with the Hromada-staffed newspaper *Kievskii Telegraf* (Kiev Telegraph).

Ukrainians in Geneva

By making the use of the language an act of political opposition to the autocracy, the Ems Ukase became a watershed in the development of the Ukrainian national movement, driving the politically inclined Ukrainians abroad and encouraging the shift of the centre of the Ukrainian movement from Kiev to Lvov (Lemburg) in Austria-Hungary. M. P. Drahomanov, a history professor at the University of Kiev, was exiled to Geneva, where he developed his ideas within a small but influential group of Ukrainian socialists and aired them among émigré Russian and Polish socialists. Drahomanov asserted that socialism and democracy were inseparable and could be attained only through political freedom which guaranteed individual and national rights. A federal structure, 'a community of communities', where the members of each nationality would be free to develop and participate in self-government, was to be the aim of socialist activity.

The Ukrainians' emphasis on national concerns became a central, complicating factor in their relations with other socialists. It brought them into conflict initially with the Polish socialists in Geneva and alienated them from PLEKHANOV and his group. While their ideas were later echoed by other socialists, they received little support at the time.

Before 1918, the Ukrainian publishing house established by Drahomanov in Geneva put out 112 publications in Ukrainian and other languages of Eastern Europe, many of them smuggled into Russian Ukraine and distributed around Europe. The journal *Hromada* and its affiliated publications were the first in the émigré Ukrainian language to be devoted to politics and sociology.

Ukrainian political parties

The 1890s saw the establishment of the first Ukrainian political organizations. These groups pursued a combination of nationalist and socialist ideals. In Austrian Galicia, the Ukrainian-Ruthenian Radical Party held its founding congress in Lvov in October 1890, where, in Marxist terms, Vyacheslav Budzynovsky first proposed the ideal of political independence which the older generation of national populists rejected. Within two years another member, Julian Bachynsky used Marxist arguments to propose in *Ukraina Irridenta* the formation of an independent Ukraine 'from the San to the Caucasus'.

In Russian Ukraine the Brotherhood of Taras (1891/1892), functioned as a secret group of nationally conscious civic leaders and students. Its goals, expressed in its programme published in the Galician journal, *Pravda* (Truth), included full autonomy for Ukraine and social justice for all the peoples of the Russian empire. The Revolutionary Ukrainian Party (RUP) (founded in Kharkov February 1900), had a more substantial following of young Ukrainian students. In the absence of an agreed platform the founder members adopted Mykola

Figure 29 Ukrainian Students' Club, St Petersburg 1905.

Mikhnovsky's pamphlet *Samostiina Ukraina* (Independent Ukraine) as their programmatic statement. Although Mikhnovsky's pamphlet expressed some extreme nationalist ideas most RUP members considered themselves socialists. The party was the forerunner of many Ukrainian political parties, and a number of its members were to become prominent during the revolution: Mykhailo Rusov, Dmytro Antonovych, Volodymyr VYNNYCHENKO, Simon PETLIURA, Mykola Porsh.

The conflict between socialist and nationalist priorities soon split the party. In 1902 the nationalist elements in the RUP joined Mikhnovsky to form the Ukrainian People's Party (UNP), whose aim was an independent and socialist Ukraine. In 1917–1919, the party would take on new form as the Ukrainian Party of Socialist Independentists. The left-wing elements in RUP broke away in 1904 over the national question to form the Ukrainian Social Democratic Union, or Spilka, aligned with the RSDRP. Although the Spilka enjoyed some influence, winning fourteen seats in the Second Duma, it ceased activity in 1907 because it found itself unable to compete with the RSDRP in the urban areas.

The RUP now reconstituted itself as the Ukrainian Social Democratic Workers' Party (USDRP) in 1905, differing from the RSDRP on two major points: it rejected the

dictatorship of the proletariat and it demanded the recognition of the nationality principle in the organization of socialist parties. At its peak in 1907 it had some 3,000 members. Until 1917 the Ukrainian social democrats carried on an intermittent debate with the Russian socialists and LENIN who rejected all such demands (see RUSSIAN SOCIAL DEMOCRATIC LABOUR PARTY; BUND).

The Ukrainian Socialist Revolutionary Party (UPSR) focused on the peasantry, and echoed many of the concerns of its Russian counterpart (SRs), differing in its demands for a federal Russian republic and free development for the Ukrainian language. Convened on an all-Ukrainian basis in 1907, it was active during the FIRST WORLD WAR and came to prominence after the FEBRUARY REVOLUTION.

The Ukrainian Democratic Party was an organization of moderates formed in Kiev in 1904. Early in 1905 the more radical members split away to form the Ukrainian Radical Democratic Party (URDP) when the older members objected to the programme, which included such demands as social welfare, constitutional government and national autonomy for Ukraine within a federated Russian state.

In 1908 members and sympathizers of the Radical Democratic Party formed the Society of Ukrainian Progressivists (TUP) and adopted more conservative views. In 1917 the TUP was to reconstitute itself as the Party of

Ukrainian Socialist Federalists.

In many respects the group around the URDP was the most influential before 1917. Radicals and democrats cooperated in a wide-ranging programme of publications once restrictions on publishing were lifted in 1906. The new Ukrainian daily *Hromadska Dumka* (Social Thought) was an initiative of this group. In the Second Duma more than 30 of the 40 Ukrainian deputies came from this milieu.

Ukrainians in the Dumas

The First Duma contained 44 Ukrainian deputies sponsored mainly by Russian parties. Only one, the Democratic Radical Volodymyr Shemet, had been elected from a Ukrainian party. The RUP and other Democratic-Radicals had boycotted the elections because the suffrage was not general, equal, and direct, but they had cooperated with Jewish and Russian parties nevertheless in electing deputies. Under the leadership of Elias Shrah, the Ukrainian faction published *Ukrainskii Vestnik* (Ukrainian Messenger) in fourteen issues through the duration of the First Duma, and took part in the Union of Autonomists (Elias Shrah was vice-president), consisting of over 100 deputies from the national minorities in the empire. The Second Duma contained 47 Ukrainian deputies, none from a Ukrainian party. A separate Ukrainian faction was organized and published *Ridna Sprava-Dumski Visti* (Our Cause – Duma News). Members of the Ukrainian faction made demands on agrarian, social, and educational matters in the Second Duma although none was specifically Ukrainian in its content. The Third and Fourth Dumas, elected on a restricted franchise, contained few nationally conscious Ukrainian deputies and no Ukrainian caucus or representation was formed.

Ukrainian cultural life after 1905

The immediate benefits for Ukrainian cultural life after the 1905 REVOLUTION came from the lifting of the ban on the Ukrainian language in March 1906 after a recommendation by the philologists F. E. Korsh, A. A. Shakhmatov and other members of the Academy of Sciences in St Petersburg.

The more generous intellectual atmosphere of the post-1905 period encouraged Ukrainian literary and academic life, benefitting Ukrainian journalism in particular. The first Ukrainian daily to be published in Kiev, *Hromadska Dumka*, focused on workers' and peasants' concerns. The monthly *Nova Hromada* (New Society) represented a more intellectual approach. When *Hromadska Dumka* was closed down after the dissolution of the First Duma virtually the same newspaper resumed publication by mid September 1906 under the name *Rada* (Council) until it was also closed down as part of wide-ranging anti-Ukrainian measures taken in 1914.

The journal *Literaturno-naukovyi visnyk* (Literary and Scientific Herald) transferred from (Austrian) Lvov to Kiev

in 1906, and one of its editors, the historian Mykhailo HRUSHEVSKY moved with it. The RUP was given some funding by the wealthy benefactor Evhen Chykalenko to publish *Selianin* (Villager). The journal *Khliborob* (Harvester), edited by the brothers Volodymyr, Serhii and Mykola Shemet, first appeared in November 1905 but saw only five issues.

Under the new conditions the journal *Kievskaya Starina* (Kievan Antiquity), published since 1883, changed its name to *Ukraina* in 1907 and encouraged articles in Ukrainian. The journal *Ukrainskaya Zhizn* (Ukrainian Life), published in Russian in St Petersburg, included discussions on Ukrainian society and articles on the distinctiveness of the Ukrainian cultural heritage.

The Ukrainophile tendency which had concentrated on non-political aspects of the Ukrainian question for much of the nineteenth century also expanded its ambitions at this time. In 1904, the historian Hrushevsky delivered his seminal lecture published later under the title 'The Traditional Scheme of "Russian" History and the Rational Organisation of the History of the Eastern Slavs'. He challenged the traditional presentation of Russian history which shifted its geographical focus from Kiev to Moscow, arguing that the descendants of medieval Kievans were Ukrainians not Russians. He proposed a rigorous delineation between the histories of Great Russia, Ukraine and Belorussia.

The Ukrainian Scientific Society was formed in Kiev in 1906, with sections devoted to philology, history, natural sciences, ethnography and statistics, and published its proceedings four times a year. The membership included intellectuals who were to take up influential posts during the Revolution. The Society became the Ukrainian Academy of Sciences in 1917 and the All-Ukrainian Academy of Sciences under Bolshevik rule in 1921.

The Ukrainian movement before and during the First World War

The increasing self-assertiveness of the Ukrainians was further encouraged by the spread of the Prosvita societies. Set up in villages and small towns, these self-help and educational societies became civic and cultural centres for the Ukrainian people. The movement's strength grew further particularly through the flourishing cooperative movement.

The authorities attempted to suppress Ukrainian activities: the transport of Ukrainian newspapers into the villages was restricted, the first publication of Shevchenko's complete works was suspended in 1911, and public commemoration of his centenary in March 1914 was prohibited. The ensuing protest demonstrations brought the Ukrainian movement into the streets for the first time, mounted police and Cossack detachments being used to disperse the crowds.

In the milder conditions of Galicia, émigrés, including

Marian Melenevsky, Alexander Skoropis-Ioltukhovsky and Dmytro Dontsov, formed the Union for the Liberation of Ukraine (SVU). When the Russian army advanced to occupy Galicia in the first days of war they closed down the Prosvita and arrested leaders of the national movement. Others fled or went underground or into exile. The Union moved to Vienna and began to urge that the defeat of the tsarist armies was the only salvation for Ukraine. Its publication, *Visnyk Soiuzu Vyzvolennia Ukrainy* (Union of Free Ukraine Messenger), came out regularly in Vienna. Once its views became known, the Germans and Austrians began to lend support for Ukrainian separatism as a tactic for weakening the enemy's war effort and ultimately breaking up the Russian Empire. During the War some members of the USDRP, notable among them Lev YURKEVYCH, carried on their work in Switzerland (see REVOLUTIONIERUNGSPOLITIK).

The several small Ukrainian parties in the period before the fall of tsarism could be characterized as revolutionary parties with different political ideologies but each advocating the common goal of national liberation.   ND

The Ukraine: Revolution and Civil War

Some measure of national autonomy for the Ukrainian people was the least that was expected by the various groups and parties that had come to identify themselves as both revolutionary and Ukrainian, and the main actors had often to choose between the social and the national in difficult circumstances. Occasionally it was necessary to form alliances with external powers and factions that had entirely opposite motives for their support. The ignorance of the Ukrainian question in western Europe and the United States and the lack of any notable figures, such as Masaryk for Czechoslovakia or Paderewski for Poland, to act as spokesmen for Ukrainian interests in an international forum contributed to the defeat of the national revolutionary movement.

The shifting loyalties of key segments of the population were another obstacle to independence. Although many voted for the Ukrainian parties in the election to the CONSTITUENT ASSEMBLY, it proved difficult to sustain a commitment to the Ukrainian parties in the absence of a stable government, administration and consistent policies. The predominantly Russian, Polish and Jewish presence in the towns impeded the development of an integrated Ukrainian movement. Thus the loyalty of much of the peasantry was precarious at the best of times and often, in the turmoil of the military conflict, reverted to support of the party offering the most land, or even more pragmatically, to whatever army was approaching on the horizon.

The Central Rada: March 1917–April 1918
Once the constraints imposed by tsarism disappeared the movement for national self-government grew rapidly. The lead was taken by the members of the Society of Ukrainian Progressivists (TUP) in Kiev. The Ukrainian Central Council, or Rada (SOVIET, in Russian) as it is more commonly known, was organized in Kiev on 17 March 1917, initially as an advisory body and coordinating centre, but rapidly evolved into a representative body for the Ukrainian people as a whole, as different political parties and groups joined in.

Plans and programmes were being reassessed at this time to meet the new circumstances. Following Drahomanov's ideas, TUP reorganized itself into the Ukrainian Party of Socialist-Federalists, adopted a programme of evolutionary socialism, and opposed revolutionary experiments and the expropriation of large estates without compensation. The social democrats of the Ukrainian Social Democratic Workers' Party (USDRP), who included many of the Ukrainian intellectuals, were the most influential in formulating policy. Without abandoning revolutionary ideals or their faith in proletarian revolution, like most other Ukrainian parties they proposed that the Ukraine should aim for autonomy within a future federated Russian state. The newly revived Ukrainian Socialist Revolutionary Party (UPSR) voiced radical proposals for land reform and at its congress, 17–18 April 1917, called for broad national territorial autonomy for the Ukraine and the guarantee of rights for national minorities within a future democratic federal republic. This party rapidly became the largest and most popular of the Ukrainian political parties, particularly after Hrushevsky left the TUP to join its youthful ranks.

As support for the Rada grew, plans were made to extend and consolidate its representation. An All-Ukrainian National Congress was convened in Kiev 17–21 April, with 900 mandated delegates and a further 600 observers. An atmosphere of sheer euphoria prevailed among all present. While they considered themselves to be part of the broad revolutionary movement towards a democratic Russian Republic, the Congress decided that only the legal recognition of Ukraine's national territorial autonomy would satisfy the demands of the Ukrainian people it now felt it represented. The forthcoming All-Russian Constituent Assembly should sanction the new order, while confirmation of territorial boundaries, with the consent of the border populations, was left to a future international peace conference.

The Congress unanimously elected Hrushevsky as president of the Rada and two vice-presidents, the Ukrainian Social Democrats V. K. Vynnychenko the writer, and the publicist and military affairs specialist S. V. Petliura. The Rada, emerging as a body of 150 members representing a wide range of organizations and local groups, expressed the transition between the 'national-cultural' and the 'national-political' stages of the revolution.

Over the next few months the Rada increased its size steadily to approximately 600 by incorporating members

Figure 30 Ukrainian delegates to a military congress, 1917. (Insert of unknown figure.)

elected and appointed by numerous organizations. The Peasants' Congress, 23–29 June, yielded more than 200 delegates, the First Ukrainian Military Congress, 18–21 May, provided 150 and the First Ukrainian Workers' Congress, 24–27 July, provided 100. The Rada held plenary sessions once a month and an interim committee, the Mala Rada (Little Rada), composed of a presidium and some twenty other members, met continuously to conduct the day-to-day business.

From its inception, one of the Rada's preoccupations was to define its relationship to the PROVISIONAL GOVERNMENT in Petrograd. Negotiations between the two bodies were fraught with tension and misunderstandings. A delegation of ten, headed by Vynnychenko, arrived in Petrograd at the end of May and presented to the Provisional Government and the Petrograd Soviet the Rada's current demands: recognition of Ukrainian autonomy; representation of Ukrainian delegates at the forthcoming peace conference, especially in relation to the proposed disposition of Eastern Galicia; the introduction of Ukrainian language and subjects in schools in Ukraine; separate Ukrainian military formations in the army; a post in the Provisional Government for Ukrainian affairs.

Lack of a satisfactory response from the Provisional Government deepened the atmosphere of mistrust and prompted the Rada to issue the First Universal 23 June 1917. Addressed to the 'peasants, workers and toiling people' of the Ukraine, the Universal proclaimed: 'Let law and order in Ukraine be given by the all-national Ukrainian parliament elected by universal, equal, direct and secret suffrage . . . From this day forth we shall direct our own lives.' Despite the pretensions of independence, links with Russia were not to be severed and again confirmation of the new order was deferred to the Constituent Assembly. A General Secretariat of nine, headed by Vynnychenko and established as the executive of the government shortly after, was regarded by the Provisional Government as a serious challenge, as was the First Universal. Three representatives led by A. F. KERENSKY were dispatched from Petrograd to Kiev to continue negotiations with the Rada.

The Second Universal, amended in the light of the negotiations, was issued on 16 July 1917. The membership of the Rada was increased to over 800; a quarter of these to be representatives of non-Ukrainian minorities living in the

Ukraine. The General Secretariat was increased to fourteen to include representatives for the non-Ukrainians. On the inclusion of the national minorities the Rada claimed to be the 'sole supreme organ of revolutionary democracy in Ukraine'.

Meanwhile in Petrograd, dissatisfaction with the terms of the Second Universal precipitated a crisis in the Provisional Government leading to the resignation of four of the Kadet ministers, and the issuance on 4 August 1917, of an 'Instruction for the Provisional Government's General Secretariat in Ukraine' as an attempt to limit and define the powers of the Rada: the General Secretariat was to be subordinate to the government in Petrograd, the number of secretaryships was to be reduced to nine, four of them for the minorities, and the territory under the General Secretariat's jurisdiction was to be limited to the Kiev, Poltava, Volynia, Podolia and Chernigov provinces. The Rada's reluctant capitulation to some of these demands served only to increase hostility towards the Provisional Government.

As weakness and disorder grew in the north, the Ukrainians thought more seriously of independent action. At the Third All-Ukrainian Military Congress attended by 3,000 delegates on 2 to 12 November (NS), Vynnychenko proposed the establishment of the Ukrainian National Republic and the convening of a Ukrainian Constituent Assembly. News of the Bolshevik coup, which came in the middle of the congress, put an end to negotiations with the Provisional Government and created a new framework for the Rada's strivings for legitimacy.

The October Revolution to the demise of the Central Rada

The Third Universal, which codified the new state of affairs and proclaimed the Ukrainian People's Republic, was issued on 20 November 1917. It stated that in the absence of an organized government in Petrograd, the Rada was to be the sole authority in Ukraine until the convocation of the Constituent Assembly of Ukraine on 22 January 1918. None the less, it expressed the hope of retaining links with a democratic Russia within a federation of 'equal and free peoples'.

The terms of the Universal provided for an independent government and claimed jurisdiction over the nine provinces with a Ukrainian population. Freedom of speech, press, religion, assembly, strikes and the individual were guaranteed and the principle of 'national-personal' autonomy was to ensure the rights of all the minorities in Ukraine. Social and economic legislation was proposed, including the guarantee of an eight-hour work day and 'state control over production in the interests of Ukraine as well as Russia'. Lands not directly worked by the owners were to become 'the property of all the toiling people' without compensation to the owners.

A fairly accurate test of the real extent of support for Ukrainian political parties and the mandate for the Rada's action came in the returns to the All-Russian Constituent Assembly elections at the beginning of December 1917. In the Ukraine, where 7,580,000 votes were cast, 61.5 per cent were for the Ukrainian parties (the Ukrainian SRs took 45.3 per cent of these); 24.8 per cent for the Russian SRs; 10 per cent for the Bolsheviks; and 3.7 per cent for the Kadets. The strongest support for Ukrainian parties was outside the cities. In Poltava province, for example, the Ukrainian SRs polled 83.2 per cent of the vote. In Kiev province, the Ukrainian Socialist bloc of the Ukrainian SRs, and the USDRP together received 77 per cent of the total vote and 83 per cent of the vote outside the towns. In Podolia province a similar slate received 79 per cent of the vote and in Volynia, the Ukrainian SRs polled 71 per cent. The Ukrainian SRs won 9.5 per cent of the total votes cast throughout the territory of the former Russian Empire; the Ukrainian Social Democrats gained 0.26 per cent; and the Ukrainian socialists (the name used at the front by the joint slate of Ukrainian SRs and Ukrainian SDs) won 1.4 per cent.

The Bolsheviks made an effort to circumvent the Rada even though they had little support at this time. An All-Ukrainian Congress of Workers', Soldiers', and Peasants' Soviets was called by the Bolsheviks in Kiev on 17 December 1917. The effort failed as only 80 Bolshevik supporters could be mustered to counter the 2,500 who turned out to support the Rada. The Bolsheviks then withdrew to Kharkov where they called the first Ukrainian Congress of Soviets.

Tension between the Rada and the newly formed Council of People's Commissars (Sovnarkom – see LENIN'S GOVERNMENT) in Petrograd escalated quickly into a declaration of war after the Bolsheviks issued an ultimatum on 17 December 1917. Meanwhile the Bolshevik representatives at the peace negotiations in Brest-Litovsk had concluded an armistice with the Central Powers on 15 December in the name of all of Russia, including Ukraine. Despite the presence of a Soviet Ukrainian delegation from Kharkov, the Central Powers approved the delegation from the Rada which sought to procure a separate peace.

On 22 January 1918 in Kiev, halfway through the Brest-Litovsk negotiations, the Ukrainian National Republic with the Rada as its representative body proclaimed Ukraine's independence in the Fourth Universal: 'On this day the Ukrainian People's Republic becomes independent, dependent upon no one, a free sovereign state of the Ukrainian people.' On 9 February 1918 a treaty between the Central Powers and the Ukrainian National Republic was signed despite the protests of the Soviet delegation. The terms provided for future discussions on the precise boundaries between Austria-Hungary and the Ukrainian National Republic; the establishment of diplomatic relations; return of prisoners of war; and the immediate resumption of economic relations and trade. Under the

Figure 31   Departure of the Blue Coat Division to Ukraine.

terms of the treaty, Ukraine undertook to provide the Austrians with grain.

On the day the treaty was signed, Bolshevik forces entered Kiev and occupied the city for three weeks until the Rada called for German military assistance, which when it came was concerned only with maintaining a government that could guarantee the delivery of food supplies. The increasingly radical measures of the Rada, illusorily believing it could maintain unlimited Ukrainian sovereignty, began to jeopardize the collection of foodstuffs and also proved more and more unpopular with the landowners and wealthier peasants.

This dissatisfaction was harnessed by the German command to support several initiatives. On 28 April 1918, the day the new constitution was to be read, the Rada chamber was invaded by German troops. Potential sources of defence were immobilized. The most loyal Ukrainian military detachment, the 'Blue Coat' division, composed of former Ukrainian prisoners of war in Germany, had already been disarmed. The following day, the League of Landowners proclaimed General Pavlo SKOROPADSKY 'Hetman' of Ukraine.

The government of Hetman Pavlo Skoropadsky: April–October 1918

Although Pavlo Skoropadsky was descended from the last

elected Ukrainian hetman of the Zaporozhian Cossacks, the subsequent russification of his family and his close identification with the imperial regime hardly recommended him to the leaders of the Ukrainian movement.

The Ukrainian State superseded the Ukrainian National Republic and all authority was vested in the Hetman until an electoral law was passed to prepare for the election of a Ukrainian parliament. Skoropadsky quickly appointed a cabinet headed by Fedir Lyzohub consisting of men who were 'Ukrainian by blood but Muscovite in spirit', as the new Ukrainian opposition described them.

One of Skoropadsky's first moves was to repeal all the land reform enactments of the Rada and Provisional Government, thus restoring the right of private ownership. But the problems inherited from the Rada persisted especially in agriculture. Moreover, his agrarian policy, more than any other, was constrained by the economic demands of the Central Powers. A succession of agreements signed by the Hetman provided for the delivery of more than a million tons of grain, 400 million eggs, 50 thousand tons of horned livestock, 27 thousand tons of potatoes, two million fowl, butter, fruit and more than 45 thousand tons of sugar.

The Hetman intended to enact gradual agricultural reform to create a larger number of small landholdings for the peasants. The State Land Bank was to have supervised the purchase and resale of land. Despite this ambitious plan, failure to provide for the division of large estates finally drove the peasants and potential supporters of such a policy to join the uprising against the Hetman.

Skoropadsky attempted to bring former members of the Rada into his government but none, apart from Dmytro Doroshenko, would join. Even though the Hetman's cabinet was made up of men who had difficulties with the Ukrainian language, there were genuine attempts to carry on the policies of Ukrainianization begun by the Rada. This policy was actively supported also by the German representatives once they saw that it could promote the government's credibility and thus help to prevent the reunion of Ukraine with Russia. Summer courses in the Ukrainian language and culture were set up for teachers and Ukrainian began to be taught in some schools. By the autumn of 1918, 150 Ukrainian high schools had been set up. The law of 3 July 1918, which repeated the principles of the Rada's Law of March 1918, conferred Ukrainian citizenship on all who resided in Ukraine, unless they specifically asked to be excluded. The oath of citizenship was pledged to the Ukrainian State.

Despite the Hetman's honest intentions in appointing an efficient administration and attempting to conduct the affairs of his state in an independent manner, he encountered constraints and opposition from many sources. The German demands hampered a viable domestic policy and undermined attempts to establish diplomatic relations with other states. Opposition came also from the former members of the Rada who organized the Ukrainian National Union, which included Social Democrats, moderate Socialist Revolutionaries, Socialist Federalists, Democratic Agrarians, Independent Socialists and members of postal telegraphic, railway and other labour, professional, peasant and student groups. Passive opposition existed in Kiev among the many Russians fleeing from the Bolsheviks and who at best considered their present location as temporary and the Hetman regime as something to be tolerated for the short term.

The Ukrainian National Union, headed by Vynnychenko, had been planning to overthrow the Hetman throughout the late summer and autumn. The Sich Riflemen, who formed the core of the Ukrainian military forces throughout 1917–1919, were to provide the military backing for the coup and the leadership was to be the Directory, formed on 13 November 1918 and consisting of Vynnychenko, an SD; Petliura, SD and the military; Fedir Shvets from the SRs; Opanas Andrievsky and Andrii Makarenko.

As the German defeat drew closer, the Skoropadsky government began negotiations with the Allies in an attempt to maintain its independence and power. These produced little response however and the regime began to disintegrate. On the withdrawal of the German military the Directory's forces, led by Petliura, entered Kiev on 14 December 1918.

Ukrainian National Republic from the Directory to Petliura

The Directory suffered all the ills of a government convened in the heat of revolution. On 26 December 1918 a new Council of National Ministers was established under the Directory with V. Chekhivsky (USDRP) as prime minister. Skoropadsky's legislation on land was revoked, Ukrainian reestablished as the official language and the autocephaly of the RUSSIAN ORTHODOX CHURCH restored.

The Directory's tasks were complicated by the Bolshevik invasion of Ukrainian territories in late December 1918, giving support to the Directory's adversary, the Bolshevik Provisional Workers' and Peasants' Government of Ukraine led by G. L. Pyatakov. On 16 January 1919 the Directory declared war on Soviet Russia.

The Directory's jurisdiction increased when the Western Ukrainian Republic joined the Ukrainian National Republic in the Act of Union on 22 January 1919. The Western Ukrainian Republic, formed from the Ukrainian territories of Eastern Galicia on the collapse of Austria-Hungary, and centred in Lvov, had declared itself an independent entity on 1 November 1918. It retained some autonomy, in its separate foreign ministry, for example.

The Labour Congress which was to define the status of the new Council was held 23–28 January 1919. It empowered the Directory to act as the supreme power and enact laws that were necessary for the defence of the Republic, and it invested the Council of Ministers with executive powers. Political factions and individuals, however, grew suspicious of one another, e.g. Vynnychenko for proposing negotiations with the Bolsheviks, although his idea was a non-Bolshevik 'soviet' Ukraine, and Petliura, who was against any kind of cooperation with the Bolsheviks, could not command enough support for his views to prevail.

When the RED ARMY entered Kiev on 4 February 1919, the Directory and its government fled to Vinnitsa where it formed a new, more right wing and non-partisan Council excluding the USDRP and UPSR, to negotiate with the Entente. The new prime minister was S. Ostapenko. Petliura left the USDRP to head the government and Vynnychenko resigned, disappointed with the view that the independent military commanders now constituted the only government that was left.

Vinnitsa fell to the Bolsheviks in early March and the government fled to Proskurov. The Second Labour Congress, initiated by Hrushevsky, met in Kamenets-Podolsk on 21 March 1919 to discuss a possible agreement with Moscow, in opposition to Petliura's focus on the Entente.

Throughout 1919 the decline of the Directory and the disintegration of any kind of stable government was accompanied by the spread of anarchy and anti-Jewish pogroms (see JEWS), condemned by the Directory, which appropriated large sums of money to aid pogrom victims in an attempt to persuade Jews to support the Ukrainian government. Although orders were issued censuring the instigators of the pogroms, many atamans, nominally under Petliura, were a law unto themselves and the government was unable to have such persons apprehended and brought to justice (see ATAMANS).

The Entente was of little help to the Directory. When the French forces in the strategic city of Odessa were withdrawn suddenly on 3 April 1919, the Ukrainian government's policy was thrown into further disarray. Petliura withdrew to Rovno to form a new Council on 9 April 1919, including members of the USDRP, UPSR and Western Ukrainian SD Party. B. Martos was elected prime minister and P. Krasny of the Poalei-Tsion party minister for Jewish affairs. Then military commander Oskilko, age twenty-six, supported by Directory member Andrievsky, made an unsuccessful attempt to arrest Petliura and the other members of the Directory and the government retreated to Galicia, unable to hold any positions in Eastern Ukraine. By 4 June 1919 Petliura had recovered sufficiently to return across the Zbruch River (the natural dividing line between Western and Eastern Ukraine) and retake Kamenets-Podolsk in preparation for a march on Kiev. In mid July he was joined by Galician troops who were in retreat from the Polish offensive. They were joined en route by peasants escaping from WAR COMMUNISM. Ukrainian forces entered Kiev on 30 August 1919 and a Council was organized under Izaak Mazepa.

Meanwhile, in the absence of Ukrainians representatives, the Allied Powers at the Paris Peace Conference in 1918 were uncertain about who the Ukrainians were or what they wanted, despite the Directory's efforts at publicity and diplomacy. By the autumn of 1919 Polish armed forces had moved into Volynia and Podolia. Suspecting that Petliura was planning concessions to the Poles in return for aid to fight against the Bolsheviks, the Galicians entered into their own secret negotiations with DENIKIN in November, causing a rift between the government of Western Ukraine and the Ukrainian National Republic. By early December most of the Ukraine, including the cities of Kiev, Poltava, and Kharkov, was in the hands of the Red Army.

On 15 November 1919 Petliura was vested with the supreme authority as head of the Directory and Supreme Ataman but, faced with revolt, left on 6 December 1919 for Warsaw where negotiations with PIŁSUDSKI led to the Polish-Ukrainian Treaty of 21 April 1920. Their joint forces then entered Ukraine and on 7 May recaptured Kiev from the Bolsheviks, for which Piłsudski was given wide powers on the Right-Bank. Mazepa resigned, a new Council was formed on 26 May 1920 comprising mainly right-wing social democrats, the UPSF and independentists and headed by V. Prokopovych and A. Livytsky. When the remaining two members of the Directory, Shvets and Makarenko, failed to return from abroad where they had been rallying support for the Ukrainian cause, all the Directory's power formally passed to Petliura on 21 May

1920. The Bolsheviks retook Kiev 11 June 1920, however, and what was left of the government retreated with Petliura to Tarnow in Poland where the one-man Directory was formally sanctioned on 12 November 1920. The government of the UNR went into exile at the beginning of 1921.

The failure of the Ukrainian revolution exposed the uneven development of the population. The results of the elections demonstrated that despite the lack of an infrastructure to propagate the national idea, in a few short months the Ukrainian peasantry (the majority of the Ukrainian population) had learned to link economic interests to national ideas in politics. The weakness of Ukrainian party successes in the urban areas, particularly among the predominantly Russian industrial workers, contributed to the undoing of the Ukrainian revolution, as did lack of ability to organize, lack of resources, the absence of sufficient intelligentsia and tactical errors, including a delay in creating a standing Ukrainian army.   ND

Further Reading

Borys, Jurij: *The Sovietization of Ukraine, 1917–1923*, rev. edn. Edmonton: 1980.

Guthier, Steven L.: The popular base of Ukrainian nationalism in 1917. *Slavic Review* 1 (1979).

Ivanova, R.: *Mykhailo Drahomanov u suspil'nomu rusi rosii ta ukrainy*. Kiev: 1971.

Khrystiuk, P.: *Zamitky i materialy do istorii ukrainskoi revoliutsii, 1917–1920*, 4 vols. Vienna: 1921–22.

Krawchenko, B.: *Social Change and National Consciousness in Twentieth Century Ukraine*. London: Macmillan/St Antony's College Oxford, 1985.

Mace, James E.: *Communism and the Dilemmas of National Liberation, National Communism in Soviet Ukraine, 1918–1933*. Harvard: 1983.

Pidhainy, Oleh S.: *The Formation of the Ukrainian Republic*. New York: 1966.

Pipes, Richard: *The Formation of the USSR*, rev. edn. New York: 1968.

Reshetar, John: *The Ukrainian Revolution, 1917–1920*. Princeton, NJ: 1952.

The Baltic before 1917

Finland and the lands of the eastern Baltic only came under Russian control with the decline of Sweden in the eighteenth century. The provinces of Estland and Livland, and the Karelian borderland, were formally surrendered by Sweden in 1721. Kurland passed under Russian control with the third partition of Poland in 1795. Finally, in 1809, the Finnish provinces were ceded by Sweden to Alexander I. The rights and privileges of the Baltic German nobility and the Finnish Estates were confirmed by the new rulers, and it was not until the end of the nineteenth century that local control of affairs began to come under serious attack from St Petersburg.

The Finnish lands had formed an integral part of the Swedish realm since the middle ages and the laws, institutions and customs of that kingdom had taken firm root. The convening of the four Estates by Alexander I in February 1809 (Diet of Porvoo) and his confirmation of their rights and privileges, religion and laws, was a recognition of this fact. Although the official language and that of the educated classes was Swedish, Finnish was the language of the great majority of the population, and had been given written form as a result of the Reformation. The predominantly Finnish-speaking peasantry played an active part in public life, and there was a strong link between the rural population and the clergy, most of whom were recruited from that milieu. Serfdom had never existed in Finland, and there was a substantial number of freehold farmers who were to join the ranks of the nationalist movement from the 1870s, with the acceleration of economic life and the spread of organized political activity into the countryside.

In the Baltic lands the military order of the Teutonic knights had imposed its rule over the indigenous population in the thirteenth century and, although the order disappeared with the Reformation, the dominance of the Baltic German landowners remained. Serfdom was abolished in 1816–19, but the peasantry were still subject to the overlordship of the landowners until the reign of Alexander II. The political and economic grip of this numerically small and rigidly exclusive caste did not begin to slacken appreciably until the second half of the nineteenth century, partly as a result of the actions of the imperial government, partly as a consequence of economic change, which helped create a more diverse social stratification of the Latvian and Estonian population.

On the eve of the FIRST WORLD WAR, the provinces of Estland and Livland were ranked fourth and fifth respectively in terms of per capita industrial production and the relative number of industrial workers of the fifty provinces of European Russia. With a population of over half a million, Riga was the fifth largest city in the empire. Although Latvians constituted the largest single ethnic group in the city (57 per cent), there were also sizeable German (15 per cent), Russian (18 per cent) and Jewish communities (7.9 per cent). Latvians constituted three quarters of the population of southern Livland and Kurland, with a further 19 per cent, mostly Catholic peasants, in the Latgale region of Vitebsk province. Estonians made up 91 per cent of the population of Estland and northern Livland, and almost three quarters of the population of the cities of Reval and Dorpat. The university of Dorpat, although remaining primarily a German institution for much of the nineteenth century, attracted an increasing number of Estonian students by the turn of the century. It also served as a focal point for Estonian intellectual and political life, as did the university in Finland (transferred from Turku to Helsinki in 1827).

By contrast, St Petersburg became the centre of the early Latvian national awakening.

The tempo of urbanization was slower in Finland where the main marketable commodity, timber, was processed in rural areas. During the course of the nineteenth century, the autonomy of the Grand Duchy was significantly strengthened, and political life was altogether freer than elsewhere in the Empire. The four-estate Diet met regularly after 1863. The government, or Senate, was manned by native-born Finns. A series of reforms and measures which strengthened autonomy, such as the creation of a Finnish army, were passed during the reign of Alexander II. The principal political issue of the latter half of the nineteenth century, the language conflict, was characterized by a degree of flexibility and common understanding which was lacking in the non-Finnish Baltic lands. By the time serious efforts were undertaken to whittle away some of Finland's autonomous status, under the governor-generalship of N. I. Bobrikov (1898–1904), the cause of Finnishness was in the ascendancy, even if the language conflict still continued to exercise an influence on political debate.

Bobrikov's measures aroused opposition from a hitherto loyal population. This took the form of a passive resistance, principally directed against conscription into the Imperial army, a measure which was abandoned by the Imperial government before the 1905 REVOLUTION. The passive resistance was led by the Swedish party and the Young Finn wing of the nationalist movement which placed the defence of constitutional liberties before the demands of linguistic nationalism. A section of the Old Finn party favoured negotiations with moderate elements in St Petersburg, and regarded the constitutionalist alliance as something of a betrayal of the cause of unitary monolinguistic nationhood. A few, mainly Swedish-speaking intellectuals, collaborated with the Russian revolutionary movement and followed a policy of active resistance, in which some elements of the labour movement were also involved. The assassination of Bobrikov in June 1904 was the work of a lone patriot, unconnected with the active resistance.

Russification measures in the Baltic lands were more far-reaching than in Finland, and in so far as these undermined the hegemony of the Baltic Germans, were supported by the Latvian and Estonian national movements. The reform of municipal election procedures in 1877 and 1892 was of particular benefit to the ethnic majorities, and a number of towns, especially in Estland, fell under their control by 1914. Political opinion was not so easily translated into organized activity, in comparison with Finland, largely because of the repressive nature of Imperial Russia, but also because of the rivalries and regional fragmentation within the ethnic communities. Estonians and Latvians were also more intimately affected by and involved in the political currents prevalent in Russia than were the Finns, whose strong traditions of self-government and the inheritance from Swedish times insulated them from events in the rest of the Empire. Social democracy in Finland, for example, drew its inspiration from Germany and Sweden rather than from Russia, and was careful not to compromise Finland's special status by too close an involvement with the revolutionary movement.

Nationalism and socialism

The initial task of the Finnish, Estonian and Latvian national movements was the creation of a distinct cultural identity for the indigenous peasant population. A singular feature of the nationalist movements was that they sought to supplant the dominant linguistic culture of the local ruling elites. Resistance to russification occurred relatively late in the nineteenth century, and was prompted primarily by the measures which Imperial authorities wished to enforce. Indeed, for much of the nineteenth century these national movements tended to look to Imperial Russia as a potential ally in breaking down the cultural and political dominance of the Swedish- and German-speaking minorities. It was only during the reigns of the last two Emperors, when russification measures began to be implemented at the same time as mature native nationalist movements took shape, that serious conflict arose between Imperial Russia and the Baltic borderlands.

The task of the pioneers of the national awakening was made difficult by the absence of any historical tradition of political independence (as in Poland), or high culture (as in Armenia), and the numerical smallness and linguistic isolation of the respective ethnic groups. On the other hand Lutheranism had ensured relatively high levels of literacy, and had fostered the development of the written languages. The universities in Turku and Dorpat, founded in the seventeenth century, were important centres for the awakening of interest in the culture of the indigenous peoples, and many of the early pioneers of the national movement were products of these two centres of learning.

The initial phase of cultural awakening began to acquire a harder political edge in Finland from the mid-nineteenth century, in the Baltic lands at the end of the century. The emergence of a stratum of prosperous peasant landowners among the indigenous majority population from the 1870s helped provide a mass basis for the nationalist movements; but it also added a further dimension to the class antagonisms of the area. The existence of an impoverished rural proletariat to whom radical solutions had a definite appeal, posed problems for the nationalist movements and Marxist socialists (see MARXISM IN RUSSIA). The former tended to divide into a patriarchal, conservative wing and a section which recognized the need for radical social reforms. Both the Latvian and the Finnish social democratic parties enjoyed wide support amongst the landless poor, especially at times of revolution. Unlike the Latvian and Estonian BOLSHEVIKS, who alienated much peasant

support in 1917–19 by their doctrinaire approach to the land question, the Finnish socialists adopted a rather pragmatic line. The Red government simply decreed the freeing of leasehold farmers from their obligations, and took no steps to collectivize the land.

The Finnish social democratic party was also unusual in that it functioned legally from its foundation in 1899. It drew its ideological inspiration from German Marxism and played little part in the Russian revolutionary movement. The Latvian social democrats affiliated with the RSDRP in 1906, but retained a considerable degree of independence, as a large and well-organized party, in which Bolsheviks and MENSHEVIKS coexisted until 1917. Social democracy was less well organized in Estonia, where the Estonian social democratic party suffered from the loss of leaders, forced to flee abroad after the 1905 revolution.

The support enjoyed by the left in Finland and the Baltic lands may be ascribed to the impetus of the 1905 revolution, and local class antagonisms which the lack of effective social reforms and an intractable land question further exacerbated. In the Baltic lands, the left had to contend with repression and persecution. In Finland, on the other hand, the labour movement was able to establish an impressive legal organization, providing a cultural and political home for thousands of industrial and rural workers. In this respect it resembled the mass movements of western Europe, though it too was overwhelmed by the sudden upsurge of revolutionary discontent in 1917.

The unrest sparked off by 'Bloody Sunday' spread rapidly to the cities of the Baltic provinces, as did the massive strike movement in October 1905. The events of 1905–6 were more violent in the Baltic lands than in Finland. Many estates were attacked, and a number of landowners and clergymen murdered. In some areas, notably in Kurland, pitched battles were fought between armed insurgents and troops. Punitive expeditions were launched in the winter of 1905–6, with many executions and the imprisonment or deportation to Siberia of thousands of people. The Baltic German provincial diets remained, and the only significant political concession was the creation of the Imperial Duma, in which a number of Estonian and Latvian politicians were able to gain experience.

Estonia: The Estonian liberals proved to be rather better organized than their Latvian counterparts. The main demands put forward by the liberals, led by Jaan Tõnisson (1868–19–?), at the All-Estonian congress held in November 1905 were for civil rights, administrative and educational reform, with a wide measure of devolved local autonomy. The radical-democrat majority was prepared to resort to armed insurrection to overthrow the autocracy, and their perspective was All-Russian, rather than Baltic. They were nevertheless committed to Estonian autonomy in addition to expropriation of the lands of the Baltic barons and the state, and the right of workers to organize trade unions and to strike.

Finland: The Finnish experience of 1905 was rather different. A patriotic national strike broke out several days after the outbreak of revolution in the capital, at the end of October. The labour movement played an important role in organizing the strike, and membership of the social democratic party rose from 16,000 to almost 100,000 in 1906. The relative unanimity of the early days of the strike was soon shattered, with the social democrats claiming that they had been excluded from discussions with the governor-general. The constitutionalists were able to obtain a manifesto from the Emperor, and a mandate to form a new government. The decrees introduced during the Bobrikov era were rescinded, and provision made for the reform of the four-estate Diet. In the elections of 1907 to the new unicameral assembly (Eduskunta), on the basis of direct and universal male and female suffrage, the social democrats obtained eighty of the two hundred seats. The Swedish people's party was reduced to a minority defending the interests of Swedish speakers, and their Young Finn allies lost support to the Old Finns and a new farmers' party in the north and east of the country.

The new assembly failed to bring about significant reforms, especially on the pressing land question, partly as a consequence of internal party political strife, partly because of the blocking tactics of the autocracy. By 1914 the government was filled with nonentities appointed by the Emperor; the assembly had been frequently dissolved because of the protests of the Speaker against russification measures; and the Imperial government and its representatives in Finland had begun a new series of measures designed to diminish Finland's autonomous position. The publication of a plan to reduce Finland's autonomy even further in November 1914 did little to rally Finnish opinion to the Imperial war effort. Conscription did not apply in Finland, and rather more Finns (around two thousand) opted for military training in Germany than volunteered for service in the Russian army (though there were still a number of professionals, such as General C. G. Mannerheim (1867–1951), in the armed forces).

The activists who organized the setting up of the JÄGER MOVEMENT in Germany were, however, on the fringes of Finnish political life. Before 1917 there was no movement for national independence, and the same holds true for the Baltic provinces. The German assault further undermined the status and power of the Baltic Germans, and caused widespread disruption. In 1915 much of Kurland was occupied by the German army, with half a million refugees fleeing to Russia. The war economy also brought large numbers of Russian workers into the Baltic cities. The organization of the war effort and relief work provided an opportunity for creating recognizable national bodies, and the formation of two Latvian light infantry battalions in

1915 (which were eventually brought up to a complement of 130,000 men in eight battalions) was to have an important consequence in the revolution of 1917.   DGK

The Baltic: Revolution and Civil War

The collapse of the old order in March 1917 opened up new prospects for the aspirations of the Finns, Estonians and Latvians: but it also raised the question of who would now exercise power and maintain order. The presence of large numbers of troops and the sailors of the Baltic Fleet in what was a front-line war zone added a further dimension to this problem.

Figure 32 Labour leaders of Pori 'fraternizing' with Russian sailors.

Estonia: The aspirations of the Estonians were given a boost by the PROVISIONAL GOVERNMENT's decree of 30 March, which established a single administrative unit for Estland, the islands and northern Livland, under the jurisdiction of the government-appointed commissar, Jaan Poska (1866–1922), the former mayor of Reval. District councils were also established, with an indirectly elected provincial assembly (Maapäev).

Initially, elections to the Maapäev were held only in rural areas; elected members from Reval and Dorpat did not join the assembly until the autumn. The Maapäev, which convened on 1 July, was divided into two roughly equal blocs – the democrats (Tõnisson's democratic party, the radical democrats led by Konstantin Päts (1874–1955)) and the agrarians and the socialists (Estonian social democrats, SRs, labour and one Bolshevik). During the course of the summer the Maapäev and its administrative board clashed with the Provisional Government on a number of issues, such as the control of education and local government. On 25 August, faced with the threat of a German occupation, the members of the Maapäev declared themselves to be the representatives of the Estonian nation and resolved to send delegates abroad to defend Estonian interests in the event of occupation.

The Bolsheviks, though poorly organized outside the cities, made steady advances in the soviets of Reval, Narva and Dorpat, and with the left SRs, captured control of the executive committee of the Estonian soviets in October. Russian troops and workers were strongly represented in these city soviets, which adopted a hostile attitude towards the Maapäev and the government commissar. On the eve of the OCTOBER REVOLUTION, there were thus two main contenders for power in Estonia: the soviets and the Maapäev, still struggling to gain a grip on the administration of local affairs.

The soviets' executive set up a military revolutionary committee on 22 October. This committee compelled the government commissar to resign, and claimed the right to executive authority in Estonia after the October revolution. This claim was challenged by the Maapäev, and before its forcible dissolution on 15 November, it proclaimed itself to be the supreme authority in Estonia and vested full powers in its council of elders. In the winter of 1917–18, members of this council secretly established contact with representatives of foreign countries to seek support for Estonian independence. Elections for an Estonian constituent assembly decreed by the soviet executive were suspended in January 1918 on the pretext of a feared anti-soviet coup. In the elections which were held, the Bolsheviks claimed 37 per cent of the vote, with the labour party (Tööerakond) winning nearly 30 per cent. The Bolsheviks lacked an effective rural organization, and alienated many peasants by their doctrinaire approach to the land question. The soviets were still attempting to consolidate their power in the Baltic when the area was overrun and occupied by German troops in February 1918.

Latvia: The revolutionary left was far more powerful on Latvian territory, and the Latvian Bolsheviks were strongly supported in rural areas, where peasants' soviets were set up. Two rival provincial assemblies for Livland were established in the spring of 1917, and although the two fused in May, friction between the socialist and democratic blocs continued.

The Latvian bourgeois parties were slow to organize, and lacked much of the verve and organizational ability of the Latvian social democrats. The cause of united Latvia was seriously hindered by the war, the dispersal of thousands of refugees, and the conflict between Russians and Latvians of Latgale. Nevertheless, a conference called by the Livland provincial assembly on 30 July, attended by representatives of bourgeois and soviet organizations, unanimously endorsed the right of the Latvian people to self-determination, within the framework of the Russian democratic republic.

The initiative from the summer of 1917 lay firmly with the Bolsheviks, who secured majority support in elections to the district land councils in the autumn, and held 60 per cent of the seats in the Livland provincial assembly elected on 20 August. The first congress of Latvian soviets, meeting in Riga at the end of July, was overwhelmingly Bolshevik in composition, and the executive committee (Iskolat) that it elected was to become the chief instrument of revolutionary rule in unoccupied Latvian territory. Iskolat was in effective control from the fall of Riga (22 August). The seizure of power in Petrograd simply ensured the transfer of power to the soviets in the Baltic lands. Iskolat, better organized and led than its Estonian counterpart, sought by strict measures to ensure control of the economy and distribution of commodities and foodstuffs, and instituted a programme of expropriation of large estates which were run by local committees.

The Latvian bourgeois parties were not entirely inactive. At the instigation of the Latvian refugee committee in Petrograd, an assembly was convened in Walk on 4 November. This elected a national council, which called on the Soviet government to authorize the incorporation of Latgale into Latvia and to respect the right of the Latvian people to determine their own internal government. Though recognizing the incorporation of Latgale, the Soviet government rejected the other demands and ordered the dissolution of the council. Its members continued to operate clandestinely but in the meantime, the second congress of Latvian soviets (16–18 December) vested supreme power in the soviets and elected a new executive committee, of which Fricis Rozins-Azis (1879–1919) was the chairman.

Finland: The course of events in Finland was very different. The country's internal administration and political institutions were not swept away by the revolution, but were given scope to function effectively with the abolition of tsarist restrictions. The problem of the exercise of supreme authority, however, remained unresolved though there was no challenge in this regard from the soviets, which were concerned with military matters and the course of the revolution in Petrograd. No Finnish soviets were created. The social democratic party, with an absolute majority in the Eduskunta, preferred to follow a parliamentary tactic, even reluctantly entering the coalition government which replaced the deposed appointees of NICHOLAS II. By June the social democrats were pressing for complete internal independence which the Provisional Government was not prepared to concede. The first All-Russian congress of soviets was more sympathetic, though it too insisted that the Finnish question could only be settled by the All-Russian CONSTITUENT ASSEMBLY. A short bill pushed through parliament on 18 July (NS) by the social democrats and bourgeois supporters of independence proclaimed the sovereignty of the Eduskunta in all matters except defence and foreign affairs. The Provisional Government, which was also facing a crisis in relations with the Ukrainian

Rada, responded by ordering the dissolution of the Eduskunta. The social democrats protested, but were powerless to offer any resistance. In the October elections they won ninety-two seats, but lost their overall majority. The party had also withdrawn from government by the late summer.

The spring and summer were characterized by rising unemployment, inflation and food shortages, with a wave of strikes on the land. Conscious of rising discontent, the labour movement now sought to push through a package of political and social reforms. The refusal of the bourgeois majority in parliament to discuss these demands sparked off a general strike on 13 November (NS). Workers' guards – officially sanctioned by the party and unions in September – exercised *de facto* control over much of the country, but the specially-formed revolutionary council shrank from a full-blooded seizure of power after the Eduskunta had approved reform of local suffrage and the eight-hour working day. Dissatisfied Red Guards broke away from party control and began preparations for armed struggle. The violent excesses of the strike week, in which some Russian troops were involved, prompted the bourgeois majority on 26 November to vote in a non-socialist government, committed to independence for Finland and the restoration of order.

The first objective was realized on 6 December, when the Eduskunta gave its approval for the Svinhufvud government to seek recognition of Finland's independence. Formal recognition of independence was given by the Soviet government three weeks later. To restore order which the workers' militias had proved incapable of maintaining in the towns, and which marauding bands of soldiers and Red Guards were threatening in the countryside, the government drew upon paramilitary units established to fight for independence in the autumn of 1917, the Jäger troops whose return was negotiated in Germany, and ex-Imperial army officers. This was seen by the left as a measure to repress the working class, and with fighting breaking out between Red and White militias, and an almost total lack of communication between government and the labour movement, the social democratic party leadership authorized a seizure of power at the end of January.

The civil war which followed lasted three months. It was largely a Finnish affair, with the Russians providing arms and some military assistance to the Reds, and a German expeditionary force landing in southern Finland in April to help the Whites. The Red government's ideal was a democratic rather than a soviet socialist republic, and it was careful to establish Finnish national claims in the treaty concluded with Soviet Russia on 1 March 1918.

Only in exile did the social democratic party split, when a group of radicals formed the Finnish Communist Party in Moscow in August 1918. The social democratic party was revived in Finland by moderates who had stayed on the sidelines during the civil war. In spite of the White terror in the aftermath of hostilities, its legality was acknowledged and in the elections of March 1919 the party succeeded in winning eighty seats. The Whites were split by a number of issues – control of the armed forces, the language question, and whether or not Finland should become a monarchy – and this undoubtedy helped the labour movement to regain political momentum.

The collapse of Germany, which had held Finland in a powerful economic and political grip after the civil war, compelled a hasty reorientation of policy in order to secure Allied recognition of independence. *De jure* recognition of Finland by the Allies was accorded on 3 May 1919. Relations with Russia still remained to be settled. The White Russians refused to acknowledge Finnish independence, thereby creating an obstacle to plans to secure Finnish support for intervention. General Mannerheim actively supported such plans, but failed to rally the politicians. His defeat in the first presidential elections under the new constitution on 25 July 1919 was a blow to the hopes of the interventionists, though he continued to plot behind the scenes.

The main bone of contention between Finland and Russia was East Karelia, to which Finland laid claim. The withdrawal of British troops from northern Russia in autumn 1919 and the collapse of the White Russian army ended the brief and tenuous existence of the provisional Karelian government, set up in February 1919. Five days before peace talks between Finland and Russia were due to begin on 12 June 1920, the Karelian Workers' Commune was established. The Soviet negotiators could thus claim that the new regime was an expression of Karelian self-determination, though in fact it was to become an instrument for Finnish communist rule in the 1920s.

The peace talks in Dorpat took place against the background of the Russo-Polish War, and peace was not signed until 14 October 1920. Finland gained Petsamo on the Arctic Ocean, returned two Karelian communes which it had annexed, and failed to persuade the Russians to agree to an article in the treaty guaranteeing the Karelians the right to self-government.

The Estonians and Latvians had to contend with a number of major obstacles on their road to independence. The occupying Germans sought to establish colonies in Kurland, and to incorporate the Baltic area into the Reich. The collapse of the Reich did not lead to German withdrawal, since considerable numbers of troops were allowed to stay in the Baltic area to counter the threat of the RED ARMY, which began advancing in November 1918. A Soviet Latvian republic was proclaimed in Moscow on 14 December, one month after the proclamation of Latvia's independence in Riga by the Latvian people's council. Red Army units drove the Latvian government out of Riga at the beginning of January 1919. The Red Army was less successful in penetrating Estonia on behalf of the Workers'

Figure 33 General Mannerheim salutes the Jägers in a parade in the square at Vaasa on 26 February 1918.

Commune, and by 24 February 1919 – the first anniversary of the proclamation of the Estonian republic by the liberation committee of the Maapäev – the invaders had been ejected, with assistance from White Russian forces, British naval units and Finnish volunteers.

The Soviet Latvian government, led by P. I. Stučka (STUCHKA), managed to retain power for a longer period, but its actions and policies did not endear it to the populace. The situation in Latvia was made complicated by the intrigues of the German forces, which overthrew the refugee Latvian government of Karlis Ulmanis (1877–1942) and replaced it with a puppet regime. With support from the Latvian Balodis brigade, White Russians and the Allied fleet commander Admiral Sinclair, the German troops stormed Riga on 22 May 1919, and met up with advancing Estonian units to the north. German refusal to withdraw led to open conflict and victory for the Estonian troops, who began to advance on Riga. The Germans were now forced to evacuate the Baltic, and the Ulmanis government was restored.

A further threat to the stability of the area was posed by the presence of numbers of White Russian troops, whom the British military representative General Marsh sought to weld into a force capable of invading Russia. When the Latvian government refused to grant transit rights to Bermondt-Avalov, commanding the Western army, he attacked Riga (8 October 1919), only to be driven out of the country a month later. The failure of the Yudenich offensive against Petrograd in the autumn brought to an end hopes for intervention, and opened the way for negotiations. Talks between Estonian and Soviet representatives began in Dorpat on 4 December 1919, and peace was concluded on 2 February 1920. Russia recognized Estonia's independence, and allocated the Petseri district and strip of land on the eastern bank of the river Narova (Narva) to the new republic.

In January 1920, a combined Latvian-Polish force liberated Latgale. An armistice was concluded with Russia on 1 February, and peace was eventually signed in Riga on 1 August 1920, Latvia acquiring the Latgale area. *De jure* recognition of Estonia and Latvia by the Allied Supreme Council was only given in January 1921, a measure of the

231

scepticism with which the western powers regarded the viability of the new states in the confused period following the collapse of the Russian Empire. Although Estonia and Latvia managed to establish economic stability, both states ended up with authoritarian regimes in the 1930s, and fell victim to the Soviet Union in 1939–40. Finland, with its older and better-established political traditions, managed to preserve its democratic constitutional forms, and was able to resist the demands of the Soviet Union and preserve its independence during the Second World War.   DGK

Further Reading

Ezergailis, Andrew: *The 1917 Revolution in Latvia*. Boulder, Col.: 1974.

Ezergailis, Andrew and von Pistohlkors, Gert eds.: *Die baltischen Provinzen Russlands zwischen den Revolutionen von 1905 und 1917*. Cologne and Vienna: 1982.

Kirby, David: *Finland in the Twentieth Century*. London: 1979.

von Rauch, Georg: *The Baltic states. The years of independence*. London: 1974.

Thaden, Edward C. ed.: *Russification in the Baltic Provinces and Finland, 1855–1914*. Princeton, NJ: 1981.

Upton, A.F.: *The Finnish Revolution 1917–1918*. Minneapolis, Minn.: 1980.

Transcaucasia before 1917

Transcaucasia comprises the area now occupied by the Soviet republics of Armenia, Azerbaijan and Georgia. Situated on the broad and strategically important isthmus between the Black and Caspian Seas, it was a major thoroughfare for the migrating populations of north and south, east and west, and the focus of warring empires. Due to the weakness of local states and the fluidity of political borders, the area became a patchwork of different ethnic groups characterized by a complex pattern of inter-ethnic dispersion. Three major ethnographic groups emerged in the region. The Turkic Azerbaijanis who by 1917 belonged largely to the Shi'ite sect of Islam, the Orthodox Georgians who spoke an Ibero-Caucasian language and the Armenians who spoke a language of Indo-European origin and belonged to the Gregorian branch of the Eastern church.

In the first half of the nineteenth century, Russian administration in Transcaucasia was an *ad hoc* affair, its main purpose being strategic (there was little economic exploitation), and beyond a tsarist concern for uniformity, the local peoples were left alone. However Russian rule set in motion a process of modernization which intensified in the second half of the century and culminated in strong Transcaucasian national movements. Tsarist administration, growth of communications, urbanization, the market economy, and the introduction of large numbers of schools all increased the interrelation between the previously isolated villages and the towns, and promoted social and ethnic integration, compelling local elites to become more educated and urban. By the second half of the nineteenth century, increasingly confident national intelligentsias under the influence of European ideas were demanding a greater say in their own national affairs. They were supported by a growing working class which accompanied the massive spurt in Transcaucasian industrial growth in the 1880s, and by 1905 national parties began to acquire a popular base among their own ethnic communities. The growth in national consciousness also led to ethnic animosities which exploded into bloody strife during 1905 and 1917.

The Azerbaijanis

Before the Russian conquest, the territory of Azerbaijan was part of the Persian empire occupied by a turkified people with no tradition of unity or separate statehood. The Azerbaijanis had no distinct national identity before the Russian annexation in the 1820s. Their loyalty was to a supranational Islam and to their co-religionists in the multi-ethnic empires of either Persia (Shi'ites) or Ottoman Turkey (Sunnis). Russian penetration of the region began in the eighteenth century but was not consolidated until 1828 when the Russo-Persian treaty of Turkomanchai gave Russia the northern regions of Persia comprising almost half of Azerbaijani territory and half a million Azerbaijani-speaking Muslims. The Russian victory over Turkey in 1829 and later in 1878 resulted in the annexation of further Muslim territories and by 1917 the Muslim population in the region amounted to almost two and a quarter million out of a total Transcaucasian population of approximately seven million.

Of the three Transcaucasian national groups, the Azerbaijanis were the least nationally conscious by 1917. Like other Russian Muslims they were loyal to the *umma*, the worldwide community of Muslims, and did not share the territorial imperative of their Transcaucasian neighbours. However, the more secularly oriented Azerbaijani intelligentsia, products of a new-style Russian education and enriched by a native bourgeoisie from the oil-producing city of Baku, were influenced by the ideas current in Turkey and Persia such as Pan-Turkism, Turkism, and Pan-Islamism, by reform movements like Jadidism (a 'new method' of teaching in schools), by the Russian Muslim cultural revival led by the Kazan Tatars, by the revolutionary events in Persia (1906) and the Ottoman empire (1908), and by the Europeanized Russian radical intelligentsia. A new breed of Russian Muslim journalists such as Ismail bey GASPRALI (Gasprinsky 1851–1914), who along with leading 'Russian' Azerbaijanis such as Ali bey Huseynzada (1864–1941) and Ahmed bey Aghayev (1870–1938) took part in the Young Turk movement, propagated the ideas of Pan-Turkism and Turkish nationalism. They attacked the traditional Shi'a and hence pro-Persian stance of the Azerbaijani intelligentsia, and emphasized ethnic and linguistic ties over religious ones. Gasprinsky's newspaper *Tarjuman* (Interpreter), which attempted to develop a simplified Osmanli-based language for all Turks in Russia, had as its slogan 'unity of language, thought and work'.

Azerbaijani literati spearheaded the modernist trends among Russian Muslims. The first Turkic language Russian newspaper, *Akinchi* (The Ploughman) was published by an ex-Moscow University student in Baku (1875–1877). Clearly influenced by Russian POPULISM, it was addressed in simple style to the peasant reader and fiercely attacked the Shi'ite clergy's hold over the Azerbaijani peasantry. Thereafter the Azerbaijani press multiplied and by 1914 the largest number of Muslim periodicals in Russia was published in Baku.

The growing ethnic consciousness of Azerbaijani intellectuals was not shaped simply by ideas, but also by their rapidly changing environment. As a result of the oil boom, Baku increased its population from 14,000 in 1863 to 206,000 in 1903 and became the largest city in Transcaucasia. It was flooded by Armenian and Russian workers, and non-native businessmen took over most of the oil industry from the nascent Azerbaijani bourgeoisie. As backward Azerbaijani workers were squeezed to the bottom of the labour hierarchy, ethnic differences became accentuated by economic and social divisions. In this multi-lingual and competitive commercial environment, ethnicity, with 'its implied claim to privilege' (Karl Deutsch), became an important means of identification, although loyalty to Islam continued to dominate Azerbaijani consciousness. Political discrimination (limiting Azerbaijanis, as non Christians, to half the city Duma seats) also underlined for the Azerbaijani intelligentsia its ethno-religious distinctness.

In the tense atmosphere of 1905, religious, social and economic antagonisms between the Muslim and Armenian communities in Transcaucasia exploded into inter-communal violence. Azerbaijani political associations emerged for the first time. Azerbaijani leaders took an active part in the three All-Russian Muslim congresses of 1905–1906 leading to the formation of the Muslim Union Party. Closely aligned to the Kadets it demanded equal rights for all Russia's Muslims. After the October Manifesto, a group of Azerbaijani liberals demonstrated a greater regional particularism by forming a Muslim Constitutional Party in Baku. Socialist organizers also had some success among the only significant Muslim proletariat in Russia. In 1904 the Himmat, a Muslim social democratic organization affiliated to the RSDRP, was formed. Its socialism, however, was tempered with a strong Muslim Turkic particularism.

Although 1905 proved a watershed in the development of Azerbaijani political consciousness, the majority of Muslim peasants and semi-proletarians in the oil fields remained untouched by party ideologies. Azerbaijanis were the least revolutionized of the Transcaucasian population. Tsarist restrictions on political life between 1906 and 1914 diverted much Azerbaijani political attention to revolutionary events

in Persia and Turkey. Only the formation of Equality (Musavat) in 1911–1912, which soon developed from a vaguely socialist into a modern nationalist party, demonstrated that 1905 had proved an irrevocable step on the path of Azerbaijani nationhood.

The Armenians

Although Armenians lost the last vestiges of independent statehood in the fourteenth century and had their territories divided up between the Ottoman and Persian empires in the seventeenth century, they retained a strong sense of ethnic identity, and despite discrimination against them as a Christian minority, maintained peaceful relations with their Muslim neighbours until the nineteenth century. Of the approximately two million Armenians in the Ottoman empire in the mid nineteenth century, the majority were gathered in the six eastern *vilayets* (provinces) known collectively as Turkish Armenia. The Ottoman *millet* system allowed the Armenian community a degree of self-rule under the direction of their own national church and in Constantinople they played a dominant role in commercial life.

The Russian conquest of Transcaucasia was welcomed by the Armenians. They had long requested Russian (and European) protection against Muslim mistreatment and the Russo-Turkish treaty of Kutchuk Kainardji in 1774 established Russia's right to protect all orthodox christians in the Ottoman empire. Systematic Russian expansion into Transcaucasia in the first half of the nineteenth century led to the creation of an Armenian province, but it was not until the 1870s, after further annexation of Turkish territory, that the Armenian population grew significantly, reaching 1.75 million, or 22 per cent of the Transcaucasian population by 1917.

The rise of nationalism in the nineteenth century was disastrous for the Armenians. Stateless and in a minority in nearly every region they inhabited, they became the victims of national and religious intolerance. By 1917 Turkish Armenia, their traditional homeland, had been denuded of its Armenian population of more than two million by a brutal and systematic policy of turkification. Armenians were a threat to the increasingly nationalistic empire-builders in Asia Minor and the Caucasus because of their strong sense of ethnic separateness, their domination of trade and industry in the region, and their status as an international 'cause'.

By the second half of the nineteenth century, literacy, urbanization and increased communications, the impact of European revolutions and the anti-Ottoman national liberation struggles in the Balkans, provided the social and intellectual bases for a modern sense of nationhood among Armenians. The physical security of the Armenian community in Russia encouraged an educational and cultural renaissance. The Armenian church, permitted to expand its network of parochial schools (which provided an

233

increasingly secular education by the 1880s when they were closed down) promoted Armenian national culture, and children of the economically secure Armenian bourgeoisie, fired by ideas received in Russian and European universities, made Transcaucasia the centre of Armenian nationalism. Enraged by the oppression of Ottoman Armenians which after a series of massacres in the 1890s was perceived as a threat to the physical survival of the Armenian people, Armenians in Transcaucasia organized political parties dedicated to the liberation of their co-ethnics in Turkey.

Although the first political associations were among Ottoman Armenians, by the 1880s, disillusioned with the russification policies of Alexander III and by the failure of Armenian liberals and Western powers to ameliorate the position of the Turkish Armenians, the Transcaucasian Armenians began to organize revolutionary parties with programmes aimed at the Armenian peasantry and working class. Influenced by Russian Populism, Armenian activists led their own 'to the people' movement (the 'Depi Yerkir') and formed revolutionary parties dedicated to the Turkish Armenian cause, the most prominent of which were the Tocsin (Hnchak) and the Armenian Revolutionary Federation (Hai Heghapokhakan Dashnaktsutiun). Both parties split in attempting to straddle the Turkish and Transcaucasian Armenian communities as well as the opposing ideologies of socialism and nationalism, although by 1917 the Transcaucasian-nationalist axis had plainly won. Both parties adopted Russian socialist methods of organization and political terror, which was turned against tsarism following the sequestration of Armenian church property by the Russian state in 1903. This measure mobilized all sections of Armenian society around the Dashnaktsutiun and turned a loyal Armenian community into a hostile one ready to take advantage of tsarism's disarray in 1905.

By 1905, the Dashnaktsutiun was the leading party in both the Turkish and Transcaucasian Armenian communities; it was backed by a strong Armenian bourgeoisie which dominated Transcaucasian economic life and had penetrated the growing Armenian working class, particularly in Baku where Armenians made up approximately one quarter of the workforce. Armenian control of city life in Baku and Tiflis led to serious antagonism with the Azerbaijanis (in 1905) and Georgians (in 1917). 1905 politicized the Transcaucasian Armenian community and radicalized the Dashnaktsutiun, which after 1907 alienated much of its middle class support with its socialist rhetoric. In 1911 most of the party's leaders were arrested and put on trial.

The nationalistic mood of 1905 isolated the small Armenian social democratic organizations. One group, the Armenian social democratic workers' organization, tried to overcome this by crafting a programme specifically related to Transcaucasian problems and became known as the 'specificists'. They, along with all Armenian parties except the Hnchak, advocated not an independent Armenia, but

administrative and economic autonomy for a united Armenia within some form of socialist federation, aspirations that were thwarted by the realities of revolution and civil war.

The Georgians

Georgians, like Armenians, had a long history of independent statehood but after the thirteenth century, overrun by successive Mongol and Seljuk invasions, the Georgian kingdom lost its political and economic unity and became a loose conglomeration of independent feudatories subject to the Muslim Persian and Ottoman empires.

By the early decades of the nineteenth century, when Russia annexed Georgian territories, Georgians were a divided and defeated people reduced to a little over half a million with little sense of national identity. Like the Armenians they welcomed Russian protection against their traditional Muslim enemies and under Russian rule increased their population by 1917 to over two million. Of the three Transcaucasian nationalities, the Georgians were the most compact geographically, concentrated in a reasonably distinct geographical area in the western Transcaucasus.

Under Russian rule, bureaucratic organization, western style education and the commodity market transformed Georgians from a divided pre-modern people into a socially integrated nation. By the second half of the nineteenth century Tiflis (now Tbilisi), the capital of Georgia, was the commercial and administrative centre of a rapidly industrializing Transcaucasia. Between 1865 and 1902, its population increased from 67,000 to 190,000 with the Georgians making up just over a quarter. The total urban population of Georgia stood at 15.5 per cent at the turn of the century, an increase of over 10 per cent since 1830.

The abolition of serfdom in Georgia in the 1860s promoted mobility and hence national integration. In the new urban ethnic market-place Georgians were confronted by a powerful Armenian middle class which controlled city government, and by a Russian bureaucracy which directed administration and the courts in a foreign language. In this alien social environment where Georgians were a minority in their own native city and occupied low status positions (Georgians made up the majority of the factory workers), the Georgian intelligentsia inevitably raised national concerns.

Social and class issues became inextricably bound up with the national question. The intelligentsia's calls for democracy meant greater participation for Georgians in the direction of their own national life. Until the late 1890s when Georgian social democracy dominated political debate, the major concerns of the Georgian intelligentsia were, apart from civil reforms within the all-Russian context, the creation of a simplified Georgian 'people's' language, the promotion of literacy, the exploration of Georgian history and the formation of national solidarity.

From the 1860s onwards, an explosion of Georgian newspapers, journals, clubs and societies laid the ideological groundwork for Georgian nationalism. The outstanding proponents of the Georgian national idea were Ilya Chavchavadze (1837–1907) and Giorgi Tsereteli (1842–1900), leaders respectively of what later became known as the 'first' and 'second' groups.

In the last decade of the nineteenth century, a 'third group' of young Marxists emerged. Led by the future president of the Georgian Democratic Republic, Noi ZHORDANIA, by 1905 they had created a mass socialist (MENSHEVIK) party with broad social support. Within the Georgian context where a Georgian working class faced an Armenian bourgeoisie and a Russian colonial administration, national struggle reinforced the Marxist doctrine of class warfare. Georgian workers and peasants, anxious to avoid a national independence which would leave them vulnerable to their old Turkish enemy, but keen to be rid of foreign exploiters and attain economic security, found the socialist solution of Georgian self-rule in a democratized Russian state the most appealing. By 1905, the Georgian social democratic party, although part of the RSDRP, had become in effect one of the first Marxist national-liberation movements this century.

The 'general rehearsal' in Georgia was dominated by the Georgian social democrats. They organized massive support among the Georgian workers and peasants around a socialist platform (particularly in west Georgia where the peasant 'Gurian Republic' successfully excluded the tsarist administration from 1904 to 1906). Their strength was recognized by the Caucasian Viceroy who distributed arms to the party in November to help prevent bloodshed between Armenians and Azerbaijanis. The party directed general strikes and trade unions and led a workers' uprising in Tiflis in December. At the same time, in contrast to the BOLSHEVIKS, they enthusiastically pursued legal avenues and despite a decline in their support between 1906 and 1917, dominated Georgian representation in the Duma until the revolution. This period also witnessed the development of a specifically Georgian form of social democracy which eventually led to secession from the RSDRP in 1918.

SFJ

Transcaucasia: Revolution and Civil War

For the divided Armenian nation, the war proved a calamity. They suffered a million dead and were cruelly deceived with wartime promises of a free and autonomous Armenia by Russia and the Allies. The Armenian community in Turkey was extremely vulnerable and despite professions of loyalty to the Ottoman state, was decimated by Turkish armies answering the call for a holy war. The Azerbaijanis faced a dilemma in a war against their co-religionists, but on the whole their political leaders supported the Russian war effort, despite secret negotiations with Ottoman rulers concerning a possible independent Azerbaijan under Turkish protection (the Ottoman leaders also attempted secret pacts with the Dashnaktsutiun and Georgian nationalists). Ottoman hopes of an Azerbaijani revolt behind Russian lines were not fulfilled and when Turkish forces briefly occupied Persian Azerbaijan, Russian Azerbaijanis remained indifferent.

For the Georgians the war was a straightforward defence of Georgian territory against Turkey. There was initial disagreement among Georgian Mensheviks on whether to adopt an 'internationalist' or 'defensist' stand, but by October 1915 they had adopted the latter position. The Georgian Bolsheviks adopted a 'defeatist' policy which, given Georgian anti-Turkish feeling, minimalized their influence.

The February Revolution: Between December 1915 (when Russian forces inflicted a decisive defeat on the Turks) and February 1917, the Caucasian army gained successive victories, and the fall of the Romanov dynasty was a shock to Transcaucasians. Although all major political parties and SOVIETS, which sprang up in Transcaucasian cities, rallied behind the PROVISIONAL GOVERNMENT, the conflicting interests of the Transcaucasian nationalities were soon reflected in fractionalization of authority along ethnic as well as class lines. This was accentuated by the social structure of the Transcaucasian cities in 1917 where social and ethnic groups were mutually reinforcing. In Tiflis, for example, the working class was largely Georgian, the middle class, Armenian, and the peasantry – the 100,000 men in the Tiflis garrison – Russian. Thus the major parties, whatever their claims, inevitably acted for both social and ethnic interests; the Dashnaktsutiun for the bourgeois Armenians, the Social Democrats for the Georgian working class and the SRs for the Russian peasants. (See FEBRUARY REVOLUTION.)

The ethnic pattern was different in Baku, where Russians and Armenians were the majority of the skilled working class and the Azerbaijanis the unskilled. The small bourgeoisie was primarily Armenian. Despite the Baku soviet's appeal across national lines, the Dashnaktsutiun and the Musavat developed into 'mono-ethnic' parties with the Russians divided up between the Bolsheviks, Mensheviks and SRs. By autumn 1917, class loyalties had given way to ethnic allegiances.

The sudden political vacuum in February led to a scramble for power among a myriad of groups, organizations and institutions. Town, army and regional soviets with powerful executive committees sprang up alongside the parties; local government organizations such as the city Dumas claimed administrative powers, and the Provisional Government set up the multi-ethnic Special Transcaucasian Committee (Ozakom) with sovereign powers in the region. The Ozakom, however, had no power base and relied on rhetoric. It was in constant conflict with the local soviets and was undermined by the Provisional Government's failure to tackle the national question before the CON-STITUENT ASSEMBLY.

Throughout the spring and summer of 1917 these various organs competed for influence among the population. Real power lay with the Menshevik (Georgian-dominated) Tiflis Workers' Soviet and the SR (Russian-dominated) Tiflis Soldiers' Soviet (superseded by the Caucasian Army Regional Soviet in April). Both, despite formal unity in May, jealously maintained their autonomy.

In Baku, the Dashnaktsutiun-backed soviet, controlled by Mensheviks and SRs, shared power with an all-party Executive Committee of Public Organizations (IKOO) and the city Duma. The Azerbaijanis were the least revolutionized group in Baku and did not participate fully in the soviet until the autumn. However, by the summer of 1917, under the leadership of the Musavat and the Muslim National Council (formed in April 1917), they became an important political force, galvanized into mass action by food shortages and unemployment. Elections to the soviet in October (subsequently cancelled) and the Constituent Assembly in November showed the Musavat to be a leading party in Baku with support from both Muslim workers and peasants.

Throughout 1917 moderate socialists committed to the bourgeois revolution, unity with Russia, and the war held power in Transcaucasia (although the Musavat adopted an anti-war position after the failure of the June offensive). Divided on land and labour reform, the parties were united in avoiding inter-ethnic strife which could lead to a bloodbath. The Tiflis Soviet threatened to expel any parties agitating for political autonomy, and agitation at the front by any party was forbidden. The Transcaucasian Bolsheviks (except in Baku under Stepan SHAUMYAN) also participated in united front policies and were reluctant to split from the Mensheviks, despite party policy. They had little support among the civil population, for example performing poorly in elections to the Tiflis city Duma (July) and various soviets; however, events in Russia, and a deteriorating military and supply situation at home combined to work in their favour, particularly in the army. The soldiers, led more by their own committees than their officers, rapidly swung to the left. At a re-election of the soldiers' section of the Tiflis Soviet in June, the Bolsheviks attained the highest number of seats and by December they achieved a majority at the second Caucasian Army Congress. From June onwards, soldiers' meetings under Bolshevik guidance called for unconditional peace and 'all power to the soviets'. The Bolsheviks, however, did not attempt to use the army to achieve power, and by January 1918, their power base had vanished along with the soldiers departing for Russia.

Between February and October 1917 the major parties consolidated their ethnic bases. Separate 'national' bureaux or councils appeared with armed national militias at their disposal (in the Azerbaijani case, not until May 1918). Although none of these 'national' organs demanded independence, their political and territorial claims were often incompatible with those of their neighbours. After October, faced by an increasingly threatening Turkey, Transcaucasian parties began to think urgently of national self-defence; in these conditions, mutually incompatible national demands became real problems of power.

The October Revolution: Georgian Mensheviks envisaged national cultural autonomy for Georgia within a unitary Russian state and, although disillusioned with the Provisional Government, were committed to defending the bourgeois revolution from foreign attack. In response to the Bolshevik coup, they called for a socialist coalition government and the peaceful liquidation of the new Sovnarkom (see LENIN'S GOVERNMENT). The Dashnaktsutiun adopted a similar position. The Armenians feared that Bolshevik defeatism would end their dream of an autonomous Turkish Armenia. At the same time, still pro-Russian in orientation, they secretly negotiated with Bolshevik leaders to try to obtain some form of protection against the Turks. This ambivalent attitude to Bolshevism was shared by the Musavat (who recognized the Sovnarkom), but for different reasons. Like the Bolsheviks, the Azerbaijani leaders wanted an end to a war against their co-ethnics and found the Bolshevik nationality programme, which stressed both national self-determination and liberation for the Muslims, compatible with their idea of an autonomous Azerbaijan. This changed when Soviet power began its struggle with the numerous autonomy-seeking Muslim authorities in Russia, and during the 'March days' in Baku the Azerbaijanis fought against the Bolshevik soviet.

Transcaucasian federalism

Between October 1917 and April 1918, Transcaucasian leaders both repudiated and practised independence at the same time. In conditions of inter-ethnic strife, war with Turkey, and an impossible supply situation, an attempt was made to bury national differences in a Transcaucasian federation, but the intensified demands of national self-interest proved too strong.

The first attempt at cooperation after the Bolshevik coup was the creation of the Transcaucasian Commissariat (November), with eleven members from various parties and national groups. The Commissariat, under Georgian Menshevik influence, put forward an ambitious programme of reform but was powerless to impose its will on strong national councils, and in the five months of its existence failed to implement it. The most divisive issue was the war, and the failure of the Transcaucasian leaders to agree on peace terms with Turkey eventually brought down the fragile federal edifice. Before this, however, the Commissariat faced two major challenges from the Bolsheviks.

The first was from the Bolshevik-oriented soldiers returning from the Caucasian front who presented a potential military threat to the Commissariat. A serious conflict was narrowly averted when a refusal to distribute arms to the Commissariat by the local Artillery Committee was followed by a Menshevik seizure of the Tiflis Arsenal. The military threat was only removed when troops began to return home encouraged by a Commissariat order to demobilize in mid December. The second challenge to the Commissariat came with the dispersal of the Constituent Assembly in January 1918. The question of supreme authority in the region became urgent and the Georgian Mensheviks, rapidly losing hope of continued union with Russia, proposed a Sejm (parliament) based on the local results of the elections. Despite opposition from the SRs, Dashnaktsutiun and Bolsheviks, who all saw the move as separatist, a Menshevik-Musavat alliance secured its formation in February 1918. Of the 112 representatives in the Transcaucasian Sejm there were 33 Menshevik, 30 Musavat, 27 Dashnaktsutiun, seven Muslim Socialist Bloc, four Himmat, three Muslims of Russia and one each from the Georgian National Democrats, the Social Federalists and the Kadets. The Sejm, which lasted 105 days, proved as powerless before the national soviets as the Commissariat. It failed to introduce urgent reforms essential for regional stability and foundered on national conflicts over peace negotiations with Turkey.

Relations with Turkey: The collapse of the Caucasian army and the disintegration of Russia revived Turkey's expansionist goals. Ottoman leaders, wanting a weak and manipulable state on their north-eastern borders, proposed that peace negotiations be preceded by a declaration of Transcaucasian independence. Having rejected an invitation to attend the Brest-Litovsk negotiations as a separate delegation, Transcaucasian leaders lamely repeated the argument that such a decision rested with the Constituent Assembly. In February 1918, Ottoman army leaders, taking advantage of Transcaucasian prevarication and Russian weakness, advanced into territory lost to Russia during the war on the pretence of defending Muslims from Armenian brutality. Recently formed Armenian and Georgian national corps were powerless. In early March, when a Transcaucasian peace delegation had finally assembled, Ottoman leaders presented the Transcaucasians with new demands (the annexation of Kars, Ardahan and Batumi districts) based on the Brest-Litovsk negotiations. After acrimonious debate in a divided Sejm, a delegation was sent to negotiate, but further Ottoman advance into Transcaucasian territory and an ultimatum to evacuate Batumi pushed the Sejm into a declaration of war (despite Musavat dissent). After eight days of resistance, the defeated Transcaucasians were forced to return to the negotiating table in Turkish-occupied Batumi. Under intense Turkish pressure, on 22 April, the Rejm reluctantly declared the

independent Democratic Federal Republic of Transcaucasia with Akaki Chkhenkeli, a Georgian Menshevik, its first premier. He rapidly conceded Transcaucasian territories agreed at Brest-Litovsk, arousing Armenian recriminations, but was unable to hold together either the peace delegation or the new federation when Turkey advanced deep into (Armenian populated) Erevan and Tiflis provinces, assisted by local Muslims. In the face of such intolerable pressures, both the peace delegation and the cabinet began to disintegrate amid mutual accusations of betrayal.

The March Days, 1918: In Baku, where the Bolsheviks had skilfully taken control of the soviet, Armeno-Muslim hatred erupted in the 'March Days', when the two groups indulged in mutual slaughter resulting in over three thousand dead. It was both an ethnic collision and a clash between a Dashnaktsutiun-Bolshevik alliance defending the revolutionary soviet and a conservative force of Muslims backed by Turkish units intent on retrieving Baku for the Islamic world.

'Balkanization': independent republics

During the Batumi peace conference, Georgian Mensheviks, fearing Turkey, made a secret agreement with the German Reich offering wide economic and political concessions in return for the recognition and defence of Georgian independence. On 26 May, the Sejm met for the last time and Irakli TSERETELI of Petrograd fame declared Transcaucasian unity a fiction and announced Georgia's intention to declare independence (which it did that same day). The Azerbaijanis did so two days later and the Armenians, reduced to a tiny landlocked area of 4,500 square miles, reluctantly followed suit on 30 May, manifesting their doubts about losing Russian protection by making no reference to an independent republic until June.

The new governments were confronted by the problems of chronic food shortages, empty treasuries, industrial collapse, peasant unrest, foreign rule, inter-ethnic strife, and lack of experienced personnel. Territorial squabbles (including wars) characterized their relations and damaged their standing among Western powers determining their future: each republic needed skilful diplomacy in relations with the powers contending for domination in Transcaucasia.

A major factor in Transcaucasia following the Central powers' defeat was the British occupation. British policy in the region was confused and despite official statements in support of self-determination, the interests of the Transcaucasian nationalities were never taken seriously. There were wide disagreements within the cabinet and among officers in Transcaucasia as to their purpose in the region. Commercial gain, the Indian border, anti-Bolshevik aid, a revived Turkish threat to British interests were all cited to justify occupation, yet British troops were withdrawn by

July 1920. The British spent much of their time in the region mediating between the territorially aggressive republics; the latter, although disillusioned by British rule and suspicious of their championship of DENIKIN, attempted to persuade them to adopt a Transcaucasian mandate. The British remained unconvinced, and although they and the Allies recognized the *de facto* independence of the republics, they provided no real aid, civil or military.

Independent Azerbaijan

Independent Azerbaijan, which lasted just under two years, was the most politically heterogeneous of the republics, reflected by the instability of its political executive (five coalition cabinets in twenty-three months). The Musavat predominated, with the Muslim Socialist Bloc and the Himmat (Menshevik) comprising the second largest parliamentary group. The conservative coalition of landowners and industrialists, however, blocked most attempts at economic or social reform. Chronic economic problems beset the new state. Cut off by the CIVIL WAR from Russian and foreign markets, reduced oil revenues and deficit financing caused rocketing inflation and high unemployment; postponement of land reform caused peasant unrest. The government nevertheless expanded education and led an effective campaign of turkification.

Azerbaijani foreign relations: Baku oil, coveted by the Bolsheviks, Turks, Germans, British and the VOLUNTEER ARMY, made Azerbaijan a strategically vital area. After the Ottoman defeat, the greatest threat came from the Volunteer Army. Hostile to Muslim separatism, in 1918–19 General Denikin invaded the North Caucasus Mountain Republic and Daghestan, and stopped at the Azerbaijani border only on British insistence. Yet British attitudes were unclear; many senior officers in Transcaucasia sympathized with the Azerbaijani government but the politicians at home, suspicious of its Pan-Turkic leanings, were generally hostile. Seeking security, the Azerbaijanis entered negotiations with both Mustafa Kemal's new nationalist Turkey and the Bolsheviks, and also made a mutual defence pact with Georgia. Relations with Armenia proved intractable and were characterized by intermittent war.

Independent Armenia

Armenia, the most disadvantaged of the republics geographically and economically, was in a catastrophic position on the eve of its independence. War had decimated its economy, population and territory; the tiny landlocked area left under its control, lacking commercial, administrative or transport facilities, was crowded with starving refugees and in the first year over 200,000 Armenians died of disease and famine. The first Armenian government, a coalition dominated by the Dashnaktsutiun, attempted to construct administrative and financial order. A multi-party legislature (Khorhurd) was elected in the summer of 1919 and democratic reforms were introduced into the judiciary and local government. Vital land reforms were not implemented, however, and the agricultural crisis remained so acute that only American relief prevented unbearable human cost. In the fight for political and economic survival, socialism was forgotten; even democracy seemed superfluous, and in the final government crisis before Sovietization the Dashnaktsutiun bureau simply took over from the cabinet.

Armenian foreign relations: Despite Allied wartime pledges (particularly from the USA) to free Armenia from Ottoman oppression, the new republic received little aid from Western governments, but the Armenians' expectations led to their local isolation. They rejected policies of Transcaucasian solidarity and refused to compromise their territorial demands. The Georgians and Azerbaijanis were equally stubborn, and Armenia fought wars against both its neighbours when it could least afford it. The bitterness of the Transcaucasian territorial struggles not only undermined the republics' political and economic stability but alienated the Allied powers. Armenian leaders anticipated that Versailles would establish an independent state incorporating Turkish Armenia, but Armenia's fate was forgotten as the Allies squabbled over spheres of influence in the decaying Ottoman empire. By 1920, as Mustafa Kemal's star rose in eastern Turkey, Armenian leaders feared that Western promises of salvation were illusory, a fear confirmed in 1922 when Turkey and the Allies signed the Lausanne Treaty, in which no mention of Armenia was made at all.

Independent Georgia

The Georgian Democratic Republic is the only example of a Menshevik state. Committed to orthodox Marxist principles of revolutionary stages, the Georgian Mensheviks declared the revolution bourgeois and encouraged a mixed economy and political pluralism. Soviet power was peacefully transferred to a multi-party parliament in which the Mensheviks enjoyed an overwhelming majority although the Georgian Red Guard (later renamed the National Guard) remained a volatile and radical element. The Mensheviks had much wider national support than either the Dashnaktsutiun or Musavat, with a firm base in both the working class and peasantry (the party's membership was 80,000 in 1920). However, they faced serious problems of disaffection among their own minorities such as the Ossets, Adzhars (Muslim Georgians) and Abkhazians. The Georgian National Guard dealt harshly with minority unrest which led to accusations of national chauvinism against the Georgian leaders. Georgianization of government and the courts was also a key element in Georgian Menshevik policy.

Like their neighbours, the Georgians faced a catastrophic economic situation aggravated by the Allied blockade and the Civil War. Serious unemployment, inadequate supplies to the city and deficit financing led to hyper-inflation. Nevertheless, the government introduced social and economic reforms, although many remained on paper. The workers (4 per cent of the population in 1918–21) were helped to form trade unions and cooperatives, although strikes were discouraged and industrial arbitration courts were set up; land reform (selling confiscated land to the peasantry) was tardy but reasonably successful, although there was insufficient land to satisfy peasant expectations.

Georgian foreign relations: Georgia's independence depended on its leaders' diplomatic skill. The Georgians, like their neighbours, had difficulty in convincing the Allies of the validity of independent republics in Transcaucasia. Hampered by their socialist status and their cooperation with Germany at the end of the war, their relations with British officers were poor and the young state got little from the Allies beyond recognition (*de facto* in January 1920, *de jure* in January 1921).

Georgian leaders, although Marxists, proved inflexible on territorial issues, and wars ensued with both the Volunteer Army (early 1919) and Armenia (October 1918). Relations with Azerbaijan, despite territorial disputes, were better. With Denikin's reversals and the British departure in 1920, Georgian leaders attempted diplomacy to deflect the new Bolshevik threat; a treaty recognizing Georgia's independence was negotiated with Soviet Russia in May 1920 but it did not prevent the Bolshevik invasion ten months later.

End of independence
Bolshevism was never strong among Transcaucasian natives with the exception of Baku where there was a sizeable Armenian cadre. Between 1917 and 1921, particularly after the fall of the Baku Commune, the Bolshevik organizations, coordinated by the Caucasian Regional Committee (Kavkraikom), were cut off from the centre. They had almost no influence although they attempted to incite rebellion against the Transcaucasian government several times.

Despite Soviet statements on the right to self-determination, Soviet practice soon threatened Transcaucasian independence. The Kavkraikom rejected all plans of federalism or autonomy, although by 1920, thanks to Anastas Mikoyan, a new policy of independent Soviet republics was enforced.

The fall of the three republics, Azerbaijan in April 1920, Armenia in December 1920 and Georgia in February 1921, was achieved by the RED ARMY; the local Bolshevik organizations were too weak to seize power. Internal weakness in Azerbaijan and Armenia, and Turkish cooperation with Soviet Russia, made them easy prey. The decision (later sanctioned by the Bolshevik Central Committee) to invade Georgia was made by the Caucasian

Bureau (Kavburo) led by the Georgian Bolshevik Sergo Ordzhonikidze. The Georgian government was overthrown by a purely military operation lasting approximately five weeks.   SFJ

Further Reading
Bennigsen, Alexandre and Lemercier-Quelquejay, Chantal: *Islam in the Soviet Union.* London: Pall Mall Press, 1967.

Blank, S.: Bolshevik organizational development in early Soviet Transcaucasia: autonomy vs. centralization, 1918–1924. In *Transcaucasia: Nationalism and Social Change*, ed. R.G. Suny. pp. 305–38. Ann Arbor: University of Michigan, 1983.

Hovannisian, R.G.: *Armenia on the Road to Independence.* Berkeley and Los Angeles: University of California Press, 1967.

Jones, S.F.: Russian Imperial administration and the Georgian nobility: the Georgian conspiracy of 1832. *The Slavonic and East European Review* 65.1 (1987) 53–76.

Suny, R.G.: *The Baku Commune 1917–1918: Class and Nationality in the Russian Revolution.* Princeton, NJ: Princeton University Press, 1972.

Swietochowski, T.: *Russian Azerbaijan 1905–20. The Shaping of National Identity in a Muslim Community.* London and New York: Cambridge University Press, 1985.

Central Asia before 1917
Central Asia, or more accurately, Russian/Soviet Central Asia is the physical-geographic and administrative-cultural entity occupying the Eurasian heartland of the Soviet Union and stretching from the Caspian Sea (in the west) to the Sino-Soviet border (in the east); from the borders with Afghanistan and Iran (in the south) to the Aral-Irtysh line, the Balkash basin, and the Kazakh Steppes (in the north). This area, which until 1924 was known as Turkestan, today roughly corresponds to the territories of the Uzbek, Turkmen, Kirghiz, Tadzhik, and Kazakh republics.

The remarkable cultural unity of Central Asia, defying its turbulent past and its more recent administrative fragmentation, has its roots in the early middle ages and rests on the twin pillars of ethnicity and religion. With the exception of the Tadzhiks, the majority of the people of the vast area of the heart of the Eurasian continent are of Turkic stock and their history has been shaped by Islam since the seventh century. Although grouped in separate territorial units drawn along ethnic lines, the peoples of the Kazakh, Uzbek, Kirghiz, and Turkmen republics have a keen awareness of belonging to a Turkic commonwealth and of sharing its world outlook.

Throughout the centuries, Central Asia's history has been shaped by the tensions between two patterns of life: nomadic and settled (villages and cities). In the nineteenth century, both ways of life experienced the increasing pressures of the eastward push of the Russian empire. The three khanates of Bukhara, Khiva and Kokand, which had emerged in the seventeenth century as the chief political,

Muslim entities, eventually succumbed to the Russian armies because, in addition to their military inferiority, their rivalries and their never-ending internecine strife had rendered them powerless.

With the exception of the protectorates of Khiva and Bukhara, the conquered lands were integrated into the administrative structure of the Russian empire without delay. The conquest of the Syr Darya and the Semirechye region led to the organization in 1867 of the General Governorship of Turkestan (with the centre at Tashkent) which was placed under a military administration responsible to the War Ministry.

The conquered Transcaspian lands were organized in 1874 as the Transcaspian Military Region under the jurisdiction of the Caucasian Board. In the 1880s, the area was subject to two administrative reorganizations only to be integrated later into the General Governorship of Turkestan. The fall of Kokand led in 1876 to its annexation as the Fergana region.

By the time of its conquest of Central Asia, the Russian state had had three centuries of experience in dealing with a conquered Muslim population and adopted a typical colonial policy. The Muslims were not considered subjects, but aliens, and were allowed to conform to the norms of *Shariat*, the Muslim law. St Petersburg did not pursue a planned policy toward the native population, yet certain long-term goals can be identified. There was no attempt to 'westernize' or russify Central Asia. The only islands of European culture were those of the Russian settlers and colonizers who lived among but apart from the Central Asians, in their own enclaves. On the contrary, Russian adminstrators encouraged scholasticism and religious conservatism, isolated the country from outside influences whether from other Muslim areas of the Russian empire or from other Muslim countries, for fear of contaminating the region with ideas of modern nationalism. They adopted similar policies in the Kazakh Steppes which were incorporated even earlier.

In the Steppe region, a number of tribes (the future Kazakhs) which had emerged as a result of the biological assimilation between the Turkic tribes and the Mongols, broke off from the declining Golden Horde in 1456, and formed three distinct hordes occupying the territory of present-day Kazakhstan: Great in Semirechye, Middle in the Central Steppe region and Little in the area between the Aral and the Caspian Seas. The energies of the hordes were spent as much in fighting each other as in responding to the challenges posed by intruders; *Manas*, the national epic of the Kazakhs, praises the deeds of the heroes who rose to meet those challenges.

The incursions of the Dzhungarian Oirots (Kalmyks) from Mongolia into the Kazakh lands brought devastation and prompted the Khans of the three hordes to ask for Russian protection, their outright incorporation into the Russian state being accomplished in the first half of the nineteenth century. The Russian garrison established in Vernyi (now Alma-Ata) in 1854, and the arrival of the first Russian settlers were the most tangible testimonies of the dramatic change in the status of the Steppes. Unlike some other groups of aliens, for example the Jews, Tatars, Azeris, the Kazakhs were not liable to military service under Russian law; they retained a degree of self government and continued to adhere to their traditional customary law.

Kazakh reformism

Only a few decades after the annexation, however, the Russian government identified with concern the role which the Volga Tatar merchants, teachers, and mullahs were playing in acquainting the Kazakhs among whom they had settled with ideas of Turkic kinship and unity and Islamic brotherhood, and in response devised a policy aimed at eliminating the danger of 'tatarization' while promoting russification. The government plan included some measures barring Tatar teachers from Kazakh educational institutions while others provided the creation of Russo-Kazakh schools.

Ironically, the first generation of Kazakhs (mainly belonging to the nobility) educated in these schools were to become the 'Kazakh enlighteners' who would lay the foundations for the process of reform and renewal known as jadidism. By questioning the value of the unchallenged acceptance of tradition, educated Kazakhs such as Ch. Valikhanov (1835–65), I. Altynsarin (1841–89) and A. Kunanbaev (1845–1904) searched for answers in their quest for progress. Whatever their specific contributions, they all agreed on the importance of education. Altynsarin was responsible for introducing Kazakh as the language of instruction in the Russo-Kazakh schools.

The pioneering work of the enlighteners was continued by the generation of the jadid reformers, represented by A. Bukeykhanov (1869–1932), M. Dulatov (1885–1937) and A. Baytursun (1873–1937). The lives and careers of these Kazakh intellectuals illustrate eloquently the transition of jadid reformism from a purely cultural phenomenon to a movement increasingly interested in social reform and political change. The Kazakh press which was born in the years after the 1905 Revolution articulated the most urgent concerns of the Kazakhs. Newspapers such as *Kazakhstan, Ishim dalasï* (The Steppe of Ishim), *Ay-Kap* (Flight), and *Kazak* addressed the issue of land, Russian colonization and its impact, and were increasingly sensitive to a nascent nationalism. The best illustration of the immense gap the Kazakhs had closed in 'entering the twentieth century' was their political socialization.

As ephemeral and limited as the political experience of all the peoples of the Russian empire was, it is remarkable that the Kazakhs sent four representatives to the First and Second Dumas and when they finally joined the third Muslim Congress (1906), their delegate, Sh. Koshchegulov, was elected to the presidium. Most of the jadids advocated using the best of what the west and Russia had to offer, 'working within the system' in order to advance the progress of their people. Their position was challenged by the conservative clergy which regarded jadidism as a 'heresy' and a betrayal of the values of Islam. The Russian authorities supported the conservatives who were advocating isolationism, since it posed no challenge to their monopoly of power.

Turkestan reformism

In Turkestan and the two protectorates, as in the Kazakh Steppes, the jadids and the conservatives confronted each other on the issue of schools and the jadids ultimately prevailed due to the financial support they received from a wealthy commercial bourgeoisie which welcomed new ideas conducive to enlightenment and progress. Interestingly enough, a purely cultural organization, the Union of Holy Bukhara, initially organized to promote the jadid system of education, became the nucleus from which in 1909 the secret revolutionary society of the Young Bukharans would be born. Its programme included demands for reform and criticisms of the emir's policies and clergy's conservatism. The ideas of the Young Bukharans found support in the Khanate of Khiva where a Young Khivan party of jadids emerged.

Jadid newspapers such as *Tarakki* (Progress), *Tujjar* (Merchant), *Shohrat* (Fame), and *Khurshid* (The Sun) supported the cultural as well as socio-economic and political goals of the jadids who in their majority were liberals. *Khurshid* advocated that Central Asians adhere to the political party of the Muslims, Ittifak-ul-Muslimin, and Central Asian delegations to the Duma did, in fact, support Ittifak when they sent six delegates to the Second Duma. For technical reasons, Central Asians were absent from the First Duma, and the new electoral law passed after the dissolution of the Second Duma in June, 1907, deprived Central Asia of participation because of the prevailing unrest in the area.

Much of the unrest had been caused by bands of poor native peasants who until 1905–6 plundered at random, but after 1906 gained coherence, focus, and the support of the local population as they emerged as an anti-Russian movement.

1905

The 1905 REVOLUTION did not bring together the Russians and the natives. It remained a purely Russian phenomenon because the emergence of Russian political organizations had not affected in any fashion the lives of the Muslim communities.

Neither the eclectic (SR, BOLSHEVIK, MENSHEVIK) Revolutionary Group of Tashkent, nor its counterparts in, for example, Ashkhabad, Samarkand, sought to attract the native population. The SDs saw the failed 1905 Revolution

as a missed opportunity and they began emphasizing the need to work among the native population. They never closed the gap, however, and were certainly no bridge builders for, despite their radicalism, they exhibited an aloofness to the needs of the native population which was unhappy with the stand of the official Administration on the land issue, a burning issue in Turkestan and Kazakhstan, particularly in view of the pressures and the economic and social crisis caused by the arrival of the Russian settlers. It was against the background of this simmering discontent that the imperial decree of 25 June, 1916, triggered a major revolt which had a clear anti-Russian character. The decree called for a labour draft of all Central Asian *inorodtsy* in 25 age categories, thus changing their conscription-status and awakening new suspicions about the Russian government's intentions.

By the end of the year, the revolt had been quelled but thousands of Russian settlers, and as many Muslims had been killed; entire Kirghiz villages had been burned, prompting a mass exodus of the Kirghiz to China and on the eve of the FEBRUARY REVOLUTION the cloud of animosity and distrust that darkened the skies of Central Asia was not the result of class antagonism and class struggle, but rather the tangible proof of the irreconcilable interests of the natives and their Russian colonizers.

A-AR

Further Reading

Allworth, E.: *Central Asia: A Century of Russian Rule.* New York and London: 1967.

Bacon, E.: *Central Asia Under Russian Rule.* Ithaca: 1966.

Bennigsen, A. and Lemercier-Quelquejay, Ch.: *Islam in the Soviet Union.* New York: 1967.

Carrère d'Encausse, H.: *Réforme et révolution chez les Musulmans de l'empire russe: Bukhara 1867–1927.* Paris: 1966.

Suleimenov, B.S. and Basin, V.Ya.: *Vosstanie 1916 goda v Kazakhstane.* Alma-Ata: 1977.

Central Asia: Revolution and Civil War

The February revolution raised expectations of the Muslims of Central Asia and the Kazakh Steppes prompting their increased participation in the political life of the area.

One of the immediate results of the revolution in Central Asia was the arrest of Kuropatkin, the governor general of Turkestan on April 7 1917, and the organization of a nine-member Turkestan Committee of the PROVISIONAL GOVERNMENT. Its president was a Russian Constitutional Democrat, N. N. Shchepkin and its members were equally divided between Russians and Muslims, of whom two were Tatars and only two were Central Asians, M. Tanyshbaev and A. BUKEYKHANOV.

The Turkestan Committee, however, had little power, because the Provisional Government wielded no authority in Central Asia. The real authority was the Soviet of

241

Tashkent, a body mainly in the hands of the Bolsheviks and Socialist Revolutionaries which, despite it political profile, perpetuated the colonial stand of the old regime by barring Muslim participation in its affairs. The arrogance of the Tashkent Soviet was matched by the aloofness of the Provisional Government in Petrograd which continued to ignore national aspirations of the non-Russians throughout the spring and summer of 1917 and declared only on 26 September, 1917, that the issue of self-determination would be addressed by the future CONSTITUENT ASSEMBLY.

The Muslim response was to move to build its own political infrastructure. Thus in March 1917 the jadid reformers organized a Muslim Council, while the conservatives set up the Society of Scholars, their joint meeting in Tashkent, 16–23 April, being the First Congress of the Muslims of Turkestan, which brought together 450 delegates to discuss the political future of Central Asia, its relationship with the Russian state. While no decision was taken on the latter issue, the delegates passed resolutions demanding a halt to Russian colonization, a solution to the land problem, and they also elected a Central Council of Turkestani Muslims, known as the National Centre. Mustafa CHOKAEV, the leading Kazakh jadid, was elected president of the National Centre which comprised representatives of all Central Asian territories: M. Behbudi (Bukhara), U. Khodzhaev, A. Khodzhaev and N. Töre (Fergana), M. Tynyshbaev (Semirechye), and O. Sardar (the Turkmen lands).

In the Kazakh Steppes the February revolution prompted changes in the highest echelons of the administration, while leaving the lower levels untouched. Thus, Tynyshbaev and Bukeykhanov emerged as the Provisional Government's representatives in Semirechye and the Turgay region, respectively. In March 1917 a group of moderate nationalist intellectuals, including A. Bukeykhanov, A. BAYTURSUN, M. DULATOV, H. Dost-muhammedov, M. Tynyshbaev, A. Zhuzhdybaev, Ö. Ömerov and M. Zhumubaev, organized the liberal nationalist Kazakh political party ALASH ORDA, whose programme exhibited clear Menshevik and SR influence and a commitment to local Kazakh interests, rather than lofty Pan-Turkist or Pan-Islamist goals.

The Kazakh leaders who supported the Provisional Government won a victory at the First Kazakh (called Kirghiz at that time) Congress in Orenburg, April 1917. Their demands for limited administrative autonomy and increased cultural autonomy, especially in the use of the Kazakh language, were endorsed by the Congress.

The Muslims of Central Asia and the Kazakh Steppes sent representatives to the First Pan-Russian Muslim Congress held in Moscow 1–11 May, 1917. While the Congress remained divided over the administrative political relationship between the Muslims and the Russian state, the delegates from Central Asia argued for territorial autonomy for their regions. Neither the Central Asian

delegates, nor those of the Kazakh Steppes participated in the Second Pan-Russian Muslim Congress in Kazan in July 1917. The Central Asians were prevented from participating mainly because of travel restrictions imposed by KORNILOV's offensive, but the Kazakh absence from Kazan was deliberate and represented a symbolic protest to what was perceived as Tatar domination of Muslim politics in the Russian empire. Consequently, the Muslims of Central Asia and the Steppes chose to articulate their specific problems at regional congresses, thus intensifying their involvement in local politics.

At the second Kazakh Congress 21–26 July 1917 in Orenburg, preference was expressed for a federation as the basis of Kazakh-Russian relations and an autonomous religious board, as a measure of 'emancipation' from Tatar tutelage as represented by the Ufa Muftiat (religious board). Although the general tone of this congress was not hostile towards the Russians, a dissident group of more radical Kazakh nationalists from Turkestan province adopted an anti-Russian stand. A third Kazakh congress, convened by the leaders of Alash Orda in December 1917, proclaimed Kazakh autonomy and elected a committee presided over by A. Bukeykhanov, which became the nucleus of the twin governments of eastern and western Alash Orda.

By the spring of 1919, having failed to attract any support from the White forces, the jadid leaders of both governments had accepted an alliance with the Bolsheviks. On 10 July 1919, the Kirghiz (i.e. Kazakh) Revolutionary Commitee (Kirrevkom) was organized as a first step towards setting up the new Kazakh government which included Russians as well as former Alash Orda leaders, such as Baytursun and Bukeykhanov. After liquidating the entire Alash Orda apparatus on 9 March 1920, Kirrevkom proclaimed the organization of the Kazakh Autonomous Soviet Socialist Republic on 26 August 1920.

As for Central Asians, the Second Congress of the Muslims of Turkestan opened in Tashkent on 3 September 1917, representing the broadest spectrum of the population from workers to religious scholars. In order to end Central Asia's dependence on European Russia for food, the Congress called for a harmonious balance between cotton and grain cultivation, while the political goals of the Turkestanis were defined as the organization of an autonomous republic of Turkestan which, though linked to Russia on a federative basis, would nevertheless enjoy its own institutions based on Islamic law.

Events taking place almost simultaneously in Tashkent, however, were to overwhelm these aims. On 12 September 1917 an uprising was organized by Russian Bolsheviks against the Provisional Government. Despite claims to the contrary by Soviet historiography, there was no Muslim participation in this uprising, it was a purely Russian affair and the resolutions adopted at its 13 September meeting were Bolshevik in nature: nationalization of banks, confiscation of landed estates and the transfer of all power to the Soviets.

1917 and after

The Tashkent uprising was quelled in a few days, but the Provisional Government, which had not established effective control over Central Asia even before this open challenge, was virtually paralysed. News of the OCTOBER REVOLUTION gave further impetus to the Soviets of Central Asia who rejected the Provisional Government and supported a Bolshevik-led uprising and the proclamation of Soviet power on 1 November 1917. This, too, was a purely Russian affair. On 2 November, SRs and Mensheviks of the Tashkent Executive Committee tried to counterbalance the almost unchallenged power of the Bolsheviks by proposing that the nine-member Coalition Committee make room for two Central Asians. A Revolutionary Coalition Committee, did eventually emerge, but without a single Muslim among its members.

The proclamation of Soviet power in Central Asia was followed by the meeting of the Third Congress of Turkestan Soviets. This gathering, in addition to proclaiming that throughout Southern Central Asia power was vested in the Soviets, announced the formation of the Turkestan Soviet of People's Commissars (Sovnarkom, see LENIN'S GOVERNMENT), and also addressed some proposals put forward by the Third Congress of Central Asian Muslims which was meeting at the same time. The conservative Ulāma Jamiyäti expressed willingness to join a coalition, while the moderate jadid Shura-i-Islam demanded local autonomy. The decision of the Congress was negative on both matters and reflected the Bolshevik view as expressed by the Sovnarkom chairman, Kolesov: 'It is not possible to admit the Muslims into the supreme organ of revolutionary power because the attitude of the local population towards us is uncertain and because it does not possess any proletarian organization.' This response reflected the political arrogance of the Tashkent Soviet, its political myopia and its failure to understand and capitalize on the weaknesses of the Muslim political groups.

Kokand: The immediate effect on the Muslims was twofold: further alienation from the Russians and an increased awareness of the urgency of unity around the Central Council of Turkestani Muslims. Consequently, Kokand, the old capital city of the Fergana Khanate became the seat of an All-Turkestani Muslim Congress which opened on 22 November 1917. Of the 200 delegates present, 150 were from Fergana, 22 from Syr Darya, 23 from Samarkand, four from Bukhara and one from the Transcaspian region.

The Kokand Congress entered negotiations with the Bolshevik leadership in Tashkent on the issue of autonomy, but at the end of November, discouraged by the response, the Congress declared Southern Central Asian autonomy. A twelve-member government (People's Council) was organized, with M. Chokaev as president, after a brief tenure of office by M. Tynyshbaev. The example of Kokand proved a powerful magnet for the Muslims of Tashkent and elsewhere in Central Asia who began agitating for autonomy. Encouraged by these developments, the Kokand Government approached Moscow and demanded official recognition, thus precipitating Moscow's decision to liquidate Kokand.

On 6 February 1918 Bolshevik forces, including Red Guards, the armed militia of the Armenian Dashnaktsutyun and units of the Tashkent garrison, launched the assault on Kokand. The Kokand Government was virtually powerless. Its attempts at securing allies and money had failed: the decision to float a loan in January 1918 had led to a domestic crisis, negotiations with Alash Orda and Ataman Dutov had proved futile and the emir of Bukhara maintained a safe distance from the jadid-dominated Kokand Government. The small Muslim detachment that was Kokand's only defence force was easily overcome by the superior Red forces which, after a three-day massacre that annihilated almost sixty per cent of the population, burned the city. The fall of Kokand triggered the beginning of armed resistance, the BASMACHI guerrilla movement against the Bolshevization of Central Asia.

The Basmachis and the overall volatile situation caused by the Red troops in Central Asia, prompted the Bolshevik government in Moscow to open an investigation in Tashkent. Moscow's envoy was P. A. Kobozev, whose presence precipitated the proclamation of the Turkestan Autonomous Republic on 30 April 1918, by the Fifth Congress of the Turkestan Soviets. Kobozev was also instrumental in changing the composition of the Turkestan Central Executive Council which now included ten Central Asians, among whom Turar RYSKULOV was one of the most prominent. This was a first major step towards integrating the liberal-minded and the radical Muslims in the party and government structure.

In many ways, the history of the Muslim areas was a replay between 1917 and 1921 of the brief Kokand experience, as it was replete with failed attempts at autonomy and independence. In February 1918, just as Kokand was being crushed, Kolesov's army was defeating the Turkmens and establishing Soviet power in Ashkhabad and the Transcaspian region. The government which represented the rebels after the fall of the soviets in Ashkhabad and Kyzyl-Arvat on 12 July 1918 was headed by the Russian SR Funtikov; its armies controlled the territory between Ashkhabad and Krasnovodsk, and were commanded by Colonel Oraz Sardar, former leader of the defunct Turkmen Executive Committee which had emerged after the fall of the National Provisional Government. The challenge posed by the government of the Transcaspian region to Tashkent lasted until 6 February 1920, when the RED ARMY re-established Soviet rule in the last rebel stronghold, Krasnovodsk. Most of the rebel-held

Transcaspian region had been pacified in 1919 by the Red Army units fighting on the Turkestan front under M. V. FRUNZE and V. V. Kuibyshev.

Challenges to Soviet rule in Central Asia were serious enough in 1918 to prompt the Bolshevik leadership to consider the political integration of the Muslim liberal elements by advancing the idea of a local party at the first regional conference of the Bolshevik Party held in Tashkent in June 1918. Once integrated into the political structure of the Bolshevik Party, it was believed, the liberal jadids would have to abandon other political commitments, thus becoming more manageable entities subject to strict scrutiny by the party leadership.

Political arrogance and Russian chauvinism, however, prevented the Tashkent authorities from moving on these recommendations. It was only in March 1919, at the second regional conference of the Bolshevik party, that a regional bureau of the Muslim organizations was established and the call launched to all Central Asians of liberal persuasion to join. Very soon many jadids, including Ryskulov and Tursun Khodzhaev, joined the bureau, airing their ideas about the specific needs and problems of colonial nations.

Turkkomissiya: The tensions between the nationalist aspirations of the jadids and the arrogance of the Russian Communists were perceived by the Bolshevik leadership in Moscow as threatening enough to justify the organization of a Commission for Turkestani Affairs, known as Turkkomissiya. The Commission's task was not an easy one, for in 1920 Central Asia was in ferment. In January, the third conference of the Communists of Turkestan passed a series of bold resolutions calling for the formation of a Turkic Communist Party, a Muslim national army, an end to Russian colonization, removal of Russian settlers, and the creation of a Turkic republic in Central Asia. One of the leading figures behind these resolutions was Turar Ryskulov.

Between 1919 and 1923, under Kuibyshev and Frunze, Turkkomissiya accomplished the sovietization of Central Asia, and to a great extent became a mechanism of coercion which barred Muslims from party affairs. It also purged the more daring jadids whose conversion to communism had not affected their commitment to nationalist ideals. Thus it was an All-'Russian' Turkkomissiya composed of Frunze, M. V. Kaganovich, Kuibyshev, G. V. Safarov, Ya. Kh. PETERS that presided over the purges of nationalists and the dismantling of the regional Muslim bureau in 1920.

Khiva and Bukhara: By 1920 southern Central Asia was under Soviet rule, but in order to extend Soviet power over the entire territory, Moscow had to address the issue of Khivan and Bukharan independence, and that of the ongoing Basmachi movement. On the eve of the October Revolution, the Khivan Khanate had been weakened by clashes between Uzbeks and Turkmens which had resulted

Figures 34 and 35 The 1st Congress of the Peoples of the East, Baku, summer 1920, was convened to organize the Muslim world against colonial imperialism. 1,891 delegates – two thirds of them already Communist, and 44 women – came from 32 oriental nations, ranging from Morocco to Manchuria. *See above* Zinoviev (centre, in dark jacket), the President of the Comintern, and Bela Kun (to right). *See below* Harry Quelch, a British delegate to the 2nd World Congress of Comintern, who attended as did the American journalist John Reed, who died shortly after his return to Moscow.

in the rise of Junaid Khan as master of Khiva, overshadowing Sayid Abdullah, the legitimate ruler, but mere figurehead. The serious opposition to Junaid Khan came from the jadid Young Khivans who, having secured the military assistance of the Turkestan republic, succeeding in ousting him on 1 February 1919. The abdication of Sayid Abdullah cleared the way for the proclamation of a Khivan (Khwarazmian) People's Republic.

The president of the jadid-dominated first Khivan

government was Pahlavan Niyaz, whose tenure of office was marked by ethnic tensions between Turkmens and Uzbeks, and political tensions between the Khivan Communist Party and the jadid government, leading to the latter's fall on 4 March 1921 and its replacement by a coalition of Uzbeks, Turkmens and Kirghiz, which in 1921 became the object of a first major purge, which so depleted the party and government apparatus of those most capable of resisting increasing sovietization, that the final liquidation of the Khivan republic was almost anticlimactic. In October 1923, in an attempt to give legitimacy to a decision which had originated in Moscow, the fourth Khivan congress adopted a decision to integrate the Khivan republic into the Soviet federation after first announcing its metamorphosis into a socialist republic.

Bukhara: After the October Revolution, the Khanate of Bukhara saw clashes between conservative forces led by the Khan/emir and the liberals and radicals represented by the Young Bukharan jadids and the Bukharan Communist Party founded in Tashkent in 1918. Despite their hostility towards the emir, the Young Bukharans were not in favour of military intervention to oust him. Nevertheless, having sought support from the Turkestan republic, the Young Bukharans brought upon the khanate the assault launched by the Turkestan Red Army under Frunze in the autumn of 1920. The capture of Bukhara on 2 September 1920 led to the emergence of a revolutionary committee led by F. KHODZHAEV and on 8 October to the proclamation of a Bukharan People's Republic. On 4 March 1921 a treaty of friendship and economic cooperation was signed with the RSFSR.

The sovereignty of the young republic was nevertheless severely violated by the continued presence of Frunze's army on Bukharan territory, creating a source of tension between the Young Bukharans and their Bolshevik allies. A further irritant for both Tashkent and Moscow was the shift of the Young Bukharans' focus from social to cultural reform, inspired by A. FITRAT who played a major role in stimulating interest in the Turkic dimension of Central Asian identity.

Clearly, Young Bukharan radicals remained loyal to their jadid roots as their commitment to nationalism and traditional values grew at the expense of their concern with the ideals of socialism. Only thus can the 1921 mass defections of the jadid leaders to the Basmachis be understood. The guerrilla movement gained strength (at least temporarily) in 1921 when most of the members of the young Bukharan government defected: M. Maksumov (minister of police), A. Hamid (minister of war), Ali Riza Bek (minister of interior) and even the president of the republic, U. Khodzhaev.

The new Bukharan government, led by F. Khodzhaev and A. Fitrat, faced the impossible task of reconciling the republic's national goals with its pursuit of independence.

The demise of Bukharan independence came on 19 September 1924, when, freed of the challenges of foreign intervention and the Basmachis, Moscow could move to liquidate the Young Bukharan experiment. On that day, the People's Republic of Bukhara was abolished and in its place a Soviet republic emerged.

Postscript

The sovietization of Central Asia and the Steppe region thus completed, after 1924 the leadership in Moscow proceeded to reshape the administrative structure of the area until 1936, when it acquired its present form. In October 1924, two union republics were approved: Uzbek and Turkmen; two autonomous republics: Tadzhik and Kazakh, which acquired union status in 1929 and 1936, respectively; two autonomous regions: Kirghiz and Karakalpak. In 1936, the Kirghiz region became a union republic, while the Karakalpak region became an autonomous republic of Uzbekistan in 1932.

The new territorial divisions of Central Asia and of the Kazakh Steppes epitomized the shattered hopes of the jadids who had failed to achieve lasting political unity. The tide of national communism which swept across Central Asia and the Kazakh Steppes until the 1930s, however, was proof that the cultural unity of the area was greatly enhanced by the jadid reformers' efforts. A-AR

Further Reading

Allworth, E.: *Central Asia. A Century of Russian Rule.* New York: Columbia University Press, 1967.

Becker, S.: *Russia's Protectorates in Central Asia: Bukhara and Khiva, 1865–1924.* Cambridge, Mass.: Harvard University Press, 1968.

Bennigsen, A. and Lemercier-Quelquejay, C.: *Islam in the Soviet Union.* New York: 1967.

Bennigsen, A. and Wimbush, S. Enders: *Muslim National Communism in the Soviet Union.* Chicago: University of Chicago Press, 1979.

Polyakov, Yu.A. and Chugunov, A.I.: *Bor'ba s Basmachestvom v Sredneaziatskikh respublikakh SSSR.* Moscow: 1983.

Programmnye dokumenty musul'manskikh politicheskikh partii 1917–1920, repr. series no. 2. Oxford: Society for Central Asian Studies, 1985.

Revolyutsiya v Srednei Azii glazami musul'manskikh Bol'shevikov, repr. series no. 3. Oxford: Society for Central Asia Studies, 1985.

The Alash Orda

Enlightened jadids (reformers), such as Ahmed BAYTURSUN and Ali-Khan BUKEYKHANOV, addressed the issue of the political future of the Kazakhs as early as 1905 (see CENTRAL ASIA BEFORE 1917), but moved to set up an organization of their own, Alash Orda, only in March 1917. The First Congress of Alash Orda which met 2–8 April, 1917 in Orenburg, debated issues concerning education, courts, administration, and local autonomy. The Second Congress, held also in Orenburg, 21–26 July, 1917, adopted resolutions demanding an immediate halt to Russian immigration into Turkestan, a return of the land distributed to Russian immigrants, separate administrative and judicial structures for Russians and Kazakhs, as well as others dealing with education and military service. Of all newspapers and journals, the newspaper *Kazakh* seems to have emerged as the organ of Alash Orda, covering in detail the resolutions of the Third Congress held in Orenburg 8–13 December, 1917.

The delegates who came from eight provinces of Turkestan proclaimed Kazakh autonomy, elected an executive committee presided over by A. Bukeykhanov and established the framework of the Alash Orda government, located in Semey, renamed Alash (now Semipalatinsk).

The CIVIL WAR and the complexity of tribal relations prompted the government to adopt a twin administration policy whereby the western Alash Orda (the Uralsk province) would be headed by the Dostmuhammedov brothers and the eastern Alash Orda (Semirechye, Semipalatinsk, Akmolinsk) would be under the leadership of A. Bukeykhanov.

The Bolshevik occupation of Orenburg and the advance of the RED ARMY along the Orenburg-Tashkent line at the beginning of 1918, forced western Alash Orda to seek an alliance with the anti-Bolshevik forces of the Bashkirs and Orenburg COSSACKS, whereas eastern Alash Orda sought to join the forces of KOLCHAK. Both attempts failed and Kolchak's decision to order the suppression of Alash Orda swung the pendulum toward a compromise with the Bolsheviks. By the end of 1918, the leaders of both eastern and western Alash Orda were won over to the Bolsheviks and given assurances about participating in the political future of the Kazakhs.

On 9 March, 1920, the Kirghiz (i.e. Kazakh, since the Kirghiz proper were called Kara-Kirghiz) Revkom (revolutionary committee) adopted a resolution to dismantle the Alash Orda government and liquidate its administrative structures. August 26 1920 marks the creation of the Kazakh Autonomous Soviet Socialist Republic. Despite the demise of the political entity which they had created, the leaders of Alash Orda remained influential in the new government until the purges of the 1930s when they were eliminated for the sins of nationalism and pan-Turkism.

A-AR

Further Reading

Oraltay, H.: The Alash Movement in Turkestan. *Central Asian Survey* 2 (1985) 41–59.

The Basmachi

One of the most complex and elusive components in the equation of Soviet integration of Central Asia was the Basmachi movement, which between 1918 and 1923 challenged the Sovietization of Turkestan in a remarkably resourceful armed resistance (see CENTRAL ASIA: REVOLUTION AND CIVIL WAR).

Bandit or brigand was the original meaning of the word basmachi, but in 1918 the old term acquired a new meaning when applied to those who took up arms against the BOLSHEVIKS: warriors defending the Muslims wronged by the Russians.

The Basmachi movement began in 1918 in Fergana in response to the crushing of Kokand autonomy but it spread rapidly to other regions as the number of Central Asians whom the Bolsheviks alienated grew to include even some of their former allies and supporters.

The political and national aspirations of the Central Asian Muslims were debated at four conferences held between March and December 1917. The fourth conference held at Kokand in early December, 1917, organized a Provisional Government which on 10 December proclaimed the autonomy of Turkestan and made an appeal to the Central Soviet government for recognition. In response, on the night of 11–12 February, 1918, the Bolshevik government engineered a coup and within a week the Red Guards were in full control of Kokand having executed and deported the supporters of the Provisional Government, after literally burning down the town. By the end of spring the entire Transcaspian region was pacified and in May a Soviet Congress in Tashkent declared the birth of the Turkestan Soviet Republic.

The Muslims in Fergana responded by taking up arms against the Tashkent Soviet, thus launching the Basmachi movement. In the early stages, the Basmachi leaders were Irgan Bek (Irgash) in the Kokand area, and Madamin in the Margelan region. They set up an organizational infrastructure which replaced Soviet administration in the countryside, bringing it almost totally under the control of Basmachi forces.

In the spring of 1918 the Tashkent Soviet responded to the Basmachi challenge by setting up Turk Front and by sending three divisions to Fergana. Yet, the Basmachis under Irgash continued to pose a serious threat until the summer of 1919, when Irgash's defeat projected Madamin to the position of supreme commander of Basmachi forces and led to an alliance with the Russian 'Peasant Army' which had taken up arms against WAR COMMUNISM policies of the Tashkent Soviet. The result of this alliance was the proclamation on 24 September 1919, of a Provisional Fergana Government which failed, however, to win the recognition of other Basmachi leaders.

By late 1919, the Basmachi movement entered a new phase. The Tashkent Soviet, exorcized of its blatant Russian chauvinism by the Turkestan Commission which arrived from Moscow on 4 November, 1919, adopted a policy of conciliation and launched an appeal to the Basmachi, the Fergana Provisional Government and the

Russian Peasant Army, offering them an opportunity to surrender. The head of the Russian Peasant Army and minor Basmachi leaders surrendered but Madamin fought on. He was eventually eliminated when he fell victim to internal Basmachi rivalries.

By 1920, the strict enforcement of labour and military conscription and the attack on Muslim religious institutions contributed to the growth of the Basmachi movement and to its acquiring a more pronounced Islamic character. In May 1920, the Basmachis proclaimed another Provisional Government, this time covering not only Fergana but the entire territory of Turkestan. Throughout 1920, they remained in control of the countryside as the Red Army was completing the invasion and annexation of the Khanates of Khiva and Bukhara.

The Sovietization of Khiva and Bukhara led to a new phase in the evolution of the Basmachi movement, whereby the guerrilla forces came to control the countryside in Fergana and Bukhara where they set up their own administration, and the Soviets controlled the cities, where they imposed their own system of administration. The entities of this parallel structure were not only divorced from each other, but were in an adversary relationship made worse by the offensives of the special Turk Front forces (under FRUNZE) against the Basmachis.

In early 1921, Soviet troops seemed to have gained the upper hand. By the end of 1921, however, despite dissension and internal rivalries which had plagued them all along, the Basmachi forces had grown stronger. The arrival of Enver Pasha (the former Ottoman War Minister) who joined the Basmachis in November 1921, and the subsequent defection of the Bukharan government to the Basmachis briefly revitalized the movement which in 1923 succumbed to the pressures of internal dissent (brought about by Enver Pasha's death in 1922), Soviet military offensive led by Budenny and the economic and cultural offensive which permitted a rapid economic recovery and repealed the laws restricting the observance of Muslim practices and traditions.   A-AR

Further Reading

Castagne, J.: *Les Basmatchis*. Paris: 1925.

Fraser, G.: Basmachi. *Central Asian Survey* 1 (1987) 1–73.

Yusupov, E.Yu.: *Basmachestvo. Sotsial'no-politicheskaya sushchnost'*. Tashkent: 1984.

The Crimean and the Volga Tatars before 1917

The Kazan and Crimean Khanates emerged in the middle of the fifteenth century in the lands extending west and southwest of the Ural mountains. The populations which absorbed the wave of newcomers comprised a Mongol minority and a significant contingent from the conquered lands of Central Asia.

The Crimean Khanate

The history of the Crimean Khanate can be divided into four periods: end of Golden Horde rule and emergence of an independent Khanate (1452–1588); Vassalage to the Ottoman Sultan (1588–1788): 'Independence' (1774–83); Russian conquest (1783).

The eighteenth century marked the demise of Crimea as an independent socio-political and cultural unity and brought the Khanate under the rule of the Russian tsars. Crimea was of utmost economic and political interest to Russia and in the eighteenth century its rulers took military and diplomatic action aimed at achieving control of the Crimea. Devastated by the forces of Count Münnich in 1736, and ravaged by the armies of General Lassy from 1737 to 1938, the Crimea was completely occupied by General Dolgoruky's large army in 1771. The Treaty of Küchük Kaynarja (1774), ended Crimean vassalage to the Ottoman sultan who, in his role as caliph, remained the spiritual head of the Khanate.

The brief period of Crimean independence was marked by attempts of the Crimean elite to test the limits of their independence from both the Russian and Ottoman states and by rivalries between pro-Russian and pro-Ottoman elites. These rivalries rendered the Khanate vulnerable, opened the door to Russian intervention and outright annexation in 1783.

On 19 April, 1783, a manifesto of Catherine II proclaimed the outright annexation of the Crimean Khanate to the Russian empire but at the same time guaranteed to the Muslim population the retention of its property, equality of status with the Russians and the right to pursue its religious practices and traditions. In reality, pushed by the tide of new settlers from Russia and deprived of their lands and economic opportunities, Crimean Tatars could hardly experience this equality. Survival, not equality, became their primary concern and in order to survive, many chose the road of exile, thus triggering the first of a tragic succession of migrations from the Crimea.

Immediately after annexation, the Russian government took measures to incorporate the Khanate into its administrative structure, a task which was accomplished by leaving almost intact the Crimean administrative institutions and by replacing the authority of the Khan with that of the new Russian governor. Incorporated into the Novorossiya Province in 1796, Crimea was reorganized as Tavride Province in 1802, and retained this administrative structure until 1917.

Russian annexation of Crimea brought the pressures of Slavic colonization on the Tatar population. Peasants suffered from the land seizures, the nobility from loss of wealth and erosion of power and prestige, urban culture deteriorated as Tatars with the exception of those in Bakhchisarai and Kerch were prevented from taking part in urban government. Altogether, the policies of the Russian government in the Crimea led to the demise and impoverishment of the Tatar nobility (with the exception of those few who had become fully russified and joined the Russian nobility), the deterioration of the Tatar urban class, the impoverishment of the peasantry and mass migrations (by 1860 100,000 Tatars had left) that amounted to the ruin and uprooting of the traditional Tatar society and culture.

The Kazan Khanate

The conquest of Kazan in 1552 projected Muscovite Russia, still in its infancy as a centralized national state, into the orbit of multinational empires. At the same time it added to the fabric of Russian society its first non-Slavic and non-Christian population, while also bringing about the acquisition of a socio-economic, cultural and political entity that had developed its own political institutions, social systems, economic practices, religious and cultural values.

When in 1552 Kazan was conquered and destroyed by the armies of Ivan IV, the very existence of its people as a distinct national, cultural, and religious entity was in danger. This was nowhere better illustrated than by Ivan IV's own statement: 'Let the unbelievers receive the True God, the new subjects of Russia, and let them with us praise the Holy Trinity for ages unto ages.' Ivan's attitude shaped to a great extent the developments of the ensuing centuries when the Russian state pursued toward the Volga Tatars a policy of national integration that meant conversion to Christianity and cultural assimilation.

Jadidism among the Crimean and Volga Tatars

Volga Tatar society and culture underwent significant change at the end of the nineteenth and beginning of the twentieth century. The movement of reform that came to be known as jadidism had a broad scope. It began as early as the end of the eighteenth and beginning of the nineteenth centuries with a reassessment of their religious thinking, then turned toward cultural and educational reformism, and finally reached the realm of politics at the beginning of the twentieth century. The earliest Volga Tatar reformers were G. Utyz Imani (1754–1815), Abu-Nasr al-Kursavi (1776–1813), and I. Khalfin (1778–1829).

The father of reformism in the middle Volga area was Shihabeddin MERJANI (1818–89), religious scholar, teacher, historian, who advocated individual interpretation of the dogma, took a stand against the conservative religious educational system of Central Asia and strongly believed that the salvation of Muslims was in a return to the purity of pristine Islam and in the acquisition of the best achievements of western science and culture.

Rizaeddin Fahreddin (1858–1936) and Musa Jarulla Bigi (1870–1949) added new dimensions to the Volga Tatars' religious thinking. Central to Fahreddin's philosophy was his belief in the compatibility of Islam and science; he advocated reform of the religious administration whereby

the Mufti would be placed in a subordinate position to the Council. He also argued that the Mufti should be elected and not nominated by the government and that his competence should be equally strong in religious and secular sciences. Bigi did not believe in blind adherence to religion, but in a conscious and active participation in it; hence he advocated translation of the Koran into Tatar which, he believed, would contribute to making every individual's religious experience a more meaningful and conscientious act.

Merjani made a significant contribution to the shaping of Tatar national consciousness by presenting his people with their own history and by being the first to use the name Tatar when writing about the Volga Muslims. A contemporary of his, Kayyum NASIRI (1825–1902) enriched the reform movement by becoming the first to raise the issue of preservation of the Tatar language and to emphasize the importance of language in shaping and maintaining one's identity. The Tatar vernacular was promoted by the new generation of jadid writers; its purity was defended in the press by all who were concerned with the preservation of their national identity.

The symbiosis between tradition and secularism advocated by the reformers underwent a crucial test in the field of education. The Volga Tatars had always attached great importance to education and had promoted it in the traditional Islamic schools where children learned the fundamentals of literacy in mektebs and furthered their knowledge in medreses. In the nineteenth century, Tatar intellectuals became increasingly aware that mektebs and medreses were not keeping pace with changing times. They rejected the Russian schools which were secular but aloof to the national needs of the Tatar students and embarked on the difficult task of establishing a network of new schools which would meet the task of balancing tradition and the requirements of modern education. The reformers were so successful that by 1912, 90 per cent of the 1,088 Tatar schools functioning in Kazan Province were jadid. Some medreses became known beyond the confines of their cities for the quality of education they provided. A network of girls' schools was the result of the jadids' concern for the education and enlightenment of women as a prerequisite for the advancement of the nation as a whole.

Book publishing and book printing, the emergence of benevolent societies, of a dynamic press, and the growth of national literature characterized the cultural jadidism that preceded and accompanied political jadidism.

Political ideas were not alien to the works of writers and poets, such as the national poet of the Tatars, Abdulla TUKAY; they were debated in the pages of newspapers and journals such as *Kazan Mukhbiri* (Kazan Messenger), *Vakt* (Time), *Shura* (Council, i.e. Soviet), but they were put in practice by the generation of jadids that rose to prominence after the 1905 REVOLUTION. To be sure, rudiments of Tatar political activity can be traced to 1895, to the organization of a literary-political circle by a few Tatar youths.

Political jadidism found expression in Tatar participation in the political life of the Russian state by using the framework of Russian political parties (Consitutional Democrats, PSR, and RSDRP) and Russian institutions (the Duma), as well as in the effort aimed at building a political infrastructure which would represent the interests of the Tatars and all Muslims.

The radical wing of the jadids adhered to the programmes of the Russian radical parties. In 1906, A. Ishaki, F. Tuktarov and other members of the radical student organizations Shakirdlik (Student Life) and Brek (Union), organized a Tatar Socialist Revolutionary Party, Tangchy, whose organ was the newspaper *Tang Yulduzy* (The Morning Star). At about the same time, H. Yamashev, another former member of Shakirdlik, joined the Russian SD party of Kazan and actively promoted it among the Tatars. His efforts were not successful and two years after the 1905 police raid of the SD party of Kazan, Yamashev organized in Orenburg a legal Tatar Social Democratic group called the Uralists which published its own paper, *Ural*.

The ideas of the radical jadids who emphasized the need for class, rather than national consciousness, did not appeal to the Volga Tatars, and after 1905 it was the liberal nationalist jadids who emerged almost unchallenged as the Spokesmen for the Tatars on the Russian political scene. Those Tatars for whom ethnic and religious concerns took precedence over class issues chose to become a part of the Union of all Russian Muslims, regardless of their social class, and set forth to organize Muslim congresses as a means of identifying the priorities of their communities and articulating plans for action.

The three Muslim Congresses which met between 1905 and 1914 (August 1905; January 1906; August 1906; June 1914) addressed mainly issues concerning education, religious reform, affiliation to Russian political parties, and stressed the need for a political union, for the organization of a party Ittifak-al-Muslimin (Muslim Union) based on the principles of nationalism and religion. Yusuf AKCHURA, who was a leading figure at these congresses, had a strong emotional commitment to the political future of the Russian Muslims; having lived most of his life abroad, however, he knew little about the details of Russian political life and much too often he gave literal interpretations to the promises of the Russian liberals and his achievements registered a gap between ideal and performance.

The conservative backlash which began in 1907 struck a major blow to the political leadership of the Tatars as many intellectuals (Akchura included) emigrated to Turkey, Europe, or the Middle East. Poor in human resources and handicapped by an almost exclusive commitment of education and religion, the Tatars did not succeed in developing an independent political life. Their 'apprentice-

ship' in politics and above all, the ideas which political and cultural jadidism had brought into the scene of Tatar national life, were to become the foundation upon which the next generation of jadids, those under Soviet rule, would build their dreams and forge their plans for action.

In the Crimea, the undisputed leader of the jadid movement was Ismail Bey GASPRALI (Gasprinsky) (1851–1914) who called for a national revival and renewal which, according to him, could only be achieved through education. He launched a new method for education which combined the best of the traditional curriculum with a new curriculum consisting of secular subjects, in addition to Russian and Tatar. His medrese at Zinjirli became the model for jadid schools which opened in Crimea and elsewhere. Gasprali called for a renewal of Russian Islam, for the emancipation of women (he published the journal *Alem-i-Nisvan* (Women's World) and for the rebirth of national life on the basis of a single Turkic language, under the leadership of a single Turkic elite, thus bringing to the service of one cause the Turkic elites of the Russian and Ottoman empires. His ideas on working within the Russian system and participating in the new political institutions on the side of Russian liberals, were not shared by the younger generation of Crimean jadids, such as the Young Tatars whose political aims focused on the 'national, social, and political liberation of the Crimea Tatar people'; they chose to look to the SRs rather than to the Russian liberals in their search for allies.

A more radical stand was represented by the members of the illegal society Vatan (Fatherland), whose ultimate goal was an independent Crimean state. Young Crimeans such as C. Seidahmet advanced the idea of Tatarness as a replacement of Ismail Bey's Turkicness and Turkic unity. The Vatan group perhaps exemplifies best the evolution of Crimean cultural jadidism to the point where it triggered the emergence of a Crimean (as distinct from Turkic or Islamic) identity and national consciousness. The cross-fertilization of the ideas of Ismail Bey, the Young Tatars, and the Vatan group prepared the foundation for the dynamic nationalism which Crimea witnessed after 1917.   A-AR

Further Reading

Abdullin, Ya.: *Tatarskaya prosvetitel'skaya mysl'*. Kazan: 1976.

Bennigsen, A. and Lemercier-Quelquejay, Ch.: *La presse et le mouvement national chez les musulmans de Russie avant 1920*. Paris: 1964.

Fisher, A.W.: *Crimean Tatars*. Stanford: 1978.

Milner, Th.: *The Crimea, its Ancient and Modern History: The Khans, the Sultans, and the Tsars*. London: 1855.

Rorlich, A.: *The Volga Tatars*. Stanford: 1986.

The Crimea and Middle Volga: Revolution and Civil War

The FEBRUARY REVOLUTION became a tangible reality in the Crimea on 17 March, 1917, when the PROVISIONAL

GOVERNMENT took power in Simferopol. On that day the Crimean Tatars marked the event by organizing a large demonstration under the motto 'Freedom, equality, brotherhood, and justice'. A week later, on 25 March, some 1,500 delegates from all corners of the Crimea convened in a Crimean Muslim conference which adopted measures to promote the cultural and religious life of the Tatars within the framework of an autonomous organization. The conference elected a Muslim Executive Committee of forty-five members with the task of proclaiming Tatar cultural and national autonomy. Tatar hopes would be determined by their interaction with the Provisional Government, the BOLSHEVIKS, and by the fortunes of the CIVIL WAR.

The Provisional Government disregarded Tatar quests for autonomy and by July, the tension of the previous months had become open hostility. More radical Crimean Tatars discarded ideas of accommodation and organized Milli Fïrka, a national party advocating cooperation with the socialist parties. The Provisional Government arrested two of their leading figures: Chelebi Jihan (the Mufti) and Shabarov (commander of Tatar military units) but released them the next day.

The period from November 1917 to January 1918 when the first Soviet regime came to power in the Crimea, was the brief moment of fulfilled national aspirations for the Crimean Tatars. On 26 December, 1917, the Tatar National Constituent Assembly, elected on the basis of broad franchise for all adult male and female Tatars, accepted a new constitution for the Crimean state, transformed itself into a national parliament and elected a Crimean national government (Directorate) under the leadership of Chelebi Jihan.

The Crimean experiment in statehood was killed in its infancy by the twin pressures of the Bolshevik forces in Sevastopol and those of the German armies. The first Bolshevik regime in the Crimea, based in Sevastopol, lasted from 27 January to 25 April, 1918. It was exclusively Russian in composition, extremely hostile to the Crimean Tatars and exhibited appalling political myopia when it executed Jihan, the Tatar leader most willing to work with the new Soviet government.

By the end of April 1918, units of the German army under General Kisch occupied the Crimea and on 5 June ordered General Sulkevich, a Tatar from Lithuania, to form a new administration. Right wing members of Milli Fïrka supported Sulkevich but the November German evacuation brought about another change in Crimea's fortunes. A Russian liberal government led by Salomon Krym replaced the Sulkevich administration. The right wing of Milli Fïrka supported Krym, a Karaite, and a former deputy to the first Duma. The left wing of Milli Fïrka, led by V. IBRAHIMOV, declined to support Krym and maintained ties with underground Bolshevik formations. It was this left faction that assisted the Bolsheviks and contributed to their

victory of DENIKIN in the spring of 1919.

The second Bolshevik regime that came to power in the Crimea in April 1919, proclaimed the creation of the Socialist Soviet Republic of the Crimea. The regime was more receptive to Tatar needs but it was soon ousted by the armies of General Denikin who was an outspoken foe of autonomy and independence for the non-Russians and in June he promptly dispersed the 'Tatar National Directorate', a move followed by the closing down of all Muslim newspapers in August and by the banning of Milli Fïrka, most of whose members (not only the Left wing) responded by going underground and collaborating with the Bolsheviks.

When, in early 1920, General WRANGEL took over the leadership of the White government in the Crimea, he tried to repair the damage inflicted by Denikin's highhandedness. He permitted some Tatar newspapers to resume publication and even authorized the appearance of a new Simferopol paper called *Kïrïm Musulmanlarï Sedasï* (The Voice of the Crimean Muslims). It was, however, much too late either to win back Tatar support or to stop the Bolshevik advance into the Crimea which they occupied in October 1920.

The installation of a third Bolshevik government in the Crimea renewed Milli Fïrka hopes for the fulfilment of Tatar national aspirations. In an attempt to meet the Bolsheviks half way, Milli Fïrka sent an official note to the Bolshevik leadership stating that despite many differences, they shared the same goal: the advancement of the Tatar people. The note was perhaps the best example of Milli Fïrka naiveté. While they were attempting to engage in dialogue, the Bolsheviks were launching the VECHEKA to eliminate opposition to Soviet power. A special Crimean Cheka under N. Bystrykh carried on a real war against the Crimeans and he was equally relentless with the Tatars and Russians. The struggle between the Cheka forces and the native opposition continued until late 1921. At its height, Crimean Tatar opposition to Soviet rule took the form of a guerrilla movement called the 'Green Forces', which under the leadership of Ismail Nazal controlled the mountainous regions of the peninsula.

The situation in the Crimea was serious enough for the Bolshevik leadership to dispatch M. SULTANGALIEV to investigate. His report, critical of Cheka abuses, made several recommendations, notably to attract Tatars into party membership and to reorganize Crimea as an autonomous Soviet republic. This second recommendation touched a sensitive chord in the hearts of all native inhabitants of the Crimea who met in Simferopol on 23 September, 1921 to address the issue of the Crimean future. In the aftermath of this meeting the Crimean Autonomous Soviet Socialist Republic was created. Hence, the 18 October 1921 decree of the Council of People's Commissars announcing the creation of the Crimean Republic seemed to have answered the dreams of the nationalists for territorial autonomy. The experience of the years to come would expose a remarkable gap between dream and reality. Those jadid radicals and members of the left wing of Milli Firka who had chosen to join the new regime attempted to narrow that gap in the 1920s, and strove to achieve for the Crimean Tatars genuine political and cultural autonomy. Among them, Veli IBRAHIMOV stands out as the most daring Crimean national communist who used to the utmost the human and intellectual resources of Milli Firka to accomplish the tatarization of Crimea in the late 1920s.

Middle Volga

The Volga Tatars welcomed the fall of the monarchy with great expectation, and they responded to the promises of the February Revolution with an explosion of organizational activity. On 7 March 1917, the Kazan Muslim Committee was organized. It was a regional chapter of the Muslim Central Executive Committee (acronym: Iskomus) which had been organized immediately after February in order to coordinate Muslim political action, and it became the voice of the Tatar nationalist forces which organized similar committees in the cities of the Volga-Ural region. On 7 April 1917, a Tatar Socialist Committee was organized in Kazan. Dominated by people from the entire spectrum of radical politics, the committee maintained ties with the Tatar organizations, and although it was not affiliated to the Bolshevik party, it adhered to the Bolshevik platform on the issues of war, land, and transfer of power to the Soviets. Its ideology was a mélange of Marxism and pan-Islamism which proved to be no obstacle in gaining Bolshevik support. Disregarding ideological incongruities, the Bolsheviks chose to gamble on the opportunity to use the Kazan Socialist Committee as the training camp for converting the Tatars to genuine Marxism. They failed to see, however, that even for the most ardent self-acknowledged socialists and communists of the committee, such as M. VAKHITOV (president) and M. Sultangaliev (presidium member) commitment to Marxism was only secondary to nationalist goals.

On 1 May 1917, the First All-Russian Congress of Muslims brought to Moscow some 900 delegates representing the broadest political spectrum from the conservative Right to the revolutionary Left, the single exception being the small minority of Muslims who had formally joined the Bolshevik party and declined participation. The proceedings of the congress unfolded under the banner of unity, religious and ethnic solidarity, with the exception of the issues of state organization and the role of women in the new society, which strained Muslim unity. On both issues the Volga Tatars swam against the tide: they defended the equality of the sexes and extra-territorial cultural autonomy within the confines of a centralized, but democratic, Russian republic. To salvage Muslim unity the congress established a National Council which, together with

Iskomus set out to coordinate Muslim political actions.

The Second All-Russian Congress (21 July–2 August, 1917) was an almost exclusively Volga Tatar event, attended by delegates from Crimea, Bashkiria, and North Caucasus with common views on extraterritorial autonomy. On 22 July 1917, the congress proclaimed the extraterritorial autonomy of the Muslims of Inner Russia and Siberia; the Muslim Military Congress which was being held simultaneously at the initiative of the Military Council, organized in April 1917, decided to proceed with the organization of Muslim Military units. In order to coordinate the implementation of extraterritorial cultural autonomy and complete the preparatory work for convening a Muslim deliberative body, (National Assembly), a National Board was organized.

The handful of Tatars who had joined the Bolshevik party were only bystanders in the flurry of organizational activity marked by the unity of purpose of the socialists and liberals alike in the spring and summer of 1917. The Bolshevik leadership, however, was not oblivious to the manifest strength of nationalist forces. In an effort to win the allegiance of the Muslims and weaken the nationalist forces, on 20 November 1917, the Soviet of People's Commissars launched an Appeal to the Muslim Workers of Russia and the East which promised them freedom to 'build their national lives without hindrance'. The Appeal was an attempt to counteract the fact that the Revolution had been a 'Russian affair', while the Muslim nationalist organizations were the creation of the Volga Tatars and of other Muslims.

Since the July Congress, the Volga Tatars' view on the issue of autonomy had changed drastically. The National Assembly of the Muslims of Inner Russia and Siberia that convened in Ufa, 20 November 1917–1 January 1918, assessed the new conditions that had emerged after the Bolshevik revolution and opted for territorial autonomy, proclaiming on 19 November 1917 an autonomous Idil-Ural state.

The parallel Muslim infrastructure which had emerged since the spring of 1917 threatened to evolve into a *de facto* dual power. The Bolshevik leadership could not tolerate this and moved swiftly to eliminate the hold of the nationalists on Tatar politics. On 17 January 1918 a decree of the Council of People's Commissars created the Central Muslim Commissariat (under M. Vakhitov) whose task was the 'Bolshevization' of the Tatar masses and the weakening of the nationalist organizations. The crisis of the Civil War prompted the Bolshevik leadership to increase its efforts to win Muslim allegiance. On 28 April 1918, these efforts were translated into the decision to organize the Central Muslim Military Collegium whose president, after the death of M. Vakhitov on 19 August 1918, was M. Sultangaliev.

The main goal of the collegium was to assist the war effort of the People's Commissariat of War (Narkomvoen)

by organizing Muslim units of the RED ARMY and by assuming leadership in the Communist political education of the Muslim soldiers. The Muslims genuinely believed in a symbiosis between communism, Islam, and nationalism, and viewed their national units and the collegium as the catalysts of this symbiosis. Neither the party nor the government leadership considered the needs and specific problems of the Muslims to be a priority and as a result, from its inception the precarious existence of the collegium was governed by a peculiar *quid pro quo*.

When the dangers of the Civil War were removed, the Bolshevik leadership proceeded to eliminate those institutions and organizations which had been set up for tactical reasons only and had outlived their purpose. On 1 October 1920, order no. 2005 of the Revolutionary Military Council dismantled the military collegium. Despite its short life, the collegium's most important achievement was in the area of basic and political literacy. Because no other texts were available, Tatar primers were used for all Muslim soldiers, and it was the Tatar theatre that was mobilized to rally the Muslim soldiers to the new regime, a dimension which testified once more to the cultural resourcefulness of the Volga Tatars, and revealed their potential for assuming the leadership of a Turkic commonwealth in Russia.

In response to the emergence of Volga Tatar nationalist organizations in the spring and summer of 1918, the Bolsheviks organized the Central Muslim Commissariat and the Central Muslim Military Collegium. In response to the proclamation of the autonomous Idil-Ural state (19 November 1917) by the Muslim National Assembly, the People's Commissariat of Nationalities (Narkomnats) issued, on 23 March 1918, a decree proclaiming a Tatar-Bashkir Soviet Republic of the Russian Soviet Federation in the Middle Volga and Southern Ural region, which, however, was postponed by the outbreak of the Civil War in May, 1918.

On May 25, the Czech Legion's uprising and support of the Whites along the Trans-Siberian railway became the catalyst for the anti-Bolshevik forces which rallied around the Komuch, a body that had emerged as a *sui generis* provisional government at the initiative of Menshevik and SR partisans of the Constituent Assembly (see COMMITTEE OF MEMBERS OF THE CONSTITUENT ASSEMBLY). On 6 August, 1918, aided by Muslim volunteers and White Russians, the Czechs took Kazan. Some Muslim nationalist leaders therafter allied themselves with Komuch in the hope that this body would be more receptive to their needs. Ataman Dutov's control of the Orenburg area enabled the Bashkirs to establish in August, 1918, a National Government of Bashkiria, presided over by A. Zeki Validov.

It was the insensitivity of the extreme-right leadership of the Whites to the needs of the Muslims that ultimately prompted the latter to rally around the Bolsheviks whose political astuteness paid high dividends in the critical years of the Civil War. Following the amnesty which the Council of People's Commissars granted on 6 February 1919, to all Bashkirs who deserted from KOLCHAK, nationalist commanders at the head of a force of 2000 soldiers joined the Bolsheviks and Zeki Validov signed a preliminary agreement with Moscow for a Provisional Government of Bashkiria which, however, never materialized.

The nationalists' hopes (shared by the people of the Volga-Ural region) for a large Turkic state on the Middle Volga were shattered by the 23 March 1919 decree announcing the formation of the Bashkir Autonomous Soviet Socialist republic. It was the strong tide of nationalism among the Volga Tatars that prompted the Bolshevik leadership to revise its plans for a Tatar-Bashkir republic. To prevent Turkic unity and the emergence of a dynamic republic in the Middle Volga, to eliminate the possibility of Kazan retaining its role as the political and cultural centre of the Muslims of Russia, the Soviet government chose to erect administrative barriers between the Tatars and Bashkirs; sponsoring the creation of smaller republics, the party and government leadership fostered isolation, nourished old jealousies and rivalries and facilitated its control over the people of the area guided by the dictum '*divide et impera*'.

After the emergence of the Bashkir republic, the creation of a separate Tatar republic became a certainty and indeed on 27 May 1920, the government proclaimed the formation of the Tatar republic as an autonomous entity of the Russian republic. The territory of the republic, some 68,000 square kilometres, represented merely one third of the area that would have been the territory of the Idil-Ural state. Moreover, the borders of the republic as they stood in 1920 left 75 per cent of the Tatar population outside its boundaries, creating a paradox whereby Tatars represented the ethnic majority in the Bashkir ASSR.

The creation of the Tatar ASSR, instead of alleviating some of the national tensions and healing the wounds of past inequities, led to growing discontent and bitterness on the part of nationalists and Communists alike and seriously tested the loyalties of the radical jadids such as Sultangaliev who had joined the new regime.

The 1920s were dominated by Tatar Communists who in their efforts to create a Nationalist-Communist symbiosis attempted to revive some of the hopes that were shattered in 1920. These attempts took the form of Sultangaliev's militant National Communism and bold plans for a state that would gather within its borders all the Turkic peoples of the Soviet Union. They were equally translated in the efforts of an orthodox Bolshevik such as G. Ibragimov who rose to the defence of the Tatar language and sought to rescue the culture where hope for independent statehood had vanished.

A-AR

Further Reading

Bor'ba za sovetskuyu vlast' v Krymu: Dokumenty i materialy, vols. 1 and 2. Simferopol: 1957; 1961.

Davletshin, T.: *Sovetskii Tatarstan. Teoriya i praktika Leninskoi natsional'noi politiki.* London: 1974.

Elagin, V.: *Revolyutsiya i grazhdanskaya voina v Krymu.* Simferopol: 1927.

Fisher, A.W.: *Crimean Tatars.* Stanford: 1978.

Klimov, I.M.: *Obrazovanie i razvitie Tatarskoi ASSR.* Kazan: 1960.

Rorlich, A.: *The Volga Tatars.* Stanford: 1986.

The Central Muslim Commissariat

One of the most important tasks of the Bolshevik leadership in the spring of 1918 was to rally the support of the Muslims to the cause of the new regime in the unfolding Civil War. The task was made ever more urgent by the existence of an infrastructure of Muslim organizations which had emerged since the spring of 1917 and were commanding Muslim allegiance. (See CRIMEA AND MIDDLE VOLGA: REVOLUTION AND CIVIL WAR.)

On 17 January 1918, a decree of the Sovnarkom (see LENIN'S GOVERNMENT) and of the Commissariat of Nationalities (Narkomnats) announced the organization of the Central Muslim Commissariat (Muskom) which was entrusted with the 'Bolshevization' of the Muslim masses. Mullanur VAKHITOV, the chairman of the Kazan Socialist Committee, accepted the Chairmanship of Muskom and was aided by G. IBRAGIMOV and Sh. Manatov who became its first vice-chairman. Muskom had not been sanctioned by the Tatar National Assembly and the decision of Ibragimov and Manatov to take positions of leadership in its hierarchy created a serious rift in Tatar unity. The creation of Muskom was the first tangible proof that the government was determined not to tolerate any longer the rivalry of the national Muslim organizations. Unable to dismantle the Muslim agencies yet, the government set out to weaken them by creating rival organizations such as the Central Muskom.

In March 1918, Muskoms were organized by province. They embarked on the urgent task of shaping the political education of the Tatar masses by setting up their own press organs such as *Esh* (Labour) of Kazan and *Mamadysh Tavyshy* (The Voice of Mamadysh).

The Central Muslim Commissariat enjoyed extensive powers from its inception. Its jurisdiction extended over all facets of Muslim life: economy, education, press, justice, propaganda, and even the army. The Central Muskom had a military section led by I. I. Ibragimov, a member of the Executive Committee of Muslim soldiers on the Northern front. Its main task was to assist local Muskoms 'in organizing battalions of the Worker-Peasant Red Army'. On 28 April 1918, the military section was reorganized under the name of Central Muslim Military Collegium and was staffed by four Tatars and two Russians. Mirsaid SULTANGALIEV became its first president.

The declared task of the Muskoms was to awaken the Muslim masses to political consciousness and rally them to the support of the Bolshevik regime. Sultangaliev and Vakhitov, however, sought to use their framework to achieve the goals of the national movement as articulated by various organizations and individuals since pre-revolutionary times. They sought to achieve extraterritorial autonomy through a Muslim administration and a Communist party; and territorial autonomy through a Tatar-Bashkir state which would extend over the territory of the Kazan Khanate in the Middle Volga and Ural region.

The goals of the leaders of Central Muskom clashed with those of the Bolshevik leadership in Moscow and as soon as the most imminent dangers of the Civil War were over, Moscow moved to end the experiment in Muslim autonomy. The tide of centralization swept most of the Muslim organizations in 1919. The Eighth Congress of the Russian Communist (Bolshevik) Party held in Moscow 18-23 March 1919 brought the Central Muskom under its control by reorganizing it as the Tatar-Bashkir Commissariat. This decision left no doubt that Moscow had halted the process of organizational independence set in motion by the Tatar national Communists in 1918.   A-AR

Siberia before 1917

Siberia is the name historically given to that part of the Russian Empire which stretches across the continent of Northern Asia from the Ural mountains to the Pacific coast, and from the Arctic Ocean to the borders of Kazakhstan, Mongolia and China. The traditional date for the beginning of Russia's penetration, conquest and colonial settlement of Siberia is 1582, when the Cossack adventurer, Ermak Timofeevich, acting as agent for the wealthy merchant family of the Stroganovs, led a military expedition across the Urals against the small Tatar khanate of Sibir, and thereby paved the way for the ultimate establishment of Muscovy's military and political control over the basins of the rivers Irtysh and upper Ob. From there the Russians' eastwards advance was remarkably swift, facilitated by a largely familiar type of terrain, superior fire-power, skilful use of the river-systems and the construction of a network of fortified stockades which formed the nuclei of Siberia's future administrative centres and major towns: Tyumen (founded in 1586), Tobolsk (1857), Tomsk (1604), Eniseisk (1619), Yakutsk (1632), Okhotsk (1647) and Irkutsk (1661). The territorial advances were matched by the rapid demographic expansion of the Russian settlers, illustrated in table 8.

Historical debate still continues over the social composition of the Russian and other immigrant population, but it seems clear that in the early period it was military and other service personnel which formed the great majority, and only later did the voluntary immigration and settlement of peasants on the land become a major factor (see p. 254). The most important economic determinant in the process

Table 8 Composition of Siberia's population, 1662–1911

Year	Native Peoples	Russians and other immigrants	Total
1662	288,000	105,000	393,000
1796	363,362	575,800	939,162
1815	434,000	1,100,500	1,534,500
1897	870,536	4,889,633	5,760,168
1911	972,866	8,393,469	9,366,335

Source: *Aziatskaya Rossiya*, vol. 1, St Petersburg, 1914.

of Russia's expansion in the seventeenth century was the quest for fur, in particular the pelt of the sable, which formed the most valuable trading commodity in Moscow's internal and external market. The general direction of Russia's advance was northwards and eastwards where the more primitive native peoples had little to match the superior military organization, weaponry and gunpowder of the occupying Russians. Only when the latter came up against the power of the Chinese Manchu Empire was their progress in the Far East checked, and the Amur and Ussuri river regions were not annexed by Russia until the mid nineteenth century (treaties of Aigun 1858, and Peking 1860). Russia's permanent position on the Pacific at this time was marked by the founding of the city and port of Vladivostok in 1858. Further north, across the Bering Straits, the government divested itself of its possessions in Russian America by selling off the territory of Alaska to the United States for 7,200,000 dollars in 1867.

Apart from commercial and imperial interests, the scientific exploration of Siberia gained momentum during the eighteenth century, much of it sponsored by the Imperial Academy of Sciences. Of particular significance were the expeditions of V. I. Bering, I. G. Gmelin, G. Müller, S. P. Krasheninnikov and P. S. Pallas. In the nineteenth century the process was continued by such people as N. G. Potanin and P. P. Semenov-Tyan-Shansky, and in the Far East by N. N. Muraviev-Amursky, G. I. Nevelskoy and V. K. Arsenev.

The governorship of Siberia was marked over the centuries by a series of institutional and administrative changes. At first the country came under the jurisdiction of the equivalent of the Foreign Office, and the Office of the Court of Kazan, until the Siberian Office was established in 1637. Local power in the seventeenth century was largely in the hands of temporarily appointed military commanders and a mixed civilian and military bureaucracy. Opportunities for graft, corruption and exploitation of the local population were plentiful, and the tyrannical and oppressive regime of the tsars' 'Siberian satraps' became legendary. The plundering of Siberia's natural and human resources by the agents of Moscow and St Petersburg lay at the root of the later concept of Siberia as the victim of systematic colonial exploitation which inspired the Siberian regionalist and separatist movement in the late nineteenth century (see below). In 1708 the Province of Siberia was established as part of Peter the Great's provincial government reform, with Tobolsk as its administrative capital. In 1764 the region was divided into the two Provinces of Tobolsk and Irkutsk. These were later administratively reunited with the establishment of the Governor-Generalship of all Siberia in 1803. This post was held between 1819 and 1822 by Count M. T. M. Speransky who introduced a thorough-going reform of the region's entire administrative structure, including the exile system and policies governing relations with the non-Russian native peoples. Once more Siberia was divided into the Governor-Generalships of Western and Eastern Siberia, their respective administrative centres being Tobolsk (from 1839, Omsk) and Irkutsk, an arrangement which lasted until the onset of the Revolution and Civil War.

Economic development

As early as the eleventh century hunters and merchants from Novgorod had crossed the northern Urals into the regions of the lower Ob in pursuit of fur. This area, then known as the land of Yugra, fell into Moscow's hands after her defeat of Novgorod in the late fifteenth century, providing her with a valuable trans-Uralian entrepôt well before Ermak's campaign of 1582. It was, however, in the seventeenth century that the economic exploitation of Siberia began in earnest. Through a mixture of state initiative and private enterprise, trappers, hunters and traders, alongside government agents, administrators and military personnel, expanded throughout Siberia in the rush to profit from the region's initially abundant supply of fur-bearing mammals. Over-killing and exhaustion of reserves led to further territorial advances and more distant hunting grounds. Apart from direct hunting by the Russians, a large proportion of their fur revenue came from the imposition of the pelt-tribute on the native Siberian tribes in the conquered territories. It has been estimated that in the seventeenth century the fur trade may have accounted for as much as one third of the total state revenue.

The establishment of settled administrative centres, tribute-collecting points and fortresses brought with it a demand for increased food resources, and the incoming Russians introduced into Siberia a comparatively advanced level of agricultural production to supplement the supply of imported foodstuffs. In many cases the new farming techniques, both of crop production and livestock rearing, were adopted by the indigenous peoples, which successfully complemented their basically hunting economy.

The wave of voluntary migration and the flight of large numbers of peasant fugitives from the serf-owning provinces of European Russia in the late seventeenth and early eighteenth centuries greatly accelerated the agricultural development of the region, particularly in western Siberia and the southern forest-steppe and steppe zones. Increased population stimulated the demand for manufactured goods, which was originally met exclusively by imports from European Russia. However, the discovery of valuable mineral resources (for example of silver, lead, copper, iron, mica) and the establishment of small industrial enterprises led to the growth of a primitive manufacturing economy. The mining and metallurgical industries in eastern Siberia and the Altai were particularly important in the production of ordnance and other military material. Salt-workings, shipbuilding and the needs of the overland transport network (including horse breeders, leather workers, blacksmiths and cartwrights) as well as the growth of minor service industries led to a steady diversification of the region's economy. Siberia's major towns, too, especially Tobolsk, Eniseisk and later, Irkutsk, developed into vigorous centres of trade and industry.

Although tiny vestiges of serf-ownership did exist, the development of Siberian agriculture was marked by an overall absence of landlord property relationships; the majority of the rural population was transformed into state peasants, and an agrarian market economy quickly developed. Although Siberia's peasantry was organized on the communal pattern, it did not generally adopt the system of periodic land redistribution or crop rotation characteristic of European Russia (see PEASANTS). In the late nineteenth and early twentieth centuries the rate of peasant migration into Siberia increased enormously, the abundant availability of cultivable land contrasting favourably with the scarcity in the central European provinces. Between 1861 and 1895, 750,000 new colonists settled in western Siberia and along the southern tract, contributing significantly to the rapid growth of large-scale capitalist farming operations. After the building of the Trans-Siberian Railway (1894–1904), the rate of immigration increased even more spectacularly, peaking during the period of STOLYPIN's agrarian reforms (1906–11). Between 1895 and 1914 over four million settlers arrived in Siberia and continued the transformation of the country into one of the Empire's major agricultural regions, dairy-farming and butter production being particularly important. At the same time, in some areas the amount of sown land and cereal production more than trebled. On the whole, the Siberian peasantry was more prosperous, their farms much larger and their work more highly mechanized than in European Russia.

Not only agriculture, but also industry expanded steadily around the turn of the century, stimulated by the construction of the Trans-Siberian Railway and the influx of foreign capital into the region's economy. State-run enterprises gradually gave way to more private capitalist production both in the manufacturing and extractive industries. Large-scale industrial enterprises were, however, rare in Siberia, the majority of those which did

exist being mines and pits for the exploitation of gold, silver and coal – gold making the most important contribution to the region's industrial output. However, Siberia still lagged behind European Russia in industrial development, accounting for only two per cent of the nation's total industrial production and containing an industrial working class of no more than half a million at the time of the 1917 Revolution. Despite these small numbers, Soviet historians emphasize the leading role played by the Siberian proletariat (for example the Lena goldfield strike of 1912) and the activities of Marxist Social-Democratic organizations and political exiles in the growth of revolutionary consciousness in Siberia immediately before 1917.

The non-Russian peoples of Siberia

At the time of Russia's original conquest of Siberia, the region was inhabited by a thinly-scattered population of multi-ethnic and multi-cultured indigenous peoples. The major ethno-linguistic groupings were the Finno-Ugric, Turkic, Mongol, Tungus-Manchu and Paleo-Asiatic, which were further subdivided into over fifty separate peoples ranging in size from the Buryat and Yakut whose numbers had risen to around a quarter million each by 1917, to the numerically insignificant Kamasintsy of the Kansk district, of whom only 137 were counted in a census of 1890. By the mid nineteenth century other small nationalities, particularly in the far north, had disappeared completely as a result of exploitation, physical destruction or assimilation. The technological level of the Siberian natives was primitive, some of them being only at the Neolithic stage of development when encountered by the Russians; the majority were nomadic, and the predominant occupations were hunting, trapping, fishing, gathering and reindeer herding. Under the influence of the Russian immigrants more sedentary patterns of existence were gradually established and agricultural activities developed. However, it was the combination of inferior technology (including weapons), loose political organization and a divisive tradition of inter-tribal hostility and warfare which facilitated the rapid subjugation of the natives to the incoming Slavs.

The nature of the Russian impact on the native peoples of Siberia has been the subject of long historical debate. Some writers consider Russia to have been the bearer of advanced civilization, superior technology and social harmony to a host of mutually belligerent and ignorant savages. Others, like the nineteenth century Siberian regionalists, saw the natives merely as the hapless victims of ruthless military conquest, economic exploitation, forced labour policies, extortion, rape and systematic cruelty. More recent Soviet historiography has sought to combine criticism of oppressive tsarist colonial policies with a belief in the predetermined and largely beneficial nature of the Russians' 'assimilation' of the Siberian lands and peoples, a process which was entirely governed by the laws of historical development.

There is of course no doubt that the aboriginal peoples were subjected to violent, inhumane and brutal treatment. Apart from mass slaughter in unequal combat or in acts of reprisal, the Siberian natives suffered a whole gamut of persecutions and humiliations at the conquerors' hands. Most obviously, the imposition of the notorious fur-tribute not only kept them in a state of ruinous fiscal obligation to the state, it also diverted them from other traditional pursuits and greatly accelerated the exhaustion of natural reserves of Siberian fauna. Only during the eighteenth century when the national economy became less dependent on the fur trade did the tribute system become less onerous and widespread. There were, however, other burdens. The practice of hostage-taking, either in exchange for immediate ransom or else to ensure the long-term docility of the rest, often denuded whole villages and tribes of their ablest hunters, chieftains and religious leaders (shamans) with disastrous consequences on the social fabric of the clan. Native males were also removed from their families for long periods as a result of forced labour recruitment or military conscription. Postal and transport duties were especially demanding in the provision of both man- and horse-power from native resources. The aborigines' plight was further aggravated by the introduction of virulent diseases, in particular smallpox and syphilis, which frequently reached epidemic proportions, and by the forcible abduction of native women and girls into conditions of near-slavery. Despite various official attempts at prohibition, widespread alcohol abuse further debilitated the native community.

On the other hand the government in Moscow or St Petersburg did on occasion take positive steps to safeguard the natives' interests and to protect them from the more gross forms of exploitation. State-interest rather than genuine altruism, however, was often the motive which lay behind the various measures designed to prevent any decrease in the tax-paying capabilities of the subject races, and in any case legislation passed in the distant capital could do little to ameliorate the flagrant abuses of the colonial system by its officers and agents in the field. On the more positive side, there was never any official policy of deliberate genocide, nor any sustained campaign of compulsory russification or christianization, although natives who did convert to Orthodox christianity were relieved of the obligation to pay the tribute. Genuine attempts were also made to incorporate native leaders into the local administrative structure of Siberia, many of them even being rewarded with the rank of hereditary noble – a practice which Soviet historians regard as a cynical alliance between the Russian and native ruling classes, the more effectively to exploit the masses. As long as the once-pacified nationalities remained docile, little attempt was made to interfere with their traditional social, judicial and religious customs. Also, some kind of peace was gradually brought to the territory as internecine warfare between the tribes was halted and sporadic anti-Russian insurgencies steadily gave way to passive acceptance or active collaboration. The aboriginal peoples benefited, too, from the adoption of superior tools, weapons and skills which helped to modernize and diversify the native economies. As well as the more distressful forms of sexual miscegenation, there was also a good deal of free intermarriage between the Russian and native populations, and despite the disappearance of some smaller nationalities, other peoples thrived and multiplied under Russian rule.

From 1822 until the Revolution relations between the native and the Russian communities were theoretically governed by Speransky's legislation which sought to bring about the 'organic' assimilation of the Russian and Siberian peoples. In practical terms, however, there was little departure from the traditional pattern of Russo-aboriginal relations which had been established over the previous centuries.

Siberian regionalism

During the latter half of the nineteenth century, a movement aimed at securing a greater degree of regional autonomy for Siberia was formed out of a variety of economic, political and cultural factors. A more emotional colouring was also provided by the theories of some regionalists, notably A. P. Shchapov and N. M. Yadrintsev, that a combination of historical and environmental circumstances had resulted in the evolution of an identifiably Siberian national 'type' that was physiologically, psychologically and behaviourally quite distinct from the European Russian, with its own specific and separate interests.

The origins of Siberian regionalism lay in the activities of regional fraternities of Siberian students in St Petersburg in the period 1859–63. Stimulated by earlier contacts with the exiled Decembrists (officer-conspirators of 1825) and Petrashevtsy (radical writers and thinkers of the 1840s) in Siberia, and influenced by the radical intellectual climate in the capital, their main concern was for the welfare and future development of their homeland; as yet no plans or aspirations for the political independence of a separate Siberian state had developed. In addition to intellectual and emotional factors which encouraged the burgeoning of a regional self-consciousness, Soviet historians have drawn attention to the growth of capitalist relationships in Siberia and the appearance of a powerful local business community with rooted economic and fiscal grievances against the central authorities who, they considered, regarded Siberia merely as a source of raw materials and a profitable market for goods manufactured in European Russia. The continuing malpractices of centrally appointed officials, and the running grievance over the use of Siberia as a vast penal settlement added further grist to the regionalists' mill, and provided more evidence to support their contention that

Siberia was simply an exploited colony of the tsarist government.

Shchapov's views on regionalism as opposed to statism as the major motivating factor in Russia's historical development offered further intellectual content to the regionalists' growing preoccupation with the struggle between the periphery and the centre, the colony and the capital, the Siberian people and the central government authorities. Although they never formed an organized movement, still less a political party, the regionalists did formulate and articulate a series of demands which amounted to a rudimentary programme for the future civic development of Siberia. A most urgent and important item among their demands was for the abolition of the exile system which they saw as the most serious obstacle to the social and economic progress of the country (see below). Secondly, in the economic sphere, the regionalists fully incorporated into their 'programme' the interests of the Siberian merchant class which resented the maintenance of a kind of internal customs barrier between European and Asiatic Russia; this not only adversely affected their mercantile and trading interests, but also financially exploited the Siberian consumer. Thirdly, a policy of more equitable and rational distribution of the land and an agricultural policy which would encourage the orderly settlement of the country by peasants from European Russia was called for. Fourth was the desire to satisfy the needs of the Siberian intelligentsia with the establishment of a Siberian university and a general improvement in the educational, scientific and cultural amenities in the region. Finally, the regionalists' special concern for the plight of the Siberian native peoples led them to demand not only the preservation of the aborigines' residual rights but also an improvement in their material circumstances and their total integration in the future development of a more independent Siberia.

In this minimal, reformist programme there were no calls for the political separation of Siberia from metropolitan Russia. However, in 1865 the discovery in Omsk of two inflammatory manifestos calling for the establishment of an independent Siberian republic led to a wave of arrests, an official inquiry and a series of imprisonments and sentences of exile in which several leading regionalists were involved. In 1866 an insurgency among the thousands of Polish exiles in the region of Lake Baikal was brutally suppressed by government troops. The rebels had hoped that their mutiny would attract the wide participation of the exploited classes of Siberian society, free all political prisoners and exiles, overthrow the tsarist government, liberate the subject peoples of the Empire and lead to the establishment of an independent Siberian republic, to be renamed Svobodoslavia, with the exiled radical theorist, N. G. CHERNYSHEVSKY, among the leaders of a new revolutionary government.

Towards the end of the century most of the regionalists' minimal demands were more or less satisfied, and their later activities, though still concentrated on Siberia's welfare, lacked the more radical coloration of the movement's infancy. This has led to a controversy among both Western and Soviet historians as to the socio-political orientation of the regionalists, some seeing them as genuine 'revolutionary democrats', others as 'bourgeois nationalists' with little popular support, and others even as forerunners of the Siberian 'counterrevolution' during the CIVIL WAR. It is noteworthy in this respect that during the revolutionary events of 1917 renewed calls for Siberian independence were made, and in December an Extraordinary All-Siberian Congress meeting at Omsk appointed the veteran regionalist, N. G. Potanin, as head of the Provisional Siberian Regional Council which addressed itself to the struggle against the local BOLSHEVIKS and the establishment of Soviet power.

The exile system

The annexation of Siberia in the late sixteenth and seventeenth centuries created for the Muscovite authorities both the geographical opportunity and to some extent the political necessity of using the new territories as a place of banishment and exile for both common and political criminals. Tsar Alexei's Law Code of 1649 specified exile as the punishment for eleven separate criminal offences, and over the next two and a half centuries exile to hard labour, permanent settlement or temporary residence in Siberia became the central and most characteristic feature of the tsarist penal system. Like other forms of banishment elsewhere in the world, Siberian exile originally fulfilled a dual purpose – punishment and colonization. By forcibly sending disgraced officials, criminals, prisoners-of-war and religious dissenters into exile, the Muscovite government not only rid European Russia of undesirable elements but also supplemented the manpower needed to consolidate its new possessions, populate the region with Russian stock and exploit its valuable resources. By 1662, ten per cent of Siberia's Russian and other immigrant population was made up of exiles.

During the first half of the eighteenth century, Peter the Great's insatiable demand for forced and convict labour in European Russia slowed down the rate of Siberian exile to some extent, but it increased again enormously in the second half as a result of Empress Elizabeth's de facto abolition of the death penalty for criminal offences in 1753, and the granting to serf-owners of the right to send their insubordinate serfs and their families to permanent settlement in Siberia in exchange for a military recruit quittance. Despite positive evaluations of the exile system – on both humanitarian and practical grounds – during the seventeenth century, by the early nineteenth century it had become clear that the operation had become grossly overburdened, underfinanced, vicious, corrupt and totally incapable of fulfilling either its penal or colonizing purposes. Far from being of demographic or economic

Figure 36 Cottage shared by 'politicals' in the Kara penal settlement.

benefit to the region, the exile population was proving to be a grave and ungovernable incubus on the Siberian community, inseminating the territory with the seeds of devastating social ills. The fact that the great majority of exiles were, almost by definition, criminally inclined, anti-social and intractable, and contained a large proportion of murderers, rapists, arsonists, vagrants and bandits was the cause of obvious concern for the local government authorities and of considerable peril for the free, settled population.

In 1822 Speransky's new Exile and Convoy Regulations sought to make the system more manageable, humane and efficient, but the rapidly increasing numbers of deportees and the continuing underprovision of finance and of administrative and supervisory personnel thwarted his efforts from the start. As the century wore on, so did the numbers continue to rise, from an average rate of around 8000 per year in the 1830s to over 14,000 in the 1870s, peaking at 20,000 in 1875 (not including those sentenced to hard labour). At the turn of the century the exile population averaged around one third of a million, and accounted for about six per cent of Siberia's total population. The overwhelming majority were common criminals sentenced by the courts or expelled by adminis-

trative process from the peasant communes for 'bad behaviour' or 'non-acceptance' after completion of a custodial sentence.

A particularly difficult problem for the authorities, and a plague for Siberian society, was the high incidence of escape and vagrancy among the exile population. As many as one third of the exiles were officially listed as 'whereabouts unknown' at any one time. Large gangs of escapees and fugitives permanently terrorized the villages and towns of Siberia, and accounted for most of the very serious and violent crimes committed in the territory. The incidence of vagrancy and vagrant-associated crime was, however, dramatically reduced after 1895 when the government introduced the expedient of dispatching all convicted vagrants to the dreaded penal colonies on the island of Sakhalin.

Political exiles only made up a small fraction (approximately one per cent) of the total exile population at the turn of the century. Apart from the Polish nationalists exiled in the 1790s, the first mass deportation of offenders against the state was that of the Decembrists in 1826, followed by the members of the Petrashevsky circle in 1849, the radicals of the 1860s, and hundreds of POPU-LISTS, terrorists and other 'untrustworthy' elements in the

258

Figure 37 Attaching chains to a new arrival, c. 1900.

1870s and 80s. The circumstances in which political exiles were detained varied from the relatively comfortable, if spartan, surroundings in which LENIN, for instance, spent the years 1897 to 1900 at Shushenskoe in southern Siberia, to conditions that were so insufferable as to drive many to the point of insanity or suicide. Despite their relatively small numbers and severe restrictions on their activities, political exiles from the Decembrists on made significant contributions to the social, intellectual and cultural life of Siberia.

After a lengthy official inquiry an Exile Reform Law was passed on 12 June 1900 which greatly curtailed the peasant communes' rights of administrative banishment, and thereby sought to reduce the numbers of deportees. However, the growing tide of industrial, agrarian and political unrest in the early years of the new century meant that the hoped-for reduction was offset by large numbers of striking workers, rebellious peasants, members of left-wing and nationalist political parties exiled for revolutionary activities. While this policy successfully isolated many such activists from their comrades and class base in European Russia, Siberia absorbed a politically conscious and experienced cohort of revolutionaries which ensured the geographical, organizational and ideological spread of the revolutionary movement into the remotest parts of the Empire, with far-reaching consequences for the events of 1917 and after. Despite the government's awareness of the deleterious penological, economic, social and, increasingly, political consequences of Siberian exile, it was not until April 1917 that the system of punitive exile to Siberia was finally abolished by the first PROVISIONAL GOVERN-MENT.   AW

Further Reading

Armstrong, T.: *Russian Settlement in the North*. Cambridge: 1965.

Dmytryshyn, B., Crownhart-Vaughan, E. and Vaughan, T. eds.: *Russia's Conquest of Siberia: A Documentary Record, 1558–1700*. Oregon: 1985.

Kennan, G.: *Siberia and the Exile System*. New York: 1891.

Levin, M.G. and Potapov, L.P.: *Narody Sibiri*. Moscow and Leningrad: 1956. Trans. *The Peoples of Siberia*. Illinois: 1964.

Okladnikov, A.P. ed.: *Istoriya Sibiri v pyati tomakh*, vols 2 and 3. Leningrad: 1968–9.

Treadgold, D.W.: *The Great Siberian Migration*. Princeton, NJ: 1957.

Wood, A. ed.: *Siberia: Problems and Prospects for Regional Development*, ch. 2. London: 1987.

Yadrintsev, N.M.: *Sibir kak koloniya*. St Petersburg: 1882.

Revolution in Siberia

The railway

Siberia was once described as lying '. . . at the back of Russia's house like a vast store-cellar, a cellar half-filled with ice and with only one door – the Urals – and in place of windows two narrow slits, Kyakhta and Okhotsk.' The physical characteristics of the region, together with the attempts at developing it, had, possibly more than in any other region in Russia, an immense influence on the political forms that took shape there during the turbulent years of the revolution. As with the American West, the construction of a railway was to have been the basis for the opening up of difficult, but potentially bountiful, terrain to colonization and exploitation. Because of the capital-intensive nature of the project, Sergei WITTE, finance minister from 1892 to 1903 and its instigator and chief visionary, looked to the extension of the line into China, thereby forming a link of steel which would draw the Russian Far East into a single economic entity with the fertile plains of NORTHERN CHINA, as well as opening up markets there for Russian entrepreneurship. Hastened by the downturn in funds available for the push to the east, and in Witte's own political fortunes in the early 1900s, the symbiotic relationship that the finance minister had hoped would underwrite the development of the region did not materialize. Instead of a link of steel, Russia acquired a brittle bridge spanning the 5,000 miles of an under-developed Siberia. The line created a relatively narrow corridor of development, but even this quickly revealed the inadequacies both of the Trans-Siberian itself (westward freight creating a bottleneck at the mouth of the line and its entire western section) and Russia's railway network as a whole. (In 1918 A. A. Bublikov, a former member of the Duma, estimated that Russia urgently required at least 9,750 miles of new trunk line in order to allow fresh increases in freight and production in Siberia.)

The settlements

The lopsided development of the railway was starkly reflected in the nature of settlements in Siberia: the pocket grandeur of cities such as Omsk, which in their '. . . breadth, sweep and western spirit . . .' reminded visitors of the major cities in European Russia, surrounded by the desolate, often impenetrable taiga and strung out along the lifeline of the railway. Or the natural beauty of Khabarovsk on the eastern seaboard, where the wretched muddy streets in combination with the confluence of humanity gave it the air of a 'Wild-West' town. These pockets of European Russian civilization were also the embodiment of Russian politics in miniature. In the generally conservative populations there was a vociferous representation of the more radical elements of the Russian political spectrum. Siberia had, after all, been a place of exile for criminals and political prisoners since the eighteenth century.

However, what was absent from the Siberian arena on the eve of 1917 was the mass base that political parties could tap, namely a disaffected peasantry and proletariat. The development of Siberian agriculture had been facilitated by the Trans-Siberian Railway and STOLYPIN's reforms: it was relatively prosperous and had not suffered serfdom. Modern industrial development in Siberia had begun with the FIRST WORLD WAR and intensified sharply only in the 1930s. Thus the debates and political machinations that took place after 1917 were in a sense those of 'revolution in a tea cup': the slogans and the political arguments employed were much the same as in European Russia, but the material conditions and the issues at stake, at least initially, were significantly different. The population of Siberia was small, its towns well stocked with food and essential goods throughout the year of revolutionary change that gripped western Russia; the latter in some measure directly as a result of such shortages. The overspill of revolution did cause a steep rise in the numbers of urban dwellers as a mixture of refugees and military personnel flooded in – trains bound for the east from Petrograd frequently could be boarded only by squeezing through carriage windows – which resulted in a chronic shortage of new accommodation in the Siberian centres (Chelyabinsk doubled its population in a year). Conditions for the new arrivals were dire. Yet native populations continued to lead a life of comparative normality: charity events thrived and the inhabitants of the larger settlements remained '. . . remarkably well dressed'.

Siberian Bolsheviks in 1917

The FEBRUARY REVOLUTION brought with it, as in the rest of Russia, the problem of political power: who was to dispense it and how was it to be dispensed? The restoration of a semblance of order to Russian life by the PROVISIONAL GOVERNMENT was barely able to disguise the struggle that emerged after the collapse of tsarism in the form of the dual power. During the course of 1917 the Siberian settlements became a political labyrinth in the contest between the recalcitrant far right, the moderate right and the moderate left: the latter composed of the Right SOCIALIST REVOLU-TIONARIES, the party closest to the interests of the Siberian peasantry, who, as a contemporary observer commented, wanted neither BOLSHEVIKS nor tsar, but '. . . good business conditions and the development of cooperatives'. For the Siberian Bolsheviks the immediate tasks perforce lay elsewhere: consolidating their own ranks, securing the left-wing platform and gaining control of the soviets.

Although numerous members of the Bolshevik elite were in exile in Siberia, their principal interests lay far from the region itself. After the events of February, and the Provisional Government's repeal of tsarist laws on corporal punishment and exile, its members returned to Petrograd and other centres in European Russia. As a result, the organization of the struggle in Siberia was left very much to diffuse local forces. There was little evidence of preliminary planning for or coordination of these Bolshevik elements. Preparation, in so far as it existed, was improvised (Ya. M. SVERDLOV, for example, stopped in KRASNOYARSK on his way from exile in Eniseisk to consult local Bolsheviks on their unification at district level and that of Siberia as a whole). The process of uniting and reinforcing Siberian Bolsheviks was relatively slow. In April 1917 a conference was held of Bolshevik groups in Krasnoyarsk, Achinsk, Kansk and Eniseisk, which instructed the Krasnoyarsk District Bureau to establish communications with all Bolsheviks in Siberia. In August the Central Siberian Regional Conference of the Bolshevik Party was held in Krasnoyarsk, with about 5,000 members in attendance, at which the Central Siberian Regional Bureau was established to direct party activity in Siberia. Only by mid September had the Bolsheviks of major Siberian centres such as Tomsk and Omsk come into line by splitting the united Social Democratic organizations they belonged to (those of Krasnoyarsk had withdrawn as early as May, while the Bolsheviks of Irkutsk would do so as late as October). The reorientation initiated by the Krasnoyarsk conference was accompanied by extensive agitation amongst the SOVIETS and party organizations, as well as the encouragement of the unification of soviets; a measure vital for the creation of a Bolshevik power base.

Their efforts in merging the soviets of workers and soldiers were in most areas problematic in themselves (in Irkutsk, for example, a representative of the Bolshevik Party's Central Committee was sent out in early October to assist local operatives in bringing the respective soviets closer together), let alone aligning them with peasant organizations. Equally, the process of gaining control of the soviet policy was frequently acrimonious and dependent on makeshift alliances with left SRs, Internationalist SRs and MENSHEVIKS. The competition with right SRs, even when the Bolsheviks were in alliance, was closely fought. Success often depended on bitter, divisive debate, leading ultimately to a walk-out of a frustrated moderate opposition, thereby allowing by default Bolshevik dictation of policy and an increasingly leftward drift of the soviets.

There was also general, and consistent, opposition from the parties of the left to Bolshevik proposals for the arming of workers; proposals that had been made as early as May 1917. However, the Bolsheviks began to create small combat groups unilaterally, employing returning soldiers to train them.

Although the stage was gradually set for the seizure of power after the OCTOBER REVOLUTION, it was a flimsy one. The Bolshevik leaders in Siberia had largely emerged from within the region itself, often through recent defections from the left SRs and Internationalists. Their efforts to bring a maturity to the party's infrastructure in the region suffered considerably from the physical remoteness of many of the Siberian settlements and their own intellectual remoteness from the Bolshevik nerve-centre in European Russia. Above all, they suffered from having to function in small, largely conservative, urban areas where much of the Bolshevik rhetoric that proved so potent in Petrograd and Moscow frequently fell on the deaf ears of an unsympathetic – at times uncomprehending – audience. Often, Bolshevik leader-agitators such as Ada LEBEDEVA were reduced to having '. . . to explain in plain terms . . .' slogans issued by LENIN in Petrograd. The uphill struggle resulted in some immediate benefit however, particularly with elements of the military (Siberia provided large numbers of men to Russia's war effort) and left-wing Hungarian prisoners-of-war interned in Siberia (who played a key role in securing Bolshevik successes at Krasnoyarsk, Omsk and in the initial routing, under the leadership of Sergei LAZO of ATAMAN G. M. SEMENOV's forces at Karimskaya).

October revolution, intervention and counter-revolution

Through a combination of political manoeuvre and a limited military force (including elements of the nascent RED ARMY), the Bolsheviks gained control of Siberia. After the fall of Krasnoyarsk, three days after Petrograd, the gains came slowly. In some centres (Tomsk and Irkutsk), the transition was relatively peaceful; in others (Omsk, Chita) the Bolsheviks had to fight. The drive eastwards was completed when, in December 1917, Vladivostok and Khabarovsk acknowledged Bolshevik authority and – in February 1918 – the nationalist Buryats were driven from Ulan Ude (south of Lake Baikal). However, while the Bolshevik revolution had finally reached the eastern periphery of the old tsarist empire, the task of consolidating the gains rapidly proved beyond the resources of the party (both at regional and national levels). The initial success was provided not so much by the strength of the Bolshevik organization of revolt as the absence of a coherent line of opposition to it. This allowed the Bolsheviks' limited resources to make the gains they did, but in asserting their control over segment after segment of Siberia via the soviets they were also the catalyst for the emergence of broad lines

of resistance. The Bolsheviks' push into the Russian Far East was seen by Japan as an encroachment on its own interests in that region (notably in Manchuria) and a reason for employing military force directly against them, as well as providing material support to White forces under Semenov in Mongolia. For the other allies the unease created by the Siberian Bolsheviks' use of Hungarian POWs in armed combat provided added impetus for intervention.

Finally, the revolt of a 15,000-strong section of the Czech Legion against the Bolsheviks in May 1918 sparked the transformation of the strands of opposition into direct force (beginning with the Allied intervention). The events leading to the Czechs' action had shown that the Bolshevik central command was quite clearly out of touch with the Siberian Bolsheviks' actual circumstances. TROTSKY in his Order No. 377 had demanded that local soviets disarm the Czech soldiers and that 'reliable forces' be sent to the rear of the Czech units '. . . with the assignment of teaching a good lesson to those who did not comply'. This greatly overestimated the capacity of local soviets and Bolsheviks to enforce their authority and provided a reason for the Czechs to broaden their military activities. The Czech units quickly spread their influence along the Trans-Siberian. On 30 June 1918 they occupied Vladivostok '. . . amidst the cheers of a joyful populace'. Subsequently, Trotsky showed further disregard, and ignorance, of the underlying strengths of the Bolsheviks in Siberia by ordering the immediate disarmament of German POWs, some of them sympathizers (mostly Hungarian) who had served as vital military support to Bolshevik authority in the region.

Under the cover of the Czechs' policing of the railway and the Allied intervention, the Siberian right began to regroup. It was a troubled and ultimately incomplete process leading to a military coup at Omsk and the designation of Admiral A. V. KOLCHAK as the Supreme Ruler of Russia. From the start there were serious problems in converting his nominal control of anti-Bolshevik forces operating inland to an actual one. While the leaders of White divisions, such as Atamans Semenov, B. V. ANNENKOV, A. I. Dutov and Captain Baron R. F. VON UNGERN-STERNBERG, were intent to the point of obsession on crushing Bolshevism, their approach to the task was wilful and often diverged from the overall plan of campaign (in so far as there was one). Early in the CIVIL WAR these shortcomings were of little significance. There was an immense amount of human traffic moving through the 'doorway' of the Urals after October 1917, most of it in an easterly direction and ripe for recruitment into the White armies. This culminated with the return of thousands of Siberian POWs, from Austria and Germany in the winter of 1918, many of whom were hostile to the Bolsheviks. The Siberian Bolsheviks, with their counterparts in European Russia coming under increasing pressure, had little choice but to withdraw to the countryside and reorientate themselves to wage a protracted guerrilla war.

Revolution in Siberia

Economics and revolution

The war and the February Revolution brought with them even greater differentials between rich and poor in Russia: shrinking supplies of goods, rising prices and the fall in the value of the ruble ensured that a wide cross-section of the population would suffer deprivation. Yet for some it was also a time for the making of money: the February days forced owners of enterprises to reconsider their positions; the more timid selling out, frequently at a considerable discount. Those who took the risk of buying were, using loans, able to take advantage of the chronic shortages to force a large (and more profitable) turnover in the space of months, thereby being in a position to repay the principal or go on to buy up further enterprises. Such economic opportunism and broadening of speculation had its costs. For the ordinary consumer it invariably led to faster price rises. For the less adventurous members of the bourgeoisie it resulted in confusion, further financial (and political) entrenchment and, finally, despair. In Siberia this process was partly translated into lost opportunities: the returning POWs of 1918, rather than being sheltered by local social organizations, were in most cases left to fend for themselves (often with grossly inadequate provisions of clothes, housing, food and money) in the depths of a Siberian winter. The Bolshevik government quickly took advantage of this situation: in place of the financial incentive it was offering at first to the trainloads of POWs on their way into Siberia (in return for their enlistment in the RED ARMY; an offer which held little appeal), it began to issue money and clothing unconditionally instead. In addition to the aid, by mid-January 1919 returnees brought with them Bolshevik newspapers '. . . singing "To the Hour" with . . . conviction that world revolution is at hand'. Kolchak's regime, dependent on the generosity and motivation of the communities it loosely presided over, could not match this systematic onslaught. Against this backdrop of the Siberian bourgeoisie's inertia, the early victories of Kolchak's armies – even as they pushed the front to the Urals – could do little to prevent the steady erosion of confidence that took place in the settlements behind them as the country's economic disorder took a firmer grip, compounded by a constant stream of rumours and reports filtering through along the railway of fearsome clashes with Bolshevik partisans.

Vladivostok and the Far Eastern republic

By late 1919 Kolchak's forces were on the defensive: the Red Army had relaunched its offensive in Siberia, while the brittle White military confederation began to break down. Through a combination of worsening material conditions and the Bolsheviks' guerrilla campaign (which elicited increasingly brutal measures from the White forces, thereby dislocating and alienating the peasantry), the Siberian countryside became awash with peasant unrest. On 10 November, the Kolchak administration evacuated Omsk and it fell to the Bolsheviks shortly after. By early January 1920 the Kolchak government was at an end (replaced briefly by a local 'political centre' at Irkutsk, where Kolchak had moved after Omsk).

Although the Bolsheviks regained their ground swiftly following Kolchak's collapse and the evacuation of part of the interventionist forces, Lenin's government was faced with a problem in the region of Siberia's 'windows' to the East. Borders there had to be secured both physically (the need to eliminate the last White divisions: some based in Mongolia, others threading their way through Northern China to the Russian maritime province) and diplomatically (dealing with local minority interests, together with the thornier issue of those of Japan, which was militarily still in a position to make the final consolidation of revolution in eastern Siberia difficult). The solution was the creation of the Far Eastern Republic on 6 April 1920: a plan – originally proposed by the Irkutsk 'political centre' – that would place a buffer zone between Russian Bolshevism and the capitalist (notably Japanese) East. Following the final withdrawal of Japanese troops from the maritime province in May 1921, and the subsequent collapse of White authority there, the Far Eastern Republic extended its administration into that region, too. In late 1921, with the immediate threat to the Soviet border gone, all of Eastern Siberia was returned to the control of the RSFSR.

Vladivostok acted as an important incentive for the Bolsheviks to stabilize the region politically. Thanks to the extension of the Trans-Siberian into Manchuria (via the South Manchurian and CHINESE EASTERN RAILWAY), Vladivostok had prior to the Revolution grown rapidly as a trans-shipment centre, primarily for Manchurian soya beans. The Bolshevik government was anxious that this role should be restored and, indeed, increased. Through its early commercial links with the Chinese markets the port provided the Bolsheviks with a source of contact with Western financial services and export channels (through banks and companies involved in trade both in Manchuria and Vladivostok). Furthermore, Vladivostok was regarded as a potential catalyst for the development of the entire region (much like Witte's thoughts on the uses of the Trans-Siberian and its Manchurian extension). For all these reasons the Bolsheviks from the start pursued a markedly pragmatic policy in the area. On occasions the central government would overrule the directives of the local Bolshevik administration if they were seen to be too radical for the economic priorities of the region. This pragmatism – which figured prominently in Soviet policy in North-eastern China as a whole – was very much at odds with the more orthodox insurrectionist approach adopted by Soviet agents in the southern parts of China in the 1920s.   FP

Further Reading

Carr, E.H.: *The Bolshevik Revolution*, vol. 1. London: Macmillan, 1950.

262

Gorky, M. et al. eds.: *The History of the Civil War in the USSR*. Vol. 2, *The Great Proletarian Revolution*. Florida: Academic International Press, 1975.

Heald, Edward T.: *Witness to Revolution*. Kent State University Press, 1972.

Patrikeeff, Felix: Russian and Soviet economic penetration of Northern China, 1895–1933. In *Essays on Revolutionary Culture and Stalinism*, ed. J. W. Strong. Columbus, Ohio: Slavica, 1990.

Serge, Victor: *Year One of the Russian Revolution*. London: Allen Lane, 1972.

Krasnoyarsk

Located on the banks of the Enisei, this Siberian settlement was an important centre of Bolshevik activity. It was here that Ya. M. SVERDLOV stopped briefly – to discuss Bolshevik activities in the region – on his way to European Russia after the FEBRUARY REVOLUTION had ended his exile. Bolshevik organization in Krasnoyarsk was strong: it was rich in leadership (S. LAZO, A. LEBEDEVA, V. N. YAKOVLEV et al.), had firm links with the local SOVIET (its newspaper, *Krasnoyarskii Rabochii* (Krasnoyarsk Worker), was under Bolshevik influence) and published the only Bolshevik newspaper in Siberia *Sibirskaya Pravda* (Siberian Truth). In the spring and summer of 1917, the town became the main vehicle for the reorganization of the Siberian Bolsheviks (in April 1917 it became the communications centre for all Bolshevik groups in Siberia, while in August it convened a conference of Central Siberian organizations). With the Bolshevik seizure of power in Petrograd, it became the first Siberian centre to fall to the party. For some time, as one description has it, it was '. . . one red spot on the white vastness of Siberia'. Indeed, it regained this status soon after the start of the Allied intervention when, in July 1918, it became one of two remaining Bolshevik strongholds (together with Irkutsk) along the Trans-Siberian.   FP

The Atamans: Annenkov, Boris Vladimirovich (1889–1927); Semenov, Grigory Mikhailovich (1890–1946); Ungern-Sternberg, Baron Roman Fedorovich von (1886–1921)

The part played by the atamans in the initial failure and eventual success of the Bolshevik Revolution in Siberia is clouded by the emotions stirred by their exploits during the CIVIL WAR, when their armies roamed areas of central Siberia (see SIBERIA: REVOLUTION AND WAR) and, finally, represented the last military elements of anti-Bolshevism on the periphery, (especially Mongolia and Manchuria). The atamans took this customary title from the COSSACK term for headman or general (hetman), although they were not always native Cossacks themselves (Annenkov, for example, was born in the province of Voronezh ·and assigned to the Cossack Hundreds at Verno only after

leaving military academy). They jealously guarded the independence of their command – and equally their self-appointed roles as military saviours to the Russian people. This attitude was frequently counterproductive to the anti-Bolshevik cause. Semenov did much to hinder the passage of supplies to KOLCHAK at crucial stages of the Civil War because of a strong sense of rivalry he felt for the Supreme Ruler. Annenkov built up his army from a partisan detachment in 1917 to a force of 12,000 in 1918, but engaged in little coordinated action with Kolchak's armies at a time when the latter needed reinforcement (although in fairness to Annenkov it must be said that Kolchak paid scant attention to his forces, which he consistently dismissed as being composed of brigands and therefore unfit to fight alongside his own regulars, even had they wished to do so). As the lines of authority between the White Command and the atamans was (at best) ill-defined, virtually no pressure could be exerted to rectify the situation.

The atamans' forces were built up informally, and were held together by a strong sense of loyalty to the leader himself and with ruthless, often savage discipline. A core of Cossacks was supplemented by a rank-and-file ranging from the illiterate peasant to the Petrograd bourgeois. Conscripts would gravitate to the atamans' divisions by word of mouth or chance. For those with little or no military training who fled from European Russia ahead of the Bolshevik surge, this represented the clearest and simplest way of opposing the new regime. To many potential conscripts, these divisions actually represented the true army of resistance. Because the atamans gave little formal support to any authority except their own, they got virtually no material support in return. Food and supplies had to be forcibly requisitioned. The cost of this self-reliance was the instilment of fear into the civilian population that these forces came into contact with. As the fortunes of the Siberian Whites declined, so the methods of the atamans' forces intensified in their violence, resulting in a trail of retreat into Eastern Siberia and beyond that was littered with atrocities. It is here that the ambiguity of the atamans' contribution to the counter-revolution looms largest. There is little doubt that after the Civil War began to turn in the Bolsheviks' favour, the atamans through their violent methods succeeded in turning vast numbers of Siberian peasants against the White cause (in his activities around Omsk in the summer of 1919, Annenkov is said to have created more Bolsheviks than he killed). And yet these men had soon after the OCTOBER REVOLUTION built up vast forces virtually from scratch. Those who worked at Annenkov's headquarters remember him as a man of iron discipline who nevertheless was extremely conscious of the need to keep irregular behaviour towards civilians to a minimum. He was said to have issued strict orders to his Cossacks and soldiers alike not to harm civilians in any way. As his strength was dependent, at least initially, on popular appeal this seems quite plausible. The truth may be, as those who fought with him suggest, that his main contribution could have come at the time of the Bolshevik counter-offensive in the Urals in the first half of 1919 when he was in a position to help regular forces ward off the initial thrust of the Red Army and, on the back of his initial successes in Western Siberia, might have attracted fresh recruits to the White cause. As it was, this opportunity was fleeting and unlikely to have been taken up because of the differences between Kolchak and the ataman himself.

Annenkov had served in General P. N. Krasnov's Regiment prior to the FIRST WORLD WAR, commanding the Cossack Hundreds. In 1914 his Cossacks were sent to the German front, where he organized a separate detachment and rose to the rank of colonel. With the outbreak of revolution Annenkov moved to Siberia and began to organize his forces at Omsk. His run of victories over Bolshevik forces took him to Semipalatinsk where he was eventually made commander-in-chief of the entire Semipalatinsk front. Although he was a talented military leader he had little conception of ultimate objectives: from June 1919, his drive to destroy the Siberian Bolsheviks turned into a hopeless cut-and-run as the White army began its retreat into the depths of Siberia. With no food (except for meat from their own pack animals) and ranks sharply depleted by typhus, his troops moved from their first point of retreat in the Altai Mountains (where a military camp, Orlinoe Gnezdo (Eagles' Nest), was formed) into Sinkiang (Xinjiang) Province in China. Their expedition took them through the Gobi Desert to Peking (Beijing), Tientsin (Tianjin) and finally to HARBIN, where the local authorities refused to allow them to remain. Over six months after they left Russian territory in May 1920, Annenkov's men were forced to return to it as they made their way to Vladivostok. Their last stand against Bolshevism (as the Annenkovskaya Diviziya, made up of three Hundreds, under the general command of General M. K. Dieterichs) was at the village of Vladimiro-Aleksandrov. In late autumn 1921 the remainder of Annenkov's men had returned to the Chinese border. There they handed over their weapons to the Chinese authorities and slipped into China to their final exile. Annenkov himself returned to Russia in 1926, was arrested, tried for atrocities committed during the Civil War, and executed in 1927.

Annenkov's division skirted territory controlled by the two most notorious White commanders of the Civil War: Ataman Semenov and the Baron von Ungern-Sternberg. Between them, Semenov and the Baron held sway over much of Trans-Baikalia and Outer Mongolia, basing themselves at Chita and Urga (Ulan Bator) respectively. Semenov was a Cossack leader from Eastern Siberia who had been commissioned by the PROVISIONAL GOVERNMENT to form a military unit for the Western Front. Instead, he created a private army (the Special Manchurian Detachment) and established himself, with Japanese sup-

port, as the dominant White Russian force east of Lake Baikal. The Baron Ungern, a Baltic German, was originally a member of Semenov's group, but broke away in 1920 to create his own sphere of influence in Mongolia. Between them, Semenov and the 'Bloody Baron' presided over a political cesspool (much aided by the Allied intervention and the region's tangled set of relations between the Chinese, Japanese, Mongols and the Russian refugees) until their fall in 1921. In Outer Mongolia those on the fringes of White politics were able to nurture their daydreams of a triumphal return to Russia: General A. P. Baksheev (leader of the remnants of the Orenburg Army), who attempted to reconcile his conservative politics with the popular revolution by issuing appeals to the Siberian peasantry under a huge red banner, occupied in one corner by the old national colours; the half-Altai Kaigorodov, uninterested in politics and bent only on ridding his beloved Altai of the evil of Communism, leaving future policy to be discussed after this had been achieved; Ataman Kazantsev (from the Enisei Province), a man '. . . not gifted with extraordinary diplomatic talents . . .' whose attempt to enlist the support of the Soyot tribe in 1921 succeeded only in causing a raid by tribesmen on his own camp, depriving him of thirty camel-loads of valuable supplies. Along with the militarists were wielders of informal power such as the shadowy, anti-Semitic Professor Ossendowsky regarded as the 'real pretender' at Ulyastay and who produced Order No. 15 (calling for an offensive against Russia, in which '. . . Commissars, Communists, and Jews shall be destroyed along with their families'.)

Neither Semenov nor Baron Ungern were capable of (or especially interested in) moulding political disparates such as these into a fluent, unified force to resist the Bolshevik counter-offensive. Military operations for these elements took the form of fierce raids into hostile territory, with little heed paid to general strategy and less still to an ultimate goal (excepting, of course, the idée fixe of eradicating Bolshevism). More often than not, their energies were further squandered on intrigues against one another as they vied to establish their individual niches of power on the barren Mongolian plains. The Baron Ungern's brutal overlordship was finally brought to an end by the Red Army in August 1921 (he was tried by Revolutionary Tribunal and executed in Novonikolaevsk the following month). The more pragmatic Semenov, who had retreated from Trans-Baikal to the Maritime Province between November 1920 and September 1921, fled to shelter under Japanese protection in Manchuria where he remained until September 1945 when he was captured by Soviet troops and executed the following August.   FP

Northern China before 1917

Russian trading relations with China in the border region between Siberia and Northern China gathered pace in the seventeenth century and were formalized by the Treaties of Nerchinsk (the first such document signed by China with a non-Asian power) in 1689 and Kyakhta in 1727. These relations formed the basis of contact between Russia and Northern China until the late nineteenth century, when, guided by finance minister S. Yu. WITTE's plans for the development of SIBERIA, the tsarist government proposed that a physical link be created between the sparsely-populated areas of the Russian Far East and those of Manchuria. Ostensibly the CHINESE EASTERN RAILWAY (the result of these proposals) was intended to shorten the Trans-Siberian's route to Vladivostok. Running through the heartland of one of China's most fertile and least exploited regions, it also represented vast potential for Russian trade and commerce. This potential was never realized. It had been Witte's intention that Russian economic predominance in Northern China should evolve naturally and peacefully (if only to preserve the delicate political balance in the region). Instead, under the aggressive policies of the Bezobrazov clique (which replaced those of Witte in 1903), the long-term interests of Russian commercial communities along the CER (the chief of these being the quintessentially Russian town of HARBIN) were sacrificed to more conventional forms of militaristic imperialism. This resulted in the isolation and debilitation of the Russian colonies in Manchuria (which had previously sheltered under the wing of the Ministry of Finance). Furthermore, it led to increased fears on the part of Japan, China and the Western powers concerning Russian intentions for the region. The friction soon gave way to military conflict, in the shape of the Russo-Japanese War (this cost Russia the southern branch line of the CER – which became the Japanese operated South Manchurian Railway – and formally divided Manchuria into Russian and Japanese spheres of influence). The war revealed that neither the railway nor the Russian settlements in the interior were capable of sustaining a large Russian military presence, let alone a major war effort, in Manchuria. Recriminations were freely exchanged between military and railway authorities for the poor conditions under which Russian forces fought and, in late 1905, awaited evacuation.

The mood of isolation and, through the war, of dislocation was mirrored in the effect of the 1905 REVOLUTION on the region. Little of the revolution's elemental character was in evidence prior to the Imperial Manifesto of 17 October (OS), news of which reached Manchuria only about a week later. Although meetings and political processions did follow (chiefly in Harbin) and there was some disorderly conduct amongst the troops (the army, as in Russia itself, remained loyal on the whole), the only concerted political action to speak of was the formation of a railway strike committee. This body, composed largely of railway workers (some of them SOCIAL DEMOCRATS) and engineers (mainly liberal or MENSHEVIK), succeeded in rousing a very brief general strike and for a short time seizing the entire CER. However, it had few well-formed political objectives and drew only hostility from the army because this action threatened to delay the evacuation of troops from Manchuria. General D. L. HORVATH, the Director of the CER and Russia's *de facto* plenipotentiary in Manchuria, regained control of the railway on 19 December, only eight days after he had been deprived of it.

The origins of party activity in Manchuria can be traced to late 1905, when BOLSHEVIK and Menshevik organizations first made their appearance at Harbin. The Bolsheviks, under the guidance of a representative of the Chita organization, formed the Harbin Workers' Group in November. At about the same time the Mensheviks, whose initial membership was made up of middle class railway employees and elements of the army medical corps, also became active. Over two years later a Harbin SR group came into existence (comprising largely the lower ranks of the railway guard force). There is little evidence to suggest that any of these parties succeeded in building up a mass base in Manchuria, or attracting Chinese support for their activities prior to 1917. The Manchurian Bolsheviks, in this last respect, were less Russocentric in their approach, having at least attempted to break the racial barrier by encouraging Chinese workers in the Russian railway zone to embark on industrial action (sporadic successes after 1911 have been attributed to Bolshevik efforts, notably through the work of B. Z. SHUMYATSKY). Even this, however, was little more than 'itinerant Bolshevism', based on essentially Russian revolutionary principles translated via interpreters or pidgin Russian into efforts to raise the political consciousness of Chinese workers. Yet without the involvement of the Chinese inhabitants of the CER Zone there could be no thorough-going political change there (let alone Northern Manchuria as a whole), except at most within the political microcosm of the Russian community itself. Activism in the latter was problematic. After the events of 1905 Horvath produced a policy of mild reform to answer grievances that had in part been responsible for the strike movement on the CER. A few years later he created a system of political vetting for new employees of the railway. By introducing these measures Horvath tightened his grip on the railway and, because the CER was the dominant element in Russian economic life in Northern Manchuria, checked the proliferation of imported political activists. His work in keeping the Manchurian radical groups in check prior to 1917 was assisted by their seclusion from parent bodies in Russia, to whom Manchuria represented something of a political backwater. For the Bolsheviks this proved to be a relatively serious underestimation, as the region (and its railway) degenerated from a relic of tsarist policy to an area of stubborn White opposition and, finally, a conundrum for Soviet foreign policy in Asia.   FP

Northern China: Revolution and Civil War

The political effects of the FEBRUARY REVOLUTION in European Russia filtered through to HARBIN in early March 1917 (the Provisional Government made somewhat circuitous contact with authorities there on 3 March (OS). News of the revolution was favourably, and peacefully, greeted by a cross-section of the community. An Executive Committee was quickly formed (principally by liberal, middle class elements) to pave the way for an orderly transition to elections and a new body of authority responsive to the PROVISIONAL GOVERNMENT for the railway zone. At the same time a SOVIET came into existence, although its precise origins and composition are unclear (almost certainly because it appeared as a spontaneous response to events in Russia rather than a manifestation of strong, politically fashioned working-class consciousness). Despite the emergence of these bodies and the open activities of the political parties (in addition to the SDs and SRs, the Kadets and National Socialists established their official presence in Harbin in the spring of 1917), the bulk of power in the railway zone resided with HORVATH. His power base had suffered initially, but through a combination of political trading (Horvath acceded, as he did in 1905, to the introduction of limited reforms and drew closer to the political platform of the Kadets) and support from the foreign powers in China he was able to retain his position of influence in local politics through the early months of uncertainty.

It was only in the summer and early autumn of 1917 that the radical groups in Harbin began to make their presence felt, aided by the delayed effect of Russia's economic problems on the local economy. However, while these groups were starting to enjoy the benefits of a radicalization of certain sectors of the working class, their potency in the Russian community as a whole remained minimal. Much of their attention, as a result, was directed at finding common ground with more moderate political elements. Taking advantage of the growing confusion in the Russian camp, the Manchurian warlord Chang Tso-lin (Zhang Zuolin) began to force the limits of Russian military influence in Northern Manchuria back from its pre-revolutionary boundaries to within the railway zone itself.

At the time of the Bolshevik seizure of power in Petrograd, the Harbin Bolsheviks were a minority in the local soviet (and remained so) and had the backing of only a small proportion of the lower ranking railway guards. Despite this, their leaders demanded a transfer of all power to the soviets at a demonstration on 25 October (OS). Receiving only limited support for this proposal (a Menshevik-dominated Provisional Revolutionary Committee was formed by the Harbin Soviet instead), the Bolshevik group were left with little choice but to perform a token seizure of the telegraph office the following day. Although support increased in subsequent weeks (culminating in the Bolshevik candidate coming second –

(behind the Menshevik candidate and ahead of Horvath, the latter representing the Kadets) – in the election to the CONSTITUENT ASSEMBLY held in the latter part of November), the Harbin Bolsheviks' chief contribution to the revolutionary effort was as an unwitting vehicle for reaction against the new Soviet government. On 8 December LENIN sent a telegram to the head of the Harbin Bolshevik group, instructing them to seize control of the railway zone in the name of the Russian proletariat and the Bolshevik government (a few days later a similar communication arrived from TROTSKY). The Harbin Bolsheviks had had neither the intention nor the military ability to do so. Nevertheless, this led to a run of events (in late December) whereby Horvath, under a certain amount of pressure from representatives of the foreign powers, invited the intervention of Chinese troops to stem the Bolshevik threat. Lenin's initial directives provided good reason for the Chinese response: his call (and Trotsky's subsequent message) for Bolshevik action in Manchuria strongly suggested that as far as the Bolshevik leadership was concerned the CER issue was an internal Russian one. In doing so Lenin had seemingly concurred with the well-established view (laid down by the tsarist government and preserved by the Provisional Government) that the railway zone was a Russian colony in all but name. Little that the Bolshevik government subsequently said (the Soviet Commissariat of Foreign Affairs initiated a series of talks on the CER and diplomatic representation with the Secretary of the Chinese legation at Petrograd in January/February 1918) could sway the Chinese from the conviction that such attitudes guided its policy towards China.

Émigrés, consuls and advisers: the overspill of revolution into Chinese politics

The stationing of Chinese forces at key locations in the railway zone temporarily halted the chaos caused by the revolution. The Chinese had, at the same time, taken a firm step in asserting their sovereignty over the railway and its zone. Their support had come at a price: Horvath's personal power base in Manchuria underwent a process of steady erosion by the Chinese authorities until, in late 1920, he was reduced to the role of 'High Adviser' to the CER (but based at Peking). However, in using Horvath's request as the pretext to act, the Chinese government had also helped to establish an anti-Bolshevik platform in Manchuria. At first this was dominated by Horvath himself (in July 1918 he formed a 'Business Cabinet' and declared himself 'Ruler of All Russia', but soon allowed himself to be demoted to the more modest station of Administrator of the Far East under KOLCHAK's regime). Later, as his power waned, it became an amorphous body of opposition fuelled by the dramatic influx of refugees into Manchuria during the Civil War. In many respects, the émigré society that emerged proved to be a thornier problem to the Soviet government than either Horvath or ATAMAN SEMENOV (the latter commanding areas of Northwestern Manchuria after October 1917) had been. Although the warlord Chang's Mukden government provided a very crude form of political shelter to the émigrés, the latter were increasingly exposed to economic privations (especially the most recent arrivals), often through the machinations of Chang and his local officials. As a consequence the Russian communities became politically volatile. Conditions did not improve for them during the 1920s, while at the end of that decade (when the effects of the Sino-Soviet conflict and the Great Depression gripped the region) they deteriorated even more sharply.

The anti-Bolshevism of local Russians took numerous forms, ranging from anti-Soviet publications to street brawls with Soviet citizens, or those who were suspected of sympathizing with their forsaken country. Soviet efforts to generate trade and develop the activities of the CER (after Moscow signed treaties with the central Chinese government and that of Chang in 1924) were constantly scrutinized for possible political motives. So sensitive was the Soviet position in Manchuria that two distinct policy lines emerged in its dealings with China during the 1920s: the northern characterized by an almost complete devotion to economic tasks; the southern by a militancy (in the work of A. P. Borodin and the Soviet advisers to the Chinese Communist Party and the Kuomintang) that embodied the very spirit of Communist internationalism. Such well-defined dualism was impossible to perpetuate. In 1927 the Soviet advisers' status in southern China was abruptly terminated (after the events in Shanghai and Canton (Guangzhou) (see THE IDEA OF WORLD REVOLUTION). In the north, however, Soviet economic operations for a time continued apace, although there had been increasing concern expressed by Soviet representatives about the pressure being exerted on the Soviet side of the CER partnership (so much so that Soviet complaints resembled, as a British banker noted, a defence of foreign rights in China!). Tensions continued to grow until mid 1929, when (after a raid on the Soviet consulate in Harbin and the arrest of Soviet citizens, together with the closure of Soviet trading organizations there) Chinese authorities seized the CER. The Soviet military response a few weeks later completed the collapse of its twin-sided China policy. FP

Further Reading

Glatfelter, R.E.: Horvath, Dimitrii Leonidovich (1858–1937). In *Modern Encyclopedia of Russian and Soviet History*, ed. J.L. Wieczynski. USA: Academic Press International, 1978.

Patrikeeff, F.: Russian and Soviet economic penetration of North China, 1895–1933. In *Essays on Revolutionary Culture and Stalinism*, ed. J. W. Strong. Columbus, Ohio: Slavica, 1990.

Quested, R.K.I.: *'Matey' Imperialists? The Tsarist Russians in Manchuria, 1895–1917*. Hong Kong: University of Hong Kong Centre of Asian Studies, 1982.

Scalapino, R.A and Yu, G.T.: *Modern China and its Revolutionary Process*. Berkeley: University of California Press, 1985.

Stephan, J.J.: *The Russian Fascists: Tragedy and Farce in Exile, 1925–1945*. London: Hamish Hamilton, 1978.

The Chinese Eastern Railway

The scheme for the construction of the railway rapidly unfolded in the aftermath of the Sino-Japanese War of 1894–5 when, in an elaborate series of diplomatic manoeuvres, Russia's path was cleared through the Liao-tung (Liaodong) Peninsula to Port Arthur. This permitted the broadening of the initial plan of a shortened link between the Trans-Siberian and Vladivostok to take in the entire hinterland of Manchuria rather than simply cutting across its northern plains (see SIBERIA BEFORE 1917; NORTHERN CHINA BEFORE 1917), thereby allowing Russia to take advantage of another port (with great strategic value) on the eastern seaboard and the commercial potential of Manchuria itself. The terms of an agreement were negotiated by Russia with the Chinese plenipotentiary Li Hung-chang (Li Hongzhang) at St Petersburg in 1896. Although the agreement was subsequently (and frequently) cited by Chinese authorities as being unequal – supported by the accounts of Li's angry scenes with his Russian counterpart at the injustices being perpetrated against China – there is some suggestion that the terms were arrived at more through financial incentive to Li himself than by irresistible force. The project was financed by the Russo-Chinese Bank (especially formed for this purpose, and heavily reliant on French capital) and work began in the same year. The line was completed in 1903. Two years later, after Russia had been defeated by the Japanese, the southern line was formally handed over to Japan's control and became the South Manchurian Railway, with its central administration at Dairen (Ta-lien, Dalni).

The CER formed the backbone of Northern Manchuria's economy and politics. As a consequence the struggle for its control became the focus of the Revolutions of 1905 and 1917, and in particular the attempts to dislodge General HORVATH (the first manager of the CER) from his seat of power. After his removal in 1920 the railway was run by the Allies (Japan and the United States) for the remainder of the CIVIL WAR. Only in 1924 did the Soviet Union succeed in securing Russian rights on the railway (but even then at a much reduced level from those enjoyed by the tsarist officials). From then on the railway acted as a constant source of friction between the Soviet and Chinese governments. Finally, the Sino-Soviet Conflict of 1929 precipitated a political process leading to Japanese intervention in Manchuria. The railway was sold to the Japanese in 1935 for a fraction of its original cost (the latter has been estimated as 350,000,000 gold rubles; after much bargaining, it was sold for 60,000,000). By then, however, the CER – which had been troubled financially for most of its existence – was a broken concern. FP

Harbin

By the terms of the original CHINESE EASTERN RAILWAY contract (signed in 1896), the railway was to receive *gratis*, or in some areas upon the payment of an annual rent, lands '. . . actually necessary for the construction, operation and protection of the line'. This guideline was subsequently interpreted in the broadest possible sense by Russia. Besides the one hundred feet either side of the track granted by the agreement, the CER acquired large areas encompassing a number of stations along the line. These acquisitions became the major towns of which Harbin was the most significant. The settlement at Harbin was founded on the banks of the River Sungaria (Songhua Jiang) in Heilungkiang (Heilongjiang) Province, in the heart of Manchuria. Harbin grew quickly: on the eve of the Russo-Japanese War it already had a Russian population of about 20,000 (out of a total of 60,000; the remainder being Chinese living in the Chinese settlement of Futiatien, which adjoined the Russian town). In 1917 the figure stood at 30,000, but was soon boosted by 14,000 refugees escaping revolutionary turmoil and the early stages of the CIVIL WAR in Russia. By the time the Civil War was at its height, the Russian population had doubled (at the very least). Despite the fact that the population of Harbin was still predominantly Chinese, the character of the railway town itself, in its administration, architecture, language, culture and commerce, was very much Russian (allowed by the physical distancing of the Chinese community and its style of life from that of the Russians, together with the successful exclusion of other foreign influences). The Russian settlement was divided into three distinct areas: Old Harbin, a residential precinct where the first CER engineers had built their spacious wooden villas; New Town, the civic and cultural centre of Harbin dominated by the grand forms of the CER's administrative buildings; and Pristan, the thriving but ill-planned commercial district whose initially unpaved, pot-holed streets had given it the air of a frontier town. By the 1920s Harbin was not only the hub of commercial activities in Northern Manchuria, but that of Russian life and culture in China as a whole. It had also become a principal centre (another was Shanghai) for émigré politics. Fringe groups ranging from liberals to Monarchists and, later, Russian Fascists made full use of the freedom to publish diatribes and manifestos, to establish educational institutions that might inculcate old Russian values in the new generation of émigrés, or simply

Figure 38 Market place, Harbin, with St Sophia Russian Orthodox Church.

to indulge in café and pavement politics. All within a tantalizing stone's throw of the Bolshevik state (during the Sino-Soviet conflict in 1929, however, this proximity was to create a great nervousness in the community, as it received daily reports of Soviet troops moving along the CER, seemingly towards Harbin). Politics continued to thrive among the émigrés in Harbin until the Japanese occupation following the Far Eastern Crisis of 1931–2, after which much of their vitality was lost through thorough surveillance and 'guidance' by units of Japanese military intelligence.   FP

The Cultural Impact of the Revolution

The debate on what should constitute the culture of the working class and the dictatorship of the proletariat had been engaged before 1914 and it continued after 1917. Was working class culture to be purged of all bourgeois influences? Or was it to be a pragmatic blend that would establish the psychological independence of the new workers' society and at the same time enhance its stability by preserving the best of what had been achieved by previous generations? In the euphoria following October 1917 a fierce dichotomy emerged, both sides of which sought to gain the state's material and ideological support. The issue may be best, if crudely, demonstrated by the question: what was to be done with museums?

The Russian revolution occurred at a moment in European cultural and intellectual history when creative human activity was dominated by the influences of Modernism and experiment. Artists and intellectuals readily saw in the coming revolution the opportunity to sweep away the out-dated and false values that still resisted the forces of change and innovation. The OCTOBER REVOLUTION reinforced these attitudes, and writers and artists flocked to support the new regime.

Their perception of its purposes was, however, flawed. The Bolshevik government, with few exceptions, was made up of men and women whose aesthetic and cultural outlook was strongly anti-elitist, and the effusions of modern art in all its forms, whatever its claims, appeared to be aimed at the cultivated taste of a minority. The new regime expected artists and writers to perform a useful function, to express the needs of the moment, not those of artistic progress.

Before the full impact of this conflict emerged, however, Russian artists in all fields produced an explosion of invention and innovation that made of the early Soviet years an episode of unprecedented originality and verve, whether in painting and sculpture, or theatre and music. As soon as the state began to demand artistic norms that suited its own pragmatic purposes, however, the freer spirits emigrated, returning from about 1922 to their pre-revolutionary habitats in Berlin and Paris. Artistic inventiveness in Soviet Russia thereafter found expression in more functional forms such as cinema, photography and architecture, but consideration of the later period falls outside the scope of the present work.   HS

Cultural Revolution

Before the Russian Revolution of 1917 the transition from capitalism to socialism was conceived of by European Social Democrats primarily in terms of political and economic change and even the German Social Democratic Party, the leading Marxist party in Europe, whilst it sought to provide workers with a socialist alternative to capitalist culture, tended to view the seizure of state power as a necessary precondition of cultural change and to subordinate its cultural activity to political and trade union work.

In Russia the analytical distinctions between political, economic and cultural, and the hierarchy of priorities between them were challenged during the 1900s by Alexander BOGDANOV, a co-founder with LENIN in 1904 of the BOLSHEVIK fraction of the RSDRP. When, during the crisis of Russian Social Democracy which followed the failed 1905 REVOLUTION, new methods of rallying the working class were judged necessary and Lenin advocated exploitation of the Duma and a reconciliation with the MENSHEVIKS, Bogdanov and his followers, without abandoning the Bolshevik strategy of insurrection, argued that in a period of reaction the energies of socialists should be devoted not to parliamentary activities but to the cultural development of the working class.

Bogdanov's ideas on cultural revolution were expounded in 'The current position and tasks of the party', the platform of the Vpered (Forward) Group, which he founded in 1909; they were further developed in his 'Cultural tasks of our time' in 1911 and incorporated in his general theory of the genesis and development of ideologies, 'The science of social awareness', in 1913. Before 1917 these and other writings of Bogdanov formed the basis of a debate upon the question of cultural revolution which anticipated the controversies of the Soviet period. Lenin in his campaign against Bogdanov between 1909 and 1917 chose to criticize not Bogdanov's cultural theories but his epistemology. However, when the Bogdanovist worker F. I. Kalinin argued in *Parizhskii Vestnik* (Paris Messenger) in 1913 that an authentic working class literature was needed to give expression to the varieties of working class experience, G. A. ALEXINSKY of the now divided Vpered group re-asserted the conventional priorities of the RSDRP by denouncing cultural activity as an accommodation to the capitalist system and by insisting on the primacy of the political struggle. When A. V. LUNACHARSKY sprang to Kalinin's defence and accused Alexinsky of favouring a dominant role for the intelligentsia within the labour movement Alexinsky returned the compliment by maintaining that the movement for proletarian culture was in reality a plaything in the hands of intellectuals like Lunacharsky himself. The charge of elitism was one to which even some Bogdanovists were prone and Lunacharsky's defence, outlined in the journal *Borba* (Struggle) in 1914, was as equivocal before the revolution as it would be after: proletarian culture, he argued, was not simply the expression of working class experience; it also comprised a particular 'world view'. The socialist intellectual could therefore 'render an enormous service to the proletariat in its quest for self-definition, in its efforts at organizing its feelings'.

Disagreements between Russian Marxists over the theoretical implications of 'cultural revolution' became further evident in 1913 when the Menshevik A. N. Potresov, writing in *Nasha Zarya* (Our Dawn), pointed to the apparent paradox that the most interesting literature of the epoch was the 'decadent' literature of a bourgeoisie in decline, whereas no worthwhile literature had been produced by the ascendant working classes. Identifying 'culture' with 'high culture' or the culture of the elite, Potresov argued that under capitalism the working classes lacked leisure, the essential prerequisite of cultural creation; working class consciousness was fragmented and expressed mainly in the political and economic struggle; consequently it was a 'Spartan' rather than an 'Athenian' culture. In general 'the culture of any class-divided society was produced by the ruling class of that society' and under capitalism the everyday life, habits and taste of the working class were conditioned by the urban bourgeoisie and petty-bourgeoisie who, through their control of art exhibitions, architecture, the theatre and variety theatre, feuilleton literature and the press, shaped the understanding of the working class of what was pleasurable and beautiful. However, the cultural domination of the working class by the bourgeoisie was not an entirely negative phenomenon: bourgeois culture embodied elements of universal humanistic culture and this was one reason why it was so readily assimilated by the working class. It was the task of socialist

critics to distinguish between the universal and specifically bourgeois elements in the culture of the present day.

In default of a reply by Bogdanov himself (an anthology to which he had contributed was banned by the Russian censor and his commentary was not published until 1925) the Bogdanovist response to Potresov came from Bogdanov's disciple, another worker Bolshevik and future President of the PROLETKULT, V. F. Pletnev. Rejecting Potresov's definition of culture, Pletnev argued that by 'culture' Marxists should understand all expressions of the value system of a social group or society and all aspects of human self-awareness. Moreover, cultural activity should be understood not as a reformist accommodation to the capitalist order but as an aspect of the class struggle which was both material and psychological. The proletariat had to 'gather together' its own ideas, logic, and methods of persuasion to resist the cultural domination of its adversary. For Potresov a working class culture could only develop after the socialist revolution, but for Pletnev the existence of working class orators, organizers, cultural associations, schools, clubs and theatres were proof of the vitality of an embryonic proletarian culture even under capitalism.

This debate over what should be understood by 'culture', over the relationship between political, economic and cultural change, over differences between proletarian culture and socialist culture, and over the putative vanguard role of socialist intellectuals was to be continued in the Soviet Union after 1917 both inside and outside the Proletkult (the workers' educational association formed by the Bogdanovists before October 1917). On one aspect of the question, however, pre-revolutionary Marxists at least were united: for Bogdanov, Lunacharsky and Pletnev, as for Potresov, the construction of a socialist culture would entail not the destruction, but the critical assimilation of previous cultures, the culture of the bourgeoisie included. Nihilism and iconoclasm were alien to pre-revolutionary Marxist theories of cultural revolution.   JB

Further Reading

Biggart, John: 'Anti-Leninist Bolshevism': the Forward Group of the RSDRP. *Canadian Slavonic Papers* 23.2 (June 1981).

Williams, R.C.: Collective immortality: the sydicalist origins of proletarian culture 1905–1910. *Slavic Review* 39.3 (September 1980).

Proletkult (The Russian Proletarian Cultural-Educational Association)

In Eastern and Western Europe during the nineteenth and early twentieth centuries the rise of the labour movement was a matter not only of party political and trade union organization. Through the formation of study-circles, self-help associations, free-schools, people's universities and the organization of libraries, choirs, drama groups and sports clubs, labour movement activists strove to build up working class solidarity and create an alternative system of values to those which prevailed under industrial capitalism. Continuing this tradition, Russian intellectuals during the Revolution of 1917 associated themselves with the spontaneous desire of the working classes for cultural improvement, perceiving in the cultural activities of the proletariat the beginnings of a socialist CULTURAL REVOLUTION.

A unification of the cultural and educational activities of the labour movement was first proposed in the Petrograd Soviet during the critical 'July Days' of 1917. Similar proposals were made at the Second Conference of FACTORY COMMITTEES of 7–12 August 1917, notably by A. V. LUNACHARSKY, and from 16–19 October 1917 208 delegates attended a 'Conference of Cultural-Educational Societies' in Petrograd. On 28 November 1917 the Central Committee created by this conference resolved to adopt the title 'Proletkult'. A Moscow branch of the Proletkult was founded in February 1918 at a conference attended by 288 delegates, mostly from factory committees and trade unions; and the First All-Russian Conference of the Proletkult was held from 15–20 September 1918. By 1919 the Proletkult claimed an enrolment of 80,000 students; by 1920 it was publishing no fewer than 20 journals; 80 per cent of members in 1922 were either production workers or of working-class origin. On the occasion of the Second Congress of the Comintern in July/August 1920 an International Bureau of the Proletkult or 'Kultintern' was formed to coordinate activities in France, Germany, Austria, Switzerland, Italy, Czechoslovakia and England.

The educational and recreational facilities offered by the Proletkult varied from locality to locality. General educational activities (including the provision of libraries) absorbed one third of the budget of the Proletkult in 1918 and courses were offered in mathematics, in the natural and social sciences, and in the history of literature and of the labour movement. In the same year the largest share of its budget was allocated to theatrical and literary activities. Plays were produced from both the classical and revolutionary repertoires; classes were offered in painting, sculpture and the writing of poetry; handicraft circles, choirs and balalaika orchestras also provided facilities for the development of a working-class leisure culture. Avant-garde writers, artists, designers, film and stage directors were eager to provide tuition in Proletkult studios, but for the most part Proletkult students were more concerned with the acquisition of useful knowledge and the assimilation of traditional culture than with cultural iconoclasm and experiment.

In the history of the Proletkult, as in the history of the factory committees and the TRADE UNIONS, we witness the demise of pluralistic tendencies within the Russian Revolution. As early as the spring of 1918 the autonomy of the Proletkult was challenged by KRUPSKAYA and others in the Extra-Mural Department of the Commissariat of Education (Narkompros) who favoured a state monopoly in adult education. For a time the autonomy of the Proletkult was preserved by Education Commissar Lunacharsky, a long-standing theorist of proletarian culture, for whom the assumption of social responsibilities by institutions such as the Proletkult was entirely appropriate under the 'commune-state'.

A more serious and ultimately fatal threat to the Proletkult came from the Communist Party. Even before the First All-Russian Congress on Extra-Mural Education of 8–19 May 1919 the Proletkult had been under suspicion as a haven for the 'bourgeois intelligentsia' (a category which included members of the MENSHEVIK and SR parties) and in his speech to this Congress LENIN expressed his disapproval of the intellectuals' infatuation with proletarian culture-building. Though Communists were at all times predominant in the Congresses and leadership of the Proletkult it had from its inception been led by Alexander BOGDANOV and his disciples LEBEDEV-POLYANSKY, Pletnev, Kerzhentsev and Kalinin. So considerable was Bogdanov's reputation as a Marxist after 1917 (his writings had influenced the Party's leading theoretician, BUKHARIN) that Lenin felt compelled in 1920 to re-publish his anti-Bogdanovist tract of 1909, *Materialism and Empiriocriticism*. A pronouncement of 1 December 1920 of the Central Committee of the RKP(b), 'On the Proletkults', which ruled that scientific and political education should be the preserve of the Commissariat of Education and that the activities of the Proletkult in the artistic field should be monitored by the Communist Party, signalled an end to the autonomy of the Proletkult. Its funding was reduced and it made only a minor contribution to adult education in the period until 1932 when it was abolished.

Despite this setback, Proletkult leaders continued after 1920 to exercise influence in other institutions and on Soviet intellectual life. The Bogdanovists considered the Soviet regime to be not a 'dictatorship of the proletariat' but rather a coalition of the proletariat, the poor peasantry and the bourgeois intelligentsia. Given the cultural backwardness of the first two strata they considered it likely, under prevailing conditions of state capitalism, that the intelligentsia would emerge as the ruling class. Without challenging the role of the Party as custodian of the political interests of the working class or of the trade unions as custodian of their economic interests, the Proletkult had reserved for itself the role of guardian of the cultural development of the working class, arguing that the transition to socialism required the formation of a new proletarian intelligentsia.

The Bogdanovist analysis of social relations under the Soviet regime was taken up by a number of BOLSHEVIK OPPOSITION groupings within the Communist Party during the 1920s, in particular the 'Collectivists', the 'Workers' Opposition' and 'Workers' Truth'. Bukharin, although he distanced himself politically from Bogdanov in 1922, conceded that the Bolsheviks lacked a cultural understanding of the transition to socialism and initiated a theoretical

271

debate on the subject in that year to which both TROTSKY and Lenin (in his last writings) contributed. Associated with this debate during the years of the New Economic Policy (NEP) were measures of positive discrimination designed to foster working class social mobility and the accelerated recruitment of workers off the shop floor in an attempt (later abandoned) to create a proletarian 'vanguard' within the Communist Party. As the Proletkult declined, the Russian Association of Proletarian Writers (RAPP) emerged from under its wing as a zealous proponent of the class war in artistic literature. In other institutions too (for example the Komsomol, the teaching profession and in economic research and administration) Communists who wished to break through what they considered to be the impasse of the NEP employed the rhetoric of 'cultural revolution'.

In 1928 STALIN enlisted the support of these 'left' factions in order to launch his own version of the cultural revolution. Bogdanovism may be said to have contributed to Stalinism an awareness of the need for a normative system which would regulate the behaviour of the working class during the transition to socialism, for a socialist equivalent of the 'Protestant ethic'. However Bogdanov, who had viewed the NEP as a system of 'moving equilibrium', had thought in terms of gradual, 'organic' change. His model of development had envisaged the end of individualism and authoritarianism and the free acquisition by workers and intellectuals of the habits of social cooperation. Stalin, by contrast, exploited the inherent contradictions of NEP as the driving force of a revolution from above, in the course of which the solidarity of working class communities was undermined both by the pace of industrialization and by the migration of peasants into the cities. For Bogdanov's spontaneously acquired behavioural norms Stalin substituted a coercive system of social control.   JB

Further Reading

Fitzpatrick, Sheila: *The Commissariat of Enlightenment*. Cambridge: Cambridge University Press, 1970.

—— ed.: *Cultural Revolution in Russia 1928–1931*. Bloomington and London: University of Indiana Press, 1978.

Gorbunov, V.V.: *V.I. Lenin i Proletkul't*. Moscow: 1974.

Gorzka, Gabriel: *A. Bogdanov und der russiche Proletkult*. Frankfurt: 1980.

Mänicke-Gyöngyösi, Krisztina: *'Proletarische Wissenschaft' und 'sozialistische Menschheitsreligion' als Modelle proletarischer Kultur*. Berlin: 1982.

Susiluoto, I.: *The origins and development of systems thinking in the Soviet Union*. Helsinki: 1982.

Writers and the Revolution

While many writers welcomed the coming of revolution in February 1917, and a number of them also became identified with the Soviet regime in due course, three major figures of Russian literature stand out and have been chosen here to represent their profession not on literary grounds alone: Blok as a poet was granted an opportunity to observe the events from a unique vantage point; Gorky had close relations with LENIN and the BOLSHEVIKS since 1905 and was consciously a 'political' writer whose world reputation was to prove an asset to the Soviet regime; Mayakovsky's explosive talents as a poet and artist of the avant-garde were quickly put into service after 1917 and became the chief influence in terms of style and content of the earliest efforts of Soviet propaganda.

Blok, Alexander Alexandrovich (1880–1921)

One of the greatest Russian poets, Blok was the most magical figure in the dazzling and complex early twentieth-century literary movement known as Russian symbolism. Both as man and writer his life and work expressed all the tensions of his time: now immersed in mysticism, now enchanted by nature; now intoxicated with passion, now ravaged by intuitions of doom or possessed by mockery. Like his wife and their close friend Andrey Bely, the more cerebral other star of symbolism, Blok was involved in incandescent relationships (platonic and otherwise) of unsurpassed rapture and anguish. He welcomed the revolutions of 1917 ecstatically, writing then the most famous and controversial of all Russian poems. He died prematurely in physical and mental agony. Not surprisingly Blok has continued to fascinate. Here, he is considered in relation to the events of 1917 (which he had clairvoyantly foreseen) and their aftermath.

Blok grew up in the cultured intellectual elite: his grandfather was Rector of St Petersburg University, his father a professor, his wife the daughter of the great chemist D. I. Mendeleev. To increasing acclaim, from his early twenties he published inspired poetry; but through witnessing the harsh life of the urban masses, the revolutionary events of 1905 in St Petersburg, and the subsequent reassertion of authority by the rigidified ruling class to which he belonged, he realized that the Russia in which he lived would perish and that his own poetic vocation was problematic. As his biographer Pyman puts it: 'The Tsar was an idol who would topple . . . . The individual was doomed to be overwhelmed and destroyed by the masses.'

Though always patriotically cherishing rural elements in Russian tradition, after 1914 Blok became sceptical and gloomy about Russia's participation in the war. He was himself actively involved for a few months supervising military construction work. (A sometimes overlooked aspect of his rich personality was that he was not only strikingly handsome but also strong and even athletic, a keen walker, rider and swimmer.) He rejoiced at the FEBRUARY REVOLUTION of 1917: 'a miracle has taken place . . . freedom has an extraordinary majesty'. Then suddenly this visionary poet found himself in an exceptional historical vantage point: he was appointed secretary to the special commission set up by the PROVISIONAL GOVERNMENT to investigate the alleged unlawful acts of high officials and dignitaries of the tsarist regime. Blok was also an experienced scholar and editor, and for almost a year he was occupied first with recording and then with editing the commission's examinations of the old regime's principal personages. (An exception was NICHOLAS II and his consort, though their correspondence was read – 'mutually loving', Blok commented.) His book about it all, *Poslednie dni tsarskogo rezhima* (Last Days of the Imperial Regime), was eventually published in 1921. As he wrote to his wife: 'I am now seeing and hearing something that almost no one hears or sees, that only the very few have the opportunity to observe once in a hundred years.' What Blok heard and saw seemed like a 'novel with a thousand characters and the most fantastic combinations, mainly in the spirit of Dostoevsky'; but the culture of which he was a brilliant representative was itself part of the house of cards that had collapsed. After attending the First All-Russian Congress of Soviets in the hectic summer of 1917 with its accelerating political and social confrontations, Blok realized that 'the brain of the country' might be 'ripped out quickly, cruelly, and authoritatively . . . How to overcome chaos? To overcome ourselves.' But the task of Russian culture was to assist in organizing the force of the fire which would burn 'what must be burnt'.

Soon after the OCTOBER REVOLUTION, Blok was one of the few writers who (like Mayakovsky) declared readiness to cooperate with the Bolshevik government. 'He walked about young and merry and wide-awake, with shining eyes', wrote a relative. As the CONSTITUENT ASSEMBLY met and was dispersed by the Bolsheviks in January 1918, Blok proclaimed in an article 'The Intelligentsia and the Revolution': 'Russia is storm . . . but she will emerge renewed and – in a new way – great'. And he wrote two famous poems, 'The Twelve' and 'The Scythians'.

'The Twelve' was the climax of Blok's inspiration and, many believe, the supreme pinnacle of Russian poetry; but what particularly astounded and bewildered and continues to divide its readers was the ending where, before the twelve ruffianly Red Guards tramping through the blizzard and bearing the red flag, hovers Jesus Christ – an image the author could never explain. 'The Scythians' was a warning to the West; as Blok summarized his thought: 'if you destroy our revolution . . . we shall open wide the gates to the East . . . your skins will go for Chinese tambourines', and again: 'it is hard to fight against the "Russian infection", because Russia has already infected mankind with health'.

That was almost the end of Blok the poet; the man lived on through three years of the Soviet regime and civil war. A foretaste of the future was a commissar's reluctance to allow 'The Twelve' to be read aloud at public gatherings;

Blok noted: 'they may be right. But where – again – is the artist and his homeless calling?'

Blok devoted himself to lecturing and to organizational work in theatre and publishing, conscientiously earning a bare subsistence during the hardship and deprivation of CIVIL WAR, shunned by many of his old friends. In 1919 he wrote an article, 'The Collapse of Humanism', in which he equated humanism with a decayed civilization, and contrasted both to the vitality of true culture, an elemental force that he likened to 'the spirit of music': to survive the artist must adapt himself to 'the age of whirlwind and storm that is opening up before us'. To a young poet he explained his thoughts about the revolution: 'it is the birth of a new kind of man . . . cosmos is born out of chaos'.

His colleague Gorky, now the most influential organizer and rescuer of culture under the new regime, was dismayed by what he called Blok's 'tragic forebodings'. Tragic indeed, for civil war chaos was ever-present, and a new cosmos still in the future; walking in the now derelict and desolate outskirts of the Petersburg he knew so well, Blok noted: 'one thing one must accord the Bolsheviks and that is their quite unique ability to stamp out custom and to liquidate the individual'.

Struggling with bureaucratic officialdom, convinced that 'art is incompatible with any forcible measures whatsoever on the part of the powers that be' and that 'what the poet is trying to do cannot be defined in advance, either by himself or by anyone else', early in 1921 Blok made his last major statement 'On the Calling of the Poet'. Appealing to officials to leave the poet that 'secret freedom' and 'peace and independence' that the greatest Russian poet Pushkin had sought under Nicholas I, he concluded with an acknowledgement and an affirmation of faith: 'We are dying, but art will remain.'

Blok was indeed dying. Though often ascribed to despair and malnutrition, the physical and psychological crumbling of his last months and his early death in August 1921 were probably consequences also of long-suffered venereal disease. Among his last comments were: 'She's gulped me down at last, that filthy, grunting, own-mother of mine Russia, like a sow her piglet . . . .'

The literature on Blok is dominated by, and any approach to his life and work must begin with, the comprehensive biography by Avril Pyman which combines exhaustive scholarship with breadth and depth of understanding unique in English-language biography of Russian authors.

Gorky, Maxim (1868–1936)

By the beginning of the twentieth century Gorky was already internationally famous as an eloquent portrayer of suffering and protest and as a sympathizer with and supporter of revolution. During his last years he was glorified in Stalin's Russia as father of socialist realism and wise guide of Soviet culture, and in some parts of the world admired as the supreme revolutionary author of modern times. Nevertherless as a writer Gorky (real name Alexei Maximovich Peshkov) remains controversial: assessment depends on the criteria adopted. Much of his fiction and drama seems crude and strident to cultivated literary taste. Gorky himself subsequently expressed dislike for his renowned novel *Mother* (1907) which extols proletarian heroism and self-sacrifice, but some revolutionaries and writers, concerned with literature as effective denunciatory and inspirational propaganda, have prized it.

Gorky was emotional rather than analytical. He came from an impoverished petty bourgeois family, and following a teenage suicide attempt ever after suffered from tuberculosis. In his youth he wandered through the turmoil of Russia's lower classes, colourfully depicting in the stories of the 1890s that made him famous both the misery and the energy of social outcasts, misfits and rebels. In the years leading to the 1905 REVOLUTION, he assisted with money and pen not only Bolsheviks but revolutionaries of all kinds. He declared in 1917 that for seventeen years he had considered himself a Social Democrat, but at the same time a heretic in every party and group (in 1925 he affirmed that he had never belonged to any political party). In 1908, not long after the prototypical socialist-realist *Mother*, he manifested his imprecise but profound conviction of the creative potential of the tormented and tormentingly contradictory Russian people in an extraordinary novel, *Confession*, where, amid the decay and corruption of conventional religiosity, popular faith generates miracle. Gorky has been called religious; both the harsh formality of dogma and the warmth of spontaneous compassion are memorably conveyed through the figures of (respectively) his grandfather and his grandmother in the autobiographical *My Childhood* (1913), often considered his masterpiece.

Not surprisingly Gorky's relations with Lenin were complex. Lenin, whom he met in London in 1907, was disgusted by the 'god-building' development in Gorky, and by the latter's attempt in 1909 (together with some well-known Bolsheviks, including V. A. BAZAROV, A. A. BOGDANOV and A. V. LUNACHARSKY who were likewise diverging from Lenin's rigorous materialism) to set up on Capri (where Gorky lived from 1906 to 1913) a non-Leninist school for selected Russian workers – which Lenin determinedly sabotaged. In one of the strongest of Lenin's published letters he asserted to Gorky: 'Every bloody little god is copulation with a corpse.'

From the February Revolution of 1917, through the October Revolution, and until the summer of 1918, Gorky occupied an independent position, condemning violence and extremism of every kind. Throughout this period he published in the MENSHEVIK-oriented newspaper *Novaya Zhizn* (New Life) many articles under the rubric 'Untimely Thoughts'; shortly after the Bolshevik seizure of power he wrote:

The working class cannot fail to understand that Lenin is only performing a certain experiment on their skin and on their blood . . . Lenin is not an omnipotent magician but a cold-blooded trickster who spares neither the honour nor the life of the proletariat.

Gorky continued to speak out until Lenin closed the paper in July 1918.

However, the next month an attempt was made on Lenin's life. Gorky visited the wounded Lenin, and the two were sufficiently reconciled for Gorky to devote himself – until the end of the Civil War in 1921 – to the colossal task of preserving Russian culture from destruction, not merely monuments and artefacts, but people. Writers and intellectuals of all kinds were found employment, and rations, in numerous literary and cultural organizations and enterprises (such as vast translation projects) devised by Gorky, exploiting to the utmost his special relationship with Lenin.

In 1921 Gorky left Soviet Russia, ostensibly for health reasons though he was certainly distressed by continuing Bolshevik ruthlessness after the end of the Civil War. Until 1928 he lived first in Germany and then in Italy. In 1922 he published in Berlin an essay 'On the Russian Peasantry' containing his most sombre reflections on the cruelty of Russian history and Russian life, citing many gruesome instances – 'I explain the cruel manifestations of the revolution in terms of the exceptional cruelty of the Russian people' – though concluding with hope for the gradual enlightenment of the rural masses.

Gorky's essential humanitarianism is underlined by his anguished concern over the Russian famine of the early 1920s. In 1922 he wrote to Herbert Hoover, chairman of the American Relief Administration which had contributed massive aid: 'In all the history of human suffering I know of no accomplishment which can be compared in magnitude and generosity with the relief that you have accomplished'. In the same year he protested to Lenin's deputy Rykov about the trial of leading SOCIALIST REVOLUTIONARIES: 'During the entire revolution I have indicated a thousand times to the Soviet government how senseless and criminal it was to exterminate the intellectual forces in our illiterate and uncultured land'. Twelve SRs were actually sentenced to death, with suspension of execution (eventually carried out under STALIN). Gorky was revolted, and is believed to have broken off all relations with Lenin.

However in 1924 Lenin died, and Gorky composed a moving obituary: Lenin was 'a hero of legend', will-power incarnate, 'a man who contrived to prevent people living their customary life as no one before him was ever able to do', who 'awakened Russia and now it will not fall asleep again'.

In 1928 Gorky visited Soviet Russia, was honoured and feted; he visited again in 1929, and returned for good in

Figure 39 Vladimir Mayakovsky, seated with Lily Brik; Boris Pasternak and Sergei Eisenstein behind.

1931. His death in 1936 remains obscure; at a trial in 1938 the former police chief, Yagoda, and Gorky's doctors confessed to having poisoned him.

In his last years Gorky was a prominent figurehead and spokesman of Stalinism, a role which has earned him contempt from many of those acquainted with the realities of Stalinist Russia. However there are some suggestions that he may not have been totally convinced that Stalin was realizing the ideals of enlightened progress that had always been his own; and he may have squashed doubts by seeing Stalinism – however mistakenly – as an energizing myth comparable to the life-enhancing lie shown as superior to dismal fact in some of his early imaginative writings.

Mayakovsky, Vladimir Vladimirovich (1893–1930)

Politically and creatively precocious, Mayakovsky was a Bolshevik at fourteen, three times arrested (and imprisoned for six months) by the time he was sixteen, a poet of brilliant and socially scandalous originality at the age of twenty, one of the few well-known writers who (like Blok and unlike Gorky) welcomed the October Revolution, then devoting much of his prodigious talent to versified Soviet propaganda; in the late 1920s he composed two provocative satirical plays, and then committed suicide. The flamboyantly aggressive Mayakovsky was at the same time naively forlorn and queasily complex. 'His suicide in 1930 could come as a shock only to those who had not studied his life and work' (Brown).

Turning from the Bolshevism of his mid teens first to painting and then to poetry (later he also wrote, and acted in, films), Mayakovsky became prominent among the avant-garde artists and writers in the movement of Russian futurism. The futurists' ebullient clowning and successfully outrageous performances, and their 1912 manifesto 'A Slap at Public Taste', represented an uncompromising repudiation of tradition and a genuinely revolutionary aesthetic, often oriented to the modern city and the machine, parallel to similar movements in Western Europe at the time.

Mayakovsky generated volcanic energy and gargantuan self-dramatization, rejoicing in titanic blasphemy, superhuman scale and cosmological sweep; he was one of the most fertile and ingenious poetic virtuosos the modern world has seen. His apparently irregular verse was an intricate coruscating mesh of invention, bold, startling, often brutal; yet his major pre-revolutionary poems 'A Cloud in Pants' and 'The Backbone Flute' are confessional, focusing on the disappointment of love, foreshadowing the frustration of his later life.

In 1915 he met his great love, Lily Brik, with whom he established a triangular relationship (she was married to the writer and critic Osip Brik) that lasted (through many vicissitudes) to his death. Reluctantly drafted for military service in the same year, Mayakovsky managed to get a light job in the capital where he continued writing, producing two verse epics: 'War and the World', a vision of horror and universal guilt (redeemed by a concluding Utopia); and 'Man', a vision of cosmic pessimism, ultimate solitude and potential suicide.

After the October Revolution of 1917, the futurists were the only literary group to support the Bolsheviks, extending a broad notion of 'revolution' to cover breaking with the past in the arts as in politics and society – an illusion soon dented by the manifestly conventional tastes both of most Bolshevik leaders (Lenin not least) and of the proletariat. During the Civil War the painter-poet Mayakovsky turned out hundreds of propaganda posters that included simple versified texts; they were typically displayed in empty storewindows instead of the goods that were lacking.

Mayakovsky and his futurist friends attempted to organize their alliance with the regime. In 1922 they set up Lef (the Left Front of Art) and published a journal of the same name, with the aim of 'encompassing the social theme by all the instruments of futurism'. The project was doomed not only by the philistinism of the masses and of most of the leaders, by controversy within Lef and with other groups, but also by Mayakovsky's own unresolved contradictions: his great poem 'About That', in the first issue of *Lef*, stems from his complex relations with Lily Brik. ('That' is love, not the building of socialism; and love, in the present, frustrated by convention.) After Lenin's death in 1924 Mayakovsky wrote a verse epic – not his most inspired – on the dead leader as a human being who became a mythical saviour, a Marxist messiah.

In the mid 1920s Mayakovsky churned out quantities of illustrated advertising jingles for a wide variety of Soviet products from macaroni through cigarettes to galoshes and infant pacifiers. It was as a 'commercial artist' that in 1925 he was admitted to the USA, his most distant foreign trip; he stayed three months and Brooklyn Bridge inspired one of his finest poems. In the 1920s he also several times visited Berlin and Paris, in the latter city seriously complicating his generally agitated love life.

From 1926 Mayakovsky, though still composing some remarkable personal poems, conscientiously devoted himself largely to useful verse, writing on current political, social, and economic topics; but he remained an innovator, at odds with Gorky and his influence.

The philistinism that was Mayakovsky's constant target is assailed in his striking play *The Bedbug* (1928), and in its less effective successor satirizing Soviet bureaucracy, *The Bathhouse* (1929). The second part of *The Bedbug* is set fifty years ahead in a rational, hygienic and antiseptic future, where a resuscitated vulgarly passionate man of the 1920s appears as a degenerate; the Rip van Winkle from 1928 is told that 'only textbooks on horticulture have anything about roses, and daydreams are dealt with only in medical works', and he is caged and displayed as a freak. But the satire is double-edged and personally ambiguous, for the emotionally unbridled Mayakovsky was the last person one could imagine happy in a sterilized Utopia. In 1928, in Paris and in love with a young Russian émigrée, he sent to his Soviet editor a poem 'on the nature of love', ending: 'Who can control this? Can you? Just try . . . .' The romance was thwarted, possibly by machinations of the Briks, and she married another.

Back in Russia Mayakovsky attached himself to an actress who reminded him of his lost Russian Parisienne. Increasingly isolated amid endless literary polemics, weary of spreading bureaucracy and deepening conformism, he wrote his last major poem 'At the Top of My Voice', telling how 'I subdued myself, setting my heel on the throat of my own song'.

At the age of twenty-two, the 'cloud in pants' shook 'the world with the might of my voice'; fifteen years later, in 1930, he wrote in a last fragment, 'Love's boat has smashed against the daily grind' and shot himself. The poet who had tried to place his supremely individual gifts at the service of a collective society lay with a bullet through his heart.

Lenin, with his thoroughly bourgeois literary taste, had disliked Mayakovsky. Stalin liked Mayakovsky's propaganda so, as Boris Pasternak wrote, Mayakovsky after his death 'began to be introduced forcibly, like potatoes under

Catherine the Great. This was his second death. He had no hand it it.'

MHF

Further Reading

On Blok

Pyman, Avril: *The Life of Aleksander Blok*, 2 vols. Oxford: Oxford University Press, 1979–80.

On Gorky

Borras, F.M.: *Maxim Gorky the Writer*. Oxford: Clarendon Press, 1967.

Gorky, M.: *Untimely Thoughts*, trans. H. Ermolaev. New York: Eriksson, 1968.

Kaun, Alexander: *Maxim Gorky and His Russia*. New York: Cape, 1931.

Hare, Richard: *Maxim Gorky: Romantic Realist and Conservative Revolutionary*. London: Oxford University Press, 1962.

Wolfe, Bertram D.: *The Bridge and the Abyss: The Troubled Friendship of Maxim Gorky and V.I. Lenin*. London: Pall Mall Press, 1967.

On Mayakovsky

Brown, Edward J.: *Mayakovsky: A Poet in the Revolution*. Princeton, NJ: Princeton University Press, 1973.

Markov, Vladimir: *Russian Futurism: A History*. Berkeley: California University Press, 1968.

Mayakovsky, V.: *The Bedbug and Selected Poetry*, ed. Patricia Blake; trans. Max Hayward and George Reavey. London: Weidenfeld and Nicolson, 1960.

Terras, Victor: *Vladimir Mayakovsky*. Boston: Twayne, 1983.

Woroszylski, Wiktor: *The Life of Mayakovsky*. New York: Orion Press, 1970.

Cinema

Agitation and propaganda had been of long-term importance to the pre-revolutionary Russian socialist movement in its underground years because it had provided the only means by which a minority party could arouse the working-class mass to revolutionary consciousness. It was no accident that the newspaper *Iskra* proclaimed from its masthead, 'From this spark shall arise a flame.'

The nature of the BOLSHEVIK coup in October 1917 meant that the new regime was equally dependent on agitation and propaganda, first to maintain itself in power and later to mobilize the population behind its ideology and authority (see OCTOBER REVOLUTION; PROPAGANDA). When the Bolsheviks came to power the cinema was already the most popular form of entertainment for the urban masses of the Russian Empire and it is therefore not surprising that LENIN is said to have described the cinema as 'for us the most important of all the arts'.

In a country where the population was still largely illiterate and where more than a hundred different languages were spoken, a country that stretched from the Baltic to the Pacific and from the Arctic to the Black Sea, a country that encompassed peoples of widely differing cultural levels and experience, the Bolsheviks needed a medium that would appeal to everyone. In these circumstances written and printed propaganda were clearly of little value and the spoken word was, by its very nature, of very limited use. The visual media were ideal: hence the importance of both the poster (see ART) and the film. The film's particular advantage was, of course, that it moved and that its appeal to the audience was direct: it did not have to be mediated by previous cultural experience. One contemporary remarked:

> In the East, where people have grown accustomed to thinking primarily in images, the cinema is the sole possible means of propaganda because it does not require the preliminary, gradual preparation of the masses. The Eastern peasant accepts everything he sees on the screen as the most fundamental and genuine reality.

But despite its mass appeal and its existing popularity, cinema in 1917 was, like the regime itself, in a rather fragile and vulnerable state.

The cinema in Russia before the Revolution was, of course, commercially orientated. Until the FIRST WORLD WAR Russian cinema had been dominated by foreign imports, predominantly French. While the war had increased cinema audiences, because cinema had provided a much needed avenue of escapism, it had also cut off the supply of imported films, raw film stock and studio and projection equipment. By 1917 the Russian cinema had almost exhausted its existing supplies of these materials and the interruptions in essential electricity supplies had made things even worse. The Revolution exacerbated these problems because the entrepreneurs who controlled the industry saw their commercial interests threatened by the Bolsheviks. Some of them buried their supplies in the hope that the revolutionary regime would be overthrown after a few months and the situation would return to what they regarded as normal. Others fled south to the Crimea, where they continued to make the kind of rather sensational, and sometimes salacious, films that they had been making before the Revolution. Both reactions seriously reduced the cinema's potential as a propaganda weapon for the new government. If there were no films, the cinemas themselves had to close: if the cinemas were closed, there would be nowhere to show the films.

LUNACHARSKY, whose People's Commissariat of Enlightenment (Narkompros) was nominally responsible for cinema organizations, realized that progress towards the effective and widespread use of the medium for government propaganda purposes could only be gradual. Too rapid a process of centralization and control would provoke an even less helpful reaction from those who were active in the industry.

Towards nationalization

The first steps towards controlling the cinema for propaganda purposes were therefore taken at the local level. In both Moscow and Petrograd the local soviets established Cinema Committees, and in April 1918 Lunacharsky announced that, at most, only one cinema theatre in each town would be nationalized in order to secure an outlet for the films produced by these and other official organizations and to protect these films against abuse or sabotage by opponents of the new government. He hoped that this announcement would calm the fears of commercial interests and encourage them to collaborate with the Bolsheviks. In late 1918 he ordered the registration of all stock and equipment: such an inventory was however widely and correctly interpreted as a prelude to nationalization. None the less a considerable number of entrepreneurs did cooperate with the new regime. In some ways they had little alternative if they wanted to remain in business because in April 1918 the authorities had created a government monopoly of foreign trade: the desperate shortage of films and equipment could only be relieved by imported supplies and these were henceforth at the disposal of the Bolshevik authorities. Since the emerging Soviet film organizations did not yet have the wherewithal or the expertise to engage in significant film production, the government largely relied on cooperation with the private sector. The studios of the Moscow and Petrograd Cinema Committees concentrated on the production of short punchy agitational films known as *agitki*: of the 92 films produced by Soviet film organizations in the 1918–20 period, 63 were classified as *agitki*. But a considerable number of *agitki* were commissioned from private firms.

Nevertheless the drain of talent and expertise to the south continued so that by the winter of 1918/19 Lunacharsky was to blame it for what he described as the 'catastrophic' state of Soviet cinema. In December 1918 Narkompros convened a meeting with the two Cinema Committees: Lunacharsky, KRUPSKAYA, Meyerhold and Tatlin were among those present. The conference recommended that all cinema organizations should be gathered under the umbrella of Narkompros and that a centralized organ of control should be established within that framework. The Eighth Party Congress, meeting in March 1919, adopted a resolution on propaganda work in the countryside which stated that the cinema and other forms of communication 'must be used for communist propaganda'. These pressures combined with the deteriorating situation within the industry to force the government to think again about its policy of gradualism. If Lunacharsky did not act swiftly and effectively, so the argument went, there would be little or nothing left to nationalize. On 27 August 1919 Lenin therefore signed the decree nationalizing Soviet cinema. The decree was itself only a first step, however, and it was some time before the process of nationalization was effectively completed: in March 1920 Lenin sent a telegram to local authorities asking them for a progress report on the steps that they had taken.

On the Red Front

The problems at the centre were only half the story. Bolshevik support was in any case strongest in the larger towns. It was in the countryside where the propaganda effort had to be concentrated, partly because of widespread support for the SOCIALIST REVOLUTIONARIES and other non-Bolshevik groups and partly because of the devastating effects of the CIVIL WAR that was raging at the time. Against this background of chaos and confusion the Bolsheviks had almost to create their own constituency. A vast country with a widely scattered population and a rapidly changing military front required above all a mobile, flexible and reliable medium of political communication between the centre and the regions, at least until those regions had become stable enough to allow the establishment of more permanent and conventional organizations. The dynamic visual medium of cinema would have been ideal. The problem was that in the years before the Revolution the cinema had scarcely penetrated on any consistent basis beyond the towns. In addition, the films that were available were those that had been made before 1917 and that reflected the cultural and ideological values that had then prevailed: these films were certainly not the sort of material that would convert the peasantry to Bolshevism.

The Bolsheviks came up with an ingenious solution. They combined a network of stationary agitational centres (*agitpunkty*), usually situated at strategic points like railway junctions or large settlements where they would be at their most effective, with a growing number of agitational trains. In the short term of the Civil War period it was these agitational trains that were more important. Their importance lay not just in their mobility and their flexibility but also in their novelty and in the variety of modes of presentation and communication that they were able to offer to the propagandist.

Agit-trains

In the early days after the Revolution the Bolsheviks had set aside a compartment in their troop trains for the propaganda section of the RED ARMY: morale was after all absolutely crucial in the struggle of those years. The agit-

Figure 40   Cinema coach on agit-train. *Above doors*: 'Theatre of the People'; *bottom right*: 'He who knows, wins.'

trains represented an extension of this idea. The first train, named *Lenin*, left Moscow for a trial run to Kazan in August 1918. It had been hurriedly prepared and painted with somewhat abstract pictorial slogans to give it a distinctive appearance. The interior of the coaches had been re-fitted to provide a bookshop, a library, an office and living quarters for the crew who spent two weeks distributing pamphlets and newspapers to the Red Army units stationed along the track. The experiment proved so successful that TROTSKY, the Commissar for War, ordered five more so-called 'literary-instructional' trains and these formed the core of the fleet.

In January 1919 a special commission was created to run the planned fleet of agit-trains and steamers. Each train carried with it a skilled team of agitprop officials, some of whom were specialists in particular fields appropriate to the areas that they were visiting. The trains had both an internal telephone link and a radio transmitter-receiver so that they could communicate with their home base in Moscow and receive up-to-the-minute information from the central authorities. Each train was equipped with a printing-press, a coach fitted out for meetings, a book shop, an exhibition space and, last but not least, facilities for projecting the short agitational *agitki*. The entire organization of the train was supervised by a political commissar: M. I. Kalinin, the future Soviet president, held this post on the train *October Revolution*, while V. M. MOLOTOV acted as commissar on the steamer *Red Star* which sailed down the Volga with Krupskaya, Lenin's wife, as Lunacharsky's representative. The presence of such prominent political activists was a further sign of the importance attached to the fleet by the central authorities.

Much of the success of the agit-trains can be attributed to the role played by the film shows in the campaign. Once the written, printed and spoken word were unleashed on the population, they encountered the problems outlined above. The striking decorations painted on the railway coaches were often misconstrued by a peasant audience unfamiliar with the conventions of contemporary art. But the *agitka*, with its simple, direct visual appeal attracted and fascinated the large numbers of people in the rural areas who had never before seen a moving picture. The *October Revolution*, which had by the end of 1920 travelled as far and wide and Minsk and Irkutsk, Petrograd and the Don Basin, had also provided more than 430 film shows for a total audience exceeding 620,000 people. Some of the films were straightforward instructional works depicting more efficient agricultural methods or ways of improving health and hygiene, but others had a more specifically ideological purpose and roused audiences with such stirring titles as *The Saviours of the Homeland*, *For the Red Banner*, *For a New World* and *Workers of the World, Unite!* For these relatively unsophisticated audiences cinema still seemed like magic: pictures of the new leaders – moving pictures – made them appear almost god-like. After the

attempt on Lenin's life in 1918 (see LENIN) he was shown in a widely distributed newsreel walking in the Kremlin grounds: this sequence was intended to scotch rumours that Lenin was dead but the context implied that he was almost superhuman, if not actually immortal.

The film sections of the trains were also important in other ways. The limited supplies of raw film stock were used to shoot actuality footage at the front and in various parts of the country: this was taken back to Moscow and edited into newsreels and documentaries. For the first time the Soviet people, albeit in limited numbers, could see what other parts of their vast country looked like. On the other hand, the *agitka*, shot at the centre for use in the regions, was also important: its terse, dynamic visual editing was to influence the style of future Soviet films and make film-makers aware of the centrality of montage. It is no coincidence that some of the leading figures to emerge in the golden era of Soviet cinema cut their cinematic teeth in the agitational campaigns of the Soviet Civil War: Lev Kuleshov, Dziga Vertov, Esfir Shub and Eisenstein's cameraman, Eduard Tisse. In this respect the agit-trains were a formative experience.

Blueprint for the future: In the maelstrom of Revolution and Civil War it is perhaps surprising that Lunacharsky had time to contemplate guidelines for the future. None the less in 1919 he introduced a collection of essays entitled *The Cinematograph*, which examined various aspects of the role of the cinema in the creation of a new post-revolutionary

Figure 41 Scene from agit-film, depicting figures emerging from 'Karl Liebknecht Workers Club'.

Soviet society. Lunacharsky's own contribution dealt specifically with 'The Tasks of the State Cinema':

> It is not simply a matter of nationalizing production and film distribution and of the direct control of cinemas. It is a matter of fostering a completely new spirit in this branch of art and education. We must do what nobody else is either able or willing to do.

The other articles in this collection laid down the guidelines for various aspects of revolutionary cinema, but Lunacharsky's views were of course central.

In order to 'foster a completely new spirit' the world's first state film school was established in Moscow in 1919 under the direction of the pre-revolutionary director and actor Vladimir Gardin. Most of the leading figures in later Soviet cinema have in some way been associated with this school and it continues to the present day to train new generations of film-makers.

An end and a beginning: By the time the Civil War came to an end and the New Economic Policy was adopted in the spring of 1921 Soviet cinema was in the process of finding its feet. Although the deprivations of the time were to cast a shadow over the next few years, it was in this period that the basic outlines of future Soviet cinema were sketched out. Most important of all, cinema was already clearly designated as 'the most important of all the arts'.   RT

Further Reading

Leyda, J.: *Kino. A History of Russian and Soviet Film*. London: Allen & Unwin, 1960.

Taylor, R.: *The Politics of the Soviet Cinema, 1917–1929*. Cambridge: Cambridge University Press, 1979.

Taylor, R. and Christie, I. eds: *The Film Factory. Russian and Soviet Cinema in Documents*. London: Routledge & Kegan Paul; Cambridge, Mass.: Harvard University Press, 1987.

Youngblood, D.J.: *Soviet Cinema in the Silent Era, 1918–1935*. Ann Arbor: University of Michigan Press, 1985.

Theatre

The fall of tsarism in March 1917 was greeted with widespread relief throughout the Russian theatre. It marked the end of repressive censorship, and was seen by the Imperial companies in Moscow and Petrograd as the opportunity to achieve the artistic autonomy for which they had long been agitating. May Day saw the renamed 'State Theatres' decked with red bunting and the evening performances were preceded by celebratory speeches and the singing of the *Marseillaise*. For the first time, the autumn season at the Mariinsky Opera opened not with Glinka's *A Life for the Tsar* but with Borodin's *Prince Igor*.

Generally speaking, however, theatres saw little need to modify their repertoires and there was no rush to stage the work of proscribed dramatists. Thus, Gorky's *Philistines* was presented by the Alexandrinsky Theatre in Petrograd in April 1917 but given only three performances. At the Maly Theatre in Moscow the only new work of any significance in its first post-revolutionary programme was *The Decembrists*, a previously banned work by the popular contemporary dramatist, Gnedich. The Moscow Art Theatre's response to the momentous events of the day was one of artistic paralysis, from which it took some years to recover.

With few exceptions, responses to the OCTOBER REVOLUTION varied from watchful neutrality to overt hostility. Anticipating the early collapse of the new regime, the three State companies in Petrograd and several theatres in Moscow went on strike in protest against the violence of October. The Moscow Art Theatre suspended performances for over three weeks and formally dissociated itself from any political alignment.

However, as early as 9 November 1917 LENIN signed a decree transferring all theatres to the control of the newly-created Commissariat for Enlightenment under LUNACHARSKY. Gradually, companies conceded the inevitable and entered into reluctant negotiations with Lunacharsky to salvage what they could of their artistic independence. For established theatres with proven repertoires this was surprisingly easy, for the Party's policy was to safeguard and subsidize the traditional arts while rendering them more accessible to the new mass audience. This policy was reinforced in 1919 with the creation of the category of 'Academic Theatres', comprising initially the Bolshoi, the Maly and the Moscow Art Theatre in Moscow and the Alexandrinsky, the Mariinsky and the Mikhailovsky in Petrograd. Two years later these were augmented by the Kamerny Theatre and the Moscow Children's Theatre.

Despite such reassurances from the Soviet state a number of prominent figures from the theatre chose to emigrate within a few years of the Revolution. They included the dramatists Leonid Andreev, Merezhkovsky and Chirikov, the innovative director, theorist and writer, Evreinov, the director, Fedor Komissarzhevsky, and the celebrated operatic bass, Fedor Chaliapin. Those who declared themselves unequivocally for the BOLSHEVIKS were few in number; foremost amongst them were the poet and dramatist Vladimir MAYAKOVSKY, and the director, Vsevolod Meyerhold. Originally an actor with the Moscow Art Theatre, Meyerhold had divided his time since 1908 between mounting lavish productions on the Imperial stages and running a series of private studios and experimental theatres in Petrograd. By common, if reluctant, consent he was acknowledged as Russia's leading theatrical innovator. Alienated from the Alexandrinsky company by his political commitment, Meyerhold accepted a commission from Lunacharsky to stage Mayakovsky's newly completed *Mystery-Bouffe* in Petrograd to mark the first anniversary of the October Revolution. They were joined by the Suprematist painter Kazimir Malevich, who was to design settings and costumes for the production (see ART). Despite public appeals, the project was boycotted by the vast majority of professional actors and eventually all but a few of the seventy-odd parts were played by students, with Mayakovsky himself filling three roles. Written in a style later defined by Lenin, not without affection, as 'hooligan communism', the plot parodied the biblical story of the ark, with seven proletarian couples surviving the flood to reach the promised land of utopian socialism. Meyerhold based his production on the knockabout gags and acrobatic skills of traditional popular theatre, lampooning the stock characters of the exploiters and celebrating the youthful vigour of the working class. The most problematic aspect of the production proved to be the cubist abstractions in which Malevich set the action; doctrinaire in conception, they did little to enhance Mayakovsky's rough satire and contributed largely to the reception of cool puzzlement at each of the three performances.

Mystery-Bouffe exemplified a problem that was soon to dominate Soviet artistic debates: how could the undoubted revolutionary commitment of 'left' artists be reconciled with the uncompromising and often obscure forms of their work, which threatened to alienate the mass audience and foster a new intellectual elite? Despite this, the fact remains that *Mystery-Bouffe* inaugurated a dramatic style that was soon to influence the whole Soviet agitprop movement. The true vitality of the play was revealed when Meyerhold revived it in rewritten form three years later in Moscow, after which it was staged throughout the Soviet Union and abroad.

It is a measure of the Revolution's slight initial impact on the theatre that *Mystery-Bouffe* was the only professional contribution to the celebrations of November 1918. At the same time numerous amateur groups throughout Petrograd gave agitatory performances in soldiers', workers' and students' clubs. In Moscow the occasion was marked by the presentation of *A Pantomime of the Great Revolution*, the first of the mass spectacles that were soon to be organized for every festival in the 'red calendar' throughout the country (see Figure 42, p. 282). The most celebrated was undoubtedly *The Storming of the Winter Palace*, re-enacted on the third anniversary and at the actual scene of the event in Petrograd, involving some ten thousand participants (and more casualties than the event itself!) plus the cruiser *Avrora* on the nearby Neva. Such performances became rare after the Civil War, but they did much to influence the form of early Soviet propagandist theatre, in particular its treatment of documentary material, its caricaturing of capitalist archetypes and its use of startling sound and visual effects.

Proletkult: The first concerted opposition to the attitudes and conventions of the established theatre was mounted by the PROLETKULT organization. Formed immediately prior to the October Revolution in Petrograd and soon extended throughout Russia, it regarded drama as the art form best suited for agitation and propaganda amongst the masses. The first of its numerous theatres, the Proletkult Arena, opened in Petrograd in May 1918, and celebrated the first anniversary of the Revolution with a production of *The Storming of the Bastille* by Romain Rolland. Depending largely on new writing and using either semi-professional or amateur performers, Proletkult sought to express the themes of mass movements and class struggle by using allegory and symbolism. It also worked in the broad satirical manner of Mayakovsky, producing numerous sketches to ridicule the Whites during the CIVIL WAR. Before making his debut in CINEMA in 1925, Sergei Eisenstein worked as a director at the First Workers' Proletkult Theatre in Moscow, employing circus tricks and clowns' costumes to transform the work of Ostrovsky and Tretyakov into 'agitgrotesque'. The principal statement on Proletkult theatre, *Creative Theatre* by Platon Kerzhentsev, ran into several editions when it was published in 1918 and there is no doubt that the movement was instrumental in stimulating the first effective critique of dramatic orthodoxy at a time when the Party itself had little to offer of theoretical value beyond a narrow-minded defence of the status quo.

Meyerhold

As even the first production of *Mystery-Bouffe* indicated, Meyerhold was close in spirit to Proletkult and no less radical in his aspirations. In the autumn of 1920 he was recalled by Lunacharsky from service with the RED ARMY to take charge of the Theatre Department of the Commissariat for Enlightenment, with power over the entire Russian Federation. Under the banner 'October in the Theatre' he proclaimed the mobilization of all theatrical resources, starting with the reorganization of the Academic Theatres. His eventual aim was a complete network of 'RSFSR Theatres', though in the event only his own RSFSR Theatre No. 1 in Moscow came to anything. His demolition plans were summarily rejected by Lunacharsky who stated:

> I can entrust comrade Meyerhold with the demolition of the old and bad and with the construction of the good and new. But I am not prepared to entrust him with the preservation of the old and good, the vital and strong which must be allowed to develop in its own way in a revolutionary atmosphere.

The Art Theatre

Thus, Meyerhold was prevented from getting his hands on either the Moscow Art Theatre or Alexander Tairov's Kamerny Theatre. The Art Theatre was still in deep crisis; between 1917 and 1922 it managed only two new productions, Gogol's *The Government Inspector* and Byron's

Figure 42 *Street decorations around the Alexander Column, Petrograd 1918*, by Natan Altman. (Photograph)

'mystery' *Cain* which survived just eight performances. The next two years were spent on tour abroad and the theatre waited until 1925 before staging its first play by a Soviet author. Meanwhile, it depended on its various studio affiliates to maintain its vitality. There its development was hampered by the tragic death from cancer at the age of thirty-nine of its finest director, Evgeny Vakhtangov. His style, whether applied to Maeterlinck or Gozzi or Strindberg, was imbued with a humanity and lightness of touch that for years to come endeared his productions to the widest audience (see MOSCOW STATE JEWISH THEATRE).

Tairov

By contrast, Tairov's work at the Moscow Kamerny ('Chamber') Theatre, which he founded in 1914, was refined to a degree and closely allied to the Futurist movement in painting with such stage designers as Larionov, Goncharova, Yakulov and, above all, Alexandra

Exter. Remarkable for its visual taste and its evocation of atmosphere through total artistic synthesis, Tairov's theatre conceded nothing to the clamouring of the rude outside world. As for the exhortations of Meyerhold and the Proletkult, Tairov had this to say in December 1920: 'An agitational theatre after a revolution is like mustard after a meal.' The point is reinforced by the Kamerny's repertoire for that year, which included Annensky's Grecian tragedy, *Thamyras the Lyrist*, Oscar Wilde's *Salome*, the Indian classic *Sakuntala* by Kalidasa and E. T. A. Hoffmann's 'capriccio', *Princess Brambilla*.

RSFSR Theatre No. 1

In this period the Kamerny played invariably to full houses, but so did the RSFSR Theatre No. 1, proof of the insatiable appetite for theatre of a Soviet public slowly emerging from the trauma of the Civil War. Helped by an unusually high proportion of trade-union sponsored free performances, Moscow theatres could claim an overall attendance figure of 97.2 per cent for the 1920/21 season.

The RSFSR Theatre No. 1 opened on 7 November 1920, the third anniversary of the Revolution, with *The Dawn*, an epic verse drama written in 1898 by the Belgian symbolist, E. Verhaeren, and depicting the transformation of a capitalist war into an international proletarian uprising. It was hurriedly adapted by Meyerhold and his assistant, V. M. Bebutov, in an attempt to bring out its relevance to recent political events, and performances were regularly interrupted with the latest bulletins from the Civil War front in the Crimea. Despite the obscure cubo-futurist designs of the costumes and settings and the political naiveté of the hastily rewritten script, scathingly criticized in *Pravda* by KRUPSKAYA, *The Dawn* played to packed houses often augmented by parties from local Red Army barracks. It ran for over a hundred performances and in effect inaugurated the professional agitprop theatre in Europe.

On May Day 1921 *The Dawn* was joined in the repertoire by *Mystery-Bouffe*, completely rewritten by Mayakovsky to make it relevant to the course of events since 1917. The production was a hilarious, dynamic caricaturist rough-and-tumble, a carnival celebration of the Civil War victory in total contrast to the hieratic solemnity of *The Dawn*. In his production Meyerhold dispensed finally with the front curtain and flown scenery, the dominant element of the set being a huge hemisphere that projected far into the auditorium. The theatre was bursting at the seams, no longer able to accommodate the kind of popular spectacle that he was striving for. The Bolshevik writer Dmitry Furmanov wrote:

> This new theatre is the theatre of the stormy age of the Revolution; it was born not of the tranquillity of *The Cherry Orchard* but of the tempests and whirlwinds of the Civil War . . . This new theatre of storm and stress undoubtedly has a great future. It can't be dismissed as a mere aberration: it has its roots in our heroic proletarian struggle.

The next four years saw the adoption of the new Soviet repertoire by every major theatre except the Kamerny, and even the reticent Moscow Art Theatre finally took the plunge by opening its 1925 season with Trenev's *The Pugachev Rising*. There followed the widespread success of such works as Trenev's *Lyubov Yarovaya*, Gladkov's *Cement*, Bulgakov's *The Days of the Turbins* and Vsevolod Ivanov's *Armoured Train 14-69*.

By the mid 1920s the new Soviet theatre was setting standards of skill and invention that challenged writers, directors, designers and performers throughout the world, drawing many of them to Moscow and Leningrad to study the work of Meyerhold, Stanislavsky, Tairov, Mikhoels and the surviving legacy of Vakhtangov.   EB

Further Reading

Braun, E.: *The Theatre of Meyerhold*. London and New York: 1979.

Fülöp-Miller, R. and Gregor, J.: *The Russian Theatre, Its Character and History*. London: 1930.

Houghton, N.: *Moscow Rehearsals*. New York: 1936.

Rudnitsky, K.L. ed.: *Istoriya sovetskogo dramaticheskogo teatra*, vol. 1. Moscow: 1966.

Zolotnitsky, Z.I.: *Zori teatralnogo oktyabrya*. Leningrad: 1976.

The Moscow State Jewish Theatre (Goset)

Originating from a modest Yiddish-speaking studio theatre set up in Petrograd in 1919 under the Theatre Department of Narkompros (see LUNACHARSKY), Goset moved to Moscow in 1920 and merged with another small Jewish theatre group, started by A. M. Granovsky, to become the 'State Jewish Chamber Theatre' (acronym: Gosekt), so called until 1925, when it had grown to the point where the word 'Chamber' was dropped from the title. Goset was managed and all its plays directed by Granovsky until 1929, when he failed to return from one of the theatre's tours abroad. From its very first production (*An Evening with Sholom Aleikhem*) in 1921, however, two actors stood out as the artistic mainstays of the theatre, S. M. Mikhoels and V. L. Zuskin. The theatre's early production style aimed to get away from the shallow melodrama and tinsel of the commercial Yiddish theatre, replacing it as an Expressionist theatricality that stressed mime, rhythmic movement, caricature, stylized sets and costumes, although the repertoire (at first mainly adaptations of literary texts), still harked back to a satirical view of Jewish life in the *shtetls* of the pre-1917 Pale of Settlement, evoked by such writers as Goldfaden, Sholom Aleikhem and Mendele Moikher-Sforim. After Granovsky's emigration, Mikhoels, while still continuing to act, took over as artistic director; this inaugurated the period of Goset's greatest success and international acclaim, in which it adopted a much wider repertoire, ranging from translations of foreign classics to contemporary plays in Yiddish by, among others, the poet Peretz Markish, and imaginative dramatizations of such Russian-Jewish classics as *Tevye the Milkman* (the original of *Fiddler on the Roof*). The pinnacle of the theatre's worldwide fame was attained in Radlov's brilliant production of *King Lear* in Yiddish with Zuskin as the Fool and Mikhoels in the title role. Evacuated to Tashkent from 1941 to 1943, the post-war Goset suffered increasingly from the effects of STALIN's anti-Semitic policies, until Mikhoels was murdered on Stalin's orders in Minsk, January 1949, an event shortly followed by the final closure of the theatre. In its twenty-eight-year history Goset faithfully reflected the brilliant rise and subsequent disgraceful repression of the Yiddish-language culture of Soviet Jewry.   MVG

Art

The outbreak of the war with Germany in August 1914 brought to an end a long period of close Russian involvement with art in Western Europe. In the late nineteenth century Russian responses to French Impressionism were evident in the work of Serov, Korovin and Grabar; the symbolist movements of the 1890s were echoed by Borisov-Musatov, Vrubel, Bakst and many others, and on the eve of the war the seminal contribution of Russian artists to Expressionism in Germany, particularly by Kandinsky and Jawlensky, and to Cubism in Paris (Lipchitz, Zadkine, Archipenko, Chagall and others) had made a great impact. The Ballets Russes, founded by Diaghilev in 1909, was at the height of its activity bringing new and vigorous Russian art, as well as Russian music and dance, to the heart of Paris.

The coming of war halted this elaborate exchange in the visual arts. It was followed by a period of intense cultural ferment and isolation in which distinctly Russian traditions and trends came once more to the fore as Russian artists were brought together away from the stimuli of Paris, Munich and Berlin. This period of isolation continued until the re-establishment of cultural relations with western European countries in the early 1920s. During that period every aspect of Russian cultural life was profoundly affected by the OCTOBER REVOLUTION which swept away conventional patronage and requisitioned private collections including those of Shchukin and Morozov, so rich in Impressionist, Post-Impressionist, Fauve and Cubist art from Paris, and now among the glories of the Pushkin Museum in Moscow and the Hermitage Museum in Leningrad.

If Russian art had been vigorously international before 1914, many artists nonetheless were already turning to distinctly Russian sources in search of their artistic identity. With the advent of the revolution those sources were to play a formative role in the establishment of an explicitly Revolutionary art. Russian Revolutionary art had its origins in the period 1913–16. The revolution spurred on the artists' iconoclastic tendency, and subsequently their constructive tendency, adding in the process a new dimension which was essentially the politicization of creativity. To create a specifically communist culture required much ideological debate together with the total reorganization of patronage, teaching, exhibitions and even the artist's means of working. Russian Futurism, Suprematism and Constructivism were distinctly Russian and pre-Revolutionary in origin. Russian Futurism was diverse and anarchic, vigorously iconoclastic in its rejection of artistic conventions; it was equally innovative in both the literary and the visual arts. The painter-poet Vladimir MAYAKOVSKY was a central participant, as was the visionary poet Velimir Khlebnikov, and both were crucially influential in the early revolutionary years. Among the plethora of visual artists associated with Russian Futurism were Larionov, Goncharova and Malevich whose up-to-date knowledge of western art was counterbalanced by a determination to find a distinct Russian identity. This ambivalence characterized the development of most Russian artists of the period; it reflected an intense and simultaneous excitement at western innovations, especially Parisian Cubism and Italian Futurism, and also in Russian cultural separateness, manifest in the traditions of icon painting, folk art and popular prints (*Lubki*).

The same ambivalence was evident in exhibitions. In January 1912 the second 'Jack of Diamonds' exhibition in Moscow included a wealth of recent western art while in March 'The Donkey's Tail' exhibition, also in Moscow, vociferously stressed its independence by embracing Neo-Primitive art and searching for non-European sources of inspiration. Similarly, Chagall worked in Paris on themes of Russian inspiration, embracing folk art and Cubism simultaneously. The year 1913 saw a major display of icons, and the painter Larionov also exhibited icons and *lubki*. Russian futurist poets and painters paraded the streets with painted faces and produced radical publications. As painters examined their means so did the poets with whom they collaborated, investigating the structure of language, the roots and phonetic material of words. In October 1913 Alexei Kruchenykh and Velimir Khlebnikov published *The Word as Such* with illustrations by Malevich and Rozanova. Collaboration was at its closest and produced in December 1913 the Russian Futurist opera *Victory Over the Sun* (libretto Kruchenykh, music Matyushin, design by Malevich), cited by Malevich as the date at which his concept of Suprematism began. It was also in 1913 that Vladimir Tatlin, the central innovator of Constructivism, visited Picasso in Paris, learnt of the latest Cubist and Italian Futurist art, and upon his return to Moscow began to construct reliefs from found materials. These experimental constructions were to prove seminal works of widespread significance in the early years of the revolution.

The outbreak of war brought the Russian artists of Paris, Munich and Berlin home to Moscow and Petrograd, where the assimilation of their foreign experiences collided with overtly Russian developments in art. The icon, folk art and the speculations of Khlebnikov blended with Cubism and Italian Futurism. Kandinsky returned from Munich with a system of expressive and spiritual abstraction. Many exhibitions followed. Tatlin launched his reliefs at 'Tramway V' in Petrograd in 1916 while Malevich exhibited irrational superimpositions of images (the so-called 'alogist' paintings) with features of Cubism and the trans-sense, or *zaum*, theories of Russian Futurist poets incorporated (his *Englishman in Moscow* now in the Stedelijk Museum, Amsterdam, is an example). Tatlin again showed reliefs at the exhibition 'The Year 1915' in Moscow, and in December 1915 at '0.10. The Last Futurist Exhibition' Malevich formally launched Suprematism, an unprecedented system of painting, comprising geometric forms against a white background, which totally rejected the role of representation in painting. At this exhibition Malevich emerged as a challenger to Tatlin whose exhibits included a series of 'corner counter-reliefs' hung on wires across corner spaces and assembled from found materials. They were partly constructed by reference to the proportions of constituent elements of metal, wood and wire, partly by an underlying geometric scheme, and partly determined by the material qualities of his elements. Both Malevich and Tatlin had separate rooms at this exhibition and their antagonism was evident. Their innovations, however, provided two reference points of the greatest importance to many other artists, and the development of post-Revolutionary art cannot be fully understood without reference to them. In this sense Russian Revolutionary art began in 1915, for the forms and techniques politicized after 1917 owe their origins substantially to these developments by Malevich and Tatlin.

At '0.10' Malevich exhibited a canvas of a *Black Square*, centrally placed with a narrow margin of white around it. It can be seen as the characteristically nihilist gesture of a Russian Futurist. Certain poems, for example, recently written and performed, were one word or even one letter long. Similarly Malevich's *Black Square* resolutely obliterated pictorial conventions. It had no narrative, no representational imagery, no window-like picture-space; it was a confrontation with expectation and convention. Malevich called it 'the zero of form'. It was deliberately boring and unyielding to the conventional view; its meaning was problematic seen in conventional terms. Yet hung across a corner it assumed the position of an icon, and Malevich immediately developed from it increasingly complex and colourful assemblages of geometrical forms which articulated their white surroundings to generate a feeling of dynamic and weightless flight. This was Suprematism as first unveiled at '0.10' and viewed with unsympathetic antagonism by Tatlin whose own room abandoned even more thoroughly the illusionistic world of picture-space for reliefs, some also hung across the icon's corner-space, which were assembled with real materials in actual space. Tatlin by contrast appeared to proffer the abandonment of illusion for reality, quitting the illusions of art for the exploration of materials, identifying art and work in the process and to an extreme degree replacing aesthetic predilection and self-expression with an investigation of construction defined in material terms. Syntheses of these extreme positions followed rapidly: in 1916 Alexander Rodchenko at the exhibition 'The Store' showed drawings and gouaches executed impersonally with ruler and compass, adapting Malevich's geometric forms to a sense of construction, while in 1916 Lyubov Popova exhibited 'Pictorial Architectonics' which slotted geometrical forms dynamically together in a shallow and contradictory picture-space, her surfaces stressing the material of their construction in thickly impastoed paint.

These radical innovations denied the importance of style, personal handling and self-expression, proposing instead an analytical investigation of the artist's means. In abandoning depiction they focused attention upon the articulation of form and material, shifting attention from what was depicted to the means employed. This entailed an examination of syntax and implied a thorough investigation of both the means and the purpose of art. It was to have far-reaching consequences.

1917 and after

With the establishment of the BOLSHEVIKS under LENIN the cultural expression of Communism became of immediate concern. Under the Commissariat of the Enlightenment, headed by the widely-travelled and culturally well-informed Bolshevik revolutionary A. V. LUNACHARSKY, a broad range of artistic endeavour was possible, but with the collapse of the customary roles of patronage, exhibitions and art-teaching in the face of Communist ideology, many artists and writers began at once to accept and explore the implications of the ideology for their own art. Malevich, Tatlin, Rodchenko, Popova and very many others wanted to place their artistically revolutionary discoveries at the service of the political revolution. This took two obvious forms: it was manifest either as service to the party, evident in the PROPAGANDA role, or as a search to define the nature of creative activity within the envisaged Communist culture. Both approaches tended to define the characteristics of the new art as communal in evolution, public in expression, politically committed and requiring a rejection of tastes associated with the old regime. Mayakovsky called for artists to abandon the solitary isolation of their studios, implying that artists engaged in self-delusion, thereby creating luxury objects evocative of good taste and an imaginary world; instead they should make the streets their brushes and the squares their palettes. Two politically inspired developments encouraged this attitude in 1918: Lenin called for Monumental Propaganda to commemorate the forerunners and heroes of the revolution, and secondly the first anniversary of the revolution was marked with street pageants, mass plays and demonstrations. The agitational art which resulted frequently made use of artistic innovations, e.g. the painter-sculptor Altman used a dynamic adaptation of suprematist forms strongly suggestive of the flags of a marching RED ARMY in order to mask the Alexander Column in Petrograd in his designs for the First Anniversary celebrations (see Figure 42). The recent advent of noise music similarly made possible a concert of factory sirens in Petrograd in 1918 (see MUSIC). The recent development evident in Tatlin's constructions, which encouraged the abandonment of illusion in art, was increasingly reflected in street theatre and mass demonstrations. The director Evreinov (see THEATRE) for example in 1920 re-enacted the storming of the Winter

Palace with a cast of 10,000 and an audience of 100,000. Mayakovsky produced hand-stencilled posters; propaganda trains and boats were decorated with agitational design, kiosks and tribunes were erected and in due course even the elegant products of the Lomonosov porcelain factory in Petrograd (now Leningrad) were decorated with slogans declaring 'Feed the hungry' or 'He who does not work shall not eat'.

Among the visual artists who responded to the search for a communist culture beyond the requirements of propaganda, Tatlin in particular played a crucial role. Appointed head of the Moscow section of the Art department of Lunacharsky's Commissariat in 1918, he responded to the call for monumental propaganda with a visionary and utopian project for a monument to the revolution. Later renamed the 'Monument for the Third International', this design consisted of an immense tower with a double conical spiral structure which appeared to lean and which was envisaged for construction at a height considerably exceeding that of the Eiffel Tower in Paris, straddling a branch of the River Neva in Petrograd on gigantic arches through which ships could sail. Tatlin constructed a large maquette with the assistance of a collective of students. With its spine-like main girder containing lifts, and with its striding arches, it represented the communal image of mankind, the colossus of Communism intent upon world government. Within its girders it was to house immense halls, a cube, a pyramid, a cone and a hemisphere, suspended one above another as gigantic insulated glass forms. These were to house the organs of world government ascending to a radio station and cloud projection facilities for the dissemination of the world-government's decisions back to the terrestrial globe. Tatlin here produced a barely feasible project which was widely influential, efficient only as a utopian reference point, an image of harmony under Communist world rule. The conflicts of the globe would be resolved within its chambers. In this sense it recalls cosmological themes in the writings of Khlebnikov and Mayakovsky, and in much earlier utopian visions of Campanella, particularly as its great halls were to revolve in time with the apparent motions of the sun, moon and stars in the sky, its main axis resolutely pointing at the Pole star.

In this monument, Tatlin envisaged the cockpit of planet Earth travelling the solar system, its social conflicts resolved by world government, history becoming the story of planetary evolution. It is the adaptation of Constructivism to a political creed which in this project is literally incorporated. It was communally evolved, essentially public and politically committed.

Tatlin also became active as a teacher, and the experiments of pre-revolutionary years evolved as the Culture of Materials. Art schools, reorganized in 1919 as Free Studios (acronym: Svomas) in Moscow and Petrograd became centres of debate in which ideological issues were pursued in the context of practical work. The forms of

Figure 43 *Monument for the Third International*, (finished model), by Vladimir Tatlin, on view 1920. Wood, about 15′ high.

Suprematism and the study of construction with materials were recurrent features of the teaching but now they also had an ideological dimension. Answers to pre-revolutionary questions concerning the role and nature of creative activity were sought within the ideology of Communism. By January 1919 when the Tenth State Exhibition: Nonobjective Creation and Suprematism opened in Moscow displaying 220 works, the identification of non-representational art with the revolution was already being vigorously assessed. It was criticized essentially from two viewpoints. To some critics it appeared to be the unintelligible product of small groups of artists working to their own ends. An aspect of the debate concerning the nature of Communist culture revolved around the question of whether art should be proletarian in which case many of these artists appeared as insecure and obscure intellectuals, or whether it should be classless in which case the emphasis upon geometry and investigative approaches could be reconciled with ideology. A number of these issues came to a head in 1920 with the formation of the Institute of Artistic Culture (acronym: Inkhuk) for which Kandinsky evolved the initial plan. By the end of the year his plan had been rejected as mystical and too psychologically inclined. Expressive and spiritual abstraction had become intolerable to many committed communist painters and ideologists. Rodchenko, Stepanova and the sculptor Babichev who replaced Kandinsky at Inkhuk, instituted a study of materials and construction in creative work which cast serious doubts upon the survival of art within communism. Rodchenko in particular began to attack art through his own painting, consistently undermining its convention and values. Despising the mysticism which led Malevich to exhibit all-white paintings in 1918, he displayed all-black works in response. This is an example of the second standpoint which questioned the significance of non-representational art in the context of communism: it came from critics and ideologists but it was equally evident among painters and sculptors.

By December 1918 the critics Nikolai Punin and Osip Brik were demanding the overthrow of art in articles in the anarchic periodical *Iskusstvo Kommuny* (Art of the Commune). Punin worked closely with Tatlin; Osip Brik worked with Mayakovsky and Rodchenko. The nihilism that Malevich embodied in his *Black Square* of 1915 Rodchenko subsequently pursued more ruthlessly, undermining the role of individual expression, fine art materials and aesthetic values in his painting. In this respect Rodchenko's work of 1919–21 is problematic in that his paintings endeavoured to undermine painting as a fine art activity. These studies culminated in two exhibitions to which Rodchenko contributed in 1921. In May he displayed hanging constructions assembled from concentric plywood shapes (circle, square, triangle, octagon, ellipse) – impersonal works which anyone could construct, without uniqueness, financial value, self-expression or taste. In September, at the exhibition '5 x 5 25' he displayed monochrome canvases, one red, one yellow, one blue, entitled *The Last Painting*, undermining composition, picture space, value and uniqueness by this single gesture. Such painting, once the gesture was made, was redundant and its role fulfilled and supplanted. When Inkhuk met in plenary session in Moscow two months later, Osip Brik called for the condemnation of easel painting as useless self-delusion and self-indulgence. Rodchenko was among the many signatories of this declaration of the death of art. Non-objective art as much as the academic illusions of easel-painting were condemned as irrelevant to communist culture. Ideological texts followed attacking art as a speculative activity. Brik voiced his views in *Iskusstvo v Proizvodstve* (Art in Production) (O. Brik, S. Filippov and D. Shterenberg, Moscow 1921) while Alexei Gan repeatedly proclaimed Death to Art! in his book *Konstruktivizm* (Tver 1922). The Inkhuk theorist Nikolai Tarabukin produced a more reasoned theoretical discussion proclaiming the need for creative work to utilitarian ends in *Ot Molberta k Mashine* (From the Easel to the Machine) (Moscow 1923) and Boris Kushner in *Iskusstvo i Klassy* (Art

and the Classes) explored the history and theory of the relation of art to work. Politically aligned, the constructivism of Tatlin, Rodchenko and others by 1921 had rejected not only the artist's aloof isolation but denied on ideological grounds his right to paint or sculpt. Lunacharsky was careful to avoid official endorsement of this position. In an article 'A Spoonful of Medicine' he warned against any group speaking as exclusive interpreters of communist art and culture. It is a curious fact that constructivists rejected non-objective art as redundant just as an increasing volume of opinion rejected it in favour of realistic academic art.

The utilitarian phase, inaugurated in 1921, witnessed former painters working in many fields. Tatlin designed stoves, clothing, ceramics, stage designs, and in the early 1930s his glider Letatlin. Rodchenko produced photomontage book illustrations for Mayakovsky's *Pro Eto* (About This) (Moscow 1923), numerous book covers, posters and even politicized sweet wrappers and hoardings for government stores together with Mayakovsky, as well as the stage designs for Mayakovsky's *Bedbug* produced in 1929 by Meyerhold with music by Shostakovich. In addition he designed furniture, textiles, ceramics, clothing and films. Popova and Stepanova and many others turned to stage design in collaboration with the directors Tairov and Meyerhold.

In the West little was known of Russian Revolutionary art until 1922 when 'The First Russian Art Exhibition' opened at the Van Diemen Gallery in Berlin, a survey of Soviet art up to and including the first utilitarian works. With this exhibition the long period of isolation and cultural ferment came to an end before resuming in a different form in the later 1920s. One result of renewed contacts was a substantial wave of emigration. Gabo, a constructivist whose belief in art remained unshaken, emigrated, as did Chagall and many others. In addition some artists travelled as spokesmen for Soviet art, particularly El Lissitzky who had been much inspired by Malevich with whom he had worked in Vitebsk. He systematically sought contacts throughout Europe collaborating with De Stijl in Holland, and with Dadaists and the Bauhaus in Germany in particular. In 1925 Rodchenko travelled to Paris where his Workers' Reading Room, agitational in its simplicity and overt political commitment among the luxurious goods of the Paris 'International Exhibition of Decorative Arts', was displayed in the Soviet Pavilion designed by Konstantin Melnikov. Malevich travelled to Poland and Germany in 1927 with the exhibition of works which now provide the substantial holdings of his paintings at the Stedelijk Museum in Amsterdam. His book *Die Gegendstandslose Welt* (The Non-Objective World) was published by the Bauhaus in 1927.

In the West the political context of the early Soviet cultural experiment was only to be imagined and its products were received as art: Constructivism was frequently seen as a style of art, for example, in a manner which would not have been comfortable to Inkhuk constructivists in Russia, as the ideological dimension of their work by 1921 overrode its visual qualities and aestheticism had been systematically rejected. For this reason George Grosz could be vaunted in Russia as a constructivist on ideological grounds, while in Germany the 'machine art' of Tatlin was discussed. Russian Revolutionary art was so closely tied to its context that it could not effectively be exported, except perhaps in the form of film or propaganda specifically designed for Western eyes.

In Russia 1922 saw the formation of The New Society of Painters which encouraged a return to easel painting, and in 1925 The Society of Easel Artists promoted a return to popularly intelligible easel painting with an overtly communist subject matter. In the same year the Communist Party Central Committee called for a style comprehensible to the millions and the cultural experiment entered a new phase leading to Socialist Realism.

Constructivists had abandoned abstract painting in any case. Their utilitarian designs in many fields were the fruit of an unprecedented analysis of the means and purpose of creative activity. Increasingly their fundamentalism gave way to specialized professionalism spreading the principles of constructivism widely, whilst diluting its essential critique in the process, with the emergence of professional constructivist stage designers (the Stenberg brothers, for example), constructivist architects (Vesnin brothers, Ginzburg and Leonidov) and constructivist film directors (Dziga Vertov). In this way constructivism in particular became a pervasive and subtle feature of later Soviet culture.   JM

Further Reading

Gray, Camilla: *The Great Experiment: Russian Art, 1863–1922.* London: Thames & Hudson, 1962.

Karginov, German: *Rodchenko*, trans. Elizabeth Hoch. London: Thames & Hudson, 1979.

Lodder, Christina: *Russian Constructivism.* New Haven and London: Yale University Press, 1983.

Milner, John: *Vladimir Tatlin and the Russian Avant-Garde.* New Haven: Yale University Press, 1983.

────── : *Russian Revolutionary Art.* London: Jupiter (Oresko) Books, 1979.

Rudenstine, Angelica: *Russian Avant-Garde Art: The George Costakis Collection.* London: Thames & Hudson, 1981.

Music

Seen in retrospect, many of the developments in the 1917 Revolution as they affected music were neither unprecedented nor unexpected. For centuries the rich heritage of Russian folk-lore had been handed down to the upper classes through songs of the peasant nurse. Catherine the Great (despite her lack of musicality) nevertheless included folk elements in the libretti she wrote for some of the first Russian national operas in the last quarter of the eighteenth century, and from that time onwards, collections of Russian folk-songs began to appear in a steadily increasing stream, in many of which were included songs expressing the sufferings of the peasants and commemorating the names of leaders of popular uprisings, especially Stenka Razin and Emilyan Pugachev. Revolutionary songs feature in a number of folk-song collections of the late nineteenth and early twentieth centuries, whose sentiments were often conveyed in allegorical terms. For the most part, although all publications were subject to censorship, the attitude of the tsarist authorities towards music was relatively tolerant. The fate of the aristocratic composer, Alexander Alyabiev (1787–1851), exiled for many years to Siberia almost certainly on account of his association with the revolutionary Decembrist movement, was an unusual one for a musician. Nicholas I personally involved himself in the composition of Glinka's opera *Ivan Susanin* (1836) to such an extent that the title was changed at his suggestion to that of *A Life for the Tsar*, though no objections were made to the inclusion of many scenes in the folk idiom or the appearance of peasant characters. The significance of Glinka's first opera was a great one for the subsequent development of Russian nationalism, for not only were the peasants shown to be living people with identifiable human emotions but musically it revealed that the folk element could be treated operatically and symphonically – factors of considerable importance to his musical successors.

During the second half of the nineteenth century, Russian national music responded strongly to current ideological trends. CHERNYSHEVSKY's dissertation *Aesthetic Relations of Art to Reality* (1853–5) was a fundamental work in the creation of POPULISM, which influenced the aesthetic outlook of the critic Vladimir Stasov and the musical compositions of Modest Mussorgsky. Indeed, Mussorgsky's masterpiece *Boris Godunov* (1869, rev. 1872) remains unsurpassed to this day in its mixture of human tragedy, pathos and realism, while his many songs are outstanding in their depiction of folk characters and their reflection of peasant life. The writings of HERZEN, Dobrolyubov and Belinsky also left their mark on Russian culture, while at the end of the century Tolstoy in his essay *What is Art?* (1897) reiterated the eighteenth-century view that art should have a moral purpose, a factor that was to be of importance in the subsequent development of Soviet musical ideology. Of significance, too, in the nineteenth century were the opposing doctrines of 'Slavophils' and 'Westerners', who saw Russia's association with the outside world as being respectively either detrimental or beneficial to her future development. This question, too, was to occur constantly in the subsequent history of Soviet music.

Questioning of authority and accepted tradition was no new phenomenon in Russian culture. The establishment of the St Petersburg Conservatory under the aegis of the Government-supported Russian Musical Society in 1862 brought an immediate reaction from Slavophils such as Balakirev, who, believing that the Conservatory would cater only for the wealthier echelons of society and would do little to support national culture, founded his own Free School of Music in the same year which, despite recurring financial problems, nevertheless survived until 1917. The group of artists known as the Peredvizhniki (Society for Travelling Art Exhibitions), refusing to accept the examination tasks set them at the Petersburg Academy of Arts in 1863, embarked on a series of excursions throughout Russia where they exhibited realist works of art, often critical of the social order. Among the members of Peredvizhniki were Repin, Perov and Kramskoy. At the end of the century new trends in painting and the arts, manifest in the journal *Mir Iskusstva* (The World of Art) founded initially in 1898 by Diaghilev and Benois, broke with existing academic canons, favouring freedom of expression. Diaghilev's revolutionary innovations in ballet (brilliantly reinforced by the music of the young Stravinsky), the startling décors, the novelty and freshness of the artistic concepts, found expression in his remarkable series of concert seasons in Paris from 1907 to 1914 and thus presented Russian culture to the western world in a new and startling light. The 'Evenings of Contemporary Music' inaugurated by the composer Ivan Kryzhanovsky, the music critics Vyacheslav Karatygin and Alfred Nurok and others in St Petersburg from 1900 to 1912, were devoted to the study and performance of contemporary music, and included premières of works by Stravinsky, Prokofiev and Myaskovsky as well as pieces by the French and German avant-garde. Concerts of a similar nature were established in Moscow in 1909.

Although Russian musicians were partisan in the sense that some were passionate devotees of contemporary western music while others zealously supported Russian tradition, for the most part they avoided open confrontation with the government or personal political involvement. In 1905, however, one of the most distinguished figures of Russian music, Rimsky-Korsakov, found himself in the centre of a political storm. Not long after the events of 'Bloody Sunday' (see 1905 REVOLUTION), the Conservatory students went on strike in an effort to obtain educational and political reform. Shocked by the repressive measures taken against the students, Rimsky-Korsakov demanded the resignation of the Director of the Conservatory, August Bernhard, and, although Bernhard resigned, on 15 March Rimsky-Korsakov was dismissed. In the ensuing uproar Glazunov and Lyadov likewise tendered their resignations and letters of protest were published in many of the leading papers. A performance on 27 March of Rimsky-Korsakov's opera *Kashchey the Deathless* was turned into a political demonstration and had to be abandoned, the composer himself being placed under police surveillance. Eventually concessions were made to the Conservatories, which were granted some independence, including the right to elect

their own Director, as a result of which Glazunov was appointed to that post and Rimsky-Korsakov was permitted to return. Some idea of Rimsky-Korsakov's state of mind at this period is seen from the fact that he made two versions of the revolutionary song 'Dubinushka' (The Cudgel) in 1905 and 1906 and completed his opera *The Golden Cockerel* which satirizes the concept of autocracy. The opera was never performed in the composer's lifetime, its première taking place in Moscow in 1909 with changes to the libretto by the censor. Nor was any performance of *The Golden Cockerel* ever permitted on the Imperial stage, though his opera *The Tale of the Invisible City of Kitezh and the Maiden Fevronya* was given at the Mariinsky Theatre in 1907. Friction also occurred at the Moscow Conservatory, as a result of which the Director, Safonov, resigned, to be replaced by Ippolitov-Ivanov who held that post until 1922. Taneev, a political activist, also resigned, and along with D. I. Arakishvili, A. T. Grechaninov, E. E. Lineva, A. G. Chesnokov, Yu. D. Engel and others, helped to form a People's Conservatory (1906) of which the purpose was to provide mass musical education at a minimal cost. The staff included Glière, A.D. Kastalsky, Goldenveyzer and Yavorsky as well as Taneev. Similar institutions were subsequently opened in other cities. The 'Historical Concerts' organized in Moscow in 1907 by Sergei Vasilenko also endeavoured to make music generally accessible.

Special mention should be made of the concern in this period for national traditions manifest both by the State and private patrons. The Ethnological Commission of the Imperial Russian Geographical Society did much to assist folk-song research at the end of the nineteenth century by sponsoring annual expeditions to remote parts of Russia to collect folk-song texts and melodies of which many were subsequently published, as well as arranging public performances by outstanding folk-singers such as the family Ryabinin. The Conservatories continued to produce highly trained composers, conductors, performers and teachers, the quality of whose work was to remain evident long after the Revolution. The State Theatres continued to perform outstanding operas by Russian composers, while an important part was played by private organizations such as those of Mamontov, Solodovnikov and Zimin. The publishing house of Belaieff (Belyaev), founded in Leipzig in 1885 specifically for the purpose of publicizing Russian music abroad, continued to flourish, as did that of Jurgenson (Yurgenson) in Moscow. The firm of Gutheil (Gutkhevl) was taken over in 1915 by Serge Kussevitsky whose Édition Russe de Musique did much to encourage young composers. Throughout the nineteenth century song, too, served as a powerful ideological cohesive force in Russian revolutionary circles, favourite pieces being songs from the French Revolution such as 'Ça ira', 'La Carmagnole' and the Marseillaise, as well as soldiers' songs, students' songs, prison songs, songs of protest, exile and many others. Several members of the Decembrist Movement wrote revolutionary verses to popular tunes of the day. In some cases inflammatory verses replaced the words of well-known operatic arias (for example the *stretti* from the prologue to Donizetti's *Lucrezia Borgia*), while at a later date both texts and music were composed afresh.

1917 and after

The new government announced by LENIN on 8 November (NS) was notable in that it included from the very beginning a People's Commissar for Education, this being A. V. LUNACHARSKY (1875–1933). As the occupant of an important and significant post, Lunacharsky was well chosen. Highly educated and widely travelled in addition to his political skills, he was a well-informed and witty writer on music. Though by no means sharing an identical outlook with Lenin on the relative importance of cultural issues, by and large the relationship between them was a good one.

Following the establishment of the People's Commissariat for Public Education (Narkompros), Lunacharsky established a new organization which was divided into three sections – THEATRE, ART and music, one of his first publications being a paper entitled 'On Popular Education' in which he made important distinctions between instruction (the handing down of knowledge) and education (a creative process). Under Lunacharsky the music section of Narkompros organized schools for a broad spectrum of society, these often being placed near factories, whereby well-known performers could carry music to the masses. From the very beginning, however, the new government came under pressure from extremist groups, some of whom considered that all previous traditions should be abandoned and that the new revolutionary music should start afresh, while others took a more moderate view, feeling that the new music should be a logical outgrowth from the old. The fact that it was desirable to make a new start in so far as artistic creativity was concerned, but that it was not necessary to abandon all that had previously been produced, is something that occurs several times in Lenin's writings, and on occasion Lenin speaks of the necessity 'to assimilate critically everything that was best in the cultural heritage of the past and on this basis, and not on an empty place, to create our new Soviet culture'. Lenin himself was fond of music, being particularly attracted to choral singing and revolutionary songs of various nations, which he saw could serve a valuable ideological role: 'the propaganda of socialism by means of the workers' song' is a phrase that occurs several times in Lenin's literary works. He was also concerned with folk culture which he saw as embodying 'the whole essence of the age-old struggles, desires and expectations of the broad folk-masses', while of the Western-European classics he favoured Beethoven's Overtures to *Egmont* and *Coriolanus*, the 'Appasionata' and 'Pathétique' sonatas, Chopin's *Préludes*, some Wagner operas, Bizet's *Carmen*, Halévy's *La Juive*, Valentine's aria

from Gounod's *Faust*, Tchaikovsky's Sixth Symphony and the opera *Evgeny Onegin*, all of which illustrate to varying degrees the concept of courage and determination in wrestling with adversity. Above all, music to Lenin was an ideology, a means of education of the masses. As he himself said:

> Art belongs to the people. It must penetrate with its deepest roots into the very midst of the broad working masses. It must unite the feeling, thought and will of these masses, must elevate them. It must awaken the artists among them and stimulate them.

Such a view was shared also by Lunacharsky. The Heraldic Hall of the Winter Palace was transformed into a public hall, more than fifty concerts being given in the course of the first season alone. Concerts and theatrical performances continued to be given in the traditional venues, though for a time members of the intelligentsia were forbidden to attend, admission being by tickets provided by factories and other organizations. Performers thus had to cope with a new type of unsophisticated audience. By July 1918, fearing the threat of foreign invasion, the whole country was placed on a state of alert, music being used to boost popular morale and artists being sent to the front lines.

Organization: An important development of this period was that of nationalization. Whereas the Moscow Bolshoi and Stanislavsky Theatres and the Petrograd Mariinsky Theatre had been taken over by the state early in 1918, by a decree issued in *Pravda* on 18 July of that year and signed by V. Ulyanov (Lenin), the Moscow and Petrograd Conservatories were placed under State control and made institutions of higher learning. Nationalization was further extended to cover the former Imperial Court Chapel (eventually named the Leningrad Academic Capella) and the Moscow Synodal Choir (renamed the People's Choral Academy), along with all private music schools, music publishing houses, musical instrument factories, libraries, archives, concert organizations and works of composers no longer living. By 1919 Narkompros had established control over all aspects of musical life. For those who were unwilling to accept the new conditions no difficulties were raised in the matter of emigration, among those leaving the country then or over the following years being the composers Grechaninov, Lyapunov, Prokofiev and the Cherepnins, the conductors Dobrowen, Kussevitsky, Malko and Ziloti, the singer Chaliapin, the pianists Horowitz and Borovsky, the violinists Heifetz, Akhron and Milstein, the distinguished violin teacher Leopold Auer, the cellist Pyatigorsky and many others.

Despite the departure of so many gifted musicians, many new organizations came into being under the aegis of Narkompros. The former Imperial Court Orchestra was transformed in 1917 into the State Symphony Orchestra; on

19 October 1920 its name was changed to that of State Philharmonic Orchestra. In 1921 the term 'Philharmonic' was expanded to embrace not only the orchestra but chamber music, the music library, the museum, lectures and publications of booklets and programmes. Philharmonic organizations were subsequently established in other cities of the Soviet Union. Another new body was that of the Russian Folk-Orchestra founded in 1919, which in 1946 became the N. P. Osipov Folk-Ensemble though V. V. Andreev's Great-Russian Orchestra, founded in 1887, continued to flourish as before. In the world of chamber music the Lunacharsky Quartet was established in late 1917, being renamed the Glazunov Quartet two years later. The Lenin Quartet was founded in 1919. The Beethoven and Komitas Quartets both arose in the 1920s. Another ensemble using four Stradivari came into being in 1919 playing instruments from the rare musical instrument collection founded by Lunacharsky in the same year.

It would be a mistake, though, to consider that Lunacharsky's policies were accepted in all quarters. Desire for a new 'proletarian culture' was characterized by PROLETKULT, which, under the leadership of such activists as Alexander Kastalsky, set up in direct competition to Narkompros through its own programme of mass music education. Proletkult's existence was only of limited duration, however, it being publicly denounced by Lenin in October 1920. The same period is important ideologically, for it saw the appearance of a document issued by Lunacharsky entitled 'Basic Policies in the Realm of Arts', in which it reasserted the authority of the Party in all matters concerning the arts, a fundamental tenet which has remained effective to the present day.

By 1921 the CIVIL WAR had ended but the country was in a state of chaos and economically exhausted. The period of the New Economic Policy (NEP) 1921–8 is notable in that it saw a lessening of state control in the arts, and the resumption of cultural links with the West. A special agreement was drawn up between the State Publishing House and Universal Edition, Vienna, as a result of which scores by Soviet composers were made available to the outside world. Russia again began to be visited by a steady stream of prominent western musicians – the composers Casella, Hindemith, Milhaud and Schreker; the conductors Otto Klemperer, Pierre Monteux, Hermann Scherchen and Bruno Walter; the pianists Wilhelm Backhaus, Edwin Fischer, Egon Petri, Artur Schnabel; the violinist Joseph Szigeti. Russian audiences were enabled to make the acquaintance of works by Bruckner, Mahler, Honegger and Křenek, while indigenous artists began to concertize abroad.

Musicology: The establishment in 1921 of two important research centres, the Russian Institute for the History of Arts in Petrograd and the State Institute for Musical Science in Moscow, did much to place Soviet musicology on a firm footing, a prominent part in the Petrograd section being played by the young musicologist Boris Asafiev. At the Russian Institute, too, the specialist publishing house 'Academia' was opened in 1923, one of its few publications being Preobrazhensky's book on Russian Liturgical Music in 1924, the last major study of Russian sacred music to be printed in Russia for nearly half a century. Though a number of music periodicals lasted for several years at this period only one journal *Zhizn iskusstva* (Life of Art) covers the span 1918–29. In 1922 fresh legislation was introduced affecting the Conservatories, while further efforts were made to facilitate the entry of students from proletarian backgrounds and allow them greater say in administration. Under a decree of 5 December 1925 the teaching of musicology was transferred from the Leningrad and Moscow Institutes to the Conservatories, and emphasis was placed on the need for students' ideological training.

Composition: The NEP period also saw notable developments in the field of creativity. Even before the Revolution the composer Roslavets had composed an atonal Violin Sonata (1913), while his Third String Quartet (1920) utilized serial elements. Following on from the experiments of Vishnegradsky, Georgy Rimsky-Korsakov (grandson of the composer) founded a Society for Quarter-tone music in 1923. The Termenvox, invented by the acoustics engineer Lev Termen in 1920 and demonstrated to Lenin in 1921, was one of the first electronic instruments and was exhibited abroad. The First Symphonic Ensemble (acronym: Persimfans) endeavoured to emulate the egalitarian concepts of the time by dispensing with a conductor and played primarily in Moscow from 1922 to 1932.

Following the establishment in 1922 of the International Society for Contemporary Music (ISCM), a Russian Association for Contemporary Music (ASM) was formed in Moscow by Myaskovsky and others, whose aim, as stated in the first issue (1923) of their unofficial journal *K Novym Beregam* (To New Shores) edited by V. V. Derzhanovsky, was to keep abreast of current musical events. Despite its short-lived duration (only three numbers appeared April–August 1923) the journal was truly international in substance, contributions including articles on microtonal music by Hàba, monographs on atonality and polytonality by Milhaud, reports from Vienna, New York and elsewhere. The antithesis of the ASM was the far more militant organization, The Russian Association of Proletarian Musicians (RAPM), likewise founded in 1923, which, largely based in Moscow, was anti-western in its outlook. Showing similar ideas to the former Proletkult and related to the powerful Russian Association of Proletarian Writers, RAPM's fundamentalist extremist attitudes did not at that stage find favour with the Party, which in 1925 was still pursuing a policy of tolerance towards creative groups, while still preserving the authority of the Party as the final arbiter. Yet another group, the Organization of

Revolutionary Composers and Musicians (ORKiMD) was formed in 1925.

Despite all the intense activity, however, the first years of the Revolution were not notable for their quality of musical composition. Notwithstanding the presence of the older generation of composers such as Glazunov, Glière, Ippolitov-Ivanov and many others, the most notable developments took place in the field of popular songs, some of which were written to original music, while others were based on already existing folk-tunes or well-known tunes of the day. The *chastushka*, a witty folk ditty often with satirical overtones, was especially popular, while throughout the whole country sounded a motley medley of revolutionary songs, peasant songs, workers' songs, and songs of the RED ARMY and NAVY, all of which had their counterparts among the anti-revolutionary factions. The 1920s saw the formation of many amateur circles and collective groups, which created an incessant demand both for new music and for arrangements of already existing works by Russian composers, or by composers such as Beethoven and Gluck. Many songs, too, were written for the Young Communists' League (acronym: Komsomol).

Orchestral: While the music of Skryabin (1872–1915) in its vague mystical yearnings, continued to exercise an appeal on many of the intellectuals, including Lunacharsky, a notable achievement was Myaskovsky's Fifth Symphony of 1918, which incorporated a number of folk tunes. Myaskovsky's Sixth Symphony of 1922–3 reflects the diverse tendencies of the time in that the finale employs two folk-songs of the French Revolution, as well as the medieval plainchant from the Mass for the Dead, the *Dies Irae*, and a sacred Russian chant 'On the Parting of Body and Soul'. His Eighth Symphony of 1924–5, in which he claimed he was inspired by the story of Stenka Razin, uses a Bashkir melody in the Adagio. Reflecting similar trends in western music (for example Milhaud's *Machines agricoles*), Kastalsky produced his own *Agricultural Symphony* (1923), while Gnesin wrote a 'Symphonic Movement 1905–1917' in 1925. None of these works, however, can compare with those of Dmitry Shostakovich (1906–75) whose First Symphony, written in the years 1924–5, may truly be regarded as 'the first Soviet symphony', its première taking place in Leningrad under Nikolay Malko in 1926.

Theatre: To many, THEATRE seemed the symbol of the aristocratic era, with its tsarist associations and elitist attributes. However, through skilful persuasion, Lunacharsky managed to surmount all problems and opera and ballet continued to be performed. It is notable that some of the most famous stage directors occupied themselves with opera, while a number of mutual projects between the Bolshoi Opera and the Moscow Art Theatre also took place. A notable event was the opening of the Maly Theatre in Petrograd in 1918, this being located in the former Mikhailovsky Theatre. In so far as the repertoire was concerned, while many of the standard Russian and West European works continued to be given in their original form (including works by Wagner), others were adapted to reflect the new ideology. Alterations were made to libretti so that Puccini's *Tosca*, for instance, became *The Battle for the Commune*, Meyerbeer's *Les Huguenots* was renamed *The Decembrists* (in no way connected with Shaporin's opera of the same name performed in 1953), Glinka's *A Life for the Tsar* was metamorphosed into *Hammer and Sickle*. Auber's *La Muette de Portici* was revised by the stage director Meyerhold as a revolutionary drama, *Fenella*. Wagner's *Rienzi* and Mozart's *Don Giovanni* acquired new texts and emphasis, while Bizet's *Carmen* was given in a completely new guise entitled *Carmencita and the Soldier*. The first opera to utilize revolutionary subject matter is generally considered to be *For Red Petrograd* composed by A. Gladkovsky and E. Prussak in 1925, which, subtitled 'The Year 1919', had as its theme the defence of Petrograd against the forces of General YUDENICH. The opera was poorly received, however, and was of short-lived duration. More successful was the opera *The Eagle's Revolt* (1925), composed by Andrei Pashchenko, based on the story of the Pugachev Rebellion. Performances of Prokofiev's operas were not given until 1926. Curiously, some of the most successful operas written in the early years were those utilizing 'exotic' subject matter. Such were the two operas *Absalom and Eteri* (1919) and *Daisi* (1923) by the Georgian composer Zakhary Paliashvili (1871–1933), both of which utilized Georgian folk melodies and were based on national themes. Mention, too, should be made of Glière's colourful opera *Shakh-Senem* (1924), written for the State Opera Theatre, Baku, which skilfully incorporated Azerbaijan national melodies and dances. Like many Russian composers of this period, who were sent to the newly formed Soviet Republics to achieve a synthesis of Russian Romantic Music and local musical traditions, Glière spent many years in Azerbaijan, then in Uzbekistan, as did Zataevich in Kazakhstan and V. A. Uspensky in Turkmenistan.

Summary

From the foregoing, therefore, it will be seen that music in the years following the 1917 revolution reflected a number of trends already evident in the preceding period. The demand for general education, the need to elevate public taste, the composition of mass song, the concept that art should serve a higher purpose, together with the conflict between the desire for personal freedom and the authority of the State, were factors common to both eras. The new social conditions, the loss of many talented composers, teachers and performers, along with the serious economic problems created by the Civil War, all imposed immense difficulties for the arts. Ideological struggles became intense, and that so much was done to preserve Russia's artistic heritage and at the same time to stimulate the quest for a new creative culture was due to no small extent to the skill and foresight of Lunacharsky. The advent of the NEP in 1921 saw a temporary relaxation of state control and a more liberal attitude towards relations with the West, a factor which was to have a largely beneficial effect on the subsequent development of Soviet music. GS

Further Reading

Abraham, Gerald: Music in the Soviet Union. In *The New Oxford History of Music*, vol. 10. London: Oxford University Press, 1975.

Bakst, James: *A History of Russian-Soviet Music*. New York: Dodd, Mead, 1962; repr. 1966.

Brown, David: Russia. In *A History of Western Music*, vol. 5, pp. 21–46. Ed. F.W. Sternfeld. London: Weidenfeld & Nicolson, 1973.

Gray, Camilla: *The Great Experiment: Russian Art, 1863–1922*. London: Thames & Hudson, 1962.

Krebs, Stanley: *Soviet Composers and the Development of Soviet Music*. New York: Norton, 1970.

Olkhovsky, Andrey: *Music Under the Soviets*. London: Routledge & Kegan Paul, 1955.

Schwarz, Boris: *Music and Musical Life in Soviet Russia. Enlarged edition, 1917–1981*. Bloomington: Indiana University Press, 1983.

Soviet Ballet

The revolution affected the world of ballet much as it did the other arts. Whereas in the early part of the century, thanks to the brilliant productions of Diaghilev, Fokine and a host of performers, stage designers and composers, Russian ballet was at an unprecedented height, by 1917 many of the outstanding artists had left the country and there was a shortage of balletmasters and teachers. Furthermore, supporters of the PROLETKULT considered that classical dance and ballet epitomized the artificial world of the tsarist regime and had outlived their purpose. This extremist viewpoint did not prevail, however, and, following the nationalization of the THEATRE, though the standard classical repertoire was retained, the following decade saw experimentation in all aspects of ballet, which indeed was to play an important part in the life of the Soviet Union and, far from being restricted to the two main theatres in Leningrad and Moscow, flourished in various studios, theatres attached to workers' institutions and at mass demonstrations.

Among the first ballets of the Soviet period is Asafiev's *Carmagnole*, which was performed regularly at workers' organizations in the winter of 1917–18 to piano accompaniment, though little is known of the music since the score and scenario are missing. Through his literary writings, Asafiev did much to foster support for the classical ballet heritage. In Moscow an important part was played by Alexander Gorsky (1871–1924), who in addition to staging traditional ballets, such as Tchaikovsky's *Casse-noisette* (1919) also presented new ballets such as Glazunov's *Stenka Razin* (1918) and Asafiev's *Immortal Flowers* (1922). In Leningrad, Goleyzovsky was responsible for the full-length ballet *The Handsome Joseph* (1924), with scenario by Lopukhov and music by Vladimir Deshevov (1889–1955). Staged at the Mariinsky Theatre, the ballet was conceived as a picture of the Revolution using symbolic and allegorical language, in which elements of dancing, singing and acrobatics were combined with cabaret and mime. Not one of these ballets, however, is preserved in the current repertoire, the first ballet to survive being Glière's *The Red Poppy*, first performed in 1927. The period 1917–25 is also important in that not only did it see the establishment of ballet companies in the cities of new Soviet Republics such as Baku (1922) and Tashkent (1925), but it provided the background for the training of a whole number of Soviet choreographers and dancers, who were to play an important part in the subsequent development of Soviet ballet. GS

Further Reading

Roslaveva, Natalia: *Era of the Russian Ballet*, pp. 190–218. London: Victor Gollancz, 1966.

PART 2

Biographies

In the alphabetical ordering of this section, individuals appear under the name by which they are most commonly known, whether this is their real name or a pseudonym. For discussion of the use of pseudonyms, see Editorial Notes.

Abramovich, Raphael (1880–1963)

While a student at the Riga Polytechnic, Abramovich (real name A. Rein) became interested in the revolutionary movement, joining the Jewish BUND in 1901. In 1905 he was co-opted into the Central Committee, served briefly as the Bund's representative in the St Petersburg SOVIET and edited the Russian language journals, *Evreiskii Rabochii* (Jewish Worker) and *Nashe Slovo* (Our Word). He was a candidate for election to the Second Duma and participated in the major conferences of the Bund and RSDRP in 1906 and 1907. From 1911, he lived in western Europe after fleeing arrest in Russia. In May 1917 he returned to Russia with German permission and served as a central committee member of the Petrograd Soviet. After the OCTOBER REVOLUTION he sought cooperation between the BOLSHE-VIKS and the other socialist parties. From 1918 on, he was heavily involved with the Social Democratic minority. In 1920 he went to Berlin where, with Yu. O. MARTOV and F. I. DAN, he helped found the journal *Sotsialisticheskii Vestnik* (Socialist Messenger). In 1940 he emigrated to the United States and participated in writing in the Yiddish daily *Forverts* (Forward). He wrote two volumes of memoirs in Yiddish, and a history of the revolution in English.   HJT

Akchura, Yusuf (1879–1935)

Born in Simbirsk on the Volga to a wealthy Tatar industrialist family, Akchura was seven years old when his mother took him, five years after his father's death, to Istanbul. There, he entered the military school in 1887, and after graduation continued his studies at the military academy. He was imprisoned several times for his affiliation with Young Turk circles. Released in 1900, Akchura left for Paris, where he attended the École Libre des Sciences Politiques, from which he graduated in 1903.

Banned from the Ottoman empire, he returned to Russia where he lived between 1903 and 1908, when he moved to Istanbul. Despite its brevity, Akchura's 'Russian period' is of utmost significance for the contributions he made to the new reformist education among the Volga Tatars, not least among women.

1905 marked the beginning of Akchura's involvement in the political life of Russian Muslims. He was involved in preparing the First Congress of the Muslims of the Russian Empire (August, 1905), and shared its presidency with the Crimean I. GASPRALI and the Azeri A. M. Topchibashev.

The Union of all Russian Muslims which emerged was not, however, a recognized political party, and could therefore not participate in the Duma elections. The leadership decided to affiliate with the Kadet party, which elected Akchura to its Central Administrative Committee. Akchura's adherence to the Kadet programme was aimed at gaining access to political participation in order to integrate the specific demands of the Volga Tatars into the programme the Russians themselves were advancing (see CRIMEAN AND VOLGA TATARS).

The post-1907 repression drastically curtailed political activities for Russians and non-Russians alike, and when in 1908 news of the Young Turk revolution in the Ottoman empire reached him, Akchura decided to leave Russia for Turkey, where he lived until his death in 1935.   A-AR

Alexeev, Mikhail Vasilievich (1857–1918)

Born into the family of an army captain, Alexeev received his initial education at the Tver classical gymnasium and thence the Moscow Infantry Junker school. Commissioned in 1876, he fought in the Russo-Turkish war a year later as a junior officer and held a variety of minor commands until his promotion to captain in 1887. Alexeev graduated from the General Staff academy in 1890 and served in the headquarters staff (from 1900 as the head of its operational section) until 1904 whilst lecturing in the academy's department of military history. On the outbreak of the Russo-Japanese war he was appointed head of operational staff to the III Manchurian army and from 1905 first quartermaster-general of the newly formed main administration of the General Staff and a permanent member of the fortresses committee.

In 1908 he became chief of staff of the Kiev military district and a participant in the war ministry's strategic conference preceding the FIRST WORLD WAR. There he argued unsuccessfully for the concentration of Russian forces against the Austrians whose army he judged the weaker in morale, discipline, fire-power and ethnic cohesion.

For eighteen months until August 1914 Alexeev commanded the XIII army corps when he was promoted infantry general and made chief of staff of the South-Western Front. After a short period as commander of the North-Western Front he succeeded General N. N. Yanushkevich in August 1915 as chief of staff to the commander-in-chief, NICHOLAS II, and the effective director of Russia's military campaigns on all the fronts until March 1917.

Alexeev cannot be numbered as one of Russia's most imaginative military intellectuals but his reputation for enterprise, hard work and attention to detail has never been challenged. An exemplary product of the opportunity D. A. MILYUTIN had afforded to the sons of soldiers and to the diligent commoner for professional military advancement, Alexeev eschewed all considerations of dynastic and party preference in his commitment to his colleagues, the army and what he believed to be the honour of Russia. He served both Nicholas and the PROVISIONAL GOVERNMENT, becoming senior military adviser to KERENSKY and once again chief of staff at the end of August 1917. In the latter capacity Alexeev almost certainly preserved Kornilov from indictment before a revolutionary court by sending him to Bykhov under the guard of troops who had been assigned personally to the chief of staff.

After the OCTOBER REVOLUTION and a brief period of detention, Alexeev fled south to Novocherkassk where in November he organized an officers' association which was to become the nucleus of the VOLUNTEER ARMY. From December until his death from a heart attack in September 1918 in the city of Ekaterinodar, Alexeev concentrated upon developing his nascent army's financial and political organization, leaving operational matters to KORNILOV.

MP

Further Reading

Katkov, G.: *Russia 1917: The February revolution*. London: Longman, 1967.

Shchegolev, P.E.: *Padenie tsarskogo rezhima. Po materialam chrezvychainnoi komissii vremennogo pravitelstva.* 7 vols., Moscow-Leningrad: 1924–27.

Sovetskaya voennaya entsiklopediya, vol. 1, Moscow: 1976.

Zayonchkovskii, A.M.: *Podgotovka Rossii k imperialisticheskoi voine.* Moscow: 1926.

Alexinsky, Grigori Alexeevich (1879–1965)

Born in Dagestan, Alexinsky studied in the Historical-Philological Faculty of Moscow University, was arrested in 1902 and exiled as a student organizer (his group included KAMENEV and TSERETELI). During the 1905 REVOLUTION he worked as a propagandist for the RSDRP Moscow Committee. After October 1905 he became a member of the St Petersburg Committee and contributed to the papers *Novaya Zhizn*, (New Life), *Vestnik Zhizni* (Messenger of Life) and *Volna* (The Wave).

In 1906 Alexinsky was elected by the St Petersburg workers' curia to the Second Duma. He represented the Ekaterinoslav Committee at the Stockholm Congress of the RSDRP (1906) and was spokesman for the BOLSHEVIK minority of the Duma group at the London Congress of the RSDRP (1907). Following the dissolution of the Second Duma, he favoured, first, a policy of boycotting the Third Duma and, later, that of 'ultimatum' (accountability of the RSDRP Duma group to the party Central Committee). Over this issue he parted company with LENIN.

With BOGDANOV and LUNACHARSKY, Alexinsky founded the RDSRP Forward group (Vpered) in December 1909 and taught at the Party Schools on Capri (1909) and in Bologna (1910). Following the departure of Bogdanov (1911) and Lunacharsky (1913) from Vpered, Alexinsky and D. Z. Manuilsky assumed the leadership of the group in Paris where they abandoned its emphasis on 'cultural revolution' in favour of technical planning and propaganda in the army. Alexinsky represented Vpered at the 'August Bloc' conference of RSDRP fractions in 1912 and at the 'unification' conference convened by the International Socialist Bureau in Brussels in July 1914.

On the outbreak of war Alexinsky became a 'defensist', arguing in the anthology *Voina* (War) (Paris, 1915) to which PLEKHANOV and AXELROD also contributed, that 'defensism' was a legitimate policy for socialists since a revolution imposed by a foreign power would be a revolution 'from above'. In August 1915 he produced his own journal *Rossiya i Svoboda* (Russia and Freedom) which included Benito Mussolini amongst its contributors. In October 1915 Alexinsky merged this journal with the SD and SR paper *Prizyv* (Call-up) but was subsequently banned from its columns for contributing to *Russkaya Volya* (Russian Freedom), a paper funded by the tsarist Interior Ministry.

As early as November 1914 Alexinsky had argued that socialist 'internationalists' and 'defeatists' were playing into German hands and by 1915 he was alleging that both the

Lenin group in Zurich and the *Nashe Slovo* group in Paris were being funded by Alexander HELPHAND (Parvus) on behalf of the German government (see REVOLU-TIONIERUNGSPOLITIK). In July 1917, Alexinsky and the SR V. Pankratov (also a former member of the Second Duma), conspired with the Justice Minister Pereverzev to discredit Lenin and the Bolsheviks by repeating these allegations in the St Petersburg newspaper *Zhivoe Slovo* (Living Word).

After October Alexinsky fled to France where he contributed to BURTSEV's *Obshchee Delo* (Common Cause) and the monarchist *Russkaya Gazeta* (Russian Gazette). In August 1920 he was tried *in absentia* and found guilty of counter-revolutionary activity and of assisting Allied Intervention. He was proclaimed an enemy of the people and denied entry to the Soviet Union.   JB

Further Reading

Alexinsky, G.: *Russia and the Great War*. London: T. Fisher Unwin, 1915.

Senn, A.E.: *The Russian Revolution in Switzerland, 1914–1917*. Madison, Milwaukee and London: University of Wisconsin Press, 1971.

Annensky, Nikolai Fedorovich (1843–1912)

Economist, statistician and publicist, Annensky was born in St Petersburg where he became involved in the revolutionary movement during the late 1860s. By the 1870s, he had developed a liberal POPULIST orientation which found expression in his contributions to such radical journals as *Otechestvennye zapiski* (Notes of the Fatherland) and *Delo* (The Cause).

Annensky's contacts with Populist circles led to several arrests and finally to administrative exile in Siberia in 1880. Upon his release in 1883, he was employed as a zemstvo statistician in Kazan and in 1887 became head of the statistical bureau of the Nizhni Novgorod provincial zemstvo. His next political involvement came during the early 1890s, when he assisted in the establishment of the People's Right Party.

Following his return to St Petersburg, Annensky went to work in the statistical section of the city administration and in 1895 became head of that department. In this period he joined the Imperial Free Economic Society as well as the radical St Petersburg Writers' Union. In 1901 he was arrested again and exiled for participating in an anti-government demonstration. For the next several years, he resided in Finland where he took part in the formation of the Union of Liberation and then served as vice-chairman of its Council. Arrested again in 1904 and briefly exiled to the provinces, Annensky soon returned to the capital. There he was instrumental in organizing the Union of Unions which elected him to its Central Bureau.

After the 1905 REVOLUTION, Annensky, who was then chief editor of the liberal Populist journal *Russkoe bogatstvo*

(Russian Wealth), was initially sympathetic to the SOCIAL-IST REVOLUTIONARIES. He soon broke with the SRs over the issue of terror, however, and in 1906 helped to found the Popular Socialist Party. He remained one of that Party's principal spokesmen until forced by ill health to withdraw from public life shortly before his death in 1912.   BTN

Metropolitan Antoni (1863–1936)

Of aristocratic birth, Antoni Khrapovitsky decided to dedicate his life to the CHURCH under the influence of the Slavophiles. Dostoevsky's *Brothers Karamazov* and his own pilgrimages to the famous Optina elders (models for Dostoevsky's Zosima and Alesha) sealed his choice to take the monastic vows while a student at the St Petersburg Theological Academy. He and Bishop Sergi (Stragorodsky, Antoni's chief antagonist after 1926 as the *de facto* patriarchal *locum tenens*) were probably the two most influential theologians in the ranks of Orthodox bishops of their time. Both contributed significantly to the Russian pastoral and theological renewal, as seminary and academy teachers, administrators and bishops. Antoni openly preached monastic renewal, restoration of the patriarchate and of Church autonomy, and, later, vehemently opposed RASPUTIN. This cost him several reversals in his professorial and episcopal careers. In politics, however, he was a staunch reactionary monarchist.

At the Moscow All-Russian Local Council (*Sobor*) Antoni gained the majority of votes (159 to 125 for Tikhon) as a patriarchal candidate; but the casting of lots favoured Tikhon. As Metropolitan of Kiev Antoni found himself on the White side of the front, chaired the Provisional Higher Church Administration of South Russia, subsequently emigrated and presided over the 'Synod' of the Russian Church Abroad in the Yugoslav town of Karlovci. Although canonically invalid and repeatedly condemned by Patriarch Tikhon and his successors, the 'Synod' survived, commanded the loyalties of a sizeable section of Russian émigrés, and even enjoyed the semi-official recognition of most local Orthodox Churches, predominantly because of the Metropolitan's exceptional personal prestige as an ecclesiastic authority.   DP

Antonov-Ovseenko, Vladimir Alexandrovich (1884–1939)

The son of a junior officer, Antonov-Ovseenko completed his education at the Voronezh Cadet Corps, enrolled in the military-engineering school at Nikolaevsk and was expelled a month later for refusing to take the oath of allegiance. He worked briefly as a labourer and coachman, and had contact with the SOCIALIST REVOLUTIONARIES. In 1902 he moved to St Petersburg where he resumed hs military training, transferred his loyalty to the Social Democrats and, in August 1904, spent ten days in gaol for possession of illegal literature. Before being posted to the 40th Kolivansk Infantry Corps in Warsaw, he forged links with the party organizations of Moscow, Ekaterinoslav, Odessa, Kiev and Vilna. In Warsaw he created a RSDRP military committee and developed contacts with workers' circles and the Jewish BUND.

He evaded posting to the Far East in early 1905 by becoming a full-time revolutionary. He incited an unsuccessful uprising of the garrison at Novaya-Alexandriya and was assigned by the Mensheviks to their branches at Kronstadt, followed by work in the illegal publication *Kazarma* (Garrison) and (in June 1906) the organization of an armed uprising in Sevastopol. By the autumn of 1907, he had spent over eighteen months in custody, been condemned to death for armed resistance to arrest (commuted to 20 years imprisonment because the authorities were unfamiliar with his new alias) and taken part in two spectacular escapes.

For the next three years Antonov-Ovseenko operated in and out of Moscow under varying degrees of surveillance. In late 1908 he organized workers' cooperatives, led a workers' occupation of the Temperance Society, and founded a Club for Sensible Amusements, which for a short time afforded him a broad base for his political work. In 1909 he became the editor of a new Plekhanovist newspaper and was arrested twice more before finally leaving the country in July 1910, making Paris his home thereafter. He was secretary of the Parisian Labour Bureau (made up of representatives from Russian cells of workers' syndicates), but his major achievement was the publication with D. Z. MANUILSKY of *Golos* (Voice) from September 1914. The paper was published for only a short time (and under various titles), but rapidly gained stature and attracted contributions from prominent internationalists.

On returning to Russia in May 1917, Antonov-Ovseenko joined the MEZHRAYONKA and soon also the BOLSHEVIK Central Committee. The ensuing months were devoted to journalism and various administrative and military committees in Finland. On 25 October 1917 (OS), he organized (with N. I. Podvoisky and M. M. LASHEVICH) and directed the seizure of the Winter Palace and the arrest of the PROVISIONAL GOVERNMENT, and became Commissar for Military Affairs and commander-in-chief of the Petrograd military district.

During the CIVIL WAR he commanded the campaign against Ataman A. M. Kaledin in UKRAINE and, between March and May 1918, led the forces of the Southern Republics. He saw action in the provinces of Tambov (where he aided TUKHACHEVSKY in putting down the (A. S.) Antonov Rising in May 1921) and Perm, and after October 1921 organized famine relief in Samara province. Chief of Political Administration of the RED ARMY from late 1922, as a leading Trotskyite his authority quickly waned and he lost his military command in 1923. After TROTSKY was defeated in 1925, Antonov-Ovseenko was

sent to Czechoslovakia (and later to Poland) as ambassador. His last post was that of Soviet representative in Spain during the civil war. He disappeared during the Great Purge and was rehabilitated after the death of STALIN.

FP

Armand, Inessa (1874–1920)

Russian revolutionary and feminist, close associate of Lenin's, first head of Zhenotdel (the Women's Section of Central Committee established in August 1919).

Inessa Armand was born in Paris of a French father and English-French mother on 8 May 1874. Shortly after the death in 1879 of her actor-father, Theodore Stefan, she was taken to Moscow by a maternal aunt and raised in the home of Evgeni Armand, a wealthy textile manufacturer of French extraction. On the family estate at Pushkino, where her aunt served as tutor and governess for the seven Armand children, Inessa acquired a facility for foreign languages, an ability to play the piano, and a growing social consciousness. At the age of nineteen she married the second eldest son, Alexander Armand, and with him opened a school for peasant children. In 1899 she joined the Moscow Society for Improving the Lot of Women, a philanthropic and charitable organization dedicated to helping destitute women. It was here that she developed a life-long interest in feminist issues. Elected president of the Society in 1900, she was soon frustrated by tsarist authorities in her efforts to set up a Sunday School for working women and to edit a newspaper that could discuss the broader aspects of the women's question.

In 1903, in search of more radical solutions and under the influence of her brothers- and sisters-in-law, she joined the RSDRP and for the next four years served as an effective underground propagandist in Moscow and Pushkino. Arrested for a third time in June 1907, she was sentenced to two years exile north of Archangel. She escaped in time to attend the December 1908 Women's Congress in St Petersburg before fleeing abroad. In 1909 she met LENIN and, after studying for a year at the New University in Brussels, settled in Paris where she became an active member of the Bolshevik émigré colony. She used her knowledge of French to act as the Social Democrats' liaison with the French Socialist Party; she spent Armand money to help finance a party school for underground workers which Lenin set up at Longjumeau in 1911; and she served as secretary for the Committee of Foreign Organizations established to coordinate all Bolshevik groups in Western Europe.

In July 1912 Armand returned illegally to Russia at Lenin's behest to help re-establish the party's Petersburg Committee and to assist in the forthcoming elections to the Fourth Duma. These efforts led to her arrest in September, to six months in prison, and to her eventual flight in August 1913. After a brief stay with the Ulyanovs (i.e.

Figure 44 Armand.

nomic council). She also was involved in the work of the French Section of the Russian Communist Party and was part of the Russian Red Cross Mission sent to France in February 1919 to repatriate Russian prisoners of war and to stir up unrest in the French labour movement.

On her return to Russia in May 1919, Armand devoted herself to organizing and propagandizing Russian factory women. As the first director of Zhenotdel she sought to increase female participation in the labour force by relieving many of the household responsibilities which normally fell to women and she fought for female equality in the party and labour movements. Almost single-handed, she organized and chaired the First International Conference of Communist Women which met in conjunction with the Second Congress of the Comintern in the summer of 1920. Shortly thereafter, while on a vacation in the Caucasus, she contracted cholera and died at the age of 46. She is buried next to the Kremlin Wall.

It is ironic that much of Armand's pioneering work among Russian factory women was soon undone and forgotten when the Soviet state abandoned its early social experiments in the late 1920s (see WOMEN IN 1917 AND AFTER). She is instead remembered in the West primarily for her close association with the first leader of that state. The fact that she lived in close proximity to Lenin from 1910 to 1916 and received more than 135 letters from him has led recent writers to conclude that she was Lenin's mistress. Of more significance and perhaps validity is the ample evidence that she was one of the few members of his entourage who had the courage and the ability to oppose him on personal and political matters.

RCE

Further Reading

Armand, I.F.: *Stat'i, rechi, pis'ma*. Moscow: 1975.

Elwood, R.C.: *Inessa Armand: Revolutionary and Feminist*. Cambridge: 1992.

Podlyashchuk, Pavel: *Tovarishch Inessa*. Moscow: 1984.

See also Volkogonov, D.: *Lenin: Life and Legacy*. London: 1994.

Arshinov, Peter Andreevich (1887–1937)

A metal worker from a Ukrainian working class family, Arshinov (also known as Marin), became a Social Democrat in 1905, favouring the BOLSHEVIKS, then an ANARCHIST communist in 1906. He was involved in terrorist activity, being frequently arrested and finally imprisoned in 1910 in Moscow, where he formed a close personal and political friendship with MAKHNO. When he was released in 1917 he became a leading figure in anarchist communist groups first in Moscow, then in Ukraine.

In 1918, Arshinov and VOLIN were leading members of the Nabat (The Tocsin) organization, and in 1919 they joined Makhno. In 1921 Arshinov went into exile, living first in Germany and then in France. He favoured a

Lenin and his wife) in Galicia, she was instrumental in establishing and editing *Rabotnitsa* (Woman Worker), a legal Social Democratic newspaper published in St Petersburg, which for the first time addressed questions of interest to proletarian women. She also was given the unenviable task of trying to defend Lenin's interests at the Brussels 'Unity' Conference called by the International Socialist Bureau in July 1914.

Inessa spent the war years in Switzerland. In March 1915 she helped to organize the International Conference of Socialist Women called in Bern to protest against the war. She also attended the International Conference of Socialist Youth, and the Zimmerwald and Kienthal Conferences, as well as going to Paris in an unsuccessful attempt to line up support for the defeatist position of Lenin's Zimmerwald Left movement. She was one of nineteen Bolsheviks to join the Bolshevik, leader on the 'sealed' train trip back to Russia in April 1917.

Following the OCTOBER REVOLUTION, in which she played only a minor role, Armand supported the Left Communists in protesting against the Brest-Litovsk peace. She was a member of the Executive Committee of the Moscow province Soviet, of the All-Russian Central Executive Committee (VTsIK), and for a year served as chairwoman of the Moscow province Sovnarkhoz (eco-

Figure 45   Arshinov, c. 1925.

militant and indeed military anarchism, and after the débâcle of the movement he proposed that the anarchists should form a virtual political party, culminating in the *Organizational Platform* (1926). But he won almost no support from other anarchists, and in 1930 he returned to his original Bolshevism and also in 1932 to Russia, where he disappeared in the purge. Arshinov wrote the first history of the Makhno movement (1923).   NW

Avksentiev, Nikolai Dmitrievich (1878–1943)

One of the most forceful politicians of the PARTY OF SOCIALIST REVOLUTIONARIES (PSR) and one of the few who could really move the masses, Avksentiev was the son of a Penza lawyer, who studied at Moscow University, but was expelled in 1899 for leading a political strike. He continued his studies in Germany, at the universities of Berlin, Leipzig and Halle, where he formed a group of young neo-Kantians who would eventually constitute the organizational nucleus of the PSR (i.e. I. I. BUNAKOV-FONDAMINSKY, A. R. GOTS, Dmitry Gavronsky and V. M. ZENZINOV). In 1905, Avksentiev returned to Russia, participating with Fondaminsky in the 'banquet' campaign

staged by liberal society. During the brief period of political liberty following the 1905 October Manifesto, Avksentiev became a popular orator in the St Petersburg factories and, with L. D. TROTSKY and others, a leading member of the Petersburg SOVIET of Workers' Deputies until his arrest and exile. Co-opted to the Central Committee in 1907, he edited its popular journal *Znamya Truda* (Labour Banner) in Paris. After AZEF's exposure as a police spy, Avksentiev strongly opposed terrorism and in 1912, he led the Pochin (Initiative) Group, whose newspaper of the same name demanded an end to terror and participation in the State Duma. He gave critical support to the activities of his fellow-Freemason, A. F. KERENSKY, in the Fourth Duma, thereby facilitating their collaboration in 1917. During the war, Avksentiev belonged to the patriotic Prizyv (Call-up) group in Paris.

After his return from exile in 1917, Avksentiev became a leading member of the Petrograd Soviet and the All-Russian Central Executive Committee of Soviets and simultaneously Chairman of the All-Russian Peasant Soviets. In July–August 1917, he served as minister of the interior in the PROVISIONAL GOVERNMENT. As Chairman of the 'Pre-Parliament', he tried to rally the Petrograd garrison against a BOLSHEVIK seizure of power. An active participant in the anti-Bolshevik 'democratic counter-revolution', he became leader of the Directory in Omsk before its overthrow by KOLCHAK in November 1918. Subsequently, he helped to coordinate support for the 1921 KRONSTADT REVOLT. An active participant in émigré life and letters, Avksentiev died in 1943, shortly after his arrival in New York.   RA

Axelrod, Pavel Borisovich (1850–1928)

Born in Chernigov, Axelrod began his revolutionary career in the autumn of 1872 when, under the impact of Lassalle's writings, he organized Kiev's first socialist circle and participated in 1875 in the 'To the People' movement. A follower of BAKUNIN in the later 1870s, he tried to stir up peasants and workers and contributed to the Bakuninist *Rabotnik* (Worker) and its successor, *Obshchina* (Commune), until in 1879 he joined BLACK REPARTITION. In the early 1880s, in exile in Switzerland, he and PLEKHANOV were co-founders of the Marxist Emancipation of Labour Group. In the 1890s, Axelrod published a series of pamphlets in which he worked out the tactical implications of Plekhanov's revolutionary strategy, highlighting the leading role of social democracy, as the party of the proletariat, in Russia's future 'bourgeois' revolution.

A co-founder and editor of *Iskra* (The Spark) in the early 1900s, Axelrod was one of MARTOV's chief supporters at the Second Congress of the RSDRP in 1903, when he argued for a more open and inclusive party. His articles in (the now Menshevik) *Iskra* (December 1903, January 1904) sharply attacked the 'organizational fetishism' of *Iskra* (and, by implication, LENIN) for having turned the party and its members into an 'apparatus run by an omniscient centre', and were, more than any other single factor, influential in the self-definition of MENSHEVISM, and its fencing off from 'Jacobin' Leninism.

Influenced by the example of German social democracy, which he knew intimately and admired, Axelrod's major aspiration was to turn the RSDRP into a revolutionary social democratic party of the advanced working masses. It was that ambition which inspired his 1905–7 campaign for a workers' congress and his unflinching support for the Menshevik 'praktiki' (denounced by Lenin and Plekhanov as 'liquidators') during the years of reaction preceding the FIRST WORLD WAR. Much less of a politician than the impulsive Martov or the imperious DAN, Axelrod never identified with any of the Menshevik factions, but did his best to conciliate and keep them together.

During the war years, Axelrod, together with Martov, was Menshevism's representative in the Zimmerwald socialist peace movement, attending the Zimmerwald (1915), Kienthal (1916) and Stockholm (1917) conferences. Defining himself as a 'Zimmerwaldist', as distinct from a 'Kienthaler', Axelrod, unlike Martov, refused to vote for the very radical Kienthal Manifesto and clashed violently with the Leninist Left (notably Karl RADEK and Vatslav Vorovsky) at the abortive Third Zimmerwald Conference in Stockholm in September 1917. Returning to Petrograd on 10 May 1917, after 34 years in exile, Axelrod, though critical of the policies of the TSERETELI-led Menshevik majority, nevertheless held aloof from the Menshevik-Internationalists, striving instead for party unity as a member of the Menshevik Organizational Committee and even as honorary chairman of the Petrograd party organization which was dominated by the Menshevik-Internationalists.

After the OCTOBER REVOLUTION, which he denounced as a 'historical crime without parallel in modern history', Axelrod was the Mensheviks' emissary abroad, mobilizing socialist public opinion for 'socialist intervention' against the Bolshevik terror and the persecution of socialist parties in Soviet Russia. At the same time, he appealed to his Menshevik comrades not to let themselves be hoodwinked by 'the revolutionary exterior and socialist past' of the Bolshevik 'autocrats', but to write off the Bolshevik regime as simple counter-revolution.

Founder and father-figure, Axelrod personified Menshevism's aspiration to civilize and Europeanize the RSDRP into a genuine social democratic and revolutionary workers' party. For him, continuous fencing off from Lenin, his October revolution and the Bolshevik regime was an integral part of that effort.   IG

Further Reading
Ascher, Abraham: *Pavel Axelrod and the Development of Menshevism.* Cambridge, Mass.: 1972.

Perepiska G.V. Plekhanovva i P.B. Akselroda. Moscow: 1925.
Pis'ma P.B. Akselroda i Yu.O. Martova 1901–1916. Berlin: 1924.

Azef, Evno Fishelevich (1869–1918)

A highly acclaimed SOCIALIST REVOLUTIONARY leader, head of the Battle Organization, who betrayed his comrades and the police at one and the same time, Azef, more than any other undercover agent in the annals of the revolutionary movement, came to epitomize provocation at its worst both to his party and the police. His exposure in 1908 was to leave a lasting mark on the SR party and on the entire revolutionary movement.

Azef was born in Lyskovo, Grodno province, the second of seven children in an impoverished Jewish family. In 1874 the family moved to Rostov-on-Don in search of a better future, but met with no greater success. Nevertheless Azef was sent to high school, from which he graduated around 1890. Short of means to continue his education, he earned his living through tutoring, writing for a small local paper, office work and finally as a travelling salesman. In early 1892, faced with arrest for revolutionary activity, he took the opportunity to abscond with 800 rubles and go abroad. He settled in Karlsruhe, Germany, and entered the Polytechnic, moving to Darmstadt, where in 1899 he received his diploma as an electrical engineer. Shortly after arriving in Karlsruhe he joined a group of Russian Social Democrats, and in April 1893 made his first contact with the Police Department, offering them his services as an informant.

Following his recruitment by the police, Azef began to radicalize his views, and by the end of 1894 became known as an ardent supporter of terrorism. Accordingly he left the Social Democrats and joined the Union of Russian Socialist Revolutionaries. He also tried to extend his contacts among Russian revolutionary émigrés and travelled to Zurich and Bern, where he made the acquaintance of Kh. O. Zhitlovsky. The latter was instrumental in paving Azef's way to a position of prominence in the future SR party. By 1899 Azef had sufficiently proved his value to the Police Department to earn a wage-rise to 100 rubles per month plus special bonuses at New Year and Easter (see AGENTS PROVOCATEURS). The police now suggested he return to Russia, promising their help in finding a position as an electrical engineer and a further increase in his salary.

In 1899 Azef made his way to Moscow well equipped with warm recommendations both to the chief of the Moscow OKHRANA, S. V. ZUBATOV, and to the Moscow revolutionaries. He joined the Northern Union and was soon to represent it in discussions with the southern groups which led to the formation in 1901 of the united SR party. From then on he was a member of the Central Committee, organizing the transport of illegal literature and travelling widely throughout Russia and abroad. At the same time he became a close associate of G. A. GERSHUNI, whom after his arrest in 1903 he succeeded as head of the Battle Organization. Thus in addition to a remarkable vantage-point over the organizations of the entire party, he now also acquired a unique power over that sphere of activity which was constantly gaining in importance in the eyes of the SRs as well as in those of the police. Using this position he could make himself indispensable to both sides: neither could hope to achieve a major success without him. Consequently his worth to the police rose first to 1,000 rubles a month and later to twice that much, while in the party he became a byword for organizational and technical skills. His key role in planning the most spectacular terrorist assaults, like the assassinations of the minister of the interior, V. K. Plehve, in 1904, and of the Grand Duke Sergei Alexandrovich in 1905, and his efforts at perfecting the methods of terrorist combat won him the admiration of the entire party. Little wonder that the several warnings that were leaked by former police sources to SR leaders throughout the years about Azef's true role were stubbornly rejected as police intrigues.

Azef's fortunes began to change in 1907. To many SRs the severe blows dealt to the party by the police were proof of the fact that an agent provocateur had wormed himself into the very centre of the party. V. L. BURTSEV, convinced of Azef's guilt and aided by M. Bakai, a police defector, led the struggle to expose Azef, bringing himself into severe conflict with the SR leadership that stood firmly by Azef and sued Burtsev before a court of honour. During the trial Burtsev managed to meet A. Lopukhin, a former director of the Police Department, who confirmed the allegations. Lopukhin later repeated these accusations to a dumbfounded delegation of the party leadership. Azef managed to escape into hiding, with both his former comrades and the police hard on his heels. In 1912 he contacted the party leadership from his hiding place in Germany, offering to stand trial before the party on condition that his safety be guaranteed pending the outcome. His request caused uproar in the party but remained unanswered. In 1915 he was arrested by the Germans as a revolutionary, was released in December 1917, and died in Berlin in 1918.   NS

Further Reading

Hildermeier, Manfred: *Die sozialrevolutionäre Partei Russlands.* Cologne: 1978.

Nikolajewsky, Boris: *Azeff the Spy: Russian Terrorist and Police Stool.* Garden City, NY: 1934.

Savinkov, Boris: *Memoirs of a Terrorist.* New York: 1931.

Bakunin, Mikhail Alexandrovich (1814–1876)

Russian (and pan-European) revolutionary leader and the principal exponent of anarchism, Bakunin was of gentry origin. At Moscow University he joined the circle of N. V.

Figure 46 Bakunin.

Stankevich, whom he succeeded as its leader in 1837. Initially a Hegelian who preached reconciliation with reality, he broke with the master on emigrating in 1840 and shocked contemporaries by hailing the destructive urge as a creative act. Caught in the revolutionary events of 1848–9, he espoused the cause of an anti-Germanic Slav federation. He was arrested for his part in the Dresden uprising and extradited to Russia. From prison he addressed an ambiguously worded confession to Nicholas I. In 1861 he escaped from Siberian exile via Japan to western Europe, where he collaborated with A. I. HERZEN on *Kolokol* (The Bell). As Herzen's prestige with younger radicals declined after 1863, so Bakunin's rose. He now stood unequivocally for social revolution, and in 1868 founded a semi-fictitious international organization, the Alliance of Socialist Democracy, as a platform for his anarchist teaching. His attempt to place his stamp on Karl Marx's rival body (the First International) led to a bitter personal and doctrinal feud between the two leaders and to the collapse of both organizations. This was a major setback to the revolutionary cause. Bakunin's enthusiastic but misguided efforts to stir up revolt in France, Spain and Italy failed, as did those of his followers, known as 'rebels' (buntari), in Russia, where he was further discredited by his close association with S. G. NECHAEV (1869–70).

In *Statism and Anarchy* (1873) and other works Bakunin maintained that man was a natural rebel. He virulently condemned Church and state for shackling human freedom. For the same reason he opposed Marxian state socialism. The revolutionaries' task was to unleash the potential for spontaneous revolt already present among the masses (including peasants and especially marginal elements such as bandits), not to replace one oppressive form of state by another, a centralized proletarian dictatorship. The future society should be an international federation of autonomous communities (which were, however, expected to follow Bakuninist precepts). Only in such a society, with production carried on by voluntary associations of workers, would man be freed from all external restraints, including the tyranny of scientific abstractions. Essentially a Romantic, Bakunin exuded great personal charisma, but his views were exceedingly naive.

He spent his last years active among the anarchist elements in the Jura and the Russian student colony in Zürich. He died in Bern in 1876.   JLHK

Further Reading

Avrich, Paul: *The Russian Anarchists*. Princeton, NJ: 1967.

Carr, E.H.: *Michael Bakunin*. London: 1937, repr. 1961.

Kelly, Aileen: *Michael Bakunin: A Study in the Psychology and Politics of Utopianism*. Oxford: 1982.

Lehning, A. ed.: *Archives Bakounine*, 5 vols. Leiden: 1961–77.

Pyziur, E.: *The Doctrine of Anarchism of Michael A. Bakunin*. Milwaukee: 1955.

Baytursun, Ahmed (1873–1937)

Born in Sartubek, northeast of the Aral Sea, the son of a Kazakh aristocratic family, Baytursun was tutored by Tatar mullahs in the fundamentals of traditional education before enrolment at the Russo-Kazakh school of Turgay. Graduating in 1895 from the Orenburg Teachers' Institute for Kazakhs he embarked on a teaching and literary career that would eventually make way for political pursuits. His involvement in education, literature, and journalism placed Baytursun in the midst of the jadid effervescence and gained him the prestige of those involved in the Kazakh cultural revival. Thus, in 1905, in Verny (now Alma-Ata), he chaired the Congress of the Kazakh Intellectuals of the Eastern Steppe Area, an event responsible for the metamorphosis of the Kazakh cultural jadidism into the Kazakh national movement. His involvement with the Kazakh underground political organizations which emerged in the following years, led to his arrest, expulsion from the Steppe Territory in 1909, and to his further radicalization.

Following the FEBRUARY REVOLUTION, Baytursun became one of the founding members of the ALASH ORDA, the Kazakh national party which held its first congress April 1917, in Orenburg. The failure of the Kazakh nationalists to forge an alliance with the anti-Bolshevik forces in the Volga area and western Siberia, brought about a rapprochement with the BOLSHEVIKS. Baytursun represented Alash Orda in the discussions with LENIN and STALIN which led to the signing of an agreement (May 1919) to lay the foundation of an autonomous government of Kazakhstan by establishing Kirrevkom (the Kirghiz Revolutionary Committee), of which Baytursun became a member in 1920, embarking on a political career which would include membership in the Central executive Committee of the Kirghiz ASSR, the position of the People's Commissar for Education, and Chairman of the Scientific Commission of the Commissariat for Education. Throughout his political career, Baytursun remained loyal to his nationalist credo, and did his utmost to 'use the legal channels for the best interests of the Kazakh people'. Such an approach to the realities of the Soviet state was not acceptable to Moscow and in 1930 Baytursun was arrested, expelled from the Party, and in 1937 executed in the purges.   A-AR

Bazarov, Vladimir Alexandrovich (1874–1939)

Best known for his work in the Soviet STATE GENERAL PLANNING COMMISSION (Gosplan) during the 1920s, Bazarov (real name Rudnev) was one of Russia's leading Marxist theorists and an active participant in the revolution of 1917. Born in Tula, the son of a doctor, Bazarov entered Moscow University in 1892. Following his arrest in 1896 for membership of the Moscow 'Workers' Union', he shared his exile first in Tula (1896–99) and then in Kaluga (1899–1901) with A. A. BOGDANOV and I. I. SKVORTSOV-STEPANOV with whom he formed a long-standing intellectual relationship. In 1901 Bazarov joined a group in Berlin which sought to reconcile the Rabochee Delo and Iskra groups of the RSDRP. Re-arrested in the same year shortly after joining the Moscow Committee of the RSDRP, he was sentenced to three years exile in Siberia. In 1904 together with other members of the Bogdanov circle, Bazarov joined LENIN in the formation of the BOLSHEVIK fraction of the RSDRP. During the 1905 REVOLUTION he worked for the fraction in St Petersburg and wrote for its newspaper *Novaya Zhizn* (New Life).

In the debate within Bolshevism after 1907 over policy towards the Third Duma Bazarov, by now a member of the editorial board of *Proletarii*, supported Lenin's policy of participation but in 1908, his philosophical views having been denounced as un-Marxist in Lenin's *Materialism and Empiriocriticism*, he left the Bolshevik fraction, though he did not join Bogdanov. In 1911 he was arrested and exiled for three years to Astrakhan.

In 1917 Bazarov joined the informal grouping of Social Democrats who wrote for Gorky's newspaper *Novaya*

Zhizn, and around the time of the Bolshevik seizure of power entered a new grouping of Social Democrat Internationalists, which included V. A. Desnitsky and B. V. Avilov. They called for the formation of a socialist coalition government and convention of the CONSTITUENT ASSEMBLY. During the CIVIL WAR Bazarov collaborated on Martov's journal *Mysl* (Thought) (Kharkov 1919) in which he expressed scepticism about the socialist content of WAR COMMUNISM. In 1922, however, he joined Gosplan as an 'honest non-Party man standing on the Soviet platform'.

Before 1917 Bazarov was known as a translator, with Skvortsov-Stepanov, of Marx's *Capital* (1907–8); as an economist and economic historian; for his contributions to positivist epistemology; and for his writings on social psychology in which he contrasted, as did Bogdanov, the individualism and authoritarianism of capitalist societies with the collectivism and moral altruism which would prevail under socialism. A scientific approach to social problems and a rejection of authoritarianism also underlay Bazarov's philosophy of economic planning during the 1920s.

Bazarov was one of a number of 'bourgeois specialists' arrested in 1930 during the second phase of the industrialization campaign. In the 'Menshevik Trial' of March 1931 it was alleged that Bazarov together with V. G. Groman had led a counter-revolutionary organization inside Gosplan since 1923. Bazarov was not tried publicly, but was imprisoned for eighteen months and exiled to Saratov. In 1935 he joined his son, A. V. Rudnev, in Gagri, Abkhazia. When the son was killed in an avalanche, Bazarov returned to Moscow, where he translated German philosophy until his own death from natural causes on 16 September 1939.   JB

Further Reading

Erlich, Alexander: *The Soviet Industrialization Debate*. Cambridge, Mass.: Harvard University Press, 1967.

Jasny, Naum: *Soviet Economists of the Twenties. Names to be Remembered*. Cambridge: Cambridge University Press, 1972.

Information communicated to the Editor by Francis King of the University of East Anglia, based partly on the unpublished memoirs of Bazarov's grandson, E. A. Rudnev.

Williams, Robert C.: *The Other Bolsheviks. Lenin and his Critics 1904–1914*. Bloomington: Indiana University Press, 1986.

Berkman, Alexander (1870–1936) and Goldman, Emma (1869–1940)

Both born into upper-middle-class Jewish families in Russian Lithuania and well educated, they both emigrated to the United States and became ANARCHISTS during the 1880s. They met in 1889, became lovers for a time and friends and comrades for life. They were active in the German-speaking movement, associated first with Johann Most and then with Joseph Peukert. In 1892 Berkman tried to assassinate Henry Clay Frick, the employers' leader in a

Figure 47   Berkman, Moscow 1920.

bitter steel dispute in Pennsylvania, and was sentenced to 21 years' imprisonment, later described in *Prison Memoirs of an Anarchist* (1912). Goldman soon became a leading speaker and writer, moving to the English-speaking movement. In 1906, with the death of Most and the release of Berkman, Berkman and Goldman became the best-known anarchists in the country. In 1906 she began the influential paper *Mother Earth*, which he edited from 1908. She represented the American movement at international anarchist conferences and produced *Anarchism and Other Essays* (1911). They took a leading part in struggles for free speech and birth control and then against the FIRST WORLD WAR and the imposition of conscription. As a result they were arrested in 1917, imprisoned for two years, and deported to Russia where they remained from the beginning of 1920 until the end of 1921. At first they supported the BOLSHEVIK regime and worked with it in various cultural activities, in the capitals and in UKRAINE, but eventually they became disillusioned and took the lead both in private pressure and in public protests on behalf of persecuted anarchists and other revolutionaries. Eventually they emigrated again, travelling through Latvia and Sweden to Germany, and took the lead in the left-wing

Figure 48   Goldman (centre) with Berkman (in front) and Maximov (behind, to left) at Kropotkin's funeral, February 1921, Moscow.

opposition to the growing dictatorship. They spoke at meetings, wrote articles and pamphlets, and produced periodicals and books, especially her *My Disillusionment in Russia* (1923–5) and his *The Bolshevik Myth* (1925). During the 1920s they settled in France, after she had stayed in Britain and Canada, and wrote more books, his *What Is Communist Anarchism?* (1927) and her *Living My Life* (1931). He committed suicide, but she worked for the Spanish anarcho-syndicalists during the Civil War, and later died in Canada during yet another speaking and writing tour. Neither of them contributed much to anarchist theory, but both of them were exemplary representatives of anarchist practice, and their involvement with the Russian Revolution well expressed the anarchist encounter with that complex phenomenon.   NW

Bochkareva, Maria Leontievna (1889–?)

Emmeline Pankhurst called Bochkareva 'the greatest woman of the century'. She was the commander of the first,

and most successful, of the volunteer women's battalions formed in 1917 by the PROVISIONAL GOVERNMENT.

Bochkareva's memoirs, dictated to the American journalist Isaac Don Levine in the summer of 1918, provide a vivid insight into the lives of the Russian poor, especially women, before the 1917 Revolution. She was also a privileged witness of the 'Kornilov Affair' (see KORNILOV).

The daughter of a serf who achieved the rank of sergeant during the 1878 Russo-Turkish War, Maria Bochkareva (née Frolkova) was brought up by her mother in Tomsk, Siberia. Her father was frequently absent, drunk or violent. At eight she was sent out to work as a nursemaid, and later a grocer's assistant. Seduced by a young officer with promises of marriage in 1905, she escaped further beatings from her father by marrying Afanasi Bochkarev, exchanging, as she soon realized 'one form of torture for another'. To escape Bochkarev she stole her mother's passport. A gendarme officer offered to take no action against her in return for sexual relations. A physically strong woman, she worked successfully as a builder, so her husband repeatedly

307

followed her to live off her earnings. Whenever she tried to escape, men in authority offered to help her, on one condition . . . Around 1910, she met Yakov Buk who seemed nicer; they even set up a successful business together, yet all was ruined when they sheltered an SR terrorist. To save Buk from lonely exile, Bochkareva had to sleep with Governor Kraft of Yakutsk, but Buk then beat her out of jealousy.

Inspired by patriotism and a desire to escape Buk, in 1914 Bochkareva volunteered for the army. The recruiters laughed at her, but her petition to NICHOLAS II was successful. As a soldier, Bochkareva was a brilliant success. She fought on the South-West Front from 1915–17. She was four times wounded and three times decorated, 'but, being a woman I received only a medal of the 3rd degree'. She was captured and escaped; promoted corporal and then sergeant. In 1917, she was 'discovered' by M. V. Rodzyanko, President of the State Duma, who brought her to Petrograd and introduced her to A. F. KERENSKY and General A. A. Brusilov. In May she formed a Women's Death Battalion, insisting on traditional forms of discipline, to shame the men into continuing the war. These efforts earned the admiration of Emmeline Pankhurst, who came to Petrograd to support her enterprise, the critical friendship of Louise Bryant, and the bitter hatred of the BOLSHEVIK soldiers. She became a warm supporter of General L. G. KORNILOV. In July, her Battalion attacked the Germans on the South-West Front taking 2,000 prisoners. This brought reprisals from Bolshevik soldiers who blamed her for provoking German counter-attacks. She was beaten up and forced to disband her Battalion. She rejected the suggestion of LENIN and TROTSKY that she cooperate with them and in February 1918 she narrowly escaped execution while visiting General Kornilov in Novocherkassk. She then left Russia for the United States where she asked President Wilson to intervene in Russia. In England she met Emmeline Pankhurst once more before returning to Russia. Her fate is unknown.   RA

Further Reading

Bochkareva, M.L.: *Yashka: My Life as Peasant, Officer and Exile* (as set down by Isaac Don Levine). New York: Stokes, 1919.

Bryant, Louise: *Six Red Months in Russia.* New York: Doran, 1918.

Pankhurst, Emmeline: In *Britannia* 13 July, 16 November, 1917.

Solonevich, Boris: *Zhenshchina s vintovkoi* (the slightly fictionalized memoirs of Lt. Nina Krylova). Buenos Aires: 1955.

Bogdanov, Alexander Alexandrovich (1873–1928)

Born in Sokolko, in the Province of Grodno, the son of a village school teacher, Alexander Bogdanov (real name Malinovsky) was a co-founder with LENIN of the BOLSHE-

VIK fraction of the RSDRP in 1904. Following the 1905 REVOLUTION the paths of Bogdanov and Lenin diverged when Lenin argued that the RSDRP could play a role in the newly created State Duma similar to that played by the German SPD in the Reichstag. Bogdanov, following STOLYPIN's emasculation of the franchise in 1907 considered the Duma to be a pseudo-parliament and participation in it to be a dissipation of the energies of the labour movement. Although unable to obtain a majority for the boycott of the Third Duma, or for the recall of the SD deputies in it, Bogdanov succeeded in December 1908 in convincing an All-Russian Conference of the RSDRP to place the Social Democratic faction in the Duma under Party discipline (or 'ultimatum'). The Bolshevik fraction now split into two sub-fractions, each of which claimed to be the legitimate successor of the fraction of 1904. In 1908, in his *Materialism and Empiriocriticism*, Lenin sought to discredit Bogdanov as a Marxist and in June 1909 he contrived his exclusion from the editorial board of *Proletarii* (the steering committee of the Bolshevik Centre). Bogdanov and his supporters then founded the Forward group (Vpered), which, however, Bogdanov left in 1911. Thereafter he devoted himself to his writings in philosophy, sociology, and economics and to the idea of a 'Union of Socialist Culture' which he considered to be a necessary adjunct to the political and trade union wings of the labour movement. This project was realized in 1917 with the founding of the Russian Proletarian Cultural Educational Association (PROLETKULT).

Although no longer a member of the RSDRP by 1917 Bogdanov remained faithful during the Revolution to the party's longstanding policy that the autocracy should be succeeded by a democratic republic or 'people's state' based upon universal, equal, direct and secret suffrage. While prepared to support the idea of a socialist coalition government responsible to the SOVIETS pending the convening of a CONSTITUENT ASSEMBLY he condemned, in June 1917, Lenin's 'maximalist' demand for the transfer of 'All Power to the Soviets'. For Bogdanov, conflicts of interest between the two principal social classes represented in the Soviets, industrial proletariat and peasantry, were more likely to result in civil war than in a 'dictatorship of the proletariat'. The idea that the working classes of Europe, who had followed their own ruling classes into war, would overcome their domination and inaugurate a 'permanent revolution' he considered to be wishful thinking.

Bogdanov also took issue with the 'maximalist' argument that the WAR ECONOMY and resulting 'state capitalism' would facilitate a transition to socialism. In what appears to have been the first use of the term, Bogdanov described WAR COMMUNISM as an adaptation of economic activity to the consumption needs of the army. As the war progressed, 'military consumers' communism' spread throughout society by way of state control of supplies, prices and distribution. Simultaneously, military authoritarianism spread into civil society where it made for government dictatorship and the subjugation of the masses. As these effects multiplied the economy was transformed into a system of 'state capitalism', characterized by the formation of syndicates and trusts. While many of the features of state capitalism might disappear in peace-time it was more likely that the government's need to coordinate economic demobilization would make for a conservation of the new system. Bogdanov denied, however, that this system would facilitate the transition to socialism. Whereas the war economy had been an authoritarian system of state-bureaucratic regulation which had destroyed resources on a massive scale, socialism was the very opposite: a system of production based upon the principle of labour cooperation.

Socialist planning would treat societies as cultural and not merely as economic entities. The World War had highlighted the cultural backwardness of the working class: inadequately organized and captives of tradition, workers had succumbed to the primitive nationalism of the petty-bourgeoisie and the peasantry. However, the intelligentsia was no better equipped to effect a transition to socialism: most social scientists, as members of the ruling class, were imbued with the individualism of private enterprise. The cultural development of the socialist planners themselves was also a precondition of socialism. Finally, since socialist planning would be not only economic but socio-economic, it would require an appropriate level of development of both the technical and the social sciences. Above all, a 'universal organizational science' or science of planning would be needed which would combine and coordinate all the individual disciplines.

Why was it, Bogdanov asked, that in the face of these facts radical theorists nevertheless insisted upon an immediate transition to socialism? As early as May 1917 Bogdanov, commenting upon Lenin's return to Russia, had identified in him the embodiment of authoritarianism within the labour movement. Later that year he wrote of the tendency of new classes and especially of their leaders or 'ideologues' to borrow organizational forms from the old regime. It was this 'conservatism of thought' which explained the 'utopia of an immediate transition to socialism'. And yet any attempt prematurely to lead the working class into the realm of socialist reconstruction was doomed to failure. Prophetically, Bogdanov warned of

> . . . the emergence of a new Arakcheev [Alexander I's despotic war minister], only on a grander scale. Having acquired sufficient power he would appoint an official in every enterprise and subordinate the entire economy to the required number of departments. There would then ensue a rapid dissipation of the forces of production and, in due course, the collapse of the entire system.

The OCTOBER REVOLUTION Bogdanov interpreted not as a conspiracy but as a 'workers'-soldiers' revolt' rendered inevitable by Russia's continuing involvement in the war. The Bolsheviks he defined as the 'War Communist' party whose constituent elements, the 'proletarian-socialist' and 'soldier-communist', were bound to part company. Lenin's assertion that socialism could be built by a 'proletarian-peasant' alliance he dismissed as un-Marxist. Bogdanov looked forward to the formation at the end of the war of a new workers' political party which would be joined by 'those elements of the social democratic intelligentsia whose ideals have remained intact'. He was associated during 1917 with the United Social Democratic Internationalists and with the newspaper *Novaya Zhizn* (New Life) but during the Revolution and Civil War most of his work was with the Proletkult.

Bogdanov was a member of the Presidium of the Socialist (Communist) Academy from 1918 to 1926 and following his exclusion from the Proletkult in 1921 he continued lecturing on economics and organizational science. A graduate in medicine of Kharkov University (he had been enlisted as a doctor during the First World War) Bogdanov devoted the last years of his life to research into blood transfusion and the ageing process. In 1926 he helped found the Institute for Clinical and Experimental Haematology and Blood Transfusion and he served as its Director until April 1928 when he died in the course of an experiment in exchange transfusion.   JB

Further Reading

Bogdanov, A.A.: Autobiography. In *Makers of the Russian Revolution*, eds Georges Haupt and Jean-Jacques Marie. London: Allen & Unwin, 1974.

———— : Fortunes of the workers' party in the present revolution. *Sbornik (Newsletter of the Study Group on the Russisan Revolution)* 1984.

———— : What have we overthrown? *Scottish Slavonic Review* 2 (1984).

———— : *Red Star*. Bloomington: Indiana University Press, 1984.

Socher, Zenovia: *Revolution and Culture: The Lenin-Bogdanov Controversy*. Ithaca: Cornell University Press, 1988.

Bogrov, Dmitri (1887–1911)

A former anarchist, undercover agent of the Kiev OKHRANA section, Bogrov's claim to fame is as the assassin of the Russian prime minister, P. A. STOLYPIN, at the local opera on 1 September 1911. The nature of his contacts with the police and the motivation for his deed remain unresolved to this day: did he enter the service of the police for revolutionary purposes, or was he an ordinary undercover agent, whose sudden remorse led him to the act for which he was to pay with his life?

Bogrov was born in 1887 into a wealthy and distinguished Jewish family in Kiev. His father was a successful local attorney with wide social contacts, which gave Bogrov the opportunity to become acquainted with the heads of the Kiev political police and to travel widely in Russia and abroad. After completing his studies at the local high school in 1905 he entered the faculty of law of Kiev University, and by the end of the year enrolled also at the law faculty in Munich. Already during his high-school years he associated with revolutionary circles and in 1906, on his return from abroad, he joined the ANARCHISTS. His revolutionary activity lasted until 1909. Simultaneously, from February 1907 until March 1910 he was on the police payroll, and under the code name 'Alensky' regularly reported to Kulyabko, chief of the Kiev Okhrana section. He received a salary of 100 rubles per month. Rumours about his connections with the Okhrana began circulating in 1908. Although he was cleared by a court of honour, suspicions against him did not abate.

In February 1910, after graduating from Kiev University, he moved to St Petersburg, and on Kulyabko's recommendation, was hired by von Kotten, head of the St Petersburg Okhrana. From February to June he reported regularly for a salary of 150 rubles per month. In the summer of that year, after returning from a short journey abroad, Bogrov approached E. Lazarev, a SOCIALIST REVOLUTIONARY leader and editor of *Vestnik Znaniya* (Messenger of Knowledge) offering to carry out an attempt on Stolypin's life in the name of the SR party. His suggestion was turned down, whereupon he returned to Kiev, approached Kolyabko and was rehired by him. Using false information about a revolutionary plot against the tsar during the forthcoming visit to the city, he obtained a police pass into the strictly guarded opera house, where a gala performance was to be held in honour of the Imperial entourage. In the presence of the tsar he fired two shots at Stolypin, fatally wounding him. Bogrov was hanged on 11 September 1911.   NS

Further Reading

Lazarev, E.: Dmitrii Bogrov i ubiistvo Stolypina. *Volya Rossii* 5 no. VI–VII (1926) 53–98; no. VIII–IX 28–65.

Mushin, A.: *Dmitrii Bogrov i ubiistvo Stolypina*. Paris: 1914.

Bogucharsky, Vasili Yakovlevich (1861–1915)

Principal pseudonym of Vasili Yakovlevich Yakovlev, historian and publicist. Born in Boguchar, in Voronezh Province, Bogucharsky became involved in the revolutionary movement as a student when he participated in POPULIST circles of the late 1870s. His contacts with the People's Will, while serving as an officer in a COSSACK regiment, led to his arrest and exile to Siberia in 1884.

Upon his return to Voronezh in 1890, Bogucharsky helped lay the organizational groundwork for the People's Right Party. Toward the end of the decade, he moved to St Petersburg where he aligned himself with the Marxists around the journal *Novoe slovo* (New Word) and its

successor *Nachalo* (The Beginning). Serving as a member of the latter's editorial staff, he also contributed to other radical journals. In the final years of the decade, he began publishing the historical studies that were to make his reputation as a major historian of the Russian revolutionary movement.

An undogmatic and non-party Marxist, Bogucharsky was instrumental in establishing the journal *Osvobozhdenie* (Liberation) in 1902 and was a founding member of the Union of Liberation. He served on the Union's Council, worked actively to promote the organization's political ideas among the working class, and helped to create the Union of Unions.

He was elected to the Central Committee of the Constitutional Democratic Party at its founding congress in 1905, but he left the Party almost immediately. In early 1906 he joined several other radicals with the intention of resurrecting the Union of Liberation. Together they established the newspaper *Bez zaglaviya* (Without A Title).

Much of Bogucharsky's time following the 1905 REVOLUTION was devoted to his scholarship. During 1906–7, he was one of the editors of the historical journal *Byloe* (The Past) and contributed to its several successors. In 1909, he went abroad where he continued his scholarship and produced two of his most important studies on Russian Populism. He returned to Russia in 1913 and was a prominent figure in POLITICAL FREEMASONRY until his death in 1915.   BTN

Bonch-Bruevich, Vladimir Dmitrievich (1873–1955)

Born in Moscow on 11 July 1873, his father a land surveyor, Bonch-Bruevich was expelled from the Land Survey Institute in Moscow in 1889 and exiled from the city for revolutionary activities. He returned to Moscow in 1893 and became involved in Marxist circles and met LENIN. He edited several books for workers, became a member of the Workers' Union in Moscow, was group organizer and wrote and distributed illegal literature. In 1896 he became a student in the natural sciences faculty of the University of Zurich and soon became active in the LIBERATION OF LABOUR GROUP. In 1899 he accompanied the religious sect of the Dukhobors to Canada and this afforded him the opportunity to study their beliefs and way of life at close quarters. He joined the BOLSHEVIKS after the 1903 congress and was active in literature work and co-founded *Vpered*. During the 1905 REVOLUTION he co-founded many newspapers and in 1907 became director of the legal Bolshevik Party press, *Zhizn i Znanie* (Life and Knowledge). He worked on *Pravda* from its inception in 1912, was arrested several times, and after the FEBRUARY REVOLUTION became a member of the editorial board of the Petrograd SOVIET's *Izvestiya* and worked closely with Lenin. After the July Days Lenin hid in Bonch-Bruevich's dacha in Finland. During the OCTOBER REVOLUTION he was commandant of the Smolny district, was a member of the Petrograd Military-Revolutionary Committee; a member of the committee for revolutionary defence of Petrograd; chairman of the Petrograd VECHEKA. When LENIN'S GOVERNMENT (Sovnarkom) was founded, Bonch-Bruevich became its executive secretary; he drafted the decree on the nationalization of the banks. He organized the transfer of Sovnarkom and the party from Petrograd to Moscow in February 1918. He was entrusted with many special assignments by Lenin, becoming in 1918 a member of the Supreme Military Council. He nevertheless continued his academic work and did further research on Russian religious sectarianism, on which he was an expert; in 1913 he had conducted a day-long interview with RASPUTIN. He became a director of various publishing houses and of the Socialist Academy of Social Sciences. He founded the Lesnye Polyany state farm in 1920 and remained its director until 1929, adapting the name from Tolstoy's home, thus reflecting his great interest and love of Tolstoy's work. Between 1925 and 1939 he worked as editor of Tolstoy's collected works. His wife, Vera Mikhailovna, was also a revolutionary and played a key role in organizing Soviet health care. His brother, Mikhail, was a tsarist military commander, and though he never joined the Communist Party, became the first prominent officer to go over to the Reds. MMcC

Breshko-Breshkovskaya, Ekaterina Konstantinovna (1844–1934)

Almost unique in having witnessed at first hand the evils of serfdom and the disappointment of the peasantry at the terms of their liberation in 1861, in participating in all subsequent phases of the liberation movement, and in taking an active role in 1917 and beyond, Breshkovskaya's political longevity earned her the sobriquet 'Babushka' – 'Grandmother' of the Russian Revolution.

The daughter of enlightened serf-owning parents, called Verigo, Breshkovskaya's strong religious convictions led her to reject serfdom and she threw herself into legal, educational and social work for the peasantry when this became possible in the liberal 1860s. When this work was suppressed as subversive in 1871, she abandoned her family (including the husband she had married to escape the tutelage of her parents), to join her widowed sister, Olga, and friend, Maria Kolenika, in Kiev. The three women founded a socialist commune equipped with craft workshops which became a magnet for the libertarian youth of Kiev. Breshkovskaya met P. B. AXELROD and A. I. ZHELYABOV and listened to debates between the followers of P. L. LAVROV and M. A. BAKUNIN. Though she believed in the necessity of terror, she took part in the mass 'To the People' movement in 1874. After three months' agitational work, she was arrested and, at the 'trial of the

193' in January 1878 she became the first woman to be sentenced to hard labour in Siberia. She was visited by the American journalist, George Kennan, in 1885, and his account of her sufferings made her internationally famous. In 1896, she was allowed to return to Russia, where she spent seven years agitating illegally and playing a key role in the revival of the POPULIST organizations that in 1901 coalesced into the PSR (see SOCIALIST REVOLUTIONARIES). In 1904, she toured the USA to raise political and financial support for the party, returning to Russia in 1905, only to be arrested in Simbirsk two years later. This time she was sentenced to perpetual exile in Siberia, where in 1912, she was visited by A. F. KERENSKY, whom she adopted as her political heir. On her triumphal return to Petrograd in 1917, she demonstrated her support for Kerensky by resigning from the CC of the PSR in protest at his non-election to the CC, and by taking up residence with him in the Winter Palace. In 1918, she actively supported the 'democratic counter-revolution' against the BOLSHEVIKS. In exile in Czechoslovakia, she founded Russian-language schools in Ruthenia, before retiring to the farm at Khvaly, Prague, where she died at the age of 90 in 1934. RA

Further Reading

Breshko-Breshkovskaya, E.K.: *Hidden Springs of the Russian Revolution. Personal Memoirs of Katerina Breshkovskaya.* Stanford: Stanford University Press, 1931.

Bukeykhanov, Ali-Khan (1869–1932)

A descendant of the Khans of the Inner (Bukey) Horde, Bukeykhanov was born in Samara. One of the handful of Kazakhs to acquire higher education in the nineteenth century, he graduated from the Omsk Forestry Institute in 1894 but he left his mark less as an engineer, than as historian, folklorist, journalist and leading jadid nationalist who shaped Kazakh politics at the beginning of the twentieth century.

Bukeykhanov's political nationalism was catalysed by his association with Sh. Kanaev's anti-Russian literary group, Zar Zaman (Hard Times) and found an early expression in the articles he published under the pen name Kir Balasi in the official Kazakh-language paper *Dala vilayatining gazeti* (Steppe Region Gazette). His journalistic activity also included contributions to Russian SR and SD newspapers published in Omsk, to the Tatar newspaper *Fiker* (Thought) of Uralsk, and the Kazakh papers *Ay-Kap* (Flight) of Troitsk, *Kazakhstan* of Uralsk, and *Kazakh* of Orenburg. Bukeykhanov's national political career was launched with his election to the First and Second Duma, where he represented Semipalatinsk.

In March 1917, together with BAYTURSUNOV, DULATOV and Dostmuhammedov he organized the Kazakh national party, ALASH ORDA. When in April 1917 a Turkestan Committee of the PROVISIONAL GOVERNMENT was set up, presided over by N. Shchepkin, a former Kadet delegate, Bukeykhanov was one of the four Muslims elected to that Committee although he was not a Central Asian. In July 1917 he represented the Provisional Government in the Turgay region.

In the aftermath of the OCTOBER REVOLUTION Bukeykhanov spearheaded the Kazakh demand for immediate autonomy. When the third Kazakh congress met in Orenburg from 5 to 13 December, 1917, and proclaimed Kazakh autonomy, Bukeykhanov was elected president of the new government. He eventually became the head of the Eastern Alash Orda (in Semipalatinsk) when due to the imperatives of Civil War, the Kazakh lands were divided into two administrative zones.

Bukeykhanov and Alash Orda's failure to forge an alliance with the anti-Bolshevik forces, led to acceptance of the new regime in 1919. Despite the fact that Bukeykhanov joined the Bolshevik party in 1920, he remained committed to his nationalist goals and played no active role in the life of Soviet Kazakhstan. This in itself seems to have been sufficient to justify his arrest and most likely his demise in 1932.

A-AR

Bukharin, Nikolai Ivanovich (1888–1938)

Born in Moscow where he spent nearly all his life and where eventually he also made his political career, Bukharin was perhaps the most urban and Russian of the BOLSHEVIK leaders and one of the few not to assume a pseudonym (see Editorial Note). He was the youngest prominent Bolshevik in 1917 and, following Lenin's death in 1924, together with TROTSKY and STALIN, a potential successor to Bolshevik and Soviet leadership who, nevertheless, fell victim to the Stalin purges leaving behind merely the memory of a possible alternative to Stalinism. A man of considerable personal appeal and political intelligence, he was also a serious and independent Marxist theoretician whose writings retain their interest today.

Bukharin's father was a university graduate and both parents were schoolteachers who fostered in him a love for literature, art, and natural history. He was drawn by the events of 1905 into student revolutionary activities and in the following year joined the Bolsheviks whose militancy attracted him and who enjoyed greater strength in Moscow than the MENSHEVIKS. In the years that followed he plunged fully into the party's activities and rose quickly in its ranks in Moscow. After being arrested he was exiled but escaped and left Russia in 1911. During the next six years he devoted himself to study and writing and published some of his major theoretical work, including an influential interpretation of imperialism. While abroad he also came into contact with LENIN: their relations were on the whole amicable but they differed on various matters, particularly on the national question on which Bukharin took a stand

similar to that of ROSA LUXEMBURG's repudiation of national self-determination.

When the FEBRUARY REVOLUTION broke out Bukharin was in New York. Like Trotsky, whom he came to know well there though they disagreed as often as not, he made his way back to Russia by May. In the turbulent events that followed his standing in the Moscow branch of the party and his advocacy of a militant left-Bolshevik position cemented his collaboration with Lenin and catapulted him into the front ranks of the Bolshevik hierarchy. But in 1918 he found himself in opposition for the first time, and at odds with Lenin, by becoming the main spokesman for the Left Communists and their advocacy of both internal economic and external revolutionary radicalism. The group did not last long for Bukharin and others, roundly denounced by Lenin and a generally hostile party, recanted before the year was out. At this stage, the 'oppositionist' label did Bukharin no harm. He remained a leading member of the Central Committee and a major strategist of economic and social policy. In 1924 he was made a member of the Politburo and in 1925 the chairman of the Comintern. This was the heyday of his power, made possible by a coalition of convenience with Stalin.

By now, however, the struggle for the succession to Lenin was the dominant political reality, though it revolved around the primary issue of the economic future of the Soviet Union. Bukharin, the once left-wing Bolshevik and Left Communist, now emerged as the leading spokesman for the right wing of the party, advocating moderation, gradualism and, in the view of some latter-day interpreters, a liberal political alternative to the radical collectivism which characterized Trotsky's views and which, in a more extreme and uncompromising fashion, was to be eventually embraced by Stalin (who for the time being was in the same right-wing ideological camp). Bukharin's position was now that socialism in the Soviet Union could evolve only over a long period of gestation and by giving precedence initially to agriculture, to market forces and to material and capital accumulation. These views were so unlike his earlier ones that they can only be attributed to a new-found pragmatism and the impact of the stark exigencies that characterized the Soviet economy after the period of WAR COMMUNISM, and the realities coming to the fore with the advent of NEP. Given the dilemma of a backward, weak and war-ravaged society, Bukharin's advocacy of sobriety – for this is what his position amounted to – appears certainly in retrospect, and on the face of it, highly sensible. He became convinced that there was no short-cut to industrialization, that a necessary pre-condition for it was the fostering of agriculture through a free market for the peasants' produce, even if this would mean the state's paying relatively high prices and thereby becoming both dependent on the peasantry and unable to go ahead immediately with the development of other sectors. Whatever the detriments of this agricul-

Figure 49 Bukharin, 1920, at John Reed's funeral.

ture-first policy, Bukharin believed that the alternative was far more dangerous, namely further civil war and chaos. He thus urged an economic road that would avoid conflict with the peasantry and mobilize it instead for the long-term interests of the Revolution. The underlying assumption of this approach was that capital accumulation among the peasantry would create demand for industrial goods and that if this process indeed emerged the goal of gradual industrialization would be assured with one sector of the economy cultivating the other. However, as the left did not cease pointing out, this economic *smychka* (alliance) was wishful thinking: by the mid 1920s Soviet industry was in such shambles that it could not possibly meet whatever demands agriculture brought forth and thus the priority for the Soviet economy was the reconstruction of industry at the expense of the countryside. Whatever the validity of the left's criticism, Bukharin's views were also governed by considerations other than economic; he genuinely dreaded, it seems, the consequences of rapid industrialization – the regimentation of society, the total power of an omnipotent state, and the inevitable recourse to repression and terror.

We shall never know for certain whether Bukharin's position did amount to a viable alternative for the Soviet Union since it did not, in the event, prevail either politically or ideologically and Stalin, now making his final programmatic shift, opted for the left strategy. The internal party alliances and manoeuvrings that characterized the period 1924–29 were so complicated and unstable as to defy any brief summary, but Bukharin ultimately found himself in the defensive stance of an oppositionist once again, this time from the right but concurrently somehow associated with the 'official arch-enemy' Trotsky and hampered, like the latter, by political weaknesses and insufficient talents as a 'politician' to stave off Stalin's assaults and the inevitable consequences thereof. These followed in short order: in 1929 Bukharin was deprived of the chairmanship of the Comintern, expelled from the Politburo and forced to recant through a statement of complete capitulation. In subsequent years he was allowed to confine himself to writing on theoretical and cultural matters and was even given a position of some stature as the editor of *Izvestiya*. But all that he now wrote was in strict accordance with the Stalinist line. This was to no avail, however, for with the advent of the Great Purge he was arrested and put on trial in Moscow in March, 1938. More so than others faced with a similar fate he conducted himself with dignity at the trial. Executed on 15 March, he was officially rehabilitated in early 1988.   BK

313

Further Reading

Bukharin, N.I.: *Imperialism and World Economy*. New York: 1929.
—— and Preobrazhensky, E.: *The ABC of Communism*. Harmondsworth: 1969.
Cohen, Stephen F.: *Bukharin and the Bolshevik Revolution: A Political Biography, 1888–1938*. New York: 1973.
Daniels, R.V.: *The Conscience of the Revolution: Communist Opposition in Soviet Russia*. Cambridge, Mass.: 1960.
Katkov, George: *The Trial of Bukharin*. New York: 1969.

Bunakov-Fondaminsky, Ilya Isidorovich (1880–1942)

The son of a rich Jewish merchant from Moscow, Ilya Fondaminsky (Bunakov was his conspiratorial pseudonym) became one of the key figures in the party of SOCIALIST REVOLUTIONARIES. His studies in Heidelberg and Halle made him the intimate of the younger neo-Kantians in the PSR leadership (N. D. AVKSENTIEV, V. M. ZENZINOV, A. R. GOTS), while his marriage to Amalia Gavronskaya, an heiress of the Vysotsky Tea Company, made him one of the 'bankers' of the PSR. An emotional orator, he played a key role in the unsuccessful attempt to provoke an uprising in the Baltic Fleet in 1906. He supported the Pochin (Inititative) group in 1912 and the patriotic wing of the PSR in 1914–18. In emigration in Paris, Fondaminsky subsidized émigré publications and maintained a fascination for religious ideas that led him, with Zenzinov and others, to form the 'Secular Order of the Russian Intelligentsia'. Deported by the Gestapo to Auschwitz, Fondaminsky embraced Russian Orthodoxy before his death in 1942.   RA

Further Reading

Berberova, Nina: *The Italics are Mine*. London: Longmans, 1969.
Pachmuss, Temira ed.: *Intellect and Ideas in Action. Selected Correspondence of Zinaida Gippius*. Munich: Wilhelm Fink Verlag, 1972.

Burtsev, Vladimir Lvovich (1862–1942)

An independent revolutionary, journalist and writer, editor of the historical journal *Byloe* (The Past), Burtsev became known as a hunter of police agents. His most famous in a long series of exposures between 1908 and 1914 was that of E. AZEF, head of the SR Battle Organization. Dubbed 'the Sherlock Holmes of the Russian Revolution' by the foreign press of his day, and more recently as a 'one-man espionage agency', the expertise and knowledge that he acquired during the many years of his stubborn struggle against the Russian political police earned him the respect of all the revolutionary parties. Nevertheless to the last day of his life he remained controversial in their eyes.

Burtsev was born in 1862, in the province of Ufa, where he spent his childhood and early youth. After attending high-school first in Ufa and then in Kazan, he enrolled at the University of St Petersburg, and soon after became involved in the capital's student movement. At the end of his first year at university, he was arrested for participating in a student demonstration, but was soon realeased only to engage in revolutionary activity, though not as a member of any organization. At the beginning of 1885 he was again arrested, and after spending almost three years in prison, was banished to Siberia, from where he escaped to Switzerland in 1888.

Burtsev's activities against police infiltration of the revolutionary movement were part of his enduring efforts to bring about the participation of all oppositional forces in the country in a 'constitutional struggle in the name of all-national objectives', i.e. the attaining of full civil liberties in Russia. To this end in the late 1880s he advocated the use of People's Will terrorist tactics and sought the cooperation of revolutionaries and liberals in the publication of a journal which would wage war against the tsarist autocracy. In 1889 he set up *Svobodnaya Rossiya* (Free Russia) together with M. P. Dragomanov (DRAHOMANOV) and Debagory-Mokrievich, but the partnership soon collapsed due to the constant tension between the liberal and the terrorist components. In 1897 he began to publish in London *Narodovolets* (Member of People's Will), but shortly afterwards was arrested and convicted of instigating regicide, and sentenced to eighteen months imprisonment. Having failed in all his endeavours to reestablish a periodical along the lines of *Svobodnaya Rossiya*, he finally started in 1909 his own *Obshchee Delo* (Common Cause), which soon folded, and in 1911 *Budushchee* (The Future). The latter became not only a platform for his ideas, but also (combined with anti-provocation investigations) an instrument to further his political aims. He pressed for an all-oppositional struggle in the Duma, while in his inquiries against the OKHRANA he sought to create political storms that would force the reluctant revolutionary parties to join in. He set up his own machinery of information and detection to expose police agents in the ranks of the revolutionaries. He used his own private resources in his work and ran publicity campaigns to drum up additional funds. Meticulously he gathered information about persons who had aroused his suspicion. He employed detectives to trail his subjects and exerted heavy pressure on the parties to conduct their own inquiries to prove the suspect's guilt. He thus became a standing threat to the Foreign Agency, the terror of all undercover agents abroad. To many his methods appeared unethical and were condemned.

With the outbreak of the FIRST WORLD WAR he returned to Russia where he resumed the publication of *Byloe*. After the OCTOBER REVOLUTION he again left Russia, settled in Paris and conducted his anti-Bolshevik struggle through his new *Obshchee Delo* and the 'National Committee' of which he was one of the founders.   NS

Further Reading

Burtsev, V.L.: *Bor'ba za svobodnuyu Rossiyu, Moi vospominaniya 1882–1924 gg*. Berlin: 1924.

Chemerisky, Alexander I. (dates unknown)

Having begun his revolutionary career in the Jewish BUND, Chemerisky was a member of the Minsk Bund Committee when he fell into ZUBATOV's net in 1900. The most famous victim of Zubatov's eloquence and charm, he was supplied books from the OKHRANA collection, was treated to an expense-account lunch at a restaurant by Zubatov, and sat for as long as six hours at a time disputing politics and theory with his captor, in the manner typical of the intelligentsia. Zubatov did not require him to betray his comrades and his conversion to the idea of a reforming Autocracy and economistic labour movement was sincere and wholehearted. He then applied himself with his usual vigour to the ZUBATOV MOVEMENT in Minsk, became a founding member of the Independent Jewish Labour Party, and was permitted to publish a Yiddish chronicle, *Arbaytsmark* (The Labour Market) to give regular news of strikes and the labour movement generally. In 1902 he was selected to carry the movement to Vilna, which he did against heavy odds. There the Bund was particularly well-entrenched, and workers' feelings against the governor, Viktor von Wahl, were venomous after the hanging of Girsh Lekert for an assassination attempt. His only real success was among the shoemakers there; and, in February 1903, after nine months of frustrating effort, the movement was formally withdrawn. He was then sent to Odessa, where he worked with G. I. SHAEVICH, this time with greater success. With all the energy and resilience of a youth in his twenties, he worked hard, often went hungry, slept at party headquarters without a blanket, and was at the labour exchange taverns every morning by 4 or 5 a.m. to contact workers. Finances were slender and there were no regular payments from government. After the dissolution of the party in July 1903 he returned, sadder and wiser, to the Bund where he was welcomed by his comrades who freely forgave him his 'confusion'. After the OCTOBER REVOLUTION he was a member of the Russian Communist Party, became secretary of the Central Bureau of the Jewish Section (Yevsektsiya) of the Party, and was active in peasant affairs. Expelled from the Party in 1933, Chemerisky was arrested and sentenced to three years in a prison camp. He was never heard of again.   MKP

Chernov, Viktor Mikhailovich (1873–1952)

Theoretician and co-founder of the Party of SOCIALIST REVOLUTIONARIES (PSR), Chernov's leadership helped to make it briefly the most popular party in Russia, and contributed to its tragic demise. The grandson of a serf,

Viktor Chernov was born in Novouzensk, Samara Province, and grew up on the banks of the Volga in Kamyshin and Saratov where he attended the gymnasium. The young Chernov's friendship with exiled Populists, including V. A. Balmashev and M. A. NATANSON, resulted in his expulsion from Saratov gymnasium. He enrolled in the law faculty of Moscow University, where he rapidly became leader of the illegal students' union, meeting leading oppositional figures, such as N. K. MIKHAILOVSKY, P. L. LAVROV, and the German Revisionists. By asserting that relations of distribution were more ZUBATOV and imprisoned in the Peter-Paul Fortress in St Petersburg. Exiled to Tambov, he and his future brother-in-law, S. V. Sletov, fostered the first independent socialist peasant brotherhoods. In 1899 he departed for Switzerland where he studied neo-Kantian philosophy at Bern University. After crossing swords with G. V. PLEKHANOV, Chernov joined Kh. O. Zhitlovsky's Union of Socialist Revolutionaries, while his contributions to the legal POPULIST journal *Russkoe Bogatstvo* (Russian Wealth) earned him widespread admiration at home. In 1901 G. A. GERSHUNI visited him to inform him of the formation of an underground Party of Socialist Revolutionaries (PSR) in Russia and inviting him to edit its journal *Revolyutsionnaya Rossiya* (Revolutionary Russia). It was in its columns that Chernov developed the programme and justified the tactics of the PSR.

In refurbishing the ideology of Russian Populism, Chernov had to take account of recent capitalist developments in the Russian economy, to contest the prevailing MARXIST view of the peasantry as a totally reactionary social class, and to align the PSR with the Second Socialist International. Chernov drew on the works of Marx, Engels and Bebel, but the voluntarist and subjectivist aspects of his philosophy were closer to those of N. K. MIKHAILOVSKY, P. L. LAVROV, and the German Revisionists. By asserting that relations of distribution were more important than relations of production, Chernov rationalized the traditional Populist view that the interests of industrial worker and peasant were almost identical. From this it followed that the essential struggle in Russia was between Autocracy and 'People' (guided by the intelligentsia), and not, as the Marxists argued, between social classes. However, the PSR Minimum Programme which included the demand for the 'socialization' of all land, was in line with equivalent sections of the German Social Democrats' programme and the PSR was welcomed into the Socialist International in 1904.

Chernov returned to Russia in 1905 but made little impression on events in St Petersburg, though his leadership of the SRs was triumphantly confirmed at the First PSR Congress in Imatra in 1906. Abroad once more after 1907 he failed to provide any sense of direction to a party faced with new dilemmas. During the FIRST WORLD WAR he adopted 'Centrist' internationalist views,

Figure 50 Chernov.

participating in the Zimmerwald (1915) and Kienthal (1916) conferences. On his return to Petrograd in 1917 he became Minister of Agriculture in the PROVISIONAL GOVERNMENT (May to September). He was unsuccessful politically and as an administrator, and in September he resigned and denounced his ex-colleagues. As leader of the largest Russian party, Chernov was elected Chairman of the CONSTITUENT ASSEMBLY in January 1918, but he played little part in SR preparations for the 'democratic counter-revolution' that summer. He actively supported the 1921 KRONSTADT REVOLT, before retiring to Czechoslovakia and then the USA where he developed his theories of 'constructive socialism' and analysed the reasons for the failure of his party in 1917. He died in New York in 1952.

RA

Further Reading

Chernov, V.M.: *Pered burei. Vospominaniya.* New York: Chekhov, 1953.

Radkey, Oliver, H.: *The Agrarian Foes of Bolshevism, Promise and Default of the Russian Socialist Revolutionaries. February to October 1917.* New York: Columbia University Press, 1958.

Tchernoff, Olga: *New Horizons: Reminiscences of the Russian Revolution.* London: Hutchinson, 1936.

Chernyshevsky, Nikolai G. (1828–1889)

The son of a priest, Chernyshevsky was educated at the University of St Petersburg where he earned a master's degree, and after briefly teaching in his native Saratov turned mainly to journalism. In 1855 he joined the staff of N. A. Nekrasov's *Sovremennik* (The Contemporary), first as a literary critic – his reviews often skilfully masked radical political statements – and from 1857, when this function passed to his colleague N. A. Dobrolyubov, as a political economist. He was scornful of liberalism both as an economic and a political theory, regarding it as serving only the interests of the well-to-do, and subtly pleaded for dynamic measures to further the interests of the peasant masses, and in particular to develop the traditional redistributive PEASANT COMMUNE (*obshchina*) as a genuinely popular institution; for, like A. I. HERZEN, but more prosaically, he hoped this might pave the way to an egalitarian socialist order.

Chernyshevsky's learning and his abrasive manner impressed many young radicals, not only students but also army officers (in 1858 he briefly edited a reformist military periodical), and he encouraged the formation of clandestine organizations. The authorities intercepted a letter from the émigré Herzen, which provided a pretext for his arrest (July 1862). While in preliminary detention Chernyshevsky smuggled out of prison a novel, *What's to be Done?* which, though deficient in literary quality, presented an attractive picture of the 'new people' ('men of the sixties') as stalwart, rationally thinking supermen (or -women), devoted to the common good. Published in *Sovremennik*, it had an immense impact at the time and later: V. I. LENIN would borrow the title for a seminal early work. In 1864 Chernyshevsky was sentenced, in part on forged evidence, to seven years' forced labour and lifelong exile in northern Siberia – a harsh fate, courageously borne, which undermined his health; but not until 1883 was he allowed to return to European Russia. Then and later he was something of a bogeyman to the right (and centre!), a reputation not entirely deserved, for although a determined foe of tsarism and privilege, he was not wild extremist à la BAKUNIN.

Chernyshevsky's utilitarian aesthetics were taken further by G. V. PLEKHANOV and, in over-simplified form, by Soviet critics. In philosophy he developed L. Feuerbach's materialism and believed that, by pursuing their own egoistic interests, rational men were naturally led to altruistic, cooperative social conduct. He was also a historical determinist, but (like Marx) interpreted the laws of societal development flexibly enough to allow Russia, as a latecomer to the modern world, a chance to skip foreordained socio-economic phases. This became an article of faith for many POPULISTS. Soviet historians classify Chernyshevsky as a 'revolutionary democrat' rather than as a Populist; but for him political democracy and human rights were much less important than 'social justice'. In this respect he left an ambiguous legacy.   JLHK

Further Reading

Keep, J.L.H.: Chernyshevsky and the military miscellany. In *Felder und Vorfelder russischer Geschichte: Studien zu Ehren von Peter Scheibert*, pp. 11–33, eds I. Auerbach et al. Freiburg: 1985.

Pereira, N.G.O.: *The Thought and Teachings of N.G. Černyševskij.* Paris and The Hague: 1975.

Scanlan, J.P.: N. Chernyshevsky and philosophical materialism in Russia. In *Journal of the History of Philosophy* 8 (1970) 65–86.

Valentinov, N.V: Chernyshevsky i Lenin. *Novyy zhurnal* 26 (1951) 193–216; 27 (1951) 225–49: New York.

Woehrlin, W.F.: *Chernyshevsky: the Man and the Journalist.* Cambridge, Mass: 1971.

Chicherin, Georgi Vasilievich (1872–1936)

Best described by TROTSKY as a 'learned old Russian nobleman who brought his many-sided education to the service of the revolutionary organization', Chicherin could indeed trace his ancestors to Athanasi Cicerini, who had come to Moscow from Italy in the suite of the Byzantine Princess Zoe Paleologue in 1472. Allied to the Naryshkin family, he was the grandson of the prominent diplomat Count Stakelberg, the nephew of a well-known law historian and the son of a professional diplomat. Though he had received an excellent education (he loved history and music, spoke French, German, Italian, Polish and Serbian in addition to his native Russian), his family's impoverishment and his own complex psychology alienated him from St Petersburg high society.

After working in the archives section of the Ministry of Foreign Affairs (1895–1904), he left Russia to travel abroad and became active in the socialist parties of France, Belgium and Germany. As secretary of the Central Foreign Bureau of the RSDRP (1907–1914), he supported the MENSHEVIKS. The war brought him closer to LENIN through pacifist ideas which he defended first in France and then in England where he was arrested in August 1917.

In January 1918, freed from his British gaol, Chicherin became Deputy Commissar for Foreign Affairs under Trotsky. After Trotsky's clever but dangerous course during the peace negotiations with Imperial Germany (Brest-Litovsk, November 1917–February 1918), Lenin felt he needed a faithful and able executant in the post, an expert in the formulation of official positions. In a letter to A. A. IOFFE, Lenin characterized Chicherin as 'an excellent worker, extremely conscientious, intelligent and learned'; he added significantly: 'That his weakness consists in his lack of leadership is no great defect. There are so many people endowed with the opposite weakness in this world!'

Thus Chicherin was all but a 'political' leader in the Soviet apparatus. He was selected precisely for that reason

and was only elected to the Central Committee in 1925 and 1927 (Fourteenth and Fifteenth Congresses of the CPSU). Yet, under Lenin's initial guidance, his role was decisive in the organization of the Commissariat for Foreign Affairs (Narkomindel), which he headed from May 1918 until his retirement in July 1930), and in the implementation of Soviet Foreign policy.

A strong advocate of Soviet interests at the Genoa Conference, Chicherin always favoured rapprochement with Germany which he helped to initiate with the Rapallo Treaty (April 1922). This alliance meant for him a counterweight to France, but also to England in which he saw the main danger for the Soviet state in Europe and in Asia. At the Lausanne conference (1923), he proved to be 'more Turkish than the Turks' when he proposed no less than the closure of the Straits.

After the end of the CIVIL WAR, Chicherin contributed to the formulation of Soviet foreign policy in that he emphatically repudiated any connection between diplomatic, military and Comintern activities (as happened in Poland in 1920 and Germany in 1921 and 1923).

After Lenin's death in January 1924, his role declined steadily. The Locarno Treaty (1925) and the setback it implied for the Soviet Union in its relations with Germany, and the growing influence of M. M. LITVINOV led him to relinquish almost all public activities after 1927.

Bad health increased his isolation which he compensated by playing the piano music of his beloved Mozart to whom he devoted a study of high quality. This was finally published in Moscow in 1973 at a time when his pioneering role in Soviet diplomacy was again acknowledged.   FC

Chokaev, Mustafa (1890–1941)

Born in a prestigious Kazakh aristocratic family which had ties to the rulers of the Khivan Khanate, Chokaev belonged to the select group of jadids who acquired degrees in Russian or western European universities. A graduate of the Law Faculty of St Petersburg University, Chokaev held the position of the Secretary of the Turkestani Section of the Muslim Faction of the Duma until February 1917.

In February 1917, Chokaev left Petrograd for Central Asia where he emerged as the Chairman of the National Centre (Milli Merkez), a body organized in March as a counterpoise to the Soviet of Tashkent which was dominated by BOLSHEVIKS and SOCIALIST REVOLUTIONARIES and ignored the needs of the Muslims. Between April and November, 1917, Chokaev was an active member of the editorial boards of *Ulug Turkistan* (Great Turkestan) and *Berlik Tuny* (The Banner of Unity), Muslim newspapers of pan-Islamic and pan-Turkic orientation.

In response to the emergence in Tashkent, on 16 November 1917, of the Turkestan Council of People's Commissars (Sovnarkom) which did not include a single Muslim member, a week later the Muslim organizations of

Turkestan convened in Kokand and formed a government called People's Council. Chokaev was the second president of that government which, on 5 February 1917, was ousted by the RED ARMY after fierce fighting that reduced the city to ruins in three days. Having escaped the massacre Chokaev joined the BASMACHIS moving to Georgia in 1919. When the Red Army occupied Georgia in 1920 he went into exile, living in Turkey, France and Germany.

A leading figure in the political awakening of the Muslims of Central Asia, Chokaev became the uncontested leader of the Russian Muslim emigration; his articles and monographs are valuable sources for the study of the revolution in Central Asia.   A-AR

Further Reading

Chokaev, M.: *Chez les Soviets en Asie Centrale*. Paris: 1928.

Dan, Fedor Ivanovich (1871–1947)

Born in St Petersburg, Dan (real name Gurvich) began his revolutionary and social democratic career in October 1895 in the Petersburg UNION OF STRUGGLE FOR THE EMANCIPATION OF THE WORKING CLASS in which he was very active until August 1896, when he was arrested and exiled to Orlov for three years together with A. N. Potresov. From March 1901, he led the Berlin *Iskra* group and was active (as a member of the Organization Committee) in preparing the Second Congress of the RSDRP. After the split in the party, Dan was active in its MENSHEVIK wing, in the Menshevik-dominated League of Social Democrats Abroad and on the editorial board of the (now Menshevik) *Iskra*, and, after his return to St Petersburg in October 1905, of *Nachalo* (Beginning), where for some time he shared TROTSKY's views on the Russian revolution.

Dan was a Menshevik delegate to the Stockholm (1906) and London (1907) congresses of the RSDRP. In 1908 he became co-editor with Yu. O. MARTOV of the *Golos sotsial demokrata* (Voice of the Social Democrat) in Paris and the major organizer, or 'chief of general staff', of the Menshevik wing of the party. He returned to St Petersburg again in January 1913 and became the chief editor of the Menshevik paper *Luch* (Ray) (and its successors) and adviser to the Menshevik fraction of the Duma.

Following his arrest at the outbreak of the war, Dan was exiled to Minusinsk and then drafted at the end of 1915 as a military surgeon in Irkutsk. There he joined the 'Siberian Zimmerwaldists', I. G. TSERETELI and V. Voitinsky, writing for their *Sibirskii zhurnal* (Siberian Journal) and its successor, *Sibirskoe obozrenie* (Siberian Review).

Dan returned to Petrograd on 19 March 1917. He remained a close associate of Tsereteli and a leading spokesman for the policies of 'revolutionary defensism' and of 'coalitionism' of the Menshevik-SR bloc. He served as deputy chairman of the Central Executive Committee of the Soviets (TsIK) and as the chief editor of its *Izvestiya*.

Together with the very articulate and aggressive M. I. LIBER, Dan became the main butt of the Bolshevik attack on 'Liberdanism'.

After the OCTOBER REVOLUTION, Dan supported Martov – he was married to Martov's sister, Lydia – and the Menshevik-Internationalist majority at the Extraordinary Congress of the Mensheviks at the end of November. Thereafter he distinguished himself as the major speaker, after Martov, of the semi-legal and hounded Menshevik opposition.

Dan was arrested in 1921 and exiled abroad in January 1922. He joined Martov and R. A. ABRAMOVICH on the *Sotsialisticheskii vestnik* (Socialist Messenger). After Martov's death Dan, Abramovich and A. Yugov became the leaders of the Mensheviks in exile and of a left-wing majority faction which, encouraged by the NEP, hoped during the 1920s for a democratic transformation of the BOLSHEVIK regime.

Dan was close to Otto Bauer and, with him, moved towards the left in the 1930s. Together with Yugov, Olga Domanevskaya and A. Shifrin, Dan accepted STALIN's Five-Year plans and collectivization, welcomed the Constitution of 1936 and recognized the Soviet Union as the main bulwark against the spread of fascism.

By 1939 Dan found himself in a minority on *Sotsialisticheskii vestnik* and published, first, *Novyi mir* (New World) in Paris and, following his escape in March 1940 to New York, *Novyi Put* (New Way). By 1943 his break with majority Menshevism was complete. So was his reconciliation with (if not capitulation to) Bolshevism. His *Origins of Bolshevism* – which he termed his swan song – recognized in Bolshevism the legitimate heir of Russian social democracy, chosen 'by history' to be 'the carrier of socialism, the key idea of our epoch' and of its 'practical realization'. But, he wrote, he still hoped for the Soviet Union's 'humanization' and 'democratization'; a sad 'swan song' for Menshevism's former chief of general staff.   IG

Further Reading

Dan, F.I.: *Dva goda skitanii (1919–1921)*. Berlin: 1922.
———— : *The Origins of Bolshevism*. New York: 1964.
Liebich, André: I menscevichi di fronte alla costruzione dell'Urss. In *Storia del Marxismo*, vol. III/2, Turin: 1981.
Sapir, Boris ed.: *Theodore Dan, Letters (1899–1946)*. Amsterdam: 1985. [An outline of Dan's political biography is included.]

Deich, Lev Grigorievich (1855–1941)

The son of a Jewish merchant, Deich was first a POPULIST and later a MARXIST revolutionary. He took part in the movement 'To the People', making propaganda among religious sectarians in southern Russia. In 1875 he was arrested but escaped from custody and in June 1876 helped to perpetrate one of the first terrorist acts, an unsuccessful attempt on the life of a suspected AGENT PROVOCATEUR, N. E. Gorinovich, who was stabbed and had his face disfigured with sulphuric acid. The next year, as one of the 'southern rebels' (Kiev), Deich took part in Ya. V. Stefanovich's scheme to provoke a peasant insurrection by distributing a forged Imperial manifesto. In May 1878 he again fled from prison, but when Land and Liberty came under the control of its terrorist faction (1879) Deich sided with the opposing minority led by G. V. PLEKHANOV – perhaps because his associate V. I. ZASULICH was Deich's common-law wife. Deich emigrated with others in the BLACK REPARTITION group to Switzerland where in 1883, following conversion to Marxism, they took the title LIBERATION OF LABOUR GROUP. As chief technical organizer of the group, Deich went to Germany in 1884 to arrange for its publications to be smuggled into Russia, but he was arrested and extradited for trial by a Russian court for his attempted murder of Gorinovich. He was sentenced to 13 years' forced labour in eastern Siberia.

After completing his sentence Deich was transferred to 'settler' status and in 1901 escaped a third time. After travelling halfway round the world he reached Western Europe, where he aided V. I. LENIN and the other editors of the Social Democratic newspaper *Iskra* and worked to ensure that the RSDRP's Second Congress (1903) reflected the organizational principles later associated with BOLSHEVISM. But when the infant party split, Deich (like Zasulich, from whom he had now parted) joined the MENSHEVIKS. In 1905 he returned to Russia, was arrested, and again sentenced to exile – but yet a fourth time he managed to escape, while *en route* to Siberia. He settled in London where he participated in the Fifth Party Congress (1907), and then in New York (1911–16). He continued to support the Mensheviks and during the FIRST WORLD WAR adopted a 'defensist' position.

After the FEBRUARY REVOLUTION Deich returned to Petrograd and assisted Plekhanov in editing his paper *Edinstvo* (Unity), which called for continuation of the war until victory. Under Bolshevik rule he earned his living by scholarly and literary work. He co-edited a volume of documents on the Liberation of Labour group (6 vols, 1923–8) and also published interesting memoirs.   JLHK

Further Reading

Deich, L.G.: *Za polveka*, 3rd edn. Moscow: 1924. (Earlier edn. trans. as *Sixteen Years in Siberia*. London: 1905.)

Dickson, R.A.: L.G. Deich. In *Modern Encyclopedia of Russian and Soviet History*, pp. 30–33, vol. 9, ed. J. L. Wieczynski. Gulf Breeze, Fla.: 1978.

Denikin, General Anton Ivanovich (1872–1947)

The most important of the White commanders, Denikin led the main forces in southern Russia, the VOLUNTEER ARMY from April 1918, and the ARMED FORCES OF SOUTH RUSSIA (AFSR) from January 1919 to April 1920.

Denikin came from a humble background but passed through the General Staff Academy and fought in the Japanese War. In the FIRST WORLD WAR he was a talented and brave infantry commander. This, combined with his origins, helped his rapid promotion after February 1917; in August 1917, aged only forty-five, he was Commander-in-Chief of the South-Western Army Group. He was imprisoned after supporting General KORNILOV's attempt to move against Petrograd, and he only escaped after October 1917.

Denikin joined the Volunteer Army in south-eastern Russia under Generals Kornilov and ALEXEEV. When Kornilov was killed in April 1918 Denikin replaced him; after Alexeev's death in October he was in sole charge. Under Denikin the Volunteers won victories in the north Caucasus. Thanks to this, to the defeats suffered by the COSSACKS of the Don, and to his pro-Allied policy, Denikin was able in January 1919 to subordinate to himself the Cossack armies and emerge as Main Commander-in-Chief of the Armed Forces of South Russia.

Denikin was most successful with small forces. Although his AFSR mounted the most successful campaign against Soviet Russia, Denikin lost control of it; his 'Moscow Directive' of July 1919 was over-ambitious. In the political sphere he was not a narrow reactionary, but he saw himself as above politics, distrusted civilians, and showed little political imagination, stressing his own military dictatorship; he had no sympathy for the minorities. After the defeat of the AFSR, when the remnants fled to the Crimea, Denikin resigned and was replaced by Baron P. N. WRANGEL. In exile, mostly in France, he produced multi-volume memoirs.   EM

Drahomanov, Mykhailo (1841–1895)

Historian and publicist, Drahomanov (Russian form: Mikhail Petrovich Dragomanov) was the most influential Ukrainian political thinker before 1917. His ideas on socialism and federalism formed the framework for the development of Ukrainian political parties (see UKRAINE). Born in Poltava, he graduated as a student of history in Kiev and taught there until his exile in 1876. Taking up residence in Geneva he took an active part in the Russian émigré community at first, but later grew apart through political differences. He moved to Sofia to take up a position teaching history in 1889 and died there six years later. (See photograph on p. 320.)   ND

Dulatov, Mir Yakub (1885–1937)

Born into a Kazakh aristocratic family, Dulatov was educated by a Tatar village mullah, and then in the Muslim school in Turgay, the famous Galiye medresse of Ufa, and

Figure 51   Drahomanov.

the Russo-Kazakh school of Gaurgan. He belonged to the young generation of Kazakhs whose militant nationalist outlook flourished in a soil enriched by the ideas of the previous generation of Kazakh enlighteners.

Like many jadids of his generation, Dulatov embraced a career as a teacher and journalist, and became a poet and novelist in his own right. His literary debut occurred in 1906, when he published some poems in the St Petersburg Kazakh newspaper *Serke* (The Guide). The publication of his collected poems *Uyan Kazakh* (Wake up, Kazakh!) in 1909 gained him recognition both for the militantly nationalistic tone of his verses, and the mastery of his literary craft. There followed another collection in 1913, entitled *Azamat* (The Brave), the novel *Bahtsïz Jamal* (The Unhappy Jamal), which he called 'the first novel of Kazakh life', as well as contributions to the Kazakh periodicals *Ay-Kap* (Flight), *Kazakh*, *Berlik Tuny* (The Banner of Unity), and *Ak Zhol* (The White Road).

Dulatov was one of the founders of ALASH ORDA and when the hopes for Kazakh autonomy were shattered by

the CIVIL WAR, he, like many other leading Kazakh jadids, joined the Soviet regime and became a member of the Communist Party in 1919. His impact on the life of Soviet Kazakhstan, however, was not due to his activities in the party and government hierarchy but rather to his writing and teaching activities.

As a professor at the Communist University of the Toilers of the East in Moscow, he shaped an entire generation of Kazakh intellectuals, but the nationalist ideas he had embraced long before the revolutions of 1917 led to Dulatov's purge in 1934 and his liquidation in 1937.

A-AR

Dzerzhinsky, Felix Edmundovich (1877–1926)

First chief of the Soviet political police, Dzerzhinsky (in Polish: Dzierżyński) was born into a Polish landed gentry and intelligentsia family, joined the Lithuanian Social Democratic Party in Vilna in 1895 and soon turned professional revolutionary, agitating among factory workers. Arrested in 1897, he escaped in August 1899 from Siberian exile. In Warsaw he resurrected Rosa LUXEMBURG's defunct Social Democratic Party of the Kingdom of Poland, negotiating its fusion with two Lithuanian socialist splinter groups to form, shortly after his second arrest in January 1900, the Social Democratic Party of the Kingdom of Poland and Lithuania (SDKPiL), precursor of the Polish Communist Party. Escaping again from Siberia in mid 1902, he was elected, at the SDKPiL's 1903 Berlin Congress, to its Central Committee; as the party's chief representative on Polish soil he greatly increased its membership and activity. In 1906 he first met LENIN in Stockholm at the RSDRP's Fourth (Unity) Congress, gaining election to its Central Committee upon the Russian party's ensuing brief merger with the SDKPiL.

Repeatedly arrested and incarcerated, Dzerzhinsky had spent over eleven years in prison and Siberian exile when the FEBRUARY REVOLUTION freed him from a Moscow gaol. He sat continuously on the BOLSHEVIK Party Central Committee from July–August 1917 until his death. Prominent in the October coup d'état, he concentrated thereafter on promoting the Soviet regime's internal security. Dzerzhinsky was appointed by Lenin on 7(20) December 1917 as chairman of the All-Russian Extraordinary Commission for Combating Counter-Revolution and Sabotage (see VECHEKA). He developed this political police agency into a vast, ubiquitous, multi-faceted apparatus, formally attached to the Sovnarkom (see LENIN'S GOVERNMENT), but in reality answerable to the Communist Party Central Committee or its Politburo. Dzerzhinsky implemented the Red Terror decree of 5 September 1918 in massive reprisal for the attempt on Lenin's life. His additional appointment in March 1919 as People's Commissar for Internal Affairs (NKVD), resulted in coordination of effort and strengthened the Vecheka's hand. His dynamic drive and organizational talents were much in demand, and he served as chairman on such bodies as the Main Committee for Universal Labour Conscription (acronym: Glavkomtrud), and the Commission for Betterment of Children's Lives which was formed in January 1921 on his initiative. He brought formidable Vecheka and NKVD resources to bear on these and many other problems. During the Soviet-Polish conflict of 1920, he commanded the Rear of the South-West Front, and figured in the abortive Provisional Revolutionary Committee of Poland. On his appointment, in April 1921, as People's Commissar for Transport (NKPS), he devoted himself to the restoration of Russia's shattered transport system. When, in February 1922, the terror-tainted Vecheka was transformed into the State Political Administration (GPU), incorporated in the NKVD, he conveniently headed both GPU and NKVD. In 1923 the GPU was upgraded to OGPU status, ranking with People's Commissariats and formally subordinated to the USSR Sovnarkom, but still under direct Communist Party centrol with Dzerzhinsky as its chairman.

Dzerzhinsky's loyalty to Lenin was unquestioned, but their relationship was strained by Dzerzhinsky's handling, in 1922/3, of the Georgian leadership crisis (see TRANSCAUCASIA). Lenin valued his administrative ability and his

Figure 52 Dzerzhinsky.

communist zeal, but not his political qualities, seeing him as a doer more than as a thinker. Within ten days of Lenin's death on 21 January 1924, Dzerzhinsky was appointed chairman of the Supreme Council of National Economy, relinquishing his NKPS (but not his OGPU) post, and in June 1924 he was elevated to Politburo candidate-member standing; he doubtless owed this sudden double advancement to STALIN, Party General Secretary since April 1922. Dzerzhinsky devoted his remaining years to reviving the country's stricken economy. He died of a heart attack on 20 July 1926.   GHL

Figner, Vera Nikolaevna (1852–1943)

Born into a well-to-do Kazan gentry family, Figner spent her early years in rural seclusion and six further years in a private institute for girls. Released in 1869, she decided to go to Zurich to train as a doctor. Failing to get her father's approval, she found another route, via marriage. Her infatuated husband was easily persuaded to give up his position as a lawyer and go with her and a younger sister to Zurich. Once there, ambitions to be a doctor were instantly challenged by the radical politics of the Russian colony. Vera Figner refused to be diverted from medical studies as her sister was, and did not join her comrades when they returned to Russia and went 'to the people'. But in 1875, Mark NATANSON induced her to give up her studies, though she was close to graduation. She returned to Russia and spent many dispiriting months working for the people as a medical aide, first in Samara province, then in Saratov. In both places she was watched closely, and after an assassination attempt on the tsar, was forced to leave. She went to St Petersburg, and in the summer of 1879 reluctantly decided that no realistic alternative existed to the terrorism of People's Will. In that organization she worked as a conspirator, preparing assassination attempts, and as a legal propagandist. She evaded arrest after the tsar's assassination and remained at large until 1883, keeping the remnants of the party together. She was tried in 1884 and sentenced to death, commuted to life imprisonment. She was incarcerated for the next twenty years in the Schlüsselburg fortress.

Figner was released in 1904, frail but still in full command of her faculties. Readjustment was painful, and though treated as a heroine by feminists (see WOMEN) and the intelligentsia generally, she did not assume an active role in radical politics, as BRESHKOVSKAYA did. Figner joined the SRs in 1908, but left after the AZEF affair. Before 1914 she wrote intermittently for the feminist press and in March 1917 headed a women's suffrage procession in Petrograd. She remained in Russia after the Bolshevik Revolution, but never became a communist. She wrote her memoirs, worked for the Society of Political Exiles, and lived out her remaining years. She died at the age of ninety and was buried in the Novodevichi cemetery.   LE

Fitrat, Abdurrauf (dates unknown)

The son of a petty merchant from Bukhara, Fitrat belonged to the radical wing of the jadid movement which took an active part in the life of Soviet Turkestan during the first two decades after the revolution. His radicalism can be traced to his early works, in which he chastised the Muslim clerics for having replaced the dynamic faith of the early generations of Muslims with a diseased religion that hindered progress and education. His final goal was to liberate the world of Islam from the domination of the infidels, while emphasizing the need for internal reform and renovation.

The paucity of Muslim Marxist cadres prompted the BOLSHEVIK authorities to enlist the radical jadids in the effort to pacify and Sovietize CENTRAL ASIA. As a result, at least until the middle of the 1920s, militant jadid nationalists such as Fitrat had an overwhelming influence in matters concerning culture and education in particular.

In 1922 Fitrat became a member of the State Council of Sciences of Uzbekistan and in 1923 the minister of foreign affairs of the People's Republic of Bukhara. Throughout the 1920s, he was active in literary societies such as Chagatay Gurungi (The Chagatay Society) (1920) and Kïzïl Kalam (Red Pen) (1927) which functioned as efficient vehicles for the spread of nationalist ideologies.

Despite the fact that the first measures aimed at eliminating nationalist influence in Turkestan were taken in 1928, it was only in the years 1932–38 that the frontal attack on the jadid intelligentsia began. Fitrat fell victim to the purge of the local communist parties of Central Asia. He was arrested for nationalism in 1938 but there is no information on his ultimate fate.   A-AR

Frunze, Mikhail Vasilievich (1885–1925)

Born in Pishpek (later Frunze) in Turkestan, the son of a russified Rumano-Moldavian peasant father who was a soldier turned medical orderly, and Russian mother, Frunze studied at a local school, later moving to a school in Verny (now Alma-Ata). There, in study circles, he was first acquainted with revolutionary thought. In 1904 he entered a polytechnic in St Petersburg, where he took part in student and worker revolutionary circles and became a member of the RSDRP, joining the BOLSHEVIK faction. Arrested and expelled from St Petersburg in November 1904 for taking part in a demonstration, he worked for a while in Moscow and then moved on to Ivanovo-Voznesensk, where he was a leader of the 1905 textile workers' strike which paralysed the industry in the entire area for six weeks. Later that year he took to the barricades of Krasnaya Presnya during the December rising in Moscow, for which he was sentenced to ten years hard labour, followed in 1914 by exile to Irkutsk province. In 1915 he escaped to Chita where he edited *Vostochnoe Obozrenie* (Eastern Review), a Bolshevik weekly.

During 1917 Frunze assumed leadership of the revolutionary movement in Minsk, Belorussia and the entire Western Front, as well as becoming the chief of the Minsk civilian militia. In October 1917 he led a 2,000-strong force of workers and soldiers in the Bolshevik struggle for Moscow. Frunze was subsequently sent to the Ural front where in 1919, leading the southern group of the RED ARMY, he dealt one of the decisive blows to KOLCHAK's forces and was rewarded with the Bolshevik command for the whole of the Eastern Front. He went on to clear Turkestan of White forces and helped to consolidate the revolution in Bukhara. His last major military success came in November 1920, when he captured Crimea and (together with STALIN) routed WRANGEL. He died on 31 October 1925, after a prolonged illness.   FP

Gapon, Father Georgii Apollonovich (1870–1906)

An Orthodox priest and leader of considerable personal magnetism, whose effect on gathered crowds, and especially those of peasants and artisans, '. . . bordered on the marvellous'. Probably born in the Ukraine, the son of a priest, Gapon's simple manner helped him to gain the confidence not only of the masses, but equally of some highly-placed officials, including the Governor of St Petersburg. The attractive features of his personality were balanced by periods of morbid introspection, bouts of emotional temper and a liability to sudden shifts from the heights of exaltation to the depths of despair.

Gapon's rise to prominence in the early 1900s coincided with a period of great political foment and radicalization, his work and fate intertwining with that of the police, as represented by V. K. PLEHVE and S. V. ZUBATOV. He became an active promoter of the phenomenon known as Police Socialism, whereby workers agitated for rights within a closely-monitored environment. His organization, the Assembly of Russian Workers (founded in St Petersburg in 1903), carried on the work of the Mutual Aid Society for Workers in Mechanical Production (founded by Plehve and Zubatov), which resembled a trade union functioning under police protection. Gapon's Assembly was quickly penetrated by Social Democratic agitators, thus giving rise to ambiguous views of both the organization and its founder; particularly so, given that within a year of its formation the organization had expanded to 11 branches in the capital, 9,000 members and perhaps ten times that number of sympathizers. Moreover, through the work of the revolutionary groups within it, it quickly showed signs of encouraging militancy in addition to advocating peaceful economic demands.

This uneasy mix was particularly evident in the events of winter 1904–5, when Gapon and the Assembly took on a more mass-based political rôle. In December 1904, when four of the organization's members were dismissed by an unpopular foreman at the Putilov Works, the Assembly

322

encouraged strike action, which within days brought the entire factory to a halt and spread to nearly 150 other firms and 100,000 workers in St Petersburg as a whole. As the movement grew, so too did Gapon's political ambitions. He drew up a petition to Tsar NICHOLAS II, appealing for the protection of workers and the introduction of 'just reforms'. The demands were a confused mixture of Populist (see POPULISM, liberal and Marxist thought, expressed together in the mystical tone of Holy Russia and love for the Tsar. Such was its appeal, however, that within three days of its release the petition had received 150,000 signatures. On Sunday, 9 January 1905 Gapon led a large procession of workers to the Winter Palace with the intention of presenting the petition to the Tsar. Members of the procession were fired upon by the police and whipped by Cossacks, with over 100 workers killed and some 300 wounded. The incident, which became known as 'Bloody Sunday', shook the very foundations of the autocracy, signalling the start of the 1905 REVOLUTION.

The experience embittered Gapon himself. He learned to ride and shoot, issued revolutionary appeals to the country and attempted for a time to take on the leadership of the revolutionary movement. However, his eventual re-establishment of contacts with the tsarist police and his apparent involvement in some of their schemes resulted in distrust by the revolutionary parties. In March 1906 these misgivings led to Gapon's execution (by SOCIALIST REVOLUTIONARIES under instructions from E. F. AZEV) as an agent-provocateur in a small village near the Finnish border.

Gapon's legacy was best summed up by TROTSKY, who wrote in 1905: 'History used the fantastic plan of Gapon for the purpose of arriving at its ends, and it only remained for the priest to sanction with priestly authority its [history's] revolutionary conclusions.' He had, indeed, done more than any other to shatter the power of autocracy in 1905.   FP

Further Reading

Dillon, E.J.: *The Eclipse of Russia*. London: J.M. Dent, 1918.
Gapon, G.: *The Story of My Life*. New York: 1906.
Shukman, H.: *Lenin and the Russian Revolution*. London: Longman, 1977.

Gasprali, Ismail bey (1851–1914)

The father of Pan-Turkism among Russian Muslims, Ismail bey Gasprali (Gasprinsky) was born in the Crimean village of Gaspra in the family of an impoverished Tatar nobleman. After early schooling in the village, he entered the Moscow Cadet Corps school where he became acquainted with Slavophilism which he would later use as a model in developing his own ideas of Pan-Turkism.

Gasprali travelled to France (1871–75) and Ottoman Turkey (1875–77) where he absorbed liberal and reformist ideas. Convinced that education was a fundamental prerequisite of progress, he devised a new system of education, and in 1882 opened the Zinjirli medrese in the Crimea as the first medrese which employed a new method (Usul-u-jadid). In time this humble term would come to designate an entire movement of renewal and reform among the Muslims of Russia.

Championing his schools in the Crimea and elsewhere in the Russian empire, Gasprali travelled to the Volga region, to the Kazakh Steppes and even to the emir of Bukhara to lend support to the jadid reformers and to persuade the conservatives of the futility of their resistance.

Gasprali's Pan-Turkist philosophy was expressed in his motto: 'Unity in language, deeds and thought'. He promoted linguistic unity in the newspaper *Terdzhuman* (Interpreter) which he launched in 1883 and where he used a language that was supposed to be understood 'from the Bosphorus to the Chinese borders'. Until its demise in 1918, it remained a model of linguistic, literary, and journalistic excellence. Also, in 1883, he started three other periodicals: *Alem-i-Nisvan* (Women's World), *Alem-i-Sibyan* (Children's World) and the satirical *Kha Kha Kha* (Ha, Ha, Ha).

An active participant in the three Muslim congresses where he defended Turkic unity, Gasprali advocated cooperation with the Russian state on the basis of mutual understanding which could be achieved only if conditions were created for the development of the Muslim national culture. Rejected by the younger generation, his most enduring legacy was that of cultural jadidism and the jadid school network that extended from the Crimea and Volga, through the Kazakh Steppes and Central Asia to Kashgar.   A-AR

Gavrilov, Nikolai Andreevich (1886–1919)

Of peasant background and a provincial schoolteacher by profession, Gavrilov was arrested for smuggling revolutionary literature shortly after the 1905 REVOLUTION and exiled to the Irkutsk region. He joined the Irkutsk RSDRP soon after February 1917 and became Secretary of its Provincial Committee in October (his work within the BOLSHEVIK faction of that organization had been instrumental in bringing about its split in early October 1917). In February 1918 he became a member of the Tsentrosibir Presidium and two months later took an active role in the Military-Revolutionary Headquarters of the Trans-Baikal Oblast. From September 1918, until his capture (and death) near Chita in May 1919, he was involved in clandestine activities at Blagoveshchensk and Khabarovsk.   FP

Gershuni, Grigori Andreevich (1870–1908)

A founding member of the Party of SOCIALIST REVOLUTIONARIES (PSR), and one of the most influential figures within it, Gershuni's premature death in 1908 deprived the PSR of its 'living hero' and, in organizational terms, possibly of its counterpart to LENIN.

Gershuni was the son of Jewish peasants in Kovno Province, and trained as a pharmacist at Kiev University. In 1898 he opened a bacteriological laboratory in Minsk and simultaneously founded the Workers' Party for the Political Liberation of Russia. He was arrested two years later but secured his release by persuading the Moscow OKHRANA chief, S. V. ZUBATOV, of his intention to collaborate with the latter's officially-inspired loyal trade unions. In 1901–2, Gershuni worked with Ekaterina BRESHKO-BRESHKOVSKAYA to secure the adhesion of the POPULIST groups inside Russia to the new Party of Socialist Revolutionaries.

As a persuasive exponent of the ethical and political efficacy of terror, Gershuni was the founder and first head of the SR Military Organization or 'Central Terror'. He was responsible for the organization's first success, the assassination in 1902 of Minister of the Interior, D. S. Sipyagin. This was followed by an attempt on the life of Governor I. M. Obolensky of Kiev, and in the following year, by the assassination of Governor N. M. Bogdanovich of Ufa. Shortly thereafter Gershuni was arrested in Kiev and transferred to the Peter-Paul Fortress in St Petersburg. At his trial in 1904 he was sentenced to death, a sentence subsequently commuted to life imprisonment and hard labour. In the autumn of 1905 he was transferred to Akatui Prison in Eastern Siberia. A year later he escaped via China and the USA to Western Europe. His unexpected appearance at the Second Extraordinary Congress of the PSR in February 1907 came as a sensation to most of the delegates. In exile he demanded the resumption of a campaign of terror against leading figures in the tsarist government, while he strongly defended his former deputy Evno AZEF against accusations of treason to the party. At his comrades' urging he wrote his memoirs before dying of tuberculosis in Zürich in 1908. All sections of the Socialist International paid lavish tribute to him at his funeral.   RA

Further Reading

Gershuni, G.A.: *Iz nedavnego proshlago*. Paris: PSR, 1908.

Hildermeier, M.: *Die Sozialrevoluzionäre Partei Russlands: Agrarsozialismus und Modernisierung im Zarenreich (1900–1914)*. Cologne and Vienna: Böhlau Verlag, 1978.

Gots, Abram Rafaelovich (1882–1937?)

The Gots brothers, sons of a wealthy Moscow Jewish merchant and relatives of the Vysotsky family with its tea interests, provided the Party of SOCIALIST REVOLUTIONARIES with essential organizational talents.

Abram Gots studied in Halle and Heidelberg, providing a link between the older Populist comrades of his brother

and the younger neo-Kantians (N. D. AVKSENTIEV, V. M. ZENZINOV, I. I. BUNAKOV-FONDAMINSKY and D. O. Gavronsky) in the PSR. Gots revived the Moscow Committee and joined the Fighting Organization until his arrest in 1906. After his return from Siberian exile in 1917 he led the PSR factions in the Petrograd SOVIET and the All-Russian Soviet Executive Committee. As an active participant in the 1918 'democratic counter-revolution' against Bolshevism, Abram Gots was the main accused in the 1922 Show Trial of the PSR in Moscow. According to Zenzinov he was shot in Alma-Ata in 1937.   RA

Gots, Mikhail Rafaelovich (1866–1906)

Described as 'the conscience of the PSR' by V. M. CHERNOV, Mikhail Gots studied at Moscow University and then joined People's Will (Narodnaya Volya) in 1884. Two years later he was arrested and exiled to Siberia. After an amnesty in 1895 he emigrated to Paris where, together with I. A. Rubanovich and N. S. Rusanov, he edited *Vestnik Russkoi Revolyutsii* (Russian Revolution Messenger). In 1901 Russian demands for his extradition from Italy caused an Italian political crisis and resulted in the withdrawal of an invitation to the Tsar to visit Italy. From 1902 Mikhail Gots edited the PSR journal *Revolyutsionnaya Rossiya* (Revolutionary Russia) with Chernov, until his death from cancer in 1906.   RA

Guchkov, Alexander Ivanovich (1862–1936)

Born in Moscow on 14 (26) October 1862, Guchkov was a major industrialist, freemason and the Chairman of the Octobrist Party (see OCTOBER MANIFESTO) (and, after September 1915, when the Octobrists merged with the KADET PARTY, a leading member of the Progressive Bloc (see pp. 112–13)). He played a key rôle in shaping the political topography of the revolutionary period, coming to prominence in the Third Duma (1907–12), where he held the position of Speaker, and was a strong supporter of P. A. STOLYPIN. This support included Stolypin's measures to dissolve the Second Duma and to introduce a retrograde reform of the electoral law in June 1907; support that earned for Guchkov the suspicion of Russia's radical politicians. Guchkov's advocacy of Stolypin and his reactionary measures was also responsible for the former's shift away from open political struggle, where he had little credibility, to conspiracy and plotting, which became his strengths. One historian, indeed, has depicted him as '. . . a man who was notorious for originality rather than democratic conviction'. A favourite tactic was to spread rumours using copies of private correspondence reproduced in typewritten or mimeographed form. His 'originality' was best demonstrated in his protracted struggle with NICHOLAS II and the Empress Alexandra Fedorovna, both of whom Guchkov regarded as a hindrance to Russia's possible future as a constitutional monarchy. As early as 1912, when Guchkov (along with M. V. RODZYANKO) first broached the subject of the monarchy's relationship with RASPUTIN, he had begun to circulate copies of private letters written by the empress and her children to Rasputin some years before. After the outbreak of the First World War the effect of these rumours had peaked, with accusations of treason, preparations for a separate peace and the link between the empress and 'dark forces' being talked about not only in the political sphere, but also by the army and the masses.

Guchkov's own political fortunes had from the start been closely associated with this process by the tremendous onslaught he had launched against Rasputin in the chamber of the Fourth Duma in April 1912. His attack, which did more than anything else to give Guchkov 'extraordinary popularity', inextricably tied Rasputin to the court that protected him. It was through his efforts that the notion of Rasputin as an 'ignoble deceiver' and 'dangerous adviser', whose influence swayed the empress, first gained currency. In return, Alexandra developed an enduring hatred for Guchkov, suggesting to the tsar from time to time that he might be hanged, or, when in a more charitable mood, banished to Siberia. It is hardly surprising that in February 1917 Guchkov, sensing that Nicholas II was in a precarious position, embarked upon a plan (which became known as the 'Guchkov Plot') to force the tsar to abdicate in favour of his son, Alexei, whose power would be wielded by a Regent (Grand Duke Michael, the tsar's brother) until he reached his majority. And it was Guchkov, together with the monarchist V. V. Shulgin, who in March 1917 travelled to GHQ at Pskov on a mission to convince the tsar to abdicate.

Guchkov's rise to the highest levels of power began during the First World War, when he became the chairman of the Duma Committee on Military and Naval Affairs, and subsequently chairman of the non-governmental Central War Industries Committee (in the summer of 1915). He was also the Red Cross commissioner for the Union of Zemstvos at the beginning of the war, and later President of the Russian Red Cross. Together with P. N. MILYUKOV and Rodzyanko, Guchkov achieved in the immediate pre-revolutionary period a status that meant his 'utterances were eagerly sought after and . . . counsels were generally followed', although, as one commentator puts it '. . . with deplorable results'. His connections were particularly strong in the military, where he was able to maintain influence on a large number of senior officers, ranging from Generals V. I. Gurko, A. A. Brusilov and N. V. RUZSKY to the Chief of Staff, General M. V. ALEXEEV. When the First PROVISIONAL GOVERNMENT came into being, Guchkov was made its Minister of War and the Navy. Owing to his differences over the notorious Order No. 1,

however, he resigned on 2 May 1917 and was replaced in that post by A. F. KERENSKY.

One of Guchkov's main failings was that, despite the impressive power base he had created for himself by 1917, he failed to piece together a coherent political programme that reflected the mood of the country. In September 1915 a document entitled 'Disposition No. 1', signed by a 'Committee of Public Safety', had begun to circulate around the Russian centres of power. This document (possibly leaked by Guchkov himself) identified two wars that had to be fought by the Russian people: one against the Germans, the other against the 'internal enemy'. The three persons represented as being at the centre of the struggle against the latter were PRINCE G. E. LVOV, Guchkov and Kerensky. Guchkov's rise in the next two years, occupying as he did a key position of influence with the military, together with his rôle in the WAR INDUSTRIES COMMITTEES (which had also allowed him potentially to exert considerable influence on the national economy), permitted him to bring that view to life. However, his stubborn campaign to maintain the centre-right of the political situation (which meant that he neither supported a full republic, nor a simple monarchy) ensured that he joined, as LENIN put it in March 1917, a political line that was little more than '. . . the "old" European pattern . . .' He was, like Lvov and, ultimately, Kerensky himself, eclipsed by conditions that were at variance with that pattern. He continued to work against the Bolsheviks after they took power in October, and in 1918 left Russia for self-exile in Paris, where he died on 14 February 1936.   FP

Further Reading

Ferro, M.: *Nicholas II: The Last of the Tsars*. London: Penguin, 1991.

Katkov, G.: *Russia 1917: The February Revolution*. London: Fontana, 1969.

Schapiro, L.: *The Russian Revolutions*. London: Pelican, 1966.

Herzen, Alexander Ivanovich (1812–1870)

Political philosopher and journalist, a leading 'westernizer' under Nicholas I. Strongly opposed to autocracy and serfdom, Herzen emigrated to Western Europe (1847) where he became disenchanted at the failure of the 1848 revolutions and developed a Romantic theory of 'Russian socialism', later widely known as POPULISM, according to which the Russian PEASANT, with his egalitarian communal instincts, could take the lead in solving the social question if only he were freed from the constraints of serfdom and tradition under the tutelage of progressive-minded intellectuals. In the early years of Alexander II's reign Herzen's periodical *Kolokol* (The Bell), published in London from 1857, helped to promote a critical attitude in educated society. It put forward a pragmatic, moderate reform programme which, however, drew objections from N. G. CHERNYSHEVSKY and other younger radicals, sometimes called 'men of the 1860s'. The disagreement was in part a generation problem, as illustrated in I. S. Turgenev's *Fathers and Sons*, but also one of style and substance. Herzen's endorsement of the Polish insurrection in 1863–4 cost him support on the right, and in his last years, although still politically active, he became increasingly isolated. Yet his legacy is an enduring one. Herzen is remembered as a courageous champion of the oppressed and a trenchant critic of all ideologies or institutions that cramp the individual spirit. A figure of European stature, he embodied the greatness as well as some of the weaknesses of nineteenth-century liberalism. JLHK

Further Reading

Acton, E.: *Alexander Herzen and the Role of the Intellectual Revolutionary*. London and New York: 1979.

Berlin, I.: *Russian Thinkers*, intro. A. Kelly. London: 1978; repr. Harmondsworth and New York: 1979.

Herzen, A.: *From the Other Shore* and *The Russian People and Socialism*, trans. M. Budberg and R. Wollheim; intro. I. Berlin. London: 1956; repr. Oxford and New York: 1979.

Malia, M.: *Alexander Herzen and the Birth of Russian Socialism, 1825–1855*. Cambridge, Mass.: Harvard University Press, 1961.

Horvath, Dmitri Leonidovich (1858–1937)

Director of the CHINESE EASTERN RAILWAY (CER) from 1902 to 1920, General Horvath was born in Poltava Province. He was an engineer by training, but went on to join the army (serving in the Russo-Turkish War of 1877–78). His first contact with railway building came some years later, when he was involved with the construction of the Trans-Caspian. His appointment to the CER followed seven years as the director of the Ussuri Railway. As the head of the CER, Horvath became a self-styled autocrat whose political influence in the railway zone endured for much of his time there. His style of leadership caused some unease in the Russian government, as indeed it did with Russian military commanders who had to deal with him during the Russo-Japanese war (when it was felt he was placing the interests of the CER ahead of those of the Russian army). The real tests to his rule in the railway zone came during the revolutions of 1905 and 1917. The first he contained with a degree of political dexterity. Those of 1917, however, gradually proved to be beyond his capabilities (See NORTHERN CHINA). His goal of preserving the railway zone as a little corner of Russia against the tide of Bolshevism made him increasingly reliant on the support of foreign powers (Japan, Britain, America and France) and the Chinese authorities. As with many of the White commanders on the periphery, Horvath felt most at ease and performed best within his own territorial limits. His

attempts to broaden his ambitions during the early stages of the CIVIL WAR failed and he agreed finally to working under Admiral KOLCHAK. This led him into a troubled association with Ataman SEMENOV, which, after the collapse of Kolchak's leadership, ended in an open rivalry between the two men. After Horvath was removed from his authority over the railway by the Chinese government in April 1920, he moved to Peking where he spent most of his remaining years as the titular head of the Russian EMIGRATION in the Far East. FP

Hrushevsky, Mykhailo (1866–1934)

Renowned Ukrainian historian and publicist, Hrushevsky was the author of over 1,800 scholarly works. He studied in Kiev and was appointed to the first professorship of East European history in Lvov in 1894. In Lvov he was active in encouraging the development of academic life and institutions among the Ukrainians. On his return to Kiev in 1906 he took part in the establishment of the Ukrainian Scientific Society and published many works of a publicistic nature on the situation of the Ukrainians as well as continuing his historical work. He was a leading member of the Society of Ukrainian Progressivists before his arrest and exile to Kazan at the outbreak of the FIRST WORLD WAR. Returning to Kiev in 1917, he was unanimously elected president of the Central Rada. On its demise he returned to academic work and went into emigration in 1919. He returned to Kiev in 1924 to work in the Ukrainian Academy of Sciences, only to see all his work destroyed and outlawed at the end of the 1920s before his death in 1934. ND

Ibragimov, Galimdzhan (1887–1938)

Born to the mullah of the village Sultanmuratovo, Ibragimov was a complex and many-sided intellectual who equally concerned himself with politics, the subtleties of the Tatar language, the methodology of language teaching and textbook writing, the development of the Tatar press and literature; in a word, with the whole of Tatar culture. A medrese student in Ufa (a centre of jadid thinking and activity), Ibragimov joined the radical 'Islah' group, which led to affiliation with Russian radical groups and eventually his membership in the SR party which he represented as a deputy to the CONSTITUENT ASSEMBLY and to the Third All-Russian Congress of the Soviets in 1918. Also in 1918 he was appointed president of the commission charged with the translation of the works of LENIN into Tatar, was invited by STALIN to direct the Central Commissariat for Muslim Affairs and founded the first Tatar pedagogical journal *Madarif* (Instruction, now called *Sovet Maktabe*, Soviet school).

Ibragimov joined the Russian Communist (Bolshevik) Party in 1918 and 1920–1929 was chairman of the

Academic Centre of the People's Commissariat for Education of the Tatar republic. He did not, however, abandon his nationalist beliefs. On the contrary, as a component of the new bureaucratic machine he could observe more directly the continuation of the russification process, even if the ideology which sanctioned it was new. He opposed russification and at the First Turkology Congress held in 1926, in Baku, he rose against the Latin alphabet, standing almost alone in the defence of the Arabic alphabet used by the Tatars for centuries, and seen by him as a vital dimension of the Tatar identity.

In 1927 Ibragimov published an essay entitled 'Which Way Will Tatar Culture Go?', perhaps his boldest stand against russification. In it he developed the thesis of tatarization as the only road for Tatar culture and argued that the Tatar language and literature were not disappearing. 'They will not be russified, they will grow on their own Tatar foundations, enriched by their proletarian essence.' The essay was condemned by the regional party committee of the Tatar republic on 14 June, 1927.

Though never associated with the national communists who advanced political solutions to the Tatar-Russian relationship, Ibragimov's defence of Tatar particularism and condemnation of Great Russian claims of superiority were serious enough sins to prompt his arrest in 1937. He died in prison a year later but is one of the few Tatar nationalists who was rehabilitated after Stalin's death.

A-AR

Further Reading

Rorlich, A.: Which way will Tatar culture go? A controversial essay by Galimdzhan Ibragimov. In *Cahiers du monde russe et soviétique* 3–4 (1974) 363–71.

Ibrahimov, Veli (?–1928)

The son of a poor Crimean artisan, in the years before 1914, Ibrahimov joined the Tatar Cultural Society of Akmesjit (Simferopol), one of many such societies organized in the Crimea at the height of the jadid reform movement. He belonged to the more restless young generation of Tatar radicals who advocated withdrawing Muslim support of Russian liberals.

In the summer of 1917 Ibrahimov and other Crimean Tatar liberals organized a Crimean National Party advocating closer cooperation with the socialist parties. When in July, 1917, the Central Executive Committee and the left wing of the party began publishing newspapers which criticized the PROVISIONAL GOVERNMENT's aloofness to the problems of non-Russian nationalities, Ibrahimov (together with M. Kurtmehmet) became the editor of *Kïrïm Odzhaghï* (The Crimean Hearth).

Ibrahimov eventually joined the BOLSHEVIK party in 1919, though he had advocated supporting them as early as 1918. He was one of the organizers of underground

Bolshevik actions in the Crimea during its occupation by DENIKIN and WRANGEL. Once Crimea was cleared of the White armies and a Crimean ASSR was organized in October, 1921, Ibrahimov became Chairman of the Central Executive Committee, and president of the Sovnarkom of the Crimean ASSR, and was able to promote what is regarded today as the Golden Age (1923–27/8) of the Crimean people under Soviet rule.

The policies pursued by Ibrahimov between 1923 and 1928 were launched within the context of two national policies: NEP and nativization. They can be summarized as a three-pronged tatarization affecting the political, cultural and economic life of Crimea. Despite the fact that his party had been outlawed in 1921, Ibrahimov contributed to the endurance of its ideas and influence by staffing the government apparatus of the new republic with former members. Land distribution focused primarily on the needs and rights of Crimean peasants while cultural policies were aimed at achieving a true renaissance of Crimean culture in its broadest definition. The 'Golden Age' ended in 1927 when Ibrahimov was arrested and together with his associates accused of nationalist deviation and executed in May 1928. Some of those thus accused in the 1930s have been rehabilitated. Veli Ibrahimov is not among them.

A-AR

Ioffe, Adolf Abramovich (1883–1927)

Born in Simferopol, Crimea, to a prominent merchant family of Karaite Jewish descent, Ioffe was active from the age of sixteen in the revolutionary movement which had developed in the Crimea, and he became a member of the RSDRP in 1902. Barred from Russian universities, he left for Western Europe where he studied medicine and law at Berlin, Zurich and Vienna. Back in Russia to take part in the 1905 REVOLUTION Ioffe fled arrest and returned to Berlin where he joined the Foreign Bureau of the Central Committee of the RSDRP after the Fourth Party Congress (1906).

Ioffe was a close political friend of TROTSKY from 1908, and helped him set up *Pravda* which they published in Vienna. After working for its distribution within Russia, Ioffe was arrested in 1912 and exiled to Tobolsk Province until the FEBRUARY REVOLUTION. Together with Trotsky's group, the MEZHRAYONKA, he joined the Bolshevik party in July 1917 and was elected to its Central Committee. Very active in the October seizure of power as a member of the Soviet Military Revolutionary Committee, he was to become one of the first Soviet diplomats for whom revolution and diplomacy had to progress hand in hand.

At the head of the first Soviet delegation which negotiated peace with Imperial Germany (December 1917), Ioffe supported Trotsky's idea that 'neither war nor peace' was a solution to end hostilities and he spoke to the German proletariat over the heads of both German military and diplomats. After the signing of the Brest-Litovsk Treaty which (together with Trotsky, DZERZHINSKY and Krestinsky) he declined to approve, Ioffe strove to enact his ideas of revolutionary diplomacy: when he was appointed Soviet representative in Berlin (April–November 1918) the Embassy openly served as a basis for the revolution, a situation which led to his expulsion.

After working in UKRAINE during the CIVIL WAR, Ioffe led the Soviet peace delegations which negotiated with the BALTIC countries in 1920 and with Poland in 1921. At the time of the Genoa conference (spring 1922) he was one of the leading negotiators of the Rapallo treaty with Germany. A year later he was appointed ambassador to China, where he signed a declaration of non-interference with the nationalists headed by Sun Yat-sen. Instrumental in the rapprochement between the Soviet Union and Japan (1923), he had a less influential role as a diplomat in England and in Austria (1924–5). Back in Moscow he was appointed rector of the Chinese University and served as a member of the STATE GENERAL PLANNING COMMISSION. He devoted the last two years of his life to backing the political opposition to STALIN, clearly realizing the danger of the situation.

Precarious health, the expulsion of Trotsky and ZINOVIEV from the party (November 14, 1927), the realization that Trotsky did not possess 'that strength of character', the 'ability to stand alone' that was so specific to Lenin, led Ioffe to conclude that the Opposition was doomed to collapse under Stalin's unremitting pressure. As an ultimate sign of protest he committed suicide three days later. His widow survived twenty years in Siberian exile and emigrated to Israel.

Kamenev, Lev Borisovich (1883–1936)

Leading member of the BOLSHEVIK Party and close associate of LENIN, Kamenev was a loser in the power struggle with STALIN and a victim of the Purges.

Kamenev (real name Rosenfeld) was born in Moscow in July 1883. He was educated briefly in law at Moscow University and was active as a Social Democratic propagandist in Tiflis and St Petersburg from 1902 until his third arrest in April 1907. Shortly thereafter he emigrated to western Europe where he became a member of the Bolshevik 'Centre', an active participant in most of the party's foreign newspapers, and one of Lenin's most trusted lieutenants. In January 1914 he was sent back to St Petersburg to oversee the operations of the Bolsheviks' *Pravda* and of their six-man DUMA FRACTION. Ten months later he and the deputies were arrested while discussing Lenin's anti-war instructions.

Early in 1917 Kamenev advocated cooperation with the PROVISIONAL GOVERNMENT, sanctioned a defensist war effort, and was agreeable to some form of unity with the MENSHEVIKS. Kamenev continued to lead the right wing of

Figure 53   Kamenev and his wife at kitchen, with US relief agent (extreme right).

the party in pursuit of a more conciliatory and cautious policy than that favoured by Lenin and the Bolshevik majority. On the eve of the OCTOBER REVOLUTION, Kamenev and G. E. ZINOVIEV argued unsuccessfully for a postponement of the seizure of power until the Second Congress of Soviets and the CONSTITUENT ASSEMBLY could broaden the party's base of support and provide a means for the peaceful transfer of power to a socialist coalition. This same belief in the need for a broad socialist coalition caused him to resign as chairman of the Soviets' Central Executive Committee (VTsIK) and temporarily from the party's Central Committee in November 1917.

Kamenev was at the pinnacle of his power from 1920 to mid 1925. In addition to his position as chairman of the Moscow Soviet, he was a member of the party's five-man ruling Politburo and frequently chaired that body during Lenin's illness. In recognition of his administrative abilities, he was appointed first deputy chairman of the Council of People's Commissars and chairman of the Council of Labour and Defence. In 1922 he formed a 'triumvirate' with Zinoviev and Stalin to keep Trotsky from taking over the mantle of Lenin's power. In doing so, Kamenev paved the way for his own downfall: four years later he lost his posts in the Moscow Soviet and the Politburo; in 1927 he was expelled from the party; and in 1936 he perished in the aftermath of the first great 'show trial'. RCE

Further Reading

Elwood, R.C.: L.B. Kamenev. In *Modern Encyclopedia of Russian and Soviet History*, vol. 15, ed. J. L. Wieczynski, pp. 212–17. Gulf Breeze, Fla.: 1980.

Haupt, Georges and Marie, J.-J. eds: *Makers of the Russian Revolution*. Ithaca: 1974.

Karakhan, Lev Mikhailovich (1889–1937)

The son of an Armenian lawyer, Karakhan was born in Georgia in January 1889. After early participation in student anti-tsarist agitation, he joined the RSDRP in 1904, first in Tiflis and later in HARBIN and Vladivostok. As a student at the Law Faculty of St Petersburg (1910–15) he was active in the trade union movement and was a member of MEZHRAYONKA in 1913. Exiled to Tomsk during the war for pacifist agitation, he could only return to Central Russia after the FEBRUARY REVOLUTION. At that time he contributed to GORKY's periodical, *Novaya Zhizn* (New Life).

Elected first to the Petrograd City Council (Duma) and then to the Presidium of the Petrograd Soviet of Workers' and Soldiers' Deputies, Karakhan joined the BOLSHEVIK party at its Sixth Congress (July 1917). In October he took an active part in the Bolshevik seizure of power as a member of the Petrograd Military Revolutionary Committee.

In November 1917 LENIN first appointed Karakhan Secretary of the Soviet delegation in charge of the peace negotiations with Germany (Brest-Litovsk). This determined his career in the Soviet apparatus and he served as a diplomat for the next twenty years. Deputy Commissar for Foreign Affairs and member of the Collegium of the Foreign Commissariat (1918–20; 1925–34), he became the best Soviet specialist on Asian Affairs. The so-called 'Karakhan Manifestos' of 1919 and 1920 are typical both of Karakhan's initiatives and of the revolutionary diplomacy which characterized the new Soviet state. Proclaiming the repudiation of the tsarist unequal treaties, the first of these Manifestos was so magnanimous that it was soon denounced by the Soviet state as a forgery: it later proved to be genuine.

After a difficult stay as ambassador in Poland due to the fresh wounds of the Soviet-Polish war (1921), Karakhan was appointed to Peking (1923–7). He negotiated simultaneously with the different powers which existed at that time in China: the Kuomintang under Sun Yat-sen, and the warlords of the Northern and Central parts of the country (see NORTHERN CHINA). He was also instrumental in the rapprochement between Japan and the USSR which

materialized with the treaty of *de jure* recognition (January 1925).

As Deputy Commissar for Foreign Affairs for more than nine years, Karakhan became one of the top Soviet advisers in matters of foreign policy together with M. M. LITVINOV. From 1934 he was Soviet representative in Turkey. Three years later he was called back to Moscow, tried and executed at the height of the Stalinist purges. Karakhan was fully rehabilitated after the Twenty-first Congress of the CPSU in 1956. FC

Karelin, Apollon Andreevich (1863–1926)

Born into the St Petersburg intellectual milieu, Karelin was an active POPULIST at school and university, being frequently imprisoned and exiled. In 1905 he escaped from Siberia and took refuge in France, where he became the founder of the Brotherhood of Free Communists and a leading figure in the ANARCHIST movement. In 1917 he returned to Russia and became the best-known anarchist communist, first in Petrograd and then in Moscow, following P. A. KROPOTKIN in both matter and manner. But he accepted the OCTOBER REVOLUTION, participated in the SOVIETS, and formed a national Federation of Anarchist Communists which supported the new regime. He soon became disillusioned, however, criticized the excesses of repression, and saw his organization destroyed and his comrades scattered. He died before he could fall foul of the growing dictatorship. NW

Kedrov, Mikhail Sergeevich (1896–1938)

Born into a wealthy bourgeois family, Kedrov was expelled in 1899 from Moscow University for subversive activity. Joining the RSDRP in 1901 he became a militant revolutionary, spending long periods in prison and Siberian exile. During 1912–16 he pursued medical studies in Switzerland, consorting there with LENIN; in 1916 he returned to Russia to serve as an army doctor. Appointed Deputy Commissar for Military Affairs in November 1917, he supervised the tsarist army's demobilization. Joining the VECHEKA in September 1918, he was made responsible for RED ARMY security until August 1919. As a member of the Vecheka Collegium from March 1919, his assignments included a punitive expedition, notorious for its cruelty, undertaken in spring 1920 to the Murmansk and Archangel areas. He also sat on the Commissariat of Internal Affairs Collegium and, as at January 1920, headed its department for forced labour. After 1921 Kedrov worked in the Commissariat for Transport, in the SUPREME COUNCIL OF THE NATIONAL ECONOMY, the STATE GENERAL PLANNING COMMISSION, and the USSR Supreme Court's Procuracy. Arrested in April 1939, and tortured to make him falsely confess to having been an OKHRANA agent, Kedrov was executed in December 1941. His tragic end was blamed on

Beria in Khrushchev's secret speech at the Twentieth Party Congress.   GHL

Kerensky, Alexander Fedorovich (1881–1970)

Born in Simbirsk (now Ulyanovsk) on the Volga, Kerensky was the elder son of F. M. Kerensky who was headmaster of Vladimir and Alexander ULYANOV (i.e. LENIN and his brother), and subsequently head of the Turkestan educational administration. From 1900–4 Kerensky studied history and law at St Petersburg University, coming under the influence of the Neo-Kantian N. O. Lossky and the liberal jurist L. I. Petrazhitsky. In 1904 he married Olga Baranovskaya, granddaughter of the Sinologist Academician V. P. Vasiliev and cousin of several active SOCIALIST REVOLUTIONARIES. In 1905 Kerensky himself joined the PSR, becoming editor of the SR newspaper *Burevestnik* (Stormy Petrel) and volunteering to join the Battle Organization.

After a brief period of imprisonment and exile in 1905–6, Kerensky returned to the capital to begin a distinguished career as defence lawyer in political cases. In 1912 he defended the Armenian Dashnak Party before the Senate (the Russian Supreme Court); later the same year, he travelled to Siberia to investigate the massacre of 170 miners during a strike at the Lena goldfields. In the same year he was elected to the Fourth State Duma as Trudovik (Labour Group of PSR) deputy for Volsk, Saratov Province. Although his membership of the Duma was against PSR policy, his action was effectively condoned by N. D. AVKSENTIEV and the Pochin group.

Kerensky's membership of the Duma made his speeches widely available and secured him a mass working class following, particularly after the exposure of the BOLSHEVIK, R. V. MALINOVSKY, as a police spy in 1914. Kerensky was also co-opted into the Russian POLITICAL FREEMASONRY.

In 1914 Kerensky was sentenced to exile for initiating a protest by the St Petersburg Bar against the anti-Semitic 'Beilis Affair', but parliamentary immunity saved him. He justified the Trudoviks' abstention in the vote on war credits on 26 July 1914. During the following summer he and V. M. ZENZINOV tried to rebuild the underground PSR and to trigger a working class revolution around bourgeois leadership. The movement failed, partly because of the resolute hostility of the Kadet leader, P. N. MILYUKOV. In 1916 Kerensky retired from politics for several months for an operation for a tubercular kidney in Finland. On his recovery he travelled directly to Central Asia to investigate the rising there (see REVOLUTION IN CENTRAL ASIA). He also became Secretary of the Political Freemasonry. On the eve of the FEBRUARY REVOLUTION he publicly announced his membership of the PSR and demanded the assassination of NICHOLAS II.

Kerensky was the central figure of the 'February Days'

and the major personality in the PROVISIONAL GOVERNMENT of 1917. As minister of justice in the First Provisional Government, he presided over the abolition of ethnic and religious discrimination and of the death penalty. During April he publicly debated war aims with foreign minister Milyukov, while he and N. V. Nekrasov masterminded the creation on 5 May of a Coalition of liberal and socialist forces in which they, together with their Masonic 'brother' M. I. Tereshchenko and the MENSHEVIK leader, I. G. TSERETELI, constituted an 'inner cabinet'. As war minister in the Coalition Kerensky toured the fronts, earning the sobriquet 'Supreme Persuader-in-Chief' with his emotional appeals to the troops to join his planned offensive. The offensive took place in late June. Its failure helped to precipitate the government's 'July Crisis'. As a result of this crisis Kerensky became prime minister on 7 July, moving into Alexander III's suite in the Winter Palace to enhance the dignity of his office, but merely thus inviting malicious comment.

Kerensky's attempts to re-constitute a coalition of Kadets and moderate socialists were rebuffed by all parties until 21 July when he offered his resignation. Reluctantly the parties agreed to a new coalition. Kerensky's premiership was wrecked by his dispute with the new Supreme Commander, General L. G. KORNILOV, about the means required to suppress Bolshevism and restore discipline in the armed forces and in war production. Kerensky's histrionic appeals at the Moscow State Conference in mid August failed to avert the polarization of Russian society. On 27 August he was approached by the conservative ex-minister, V. N. Lvov, with what appeared to be a mutinous ultimatum by Kornilov instructing him and B. V. SAVINKOV to join a Directory with Kornilov and others at GHQ. Kerensky demanded the resignation of the ministers so that he could sack Kornilov. In declining to accept demotion Kornilov mutinied, but the army despatched by him to overawe Petrograd was peaceably disarmed by Soviet agitators, alerted to Kornilov's 'treason' by minister Nekrasov.

On 1 September Kerensky assembled a 'Directory' of two ministers and the two new service chiefs to oppose Kornilov; he himself became Supreme Commander-in-Chief. To quieten public tempers he also appointed a commission of enquiry into the 'Kornilov Affair'. This was intended to keep the whole subject *sub judice* and therefore out of the public domain. The commission's members refused to go along with a whitewash and leaked documents suggesting Kerensky's complicity in Kornilov's plans for a 'dictatorship'. This enabled Lenin to convince the industrial proletariat and Petrograd garrison of Kerensky's hostility and ensured the success of the Bolshevik OCTOBER REVOLUTION. On 25 October Kerensky left Petrograd by car to summon loyal troops from the Northern Front. His pathetic band of 'Kornilovite' COSSACKS was held by Bolshevik forces at Pulkovo, and Kerensky narrowly escaped capture by Bolshevik sailors under P. E. Dybenko at Gatchina Palace.

Kerensky remained 'underground' in Russia and Finland until May 1918, when he was sent by the PSR and the liberal-socialist 'Union of Regeneration' to London and Paris to canvass Allied intervention in favour of a democratic Russia. When Clemenceau and Churchill backed the reactionaries under KOLCHAK instead, Kerensky denounced intervention. He was active in efforts to assist the KRONSTADT REVOLT of 1921. Thereafter, he edited the Russian daily *Dni* (Days) in Berlin and Paris, condemning Communists and fascists alike. In 1927 he visited the United States on a speaking tour and, with the assistance of the *New York Times*, published the first version of his memoirs. In 1939–40 he urged the democracies to intervene against both Nazism and Communism simultaneously and sent Zenzinov to Finland, probably to urge the creation of an anti-Communist Russian Legion.

Kerensky himself remained in Paris, helping fellow Russians escape, until the eve of the German occupation in 1940 and was barely saved from capture by the presence of mind of his Australian second wife Nel, née Tritton. From 1940 Kerensky lived in the United States, though from 1949 to 1953 he frequently visited West Germany to canvass support among new émigrés (i.e. Displaced Persons) for US-sponsored anti-Soviet activities. Subsequently, Kerensky worked at the Hoover Institution, Stanford, California, on a collection of documents presenting the Provisional Government in a positive light. He wrote a final version of his memoirs before dying of cancer in New York in 1970, at the age of 89.   RA

Further Reading

Abraham, Richard: *Alexander Kerensky, the First Love of the Revolution*. New York: Columbia University Press, 1987.

Carmichael, Joel: Kerensky. In *The Russian Revolution: The CBS Legacy Collection*. New York: Macmillan, 1967.

Kerensky, A.F.: *The Catastrophe*. New York: Appleton, 1927.

— : *The Kerensky Memoirs: Russia and History's Turning Point*. New York: Duell, Sloan & Pearce, 1965.

Khatisian, Alexander (1876–1945)

Khatisian was born in Tiflis, son of a high-ranking tsarist official. After attending the Tiflis gymnasium, he studied medicine at Moscow University and in Germany. On his return to Tiflis he abandoned medicine in favour of a government career. In 1906 he became the Deputy Mayor in Tiflis and subsequently Mayor. He was also President of the Union of Caucasian Cities and a member of the self-appointed Armenian National Bureau formed in 1912. In February 1917 he was one of the 'troika' (with N. ZHORDANIA and D. Popov) appointed by the Tiflis SOVIET

to supervise the transfer of power. He joined the Dashnaktsutiun in 1917 and became a member of the Armenian National Congress. He was an Armenian representative at both the Trebizond and the Batumi peace negotiations with the Turks. In April 1918 he was made Minister of Finance in the Transcaucasian cabinet of Akaki Chkhenkeli and in June 1918 he became the Minister of Foreign Affairs in the first government of independent Armenia. He subsequently became the Minister of Interior and in February 1919 acting premier after the departure of prime minister Hovhannes Kachazuni to Europe to seek Western aid. In August 1919 he was appointed premier, a position he held until his cabinet was replaced by the Dashnaktsutiun Bureau in May 1920. He was chief negotiator at the Alexandropol conference with Turkey after the latter's invasion of Armenia in September 1920. He left for Paris after the sovietization of Armenia and died there in 1945.   SFJ

Khodzhaev, Faizullah (1896–1938)

Born in Bukhara into a wealthy Uzbek merchant family, Khodzhaev witnessed and later took part in the struggle of the jadid reformers against the inertia of the conservatives. Thus one jadid organization, the Union of Holy Bukhara, although limited in scope, was responsible for laying the foundation for the radical Young Bukharan Party. Khodzhaev joined the underground Central Committee of the Young Bukharan Party and was forced to flee to Tashkent together with other Young Bukharans whom the emir condemned to death for radical activities.

From early 1918 until late 1919 Khodzhaev represented the Young Bukharan Party in Moscow, returning to Tashkent to take part in the organization of the anti-emir uprising of the Young Bukharans. When on 2 September, 1920 the RED ARMY captured Bukhara, it brought to power a revolutionary committee (mostly Young Bukharans) headed by Khodzhaev. In the same month, the Young Bukharans decided to dismantle their party and join the Bukharan Communist Party (founded in 1918), of which Khodzhaev became a member and in the ensuing years supported Moscow's efforts to eliminate the BASMACHI resistance from Central Asia.

Between 1922 and 1924 Khodzhaev lived in Moscow where he was a member of the Central Asian Bureau of the Party Central Committee. He returned to Central Asia in 1924 and became chairman of the Council of Peoples' Commissars of Uzbekistan, a position he held until his arrest in 1937. He was tried in the show trial of the Trotskyite and Rightist Blok of 21, and executed on 13 March, 1938. A dedicated communist, after 1930 he increasingly emerged as an Uzbek nationalist who reacted not only against the perils of economic dependency, but also defended Uzbek cultural integrity.   A-AR

Khoiski, Fath Ali Khan (1876–1920)

A lawyer by profession, Khan Khoiski first entered Azerbaijani politics in 1905 and was elected to the second Duma in 1907 where he acted as a spokesman for the Union of Russian Muslims (Ittifaq), the official organization representing Russia's Muslims. In 1917 along with another lawyer, Ali Mardan bey Topchibashev, he led a small Independent Democratic Group. That same year he became a member of the Muslim National Council and was elected to the Muslim National Committee in July 1917. He was also chairman of the Baku city soviet and leader of the Musavat-Non Partisan bloc in the Transcaucasian Sejm. He was Minister of Justice in Akaki Chkhenkeli's Transcaucasian cabinet and was an Azerbaijani representative at the Batumi peace conference in May 1918.

Khan Khoiski became the first prime minister of the Republic of Azerbaijan on 28 May 1918. He also retained his post as Minister of Justice. His government welcomed the Turkish occupation of Muslim districts in Transcaucasia in June–July 1918 and when Baku was captured by the Turkish army in September 1918, transferred his government there on the invitation of the Turkish commander, Nuri Pasha.

In the Azerbaijani parliament he led the moderate National Democrats (seven deputies) and remained head of a centrist government until April 1919 when the illegal oil dealings of a member of his cabinet forced his resignation. He was replaced by N.B. Ussubekov, a Musavatist with leftist leanings, but continued to serve as Foreign Minister in the new cabinet. When the RED ARMY invaded Azerbaijan in 1920, he was arrested but soon released. He left for exile in Tiflis where he was assassinated that same year.

SFJ

Figure 54 Khoiski.

Kolchak, Admiral Alexander Vasilievich (1873–1920)

The senior White leader in eastern Russia and nominal head of the whole White movement from November 1918 to the end of 1919, Kolchak was a hero of the Japanese and German wars; after successful operations in the Baltic he was in August 1916 (at the age of 43) given command of the Black Sea Fleet. In the first months after February 1917 he held the fleet together but finally resigned in the face of growing democratization.

Kolchak was abroad on a government mission in October 1917. He spent twelve months in the Far East without employment, but travelled into Russia after the Trans-Siberian Railway was cleared. Because of his war record and seniority he was in early November 1918 made War Minister in the Omsk-based PROVISIONAL ALL-RUSSIAN GOVERNMENT. He was seen as a figure of conservative views and with good Allied connections, and when the right overthrew the PA-RG in November 1918 Kolchak became 'Supreme Ruler'.

Kolchak was an ineffective military commander; the young officers he chose as subordinates, Generals D. A. Lebedev, N. A. Stepanov, R. Gajda and K. V. Sakharov, produced neither victories nor effective armies. He devoted little attention to internal affairs, and was temperamentally unsuited to politics. He achieved little as ruler of SIBERIA, and as the nominal all-Russian leader he refused to make vital concessions to win over the western border nationalities. By the end of 1919 failure at the front was matched by the political bankruptcy of the *Kolchakovshchina* and by peasant uprisings. Faced with a decisive RED ARMY offensive Kolchak left Omsk in

November 1919. The Supreme Ruler, travelling east with his gold reserve, became separated from both the remains of his armies and his government. Czechoslovak troops handed Kolchak over to an anti-Kolchak government created at Irkutsk, and on 4 January he was executed.

EM

Kollontai, Alexandra Mikhailovna (1872–1952)

Probably more significant as a pioneer European feminist (the first woman to join a government and the first woman ambassador) than as a Russian revolutionary, Kollontai (née Domontovich) had a comfortable and privileged early life; her father, of liberal orientation, was a Tsarist general from an old Ukrainian family, and her mother was the daughter of a Finnish timber merchant. In 1893 she married Vladimir Kollontai (an engineer and a distant relative) and had a son Mikhail.

According to Kollontai 1896 was the decisive year of her life, when she visited a large textile factory: 'the enslavement of the 12,000 workers had a shattering effect on me'. Plunging into MARXISM, she left her husband and visited PLEKHANOV, Kautsky, Rosa LUXEMBURG and other prominent Marxists in Europe; particularly concerned with Finland, in 1903 she published a substantial Marxist analysis *The Life of Finnish Workers*.

Until 1915 Kollontai allied herself mostly with the MENSHEVIKS. Visiting or residing in many European countries, she was an energetic speaker and prolific writer, combining Marxism with concern for women, believing that the liberation of women was only possible with the achievement of a socialist society.

From the outbreak of war in 1914 until the FEBRUARY REVOLUTION, when she returned to Russia, Kollontai lived mostly in Scandinavia (making two long tours in the USA as a propagandist); soon expelled from Sweden, she settled in Norway. From 1915 she was associated with LENIN and the Bolsheviks, collaborating with Alexander SHLYAPNIKOV (who became her intimate friend) in the SCANDINAVIAN CONNECTION.

After the OCTOBER REVOLUTION Kollontai became Commissar for Social Welfare, and during the tumultuous years of CIVIL WAR in Russia was – alongside Lenin's close friend Inessa ARMAND – the most prominent woman Bolshevik, devoting herself particularly (in the male-dominated party and government) to the realization of her conviction that female emancipation was an integral part of the construction of communism. In 1919 the Section for Work among Women (Zhenotdel) was established, headed by Inessa, who however died the next year and was succeeded by Kollontai. During 1918–23 she was married to the Bolshevik sailor Pavel Dybenko (the first Commissar for the Navy, executed in 1938).

In 1921 Kollontai joined Shlyapnikov in criticizing Bolshevik bureaucracy, publishing an eloquent pamphlet 'The Workers' Opposition'. The defeat of this movement (see BOLSHEVIK OPPOSITION) effectively ended Kollontai's political career, though while being shunted into diplomacy she published several works of fiction poignantly depicting the exploitation of sensitive women by insensitive men. As a diplomat, she was for several years Soviet representative in Norway, briefly in Mexico, and from 1930 to 1945 Soviet ambassador in Sweden. She died in retirement in Moscow, the only surviving former oppositionist of distinction.

Kollontai's vision of social revolution in Russia being a female undertaking was a mirage. The Bolshevik government's policy, as distinct from its rhetoric, was from the outset opposed and, recently, Russian women proclaiming what Kollontai so vividly pioneered under the last Tsar have been persecuted in the Soviet Union. Elsewhere the growth of feminism in recent years has led to renewed interest in Kollontai's efforts to elucidate and resolve 'something that all women shared, this conflict between love and work'.

MHF

Figure 55   Kollontai, Russian envoy 'extraordinaire', 22 September 1936, Geneva.

333

Further Reading

Björkegren, Hans: *Ryska Posten*. Stockholm: Bonniers, 1985 (in Swedish).

Clements, Barbara Evans: *Bolshevik Feminist*. Bloomington and London: Indiana University Press, 1979.

Farnsworth, Beatrice: *Aleksandra Kollontai*. Stanford: Stanford University Press, 1980.

Futrell, Michael: *Northern Underground*. London: Faber, 1963.

Holt, Alix ed.: *Selected Writings*. London: Allison & Busby, 1977.

Schapiro, Leonard: *The Origin of the Communist Autocracy*. London: Bell, 1955.

Kornilov, General Lavr Georgievich (1870–1918)

Born in Ust-Kamenogorsk, which was then in SIBERIA, of a COSSACK father and allegedly, a Buryat mother, Kornilov graduated from the Mikhailovsky Artillery Training Corps, was commissioned in 1892 and posted to Turkestan. From 1895 to 1898, he studied at the General Staff Academy, St Petersburg. On his return to Central Asia he conducted undercover espionage in Iran and India, protected by his Asiatic appearance and gift for Asian languages. Decorated in the Russo-Japanese War, he served as military attaché in China from 1907 to 1911. During the first year of the FIRST WORLD WAR he commanded Infantry divisions on the Russian Western Front. In 1915 he was captured by Austrian forces in Galicia, but escaped in the following year to command the 25th Army Corps on the South-West Front.

In March 1917 A. I. Guchkov, minister of war in the PROVISIONAL GOVERNMENT, appointed Kornilov Commander-in-Chief of the Petrograd Garrison. Disillusioned by the refusal of the Provisional Government to authorize the use of force to restore order during the disturbance known as the 'April Days' (20–22 April 1917), Kornilov asked to be sent back to the Front. During the offensive in June he commanded the VIII Army on the South-West Front with only limited success. It was his conduct during the subsequent German counter-offensive that attracted public attention; he illegally shot 14 looters out of hand and displayed their bodies as a warning to others. Encouraged by Commissar B. V. SAVINKOV, Kornilov successfully urged the restoration of the death penalty and the suppression of meetings at the Front. On 18 July 1917, he was promoted Supreme Commander-in-Chief, making his acceptance conditional on being given a free hand by the Provisional Government. On 3 and 10 August Kornilov visited Petrograd to urge the Provisional Government to restore the death penalty in the rear, to militarize the factories and railroads and to reconstitute the cabinet. KERENSKY and his closest colleagues fobbed Kornilov off with vague assurances, while publicly warning against a coup d'état. Tension mounted as the political elite gathered in Moscow on 12 August for a State Conference. On this occasion the Allies vigorously discouraged Kornilov, in the hope that Kerensky himself could be induced to adopt Kornilov's programme. Savinkov, now deputy war minister, also encouraged Kornilov in these hopes. Kornilov anticipated that the BOLSHEVIKS, and perhaps other socialists, would resist his proposed measures. With Kerensky's approval, he drew up plans to post a Special Army in (or near) Petrograd. He also concocted a secret conspiracy to fake a 'Bolshevik Rising' in Petrograd as a pretext for vigorous action against the soviets. Relations between government and Supreme Commander were further complicated by the ham-fisted attempts at mediation undertaken by the conservative politician V. N. Lvov. On 27 August Lvov presented himself to Kerensky with what appeared to be an ultimatum from Kornilov instructing Kerensky and Savinkov to join Kornilov at GHQ in Mogilev in a directory. At this point Kerensky decided to denounce Kornilov and demand his resignation. When Kornilov refused to comply, he became a mutineer. His pathetic 'Appeal to the Russian People' went unanswered, while the reaction of the masses was so hostile that Kornilov's forces were peacefully disarmed. Kerensky then appointed the Shablovsky Commission of enquiry. When it began to leak details of Kerensky's previous dealings with Kornilov, Kerensky's reputation was destroyed and the path made clear for LENIN. Kornilov himself escaped from custody during the OCTOBER REVOLUTION to become one of the commanders of the 'White' VOLUNTEER ARMY in South Russia. On 13 April, 1918, he was killed in action at the siege of Ekaterinodar. RA

Further Reading

Abraham, Richard: *Alexander Kerensky: The First Love of the Revolution*. New York: Columbia University Press, 1987.

Katkov, George: *Russia 1917: The Kornilov Affair: Kerensky and the Break-up of the Russian Army*. London: Longmans, 1980.

Kerensky, A.F.: *The Prelude to Bolshevism: The Kornilov Rebellion*. London: Unwin, 1919.

Kornilov, General L.G.: Statement in the Papers of R.R. Raupakh. Columbia University Libraries, New York.

Savinkov, B.V.: *K delu Kornilova*. Paris: Union, 1919.

Velikaya Oktyabr'skaya Sotsialisticheskaya Revolyutsiya: revolyutsionnoe dvizhenie v Rossii v avguste 1917 goda: razgrom Kornilovskogo myatezha. Moscow: AN SSSR, 1959.

Korolenko, Vladimir Galaktionovich (1853–1921)

Belletrist and publicist, born in the Ukrainian city of Zhitomir into a gentry family, Korolenko was attracted to the revolutionary movement in the early 1870s. While a student in Moscow he intended to join the 'To the People' movement but was arrested in 1875 and exiled to Kronstadt for his involvement in a student protest. After his release from exile in 1877 he went to St Petersburg, there to resume his studies and begin a literary career.

In 1879 Korolenko was arrested for revolutionary activities and exiled to Vyatka (now Kirov), remaining in prison there until 1890. The following year, because he refused to swear allegiance to Alexander III, Korolenko was arrested once more and exiled to Yakutiya. Upon his return from Siberia he settled in Nizhni Novgorod (now Gorky) where he resumed his literary activity. In 1893 he took part in organizing the People's Right Party but escaped arrest when the Party was destroyed the following year.

In 1895 he was allowed to return to St Petersburg. In the capital he became a leading democratic publicist, contributing to, among other journals, the liberal Populist *Russkoe bogatstvo* (Russian Wealth), which he was later to edit. Following a move to Poltava in 1900, he joined the radical-liberal coalition that created the UNION OF LIBERATION. During the 1905 REVOLUTION, he took part in the formation of the All-Russian Union of Journalists and Writers.

In 1906 Korolenko cooperated briefly with the Party of SOCIALIST REVOLUTIONARIES and then supported the faction that formed the Popular Socialist Party. He subsequently considered himself a non-party socialist and confined his opposition to the government to literary protests. Korolenko took no direct part in the FEBRUARY REVOLUTION of 1917. At the time of the OCTOBER REVOLUTION, he refused to support the BOLSHEVIK seizure of power and remained an opponent of the new regime until his death in 1921. BTN

Kosovsky, Vladimir (1868–1941)

Born in Dvinsk, Kosovsky (Nahum Mendel Levinson) was expelled from the gymnasium in Kovno for his radical activities. In 1894 he became linked to Social Democratic circles in Vilna and soon emerged as one of the leaders of the budding Jewish Marxist movement there. As a writer and thinker, Kosovsky became an editor of the early Yiddish journals published by the Jewish BUND, as well as serving on its Central Committee. It was Kosovsky who defended the Bund against the criticisms of the Polish Socialist Party in the 1890s (see POLISH MARXISM) and was the chief polemicist for the Bund against the early attacks of *Iskra* in the years 1901–3 (see RUSSIAN SOCIAL DEMOCRATIC LABOUR PARTY). After spending some time in prison in the late 1890s, he worked in the Foreign Committee of the Bund from 1900 to 1905. He returned to Russia during 1905 and wrote extensively for the Bund's daily press in 1906 to 1907 and returned abroad in 1907. He was elected to the Central Committee at the Tenth Conference of the Bund in April 1917, although he was still abroad and refused the German offer to return to Russia. After spending a decade in Berlin, he rejoined the Bund in Warsaw in 1930 and managed to emigrate to the United States with the outbreak of the Second World War. In New York he wrote for the Bundist journal *Unzer Tsait* (Our Times) until his death. HJT

Krasin, Leonid Borisovich (1870–1926)

Born in Kurgan, Tobolsk province in Western Siberia, educated at St Petersburg Technological Institute and Kharkov University, Krasin studied MARXISM, and for spreading revolutionary propaganda was imprisoned and exiled at intervals from 1892 to 1898, when he joined the RSDRP. He built and operated an electric power station in Baku 1900–4, simultaneously designing and running a successful underground press printing SD literature. In 1903 he was co-opted *in absentia* into the BOLSHEVIK Central Committee. Leaving Baku he worked as an engineer at the Morozov textile mills and attended the Third Congress of the RSDRP in London, May 1905, where his seat on the Central Committee was confirmed by election. While laying the cable network for the electrification of St Petersburg, he also carried on intensive underground preparations for an armed uprising. Krasin was arrested in 1908; on release he spent five years in Berlin with Siemens-Schuckert AG who in 1913 appointed him manager of their Russian subsidiary. During the FIRST WORLD WAR Krasin was also chairman of a WAR INDUSTRIES COMMITTEE, director of a bank and a munitions factory; in this period he left the Bolshevik Party on the issue of 'defensism'. On rejoining the Party in 1918, he took part in the Brest-Litovsk peace talks and negotiated the Supplementary Treaties (i.e. economic terms) of the peace settlement with Germany. In 1919 he was a key organizer of the defence of Petrograd against Yudenich and signed a peace treaty with newly-independent Estonia. Sent on a mission to London in 1920, he negotiated the Anglo-Soviet Trade Agreement (March 1921), thereby gaining the first post-Versailles *de facto* recognition of the Soviet government by a victor power. A member of the Soviet delegation to the Genoa Conference and a signatory of the Rapallo Treaty with Germany (1922), Krasin also served as the first Soviet 'plenipotentiary representative', i.e. ambassador, to Britain until 1924, when he was transferred to Paris. In 1925, following the crisis in Anglo-Soviet relations caused by the forged 'ZINOVIEV letter', Krasin was re-appointed to head the Soviet mission in London where he died *en poste* in 1926. By temperament and training a pragmatic technocrat rather than a politician, his outstanding diplomatic skills were nevertheless instrumental in breaking the economic and political boycott of Soviet Russia by the major European powers. (See photograph on p. 336.) MVG

Kremer, Arkadi (1865–1935)

The father of the Jewish BUND, Kremer attended the Vilna Secondary School, St Petersburg Technological Institute and

Figure 56 Krasin, seated second from left; to right, front row, are Litvinov and Chicherin.

the Riga Polytechnic. Drawn early to the POLISH MARXIST party Proletariat, he was imprisoned for his radical activities, received a sentence of administrative exile and went to Vilna where he joined radical circles in 1890, soon emerging as a leading local Social Democrat and remaining for many years the driving force behind the movement to create the Bund. A major organizer of the First Congress of the RSDRP, he also served on its Central Committee during its brief existence until his arrest in 1898. While in prison he developed a system of cryptography and a coding machine which became widely used in the revolutionary underground. Following his release, he went abroad and worked with the Bund's Foreign Committee. He attended Bund conferences and congresses although he never made his mark as an orator. In 1905 Kremer participated in the St Petersburg SOVIET. Arrested in 1907, he ceased to be a party professional upon release in 1908, although he continued to serve the Bund in many ways. Kremer went to France in 1912 and worked as an engineer until 1921. He returned to Vilna, taught mathematics, and played an active role in Bundist activities until his death in 1935.

HJT

336

Kropotkin, Prince Peter Alexeevich (1842–1921)

Born into an old aristocratic family in Moscow and educated at an elite military school in St Petersburg, Kropotkin served in the army in the Far East, where he made pioneering explorations and became a POPULIST, resigning his commission in 1867. Well-known as a leading geographer, he became a socialist and in 1872 an ANARCHIST, and joined the revolutionary movement. He was a leading member of the Chaikovsky Circle, agitating among workers in St Petersburg and advocating an anarchist insurrection and social revolution. He was arrested in 1874, but escaped in 1876, and spent more than 40 years in Western Europe. He became the best-known propagandist in the international anarchist movement, adopting the new theory of anarchist communism based on the biological and sociological doctrine of mutual aid as a factor of evolution. He spoke at lectures and discussions, wrote articles in the anarchist and liberal press, and produced pamphlets and books.

Kropotkin always maintained a close interest in Russian

affairs, participated in several attempts to direct anarchist propaganda into Russia, and inspired the more moderate wing of the growing anarchist movement within Russia. He returned to Russia in 1917, but his influence was reduced by his support for the war effort and the PROVISIONAL GOVERNMENT, and he concentrated on encouraging the cooperative and federalist movements and on studying ethics. However, after the OCTOBER REVOLUTION he became the focus of attention as the voice of anarchist conscience, and he did what he could to oppose both the foreign intervention in the CIVIL WAR and the growing excesses of the new regime, both through private pressure and public protests. When he died his funeral was the occasion of the last open anarchist demonstration in Moscow, and his birthplace was converted into a museum which lasted until 1938. Kropotkin was and remains the most widely read anarchist writer, and his version of anarchist theory was the most influential contribution to the anarchist movement in Russia as elsewhere, though his direct participation was only slight.   NW

Krupskaya, Nadezhda Konstantinovna (1869–1939)

Although legally married to LENIN on 10 July 1898, she was usually known by her maiden name. Born in St Petersburg on 26 February 1869, the child of impecunious nobility, her father a military officer and secret radical, Krupskaya was from an early age drawn to the idea of social uplift. For a time she was a Tolstoyan, then Marxist. Through Social Democratic underground circles in St Petersburg she met Vladimir Ilyich Ulyanov (Lenin) in 1894. Both were arrested in 1895–6, and in Siberian exile Lenin proposed that she persuade the police to allow her to join him, claiming to be his fiancée. The authorities allowed this, providing that the couple marry at once, which they did. She then followed Lenin into emigration, moving with him from place to place in 1901–16. In this period she made an important contribution to the building of the BOLSHEVIK faction by serving as Lenin's main secretarial assistant. She also kept her lifelong interest in education and the movement for the emancipation of WOMEN.

Returning with Lenin from Switzerland in April 1917, the couple settled in Petrograd with the Elizarovs, Lenin's sister Anna and her husband. From this time until October their lives diverged to some extent, possibly because Krupskaya did not share Lenin's zeal for an early Bolshevik revolution. For a few weeks she tried working in the party Secretariat, but she was not given much to do. She then shifted her main attention to the reform of education, which was not immediately pertinent to the preparation of an armed insurrection. Much of this activity occurred in the duma of the Vyborg District of Petrograd, a newly-elected body formed under the aegis of the PROVISIONAL GOVERNMENT. In a somewhat more specifically socialist, but not narrowly Bolshevik, spirit, she also worked for the establishment of a Union of Working Youth of Russia.

The July Uprising began a period of about four months during which Lenin and Krupskaya lived apart. She was not with him on holiday in Finland when the crisis began, and she saw him only twice, briefly, before his departure from Petrograd. There she was present when cadets representing the government searched the Elizarovs' flat, taking Krupskaya into custody for a few hours. After Lenin had taken up residence in Helsinki Krupskaya came to visit him twice, carrying false identity papers and crossing the Finnish border on foot in a forest. There is no evidence, however, that this meeting or any letters that Lenin may have sent to her from his refuge were important political documents.

Lenin and Krupskaya were reunited, reconciling whatever political differences they had, soon after the OCTOBER REVOLUTION. They were once again sharing a domicile by the time the government moved to Moscow in March 1918, and Krupskaya was serving the Soviet government as Deputy People's Commissar of Enlightenment, specializing in education. She remained devoted to Lenin through the rest of his life and, as a widow, tried, with little success, to influence the management of the Lenin cult. She died on 27 February 1939, well into the STALIN era.   RHMcN

Further Reading

Krupskaya, N.K.: *Memories of Lenin*. New York: 1930.

McNeal, R.H.: *Bride of the Revolution. Krupskaya and Lenin*. Ann Arbor: University of Michigan Press, 1972.

Obichkin, G.D. et al.: *Nadezhda Konstantinovna Krupskaya. Biografiya*. Moscow: Politizdat, 1978.

Krylenko, Nikolai Vasilievich (1885–1938)

From his arrest in 1937 and execution, probably in Moscow's Lefortovo prison the following year, to the Khrushchev period, Krylenko was virtually written out of Soviet historiography. He was born in the village of Bekhteevo near Smolensk into the family of a former government official and political exile. Until he graduated from the faculty of history and philosophy of St Petersburg University in 1909 and subsequently from the law faculty of Kharkov University, little has been recorded of his education or early experiences.

Recruited into the RSDRP allegedly in 1904, Krylenko became a student activist in 1905–7 in both Moscow and St Petersburg and a member of the party's so-called 'military organization' in the capital, for which he was arrested and briefly exiled in Lublin in Russian Poland. From 1911 until his call-up for military service he contributed to and took part in editing the pro-BOLSHEVIK paper, *Zvezda* (The Star). In 1913 he re-entered civilian life with the rank of ensign of the reserve as befitted a serviceman with higher education and returned to St Petersburg as member of the editorial board of *Pravda* and instructor to the Bolshevik fraction of the fourth Duma.

Krylenko was sent to Kharkov in March 1914 whence he travelled to Bern, Switzerland, in the summer to participate in the conference of émigré Russian Social Democratic sections. On his return to Russia in the summer of 1915 he was re-arrested and in April 1916 drafted into the active army on the South-Sestern Front. Between February and March 1917 Krylenko was elected regimental, divisional and later XI army committee chairman and in May a delegate to then chairman of the first all-army congress. The following month he became a member of the central executive committee of the first congress of soviets and of the presidium of its Bolshevik fraction. LENIN also appointed him a member of the bureau of the all-Russian military organization of the Bolshevik central committee.

As a member of the Petrograd Military-Revolutionary Committee and representative for military and naval affairs, Krylenko joined the first Council of People's Commissars (Sovnarkom). On 9 November he was given the post of military commissar and commander-in-chief. In this role he is usually given the credit for seizing the Stavka, the command headquarters of what remained of the active army. In fact, control of the Stavka had been accomplished on 20 November, prior to Krylenko's arrival, by the Mogilev Military-Revolutionary Committee formed two days earlier. The former senior personnel of the Stavka had already fled. Though his forces were not to reach the Stavka in full until six days later and the acting commander, General Dukhonin, had been murdered (originally ordered removed 'without force'), Krylenko took over the high command insisting on the absolute authority of the Sovnarkom over all local revolutionary committees.

With the demobilization of the old army in March 1918 Krylenko played a key role in setting up the SOVIET LEGAL SYSTEM and in drafting the RSFSR (All-Russian Soviet Federative Socialist Republic) and later the USSR CONSTI-TUTIONS. As president of the supreme tribunal under the central executive committee of the congress of soviets and chief procurator of the RSFSR from 1922 to 1931, Krylenko prosecuted the major political trials of 1921–22 and the infamous Shakhty case of 1928 in which he demonstrated an almost unequalled capacity for arrogance and venom towards the victims. In 1931 Krylenko became Commissar for Justice of the RSRSR and of the USSR in 1936. Between 1928 and 1934 he took part in two Academy of Science expeditions to the Pamir mountains and also presided over the Soviet national chess organization.

Krylenko typified a particular section of the Old Bolsheviks by his relative intelligence, capacity for organiz-ational work, unquestioning loyalty to the party leadership, ambition and ruthlessness. Though the author of several treatises on the principles of Soviet law and procedure, he

resorted to torture and forcibly extracted confessions as the mainstay of his courtroom tactics. Executed in 1938, Krylenko, like others of his type, was destroyed by the inhuman methods he had promoted and by the very system he had helped to found.   MP

Kuskova, Ekaterina Dmitrievna (1869–1958)

Publicist and publisher (wife of S. N. PROKOPOVICH), Kuskova was born in the Ural provincial capital of Ufa. She was first exposed to revolutionary ideas as a youngster in Saratov during the 1880s. In the early 1890s she partici-pated in radical circles in Moscow, where she went to study midwifery. In 1893 she was arrested for her revolutionary associations and exiled to Nizhni Novgorod (now Gorky). The following year, after her release from exile, she left Russia for Europe.

Already a MARXIST before she left Russia in 1897, she joined the Berlin section of the UNION OF RUSSIAN SOCIAL DEMOCRATS ABROAD. There, as a proponent of Bernstein-ian Revisionism, she was identified with the so-called ECONOMIST faction. The next year, she withdrew from the Union Abroad and returned to Russia to settle in St

Figure 57 Kuskova.

Petersburg, where in 1899 she penned her famous 'Credo' criticizing the theory and practice of Russian Marxism. Following this, she left the RUSSIAN SOCIAL DEMOCRATIC movement.

A founding member of the Union of Liberation at the beginning of the twentieth century, Kuskova helped launch the paper *Nasha zhizn* (Our Life) to articulate its programme. In 1905, after a brief arrest for her association with Father Gapon, she took part in organizing the Union of Unions. She was one of the creators of the Constitutional Democratic Party and was elected to its Central Committee. She withdrew from the party almost immediately, however, and subsequently remained without party affiliation.

From 1906 to 1917 Kuskova was a major contributor to the oppositional press. She also published or edited several short-lived radical journals and papers, including *Bez zaglaviya* (Without a Title) and *Tovarishch* (Comrade). She was active in the cooperative moment and in the campaign for women's rights, and she played a prominent role in Russian POLITICAL FREEMASONRY, especially following her move to Moscow in 1910.

In 1917 Kuskova participated in the Democratic Conference and the Pre-Parliament, and was a candidate for the CONSTITUENT ASSEMBLY. An opponent of the BOLSHEVIK seizure of power, she became a leading figure among the democratic opposition. In 1921 she took part in the Public Committee for Famine Relief, was arrested for alleged anti-Soviet activities and expelled from the country. She remained in emigration until her death in Geneva in 1958. BTN

Lashevich, Mikhail Mikhailovich (1884–1928)

Born in Odessa and initiated into radical politics while at school, in 1901 Lashevich became a member of the Iskra tendency of the RSDRP and later joined the BOLSHEVIKS. Conscripted during the war and twice wounded, after February 1917 he was in the Petrograd SOVIET of Workers' and Soldiers' Deputies and later in the city's Revolutionary Military Soviet (MRC).

On 23 October 1917 Lashevich accompanied TROTSKY to the Peter-Paul Fortress, where they succeeded in convincing its anti-Bolshevik garrison to transfer allegiance to the RMC. Had they failed, the fortress (with artillery overlooking the Winter Palace and 100,000 rifles in the armoury) might have served as a formidable command point for further PROVISIONAL GOVERNMENT resistance. Then on the night of 25 October he was involved in planning the capture of the Winter Palace, as well as directing the seizure of the government bank, treasury, telegraph and post offices and the Pavlovsk Military Academy.

During the CIVIL WAR Lashevich was commander of the III and VII Armies, as well as those of the Eastern and Southern Fronts, and contributed to the defeat of KOLCHAK, DENIKIN and YUDENICH. From 1920 he served

in the Presidium of the Leningrad Executive Committee of the Soviet and went on to become a member of the MRC and commander of forces in SIBERIA. In August 1921 he was transferred to the MRC of the XV Army and saw action in Poland. He was twice decorated with the Order of the Red Banner.

'A good-natured, fat little fellow', Lashevich was undaunted by any problem set before him: if a solution could not be finessed, it could be forced. It was an attitude shared by many of the Bolshevik old guard in the early Soviet years of improvisation. Subsequently he supported the Leningrad Opposition and later the Joint Opposition. A member of the Central Committee since 1923, he was demoted to candidate member in 1925 and removed altogether in 1926. Later that year he was sent by CHICHERIN to HARBIN to act as chairman of the CHINESE EASTERN RAILWAY, a post cruelly combining political exile and delicate diplomacy. His task was to reinforce Soviet interests in a railway management crippled by heightened Chinese nationalism, Japanese rivalry and Russian 'émigré' hostility. With considerable tact Lashevich succeeded in temporarily restoring a veneer of order to the railway operation, but at great personal cost. In late August 1928 he committed suicide. FP

Latsis, Martyn Ianovich (1883–1938)

Prominent Chekist. A Latvian peasant by birth, schoolteacher by profession, Latsis (real name Sudrabs, Ian Fridrikhovich) joined the Latvian Social Democratic Party in 1905, engaging in revolutionary activity. In 1911 he changed his name to Latsis and left Riga for the Caucasus, moving to Moscow in 1913. Exiled to Siberia in 1916, he escaped to Petrograd; in 1917 he entered the BOLSHEVIK Party's Petrograd Committee, and in the OCTOBER REVOLUTION he headed the Bureau of Commissars of the Petrograd Soviet's Military Revolutionary Committee. A member of the People's Commissariat for Internal Affairs Collegium from mid November 1917 until 1919, initially directing its department of local government, Latsis also served in the VECHEKA Collegium from May 1918 to 1921. Whilst commanding the Eastern Front Cheka during July to November 1918, he made notorious pronouncements on waging war mercilessly, unrestrained by any rules of conduct, and on exterminating the bourgeoisie as a class, the fate of the accused persons being dictated by their social origin. During April to August 1919 he headed the Ukrainian Cheka, famed for its cruelty, and he thereafter directed the Vecheka's Secret-Operational Department. His two handbooks on Vecheka policy and practice were published in 1920 and 1921. He became chairman of the Salt Industry Board in 1921, and later held important appointments in the coalmining industry, in agriculture, etc., also working in the Communist Party's Central Committee apparatus. From 1932 he directed the

Plekhanov Institute. Arrested in 1937, Latsis was executed on 20 March 1938. He was posthumously rehabilitated.

GHL

Lavrov, Peter Lavrovich (1823–1900)

Leading theorist of POPULISM, Lavrov was an army officer of gentry origin whose reformist leanings brought him into contact with St Petersburg radical circles after 1855. Arrested in 1866 and banished to Vologda province, he wrote his influential *Historical Letters* which were really essays in social theory (first published 1868–9, in book form 1870). An émigré for the last thirty years of his life, Lavrov edited from 1873 to 1876 the periodical *Vpered!* (Forwards!), in which he preached a moderate tactical line; but in 1881, under the impact of Alexander II's assassination by terrorists of the People's Will group, he lent these methods his support. A similar vacillation characterized his philosophical views. He began as an advocate of 'subjectivist sociology', arguing that progress came about from the deliberate action of 'critically thinking individuals', i.e. intellectuals, who were morally obligated to promote it until all social institutions were based on truth and justice. Later, in part under Marxist influence, he came to allot a greater role to the supposed objective laws of social development; however, he never became a thorough-going historical determinist and his rationalistic secular progressivism rested on a suppressed ethical, indeed religious, impulse. Lavrov was a gentle, humane westernizer, widely respected on the Russian left.

JLHK

Further Reading

Lavrov, P.L.: *Historical Letters*, ed. J. Scanlan. Berkeley: 1967.
Pomper, P.: *Peter Lavrov and the Russian Revolutionary Movement*. Chicago: 1972.

Lazo, Sergei Georgievich (1892–1920)

A Moldavian of Swiss descent, Lazo played an important part in the initial spread of the Bolshevik Revolution into SIBERIA, through both party and military work. A former tsarist army officer, he joined the BOLSHEVIK Party in the latter half of 1917, having shifted rapidly across the SOCIALIST REVOLUTIONARY political spectrum and finally broken with it totally. His first major political test came in mid October 1917 at the First Congress of Soviets of Siberia, where his impassioned speech to delegates helped to shift sentiment to an immediate transfer of power to the Soviets. Under his leadership a force of Hungarian prisoners-of-war and regular troops took control of Krasnoyarsk soon after Petrograd had fallen to the Bolsheviks. His role then extended to furthering and consolidating Bolshevik military gains over a large area of Siberia, including the suppression of an attempted White coup at Irkutsk in December 1917 and the initial defeat of Ataman Semenov at Karimskaya. As political commissar (based at Irkutsk), Lazo took part in unsuccessful negotiations with Chinese officials in April 1918 at Matsiyevskaya (on the Manchurian border) in an attempt to isolate and eliminate Semenov's forces (which were by now based in Mongolia). Once the Bolsheviks had lost control of Siberia, Lazo went on to become a partisan leader. After the massacre of 600 Japanese by partisans at Nikolaevsk in March 1920, he was captured by Japanese forces in Vladivostok and handed over to White troops, who burnt him alive in a locomotive furnace. His exploits (and gruesome end) made Lazo a folk hero in the Soviet Far East, as well as a rallying point for Russian recruitment against Japanese militarism.

FP

Lebedev, Pavel Ivanovich (1881–1948)

Born the son of a petty official in Melenki, Vladimir province, Lebedev (known as Lebedev-Polyansky) was educated first in a religious seminary, and then studied medicine in the University of Dorpat (now Tartu). Exiled to Vladimir in 1904 for distribution of political propaganda he became a professional revolutionary. Imprisoned in 1905, he escaped in 1907 to Finland where he met LENIN and BOGDANOV. A critic of the sectarianism and authoritarianism of the Leninists, Lebedev-Polyansky in 1911 became secretary of the Geneva branch of the left-Bolshevik fraction Vpered (Forward). With LUNACHARSKY he edited the internationalist *Vpered* (1915–17) in Geneva and in May 1917 accompanied him in the second 'sealed train' from Zurich to Petrograd where they joined the MEZHRAYONKA. Lebedev-Polyansky became an editor (with MANUILSKY and URITSKY) of the group's newspaper, also named *Vpered* and played an organizing role during the 'July Days'. Arrested as a 'German spy' (see REVOLUTIONIERUNGSPOLITIK), he was released on payment of bail by workers of the 'Amchar' factory.

As head of the Literary Publishing Department at the Commissariat of Education (Narkompros) under Lunacharsky, Lebedev-Polyansky introduced the decree of 4 January 1918 'nationalizing' publication of the classics, the first Soviet measure of state intervention in literature. From 1917 to 1920 he was Chairman of the All-Union Council of PROLETKULT but resigned when the fierce political battle to retain its autonomy was lost to Narkompros and to the Communist Party in 1920. In November 1921 he became chairman of the Chief Directorate for Literature and Publishing (acronym Glavlit), a position which he held until 1930 and which gave him considerable influence over literary policy and in defining the literary heritage. A specialist on the democratic writers of the nineteenth century, and a strict 'realist', Lebedev-Polyansky had no time for the Futurists, the Imaginists or the Constructivists (see ART). Among the first to attach importance to Lenin's literary opinions, he also enlisted Bogdanov's theory of the 'organizing' function of literature in writings which made a significant contribution to the doctrine of 'socialist realism'. In addition to his position in Glavlit Lebedev-Polyansky was a Professor of the Communist Academy and of Moscow State University; director of the Institute of Literature of the Academy of Sciences of the USSR (1937) and the department of Literary Criticism of the publishing house Academia. Throughout his career he was an active editor of literary and cultural journals, the Literary Encyclopedia; the first Great Soviet Encyclopedia; the documentary series *Literaturnoe Nasledstvo* (Literary Heritage). In his last years he was awarded the Order of Lenin.   JB

Lebedeva, Ada (1870–1924)

Born in Irkutsk of a Polish father (who was in exile in Siberia) and a native Siberian mother, Lebedeva began her political career as a SOCIALIST REVOLUTIONARY, but in May 1917 split from the mainstream of the party to form an independent left-wing SR group (led by LAZO) at Krasnoyarsk. As her political stance became more radical between February and October 1917, she was increasingly drawn to the BOLSHEVIK line, which she formally adopted (breaking with the SRs completely and joining Bolshevik ranks with Lazo) soon after the SR Congress in Petrograd. Like ROSA LUXEMBURG, her diminutive physical stature was greatly outweighed by her oratorical power and energy as an agitator. Also like Luxemburg, Lebedeva showed a particular talent at translating complex ideas into the language of the politically primitive. As with many of the Siberian Bolshevik leaders, Lebedeva's period of revolutionary activity was intense and short-lived. In 1918 she was caught (near Krasnoyarsk) and hacked to death by COSSACKS.   FP

Lenin, Vladimir Ilyich (1870–1924)

First head of the Soviet government, founder of the Communist Party of the Soviet Union and the Communist International. Lenin (real name Ulyanov) was born on 23 April 1870 in the provincial town of Simbirsk (now Ulyanovsk) on the Volga. His father, Ilya Nikolaevich Ulyanov (1831–1886) was provincial schools inspector. His mother, Maria Alexandrovna Ulyanov (1835–1916) was the daughter of an army doctor of Jewish extraction called A. D. Blank. There were six children. The eldest was Anna (1864–1935), Vladimir's first official biographer; the second was Alexander (1866–1887) (see Alexander ULYANOV), a member of People's Will whose hanging for an attempt on the life of Alexander III had a dramatic effect on Lenin's political development; Vladimir was the third child and was followed by Olga (1871–91), Dmitri (1874–1943) and

Maria (1878–1937). All, except Olga who died young and Alexander who died for his own cause, became revolutionaries in Vladimir's service.

Influenced by POPULISM and his brother's execution, Vladimir was expelled from Kazan University in his first year for participating in a student demonstration, and he graduated in Law in 1891 as an external candidate at St Petersburg University. In Kazan and Samara he joined the revolutionary circles of Fokin and Bekaryukov, which were evolving from Populism to MARXISM, and in 1893 moved to St Petersburg where he practised law for a year (see 'Lenin as a lawyer' below) and joined S. I. RADCHENKO's group. His attacks on Populism and Legal Marxism earned him an early reputation as a formidable debater. He went abroad for the first time in 1895, partly for medical treatment, partly to establish contact with the LIBERATION OF LABOUR GROUP in Switzerland. On his return to St Petersburg he set up a group with MARTOV which, after their arrest in December 1895 and January 1896 respectively, became known as the St Petersburg UNION OF STRUGGLE FOR THE EMANCIPATION OF THE WORKING CLASS.

In 1894 Lenin met Nadezhda Konstantinovna KRUPSKAYA in St Petersburg, where she had been involved since 1891 in the first Marxist circle. Arrested in 1896 and sentenced to three years exile, she was permitted to join Lenin (who had been similarly sentenced) in Siberia where they were married in July 1898. During his exile in Siberia from February 1897 to February 1900 Lenin, who took his party name from the river Lena, wrote *The Development of Capitalism in Russia* as well as reviews for various journals. He also produced his first response to the formation of the RSDRP in 1898 and in 1900 adumbrated his ideas for a more effective kind of party organization. In early 1900 he went abroad to set these ideas in motion (see THE RUSSIAN SOCIAL DEMOCRATIC LABOUR PARTY).

By means of his *Iskra* (The Spark) newspaper and network of agents, Lenin had enough support by summer 1903 to convene the Second Party Congress which, he believed, would expel his critics and create a disciplined party of like-minded professional revolutionaries. In the event the Congress, *Iskra*, and Lenin and Martov were divided on a number of issues, but chiefly on organization, and a majority and minority ensued who became known as BOLSHEVIKS and MENSHEVIKS respectively. Lenin lost control of *Iskra*.

Following the Congress Lenin lost the support of Plekhanov, but rallied his strength and in January 1905 launched his own newspaper, *Vpered* (Forward). At the same time his persistent call for a purely Bolshevik 'Third' Party Congress alienated many supporters and even led to his expulsion from 'his own' Central Committee. Having returned to Russia in October 1905 he did not emerge as a national figure during the events of that year, and up to 1914 his biography is one of constant feuding, not least within his own faction (see BOLSHEVIK PARTY: 1905–April 1917).

The outbreak of the FIRST WORLD WAR found Lenin in Austrian Galicia, near the Russian border, and in close touch with his agents in St Petersburg where an upsurge in labour unrest since 1912 had aroused new hope of revolutionary activity. Instead, the workers in the belligerent countries greeted the declaration of war with patriotic enthusiasm. In the Duma only the Bolsheviks and Mensheviks opposed war credits, but in all other belligerent countries (except Serbia), the anti-war platform of the Second International crumbled as both leaders and rank and file voted to support the war effort and flocked to the colours. In Russia and in the Russian émigré colonies, especially in Paris, all brands of revolutionaries did likewise.

Arrested briefly in August 1914 by the Austrians as a Russian spy, Lenin was permitted with Krupskaya to leave for Zurich where they survived on remittances from his mother's dwindling estate in Russia. During this period Lenin analysed the causes of the war and published his findings as *Imperialism: The Highest Stage of Capitalism*. Contacts with Russia were practically impossible (see SHLYAPNIKOV) and assisted by ZINOVIEV he devoted his efforts to creating an anti-war, revolutionary wing in the Second International. Unlike the mainstream socialist movement which called for peace without annexations and reparations, Lenin's Left Zimmerwald movement – named after one of the two Swiss villages where it was launched in 1915, the other being Kienthal – called for the transformation of the imperialist war into civil war (see THE IDEA OF WORLD REVOLUTION). Also out of step with the majority of socialist opinion, Lenin regarded a defeat for Russia as a 'lesser evil' than a victory for Germany. The Zimmerwald Left attracted minuscule support. Efforts were made to distribute propaganda urging Allied troops to turn their rifles against their officers and start a socialist revolution, but this programme was unsuccessful until after the downfall of the tsar in March 1917.

Lenin, like everyone else, was taken by surprise when the tsar abdicated and a liberal PROVISIONAL GOVERNMENT took over. His fear that this event would not be fully exploited by the revolutionaries was confirmed when the SOVIET of Workers' and Soldiers' Deputies in Petrograd (as St Petersburg had been renamed in 1914) announced its support for the new government, as long as the latter conducted the war in a purely defensive manner. He became desperate to return to Russia when the two senior Bolsheviks in the captial, I. V. STALIN and V. M. MOLOTOV, having returned from Siberia in March, ratified this position.

The German Foreign Ministry, which had monitored Lenin's anti-war utterances expectantly (see REVOLUTIONIERUNGSPOLITIK), provided a special train and Lenin, with thirty-two others, travelled via Stockholm and Finland, arriving in Petrograd on 16 April 1917 (NS). He immediately declared publicly that the revolution was being betrayed by its leaders, and called on the Bolsheviks to begin preparing for a new revolution. They thought he was out of touch and that his speeches would isolate them. Lenin's perceptions, however, were based on his conviction that the war had provided both the cause and the opportunity for socialist revolution. His efforts were now to be shared between galvanizing the Bolsheviks into an insurrectionary state of mind, and organizing defeatist propaganda among the front-line troops and anti-government disorders among the Petrograd mobs.

As the Provisional Government went from crisis to crisis, and the cabinet coalitions shed parties from the right, Lenin heightened his call for increased militancy. He drew derision from the other socialist parties when he claimed in June that the Bolsheviks were the only party ready to govern alone. In July, however, mass demonstrations came close to a Bolshevik take-over, but Lenin was not sufficiently confident that the Provisional Government had lost the support of the army. The government now moved against the Bolsheviks, using as their weapon evidence of German financial support. A timely leak from the Ministry of Justice, however, allowed Lenin to escape to nearby Finland, where he was kept in hiding by the Helsinki chief of police, a Bolshevik.

While in hiding Lenin completed *State and Revolution*, which he had begun in 1915 in Switzerland and in which he developed his ideas on the nature of the state as it would evolve after the socialist revolution. In this he laid emphasis on the efficiency of modern capitalist administration, in which any worker would be capable of taking part. As exploitation and class and personal antagonisms diminished, so also would the law and order functions of the state. This work was not published until the middle of 1918, paradoxically at a time when the repressive role of the state, in the form of the VECHEKA, was unprecedented in its extent and degree.

Meanwhile the KORNILOV 'affair' had the effect of re-arming the Bolshevik Red Guards who, as the MILITARY-REVOLUTIONARY COMMITTEE (MRC) under TROTSKY (now chairman of the Petrograd Soviet), became the *de facto* armed force of the Soviet. KERENSKY having thus prepared his own political demise, it was plain to Lenin that nothing stood between the Bolsheviks and power, except the will to take it. At the end of September he returned in secret to Petrograd against the orders of his Central Committee, who feared premature action, and there, in his clean-shaven disguise, he urged the Bolshevik Central Committee to seize power 'before it was too late'.

Trotsky argued that the forthcoming Second Congress of Soviets be used as the occasion for declaring the seizure of power. The government's closure of *Pravda* and Trotsky's blatant challenge by using Red Guards to reopen it provided the setting, a blank shot from the cruiser *Avrora* at anchor opposite the Winter Palace provided the signal, and a token assault by Red Guards against the government's few remaining supporters, among them a battalion of WOMEN SOLDIERS, provided the action. On the night of 24/25 October (OS) (6/7 November, NS), the virtually bloodless OCTOBER REVOLUTION had taken place and Trotsky could announce to the Congress that the government had fallen and that power had now passed to the Soviets.

On 9 November (NS) Lenin became the Chairman of the Council of People's Commissars. His government's first acts were to nationalize the land, demobilize the army, establish the Vecheka, disperse the CONSTITUENT ASSEMBLY and launch the elimination of organized opposition. In February 1918, as the Germans renewed their advance, Lenin moved his government to the Kremlin in Moscow, and on 3 March concluded the Treaty of Brest-Litovsk.

In August 1918 Lenin was shot and wounded by the SR terrorist Fanny Kaplan but, though his health was permanently affected, by March 1919 he was able to open the First Congress of the Communist International (Comintern) in Moscow. The CIVIL WAR and Lenin's policy of WAR COMMUNISM created severe stress both in the country at large and among the Bolsheviks, leading to revolts and riots, strikes and demonstrations, as well as the formation of numerous BOLSHEVIK OPPOSITION platforms. By March 1921, faced with the uprising at KRONSTADT, Lenin was ready to reverse his revolutionary policy and to introduce a measure of free trade and small-scale manufacture by means of his New Economic Policy (NEP).

Lenin's health began to decline at the end of 1921, and it was decided he should seek rest at Gorki, just outside Moscow. While there, from January to February 1922, he continued to be actively involved in government business, as testified by the 200 or more letters, memoranda and telegrams extant from that period. In May 1922 Lenin suffered a stroke, and on 20 November 1922 he gave his last public speech. He was partially paralysed by a second stroke on 16 December 1922; four days later Lenin dictated his famous 'testament' assessing the party leaders, following it on 4 January 1923 with an attack on Stalin's personality and the harmful effects of his role as General Secretary. His last writings express his disillusionment with the heavy-handed bureaucracy created by the party. A third stroke in March deprived him of the power of speech, and on 21 January 1924 he died. His embalmed body was placed in a specially designed mausoleum, a rare example of surviving avant-garde architecture in Moscow on Red Square. Its removal to St Petersburg for reburial was expected in 1994, when the mausoleum was closed.

Lenin as a lawyer

Lenin's legal training and career as a practising advocate in Russia have been slighted by his biographers. His determination to become a lawyer was manifest as early as the eighth form in the Simbirsk gymnasium when he completed a questionnaire as to his future intentions and wrote: 'I want to enroll at the Law Faculty of Kazan University.' This came as a surprise to his teachers, who had encouraged him to pursue his gift for languages and mathematics and perhaps become a school teacher. The law evidently appealed to Lenin as one of the freer professions, and as his thoughts matured with respect to the autocratic government in Russia, law as a social science seemed to offer insight into Russian political and socio-economic forces and an opportunity to do something tangible in furtherance of revolutionary change. It was, in short, a deliberate and calculated choice of profession single-mindedly pursued from early youth.

In September 1887 Lenin enrolled as one of 264 students in the Law Faculty of Kazan University. He joined a secret student group, one of several in the University, and later in the year was expelled for his part in protests against the onerous regime imposed on students by the 1884 University Statute. A year's exile in the village of Kokushkino in the Kazan Province, under close observation, gave Lenin time to read Korkunov's lectures on the general history of law, Vladimirsky-Budanov's history of Russian law, CHERNYSHEVSKY, Nekrasov, and others. Returning to his parents' home in autumn 1888, Lenin accompanied them the following May to his mother's small estate at Alakaevka and spent the winters with them in Samara, preparing for the entrance examinations at St Petersburg University. Delays in the processing of his application and economic pressures forced him to seek permission to sit the examinations externally and the ministry of education finally authorized this in May 1890. During the spring and autumn 1891 Lenin sat examinations in eighteen subjects including the history of Roman law, the history of Russian law, political economy, statistics, encyclopedia of law, history of legal philosophy, dogma of Roman law, financial law, canon law, and public international law. Of 33 external candidates, eight passed of whom only Lenin was awarded a diploma with distinction.

A diploma in law from St Petersburg University carried with it the right to practise law in all the courts of Russia. In November 1891 Lenin returned to Samara, where in 1892 he became a member of the local Bar, initially as an associate of A. N. Khardin. There, notwithstanding some delay in securing the court certificate authorizing him to appear in 'all cases', during 1892–3 Lenin appeared as defence counsel and, occasionally, as prosecutor in a number of criminal and civil cases. In August 1893 he moved to the capital, immediately enrolling in the St Petersburg Bar under the sponsorship of a well-known radical Petersburg advocate, M. F. Volkenstein. Court archives of the period have disappeared, but substantial circumstantial evidence discloses that Lenin practised law actively in civil and criminal matters while in St Petersburg

343

(1893–6). Although this ceased with his arrest by the authorities for revolutionary activities, he remained a member of the St Petersburg Bar until 1899, when his name was dropped by reason of his 'unknown whereabouts' and failure to 'submit reports about his work'. In Siberian exile Lenin became an 'underground advocate', unofficially advising peasants, workers, and other exiles on a range of legal matters.

In the post-exile years Lenin had reason on several occasions to draw upon his legal background. Often, including his reader registration at the British Museum, he described himself as a 'doctor of laws', i.e. possessing a diploma in law from St Petersburg University. From time to time he advised party members on legal matters. After the October Revolution he devoted significant time to drafting or redrafting Soviet legislative acts, often introducing quite technical alterations as well as fundamental policy provisions; these are exhaustively documented in *Dekrety sovetskoi vlasti* (Soviet Decrees) (1957–) and accompanying index volume.

How Lenin's legal training may have influenced him as a revolutionary leader and State official remains to be thoroughly explored. There is every reason to suppose the law sharpened his analytical, drafting, and oratorical skills, gave him a more profound understanding of the socio-economic and political forces of his day, brought him into direct contact with both the day-to-day existence and the psychology of the peasantry and low-income urban folk and, as Lenin himself suggested, affected his perception of and approach to events, to people, to doubtful or ambiguous situations.　　　　　　　　　　　　　　　WEB

Further Reading

Katkov, G. and Shukman, H.: *Lenin's Path to Power*. London: Macdonald, 1971.

Lewin, M.: *Lenin's Last Struggle*. London: Faber & Faber, 1968.

Service, R.: *Lenin: A Political Life*, vol 1. London: Macmillan, 1985.

Shub, D.: *Lenin*. London: Penguin, 1966.

Shukman, H.: *Lenin and the Russian Revolution*. London: Longmans Green, 1977.

Sternik, I.B.: *Lenin – Yurist*. Tashkent: 1969.

Volkogonov, Dmitri: *Lenin: Life and Legacy*. London: 1994.

Liber, Mark (1880–1937)

Born in Vilna, Liber (real name Mikhal Goldman) was the son of a Hebrew poet, but was raised without any special Jewish education. He entered revolutionary activity early, probably influenced by his older brothers, Boris (best known by the pseudonym Gorev) and Leon (an underground organizer for *Iskra*, known as Akim), who were both already active in Social Democratic circles in Vilna and St Petersburg in the early 1890s. Although he always maintained strong ties with the Russian Marxist movement, he tied himself specifically to the BUND at the turn of the century.

Liber's talents and education brought him into the leadership of the Bund quite early. At the Bund's Fourth Congress in 1901 he emerged as a skilled speaker and defended the position proposed there that the Bund needed a plank for Jewish national as well as civil rights. At the Second Congress of the RSDRP in 1903 Liber came forth as the most frequent spokesman for the Bund (and third most frequent speaker of the Congress after LENIN and TROTSKY). He also strongly advocated introducing into the party programme the demand for cultural self-determination for nations, and it was Liber who delivered the notice of withdrawal when the Bund left the Congress.

During the 1905 REVOLUTION, Liber served as a major figure in the Bund, becoming a member of the central committee. He attended the Fourth and Fifth Congresses of the RSDRP and at the latter became the Bund's representative on the party central committee. After the 1905 Revolution he married and leaned more towards legal activities, while continuing to work for the Bund.

Following the FEBRUARY REVOLUTION, he worked as both Bundist and MENSHEVIK. Shortly after his arrival in Petrograd he became one of the Bund's representatives in the Executive Committee of the Petrograd SOVIET. In the Soviet he fought for a coalition government of socialists and liberals and he justified the existence of the PROVISIONAL GOVERNMENT. From that viewpoint he fought both BOLSHEVIKS and Internationalists. He also refused to take a ministerial position in the Provisional Government, although it may have been his Jewish background that played a part in his attitude here.

Following the Bolshevik seizure of power, Liber rejected the party position of seeking a unified government and resigned from the Menshevik central committee, maintaining that negotiations with the Bolsheviks would be fatal to the revolution. He held the same position at the Bund's Eighth Congress and, probably as a direct result, he was not elected to the central committee. He spent a considerable part of the CIVIL WAR in the UKRAINE, returning to Moscow in 1920.

Along with F. I. DAN and Abram GOTS, Liber was often linked to counter-revolution by the Bolsheviks during the Civil War period, their names often appearing bound together in combined form as 'Gotsliberdan'. That Liber subsequently fared as well as he did has been ascribed to his lifelong friendship with Felix DZERZHINSKY, then head of the VECHEKA, who had been married to Liber's sister until her death.

In 1922 Liber again returned to Menshevik work, now illegal, and suffered arrest and exile. In 1947 it was learned that, along with Gots, he had been put to death in 1937 on Stalin's orders.　　　　　　　　　　　　　　　HJT

Figure 58 Litvinov (extreme left), with Krasin (extreme right) and others, Geneva 1922.

Litvinov, Maxim Maximovich (1876–1951)

Born to a middle class Jewish family, Litvinov (real name Vallakh) left school at the age of seventeen to enlist in the army. There he gained a basic grounding both in soldiers' skills and socialist theory, and on his release in 1900 he began work as an RSDRP activist in Chernigov province and Kiev, where he was soon arrested. After eighteen months in captivity he escaped to Switzerland, where he became a member of *Iskra*'s editorial board and was later elected to administer the League of Russian Revolutionary Social Democrats Abroad.

Returning clandestinely to Russia in 1903, he was the Central Committee's plentipotentiary for the north-western region based in Riga, where he was involved in arms-smuggling (see SCANDINAVIAN CONNECTION). In 1905, together with KRASIN, he established *Novaya Zhizn* (New Life) in Petersburg, Russia's first legal SD newspaper. After a brief spell of journalism under the pseudonym 'Nits', he returned abroad in the general post-1905 exodus and spent the next ten years in London, combining a job as a clerk with a host of political activities. He was secretary of the London BOLSHEVIKS and played an active part in the work of the International Socialist Bureau. By 1917 he was threatened with arrest in virtually every country in Europe. After the OCTOBER REVOLUTION Litvinov represented the Soviet Government in Britain. Ten months later he was held by British authorities in retaliation for the Soviet detention of BRUCE LOCKHART and subsequently expelled.

Litvinov worked for Narkomindel and Rabkrin, acted as a roaming ambassador and headed early trade delegations. Through his efforts the exchange of prisoners of war was agreed, Britain was persuaded to end its economic blockade of the Soviet Union and the first Soviet trade agreements with Europe were signed. In 1921 he became the Deputy Commissar for Foreign Affairs and in 1930 formally replaced G. V. CHICHERIN as Commissar.

Of Jewish origin, and associated with the League of Nations 'collective security' policy, Litvinov was unsuitable as the Soviet partner to the Nazi-Soviet Pact of 1939 and he left office shortly before, being replaced by the Russian V. M. MOLOTOV. Although he was eventually reappointed Deputy Commissar (1941–6), a post held in part concurrently with an ambassadorship to the United States (1941–43), he had little further influence on the shaping of Soviet foreign policy.

His fierce, ambitious nature did not endear Litvinov to the Party, and as a result he hovered about the heights of Bolshevik politics without ever entering their inner sanctum (he was never a Politburo member). This distance from the party's core may explain why the purges ravaged Narkomindel but left Litvinov himself unscathed.   FP

Lobkov, Z. I. (1898–1919)

A prominent BOLSHEVIK agitator in Omsk, Lobkov, despite his youth – he was only 19 at the time of the OCTOBER REVOLUTION – developed a strong platform among the soldiers and workers of the city. From May 1917, he helped to create a proto-Red Guard (consisting of peasants and workers trained by returning soldiers) and by mid October had become chairman of the united Social-Democratic organization at Omsk. This, as in many other local SD organizations, was achieved by default, following a walk-out by MENSHEVIKS over the issue of representation at the CONSTITUENT ASSEMBLY. In May 1919 he was arrested in Chelyabinsk and tortured to death by KOLCHAK'S forces.   FP

Lockhart, (Sir) Robert Hamilton Bruce (1887–1970)

Diplomat and journalist, Lockhart served as Vice-Consul and Acting Consul-General in Moscow during 1912 to September 1917; in January 1918 he returned to Russia as Head of Special Mission accredited to the Soviet Government, with semi-diplomatic status as 'British Agent'. Initially strongly opposed to Allied intervention, Lockhart began advocating it in May (it started on 2 August); in July he helped the French to subsidize the National Centre clandestine organization, and the White Army in Southern Russia. In mid August, through an agent provocateur, he met Colonel Berzin, commander of a Latvian battalion guarding the Kremlin, who was acting on VECHEKA instructions; Lockhart introduced Berzin to Sidney REILLY, a British Intelligence agent who supplied Berzin with funds and plotted the overthrow of the Soviet regime by the supposedly disaffected Latvian troops – a scheme rejected by Lockhart. Following the unconnected attempt on LENIN's life on 30 August, Lockhart was arrested and detained until 2 October, when he left Moscow with British and French personnel, to be exchanged for captive Soviet officials. The public trial took place in Moscow, on 28 November–3 December 1918, of persons implicated in the 'Lockhart case' and the 'envoys' plot' through Berzin's disclosures and by independent evidence of espionage activity and sabotage intentions on the part of Allied representatives; Lockhart, Reilly, and others were sen-

tenced to be shot if apprehended. After a posting to Prague Lockhart resigned from the Foreign Office in 1922; he practised banking and journalism until 1937. Returning to the Foreign Office in 1939, he served during 1941–5 as Director-General of the Political Warfare Executive, with status as Deputy Under-Secretary of State. He wrote *Memoirs of a British Agent*, London, 1932.   GHL

Lunacharsky, Anatoli Vasilievich (1875–1933)

First Soviet People's Commissar for Popular Enlightenment (i.e. Minister of Education and the Arts); publicist, literary critic, playwright, Lunacharsky was born at Poltava in the Ukraine, son of a notary. He joined an illegal Marxist study-circle while still at school in Kiev, also developing an interest in the philosophical teaching known as Empirio-Criticism expounded by Mach and Avenarius, under whom he studied at Zurich University. There he met and formed a friendship with Rosa LUXEMBURG. In 1896 he returned to Russia, moving to Moscow where he joined a SOCIAL DEMOCRAT group, was arrested and sentenced to internal exile in the North Russian town of Kaluga, where he met A. A. BOGDANOV, who became his close friend and associate (and later his brother-in-law), giving Lunacharsky strong moral support in his unabated efforts to achieve a synthesis between Marxism and Empirio-Criticism, resulting in his first theoretical treatise, *An Essay in Positive Aesthetics*.

Following his release in 1902 Lunacharsky was invited by Bogdanov to co-edit a BOLSHEVIK journal in Switzerland. Lunacharsky first met LENIN in Paris in 1904, and despite his support for the Bolshevik faction, he was not uncritical of Lenin. In turn Lenin was equally sceptical of Lunacharsky's penchant for Avenarius, and of his latest preoccupation, 'God-seeking'. The latter was an attempt to find in Marxism a kind of man-made substitute for theistic religion, which would not merely be a critique of social and economic conditions combined with a blue-print for political action (as Lenin chiefly saw it), but would also satisfy the needs of the deeper layers of man's nature. Soon, in Geneva, Lunacharsky began working with Lenin in editing *Vpered* (Forward) and *Proletarii* (The Proletarian), Bolshevik publications for smuggling into Russia.

Returning to Russia when the 1905 REVOLUTION was virtually over, Lunacharsky joined Gorky in St Petersburg to co-edit *Novaya Zhizn* (New Life), the first overtly Bolshevik daily newspaper to appear in Russia under the liberalized press laws following October 1905.

When the Bolsheviks were later accused by the MENSHEVIKS of harbouring deviants from Marxism (in particular such 'God-seekers' and Empirio-Critics as Lunacharsky and Bogdanov), Lenin fiercely attacked the latter's views in his pamphlet *Materialism and Empirio-Criticism* (1909). This and other more practical disagreements provoked a breach with Lenin and Lunacharsky's temporary departure from the Bolshevik ranks.

In August 1914 Lunacharsky was in Paris, where with TROTSKY and MARTOV he co-edited the strongly internationalist, anti-war daily newspaper *Nashe Slovo* (Our Word). When the French authorities banned the paper and expelled Trotsky in 1915, Lunacharsky moved to Switzerland, where he remained until the FEBRUARY REVOLUTION allowed him to return to Russia. There he joined Trotsky's MEZHRAYONKA, which merged *en bloc* with the Bolsheviks in August 1917. Throughout that year Lunacharsky played a prominent role as a popular leader, revealing unsuspected militancy and compelling powers of crowd oratory second only to Trotsky's. So prominent was he, indeed, in the weeks immediately prior to the OCTOBER REVOLUTION – he had been elected Deputy Mayor of Petrograd – that when Lenin formed his first 'cabinet' or Council of People's Commissars (Sovnarkom), many were surprised to find Lunacharsky nominated to the comparatively second-rank post of Commissar for Enlightenment.

In fact the appointment was an inspired one. Despite his activity prior to October, Lunacharsky was by temperament 'not a militant politician', as Trotsky remarked, nor was he a good administrator; but Lenin knew his man: an intellectual of wide culture, creative, tolerant and open-minded, with the rare gifts of zeal for innovation combined

Figure 59 Lunacharsky (left) and Mayakovsky (right) leaving Narkompros, 1919.

with a love and respect for the cultural achievements of the past, which (in contrast to the iconoclastic, 'down-with-all-bourgeois-culture' attitudes of many 'leftist' Bolsheviks and SRs) largely coincided with Lenin's own rather conventional, schoolmasterly views on education and the arts.

In 1917–21 Lunacharsky and his colleagues in the Commissariat of Englightenment (acronym: Narkompros) struggled (with limited success in a period of CIVIL WAR, economic ruin, hunger and raging epidemics) to achieve the impossible: the total reform of education and the creation of a system for subsidizing and democratizing the arts. With the end of the Civil War and the inauguration of NEP (the New Economic Policy), the Narkompros was reorganized and began the process of imposing a unified educational system which abolished the divide between primary and secondary schooling and introduced an element of practical training in vocational skills. The urgent need to train technicians and administrators from the working class and peasantry led to the creation of so-called 'Workers' Faculties' (acronym: Rabfak), providing intensive, accelerated courses designed to propel gifted but hitherto under-educated adult students from elementary to diploma-level education in an average of two years. Perhaps the most significant long-term reform initiated under Lunacharsky was the massive campaign against adult illiteracy, known as Likbez (acronym of Likvidatsiya bezgramotnosti), which reduced illiteracy nationally from about 65 per cent in 1917 virtually to zero by the mid 1930s.

Under Lunacharsky's benevolent patronage, the 1920s were the years of an outburst of artistic creativity, in which conflicting theories and schools of literature and the visual and performing arts were enabled to flourish, a state of affairs that was to be drastically altered in the next two decades, during which STALIN dragooned writers, artists, musicians and film-makers into prescriptive, state-controlled conformity.

In the four years of intra-Party struggle for the party leadership after Lenin's death in 1924, Lunacharsky took no part. When Stalin emerged as the new leader, Lunacharsky did his best to ignore him, immersing himself in the work of Narkompros and in prolific writing on philosophy, the arts and literature, including some of his own original work as playwright and author of screenplays. From 1930 to 1932, together with LITVINOV, Lunacharsky represented the Soviet Union at the League of Nations in Geneva. In 1933 he was appointed Soviet ambassador to Spain, but died before he could take up the post.   MVG

Luxemburg, Rosa (1870–1919) and Jogiches, Leo (Jan Tyszka)

Rosa Luxemburg and her life-long comrade Leo Jogiches were one of the most remarkable political couples of modern history. Their 'folie à deux', the dream of leading

347

Figure 60   Workers' parade in honour of Rosa Luxemburg and Karl Liebknecht, Berlin.

the entire European socialist movement, came extraordinarily close to success. Their uncompromising internationalism and heroic martyrdom make them luminous figures in the history of socialism, while Luxemburg's letters are literary masterpieces. Rosa Luxemburg's polemics against LENIN, and Jogiches' attempts to assume the leadership of the RSDRP, had a considerable impact on Russian SOCIAL DEMOCRACY.

Jogiches, the son of a wealthy Vilna merchant, conducted MARXIST agitation among Jewish workers and Russian army officers at home before going into exile in Zurich. There he studied economics with Rosa Luxemburg, A. I. Helphand (see REVOLUTIONIERUNGSPOLITIK), Julian Marchlewski and Adolf Warszawski. In 1893 they founded the Social-Democracy of the Kingdom of Poland (SDKP) to combat the nationally-orientated Polish Socialist Party (PPS). Jogiches sent Rosa Luxemburg to Paris to edit their paper, *Sprawa Robotnicza* (Workers' Cause) and to canvass French socialist support.

In 1898 Luxemburg moved to Berlin where she rapidly assumed the leadership of the campaign within the German socialist party (SPD) against Eduard Berstein's 'Revisionist' ideas (see ECONOMISM). Her influence spread through the whole of Western Europe; she played a significant part in the amalgamation of the French socialists in the Section Française de l'Internationale Ouvrière. When, in 1905, the editors of the SPD central organ *Vorwärts* (Forward) betrayed their hostility to the Russian Revolution, August Bebel purged them, making Luxemburg *de facto* editor.

In 1906 Luxemburg joined Jogiches in Warsaw where they were soon arrested. Their experiences of the 1905 REVOLUTION drove them into an alliance with Lenin, and, despite Luxemburg's earlier criticisms of the RSDRP, the SDKPiL (its previous title, plus Lithuania) joined it at the 1906 Unification Congress in Stockholm. The balance between BOLSHEVIKS and MENSHEVIKS in the RSDRP was so close that for several years Jogiches became the arbiter of the Russian party. When Lenin finally broke with the Mensheviks in 1911, a bitter feud broke out between Jogiches and Luxemburg on one hand, and Lenin and his Polish protegés, such as Karl RADEK, on the other. Though their intimacy had ended in 1907, Luxemburg lent

348

her full weight to Jogiches' campaign, threatening Lenin with expulsion from the Socialist International.

In 1910 Rosa Luxemburg broke with her former ally Karl Kautsky when the latter refused to back her efforts to foster mass strikes in pursuit of parliamentary democracy in Germany. Marginalized by the SPD leaders, Luxemburg then joined Karl Liebknecht's campaign against Prussian militarism. After 1914 Luxemburg and Jogiches were forced to restrict themselves to German affairs, forming (with Liebknecht, Clara Zetkin etc.) the 'Spartacist League'. While in prison Luxemburg wrote her celebrated critique of Bolshevism, *The Russian Revolution*. On her release in November 1918 Luxemburg joined her comrades to form the Communist Party of Germany (KPD). Following the ill-fated 'Spartacist Rising' in January 1919, Rosa Luxemburg was murdered by soldiers of the SPD government; weeks later Jogiches was also murdered tracking down her killers.   RA

Further reading

Luxemburg, Rosa: *Gesammelte Werke*, 5 vols. Berlin: Dietz, 1970–5.

——— : *Gesammelte Briefe*, 5 vols. Berlin: Dietz, 1982–4.

Najdus, Walentyna: *SDKPiL a SDPRR, 1893–1918*, 2 vols. Wrocław: Polska Akademia Nauk, 1973–80.

Nettl, J.P.: *Rosa Luxemburg*, 2 vols. Oxford and London: Oxford University Press, 1966.

Pilch, Andrzej: Jogiches, Leon. In *Polski Słownik Biograficzny*, vol. 11. Wrocław: Polska Akademia Nauk, 1964–5.

Strobel, Georg W.: *Die Partei Rosa Luxemburgs, Lenin und die SPD*. Wiesbaden: Steiner, 1974.

Lvov, Prince Georgii Evgenyevich (1861–1925)

Born in Dresden on 21 October (3 November) 1861, a landowner and Constitutional Democrat, who initially came to prominence in the zemstvo movement (becoming the chairman of the All-Russian Union of Zemstva in 1915), Prince Lvov was, according to one contemporary commentator, as a politician a 'paragon of reasonableness'. Others, however, have depicted him as a windbag and 'a man without great depth', who used pompous and sanctimonious language. Nonetheless, under his leadership the zemstvo movement achieved considerable status, numbering nearly 8,000 agencies and wielding a budget of some 108 million roubles by 1916. Lvov used the movement to suggest a new political form for Russia, proposing at a zemstvo conference in the spring of 1915 that 'we must mobilize our forces, and all Russia must be welded into one military organization'; an image of strength that dovetailed with the creation, in the autumn of the same year, of a nationwide network of WAR INDUSTRY COMMITTEES. These suggestions of a clear path for Russia were supplemented by Lvov's warning that there was no longer a government in Russia (a view expressed at the December Zemstvo Congress in Moscow).

This was a political platform which Lvov employed with great success after February 1917. His rôle in the Union, and the ideological vision he propagated, brought him to the presidency of the PROVISIONAL GOVERNMENT in March 1917; a transition that was 'in itself eloquent testimony to the prestige possessed by the zemstvos in the esteem of the masses'. The make-up of the new government promised 'unlimited possibilities' for democratic reform and, for the liberals, suggested that Russia was, at last, standing side-by-side with the great democracies of Europe in their contest with Germany and its allies during the First World War. Indeed, Lvov and M. V. Chelnokov, at a meeting of the Progressive Bloc (see pp. 112–13) in Petrograd held in January 1917, expressed the opinion that Russia could not achieve final victory against Germany under the existing regime. Despite this feeling of hope, however, Prince Lvov's coalitions (which he headed from February to July 1917) brought nothing but disappointment.

Lvov's First Provisional Government, formed after the abdication of NICHOLAS II in March 1917, was mostly made up of men who were 'socially acceptable' and had no wish to overthrow the monarchy as the basic institution of government. His Second Provisional Government saw a greater representation of socialists, but nonetheless pursued relatively conventional policy lines (notably with the new government's insistence on continuing its full-scale commitment to its wartime allies; a stance that was deeply unpopular, and that led to the resignation of the other pre-eminent leader of the provisional governments, P. N. MILYUKOV). Despite maintaining an optimistic attitude, privately Lvov admitted that circumstances had carried his governments much farther than they had intended to go: 'we are tossed about like débris on a stormy sea', he once commented to General Kuropatkin. This view was reflected in the desperate attempts his governments made to find accommodation with the SOVIETS. As early as April 1917, Lvov approached N. S. Chkheidze, the President of the Petrograd Soviet, with the idea that representatives of the Soviets enter the Provisional Government. After the 'July Days' this search for a compromise form of authority was heightened by Lvov's fear of Lenin and his Bolsheviks. He considered that the Lenin 'front' was of far greater significance to Russia than the breaches made by the Germans on the south-western front.

Lvov resigned on 8 July 1917, replaced by A. F. KERENSKY. After the OCTOBER REVOLUTION he emigrated to France, where he headed an anti-Soviet émigré organization from 1918 to 1920. He died in Paris on 7 March 1925.   FP

Further Reading

Katkov, G.: *Russia 1917: The February Revolution*. London: Fontana, 1969.

Liebman, M.: *The Russian Revolution*. New York: Vintage, 1972.

Schapiro, L.: *The Russian Revolutions*. London: Pelican, 1966.

Lyadov, Martyn Nikolaevich (1872–1947)

Born the son of a Moscow merchant, Lyadov (real name Mandelshtam) was converted from POPULISM to MARXISM in 1893 and took part in the founding of the Moscow Workers' Union. After imprisonment and exile he was a delegate of the Saratov Committee to the Second Congress of the RSDRP at which he sided with LENIN. A founder member of the BOLSHEVIK fraction in Geneva in 1904, Lyadov served as as an agent of the Bureau of Committees of the Majority inside Russia. He was an executive member of the Moscow Committee of the RSDRP during the 1905 REVOLUTION.

A leading opponent in Moscow of participation in the Third Duma, Lyadov in December 1909 joined BOGDANOV's Vpered group of 'left-Bolsheviks', lecturing on party history at the Party schools on Capri and in Bologna. In 1911 he broke with Vpered, abandoned party work and moved to Baku to agitate among oil-workers while working in the industry and for the newspaper *Neftyanoe Delo* (Oil Affairs).

In February 1917 Lyadov was elected deputy chairman of the Baku SOVIET and an editor of its *Izvestiya*. His autobiography (1929) claims that he led Red Guard formations in Baku and organized the nationalization of the oil industry prior to the take-over of Baku by MENSHEVIKS and SRs, though a recent Soviet biography alleges that he joined the Mensheviks. Arrested by the Turks following their capture of Baku, Lyadov was transferred by them to Menshevik Georgia (see TRANSCAUCASIA) where he worked as a statistician. He joined the Communist Party on his return to Russia in 1920.

During the NEP years Lyadov worked in the management of the oil industry, and in the Soviet scientific and economic establishment. A critic of the various Left Oppositions, he was an important 'official of the superstructure' in his capacities as member of the councils of the Lenin Institute and of Istpart (Party History), and as Rector from 1923 to 1929 of the Sverdlov Communist University. In October 1928 his political career came to an end when he was dismissed as local head of Agitprop during Stalin's purge of the Moscow Party organization. Subsequently he worked in the Literary Department of the Society of Old Bolsheviks. His are among the most informative memoirs of the 1905 revolution. He survived the purges of the 1930s and it may be that the services which this one-time opponent of Lenin rendered to Stalin's rewriting of history enabled him to escape the fate of other

members of the 'Right Opposition' (see HISTORICAL INTERPRETATIONS OF THE REVOLUTION).   JB

Further Reading

Biggart, John: 'Anti-Leninist Bolshevism'; the Forward Group of the RSDRP. In *Canadian Slavonic Papers*. June, 1981.

Daniels, R.V.: *The Conscience of the Revolution: Communist Opposition in Soviet Russia*. Cambridge, Mass.: Harvard University Press, 1960.

Lyadov, M.N.: *Iz zhizni partii nakanune i v gody pervoi revolyutsii*. Moscow: 1926.

Machajski, Jan Wacław (1866–1926)

Born into a lower-middle-class family in Russian Poland, at school Machajski (also known as Vatslav Konstantinovich Makhaiski) became a Polish nationalist and at Warsaw University a revolutionary socialist. He got into trouble with the authorities in 1891 and became a Marxist agitator in 1892. He was soon arrested, imprisoned for three years, and banished to Siberia, escaping to Western Europe in 1903. During his exile he made his major contribution to revolutionary theory in a series of widely read essays, some of which were circulated in Siberia in 1898 and all of which were published in Geneva in 1904–5 as a book *Umstvennyi Rabochii* (The Intellectual Worker) under the pseudonym V. Volski. He argued that socialism was the ideology not of the industrial working class but of the intelligentsia, a new class of intellectual workers created by the development of capitalism; and that the revolutionary or parliamentary victory of socialism would lead not to the abolition of the class system, but to the creation of a new class system in which the owners of capital would be replaced by the administrators of industry, using their possession of education and expertise to exploit the labour power of the working class as before. He applied this critique not only to parliamentary socialists and revolutionary MARXISTS but also to the anarchist followers of KROPOTKIN, and his solution was a Workers' Conspiracy, a secret organization of genuine revolutionaries in the BAKUNIN tradition which would encourage direct action, leading to a general strike and proletarian revolution and the deliberate abolition of all class divisions. Makhaevism (*Makhaevshchina*) became an influential heresy on the Russian left, attracting dissident socialists and anarchists, and several organizations of his followers were formed during the 1905 upheaval, when he returned to Russia. In 1907 he produced a single issue of a paper called *Rabochii Zagovor* (Workers' Conspiracy), but in 1911 he was again arrested and forced to take refuge in Western Europe. In 1917 he returned to Russia again, and in 1918 he produced a single issue of a paper called *Rabochaya Revolyutsiya* (The Workers' Revolution). He accepted the BOLSHEVIK regime but argued for a much more profound 'Workers' Revolu-

Figure 61   The corpse of Machajski.

tion'. Meanwhile he earned his living as a technical journalist, and died before he could fall foul of the growing dictatorship.   NW

Makhno, Nestor Ivanovich (1889–1935)

Born into a peasant family near Hulyai-Pole in UKRAINE, Makhno (real name Mikhnenko) joined an ANARCHIST communist group when he was about 18, got into trouble with the authorities for violent activity in 1908, was sentenced to death in 1910 but reprieved because of his youth, and imprisoned in Moscow. In prison he contracted tuberculosis and formed a close personal and political friendship with ARSHINOV. When he was released in 1917 he returned to Ukraine and became a leading revolutionary agitator among the peasants and workers. When Ukraine was occupied by the Central Powers in 1918 he visited Moscow, meeting LENIN and KROPOTKIN. From July 1918 he commanded a revolutionary army based in south-eastern Ukraine, getting the title Batko (Father) in October 1918. He fought against the Austrians and Germans, the Ukrainian nationalists, the Whites, and both for and against the BOLSHEVIKS depending on circumstances. He played a leading part in the defeats of SKOROPADSKY and PETLIURA in 1918, of DENIKIN in 1919, and of WRANGEL in 1920, and in the establishment of a revolutionary regime over much of Ukraine at various times. The *Makhnovshchina* (Makhno regime) was based on his army, called the Revolutionary Insurgent Army of Ukraine, which specialized in the techniques of guerrilla warfare but also involved a profound social revolution, expressed by Councils and Congresses of peasants, workers and soldiers, and from 1919 articulated by educational and propagandist work dominated by anarchist intellectuals. From 1919 the Bolshevik regime put increasing pressure on Ukraine and by the end of 1920 destroyed Makhno's army and regime. In August 1921 he left Russian territory, and after periods of imprisonment in Romania, Poland and Danzig he settled in Paris. He supported Arshinov's Organizational Platform in 1926, but repudiated his return to the Bolsheviks in 1930, and he died in poverty and isolation. He wrote three volumes of his memoirs up to the end of 1918, which were published between 1929 and 1937. His partisan war and his

351

revolutionary regime may be seen as the most dramatic and (for a time) successful episode in the anarchist involvement in the Russian Revolution.   NW

Malinovsky, Roman Vatslavovich (1876–1918)

Russian trade unionist, member of the Bolshevik Central Committee, head of the party's group in the Fourth Duma, and tsarist police spy.

Malinovsky was born of Roman Catholic peasant parents in Russian Poland on 18 March 1876. After being orphaned at an early age he turned to petty crime before enlisting in the Izmailovsky Guards Regiment in 1902. Four years later he was back in St Petersburg working as a lathe operator in the Langenzipen Factory. He soon showed talent as a labour organizer and rapidly rose to be full-time secretary of the new Metalworkers Union. For the next three years he helped to recruit members, to edit the union newspaper, and participated in various Duma commissions and legal congresses made possible in the aftermath of the 1905 REVOLUTION. In November 1909, however, the police cracked down on the Metalworkers Union, arrested Malinovsky and expelled him from the Russian capital. The one-time trade union leader, now married with two children and unemployed, went to Moscow where he was arrested again in May 1910. This time he accepted a police deal whereby in return for his freedom and an initial salary of 100 rubles a month, he became an agent of the OKHRANA. (See also AGENTS PROVOCATEURS.)

The police were interested in Malinovsky developing his earlier ties with the RSDRP and particularly with its BOLSHEVIK faction. Using information he supplied in some fifty-seven reports on party pseudonyms (see Editorial Note), locations of party meetings and storage places for illegal literature, the police were able to curtail almost all meaningful Social Democratic activity in Moscow during 1910 and 1911. In January 1912 Malinovsky showed up without a valid mandate at the Sixth Party Conference which LENIN had called in Prague (see BOLSHEVIKS). The Bolshevik leader, who knew of Malinovsky's reputation as a trade unionist and was impressed by his forceful personality, immediately insisted that he be elected to the party's Central Committee and to the Russian Bureau. He also suggested that Malinovsky would be an excellent Bolshevik candidate for election to the Fourth Duma from the Moscow workers' curia.

Backed by both the police and the party, Malinovsky was duly elected in October 1912. To the surprise of many, the uneducated worker turned out to be an eloquent speaker from the Duma rostrum and a natural leader of the six Bolshevik deputies. He also used his immunity as a Duma deputy to raise funds for the party, to promote its publishing ventures in Moscow, and even to serve on its commission to seek out police spies in party ranks. At the same time he fulfilled police instructions to intensify

Figure 62 Malinovsky.

division within the Social Democratic Party and was instrumental in splitting its united DUMA FRACTION in November 1913. Six months later the Okhrana, uneasy about having infiltrated the nation's highest parliamentary body and unhappy about the agitational value of many of Malinovsky's militant speeches, ordered that he resign his seat. The resulting scandal and rumours about his true loyalties to the police greatly embarrassed the Bolsheviks. A tribunal appointed by Lenin came to the questionable conclusion that Malinovsky's 'political honesty' was not in doubt but removed him from all party positions and from the party itself for having deserted his post in the Duma.

During the FIRST WORLD WAR, Malinovsky fought in the Russian army until wounded and captured by the Germans in 1915. From his prisoner-of-war camp, he re-established contact with Lenin in Switzerland and assisted in spreading Bolshevik propaganda among his fellow prisoners. In October 1918, despite the uncovering of ample proof in Okhrana files concerning his pre-war treachery, Malinovsky voluntarily returned to Soviet Russia and was put on trial in the Kremlin on 5 November. No evidence was produced then or later to support recent allegations that he was a true double agent working in the first instance and with Lenin's prior knowledge for the Bolsheviks. To the contrary, Lenin, who attended the trial, did not come to his protegé's defence as he had in 1914 and then again during the war. For serving the Okhrana between 1910 and 1914 and for 'discrediting the revolution and its leaders', the Revolutionary Tribunal ordered that Malinovsky be executed.   RCE

Further Reading

Elwood, R.C.: *Roman Malinovsky: A Life Without a Cause.* Newtonville, Mass.: 1977.

Materialy revolyutsionnogo tribunala po delu provokatora Malinovskogo. In *Istoriya SSSR*, nos. 1–6, Moscow: 1991.

Manuilsky, Dmitri Zakharievich (1883–1959)

Born into a peasant family in Svyatets (now Manuilskoe) in the Ukrainian province of Volynia, in 1903 Manuilsky entered St Petersburg University, joined the RSDRP and was arrested in 1904. In 1906, with G. E. ZINOVIEV and G. A. ALEXINSKY, he took part in the KRONSTADT REVOLT in 1905. Arrested in 1906 and sentenced to five years confinement in Yakutsk, he escaped from prison and joined the RSDRP combat organization in Kiev.

In 1907 Manuilsky emigrated to Paris where in 1911 he completed his law studies at the Sorbonne. As secretary of the local Vpered group he stressed, with Alexinsky, the need for direct action against the autocracy and criticized the Geneva section of Vpered for espousing BOGDANOV's emphasis on education and CULTURAL REVOLUTION.

In 1914 Manuilsky joined ANTONOV-OVSEENKO in founding and editing the internationalist paper *Golos* (Voice), which became *Nashe Slovo* (Our Word). This resulted in a break with Alexinsky who claimed that *Golos* was being funded by the German agent Helphand (see REVOLUTIONIERUNGSPOLITIK). Active in seeking the unification of the anti-war factions of the RSDRP, Manuilsky returned to Russia in May 1917 and joined the MEZHRAYONKA.

In the spring of 1918 Manuilsky was sent with RAKOVSKY to negotiate with the nationalist Directory in UKRAINE. During 1919 he denounced the Bolshevik government in Ukraine as 'colonial' and following the temporary Soviet retreat in July 1919 he chaired the Gomel conference of dissident Ukrainian communists at which, however, he opposed 'federalism' and supported the majority demand for greater autonomy. When at the Eighth Conference of the RKP(b) in December 1919 Lenin introduced a more conciliatory policy, Manuilsky was brought into a new party-state leadership for Ukraine,

dominated by Rakovsky. Temporarily ousted in March 1920 by a Democratic Centralist majority under Sapronov, Manuilsky was reinstated and appointed First Secretary of the Ukrainian Communist Party from December 1921 to 1923. As an adherent of STALIN's concept of constitutional 'autonomy', he played a leading role in reimposing Moscow's hegemony.

Following the removal of BUKHARIN from IKKI, Manuilsky acquired a growing role, and he succeeded MOLOTOV as head of the Russian delegation in 1930 when the latter became chairman of Sovnarkom (see LENIN'S GOVERNMENT). In May 1933 Manuilsky launched the party purge in Ukraine, accusing Skrypnik and his associates of nationalist conspiracy. He led the Ukrainian delegation at the San Francisco Conference in 1945 and the Paris Peace Conference in 1946. He attended the first four sessions of the United Nations General Assembly and in 1948 became the Ukraine's permanent representative in the Security Council. In 1952, however, even this most loyal of Stalin's servants fell victim to his master's paranoia and he was divested of his UN posts. Spared deportation, Manuilsky contracted a serious illness in 1953 and lived in retirement until his death in 1959.   JB

Martov, Yuli Osipovich (1873–1923)

Born in Constantinople to a Russian Jewish middle class family, Martov (real name Tsederbaum) came to revolutionary activity by the POPULIST route.

Together with LENIN, Martov founded the Petersburg UNION OF STRUGGLE FOR THE EMANCIPATION OF THE WORKING CLASS in October 1895. In 1900 he, Lenin and A. N. Potresov together founded the revolutionary Marxist *Iskra* (The Spark) journal and group to crusade against so-called ECONOMISM and Revisionism and to battle for the unification of Russian social democracy under *Iskra* leadership (see SOCIAL DEMOCRACY) .

Martov's close personal and political friendship with Lenin broke at the Second Congress of the RSDRP in August 1903, when Martov turned against Lenin's concept of an elitist party of professional revolutionaries imbued with what Martov termed a 'state of siege' mentality. Then, and thereafter, Martov was to try to thwart Lenin's bid for personal domination of the party.

Leader of the MENSHEVIK wing of the RSDRP and, from November 1903, editor of the (now Menshevik) *Iskra* until its closure in October 1905, Martov restated Menshevik revolutionary strategy in the 1905 debate on power with Lenin, A. I. Helphand (see PERMANENT REVOLUTION) and L. D. TROTSKY. Upholding Plekhanov's concept of bourgeois revolution and its operational complement of socialist abstention from power, Martov assigned to Russian social democrats the role of militant opposition to a post-revolutionary bourgeois government. Entrenched in a 'network of organs of revolutionary self-government' such as trade unions, cooperatives, municipal and village councils and workers' SOVIETS, the socialist opposition would confront and harass the bourgeois government in an attempt to force it – despite itself – to implement 'democratic' policies, until economic and social conditions for a socialist takeover should have ripened.

During the years of STOLYPIN reaction Martov lived in exile abroad, mainly in Paris, editing the central Menshevik journal *Golos sotsial-demokrata* (Voice of the Social Democrat) and the monumental Menshevik study of modern Russian society and politics, *Obshchestvennoe dvizhenie v Rossii v nachale XX-go veka* (The social movement in Russia at the beginning of the twentieth century). He led the Menshevik faction centred around the *Golos sotsial-demokrata* which, in the post-1905 semi-constitutional conditions of Russia, sought to combine legal and underground activities and, despite its misgivings, sought unity with the Bolsheviks.

During the FIRST WORLD WAR Martov, together with N. V. ANTONOV-OVSEENKO, and later with Trotsky, edited the major Russian anti-war or 'internationalist' newspaper, *Golos* (Voice) (later *Nashe Slovo* (Our Word)) and was a co-founder of the Zimmerwald movement. Together with Robert Grimm, the secretary of the International Socialist Committee, he thwarted Lenin's attempts at Zimmerwald (1915) and Kienthal (1916) to turn the socialist peace movement, which was working for the regeneration of the Socialist International, into a Bolshevik-dominated organization pledged to revolutionary civil war and the destruction of the Socialist International.

Returning to Russia in revolution on 10 May 1917 (OS), Martov was too late to prevent the Mensheviks from joining the coalition government formed on 6 May. Henceforth, as leader of the small faction of Menshevik-Internationalists, he strongly opposed the 'defensist' and 'coalitionist' policies of I. G. TSERETELI, N. S. Chkheidze and F. I. DAN, who controlled the Menshevik party and (together with their SR allies) the soviets. He also fiercely denounced the offensive launched on 18 June, calling instead for general peace negotiations, or, should the Allies reject Russia's demand for a negotiated peace and should the Germans attack, for a 'separate war'.

It was only as late as 3 July that he began to advocate the establishment of a largely socialist popular-front type of government to replace the coalition government of 'organized collective inaction'. But to no avail. Neither at the Menshevik (Unification) Congress late in August, where no more than one third of the delegates supported him, nor at the Democratic Conference in mid September, where he had been elected as spokesman of both the Menshevik and the soviet sections, did he succeed in persuading a majority to end coalition with the bourgeoisie.

After the Bolshevik seizure of power, and having failed to negotiate the creation of a broad socialist coalition

government ranging from the Popular Socialists to the Bolsheviks, Martov became the fearless leader of a small but vociferous Menshevik opposition party.

Following the utter failure of all Martov's attempts to mediate between the Bolsheviks and the SRs, he desperately tried to find a place for a semi-implacable, semi-loyal Menshevik opposition party in the Soviet system by shaming the Bolsheviks into respect for their own Soviet CONSTITUTION. Fearlessly, he denounced the terror, whether it was directed against 'bourgeois' newspapers, the Kadets, the Romanov family, the Metropolitan Venyamin or the SRs, and thus he became 'the revolution's true voice of conscience' (M. Ferro). Yet he loyally supported the Soviet state against White restoration and foreign intervention.

At the end of 1920 when all his valiant efforts to 'straighten out' the revolution had failed, and his hitherto semi-legal party was driven into exile or underground, Martov went abroad (Lenin was glad to see him go). However his activity continued and he mobilized European socialist opinion against the Bolshevik terror, led the Mensheviks in exile and edited the *Sotsialisticheskii vestnik* (Socialist Messenger) which, thanks to his massive and incomparable contributions, received a literary and political headstart which lodged it firmly on the left-wing of European social democracy. Co-founder of the Vienna Two-and-a-Half International, he tried to stem the Bolshevik tide and block G. E. ZINOVIEV's and the Comintern's bid for a takeover of the German Independents (USDP) and the other left-wing socialist parties.

Having all along dissociated himself and the Mensheviks from the crusading anti-Communism of much of the Russian EMIGRATION and refused, in debate with P. B. AXELROD and Karl Kautsky, to write off the Bolshevik regime as simple counter-revolution, Martov in the last months of his life – having watched the suppression of the KRONSTADT REVOLT and the systematic institutionalization of the Bolshevik minority dictatorship – began to revise his position. His nightmare now was a 'counter revolutionary . . . Caesarist, Bonapartist completion of the Red dictatorship' that he feared would come from that 'military and bureaucratic apparatus' which the Bolsheviks themselves had created. Even so, he still opposed all forms of revolutionary or military activity against the Bolshevik regime, believing they would be bound to serve right-wing counter-revolution.

A beloved figure of Russian and European socialism and internationalism – even the Bolsheviks' *Pravda* and *Izvestiya* and A. V. LUNACHARSKY mourned in him their 'most sincere and selfless opponent' – Martov personified the perennial dilemma of revolutionary socialists with deep humanitarian commitments confronting the amoral authoritarianism of Lenin and the Soviet state. He died in Schomberg, Germany, in 1923.   IG

Further Reading

Aronson, G. et al. eds.: *Martov i ego blizkie*. New York: 1959.

Getzler, I.: *Martov, Political Biography of a Russian Social Democrat*. Cambridge and Melbourne: 1967.

Lunacharsky, A.: *Revolutionary Silhouettes*. London: 1967.

Martov, Yu. O.: *Zapiski sotsial-demokrata*. Berlin: 1922.

Maximov, Grigori Petrovich (1893–1950)

Of peasant background, and educated at an Orthodox seminary and then at the St Petersburg Agricultural Academy, Maximov became an ANARCHIST before military service during the FIRST WORLD WAR, and took part in the FEBRUARY REVOLUTION. He became a leading figure in the anarcho-syndicalist organization first in Petrograd and then in Moscow, maintaining a strong syndicalist position within the anarchist movement and a strong libertarian opposition to the BOLSHEVIK regime. After frequent arrests and deportation from Russia in 1922, he became active among the exiles first in Germany and then in the United States, producing a documentary account of the persecution of revolutionaries in Russia, *The Guillotine at Work* (1940), and a series of arguments for a 'Constructive Anarchism' to combine anarcho-syndicalism and anarchist communism, collected in *Constructive Anarchism* (1952). When he died in the United States, Russian anarchism had in effect returned to its roots in a synthesis of the ideas of BAKUNIN and KROPOTKIN.   NW

Medem, Vladimir (1879–1923)

Unique among the Jewish BUND leaders by background in that he was a baptized Christian, Vladimir Medem was the son of an assimilated Jewish doctor who converted to Lutheranism. He grew up in Minsk on the fringe of Jewish life, and attended gymnasium in Minsk and the University of Kiev, where he was drawn into radical circles. Expelled for his activities, he returned to Minsk where he joined the radical circles in the late nineties. Gradually, Medem identified himself as a Jew and entered the world of the Bund. In the early years of the century he devoted himself to the study of the national question, becoming one of the Bund's experts on the subject. He formulated the position of 'neutralism', arguing that Social Democracy should be neither for nor against nationalities, which should be left to decide their own future. He attended the Second Congress of the RSDRP, where he was prominent as a speaker in the Bund's defence, and thereafter he was regarded as a major figure in the party, also serving as an editor for various publications. In 1906 he became a member of the Central Committee and remained on it, when possible, until 1917. During the years 1908–13 he lived abroad and wrote for Bundist and other publications, including *Vestnik Evropy* (European Messenger), *Die Neue Zeit* (New Times), and *Den* (Day). He was in Poland during the FIRST WORLD WAR. Heavily committed to Yiddish culture by that time, he worked for the achievement of national cultural autonomy. Opposed to the BOLSHEVIKS, he stayed in Warsaw from 1918 to 1921, when he emigrated to the United States. In the United States he worked for the Yiddish daily in New York, *Forverts* (Forward). Ill health plagued him most of his life and he died in New York in 1923.   HJT

Menzhinsky, Vyacheslav Rudolfovich (1874–1934)

Born in St Petersburg into a russified Polish intelligentsia family, Menzhinsky graduated in law at St Petersburg University. Aesthete, dilettante poet and painter, he excelled as a linguist. A revolutionary since 1895, he joined the RSDRP in 1902, belonging to its BOLSHEVIK wing from 1903. Active in the 1905 REVOLUTION, and briefly imprisoned in 1906, he lived during 1907–17 as an émigré in Western Europe, often opposed to LENIN; until 1911 he adhered to the Bolshevik Party's dissenting Vpered group.

Figure 63   Menzhinsky.

After participation in the OCTOBER REVOLUTION he functioned as People's Commissar for Finance (also sitting on the VECHEKA Collegium) until March 1918, and as Soviet Consul-General in Berlin from April to November 1918. During January to August 1919 he held government posts in the Ukraine, including membership of the Ukrainian Cheka's Collegium. In September 1919 he rejoined the Vecheka, serving in its Special Department, responsible for RED ARMY security, heading it from July 1920, when he entered the Vecheka Collegium. In February 1922 the Vecheka became the GPU, and in 1923, the OGPU. In September 1923 Menzhinsky was appointed OGPU deputy chairman, and succeeded the deceased DZERZHINSKY as chairman in July 1926. During Menzhinsky's term in office, the OGPU implemented the ruthless collectivization of agriculture, and extended the system of concentration camp forced labour. Due to chronic ill health, he increasingly delegated control of the OGPU to his deputy, Yagoda; he died in May 1934. At the Fifteenth (1927) and Sixteenth (1930) but not the Seventeenth (early 1934) Party Congresses Menzhinsky was elected to the Party's Central Committee. GHL

Merjani, Shihabeddin (1818–1899)

A religious reformer above all, but also a historian and a teacher, Merjani studied at the medreses of Bukhara and investigated the manuscripts and rare materials at the Samarkand library (1838–1849). During this time his critical approach to all established truth first revealed itself. The publication in 1865 of his essay on the history of the Uighurs brought him membership of the St Petersburg Archaeological Society where he presented papers on the history of the VOLGA TATARS.

In 1886 and 1887 Merjani travelled to the Middle East where he most likely became acquainted with reformist ideas. Shortly after his return to Kazan in 1887 he was appointed language teacher at the Russo-Tatar Teachers' School. His contact with the Russian teachers at this school, as well as with the professors at Kazan University, allowed him to compare the reform prospects in two different societies, Islamic and Russian, and contributed to his critical assessment of Tatar needs.

Merjani wrote some 24 works on various issues. All were written in Arabic, with the exception of one work which was a first attempt to present the Volga Tatars with their history, written in their language. The core of his writings is contained in his religious writings where he promoted individual interpretation of the dogma.

The key to Merjani's reformist thinking was his belief that the main source of Islamic revival would spring from a return to the purity of pristine Islam, though he also advocated that medreses be purged of books on conservative scholastic philosophy which, he believed, had caused the stagnation in Muslim science and education. Emphasiz-

ing scientific knowledge for the advancement of a society, Merjani stressed the importance of learning Russian, for Russian science then offered the Tatars the shortest bridge to reach the world of modern science. With Merjani, reformist thinking moved one considerable step ahead, due largely to the impact which his re-evaluation of Islam as a religion and culture had on the evolution of Tatar life.

A-AR

Mikhailovsky, Nikolai Konstantinovich (1842–1904)

POPULIST philosopher and sociologist, Mikhailovsky took a minor part in radical agitation while a student in St Petersburg in the early 1860s, but thereafter settled down to serious journalistic work. He was associated chiefly with two 'solid' periodicals: from 1869 to 1884, *Otechestvennye zapiski* (Notes of the Fatherland) and from 1892 *Russkoye bogatstvo* (Russian Wealth). Though no revolutionary activist, Mikhailovsky flirted briefly with terrorism after 1879 and in 1881 interceded in vain with Alexander III to spare the arrested leaders of the People's Will party.

Under the influence primarily of Proudhon, Spencer and Comte, Mikhailovsky developed in 1869–70 a theory of progress according to which mankind, in the last of three historical stages, would overcome the fragmentation of human nature induced by capitalism, with its allegedly pernicious division of labour, and create a better society based on cooperation and solidarity, in which the individual's interests would nevertheless be safeguarded and harmonized with those of the collective. He saw such harmony as present embryonically in the PEASANT COMMUNE (*obshchina*) and *artel*, which like HERZEN he was prone to idealize; he was sceptical of the advantages of large-scale industrialism, although he did allow for continuing scientific-technical development. Later he explained that his scheme should be regarded as a metaphorical exercise rather than a scientific blueprint; and he criticized Marxian 'scientific socialism' as excessively deterministic, and therefore a potential threat to the integrity of the individual whose well-being should be the criterion against which all progress should be measured. Mikhailovsky's socialism was pre-eminently ethical; and for ths approach he was excoriated in the mid 1890s by Marxists such as P. B. STRUVE and, more particularly, V. I. LENIN; for the latter morality was necessarily relative and class-specific, and the idea of a 'special path' for Russia, by-passing industrial capitalism, was ruled out by 'objective' factors. As the century closed Mikhailovsky seemed to have been worsted in the debate, but with V. M. CHERNOV Populist sociology would undergo a revival. JLHK

Further Reading

Billington, J.H.: *Mikhailovsky and Russian Populism*. London: 1958.

Milyukov, Paul Nikolaevich (1859–1943)

Historian and liberal leader, Milyukov was a man of remarkable intellect and organizational ability. He was born in Moscow and attended its university where he specialized in history. At the university he became embroiled in the radical student movement yet managed to attend to his studies, displaying such ability that he was to stay on there as a teacher. During his ten years at the university he made several major contributions to Russian historical writing, notably his *Studies in the History of Russian Culture.*

As punishment for sharing his hostile feelings toward the regime with his students Milyukov was dismissed from the university and banished from the city. There followed what he called his ten years of wandering: two years in exile in Ryazan, followed by eight years abroad, which were punctuated by a brief return to Russia where he was twice arrested. During his foreign stay this remarkably energetic man lectured, taught, carried on scholarly research, and took part in the foreign activities of the liberal movement.

Milyukov was lecturing, in English, at the University of Chicago when he learned of 'Bloody Sunday' (January 1905) and decided to return home. By this time he was convinced that the tsarist regime was beyond redemption and that his country was ready for democracy. Soon after his return to Russia, he became the leading figure in the Union of Liberation and through it helped create the Union of Unions and was chosen to be its chairman. Because of his activities in this post he was arrested and spent a month in prison, using the time to catch up on his reading.

On his release he helped prepare for the founding congress of the Constitutional Democratic Party, in which he was to be the dominant figure. The congress was in session when word arrived of the October Manifesto. Like most of his colleagues he found the document unacceptable and determined to continue the struggle for a CONSTITUENT ASSEMBLY in alliance with the revolutionaries, a decision for which he was later to be criticized by more moderate colleagues. By 1907 he was forced to admit that the regime was not about to collapse and decided to use the legal weapons that were available in the fight for a democratic Russia.

Milyukov served in the third and fourth Dumas, in which he acted as the chief of his party's contingent, continuing to be a stern critic of the government. When the First World War broke out, he joined those who believed Russia's cause was just and that political differences with the regime should temporarily be laid aside. Nevertheless, by the spring of 1915, he became so convinced of the ineptitude of NICHOLAS II and his ministers that he joined a group of Duma deputies and State Council members, known as the Progressive Bloc, demanding to be permitted a share in organizing the war effort. As the country's fortunes waned, the Progressive Bloc began calling for a

Figure 64 Milyukov.

GOVERNMENT OF PUBLIC CONFIDENCE. Milyukov was increasingly critical of the way in which the war effort was being conducted (see FIRST WORLD WAR AND THE REVOLUTION. In a dramatic speech to the Duma in November 1916 he listed the shortcomings of the government, asking in each case whether the explanation was stupidity or treason, clearly implying that the government as it was constituted was not to be trusted to bring victory.

When the revolution came in February, Milyukov welcomed it and, because he had considerable knowledge of the subject, was named minister of foreign affairs of the PROVISIONAL GOVERNMENT. In 1917, in contrast to 1905, he found himself on the right because of his commitment to the war and his conviction that the monarchy as an institution should be preserved. In May, when a crisis broke out over his views concerning the country's war aims, he had to leave his post. During the next five months Milyukov sadly watched the disintegration of the Provisional Government. After its fall he helped form the VOLUNTEER ARMY under General M. V. ALEXEEV. After the failure of the Whites he left Russia to spend his remaining years in France, actively involved in Russian émigré politics, editing a newspaper, continuing his scholarly work, never in doubt that the cause he espoused was the right one. SH

Milyutin, Dmitri Alexeevich (1816–1912)

Born in Moscow into the family of an insolvent factory owner, Milyutin received his secondary education at the Moscow provincial gymnasium and the pension of Moscow University, from which he graduated with a silver medal in 1832. The following year he was commissioned as a junior officer in the 1st Guards artillery brigade. In 1836 he entered the Military Academy and was later posted to the Guards general headquarters with the rank of staff-captain. During this period his scholarly aptitude and commitment to the value of military education found expression in a variety of published articles. He was one of the founders of the historical *Voennyi zhurnal* (Military Journal) and subsequently, in 1858, of *Voennyi sbornik* (Military Miscellany).

After active service in the Caucasus, Milyutin embarked in 1840 on an extended tour of Western Europe from which he developed an intense interest in political economy, law and administration to add to his existing penchant for history and geography. From 1845 to 1856 he taught at the academy and continued to publish while also devising operational plans for the impending campaign against Turkey. After further service as chief of staff to the Caucasian armies, he became deputy war minister in 1860 and minister in November 1861.

In administrative skill and determination Milyutin was outstanding among Russia's nineteenth century reformist bureaucrats. Courteous and reserved according to most contemporary accounts, he pursued his reforms with a conviction and energy which earned him many political enemies and the wholly undeserved reputation of democrat. As a great Russian nationalist, he resolutely defended the brutal suppression of the insurgency in Poland in 1863.

His experiences had convinced him that future wars would be national, between peoples rather than merely princes, and he thus aspired to create a national army which transcended class divisions. If his aspiration was not to be entirely fulfilled, he at least had set the Russian army on the path to professionalism and modernity.

Although promoted to field-marshal and awarded the title of count in 1878, Milyutin came under severe political pressure after the assassination of his protector, Alexander II. In May 1881 he resigned and was rewarded with a seat on the State Council, the highest consultative body of the empire until its reform as the upper chamber to the Duma in 1905. Together with other administrators of the reform era he continued in this capacity to maintain an albeit toothless opposition to the more extreme and obscurantist policies of the new regime. MP

Mirovich, Zinaida Sergeevna (1865–1913)

A leading figure in the Union of Equal Rights for Women between 1905 and its demise in 1908, Mirovich (real name Ivanova) remained active in the movement for women's rights up to her death in 1913. A graduate of the women's higher courses in Moscow in 1887, she began a career as a freelance writer specializing in the French Revolution, and later as a translator, particularly of Ibsen. As a fluent speaker of several languages she travelled abroad and became well acquainted with the women's movement in the West at a time (the late 1890s) when feminist organization in Russia was at a low ebb. After 1905 she continued to be an ambassador for Russian women and reported on feminism in Russia and the West for Russian and international feminist journals. Her articles on the Russian movement include one of the important sources for the history of feminism in 1905. She was an outspoken critic of both liberal and social-democratic opponents of the Union of Equal Rights and later of the League of Equal Rights, of which she was a member. She made some enemies, including a fellow member of the League in Moscow, with whom she carried on a feud which erupted into the daily press in 1911. She withdrew from public life soon after and died at the age of forty-eight in 1913. (See THE WOMEN'S MOVEMENT BEFORE 1917). LE

Molotov, Vyacheslav Mikhailovich (1890–1986)

Born into a middle-class family, Molotov (real name Skryabin) became politically active after 1905 and soon joined the BOLSHEVIKS, helping to found and edit *Pravda*, the newspaper on which STALIN was also active. In 1917 he was a member of the MILITARY-REVOLUTIONARY COMMITTEE which oversaw the insurrection, and one of the leaders of the pro-LENIN left wing of the party. During the CIVIL WAR he was engaged mostly in party committee work but from 1920 he began to rise in the organizational hierarchy, primarily through the advocacy of Stalin. In 1921 he was made a member of the party Central Committee and of the Secretariat (the latter with the title of 'responsible secretary') and in 1925 he was appointed to the Politburo. He became Premier of the Soviet state in 1931 and succeeded M. M. LITVINOV as commissar for foreign affairs in May 1939. It is in this latter post that he played host to the German foreign minister Ribbentrop when the Nazi-Soviet non-aggression pact was signed in August of that year. In subsequent years he was a familiar figure at Stalin's side during the Teheran, Yalta and Potsdam conferences (American diplomats referred to him as 'Old Stone Bottom'). Although he was replaced by A. Ya. Vyshinsky, a former MENSHEVIK, as Foreign Minister in 1949, he remained a member of the Politburo and of the Central Committee, and between 1953 and 1956 served again as

Foreign Minister. It was not until 1957, with the rise of Khrushchev, that his demise began. Stripped of his official party positions he was first made ambassador to Mongolia and then Soviet representative at the International Atomic Energy Agency. Denounced as a collaborator in the Stalin purges he was expelled from the party in 1964. He then receded into total obscurity, perhaps the last and most infamous of the survivors of the Stalinist era, and only his death in 1986 reminded the world of the prominent political and diplomatic role he had played as the dour spokesman and pre-eminent functionary of that era. There is little in his long career and life to suggest any outstanding talents except an uncanny ability to survive and a steadfast readiness to serve his master well, though he must have done the latter with a clear conscience for he was himself a hardliner on most issues in 1917 and after.   BK

Nasiri, Kayyum (1825-1902)

Often called a 'Tatar Lomonosov' or 'Tatar Encyclopedist', Nasiri was the first to raise the issue of preservation of the Tatar language and to underline the importance of language in shaping and maintaining one's identity. He wrote textbooks on a variety of secular subjects in an effort to spread science among the Tatars and was also interested in ethnography and anthropology. Most of all, however, Nasiri was a pioneer who urged building the Tatar literary language on the basis of the vernacular of the Volga region.

Knowledge of Russian stimulated Nasiri's curiosity about the secular sciences and prompted his decision to register as an auditor at the University of Kazan where he became acquainted with leading intellectuals such as the orientalist V. V. Radlov and jurist N. P. Zagoskin. Knowledge of Russian secured him a post in 1850 as a teacher of Tatar at the Kazan Theological Seminary, and in 1873 the same appointment at the newly opened Russo-Tatar Teacher's Seminary.

During this time Nasiri wrote grammars, dictionaries, stylistic studies of the Tatar language, and translated Arabic and Ottoman literature into Tatar, efforts rewarded in 1885 by his election to membership of the Kazan Archeological Society. A vocal opponent of his ideas was Ismail Bey GASPRALI who advocated a common Turkic language for all Russian Muslims.

Through Nasiri's linguistic endeavours Tatarism became an intrinsic part of the identity of the Volga Muslims. The move toward a Tatar literary language was also perhaps the key point in the transition from a purely Islamic identity to a still Islamic but also national, Tatar identity.   A-AR

Natanson, Mark Andreevich (1850-1919)

Professional political activist and revolutionary, Natanson was born into a prosperous Jewish merchant family in Vilna Province. He became involved in the revolutionary movement during his youth and his first arrest came when, as a medical student in St Petersburg, he took part in student disturbances in 1869. Following a brief imprisonment he helped organize a student circle of 'self-education' that in 1871 formed part of the nucleus of the Chaikovsky Circle.

Arrested again in 1870 and 1871, Natanson was exiled to Archangel Province in early 1872 but escaped to St Petersburg. There he was instrumental in establishing the revolutionary circle that was transformed into Land and Liberty in 1876 (see POPULISM). The following year, he was arrested once more, and at the end of 1879 he was exiled to Siberia where he remained for the next eleven years.

On release from exile in 1890 Natanson settled in Saratov where he founded the People's Right Party. He was arrested in this connection in 1894 and sent to Siberia, once again remaining there until 1903. After his release he worked briefly as an accountant in the Nobel oil fields in Baku and then went abroad to avoid further arrest. As an exile in Europe he remained in touch with the Russian revolutionary movement through his membership in the Central Committee of the Party of SOCIALIST REVOLUTIONARIES.

Natanson sided with the Left SRs at the time of the FIRST WORLD WAR. Abroad in 1917, he returned to Russia after the FEBRUARY REVOLUTION to take a leading role in directing the activities of the Left SRs. Following the OCTOBER REVOLUTION he was elected to that party's Central Committee and acted as its main intermediary with the BOLSHEVIKS. In 1918 Natanson helped to found the Group of Revolutionary Communists. Shortly thereafter he returned to Europe and died in Switzerland in 1919.

BTN

Nechaev, Sergei Gennadievich (1847-1882)

A revolutionary fanatic, Nechaev was the son of a waiter in Ivanovo. While a student in St Petersburg in 1868-9 he participated in disturbances and then emigrated. In Geneva he impressed M. A. BAKUNIN with his claims to be the head of a powerful clandestine organization. They wrote several propaganda brochures together but Nechaev, it seems, was mainly responsible for a coded document generally known as 'The Catechism of a Revolutionary'. The true revolutionary, he taught, was 'absorbed by a single exclusive interest, a total concept, a total passion: revolution . . . He knows only one science, the science of destruction.' For the sake of the cause he should suppress all moral inhibitions and be prepared to kill opponents, to manipulate influential personages and compromise vacillating reformists. Nechaev set out organizational rules that provided for dictatorial centralization, secrecy and strict subordination.

Following his return to Moscow in August 1869 Nechaev

set up a body called 'People's Retribution' (Narodnaya rasprava). One member, the student I. I. Ivanov, protested against his fraudulent techniques. With four comrades Nechaev murdered him, (this event figures in Dostoevsky's novel *The Possessed*), and fled abroad again. Most radical émigrés, including eventually Bakunin, repudiated him and in 1872 he was extradited from Switzerland as a common criminal. Eighty-four associates had previously been convicted (1871). Sentenced to twenty years' hard labour, Nechaev was instead kept in solitary confinement in St Petersburg's grim Peter-Paul Fortress where he succeeded in winning over some of his guards to try, in vain, to help him escape. He may have died by his own hand. Nechaev's unscrupulous amoralism ('the ends justifyy the means') resurfaced in the teachings of P. N. TKACHEV, a former associate, and in the terrorist activities of the People's Will group. How far LENIN's followers displayed similar pathological traits is debatable.   JLHK

Further Reading

Pomper, P.: *Sergei Nechaev*. New Brunswick: 1979.

Nikolaeva, Klavdiya Ivanovna (1893–1944)

One of the relatively small number of working-class women who achieved prominence in the Bolshevik hierarchy, Nikolaeva became a factory worker at the age of eleven and was politicized while still a young girl. At the age of fourteen she was working in the women's club which Alexandra KOLLONTAI set up in 1907, the Mutual Aid Society for Working Women, and a year later spoke for the Social Democrats at the feminist congress of women. In 1914 she was one of the collaborators on the Bolshevik women's journal *Rabotnitsa* (The Woman Worker), and again in 1917, when the journal was revived. In 1924 she became the first working-class woman to head the women's section of the party (Zhenotdel), a post which had earlier been held by Inessa ARMAND and Kollontai. In later years she was elected to the central committee of the party and was a deputy on the Supreme Soviet.   LE

Nicholas II (1868–1918)

The last of the Russian Tsars, Nicholas Alexandrovich Romanov, was born in St Petersburg on 5 (18) May 1868, the first son of Alexander III and of Maria Fedorovna, daughter of King Christian IX of Denmark. He had two brothers, George (1871–99) and Michael (1878–1918) and two sisters, Xenia (1875–1960) and Olga (1881–1960). He succeeded to the throne following his father's death from liver disease on 20 October (1 November) 1894. On 14 (26) November 1984 he married Princess Alix (born 25 May 1872) of Hesse-Darmstadt, daughter of Princess Alice of England and of Grand Duke Louis of Hesse. The couple

Figure 65   Nechaev, Switzerland 1869/70.

had five children: Olga (1895), Tatyana (1897), Maria (1899), Anastasia (1901) and Alexis (1904). The coronation of Nicholas and Alexandra took place on 14 (26) May 1896.

A man of retiring disposition and limited imagination, Nicholas was ill-endowed by nature to serve as absolute monarch of the Russian Empire. Nor was he well equipped by education to cope with the challenges he would encounter during a period of rapid social and economic change: from 1885 to 1890 his studies, under a composite syllabus of the Law Faculty of St Petersburg University and of the Academy of the General Staff, were supervised by Konstantin Pobedonostsev, Procurator of the Holy Synod and enemy of all reform. Between 1887 and 1893 he gained military experience in summer manoeuvres. He served on the State Council and the Committee of Ministers in 1889; toured the Near East and Asia in 1890–1; and in 1891 he chaired the Siberian Committee and the Special Committee on Family Relief. However, his early manhood was essentially that of an idle socialite and he displayed little interest in or understanding of affairs of state.

In his political thought Nicholas looked back to the reign of Tsar Alexis (1629–76), after whom he named his son, idealizing the unity of church, monarch and people which he considered to have been characteristic of the Muscovite era. A cultural nationalist, he deplored in the Westernization of Peter the Great the suppression of 'Russian habits, the good customs, the usages bequeathed by a nation'. Despising the social classes of urban Russia (bourgeoisie, industrial workers and dissolute aristocracy), he moved his residence in 1895 from the Anichkov Palace in St Petersburg to the Alexander Palace in Tsarskoe Selo where he lived a secluded life, sustained by the illusion that he enjoyed the undying trust and affection of the 'real Russia' – the peasantry. A futher component of this 'Slavophilism' was a mistrust of the non-Russian peoples of the Empire, especially those of the Western frontiers. Russification policies during his reign aggravated relations with the non-Russians and Nicholas had no hesitation in approving the use of force to maintain Great Russian hegemony. Persecution of the non-Orthodox intensified and in the case of the Jews his anti-Semitism, and that of the Court, made for continuing racial discrimination and government sponsored pogroms, i.e. organized massacres.

A firm believer in the principles of divine right monarchy, Nicholas laid down his attitude to reform in a speech of 17 January 1895 (OS) in which he denounced as 'senseless dreams' proposals to involve public bodies, such as the zemstvos, in government. He was never reconciled to the existence of the Duma founded after the 1905 REVOLUTION, notwithstanding the reaffirmation of his autocratic powers in the Fundamental Laws of April 1906; and in the euphoria which attended the tercentenary of the Romanov dynasty in February 1913, he considered abolishing the Duma's limited legislative powers. Only at the moment of abdication in March 1917 did Nicholas concede the wartime demand of the Duma politicians that he should appoint a 'GOVERNMENT OF PUBLIC CONFIDENCE' from their ranks, even though this government would have remained accountable to him alone. One consequence, fatal for the monarchy, of his stubborn refusal to allow the political integration of Russia's rising social classes was the discrediting by 1917 of those parties (Octobrists, Kadets) who considered constitutional monarchy a sufficient means to this end.

In foreign affairs, in which he was more interested, Nicholas saw himself as a 'man of peace' and he took pride in his sponsorship of the Hague Conference on arms limitation in 1899 (the idea originated with S. Yu. WITTE). However his sense of Russia's imperial destiny had made him an enthusiastic supporter in 1896–7 of plans to seize Constantinople; and his conception of Russia as a Eurasian power led to expansion in Manchuria and Korea and war with Japan in January 1904. Though not a Pan-Slav, Nicholas objected to German expansion in the Balkans and (in ignorance of the diplomacy of his foreign minister Izvolsky) opposed Austria's annexation of Bosnia in 1908. When Austria issued its ultimatum to Serbia in 1914, however, he sought to avoid conflict and pleaded with Wilhelm II to restrain Austria.

Briefly, during the FIRST WORLD WAR, both Nicholas and Alexandra shared the experience of the common people of the Empire; he through his involvement with the army and she through her contribution to hospital work. In August 1915, however, the decision of Nicholas, following the loss of Warsaw, to appoint himself Commander-in-Chief placed the prestige of the monarchy at risk and sorely tested the loyalty of the High Command. Futhermore, the absence of Nicholas at Military Headquarters now made for an increasing interference of Alexandra in affairs of state and, through her, of the wandering priest and 'Man of God' (*starets*) Gregory RASPUTIN. Engaged originally to heal the effects of the tsarevich's haemophilia, Rasputin's influence over not only religious but also political appointments and his interference in military policy (the termination of Brusilov's offensive of September 1916) seriously eroded support for Nicholas among the aristocracy, officialdom, the High Command, the Duma politicians and Allied diplomatic representatives.

The attempt by Nicholas forcibly to repress the industrial and military revolt in Petrograd in February 1917 was characteristic of a ruler whose methods of dealing with social protest had earned him the title 'Nicholas the Bloody' (*Nikolai Krovavy*). Whereas the success of these methods had earned Nicholas a reprieve in 1905, his departure in 1917 was the very least that was required to secure the cooperation of High Command, Duma leaders and Petrograd SOVIET in managing the crisis. The equanimity with which Nicholas accepted abdication at Pskov on 2 (15) March may be attributed to physical and mental exhaustion, as much as to his reputed 'fatalism' or any failure of nerve. This same condition and a realization that exile would separate him from his son may explain his unconstitutional 'second abdication' in favour of his brother, the Grand Duke Michael.

Following the abdication Nicholas and Alexandra were held in custody for five months in Tsarskoe Selo where they were interrogated by A. F. KERENSKY concerning their alleged collaboration with Germany. On the initiative of P. N. MILYUKOV, an offer of political asylum in the United Kingdom was made by Lloyd George and then withdrawn on the insistence of King George V who feared popular protest. In mid August 1917 Kerensky arranged for the removal, for their own safety, of the royal family to Tobolsk. In April 1918 they were taken into custody in Yekaterinburg and held there while the Bolshevik government in Moscow pondered their fate. The case for a trial of Nicholas, and perhaps his wife, had strong appeal, but the surviving children would remain as no less of a political liability. The tsar's brother, Michael, and many other Romanovs were executed in June 1918, and, according to

Dmitri Volkogonov, a month later the Bolsheviks in Yeka-terinburg were given the signal for which they had been waiting: the government had decided the tsar and the rest of his family be similarly dealt with. On 17 July the tsar, his wife, his son, certainly three, possibly all four daughters, and their few remaining personal servants were executed, their bodies were stripped and thrown into a disused mineshaft outside the town, where they were discovered some sixty years later and scientifically authenticated in 1993.

JB

Further Reading

Dillon, E.J.: *The Eclipse of Russia*. London and Toronto: 1918.

Massie, Robert K.: *Nicholas and Alexandra*. New York: 1967.

Pares, Bernard: *The Fall of the Russian Monarchy*. New York: 1939.

Rogger, Hans: *Russia in the Age of Modernization and Revolution 1881–1917*. London and New York: 1983.

Summers, Anthony and Mangold, Tom: *The File on the Tsar*. London: 1976.

Volkogonov, Dmitri: *Lenin: Life and Legacy*. London: 1994.

Novitsky, Vasili Fedorovich (1869–1929)

A representative of that group of technocratic and professionally-minded staff officers who sustained the military reform movement between 1905 and 1914, Novitsky was a graduate of the Mikhailovskoe artillery school and of the General Staff academy in 1895. He first saw active service as an officer for special assignments to the commander of the II Manchurian Army in the Russo-Japanese war. In 1914 and 1915 he was to command a brigade of rifles and then an infantry division. Promoted lieutenant general in 1916, Novitsky became assistant war minister in February 1917 and subsequently commander of the unruly XII Army. In November he was appointed commander-in-chief of the rapidly disintegrating Northern Front.

Novitsky proved an accomplished historian and publicist. In 1906 he collaborated in the publication of an independent journal, *Voennyi golos* (Military Voice), which campaigned against the incompetence, toadyism and haphazard organization its authors believed lay at the root of Russia's humiliation in the Russo-Japanese War. The journal was soon suppressed by the authorities but Novitsky was to return to the latter theme in 1909 and in a collection of critical articles in 1911.

Novitsky served on the general staff from 1906 to 1911 when he was transferred to a regimental command. In that capacity he edited with others the *Voennnaya entsiklopediya* (Military Encyclopedia) until the outbreak of war. His other works included military geographies of India, Afghanistan and Mongolia, an operational history of the Russo-Japanese war and a major treatise on the 1914 campaign in Belgium and France, published posthumously.

In 1918 Novitsky joined the RED ARMY as deputy and then head of the higher military inspectorate. From October 1919 until his death he taught military history at the Soviet military academy. The motives of Novitsky and others like him in serving the BOLSHEVIKS stemmed from their absolute commitment to military life rather than any ideological affinity with the Communist Party. After 1905 Novitsky had opposed civilian meddling and amateurism, and he disparaged monarchical privilege. Personal ambition apart, it would have been entirely in character for him to have perceived in the formation of the Red Army an opportunity to help create a new professional and national war machine.

MP

Olminsky, Mikhail Stepanovich (1863–1933)

Born in Voronezh into a poor family of noble extraction, Olminsky (real name Alexandrov) was admitted to the Law Faculty of St Petersburg University in 1883 and expelled in 1885 for political activity. After two years of military service, he returned to St Petersburg and helped form the People's Will Group which cooperated with SOCIAL DEMOCRATS in workers' study circles. Arrested in 1894 he spent four years in prison before being exiled to Olekminsk (from which he derived his pseudonym), Yakutsk Province.

A convert to Social Democracy, in 1904 Olminsky joined the BOLSHEVIKS in Geneva and embarked on a career in party journalism. Using the alias 'Galerka', he edited and contributed to *Vpered* (Forward), *Proletarii*, the legal papers *Novaya Zhizn* (New Life) and *Vestnik Zhizni* (Messenger of Life) in St Petersburg and was an editor of *Nasha Mysl* (Our Thought), *Volna* (The Wave) and *Ekho* and of the illegal army journal *Kazarma* (Barracks).

Following the 1905 REVOLUTION Olminsky worked in local government in Baku, joined the local Social Democrats and worked with the union of clerical workers. In 1909 he was employed by the statistical department of the St Petersburg city council and in 1911–12 he joined the editorial board of the St Petersburg *Pravda*. Factionally unaligned, Olminsky resisted LENIN's campaign against the 'Liquidators' until April 1913 when Lenin had KAMENEV appointed to the board. With the outbreak of war and closure of *Pravda*, Olminsky moved to Saratov where he joined the 'Mayak' company and helped publish *Nasha Gazeta*.

From Moscow, where in 1916 he edited the printers' union journal, Olminsky returned to St Petersburg in 1917 and, as a member of the editorial board of *Pravda*, gave support to the policy of 'democratic revolution'. Following the dispute over Kamenev's cooption on to the newspaper, he returned to Moscow to edit *Sotsial Demokrat*. Olminsky was chairman of the Bolsheviks' 'Sixth' Congress and a Bolshevik delegate to the CONSTITUENT ASSEMBLY. Following his resignation as deputy commissar for finance in mid 1918 for health reasons, he wrote several articles in *Pravda* protesting against the excesses of the VECHEKA and in particular against the reprisals following the assassination of URITSKY.

In October 1919 Olminsky was appointed to a state commission for the publication of Lenin's works; in August 1920 he obtained Lenin's agreement to a new project on the history of the Communist Party. The introduction of this project into the terms of reference of a commission on the history of the October Revolution (Istpart), already set up under the chairmanship of POKROVSKY, led to the latter's resignation and his replacement by Olminsky. Whereas Pokrovsky had favoured the appointment of professional archivists and the use of a broad documentary base, Olminsky surrounded himself in Istpart with Leninists of his Geneva and pre-war *Pravda* days and concentrated on the collection of memoir material. By December 1921 Istpart had become a department of the Party Central Committee.

Olminsky compromised the factional impartiality of *Istpart* as early as 1921 when he denounced BUKHARIN's *Economics of the Transition Period* for 'Left-revisionism and equated ideological 'unorthodoxy' with political opposition. In 1924 he assisted STALIN in the succession struggle by editing the anthology *Lenin on Trotsky and Trotskyism*. His seniority as a revolutionary, his involvement with the Party press at all stages of its development and his later role in Istpart gave him special status as a witness and custodian of the Party's memory. It was perhaps for this reason that Stalin, on Olminsky's death in 1933, forbade publication of an official biography, setting a precedent which was to apply to other Old Bolsheviks.   JB

Perovskaya, Sofiya Lvovna (1854–1881)

A leading member of People's Will, Perovskaya took part in the tsar's assassination and was the first woman in Imperial Russia to be executed for a political crime. Her death made her a martyr and a heroic example to future generations of revolutionaries, the best remembered of the several hundred female populists of the 1870s.

She was born into a gentry-officer family, the granddaughter of a minister of state and daughter of the then governor-general of St Petersburg. Family life was unhappy and she grew up with a lasting deep antipathy towards her overbearing father, who mocked his wife and played the despot with his children. In 1866 he lost his post after Karakozov's attempt on the tsar's life. After his demotion Perovskaya spent some time on her mother's estate in the Crimea, where she led a less restricted life, reading freely and educating herself.

In 1869, at the age of fifteen, Perovskaya enrolled in the Alarchin women's preparatory courses which had just opened in St Petersburg. Contact with other students transformed her from a 'patriot of women' into a political radical. At first a member of a women's circle, she was finally persuaded to join the Chaikovsky circle in 1871, went 'to the people' and was arrested with other Chaikovtsy in spring 1874. While on bail awaiting trial, she trained as a medical aide. Acquitted in the Trial of the 193, in 1878, she immediately went into hiding. Rearrested, she escaped, returned to the capital and engaged in the POPULIST debate over terror. Reluctant to give up work with 'the people' for the sake of terror, yet impatient for decisive political action, she tried at first to work with both BLACK REPARTITION and People's Will, finally committing herself to People's Will and the terrorist campaign. Single-minded, controlled and quick-witted in an emergency, she participated in the planning and implementation of all the attempts on the tsar between 1879 and 1881. During 1880 she fell in love with her fellow-conspirator, ZHELYABOV, breaking a vow of celibacy and surprising her comrades who believed that she despised men. After his arrest on 27 February 1881 she took over control of the assassination plot, and gave the signal to the bomb-throwers on 1 March. Arrested nine days after the assassination, she was tried with five other conspirators, including Zhelyabov. All, with the exception of the pregnant Gesya Gelfman, were sentenced to death, and Perovskaya was hanged with them on 3 April 1881.

LE

Peters, Yakov Khristoforovich (1886–1938)

A Latvian peasant by birth, Peters joined the Latvian Social Democratic Party (LSDP) in 1904, suffering imprisonment during 1907–8. He arrived in London in October 1909 and worked as a tailor's presser. Arrested on 22 December 1910 on suspicion of involvement in the Houndsditch murders committed by Latvian ANARCHISTS, he was acquitted in May 1911. Returning to Russia in spring 1917, he entered the LSDP Central Committee, and participated in the OCTOBER REVOLUTION. A key member of the VECHEKA from its formation in December 1917, Peters helped to suppress the Left Socialist Revolutionary insurrection in Moscow on 6–7 July 1918, and officiated as Vecheka chairman during DZERZHINSKY's subsequent six weeks suspension. He investigated the 'LOCKHART case' and 'envoys plot'. As Dzerzhinsky's deputy from late August 1918 to spring 1919, he earned a reputation for mercilessness. In 1920–2 he was Vecheka/GPU plenipotentiary for Turkestan. As a Collegium member of the OGPU (Unified State Political Administration) from 1923 onwards, he headed its Eastern Department, but became increasingly absorbed in political and public administration. Elected member of the Communist Party Central Control Commission at the Twelfth (1923) to Seventeenth (1934) Party

Congresses, Peters also served as Collegium member of the People's Commissariat of Worker-Peasant Inspection (Rabkrin); from 1930 he held important Party and Soviet posts in Moscow City and Region. Arrested in early December 1937, he was executed on 25 April 1938; posthumously rehabilitated.   GHL

Petliura, Simon V. (1879–1926)

Ukrainian publicist and military affairs specialist, Petliura was active in Ukrainian socialist groups from an early age leading to his expulsion from an Orthodox seminary. He worked in Tiflis and Lvov, and moved to Kiev in 1905 where he edited *Slovo* (The Word), a socialist newspaper. Taking up residence in Moscow, then St Petersburg, in 1911, he continued his publicistic work in the Russian-language journal *Ukrainskaya Zhizn* (Ukrainian Life). During the FIRST WORLD WAR he organized aid for the troops on the Western Front.

Petliura was Secretary for military affairs in the Central Rada, and attempted to organize Ukrainian armed forces in the face of opposition from his fellow Social Democrats and members of the Rada. He spent four months under arrest during the SKOROPADSKY regime, then became a member of the Directory and Supreme Ataman, or Leader, of the Ukrainian National Republic's Army. Fighting a difficult war against the BOLSHEVIKS, with dwindling troops and resources, Petliura failed to hold Kiev after a joint campaign with Polish forces (see THE UKRAINE: REVOLUTION AND CIVIL WAR). He moved to Poland in 1920 and settled in Paris in 1924, where he was assassinated two years later by Samuel Schwartzbard, commonly believed to have been a Bolshevik agent.   ND

Piłsudski, Józef (1867–1935)

A co-founder of the Polish Socialist Party (PPS) (see POLISH MARXISM, Piłsudski became first Head of State in 1918 and the most powerful politician in Poland between the wars.

Józef Piłsudski was the oldest of the eleven children of an impoverished *szlachta* (gentry) family in Zułowa, Lithuania, who attended the Russian gymnasium (which he loathed) in Wilno (Russian, Vilna). His contacts with the People's Will organization led to his first arrest in 1887, and to exile in Siberia. On his release in 1892 he set up a conspiratorial socialist group in Wilno which in 1893 conducted the First Congress of the PPS, approving the Draft Programme by Stanisław Mendelson which had been adopted at the Paris Conference in 1892. Piłsudski became editor and printer of the PPS's underground paper *Robotnik* (Worker), which published an unprecedented 35 issues before its (temporary) suppression in 1900. On that occasion, Piłsudski escaped from prison by feigning mental illness. Between 1895 and 1905 he was a member of the ruling Central Workers' Committee (CKR) of the PPS.

Piłsudski always hoped for a war between Russia and her enemies leading to a national uprising in Poland. In 1904 he travelled to Japan to seek support for a rising; the Japanese merely offered a small subsidy. On 13 November 1904 he organized an open demonstration on Grzybowski Square in Warsaw which ended in an exchange of gunfire. Piłsudski was infuriated when, at the Seventh PPS Congress in Warsaw in March 1905, the party's left-wing 'youth' voted to accept autonomy for Poland within a democratized Russia. For a while he remained in the party, as it still allowed him to form a Military Organization (OB). The OB conducted a series of 'expropriations' (bank raids, etc.) and killed tsarist police and officials during the revolutionary years 1905–8. At the Ninth Congress of the PPS in Vienna in 1906 the PPS 'elders', led by Piłsudski, walked out and created their own party, the PPS-Revolutionary Fraction, though he did not seek election to its central committee. He organized the raid on a mail train in Bezdany on 26 September 1908, which secured 200,000 rubles, assuring the future of the new party and of his secret Union of Active Struggle (ZWC). From then until 1914 he devoted his efforts to the creation of a Polish military cadre.

During the FIRST WORLD WAR Piłsudski was permitted by the Austrians to form a Polish Brigade to fight against Russia. To assert his independence from the Central Powers, he resigned his command in July 1916, but accepted the military portfolio in the Provisional Council of State established by the Central Powers in Warsaw. After the Russian FEBRUARY REVOLUTION, Piłsudski incited the Polish legionaries to refuse to give an oath of allegiance to the Austrian Kaiser. On 22 July 1917 he was arrested and eventually imprisoned in Magdeburg castle.

With the collapse of the Central Powers in November 1918, Piłsudski returned to Warsaw, where he was invited to become Provisional Head of State. He appointed his former PPS comrade Jędrzej Moraczewski head of a Provisional cabinet, which promised egalitarian social reforms and prepared the democratic elections to the Constituent Sejm (Assembly) in January 1919. Piłsudski hoped to create a federation of the Polish, Lithuanian and Belorussian peoples, broadly corresponding to the eighteenth century Polish Commonwealth in alliance with an independent UKRAINE. On 7 May 1920 his forces reached Kiev, but were soon forced to retire. The RED ARMY under TUKHACHEVSKY then advanced to the gates of Warsaw by August before it was repulsed in turn. The Soviet-Polish Treaty of Riga (1921) left Poland in control of substantial areas of Lithuania, Belorussia and Ukraine.

In Poland's inter-war system of guided parliamentary democracy, Piłsudski was almost permanent defence minister and armed forces minister. In 1926 he carried out a coup d'état to clip the powers of his right-wing enemies in the Sejm. In 1930, he ordered the detention and torture of

80 deputies opposed to him. Nevertheless, he refused to become a totalitarian dictator. He died as the 'father of his people' in 1935.   RA

Further Reading

Dziewanowski, M.K.: *Joseph Piłsudski: A European Federalist, 1918–1922*. Stanford: Hoover Institution, 1969.

Garlicki, A.: Piłsudski, Józef. In *Polski Słownik Biograficzny*, vol. 26. Wrocław: Polska Akademia Nauk, 1981.

Piłsudski, J.: *The Memories of a Polish Revolutionary and Soldier*, ed. D. R. Gillie. London: Faber, 1931.

Rothschild, J.: *Piłsudski's Coup d'État*. New York: Columbia University Press, 1966.

Plehve, Vyacheslav Konstantinovich (1846–1904)

Born in Meshchovsk in the province of Kaluga, Plehve specialized in jurisprudence at the University of Moscow, served in the Ministry of Justice from 1867 to 1880, then the Ministry of Interior, where he held the position of director of the Department of Police till 1884, was promoted to the rank of assistant minister and remained in that post until 1894 when be became imperial secretary, in effect chief of staff of the State Council. From 1889 he also served as state secretary for Finland. In 1902 he was appointed minister of interior.

Plehve was an able and intelligent, but very narrow bureaucrat who early on proved himself more adaptable than most officials in identifying himself with the policies of his superiors. In the period after 1881 this meant identifying himself with the programme of buttressing the autocracy (which included buttressing the landed nobility), continuation of heavy-handed russification of the Kingdom of Poland and Finland, the attack on the Armenian Orthodox Church, and persecution of the Jews. Also, he supported the clique that favoured an aggressive policy in the Far East.

On becoming minister of interior at a time of growing opposition, Plehve was convinced that he could hold back the revolutionary tide by a combination of stern measures and conciliatory gestures, even taking the extraordinary step of visiting P. N. MILYUKOV in jail to offer him the post of minister of education as a way of calming the students. When such gestures were rebuffed and as opposition mounted, he resorted increasingly to the use of police power, so much so that even the director of the Department of Police fell into despair. Plehve's image as the personification of repression was heightened by the mindless policy of Russification with which he was associated and the horrific Kishinev pogrom in 1903 which he was accused of having instigated and for which, though the accusation was unfounded, he bore a moral responsibility because of his open hostility toward Jews whom he considered to be the chief source of revolutionary agitation. By the end of his tenure Plehve had lost the support of his colleagues and driven even those liberals who anxiously sought to avoid open conflict with the government to the sad conclusion that peaceful reform was impossible as long as Plehve remained in office.

And yet Plehve was not blind to the facts of life, eventually admitting privately that concessions would be necessary. For example, he considered easing some of the onerous restrictions on the Jews; tried to deal with some of the more moderate elements in Finland; and he was worried about the drift toward war with Japan, although he was confident that if fighting broke out there would be no untoward domestic consequences and that Russia would win. (The assertion ascribed to him by S. Yu. WITTE that Russia needed 'a little, victorious war to stem the revolution' does not represent Plehve's thinking in the last months before the war and possibly was taken out of context by Witte or Witte's source.)

No matter. The terrorist arm of the SOCIALIST REVOLUTIONARIES, directed by Evno AZEF, one of Plehve's own secret agents, had decided to put an end to him, and on 15 July 1904 he was killed by a bomb thrown by Egor Sazonov, a former student. For the most part the news was received with joy by the public and indifference by most high officials, who felt that he had brought his death upon himself. NICHOLAS II was one of the few who felt sorrow at the loss of a man whom he considered a friend and an invaluable minister. (See photograph, p. 366.)   SH

Plekhanov, Georgi Valentinovich (1856–1918)

Born in Gudalovka, Tambov province, Plekhanov joined the revolutionary cause and its populist Land and Liberty (Zemlya i Volya) organization in autumn 1876, shortly after its foundation, and was the chief speaker at the famous Kazan Square demonstration in St Petersburg on 6 December 1876. When Land and Liberty broke up in October 1879, with the majority forming the terrorist People's Will (Narodnaya Volya), Plekhanov founded and led the BLACK REPARTITION (Chernyi Peredel) minority, which rejected all-out terrorism and insisted on propaganda work among workers and peasants.

Escaping abroad in January 1880, Plekhanov soon abandoned POPULISM and wrote his first clearly MARXIST work in 1882 (an introduction to the second Russian edition of the *Communist Manifesto*). A year later, in Geneva, together with Chernyi Peredel colleagues P. B. AXELROD, Vera ZASULICH and L. G. DEICH, he founded the Liberation of Labour group to propagate 'the ideas of scientific socialism' in Russia and re-examine Russian

365

Figure 66   Assassination of Plehve.

revolutionary theory and society 'from its own viewpoint'.

While it was Plekhanov's deep hatred of tsarist despotism (and of Russian backwardness on which, he believed, it rested) that made him into a revolutionary, his revolutionary theory and strategy (his most original and influential contribution to Russian Marxism) was above all informed by an overriding fear that a premature socialist seizure of power in Russia could only end in a restoration of despotism. That fear led him to reject all maximalist schemes, whether the 'now or never' Jacobinism of P. N. TKACHEV, the 'Blanquism' of Narodaya Volya, or LENIN's 1905 and 1917 programmes of revolutionary dictatorship.

Nevertheless, seeing himself to the very end of his life as 'a revolutionary and nothing but a revolutionary', Plekhanov fiercely battled all attempts by Revisionists, Legal Marxists, 'Economists' and so-called (MENSHEVIK) 'Liquidators' to strip socialism of revolution. Thus it was Plekhanov who was largely responsible for the insertion of a militant (and 'somewhat sinister looking') commitment to the 'dictatorship of the proletariat' in the draft programme of the RSDRP in 1902. It was he, too, who, in his famous (or notorious) Jacobin speech on the theme of *salus revolutionis suprema lex* to the RSDRP's Second Congress in 1903, expounded a theory of revolutionary expediency to which all 'democratic principles', political liberties and even the duration of parliaments must be subordinated.

Already in his first Marxist tracts, 'Socialism and the Political Struggle' (1883) and 'Our Differences' (1884), Plekhanov faced and came to grips with the basic dilemma of Russian socialists who strove for a post-bourgeois and post-capitalist socialist society, yet were fated to make their revolution in pre-bourgeois, pre-capitalist tsarist Russia. His strategy was to divide a future Russian revolution into two consecutive stages: the first, liberal-bourgeois stage (or revolution) must topple tsarism and, though made largely by the working class, would put the liberal bourgeoisie in power and, creating free liberal-democratic institutions, would promote capitalist development and thus Europeanize backward Russia. Once that was achieved, and with the help of mentors from the socialist intelligentsia armed with 'revolutionary theory', the growing, maturing working class would acquire the political consciousness, organization and power (and possibly peasant support) needed to make its own revolution and establish a socialist government for the realization of socialism. Since Russia was an industrial latecomer, its bourgeoisie relatively weak and its working class quite strong, the first stage of bourgeois rule and capitalist development would be of short duration and thus hasten the advent of the second, socialist stage.

Most important, the practical message of Plekhanov's revolutionary strategy was a socialist self-denying ordinance during Russia's bourgeois revolution. Any premature attempt at seizure of power for the establishment of socialism in backward Russia was doomed to end in a 'most shameful fiasco', he warned. If such self-denial was ignored, then, at best, a socialist minority would maintain itself in power as some 'socialist caste' in a system of 'patriarchal authoritarian communism'. The minority certainly could not build socialism, for that 'must be the business of the workers themselves'. The final outcome of any gamble and experiment 'from above' would be 'tsarist despotism with a communist lining', a 'political monster similar to the ancient Chinese and Peruvian empires', indeed, the very opposite of what they had intended. Plekhanov's revolutionary strategy enabled a large section of the revolutionary intelligentsia, who had despaired of an 'exceptional' 'Russian' road to socialism (based on the peasant and the PEASANT COMMUNE), to become Marxist social democrats and leaders of the burgeoning working class, Plekhanov's 'people in the European sense'.

If Plekhanov's tracts of the 1880s deservedly earned him the title of 'father of Russian Marxism', his philosophical works of the 1890s, notably 'On the Development of the Monist View of History' (1895), established his place in European socialism as a leading theorist and expositor of Marxism as an 'integrated, harmonious and consistent world-view' which included dialectical materialism (he is credited with having coined the term) and Marxist political economy and sociology. His exposition owes a great deal to Engels's 'Anti-Dühring' and Ludwig Feuerbach and to that elaboration of Marxist doctrine carried on by Karl Kautsky, Paul Lafargue, Antonio Labriola and himself in the 1890s. Plekhanov's Marxism however is singularly deterministic and 'necessitarian'; its claim for scientific certainty is almost absolute; its rejection of 'moralism' and 'subjectivism' is most passionate and its insistence on 'orthodoxy' and doctrinal purity is most intransigent. Small wonder he became Europe's fiercest champion of Marxist orthodoxy and injected into Russian Marxism and social democracy that spirit of combative dogmatism and intolerance that have characterized it ever since.

While Plekhanov's political performance (notably in the Menshevik-BOLSHEVIK running feud in which he changed sides too often to remain credible) was singularly unimpressive, his theoretical authority, too, was severely dented

during the 1905 REVOLUTION and thereafter. It was then that Lenin and TROTSKY (and to a lesser extent the Mensheviks) developed their own revolutionary strategies, and a group of Marxist intellectuals – the Empiriomonists – questioned his dialectical materialism.

The FIRST WORLD WAR and the Russian revolution of 1917 spelt the end of whatever was left of Plekhanov's authority. Arriving in Petrograd at the end of March 1917, after 37 years in exile, he who had been a 'defeatist' in 1904/5, now preached with zest from the pages of *Edinstvo* (Unity) the pursuit of war 'until final victory', calling for an offensive that would be 'Russia's salvation'. In a similar vein – and *pace* his time-hallowed self-denying ordinance – he urged socialist participation in a broad coalition government with bourgeois parties, since 'outside coalition there is no salvation'.

While Plekhanov denounced the Bolsheviks as 'today's Bakuninists', it was against the Menshevik 'half-Leninists' that he turned the full force of his ire, castigating their collaboration with the bourgeoisie as too half-hearted and insincere. What they really wanted, he charged, was 'a bourgeois order . . . without the bourgeoisie', and that would ruin 'the revolution'. Small wonder that the Mensheviks shunned him and would not co-opt him onto the Executive Committee of the Petrograd Soviet; nor did they invite him to the Menshevik (Unification) Congress in August.

But it was Lenin who must have hurt him most when, on the eve of the dispersal of the CONSTITUENT ASSEMBLY, he published Plekhanov's 'Jacobin' speech of 1903 in full, commenting that it 'could have been written specially for today'. Even then, in what was to remain his last article, Plekhanov reiterated his Jacobin credo of revolutionary expediency – *salus revolutionis suprema lex*': the good of the revolution is the highest law.

If Plekhanov's concern and life-work was to Europeanize and civilize the Russian revolution by preventing it from turning into a premature socialist revolution and from consequent relapse into despotism, then he failed sadly.

IG

Further Reading

Baron, S.H.: *Plekhanov, the Father of Russian Marxism*. London: 1963.

Frankel, Jonathan: *Vladimir Akimov on the Dilemmas of Russian Marxism 1895–1903*. Cambridge: 1969.

Getzler, I.: Georgij V. Plechanov: la dannazione dell'ortodossia. In *Storia del Marxismo*, vol. 2. Turin: 1979.

Walicki, Andrzej: *The Controversy over Capitalism*. Oxford: 1969.

Pokrovskaya, Mariya Ivanovna (1852–?)

Born in Penza province, Pokrovskaya trained first as a teacher and then as a doctor, working after graduation in Pskov. In 1886 she moved to St Petersburg, employed by the city duma as a municipal doctor for the poor. In the 1890s she became involved in the international campaign against state-licensed prostitution, a cause which she pursued for the rest of her career. In 1904 she launched *Zhenskii vestnik* (Women's Messenger), the first and longest-lived of the three political feminist journals published between 1904 and 1917. A ceaseless campaigner for women's rights, she also used her journal to protest against poverty and social injustice (see THE WOMEN'S MOVEMENT). Though espousing a vague form of socialism, she was wary of collaborating with any male-led political organization. She did not join the main feminist organization (the Union of Equal Rights for Women) during the 1905 REVOLUTION, believing it to be too politically radical and too dependent on the liberation movement. At the end of 1905 she set up the Women's Progressive Party. Though it existed until 1917, it never gained much following and was sustained by Pokrovskaya's unflagging devotion to it. Like many feminists before 1914 she believed that women were natural pacifists and men were solely responsible for war. But this did not lead her to speak out against either the Russo-Japanese or the FIRST WORLD WAR. In 1917 she was increasingly outspoken against the BOLSHEVIKS, but nothing is known of her life after the OCTOBER REVOLUTION, not even whether she stayed in Russia or emigrated.   LE

Pokrovsky, Mikhail Nikolaevich (1868–1932)

Born in Moscow the son of a state official, in 1891 Pokrovsky entered Moscow University where he was a pupil of the historians V. O. Klyuchevsky and P. G. Vinogradov. Following a dispute with Klyuchevsky during his Master's examination he abandoned his academic career for involvement in the 'University Extension' movement founded by P. N. MILYUKOV and E. N. Orlova. A member in 1904 of both the Union of Liberation and the MARXIST 'Literary-Lector Group', in 1905 Pokrovsky joined the RSDRP and was active in the Moscow rising of December 1905. At the London Congress of 1907 he became a member of the 'BOLSHEVIK Centre', but broke with LENIN in 1909 over Duma policy. A founder member of the 'left-Bolshevik' Vpered group, he lectured at the Party Schools in Capri and Bologna, resigning in May 1911 and returning to historical research in Paris where in 1915–16 he edited the internationalist *Nashe Slovo*.

Pokrovsky returned to Russia in August 1917, after the MEZHRAYONKA, with which he had been associated, had merged with the Bolsheviks. He was chairman of the Moscow SOVIET, a member of its MILITARY-REVOLUTIONARY COMMITTEE, editor of its *Izvestiya* and chairman of the short-lived Moscow Regional Sovnarkom. Pokrovsky was a member of the Bolshevik delegation at Brest-Litovsk, and on 22 February 1918 he signed the letter to the Central Committee of the 'Left Communists' who opposed the terms of the peace settlement and advocated revolutionary war.

From May 1918 until his death he was Deputy Commissar for Education. As chairman of the State Academic Council (GUS) Pokrovsky presided over the incorporation of university history departments into new departments of social science, also introducing in 1918 the 'Workers' Faculty' (Rabfak) as a means of preparing worker-students for university entrance. A state centralist in outlook, in 1920 he opposed the bid of PROLETKULT for an independent role in workers' education. By the 1920s Pokrovsky had produced a substantial body of work, much of it survey history presenting a Marxist alternative to liberal and conservative historiography. His four-volume *History of Russia from Ancient Times* (1910–15) was conceived as a reply to Klyuchevsky; his *Outline History of Russian Culture* (1915–18) as a reply to Milyukov. His best known work (which he considered his worst) was his *Brief History of Russia* (1920–3). Yielding chairmanship of the Commission on the history of the October Revolution (Istpart) to Martin OLMINSKY in 1920, in 1921 he became head of the History Sections of the Communist Academy and of the Institute of Red Professors, and in 1922 the head of Tsentrarkhiv (Central Archival Administration of the RSFSR). In 1925 he founded the Society of Marxist Historians whose purposes included a 'struggle against the perversion of history by bourgeois scholarship through critical illumination of current historical literature from the Marxist standpoint'. In 1928 'critical illumination' turned into political persecution and a purge of non-Marxist scholars in which Pokrovsky played a leading role, 'unmasking' Platonov, Petrushevsky, and Tarle. Police actions which began in September 1929 resulted in the arrest of over one hundred historians and for many in dismissal, imprisonment, exile or death.

Pokrovsky's own school of historiography, however, had come under attack as early as 1926 and he had been compelled through 'self-criticism' to revise many of his early views: essentially a social historian, by 1930 he was obliged to admit the role of will and idea in history. More ominously, from 1929 Pokrovsky was being charged with a lack of 'party-mindedness' by the head of Istpart, E. M. Yaroslavsky.

Following STALIN's letter of 28 October 1931 to the editors of the Istpart journal *Proletarskaya Revolyutsiya* (Proletarian Revolution), party authority was imposed in all spheres of intellectual life. Spared by illness from impending disgrace, Pokrovsky died in 1932 and was accorded a state funeral, although in their August 1934 guidelines for new history textbooks, Stalin, Kirov and Zhdanov condemned his 'schematic sociologizing' and 'mechanical economism' and called for more narrative history which emphasized the importance of political, military and diplomatic leadership. He was rehabilitated in 1956 and a four-volume edition of some of his works was published in the Soviet Union in 1965–7.   JB

Further Reading

Barber, John: *Soviet Historians in Crisis, 1920–1932*. London: Macmillan, 1981.

Enteen, George M.: *The Soviet Scholar-Bureaucrat. M.N. Pokrovskii and the Society of Marxist Historians*. University Park, Pennsylvania and London: The Pennsylvania State University Press, 1978.

Pokrovsky, M.N.: *History of Russia from the Earliest Times to the Rise of Commercial Capitalism*, trans. and ed. J.D. Clarkson and M.R. Griffiths. London: Martin Lawrence, 1931.

———: *A Brief History of Russia*, trans. D. Mirsky, intro. Peter von Wahlde. Orono, Maine: University Prints and Reprints, 1968.

Polivanov, Alexei Andreevich (1855–1920)

The son of a noble landowner in Kostroma province, Polivanov was to become one of the most enigmatic actors in the drama of 1917. He joined the 2nd sappers battalion as a sub-lieutenant in 1874 and served in the Russo-Turkish war of 1877–8. In 1879 and 1880 he studied at the Nikolaevskaya engineering academy. Eight years later he graduated from the academy of the General Staff and was posted to the staff of the Kiev military district.

Polivanov edited *Voennyi sbornik* (Military Miscellany) and the newspaper *Russkii invalid* (Russian Invalid) from 1899 to 1904 when he was appointed a permanent member and executive officer of the main fortresses committee. In June 1905 he became chief of headquarters staff and assistant war minister from 1906 to 1912, when he was dismissed for allegedly intriguing against his superior, V. A Sukhomlinov. While he was assistant minister and later during the war he maintained a close relationship with A. I. Guchkov, the chairman of the Octobrist party, and his Duma colleagues.

With Sukhomlinov's disgrace in 1915 Polivanov, now an infantry general, took over as war minister and chairman of the newly created Special Council for State Defence. He used this position to attack the chief of staff at the Stavka, General N. N. Yanushkevich, and his aides for their incompetence and to promote, in association with the minister for agriculture, A. V. Krivoshein, an internal policy favourable to the Duma liberals. His interventions helped secure the appointment of General M. V. ALEXEEV as Yanushkevich's successor, as they had helped Guchkov to found the central WAR INDUSTRIES COMMITTEE in May. In August 1916, after his replacement as minister by D. S. Shuvaev who was formerly head of the army's commissariat, Polivanov again supported Guchkov in his open letter campaign against ministers of the Stuermer cabinet.

In spite of his supposed liberal sympathies Polivanov was in some respects an extreme nationalist. He was an advocate, for example, of the inhuman mass deportation of Jews from the war zones into restricted locations in the interior in 1915 (see THE JEWS IN THE REVOLUTION). Yet he demonstrated what many émigré memoirists considered cynical opportunism in presiding over a commission in March 1917 to produce a declaration of soldiers' rights which, though intended to counteract the harmful effects of Order No. 1, nevertheless alarmed both Alexeev and Guchkov.

After the OCTOBER REVOLUTION Polivanov served as a member of the committee for military legislation and the military training editorial board. In February 1920 he became a member of the special advisory council to the commander-in-chief and expert consultant in the negotiation of the Soviet-Polish peace treaty in Riga where he died in September.   MP

Potresov, Alexander Nikolaevich (Starover) (1869–1934)

Born either in Moscow or Kharkov on 19 August (1 September) 1869, the son of a major-general, Potresov was one of the founding members, with LENIN and MARTOV, of the St Petersburg UNION OF STRUGGLE FOR THE EMANCIPATION OF THE WORKING CLASS. He was arrested in 1896 and exiled for two years. In 1900 he went abroad and was reunited with Lenin and Martov in their efforts to create an underground network in Russia and a party newspaper, *Iskra*, abroad. He was a member of the editorial board until August 1903, when this was reduced to Lenin and Plekhanov alone. Potresov's departure from *Iskra* was prompted by what he saw as Lenin's opportunism and lack of principle; characteristics that repelled him (at one point Potresov described Lenin as 'constitutionally incapable of digesting opinions different from his own').

He shifted to the MENSHEVIKS after the 1905 REVOLUTION and became the leader of their right wing (known at various periods as the Liquidationists or Defensist Mensheviks). His uneasy relationship with both the Bolshevik and the Menshevik parties was demonstrated in 1917, when he rejected the former by saying that 'to hope that Bolshevism can be "given a haircut" and made presentable is unfounded. It is part of the nature of Bolshevism not to let its hair be cut. It is intransigent', while the latter he described as having '. . . been swept almost entirely from the political arena'. In the March of that year, some SOCIALIST REVOLUTIONARIES, Mensheviks and Kadets formed *Soyuz Vozrozhdeniya* (League for Renewal). Its committee in Petrograd consisted of two Popular Socialists, one SR (A. R. GOTS), one Kadet (V. N. Pepelyaev, who later became a KOLCHAK minister) and two Mensheviks (Potresov and Rozanov). At the Congress of the Menshevik Party (held in Petrograd 30 November–7 December 1917), Potresov, along with M. I. LIBER, condemned the OCTOBER REVOLUTION as 'not conforming to historical

369

laws'. Together, Liber and Potresov called for a new coalition with the Kadets to overthrow the Bolsheviks.

In December 1917, the old 'defensists', led by Potresov, seceded, leaving two groups of Internationalists (led by Y. O. Martov and F. I. DAN) to reach a troubled compromise in the revolutionary process. During the Allied Intervention, the League maintained contact with the Allies, the latter approving of its political programme and promising it military assistance against the German–Bolshevik enemy; a line that concurred with Potresov's view that the Mensheviks' insistence on opposition to the Bolsheviks by only legal means was too circumscribed. In late 1924 he emigrated, but joined no anti-Bolshevik organizations. He published his memoirs, *Zapiski Sotsial Demokrata*, in Paris in 1931, and in 1937 his friends published a posthumous collection of his early and later works, including articles that dealt with 1917–18. He died in Paris on 11 July 1934.

FP

Further Reading

Medvedev, R.: *The October Revolution*. London: Constable, 1979.

Serge, V.: *Year One of the Russian Revolution*. London: Allen Lane, 1972.

Prokopovich, Sergei Nikolaevich (1871–1955)

Economist and publicist (husband of E. D. KUSKOVA), Prokopovich was born into a noble family in Tsarskoe Selo (now Pushkin). He was attracted first to POPULIST circles in Moscow in the early 1890s, but by 1894 had become a Marxist. He joined the UNION OF RUSSIAN SOCIAL DEMOCRATS ABROAD while living in Europe after 1895, and as a proponent of Bernsteinian Revisionism was identified with the so-called ECONOMIST orientation in RUSSIAN SOCIAL DEMOCRACY. In 1898 he left the Union Abroad and the Social Democratic movement. He returned to Russia the following year.

In 1900 Prokopovich published the first of several important studies of the European and Russian labour movements. Shortly thereafter he participated in the creation of the Union of Liberation and joined its Council. In 1904 he helped establish the radical-liberal daily *Nasha zhizn* (Our Life)) in St Petersburg. During the 1905 REVOLUTION he was arrested briefly for contacts with Father Gapon, and later took part in organizing the Union of Unions. Elected to the Central Committee of the Constitutional Democratic Party, he soon left it to remain without party affiliation for the next decade.

Prokopovich devoted his attention immediately after 1905 to the study of Russia's economy and to the short-lived publishing enterprises *Bez zaglaviya* (Without a Title) and *Tovarishch* (Comrade). He was also active in the cooperative movement, particularly after moving to Moscow in 1910. As a member of Russian Political Freemasonry he participated in efforts to democratize Russia in the years before 1917.

Following the FEBRUARY REVOLUTION, Prokopovich served in the PROVISIONAL GOVERNMENT as minister of commerce and industry (August) and as minister of food supplies (September–October), initially representing the MENSHEVIKS. He also functioned briefly as head of the Provisional Government in Moscow during the OCTOBER REVOLUTION.

After 1917 Prokopovich continued his scholarship and his involvement in the cooperative movement. In 1921 he was a member of the Public Committee for Famine Relief. Arrested for alleged anti-Soviet activities, he was expelled from the country in 1922 and lived in emigration until his death in Geneva in 1955.

BTN

Radchenko, Stepan Ivanovich (1869–1911)

An early Social-Democratic activist, Radchenko was the son of a timber merchant in Chernigov. While studying at the St Petersburg Technological Institute, a focus of radicalism, he joined the clandestine circle of R. E. Klasson to study Marxist ideas, and in 1893 founded a group of his own, to which belonged G. M. Krzhizhanovsky who was L. B. KRASIN's brother, and N. K. KRUPSKAYA, future wife of V. I. LENIN. It engaged in educational propaganda among skilled workers in the capital and shunned more active agitational measures as premature. A skilled conspirator, Radchenko developed elitist theories of party organization which anticipated those of Lenin, with whom he collaborated from 1894. With some reluctance he helped to found the body later known as the UNION OF STRUGGLE FOR THE EMANCIPATION OF THE WORKING CLASS, and was arrested. Soon released, he stayed mainly in the background as an adviser to less experienced activists in conspiratorial technique. In 1898 he participated in the abortive First Congress of the RSDRP (Russian Social Democratic Labour Party) and convinced P. B. STRUVE, who by then was drifting away from Marxism, to write its manifesto (a programmatic document). The police caught up with Radchenko in December 1901 and he was banished for five years to Vologda province, whence he returned broken in health; he then withdrew from revolutionary politics.

JLHK

Radek, Karl Berngardovich (1885–1939?)

Born in Lvov, in Eastern Galicia, to Jewish parents (real name Sobelson), Radek was intensively involved in the working class movements of a number of countries and he came to prominence through his activities on behalf of the International Communist movement after 1917. He was a man of both political and intellectual talents who was as much at home in the Polish and German revolutionary organizations as in the BOLSHEVIK party which he ultimately embraced as the framework for his international

Figure 67 Radek (smoking) with Chicherin (left) and Litvinov (right, light coat); delegates to Genoa, April/May 1922.

expertise. Radek joined the Polish Social Democratic Party in 1902 and soon became well known through his activities in the trade unions and his political writings (see POLISH MARXISM). Exiled, he spent the years 1908–13 in Germany where he also made a name for himself as an organizer and revolutionary strategist. He later worked with LENIN in Switzerland and, in April 1917, was on the so-called 'sealed' German train which brought them to Russia. He

joined the Bolshevik party and after October combined diplomatic with political missions, being instrumental in the founding of the German Communist Party in December 1918. From 1919 he was a member of the Bolshevik Central Committee but the main base for his activities was the Comintern in which he held various posts and whose international strategy he directed in collaboration with Lenin. In retrospect, however, it seems that both his

371

internationalist interests and a tendency to identify with radical positions were to be a source of his subsequent downfall. Already during the FIRST WORLD WAR he had expressed agreement with TROTSKY's notions of 'PERMANENT REVOLUTION' and, in 1918, he was one of the leaders of the Left Communists who urged extreme left-wing policies both in economic matters and in the fomentation of revolution abroad (thus he opposed Lenin's stand on Brest-Litovsk). Though he quickly recanted his Left Communist views, in later years he was again associated with various opposition groups and sided with Trotsky against STALIN. In 1927 he was expelled from the party but two years later he openly repudiated his 'errors', was re-admitted to the party and became a fervent propagandist for Stalin. All this was to no avail, however, for in 1937 he was put on trial for treason and sentenced to ten years in prison where, it is presumed, he was executed in 1939. (See photograph, p. 371.)   BK

Rakovsky, Christian Georgievich (1873–1941)

Born on 13 August 1873 (NS) in the Southern Bulgarian town of Kotel which his prosperous family virtually owned, Rakovsky was enabled by the considerable fortune left to him by his father to travel and study all over Europe, to become a qualified doctor, to publish pamphlets and newspapers, Bulgarian, Romanian and Russian, in particular LENIN's *Iskra* in 1900, and TROTSKY's two newspapers, *Pravda* in 1908 and *Nashe Slovo* (Our Word) in 1915.

As a leader of the Bulgarian revolutionary movement at the turn of the century, Rakovsky espoused the idea of a Balkan union of nations to achieve their independence, while rejecting the popular notion that Russia's intervention would bring liberation. In 1917, however, he based his hope for revolution in the Balkans on the might of the rising Soviet state. Until that time, his internationalism – he was expelled successively from Bulgaria, Romania, Russia, the Ukraine and France for his revolutionary activities – made him a genuine 'citizen of the world', the quality for which Lenin recruited him in 1918. No other socialist had spanned the Balkans as he had. Before the FIRST WORLD WAR he was identified with the Romanian Socialist movement, became leader of the 'Narrows' (i.e. strict Marxists) within the Bulgarian Social Democratic Party, represented both countries at the Amsterdam Congress of the Second International in 1904, while also holding a mandate from the Serbian Social Democratic Party. His energetic campaign in support of the mutinous sailors of the Russian battleship *Potemkin*, which ended up at Constanza, marked his involvement with the Russian revolutionary movement from 1905 onwards.

Close to Trotsky since the time of the Balkan wars, Rakovsky came closer to him during the First World War and adopted a more radical pacifist position under his

Figure 68   Rakovsky.

influence. He initiated a conference of all the Balkan Social Democratic parties (Romanian, Greek, Serbian and Bulgarian 'Narrows') which met in Bucharest in 1915, and which called for the establishment of a Balkan Socialist Federation, to include the parties taking part in the conference, and issued a manifesto calling for an end to the war and advocating an 'internationalist platform based on class struggle'. Rakovsky was one of the prime movers of the Zimmerwald Conference, and emerged as a supporter of the call for 'a peace without indemnities or annexations, based on the principle of self-determination of the peoples'.

Twice arrested for revolutionary activities after his return to Romania in 1916, he was taken to Jassy, a few miles from the Russian frontier, where on 1 May 1917 Russian soldiers freed him from gaol and helped him escape to Odessa. In January 1918 Rakovsky took part in the Third All-Russian Congress of Soviets on behalf of Romanian Social Democracy. During the first three months which preceded the German occupation of the Ukraine – January to March, when Odessa was occupied – he headed the so-called 'Romanian Revolutionary Council against Counter-revolution in Romania'.

Trying every possible way to provoke revolution in Romania, Rakovsky organized an expedition of Romanian and Russian soldiers to Sevastopol and sent a proclamation on 8 February 1918 'To the entire Romanian people', which linked the fate of their country with that of Revolutionary Russia. This military operation was so successful that, as early as 5 March, the President of the

Romanian Council of Ministers and Foreign Minister, General A. Averescu, signed an agreement with Rakovsky by which Romania would withdraw from Bessarabia for two months to allow a referendum to take place. A few days later, however, the Germans entered Odessa and Rakovsky was obliged to flee to the Crimea. Romanian government troops re-occupied Bessarabia and the issue remained contentious between the Romanian and Soviet governments until 1945, at least.

From June to October 1918 Rakovsky was in charge successively of negotiations between the Soviets and the Ukrainian Rada, Hetman SKOROPADSKY, and finally the Germans, in Ukraine and Berlin. In January 1919 Lenin put him at the head of the Ukrainian Soviet Government, where he replaced G. L. Pyatakov. Also in charge of the party and army, Rakovsky remained essentially in Ukraine until 1923. He was, in Souvarine's words, 'the real *khozyain* (boss) of Soviet Ukraine'. He was instrumental in the bolshevization of the entire southern region, which for a long time he considered the military base of the revolution. In March 1919, at the First Congress of the Communist International (of which he was a founding father, seated on Lenin's right at the presidium), he declared: 'In Romania, circumstances are developing favourably for the revolution; much also depends on an offensive movement of the RED ARMY: its contact would undoubtedly give a push to the strong revolutionary movement.'

With the beginning of the Hungarian revolution in spring 1919, and the entry of Soviet troops into Odessa in April, Rakovsky believed that the revolution would sweep the Balkans. In fact the situation was so disastrous for the Bolsheviks on the internal front, that most of the Red troops had to be sent to the Don against DENIKIN, despite the opposition of Rakovsky and V. A. ANTONOV-OVSEENKO, and with that died Rakovsky's hopes for Romania. He became a member of the Party Central Committee in 1919 and took part in talks leading to British and French recognition of the Soviet Union. He was Soviet ambassador to Paris from 1925 to 1927, in which year, at the Fifteenth Party Congress, he was expelled from the Party as a Trotskyist. Exiled to Central Asia, he was readmitted to the Party in 1934, having recanted his anti-Stalinist views in the wake of Hitler's rise to power. Arrested and tried in the 1938 show trial, he was found guilty of high treason and sentenced to twenty years hard labour. He was shot, with SPIRIDONOVA, in 1941.　　FC

Further Reading

Conte, F.: *Christian Rakovski (1873–1941). Essai de biographie politique*, 2 vols. Paris: H. Champion, 1975.

———— : C. Rakovsky, Commissaire aud Affaires étrangères de l'Ukraine. *Cahiers du Monde russe et soviétique* (December 1971) 439–66.

Rakovsky, Kristian (1-2). In *Cahiers Léon Trotski*, vols 17 and 18. Paris and Grenoble: 1984.

Raskolnikov, Fedor Fedorovich (1892–1939)

Born In St Petersburg to educated parents, in 1900 Raskolnikov entered Prince Oldenburg's boarding school and eight years later the St Petersburg Polytechnical Institute. Already politically active in school during the 1905 REVOLUTION, by 1910 he was a BOLSHEVIK and contributing to *Zvezda* (the Star) and *Pravda*. Arrested in 1912, he suffered a nervous breakdown after four months in solitary confinement and in 1913, as a student, was amnestied and allowed to return to the capital.

An Internationalist and defeatist from the outbreak of the war, Raskolnikov nevertheless joined the NAVY, became a naval cadet and, his political past and medical record notwithstanding, served in the Far East and Japan. After the FEBRUARY REVOLUTION he became a leading figure in KRONSTADT. As a naval officer and Bolshevik, in July 1917 he led the Kronstadt sailors when they attempted an armed uprising in Petrograd against the PROVISIONAL GOVERNMENT of KERENSKY. The revolt, influenced by ANARCHIST elements, came from within the ranks of the sailors themselves and the Bolsheviks found themselves forced to identify with their cause, but it was Raskolnikov who, together with TROTSKY and other Bolsheviks at the scene, was active in defusing the sailors' enthusiasm and in preventing the revolt from getting out of hand and thus compromising the Bolsheviks who were at the time as yet unprepared for a major initiative against the government.

Raskolnikov subsequently had an active career as commander of various fleets which fought against the Whites in the CIVIL WAR. For two years, 1921–3, he served as the Soviet representative (*polpred*) to Afghanistan, and in the late 1930s served in this capacity in Estonia, Denmark, and Bulgaria. Recalled to Moscow in April 1938, at the height of the purges, he fled instead to Belgium, coming out with an open letter accusing Stalin of tyranny etc., and died in unexplained circumstances in the south of France in late 1939.　　BK

Further Reading

Florinsky, Michael T. ed.: Raskolnikov. In *McGraw-Hill Encyclopedia of Russia and the Soviet Union*. McGraw-Hill, 1962.

Rasputin, Grigori Efimovich (1872–1916)

Born a peasant in Tobolsk, Siberia, Rasputin (real name Novykh) entered the life of the Romanov royal family in 1905. As a *starets*, or 'holy man' and 'healer', he was brought in to alleviate the condition of the tsar's last child and only son, the tsarevich Alexei (1904–18), who, as a male descendant of Queen Victoria through his mother, had been found to suffer from haemophilia. Whether by hypnosis or some other calming influence, Rasputin's presence was found to be effective and he therefore became an indispensable member of the royal entourage.

This role in itself would no doubt have remained beneficial, had it not been for Rasputin's other practices. Preaching a dubious sort of 'Orthodoxy' he counselled redemption through sin, making the claim that the more sin, the more redemption. (His adopted name is derived from the Russian for libertine.) Patronized by no less than the empress herself, his mystical oracles and charismatic presence aroused among many high-born females in St Petersburg an exalted response which, when exploited for his sexual appetite – said to be insatiable – created around him an aura of unctuous debauchery.

This behaviour would have been no more than scandalous had Rasputin not also become involved with shady financial and political operators who sought to exploit his court connections for their own gain, and had certain opposition politicians in the Duma as early as 1912 not identified in him a potential Achilles' heel in the autocracy's armour. Their public attacks on Rasputin's behaviour earned them the empress's lasting hatred and set the scene for disastrous developments when war came. (See THE FIRST WORLD WAR.)

NICHOLAS II assumed supreme command of the armed forces in September 1915 and thereafter spent most of his time at GHQ, leaving his wife the empress Alexandra Fedorovna, to deal with the ministers and in general hold the fort at home. Guided by prayer and the divinely-inspired judgement of her 'friend', Rasputin, the empress appointed and dismissed ministers and their deputies in such rapid succession – the notorious 'ministerial leapfrog' – that even the tsar complained that it made his head spin. Evidence of Rasputin's interference in military affairs, rumours that a pro-German court party, associated with the empress – she was nicknamed 'the German woman' – was seeking a separate peace which would reinforce the autocracy, and the continued gossip about financial speculation and shady deals, all associated with the unsavoury name of Rasputin, brought growing disrepute on the Romanov household. Extreme right-wing politicians together with a relative of the tsar conspired at the end of December 1916 to poison, shoot and finally drop Rasputin through a hole in the frozen canal outside his house in St Petersburg, bringing his dangerous association with the court to an end. HS

Rasul-Zade, Mehmid Emin (1884–1955)

Born to a devout family in Baku, Rasul-Zade was educated locally. He began publishing when he was nineteen, and joined the Himmat in 1904. He edited the Himmat paper *Takammul* (Perfection) from the end of 1906 to March 1907 when it was closed by the police. He escaped to Persia to avoid tsarist persecution and became a major political figure in the Persian revolutionary movement. In Tehran he edited two radical journals. The weekly *Iran-i-Nou* (New

Iran), which he founded in 1909, subsequently became the official organ of the Democratic Party of Iran.

In 1912 he was forced to leave Persia after Russian demands for his deportation and settled in Constantinople. Attracted by the Young Turk movement and the ideas of Pan-Turkism, Rasul-Zade took an active role in the Turkic nationalist paper *Turk Yurdu* (Turkish Home) founded by his compatriot Ahmed bey Aghayev. Taking advantage of an amnesty in 1913, he returned to Russia, joined the Mussavat and became the party's leading spokesman. His paper *Achik Soz* (Open World) took a moderate line during the war and was loyal to the Russian war effort. In 1917 he was elected leader of the Musavat and, as a delegate to the Transcaucasian Muslim congress in April and the All-Russian Muslim congress in May, he argued for Azerbaijani national territorial autonomy. In June the Musavat merged with the Ganja-based Turkic Federalist Party and Rasul-Zade became a leading member of the new organization's central committee. In October he was elected its chairman and maintained a moderate left position against the strong conservative elements within the party.

In December 1918 he was elected President of the Azerbaijani parliament, and in 1920 confirmed as Musavat party leader. After the sovietization of Azerbaijan, Rasul-Zade was arrested and taken to Moscow whence he escaped to Finland in 1922. Active in émigré politics, he lived in various countries before finally settling in Ankara where he died in 1955. SFJ

Reed, John (1887–1920)

Born in Oregon, USA, the son of a judge, Reed was educated at Harvard and went on to become a prominent war correspondent, covering the Mexican War of 1916–17 and the FIRST WORLD WAR when he found himself in Russia on the eve of the OCTOBER REVOLUTION (he was present at the storming of the Winter Palace). Like a small number of other foreigners of radical bent who made their way to Russia after February 1917, his sympathies lay squarely with the BOLSHEVIK government; so much so that from December 1917 he went to work for it as a member (with Boris Reinstein and another American, Albert Rhys Williams) of the Bureau of International Revolutionary Propaganda which later became Narkomindel's Press Bureau. He attended the Second All-Russian Congress of Soviets (October 1917) as an observer and spoke as a participant at the Third and Seventh Congresses (January 1918 and December 1919 respectively). In January 1918 the Soviet government proposed Reed as a replacement for the then Russian consul in New York, but his appointment was rejected by American authorities. He returned to the USA a month later and completed his eye-witness account of the revolution (*Ten Days That Shook the World*, published in March 1919) and helped to found the Communist-Labor Party (later to become the Communist

Figure 69   Reed.

Party of the USA). In October 1919 he was once again in Russia (Moscow). He became a member of the Executive Committee of Comintern and was a delegate to the organization's Second Congress in July–August 1920, travelling soon after (in ZINOVIEV's special train) to Baku for the Congress of the Peoples of the East (see THE IDEA OF WORLD REVOLUTION). In Baku he contracted typhoid from a piece of contaminated watermelon and died soon after arriving in Moscow. He is buried in Red Square, near the Kremlin Wall.   FP

Reilly, Sidney (1874–1925?)

British Intelligence agent. Born in Russia of Russian- or Polish-Jewish parents, Sigmund Georgievich Rosenblum married an Irish widow in London in 1898, changed his name to Reilly, and acquired a British passport. He carried out British Intelligence assignments in several countries, and represented a German armaments firm in St Petersburg until 1914. Returning to Russia in April 1918, he operated under assumed identities. In mid August he was introduced

by the British semi-diplomatic mission chief in Moscow, R. B. LOCKHART, to Colonel Eduard Berzin, a Latvian battalion commander guarding the Kremlin; acting on VECHEKA orders, Berzin pretended that Latvian troops serving the BOLSHEVIK regime were disaffected. Reilly subsidized Berzin, encouraging him to mount an anti-Bolshevik coup. He also participated in joint American, British and French espionage activities and sabotage preparations. The Soviet authorities suppressed and publicized these conspiracies in early September, putting a number of conspirators on trial in late November 1918; Reilly, who had meanwhile escaped to Britain, was sentenced to death. His connections with British Intelligence diminished thereafter, but his freelance anti-Soviet activity continued. He supported SAVINKOV, and was allegedly implicated in the ZINOVIEV Letter forgery in 1924. In September 1925, he re-entered Russia illegally, under the auspices of an OGPU-controlled monarchist resistance organization known as the Trust. He was promptly arrested and reportedly executed in November 1925. GHL

Figure 70   Reilly.

375

Rodzyanko, Mikhail Vladimirovich (1859–1924)

Born on 9 (21) March 1859 in the province of Ekaterinoslav, Rodzyanko was an aristocrat, a wealthy landowner, a former officer with one of the élite regiments of guards and, until 1914, closely associated with court circles. As one of the leaders of the Octobrists (see OCTOBER MANIFESTO), he cut a massive figure both in girth and politically, and for years was at the centre of the struggle over liberal reforms. However, he was, according to his critics, big 'only . . . in physical bulk', being deficient in the vision and insight necessary for true statesmanship. Despite this, Rodzyanko was a Deputy of the Third and Fourth State Dumas, and from March 1911 its leader. In that capacity, he was the one who, in March 1912, brought the RASPUTIN case before the tsar. Whilst at the beginning Rodzyanko was one of those who considered that Rasputin and his supporters were 'without doubt' collaborating with the German General Staff during the First World War, he later concluded that Rasputin was 'entirely incapable' of holding any political opinions, and was at worst the tool of 'certain sinister agents'. However, although his views regarding the danger that the 'holy man' posed to the embattled nation were eventually toned down, his pronouncements, together with those of GUCHKOV, did much to cause sustained destabilization of the Russian political system, and notably the part played in it by the monarchy. Four years later, after Rasputin had been assassinated by Prince Felix Yusupov, Rodzyanko attempted to persuade the tsar to overcome the prolonged crisis by appointing a Duma cabinet.

His lack of acumen in dealing with the increasingly complex political situation in Russia was particularly evident in his view of his Duma colleagues being the 'chosen representatives of the people'; a mantle that, arguably, had not been the case since that legislature was elected under the Law of 3 June 1907. The people he regarded as leaders, and notably the landed nobility, had even by then been forced to give way to new social and political formations. Yet his views remained fairly constant: the tsar's first visit to the Duma on 9 February 1916 was described in 'glowing terms' by Rodzyanko; indicative of a man who was loyal to a notion of Russia's future development as a constitutional government that was very closely linked to the monarchy. In the course of the FEBRUARY REVOLUTION, Rodzyanko was one of those who attempted to convince the tsar of the need to introduce a constitution. On 26 February he sent a series of telegrams to the tsar, reporting anarchy in St Petersburg, the capital, the need for a new government that enjoyed the confidence of the country, and the urgency of immediate action to save the country and the Romanov Dynasty. Upon reading these telegrams, the tsar responded by saying that 'this fat Rodzyanko has written me some nonsense to which I will not even reply'. When, on the evening of 14 March 1917, the tsar finally decided, in fact, to commission Rodzyanko to form a cabinet, the Duma Committee had already become a quasi-government. This ensured that there would be little chance of a constitutional monarchy emerging.

With the onset of the revolution, both Rodzyanko and the Duma 'were merely shadows of the past'. Rodzyanko's claim that the Duma was 'the only legal body representative of all the peoples of Russia' hardly squared with his own perceptions of the power of the Petrograd Soviet: when he wanted to visit the tsar at Pskov to discuss the latter's future, he was forced to apply to the Executive Committee of the Soviet for a permit; when the tsar wanted to speak to him from Pskov, Rodzyanko refused to go to the telephone unless he received the Soviet leaders' express permission to do so.

Rodzyanko's poorly developed sense of political judgment was visible in two other important areas. He must, to a degree at least, be viewed as responsible for the rise to the Vice-Presidency of the Duma of the deeply unpopular D. D. Protopopov; a misjudgment of which he was never able to clear himself or the Duma. The second major failing was his support of GENERAL L. G. KORNILOV and his eleventh-hour move to restore order and 'proper governance' to Russia. Kornilov received an unambiguous vote of support from Rodzyanko when the latter sent the General a telegram in which he announced that 'all thinking Russia turns towards you, full of hope and faith'. This led Kornilov to the mistaken conclusion that this was clear proof of strong support from the people of Russia, whereas in reality it was nothing more than a vote of confidence from a relatively few people (with Rodzyanko at their head) and without the necessary popular backing. In 1920 Rodzyanko emigrated to Yugoslavia, where he died on 24 January 1924.   FP

Further Reading
Florinsky, M.: *The End of the Russian Empire*. New York: Collier Books, 1961.

Golub, P.A. et al. (eds.): *Velikaya Oktyabr'skaya Sotsialisticheskaya Revolyutsiya*. Moscow: Sovetskaya Entsiklopediya, 1987.

Ruzsky, Nikolai Vladimirovich (1854–1918)

A graduate of the 2nd Konstantinovskoe military school, Ruzsky entered the army in 1872, enlisted in the Life Guards grenadier regiment as a sub-lieutenant and saw active service in the 1877–8 war with Turkey. From 1882 after further study at the General Staff academy, he held a series of staff posts until his appointment as chief of staff to the II Manchurian army in 1904. Ruzsky commanded an army corps for three years until 1909 when he was promoted general of infantry and made a permanent member of the war ministry's military council. In the latter capacity he was one of the main architects of the new army field regulations introduced in 1912. Between 1912 and September 1914 he served as assistant commander of the Kiev military districts and then commander of the North-Western Front until March 1915. After two months as head of the VI army in the summer of 1915 he took command of the northern and later both the Northern and North-Western Fronts.

Dogged by ill-health since the winter of 1915 when for eight months he relinquished his command, Ruzsky finally retired in April 1917. Patriotic, able and never on good personal terms with NICHOLAS II, Ruzsky played a key role in convincing the emperor to abdicate in the last days of February 1917. From April 1917 to September 1918 he sought treatment in the spa town of Kislovodsk where he was taken hostage by the Caucasian RED ARMY. The following month Ruzsky was executed by a squad of BOLSHEVIK sailors in Pyatigorsk.   MP

Rykov, Alexei Ivanovich (1881–1938)

Alexei Rykov, born in Saratov on 13 (25) February 1881 and from a peasant background, joined the militant wing of the RSDLP at the age of 20 and, after 1903, the Bolshevik faction of that organization. He worked for some time as an underground agent in Russia (principally in the Saratov, Moscow and St Petersburg areas) and was a participant in the 1905 REVOLUTION; in the process, however, becoming resentful of V. I. LENIN's dictatorial orders from abroad. In 1910 Rykov broke with Lenin, becoming leader of the 'Party-minded' Bolsheviks (also known as Bolshevik Conciliators); a sub-faction that adopted a conciliatory attitude to other socialist parties in the wake of the FEBRUARY REVOLUTION, and, after the Bolsheviks seized power in October 1917, advocated the formation of a coalition government involving all socialist parties. Rykov's ideological dissidence in this period earned him the label of 'inconsistent Trotskyist' from Lenin (a particularly biting slur, given that Rykov held an abiding antipathy for TROTSKY).

Following the February Revolution, Rykov became a member of the Moscow Soviet and, a few weeks later, spoke out against Lenin's April Theses, stressing in doing so that it was imperative that the West give the socialist revolution 'a push' in order for it to succeed: 'We do not have the strength or the objective conditions [to do otherwise]', he concluded. In September 1917, Rykov suggested that the Bolsheviks should adopt a more moderate political line, which again drew Lenin's criticism. Nonetheless, in the same month Rykov was called to join the party's Central Committee in Petrograd, and was made a member of the Petrograd Soviet. In the October days, he was elected a member of the Moscow Military-Revolutionary Committee, but did not work in this body because of his continuing presence in Petrograd. During the CIVIL WAR, Rykov served as Special Plenipotentiary for the supply of the Red Army and Navy.

Despite his differences with Lenin, and because of his strengths as an administrator, Rykov came to work in a number of senior posts in the Bolshevik Government, including those of People's Commissar of the Interior (1917–18) and Chairman of the Supreme Council of National Economy (1918–20). Between 1921 and 1924 he was the Deputy Chairman of the Council of People's Commissars (SOVNARKOM), becoming chairman after Lenin's death in 1924, a post he held until 1929. He was concurrently a member of the Politburo. Rykov managed throughout to maintain a highly critical, independent line. In the first month of Bolshevik rule, for example, he was one of the six original members of the Soviet Government (the others being V. P. Nogin, V. P. Milyutin, A. I. Teodorovich, A. G. SHLYAPNIKOV and D. B. Ryazanov) to resign from the Central Committee and the Council of People's Commissars. Moreover, he never abandoned his belief in the early Bolshevik slogan/position of creating a democratic dictatorship of the proletariat *and* peasantry; a belief, in other words, in a socialism founded on toilers rather than the proletariat alone.

Given this political orientation, Rykov supported N. I. BUKHARIN and M. P. Tomsky (and ultimately I. V. STALIN) against Trotsky and G. E. ZINOVIEV in the course of the inner-party conflict following Lenin's death. Later, however, he became one of the most prominent members of the Right Opposition, working against the compulsory collectivization of agriculture. After the Right Opposition was defeated, Rykov was removed from senior positions, being made for a time the Commissar for Posts and Telegraphs. In 1929 he was removed from all posts and eventually charged and tried for treason in the final show trial of the great purge. He (together with Bukharin) denied charges of having participated in the murder of S. M. Kirov, V. V. Kuybyshev, V. R. Menzhinsky, M. GORKY and Gorky's son Peshkov, but admitted (again, with Bukharin) to having had 'indirect responsibility for the terrorist acts of others'. Rykov was found guilty of having personally formed (in 1934) a terrorist group for the preparation and commission of terrorist acts against Stalin, V. M. MOLOTOV, L. M. Kaganovich and K. E. Voroshilov. He was sentenced to death and executed on 15 March 1938.   FP

Further Reading

Cohen, S.: *Bukharin and the Bolshevik Revolution.* London: Wildwood House, 1974.

Golub, P.A. et al. (eds.): *Velikaya Oktyabr'skaya Sotsialisticheskaya Revolyutsiya.* Moscow: Sovetskaya Entsiklopediya, 1987.

Ryskulov, Turar (1894–1938)

Born into a wealthy family of the Kazakh aristocracy, Ryskulov emerged as one of the leading Kazakh nationalists of the twentieth century. He made his political début in

1916 when he served a prison term for his participation in the 1916 revolt in his native Semirechye. Soon after his release from prison in early 1917, he founded the nationalist revolutionary organization, The Union of the Revolutionary Kirghiz Youth, and in September of the same year became one of the first Central Asian Muslims to join the BOLSHEVIK party. Ryskulov's political career unfolded under the twin stars of communism and nationalism. Although he remained committed to both until the end of his life in 1938, nationalism definitely took precedence over proletarian internationalism and communism in Ryskulov's concerns.

Among many important positions in the party and government bureaucracy, he was commissar of health of the Turkestan Autonomous Soviet Socialist Republic (1919–20); a member of the Turkestan Bureau of the Commissariat for Nationalities (1921–3); the Central Asian Bureau of the Central Committee of the Russian Communist Party (1923–4); the Central Committee of the Turkestan Communist Party (1924–4); deputy chairman of the Eastern Department of Comintern (1924–5); lecturer at the Communist University of the Toilers of the East in Moscow. Ryskulov's political career began to decline in 1923 and it ended with his arrest in 1937 and execution on 10 February 1938 on the grounds of treason and nationalism.

Although rehabilitated posthumously in the years following the Twentieth Party Congress (1956), Ryskulov remains shrouded in mystery, as his works are banned in the USSR. In his essays and speeches he presented his ideas on the special conditions of his native region and the relationship between native and Russian Bolsheviks. In all, he emerged as a critic of the colonialist attitude of Moscow *vis à vis* Turkestan and a defender of the special needs of the Muslims, even advocating a Turkic Communist Party and a National Muslim Army. A-AR

Samoilova, Konkordiya Nikolaevna (1876–1921)

The daughter of a Siberian priest, Samoilova attended the higher courses in St Petersburg in the late 1890s, helped to organize a student demonstration in 1897 and was arrested after the Kazan square demonstration in 1901. After being expelled from the higher courses, she went to Paris and attended the Free Russian School of Social Sciences. She became a Social Democrat and on returning to Russia in 1903, became a member of the Tver party committee. She moved to Ekaterinoslav and was arrested in 1904, spending fourteen months in prison. On her release she went to Odessa where she joined the BOLSHEVIKS. After further peregrinations she ended up in St Petersburg, on the Bolshevik party committee. From 1912 she worked for *Pravda* and was one of the editorial collective of the

Bolsheviks' journal for women, *Rabotnitsa* (The Woman Worker) in 1914. After its suppression she was arrested and imprisoned, and returned to Petrograd only after the FEBRUARY REVOLUTION. Originally an opponent of separate women's sections, her work with women during 1917 made her less amenable to the orthodox party line. After the OCTOBER REVOLUTION she continued her work with women until her death, in 1921, from cholera contracted while on an 'agitation steamer' on the Volga (see WOMEN: 1917 AND AFTER; PROPAGANDA). LE

Savinkov, Boris Viktorovich (1879–1925)

Born in Kharkov, the son of an assistant procurator of the Kharkov military district, Savinkov was educated in Warsaw before matriculating in 1897 in the Law Faculty of St Petersburg University. Expelled for political activity in 1899, he joined the Plekhanovist group Sotsialist. In 1902 he was exiled to Vologda where he converted to POPULISM.

In 1903 Savinkov escaped to Geneva where he joined the SOCIALIST REVOLUTIONARY fighting organization under Evno AZEF. He was involved in the assassination of Interior Minister V. K. PLEHVE in July 1904 and, in February 1905, of Grand Duke Sergei Alexandrovich, Governor General of Moscow. Following Azef's exposure in 1908 as an OKHRANA agent, Savinkov attempted to revive the fighting organization, but by 1911 he had abandoned politics for literature. His first works, *The Pale Horse* (1909) and *What Never Happened* (1912), express the religious populist ideas of Dmitri Merezhkovsky, Zinaida Gippius and Dmitri Filosofov (see RELIGIOUS-PHILOSOPHICAL MOVEMENT). In 1920 they were to join his Russian Political Committee in Poland.

In 1914 Savinkov joined Vladimir BURTSEV in publishing the patriotic journal *Pryzyv* (Call-up) (1914–16) in Paris and enlisted in the French Army. On his return to Russia in April 1917 he was appointed political commissar to the VII Army on the South-Western Front. By July 1917 his part in restoring military discipline and his Political Freemasonry had earned him the post of assistant war minister under KERENSKY. Savinkov now sought abolition of the Soldiers' Committees and conspired with the Commander-in-Chief General L. G. KORNILOV to replace the PROVISIONAL GOVERNMENT by a Directory in which he was to play a leading role. In August 1917, however, Kornilov moved on Petrograd and Savinkov, fearing a military dictatorship, rallied to the civilian government. His equivocal role in this affair and refusal to appear before a commssion of enquiry led to Savinkov's dismissal from the Provisional Government and expulsion from the SR party.

In January 1918 Savinkov founded the SR-based Union for the Defence of Freedom and the Fatherland which organized a series of risings in the Upper Volga towns in July. Following action with the Czech forces in Kazan he attended the State Conference at Ufa and served as foreign representative of the Directory and of Admiral KOLCHAK, notably in the 'Russian Political Conference' which attended to Russia's interests at Versailles.

Following Kolchak's collapse, Savinkov negotiated with Józef Piłsudski in January 1920 to accept a revision of Poland's frontiers in return for permission to recruit a Russian 'Third Army' inside Poland. The defeat of General Bulak-Balakhovich's advance on Moscow in November 1920, in which Savinkov took part, the collapse of WRANGEL and the growing desire for peace in Poland undermined his position. Following the Treaty of Riga (March 1921), the Soviet government obtained his expulsion from Poland.

By means of a 'Green' or peasant revolution Savinkov had hoped that the former Empire could be transformed into a democratic federal state. A Russian nationalist, he had nevertheless agreed to autonomy for UKRAINE, the Don and the Kuban (see COSSACKS). He had recognised Finnish independence and that of Belorussia in principle. In 1921 he advised that in return for recognition of the Soviet Government the European powers should demand the abolition of the VECHEKA, the reintroduction of private property (without prejudice to peasant land acquisitions) and free elections to the SOVIETS. In 1921 in Paris, aided by Russian business interests and Western secret services (see LOCKHART and REILLY), Savinkov formed a National Union for the Defence of Freedom and the Fatherland. Lenin's New Economic Policy and the suppression of the SRs during 1922, with the elimination of many of his agents, undermined his position. In August 1924 he was arrested crossing the Polish frontier and sentenced to death. The commutation of the sentence to ten years' imprisonment, and the publication of a penitent article in *Izvestiya*, suggest that Savinkov, voluntarily or otherwise, reached an accommodation with the Bolsheviks. In 1925 it was announced that on 7 May Savinkov had committed suicide in the Lubyanka prison. A film on his life, 'Krakh' (Collapse), appeared in the Soviet Union in 1969.   JB

Further Reading

Abraham, Richard: *Alexander Kerensky*. London and New York: Sidgwick & Jackson/Columbia University Press, 1987.

Radkey, Oliver: *The Agrarian Foes of Bolshevism*. New York and London: 1958.

Savinkov, Boris: *Memoirs of a Terrorist*. New York: 1931.

Serge, Victor (1890–1947)

Born in Belgium to Russian/Polish parents (real name Viktor Kibalchich) who commuted for '. . . their daily bread and . . . good libraries' between the British Museum, Paris, Switzerland and Belgium, Serge's childhood was spent in an environment filled with radical thought and tales of trials, executions and exile. In 1908 he went to Paris to find work as a draftsman. Through the Russian émigré community he was introduced to the SOCIALIST REVOLUTIONARIES, but joined the ANARCHISTS. Quickly tiring of conventional work, instead he engaged in translating Russian literature, his own writings and political activism in the French anarchist circle. As editor of *l'Anarchie* in 1910, he received a five-year prison sentence for his complicity in a previous wave of terrorism. Following his release in 1917 he made his way to Barcelona, where he mingled with Syndicalists and observed the news from Russia. In August 1917, disenchanted with the Spanish revolutionary movement, he met the Russian Consul-General, volunteered for military service in 'liberated Russia', and took over fourteen months (including a period of internment in a French concentration camp) getting there.

In Petrograd Serge made contact with Gorky (see WRITERS AND THE REVOLUTION) and ZINOVIEV, became a member of the BOLSHEVIK Party and soon, with V. O. Mazin, constituted the Comintern Executive, for it had neither personnel nor office. Their lives were spent in transit, correcting proofs on trams and conferring with Zinoviev in the evenings. Serge was invaluable to the Comintern in its early stages. His knowledge of languages ensured an important part in the preparations for its Second Congress, publication of international editions of its journal and later as one of its agents abroad.

Serge's relationship with the Soviet state was from the start a troubled one. He was uneasy about the Bolshevik exercise of power and the cruelty practised under the authority of the revolution. After his return from abroad in 1926, he became aligned with the Left Opposition and was expelled from the party in 1928. There followed imprisonment, more work for the opposition and, in 1933, exile to Orenburg. Upon release in 1936 Serge left for France (he was the last opposition member allowed to leave) where he maintained links with the opposition-in-exile. After the Nazis came to power in Germany he sought asylum in Mexico. There he remained until his death in November 1947.   FP

Further Reading

Serge, Victor: *The Case of Comrade Tulaev*. London: Hamish Hamilton, 1951.

——— : *Memoirs of a Revolutionary, 1901–1941*. London: Oxford University Press, 1963.

——— : *Year One of the Russian Revolution*. London: Allen Lane, 1972.

——— : *Conquered City*. London: Writers and Readers Cooperative, 1978.

Shabanova, Anna Nikolaevna (1848–1932)

The leading figure on the moderate wing of the WOMEN'S MOVEMENT from the late 1890s to 1917, Shabanova came from a modest gentry background, was swept up by the nihilist revolt in the 1860s and spent six months in prison at the age of seventeen for membership of an illegal women's circle. Putting this radicalism behind her, she decided to train as a doctor, failed to gain admission to medical school in Russia and went to Helsinki for two years. In 1873 she enrolled in the women's medical courses which had recently opened in St Petersburg, and was one of the small number of women doctors who graduated in 1878, though licensed to practise only in 1883. For the next decade she practised as a paediatrician. She became involved in the women's movement in the early 1890s, being one of the founders of the Russian Women's Mutual Philanthropic Society which, despite its name and its bureaucratic regulations, was the first general women's association in Russia. She became its president in 1896, a post she held until 1917. The society represented the non-political and moderate side of Russian feminism. Although it became involved in the suffrage campaign in 1905, Shabanova took care not to antagonize those in political authority. She guided the society through the vicissitudes of political life after 1905, remaining vulnerable all the while to the criticisms of more radical feminists. During the FIRST WORLD WAR Shabanova was a vigorous patriot and in 1917 supported the PROVISIONAL GOVERNMENT's policy of fighting the war to the finish. She remained in Russia after the OCTOBER REVOLUTION, without being reconciled to the new regime. But she was honoured for her work as a paediatrician, and died in 1932 at the age of eighty-four.

LE

Shaevich, Genrikh Isaevich (dates unknown)

Shaevich's origins and later fate are obscure and there is an element of the charlatan about him. He began as a ZIONIST, became chairman of an Odessa Zionist circle, Oir Tsion, and then director of a project to publish Jewish nationalist literature. He was converted by Manya VIL-BUSHEVICH when they met at a Zionist congress in Minsk in the summer of 1902 (see THE ZUBATOV MOVEMENT). He worked exclusively in Odessa, was a superb orator who could move his audience to tears, was an excellent labour organizer with a large following among Jews and non-Jews alike. Indeed his support among the Russian Orthodox exceeded that among JEWS. This was perhaps due to his capacity for self-advertisement. He claimed he had a doctoral degree from Berlin, and even that essential certificate for a radical career, an expulsion from university – both strongly doubted by contemporaries. His Orthodox followers were permitted to believe that he was a convert and a teacher at the Odessa Orphanage of the Empress Marie Fedorovna. In his hands the Jewish Odessa Independents became the largest labour movement then in Russia, recruiting Russians, Ukrainians and Jews alike, and was successful among all segments of the working class.

From early 1903 he conducted strike after strike in Odessa with official sanction as usual until he was reprimanded by A. A. Lopukhin, the director of the Department of Police, for excessive radicalism in the Restel strike of May 1903. He promised to reduce the tempo, but in fact did not; and the July general strike, a part of the great wave then sweeping the south, found him competing with the socialists, leading to such provocative demands as the eight-hour day. He was arrested and exiled for that performance. There are widely divergent opinions on his role in that strike. Perhaps he was dejected, as he acknowledged, after the atrocious Kishinev pogrom and the dissolution of the Independent Jewish Labour Party that very month, and might thus have retaliated against the autocracy; or he might not have been in a position to hold back the tide which was rising all over the south and, in order to retain any credibility among his following, had to compete with the socialists.

Shaevich did receive regular payments from ZUBATOV, but again there is controversy as to how he spent the money. At Zubatov's instance, Shaevich's Siberian exile was cancelled; but he was permitted to rejoin his family in Odessa only on condition that he forswear political activity. He is the only one of the Zubatovites to have been arrested, a point he proudly boasted of to prove his integrity.

MKP

Shaumyan, Stepan Georgievich (1878–1918)

The son of an Armenian merchant, Shaumyan was born and spent his childhood in Tiflis. He joined the RSDRP in 1901 while at Riga Polytechnic, from which he was expelled after being arrested for taking part in student disorders. Exiled to the Caucasus, he later made his way to Berlin where he continued both his formal and political education. He had met Kautsky and MARTOV in Germany, but it was his first contact with PLEKHANOV and LENIN in Switzerland that brought about a major change in his political development. His practical and theoretical skills made fertile ground for an enduring affinity to Lenin, and indeed he came to be known as 'Lenin of the Caucasus'.

On returning to the Caucasus, Shaumyan became a teacher and took on the leadership of the BOLSHEVIK group in Tiflis. In 1907 he moved to Baku where he helped to build up and lead the workers' movement. Arrested in 1909 and again in 1911, he returned in 1914 to Baku to organize strikes, only to be imprisoned and banished again, this time to Saratov. The FEBRUARY REVOLUTION brought Shaumyan back to Baku and election to chairmanship of its SOVIET. He went on to lead the small Bolshevik faction at the First All-Russian Congress of Soviets, direct the Baku Revolutionary Military Committee and, in 1918, joined the party's Central Committee as Chairman of the Baku Council of People's Commissars and as Commissar for Foreign Affairs. In these capacities he waged an intense struggle to establish Soviet power in the Caucasus, resulting in the formation of the Baku Commune and the Republic of Azerbaijan (see TRANSCAUCASIA. There was strong opposition to this, particularly from the Mussavat (Turkic Federalists) who instigated a Muslim rising in March 1918 and subsequently applied increasing pressure through a blockade of Baku and the threat of a joint-offensive with Turkish troops. In July rightist elements in the Soviet prevailed over Bolshevik protests in summoning support from British forces stationed in Northern Persia. Shaumyan and twenty-five other Baku commissars fled, only to be arrested by British troops in Krasnovodsk. In what was to become a controversial area of Anglo-Soviet relations in later years (STALIN made reference to it as early as 1919), the 'twenty-six commissars', as they became known, were shot on 20 September 1918, *en route* to internment in India. FP

Shevchenko, Taras (1814–1861)

Regarded as the greatest poet of Ukraine, Shevchenko exercised an enormous influence on the literary and political imagination of Ukrainians throughout the nineteenth and early twentieth centuries. His poetry, particularly in the collection titled *Kobzar* (The Minstrel), was a powerful call for social justice, a search for truth and demand for national liberation of the Ukrainian people. Born a serf and liberated at the age of twenty-four, he was arrested as part of the Brotherhood of Saints Cyril and Methodius and sentenced to serve in exile as a private soldier. He was pardoned in 1857 but died four years later. ND

Shlyapnikov, Alexander Gavrilovich (1885–1937)

Born in Murom, Vladimir province. Shlyapnikov's parents belonged to a sect of Old Believers persecuted by the authorities. His mother with several small children was widowed when Shlyapnikov was two and his early environment hence combined militant religious faith with extreme poverty and hardship; he wrote about his childhood: 'life taught me that there is no justice in this world . . . all this turned my childish dreams and inclinations towards struggle and martyrdom'.

After three years of primary school, he worked his way up from labouring to metal work, and by his early twenties was an experienced mechanic and BOLSHEVIK, knowing machines and factories, strikes and prisons in St Petersburg, Moscow and other cities. From 1908 he was abroad, 'wandering from factory to factory in France, England and Germany', learning French well, and some English and German.

Returning to St Petersburg in early 1914, later that year Shlyapnikov moved to Sweden, entrusted with the vital

Figure 71 Shlyapnikov.

task of organizing clandestine communications between LENIN in Switzerland and Bolshevik organizations in Russia, collaborating with Alexandra KOLLONTAI (who became his intimate friend) and several Swedish and Finnish socialists (see THE SCANDINAVIAN CONNECTION).

One of the few Bolsheviks in Petrograd during the FEBRUARY REVOLUTION, during the spring and summer of 1917 Shlyapnikov was a leading trade union organizer, becoming president of the largest union of metal-workers, and, after the OCTOBER REVOLUTION, Commissar of Labour.

During 1919–21 Shlyapnikov was a principal figure (eventually joined by Kollontai) in the group within the Bolshevik party called (by Lenin) the Workers' Opposition (advocating control of industry by the trade unions, led of course by Bolsheviks, but Bolshevik workers, not bureaucratic officials), which was branded by Lenin as deviation and condemned at the crucial Tenth Party Congress in 1921 (see BOLSHEVIK OPPOSITIONS).

This was effectively the end of Shlyapnikov's career; he had for a couple of years a diplomatic post in Paris, but more importantly compiled two books (now rare) of exceptional historical value, combining personal account and narrative with extensive documentation: *Kanun semnadtsatogo goda* (in translation *On the Eve of 1917*, published in London and New York, 1982), and *Semnadtsaty god* (The Year 1917), 4 vols, 1923–31. He was expelled from the party in 1933, imprisoned in 1935, and evidently died in prison in 1937, as a consequence of ill treatment and neglect rather than intention.

Unusual as an authentically proletarian Bolshevik of some prominence, Shlyapnikov was remembered with respect by those who knew him in Scandinavia, not only for his Bolshevik efficiency but also for his less typical integrity and good nature.   MHF

Further Reading

Björkegren, Hans: *Ryska Posten*. (In Swedish.) Stockholm: Bonniers, 1985.

Futrell, Michael: *Northern Underground*. London and New York: Faber, 1963.

Haupt, Georges and Marie, Jean-Jacques: *Makers of the Russian Revolution*. London: Allen & Unwin, 1974. (Includes short autobiography, to 1920.)

Schapiro, Leonard: *The Origin of the Communist Autocracy*. London: Bell, 1955.

Shumyatsky, Boris Zakharovich (1886–1938)

The son of a bookbinder, Shumyatsky became a party member in 1903. His initial political work was carried out in Manchuria, where he rose to prominence in his moderately successful attempts to spread BOLSHEVIK agitation to Chinese workers. His party activities in China were shortlived. In 1913 he joined the army and in 1917 became active in Siberian politics (and trade union affairs). He was at first appointed chairman of the Bolshevik Siberian regional bureau and representative of the party's Central Committee there. After the Bolshevik seizure of power in October he became chairman of Tsentrosibir and the Military Revolutionary Committee of Eastern Siberia. When Bolshevik authority collapsed in the region, Shumyatsky directed partisan activity there. From July 1919 to March 1920 he was active in the revolutionary committees in Tobolsk and Tyumen (see REVOLUTION IN SIBERIA). In 1921 he was appointed to the Far East Department of the Commissariat of Foreign Affairs and was a delegate to the Third Congress of Comintern.   FP

Skoropadsky, Pavlo (1873–1945)

A political and military activist, Skoropadsky became head of the Ukrainian State between April and December 1918. He completed officers' training in St Petersburg and took

Figure 72 Skoropadsky.

part in the Russo-Japanese War as a lieutenant in the Russian Army. Promoted to General in 1912, he was commended for bravery in battle against the Germans in the FIRST WORLD WAR. After the FEBRUARY REVOLUTION, he supervised the Ukrainianization of the 34th corps which was renamed the First Ukrainian Corps. Elected leader of the Ukrainian Free COSSACKS in October 1917, which pledged to support the Central Rada, he dissented when the Rada sought to demobilize all permanent military formations. His claim to the position of Hetman was supported by larger landowners and wealthy peasants (see THE UKRAINE: REVOLUTION AND CIVIL WAR. After the collapse of his government he emigrated to Germany where he resided until his death.   ND

Skvortsov-Stepanov, Ivan Ivanovich (1870–1928)

Born the son of a factory office worker in Bogorodsk (now Noginsk), Skvortsov (party name Stepanov) graduated from the Moscow Teachers' Institute in 1890 and taught in a Moscow secondary school before being implicated in a plot to assassinate NICHOLAS II. Experience of workers' study groups with A. A. BOGDANOV and V. BAZAROV while in exile in Tula and Kaluga (1896–1902) made for a conversion to Marxism and the formation of a long-standing intellectual relationship. In 1904 he was brought into the BOLSHEVIK fraction by Bogdanov in Geneva. He was a founder-member of the Moscow group of Marxist littérateurs and a contributor to their journal *Pravda*.

Opposed to the 'recallist' and 'ultimatist' tendencies, Stepanov contested the elections to the Second and Third Dumas. In 1911 he was arrested and exiled to Astrakhan; between 1914 and 1917 he resumed Party work in Moscow. Between the two revolutions he edited the journals *Borba* (Struggle) (1905), *Rabochee Znamya* (Workers' Banner) (1908), *Nash Put* (Our Path) (1913) and *Rabochii Trud* (Workers' Labour) (1914), but remained independent of both the LENIN and Vpered (Forward) factions. In 1907–8 he and Bazarov published a Russian translation of Marx's *Capital*; in 1910 appeared the first volume of *Kurs politicheskoi ekonomii* (A Course in Political Economy) which he co-authored with Bogdanov.

Following the FEBRUARY REVOLUTION Stepanov edited the Moscow Soviet *Izvestiya* until dismissed by its MENSHEVIK and SR majority. He then edited *Sotsial-Demokrat* for the Moscow Committee of the RSDRP and from June led the Bolshevik fraction in the Moscow City Duma. A supporter, like KAMENEV, of the 'democratic revolution', Stepanov was nevertheless appointed Commissar for Finance in the first Sovnarkom. He declined this position, assuming instead responsibilities first with Kommunist, the publishing house of the Left Communists in Moscow, and then Gosizdat (State Publishing House).

During the CIVIL WAR Stepanov was concerned with cooperation in industry and agriculture and with electrification and his writings on these subjects influenced Lenin's thinking on 'CULTURAL REVOLUTION'. During NEP he supported STALIN and BUKHARIN against TROTSKY and in 1925, during the campaign against ZINOVIEV, he was appointed editor of *Leningradskii Pravda*. In 1926 he assumed control of the Lenin Institute, which under Kamenev had become critical of the NEP, and re-edited Lenin's works in such a way as to disgrace Kamenev and Zinoviev. In 1928 he presided over the further 'Leninization' of Party history when the Lenin Institute absorbed the Central Commission for the Study of Party History and the History of the October Revolution (acronym: Istpart).

A militant atheist and critic of the sociologies of religion of Pokrovsky and LUNACHARSKY, Stepanov remained in epistemology a disciple of Bogdanov and his essay of 1924 on 'Historical materialism and contemporary natural science', in which he argued the positivist ('Mechanist') case for reducing philosophy to the natural sciences, precipitated an important debate with 'dialectical materialists' of the Deborin school.

A member of the Central Committee from 1925 until his death, Stepanov was editor of *Izvestiya* from 1925 and deputy chief editor of *Pravda* from 1927. A prolific and respected social theorist and Party veteran, Stepanov played an important part in the consolidation of Bolshevik rule during the NEP and in the construction of Marxist-Leninist ideology. He died of typhoid fever in 1928.   JB

Spiridonova, Maria Alexandrovna (1885–1941)

Born in the city of Tambov, Spiridonova began to train as a nurse in 1904, but was attracted to the Party of SOCIALIST REVOLUTIONARIES (PSR). When the Tambov PSR decided to avenge the brutal suppression of peasant unrest in the province, she volunteered to assassinate its authors. On 16 January 1906, she mortally wounded Police Inspector Luzhenovsky. The beatings, torture and violation she was subjected to shocked Russian and international opinion; her deportation to Akatui, Siberia assuming the character of a triumphal procession. On her release, in March 1917, she was briefly mayor of Chita where she blew up the prison. Spiridonova arrived in Petrograd for the Third Congress of the PSR in May, at which her intense and radical speeches soon made her a leader of the left wing. After the OCTOBER REVOLUTION she became leader of the new Party of Left Socialist Revolutionaries (Internationalists). Elected to the chair of the Second Congress of Peasants' Soviets, Spiridonova was also the Bolshevik-Left SR candidate for the chair of the CONSTITUENT ASSEMBLY. At first she supported the Brest-Litovsk Treaty, but in July 1918 she led the anti-Bolshevik rising. After twenty years of imprisonment and exile in Central Asia and Siberia, she was shot in 1941 to avert her capture by advancing German forces.   RA

Further Reading

Gusev, I.K.: *Krakh partii levykh eserov*. Moscow: 1963.

Steinberg, I.: *Spiridonova. Revolutionary Terrorist*. London: Methuen, 1935.

Stalin, Iosif Vissarionovich (1879–1953)

Though not highly visible during February–October 1917, Stalin (real name Dzhugashvili) was one of the inner circle of BOLSHEVIKS whose common commitment and political ability made possible the victory of LENIN's party. His reward for his unpublicized contributions in this period was the engagement of his great capacity for political administration with a wide range of important issues immediately following the OCTOBER REVOLUTION, leading to his eventual emergence as the dominant person in a generation of Soviet history and the most eminent Communist in the world.

Born in poverty in the Georgian town of Gori, Iosif

Vissarionovich Dzhugashvili received an incomplete secondary education in the Orthodox Christian Seminary in Tiflis (Tbilisi), where he acquired radical ideas. From the turn of the century to 1917 he remained an obscure worker in the underground organization of the Marxist movement. Although he supported the Bolsheviks and first met Lenin in 1905, it was only in 1912 that he was elevated to the Central Committee. In that year he also began using the pseudonym 'Stalin'. The following year Lenin commissioned him to write a substantial essay on the Marxist approach to the problem of minority nationalities, which he did in the course of about a month spent in Vienna. Apart from attending the party's Fifth Congress in London in 1907, this was the only time in his life that he stayed any length of time outside the boundaries of the Russian Empire or Soviet Union. Often arrested, he was completing a term of exile in Siberia at the time of the FEBRUARY REVOLUTION.

Arriving in Petrograd on 12 March (OS), Stalin and KAMENEV asserted their prerogatives as members of the Central Committee, contrary to the wishes of the local party leadership. They accepted the main lines of the Dual Power as it was then understood by the leadership of the Soviet and also accepted the necessity of continuing a defensive war. In his later career Stalin found this non-Leninist stance highly embarrassing and sought to suppress evidence of it. Only by May had Stalin clearly accepted Lenin's more radical position, but in June he was a strong supporter of the abortive armed demonstration.

Stalin did not repeat this radical belligerence in the 'July Days', but acted as liaison between the party and the Soviet leadership. He had been a member of the Central Executive Committee since 18 March, acting more as an observer than a participant. Only in the July crisis did he speak out, trying to induce the Soviet to prevent the PROVISIONAL GOVERNMENT from repressing the Bolsheviks. In particular he tried to stop publication of the treason charges against Lenin, but failed. It therefore fell to Stalin to consult with Lenin on the advisability of staying in Petrograd or of going into hiding. When Lenin opted for flight, Stalin shaved off the leader's beard by way of disguise and escorted him through the night to the railway station.

As a result of Lenin's absence, Stalin gave the major report on the work of the Central Committee to the Sixth Party Congress, which opened on 26 July. Here he tried to justify the ineffectual policy of the party in the July Uprising and Lenin's decision to drop the slogan 'All Power to the Soviets'. At the end of the Congress Stalin was elected to the new Central Committee and assumed principal responsibility for the political line of the party organ.

This was Stalin's main activity during the October Revolution. At this time he distinguished himself neither by his support for Lenin's efforts to wring from the Central Committee a commitment to armed uprising nor by his direction of the military action. In later years, however, his regime insisted that he was 'Lenin's closest associate', and that 'he had direct charge of all the preparations for the insurrection'. To buttress this claim there were many references to a 'Party Centre' that the Central Committee established on 16 October, but there is no evidence that this body ever functioned.

For Stalin the immediate result of the October Revolution was his assumption of a cabinet post, People's Commissar of Nationality Affairs. Its task was to prevent as much as possible the fragmentation of the Russian Empire along ethnic lines. Attempting to demonstrate to minority nationalities that the new regime was not Russian imperialist, Stalin and Lenin on 2 December 1917 co-signed the 'Declaration of the Rights of the Peoples of Russia'. This promised the right of national self-determination, but in his dealings with Finland and UKRAINE in the next few weeks Stalin introduced a major qualification of this right. The Moscow government would recognize as independent only those minority nationalist states that it considered proletarian. However, Stalin implied in his address to the Third All-Russian Congress of Soviets in January 1918, it was unlikely that 'proletarian' regimes would opt for independence. He now proposed a Soviet federal state, which could reabsorb national minorities to a Russo-centric order. He played a major role in the drafting of the CONSTITUTION for this state, the Russian Soviet Federative Socialist Republic (RSFSR), which was adopted on 10 July 1918.

During the CIVIL WAR Stalin served in many capacities, especially as a political-military leader in critical fronts: Tsaritsyn and the North Caucasus in June–October 1918, the Eastern Front in May–September 1919, the Southern Front and South-Western fronts in October 1919–August 1920. This work brought him into conflict with Trotsky who as People's Commissar of War found Stalin insubordinate. He also served on numerous committees, including the Revolutionary-Military Council of the Republic, the Council of Workers' and Peasants' Defence. He was elected to the Politburo and Orgburo in March 1919, bodies which played an increasingly important role in the direction of the system of government.

Thus, by the end of the Civil War Stalin probably possessed the most wide-ranging experience of any party leader with the exception of Lenin. His career in 1917–21 made him well qualified to assume the newly-created post of General Secretary of Communist Party in April 1922, opening the way for his rise to supremacy.　　　RHMcN

Further Reading

Hingley, R.: *Joseph Stalin: Man and Legend*. New York: McGraw-Hill, 1974.

McNeal, R. H.: *Stalin: Man and Ruler*. London: Macmillan, 1988.

Stalin, J. V.: *Works*, vols 3 and 4, Moscow: 1953.

Trotsky, Leon: *Stalin: An Appraisal of the Man and His Influence*. New York: Harper, 1941.

Tucker, R. C.: *Stalin as Revolutionary 1879–1929*. New York: Norton, 1973.

Ulam, A. B.: *Stalin: The Man and His Era*. New York: Viking, 1973.

Stasova, Elena Dmitrievna (1873–1966)

The daughter of a liberal lawyer who was arrested and searched more than once for his defence of revolutionaries, Stasova grew up in a cultured, enlightened household, with free access to books and ideas. Her uncle was the music and art critic, Vladimir Stasov, and her aunt one of the founders of the feminist movement, Nadezhda Stasova. Having entertained and discarded the idea of training as a doctor, Stasova began teaching at workers' Sunday schools in St Petersburg, then became involved with the fledgeling RSDRP, becoming in 1900 a full-time Iskra agent. From 1904 she took on increasing responsibility for administration in the party committee. In 1912 she became a candidate member of the central committee. Immediately after the FEBRUARY REVOLUTION she was commissioned to reorganize the secretariat of the Petrograd party committee. She served as central committee secretary until 1918, when the new Soviet government moved to Moscow. SVERDLOV replaced her in Moscow, but on his death in 1919 she resumed work under a tripartite management. She resigned in 1920 when the secretariat was reorganized. In her entire career she spent little time on women's issues (and her feminist aunt left hardly a trace of an influence). When it was proposed that she work in Zhenotdel (the Women's Section of the Central Committee) after her resignation from the party secretariat, she declined and spent the rest of her career in various branches of party administration. She was known as an efficient, reliable administrator, 'Comrade Absolute'. It is not at all clear from published sources whether her failure to achieve a more prominent position stemmed from her own limitations or from an implicit tendency in the party to promote men in preference to women, both before October and afterwards.   LE

Stolypin, Peter Arkadievich (1862–1911)

Born of a solid Russian land-owning family on 17 April 1862, Stolypin completed higher education before entering the Ministry of State Domains in 1885. Four years later he was appointed a district (in 1899 provincial) marshal of the nobility in Kovno province. In 1902 he became governor of Grodno province. The Western borderland where Stolypin served was ethnically complex and differed economically from the rest of the empire. As well as Great Russians, the area had substantial Polish, Lithuanian and Jewish populations. Agriculturally it was characterized by the predomi-

nance of the hereditary PEASANT COMMUNE and individual farming. Stolypin took a close interest in agriculture and promoted agricultural reform in this region and the close association with peasant agriculture provided the roots for his later reforms at the national level.

In 1903 Stolypin was appointed governor of Saratov province. He brought with him to this post a commitment to small-holder peasant agriculture and a conviction that the threat of rural disturbances could be significantly eased if the traditional repartitional commune (which dominated in Saratov) could be dismantled in favour of independent peasant farms. His convictions were reinforced by the revolutionary outbreak of 1905, which was particularly severe in Saratov. His success in putting down the revolutionary disturbances was rewarded with his appointment as Minister of the Interior in April 1906, and Chairman of the Council of Ministers, i.e. Prime Minister, three months later. An innovative statesman, within a conservative frame of reference, he was convinced that the existing system had to change to survive and so, while vigorously suppressing the revolutionary movement with one hand, he applied his other energies to what he saw as one of Russia's fundamental problems, peasant agriculture.

Stolypin encouraged peasant migration to under-popu-

Figure 73   Stolypin.

385

lated areas and provided extra funds for agricultural development, but his major attempt to tackle the problem was his attack upon the peasant commune. He introduced legislation in October and November 1906 to facilitate individual peasant separation from the commune and the establishment of consolidated holdings. Consolidation of all plots in the hereditary commune was made contingent upon a two thirds majority (a simple majority in 1910) of all members, instead of unanimity as previously. In the repartitional commune, in which most peasants lived and which was the main focus of his attack, individual separation and the establishment of an hereditary holding could be brought about at the will of the individual householder, providing 'no special difficulties' were involved. This constituted a major attempt to establish a class of yeoman farmers in the Russian countryside, but its results were limited (see PEASANTS AND REVOLUTION).

Stolypin also had a significant impact on Russian constitutional development. The first Duma had been dissolved in July 1906, but the second was equally unruly and it too was dissolved in June 1907. Stolypin then introduced a new electoral law, by-passing the 1906 constitution, which assured future Dumas of a conservative, right-wing majority.

Stolypin also sought to introduce reforms in local government, police, education and taxation, but he was opposed by more conservative forces at court and in the upper levels of the bureaucracy. In his last years in office, he also lacked the full support and confidence of the tsar, and his ability to bring about significant change was thus impaired. He was assassinated at the Kiev opera in the presence of NICHOLAS II on 1 September 1911 by D. BOGROV, a double-agent, in circumstances which remain unclear.

GJG

Further Reading

Atkinson, Dorothy: *The End of the Russian Land Commune, 1905–1930*. Stanford: 1983.

Levin, Alfred: *Peter Arkad'evich Stolypin: A Political Appraisal*. *Journal of Modern History* 37 (1965) 445–63.

Struve, Peter Berngardovich (1870–1944)

Economic historian and publicist, Struve was born into a Baltic German noble family in the Ural provincial capital of Perm. Initially a political conservative, he had evolved a socialist orientation by 1889 when he entered the University of St Petersburg. There he formed a Social Democratic study circle that played a major role in disseminating Marx's social and political philosophy.

Struve first articulated his radical views in a series of articles published abroad in 1892–3. The following year he published a study of Russia's economic development that established him as the leading Marxist theorist in Russia. He subsequently travelled abroad where he conferred with the LIBERATION OF LABOUR GROUP and acquainted himself with European socialist movements.

In 1897 Struve briefly became editor of the St Petersburg Marxist periodical *Novoe slovo* (New Word). During the spring of the following year Struve composed the manifesto of the nascent RUSSIAN SOCIAL DEMOCRATIC LABOUR PARTY (RSDRP). Although most of his time between 1898 and 1900 was devoted to the study of Russia's agrarian history, he assumed the role of editor of *Nachalo* (The Beginning) in early 1899 and used the journal to articulate his new Revisionist Marxism.

Struve was arrested at the beginning of 1901 in connection with an anti-government demonstration in the capital. After some months in administrative exile in Tver he went to Stuttgart where, continuing his political evolution away from Orthodox Marxism, he became the editor of the liberal-constitutionalist organ *Osvobozhdenie* (Liberation). Returning to Russia in October 1905, he joined the newly established Constitutional Democratic Party, became a prominent member of its Central Committee and in 1907 was elected to the Second Duma. Following the Duma's dissolution he effectively retired from active politics to devote himself to scholarship.

With the outbreak of the FIRST WORLD WAR Struve served in the Ministry of Trade and Industry and then headed the Economic Department of the Ministry of Foreign Affairs in the PROVISIONAL GOVERNMENT. Following the OCTOBER REVOLUTION he became a political adviser to the White Army. Emigrating at the end of the CIVIL WAR, Struve lived in Europe until his death in Paris in 1944.

BTN

Stuchka, Peter Ivanovich (1865–1932)

Born of peasant stock in the Livonian province of the Russian Empire, Stuchka graduated from the St Petersburg University Law Faculty in 1888, returned to Riga where he worked for nine years as an advocate's associate and edited a progressive daily newspaper *Dienas Lapa* (Daily News). During the 1890s his activities in *Jauna Strava* (New Current) eventually led to arrest and five years of exile in Vitebsk province. In 1903 he founded what eventually became the Latvian Bolshevik Party and three years later engineered its coalition with the Russian BOLSHEVIKS, which helped strengthen Bolshevik influence in the Social Democrats of the Latvian Territory (SDLK). The latter in turn combined with the Bolshevik Party in August 1914. After the 1905 REVOLUTION, as an advocate in St Petersburg, he took part in the trials of many who had participated in those events.

After the FEBRUARY REVOLUTION, Stuchka became a member of the editorial board of *Pravda*, was a member of the Petrograd Committee of the RSDRP(b), a delegate from the Petrograd organization of Bolsheviks to the Seventh (April) All-Russian Conference of the RSDRP(b), and a member of the Bolshevik faction in the Petrograd Soviet of Workers' and Soldiers' Deputies. He continued to be active in Latvian affairs, delivering in April 1917 an influential report on agrarian policy to the Thirteenth Conference of the SDLK in Moscow. He was a delegate to the Sixth Congress of the RSDRP(b) representing the Riga organization.

A delegate to the Second All-Russian Congress of Soviets, in November 1917 Stuchka entered the Soviet Government as People's Commissar of Justice from 15 November–9 December 1917 and again from 18 March–22 August 1918. In that position he played a key theoretical and practical role in eliminating the pre-revolutionary legal system and shaping the Soviet organs which replaced it. The initial draft of Decree No. 1 on the Courts was written by Stuchka, as was the draft decree abolishing Imperial civil ranks. His draft of Decree No. 2 on the Courts was altered by the left-Kadets, but in July 1918 he prepared the draft Instruction on Revolutionary Tribunals and in November 1918 the draft Statute on People's Court.

Returning to Latvia at the end of 1918, Stuchka headed the Provisional Soviet Government of Latvia until its collapse in January 1920. Thereafter he lived in Moscow until his death. There he was elected a member of the VTSIK of the RSFSR, from 1919 served as Deputy People's Commissar of Justice, and from 1923 until his death, as chairman of the RSFSR Supreme Court. He had a major share in drafting the Leading Principles of Criminal Law of the RSFSR, adopted in December 1919. Throughout the 1920s he served on various legislative subcommissions and had a direct part in preparing the Statute on the procuracy, on the USSR Supreme Court, legislation on the relations of central and local organs of the people's commissariat of justice, and the systematic collection of RSFSR legislation (see THE SOVIET LEGAL SYSTEM).

On 1 October 1918 Stuchka was elected a member of the Socialist (later Communist) Academy and organized the Sector therein for the general theory of State and law. That same year he published *Narodnyi sud v voprosakh i otvetakh* (The People's Court in Questions and Answers) and then a year later his *Konstitutsiya RSFSR v voprosakh i otvetakh* (The RSFSR Constitution in Questions and Answers). At the request of the Orgburo of the Central Committee of the Party, dated 24 June 1921, Stuchka wrote his *Revolyutsionnaya rol' prava i gosudarstva* (The Revolutionary Role of the Law and the State) which went through three editions in as many years; and *Uchenie o gosudarstve i Konstitutsii RSFSR* (The Doctrine on the State and the RSFSR Constitution) which was published in seven editions over ten years. He became professor at Moscow State University, first director of the Institute of Soviet Law, editor of the journal *Revolyutsiya prava* (The Revolution of the Law), and initiator and director of the three volume *Entsiklopediya gosudarstva i prava* (Encyclopedia of State and Law), 1927–29. As chairman of the RSFSR Supreme Court, he edited

Sudebnaya praktika verkhovnogo suda RSFSR (Judicial Practice of the RSFSR Supreme Court).

In 1917–20 Stuchka's learned writings were principally concerned with ascertaining the two views of Marx and Engels on law, criticizing those 'legal socialists' who in his opinion distorted those views, attacking manifestations of a bourgeois view of law, and laying the basis for a new science of Soviet law. His principal works have been translated into English.

In 1938 Stuchka was singled out by A. Ya. Vyshinsky for having ideologically harmful views. His reputation was fully rehabilitated in the post-Stalin era and his writings republished in Russian and Latvian language editions.

WEB

Sukhanov, Nikolai Nikolaevich (1882–1940)

Born in Moscow, Sukhanov (real name Gimmer) began his revolutionary career in Moscow high school and student socialist circles in the late 1890s, and was active in the Moscow organization of SOCIALIST REVOLUTIONARIES until 1907, with a one-year spell in the Taganka Prison in 1904 – after being caught in possession of a mass of illegal literature – from which he was liberated by a 1905 revolutionary crowd.

A noted economist, Sukhanov published a number of books on agricultural economics, contributed to *Russkoe Bogatstvo* (Russian Wealth) and prepared for an academic career. Arrested again in 1910 and exiled to Archangel province, he contributed to journals with POPULIST tendencies, even though he had by then embraced MARXISM. In 1913, with the period of his exile expired, he settled in St Petersburg and became editor of the radical literary-political journal *Sovremennik* (The Contemporary) and, from 1915 to 1917, of its successor, Maxim Gorky's socialist-internationalist *Letopis* (Chronicle).

With the outbreak of the FEBRUARY REVOLUTION Sukhanov, a leading member of the Petrograd SOVIET's Executive Committee, became the key figure in its negotiations with the Duma's Provisional Committee, which led to the formation of the PROVISIONAL GOVERNMENT on March 2. It was Sukhanov who drafted the guidelines for the Provisional Government's programme and initiated the establishment of the Liaison Commission of the Executive Committee which was to ensure that the government realized that programme. That continuous control, which was the Petrograd Soviet's price for its conditional support, characterized the early, vigilant phase of dual power of which Sukhanov was both architect and ideologist. He also drafted the Appeal of the Petrograd Soviet to the Peoples of the World of 14 March, and thus launched the Soviet on its peace policy.

With the arrival of Irakli TSERETELI and the takeover of the Petrograd Soviet by the Menshevik-SR bloc of revolutionary defensists by the end of March, Sukhanov and his independent socialist allies were pushed aside. From April, when he founded and became editor of Gorky's socialist-internationalist newspaper *Novaya Zhizn* (New Life) while also a member of the small faction of 'internationalists' in the Soviet and then from May as a Menshevik-Internationalist, he opposed the policies of Tsereteli and the Menshevik-SR bloc.

Thus, when the entry of socialists into the government was debated in the Executive Committee following the April crisis of MILYUKOV's foreign policy, Sukhanov (supported by Y. M. Steklov and I. P. Goldenberg) urged that only a coalition government with a socialist majority could be trusted to conduct a foreign policy pledged to peace. Late in May he again pressed for the appointment of a socialist as minister of trade and industry, after the resignation of A. I. Konovalov and his refusal to implement the economic policy of the coalition government. But MARTOV failed to support him and Sukhanov felt let down.

Nevertheless, he strongly supported Martov's 3 July call for a 'democratic' government based on the soviets and his desperate bid at the Democratic Conference in September to end 'coalitionism'.

After the OCTOBER REVOLUTION, Sukhanov castigated the Bolshevik dictatorship, its terror and 'persecution of the press' in the columns of *Novaya Zhizn* and in the Central Executive Committee of the Soviets – that 'sorry parody of a revolutionary parliament' – where he represented the United SD Internationalists. The end came in June 1918, when he was expelled from the CEC and *Novaya Zhizn* was closed down. It was then that he began to write his *Zapiski o revolyutsii* (Notes on the Revolution), completing its seventh volume in 1922.

Sukhanov spent the 1920s as an economist in Soviet institutions, ending up in the Agrarian Institute of the Communist Academy. There he annoyed his Communist colleagues when, on the eve of the 'dekulakization' drive, he postulated a very narrow definition of the kulak, having earlier extolled the socialist potentialities of the traditional Russian village commune. He was expelled from the Communist Academy in 1930 because 'his opinions were incompatible with its aims', and a year later, at the notorious Menshevik Trial, he (who had already left the Menshevik party late in 1920) was charged and convicted of being a member of 'the counter-revolutionary organization of the Menshevik-Interventionists'. He was shot on Stalin's orders in Omsk on 27 August 1939. Notwithstanding the sneers in the accounts of detractors, his honest and modest *Zapiski o revolyutsii* has immortalized him as the incomparable chronicler and historian of the Russian revolution.

IG

Further Reading

Getzler, Israel: 'Nikolai Sukhanov's *Zapiski o revoliutsii*', *Revolutionary Russia*, vol. 6, December 1993. London: Frank Cass, 1993.

Sukhanov, N.N.: *Zapiski o revolyutsii*, vols 1–7. Berlin and St Petersburg: 1919–22.

——: *Zapiski o revolyutsii*, in 3 vols., Moscow 1991–92, edited, introduced and annotated by N.N. Kornikov.

—————: *The Russian Revolution 1917: A Personal Record*, trans. and abridged by Joel Carmichael. Oxford: Oxford University Press, 1955.

Sultangaliev, Mirsaid (1880–1939?)

Born to a teacher's family in the village of Kmrskaly in Bashkiria, Sultangaliev studied first in the village mektep and then in the Russian-Tatar Teachers' School of Kazan. He worked as a teacher in his native village, then as a librarian in the first zemstvo library in Ufa, becoming actively involved in jadid reformism and advocating the transformation of zemstvo schools into national schools.

By 1911 Sultangaliev had made his journalistic debut with many articles in the zemstvo organ *Ufimskii Vestnik* (Ufa Messenger), followed over the years by contributions to many Russian and Tatar periodicals under diverse pseudonyms.

Sultangaliev took part in the Muslim congresses of May and July 1917 and became one of the most prominent figures of the Muslim Socialist Committee of Kazan, organized on 7 April 1917. He joined the Russian Communist Party (Bolshevik) in November 1917, and became chairman of the Central Muslim Commissariat organized on 17 January 1918. Among his appointments were Inner Collegium of the People's Commissariat of Nationalities (Narkomnats); editor of *Zhizn Natsionalnostei* (Nationalities' Life), its official organ; president of the Muslim military collegium; and member of the Central Executive Committee of the TASSR.

Developing his thesis on the problems of colonial nations in a revolution, Sultangaliev argued that in the Muslim lands the goal of national liberation should prevail over those of social conflict and social revolution. Equally, he emphasized the role played in Russia by Islam, where its bonds of brotherhood had pushed class antagonisms into the background and maintained a sense of community throughout the centuries. To mobilize Islam's assets in the service of the new political order, Sultangaliev advocated endowing Marxism-Leninism with Islamic qualities, giving it an identifiable 'national face', thereby laying the foundations of Muslim national communism and offering a revolutionary strategy for the colonial world.

The cornerstones of this national communist credo were an autonomous Muslim Communist Party; the creation of a Muslim Red Army with a Muslim High Command; the establishment of a state, the Republic of Turan, which would bring together all the Turkic peoples scattered from the Volga to Eastern Turkestan; and the creation of a

Colonial International, independent of Comintern, which would be able to address the problems of those 'proletarian nations' where the peasantry represented the proletariat.

Sultangaliev's ideas were tolerated until 1923 when he was purged at the Twelfth Party Congress which condemned nationalist deviations. This was followed by a brief arrest, after which he was allowed to work in Georgia and then Moscow at the RSFSR state publishing agency. He was arrested again in 1928, tried, convicted and sentenced to ten years hard labour in the Solovki camp. It is believed that he died in 1939 or shortly thereafter.   A-AR

Further Reading

Bennigsen, A. and Lemercier-Quelquejay, Ch.: *Les mouvements nationaux chez les musulmans de Russie: Le 'Sultangalievisme' en Tatarstan*. Paris and The Hague: 1960.

———: *Sultangaliev. Le père de la révolution tiers-mondiste*. Paris: 1986.

——— and Wimbush, S.E.: *Muslim National Communism in the Soviet Union*. Chicago: 1979.

Sverdlov, Yakov Mikhailovich (1885–1919)

The son of a Jewish engraver, Sverdlov joined the revolutionary movement in 1902 at the age of seventeen. After the party split in 1903 he immediately sided with the BOLSHEVIKS. He was first arrested in 1903 and restricted to his father's house. He left his home town of Nizhni Novgorod for Kostroma in 1904. Blessed with a phenomenal memory he began to build up mental lists of activists who could be relied upon. The 1905 REVOLUTION allowed him to spread his wings and he became a travelling agitator, especially among youth. Moving to the Urals in late 1905 he became a very effective speaker, noted for his passion, and his stentorian bass voice was out of all proportion to his small frail frame. He and his wife, Klavdiya, were arrested in June 1906 and sent to prison for three years. He used this time to establish contact with other 'illegals' and cross-examined every new arrival on Bolshevik-MENSHEVIK relations. His knowledge of party affairs was so extensive that E. A. Preobrazhensky later remarked that Sverdlov 'knew personally, more or less, almost all our main party workers. He knew our party better than anyone else.' After release he was very active on LENIN's behalf but was rearrested in December 1910 and exiled to the Narym region in Siberia for three years. He first met STALIN during this exile and the two shared a room, but there was considerable friction between them. Sverdlov escaped and returned to the capital where he found he had been co-opted onto the Central Committee and was an official member of the CC Russian Bureau. He worked on *Pravda* until he was again arrested, in February 1913, and exiled to Turukhansk in Siberia. He again shared with Stalin and the tension grew. After the FEBRUARY REVOLUTION he returned to Petrograd and played an important organizational role in the April Conference. He was re-elected to the CC. Lenin instructed him to stay in the capital and take over the embryonic Secretariat. His duties included supervising provincial party committees, military organizations, peasant associations, trade unions, factory and shop committees. Sverdlov was well suited to such work, paying great attention to detail. Yaroslavsky (the party historian) did not consider Sverdlov a theoretician but a 'practical leader to the core and the practical leader of the proletarian revolution'. He built up his 'tail' of trusted collaborators over the next eighteen months and they were all known to him before 1917.

At the Sixth Party Congress in July/August 1917, Sverdlov presented a detailed account of party committees and membership. However the congress rejected his motion allowing the CC to expel party members between congresses. As before the regional party committees were to retain their autonomy. Sverdlov campaigned for Lenin's plan of insurrection and such was his role that TROTSKY described him as the 'unofficial, but all the more real "secretary general" of the October uprising'.

When it came to the composition of Sovnarkom, Sverdlov, himself of Jewish origin, opposed the appointment of Trotsky as Commissar for Internal Affairs because of his Jewish background. He also was against Trotsky taking over the party press, favouring instead N. I. BUKHARIN. Sverdlov proposed that Trotsky, instead, should become Commissar for Foreign Affairs. Trotsky concurred. As Lenin was dissatisfied with L. B. KAMENEV as chairman of the CEC he lobbied Sverdlov for the task. The latter at first declined because of his workload in the Secretariat, but Lenin convinced him that the CEC job was the more important task. Sverdlov inevitably brought the CEC and the Secretariat closer together and thus began a process which led to the emasculation of the soviets. Sverdlov and Lenin became fast friends and collaborated closely. Sverdlov curtailed debate in the CEC in order to minimize the possibility of a rejection of Sovnarkom legislation. During 1918 the presidium of CEC became the actual power centre, a process carefully promoted by Sverdlov. Bolsheviks dominated the presidium. Sverdlov played a key role in ensuring soviet acceptance of the Brest-Litovsk peace treaty and enforced party discipline on those Bolsheviks who opposed its ratification.

At the Fifth Congress of Soviets in August 1918 the newly elected CEC consisted of 57 Bolsheviks and 41 others. It was very docile and a tribute to Sverdlov's surgical skills in lancing all contentious issues by not permitting adequate debate. In August 1918 he set about increasing the power of the central apparatus *vis-à-vis* local party committees in earnest. The aim was to establish secretariats within local party organizations. They were to collect the data needed to facilitate informed judgement by the CC Secretariat. So close were Sverdlov's views on organization to Lenin's, that he could often anticipate what Lenin would propose. If Lenin provided the theory, Sverdlov contributed the practice of organization.

His enormous workload gradually undermined his already precarious health and he died in the epidemic of Spanish influenza on 16 March 1919 at the early age of thirty-three. Had Sverdlov lived the Bolshevik party might not have experienced the violent conflicts over organizational questions which rent the party apart until the Tenth Congress. No successor had his intimate knowledge of party personnel in the provinces and how to deal with them. Also had he lived he would have been the natural nominee as Secretary General in 1922.   MMcC

Tikhomirov, Lev Alexandrovich (1852–1923)

The most famous renegade of his time, Tikhomirov distinguished himself both as a revolutionary and terrorist and as an ideologue of Autocracy. A typical member of the intelligentsia, he was acutely intelligent, extremely widely read on social and political matters, and a man of profound conviction and passion. After his education at Moscow university, he became a member of the Chaikovsky circle in 1872–3, did much propaganda among workers, composed revolutionary tracts, and was arrested in 1873 and convicted in the 'trial of the 193'. After four years in gaol he became member of the Land and Freedom group in 1878 and editor of their journal of that name. From 1879, and then, with P. L. LAVROV, he edited the *Vestnik Narodnoi Voli* (People's Will Messenger). It was this distinguished revolutionary past that he rejected and denounced in 1888 after deep soul-searching and a painful personal crisis. The trauma of that experience left its indelible imprint and he was, to the end of his days, gloomy and dystopian, with rarely a smile flickering across his sombre face.

Tikhomirov then devoted himself to working out the theory and practice of a conservative monarchism for Russia, writing numerous tracts, newspaper articles, and two important books on the subject. He closely studied European conservative movements, especially Christian Democracy and the new attitudes of the Church to social problems, and wrote about them, chiefly in the conservative newspaper, *Moskovskiya Vedomosti* (Moscow Gazette), of which he was eventually the editor, 1909–13. It was this concern that brought him to the ZUBATOV MOVEMENT to write on its behalf, and to secure official subsidies for the unions in Moscow. But he did not assume a directly activist role as in the past or as Zubatov himself did: he confined himself to theoretical work. During the 1905 REVOLUTION he composed his magnum opus, *Monarkhicheskaya Gosudarsvennost* (The Principle of the Monarchical State), and thereafter continued advocating conservative social reform, especially unionism for workers, corresponded with STOLYPIN on the labour reform then under way, and from

1909 was the editor of the most important conservative newspaper. With the revolution of 1917 he ceased all political activity and died in Zagorsk in 1923.   MKP

Patriarch Tikhon (1865–1925)

Born to a family of humble provincial clergy, the future Patriarch (family name Belavin) took his advanced theological degree from the St Petersburg Academy in 1888. Tonsured in 1891, he was consecrated a bishop seven years later and posted to head the Orthodox missionary Diocese of Alaska and North America. In his nine years in America (to 1907) he proved himself an excellent administrator and widely loved pastor, who restored there the conciliar structure missing in his native Russia, and drafted a model self-governing parish statute which the Moscow All-Russian Local Council (*Sobor*) of 1917–18 adopted for the RUSSIAN ORTHODOX CHURCH.

Soon after the FEBRUARY REVOLUTION Tikhon was among the first bishops to be democratically elected by a diocesan clergy-laity assembly in place of Metropolitan Makari of Moscowa (a RASPUTIN appointment). The first bishop to be elected that way was Venyamin (Kazansky) who received the Petrograd See, vacated by the Rasputinite Pitirim. Both bishops were extremely modest, humble and accessible to the common man. Both were greatly loved, both were basically apolitical, and both would be victimized by the BOLSHEVIKS, probably because their personalities so blatantly contradicted the Marxist-Leninist anti-clerical propaganda clichés. Venyamin was condemned to death and shot in August 1922, although the defence had proved his innocence. Tikhon, having survived two attempts on his life and over a year in prison (May 1922–June 1923), died in 1925. Whether he was poisoned by the VECHEKA, as popularly believed, or not, the believers of Russia consider Tikhon and the murdered Venyamin foremost among the new holy martyrs.   DP

Tkachev, Peter Nikitich (1844–1886)

An exponent of the conspiratorial 'Jacobin' tendency (sometimes called 'Blanquist' after L. A. Blanqui, 1805–81) within revolutionary POPULISM, Tkachev was born into an impoverished gentry family in Pskov province. He entered St Petersburg University in 1861, but immediately was involved in a student protest movement that led to a jail sentence and the interruption of his formal education. He earned a precarious living by journalism and in March 1869 was again arrested for revolutionary agitation. As an associate of S. G. NECHAEV, on whom he exerted a strong influence, he was sentenced in 1871 to a further sixteen months in prison. In December 1873 he emigrated, ostensibly to assist P. L. LAVROV on his periodical *Vpered!* (Forwards!); but he soon quarrelled with this advocate of moderate, propagandist tactics and in 1875 launched his own journal, *Nabat* (The Tocsin). Here he expounded the theory that in Russia state power was 'suspended in the air' and therefore could easily be seized by an organization of determined revolutionaries; to delay was to forfeit the last opportunity to avert the onset of capitalism. The peasants, he was convinced, could not by themselves bring about a social revolution. Tkachev held that his views were consistent with economic determinism, and polemicized with F. Engels on this point, maintaining that the revolution might occur first in a backward country. In this respect his ideas anticipated those of LENIN, although the latter's attitude towards Tkachev was ambivalent. The issue of ideological continuity was debated by Soviet historians in 1924–5, but it raised such delicate issues that the discussion was cut short. Tkachev became insane in 1882.   JLHK

Further reading

Hardy, D.: *Peter Tkachev: the Critic as Jacobin*. Seattle and London: 1977.

Trepov, Dmitri Fedorovich (1855–1906)

Repeatedly figuring in revolutionary demonology, the name belongs to a family of famous or notorious policemen. Trepov was educated in the Corps of Pages, served in the Guards Regiment, and from 1896 to 1905 was Police Chief of Moscow city when he gave full support to ZUBATOV (see also THE ZUBATOV MOVEMENT). on 11 January 1905 he was appointed governor-general of St Petersburg with dictatorial powers to handle the revolutionary crisis there, which he did with typical firmness and brutality. After the October Manifesto, he was appointed Commandant of the Palace, became the tsar's close confidant, and was at the heart of the 'court camarilla'. He died early in 1906. He was the quintessential policeman who could analyse situations only in terms of 'law and order'; he therefore came into his own during emergencies, as throughout 1905. For this reason he was depicted in liberal and left-wing public opinion as a 'constable by education, and a pogromist/rioter by persuasion', and he is notorious for his order in October 1905 not to use blank cartridges nor to spare bullets.

Although Trepov worked closely with Zubatov, he did not think on the same lines, nor act with the same subtlety and flexibility. But, as with so many other such tough-minded policemen, he tended to be paternalist, and he ascribed labour unrest to bad management and incompetence in the factory inspectorate. Hence his readiness to experiment with a moderate, non-revolutionary labour movement aiming to have the law enforced and to resolve industrial dispute, as in Moscow. Trepov was further inspired by the idea of bringing the tsar and people together. He therefore welcomed the idea of the loyal demonstration on 19 February 1902 in Moscow, brought a delegation of workers to meet the tsar in the Winter Palace in January 1905 in an attempted reconciliation, and finally even thought up the Shidlovsky Commission of February 1905 consisting of workers' and management representatives, along with officials, to discuss the 'labour question'. But he was essentially ham-fisted and could not countenance working-class activism as such, as Zubatov could; and, with the latter's departure from Moscow in 1902, the reform tended to an antiseptic quietism.   MKP

Trotsky, Lev Davidovich (1879–1940)

Leon Trotsky's name is as synonymous with the making of the Russian Revolution as it is with the consequences of its unmaking – with the triumph, that is, of October 1917 as with the defeat of the opposition to the course which the Revolution eventually followed. Therein lies the unique fascination of his historical record – a somewhat cruel fascination, to be sure, for it breeds upon the harsh ironies that engulfed Trotsky's life. He was initially a bitter enemy of Bolshevism, then virtually its second-in-command, and, finally, the most dramatic victim of the Stalinist regime it gave rise to. One could also formulate the ironies in the following ways: in view of his position before 1917 he should not have found himself at LENIN's side in 1917 – but he did; in view of his stature after 1917 he should have succeeded Lenin in 1924 or thereafter – but he did not. As early as 1905 he had been the originator and almost the only proponent of a theory of revolution which, twelve years later, appeared to have become vindicated better than any other analysis of events in Russia; he himself led the October insurrection and, later the RED ARMY, thus masterminding the BOLSHEVIK seizure of power and its ultimate consolidation. Yet in less than five years after this triumph he found himself divested of nearly all personal office and power, and less than five years after that, he was murdered by those who now stood at the head of the edifice whose foundations he had so assiduously prepared. His rise to fame was indeed spectacular, but perhaps no more so than his downfall. In this sense at least Trotsky's life may be seen as a personalized reflection of the Russian Revolution itself.

Life

Trotsky's name at birth was Lev Davidovich Bronstein (he assumed his pseudonym in 1902, borrowing it from a gaoler in Odessa). He was born the son of a Jewish farm-owner in Yanovka, an isolated village in the Kherson province of the southern Ukraine, on October 26 (OS) – exactly thirty-eight years before the 1917 OCTOBER REVOLUTION. Despite the intellectually unstimulating surroundings, he displayed from an early age those characteristics which were to distinguish him throughout his life: a rebellious and aggressive temperament, quickness of mind and intellectual curiosity, a penchant for the

РАКОВСКИЙ, ТРОЦКИЙ И ДОБРОДЖАНУ-ГЕРЕА
В БУХАРЕСТЕ В 1913 г.

Figure 74   Sketch of Trotsky (centre) with Rakovsky (left) and Dobrodzhanu-Gerea (right), Bucharest 1913.

dramatic, and an oral and written facility with language. His first reaction to Marxist ideas was unenthusiastic, but once converted he plunged wholeheartedly into political activity organizing workers in Nikolaev, a provincial town near Odessa. There followed the inevitable odyssey of Russian revolutionaries: prison, exile in Siberia, escape, and finally exile abroad.

He first met LENIN in London in 1902 and the two were cordially respectful of each other. But in 1903, at the Second Congress of the Russian Social Democrats, he bitterly denounced Lenin's organizational conception of the party, branding his aims as dictatorial and his personality as akin to that of the mad Robespierre. Thereafter, until 1917, he was an isolated figure in the revolutionary movement for, after rejecting Bolshevism, he also refused to join the MENSHEVIKS whose revolutionary decisiveness he doubted. Yet, his personal magnetism was such that even as a 'lone wolf' he managed to become the most conspicuous figure in the St Petersburg Soviet of October

1905. At the end of that fateful year he was imprisoned, again exiled to Siberia and again escaped. The decade before 1917 was spent abroad, travelling, writing, editing newspapers and attending Russian Social-Democrat gatherings of one kind or another in European capitals.

Trotsky was in New York when the FEBRUARY REVOLUTION broke out but managed to return to Russia by May. The sense of the possibilities in the air and his conviction now that only Lenin understood the unfolding situation and was prepared for it, drew Trotsky into the Bolshevik camp. In September he was elected President of the Petrograd Soviet and his standing in the Bolshevik party was now second only to that of Lenin. This meteoric rise to prominence culminated with his planning and execution of the October insurrection, during which his organizational skills were brilliantly revealed. As the first Soviet Commissar for Foreign Affairs he led the Russian delegation at the Brest-Litovsk negotiations and propounded a policy of 'neither war nor peace', i.e. neither an active continuation of the hostilities by Russia nor a capitulation to German demands. But Lenin's view, that Russia must withdraw from the war at all costs now and wait to regain territorial concessions at a later date, prevailed. In March 1918 Trotsky was appointed Commissar of War and President of the Supreme War Council and his career reached its zenith: he built and organized the new Red Army from its foundations, emphasizing the need for a purely military doctrine of warfare as against a nonsensical, as he saw it, 'Marxist-proletarian strategy', and he spectacularly led his forces, which eventually numbered some five million men, to victory in the CIVIL WAR. This victory, of course, is what ensured the survival of the Soviet regime.

It has often been observed that Trotsky's talents, however impressive in moments of great historical juncture, did not extend to the sphere of everyday politics, particularly within the framework of party organization and in-fighting. Even at the height of his powers he had failed to create a following within the party, partly because of his chronic inability to compromise over issues – he made many enemies over his economic positions in general and his anti-trade union, pro-militarization of labour views in particular – and partly because his anti-Bolshevik past remained forever a source of suspicion. He was already losing ground in the party hierarchy during Lenin's last years, and after the latter's death he was completely outmanoeuvred in the struggle for succession. In the years that followed he found himself pushed into an uneasy collaboration with various marginal opposition groups. He grossly underestimated both the importance and the extent of STALIN's political skills and when eventually he grasped the danger, it was too late. In 1928 he was forced into exile and wandered from one country to another until in 1937 he was given refuge in Mexico. There, in Coyoacan, a suburb of Mexico City, he played out his last role as the spokesman for the Fourth International and the bitterest, albeit inconsequential, voice in the opposition to the now impregnable Stalinist regime. On August 20 1940 he died from an ice-pick blow to his head delivered by an agent of that regime.

Ideas

Trotsky's main contribution to Marxism and to social and political theory (see PERMANENT REVOLUTION; THE IDEA OF WORLD REVOLUTION) was part of a general preoccupation with the problem of revolutionary politics in backward societies and with the possibilities and limitations of socialism in such societies. This pre-occupation is already evident in his early views of Bolshevism. His attacks in 1903–4 against Lenin's conception of party organization were governed less by a concern for democratic principles – a concern perhaps more characteristic of the Mensheviks – than by a fear that in conditions where an impoverished social and political culture prevailed, the temptations of Blanquism and Jacobinism might prove to

be irresistible. Such temptations, he believed, sought to substitute the supposedly autonomous instruments of politics for the objective necessities of mass struggle. The danger was not only that in the process a single 'dictator' would come to dominate the revolution, but that the revolution would degenerate into a purely political, rather than a social, phenomenon, devoid, that is, of the historical content it was meant to serve. Bolshevism, Trotsky believed, was endemic to Russian backwardness in the sense that it reflected politically the dark and ugly underside of the primitive foundations of Russian social life. The upper side of these foundations, however, so he thought, was also the advanced side of Russian backwardness: its industrial development, its large cities with their radicalized proletariat, its dynamic possibilities in an era of world revolution. He believed, consequently, that the Social Democratic movement should and could triumph on this side of the socio-political divide.

When Trotsky joined hands with Lenin in 1917 he either chose to forget this early analysis of Bolshevism or to argue that Bolshevism had in the meantime transformed itself. It is hardly surprising, therefore, that when in later years he formulated a critique of Stalinism he was constantly plagued by the inconsistency between his theoretical position before 1917 and the political course he followed in 1917. Try as he might, he could not in the 1930s make a clear separation between Stalinism and Leninism. He denounced the former as a 'degeneration' of the revolution, and analysed it first as the Soviet 'Thermidor', then as 'Bonapartism', and finally as a form of 'bureaucratic collectivism' – though throughout the somewhat personalized charge of 'betrayal' also figured large in his attacks on Stalin. The most convincing part of his critique of Stalinism, however, was that part which had always been the source of his theoretical preoccupations: the backwardness of Russia, he now had to admit, however grudgingly, had reappeared in the form of Stalin and of the doctrine of 'socialism in one country' with its anti-international orientation. He spent the last years of his life contemplating the consequences of what for him must have been the final irony of the Russian Revolution.   BK

Further Reading

Deutscher, Isaac: *The Prophet Armed; The Prophet Unarmed; The Prophet Outcast*, 3 vols. London: Oxford University Press, 1954, 1959, 1963.

Knei-Paz, Baruch: *The Social and Political Thought of Leon Trotsky*. Oxford: Oxford University Press, 1978.

Trotsky, Leon: *The History of the Russian Revolution*. London: Gollancz, 1965.

——— : *My Life*. New York: Scribner, 1930.

——— : *The Revolution Betrayed*. New York: 1937.

——— : *Stalin: An Appraisal of the Man and His Influence*. New York and London: Oxford University Press, 1941.

Wolfe, Bertram D.: *Three Who Made a Revolution*. Boston: Dial, 1955.

Tsereteli, Irakli G. (1881–1960)

The youngest child of Giorgi Tsereteli, a major figure in Georgian radical politics, Irakli attended Tiflis gymnasium and Moscow University where he studied Law. He was arrested in 1902 for leading student demonstrations and sentenced to five years exile in Yakutsk (Eastern Siberia). He joined the Siberian Union of Social Democrats and came out strongly against LENIN's *What is to be Done?* when it reached Siberia in 1902. Released from exile in 1903, he returned to Georgia where he joined the Tiflis committee of the RSDRP. He was a delegate to the first congress of the Caucasian Union where he argued against the centralistic plan of party organization. He was appointed editor of *Kvali* (Track) in 1903. Arrested in January 1904, he was allowed to continue his studies in Berlin. In 1905 he attended the MENSHEVIK conference in Geneva but became ill and returned to Georgia in 1906. The following year he was elected to the second Duma and was made chairman of the social democratic faction at the age of twenty-five. He had a great impact in the Duma and his fiery oratory made him into a national figure. After the dissolution of the second Duma in June 1907, Tsereteli was arrested and sentenced to five years imprisonment. He was released in 1913 and exiled to Irkutsk. During the war he became a leader of the 'Siberian Zimmerwaldist' movement which advocated an international socialist solution to the conflict.

Tsereteli returned to Petrograd in March 1917 and was co-opted onto the Petrograd SOVIET Executive Committee as an adviser. He switched to a revolutionary defensist stand on the war and advocated soviet cooperation with the PROVISIONAL GOVERNMENT. He was made a full member of the All-Russian Central Executive in June where he had great influence. He joined the first coalition government in May as Minister of Posts and Telegraphs and in July briefly became Minister of Interior under A. F. KERENSKY. After playing a major part in the organization of the Provisional Council of the Republic, he left for Georgia in October to see his family, returning to Petrograd as a delegate to the CONSTITUENT ASSEMBLY. Bolshevik orders for his arrest, however, forced him back to Georgia.

Tsereteli played an important part in Transcaucasian politics and was a member of the Transcaucasian Sejm. After Georgian independence, however, he played a modest role, although he carried out a number of diplomatic missions and represented Georgia at the Paris peace conference. He also continued to participate as Georgia's delegate at the Second International. After the fall of Georgia, he lived in exile in Paris and the USA where he died in 1960 (see TRANSCAUCASIA).   SFJ

Tukay, Abdulla (1886–1913)

Born in the village of Kushlavych of what is today the Atninsk district of the Tatar ASSR, Tukay is the leading

Figure 75 Tsereteli.

national poet of the Volga Tatars. His poetry played a crucial role in the establishment of the standards and norms of the modern Tatar literary language.

Orphaned by 1890, Tukay was raised by relatives in the villages of Sasna and Kirlay. From 1907 he lived in Kazan which was not only an outstanding Russian university centre but also the cultural centre of the Volga Tatars. In the years immediately following the 1905 Revolution, social concerns prevailed over issues such as Islamic unity or nationalism in Tukay's poetry. His enthusiasm for socialist ideas reached a peak between 1905 and 1907, when he also relentlessly criticized the Muslim clergy whom he held responsible for Muslim backwardness. By 1907, however, his poems reflected a growing concern for the endurance and growth of Tatar national culture and traditions, a renewed commitment to its defence which the political climate of Kazan stimulated.

Tukay took part in the organization of a Tatar club named Sharq (The East) which had a Social Democratic orientation. He joined a circle of Left-wing Tatar intellectuals, among them the BOLSHEVIK Kh. Yamashev, and began publishing in the Tatar paper *Azat* (Freedom) translations of articles from the Russian Bolshevik paper *Sotsial-Demokrat*. His involvement in journalism included also regular contributions to the radical paper *El Islah* (The Reform), the satirical journals *Yashen* (The Lightning) and *Yalt-Yult* (Summer Lightning).

Tukay did not, however, embrace the Social-Democratic cause. On the contrary, he began to reassess his initial enthusiasm for socialism to the point of abandoning his war against the *bays* (rich). The poems published between 1907 and his death in 1913 do not contain a wholesale criticism of the bourgeois nationalists, but focus on the narrow-mindedness of some and support the ideals of national revival. In the true spirit of jadidism, Tukay was an ardent supporter of the emancipation of women, and voiced his concerns in both poems and journal articles.

Tukay's contribution to Tatar culture was not confined to poetry, to moulding the literary language, and to journalism. He contributed to the widening of the cultural horizon of the Tatars through his activity as a translator and textbook writer. He translated from Russian, French, Turkish, Arabic, and Farsi, and wrote textbooks for subjects as diverse as language, literature, history and methodology.   A-AR

Tukhachevsky, Mikhail Nikolaevich (1893–1937)

Of noble birth and educated in Penza and Moscow, Tukhachevsky entered the Moscow Cadet Corps and successfully completed his training in 1912. On graduating from the Alexandrov Military Academy in 1914, he was posted to the Imperial Guard (Semenov Regiment) and went to war. Taken prisoner in 1915 and sent to Germany, he escaped in October 1917 at the sixth attempt, crossed into Switzerland and returned to Russia, where he was promoted to company commander. He joined the BOLSHEVIK Party on 5 April 1918.

In spring 1918 Tukhachevsky was appointed Military Commissar for the Moscow district and later in the year to the command of the First Army, which he succeeded in reorganizing by mid September, when he led them in an offensive against the Czech Legion and the capture of Simbirsk (see CIVIL WAR). Following a series of successful campaigns on the Eastern Front he was transferred to the main body of the Southern group (under FRUNZE's command), where he was responsible for a string of Bolshevik advances. After a successful Siberian campaign against KOLCHAK and the capture of Novorossiysk (26 March 1920) from DENIKIN, his next major action was on the Western Front, where he launched an offensive against Poland that brought his forces to within striking distance of Warsaw, but was thwarted through strained lines of communication and lack of support from the 1st Cavalry (under Voroshilov and STALIN). This defeat was significant in two respects: first, the offensive had been an opportunity to put into practice Tukhachevsky's belief that the RED ARMY should support revolutionary movements in other countries and, second, it brought about bad relations with Stalin.

In March 1921 Tukhachevsky was charged with the suppression of the KRONSTADT REVOLT and two months later the Antonov rising in Tambov province. In the same year he became head of the Military Academy, and in January 1922 commander of the Western Front. In 1924–5 he rose from Deputy Chief to Chief of Staff of the Red Army, was made commander of the Western military district and a member of the Revolutionary Military Council. There followed further promotion in 1931, when be became Deputy Commissar for Military and Naval Affairs and deputy chairman of the RMC. In 1935 he was created one of the first Soviet Marshals. Two years later he was accused of leading a military conspiracy, and shot without trial.   FP

Tyrkova, Ariadna Vladimirovna (1869–1962)

The first and only woman to serve on the central committee of the Constitutional Democratic party before 1917, Tyrkova was an active feminist between 1906 and 1917, a journalist and writer. She was born into an old Novgorod landowning family in 1869, and though never attracted to revolutionary politics herself, her elder brother Arkady was a member of People's Will, was imprisoned, then exiled after the tsar's assassination in 1881 and not amnestied until 1905. His arrest had a profound impact on the family, which was ostracized thereafter by neighbours and friends.

Tyrkova grew up with ambitions of becoming a doctor, like many educated women of her generation, but was frustrated by the closure of the medical courses in the 1880s. She went instead to the women's higher courses, married and had two children. She was divorced soon after. She first became involved in politics at the turn of the century. She was arrested in 1903, trying to smuggle *Osvobozhdenie* (Liberation), the journal of the liberation movement, into Russia. She escaped abroad and joined P. B. STRUVE's family in Stuttgart and Paris, returning only late in 1905. Until that time she claimed to have had no interest in feminism, assuming that sexual equality was taken for granted in the Russian intelligentsia. But her attendance at the second Kadet congress early in 1906 introduced her to the 'woman question'. Witnessing the strong opposition in the party to the incorporation of female suffrage into the party programme, she made her first political speech in defence of women's rights, and thereafter remained committed to the WOMEN'S MOVEMENT until 1917. In 1907, she was co-opted onto the Kadet central committee and served on it for the next decade. Politically on the right wing of the party, she left Russia in 1918, and worked with her second husband, the journalist Harold Williams, for the Russian Liberation Committee in London.   LE

Ulyanov, Alexander Ilyich (1866–1887)

The elder brother of the future LENIN, Alexander Ulyanov's execution for an unsuccessful plot to assassinate Alexander III in 1887 was an important and traumatic influence on the founder of Soviet Communism.

Alexander Ulyanov attended the Simbirsk Gymnasium during the directorship of F. M. Kerensky, father of Alexander KERENSKY. At his graduation in 1883, Kerensky père recommended him for a gold medal, and he proceeded to study natural sciences at St Petersburg University, winning a further gold medal for his work in zoology. Depressed by his father's enforced retirement and early death in 1886, he was also increasingly frustrated by police repression of all forms of political protest. In 1887 he joined a so-called 'terrorist fraction' of the virtually defunct POPULIST organization People's Will (Narodnaya Volya), which also included Józef PIŁSUDSKI's elder brother Bronisław. Ulyanov was the principal author of its programme, which showed some signs of the study of Marxist ideas. The group resolved to kill the tsar on the sixth anniversary of the assassination of his father, Alexander II. Instead, the conspirators were arrested. Ulyanov eloquently defended the group's ideas at the trial. Together with P. I. Andreushkin, V. D. Generalov, V. S. Osipanov and P. Ya. Shevyrev, Ulyanov was found guilty and sentenced to death. He refused to ask for clemency and was hanged on 5 May 1887 in the Schlüsselburg Fortress.   RA

Further Reading

Deutscher, Isaac: *Lenin's Childhood*. London: Oxford University Press, 1970.

Itenberg, B.S.: *Zhizn' A. Ulyanova*. Moscow and Leningrad: 1966.

Ulyanova-Elizarova, A.I.: *A.I. Ulyanov i delo 1 marta 1887*. Moscow and Leningrad: 1927.

Unshlikht, Iosif Stanislavovich (1879–1938)

A prominent political police and state official, Unshlikht was born into a Polish intelligentsia family. He joined the revolutionary Social Democratic Party of the Kingdom of Poland and Lithuania in 1900, rising to membership of its national committee. Repeatedly arrested and imprisoned during 1902–9, he spent 1913–16 in tsarist gaols and Siberian exile. After participating in the OCTOBER REVOLUTION, he served in the Commissariat for Internal Affairs from November 1917 to late 1918. He held key posts in the short-lived Republic of Lithuania and Belorussia in February to April 1919, and figured in the Provisional

Revolutionary Committee of Poland in July and August 1920. During much of the period 1919 to early 1921 he saw service as Revolutionary Military Council member on Russia's Western Front. From April 1921 until autumn 1923, as deputy to the VECHEKA/GPU chairman DZERZHINSKY, he effectively controlled the political police, Dzerzhinsky being preoccupied with duties as Commissar for Transport. Unshlikht subsequently held office: as member of the Revolutionary Military Council of the USSR 1923–5); as its deputy chairman and Deputy Commissar for the Army and Navy (1925–30); as deputy chairman of the Supreme Council of National Economy and USSR Planning Commission (1930–3); as director of civil aviation (1933–5); and as secretary to the Central Executive Committee of the USSR (1935–7). He was candidate-member of the Communist Party's Central Committee from December 1925 onwards. Arrested in June 1937, he was shot in July 1938. He was posthumously rehabilitated.

Uritsky, Moisei Solomonovich (1873–1918)

Born into a Jewish merchant family in the Ukraine, Uritsky was active in Polish socialist organizations while studying

Figure 76   Uritsky.

law at Kiev University. Graduating in 1897, he became a professional revolutionary, experiencing arrests, imprisonments and Siberian exile. A member of the RSDRP since 1898, he sided with the MENSHEVIKS after the party split in 1903. As a wartime émigré in Western Europe, Uritsky held Trotskyist views; returning to Russia in March 1917, he, together with the MEZHRAYONKA group led by TROTSKY, joined the BOLSHEVIK Party during its Sixth Congress in July–August 1917, being elected to its Central Committee. He was demoted to Central Committee candidate-member status at the Seventh Party Congress in March 1918. Meanwhile he participated in the OCTOBER REVOLUTION, and in the suppression of the democratically elected CONSTITUENT ASSEMBLY. From March 1918 onwards, he was Commissar for Internal Affairs in the Northern Region Commune, and chairman of the Petrograd Cheka (see VECHEKA), in which capacity he ordered executions of counter-revolutionaries. His assassination in Petrograd on 30 August 1918, coinciding fortuitously with the attempt on LENIN's life in Moscow that same day, provoked the Communist regime's proclamation of the Red Terror.   GHL

Vakhitov, Mullanur (1885–1918)

The Tatar Communist who is celebrated as a hero and a martyr. Vakhitov's father was a Tatar merchant from Kungur in the southern Urals. The personality of the future Communist was shaped by Russian schools and not by the traditional medreses which figured in the background of almost all jadids. Vakhitov attended the Russian gymnasium of Kazan, and the Polytechnical and Psycho-Neurological Institutes of St Petersburg, from which he was duly expelled for political activism in 1911 and 1912, respectively.

The FEBRUARY REVOLUTION found Vakhitov employed as an engineer in Kazan. Like many other Muslim intellectuals, he was caught up in the euphoria of the February Revolution and threw himself into organizing the Tatars politically. He became chairman of the Kazan Socialist Committee organized on 7 April 1917, and adhered to an ideology which, defying its socialist label, represented a mélange of Marxism and pan-Islamism.

When the dangers of the CIVIL WAR prompted the BOLSHEVIK leadership to look for an alliance with the Muslims, Vakhitov accepted chairmanship of the Central Muslim Commissariat created by government decree 17 January 1918, with the purpose of attracting the Muslims to the Bolshevik cause and also depriving the Muslim organizations (which had emerged since the spring of 1917) of popular support.

· A member of the Bolshevik party since December 1917, Vakhitov was trusted by the leadership in Moscow and offered many responsible positions. In March 1918 he signed (alongside STALIN, G. IBRAGIMOV and Manatov) the decree proclaiming the territory of Southern Ural and Middle Volga the Tatar-Bashkir republic of the Russian Soviet Federation, a republic whose existence, however, remained only on paper since in its place, at the end of the Civil War, two republics were born: Tatar and Bashkir. In April 1918, Vakhitov was made chairman of the Muslim Military Collegium, a body under the jurisdiction of the War Commissariat (see CRIMEAN AND VOLGA TATARS).

In August of the same year, Vakhitov left for the Eastern Front at the head of the Tatar-Bashkir battalion which was sent against the Whites. 1918 was also the year of the Czech uprising and their support for the Whites in the struggle for Kazan. It was in this battle that Vakhitov was captured by the Czechs and executed on 19 August 1918.

Vakhitov died too early to allow substantive comment on his evolution as a Tatar Communist under Soviet rule. It could be argued, however, that had he lived, Vakhitov would have most likely shared in the nationalism of both M. SULTANGALIEV and G. Ibragimov. After all, it was Vakhitov who, at the March 1918 conference of the Muslim Toilers of Russia, which adopted a decision to organize a part of Muslim Socialist Communists, urged the Muslims to commit themselves to a purely Muslim Communist party.   A-AR

Vilbushevich, Manya Vladimirovna (1880–1961)

Born in Grodno to a prosperous Jewish merchant, Manya Vilbushevich was early involved in intelligentsia circles, especially that of Evgeni Gershuni in Minsk, became a leading member of the Minsk Committee of the BUND, and was successful in her campaign in 1889 to restore workers' circles against the Central Committee's new policy of mass agitation. She became a committed ZIONIST at about that time, was arrested and met ZUBATOV by whom she was clearly captivated and of course converted. While working for this new cause she came close to the Poale Tsion (Workers of Zion), which had arisen simultaneously in Ekaterinoslav and Minsk in 1900 and believed that an effective class struggle could be waged only when the Jews had their own homeland. While eschewing politics altogether in the ZUBATOV MOVEMENT, she claimed that Zionism was the only possible politics for Jewish workers, clearly an attempt to square the circle. She was most successful among the printers of Grodno and the artisans of Minsk, worked closely with Colonel Vasilyev of the Minsk gendarmerie and was a founding member of the Independent Jewish Labour Party. In 1902, after a visit to St Petersburg, she secured sanction for an extension of the movement to Vilna. The Kishinev pogrom and the dissolution of the party were a severe shock to her, and there were reports that she planned to assassinate PLEHVE.

Figure 77 Volin (right) with Senya Fleshin.

She was an ardent and emotionally somewhat unstable girl, as her published correspondence with Zubatov indicates.

She had a consistently Zionist career thereafter. In 1904 she settled in Palestine, joining her three brothers there. She visited Baron Edmond de Rothschild in Paris to raise funds for Jewish self-defence in Russia, returned to Russia to promote settlement in the Golan Heights, went abroad again in 1907, to America, to raise money for Jewish migration but secured it only for Jewish self-defence in Russia; she finally married Israel Shohat and settled in Sejera in the lower Galilee. There, with her husband, she was one of the founders of Ha-Shomer, the self-defence organization. She was thus one of the pioneers of the Second Aliya, the immigration movement which, especially from Russia after 1905, reached its peak before the FIRST WORLD WAR. After deportation to Damascus and Anatolia during the War, she returned to Palestine, settled in Upper Galilee, went to the USA in 1921 on behalf of the Histradut (General Federation of Labour), was active in the twenties and thirties in the Hagana (Jewish Self-Defence), helped found the League of Jewish-Arab Rapprochement in 1929, and travelled abroad several times in the forties to encourage illegal immigration. Her last years were spent helping new immigrants in transit villages.   MKP

Volin, Vsevolod Mikhailovich (1882–1945)

Born in a professional family in Russia, Volin (real name Eikhenbaum) went to St Petersburg University where he became a SOCIALIST REVOLUTIONARY. He was arrested in 1905 and banished to Siberia, but he escaped to the West. He became an ANARCHIST in 1911, and joined the anarcho-syndicalists in the United States in 1914. In 1917 he returned to Russia and became a leading figure in the anarcho-syndicalist organization, first in Petrograd and then in Ukraine. Volin, who with ARSHINOV went into exile in 1921, first in Germany and then in France, favoured what he called a 'United Anarchism', going beyond anarcho-syndicalism to a synthesis of anarchist communism and individualism in the spirit of KROPOTKIN and the circumstances of the CIVIL WAR. He wrote a libertarian history of the Russian revolution, *The Unknown Revolution* (1947), which was published after his death in Paris. An English translation was published in part in Britain in 1954–5, and in full in the United States in 1974.   NW

Volodarsky, V. (1890–1918)

Born Moisei Markovich Goldstein into a poor Jewish family in Ostropol (in the Volyn region) and politically active in SOCIAL DEMOCRAT circles in his teens under the influence of the events of 1905, Volodarsky's life followed a course not unlike that of most Russian revolutionaries: prison, escape, prison again and exile (in his case self-imposed, to avoid police pursuit). From 1913 he lived in the United States, first in Philadelphia where he worked as a tailor and was active as a union agitator, then in New York where he continued his agitation work and contributed to the Russian revolutionary paper *Novy Mir* (New World). Following the FEBRUARY REVOLUTION he made his way back to Russia, first joined the MEZHRAYONKA and, in July 1917, together with the group, entered the Bolshevik Party in whose ranks he quickly rose to prominence as an agitator and mob orator. Active in meetings of the SOVIETS, Volodarsky was after the OCTOBER REVOLUTION appointed Commissar for the press, PROPAGANDA and agitation. A minor but militant BOLSHEVIK, Volodarsky was assassinated in July 1918 by a SOCIALIST REVOLUTIONARY in the course of a number of reprisals against the Red Terror of the time.   BK

Vratsian, Simon (1882–1969)

Educated at local Armenian and Russian schools, and at the Georgian Academy at Etchmiadzin, Vratsian joined the Dashnaktsutiun in 1898. He took a left-wing position in the party and supported its adoption of a socialist programme, which was closely based on that of the SRs, at the party's Fourth General Congress in 1907. Between 1908 and the war, he travelled widely. He studied law in St Petersburg and fled to Constantinople to escape a tsarist crack-down on the Dashnaktsutiun. He also spent time in the USA. He was in Erzerum for the party's Eighth General Congress where he was elected to the supreme party organ, the party bureau.

A strong supporter of the Russian war effort, Vratsian helped organize Armenian volunteer units in 1914–15. After February 1917 he was made editor of the Dashnaktsutiun's Tiflis organ *Horizon* and became a member of the Armenian National Council in September 1917. In the summer of 1918 he was sent on a special mission to the VOLUNTEER ARMY to gain arms and supplies. He also served as an adviser on the Batumi peace delegation. He became the major spokesman for the Dashnaktsutiun in the Khorhurd and advocated a gradualistic programme of socialism. At the party's Ninth General Congress in 1919, he resisted dictatorial demands for Dashnaktsutiun control of the state administration. He was appointed minister of the rural economy and state properties, and subsequently of labour, in KHATISIAN's

Figure 78   Vynnychenko.

cabinet. On the eve of independent Armenia's collapse, he accepted the post of premier in November 1920, and agreed to the transfer of power to the Bolsheviks to avoid decimation by the Turkish armies. After sovietization, he led the Committee for the Salvation of the Fatherland which organized a brief revolt against Bolshevik rule in February 1921. Active in émigré politics, he died in Beirut in 1969.   SFJ

Vynnychenko, Volodymyr (1880–1951)

A prominent Ukrainian writer, Vynnychenko was politically active in Ukrainian social democratic groups before the revolution. He spent most of the period 1903–17 as an émigré in Europe and returned to UKRAINE to take up the position of vice-president of the Central Rada in 1917. The Universals of the Central Rada were formulated and written under his supervision. He took an active part in the Ukrainian National Union against the SKOROPADSKY regime in 1918 and became one of the five members of the Directory which took power on the Hetman's demise. He resigned over political differences in 1919, spending a short time in Vienna but returned in 1920 to negotiate, without success, the future government of Ukraine with the BOLSHEVIKS. He settled in France in the 1920s where he spent the rest of his émigré life.   ND

Witte, Sergei Yulevich (1849–1915)

The ablest minister to serve under Alexander III and NICHOLAS II, Sergei Witte was born in Tiflis, and attended university in Odessa where he specialized in mathematics. Following his graduation in 1870 he began a career in railway management at which he proved himself an extremely competent and daring executive. He entered government service in 1889 to become Director of the Department of Railway Affairs of the Ministry of Finance. In February 1892 he was named acting minister of ways and communications. Six months later he was appointed acting minister of finance and in January 1893 he received the rank of minister.

It was as minister of finance that Witte truly made his mark, earning the reputation in many eyes of a man of genius. He accelerated the building of the Trans-Siberian Railway, was responsible for the construction of the CHINESE EASTERN RAILWAY (and as a result became deeply involved in the formulation of Far Eastern policy), placed Russia on the gold standard (1897), and helped speed up the country's industrial development, his primary aim being to give Russia the economic might commensurate with its claim to being a major power. By the end of the century this ambitious, dynamic, overwhelming man was the most powerful minister in the realm, the object of both adulation and hatred at home and abroad.

In August 1903 he fell from power when Nicholas II shifted him to the post of chairman of the committee of ministers, a dead-end position generally reserved for ministers out of favour. His fall was the result of personality and policy differences with the emperor, hostility on the part of some of the landed nobility and some of his colleagues, chief among them PLEHVE who, in his efforts to destroy Witte, passed on to the emperor letters accusing Witte of being a part of a Jewish-Masonic conspiracy, and the emperor was sufficiently convinced to terminate Witte's appointment.

A turn in Witte's fortunes came in June 1905 when the emperor, for want of any other able and willing candidate, selected him to negotiate peace with Japan. Witte's brilliant performance in this role apparently restored the emperor's confidence in him and prompted him to bestow on Witte the title of count. Moreover, he now planned to appoint him to the post of chairman of the council of ministers. Meanwhile the general strike broke out, leading to Witte's preparation of the October Manifesto and his assumption of the office that made him head of government.

Witte's six-month tenure in that office was not a glorious

Figure 79   Witte.

one. Aware of intrigues, even plots, against him at court where some held him to be a traitor, under extreme physical and mental strain, torn between the conviction that Russia would be best served by a benevolent autocrat and the realization that the turn from absolutism was irreversible, disappointed by the failure of moderates to cooperate with him, overwhelmed by the scope of disorder after 17 October, he occasionally behaved erratically and unwisely. But he managed to see the country through the turbulent transition to what was supposed to be a new era and to do the preparatory work necessary for entry into that era of constitutional experiment.

Despite repeated urgings from those close to him to dismiss Witte (one courtier even asked for permission to have Witte killed!), Nicholas II waited until his chief minister had completed his work, then, in April 1906, he 'agreed' to Witte's repeated request to be relieved of his duties. Very disappointed by the mixed results of the October Manifesto, apparently convinced that Witte had tricked him into signing the manifesto, and possibly suspecting him once more of being a Mason, the emperor vowed never again to entrust this man with any responsibility. He was as good as his word.

Witte spent his remaining years an unhappy has-been, cut off from any opportunity to use his ability and experience in the service of his country. He used his enforced leisure to write his memoirs, inspire many publications defending his record, and engage in occasional political intrigue. In death he remained almost as controversial a figure as he had been in life, reviled by some as a malignant figure and extolled by others as Russia's greatest statesman since Peter the Great.   SH

Wrangel, General Peter Nikolaevich (1878–1928)

An outstanding White commander in 1918–19, he became in 1920 the last major leader of the White movement. Wrangel commanded a cavalry corps in the World War. He took little part in the events of 1917 or early 1918, but when he reached the Kuban at the end of 1918 he proved to be a gifted commander, first in the north Caucasus campaign and then leading his Caucasus Army against Tsaritsyn, which he captured in July 1919. At the end of 1919, after the failure of the Moscow campaign, Wrangel briefly commanded the VOLUNTEER ARMY but could not reverse its panicky retreat. He never got on well with his superior, DENIKIN; although dismissed for conspiring against Denikin at the beginning of 1920, he was in early April summoned by the surviving generals to be Denikin's successor.

Wrangel took over command in the Crimea with little hope of a prolonged campaign, but thanks to his organizing abilities, the RED ARMY's preoccupation with other fronts, and the geography of the Crimean peninsula, he was able not only to hold out but even to take the offensive for five months. His policies towards the peasants and the national minorities were more realistic than those of the earlier Whites, but if he did not face the kind of internal disorder that Denikin had this was because of his smaller territory, just Tauride Province. Wrangel's defeat was inevitable, given that he only had 35,000 men against a Red Army with a nominal strength of 5,000,000. He did get French recognition, but little effective help; the British, meanwhile, had withdrawn all support. Wrangel retreated into the Crimea when the Reds attacked in November 1920 and evacuated many of his followers; until his death he was head of the émigré movement.   EM

Yakovlev, Nikolai Nikolaevich (1886–1918)

A member of the Siberian 'old guard' who joined the party in 1905 as a university student in Moscow, Yakovlev's arrival to political activism in Siberia followed the classic path of numerous radicals: revolutionary work interspersed with arrests, imprisonment, internal exile with several escapes from Siberia and a brief period of self-exile abroad. In 1916, straight from Siberian exile, he was called up for military service. On the outbreak of revolution he used his experience in the army (he was an agitator in the Tomsk Garrison) to be elected to the Presidium of the Tomsk Soviet of Soldiers' Deputies. In early October 1917 he rose to the post of chairman of the Presidium of the United Soviet of Workers' and Soldiers' Deputies and, finally, in February 1918 he became Chairman of the All-Siberian Soviet. In the latter capacity he helped to engineer the meeting between BOLSHEVIK representatives and Chinese officials at Matsiyevskaya (see LAZO). After the Bolshevik

collapse in Siberia, Yakovlev fled into the taiga. He was captured in Yakutiya in late November 1918 and shot by White forces (see REVOLUTION IN SIBERIA).   FP

Yakovlev, Valentin Nikolaevich (1892–1918)

A party member since 1912, Yakovlev became chairman of the Enisei SOVIET's executive committee in early 1917. He was also a member of the BOLSHEVIK Party's Siberian Regional Bureau and an editor of the Siberian *Pravda*. In July 1917 he secured membership of the Krasnoyarsk Regional Bureau and in August that of the Bolshevik Central Siberian Regional Bureau. Concurrently he was appointed the Bolshevik Central Committee's plenipotentiary for the whole of Central Siberia. Yakovlev was responsible for launching a broad attack on the right SRs at the Congress of Soviets of Eastern Siberia, held at Irkutsk on 10 October 1917. In his speech to the delegates he accused the right SRs of underestimating the capabilities of those manning the Soviets (after the SR right wing had argued that all power should not be transferred to the Soviets as they lacked personnel with the ability to govern) and of being in league with the bourgeoisie, concluding pointedly that '. . . behind KORNILOV stands SAVINKOV' (the latter being an eminent SR who eventually abandoned his Marxism to take up resistance against the Bolsheviks). The Bolshevik attack successfully split the Congress. Yakovlev's activities at Krasnoyarsk continued until 25 October 1918, when he was executed by the Czech Legion.   FP

Yudenich, General Nikolai Nikolaevich (1862–1933)

Yudenich was one of the most successful FIRST WORLD WAR commanders, capturing the Turks' Erzerum fortress in 1916. He retired in 1917, after briefly commanding the Caucasus Army Group. He spent 1918 underground in Petrograd but escaped to Finland in November, where he became overall commander of White forces in the BALTIC region. Yudenich's CIVIL WAR role was relatively slight. THE NORTH-WESTERN ARMY, his main field force, was small, and in any event he did not personally command it until September 1919; older than the other White leaders, he was not an active or gifted commander. Politically he failed to build a popular Great Russian administration, to attract substantial Allied support, or to get Finnish-Estonian cooperation. With his army's internment he was briefly arrested, but emigrated in 1920.   EM

Yurkevych, Lev (1881–1918)

A Ukrainian social democrat from an early age, Yurkevych was active in Kiev after 1905 and contributed financial support to political publishing. In emigration in Geneva during the FIRST WORLD WAR he wrote under the pen-name L. Rybalka. His best known polemic was with LENIN in a pamphlet entitled 'Russian Social-Democrats and the National Question' (Geneva, 1917). He moved to Moscow to continue his work after the beginning of the revolution, but died suddenly a year later. ND

Zasulich, Vera Ivanovna (1849–1919)

A POPULIST activist and later a leading exponent of Russian MARXISM, Zasulich entered history by committing a spectacular act of political violence. In July 1877 an imprisoned comrade, A. Bogolyubov, was flogged – illegally – on the orders of the St Petersburg governor, General F. F. TREPOV. The Land and Liberty organization planned to avenge the deed by assassinating Trepov, but Zasulich forestalled the attempt. Her revolver shot, which wounded the general, launched the terrorist campaign against government officials, and later the tsar, by the People's Will group. Zasulich was sent for jury trial, in the hope that public opinion would rally against left-wing extremism, but the jury, impressed by the apparent altruism of her motives, acquitted her, to the plaudits of the crowd, and friends helped her escape re-arrest. The verdict was widely seen as an indictment of autocracy. In 1879 Zasulich came out against further terroristic acts, for a mixture of pragmatic and moral reasons, and joined G. V. PLEKHANOV's proto-Marxist BLACK REPARTITION group. Four years later she helped him found its successor, the Liberation of Labour group of émigrés in Switzerland. Her heroic image was useful to the Russian Marxists in their struggle against the Populist epigones. She wrote much, despite ill health, but without showing great originality, and earned her comrades' respect for her moral qualities. During the Iskra period she tried to conciliate the warring leaders of the infant RSDRP. In 1905 she returned to Russia and withdrew from active politics. During the FIRST WORLD WAR her sympathies lay with the defensists and she opposed the OCTOBER REVOLUTION. JLHK

Further Reading

Bergman, J.: *Vera Zasulich: a Biography*. Stanford: 1983.

Zenzinov, Vladimir Mikhailovich (1880–1953)

Son of a wealthy Moscow family of Siberian background, who always retained the air of a 'Moscow-Siberian Old Believer' (CHERNOV), Zenzinov was a highly readable author and an indefatigable manager of the affairs of the Party of SOCIALIST REVOLUTIONARIES (PSR). Zenzinov studied at Moscow Classical Gymnasium and then at the universities of Berlin, Heidelberg and Halle, where he came under the influence of N. D. AVKSENTIEV. His admiration for Amalia Gavronskaya (a member of the

wealthy family of tea merchants who financed the PSR) created a lifelong association with her husband Ilya BUNAKOV-FONDAMINSKY. A founder-member of the PSR and member of its Central Committee, Zenzinov returned to Moscow in January 1904. Arrested on the eve of 'Bloody Sunday' 1905, he was exiled to Archangel Province, whence he escaped to Geneva. He returned once more after the 1905 October Manifesto and attended the First Congress of the PSR at Imatra. After a brief spell in the Fighting Organization, he took part in agitation among the Ukrainian peasantry. In September 1906 he was arrested in St Petersburg and sentenced to exile in Eastern Siberia. In the following summer he escaped to Japan after a 500 mile walk through the taiga. This became the subject of his first book. In 1908 he acted as secretary to the commission summoned by the PSR to examine the charges against AZEF and was personally blamed for Azef's escape from the vengeance of his comrades. Returning to St Petersburg, Zenzinov was re-arrested in 1910, served six months in the Peter-Paul Fortress and was once more exiled, this time to Yakutia. There he undertook serious studies of the Arctic peoples, subsequently published in three books. In 1915 he returned once more to Petrograd, where he assisted A. F. KERENSKY in his attempts to re-build the PSR and overthrow the tsarist government. In February 1917 he became chairman of the Petrograd Committee of the PSR, and subsequently served on the All-Russian Central Executive Committee of Soviets. He attended the sole session of the CONSTITUENT ASSEMBLY in January 1918, and five months later joined the Committee of the Constituent Assembly (Komuch) government in Samara. He served in the Omsk Directory until its overthrow by Admiral KOLCHAK in November 1918. Escaping to Europe via China, Zenzinov published a collection of documents discrediting Kolchak. Between 1919 and 1940 he lived in Paris, writing frequently in the SR émigré press and living with the Fondaminskys. In 1927 he published a vivid account of a journey to the United States. In 1939–40 he visited Finland at the behest of Kerensky to investigate the morale of the RED ARMY, and possibly to urge the creation of an anti-Bolshevik Russian Legion. The letters he discovered were later published as a book casting vivid light on the mentality of Soviet citizens on the eve of the German invasion. Kerensky secured Zenzinov an entry visa for the USA where he arrived in 1940. To the end of his life, he played an active part in émigré politics and letters. RA

Further Reading

Zenzinov, V.M.: *Perezhitoe*. New York: Chekhov, 1953.

Zhelyabov, Andrei Ivanovich (1850–1881)

The son of a former serf, Zhelyabov managed to enter university at Odessa, whence in 1871 he was expelled for indiscipline. Later he joined the POPULIST movement, engaged in peaceful propaganda among the peasants and was arrested (1874), released on bail and eventually acquitted for lack of evidence. Deciding that more active measures were necessary, he joined the terrorist wing of Land and Liberty (Zemlya i volya) and took a leading part in the debates of 1879 that led to the moderates' secession and the emergence of the People's Will (Narodnaya volya) group. As chief organizer of the attempts to kill Alexander II, Zhelyabov first tried to blow up a train on which the tsar was travelling (November 1879), and was involved in five other attempts before his goal was attained on 1 March 1881. Since he had been arrested two days earlier, the final arrangements were made by his accomplice (and common-law wife), Sofiya Perovskaya (1853–81). Both were among the five individuals condemned and publicly hanged for tsaricide on 3 April 1881. JLHK

Further Reading

Footman, D.: *Red Prelude: a Life of Andrey Zhelyabov*. London: 1944. Repr. with foreword by L.B. Schapiro, as *The Alexander Conspiracy*. Illinois: La Salle, 1974.

Zhordania, Noi (1870–1953)

Born in Guria (West Georgia), son of a poor nobleman, Zhordania attended the Tiflis Seminary and the Warsaw Veterinary Institute. In the 1890s he led the small group of Marxists known as the Mesame Dasi (Third Group) and was recognized as the leading Georgian Marxist theorist. Threatened with arrest, he went abroad between 1893 and 1897. In 1898 he became editor of the weekly *Kvali* (Track) which he turned into a legal Marxist journal. He was a member of the Tiflis social democratic committee and was elected to the Caucasian Union Committee in March 1903. He attended the Second Congress of the RSDRP (as an observer) and sided with MARTOV and the 'softs'. On his return to Georgia in late 1904, he swung the Georgian organization behind the MENSHEVIK line and isolated the BOLSHEVIK-dominated Caucasian Committee. By 1905 he dominated the Georgian organization and had a decisive influence on its direction and tactics. In 1905 he edited the Georgian paper *Sotsial-Demokratia* and was elected to the first Duma, where he was made leader of the social democratic fraction. He was a signatory to the Vyborg Manifesto. He regularly attended the RSDRP congresses at the head of large Georgian delegations and was elected to the RSDRP central committee in 1907.

In 1914 Zhordania collaborated with TROTSKY on *Borba* (The Struggle), but took a defensist position on the war. In 1917 he was elected chairman of both the Tiflis Soviet and the (Caucasian) Regional Centre of Soviets. He avoided work in Transcaucasian governments, preferring to lead the revolutionary organizations and the Georgian RSDRP. He was elected to the Transcaucasian Sejm in 1918 and in June 1918, a month after Georgian independence, Zhordania

Figure 80 Zhuchenko.

consented to lead the new Georgian government, and became the republic's first President (see TRANSCAUCASIA: REVOLUTION AND CIVIL WAR). He held this post until the invasion of Georgia by the RED ARMY in February 1921 when he was forced into exile in Paris. He died there in 1953. SFJ

Zhuchenko, Zinaida Fedorovna (dates unknown)

One of the most important police undercover agents in the SR party, member of the Moscow Regional Committee, active as an agent under the police code name 'Mikheev' from 1894 until her exposure in 1909, Zhuchenko (née Gerngross) volunteered her services to the police after she had made the acquaintance of Deputy Police Director, Semyakin in 1893. He introduced her to S. ZUBATOV. Thus in 1894 she began working for the Moscow OKHRANA until April 1895 when she was arrested together with I. Rasputina, I. Akimova and others. In February 1896 she was sent into exile in Siberia for five years, but already in April 1898 she was on her way to Germany, where she continued her role as an undercover agent of the Paris Foreign Agency, first in Leipzig and later in Heidelberg.

Zhuchenko found no difficulty in penetrating revolutionary circles abroad with a revolutionary past behind her, which included arrest and exile as a cover. Likewise, in September 1905, as the need grew for police agents at home, she could easily obtain the necessary references to approach members of the Fighting Organization in Russia.

403

She took part in the Moscow uprising that broke out shortly after her arrival, and in March 1906 her prominence brought her into the fighting squad of the Moscow Regional Committee, where she served as a secretary alongside Sladokoptsev – 'Kazbek' the squad leader.

Zhuchenko herself both proposed and took part in a number of terrorist acts and 'expropriations', which included an attempted murder of P. Kurlov, the then Governor of Minsk. She informed the authorities in advance about the proposed plot, thus enabling them to apprehend the would-be assassin red-handed. He was subsequently hanged.

Zhuchenko's position gave her access to all the secrets of the entire Moscow region. No suspicions were raised against her until after AZEF's exposure. The first rumours concerning her ties with the Okhrana began to filter from abroad, following the defection to the revolutionaries of L. Menshchikov, a former high-ranking police officer. The police hastened to liquidate the vestiges of the Moscow organization, while she herself fled abroad.

The SR Central Committee thought it best not to issue an immediate communique about Zhuchenko, and suggested that BURTSEV, as editor of *Byloe* (The Past), try to extract a detailed confession from her, covering everything she knew about the 'world of provocation'. Burtsev met Zhuchenko in Berlin, where she admitted to having served as an undercover agent of the Police Department, maintaining repeatedly that her motivation was purely ideological.

Zhuchenko's value to the police found expression in the monthly salaries she was paid: 150 rubles until September 1906, followed by 500 roubles until her exposure and as a token of appreciation a 200 rouble pension afterwards. NS

Zinoviev, Grigori Evseevich (1883–1936)

A close associate of LENIN before the revolution and the first President of Comintern after 1917. Born in Elizavetgrad (later Zinovievsk, now Kirovgrad), Kherson province, in 1883, where his Jewish parents owned a small dairy farm, Zinoviev (real name Radomyslsky) became a member of the RSDRP in 1901. In 1903 he met Lenin and PLEKHANOV in Switzerland and after the party split joined the BOLSHEVIKS.

In 1905 Zinoviev and a group of Bolsheviks arrived in St Petersburg at the height of the general strike, though ill health minimized his activities. He was elected to the local executive committee, and at the Fifth Congress of the RSDRP in London (1907) he was elected to the Central Committee. Zinoviev was arrested in spring 1908 but released on the grounds of ill-health. At the end of the year he joined the editorial board of Lenin's *Proletarii*, was elected to the new all-Bolshevik Central Committee (January 1912) and constituted with Lenin the Central Committee Bureau in Cracow, Austrian Poland.

Zinoviev spent the war in Switzerland and returned with Lenin to Petrograd in April 1917, the first sign of his

divergent views emerging after Lenin proclaimed his April Theses. Zinoviev joined *Pravda* as an editor, however. During the July Days he went into hiding with Lenin, but in August returned to Petrograd, writing for *Proletarii* and *Rabochii Put* (Workers' Way) which replaced the silenced *Pravda*, and continued work with the Central Committee. He became a member of the Politburo at its inception on 10 October (OS).

Opposed to an armed coup, at a Central Committee meeting on 9 October, Zinoviev and KAMENEV had been the only dissenters to Lenin's call for action. In the next two weeks the issue threatened to take on a more divisive form, but was overtaken by the events of 25 October. In early November Zinoviev opposed the exclusion of non-Bolsheviks from the new Soviet government. This time (with four others) he resigned from the committee. Within a few days he was readmitted, having published his 'Letter to the Comrades' in *Pravda*. In January 1918 he became head of the Revolutionary Committee for the defence of Petrograd. At the First World Congress of the Comintern (Moscow, March 1919), Zinoviev was elected chairman of its Executive Committee (IKKI) and in September presided over the Congress of the Peoples of the East in Baku.

Zinoviev reached the pinnacle of his power in 1923–4 as one of the Triumvirate, with STALIN and Kamenev, which prepared to take over on Lenin's death. After TROTSKY and the Left Opposition had been neutralized in 1925, however, Stalin turned on his own allies, and in 1926 Zinoviev was removed from the Politburo and IKKI and expelled from the party in November 1927. He recanted his 'mistakes' and was reinstated in 1928, only to be expelled again in 1932. His secret trial (with Kamenev) followed in January 1935, resulting in ten years' imprisonment. In August 1936 he appeared as a defendant at the first show trial, was sentenced to death for treason and executed shortly after. FP

Zubatov, Sergei Vasilievich (1863?–1917)

Born in Moscow to the manager of a block of flats on the Tverskaya, Zubatov's early days were typical of a member of the intelligentsia: he read the progressive literature of the time; at gymnasium he enrolled in a circle devoted to D. I. Pisarev, the nihilist, whose admirer he became; and, being a talented speaker, soon formed a group around himself. Through a family friend, the revolutionary V. N. Morozov, he also contacted revolutionary circles outside. For some reason his education was interrupted. He was either expelled for illegal activity or his father took him out for that reason. He worked briefly in the postal department, and then became manager of a bookshop run by Alexandra Nikolaevna Mikhina, from which vantage point he renewed his radical contacts and distributed banned literature. In the discussion circles, he met M. R. GOTS and other sympathizers of the Narodnaya Volya from 1882 onward.

Perhaps Zubatov compromised himself in some fashion; at any rate from around 1883 he began cooperating with the police and from 1886 disrupting revolutionary circles in Moscow before formally enlisting in the OKHRANA. His career in political intelligence was meteoric. This function became especially important from the mid 1890s with the growing mass movement among workers influenced by the revolutionary intelligentsia. He continuously innovated: he introduced photographic files, the systematic registration of suspects, the training of the police in revolutionary theory and conspiratorial methods, and he started the flying squad to track down suspects speedily. Brilliantly successful, he was summoned to St Petersburg in 1895 to attend the coronation festivities, and was personally congratulated by I. L. Goremykin, the minister for internal affairs. At the young age of thirty-two he was appointed chief of the Moscow Okhrana, from which position he carried out his now famous experiment.

His success aroused suspicion and envy, and Zubatov was moved to the innocuous Special Affairs Section of the Department of Police in St Petersburg in 1902 after the Guzhon crisis in Moscow. There he was involved in intrigue between WITTE and PLEHVE, who then ignominiously dismissed him in 1903 to exile in Vladimir. Thereafter he wrote articles in the newspaper *Grazhdanin* (Citizen) defending the monarchy, in *Vestnik Evropy* (European Messenger) explaining his past action, and left behind a long account of the whole affair, which was posthumously published in *Byloe* (The Past) in 1917. He committed suicide on hearing of the abdication. MKP

Index

The Editor and Publisher are grateful to Mary Norris for compiling the index.

Page references in bold type refer to major entries on a subject, those in parentheses refer to illustrations.

Conjunctions and prepositions have been ignored in determining the order of subheadings.

Individuals appear under the name by which they are most commonly known; their other name, whether real or a pseudonym, is given as a cross-reference.

The following abbreviations have been used in the index:

AFSR	Armed Forces of South Russia
MRC	Military Revolutionary Committee
NEP	New Economic Policy
PA-RG	Provisional All-Russian Government
PG	Provisional Government
RSDRP	Russian Social Democratic Labour Party
SDs	Social Democrats
SRs	Socialist Revolutionaries

Index

Vasiliev, V. P. 330
Vatan 249
Vatsetis, I. I. 142, 143, 145, 148, 187
Vecheka (see also Okhrana) 6, 89, 148,
  166, 175, **181–5**, 342, 379
  and Bolshevization 202
  Church and 140
  Civil War and 149
  in Crimea 250
  Dzerhinsky and 320
  Kedrov and 329
  Latsis and 339
  Menzhinsky and 356
  Peters and 363
  protests against 363
  Sovnarkom and 165
Venyamin, Metropolitan 354, 390
Verkhovsky, General 129, 130
Vernadskaya, Mariya 31
Vertov, Dziga 288
Vestnik Zhizn (Messenger of Life) 298,
  362
Vienna, émigrés in 220
Vikzhel 200
Vilbushevich, Manya Vladimirovna 54,
  380, **397–8**
Vinaver, M. M. 208, 209, 210
Vinnitsa 224
Vinogradov, P. G. 368
Vinogradov, V. A. 147
Viren, Robert 158
Vishnyak, Mark 210
Vitebsk 214
Vladimirsky-Budanov, M. F. 343
Vladivostok 261, 262
Voennyi golos (Military Voice) 362
Voennyi sbornik (Military Miscellany)
  369
voenspets 186, 187
Voitinsky, V. 82, 318
Volga Tatars
  before 1917 **247–9**
  revolution and Civil War 6, 142,
    249–52, 297, 356
  Volin, Vsevolod Mikhailovich 301,
    398, (398)
Volkenstein, M. F. 343
Volna (The Wave) 298, 362
Volnoe Kazachestvo (Free Cossacks)
  204
Volodarsky, V. 26, 84, **399**
Vologodsky, P. V. 147
Voloshinov, Colonel 204
Volski, V. see Machajski, Jan W.
Volsky, V. K. 146
Volunteer Army 143, 145, 146, **147**, 298,
  399
  in Azerbaijan 238
  Denikin and 319
  in Don region 206, 207
  Kornilov and 334

Wrangel and 401
Volya Naroda (The Will of the People)
  127
Voroshilov, K. E. 377, 390
Vorovsky, Vatslav, V. 67, 79, 178, 303
Vpered (Forward), group 269, 298, 308
Vpered (Forward), newspaper 67, 68,
  310, 340, 341, 362
  in Europe 340, 346
Vpered! (Forwards!), periodical 340, 390
Vperedism 70–1
Vratsian, Simon **399**
VSNKh see Supreme Council of the
  National Economy
Vtorov, N. A. 122
Vyborg Manifesto 404
Vygodsky, Dv. 215
Vynnychenko, Volodymyr 218, 220,
  221, 224, **399–400**, (399)
Vyshinsky, A. Ya. 358, 388

wages 24, 25, 119
Wahl, V. von 315
Walecki see Horwitz, Maksymilian
war communism 6, **148–50**, 172, 343
  Bogdanov on 308–9
  labour protest and 27
  Maximalists and 90
  peasants reaction to 16
war economy, importance of women in
  34
war industries, demobilization of 25
War Industries Committees 82, 112,
  115–17, 117–18, 325, 335
  Jews on 209
War Industries Council 172
Warsaw, strikes in 100
Warszawski, Adolf 100, 102, 348
Waryński, Ludwik 99
Weinstein, Gregory 209
White Army
  and Atamans 263–4
  in Civil War, 143, 144, 145, 146
  and Cossacks 206, 207
  and emigration 161
  and pogroms in Ukraine 215
  Wrangel and 401
Whites
  in Finland 230, 231
  in Volga 252
Wieczorek, F. 101
Wiik, Karl 75
Williams, Albert Rhys 374
Williams, Harold 395
Witte, Sergei Yulevich 37, 107, 108,
  265, 365, **400**, (400)
  and Trans-Siberian Railway 259
  minor refs: 63, 361, 405
Wojnarowska, C. 100, (101)
women
  in the Church 38

in industry 19
Women's Death Battalion 308
women's movement
  Armand and 300
  before 1917 3, **30–4**
  Kollontai and 333
  Mirovich and 358
  1917 and after **34–6**, 175
  Pokrovskaya and 368
  Shabanova and 379–80
  Tyrkova and 395
Women's Progressive Party 368
women soldiers: 1917–1921 34, **36**, 343
women's suffrage 33, 34
workers: February–October 1917 6, **19–
  21**, 45
workers: October 1917–March 1921
  25–8, 139
Workers' Cause see Rabochee Delo
Workers of the City of Moscow 54
workers' control: February–October
  1917 20, 21–2, **22–3**
workers' control, demise of **28–9**
workers' deputies 26
Workers' Faculties (Rabfak) 347
Workers' Group 94, 116
workers' militias **24**
Workers' Opposition **152**, 177, 381
Workers' Party for the Political
  Liberation of Russia 85, 324
Workers of Zion see Poale Tsion
working class 4, 9
  culture of 270, 271
  in First World War 111
  Marxism and 60–1
  organizations of 65
  Plekhanov on 366–7
  and soviets 135
working conditions, factory committees
  and 22
world revolution
  idea of 5, **194–8**
  Trotsky and 178, 179
Wrangel, General Peter Nikolaevich
  130, 147, **401**
  and Civil War 145, 146, 150, 161
  in Crimea 250
  and massacre of Jews 215
  minor refs: 146, 319, 322, 351, 378
Writers and the Revolution **272–6**

Yadrintsev, N. M. 256
Yagoda, G. G. 183, 275, 356
Yakovlev, Nikolai Nikolaevich **401**
Yakovlev, Valentin Nikolaevich 263,
  401
Yakovlev, V. Y. see Bogucharsky, Vasili
  Yakovlevich
Yamashev, Kh. 249, 394
Yanushkevich, General N. N. 298, 369
Yaroslavsky, E. M. 177, 370, 389

424